THE

POETICAL WORKS

OF

CRABBE, HEBER, AND POLLOK,

COMPLETE

IN ONE VOLUME.

PHILADELPHIA:
LIPPINCOTT, GRAMBO & CO.,
SUCCESSORS TO
GRIGG, ELLIOT & CO.,
No. 14, NORTH FOURTH STREET.
1852.

Printed by T. K. & P. G. Collins.

THE

POETICAL WORKS

OF

GEORGE CRABBE.

Contents.

Memoir of the Rev. George Crabbe.

If the humorous observation of Addison were founded in fact, that a reader seldom peruses a book with pleasure "till he knows whether the writer of it be a black or fair man—of a mild or choleric disposition,—with other particulars of the like nature,"—we should be in a state of some apprehension, since the Rev. George Crabbe, the celebrated author of the poems a new edition of which we here present to the public, has, from the modesty and retiredness of his life, furnished but few biographical particulars to be developed to an admiring world. Unlike so many others of his *genus*, he never intermeddled in the turmoils of politics, or mingled in the intrigues of fashion. He was, in his manners and feelings, a *child* of nature; though a *savant* in her dispositions and her laws. Contented with keeping the "noiseless tenor of his way," with the approbation of his conscience and the approval of his God,—he was willing to allow some to be the idol of the factious, and others to fawn at the footstool of power;—satisfied himself with being admired as a poet—revered as a divine,—and respected as a man.

Our poet was born at Aldborough, on the coast of Suffolk, England, on the Christmas eve of 1754. His father held the station of salt-master, or collector of the salt duties, and was a man of strong intellect, vigorous habits of business, and a remarkable faculty of calculation. Early in his boyhood, as soon, indeed, as he had learned to read, young Crabbe manifested a strong inclination towards books of all kinds; and he perused with eagerness every thing that came within his reach, especially if it were a work of fiction and romance, or treated of witches, fairies, and ghosts. But he particularly delighted in verse, and began at a very early period to imitate the humble specimens of poetry which were then accessible to him.

His father observed this bookish disposition, and although he had no higher views for the boy than that of following his own example, and being employed in some inferior department of the revenue service, he resolved to send George to a school at Bungay, on the borders of Norfolk.—Here he remained for a short time, and was then removed to a school at Stowmarket, kept by a skilful mathematician named Haddon. The boy himself had a predilection, as well as his father for mathematics; and he made considerable proficiency in the pursuit.

After leaving this latter school, George was placed as a surgeon's apprentice at Wickham-Brook; but as this situation was not a very desirable one, he left it, and concluded his apprenticeship with a Mr. Page, surgeon at Woodbridge, a market-town about seventeen miles from Aldborough. Here he met with society congenial to his own disposition, and was by this means introduced to Miss Sarah Elmy, who afterwards became his wife. Notwithstanding that he here applied himself with energy to the studies necessary to a knowledge of his intended profession, he was often beguiled into the more flowery fields of poesy, and contributed numerous pieces to the Lady's Magazine, a periodical of some repute at that period.

About the end of the year 1775, Mr. Crabbe's term of apprenticeship expired, and he returned to his native village, with the hope of finding means of finishing his professional education in London. But his father's circumstances did not permit the necessary expenditure, and the youthful aspirant was compelled to labour in the drudgery of the public warehouse wherein his parent's duties were performed. This was in the highest degree unpleasant to young Crabbe; and the irksomeness of his situation was increased by an unhappy change in the habits of his father, who had become a politician, a tavern-haunter, and a domestic tyrant.

Mr. Crabbe, at this period, devoted such leisure time as was at his disposal, to the study of botany, and the advancement of his professional knowledge; and if he still dallied with the muses, it was with the persuasion that this was not his main pursuit in the progress of life. At length, however, his father was able to afford some slight assistance, and the son journeyed to London with the view of walking the hospitals and profiting by the medical lectures. He remained in the metropolis about eight or ten months; but his means were inadequate to an effectual participation in the advantages which such a residence ordinarily affords to the student of medicine; and he was compelled once more to return to Aldborough.

Crabbe now engaged himself as an assistant in the shop of a surgeon named Maskill. This man had an imperious temper, and Crabbe's situation was a most undesirable one. But he was content to submit for a while to ill-usage, for he felt the necessity of acquiring additional knowledge in his business. After a short time, Maskill removed from Aldborough, and Crabbe was encouraged to set up for himself in his native town. He was hardly qualified for his task, however, and his practice and emoluments were scanty enough.

All this time, he improved his opportunities of acquaintance with Miss Elmy, and the young couple were understood to be affianced. But poverty barred the nuptials, and a dispassionate view of the future seemed scarcely to promise a removal of the impediment.

Brooding over the profitless life he was leading in this secluded village, our poet at length formed the bold resolution of abandoning the medical profession, and pushing his fortune in the literary world of London. He was so poor, that he had not the means of defraying the expenses of the journey thither; and all his friends were as poor as himself. In this dilemma, he addressed a letter to Mr. Dudley North, asking the loan of a small sum. That gentleman kindly advanced him five pounds; and with this fund, Crabbe settled his affairs at Aldborough, and, embarking in a sloop at Slaughton, he sailed for the great city. He was at this time about 24 years of age.

Upon his arrival in the metropolis, he took economical lodgings, and applied himself diligently to transcribing and correcting the poetical pieces he had brought with him from the country. But he applied to the publishers in vain: none of them would hazard print and paper on behalf of the unknown author. Crabbe now was soon reduced to a situation of great embarrassment and distress. He made written applications to several eminent individuals, but none would aid him, until, in an auspicious moment, he determined to address the illustrious Edmund Burke. That gentleman immediately appointed an interview, and judged so favourably of the young poet's character and attainments, that he immediately became his friend, took him to dwell in his own family, introduced him to the highest literary society of London, and assisted him in the publication of his poems. "*The Library*" was issued in 1781; and its favourable reception was such as at once to establish the poetical reputation of the author. Even the fastidious Dr. Johnson condescended to admire and commend, and indeed had lent the aid of his efficient revisal to the manuscript of the poem.

Crabbe had long felt an inclination towards the clerical profession, and the powerful influence of his present friends soon enabled him to enter the Church as one of its ministers. He was admitted to deacon's orders by the Bishop of Norwich, and soon after left London to assume the duties of a curate at his native village of Aldborough.

Mr. Crabbe retained this post only for a few months. The untiring friendship of Mr. Burke obtained for him the more advantageous situation of domestic chaplain to the Duke of Rutland; and Mr. Crabbe took up his residence, of course, at Belvoir Castle.

In 1783, our author again ventured before the public, in his "*Village*," which met with the most decided success, and materially enhanced Mr. Crabbe's poetical reputation.

His altered prospects never in the least degree influenced his habits or demeanour;—these continued to be characterized by the same simplicity and equanimity which marked the penniless student, and the rejected candidate for publication.

It was now deemed expedient that Mr. Crabbe should have a university degree; and his name was accordingly entered on the boards of Trinity College, Cambridge. Soon after this, the Chancellor Thurlow bestowed upon him the small livings of Frome St. Quintin, and Evershot, in Dorsetshire; and Mr. Crabbe obtained, at the same time, from the Archbishop of Canterbury, the degree of LL. B.

When the Duke of Rutland went to Ireland as lord-lieutenant, Mr. Crabbe did not accompany him;—for the time had arrived when he could, without incurring the imputation of imprudence, offer his hand to the long-beloved Miss Elmy. The marriage took place in December 1783, and the wedded couple took possession of apartments in Belvoir Castle, which had been kindly tendered by the Duke, on his departure from England. But from various causes, it was found that a residence here was not desirable; and, before a year and a half had elapsed, Mr. Crabbe removed to the neighbouring parsonage of Stathern. He here spent four of the happiest years of his life, and in this period became the father of four children, two of whom only (George and John) grew to maturity.

In 1785, Mr. Crabbe again appeared as a poet, and published "*The Newspaper*," which received the same emphatic approval which had attended his prior efforts.

In October, 1787, the Duke of Rutland died, somewhat suddenly, in Dublin, and his widow, returning to Belvoir, was not forgetful of her husband's *protegé*. She procured from the Chancellor the exchange of the two inconsiderable livings held by Mr. Crabbe, for the more important ones of Muston in Leicestershire, and Allington in Lincolnshire. In February, 1789, he removed, with his family, to the parsonage of Muston.

His new residence was pleasant in many respects; and it was with much reluctance, after abiding here for three years, that he yielded to another change. The death of a relative of Mrs. Crabbe rendered necessary the services of her husband as executor; and he removed to Parham, in Suffolk—again placing himself near the scenes of his boyhood and early courtship. Here he undertook the curacies of Swefling and Great Glemham, and the course of his life varied but little from what it had been in Muston. He had resided four years at Parham, when he lost by death his third son, a child of about six years. His children had been seven, and they were now reduced to two. This deprivation was severely felt by the mother, and conjoined with other circumstances to cause a removal again. Mr. Crabbe now rented Great Glemham Hall, a pleasant house belonging to Mr. North, and lived in it four or five years with great comfort and satisfaction.—But another removal then becoming necessary on account of the sale of the estate, Mr. Crabbe hired a house in the neighbouring village of Rendham, wherein he remained until the year 1805, when he left Suffolk, and resumed his clerical station at Muston.

In this tranquil course of life, attending to the care of his flock, and to the instruction of his beloved family, Mr. Crabbe long concealed himself from the gaze of the world until the year 1807; when, after an absence of about twenty-two years, he at length produced a collection of "*Poems.*" ("The Parish Register," &c.) "Laudari a laudato viro" has ever been deemed a stamp of merit; and, such has been the invariable proof of Mr. Crabbe's excellence as a Poet, that he has ever been *distinguished* by the discerning few, as he will always be admired by the reading public.

The "*Poems*" were honoured with a perusal in manuscript by the present Lord Holland, and his late illustrious uncle; and may naturally be supposed to have derived considerable advantage from their critical *acumen.*

In addition to their intrinsic merit, they will be deemed, by kindred minds, to possess an additional value, when it is considered that they tended to cheer the death-bed of the highly-gifted Charles Fox. This collection has passed through several editions.

Three years afterwards (1810) he produced the Poem of the "*Borough;*" the scene of which is his native place: and in 1812 he published his *Tales.*

In 1813, Mr. Crabbe sustained the severe affliction of losing his wife; and soon after, having obtained the living of Trowbridge, in Wiltshire, he removed to that town. From this period, our author mixed much more in society, and especially in the gay and literary world of London, than during the lifetime of his wife. In the metropolis, he met on intimate terms with most of the eminent writers of the day, and seemed to form a connecting link between the era of Johnson, Burke, and Reynolds, and that of Scott, Byron, Moore, and Campbell.

In 1819, Mr. Murray published the "*Tales of the Hall*"—and gave for the manuscript of that work, and the copy-right of Mr. Crabbe's previous poems, the liberal sum of 3000*l.* This work was not less favourably received than its predecessors.

Whilst in London upon one of his visits, in 1821, our poet had the good fortune of meeting Sir Walter Scott, and accepted a pressing invitation to visit him in Scotland. Mr. Crabbe accordingly journeyed to the north for that purpose in the following year, and found Sir Walter in Edinburgh, attending upon George IV., who was then making his famous visit to Scotland. But, notwithstanding the pressure of multifarious business, the great novelist contrived to make Crabbe's sojourn in his house pleasant and gratifying in no ordinary degree.

In the year 1821, Mr. Crabbe had a severe attack of tic douloureux, and thenceforward he was subject to that complaint, which aided the natural decay attendant upon old age. But he continued in the performance of his clerical duties, and maintained his friendly and social relations, until within a few days of the termination of his existence. This event took place at Trowbridge, on the 7th of February, 1832.

It is not our intention to enter into an elaborate criticism of Mr. Crabbe's qualities as a poet.—We shall content ourselves with observing merely

—that the characteristics of his style are, originality of thought, force, precision, truth, depth, and pathos of description; clothed frequently in the happy diction and polished versification which we so much admire in Goldsmith.

It must not, however, be supposed, from this remark, that Mr. Crabbe is a copyist of any former author. He is a bard *sui generis;* he has formed himself upon no model, and is consequently unlike other writers. He is a poet who examines man as *he is,* there is, therefore, no *illusion* in his poetry.

He is, in fact, the *Portrait-Painter* of humble life—in all its variety and detail. His portraits are exact likenesses; and are equally to be praised for the correctness of the outline, and the propriety of the colouring. His descriptions are, not like those of Thomson, of imaginary, but of *real* nature. The delineations of his rustics are, consequently, different from those which we meet with in the Georgics of Virgil, or the Idylls of Gesner: but they are such as *may be seen* every day in the country. He sees with a keen, correct, and perhaps too microscopic an eye, and all his scenes of common life are portrayed with minuteness, but with a fidelity true to nature. He is naturally and deservedly a popular poet; since all his delineations come home closely to the "business and bosoms of men." He is certainly one of the most original and pathetic poets that England has, in modern times, produced; and is a bright star in that splendid constellation of British genius that has illumined and adorned the present age.

THE

POETICAL WORKS

OF

GEORGE CRABBE.

Poems.

Ipse per Ausonias Æneia carmina gentes
Qui sonat, ingenti qui nomine pulsat Olympum;
Mæoniumque senem Romano provocat ore:
Forsitan illius nemoris latuisset in umbra
Quod canit, et sterili tantum cantasset avena
Ignotus populi, si Mæcenate careret.
LUCAN. *Paneg. ad Pisones.*

TO

THE RIGHT HONOURABLE HENRY-RICHARD FOX, LORD HOLLAND,

Of Holland, in Lincolnshire; Lord Holland of Foxley; and Fellow of the Society of Antiquaries.

My Lord,

That the longest poem in this collection was honoured by the notice of your Lordship's right honourable and ever-valued relation, Mr. Fox; that it should be the last which engaged his attention, and that some parts of it were marked with his approbation; are circumstances productive of better hopes of ultimate success than I had dared to entertain before I was gratified with a knowledge of them: and the hope thus raised leads me to ask permission that I may dedicate this book to your Lordship, to whom that truly great and greatly-lamented personage was so nearly allied in family, so closely bound in affection, and in whose mind presides the same critical taste which he exerted to the delight of all who heard him. He doubtless united with his unequalled abilities a fund of good-nature; and this possibly led him to speak favourably of, and give satisfaction to writers, with whose productions he might not be entirely satisfied: nor must I allow myself to suppose his desire of obliging was withholden, when he honoured any effort of mine with his approbation: but, my Lord, as there was discrimination in the opinion he gave; as he did not veil indifference for insipid mediocrity of composition under any general expression of cool approval—I allow myself to draw a favourable conclusion from the verdict of one who had the superiority of intellect few would dispute, which he made manifest by a force of eloquence peculiar to himself; whose excellent judgment no one of his friends found cause to distrust, and whose acknowledged candour no enemy had the temerity to deny.

With such encouragement, I present my book to your Lordship: the Account of the *Life and Writings of Lopez de Vega* has taught me what I am to expect; I there perceive how your Lordship can write, and am there taught how you can judge of writers: my faults, however numerous, I know will none of them escape through inattention, nor will any merit be lost for want of discernment: my verses are before him who has written elegantly, who has judged with accuracy, and who has given unequivocal proof of abilities in a work of difficulty;—a translation of poetry, which few persons in this kingdom are able to read, and in the estimation of talents not hitherto justly appreciated. In this view, I cannot but feel some apprehension; but I know also, that your Lordship is apprised of the great difficulty of writing well; that you will make much allowance for failures, if not too frequently repeated; and, as you can accurately discern, so you will readily approve, all the better and more happy efforts of one, who places the highest value upon your Lordship's approbation, and who has the honour to be,

My Lord,
Your Lordship's most faithful
And obliged humble servant,
GEO. CRABBE.

PREFACE.

About twenty-five years since was published a poem called "The Library;" which, in no long time, was followed by two others, "The Village," and "The Newspaper:" these, with a few alterations and additions, are here reprinted; and are accompanied by a poem of greater length, and several shorter attempts, now, for the first time, before the public; whose reception of them creates in their author something more than common solicitude, because he conceives that, with the judgment to be formed of these latter productions, upon whatever may be found intrinsically meritorious or defective, there will be united an inquiry into the relative degree of praise or blame which they may be thought to deserve, when compared with the more early attempts of the same writer.

And certainly, were it the principal employment of a man's life to compose verses, it might seem reasonable to expect that he would continue to improve as long as he continued to live; though, even then, there is some doubt whether such improvement would follow, and perhaps proof might be adduced to show it would not: but when, to this "*idle trade*," is added some "*calling*," with superior claims upon his time and attention, his progress in the art of versification will probably be in proportion neither to the years he has lived, nor even to the attempts he has made.

While composing the first-published of these poems, the author was honoured with the notice, and assisted by the advice of the Right Honourable Edmund Burke: part of it was written in his presence, and the whole submitted to his judgment; receiving, in its progress, the benefit of his correction: I hope, therefore, to obtain pardon of the reader, if I eagerly seize the occasion, and, after so long a silence, endeavour to express a grateful sense of the benefits I have received from this gentleman, who was solicitous for my more essential interests, as well as benevolently anxious for my credit as a writer.

I will not enter upon the subject of his extraordinary abilities; it would be vanity, it would be weakness in me to believe that I could make them better known, or more admired than they now are: but of his private worth, of his wishes to do good, of his affability and condescension; his readiness to lend assistance when he knew it was wanted, and his delight to give praise where he thought it was deserved; of these I may write with some propriety. All know that his powers were vast, his acquirements various; and I take leave to add, that he applied them with unremitted attention to those objects which he believed tended to the honour and welfare of his country. But it may not be so generally understood that he was ever assiduous in the more private duties of a benevolent nature, that he delighted to give encouragement to any promise of ability, and assistance to any appearance of desert: to what purposes he employed his pen, and with what eloquence he spake in the senate, will be told by many, who yet may be ignorant of the solid instruction, as well as the fascinating pleasantry, found in his common conversation, amongst his friends, and his affectionate manners, amiable disposition, and zeal for their happiness, which he manifested in the hours of retirement with his family.

To this gentleman I was indebted for my knowledge of Sir Joshua Reynolds, who was as well known to his friends for his perpetual fund of good-humour and his unceasing wishes to oblige, as he was to the public for the extraordinary productions of his pencil and his pen. By him I was favoured with an introduction to Doctor Johnson, who honoured me with his notice, and assisted me, as Mr. Boswell has told, with remarks and emendations for a poem I was about to publish.* The Doctor had been often wearied by applications, and did not readily comply with requests for his opinion; not from any unwillingness to oblige, but from a painful contention in his mind, between a desire of giving pleasure and a determination to speak truth. No man can, I think, publish a work without some expectation of satisfying those who are to judge of its merit: but I can, with the utmost regard to veracity, speak my fears, as predominating over every pre-indulged thought of a more favourable nature, when I was told that a judge so discerning had consented to read and give his opinion of "The Village," the poem I had prepared for publication. The time of suspense was not long protracted; I was soon favoured with a few words from Sir Joshua, who observed,—"If I knew how cautious Doctor Johnson was in giving commendation, I should be well satisfied with the portion dealt to me in his letter."—Of that letter the following is a copy:

"Sir,—I have sent you back Mr. Crabbe's poem, which I read with great delight. It is original, vigorous, and elegant. The alterations which I have made, I do not require him to adopt; for my lines are, perhaps, not often better [than] his own: but he may take mine and his own together, and perhaps, between them, produce something better than either.—He is not to think his copy wantonly defaced: a wet sponge will wash all the red lines away, and leave the pages clean.—His Dedication† will be least liked: it were better to contract it into a short sprightly address.—I do not doubt of Mr. Crabbe's success.

"I am, Sir, your most humble servant,

"SAM. JOHNSON.

"*March* 4, 1783."

That I was fully satisfied, my readers will do me the justice to believe; and I hope they will pardon me, if there should appear to them any impropriety in publishing the favourable opinion expressed in a private letter: they will judge, and truly, that by so doing, I wish to bespeak their good opinion, but have no design of extorting their applause. I would not hazard an appearance so ostentatious to gratify my vanity, but I venture to do it in compliance with my fears.

* See the Life of S. Johnson, by Boswell, vol. iv, p. 185, octavo edition.

† Neither of these were adopted; the author had written, about that time, some verses to the memory of Lord Robert Manners, brother to the late Duke of Rutland; and these, by a junction, it is presumed not forced or unnatural, form the concluding part of "The Village."

After these was published "The Newspaper:" it had not the advantage of such previous criticism from any friends, nor perhaps so much of my own attention as I ought to have given to it; but the impression was disposed of, and I will not pay so little respect to the judgment of my readers as now to suppress what they then approved.

Since the publication of this poem more than twenty years have elapsed, and I am not without apprehension, lest so long a silence should be construed into a blamable neglect of my own interest, which those excellent friends were desirous of promoting: or what is yet worse, into a want of gratitude for their assistance; since it becomes me to suppose, they considered these first attempts as promises of better things, and their favours as stimulants to future exertion. And here, be the construction put upon my apparent negligence what it *may*, let me not suppress my testimony to the liberality of those who are looked up to, as patrons and encouragers of literary merit, or indeed of merit of any kind: their patronage has never been refused, I conceive, where it has been reasonably expected or modestly required; and it would be difficult, probably, to instance, in these times and in this country, any one who merited or was supposed to merit assistance, but who nevertheless languished in obscurity or necessity for the want of it; unless in those cases where it was prevented by the resolution of impatient pride, or wearied by the solicitations of determined profligacy. And, while the subject is before me, I am unwilling to pass silently over the debt of gratitude which I owe to the memory of two deceased noblemen. His Grace the late Duke of Rutland, and the Right Honourable the Lord Thurlow: sensible of the honour done me by their notice, and the benefits received from them, I trust this acknowledgment will be imputed to its only motive, a grateful sense of their favours.

Upon this subject I could dwell with much pleasure; but, to give a reason for that appearance of neglect, as it is more difficult, so, happily, it is less required. In truth, I have, for many years, intended a republication of these poems, as soon as I should be able to join with them such other of later date as might not deprive me of the little credit the former had obtained. Long indeed has this purpose been procrastinated: and if the duties of a profession, not before pressing upon me; if the claims of a situation, at that time untried; if diffidence of my own judgment, and the loss of my earliest friends, will not sufficiently account for my delay, I must rely upon the good-nature of my reader, that he will let them avail as far as he can, and find an additional apology in my fears of his censure.

These fears being so prevalent with me, I determined not to publish any thing more, unless I could first obtain the sanction of such an opinion as I might with some confidence rely upon. I looked for a friend who, having the discerning taste of Mr. Burke, and the critical sagacity of Doctor Johnson, would bestow upon my MS. the attention requisite to form his opinion, and would then favour me with the result of his observations: and it was my singular good fortune to gain such assistance; the opinion of a critic so qualified, and a friend so disposed to favour me. I had been honoured by an introduction to the Right Honourable Charles James Fox some years before, at the seat of Mr. Burke; and being again with him, I received a promise that he would peruse any work I might send to him previous to its publication, and would give me his opinion. At that time, I did not think myself sufficiently prepared; and when, afterwards, I had collected some poems for his inspection, I found my right honourable friend engaged by the affairs of a great empire, and struggling with the inveteracy of a fatal disease; at such time, upon such mind, ever disposed to oblige as that mind was, I could not obtrude the petty business of criticising verses: but he remembered the promise he had kindly given, and repeated an offer, which, though I had not presumed to expect, I was happy to receive. A copy of the poems, now first published, was immediately sent to him, and (as I have the information from Lord Holland, and his Lordship's permission to inform my readers) the poem which I have named "The Parish Register" was heard by Mr. Fox, and it excited interest enough, by some of its parts, to gain for me the benefit of his judgment upon the whole. Whatever he approved, the reader will readily believe, I have carefully retained; the parts he disliked are totally expunged, and others are substituted, which I hope resemble those, more conformable to the taste of so admirable a judge. Nor can I deny myself the melancholy satisfaction of adding, that this poem (and more especially the poem of Phœbe Dawson,* with some parts of the second book,) were the last compositions of their kind that engaged and amused the capacious, the candid, the benevolent mind of this great man.

The above information I owe to the favour of the Right Honourable Lord Holland; nor this only, but to his Lordship I am indebted for some excellent remarks upon the other parts of my MS. It was not indeed my good fortune then to know that my verses were in the hands of a nobleman who had given proof of his accurate judgment as a critic, and his elegance as a writer, by favouring the public with an easy and spirited translation of some interesting scenes of a dramatic poet, not often read in this kingdom. The Life of Lopez de Vega was then unknown to me; I had, in common with many English readers, heard of him, but could not judge whether his far-extended reputation was caused by the sublime efforts of a mighty genius, or the unequalled facility of a rapid composer aided by peculiar and fortunate circumstances. That any part of my MS. was honoured by the remarks of Lord Holland yields me a high degree of satisfaction, and his Lordship will perceive the use I have made of them; but I must feel some regret when I know to what small portion they were limited; and discerning, as I do, the taste and judgment bestowed upon the verses of Lopez de Vega, I must perceive how much my own needed the assistance afforded to one, who cannot be sensible of the benefit he has received.

But how much soever I lament the advantages

* See page 26.

lost, let me remember with gratitude the helps I have obtained. With a single exception, every poem in the ensuing collection has been submitted to the critical suggestion of a gentleman, upon whose skill and candour their author could rely. To publish by advice of friends has been severely ridiculed, and that too by a poet, who probably, without such advice, never made public any verses of his own: in fact, it may not be easily determined who acts with less discretion, the writer who is encouraged to publish his works, merely by the advice of friends whom he consulted, or he who, against advice, publishes from the sole encouragement of his own opinion. These are deceptions to be carefully avoided, and I was happy to escape the latter, by the friendly attentions of the Reverend Richard Turner, minister of Great Yarmouth. To this gentleman I am indebted more than I am able to describe, or than he is willing to allow, for the time he has bestowed upon the attempts I have made. He is, indeed, the kind of critic for whom every poet should devoutly wish, and the friend whom every man would be happy to acquire; he has taste to discern all that is meritorious, and sagacity to detect whatsoever should be discarded; he gives just the opinion an author's wisdom should covet, however his vanity might prompt him to reject it; what altogether to expunge and what to improve he has repeatedly taught me, and, could I have obeyed him in the latter direction, as I invariably have in the former, the public would have found this collection more worthy its attention, and I should have sought the opinion of the critic more void of apprehension.

But whatever I may hope or fear, whatever assistance I have had or have needed, it becomes me to leave my verses to the judgment of the reader, without any endeavour to point out their merit, or an apology for their defects: yet as, among the poetical attempts of one who has been for many years a priest, it may seem a want of respect for the legitimate objects of his study, that nothing occurs, unless it be incidentally, of the great subjects of religion; so it may appear a kind of ingratitude of a beneficed clergyman, that he has not employed his talent (be it estimated as it may) to some patriotic purpose; as in celebrating the unsubdued spirit of his countrymen in their glorious resistance of those enemies, who would have no peace throughout the world, except that which is dictated to the drooping spirit of suffering humanity by the triumphant insolence of military success.

Credit will be given to me, I hope, when I affirm that subjects so interesting have the due weight with me, which the sacred nature of the one, and the national importance of the other, must impress upon every mind not seduced into carelessness for religion by the lethargic influence of a perverted philosophy, nor into indifference for the cause of our country by hyperbolical or hypocritical professions of universal philanthropy: but, after many efforts to satisfy myself by various trials on these subjects, I declined all further attempt, from a conviction that I should not be able to give satisfaction to my readers. Poetry of a religious nature must indeed ever be clogged with almost insuperable difficulty; but there are doubtless to be found poets who are well qualified to celebrate the unanimous and heroic spirit of our countrymen, and to describe in appropriate colours some of those extraordinary scenes, which have been and are shifting in the face of Europe, with such dreadful celerity; and to such I relinquish the duty.

It remains for me to give the reader a brief view of those articles in the following collection, which for the first time solicit his attention.

In the "Parish Register," he will find an endeavour once more to describe village manners, not by adopting the notion of pastoral simplicity or assuming ideas of rustic barbarity, but by more natural views of the peasantry, considered as a mixed body of persons, sober or profligate, and hence, in a great measure, contented or miserable. To this more general description are added the various characters which occur in the three parts of a Register; Baptisms, Marriages, and Burials.

If the "Birth of Flattery" offer no moral, as an appendage to the fable, it is hoped that nothing of an immoral, nothing of improper tendency will be imputed to a piece of poetical playfulness; in fact, genuine praise, like all other species of truth, is known by its bearing full investigation: it is what the giver is happy that he can justly bestow, and the receiver conscious that he may boldly accept; but adulation must ever be afraid of inquiry, and must, in proportion to their degrees of moral sensibility,

> Be shame "to him that gives and him that takes."

The verses in page 49 want a title; nor does the motto, although it gave occasion to them, altogether express the sense of the writer, who meant to observe that some of our best acquisitions, and some of our nobler conquests, are rendered ineffectual, by the passing away of opportunity, and the changes made by time; an argument that such acquirements and moral habits are reserved for a state of being in which they have the uses here denied them.

In the story of "Sir Eustace Grey," an attempt is made to describe the wanderings of a mind, first irritated by the consequences of error and misfortune, and afterwards soothed by a species of enthusiastic conversion, still keeping him insane; a task very difficult, and, if the presumption of the attempt may find pardon, it will not be refused to the failure of the poet. It is said of our Shakspeare, respecting madness,

> In that circle none dare walk but he:—

yet be it granted to one, who dares not to pass the boundary fixed for common minds, at least to step near to the tremendous verge, and form some idea of the terrors that are stalking in the interdicted space.

When first I had written "Aaron, or the Gipsy," I had no unfavourable opinion of it; and had I been collecting my verses at that time for publication, I should certainly have included this tale. Nine years have since elapsed, and I continue to judge the same of it, thus literally obeying one of the directions given by the prudence of criticism to the eagerness of the poet: but how far I may have conformed to rules of more importance must be left to the less partial judgment of the readers.

The concluding poem, entitled "Woman!" was written at the time when the quotation from Mr. Ledyard was first made public: the expression has since become hackneyed; but the sentiment is congenial with our feelings, and though somewhat amplified in these verses, it is hoped they are not so far extended as to become tedious.

After this brief account of his subjects, the author leaves them to their fate, not presuming to make any remarks upon the kinds of versification he has chosen, or the merit of the execution: he has indeed brought forward the favourable opinion of his friends, and for that he earnestly hopes his motives will be rightly understood: it was a step of which he felt the advantage, while he foresaw the danger; he was aware of the benefit, if his readers would consider him as one who puts on a defensive armour against hasty and determined severity; but he feels also the hazard, lest they should suppose he looks upon himself to be guarded by his friends, and so secure in the defence, that he may defy the fair judgment of legal criticism. It will probably be said, "he has brought with him his testimonials to the bar of the public;" and he must admit the truth of the remark: but he begs leave to observe in reply, that, of those who bear testimonials of any kind, the greater numbers feel apprehension, and not security; they are indeed so far from the enjoyment of victory, or the exultation of triumph, that with all they can do for themselves, with all their friends have done for them, they are, like him, in dread of examination, and in fear of disappointment.

Muston, Leicestershire, September, 1807.

THE VILLAGE.

BOOK I.

The Subject proposed—Remarks upon Pastoral Poetry—A Tract of Country near the Coast described—An impoverished Borough—Smugglers and their Assistants—Rude Manners of the Inhabitants—Ruinous Effects of a high Tide—The Village Life more generally considered: Evils of it—The youthful Labourer—The old Man: his Soliloquy—The Parish Workhouse: its Inhabitants—The sick Poor: their Apothecary—the dying Pauper—The Village Priest.

The Village Life, and every care that reigns
O'er youthful peasants and declining swains;
What labour yields, and what, that labour past,
Age, in its hour of languor, finds at last;
What form the real picture of the poor,
Demand a song—the Muse can give no more.

Fled are those times, when, in harmonious strains,
The rustic poet praised his native plains:
No shepherds now, in smooth alternate verse,
Their country's beauty or their nymphs' rehearse;
Yet still for these we frame the tender strain,
Still in our lays fond Corydons complain,
And shepherds' boys their amorous pains reveal,
The only pains, alas! they never feel.

On Mincio's banks, in Cæsar's bounteous reign
If Tityrus found the Golden Age again,
Must sleepy bards the flattering dream prolong,
Mechanic echoes of the Mantuan song?
From Truth and Nature shall we widely stray,
Where Virgil, not where Fancy, leads the way?

Yes, thus the Muses sing of happy swains,
Because the Muses never knew their pains:
They boast their peasants' pipes; but peasants now
Resign their pipes, and plod behind the plough;
And few, amid the rural tribe, have time
To number syllables, and play with rhyme;
Save honest Duck, what son of verse could share
The poet's rapture, and the peasant's care?
Or the great labours of the field degrade,
With the new peril of a poorer trade?

From this chief cause these idle praises spring,
That themes so easy few forbear to sing;
For no deep thought the trifling subjects ask;
To sing of shepherds is an easy task:
The happy youth assumes the common strain,
A nymph his mistress, and himself a swain;
With no sad scenes he clouds his tuneful prayer,
But all, to look like her, is painted fair.

I grant indeed that fields and flocks have charms
For him that grazes or for him that farms;
But when amid such pleasing scenes I trace
The poor laborious natives of the place,
And see the mid-day sun, with fervid ray,
On their bare heads and dewy temples play;
While some, with feebler heads and fainter hearts,
Deplore their fortune, yet sustain their parts:
Then shall I dare these real ills to hide
In tinsel trappings of poetic pride?

No; cast by Fortune on a frowning coast,
Which neither groves nor happy valleys boast;
Where other cares than those the Muse relates,
And other shepherds dwell with other mates;
By such examples taught, I paint the cot,
As Truth will paint it, and as Bards will not:
Nor you, ye poor, of letter'd scorn complain,
To you the smoothest song is smooth in vain;
O'ercome by labour, and bow'd down by time,
Feel you the barren flattery of a rhyme?
Can poets soothe you, when you pine for bread,
By winding myrtles round your ruin'd shed?
Can their light tales your weighty griefs o'erpower,
Or glad with airy mirth the toilsome hour?

Lo! where the heath, with withering brake grown o'er,
Lends the light turf that warms the neighbouring poor;
From thence a length of burning sand appears,
Where the thin harvest waves its wither'd ears;
Rank weeds, that every art and care defy,
Reign o'er the land, and rob the blighted rye:
There thistles stretch their prickly arms afar,
And to the ragged infant threaten war;
There poppies nodding, mock the hope of toil;
There the blue bugloss paints the sterile soil;
Hardy and high, above the slender sheaf,
The slimy mallow waves her silky leaf;

O'er the young shoot the charlock throws a shade,
And clasping tares cling round the sickly blade;
With mingled tints the rocky coasts abound,
And a sad splendour vainly shines around.
So looks the nymph whom wretched arts adorn,
Betray'd by man, then left for man to scorn;
Whose cheek in vain assumes the mimic rose,
While her sad eyes the troubled breast disclose;
Whose outward splendour is but folly's dress,
Exposing most, when most it gilds distress.

Here joyless roam a wild amphibious race,
With sullen wo display'd in every face;
Who, far from civil arts and social fly,
And scowl at strangers with suspicious eye.

Here too the lawless merchant of the main
Draws from his plough th' intoxicated swain;
Want only claim'd the labour of the day,
But vice now steals his nightly rest away.

Where are the swains, who, daily labour done,
With rural games play'd down the setting sun;
Who struck with matchless force the bounding ball,
Or made the pond'rous quoit obliquely fall;
While some huge Ajax, terrible and strong,
Engaged some artful stripling of the throng,
And fell beneath him, foil'd, while far around
Hoarse triumph rose, and rocks return'd the sound?
Where now are these?—Beneath yon cliff they stand,
To show the freighted pinnace where to land;
To load the ready steed with guilty haste,
To fly in terror o'er the pathless waste,
Or, when detected, in their straggling course,
To foil their foes by cunning or by force;
Or, yielding part (which equal knaves demand),
To gain a lawless passport through the land.

Here, wand'ring long, amid these frowning fields,
I sought the simple life that Nature yields;
Rapine and Wrong and Fear usurp'd her place,
And a bold, artful, surly, savage race;
Who, only skill'd to take the finny tribe,
The yearly dinner, or septennial bribe,
Wait on the shore, and, as the waves run high,
On the tost vessel bend their eager eye,
Which to their coast directs its vent'rous way;
Theirs, or the ocean's, miserable prey.

As on their neighbouring beach yon swallows stand,
And wait for favouring winds to leave the land;
While still for flight the ready wing is spread:
So waited I the favouring hour, and fled;
Fled from these shores where guilt and famine reign,
And cried, Ah! hapless they who still remain;
Who still remain to hear the ocean roar,
Whose greedy waves devour the lessening shore;
Till some fierce tide, with more imperious sway,
Sweeps the low hut and all it holds away;
When the sad tenant weeps from door to door,
And begs a poor protection from the poor!

But these are scenes where Nature's niggard hand
Gave a spare portion to the famish'd land;
Hers is the fault, if here mankind complain
Of fruitless toil and labour spent in vain;
But yet in other scenes more fair in view,
Where Plenty smiles—alas! she smiles for few—
And those who taste not, yet behold her store,
Are as the slaves that dig the golden ore,
The wealth around them makes them doubly poor.

Or will you deem them amply paid in health,
Labour's fair child, that languishes with wealth?
Go then! and see them rising with the sun,
Through a long course of daily toil to run;
See them beneath the dog-star's raging heat,
When the knees tremble and the temples beat;
Behold them, leaning on their scythes, look o'er
The labour past, and toils to come explore;
See them alternate suns and showers engage,
And hoard up aches and anguish for their age;
Through fens and marshy moors their steps pursue,
When their warm pores imbibe the evening dew;
Then own that labour may as fatal be
To these thy slaves, as thine excess to thee.

Amid this tribe too oft a manly pride
Strives in strong toil the fainting heart to hide;
There may you see the youth of slender frame
Contend with weakness, weariness, and shame;
Yet, urged along, and proudly loth to yield,
He strives to join his fellows of the field.
Till long-contending nature droops at last,
Declining health rejects his poor repast,
His cheerless spouse the coming danger sees,
And mutual murmurs urge the slow disease.

Yet grant them health, 'tis not for us to tell,
Though the head droops not, that the heart is well,
Or will you praise that homely, healthy fare,
Plenteous and plain, that happy peasants share!
Oh! trifle not with wants you cannot feel,
Nor mock the misery of a stinted meal;
Homely, not wholesome, plain, not plenteous, such
As you who praise would never deign to touch.

Ye gentle souls, who dream of rural ease,
Whom the smooth stream and smoother sonnet please;
Go! if the peaceful cot your praises share,
Go look within, and ask if peace be there;
If peace be his—that drooping weary sire,
Or theirs, that offspring round their feeble fire;
Or hers, that matron pale, whose trembling hand
Turns on the wretched hearth th' expiring brand.

Nor yet can Time itself obtain for these
Life's latest comforts, due respect and ease;
For yonder see that hoary swain, whose age
Can with no cares except his own engage;
Who, propp'd on that rude staff, looks up to see
The bare arms broken from the withering tree,
On which, a boy, he climb'd the loftiest bough,
Then his first joy, but his sad emblem now.

He once was chief in all the rustic trade;
His steady hand the straightest furrow made;
Full many a prize he won, and still is proud
To find the triumphs of his youth allow'd;
A transient pleasure sparkles in his eyes,
He hears and smiles, then thinks again and sighs:
For now he journeys to his grave in pain;
The rich disdain him; nay, the poor disdain:
Alternate masters now their slave command,
Urge the weak efforts of his feeble hand,
And, when his age attempts its task in vain,
With ruthless taunts, of lazy poor complain.*

Oft may you see him, when he tends the sheep,
His winter-charge, beneath the hillock weep;

*A pauper who, being nearly past his labour, is employed by different masters for a length of time, proportioned to their occupations.

Oft hear him murmur to the winds that blow
O'er his white locks, and bury them in snow,
When, roused by rage and muttering in the morn,
He mends the broken hedge with icy thorn:—
"Why do I live, when I desire to be
At once from life and life's long labour free?
Like leaves in spring, the young are blown away,
Without the sorrows of a slow decay;
I, like yon wither'd leaf, remain behind,
Nipp'd by the frost, and shivering in the wind;
There it abides till younger buds come on,
As I, now all my fellow-swains are gone;
Then, from the rising generation thrust,
It falls, like me, unnoticed to the dust.
"These fruitful fields, these numerous flocks I see,
Are others' gain, but killing cares to me;
To me the children of my youth are lords,
Cool in their looks, but hasty in their words:
Wants of their own demand their care; and who
Feels his own want and succours others too?
A lonely, wretched man, in pain I go,
None need my help, and none relieve my wo;
Then let my bones beneath the turf be laid,
And men forget the wretch they would not aid."
Thus groan the old, till, by disease oppress'd,
They taste a final wo, and then they rest.
Theirs is yon house that holds the parish-poor,
Whose walls of mud scarce bear the broken door;
There, where the putrid vapours, flagging, play,
And the dull wheel hums doleful through the day;—
There children dwell who know no parents' care;
Parents, who know no children's love, dwell there!
Heart-broken matrons on their joyless bed,
Forsaken wives, and mothers never wed;
Dejected widows with unheeded tears,
And crippled age with more than childhood fears;
The lame, the blind, and, far the happiest they!
The moping idiot and the madman gay.
Here too the sick their final doom receive,
Here brought, amid the scenes of grief, to grieve,
Where the loud groans from some sad chamber flow,
Mix'd with the clamours of the crowd below;
Here, sorrowing, they each kindred sorrow scan,
And the cold charities of man to man:
Whose laws indeed for ruin'd age provide,
And strong compulsion plucks the scrap from pride;
But still that scrap is bought with many a sigh,
And pride embitters what it can't deny.
Say ye, oppress'd by some fantastic woes,
Some jarring nerve that baffles your repose;
Who press the downy couch, while slaves advance
With timid eye, to read the distant glance;
Who with sad prayers the weary doctor tease,
To name the nameless ever-new disease;
Who with mock patience dire complaints endure,
Which real pain and that alone can cure;
How would ye bear in real pain to lie,
Despised, neglected, left alone to die?
How would ye bear to draw your latest breath,
Where all that's wretched paves the way for death?
Such is that room which one rude beam divides,
And naked rafters form the sloping sides;
Where the vile bands that bind the thatch are seen,
And lath and mud are all that lie between;
Save one dull pane, that, coarsely patch'd, gives way
To the rude tempest, yet excludes the day:
Here, on a matted flock, with dust o'erspread,
The drooping wretch reclines his languid head;
For him no hand the cordial cup applies,
Or wipes the tear that stagnates in his eyes;
No friends with soft discourse his pain beguile,
Or promise hope till sickness wears a smile.
But soon a loud and hasty summons calls,
Shakes the thin roof, and echoes round the walls.
Anon, a figure enters, quaintly neat,
All pride and business, bustle and conceit;
With looks unalter'd by these scenes of wo,
With speed that, entering, speaks his haste to go,
He bids the gazing throng around him fly,
And carries fate and physic in his eye:
A potent quack, long versed in human ills,
Who first insults the victim whom he kills;
Whose murd'rous hand a drowsy Bench protect,
And whose most tender mercy is neglect.
Paid by the parish for attendance here,
He wears contempt upon his sapient sneer;
In haste he seeks the bed where Misery lies,
Impatience mark'd in his averted eyes;
And, some habitual queries hurried o'er,
Without reply, he rushes on the door:
His drooping patient, long inured to pain,
And long unheeded, knows remonstrance vain;
He ceases now the feeble help to crave
Of man, and silent sinks into the grave.
But ere his death some pious doubts arise,
Some simple fears, which "bold bad" men despise,
Fain would he ask the parish-priest to prove
His title certain to the joys above:
For this he sends the murmuring nurse, who calls
The holy stranger to these dismal walls:
And doth not he, the pious man, appear,
He, "passing rich with forty pounds a year?"
Ah! no; a shepherd of a different stock,
And far unlike him, feeds this little flock:
A jovial youth, who thinks his Sunday's task
As much as God or man can fairly ask;
The rest he gives to loves and labours light,
To fields the morning, and to feasts the night;
None better skill'd the noisy pack to guide,
To urge their chase, to cheer them or to chide;
A sportsman keen, he shoots through half the day,
And, skill'd at whist, devotes the night to play:
Then, while such honours bloom around his head,
Shall he sit sadly by the sick man's bed,
To raise the hope he feels not, or with zeal
To combat fears that e'en the pious feel?
Now once again the gloomy scene explore,
Less gloomy now; the bitter hour is o'er,
The man of many sorrows sighs no more.—
Up yonder hill, behold how sadly slow
The bier moves winding from the vale below;
There lie the happy dead, from trouble free,
And the glad parish pays the frugal fee:
No more, O Death! thy victim starts to hear
Churchwarden stern, or kingly overseer;
No more the farmer claims his humble bow,
Thou art his lord, the best of tyrants thou!
Now to the church behold the mourners come,
Sedately torpid, and devoutly dumb;
The village children now their games suspend,
To see the bier that bears their ancient friend
For he was one in all their idle sport,
And like a monarch ruled their little court;

The pliant bow he form'd, the flying ball,
The bat, the wicket, were his labours all;
Him now they follow to his grave, and stand
Silent and sad, and gazing, hand in hand;
While bending low, their eager eyes explore
The mingled relics of the parish poor:
The bell tolls late, the moping owl flies round,
Fear marks the flight and magnifies the sound;
The busy priest, detain'd by weightier care,
Defers his duty till the day of prayer;
And, waiting long, the crowd retire distress'd,
To think a poor man's bones should lie unbless'd.*

BOOK II.

There are found, amid the Evils of a laborious Life, some Views of Tranquillity and Happiness—The Repose and Pleasure of a Summer Sabbath: interrupted by intoxication and Dispute—Village Detraction—Complaints of the 'Squire—The Evening Riots—Justice—Reasons for this unpleasant View of Rustic Life: the Effect it should have upon the Lower Classes; and the Higher—These last have their peculiar Distresses: Exemplified in the Life and heroic Death of Lord Robert Manners—Concluding Address to His Grace the Duke of Rutland.

No longer truth, though shown in verse, disdain,
But own the Village Life a life of pain:
I too must yield, that oft amid these woes
Are gleams of transient mirth and hours of sweet repose,
Such as you find on yonder sportive Green,
The 'squire's tall gate and churchway-walk between;
Where loitering stray a little tribe of friends,
On a fair Sunday when the sermon ends:
Then rural beaux their best attire put on,
To win their nymphs, as other nymphs are won;
While those long wed go plain, and by degrees,
Like other husbands, quit their care to please.
Some of the sermon talk, a sober crowd,
And loudly praise, if it were preach'd aloud;
Some on the labours of the week look round,
Feel their own worth, and think their toil renown'd;
While some, whose hopes to no renown extend,
Are only pleased to find their labours end.
Thus, as their hours glide on, with pleasure fraught,
Their careful masters brood the painful thought;
Much in their mind they murmur and lament,
That one fair day should be so idly spent;
And think that Heaven deals hard, to tithe their store
And tax their time for preachers and the poor.

Yet still, ye humbler friends, enjoy your hour,
This is your portion, yet unclaim'd of power;
This is Heaven's gift to weary men oppress'd,
And seems the type of their expected rest:
But yours, alas! are joys that soon decay;
Frail joys, begun and ended with the day;
Or yet, while day permits those joys to reign,
The village vices drive them from the plain.
See the stout churl, in drunken fury great,
Strike the bare bosom of his teeming mate!
His naked vices, rude and unrefined,
Exert their open empire o'er the mind;
But can we less the senseless rage despise,
Because the savage acts without disguise?
Yet here disguise, the city's vice, is seen,
And Slander steals along and taints the Green:
At her approach domestic peace is gone,
Domestic broils at her approach come on;
She to the wife the husband's crime conveys,
She tells the husband when his consort strays;
Her busy tongue, through all the little state,
Diffuses doubt, suspicion, and debate;
Peace, tim'rous goddess! quits her old domain,
In sentiment and song content to reign.
Nor are the nymphs that breathe the rural air
So fair as Cynthia's, nor so chaste as fair:
These to the town afford each fresher face,
And the clown's trull receives the peer's embrace;
From whom, should chance again convey her down,
The peer's disease in turn attacks the clown.
Here too the 'squire, or 'squire-like farmer, talk,
How round their regions nightly pilferers walk;
How from their ponds the fish are borne, and all
The rip'ning treasures from their lofty wall;
How meaner rivals in their sports delight,
Just rich enough to claim a doubtful right;
Who take a license round their fields to stray,
A mongrel race! the poachers of the day.
And hark! the riots of the Green begin,
That sprang at first from yonder noisy inn;
What time the weekly pay was vanish'd all,
And the slow hostess scored the threat'ning wall;
What time they ask'd, their friendly feast to close
A final cup, and that will make them foes;
When blows ensue that break the arm of toil,
And rustic battle ends the boobies' broil.
Save when to yonder Hall they bend their way,
Where the grave justice ends the grievous fray;
He who recites, to keep the poor in awe,
The law's vast volume—for he knows the law:—
To him with anger or with shame repair
The injured peasant and deluded fair.
Lo! at his throne the silent nymph appears,
Frail by her shape, but modest in her tears;
And while she stands abash'd, with conscious eye,
Some favourite female of her judge glides by,
Who views with scornful glance the strumpet's fate,
And thanks the stars that made her keeper great;
Near her the swain, about to bear for life
One certain evil, doubts 'twixt war and wife;
But, while the falt'ring damsel takes her oath,
Consents to wed, and so secures them both.
Yet why, you ask, these humble crimes relate,
Why make the poor as guilty as the great?
To show the great, those mightier sons of pride,
How near in vice the lowest are allied:

---

* Some apology is due for the insertion of a circumstance by no means common: that it has been a subject for complaint in any place is a sufficient reason for its being reckoned among the evils which may happen to the poor, and which must happen to them exclusively; nevertheless, it is just to remark, that such neglect is very rare in any part of the kingdom, and in many parts is totally unknown.

Such are their natures and their passions such,
But these disguise too little, those too much:
So shall the man of power and pleasure see
In his own slave as vile a wretch as he;
In his luxurious lord the servant find
His own low pleasures and degenerate mind:
And each in all the kindred vices trace,
Of a poor, blind, bewilder'd, erring race;
Who, a short time in varied fortune past,
Die, and are equal in the dust at last.

And you, ye poor, who still lament your fate,
Forbear to envy those you call the great;
And know, amid these blessings they possess,
They are, like you, the victims of distress;
While sloth with many a pang torments her slave,
Fear waits on guilt, and danger shakes the brave.

Oh! if in life one noble chief appears,
Great in his name, while blooming in his years;
Born to enjoy whate'er delights mankind,
And yet to all you feel or fear resign'd;
Who gave up joys and hopes to you unknown,
For pains and dangers greater than your own:
If such there be, then let your murmurs cease,
Think, think of him, and take your lot in peace.

And such there was:—Oh! grief, that checks our pride,
Weeping we say there was,—for Manners died:
Beloved of Heaven, these humble lines forgive,
That sing of Thee,* and thus aspire to live.

As the tall oak, whose vigorous branches form
An ample shade, and brave the wildest storm,
High o'er the subject wood is seen to grow,
The guard and glory of the trees below;
Till on its head the fiery bolt descends,
And o'er the plain the shatter'd trunk extends;
Yet then it lies, all wondrous as before,
And still the glory, though the guard no more:

So THOU, when every virtue, every grace,
Rose in thy soul, or shone within thy face;
When, though the son of Granby, thou wert known
Less by thy father's glory than thine own;
When Honour loved and gave thee every charm,
Fire to thy eye and vigour to thy arm;
Then from our lofty hopes and longing eyes,
Fate and thy virtues call'd thee to the skies;
Yet still we wonder at thy tow'ring fame,
And losing thee, still dwell upon thy name.

Oh! ever honour'd, ever valued! say,
What verse can praise thee, or what work repay?
Yet verse (in all we can) thy worth repays,
Nor trusts the tardy zeal of future days;—
Honours for thee thy country shall prepare,
Thee in their hearts, the good, the brave shall bear;
To deeds like thine shall noblest chiefs aspire—
The Muse shall mourn thee, and the world admire.

In future times, when smit with Glory's charms,
The untried youth first quits a father's arms—
"Oh! be like him," the weeping sire shall say;
"Like Manners walk, who walk'd in Honour's way;
In danger foremost, yet in death sedate,
Oh! be like him in all things, but his fate!"

If for that fate such public tears be shed,
That Victory seems to die now THOU art dead,
How shall a friend his nearer hope resign,
That friend a brother, and whose soul was thine?
By what bold lines shall we his grief express,
Or by what soothing numbers make it less?

'T is not, I know, the chiming of a song,
Nor all the powers that to the Muse belong,
Words aptly cull'd, and meaning well express'd,
Can calm the sorrows of a wounded breast;
But Virtue, soother of the fiercest pains,
Shall heal that bosom, Rutland, where she reigns.

Yet hard the task to heal the bleeding heart,
To bid the still recurring thoughts depart,
Tame the fierce grief and stem the rising sigh,
And curb rebellious passion, with reply;
Calmly to dwell on all that pleased before,
And yet to know that all shall please no more:—
Oh! glorious labour of the soul, to save
Her captive powers, and bravely mourn the brave.

To such these thoughts will lasting comfort give—
Life is not measured by the time we live:
'T is not an even course of threescore years,
A life of narrow views and paltry fears,
Grey hairs and wrinkles, and the cares they bring,
That take from death the terrors or the sting;
But 't is the gen'rous spirit mounting high
Above the world, that native of the sky;
The noble spirit, that, in dangers brave,
Calmly looks on, or looks beyond the grave:—
Such Manners was, so he resign'd his breath,
If in a glorious, then a timely death.

Cease then that grief, and let those tears subside,
If Passion rule us, be that passion pride;
If Reason, Reason bids us strive to raise
Our fallen hearts, and be like him we praise;
Or if Affection still the soul subdue,
Bring all his virtues, all his worth in view,
And let Affection find its comfort too:
For how can Grief so deeply wound the heart,
When Admiration claims so large a part!

Grief is a foe—expel him then thy soul;
Let nobler thoughts the nearer views control!
Oh! make the age to come thy better care,
See other Rutlands, other Granbys there!
And, as thy thoughts through streaming ages glide,
See other heroes die as Manners died:
As from their fate, thy race shall nobler grow,
As trees shoot upwards that are pruned below·
Or as old Thames, borne down with decent pride,
Sees his young streams run warbling at his side;
Though some, by art cut off, no longer run,
And some are lost beneath the summer's sun—
Yet the pure stream moves on, and, as it moves,
Its power increases and its use improves;
While plenty round its spacious waves bestow,
Still it flows on, and shall forever flow.

---

* Lord Robert Manners, the youngest son of the Marquis of Granby and the Lady Frances Seymour, daughter of Charles Duke of Somerset, was born the 5th of February, 1758; and was placed with his brother, the late Duke of Rutland, at Eton school, where he acquired, and ever after retained, a considerable knowledge of the classical authors.

Lord Robert, after going through the duties of his profession on board different ships, was made captain of the Resolution, and commanded her in nine different actions, besides the last memorable one on the 2d of April, 1782, when, in breaking the French line-of-battle, he received the wounds which terminated his life, in the twenty-fourth year of his age.—*See the Annual Register, printed for Mr. Dodsley.*

THE PARISH REGISTER.

PART I.

BAPTISMS.

Tum porro puer (ut sævis projectus ab undis
Navita) nudus humi jacet infans, indigus omni
Vitali auxilio, ——
Vagituque locum lugubri complet, ut æquum est,
Cui tantum in vita restat transire malorum.
Lucret. *de Nat. Rerum,* lib. 5.

INTRODUCTION.

The Village Register considered as containing principally the Annals of the Poor—State of the Peasantry as meliorated by Frugality and Industry—The Cottage of an industrious Peasant; its Ornaments—Prints and Books—The Garden; its Satisfactions—The State of the Poor, when improvident and vicious—The Row or Street, and its Inhabitants—The Dwelling of one of these—A Public House—Garden and its Appendages—Gamesters; rustic Sharpers, etc. —Conclusion of the Introductory Part.

The Child of the Miller's Daughter, and Relation of her Misfortune—A frugal Couple: their Kind of Frugality—Plea of the Mother of a natural Child: her Churching—Large Family of Gerard Ablett: his Apprehensions: Comparison between his State and that of the wealthy Farmer his Master: his Consolation—An old Man's Anxiety for an Heir: the Jealousy of another on having many—Characters of the Grocer Dawkins and his friend: their different Kinds of Disappointment—Three Infants named—An Orphan Girl and Village Schoolmistress — Gardener's Child: Pedantry and Conceit of the Father: his Botanical Discourses: Method of fixing the Embryo-fruit of Cucumbers—Absurd Effects of Rustic Vanity: observed in the Names of their Children —Relation of the Vestry Debate on a Foundling; Sir Richard Monday—Children of various Inhabitants—The poor Farmer—Children of a Profligate: his Character and Fate—Conclusion.

THE year revolves, and I again explore
The simple annals of my parish poor;
What infant-members in my flock appear,
What pairs I bless'd in the departed year;
And who, of old or young, or nymphs or swains,
Are lost to life, its pleasures and its pains.

No Muse I ask, before my view to bring
The humble actions of the swains I sing.—
How pass'd the youthful, how the old their days;
Who sank in sloth, and who aspired to praise;
Their tempers, manners, morals, customs, arts,
What parts they had, and how they 'mployed their parts;
By what elated, soothed, seduced, depress'd,
Full well I know—these records give the rest.

Is there a place, save one the poet sees,
A land of love, of liberty, and ease;
Where labour wearies not, nor cares suppress
Th' eternal flow of rustic happiness;
Where no proud mansion frowns in awful state,
Or keeps the sunshine from the cottage-gate,
Where young and old, intent on pleasure, throng,
And half man's life is holiday and song?
Vain search for scenes like these! no view appears,
By sighs unruffled or unstain'd by tears;
Since vice the world subdued and waters drown'd,
Auburn and Eden can no more be found.

Hence good and evil mix'd, but man has skill
And power to part them, when he feels the will!
Toil, care, and patience bless th' abstemious few,
Fear, shame, and want the thoughtless herd pursue.

Behold the cot! where thrives th' industrious swain,
Source of his pride, his pleasure, and his gain;
Screen'd from the winter's wind the sun's last ray
Smiles on the window and prolongs the day;
Projecting thatch the woodbine's branches stop,
And turn their blossoms to the casement's top:
All need requires is in that cot contain'd,
And much that taste untaught and unrestrain'd
Surveys delighted; there she loves to trace,
In one gay picture, all the royal race;
Around the walls are heroes, lovers, kings;
The print that shows them and the verse that sings

Here the last Lewis on his throne is seen,
And there he stands imprison'd, and his queen;
To these the mother takes her child, and shows
What grateful duty to his God he owes;
Who gives to him a happy home, where he
Lives and enjoys his freedom with the free;
When kings and queens, dethroned, insulted, tried,
Are all these blessings of the poor denied.

There is King Charles, and all his Golden Rules,
Who proved Misfortune's was the best of schools:
And there his son, who, tried by years of pain,
Proved that misfortunes may be sent in vain.

The magic-mill that grinds the gran'nams young,
Close at the side of kind Godiva hung;
She, of her favourite place the pride and joy,
Of charms at once most lavish and most coy,
By wanton act, the purest fame could raise,
And give the boldest deed the chastest praise.

There stands the stoutest Ox in England fed;
There fights the boldest Jew, Whitechapel-bred;
And there Saint Monday's worthy votaries live,
In all the joys that ale and skittles give.

Now lo! in Egypt's coast that hostile fleet,
By nations dreaded and by Nelson beat;
And here shall soon another triumph come,
A deed of glory in a day of gloom;
Distressing glory! grievous boon of fate!
The proudest conquest, at the dearest rate.

On shelf of deal beside the cuckoo-clock,
Of cottage-reading rests the chosen stock;
Learning we lack, not books, but have a kind
For all our wants, a meat for every mind:
The tale for wonder and the joke for whim,
The half-sung sermon and the half-groan'd hymn.

No need of classing; each within its place,
The feeling finger in the dark can trace;
"First from the corner, furthest from the wall,"
Such all the rules, and they suffice for all.
Their pious works for Sunday's use are found;
Companions for that Bible newly bound;
That Bible, bought by sixpence weekly saved,
Has choicest prints by famous hands engraved;
Has choicest notes by many a famous head,
Such as to doubt have rustic readers led;
Have made them stop to reason *why?* and *how?*
And where they once agreed, to cavil now.
Oh! rather give me commentators plain,
Who with no deep researches vex the brain;
Who from the dark and doubtful love to run,
And hold the glimmering tapers to the sun;
Who simple truth with nine-fold reasons back,
And guard the point no enemies attack.
Bunyan's famed Pilgrim rests that shelf upon—
A genius rare but rude was honest John:
Not one who, early by the Muse beguiled,
Drank from her well the waters undefiled;
Not one who slowly gain'd the hill sublime,
Then often sipp'd and little at a time;
But one who dabbled in the sacred springs,
And drank them muddy, mix'd with baser things.
Here to interpret dreams, we read the rules,
Science our own! and never taught in schools;
In moles and specks we Fortune's gifts discern,
And Fate's fix'd will from nature's wand'rings learn.
Of Hermit Quarle we read, in island rare,
Far from mankind and seeming far from care;
Safe from all want and sound in every limb;
Yes! there was he, and there was care with him.
Unbound, and heap'd these valued works beside,
Lay humbler works the pedlar's pack supplied;
Yet these, long since, have all acquired a name:
The Wandering Jew has found his way to fame;
And fame, denied to many a labour'd song,
Crowns Thumb the Great, and Hickerthrift the Strong.
There too is he, by wizard-power upheld,
Jack, by whose arm the giant-brood were quell'd;
His shoes of swiftness on his feet he placed;
His coat of darkness on his loins he braced;
His sword of sharpness in his hand he took;
And off the head of doughty giants stroke:
Their glaring eyes beheld no mortal near;
No sound of feet alarm'd the drowsy ear;
No English blood their pagan sense could smell,
But heads dropp'd headlong, wondering why they fell.
These are the peasant's joy, when placed at ease,
Half his delighted offspring mount his knees.
To every cot the lord's indulgent mind
Has a small space for garden-ground assign'd;
Here—till return of morn dismiss'd the farm—
The careful peasant plies the sinewy arm,
Warm'd as he works, and casts his look around
On every foot of that improving ground:
It is his own he sees; his master's eye
Peers not about, some secret fault to spy;
Nor voice severe is there, nor censure known;—
Hope, profit, pleasure,—they are all his own.
Here grow the humble cives, and, hard by them,
The leek with crown globose and reddy stem;
High climb his pulse in many an even row,
Deep strike the ponderous roots in soil below;
And herbs of potent smell and pungent taste
Give a warm relish to the night's repast:
Apples and cherries grafted by his hand,
And cluster'd nuts for neighbouring market stand.
Nor thus concludes his labour; near the cot,
The reed-fence rises round some fav'rite spot;
Where rich carnations, pinks with purple eyes,
Proud hyacinths, the least some florist's prize,
Tulips tall-stemm'd and pounced auriculas rise.
Here on a Sunday-eve, when service ends,
Meet and rejoice a family of friends;
All speak aloud, are happy and are free,
And glad they seem, and gaily they agree.
What, though fastidious ears may shun the speech,
Where all are talkers and where none can teach;
Where still the welcome and the words are old,
And the same stories are for ever told?
Yet theirs is joy that, bursting from the heart,
Prompts the glad tongue these nothings to impart;
That forms these tones of gladness we despise,
That lifts their steps, that sparkles in their eyes;
That talks or laughs or runs or shouts or plays,
And speaks in all their looks and all their ways.
Fair scenes of peace! ye might detain us long,
But vice and misery now demand the song;
And turn our view from dwellings simply neat,
To this infected row, we term our street.
Here, in cabal, a disputatious crew
Each evening meet; the sot, the cheat, the shrew:
Riots are nightly heard:—the curse, the cries
Of beaten wife, perverse in her replies;
While shrieking children hold each threat'ning hand,
And sometimes life, and sometimes food demand:
Boys, in their first-stol'n rags, to swear begin,
And girls, who heed not dress, are skill'd in gin:
Snarers and smugglers here their gains divide;
Ensnaring females here their victims hide;
And here is one, the sibyl of the row,
Who knows all secrets, or affects to know.
Seeking their fate, to her the simple run,
To her the guilty, theirs awhile to shun;
Mistress of worthless arts, depraved in will,
Her care unbless'd and unrepaid her skill,
Slave to the tribe, to whose command she stoops,
And poorer than the poorest maid she dupes.
Between the road-way and the walls, offence
Invades all eyes and strikes on every sense:
There lie, obscene, at every open door,
Heaps from the hearth and sweepings from the floor;
And day by day the mingled masses grow
As sinks are disembogued and kennels flow.
There hungry dogs from hungry children steal,
There pigs and chickens quarrel for a meal;
There dropsied infants wail without redress,
And all is want and wo and wretchedness:
Yet should these boys, with bodies bronzed and bare,
High-swoln and hard, outlive that lack of care—
Forced on some farm, the unexerted strength,
Though loth to action, is compell'd at length,
When warm'd by health, as serpents in the spring
Aside their slough of indolence they fling.
Yet, ere they go, a greater evil comes—
See! crowded beds in those contiguous rooms,

Beds but ill parted, by a paltry screen
Of paper'd lath or curtain dropp'd between;
Daughters and sons to yon compartments creep,
And parents here beside their children sleep:
Ye who have power, these thoughtless people part,
Nor let the ear be first to taint the heart.
Come! search within, nor sight nor smell regard;
The true physician walks the foulest ward.
See! on the floor what frouzy patches rest!
What nauseous fragments on yon fractured chest!
What downy dust beneath yon window-seat!
And round these posts that serve this bed for feet;
This bed where all those tatter'd garments lie,
Worn by each sex, and now perforce thrown by!
See! as we gaze, an infant lifts its head,
Left by neglect and burrow'd in that bed;
The mother-gossip has the love suppress'd
An infant's cry once waken'd in her breast;
And daily prattles, as her round she takes,
(With strong resentment) of the want she makes.
Whence all these woes?—From want of virtuous will,
Of honest shame, of time-improving skill;
From want of care t' employ the vacant hour,
And want of ev'ry kind but want of power.

Here are no wheels for either wool or flax,
But packs of cards—made up of sundry packs;
Here is no clock, nor will they turn the glass,
And see how swift th' important moments pass;
Here are no books, but ballads on the wall,
Are some abusive, and indecent all;
Pistols are here, unpair'd; with nets and hooks,
Of every kind, for rivers, ponds, and brooks;
An ample flask, that nightly rovers fill
With recent poison from the Dutchman's still;
A box of tools, with wires of various size,
Frocks, wigs, and hats, for night or day disguise,
And bludgeons stout to gain or guard a prize.

To every house belongs a space of ground,
Of equal size, once fenced with paling round;
That paling now by slothful waste destroy'd,
Dead gorse and stumps of elder fill the void;
Save in the centre-spot, whose walls of clay
Hide sots and striplings at their drink or play:
Within, a board, beneath a tiled retreat,
Allures the bubble and maintains the cheat;
Where heavy ale in spots like varnish shows,
Where chalky tallies yet remain in rows;
Black pipes and broken jugs the seats defile,
The walls and windows, rhymes and reck'nings vile;
Prints of the meanest kind disgrace the door,
And cards, in curses torn, lie fragments on the floor.

Here his poor bird th' inhuman cocker brings,
Arms his hard heel, and clips his golden wings;
With spicy food th' impatient spirit feeds,
And shouts and curses as the battle bleeds.
Struck through the brain, deprived of both his eyes,
The vanquish'd bird must combat till he dies;
Must faintly peck at his victorious foe,
And reel and stagger at each feeble blow:
When fall'n, the savage grasps his dabbled plumes,
His blood-stain'd arms, for other deaths assumes;
And damns the craven-fowl, that lost his stake,
And only bled and perish'd for his sake.

Such are our peasants, those to whom we yield
Praise with relief, the fathers of the field;
And these who take from our reluctant hands
What Burn advises or the Bench commands.

Our farmers round, well pleased with constant gain,
Like other farmers, flourish and complain.—
These are our groups; our portraits next appear,
And close our exhibition for the year.

With evil omen we that year begin:
A Child of Shame,—stern Justice adds, of Sin,
Is first recorded;—I would hide the deed,
But vain the wish; I sigh and I proceed:
And could I well th' instructive truth convey,
'T would warn the giddy and awake the gay.

Of all the nymphs who gave our village grace,
The Miller's daughter had the fairest face;
Proud was the Miller; money was his pride;
He rode to market, as our farmers ride,
And 't was his boast, inspired by spirits there,
His favourite Lucy should be rich as fair;
But she must meek and still obedient prove,
And not presume, without his leave, to love.

A youthful Sailor heard him;—"Ha!" quoth he
"This Miller's maiden is a prize for me;
Her charms I love, his riches I desire,
And all his threats but fan the kindling fire;
My ebbing purse no more the foe shall fill,
But Love's kind act and Lucy at the mill."

Thus thought the youth, and soon the chase began
Stretch'd all his sail, nor thought of pause or plan
His trusty staff in his bold hand he took,
Like him and like his frigate, heart of oak;
Fresh were his features, his attire was new;
Clean was his linen, and his jacket blue:
Of finest jean, his trowsers, tight and trim,
Brush'd the large buckle at the silver rim.

He soon arrived, he traced the village-green,
There saw the maid, and was with pleasure seen:
Then talk'd of love, till Lucy's yielding heart
Confess'd 't was painful, though 't was right to part

"For ah! my father has a haughty soul;
Whom best he loves, he loves but to control;
Me to some churl in bargain he 'll consign,
And make some tyrant of the parish mine:
Cold is his heart, and he with looks severe
Has often forced but never shed the tear;
Save, when my mother died, some drops express'd
A kind of sorrow for a wife at rest:—
To me a master's stern regard is shown,
I 'm like his steed, prized highly as his own;
Stroked but corrected, threaten'd when supplied,
His slave and boast, his victim and his pride."

"Cheer up, my lass; I 'll to thy father go;
The Miller cannot be the Sailor's foe;
Both live by Heaven's free gale, that plays aloud
In the stretch'd canvas and the piping shroud;
The rush of winds, the flapping sails above,
And rattling planks within, are sounds *we* love;
Calms are our dread; when tempests plough the deep,
We take a reef, and to the rocking sleep."

"Ha!" quoth the Miller, moved at speech so rash,
"Art thou like me? then where thy notes and cash?
Away to Wapping, and a wife command,
With all thy wealth, a guinea, in thine hand;

There with thy messmates quaff the muddy cheer,
And leave my Lucy for thy betters here."
"Revenge! revenge!" the angry lover cried,
Then sought the nymph, and "Be thou now my bride."
Bride had she been, but they no priest could move
To bind in law, the couple bound by love.
What sought these lovers then by day, by night?
But stolen moments of disturb'd delight;
Soft trembling tumults, terrors dearly prized,
Transports that pain'd, and joys that agonized:
Till the fond damsel, pleased with lad so trim,
Awed by her parent, and enticed by him,
Her lovely form from savage power to save,
Gave—not her hand—but ALL she could, she gave.
Then came the day of shame, the grievous night,
The varying look, the wandering appetite:
The joy assumed, while sorrow dimm'd the eyes,
The forced sad smiles that follow'd sudden sighs;
And every art, long used, but used in vain,
To hide thy progress, Nature, and thy pain.
Too eager caution shows some danger's near:
The bully's bluster proves the coward's fear;
His sober step the drunkard vainly tries,
And nymphs expose the failings they disguise.
First, whispering gossips were in parties seen;
Then louder Scandal walk'd the village-green;
Next babbling Folly told the growing ill,
And busy Malice dropp'd it at the mill.
"Go! to thy curse and mine," the Father said,
"Strife and confusion stalk around thy bed;
Want and a wailing brat thy portion be,
Plague to thy fondness, as thy fault to me;—
Where skulks the villain?"——
—"On the ocean wide
My William seeks a portion for his bride."—
"Vain be his search! but, till the traitor come,
The higgler's cottage be thy future home;
There with his ancient shrew and Care abide,
And hide thy head,—thy shame thou canst not hide."

Day after day was pass'd in pains and grief;
Week follow'd week,—and still was no relief:
Her boy was born—no lads nor lasses came
To grace the rite or give the child a name;
Nor grave conceited nurse, of office proud,
Bore the young Christian roaring through the crowd:
In a small chamber was my office done,
Where blinks through paper'd panes the setting sun;
Where noisy sparrows, perch'd on penthouse near,
Chirp tuneless joy, and mock the frequent tear;
Bats on their webby wings in darkness move,
And feebly shriek their melancholy love.

No sailor came; the months in terror fled!
Then news arrived—He fought, and he was DEAD!

At the lone cottage Lucy lives, and still
Walks for her weekly pittance to the mill;
A mean seraglio there her father keeps,
Whose mirth insults her, as she stands and weeps;
And sees the plenty, while compell'd to stay,
Her father's pride, become his harlot's prey.
Throughout the lanes she glides, at evening's close,
And softly lulls her infant to repose;
Then sits and gazes, but with viewless look,
As gilds the moon the rippling of the brook;
And sings her vespers, but in voice so low,
She hears their murmurs as the waters flow:
And she too murmurs, and begins to find
The solemn wanderings of a wounded mind:
Visions of terror, views of woe succeed,
The mind's impatience to the body's need;
By turns to that, by turns to this a prey,
She knows what reason yields, and dreads what madness may.

Next with their boy, a decent couple came,
And call'd him Robert, 't was his father's name;
Three girls preceded, all by time endear'd,
And future births were neither hoped nor fear'd:
Bless'd in each other, but to no excess;
Health, quiet, comfort, form'd their happiness;
Love all made up of torture and delight,
Was but mere madness in this couple's sight:
Susan could think, though not without a sigh,
If she were gone, who should her place supply;
And Robert, half in earnest, half in jest,
Talk of her spouse when he should be at rest:
Yet strange would either think it to be told,
Their love was cooling or their hearts were cold.
Few were their acres,—but, with these content,
They were, each pay-day, ready with their rent:
And few their wishes—what their farm denied,
The neighbouring town, at trifling cost, supplied.
If at the draper's window Susan cast
A longing look, as with her goods she pass'd,
And with the produce of her wheel and churn,
Bought her a Sunday-robe on her return;
True to her maxim, she would take no rest,
Till care repaid that portion to the chest:
Or if, when loitering at the Whitsun-fair,
Her Robert spent some idle shillings there;
Up at the barn, before the break of day,
He made his labour for the indulgence pay:
Thus both—that waste itself might work in vain—
Wrought double tides, and all was well again.

Yet, though so prudent, there were times of joy
(The day they wed, the christening of the boy,)
When to the wealthier farmers there was shown
Welcome unfeign'd, and plenty like their own;
For Susan served the great, and had some pride
Among our topmost people to preside:
Yet in that plenty, in that welcome free,
There was the guiding nice frugality
That in the festal as the frugal day,
Has, in a different mode, a sovereign sway;
As tides the same attractive influence know,
In the least ebb, and in their proudest flow;
The wise frugality that does not give
A life to saving, but that saves to live;
Sparing, not pinching, mindful though not mean,
O'er all presiding, yet in nothing seen.

Recorded next a babe of love I trace!
Of many loves, the mother's fresh disgrace.—

"Again, thou harlot! could not all thy pain,
All my reproof, thy wanton thoughts restrain?"
"Alas! your reverence, wanton thoughts, I grant,
Were once my motive, now the thoughts of want
Women, like me, as ducks in a decoy,
Swim down a stream, and seem to swim in joy,
Your sex pursues us, and our own disdain;
Return is dreadful, and escape is vain.

Would men forsake us, and would women strive
To help the fall'n, their virtue might revive."

For rite of churching soon she made her way,
In dread of scandal, should she miss the day :—
Two matrons came ! with them she humbly knelt,
Their action copied and their comforts felt,
From that great pain and peril to be free,
Though still in peril of that pain to be ;
Alas ! what numbers, like this amorous dame,
Are quick to censure, but are dead to shame !

Twin-infants then appear ; a girl, a boy,
The o'erflowing cup of Gerard Ablett's joy :
One had I named in every year that pass'd
Since Gerard wed ! and twins behold at last !
Well pleased, the bridegroom smiled to hear—" A vine
Fruitful and spreading round the walls be thine,
And branch-like be thine offspring !"—Gerard then
Look'd joyful love, and softly said, " Amen."
Now of that vine he'd have no more increase,
Those playful branches now disturb his peace :
Them he beholds around his table spread,
But finds, the more the branch, the less the bread ;
And while they run his humble walls about,
They keep the sunshine of good humour out.

Cease, man, to grieve ! thy master's lot survey,
Whom wife and children, thou and thine obey ;
A farmer proud, beyond a farmer's pride,
Of all around the envy or the guide ;
Who trots to market on a steed so fine,
That when I meet him, I'm ashamed of mine;
Whose board is high up-heap'd with generous fare,
Which five stout sons and three tall daughters share :
Cease, man, to grieve, and listen to his care.

A few years fled, and all thy boys shall be
Lords of a cot, and labourers like thee :
Thy girls unportion'd neighbouring youths shall lead
Brides from my church, and henceforth thou art freed :
But then thy master shall of cares complain,
Care after care, a long connected train ;
His sons for farms shall ask a large supply,
For farmer's sons each gentle miss shall sigh ;
Thy mistress, reasoning well of life's decay,
Shall ask a chaise, and hardly brook delay ;
The smart young cornet who, with so much grace,
Rode in the ranks and betted at the race,
While the vex'd parent rails at deed so rash,
Shall d—n his luck, and stretch his hand for cash.
Sad troubles, Gerard ! now pertain to thee,
When thy rich master seems from trouble free ;
But 't is one fate at different times assign'd,
And thou shalt lose the cares that he must find.

" Ah !" quoth our village Grocer, rich and old,
" Would I might one such cause for care behold !"
To whom his Friend, " Mine greater bliss would be,
Would Heaven take those my spouse assigns to me."

Aged were both, that Dawkins, Ditchem this,
Who much of marriage thought, and much amiss ;
Both would delay, the one, till—riches gain'd,
The son he wish'd might be to honour train'd;
His Friend—lest fierce intruding heirs should come,
To waste his hoard and vex his quiet home.

Dawkins, a dealer once, on burthen'd back
Bore his whole substance in a pedlar's pack ;
To dames discreet, the duties yet unpaid,
His stores of lace and hyson he convey'd :
When thus enrich'd, he chose at home to stop,
And fleece his neighbours in a new-built shop ;
Then woo'd a spinster blithe, and hoped, when wed,
For love's fair favours and a fruitful bed.

Not so his Friend :—on widow fair and staid
He fix'd his eye, but he was much afraid ;
Yet woo'd ; while she his hair of silver hue
Demurely noticed, and her eye withdrew :
Doubtful he paused—" Ah ! were I sure," he cried,
" No craving children would my gains divide ;
Fair as she is, I would my widow take,
And live more largely for my partner's sake."

With such their views some thoughtful years they pass'd,
And hoping, dreading, they were bound at last.
And what their fate ? Observe them as they go,
Comparing fear with fear, and woe with woe.
" Humphrey !" said Dawkins, " envy in my breast
Sickens to see thee in thy children bless'd ;
They are thy joys, while I go grieving home
To a sad spouse, and our eternal gloom :
We look despondency ; no infant near,
To bless the eye or win the parent's ear ;
Our sudden heats and quarrels to allay,
And soothe the petty sufferings of the day :
Alike our want, yet both the want reprove ;
Where are, I cry, those pledges of our love ?
When she, like Jacob's wife, makes fierce reply,
Yet fond—Oh ! give me children, or I die :
And I return—still childless doom'd to live,
Like the vex'd patriarch—Are they mine to give ?
Ah ! much I envy thee thy boys who ride
On poplar branch, and canter at thy side ;
And girls, whose cheeks thy chin's fierce fondness know,
And with fresh beauty at the contact glow."

" Oh ! simple friend," said Ditchem, " wouldst thou gain
A father's pleasure by a husband's pain ?
Alas ! what pleasure—when some vig'rous boy
Should swell thy pride, some rosy girl thy joy,
Is it to doubt who grafted this sweet flower,
Or whence arose that spirit and that power ?

" Four years I've wed ; not one has pass'd in vain :
Behold the fifth ! behold a babe again !
My wife's gay friends th' unwelcome imp admire,
And fill the room with gratulation dire :
While I in silence sate, revolving all
That influence ancient men, or that befall ;
A gay pert guest—Heaven knows his business—came ;
A glorious boy, he cried, and what the name ?
Angry I growl'd,—' My spirit cease to tease,
Name it yourselves,—Cain, Judas, if you please ;
His father's give him—should you that explore
The devil's or yours :'—I said, and sought the door
My tender partner not a word or sigh
Gives to my wrath, nor to my speech reply ;
But takes her comforts, triumphs in my pain
And looks undaunted for a birth again."

Heirs thus denied afflict the pining heart,
And thus afforded, jealous pangs impart ;
Let, therefore, none avoid, and none demand
These arrows number'd for the giant's hand.

Then with their infants three, the parents came,
And each assign'd—'t was all they had—a name;
Names of no mark or price; of them not one
Shall court our view on the sepulchral stone,
Or stop the clerk, the engraven scrolls to spell,
Or keep the sexton from the sermon bell.

An orphan-girl succeeds: ere she was born
Her father died, her mother on that morn:
The pious mistress of the school sustains
Her parents' part, nor their affection feigns,
But pitying feels: with due respect and joy,
I trace the matron at her loved employ;
What time the striplings, wearied e'en with play,
Part at the closing of the summer's day,
And each by different path returns the well-known way—
Then I beheld her at the cottage-door,
Frugal of light;—her Bible led before,
When on her double duty she proceeds,
Of time as frugal—knitting as she reads:
Her idle neighbours, who approach to tell
Some trifling tale, her serious looks compel
To hear reluctant,—while the lads who pass,
In pure respect, walk silent on the grass:
Then sinks the day, but not to rest she goes
Till solemn prayers the daily duties close.

But I digress, and lo! an infant train
Appear, and call me to my task again.

"Why Lonicera wilt thou name thy child?"
I ask'd the Gardener's wife, in accents mild:
"We have a right," replied the sturdy dame,—
And Lonicera was the infant's name.
If next a son shall yield our Gardener joy,
Then Hyacinthus shall be that fair boy;
And if a girl, they will at length agree,
That Belladona that fair maid shall be.

High-sounding words our worthy Gardener gets,
And at his clubs to wondering swains repeats;
He then of Rhus and Rhododendron speaks,
And Allium calls his onions and his leeks;
Nor weeds are now, for whence arose the weed,
Scarce plants, fair herbs, and curious flowers proceed;
Where Cuckoo-pints and Dandelions sprung,
(Gross names had they our plainer sires among,)
There Arums, there Leontodons we view,
And Artemisia grows, where Wormwood grew.

But though no weed exists his garden round,
From Rumex strong our Gardener frees his ground,
Takes soft Senicio from the yielding land,
And grasps the arm'd Urtica in his hand.

Not Darwin's self had more delight to sing
Of floral courtship, in th' awaken'd Spring,
Than Peter Pratt, who simpering loves to tell
How rise the Stamens, as the Pistils swell;
How bend and curl the moist-top to the spouse,
And give and take the vegetable vows;
How those esteem'd of old but tips and chives,
Are tender husbands and obedient wives:
Who live and love within the sacred bower,—
That bridal bed, the vulgar term a flower.

Hear Peter proudly, to some humble friend,
A wondrous secret, in his science, lend:—
"Would you advance the nuptial hour, and bring
The fruit of Autumn with the flowers of Spring;
View that light frame where Cucumis lies spread,
And trace the husbands in their golden bed,
Three powder'd Anthers;—then no more delay,
But to the Stigma's tip their dust convey;
Then by thyself, from prying glance secure,
Twirl the full tip and make your purpose sure;
A long-abiding race the deed shall pay,
Nor one unbless'd abortion pine away.'

T' admire their friend's discourse our swains agree,
And call it science and philosophy.

'Tis good, 'tis pleasant, through th' advancing yea
To see unnumber'd growing forms appear;
What leafy-life from Earth's broad bosom rise!
What insect myriads seek the summer skies!
What scaly tribes in every streamlet move!
What plumy people sing in every grove!
All with the year awaked to life, delight, and love.
Then names are good; for how, without their aid,
Is knowledge, gain'd by man, to man convey'd?
But from that source shall all our pleasures flow?
Shall all our knowledge be those names to know?
Then he, with memory bless'd, shall bear away,
The palm from Grew, and Middleton, and Ray:
No! let us rather seek, in grove and field,
What food for wonder, what for use they yield;
Some just remark from Nature's people bring,
And some new source of homage for her King.

Pride lives with all: strange names our rustics give
To helpless infants, that their own may live;
Pleased to be known, they'll some attention claim,
And find some by-way to the house of fame.

The straightest furrow lifts the ploughman's art,
The hat he gain'd has warmth for head and heart;
The bowl that beats the greater number down
Of tottering nine-pins, gives to fame the clown;
Or, foil'd in these, he opes his ample jaws,
And lets a frog leap down to gain applause;
Or grins for hours, or tipples for a week,
Or challenges a well-pinch'd pig to squeak:
Some idle deed, some child's preposterous name,
Shall make him known, and give his folly fame.

To name an infant meet our village-sires,
Assembled all, as such event requires;
Frequent and full the rural sages sate,
And speakers many urged the long debate,—
Some harden'd knaves, who roved the country round,
Had left a babe within the parish bound,--
First, of the fact they question'd—"Was it true?"
The child was brought—"What then remain'd to do?
Was't dead or living?" This was fairly proved,—
'T was pinch'd, it roar'd, and every doubt removed.
Then by what name th' unwelcome guest to call
Was long a question, and it posed them all;
For he who lent it to a babe unknown,
Censorious men might take it for his own.
They look'd about, they gravely spoke to all,
And not one Richard answer'd to the call.
Next they inquired the day, when, passing by,
Th' unlucky peasant heard the stranger's cry:
This known,—how food and raiment they might give,
Was next debated—for the rogue would live,

At last, with all their words and work content,
Back to their homes the prudent vestry went,
And Richard Monday to the workhouse sent.
There was he pinch'd and pitied, thump'd and fed,
And duly took his beatings and his bread;
Patient in all control, in all abuse,
He found contempt and kicking have their use:
Sad, silent, supple; bending to the blow,
A slave of slaves, the lowest of the low;
His pliant soul gave way to all things base,
He knew no shame, he dreaded no disgrace.
It seem'd, so well his passions he suppress'd,
No feeling stirr'd his ever torpid breast;
Him might the meanest pauper bruise and cheat,
He was a footstool for the beggar's feet;
His were the legs that ran at all commands;
They used on all occasions Richard's hands:
His very soul was not his own; he stole
As others order'd, and without a dole;
In all disputes, on either part he lied,
And freely pledged his oath on either side;
In all rebellions Richard join'd the rest,
In all detections Richard first confess'd:
Yet, though disgraced, he watch'd his time so well,
He rose in favour, when in fame he fell;
Base was his usage, vile his whole employ,
And all despised and fed the pliant boy.
At length, "'t is time he should abroad be sent,"
Was whisper'd near him,—and abroad he went;
One morn they call'd him, Richard answer'd not;
They deem'd him hanging, and in time forgot,—
Yet miss'd him long, as each throughout the clan,
Found he "had better spared a better man."

Now Richard's talents for the world were fit,
He'd no small cunning, and had some small wit;
Had that calm look which seem'd to all assent,
And that complacent speech which nothing meant;
He'd but one care, and that he strove to hide,
How best for Richard Monday to provide.
Steel, through opposing plates, the magnet draws,
And steely atoms culls from dust and straws;
And thus our hero, to his interest true,
Gold through all bars and from each trifle drew;
But still more surely round the world to go,
This fortune's child had neither friend nor foe.

Long lost to us, at last our man we trace,—
Sir Richard Monday died at Monday-place:
His lady's worth, his daughter's we peruse,
And find his grandsons all as rich as Jews:
He gave reforming charities a sum,
And bought the blessings of the blind and dumb;
Bequeathed to missions money from the stocks,
And Bibles issued from his private box;
But to his native place severely just,
He left a pittance bound in rigid trust;—
Two paltry pounds, on every quarter's-day,
(At church produced) for forty loaves should pay;
A stinted gift that to the parish shows
He kept in mind their bounty and their blows!

To farmers three, the year has given a son,
Finch on the Moor, and French, and Middleton.
Twice in this year a female Giles I see,
A Spalding once, and once a Barnaby;—
A humble man is he, and when they meet,
Our farmers find him on a distant seat;
There for their wit he serves a constant theme,—
"They praise his dairy, they extol his team,
They ask the price of each unrivall'd steed,
And whence his sheep, that admirable breed?
His thriving arts they beg he would explain,
And where he puts the money he must gain.
They have their daughters, but they fear their friend
Would think his sons too much would condescend;
They have their sons who would their fortunes try,
But fear his daughters will their suit deny."
So runs the joke, while James, with sigh profound,
And face of care, looks moveless on the ground:
His cares, his sighs, provoke the insult more,
And point the jest—for Barnaby is poor.

Last in my list, five untaught lads appear;
Their father dead, compassion sent them here,—
For still that rustic infidel denied
To have their names with solemn rite applied:
His, a lone house, by Deadman's Dyke-way stood
And his, a nightly haunt, in Lonely-wood:
Each village inn has heard the ruffian boast,
That he believed "in neither God nor ghost;
That, when the sod upon the sinner press'd,
He, like the saint, had everlasting rest;
That never priest believed his doctrines true,
But would, for profit, own himself a Jew,
Or worship wood and stone, as honest heathen do;
That fools alone on future worlds rely,
And all who die for faith, deserve to die."

These maxims,—part th' attorney's clerk profess'd,
His own transcendent genius found the rest.
Our pious matrons heard, and much amazed,
Gazed on the man, and trembled as they gazed;
And now his face explored, and now his feet,
Man's dreaded foe in this bad man to meet:
But him our drunkards as their champion raised,
Their bishop call'd, and as their hero praised;
Though most, when sober, and the rest, when sick,
Had little question whence his bishopric.

But he, triumphant spirit! all things dared,
He poach'd the wood, and on the warren snared;
'T was his, at cards, each novice to trepan,
And call the wants of rogues the rights of man;
Wild as the winds, he let his offspring rove,
And deem'd the marriage-bond the bane of love.

What age and sickness, for a man so bold,
Had done, we know not;—none beheld him old:
By night, as business urged, he sought the wood,—
The ditch was deep,—the rain had caused a flood,—
The foot-bridge fail'd,—he plunged beneath the deep,
And slept, if truth were his, th' eternal sleep.

These have we named; on life's rough sea they sail,
With many a prosperous, many an adverse gale!
Where passion soon, like powerful winds, will rage,
And prudence wearied, with their strength engage;
Then each, in aid, shall some companion ask,
For help or comfort in the tedious task;
And what that help—what joys from union flow,
What good or ill, we next prepare to show;
And row, meantime, our weary bark ashore,
As Spenser his—but not with Spenser's oar.*

* Allusions of this kind are to be found in the Fairy Queen. See the end of the first book, and other places.

PART II.

MARRIAGES.

Nubere si qua voles, quamvis properabitis ambo,
Differ; habent parvæ commoda magna moræ.
Ovid. *Fast.* lib. iii.

Previous consideration necessary: yet not too long Delay—Imprudent Marriage of old Kirk and his Servant—Comparison between an ancient and youthful Partner to a young man—Prudence of Donald the Gardener—Parish Wedding: the compelled Bridegroom: Day of Marriage, how spent—Relation of the accomplishments of Phœbe Dawson, a rustic Beauty: her Lover: his Courtship: their Marriage—Misery of Precipitation—The wealthy Couple: Reluctance in the Husband; why?—Unusually fair Signatures in the Register: the common kind—Seduction of Lucy Collins by Footman Daniel: her rustic Lover: her Return to Him—An ancient Couple: Comparisons on the Occasion—More pleasant View of Village Matrimony: Farmers celebrating the Day of Marriage: their Wives—Reuben and Rachel, a happy Pair: an Example of prudent delay—Reflections on their State who were not so prudent, and its Improvement towards the Termination of Life: an old Man so circumstanced—Attempt to seduce a Village Beauty: Persuasion and Reply; the Event.

Disposed to wed, e'en while you hasten, stay;
There's great advantage in a small delay:
Thus Ovid sang, and much the wise approve
This prudent maxim of the priest of Love:
If poor, delay for future want prepares,
And eases humble life of half its cares;
If rich, delay shall brace the thoughtful mind,
T' endure the ills that e'en the happiest find:
Delay shall knowledge yield on either part,
And show the value of the vanquish'd heart;
The humours, passions, merits, failings prove,
And gently raise the veil that's worn by Love;
Love, that impatient guide!—too proud to think
Of vulgar wants, of clothing, meat, and drink,
Urges our amorous swains their joys to seize,
And then, at rags and hunger frighten'd, flees:—
Yet not too long in cold debate remain;
Till age refrain not—but if old, refrain.

By no such rule would Gaffer Kirk be tried;
First in the year he led a blooming bride,
And stood a wither'd elder at her side.
Oh! Nathan! Nathan! at thy years trepann'd,
To take a wanton harlot by the hand!
Thou, who wert used so tartly to express
Thy sense of matrimonial happiness,
Till every youth, whose banns at church were read,
Strove not to meet, or meeting, hung his head;
And every lass forbore at thee to look,
A sly old fish, too cunning for the hook;—
And now at sixty, that pert dame to see,
Of all thy savings mistress, and of thee;
Now will the lads, rememb'ring insults past,
Cry, "What, the wise one in the trap at last!"

Fie! Nathan! fie! to let an artful jade
The close recesses of thine heart invade;
What grievous pangs! what suffering she'll impart,
And fill with anguish that rebellious heart;
For thou wilt strive incessantly, in vain,
By threatening speech, thy freedom to regain:
But she for conquest married, nor will prove
A dupe to thee, thine anger, or thy love;
Clamorous her tongue will be;—of either sex
She'll gather friends around thee, and perplex
Thy doubtful soul:—thy money she will waste,
In the vain rambling of a vulgar taste;
And will be happy to exert her power,
In every eye, in thine, at every hour.

Then wilt thou bluster—"No! I will not rest,
And see consumed each shilling of my chest:"
Thou wilt be valiant,—"When thy cousins call,
I will abuse and shut my door on all:"
Thou wilt be cruel!—"What the law allows,
That be thy portion, my ungrateful spouse!
Nor other shillings shalt thou then receive,
And when I die"—"What! may I this believe?
Are these true tender tears? and does my Kitty grieve?
Ah! crafty vixen, thine old man has fears
But weep no more! I'm melted by thy tears,
Spare but my money; thou shalt rule ME still,
And see thy cousins—there! I burn the will."—

Thus, with example sad, our year began,
A wanton vixen and a weary man;
"But had this tale in other guise been told,"
Young let the lover be, the lady old,
And that disparity of years shall prove
No bane of peace, although some bar to love:
'T is not the worst, our nuptial ties among,
That joins the ancient bride and bridegroom young;—
Young wives, like changing winds, their power display,
By shifting points and varying day by day;
Now zephyrs mild, now whirlwinds in their force,
They sometimes speed, but often thwart our course;
And much experienced should that pilot be,
Who sails with them on life's tempestuous sea.
But like a trade-wind is the ancient dame,
Mild to your wish, and every day the same;
Steady as time, no sudden squalls you fear,
But set full sail, and with assurance steer;
Till every danger in your way be pass'd,
And then she gently, mildly breathes her last
Rich you arrive, in port awhile remain,
And for a second venture sail again.

For this, blithe Donald southward made his way,
And left the lasses on the banks of Tay;
Him to a neighbouring garden fortune sent,
Whom we beheld, aspiringly content:
Patient and mild, he sought the dame to please
Who ruled the kitchen and who bore the keys.
Fair Lucy first, the laundry's grace and pride,
With smiles and gracious looks, her fortune tried,
But all in vain she praised his "pawky eyne,"
Where never fondness was for Lucy seen:
Him the mild Susan, boast of dairies, loved,
And found him civil, cautious, and unmoved:

From many a fragrant simple, Catharine's skill
Drew oil and essence from the boiling still;
But not her warmth, nor all her winning ways,
From his cool phlegm could Donald's spirit raise;
Of beauty heedless, with the merry mute,
To Mistress Dobson he preferr'd his suit;
There proved his service, there address'd his vows,
And saw her mistress,—friend,—protectress,—spouse;
A butler now, he thanks his powerful bride,
And, like her keys, keeps constant at her side.

Next at our altar stood a luckless pair,
Brought by strong passions and a warrant there;
By long rent cloak, hung loosely, strove the bride,
From ev'ry eye, what all perceived to hide.
While the boy-bridegroom, shuffling in his pace,
Now hid awhile and then exposed his face;
As shame alternately with anger strove,
The brain confused with muddy ale to move:
In haste and stammering he perform'd his part,
And look'd the rage that rankled in his heart;
(So will each lover inly curse his fate,
Too soon made happy, and made wise too late:)
I saw his features take a savage gloom,
And deeply threaten for the days to come.
Low spake the lass, and lisp'd and minced the while,
Look'd on the lad, and faintly tried to smile;
With soften'd speech and humbled tone she strove
To stir the embers of departed love:
While he, a tyrant, frowning walk'd before,
Felt the poor purse, and sought the public door,
She sadly following in submission went,
And saw the final shilling foully spent;
Then to her father's hut the pair withdrew,
And bade to love and comfort long adieu!
Ah! fly temptation, youth, refrain! refrain!
I preach for ever; but I preach in vain!

Two summers since, I saw, at Lammas Fair,
The sweetest flower that ever blossom'd there,
When Phœbe Dawson gaily cross'd the green,
In haste to see and happy to be seen:
Her air, her manners, all who saw, admired;
Courteous though coy, and gentle though retired;
The joy of youth and health her eyes display'd,
And ease of heart her every look convey'd;
A native skill her simple robes express'd,
As with untutor'd elegance she dress'd:
The lads around admired so fair a sight,
And Phœbe felt, and felt she gave, delight.
Admirers soon of every age she gain'd,
Her beauty won them and her worth retain'd;
Envy itself could no contempt display,
They wish'd her well, whom yet they wish'd away.
Correct in thought, she judged a servant's place
Preserved a rustic beauty from disgrace;
But yet on Sunday-eve, in freedom's hour,
With secret joy she felt that beauty's power,
When some proud bliss upon the heart would steal,
That, poor or rich, a beauty still must feel.—

At length, the youth, ordain'd to move her breast,
Before the swains with bolder spirit press'd;
With looks less timid made his passion known,
And pleased by manners most unlike her own;
Loud though in love, and confident though young;
Fierce in his air, and voluble of tongue;
By trade a tailor, though, in scorn of trade,
He served the 'Squire, and brush'd the coat he made:
Yet now, would Phœbe her consent afford,
Her slave alone, again he'd mount the board;
With her should years of growing love be spent,
And growing wealth:—she sigh'd and look'd consent.

Now, through the lane, up hill, and 'cross the green,
(Seen by but few, and blushing to be seen—
Dejected, thoughtful, anxious, and afraid,)
Led by the lover, walk'd the silent maid:
Slow through the meadows roved they, many a mile
Toy'd by each bank and trifled at each stile;
Where, as he painted every blissful view,
And highly colour'd what he strongly drew,
The pensive damsel, prone to tender fears,
Dimm'd the false prospect with prophetic tears.—
Thus pass'd th' allotted hours, till lingering late,
The lover loiter'd at the master's gate;
There he pronounced adieu!—and yet would stay
Till chidden—soothed—entreated—forced away;
He would of coldness, though indulged, complain,
And oft retire, and oft return again;
When, if his teasing vex'd her gentle mind,
The grief assumed, compell'd her to be kind!
For he would proof of plighted kindness crave,
That she resented first, and then forgave,
And to his grief and penance yielded more
Than his presumption had required before.—
Ah! fly temptation, youth; refrain! refrain!
Each yielding maid and each presuming swain!

Lo! now with red rent cloak and bonnet black,
And torn green gown loose hanging at her back,
One who an infant in her arms sustains,
And seems in patience striving with her pains;
Pinch'd are her looks, as one who pines for bread,
Whose cares are growing, and whose hopes are fled;
Pale her parch'd lips, her heavy eyes sunk low,
And tears unnoticed from their channels flow;
Serene her manner, till some sudden pain
Frets the meek soul, and then she's calm again;—
Her broken pitcher to the pool she takes,
And every step with cautious terror makes;
For not alone that infant in her arms,
But nearer cause, her anxious soul alarms.
With water burthen'd, then she picks her way,
Slowly and cautious, in the clinging clay;
Till, in mid-green, she trusts a place unsound,
And deeply plunges in th' adhesive ground:
Thence, but with pain, her slender foot she takes,
While hope the mind as strength the frame forsakes;
For when so full the cup of sorrow grows,
Add but a drop, it instantly o'erflows.
And now her path but not her peace she gains,
Safe from her task, but shivering with her pains;
Her home she reaches, open leaves the door,
And placing first her infant on the floor,
She bares her bosom to the wind, and sits,
And sobbing struggles with the rising fits:
In vain, they come, she feels th' inflating grief,
That shuts the swelling bosom from relief;
That speaks in feeble cries a soul distress'd,
Or the sad laugh that cannot be repress'd.
The neighbour-matron leaves her wheel, and flies
With all the aid her poverty supplies;

Unfee'd, the calls of nature she obeys,
Not led by profit, nor allured by praise;
And waiting long, till these contentions cease,
She speaks of comfort, and departs in peace.

Friend of distress! the mourner feels thy aid,
She cannot pay thee, but thou wilt be paid.

But who this child of weakness, want, and care?
'T is Phœbe Dawson, pride of Lammas Fair;
Who took her lover for his sparkling eyes,
Expressions warm, and love-inspiring lies:
Compassion first assail'd her gentle heart,
For all his suffering, all his bosom's smart:
"And then his prayers! they would a savage move,
And win the coldest of the sex to love:"—
But ah! too soon his looks success declared,
Too late her loss the marriage-rite repair'd;
The faithless flatterer then his vows forgot,
A captious tyrant or a noisy sot:
If present, railing, till he saw her pain'd;
If absent, spending what their labours gain'd;
Till that fair form in want and sickness pined,
And hope and comfort fled that gentle mind.
Then fly temptation, youth; resist, refrain!
Nor let me preach for ever and in vain!

Next came a well-dress'd pair, who left their coach,
And made, in long procession, slow approach:
For this gay bride had many a female friend,
And youths were there, this favour'd youth t'attend:
Silent, nor wanting due respect, the crowd
Stood humbly round, and gratulation bow'd;
But not that silent crowd, in wonder fix'd,
Not numerous friends, who praise and envy mix'd,
Nor nymphs attending near to swell the pride
Of one more fair, the ever-smiling bride;
Nor that gay bride, adorn'd with every grace,
Nor love nor joy triumphant in her face,
Could from the youth's, sad signs of sorrow chase:
Why didst thou grieve? wealth, pleasure, freedom, thine;
Vex'd it thy soul, that freedom to resign?
Spake Scandal truth? "Thou didst not then intend
So soon to bring thy wooing to an end?"
Or, was it, as our prating rustics say,
To end as soon, but in a different way?
'T is told thy Phyllis is a skilful dame,
Who play'd uninjured with the dangerous flame:
That, while, like Lovelace, thou thy coat display'd,
And hid the snare for her affection laid,
Thee, with her net, she found the means to catch,
And, at the amorous see-saw, won the match:*
Yet others tell, the Captain fix'd thy doubt,
He'd call thee brother, or he'd call thee out:—
But rest the motive—all retreat too late,
Joy like thy bride's should on thy brow have sate;
The deed had then appear'd thine own intent,
A glorious day, by gracious fortune sent,
In each revolving year to be in triumph spent.
Then in few weeks that cloudy brow had been
Without a wonder or a whisper seen;
And none had been so weak as to inquire,
"Why pouts my Lady?" or "why frowns the 'Squire?"

How fair these names, how much unlike they look
To all the blurr'd subscriptions in my book:
The bridegroom's letters stand in row above,
Tapering yet stout, like pine-trees in his grove;
While free and fine the bride's appear below,
As light and slender as her jasmines grow.
Mark now in what confusion, stoop or stand,
The crooked scrawls of many a clownish hand;
Now out, now in, they droop, they fall, they rise,
Like raw recruits drawn forth for exercise;
Ere yet reform'd and modell'd by the drill,
The free-born legs stand striding as they will.

Much have I tried to guide the fist along,
But still the blunderers placed their blottings wrong:
Behold these marks uncouth! how strange that men
Who guide the plough, should fail to guide the pen!
For half a mile, the furrows even lie;
For half an inch the letters stand awry;—
Our peasants, strong and sturdy in the field,
Cannot these arms of idle students wield:
Like them, in feudal days, their valiant lords
Resign'd the pen and grasp'd their conqu'ring swords;
They to robed clerks and poor dependent men
Left the light duties of the peaceful pen;
Nor to their ladies wrote, but sought to prove,
By deeds of death, their hearts were fill'd with love.

But yet, small arts have charms for female eyes;
Our rustic nymphs the beau and scholar prize;
Unletter'd swains and ploughmen coarse they slight,
For those who dress, and amorous scrolls indite.

For Lucy Collins happier days had been,
Had Footman Daniel scorn'd his native green;
Or when he came an idle coxcomb down,
Had he his love reserved for lass in town;
To Stephen Hill she then had pledged her truth,—
A sturdy, sober, kind, unpolish'd youth;
But from the day, that fatal day she spied
The pride of Daniel, Daniel was her pride.
In all concerns was Stephen just and true;
But coarse his doublet was and patch'd in view,
And felt his stockings were, and blacker than his shoe;
While Daniel's linen all was fine and fair,—
His master wore it, and he deign'd to wear:
(To wear his livery, some respect might prove;
To wear his linen, must be sign of love:)
Blue was his coat, unsoil'd by spot or stain;
His hose were silk, his shoes of Spanish-grain;
A silver knot his breadth of shoulder bore;
A diamond buckle blazed his breast before—
Diamond he swore it was! and show'd it as he swore;
Rings on his fingers shone; his milk-white hand
Could pick-tooth case and box for snuff command:
And thus, with clouded cane, a fop complete,
He stalk'd, the jest and glory of the street.
Join'd with these powers, he could so sweetly sing,
Talk with such toss, and saunter with such swing;
Laugh with such glee, and trifle with such art,
That Lucy's promise fail'd to shield her heart.
Stephen, meantime, to ease his amorous cares,
Fix'd his full mind upon his farm's affairs;
Two pigs, a cow, and wethers half a score,
Increased his stock, and still he look'd for more

---

* Clarissa, vol. vii. Lovelace's Letter.

He, for his acres few, so duly paid,
That yet more acres to his lot were laid;
Till our chaste nymphs no longer felt disdain,
And prudent matrons praised the frugal swain;
Who thriving well, through many a fruitful year,
Now clothed himself anew, and acted overseer.

Just then poor Lucy, from her friend in town,
Fled in pure fear, and came a beggar down;
Trembling, at Stephen's door she knock'd for bread,—
Was chidden first, next pitied, and then fed;
Then sat at Stephen's board, then shared in Stephen's bed:
All hope of marriage lost in her disgrace,
He mourns a flame revived, and she a love of lace.

Now to be wed a well-match'd couple came;
Twice had old Lodge been tied, and twice the dame;
Tottering they came and toying, (odious scene!)
And fond and simple, as they 'd always been.
Children from wedlock we by laws restrain;
Why not prevent them, when they 're such again?
Why not forbid the doting souls, to prove
Th' indecent fondling of preposterous love?
In spite of prudence, uncontroll'd by shame,
The amorous senior woos the toothless dame,
Relating idly, at the closing eve,
The youthful follies he disdains to leave;
Till youthful follies wake a transient fire,
When arm in arm they totter and retire.

So a fond pair of solemn birds, all day,
Blink in their seat, and doze the hours away;
Then by the moon awaken'd, forth they move,
And fright the songsters with their cheerless love.

So two sear trees, dry, stunted, and unsound,
Each other catch, when dropping to the ground;
Entwine their wither'd arms 'gainst wind and weather,
And shake their leafless heads and drop together.

So two cold limbs, touch'd by Galvani's wire,
Move with new life, and feel awaken'd fire;
Quivering awhile, their flaccid forms remain,
Then turn to cold torpidity again.

"But ever frowns your Hymen? man and maid,
Are all repenting, suffering, or betray'd?"
Forbid it, Love! we have our couples here
Who hail the day in each revolving year:
These are with us, as in the world around;
They are not frequent, but they may be found.

Our farmers too, what though they fail to prove,
In Hymen's bonds, the tenderest slaves of love,
(Nor, like those pairs whom sentiment unites,
Feel they the fervour of the mind's delights;)
Yet coarsely kind and comfortably gay,
They heap the board and hail the happy day:
And though the bride, now freed from school, admits,
Of pride implanted there, some transient fits;
Yet soon she casts her girlish flights aside,
And in substantial blessings rests her pride.
No more she moves in measured steps, no more
Runs, with bewilder'd ear, her music o'er;
No more recites her French the hinds among,
But chides her maidens in her mother-tongue;
Her tambour-frame she leaves and diet spare,
Plain work and plenty with her house to share;
Till, all her varnish lost, in few short years,
In all her worth, the farmer's wife appears.

Yet not the ancient kind; nor she who gave
Her soul to gain—a mistress and a slave:
Who not to sleep allow'd the needful time;
To whom repose was loss, and sport a crime;
Who, in her meanest room (and all were mean),
A noisy drudge, from morn till night was seen;—
But she, the daughter, boasts a decent room,
Adorn'd with carpet, form'd in Wilton's loom;
Fair prints along the paper'd wall are spread;
There, Werter sees the sportive children fed,
And Charlotte, here, bewails her lover dead.

'Tis here, assembled, while in space apart
Their husbands, drinking, warm the opening heart,
Our neighbouring dames, on festal days, unite
With tongues more fluent and with hearts as light;
Theirs is that art, which English wives alone
Profess—a boast and privilege their own;
An art it is, where each at once attends
To all, and claims attention from her friends,
When they engage the tongue, the eye, the ear,
Reply when list'ning, and when speaking hear:
The ready converse knows no dull delays,
"But double are the pains, and double be the praise."*

Yet not to those alone who bear command
Heaven gives a heart to hail the marriage band;
Among their servants, we the pairs can show,
Who much to love and more to prudence owe:
Reuben and Rachel, though as fond as doves,
Were yet discreet and cautious in their loves;
Nor would attend to Cupid's wild commands,
Till cool reflection bade them join their hands:
When both were poor, they thought it argued ill
Of hasty love to make them poorer still;
Year after year, with savings long laid by,
They bought the future dwelling's full supply;
Her frugal fancy cull'd the smaller ware,
The weightier purchase ask'd her Reuben's care;
Together then their last year's gain they threw,
And lo! an auction'd bed, with curtains neat and new.
Thus both, as prudence counsell'd, wisely stay'd,
And cheerful then the calls of Love obey'd:
What if, when Rachel gave her hand, 't was one
Embrown'd by Winter's ice and Summer's sun?
What if, in Reuben's hair, the female eye
Usurping grey among the black could spy?
What if, in both, life's bloomy flush was lost,
And their full autumn felt the mellowing frost?
Yet time, who blow'd the rose of youth away,
Had left the vigorous stem without decay;
Like those tall elms, in Farmer Frankford's ground,
They 'll grow no more,—but all their growth is sound;
By time confirm'd and rooted in the land,
The storms they 've stood still promise they shall stand.

These are the happier pairs, their life has rest,
Their hopes are strong, their humble portion bless'd;
While those more rash to hasty marriage led,
Lament th' impatience which now stints their bread:

* Spenser

When such their union, years their cares increase,
Their love grows colder, and their pleasures cease;
In health just fed, in sickness just relieved;
By hardships harass'd and by children grieved;
In petty quarrels and in peevish strife,
The once fond couple waste the spring of life:
But when to age mature those children grown,
Find hopes and homes and hardships of their own,
The harass'd couple feel their lingering woes
Receding slowly, till they find repose.
Complaints and murmurs then are laid aside,
(By reason these subdued, and those by pride;)
And, taught by care, the patient man and wife
Agree to share the bitter-sweet of life;
(Life that has sorrow much and sorrow's cure,
Where they who most enjoy shall much endure:)
Their rest, their labours, duties, sufferings, prayers,
Compose the soul, and fit it for its cares;
Their graves before them and their griefs behind,
Have each a med'cine for the rustic mind;
Nor has he care to whom his wealth shall go,
Or who shall labour with his spade and hoe;
But as he lends the strength that yet remains,
And some dead neighbour on his bier sustains,
(One with whom oft he whirl'd the bounding flail,
Toss'd the broad quoit, or took th' inspiring ale,)
"For me," (he meditates,) "shall soon be done
This friendly duty, when my race be run;
'T was first in trouble as in error pass'd,
Dark clouds and stormy cares whole years o'ercast,
But calm my setting day, and sunshine smiles at last:
My vices punish'd and my follies spent,
Not loth to die, but yet to live content,
I rest:"—then casting on the grave his eye,
His friend compels a tear, and his own griefs a sigh.

Last on my list appears a match of love,
And one of virtue;—happy may it prove!—
Sir Edward Archer is an amorous knight,
And maidens chaste and lovely shun his sight;
His bailiff's daughter suited much his taste,
For Fanny Price was lovely and was chaste;
To her the Knight with gentle looks drew near,
And timid voice assumed, to banish fear:—

"Hope of my life, dear sovereign of my breast,
Which, since I knew thee, knows not joy nor rest;
Know, thou art all that my delighted eyes,
My fondest thoughts, my proudest wishes prize;
And is that bosom—(what on earth so fair!)
To cradle some coarse peasant's sprawling heir?
To be that pillow which some surly swain
May treat with scorn and agonize with pain?
Art thou, sweet maid, a ploughman's wants to share,
To dread his insult, to support his care;
To hear his follies, his contempt to prove,
And (oh! the torment!) to endure his love;
Till want and deep regret those charms destroy,
That time would spare, if time were pass'd in joy?
With him, in varied pains, from morn till night,
Your hours shall pass; yourself a ruffian's right;
Your softest bed shall be the knotted wool;
Your purest drink the waters of the pool;
Your sweetest food will but your life sustain,
And your best pleasure be a rest from pain;
While, through each year, as health and strength abate,
You'll weep your woes and wonder at your fate;
And cry, 'Behold,' as life's last cares come on,
'My burthens growing when my strength is gone.'

"Now turn with me, and all the young desire,
That taste can form, that fancy can require;
All that excites enjoyment, or procures
Wealth, health, respect, delight, and love, are yours.
Sparkling, in cups of gold, your wines shall flow,
Grace that fair hand, in that dear bosom glow;
Fruits of each clime, and flowers, through all the year
Shall on your walls and in your walks appear;
Where all beholding, shall your praise repeat,
No fruit so tempting and no flower so sweet:
The softest carpets in your rooms shall lie,
Pictures of happiest loves shall meet your eye,
And tallest mirrors, reaching to the floor,
Shall show you all the object I adore;
Who, by the hands of wealth and fashion dress'd,
By slaves attended and by friends caress'd,
Shall move, a wonder, through the public ways,
And hear the whispers of adoring praise.
Your female friends, though gayest of the gay,
Shall see you happy, and shall, sighing, say,
While smother'd envy rises in the breast,—
'Oh! that we lived so beauteous and so bless'd!'

"Come then, my mistress, and my wife; for she
Who trusts my honour is the wife for me;
Your slave, your husband, and your friend employ,
In search of pleasures we may both enjoy."

To this the damsel, meekly firm, replied:
"My mother loved, was married, toil'd, and died;
With joys, she'd griefs, had troubles in her course,
But not one grief was pointed by remorse;
My mind is fix'd, to Heaven I resign,
And be her love, her life, her comforts mine."

Tyrants have wept; and those with hearts of steel,
Unused the anguish of the heart to heal,
Have yet the transient power of virtue known,
And felt th' imparted joy promote their own.

Our Knight, relenting, now befriends a youth
Who to the yielding maid had vow'd his truth;
And finds in that fair deed a sacred joy,
That will not perish, and that cannot cloy:—
A living joy, that shall its spirit keep,
When every beauty fades, and all the passions sleep.

PART III.

BURIALS.

Qui vultis Acherontis atri,
Qui Stygia tristem, non tristis, videt,—
. . . .
Par ille Regi, par Superis erit.
SENECA *in Agamem*

True Christian Resignation not frequently to be seen—The Register a melancholy Record—A dying man, who at length sends for a Priest: fo what purpose? answered—Old Collett of the Inn, an instance of Dr. Young's slow-sudden Death: his Character and Conduct—The Manners and Management of the widow Goe: her successful Attention to Business: her Decease unexpected—The Infant-boy of Gerard Ablett dies: Reflections on his death, and the Survivor his Sister-Twin—The funeral of the deceased Lady of the Manor described: her neglected Mansion: Undertaker and Train: the Character which her monument will hereafter display—Burial of an ancient Maiden: some former drawback on her Virgin-fame: Description of her House and Household: Her Manners, Apprehensions, Death—Isaac Ashford, a virtuous Peasant, dies: his manly Character: Reluctance to enter the Poor-House; and why—Misfortune and Derangement of Intellect in Robin Dingley: whence they proceeded: he is not restrained by Misery from a wandering life: his various returns to his Parish: his final Return—Wife of Farmer Frankford dies in Prime of Life: Affliction in Consequence of such Death: melancholy view of her House, etc. on her Family's Return from her funeral: Address to Sorrow—Leah Cousins, a midwife: her Character; and successful Practice: at length opposed by Doctor Glibb: Opposition in the Parish: Argument of the Doctor; of Leah: her Failure and Decease—Burial of Roger Cuff, a Sailor: his Enmity to his Family; how it originated: his Experiment and its Consequence—The Register terminates—A Bell heard: Inquiry for whom? The Sexton—Character of old Dibble, and the five Rectors whom he served—Reflections—Conclusion.

There was, 't is said, and I believe, a time,
When humble Christians died with views sublime;
When all were ready for their faith to bleed,
But few to write or wrangle for their creed;
When lively faith upheld the sinking heart,
And friends, assured to meet, prepared to part;
When Love felt hope, when sorrow grew serene,
And all was comfort in the death-bed scene.

Alas! when now the gloomy king they wait,
'T is weakness yielding to resistless fate;
Like wretched men upon the ocean cast,
They labour hard and struggle to the last;
"Hope against hope," and wildly gaze around,
In search of help that never shall be found:
Nor, till the last strong billow stops the breath,
Will they believe them in the jaws of Death!

When these my records I reflecting read,
And find what ills these numerous births succeed;
What powerful griefs these nuptial ties attend,
With what regret these painful journeys end:
When from the cradle to the grave I look,
Mine I conceive a melancholy book.

Where now is perfect resignation seen?
Alas! it is not on the village green:—
I've seldom known, though I have often read
Of happy peasants on their dying-bed;
Whose looks proclaim'd that sunshine of the breast,
That more than hope, that Heaven itself express'd.

What I behold are feverish fits of strife,
'Twixt fears of dying and desire of life:
Those earthly hopes, that to the last endure;
Those fears, that hopes superior fail to cure;
At best a sad submission to the doom,
Which, turning from the danger, lets it come.

Sick lies the man, bewilder'd, lost, afraid,
His spirits vanquish'd, and his strength decay'd;
No hope the friend, the nurse, the doctor lend—
"Call then a priest, and fit him for his end."
A priest is call'd; 't is now, alas! too late,
Death enters with him at the cottage-gate;
Or time allow'd,—he goes, assured to find
The self-commanding, all-confiding mind;
And sighs to hear, what we may justly call
Death's common-place, the train of thought in all.

"True, I'm a sinner," feebly he begins,
"But trust in Mercy to forgive my sins:"
(Such cool confession no past crimes excite!
Such claim on Mercy seems the sinner's right!)
"I know, mankind are frail, that God is just,
And pardons those who in his mercy trust;
We're sorely tempted in a world like this,
All men have done, and I like all, amiss;
But now, if spared, it is my full intent
On all the past to ponder and repent:
Wrongs against me I pardon great and small,
And if I die I die in peace with all."
His merits thus and not his sins confess'd,
He speaks his hopes, and leaves to Heaven the rest
Alas! are these the prospects, dull and cold,
That dying Christians to their priests unfold?
Or mend the prospect when th' enthusiast cries,
"I die assured!" and in a rapture dies?

Ah, where that humble, self-abasing mind,
With that confiding spirit, shall we find;
The mind that, feeling what repentance brings,
Dejection's terror and Contrition's stings,
Feels then the hope, that mounts all care above,
And the pure joy that flows from pardoning love?

Such have I seen in death, and much deplore,
So many dying—that I see no more:
Lo now my records, where I grieve to trace,
How Death has triumph'd in so short a space;
Who are the dead, how died they, I relate,
And snatch some portion of their acts from fate.

With Andrew Collett we the year begin,
The blind, fat landlord of the Old Crown Inn,—
Big as his butt, and, for the self same use,
To take in stores of strong fermenting juice.

On his huge chair beside the fire he sate,
In revel chief, and umpire in debate;
Each night his string of vulgar tales he told;
When ale was cheap and bachelors were bold:
His heroes all were famous in their days,
Cheats were his boast and drunkards had his praise
"One, in three draughts, three mugs of ale took down,
As mugs were then, the champion of the Crown;
For thrice three days another lived on ale,
And knew no change but that of mild and stale;
Two thirsty soakers watch'd a vessel's side,
When he the tap, with dexterous hand, applied;
Nor from their seats departed, till they found
The butt was out, and heard the mournful sound."

He praised a poacher, precious child of fun!
Who shot the keeper with his own spring-gun;
Nor less the smuggler who the exciseman tied,
And left him hanging at the birch-wood side,
There to expire;—but one who saw him hang
Cut the good cord—a traitor of the gang.

His own exploits with boastful glee he told,
What ponds he emptied and what pikes he sold;
And how, when bless'd with sight alert and gay,
The night's amusements kept him through the day.

He sang the praises of those times, when all
"For cards and dice, as for their drinks, might call;
When justice wink'd on every jovial crew,
And ten-pins tumbled in the parson's view."

He told, when angry wives, provoked to rail,
Or drive a third-day drunkard from his ale,
What were his triumphs, and how great the skill
That won the vex'd virago to his will;
Who raving came; then talk'd in milder strain,—
Then wept, then drank, and pledged her spouse again.

Such were his themes: how knaves o'er laws prevail,
Or, when made captives, how they fly from jail;
The young how brave, how subtle were the old:
And oaths attested all that Folly told.

On death like his what name shall we bestow,
So very sudden! yet so very slow?
'Twas slow:—Disease, augmenting year by year,
Show'd the grim king by gradual steps brought near:
'Twas not less sudden; in the night he died,
He drank, he swore, he jested, and he lied;
Thus aiding folly with departing breath:
"Beware, Lorenzo, the slow-sudden death."

Next died the Widow Goe, an active dame,
Famed ten miles round, and worthy all her fame;
She lost her husband when their loves were young,
But kept her farm, her credit, and her tongue
Full thirty years she ruled, with matchless skill,
With guiding judgment and resistless will;
Advice she scorn'd, rebellions she suppress'd,
And sons and servants bow'd at her behest.
Like that great man's, who to his Saviour came,
Were the strong words of this commanding dame:—
"Come," if she said, they came; if "go," were gone;
And if "do this,"—that instant it was done:
Her maidens told she was all eye and ear,
In darkness saw and could at distance hear;—
No parish-business in the place could stir,
Without direction or assent from her:
In turn she took each office as it fell,
Knew all their duties, and discharged them well;
The lazy vagrants in her presence shook,
And pregnant damsels fear'd her stern rebuke;
She look'd on want with judgment clear and cool,
And felt with reason and bestow'd by rule;
She match'd both sons and daughters to her mind,
And lent them eyes, for Love, she heard, was blind;
Yet ceaseless still she throve, alert, alive,
The working bee, in full or empty hive;
Busy and careful, like that working bee,
No time for love nor tender cares had she;
But when our farmers made their amorous vows,
She talk'd of market-steeds and patent ploughs.
Nor unemploy'd her evenings pass'd away,
Amusement closed as business waked the day;
When to her toilet's brief concerns she ran,
And conversation with her friends began,
Who all were welcome, what they saw, to share;
And joyous neighbours praised her Christmas fare,
That none around might, in their scorn, complain
That Gossip Goe was greedy in her gain.

Thus long she reign'd, admired, if not approved
Praised, if not honour'd; fear'd, if not beloved:—
When, as the busy days of Spring drew near,
That call'd for all the forecast of the year;
When lively hope the rising crop survey'd,
And April promised what September paid;
When stray'd her lambs where gorse and green-weed grow;
When rose her grass in richer vales below;
When pleased she look'd on all the smiling land,
And view'd the hinds who wrought at her command;
(Poultry in groups still follow'd where she went;)
Then dread o'ercame her,—that her days were spent.

"Bless me! I die, and not a warning giv'n,—
With *much* to do on Earth, and ALL for Heaven!
No reparation for my soul's affairs,
No leave petition'd for the barn's repairs;
Accounts perplex'd, my interest yet unpaid,
My mind unsettled, and my will unmade;—
A lawyer haste, and in your way a priest;
And let me die in one good work at least."
She spake, and trembling, dropp'd upon her knees,
Heaven in her eye and in her hand her keys;
And still the more she found her life decay,
With greater force she grasp'd those signs of sway
Then fell and died!—In haste her sons drew near
And dropp'd, in haste, the tributary tear;
Then from th' adhering clasp the keys unbound,
And consolation for their sorrows found.

Death has his infant train; his bony arm
Strikes from the baby-cheek the rosy charm:
The brightest eye his glazing film makes dim,
And his cold touch sets fast the lithest limb:
He seized the sick'ning boy to Gerard lent,*
When three days' life, in feeble cries, were spent
In pain brought forth, those painful hours to stay
To breathe in pain, and sigh its soul away!

"But why thus lent, if thus recall'd again,
To cause and feel, to live and die in, pain?"
Or rather say, Why grievous these appear,
If all it pays of Heaven's eternal year;
If these sad sobs and piteous sighs secure
Delights that live, when worlds no more endure?

The sister-spirit long may lodge below,
And pains from nature, pains from reason, know
Through all the common ills of life may run,
By hope perverted and by love undone;
A wife's distress, a mother's pangs may dread,
And widow-tears, in bitter anguish, shed,
May at old age arrive through numerous harms,
With children's children in those feeble arms:
Nor till by years of want and grief oppress'd,
Shall the sad spirit flee and be at rest!

* See page 22.

Yet happier therefore shall we deem the boy,
Secured from anxious care and dangerous joy!

Not so! for then would Love Divine in vain
Send all the burthens weary men sustain;
All that now curb the passions when they rage,
The checks of youth and the regrets of age;
All that now bids us hope, believe, endure,
Our sorrow's comfort and our vice's cure;
All that for Heaven's high joys the spirits train,
And charity, the crown of all, were vain.

Say, will you call the breathless infant bless'd
Because no cares the silent grave molest?
So would you deem the nursling from the wing
Untimely thrust, and never train'd to sing;
But far more bless'd the bird whose grateful voice
Sings its own joy, and makes the woods rejoice,
Though, while untaught, ere yet he charm'd the ear,
Hard were his trials and his pains severe!

Next died the Lady who yon Hall possess'd;
And here they brought her noble bones to rest.
In Town she dwelt;—forsaken stood the Hall:
Worms ate the floors, the tap'stry fled the wall:
No fire the kitchen's cheerless grate display'd;
No cheerful light the long-closed sash convey'd;
The crawling worm, that turns a summer-fly,
Here spun his shroud and laid him up to die
The winter-death:—upon the bed of state,
The bat shrill-shrieking woo'd his flickering mate;
To empty rooms the curious came no more,
From empty cellars turn'd the angry poor,
And surly beggars cursed the ever-bolted door.
To one small room the steward found his way,
Where tenants follow'd to complain and pay;
Yet no complaint before the Lady came,
The feeling servant spared the feeble dame;
Who saw her farms with his observing eyes,
And answer'd all requests with his replies;—
She came not down, her falling groves to view;
Why should she know what one so faithful knew?
Why come, from many clamorous tongues to hear
What one so just might whisper in her ear?
Her oaks or acres, why with care explore;
Why learn the wants, the sufferings of the poor;
When one so knowing all their worth could trace,
And one so piteous govern'd in her place?

Lo! now what dismal sons of Darkness come,
To bear this daughter of Indulgence home;
Tragedians all, and well arranged in black!
Who nature, feeling, force, expression lack;
Who cause no tear, but gloomily pass by,
And shake their sables in the wearied eye,
That turns disgusted from the pompous scene,
Proud without grandeur, with profusion, mean!
The tear for kindness past affection owes;
For worth deceased the sigh from reason flows;
E'en well feign'd passion for our sorrows call,
And real tears for mimic miseries fall:
But this poor farce has neither truth nor art
To please the fancy or to touch the heart;
Unlike the darkness of the sky, that pours
On the dry ground its fertilizing showers;
Unlike to that which strikes the soul with dread,
When thunders roar, and forky fires are shed;
Dark but not awful, dismal but yet mean,
With anxious bustle moves the cumbrous scene;
Presents no objects tender or profound,
But spreads its cold unmeaning gloom around.

When woes are feign'd, how ill such forms appear;
And oh! how needless, when the wo 's sincere.

Slow to the vault they come, with heavy tread,
Bending beneath the Lady and her lead;
A case of elm surrounds that ponderous chest,
Close on that case the crimson velvet's press'd;
Ungenerous this, that to the worm denies,
With niggard caution, his appointed prize;
For now, ere yet he works his tedious way,
Through cloth and wood and metal to his prey,
That prey dissolving shall a mass remain,
That fancy loathes and worms themselves disdain.

But see! the master-mourner makes his way,
To end his office for the coffin'd clay;
Pleased that our rustic men and maids behold
His plate like silver, and his studs like gold,
As they approach to spell the age, the name,
And all the titles of th' illustrious dame.—
This as (my duty done) some scholar read,
A village-father look'd disdain and said:
"Away, my friends! why take such pains to know
What some brave marble soon in church shall show!
Where not alone her gracious name shall stand,
But how she lived—the blessing of the land;
How much we all deplored the noble dead,
What groans we utter'd and what tears we shed;
Tears true as those, which in the sleepy eyes
Of weeping cherubs on the stone shall rise;
Tears, true as those, which, ere she found her grave,
The noble Lady to our sorrows gave."

Down by the church-way walk and where the brook
Winds round the chancel like a shepherd's crook;
In that small house, with those green pales before,
Where jasmine trails on either side the door;
Where those dark shrubs that now grow wild at will,
Were clipp'd in form and tantalized with skill;
Where cockles blanch'd and pebbles neatly spread,
Form'd shining borders for the larkspur's bed;—
There lived a lady, wise, austere, and nice,
Who show'd her virtue by her scorn of vice;
In the dear fashions of her youth she dress'd,
A pea-green joseph was her favourite vest;
Erect she stood, she walk'd with stately mien,
Tight was her length of stays, and she was tall and lean.

There long she lived in maiden-state immured,
From looks of love and treacherous man secured;
Though evil fame—(but that was long before)
Had blown her dubious blast at Catherine's door:
A Captain thither, rich from India came,
And though a cousin call'd, it touch'd her fame:
Her annual stipend rose from his behest,
And all the long-prized treasures she possess'd:—
If aught like joy awhile appear'd to stay
In that stern face, and chase those frowns away,
'T was when her treasures she disposed for view,
And heard the praises to their splendour due;
Silks beyond price, so rich they'd stand alone,
And diamonds blazing on the buckled zone;

Rows of rare pearls by curious workmen set,
And bracelets fair in box of glossy jet;
Bright polish'd amber, precious from its size,
Or forms the fairest fancy could devise:
Her drawers of cedar, shut with secret springs,
Conceal'd the watch of gold and rubied rings;
Letters, long proofs of love, and verses fine
Round the pinked rims of crisped Valentine.
Her china-closet, cause of daily care,
For woman's wonder held her pencill'd ware;
That pictured wealth of China and Japan,
Like its cold mistress, shunn'd the eye of man.

Her neat small room, adorn'd with maiden-taste,
A clipp'd French puppy, first of favourites graced:
A parrot next, but dead and stuff'd with art;
(For Poll, when living, lost the lady's heart,
And then his life; for he was heard to speak
Such frightful words as tinged his Lady's cheek:)
Unhappy bird! who had no power to prove,
Save by such speech his gratitude and love.
A grey old cat his whiskers lick'd beside;
A type of sadness in the house of pride.
The polish'd surface of an India chest,
A glassy globe, in frame of ivory press'd;
Where swam two finny creatures; one of gold,
Of silver one; both beauteous to behold:—
All these were form'd the guiding taste to suit;
The beasts well-manner'd and the fishes mute.
A widow'd Aunt was there, compell'd by need,
The nymph to flatter and her tribe to feed;
Who, veling well her scorn, endured the clog,
Mute as the fish, and fawning as the dog.

As years increased, these treasures, her delight,
Arose in value in their owner's sight:
A miser knows that, view it as he will,
A guinea kept is but a guinea still;
And so he puts it to its proper use,
That something more this guinea may produce:
But silks and rings, in the possessor's eyes,
The oft'ner seen, the more in value rise,
And thus are wisely hoarded to bestow
The kind of pleasure that with years will grow.

But what avail'd their worth,—if worth had they,—
In the sad summer of her slow decay?

Then we beheld her turn an anxious look
From trunks and chests, and fix it on her book,—
A rich-bound Book of Prayer the Captain gave,
(Some Princess had it, or was said to have;)
And then once more, on all her stores look round,
And draw a sigh so piteous and profound,
That told, "Alas! how hard from these to part,
And for new hopes and habits form the heart!
What shall I do, (she cried,) my peace of mind
To gain in dying, and to die resign'd?"

"Hear," we return'd;—"these baubles cast aside,
Nor give thy God a rival in thy pride;
Thy closets shut, and ope thy kitchen's door;
There own thy failings, *here* invite the poor;
A friend of Mammon let thy bounty make;
For widows' prayers, thy vanities forsake;
And let the hungry, of thy pride, partake:
Then shall thy inward eye with joy survey
The angel Mercy tempering Death's delay!"

Alas! 'twas hard; the treasures still had charms,
Hope still its flattery, sickness its alarms;
Still was the same unsettled, clouded view,
And the same plaintive cry, "What shall I do?"

Nor change appeared: for when her race was run,
Doubtful we all exclaim'd, "What has been done?"
Apart she lived, and still she lies alone;
Yon earthy heap awaits the flattering stone,
On which invention shall be long employ'd,
To show the various worth of Catharine Lloyd.

Next to these ladies, but in nought allied,
A noble peasant, Isaac Ashford, died.
Noble he was, contemning all things mean,
His truth unquestion'd and his soul serene:
Of no man's presence Isaac felt afraid;
At no man's question Isaac look'd dismay'd:
Shame knew him not, he dreaded no disgrace;
Truth, simple truth, was written in his face;
Yet while the serious thought his soul approved,
Cheerful he seem'd, and gentleness he loved:
To bliss domestic he his heart resign'd,
And, with the firmest, had the fondest mind:
Were others joyful, he look'd smiling on,
And gave allowance where he needed none,
Good he refused with future ill to buy,
Nor knew a joy that caused reflection's sigh;
A friend to virtue, his unclouded breast
No envy stung, no jealousy distress'd;
(Bane of the poor! it wounds their weaker mind
To miss one favour which their neighbours find);
Yet far was he from stoic pride removed;
He felt humanely, and he warmly loved:
I mark'd his action, when his infant died,
And his old neighbour for offence was tried,
The still tears, stealing down that furrow'd cheek,
Spoke pity, plainer than the tongue can speak.
If pride were his, 't was not their vulgar pride,
Who, in their base contempt, the great deride;
Nor pride in learning,—though my clerk agreed,
If fate should call him, Ashford might succeed;
Nor pride in rustic skill, although we knew
None his superior, and his equals few:—
But if that spirit in his soul had place,
It was the jealous pride that shuns disgrace;
A pride in honest fame, by virtue gain'd,
In sturdy boys to virtuous labours train'd;
Pride, in the power that guards his country's coast,
And all that Englishmen enjoy and boast;
Pride, in a life that slander's tongue defied,—
In fact, a noble passion, misnamed pride.

He had no party's rage, no sect'ry's whim;
Christian and countryman was all with him:
True to his church he came; no Sunday-shower
Kept him at home in that important hour;
Nor his firm feet could one persuading sect,
By the strong glare of their new light, direct;—
"On hope, in mine own sober light, I gaze,
But should be blind and lose it, in your blaze."

In times severe, when many a sturdy swain
Felt it his pride, his comfort, to complain;
Isaac their wants would soothe, his own would hide,
And feel in that his comfort and his pride.

At length he found, when seventy years were run,
His strength departed, and his labour done;
When he, save honest fame, retain'd no more,
But lost his wife and saw his children poor:

'T was then, a spark of—say not discontent—
Struck on his mind, and thus he gave it vent:

"Kind are your laws, ('t is not to be denied,)
That in yon house, for ruin'd age, provide,
And they are just;—when young, we give you all,
And for assistance in our weakness call.—
Why then this proud reluctance to be fed,
To join your poor, and eat the parish-bread!
But yet I linger, loth with him to feed
Who gains his plenty by the sons of need;
He who, by contract, all your paupers took,
And gauges stomachs with an anxious look:
On some old master I could well depend,
See him with joy, and thank him as a friend;
But ill on him, who doles the day's supply,
And counts our chances who at night may die:
Yet help me, Heav'n! and let me not complain
Of what I suffer, but my fate sustain."

Such were his thoughts, and so resign'd he grew;
Daily he placed the workhouse in his view!
But came not there, for sudden was his fate,
He dropp'd, expiring at his cottage-gate.

I feel his absence in the hours of prayer,
And view his seat and sigh for Isaac there:
I see no more those white locks thinly spread
Round the bald polish of that honour'd head;
No more that awful glance on playful wight,
Compell'd to kneel and tremble at the sight,
To fold his fingers, all in dread the while,
Till Mister Ashford soften'd to a smile;
No more that meek and suppliant look in prayer,
Nor the pure faith (to give it force) are there:—
But he is bless'd, and I lament no more
A wise good man contented to be poor.

Then died a Rambler; not the one who sails
And trucks, for female favours, beads and nails;
Not one, who posts from place to place—of men
And manners treating with a flying pen;
Not he, who climbs, for prospects, Snowden's height,
And chides the clouds that intercept the sight;
No curious shell, rare plant, or brilliant spar,
Enticed our traveller from his home so far;
But all the reason, by himself assign'd
For so much rambling, was, a restless mind;
As on, from place to place, without intent,
Without reflection, Robin Dingley went.

Not thus by nature: never man was found
Less prone to wonder from his parish-bound:
Claudian's old Man, to whom all scenes were new,
Save those where he and where his apples grew,
Resembled Robin, who around would look,
And his horizon, for the earth's, mistook.

To this poor swain a keen Attorney came;—
"I give thee joy, good fellow! on thy name;
The rich old Dingley's dead;—no child has he,
Nor wife, nor will; his ALL is left for thee:
To be his fortune's heir thy claim is good;
Thou hast the name, and we will prove the blood."

The claim was made; 't was tried,—it would not stand;
They proved the blood, but were refused the land.

Assured of wealth, this man of simple heart,
To every friend had predisposed a part:
His wife had hopes indulged of various kind;
The three Miss Dingleys had their school assign'd,
Masters were sought for what they each required,
And books were bought and harpsichords were hired:
So high was hope:—the failure touch'd his brain,
And Robin never was himself again;
Yet he no wrath, no angry wish express'd,
But tried, in vain, to labour or to rest;
Then cast his bundle on his back, and went
He knew not whither, nor for what intent.

Years fled;—of Robin all remembrance past,
When home he wander'd in his rags at last:
A sailor's jacket on his limbs was thrown,
A sailor's story he had made his own;
Had suffer'd battles, prisons, tempests, storms,
Encountering death in all his ugliest forms:
His cheeks were haggard, hollow was his eye,
Where madness lurk'd, conceal'd in misery;
Want and th' ungentle world, had taught a part,
And prompted cunning to that simple heart:
"He now bethought him, he would roam no more,
But live at home, and labour as before."

Here clothed and fed, no sooner he began
To round and redden, than away he ran:
His wife was dead, their children past his aid:
So, unmolested, from his home he stray'd:
Six years elapsed, when, worn with want and pain
Came Robin, wrapt in all his rags, again:—
We chide, we pity;—placed among our poor,
He fed again, and was a man once more.

As when a gaunt and hungry fox is found,
Entrapp'd alive in some rich hunter's ground;
Fed for the field, although each day 's a feast,
Fatten you may, but never *tame* the beast;
A house protects him, savoury viands sustain
But loose his neck and off he goes again:
So stole our vagrant from his warm retreat,
To rove a prowler and be deem'd a cheat.

Hard was his fare; for, him at length we saw,
In cart convey'd, and laid supine on straw.
His feeble voice now spoke a sinking heart;
His groans now told the motions of the cart;
And when it stopp'd, he tried in vain to stand;
Closed was his eye, and clench'd his clammy hand:
Life ebb'd apace, and our best aid no more
Could his weak sense or dying heart restore:
But now he fell, a victim to the snare
That vile attorneys for the weak prepare;—
They who, when profit or resentment call,
Heed not the groaning victim they enthral.

Then died lamented, in the strength of life,
A valued Mother and a faithful Wife,
Call'd not away, when time had loosed each hold
On the fond heart, and each desire grew cold;
But when, to all that knit us to our kind,
She felt fast-bound, as charity can bind;—
Not when the ills of age, its pain, its care,
The drooping spirit for its fate prepare;
And, each affection failing, leaves the heart
Loosed from life's charm and willing to depart;—
But all her ties the strong invader broke,
In all their strength, by one tremendous stroke!
Sudden and swift the eager pest came on,
And terror grew, till every hope was gone:
Still those around appear'd for hope to seek!
But view'd the sick and were afraid to speak.—

Slowly they bore, with solemn step, the dead,
When grief grew loud and bitter tears were shed:
My part began; a crowd drew near the place,
Awe in each eye, alarm in every face:
So swift the ill, and of so fierce a kind,
That fear with pity mingled in each mind;
Friends with the husband came their griefs to blend;
For good-man Frankford was to all a friend.
The last-born boy they held above the bier,
He knew not grief, but cries express'd his fear;
Each different age and sex reveal'd its pain,
In now a louder, now a lower strain;
While the meek father, listening to their tones,
Swell'd the full cadence of the grief by groans.

The elder sister strove her pangs to hide,
And soothing words to younger minds applied:
"Be still, be patient," oft she strove to say;
But fail'd as oft, and weeping turn'd away.

Curious and sad, upon the fresh-dug hill,
The village-lads stood melancholy still;
And idle children, wandering to and fro,
As Nature guided, took the tone of wo.

Arrived at home, how then they gazed around,
In every place,—where she—no more was found;—
The seat at table she was wont to fill;
The fire-side chair, still set, but vacant still;
The garden-walks, a labour all her own;
The latticed bower, with trailing shrubs o'ergrown;
The Sunday-pew she fill'd with all her race,—
Each place of hers, was now a sacred place,
That, while it call'd up sorrows in the eyes,
Pierced the full heart, and forced them still to rise.

Oh sacred sorrow! by whom souls are tried,
Sent not to punish mortals, but to guide;
If thou art mine, (and who shall proudly dare
To tell his Maker, he has had his share?)
Still let me feel for what thy pangs are sent,
And be my guide and not my punishment!

Of Leah Cousins next the name appears,
With honours crown'd, and bless'd with length of years,
Save that she lived to feel, in life's decay,
The pleasure die, the honours drop away;
A matron she, whom every village-wife
View'd as the help and guardian of her life;
Fathers and sons, indebted to her aid,
Respect to her and her profession paid;
Who in the house of plenty largely fed,
Yet took her station at the pauper's bed;
Nor from that duty could be bribed again,
While fear or danger urged her to remain:
In her experience all her friends relied,
Heaven was her help and nature was her guide.

Thus Leah lived; long trusted, much caress'd,
Till a Town-Dame a youthful Farmer bless'd;
A gay vain bride, who would example give
To that poor village where she deign'd to live;
Some few months past, she sent, in hour of need,
For Doctor Glibb, who came with wondrous speed:
Two days he waited, all his art applied,
To save the mother when her infant died;—
"'T was well I came," at last he deign'd to say;
"'T was wondrous well;"—and proudly rode away.

The news ran round;—"How vast the Doctor's pow'r!
He saved the Lady in the trying hour;
Saved her from death, when she was dead to hope,
And her fond husband had resign'd her up:
So all, like her, may evil fate defy,
If Doctor Glibb, with saving hand, be nigh."

Fame (now his friend), fear, novelty and whim,
And fashion, sent the varying sex to him:
From this, contention in the village rose;
And *these* the Dame espoused; the Doctor *those*:
The wealthier part, to him and science went;
With luck and her the poor remain'd content.

The matron sigh'd; for she was vex'd at heart,
With so much profit, so much fame to part:
"So long successful in my art," she cried,
"And this proud man so young and so untried!"

"Nay," said the Doctor, "dare you trust your wives,
The joy, the pride, the solace of your lives,
To one who acts and knows no reason why,
But trusts, poor hag! to luck for an ally?—
Who, on experience, can her claims advance,
And own the powers of accident and chance?
A whining dame, who prays in danger's view,
(A proof she knows not what beside to do!)
What's her experience? In the time that's gone,
Blundering she wrought, and still she blunders on:—
And what is Nature? One who acts in aid
Of gossips half asleep, and half afraid:
With such allies I scorn my fame to blend,
Skill is my luck and courage is my friend:
No slave to Nature, 't is my chief delight
To win my way and act in her despite:—
Trust then my art, that, in itself complete,
Needs no assistance and fears no defeat."

Warm'd by her well-spiced ale and aiding pipe,
The angry matron grew for contest ripe.

"Can you," she said, "ungrateful and unjust,
Before experience, ostentation trust!
What is your hazard, foolish daughters, tell?
If safe, you're certain; if secure, you're well:
That I have luck my friend and foe confess,
And what's good judgment but a lucky guess?
He boasts but what he *can* do:—will you run
From me, your friend! who, all *he* boasts, *have* done?
By proud and learned words his powers are known;
By healthy boys and handsome girls my own:
Wives! fathers! children! by my help you live;
Has this pale doctor more than life to give?
No stunted cripple hops the village round;
Your hands are active and your heads are sound:
My lads are all your fields and flocks require;
My lasses all those sturdy lads admire.
Can this proud leech, with all his boasted skill,
Amend the soul or body, wit or will?
Does he for courts the sons of farmers frame,
Or make the daughter differ from the dame?
Or, whom he brings into this world of wo,
Prepares he them their part to undergo?
If not, this stranger from your doors repel,
And be content to *be* and to be *well*."

She spake; but, ah! with words too strong and plain;
Her warmth offended and her truth was vain:

The *many* left her, and the friendly *few*,
If never colder, yet they older grew;
Till, unemploy'd, she felt her spirits droop,
And took, insidious aid! th' inspiring cup;
Grew poor and peevish as her powers decay'd,
And propp'd the tottering frame with stronger aid,—
Then died!—I saw our careful swains convey,
From this our changeful world the matron's clay,
Who to this world, at least, with equal care,
Brought them its changes good and ill to share.

Now to this grave was Roger Cuff convey'd,
And strong resentment's lingering spirit laid.
Shipwreck'd in youth, he home return'd and found
His brethren three—and thrice they wish'd him drown'd.
"Is this a landman's love? Be certain then,
We part for ever!"—and they cried, "Amen!"

His words were truth's:—Some forty summers fled,
His brethren died, his kin supposed him dead:
Three nephews these, one sprightly niece, and one,
Less near in blood—they call'd him *surly John;*
He work'd in woods apart from all his kind,
Fierce were his looks and moody was his mind.

For home the Sailor now began to sigh:
"The dogs are dead, and I'll return and die;
When all I have, my gains, in years of care,
The younger Cuffs with kinder souls shall share.—
Yet hold! I'm rich;—with one consent they'll say,
'You're welcome, Uncle, as the flowers in May.'
No; I'll disguise me, be in tatters dress'd,
And best befriend the lads who treat me best."

Now all his kindred,—neither rich nor poor,—
Kept the wolf want some distance from the door.

In piteous plight he knock'd at George's gate,
And begg'd for aid, as he described his state:—
But stern was George;—"Let them who had thee strong,
Help thee to drag thy weaken'd frame along;
To us a stranger, while your limbs would move,
From us depart and try a stranger's love:—
Ha! dost thou murmur?"—for, in Roger's throat,
Was "Rascal!" rising with disdainful note.

To pious James he then his prayer address'd;—
"Good lack," quoth James, "thy sorrows pierce my breast;
And, had I wealth, as have my brethren twain,
One board should feed us and one roof contain:
But plead I will thy cause and I will pray:
And so farewell! Heaven help thee on thy way!
"Scoundrel!" said Roger, (but apart;) and told
His case to Peter;—Peter too was cold:—
"The rates are high; we have a-many poor;
But I will think," he said, and shut the door.

Then the gay Niece the seeming pauper press'd;—
"Turn, Nancy, turn, and view this form distress'd:
Akin to thine is this declining frame,
And this poor beggar claims an Uncle's name."

"Avaunt! begone!" the courteous maiden said,
"Thou vile impostor! Uncle Roger's dead;
I hate thee, beast; thy look my spirit shocks!
Oh! that I saw thee starving in the stocks!"

"My gentle niece!" he said—and sought the wood.—
"I hunger, fellow; prithee, give me food!"

"Give! am I rich? This hatchet take, and try
Thy proper strength, nor give those limbs the lie;
Work, feed thyself, to thine own powers appeal,
Nor whine out woes, thine own right-hand can heal:
And while that hand is thine and thine a leg,
Scorn of the proud or of the base to beg."

"Come, surly John, thy wealthy kinsman view,"
Old Roger said:—"thy words are brave and true;
Come, live with me; we'll vex those scoundrel-boys,
And that prim shrew shall, envying, hear our joys.—
Tobacco's glorious fume all day we'll share,
With beef and brandy kill all kinds of care;
We'll beer and biscuit on our table heap,
And rail at rascals till we fall asleep."

Such was their life: but when the woodman died,
His grieving kin for Roger's smiles applied—
In vain; he shut, with stern rebuke, the door,
And dying, built a refuge for the poor;
With this restriction, That no Cuff should share
One meal, or shelter for one moment there.

My record ends:—But hark! e'en now I hear
The bell of death, and know not whose to fear:
Our farmers all, and all our hinds were well;
In no man's cottage danger seem'd to dwell:
Yet death of man proclaim these heavy chimes,
For thrice they sound, with pausing space, three times.

"Go; of my sexton seek, Whose days are sped?—
What! he, himself!—and is old Dibble dead?"
His eightieth year he reach'd, still undecay'd,
And rectors five to one close vault convey'd:
But he is gone; his care and skill I lose,
And gain a mournful subject for my Muse:
His masters lost, he'd oft in turn deplore,
And kindly add,—"Heaven grant, I lose no more."
Yet, while he spake, a sly and pleasant glance
Appear'd at variance with his complaisance:
For, as he told their fate and varying worth,
He archly look'd,—"I yet may bear thee forth."
"When first"—(he so began)—"my trade I plied,
Good master Addle was the parish-guide;
His clerk and sexton, I beheld with fear
His stride majestic, and his frown severe;
A noble pillar of the church he stood,
Adorn'd with college-gown and parish-hood:
Then as he paced the hallow'd aisles about,
He fill'd the sevenfold surplice fairly out!
But in his pulpit, wearied down with prayer,
He sat and seem'd as in his study's chair;
For while the anthem swell'd, and when it ceased,
Th' expecting people view'd their slumbering priest:
Who, dozing, died.—Our Parson Peele was next;
'I will not spare you,' was his favourite text;
Nor did he spare, but raised them many a pound;
Ev'n me he mulct for my poor rood of ground;
Yet cared he nought, but with a gibing speech,
'What should I do,' quoth he, 'but what I preach?'
His piercing jokes (and he'd a plenteous store)
Were daily offer'd both to rich and poor;
His scorn, his love, in playful words he spoke;
His pity, praise, and promise, were a joke:

But though so young and bless'd with spirits high,
He died as grave as any judge could die:
The strong attack subdued his lively powers,—
His was the grave, and Doctor Grandspear ours.

"Then were there golden times the village round;
In his abundance all appear'd t' abound;
Liberal and rich, a plenteous board he spread,
E'en cool Dissenters at his table fed;
Who wish'd, and hoped,—and thought a man so kind
A way to Heaven, though not their own, might find;
To them, to all, he was polite and free,
Kind to the poor, and, ah! most kind to me.
'Ralph,' would he say, 'Ralph Dibble, thou art old;
'That doublet fit, 't will keep thee from the cold:
'How does my sexton?—What! the times are hard;
'Drive that stout pig, and pen him in thy yard.'
But most his rev'rence loved a mirthful jest:—
'Thy coat is thin; why, man, thou 'rt *barely* dress'd;
'It 's worn to th' thread: but I have nappy beer;
'Clap that within, and see how they will wear!'

"Gay days were these; but they were quickly past:
When first he came, we found he couldn't last:
A whoreson cough (and at the fall of leaf)
Upset him quite:—but what 's the gain of grief?

"Then came the Author-Rector: his delight
Was all in books; to read them, or to write:
Women and men he strove alike to shun,
And hurried homeward when his tasks were done:
Courteous enough, but careless what he said,
For points of learning he reserved his head;
And when addressing either poor or rich,
He knew no better than his cassock which:
He, like an osier, was of pliant kind,
Erect by nature, but to bend inclined;
Not like a creeper falling to the ground,
Or meanly catching on the neighbours round:—
Careless was he of surplice, hood, and band,—
And kindly took them as they came to hand:
Nor like the doctor, wore a world of hat,
As if he sought for dignity in that:
He talk'd, he gave, but not with cautious rules:—
Nor turn'd from gipsies, vagabonds, or fools;
It was his nature, but they thought it whim,
And so our beaux and beauties turn'd from him:
Of questions, much he wrote, profound and dark,—
How spake the serpent, and where stopp'd the ark;
From what far land the Queen of Sheba came;
Who Salem's priest, and what his father's name;
He made the Song of Songs its mysteries yield,
And Revelations, to the world, reveal'd.
He sleeps i' the aisle,—but not a stone records
His name or fame, his actions or his words:
And truth, your reverence, when I look around,
And mark the tombs in our sepulchral ground,
(Though dare I not of one man's hope to doubt),
I 'd join the party who repose without.

"Next came a youth from Cambridge, and, in truth,
He was a sober and a comely youth;
He blush'd in meekness as a modest man,
And gain'd attention ere his task began;
When preaching, seldom ventured on reproof,
But touch'd his neighbours tenderly enough.
Him, in his youth, a clamorous sect assail'd,
Advised and censured, flatter'd,—and prevail'd.—
Then did he much his sober hearers vex,
Confound the simple, and the sad perplex;
To a new style his reverence rashly took;
Loud grew his voice, to threat'ning swell'd his look
Above, below, on either side, he gazed,
Amazing all, and most himself amazed:
No more he read his preachments pure and plain,
But lanch'd outright, and rose and sank again:
At times he smiled in scorn, at times he wept,
And such sad coil with words of vengeance kept,
That our best sleepers started as they slept.

"'Conviction comes like lightning,' he would cry,
'In vain you seek it, and in vain you fly;
'T is like the rushing of the mighty wind,
Unseen its progress, but its power you find;
It strikes the child ere yet its reason wakes;
His reason fled, the ancient sire it shakes;
The proud, learn'd man, and him who loves to know
How and from whence these gusts of grace will blow,
It shuns,—but sinners in their way impedes,
And sots and harlots visits in their deeds:
Of faith and penance it supplies the place;
Assures the vilest that they live by grace,
And, without running, makes them win the race.'

"Such was the doctrine our young prophet taught;
And here conviction, there confusion wrought;
When his thin cheek assumed a deadly hue,
And all the rose to one small spot withdrew:
They call'd it hectic; 't was a fiery flush,
More fix'd and deeper than the maiden blush;
His paler lips the pearly teeth disclosed,
And lab'ring lungs the length'ning speech opposed.
No more his span-girth shanks and quiv'ring thighs
Upheld a body of the smaller size;
But down he sank upon his dying bed,
And gloomy crotchets fill'd his wandering head.—

"'Spite of my faith, all-saving faith,' he cried,
'I fear of worldly works the wicked pride;
Poor as I am, degraded, abject, blind,
The good I 've wrought still rankles in my mind:
My alms-deeds all, and every deed I 've done,
My moral-rags defile me every one;
It should not be:—what say'st thou? tell me, Ralph.'
Quoth I, 'Your reverence, I believe, you 're safe;
Your faith 's your prop, nor have you pass'd such time
In life's good-works as swell them to a crime.
If I of pardon for my sins were sure,
About my goodness I would rest secure.'

"Such was his end; and mine approaches fast;
I 've seen my best of preachers,—and my last."—
He bow'd, and archly smiled at what he said,
Civil but sly:—"And is old Dibble dead?"

Yes! he is gone: and WE are going all;
Like flowers we wither, and like leaves we fall;—
Here, with an infant, joyful sponsors come,
Then bear the new-made Christian to its home,
A few short years, and we behold him stand,
To ask a blessing, with his bride in hand:
A few, still seeming shorter, and we hear
His widow weeping at her husband's bier:—

Thus, as the months succeed, shall infants take,
Their names; thus parents shall the child forsake;
Thus brides again and bridegrooms blithe shall kneel,
By love or law compell'd their vows to seal,
Ere I again, or one like me, explore
These simple annals of the VILLAGE POOR.

THE LIBRARY.

Books afford Consolation to the troubled Mind, by substituting a lighter Kind of Distress for its own—They are productive of other Advantages:—An Author's Hope of being known in distant Times—Arrangement of the Library—Size and Form of the Volumes—The ancient Folio, clasped and chained—Fashion prevalent even in this Place—The Mode of publishing in Numbers, Pamphlets, etc.—Subjects of the different Classes—Divinity—Controversy—The Friends of Religion often more dangerous than her Foes—Sceptical Authors—Reason too much rejected by the former Converts; exclusively relied upon by the latter—Philosophy ascending through the Scale of Being to moral Subjects—Books of Medicine: their Variety, Variance, and Proneness to System: the Evil of this, and the Difficulty it causes—Farewell to this Study—Law: the increasing Number of its Volumes—Supposed happy State of Man without Laws—Progress of Society—Historians: their Subjects—Dramatic Authors, Tragic and Comic—Ancient Romances—The Captive Heroine—Happiness in the perusal of such Books: why—Criticism—Apprehensions of the Author: removed by the Appearance of the Genius of the Place; whose Reasoning and Admonition conclude the Subject.

WHEN the sad soul, by care and grief oppress'd,
Looks round the world, but looks in vain for rest;
When every object that appears in view,
Partakes her gloom and seems dejected too;
Where shall affliction from itself retire?
Where fade away and placidly expire?
Alas! we fly to silent scenes in vain;
Care blasts the honours of the flow'ry plain:
Care veils in clouds the sun's meridian beam,
Sighs through the grove and murmurs in the stream;
For when the soul is labouring in despair,
In vain the body breathes a purer air:
No storm-toss'd sailor sighs for slumbering seas,—
He dreads the tempest, but invokes the breeze;
On the smooth mirror of the deep resides
Reflected wo, and o'er unruffled tides
The ghost of every former danger glides.
Thus, in the calms of life, we only see
A steadier image of our misery;
But lively gales and gently-clouded skies
Disperse the sad reflections as they rise;
And busy thoughts and little cares avail
To ease the mind, when rest and reason fail.
When the dull thought, by no designs employ'd,
Dwells on the past, or suffer'd or enjoy'd,
We bleed anew in every former grief,
And joys departed furnish no relief.

Not Hope herself, with all her flattering art,
Can cure this stubborn sickness of the heart:
The soul disdains each comfort she prepares,
And anxious searches for congenial cares;
Those lenient cares, which, with our own combined,
By mix'd sensations ease th' afflicted mind,
And steal our grief away, and leave their own behind;
A lighter grief! which feeling hearts endure
Without regret, nor e'en demand a cure.

But what strange art, what magic can dispose
The troubled mind to change its native woes?
Or lead us, willing from ourselves to see
Others more wretched, more undone than we?
This, books can do;—nor this alone; they give
New views to life, and teach us how to live;
They soothe the grieved, the stubborn they chastise,
Fools they admonish, and confirm the wise:
Their aid they yield to all: they never shun
The man of sorrow, nor the wretch undone:
Unlike the hard, the selfish, and the proud,
They fly not sullen from the suppliant crowd;
Nor tell to various people various things,
But show to subjects, what they show to kings.

Come, Child of Care! to make thy soul serene,
Approach the treasures of this tranquil scene;
Survey the dome, and, as the doors unfold,
The soul's best cure, in all her cares, behold!
Where mental wealth the poor in thought may find,
And mental physic the diseased in mind;
See here the balms that passion's wounds assuage;
See coolers here, that damp the fire of rage;
Here alt'ratives, by slow degrees control
The chronic habits of the sickly soul;
And round the heart and o'er the aching head,
Mild opiates here their sober influence shed.
Now bid thy soul man's busy scenes exclude,
And view composed this silent multitude:—
Silent they are, but, though deprived of sound,
Here all the living languages abound;
Here all that live no more; preserved they lie,
In tombs that open to the curious eye.

Bless'd be the gracious Power, who taught mankind
To stamp a lasting image of the mind!
Beasts may convey, and tuneful birds may sing,
Their mutual feelings, in the opening spring;
But man alone has skill and power to send
The heart's warm dictates to the distant friend:
'T is his alone to please, instruct, advise
Ages remote, and nations yet to rise.

In sweet repose, when labour's children sleep,
When joy forgets to smile and care to weep,
When passion slumbers in the lover's breast,
And fear and guilt partake the balm of rest,
Why then denies the studious man to share
Man's common good, who feels his common care?

Because the hope is his, that bids him fly
Night's soft repose, and sleep's mild power defy;
That after-ages may repeat his praise,
And fame's fair meed be his, for length of days.

Delightful prospect! when we leave behind
A worthy offspring of the fruitful mind!
Which, born and nursed through many an anxious day,
Shall all our labour, all our care repay.

Yet all are not these births of noble kind,
Not all the children of a vigorous mind;
But where the wisest should alone preside,
The weak would rule us, and the blind would guide;
Nay, man's best efforts taste of man, and show
The poor and troubled source from which they flow:
Where most he triumphs, we his wants perceive,
And for his weakness in his wisdom grieve.
But though imperfect all; yet wisdom loves
This seat serene, and virtue's self approves:—
Here come the grieved, a change of thought to find;
The curious here, to feed a craving mind;
Here the devout their peaceful temple choose;
And here the poet meets his favouring muse.

With awe, around these silent walks I tread;
These are the lasting mansions of the dead:—
"The dead," methinks a thousand tongues reply;
"These are the tombs of such as cannot die!
Crown'd with eternal fame, they sit sublime,
And laugh at all the little strife of time."

Hail, then, immortals! ye who shine above,
Each, in his sphere, the literary Jove;
And ye the common people of these skies,
A humbler crowd of nameless deities;
Whether 't is yours to lead the willing mind
Through history's mazes, and the turnings find;
Or whether, led by science, ye retire,
Lost and bewilder'd in the vast desire;
Whether the Muse invites you to her bowers,
And crowns your placid brows with living flowers;
Or godlike wisdom teaches you to show
The noblest road to happiness below;
Or men and manners prompt the easy page
To mark the flying follies of the age:
Whatever good ye boast, that good impart;
Inform the head and rectify the heart.

Lo! all in silence, all in order stand,
And mighty folios first, a lordly band;
Then quartos their well-order'd ranks maintain,
And light octavos fill a spacious plain:
See yonder, ranged in more frequented rows,
A humbler band of duodecimos;
While undistinguish'd trifles swell the scene,
The last new play and fritter'd magazine.
Thus 't is in life, where first the proud, the great,
In leagued assembly keep their cumbrous state;
Heavy and huge, they fill the world with dread,
Are much admired, and are but little read:
The commons next, a middle rank, are found;
Professions fruitful pour their offspring round;
Reasoners and wits are next their place allow'd,
And last, of vulgar tribes a countless crowd.

First, let us view the form, the size, the dress;
For these the manners, nay the mind express;
That weight of wood, with leathern coat o'erlaid;
Those ample clasps, of solid metal made;
The close-press'd leaves, unclosed for many an age;
The dull red edging of the well-fill'd page;
On the broad back the stubborn ridges roll'd,
Where yet the title stands in tarnish'd gold;
These all a sage and labour'd work proclaim,
A painful candidate for lasting fame:
No idle wit, no trifling verse can lurk
In the deep bosom of that weighty work;
No playful thoughts degrade the solemn style,
Nor one light sentence claims a transient smile.
Hence, in these times, untouch'd the pages lie,
And slumber out their immortality:
They *had* their day, when, after all his toil,
His morning study, and his midnight oil,
At length an author's ONE great work appear'd,
By patient hope, and length of days, endear'd:
Expecting nations hail'd it from the press;
Poetic friends prefix'd each kind address;
Princes and kings received the pond'rous gift,
And ladies read the work they could not lift.
Fashion, though Folly's child, and guide of fools,
Rules e'en the wisest, and in learning rules;
From crowds and courts to Wisdom's seat she goes,
And reigns triumphant o'er her mother's foes.
For lo! these fav'rites of the ancient mode
Lie all neglected like the Birth-day Ode;
Ah! needless now this weight of massy chain;*
Safe in themselves, the once-loved works remain;
No readers now invade their still retreat,
None try to steal them from their parent-seat;
Like ancient beauties, they may now discard
Chains, bolts, and locks, and lie without a guard.
Our patient fathers trifling themes laid by,
And roll'd o'er labour'd works th' attentive eye;
Page after page, th' much-enduring men
Explored, the deeps and shallows of the pen;
Till, every former note and comment known,
They mark'd the spacious margin with their own:
Minute corrections proved their studious care;
The little index, pointing, told us where;
And many an emendation show'd the age
Look'd far beyond the rubric title-page.

Our nicer palates lighter labours seek,
Cloy'd with a folio-*Number* once a week;
Bibles, with cuts and comments, thus go down:
E'en light Voltaire is *number'd* through the town:
Thus physic flies abroad; and thus the law,
From men of study, and from men of straw;
Abstracts, abridgments, please the fickle times,
Pamphlets and plays, and politics and rhymes:
But though to write be now a task of ease,
The task is hard by manly arts to please,
When all our weakness is exposed to view,
And half our judges are our rivals too.

Amid these works, on which the eager eye
Delights to fix, or glides reluctant by,
When all combined, their decent pomp display,
Where shall we first our early offering pay?—

To thee, DIVINITY! to thee, the light
And guide of mortals, through their mental night;
By whom we learn our hopes and fears to guide;
To bear with pain, and to contend with pride;
When grieved, to pray; when injured, to forgive;
And with the world in charity to live.
Not truths like these inspired that numerous race,
Whose pious labours fill this ample space;

* In the more ancient libraries, works of value and importance were fastened to their places by a length of chain; and might so be perused, but not taken away.

But questions nice, where doubt on doubt arose,
Awaked to war the long-contending foes.
For dubious meanings, learn'd polemics strove,
And wars on faith prevented works of love;
The brands of discord far around were hurl'd,
And holy wrath inflamed a sinful world:—
Dull though impatient, peevish though devout,
With wit disgusting and despised without;
Saints in design, in execution men,
Peace in their looks, and vengeance in their pen.

Methinks I see, and sicken at the sight,
Spirits of spleen from yonder pile alight;
Spirits who prompted every damning page,
With pontiff pride, and still-increasing rage.
Lo! how they stretch their gloomy wings around,
And lash with furious strokes the trembling ground!
They pray, they fight, they murder, and they weep,—
Wolves in their vengeance, in their manners sheep;
Too well they act the prophet's fatal part,
Denouncing evil with a zealous heart;
And each, like Jonas, is displeased if God
Repent his anger, or withhold his rod.

But here the dormant fury rests unsought,
And Zeal sleeps soundly by the foes she fought;
Here all the rage of controversy ends,
And rival zealots rest like bosom-friends:
An Athanasian here, in deep repose,
Sleeps with the fiercest of his Arian foes;
Socinians here with Calvinists abide,
And thin partitions angry chiefs divide;
Here wily Jesuits simple Quakers meet,
And Bellarmine has rest at Luther's feet.
Great authors, for the church's glory fired,
Are, for the church's peace, to rest retired;
And close beside, a mystic, maudlin race,
Lie, "Crums of Comfort for the Babes of Grace."

Against her foes Religion well defends
Her sacred truths, but often fears her friends;
If learn'd, their pride, if weak, their zeal she dreads,
And their hearts' weakness, who have soundest heads:
But most she fears the controversial pen,
The holy strife of disputatious men;
Who the bless'd Gospel's peaceful page explore,
Only to fight against its precepts more.

Near to these seats, behold yon slender frames,
All closely fill'd and mark'd with modern names;
Where no fair science ever shows her face,
Few sparks of genius, and no spark of grace:
There sceptics rest, a still-increasing throng,
And stretch their widening wings ten thousand strong:
Some in close fight their dubious claims maintain;
Some skirmish lightly, fly and fight again;
Coldly profane, and impiously gay,
Their end the same, though various in their way.

When first Religion came to bless the land,
Her friends were then a firm believing band;
To doubt was, then, to plunge in guilt extreme,
And all was gospel that a monk could dream;
Insulted Reason fled the grov'ling soul,
For Fear to guide, and visions to control;
But now, when Reason has assumed her throne,
She, in her turn, demands to reign alone;
Rejecting all that lies beyond her view,
And, being judge, will be a witness too:
Insulted Faith then leaves the doubtful mind,
To seek for truth, without a power to find:
Ah! when will both in friendly beams unite,
And pour on erring man resistless light?

Next to the seats, well stored with works divine,
An ample space, PHILOSOPHY! is thine;
Our reason's guide, by whose assisting light
We trace the moral bounds of wrong and right;
Our guide through nature, from the sterile clay,
To the bright orbs of yon celestial way!
'T is thine, the great, the golden chain to trace,
Which runs through all, connecting race with race
Save where those puzzling, stubborn links remain,
Which thy inferior light pursues in vain:—
How vice and virtue in the soul contend;
How widely differ, yet how nearly blend!
What various passions war on either part,
And now confirm, now melt the yielding heart:
How Fancy loves around the world to stray,
While Judgment slowly picks his sober way;
The stores of memory, and the flights sublime
Of genius, bound by neither space nor time;—
All these divine Philosophy explores,
Till, lost in awe, she wonders and adores.
From these, descending to the earth, she turns,
And matter, in its various form, discerns;
She parts the beamy light with skill profound,
Metes the thin air, and weighs the flying sound;
'T is hers, the lightning from the clouds to call,
And teach the fiery mischief where to fall.

Yet more her volumes teach,—on these we look
As abstracts drawn from Nature's larger book:
Here, first described, the torpid earth appears,
And next, the vegetable robe it wears;
Where flow'ry tribes, in valleys, fields, and groves,
Nurse the still flame, and feed the silent loves;
Loves, where no grief, nor joy, nor bliss, nor pain,
Warm the glad heart or vex the labouring brain;
But as the green blood moves along the blade,
The bed of Flora on the branch is made;
Where, without passion, love instinctive lives,
And gives new life, unconscious that it gives.
Advancing still in Nature's maze, we trace,
In dens and burning plains, her savage race;
With those same tribes who on their lord attend,
And find, in man, a master and a friend:
Man crowns the scene, a world of wonders new,
A moral world, that well demands our view.

This world is here; for, of more lofty kind,
These neighbouring volumes reason on the mind;
They paint the state of man ere yet endued
With knowledge;—man, poor, ignorant, and rude;
Then, as his state improves, their pages swell,
And all its cares, and all its comforts, tell:
Here we behold how inexperience buys,
At little price, the wisdom of the wise:
Without the troubles of an active state,
Without the cares and dangers of the great,
Without the miseries of the poor, we know
What wisdom, wealth, and poverty bestow;
We see how reason calms the raging mind,
And how contending passions urge mankind;
Some, won by virtue, glow with sacred fire;
Some, lured by vice, indulge the low desire,

Whilst others, won by either, now pursue
The guilty chase, now keep the good in view;
For ever wretched, with themselves at strife,
They lead a puzzled, vex'd, uncertain life;
For transient vice bequeaths a lingering pain,
Which transient virtue seeks to cure in vain.

Whilst thus engaged, high views enlarge the soul,
New interests draw, new principles control;
Nor thus the soul alone resigns her grief,
But here the tortured body finds relief;
For see where yonder fierce Arachnè shapes
Her subtile gin, that not a fly escapes!
There Physic fills the space, and far around,
Pile above pile, her learned works abound:
Glorious their aim—to ease the labouring heart;
To war with death, and stop his flying dart;
To trace the source whence the fierce contest grew,
And life's short lease on easier terms renew;
To calm the frenzy of the burning brain;
To heal the tortures of imploring pain;
Or, when more powerful ills all efforts brave,
To ease the victim no device can save,
And smooth the stormy passage to the grave.

But man, who knows no good unmix'd and pure,
Oft finds a poison where he sought a cure;
For grave deceivers lodge their labours here,
And cloud the science they pretend to clear:
Scourges for sin, the solemn tribe are sent;
Like fire and storms, they call us to repent;
But storms subside, and fires forget to rage,
These are eternal scourges of the age:
'T is not enough that each terrific hand
Spreads desolation round a guilty land;
But, train'd to ill, and harden'd by its crimes,
Their pen relentless kills through future times.
Say ye, who search those records of the dead,
Who read huge works, to boast what ye have read;
Can all the real knowledge ye possess,
Or those (if such there are) who more than guess,
Atone for each impostor's wild mistakes,
And mend the blunders pride and folly makes?

What thought so wild, what airy dream so light,
That will not prompt a theorist to write?
What art so prevalent, what proof so strong,
That will convince him his attempt is wrong?
One in the solids finds each lurking ill,
Nor grants the passive fluids power to kill:
A learned friend some subtler reason brings
Absolves the channels, but condemns their springs:
The subtile nerves, that shun the doctor's eye,
Escape no more his subtler theory;
The vital heat, that warms the labouring heart,
Lends a fair system to these sons of art;
The vital air, a pure and subtile stream,
Serves a foundation for an airy scheme,
Assists the doctor, and supports his dream.
Some have their favourite ills, and each disease
Is but a younger branch that kills from these:
One to the gout contracts all human pain,
He views it raging in the frantic brain;
Finds it in fevers all his efforts mar,
And sees it lurking in the cold catarrh:
Bilious by some, by others nervous seen,
Rage the fantastic demons of the spleen;
And every symptom of the strange disease
With every system of the sage agrees.

Ye frigid tribe, on whom I wasted long
The tedious hours, and ne'er indulged in song;
Ye first seducers of my easy heart,
Who promised knowledge ye could not impart;
Ye dull deluders, truth's destructive foes;
Ye sons of fiction, clad in stupid prose;
Ye treacherous leaders, who, yourselves in doubt,
Light up false fires, and send us far about;—
Still may yon spider round your pages spin,
Subtile and slow, her emblematic gin!
Buried in dust and lost in silence, dwell,
Most potent, grave, and reverend friends—farewell!

Near these, and where the setting sun displays,
Through the dim window, his departing rays,
And gilds yon columns, there, on either side,
The huge abridgements of the law abide;
Fruitful as vice the dread correctors stand,
And spread their guardian terrors round the land
Yet, as the best that human care can do,
Is mix'd with error, oft with evil too,
Skill'd in deceit, and practised to evade,
Knaves stand secure, for whom these laws were made;
And justice vainly each expedient tries,
While art eludes it, or while power defies.
"Ah! happy age," the youthful poet sings,
"When the free nations knew not laws nor kings;
When all were bless'd to share a common store,
And none were proud of wealth, for none were poor;
No wars nor tumults vex'd each still domain,
No thirst of empire, no desire of gain;
No proud great man, nor one who would be great,
Drove modest merit from its proper state;
Nor into distant climes would avarice roam,
To fetch delights for luxury at home:
Bound by no ties which kept the soul in awe,
They dwelt at liberty, and love was law!"

"Mistaken youth! each nation first was rude,
Each man a cheerless son of solitude,
To whom no joys of social life were known,
None felt a care that was not all his own;
Or in some languid clime his abject soul
Bow'd to a little tyrant's stern control;
A slave, with slaves his monarch's throne he raised,
And in rude song his ruder idol praised:
The meaner cares of life were all he knew;
Bounded his pleasures, and his wishes few:
But when by slow degrees the Arts arose,
And Science waken'd from her long repose;
When Commerce, rising from the bed of ease,
Ran round the land, and pointed to the seas;
When Emulation, born with jealous eye;
And Avarice, lent their spurs to industry,
Then one by one the numerous laws were made,
Those to control, and these to succour trade;
To curb the insolence of rude command,
To snatch the victim from the usurer's hand;
To awe the bold, to yield the wrong'd redress,
And feed the poor with Luxury's excess."

Like some vast flood, unbounded, fierce, and strong,
His nature leads ungovern'd man along;
Like mighty bulwarks made to stem that tide,
The laws are form'd and placed on ev'ry side:
Whene'er it breaks the bounds by these decreed,
New statutes rise, and stronger laws succeed;

More and more gentle grows the dying stream,
More and more strong the rising bulwarks seem;
Till, like a miner working sure and slow,
Luxury creeps on, and ruins all below:
The basis sinks, the ample piles decay;
The stately fabric shakes and falls away;
Primeval want and ignorance come on,
But freedom, that exalts the savage state, is gone.

Next, HISTORY ranks;—there full in front she lies,
And every nation her dread tale supplies;
Yet History has her doubts, and every age
With sceptic queries marks the passing page;
Records of old nor later date are clear,
Too distant those, and these are placed too near;
There time conceals the objects from our view,
Here our own passions and a writer's too:
Yet, in these volumes, see how states arose!
Guarded by virtue from surrounding foes;
Their virtue lost, and of their triumphs vain,
Lo! how they sunk to slavery again!
Satiate with power, of fame and wealth possess'd,
A nation grows too glorious to be bless'd;
Conspicuous made, she stands the mark of all,
And foes join foes to triumph in her fall.

Thus speaks the page that paints ambition's race,
The monarch's pride, his glory, his disgrace;
The headlong course, that madd'ning heroes run,
How soon triumphant, and how soon undone;
How slaves, turn'd tyrants, offer crowns to sale,
And each fall'n nation's melancholy tale.

Lo! where of late the Book of Martyrs stood,
Old pious tracts, and Bibles bound in wood;
There, such the taste of this degenerate age,
Stand the profane delusions of the STAGE:
Yet virtue owns the TRAGIC MUSE a friend,
Fable her means, morality her end;
For this she rules all passions in their turns,
And now the bosom bleeds, and now it burns;
Pity with weeping eye surveys her bowl,
Her anger swells, her terror chills the soul;
She makes the vile to virtue yield applause,
And own her sceptre while they break her laws;
For vice in others is abhorred by all,
And villains triumph where the worthless fall.

Not thus her sister COMEDY prevails,
Who shoots at folly, for her arrow fails;
Folly, by dulness arm'd, eludes the wound,
And harmless sees the feather'd shafts rebound;
Unhurt she stands, applauds the archer's skill,
Laughs at her malice, and is folly still.
Yet well the Muse portrays, in fancied scenes,
What pride will stoop to, what profession means;
How formal fools the farce of state applaud;
How caution watches at the lips of fraud:
The wordy variance of domestic life;
The tyrant husband, the retorting wife;
The snares for innocence, the lie of trade,
And the smooth tongue's habitual masquerade.

With her the virtues too obtain a place,
Each gentle passion, each becoming grace;
The social joy in life's securer road,
Its easy pleasure, its substantial good;
The happy thought that conscious virtue gives,
And all that ought to live, and all that lives.

But who are these? Methinks a noble mien
And awful grandeur in their form are seen,
Now in disgrace: what though by time is spread
Polluting dust o'er every reverend head;
What though beneath yon gilded tribe they lie
And dull observers pass insulting by:
Forbid it shame, forbid it decent awe
What seems so grave, should not attention draw!
Come, let us then with reverend step advance,
And greet—the ancient worthies of ROMANCE.

Hence, ye profane! I feel a former dread,
A thousand visions float around my head;
Hark! hollow blasts through empty courts resound,
And shadowy forms with staring eyes stalk round;
See! moats and bridges, walls and castles rise,
Ghosts, fairies, demons, dance before your eyes;
Lo! magic verse inscribe on golden gate,
And bloody hand that beckons on to fate:—
"And who art thou, thou little page, unfold?
Say, doth thy lord my Claribel withhold?
Go tell him straight, Sir Knight, thou must resign
The captive queen;—for Claribel is mine."
Away he flies; and now for bloody deeds,
Black suits of armour, masks, and foaming steeds;
The giant falls; his recreant throat I seize,
And from his corslet take the massy keys:—
Dukes, lords, and knights in long procession move,
Released from bondage with my virgin love:—
She comes! she comes! in all the charms of youth,
Unequall'd love and unsuspected truth!

Ah! happy he who thus, in magic themes,
O'er worlds bewitch'd, in early rapture dreams,
Where wild Enchantment waves her potent wand,
And Fancy's beauties fill her fairy land;
Where doubtful objects strange desires excite,
And Fear and Ignorance afford delight.

But lost, for ever lost, to me these joys,
Which Reason scatters, and which Time destroys,
Too dearly bought: maturer judgment calls
My busied mind from tales and madrigals;
My doughty giants all are slain or fled,
And all my knights blue, green, and yellow, dead!
No more the midnight fairy tribe I view,
All in the merry moonshine tippling dew;
E'en the last lingering fiction of the brain,
The church-yard ghost, is now at rest again;
And all these wayward wanderings of my youth
Fly Reason's power, and shun the light of truth.

With fiction then does real joy reside,
And is our reason the delusive guide?
Is it then right to dream the syrens sing?
Or mount enraptured on the dragon's wing?
No, 't is the infant mind, to care unknown,
That makes th' imagined paradise its own;
Soon as reflections in the bosom rise,
Light slumbers vanish from the clouded eyes:
The tear and smile that once together rose,
Are then divorced; the head and heart are foes:
Enchantment bows to Wisdom's serious plan,
And pain and prudence make and mar the man.

While thus of power and fancied empire vain,
With various thoughts my mind I entertain;
While books my slaves, with tyrant hand I seize,
Pleased with the pride that will not let them please

Sudden I find terrific thoughts arise,
And sympathetic sorrow fills my eyes;
For lo! while yet my heart admits the wound,
I see the Critic army ranged around.

Foes to our race! if ever ye have known
A father's fears for offspring of your own—
If ever, smiling o'er a lucky line,
Ye thought the sudden sentiment divine,
Then paused and doubted, and then, tired of doubt,
With rage as sudden, dash'd the stanza out;—
If, after fearing much and pausing long,
Ye ventur'd on the world your labour'd song,
And from the crusty critics of those days
Implored the feeble tribute of their praise;
Remember now the fears that moved you then,
And, spite of truth, let mercy guide your pen.

What vent'rous race are ours! what mighty foes
Lie waiting all around them to oppose!
What treacherous friends betray them to the fight!
What dangers threaten them!—yet still they write:
A hapless tribe! to every evil born,
Whom villains hate, and fools affect to scorn:
Strangers they come amid a world of wo,
And taste the largest portion ere they go.

Pensive I spoke, and cast mine eyes around;
The roof, methought, return'd a solemn sound;
Each column seem'd to shake, and clouds, like smoke,
From dusty piles and ancient volumes broke;
Gathering above, like mists condensed they seem,
Exhaled in summer from the rushy stream;
Like flowing robes they now appear, and twine
Round the large members of a form divine;
His silver beard, that swept his aged breast,
His piercing eye, that inward light express'd,
Were seen,—but clouds and darkness veil'd the rest.
Fear chill'd my heart: to one of mortal race
How awful seem'd the Genius of the place!
So in Cimmerian shores, Ulysses saw
His parent-shade, and shrunk in pious awe;
Like him I stood, and wrapt in thought profound,
When from the pitying power broke forth a solemn sound:—

"Care lives with all; no rules, no precepts save
The wise from wo, no fortitude the brave;
Grief is to man as certain as the grave:
Tempests and storms in life's whole progress rise,
And hope shines dimly through o'erclouded skies;
Some drops of comfort on the favour'd fall,
But showers of sorrow are the lot of *all:*
Partial to talents, then shall Heaven withdraw
Th' afflicting rod, or break the general law?
Shall he who soars, inspired by loftier views,
Life's little cares and little pains refuse?
Shall he not rather feel a double share
Of mortal wo, when doubly arm'd to bear?

"Hard is his fate who builds his peace of mind
On the precarious mercy of mankind;
Who hopes for wild and visionary things,
And mounts o'er unknown seas with vent'rous wings:
But as, of various evils that befal
The human race, some portion goes to all,
To him perhaps the milder lot's assign'd,
Who feels his consolation in his mind;
And, lock'd within his bosom, bears about
A mental charm for every care without.
E'en in the pangs of each domestic grief,
Or health or vigorous hope affords relief;
And every wound the tortured bosom feels,
Or virtue bears, or some preserver heals;
Some generous friend, of ample power possess'd;
Some feeling heart, that bleeds for the distress'd;
Some breast that glows with virtues all divine;
Some noble Rutland, Misery's friend and thine.

"Nor say, the Muse's song, the Poet's pen,
Merit the scorn they meet from little men.
With cautious freedom if the numbers flow,
Not wildly high, nor pitifully low;
If vice alone their honest aims oppose,
Why so ashamed their friends, so loud their foes?
Happy for men in every age and clime,
If all the sons of vision dealt in rhyme.
Go on then, Son of Vision! still pursue
Thy airy dreams; the world is dreaming too.
Ambition's lofty views, the pomp of state,
The pride of wealth, the splendour of the great,
Stripp'd of their mask, their cares and troubles known,
Are visions far less happy than thy own;
Go on! and, while the sons of care complain,
Be wisely gay and innocently vain:
While serious souls are by their fears undone,
Blow sportive bladders in the beamy sun,
And call them worlds! and bid the greatest show
More radiant colours to their worlds below:
Then, as they break, the slaves of care reprove,
And tell them, Such are all the toys they love."

THE NEWSPAPER.

E quibus, hi vacuas implent sermonibus aures,
Hi narrata ferunt alio: Mensuraque ficti
Crescit, et auditis aliquid novus adjicit auctor:
Illic Credulitas, illic temerarius Error,
Vanaque Lætitia est; consternatique Timores,
Seditioque recens, dubioque auctore Susurri.

OVID, *Metamorph.* lib. xii.

This not a time favourable to poetical Composition: and why—Newspapers Enemies to Literature, and their general Influence—Their Numbers—The Sunday Monitor—Their general Character—Their Effect upon Individuals—upon Society—in the Country—The Village Freeholder—What kind of Composition a Newspaper is; and the Amusement it affords—Of what Parts it is chiefly composed—Articles of Intelligence: Advertisements: The Stage: Quacks: Puffing—The Correspondents to a Newspaper, political and poetical—Advice to the latter—Conclusion.

A time like this, a busy, bustling time,
Suits ill with writers, very ill with rhyme:
Unheard we sing, when party-rage runs strong,
And mightier madness checks the flowing song:
Or, should we force the peaceful Muse to wield
Her feeble arm amid the furious field,

Where party-pens a wordy war maintain,
Poor is her anger, and her friendship vain;
And oft the foes who feel her sting, combine,
Till serious vengeance pays an idle line;
For party-poets are like wasps, who dart
Death to themselves, and to their foes but smart.

Hard then our fate: if general themes we choose,
Neglect awaits the song, and chills the Muse;
Or shall we sing the subject of the day,
To-morrow's wonder puffs our praise away.
More bless'd the bards of that poetic time,
When all found readers who could find a rhyme;
Green grew the bays on every teeming head,
And Cibber was enthroned, and Settle read.
Sing, drooping Muse, the cause of thy decline;
Why reign no more the once-triumphant Nine?
Alas! new charms the wavering may gain,
And rival sheets the reader's eye detain;
A daily swarm, that banish every Muse,
Come flying forth, and mortals call them NEWS:
For these, unread, the noblest volume lie;
For these, in sheets unsoil'd, the Muses die;
Unbought, unbless'd, the virgin copies wait
In vain for fame, and sink, unseen, to fate.

Since, then, the town forsakes us for our foes,
The smoothest numbers for the harshest prose;
Let us, with generous scorn, the taste deride,
And sing our rivals with a rival's pride.

Ye gentle poets who so oft complain
That foul neglect is all your labour's gain;
That pity only checks your growing spite
To erring man, and prompts you still to write;
That your choice works on humble stalls are laid,
Or vainly grace the windows of the trade;
Be ye my friends, if friendship e'er can warm
Those rival bosoms whom the Muses charm:
Think of the common cause wherein we go,
Like gallant Greeks against the Trojan foe;
Nor let our peevish chief his leader blame,
Till, crown'd with conquest, we regain our fame;
And let us join our forces to subdue
This bold assuming but successful crew.

I sing of NEWS, and all these vapid sheets
The rattling hawker vends through gaping streets;
Whate'er their name, whate'er the time they fly,
Damp from the press to charm the reader's eye;
For, soon as morning dawns with roseate hue,
The Herald of the morn arises too;
Post after Post succeeds, and, all day long,
Gazettes and Ledgers swarm, a noisy throng.
When evening comes, she comes with all her train
Of Ledgers, Chronicles, and Posts again,
Like bats, appearing, when the sun goes down,
From holes obscure and corners of the town.
Of all these triflers, all like these, I write;
Oh! like my subject could my song delight,
The crowd at Lloyd's one poet's name should raise,
And all the Alley echo to his praise.

In shoals the hours their constant numbers bring,
Like insects waking to th' advancing spring;
Which take their rise from grubs obscene that lie
In shallow pools, or thence ascend the sky:
Such are these base ephemera, so born
To die before the next revolving morn.

Yet thus they differ: insect-tribes are lost
In the first visit of a winter's frost;
While these remain, a base but constant breed,
Whose swarming sons their short-lived sires succeed;
No changing season makes their number less,
Nor Sunday shines a sabbath on the press!

Then lo! the sainted Monitor is born,
Whose pious face some sacred texts adorn:
As artful sinners cloak the secret sin,
To veil with seeming grace the guile within;
So Moral Essays on his front appear,
But all is carnal business in the rear;
The fresh-coin'd lie, the secret whisper'd last,
And all the gleanings of the six days past.

With these retired, through half the Sabbath-day,
The London-lounger yawns his hours away:
Not so, my little flock! your preacher fly,
Nor waste the time no worldly wealth can buy;
But let the decent maid and sober clown
Pray for these idlers of the sinful town:
This day, at least, on nobler themes bestow,
Nor give to Woodfall, or the world below.

But, Sunday pass'd, what numbers flourish then,
What wondrous labours of the press and pen!
Diurnal most, some thrice each week affords,
Some only once,—O avarice of words!
When thousand starving minds such manna seek,*
To drop the precious food but once a week.

Endless it were to sing the powers of all,
Their names, their numbers; how they rise and fall:
Like baneful herbs the gazer's eye they seize,
Rush to the head, and poison where they please:
Like idle flies, a busy, buzzing train,
They drop their maggots in the trifler's brain:
That genial soil receives the fruitful store,
And there they grow, and breed a thousand more.

Now be their arts display'd, how first they choose
A cause and party, as the bard his muse;
Inspired by these, with clamorous zeal they cry,
And through the town their dreams and omens fly:
So the Sibylline leaves were blown about,†
Disjointed scraps of fate involved in doubt;
So idle dreams, the journals of the night,
Are right and wrong by turns, and mingle wrong with right.—
Some champions for the rights that prop the crown,
Some sturdy patriots, sworn to pull them down;
Some neutral powers, with secret forces fraught,
Wishing for war, but willing to be bought:
While some to every side and party go,
Shift every friend, and join with every foe;
Like sturdy rogues in privateers, they strike
This side and that, the foes of both alike;
A traitor-crew, who thrive in troubled times,
Fear'd for their force, and courted for their crimes.

Chief to the prosperous side the numbers sail,
Fickle and false, they veer with every gale;
As birds that migrate from a freezing shore,
In search of warmer climes, come skimming o'er,

* The Manna of the Day.—GREEN'S *Spleen*.

† . . . . . . in foliis descripsit carmina Virgo;—
. . . . . . et teneres turbavit janua frondes.
VIRG. *Æneid*. lib. iii.

Some bold adventurers first prepare to try
The doubtful sunshine of the distant sky;
But soon the growing Summer's certain sun
Wins more and more, till all at last are won:
So, on the early prospect of disgrace,
Fly in vast troops this apprehensive race;
Instinctive tribes! their failing food they dread,
And buy, with timely change, their future bread.

Such are our guides: how many a peaceful head,
Born to be still, have they to wrangling led!
How many an honest zealot, stolen from trade,
And factious tools of pious pastors made!
With clews like these they tread the maze of state,
These oracles explore, to learn our fate;
Pleased with the guides who can so well deceive,
Who cannot lie so fast as they believe.

Oft lend I, loth, to some sage friend an ear
(For we who will not speak are doom'd to hear);
While he, bewilder'd, tells his anxious thought,
Infectious fear from tainted scribblers caught,
Or idiot hope; for each his mind assails,
As Lloyd's court-light or Stockdale's gloom prevails.
Yet stand I patient while but one declaims,
Or gives dull comments on the speech he maims:
But oh! ye Muses, keep your votary's feet
From tavern-haunts where politicians meet;
Where rector, doctor, and attorney pause,
First on each parish, then each public cause:
Indited roads and rates that still increase;
The murmuring poor, who will not fast in peace;
Election-zeal and friendship, since declined;
A tax commuted, or a tithe in kind;
The Dutch and Germans kindling into strife;
Dull port and poachers vile! the serious ills of life.

Here comes the neighbouring justice, pleased to guide
His little club, and in the chair preside.
In private business his commands prevail,
On public themes his reasoning turns the scale;
Assenting silence soothes his happy ear,
And, in or out, his party triumphs here.

Nor here th' infectious rage for party stops,
But flits along from palaces to shops;
Our weekly journals o'er the land abound,
And spread their plague and influenzas round;
The village, too, the peaceful, pleasant plain,
Breeds the Whig-farmer and the Tory swain;
Brookes' and St. Albans' boasts not; but, instead,
Stares the Red Ram, and swings the Rodney's Head:—
Hither, with all a patriot's care, comes he
Who owns the little hut that makes him free;
Whose yearly forty shillings buy the smile
Of mightier men, and never waste the while;
Who feels his freehold's worth, and looks elate,
A little prop and pillar of the state.

Here he delights the weekly news to con,
And mingle comments as he blunders on;
To swallow all their varying authors teach,
To spell a title, and confound a speech:
Till with a muddled mind he quits the news,
And claims his nation's license to abuse;
Then joins the cry, "That all the courtly race
Are venal candidates for power and place;"
Yet feels some joy, amid the general vice,
That his own vote will bring its wonted price.

These are the ills the teeming press supplies,
The pois'nous springs from learning's fountain rise;
Not there the wise alone their entrance find,
Imparting useful light to mortals blind;
But, blind themselves, these erring guides hold out
Alluring lights, to lead us far about;
Screen'd by such means, here Scandal whets her quill,
Here Slander shoots unseen, whene'er she will;
Here Fraud and Falsehood labour to deceive,
And Folly aids them both, impatient to believe.

Such, sons of Britain! are the guides ye trust;
So wise their counsel, their reports so just:—
Yet, though we cannot call their morals pure,
Their judgment nice, or their decisions sure,
Merit they have to mightier works unknown,
A style, a manner, and a fate their own.

We, who for longer fame with labour strive,
Are pain'd to keep our sickly works alive;
Studious we toil, with patient care refine,
Nor let our love protect one languid line.
Severe ourselves, at last our works appear,
When, ah! we find our readers more severe;
For after all our care and pains, how few
Acquire applause, or keep it if they do!—

Not so these sheets, ordain'd to happier fate,
Praised through their day, and but that day their date;
Their careless authors only strive to join
As many words, as make an even line;*
As many lines, as fill a row complete;
As many rows, as furnish up a sheet;
From side to side, with ready types they run,
The measure 's ended, and the work is done;
Oh, born with ease, how envied and how blest!
Your fate to-day and your to-morrow's rest.
To you all readers turn, and they can look
Pleased on a paper, who abhor a book;
Those, who ne'er deign'd their Bible to peruse,
Would think it hard to be denied their news;
Sinners and saints, the wisest with the weak,
Here mingle tastes, and one amusement seek;
This, like the public inn, provides a treat,
Where each promiscuous guest sits down to eat;
And such this mental food, as we may call
Something to all men, and to some men all.

Next, in what rare production shall we trace
Such various subjects in so small a space?
As the first ship upon the waters bore
Incongruous kinds who never met before;
Or as some curious virtuoso joins,
In one small room, moths, minerals, and coins,
Birds, beasts, and fishes; nor refuses place
To serpents, toads, and all the reptile race;
So here, compress'd within a single sheet,
Great things and small, the mean and mighty meet
'T is this which makes all Europe's business known,
Yet here a private man may place his own;

---

* How many hours bring about the day,
How many days will furnish up the year,
How many years a mortal man may live, etc.
SHAKSPEARE'S *Henry VI*

And, where he reads of Lords and Commons, he
May tell their honours that he sells rappee.

Add next th' amusement which the motley page
Affords to either sex and every age :
Lo! where it comes before the cheerful fire,—
Damps from the press in smoky curls aspire
(As from the earth the sun exhales the dew),
Ere we can read the wonders that ensue :
Then eager every eye surveys the part,
That brings its favourite subject to the heart ;
Grave politicians look for facts alone,
And gravely add conjectures of their own :
The sprightly nymph, who never broke her rest
For tottering crowns, or mighty lands oppress'd,
Finds broils and battles, but neglects them all
For songs and suits, a birth-day or a ball :
The keen warm man o'erlooks each idle tale
For "Money 's wanted," and "Estates on Sale ;"
While some with equal minds to all attend,
Pleased with each part, and grieved to find an end.

So charm the News ; but we, who, far from town,
Wait till the postman brings the packet down,
Once in the week, a vacant day behold,
And stay for tidings, till they 're three days old :
That day arrives ; no welcome post appears,
But the dull morn a sullen aspect wears ;
We meet, but ah ! without our wonted smile,
To talk of headaches, and complain of bile ;
Sullen we ponder o'er a dull repast,
Nor feast the body while the mind must fast.

A master-passion is the love of news,
Not music so commands, nor so the Muse :
Give poets claret, they grow idle soon ;
Feed the musician, and he 's out of tune ;
But the sick mind, of this disease possess'd,
Flies from all cure, and sickens when at rest.
Now sing, my Muse, what various parts compose
These rival sheets of politics and prose.

First, from each brother's hoard a part they draw,
A mutual theft that never fear'd a law ;
Whate'er they gain, to each man's portion fall,
And read it once, you read it through them all :
For this their runners ramble day and night,
To drag each lurking deed to open light ;
For daily bread the dirty trade they ply,
Coin their fresh tales, and live upon the lie :
Like bees for honey, forth for news they spring,—
Industrious creatures ! ever on the wing ;
Home to their several cells they bear the store,
Cull'd of all kinds, then roam abroad for more.
No anxious virgin flies to "fair Tweed-side ;"
No injured husband mourns his faithless bride ;
No duel dooms the fiery youth to bleed ;
But through the town transpires each vent'rous deed.

Should some fair frail-one drive her prancing pair
Where rival peers contend to please the fair ;
When, with new force, she aids her conquering eyes,
And beauty decks, with all that beauty buys ;
Quickly we learn whose heart her influence feels,
Whose acres melt before her glowing wheels.

To these a thousand idle themes succeed,
Deeds of all kinds, and comments to each deed.
Here stocks, the state-barometers, we view,
That rise or fall, by causes known to few ;
Promotion's ladder who goes up or down ;
Who wed, or who seduced, amuse the town ;
What new-born heir has made his father blest ;
What heir exults, his father now at rest ;
That ample list the Tyburn-herald gives,
And each known knave who still for Tyburn lives.

So grows the work, and now the printer tries
His powers no more, but leans on his allies,
When lo ! the advertising tribe succeed,
Pay to be read, yet find but few will read ;
And chief th' illustrious race, whose drops and pills
Have patent powers to vanquish human ills :
These, with their cures, a constant aid remain,
To bless the pale composer's fertile brain ;
Fertile it is, but still the noblest soil
Requires some pause, some intervals from toil ;
And they at least a certain ease obtain
From Katterfelto's skill, and Graham's glowing strain.

I too must aid, and pay to see my name
Hung in these dirty avenues to fame ;
Nor pay in vain, if aught the muse has seen
And sung, could make their avenues more clean ;
Could stop one slander ere it found its way,
And gave to public scorn its helpless prey.
By the same aid, the Stage invites her friends,
And kindly tells the banquet she intends ;
Thither from real life the many run,
With Siddons weep, or laugh with Abingdon ·
Pleased in fictitious joy or grief, to see
The mimic passion with their own agree ;
To steal a few enchanted hours away
From care, and drop the curtain on the day.

But who can steal from self, that wretched wight,
Whose darling work is tried some fatal night ?
Most wretched man ! when, bane to every bliss,
He hears the serpent-critic's rising hiss ;
Then groans succeed : not traitors on the wheel
Can feel like him, or have such pangs to feel.
Nor end they here : next day he reads his fall
In every paper ; critics are they all ;
He sees his branded name, with wild affright,
And hears again the cat-calls of the night.

Such help the STAGE affords : a larger space
Is fill'd by PUFFS and all the puffing race.
Physic had once alone the lofty style,
The well-known boast, that ceased to raise a smile :
Now all the province of that tribe invade,
And we abound in quacks of every trade.

The simple barber, once an honest name,
Cervantes founded, Fielding raised his fame :
Barber no more—a gay perfumer comes,
On whose soft cheek his own cosmetic blooms ;
Here he appears, each simple mind to move,
And advertises beauty, grace, and love.
—"Come, faded belles, who would your youth renew,
And learn the wonders of Olympian dew ;
Restore the roses that begin to faint,
Nor think celestial washes vulgar paint ;
Your former features, airs, and arts assume,
Circassian virtues, with Circassian bloom.

—Come, batter'd beaux, whose locks are turn'd to grey,
And crop Discretion's lying badge away;
Read where they vend these smart engaging things,
These flaxen frontlets with elastic springs;
No female eye the fair deception sees,
Not Nature's self so natural as these."

Such are their arts, but not confined to them,
The Muse impartial must her sons condemn;
For they, degenerate! join the venal throng,
And puff a lazy Pegasus along:
More guilty these, by Nature less design'd
For little arts that suit the vulgar kind:—
That barbers' boys, who would to trade advance,
Wish us to call them, smart Friseurs from France;
That he who builds a chop-house, on his door
Paints "The true old original Blue Boar!"

These are the arts by which a thousand live,
Where Truth may smile, and Justice may forgive;
But when, amid this rabble-rout, we find
A puffing poet to his honour blind;
Who silly drops quotations all about,
Packet or Post, and points their merit out;
Who advertises what reviewers say,
With sham editions every second day;
Who dares not trust his praises out of sight,
But hurries into fame with all his might;
Although the verse some transient praise obtains,
Contempt is all the anxious poet gains.

Now puffs exhausted, advertisements past,
Their correspondents stand exposed at last;
These are a numerous tribe, to fame unknown,
Who for the public good forego their own;
Who volunteers in paper-war engage,
With double portion of their party's rage:
Such are the Bruti, Decii, who appear
Wooing the printer for admission here;
Whose generous souls can condescend to pray
For leave to throw their precious time away.

Oh! cruel Woodfall! when a patriot draws
His grey-goose quill in his dear country's cause,
To vex and maul a ministerial race,
Can thy stern soul refuse the champion place?
Alas! thou know'st not with what anxious heart
He longs his best-loved labours to impart;
How he has sent them to thy brethren round,
And still the same unkind reception found:
At length indignant will he damn the state,
Turn to his trade, and leave us to our fate.

These Roman souls, like Rome's great sons, are known
To live in cells on labours of their own.
Thus Milo, could we see the noble chief,
Feeds, for his country's good, on legs of beef:
Camillus copies deeds for sordid pay,
Yet fights the public battles twice a day:
E'en now the godlike Brutus views his score
Scroll'd on the bar-board, swinging with the door;
Where, tippling punch, grave Cato's self you'll see,
And *Amor Patriæ* vending smuggled tea.

Last in these ranks, and least, their art's disgrace,
Neglected stand the Muses' meanest race;
Scribblers who court contempt, whose verse the eye
Disdainful views, and glances swiftly by:
This Poet's Corner is the place they choose,
A fatal nursery for an infant Muse;
Unlike that corner where true poets lie,
These cannot live, and they shall never die;
Hapless the lad whose mind such dreams invade,
And win to verse the talents due to trade.

Curb then, O youth! these raptures as they rise,
Keep down the evil spirit and be wise;
Follow your calling, think the Muses foes,
Nor lean upon the pestle and compose.

I know your day-dreams, and I know the snare
Hid in your flow'ry path, and cry "Beware."
Thoughtless of ill, and to the future blind,
A sudden couplet rushes on your mind;
Here you may nameless print your idle rhymes,
And read your first-born work a thousand times;
Th' infection spreads, your couplet grows apace,
Stanzas to Delia's dog or Celia's face:
You take a name; Philander's odes are seen,
Printed, and praised, in every magazine:
Diarian sages greet their brother sage,
And your dark pages please th' enlighten'd age.—
Alas! what years you thus consume in vain,
Ruled by this wretched bias of the brain!

Go! to your desks and counters all return;
Your sonnets scatter, your acrostics burn;
Trade, and be rich; or, should your careful sires
Bequeath you wealth! indulge the nobler fires:
Should love of fame your youthful heart betray,
Pursue fair fame, but in a glorious way,
Nor in the idle scenes of Fancy's painting stray.

Of all the good that mortal men pursue,
The Muse has least to give, and gives to few;
Like some coquettish fair, she leads us on,
With smiles and hopes, till youth and peace are gone;
Then, wed for life, the restless wrangling pair
Forget how constant one, and one how fair;
Meanwhile, Ambition, like a blooming bride,
Brings power and wealth to grace her lover's side;
And though she smiles not with such flattering charms,
The brave will sooner win her to their arms.

Then wed to her, if Virtue tie the bands,
Go spread your country's fame in hostile lands;
Her court, her senate, or her arms adorn,
And let her foes lament that you were born:
Or weigh her laws, their ancient rights defend,
Though hosts oppose, be theirs and Reason's friend
Arm'd with strong powers, in their defence engage
And rise the Thurlow of the future age.

THE

BIRTH OF FLATTERY.

Omnia habeo, nec quicquam habeo;
Quidquid dicunt, laudo; id rursum si negant, laudo id quoque:
Negat quis, nego; ait, aio:
Postremo imperavi egomet mihi
Omnia assentari.

TERENT. *in Eunuch.*

It has been held in ancient rules
That flattery is the food of fools;
Yet now and then your men of wit
Will condescend to taste a bit.

SWIFT.

The subject — Poverty and Cunning described — When united, a jarring couple—Mutual Reproof —The Wife consoled by a Dream—Birth of a Daughter—Description and Prediction of Envy—How to be rendered ineffectual, explained in a Vision—Simulation foretells the future Success and Triumphs of Flattery—Her Power over various Characters and different Minds; over certain Classes of men; over Envy himself—Her successful art of softening the Evils of Life; of changing Characters; of meliorating Prospects, and affixing Value to Possessions, Pictures, etc.—Conclusion.

MUSE of my Spenser, who so well could sing
The passions all, their bearings and their ties;
Who could in view those shadowy beings bring,
And with bold hand remove each dark disguise,
Wherein love, hatred, scorn, or anger lies:
Guide him to Fairy-land, who now intends
That way his flight; assist him as he flies,
To mark those passions, Virtue's foes and friends,
By whom when led she droops, when leading she ascends.

Yes! they appear, I see the fairy train!
And who that modest nymph of meek address?
Not Vanity, though loved by all the vain:
Not hope, though promising to all success;
Nor Mirth, nor joy, though foe to all distress;
Thee, sprightly syren, from this train I choose,
Thy birth relate, thy soothing arts confess;
'T is not in thy mild nature to refuse,
When poets ask thine aid, so oft their meed and muse.

In Fairy-land, on wide and cheerless plain,
Dwelt, in the house of Care, a sturdy swain;
A hireling he, who, when he till'd the soil,
Look'd to the pittance that repaid his toil;
And to a master left the mingled joy
And anxious care that follow'd his employ;
Sullen and patient he at once appear'd,
As one who murmur'd, yet as one who fear'd;
Th' attire was coarse that clothed his sinewy frame,
Rude his address, and Poverty his name.

In that same plain a nymph, of curious taste,
A cottage (plann'd with all her skill) had placed;
Strange the materials, and for what design'd
The various parts, no simple man might find;
What seem'd the door, each entering guest withstood,
What seem'd a window was but painted wood;
But by a secret spring the wall would move,
And daylight drop through glassy door above;
'T was all her pride, new traps for praise to lay,
And all her wisdom was to hide her way;
In small attempts incessant were her pains.
And Cunning was her name among the swains.

Now whether fate decreed this pair should wed,
And blindly drove them to the marriage bed;
Or whether love in some soft hour inclined
The damsel's heart, and won her to be kind,
Is yet unsung: they were an ill-match'd pair,
But both disposed to wed—and wed they were.

Yet though united in their fortune, still
Their ways were diverse; varying was their will;
Nor long the maid had bless'd the simple man,
Before dissensions rose, and she began:—

"Wretch that I am! since to thy fortune bound,
What plan, what project, with success is crown'd?
I, who a thousand secret arts possess,
Who every rank approach with right address;
Who've loosed a guinea from a miser's chest,
And worm'd his secret from a traitor's breast;
Thence gifts and gains collecting, great and small,
Have brought to thee, and thou consumest them all:
For want like thine—a bog without a base—
Ingulfs all gains I gather for the place;
Feeding, unfill'd; destroying, undestroy'd;
It craves for ever, and is ever void:—
Wretch that I am! what misery have I found,
Since my sure craft was to thy calling bound!"

"Oh! vaunt of worthless art," the swain replied
Scowling contempt, "how pitiful this pride!
What are these specious gifts, these paltry gains,
But base rewards for ignominions pains?
With all thy tricking, still for bread we strive,
Thine is, proud wretch! the care that cannot thrive
By all thy boasted skill and baffled hooks,
Thou gain'st no more than students by their books;
No more than I for my poor deeds am paid,
Whom none can blame, will help, or dare upbraid.

"Call this our need, a bog that all devours,—
Then what thy petty arts, but summer-flowers,
Gaudy and mean, and serving to betray
The place they make unprofitably gay?
Who know it not, some useless beauties see,—
But ah! to prove it, was reserved for me."

Unhappy state! that, in decay of love,
Permits harsh truth his errors to disprove;
While he remains, to wrangle and to jar,
Is friendly tournament, not fatal war;
Love in his play will borrow arms of hate,
Anger and rage, upbraiding and debate;
And by his power the desperate weapons thrown,
Become as safe and pleasant as his own;
But left by him, their natures they assume,
And fatal, in their poisoning force, become.

Time fled, and now the swain compell'd to see
New cause for fear—"Is this thy thrift?" quoth he
To whom the wife with cheerful voice replied:—
"Thou moody man, lay all thy fears aside,

I've seen a vision;—they, from whom I came,
A daughter promise, promise wealth and fame;
Born with my features, with my arts, yet she
Shall patient, pliant, persevering be,
And in thy better ways resemble thee.
The fairies round shall at her birth attend,
The friend of all in all shall find a friend,
And save that one sad star that hour must gleam,
On our fair child, how glorious were my dream!"

This heard the husband, and, in surly smile,
Aim'd at contempt, but yet he hoped the while:
For as, when sinking, wretched men are found
To catch at rushes rather than be drown'd;
So on a dream our peasant placed his hope,
And found that rush as valid as a rope.

Swift fled the days, for now in hope they fled,
When a fair daughter bless'd the nuptial bed;
Her infant-face the mother's pains beguiled,
She look'd so pleasing, and so softly smiled;
Those smiles, those looks, with sweet sensations moved
The gazer's soul, and, as he look'd, he loved.

And now the fairies came, with gifts, to grace
So mild a nature and so fair a face.

They gave, with beauty, that bewitching art,
That holds in easy chains the human heart;
They gave her skill to win the stubborn mind,
To make the suffering to their sorrows blind,
To bring on pensive looks the pleasing smile,
And Care's stern brow of every frown beguile.

These magic favours graced the infant-maid,
Whose more enlivening smile the charming gifts repaid.

Now Fortune changed, who, were she constant long,
Would leave us few adventures for our song.

A wicked elfin roved this land around,
Whose joys proceeded from the griefs he found;
Envy his name:—his fascinating eye
From the light bosom drew the sudden sigh;
Unsocial he, but with malignant mind,
He dwelt with man, that he might curse mankind;
Like the first foe, he sought th' abode of Joy,
Grieved to behold, but eager to destroy;
Round blooming beauty, like the wasp, he flew,
Soil'd the fresh sweet, and changed the rosy hue;
The wise, the good, with anxious heart, he saw,
And here a failing found, and there a flaw;
Discord in families 't was his to move,
Distrust in friendship, jealousy in love;
He told the poor what joys the great possess'd,
The great—what calm content the cottage bless'd;
To part the learned and the rich he tried,
Till their slow friendship perish'd in their pride.
Such was the fiend, and so secure of prey,
That only Misery pass'd unstung away.

Soon as he heard the fairy-babe was born,
Scornful he smiled, but felt no more than scorn:
For why, when Fortune placed her state so low,
In useless spite his lofty malice show?
Why, in a mischief of the meaner kind,
Exhaust the vigour of a ranc'rous mind?
But, soon as Fame the fairy-gifts proclaim'd,
Quick-rising wrath his ready soul inflamed,
To swear, by vows that e'en the wicked tie,
The nymph should weep her varied destiny;
That every gift, that now appear'd to shine
In her fair face, and make her smiles divine,
Should all the poison of his magic prove,
And they should scorn her, whom she sought for love.

His spell prepared, in form an ancient dame,
A fiend in spirit, to the cot he came;
There gain'd admittance, and the infant press'd
(Muttering his wicked magic) to his breast;
And thus he said:—"Of all the powers, who wait
On Jove's decrees, and do the work of fate,
Was I alone, despised or worthless, found,
Weak to protect, or impotent to wound?
See then thy foe, regret the friendship lost,
And learn my skill, but learn it at your cost.

"Know then, O child! devote to fates severe,
The good shall hate thy name, the wise shall fear;
Wit shall deride, and no protecting friend
Thy shame shall cover, or thy name defend.
Thy gentle sex, who, more than ours, should spare
A humble foe, will greater scorn declare;
The base alone thy advocates shall be,
Or boast alliance with a wretch like thee."

He spake and vanish'd, other prey to find,
And waste in slow disease the conquer'd mind.

Awed by the elfin's threats, and fill'd with dread,
The parents wept, and sought their infant's bed;
Despair alone the father's soul possess'd,
But hope rose gently in the mother's breast;
For well she knew that neither grief nor joy
Pain'd without hope, or pleased without alloy;
And while these hopes and fears her heart divide,
A cheerful vision bade the fears subside.

She saw descending to the world below
An ancient form, with solemn pace and slow.

"Daughter, no more be sad," (the phantom cried),
"Success is seldom to the wise denied;
In idle wishes fools supinely stay,
Be there a will and wisdom finds a way:
Why art thou grieved? Be rather glad, that he
Who hates the happy, aims his darts at thee;
But aims in vain: thy favour'd daughter lies,
Serenely blest, and shall to joy arise.
For, grant that curses on her name shall wait,
(So envy wills and such the voice of hate,)
Yet if that name be prudently suppress'd,
She shall be courted, favour'd, and caress'd.

"For what are names? and where agree mankind,
In those to persons or to acts assign'd?
Brave, learn'd, or wise, if some their favourites call,
Have they the titles or the praise from all?
Not so, but others will the brave disdain
As rash, and deem the sons of wisdom vain;
The self-same mind shall scorn or kindness move,
And the same deed attract contempt and love.

"So all the powers who move the human soul,
With all the passions who the will control,
Have various names—One given by Truth Divine
(As Simulation thus was fix'd for mine,)
The rest by man, who now, as wisdom's, prize
My secret counsels, now as art despise;

One hour, as just, those counsels they embrace,
And spurn, the next, as pitiful and base.

"Thee, too, my child, those fools as Cunning fly,
Who on thy counsel and thy craft rely;
That worthy craft in others they condemn,
But 't is their prudence, while conducting them.

"Be FLATTERY, then, thy happy infant's name,
Let Honour scorn her and let Wit defame;
Let all be true that Envy dooms, yet all,
Not on herself, but on her name, shall fall;
While she thy fortune and her own shall raise,
And decent Truth be call'd, and loved, as modest Praise.

"O happy child! the glorious day shall shine,
When every ear shall to thy speech incline,
Thy words alluring and thy voice divine:
The sullen pedant and the sprightly wit,
To hear thy soothing eloquence, shall sit;
And both, abjuring Flattery, will agree
That truth inspires, and they must honour thee.

"Envy himself shall to thy accents bend,
Force a faint smile, and sullenly attend,
When thou shalt call him Virtue's jealous friend,
Whose bosom glows with generous rage to find
How fools and knaves are flatter'd by mankind.

"The sage retired, who spends alone his days,
And flies th' obstreperous voice of public praise;
The vain, the vulgar cry,—shall gladly meet,
And bid thee welcome to his still retreat;
Much will he wonder, how thou camest to find
A man to glory dead, to peace consign'd.
O Fame! he'll cry (for he will call thee Fame),
From thee I fly, from thee conceal my name;
But thou shalt say, Though Genius takes his flight,
He leaves behind a glorious train of light,
And hides in vain:—yet prudent he that flies
The flatterer's art, and for himself is wise.

"Yes, happy child! I mark th' approaching day,
When warring natures will confess thy sway;
When thou shalt Saturn's golden reign restore,
And vice and folly shall be known no more.

"Pride shall not then in human-kind have place,
Changed by thy skill, to Dignity and Grace;
While Shame, who now betrays the inward sense
Of secret ill, shall be thy Diffidence;
Avarice shall thenceforth prudent Forecast be,
And bloody Vengeance, Magnanimity;
The lavish tongue shall honest truths impart,
The lavish hand shall show the generous heart,
And Indiscretion be, contempt of art;
Folly and Vice shall then, no longer known,
Be, this as Virtue, that as Wisdom, shown.

"Then shall the Robber, as the Hero, rise
To seize the good that churlish law denies;
Throughout the world shall rove the generous band,
And deal the gifts of Heaven from hand to hand.

"In thy blest days no tyrant shall be seen,
Thy gracious king shall rule contented men;
In thy blest days shall not a rebel be,
But patriots all and well approved of thee.

"Such powers are thine, that man, by thee, shall wrest
The gainful secret from the cautious breast;
Nor then, with all his care, the good retain,
But yield to thee the secret and the gain.
In vain shall much experience guard the heart
Against the charm of thy prevailing art;
Admitted once, so soothing is thy strain,
It comes the sweeter, when it comes again;
And when confess'd as thine, what mind so strong
Forbears the pleasure it indulged so long?

"Soft'ner of every ill! of all our woes
The balmy solace! friend of fiercest foes!
Begin thy reign, and like the morning rise!
Bring joy, bring beauty, to our eager eyes;
Break on the drowsy world like opening day,
While grace and gladness join thy flow'ry way;
While every voice is praise, while every heart is gay.

"From thee all prospects shall new beauties take,
'T is thine to seek them, and 't is thine to make;
On the cold fen I see thee turn thine eyes,
Its mists recede, its chilling vapour flies;
Th' enraptured lord th' improving ground surveys,
And for his Eden asks the traveller's praise,
Which yet, unview'd of thee, a bog had been,
Where spungy rushes hide the plashy green.

"I see thee breathing on the barren moor,
That seems to bloom, although so black before;
There, if beneath the gorse the primrose spring,
Or the pied daisy smile below the ling,
They shall new charms, at thy command, disclose,
And none shall miss the myrtle or the rose.
The wiry moss, that whitens all the hill,
Shall live a beauty by thy matchless skill;
Gale* from the bog shall yield Arabian balm,
And the grey willow wave a golden palm.

"I see thee smiling in the pictured room,
Now breathing beauty, now reviving bloom;
There, each immortal name 't is thine to give
To graceless forms, and bid the lumber live.
Shouldst thou coarse boors or gloomy martyrs see,
These shall thy Guidos, those thy Teniers be;
There shalt thou Raphael's saints and angels trace,
There make for Rubens and for Reynolds place,
And all the pride of art shall find, in her, disgrace.

"Delight of either sex! thy reign commence;
With balmy sweetness soothe the weary sense,
And to the sickening soul thy cheering aid dispense.
Queen of the mind! thy golden age begin;
In mortal bosoms varnish shame and sin,
Let all be fair without, let all be calm within."

The Vision fled; the happy mother rose,
Kiss'd the fair infant, smiled at all her foes,
And FLATTERY made her name:—her reign began,
Her own dear sex she ruled, then vanquish'd man.
A smiling friend, to every class, she spoke,
Assumed their manners, and their habits took:
Her, for her humble mien, the modest loved;
Her cheerful looks the light and gay approved;
The just beheld her, firm; the valiant, brave;
Her mirth the free, her silence pleased the grave;
Zeal heard her voice, and, as he preach'd aloud,
Well-pleased he caught her whispers from the crowd,

* "Myrica gale," a shrub growing in boggy and fenny grounds.

(Those whispers, soothing-sweet to every ear,
Which some refuse to pay, but none to hear);
Shame fled her presence; at her gentle strain,
Care softly smiled, and guilt forgot its pain;
The wretched thought, the happy found her true,
The learn'd confess'd that she their merits knew;
The rich—could they a constant friend condemn?
The poor believed—for who should flatter them?
Thus on her name though all disgrace attend,
In every creature she beholds a friend.

REFLECTIONS

UPON THE SUBJECT ——.

> Quid juvat errores, mersa jam puppe, fateri?
> Quid lacrymæ delicta juvant commissa secutæ?
> CLAUDIAN. *in Eutropium*, lib. ii, lin. 7.

> What avails it, when shipwreck'd, that error appears?
> Are the crimes we commit wash'd away by our tears?

When all the fiercer passions cease,
(The glory and disgrace of youth);
When the deluded soul, in peace,
Can listen to the voice of truth;
When we are taught in whom to trust,
And how to spare, to spend, to give;
(Our prudence kind, our pity just,)
'T is then we rightly learn to live.

Its weakness when the body feels,
Nor danger in contempt defies;
To reason, when desire appeals,
When, on experience, hope relies;
When every passing hour we prize,
Nor rashly on our follies spend,
But use it, as it quickly flies,
With sober aim to serious end;
When prudence bounds our utmost views,
And bids us wrath and wrong forgive;
When we can calmly gain or lose,—
'T is then we rightly learn to live.

Yet thus, when we our way discern,
And can upon our care depend,
To travel safely, when we learn,
Behold! we 're near our journey's end,
We 've trod the maze of error round,
Long wand'ring in the winding glade;
And now the torch of truth is found,
It only shows us where we stray'd:
Light for ourselves, what is it worth,
When we no more our way can choose?
For others, when we hold it forth,
They, in their pride, the boon refuse.

By long experience taught, we now
Can rightly judge of friends and foes,
Can all the worth of these allow,
And all their faults discern in those;
Relentless hatred, erring love,
We can for sacred truth forego;
We can the warmest friend reprove,
And bear to praise the fiercest foe:
To what effect? Our friends are gone,
Beyond reproof, regard, or care;
And of our foes remains there one,
The mild relenting thoughts to share?

Now 't is our boast that we can quell
The wildest passions in their rage;
Can their destructive force repel,
And their impetuous wrath assuage:
Ah! Virtue, dost thou arm, when now
This bold rebellious race are fled;
When all these tyrants rest, and thou
Art warring with the mighty dead?
Revenge, ambition, scorn, and pride,
And strong desire and fierce disdain,
The giant-brood, by thee defied,
Lo! Time's resistless strokes have slain.

Yet Time, who could that race subdue
(O'erpow'ring strength, appeasing rage)
Leaves yet a persevering crew,
To try the failing powers of age.
Vex'd by the constant call of these,
Virtue awhile for conquest tries,
But weary grown and fond of ease,
She makes with them a compromise:
Av'rice himself she gives to rest,
But rules him with her strict commands
Bids Pity touch his torpid breast,
And Justice hold his eager hands.

Yet is there nothing men can do,
When chilling Age comes creeping on?
Cannot we yet some good pursue?
Are talents buried? genius gone?
If passions slumber in the breast,
If follies from the heart be fled:
Of laurels let us go in quest,
And place them on the poet's head.

Yes, we 'll redeem the wasted time,
And to neglected studies flee;
We 'll build again the lofty rhyme,
Or live, Philosophy, with thee;
For reasoning clear, for flight sublime,
Eternal fame reward shall be;
And to what glorious heights we 'll climb,
Th' admiring crowd shall envying see.

Begin the song! begin the theme!—
Alas! and is Invention dead?
Dream we no more the golden dream?
Is Mem'ry with her treasures fled?
Yes, 't is too late,—now Reason guides
The mind, sole judge in all debate;
And thus th' important point decides,
For laurels, 't is, alas! too late.
What is possess'd we may retain,
But for new conquests strive in vain

Beware then, Age, that what was won,
If life's past labours, studies, views,
Be lost not, now the labour 's done,
When all thy part is,—not to lose:
When thou canst toil or gain no more,
Destroy not what was gain'd before.

For, all that's gain'd of all that's good,
  When time shall his weak frame destroy,
(Their use then rightly understood),
  Shall man, in happier state, enjoy.
Oh! argument for truth divine,
  For study's cares, for virtue's strife;
To know th' enjoyment will be thine,
  In that renew'd, that endless life!

SIR EUSTACE GREY.

SCENE—*A Mad-House.*

Persons—VISITOR, PHYSICIAN, AND PATIENT.

Veris miscens falsa.—
SENECA, *in Herc. furente.*

VISITOR.

I'll know no more;—the heart is torn,
  By views of wo, we cannot heal;
Long shall I see these things forlorn,
  And oft again their griefs shall feel,
  As each upon the mind shall steal;
That wan projector's mystic style,
  That lumpish idiot leering by,
That peevish idler's ceaseless wile,
And that poor maiden's half-form'd smile,
  While struggling for the full-drawn sigh!
I'll know no more.

PHYSICIAN.

—Yes, turn again;
Then speed to happier scenes thy way,
  When thou hast view'd, what yet remain,
The ruins of Sir Eustace Grey,
  The sport of madness, misery's prey:
But he will no historian need,
  His cares, his crimes, will he display,
And show (as one from frenzy freed)
  The proud-lost mind, the rash-done deed.

That cell to him is Greyling Hall:—
  Approach; he'll bid thee welcome there;
Will sometimes for his servant call,
  And sometimes point the vacant chair:
He can, with free and easy air,
  Appear attentive and polite;
Can veil his woes in manners fair,
  And pity with respect excite.

PATIENT.

Who comes?—Approach!—'t is kindly done:
  My learn'd physician, and a friend,
Their pleasures quit, to visit one,
  Who cannot to their ease attend,
Nor joys bestow, nor comforts lend,
  As when I lived so bless'd, so well,
And dreamt not I must soon contend
  With those malignant powers of hell.

PHYSICIAN.

Less warmth, Sir Eustace, or we go.—

PATIENT.

See! I am calm as infant-love,
A very child, but one of wo,
  Whom you should pity, not reprove:—
But men at ease, who never strove
  With passions wild, will calmly show
How soon we may their ills remove,
  And masters of their madness grow.

Some twenty years, I think, are gone,—
  (Time flies, I know not how, away,)
The sun upon no happier shone,
  Nor prouder man, than Eustace Grey.
Ask where you would, and all would say,
  The man admired and praised of all,
By rich and poor, by grave and gay,
  Was the young lord of Greyling Hall.

Yes! I had youth and rosy health;
  Was nobly form'd, as man might be;
For sickness then, of all my wealth,
  I never gave a single fee:
The ladies fair, the maidens free,
  Were all accustomed then to say,
Who would a handsome figure see
  Should look upon Sir Eustace Grey.

He had a frank and pleasant look,
  A cheerful eye and accent bland;
His very speech and manner spoke
  The generous heart, the open hand;
About him all was gay or grand,
  He had the praise of great and small;
He bought, improved, projected, plann'd,
  And reign'd a prince at Greyling Hall.

My lady!—she was all we love;
  All praise (to speak her worth) is faint;
Her manners show'd the yielding dove,
  Her morals, the seraphic saint;
She never breathed nor look'd complaint;
  No equal upon earth had she:—
Now, what is this fair thing I paint?
  Alas! as all that live shall be.

There was, beside, a gallant youth,
  And him my bosom's friend, I had:—
Oh! I was rich in very truth,
  It made me proud—it made me mad!—
Yes, I was lost—but there was cause!—
  Where stood my tale?—I cannot find—
But I had all mankind's applause,
  And all the smiles of womankind.

There were two cherub-things beside,
  A gracious girl, a glorious boy;
Yet more to swell my full-blown pride,
  To varnish higher my fading joy,
Pleasures were ours without alloy,
  Nay, Paradise,—till my frail Eve
Our bliss was tempted to destroy;
  Deceived and fated to deceive.

But I deserved; for all that time,
When I was loved, admired, caress'd,
There was within, each secret crime,
Unfelt, uncancell'd, unconfess'd:
I never then my God address'd,
In grateful praise or humble prayer:
And if His Word was not my jest!
(Dread thought!) it never was my care.

I doubted:—fool I was to doubt!
If that all-piercing eye could see,—
If He who looks all worlds throughout,
Would so minute and careful be,
As to perceive and punish me:—
With man I would be great and high,
But with my God so lost, that He,
In his large view, should pass me by.

Thus bless'd with children, friend, and wife,
Bless'd far beyond the vulgar lot,
Of all that gladdens human life,
Where was the good, that I had not?
But my vile heart had sinful spot,
And Heaven beheld its deep'ning stain;
Eternal justice I forgot,
And mercy sought not to obtain.

Come near,—I'll softly speak the rest!—
Alas! 'tis known to all the crowd,
Her guilty love was all confess'd;
And his, who so much truth avow'd,
My faithless friend's.—In pleasure proud
I sat, when these cursed tidings came;
Their guilt, their flight was told aloud,
And Envy smiled to hear my shame!

I call'd on Vengeance; at the word
She came;—Can I the deed forget?
I held the sword, th' accursed sword,
The blood of his false heart made wet;
And that fair victim paid her debt,
She pined, she died, she loath'd to live;—
I saw her dying—see her yet:
Fair fallen thing! my rage forgive!

Those cherubs still, my life to bless,
Were left; could I my fears remove,
Sad fears that check'd each fond caress,
And poison'd all parental love?
Yet that with jealous feelings strove,
And would at last have won my will,
Had I not, wretch! been doom'd to prove
Th' extremes of mortal good and ill.

In youth! health! joy! in beauty's pride!
They droop'd: as flowers when blighted bow,
The dire infection came:—They died,
And I was cursed—as I am now—
Nay, frown not, angry friend,—allow
That I was deeply, sorely tried;
Hear then, and you must wonder how
I could such storms and strifes abide.

Storms!—not that clouds embattled make,
When they afflict this earthly globe;
But such as with their terrors shake
Man's breast, and to the bottom probe;
They make the hypocrite disrobe,
They try us all, if false or true;
For this, one devil had pow'r on Job;
And I was long the slave of two.

PHYSICIAN.

Peace, peace, my friend; these subjects fly;
Collect thy thoughts—go calmly on.—

PATIENT.

And shall I then the fact deny?
I was,—thou know'st,—I was begone,
Like him who fill'd the eastern throne,
To whom the Watcher cried aloud;*
That royal wretch of Babylon,
Who was so guilty and so proud.

Like him, with haughty, stubborn mind,
I, in my state, my comforts sought;
Delight and praise I hoped to find,
In what I builded, planted, bought!
Oh! arrogance! by misery taught—
Soon came a voice! I felt it come;
"Full be his cup, with evil fraught,
Demons his guides, and death his doom!"

Then was I cast from out my state;
Two fiends of darkness led my way;
They waked me early, watch'd me late,
My dread by night, my plague by day!
Oh! I was made their sport, their play,
Through many a stormy, troubled year;
And how they used their passive prey
Is sad to tell:—but you shall hear.

And first, before they sent me forth,
Through this unpitying world to run,
They robb'd Sir Eustace of his worth,
Lands, manors, lordships, every one;
So was that gracious man undone,
Was spurn'd as vile, was scorn'd as poor,
Whom every former friend would shun,
And menials drove from every door.

Then those ill-favour'd Ones,† whom none
But my unhappy eyes could view,
Led me, with wild emotion, on,
And, with resistless terror, drew.
Through lands we fled, o'er seas we flew,
And halted on a boundless plain;
Where nothing fed, nor breathed, nor grew
But silence ruled the still domain.

Upon that boundless plain, below,
The setting sun's last rays were shed,
And gave a mild and sober glow,
Where all were still, asleep, or dead;
Vast ruins in the midst were spread,
Pillars and pediments sublime,
Where the grey moss had form'd a bed,
And clothed the crumbling spoils of time.

There was I fix'd, I know not how,
Condemn'd for untold year to stay;
Yet years were not;—one dreadful *now*
Endured no change of night or day;

* Prophecy of Daniel, chap. iv, 22.
† Vide Bunyan's Pilgrim's Progress.

The same mild evening's sleeping ray
 Shone softly-solemn and serene,
And all that time I gazed away,
 The setting sun's sad rays were seen.

At length a moment's sleep stole on,—
 Again came my commission'd foes;
Again through sea and land we're gone,
 No peace, no respite, no repose:
Above the dark broad sea we rose,
 We ran through bleak and frozen land;
I had no strength their strength t' oppose,
 An infant in a giant's hand.

They placed me where these streamers play,
 Those nimble beams of brilliant light;
It would the stoutest heart dismay,
 To see, to feel, that dreadful sight:
So swift, so pure, so cold, so bright,
 They pierced my frame with icy wound,
And all that half-year's polar night,
 Those dancing streamers wrapp'd me round.

Slowly that darkness pass'd away,
 When down upon the earth I fell,—
Some hurried sleep was mine by day;
 But, soon as toll'd the evening bell,
They forced me on, where ever dwell
 Far-distant men in cities fair,
Cities of whom no trav'lers tell,
 Nor feet but mine were wanderers there.

Their watchmen stare, and stand aghast,
 As on we hurry through the dark;
The watch-light blinks as we go past,
 The watch-dog shrinks and fears to bark;
The watch-tower's bell sounds shrill; and hark!
 The free wind blows—we've left the town—
A wide sepulchral ground I mark,
 And on a tomb-stone place me down.

What monuments of mighty dead!
 What tombs of various kinds are found!
And stones erect their shadows shed
 On humble graves, with wickers bound;
Some risen fresh, above the ground,
 Some level with the native clay,
What sleeping millions wait the sound,
 "Arise, ye dead, and come away!"

Alas! they stay not for that call;
 Spare me this wo! ye demons, spare!—
They come! the shrouded shadows all,—
 'T is more than mortal brain can bear;
Rustling they rise, they sternly glare
 At man upheld by vital breath;
Who, led by wicked fiends, should dare
 To join the shadowy troops of death!

Yes, I have felt all man can feel,
 Till he shall pay his nature's debt;
Ills that no hope has strength to heal,
 No mind the comfort to forget:
Whatever cares the heart can fret,
 The spirits wear, the temper gall,
Wo, want, dread, anguish, all beset
 My sinful soul!—together all!

Those fiends upon a shaking fen
 Fix'd me, in dark tempestuous night;
There never trod the foot of men,
 There flock'd the fowl in wint'ry flight;
There danced the moor's deceitful light
 Above the pool where sedges grow;
And when the morning-sun shone bright,
 It shone upon a field of snow.

They hung me on a bough so small,
 The rook could build her nest no higher;
They fix'd me on the trembling ball
 That crowns the steeple's quiv'ring spire;
They set me where the seas retire,
 But drown with their returning tide;
And made me flee the mountain's fire,
 When rolling from its burning side.

I 've hung upon the ridgy steep
 Of cliffs, and held the rambling brier;
I 've plunged below the billowy deep,
 Where air was sent me to respire;
I 've been where hungry wolves retire;
 And (to complete my woes) I 've ran
Where Bedlam's crazy crew conspire
 Against the life of reasoning man.

I 've furl'd in storms the flapping sail,
 By hanging from the topmast-head;
I 've served the vilest slaves in jail,
 And pick'd the dunghill's spoil for bread;
I 've made the badger's hole my bed,
 I 've wander'd with a gipsy crew;
I 've dreaded all the guilty dread,
 And done what they would fear to do.

On sand, where ebbs and flows the flood,
 Midway they placed and bade me die;
Propp'd on my staff, I stoutly stood
 When the swift waves came rolling by;
And high they rose, and still more high,
 Till my lips drank the bitter brine;
I sobb'd convulsed, then cast mine eye,
 And saw the tide's re-flowing sign.

And then, my dreams were such as nought
 Could yield but my unhappy case;
I 've been of thousand devils caught,
 And thrust into that horrid place,
Where reign dismay, despair, disgrace;
 Furies with iron fangs were there,
To torture that accursed race,
 Doom'd to dismay, disgrace, despair.

Harmless I was: yet hunted down
 For treasons, to my soul unfit;
I 've been pursued through many a town,
 For crimes that petty knaves commit;
I 've been adjudged t' have lost my wit,
 Because I preach'd so loud and well;
And thrown into the dungeon's pit,
 For trampling on the pit of hell.

Such were the evils, man of sin,
 That I was fated to sustain;
And add to all, without—within,
 A soul defiled with every stain

That man's reflecting mind can pain;
That pride, wrong, rage, despair, can make;
In fact, they 'd nearly touch'd my brain,
And reason on her throne would shake.

But pity will the vilest seek,
If punish'd guilt will not repine,—
I heard a heavenly teacher speak,
And felt the SUN OF MERCY shine:
I hail'd the light! the birth divine!
And then was seal'd among the few;
Those angry fiends beheld the sign,
And from me in an instant flew.

Come, hear how thus the charmers cry
To wandering sheep, the strays of sin,
While some the wicket-gate pass by,
And some will knock and enter in:
Full joyful 't is a soul to win,
For he that winneth souls is wise;
Now hark! the holy strains begin,
And thus the sainted preacher cries:—*

"Pilgrim, burthen'd with thy sin,
Come the way to Zion's gate,
There, till Mercy let thee in,
Knock and weep and watch and wait.
Knock!—He knows the sinner's cry:
Weep!—He loves the mourner's tears:
Watch!—for saving grace is nigh:
Wait,—till heavenly light appears.

"Hark! it is the Bridegroom's voice;
Welcome, pilgrim, to thy rest;
Now within the gate rejoice,
Safe and seal'd and bought and bless'd!
Safe—from all the lures of vice,
Seal'd—by signs the chosen know,
Bought—by love and life the price,
Bless'd—the mighty debt to owe.

"Holy Pilgrim! what for thee
In a world like this remain?
From thy guarded breast shall flee,
Fear and shame, and doubt and pain.
Fear—the hope of Heaven shall fly,
Shame—from glory's view retire,
Doubt—in certain rapture die,
Pain—in endless bliss expire."

But though my day of grace was come,
Yet still my days of grief I find;
The former clouds' collected gloom
Still sadden the reflecting mind;
The soul, to evil things consign'd,
Will of their evil some retain;
The man will seem to earth inclined,
And will not look erect again.

* It has been suggested to me, that this change from restlessness to repose, in the mind of Sir Eustace, is wrought by a methodistic call; and it is admitted to be such: a sober and rational conversion could not have happened while the disorder of the brain continued: yet the verses which follow, in a different measure, are not intended to make any religious persuasion appear ridiculous; they are to be supposed as the effect of memory in the disordered mind of the speaker, and, though evidently enthusiastic in respect to language, are not meant to convey any impropriety of sentiment.

Thus, though elect, I feel it hard
To lose what I possess'd before,
To be from all my wealth debarr'd,—
The brave Sir Eustace is no more:
But old I wax and passing poor,
Stern, rugged men my conduct view;
They chide my wish, they bar my door,
'T is hard—I weep—you see I do.—

Must you, my friends, no longer stay?
Thus quickly all my pleasures end;
But I 'll remember, when I pray,
My kind physician and his friend:
And those sad hours, you deign to spend
With me, I shall requite them all;
Sir Eustace for his friends shall send,
And thank their love at Greyling Hall.

VISITOR.

The poor Sir Eustace!—Yet his hope
Leads him to think of joys again;
And when his earthly visions droop,
His views of heavenly kind remain:—
But whence that meek and humbled strain,
That spirit wounded, lost, resign'd?
Would not so proud a soul disdain
The madness of the poorest mind?

PHYSICIAN.

No! for the more he swell'd with pride,
The more he felt misfortune's blow;
Disgrace and grief he could not hide,
And poverty had laid him low:
Thus shame and sorrow working slow,
At length this humble spirit gave;
Madness on these began to grow,
And bound him to his fiends a slave.

Though the wild thoughts had touch'd his brain,
Then was he free:—So, forth he ran;
To soothe or threat, alike were vain:
He spake of fiends, look'd wild and wan;
Year after year, the hurried man
Obey'd those fiends from place to place;
Till his religious change began
To form a frenzied child of grace.

For, as the fury lost its strength,
The mind reposed; by slow degrees
Came lingering hope, and brought at length,
To the tormented spirit, ease:
This slave of sin, whom fiends could seize,
Felt or believed their power had end;—
"'T is faith," he cried, "my bosom frees,
And now my SAVIOUR is my friend."

But ah! though time can yield relief,
And soften woes it cannot cure;
Would we not suffer pain and grief,
To have our reason sound and sure?
Then let us keep our bosoms pure,
Our fancy's favourite flights suppress,
Prepare the body to endure,
And bend the mind to meet distress:
And then HIS guardian care implore,
Whom demons dread and men adore.

THE HALL OF JUSTICE.

PART I.

Confiteor facere hoc annos; sed et altera causa est,
Anxietas animi, continuusque dolor.
OVID.

MAGISTRATE, VAGRANT, CONSTABLE, *etc.*

VAGRANT.

TAKE, take away thy barbarous hand,
And let me to thy master speak;
Remit awhile the harsh command,
And hear me, or my heart will break.

MAGISTRATE.

Fond wretch! and what canst thou relate,
But deeds of sorrow, shame, and sin?
Thy crime is proved, thou know'st thy fate;
But come, thy tale!—begin, begin!—

VAGRANT.

My crime!——This sick'ning child to feed,
I seized the food, your witness saw;
I knew your laws forbade the deed,
But yielded to a stronger law.

Know'st thou, to Nature's great command
All human laws are frail and weak?
Nay! frown not—stay his eager hand,
And hear me, or my heart will break.

In this, th' adopted babe I hold
With anxious fondness to my breast,
My heart's sole comfort I behold,
More dear than life, when life was bless'd;
I saw her pining, fainting, cold,
I begg'd—but vain was my request.

I saw the tempting food, and seized—
My infant-sufferer found relief;
And, in the pilfer'd treasure pleased,
Smiled on my guilt, and hush'd my grief.

But I have griefs of other kind,
Troubles and sorrows more severe;
Give me to ease my tortured mind,
Lend to my woes a patient ear;
And let me—if I may not find
A friend to help—find one to hear.

Yet nameless let me plead—my name
Would only wake the cry of scorn;
A child of sin, conceived in shame,
Brought forth in wo, to misery born.

My mother dead, my father lost,
I wander'd with a vagrant crew
A common care, a common cost,
Their sorrows and their sins I knew;
With them, by want on error forced,
Like them, I base and guilty grew.

Few are my years, not so my crimes;
The age, which these sad looks declare,
Is Sorrow's work, it is not Time's,
And I am old in shame and care.

Taught to believe the world a place
Where every stranger was a foe,
Train'd in the arts that mark our race,
To what new people could I go?
Could I a better life embrace,
Or live as virtue dictates? No!—

So through the land I wandering went,
And little found of grief or joy;
But lost my bosom's sweet content
When first I loved—the Gipsy-Boy.

A sturdy youth he was and tall,
His looks would all his soul declare;
His piercing eyes were deep and small,
And strongly curl'd his raven-hair.

Yes, Aaron had each manly charm,
All in the May of youthful pride,
He scarcely fear'd his father's arm,
And every other arm defied.—

Oft, when they grew in anger warm,
(Whom will not love and power divide?)
I rose, their wrathful souls to calm,
Not yet in sinful combat tried.

His father was our party's chief,
And dark and dreadful was his look;
His presence fill'd my heart with grief,
Although to me he kindly spoke.

With Aaron I delighted went,
His favour was my bliss and pride;
In growing hope our days we spent,
Love growing charms in either spied,
It saw them, all which Nature lent,
It lent them, all which she denied.

Could I the father's kindness prize,
Or grateful looks on him bestow,
Whom I beheld in wrath arise,
When Aaron sunk beneath his blow?

He drove him down with wicked hand,
It was a dreadful sight to see;
Then vex'd him, till he left the land,
And told his cruel love to me;—
The clan were all at his command,
Whatever his command might be.

The night was dark, the lanes were deep,
And one by one they took their way;
He bade me lay me down and sleep,
I only wept and wish'd for day.

Accursed be the love he bore,
Accursed was the force he used,
So let him of his God implore
For mercy, and be so refused!

You frown again,—to show my wrong,
  Can I in gentle language speak?
My woes are deep, my words are strong,—
  And hear me, or my heart will break.

MAGISTRATE.

I hear thy words, I feel thy pain:
  Forbear awhile to speak thy woes;
Receive our aid, and then again
  The story of thy life disclose.

For, though seduced and led astray,
  Thou 'st travell'd far and wander'd long;
Thy God hath seen thee all the way,
  And all the turns that led thee wrong.

PART II.

Quondam ridentes oculi, nunc fonte perenni
Deplorant pœnas nocte dieque suas.
CORN. GALLI, *Eleg.*

MAGISTRATE.

Come, now again thy woes impart,
  Tell all thy sorrows, all thy sin;
We cannot heal the throbbing heart
  Till we discern the wounds within.

Compunction weeps our guilt away,
  The sinner's safety is his pain;
Such pangs for our offences pay,
  And these severer griefs are gain.

VAGRANT.

The son came back—he found us wed,
  Then dreadful was the oath he swore;—
His way through Blackburn Forest led,—
  His father, we beheld no more.

Of all our daring clan not one
  Would on the doubtful subject dwell:
For all esteem'd the injured son,
  And fear'd the tale which he could tell.

But I had mightier cause for fear,
  For slow and mournful round my bed
I saw a dreadful form appear,—
  It came when I and Aaron wed.

(Yes! we were wed, I know my crime,—
  We slept beneath the elmin tree;
But I was grieving all the time,
  And Aaron frown'd my tears to see.

For he not yet had felt the pain
  That rankles in a wounded breast;
He wak'd to sin, then slept again,
  Forsook his God, yet took his rest.—

H

But I was forced to feign delight,
  And joy in mirth and music sought,—
And mem'ry now recalls the night,
  With such surprise and horror fraught,
That reason felt a moment's flight,
  And left a mind to madness wrought.)

When waking, on my heaving breast
  I felt a hand as cold as death;
A sudden fear my voice suppress'd,
  A chilling terror stopp'd my breath.—

I seem'd—no words can utter how!
  For there my father-husband stood,—
And thus he said:—"Will God allow,
  The great avenger, just and good,
A wife to break her marriage-vow?
  A son to shed his father's blood?"

I trembled at the dismal sounds,
  But vainly strove a word to say;
So, pointing to his bleeding wounds,
  The threat'ning spectre stalk'd away.*

I brought a lovely daughter forth,
  His father's child, in Aaron's bed;
He took her from me in his wrath,
  "Where is my child?"—"Thy child is dead."

'T was false.—We wander'd far and wide,
  Through town and country, field and fen,
Till Aaron, fighting, fell and died,
  And I became a wife again.

I then was young:—my husband sold
  My fancied charms for wicked price;
He gave me oft, for sinful gold,
  The slave, but not the friend of vice:—
Behold me, Heaven! my pains behold,
  And let them for my sins suffice!

The wretch who lent me thus for gain,
  Despised me when my youth was fled
Then came disease, and brought me pain:—
  Come, death, and bear me to the dead!
For though I grieve, my grief is vain,
  And fruitless all the tears I shed.

True, I was not to virtue train'd,
  Yet well I know my deeds were ill;
By each offence my heart was pain'd,
  I wept, but I offended still;
My better thoughts my life disdain'd,
  But yet the viler led my will.

My husband died, and now no more
  My smile was sought or ask'd my hand,
A widow'd vagrant, vile and poor,
  Beneath a vagrant's vile command.

---

* The state of mind here described will account for a vision of this nature, without having recourse to any supernatural appearance.

Ceaseless I roved the country round,
To win my bread by fraudful arts,
And long a poor subsistence found,
By spreading nets for simple hearts.

Though poor, and abject, and despised,
Their fortunes to the crowd I told;
I gave the young the love they prized,
And promised wealth to bless the old;
Schemes for the doubtful I devised,
And charms for the forsaken sold.

At length for arts like these confined
In prison with a lawless crew,
I soon perceived a kindred mind,
And there my long-lost daughter knew.

His father's child, whom Aaron gave
To wander with a distant clan,
The miseries of the world to brave,
And be the slave of vice and man.

She knew my name—we met in pain,
Our parting pangs can I express?
She sail'd a convict o'er the main,
And left an heir to her distress.

This is that heir to shame and pain,
For whom I only could descry
A world of trouble and disdain:
Yet, could I bear to see her die,
Or stretch her feeble hands in vain,
And, weeping, beg of me supply?

No! though the fate thy mother knew
Was shameful! shameful though thy race
Have wander'd all, a lawless crew,
Outcasts, despised in every place;

Yet as the dark and muddy tide,
When far from its polluted source,
Becomes more pure, and, purified,
Flows in a clear and happy course;—

In thee, dear infant! so may end
Our shame, in thee our sorrows cease:
And thy pure course will then extend,
In floods of joy, o'er vales of peace.

Oh! by the God who loves to spare,
Deny me not the boon I crave;
Let this loved child your mercy share,
And let me find a peaceful grave;
Make her yet spotless soul your care,
And let my sins their portion have;
Her for a better fate prepare,
And punish whom 't were sin to save!

MAGISTRATE.

Recall the word, renounce the thought,
Command thy heart and bend thy knee.
There is to all a pardon brought,
A ransom rich, assured, and free;
'T is full when found, 't is found if sought,
Oh! seek it, till 't is seal'd to thee.

VAGRANT.

But how my pardon shall I know?

MAGISTRATE.

By feeling dread that 't is not sent,
By tears for sin that freely flow,
By grief, that all thy tears are spent,
By thoughts on that great debt we owe,
With all the mercy God has lent,
By suffering what thou canst not show,
Yet showing how thine heart is rent,
Till thou canst feel thy bosom glow,
And say, "My Saviour, I repent!"

WOMAN!

MR. LEDYARD, AS QUOTED BY M. PARKE IN HIS TRAVELS INTO AFRICA:

"To a Woman I never addressed myself in the language of decency and friendship, without receiving a decent and friendly answer. If I was hungry or thirsty, wet or sick, they did not hesitate, like Men, to perform a generous action: in so free and kind a manner did they contribute to my relief, that if I was dry, I drank the sweetest draught; and if hungry I ate the coarsest morsel with a double relish."

Place the white man on Afric's coast,
Whose swarthy sons in blood delight,
Who of their scorn to Europe boast,
And paint their very demons white:
There, while the sterner sex disdains
To soothe the woes they cannot feel,
Woman will strive to heal his pains,
And weep for those she cannot heal:
Hers is warm pity's sacred glow;
From all her stores she bears a part,
And bids the spring of hope re-flow,
That languish'd in the fainting heart.

"What though so pale his haggard face,
So sunk and sad his looks,"—she cries;
"And far unlike our nobler race,
With crisped locks and rolling eyes;
Yet misery marks him of our kind;
We see him lost, alone, afraid;
And pangs of body, griefs in mind,
Pronounce him man, and ask our aid.

"Perhaps in some far-distant shore,
There are who in these forms delight;
Whose milky features please them more
Than ours of jet, thus burnish'd bright;
Of such may be his weeping wife,
Such children for their sire may call,
And if we spare his ebbing life,
Our kindness may preserve them all."

Thus her compassion Woman shows,
Beneath the line her acts are these;
Nor the wide waste of Lapland-snows
Can her warm flow of pity freeze:—

"From some sad land the stranger comes,
Whose joys, like ours, are never found;
Let 's soothe him in our happy homes,
Where freedom sits with plenty crown'd.

"'T is good the fainting soul to cheer,
To see the famish'd stranger fed;
To milk for him the mother-deer,
To smooth for him the furry bed.
The Powers above our Lapland bless
With good no other people know;
T' enlarge the joys that we possess
By feeling those that we bestow!"

Thus in extremes of cold and heat,
Where wandering man may trace his kind;
Wherever grief and want retreat,
In Woman they compassion find;
She makes the female breast her seat,
And dictates mercy to the mind.

Man may the sterner virtues know,
Determined justice, truth severe:
But female hearts with pity glow,
And Woman holds affection dear;
For guileless woes her sorrow flow,
And suffering vice compels her tear;
'T is hers to soothe the ills below,
And bid life's fairer views appear:
To Woman's gentle kind we owe
What comforts and delights us here:
They its gay hopes on youth bestow,
And care they soothe and age they cheer.

The Borough.

Paulo majora canamus.—VIRGIL.

TO HIS GRACE

THE DUKE OF RUTLAND, MARQUIS OF GRANBY;

RECORDER OF CAMBRIDGE AND SCARBOROUGH; LORD-LIEUTENANT AND CUSTOS-ROTOLORUM OF THE COUNTY OF LEICESTER; K. G. AND LL.D.

My Lord,

The poem, for which I have ventured to solicit your Grace's attention, was composed in a situation so near to Belvoir Castle, that the author had all the advantage to be derived from prospects extensive and beautiful, and from works of grandeur and sublimity: and though nothing of the influence arising from such situation should be discernible in these verses, either from want of adequate powers in the writer, or because his subjects do not assimilate with such views, yet would it be natural for him to indulge a wish, that he might inscribe his labours to the lord of a scene which perpetually excited his admiration, and he would plead the propriety of placing the titles of the House of Rutland at the entrance of a volume written in the Vale of Belvoir.

But, my Lord, a motive much more powerful than a sense of propriety, a grateful remembrance of benefits conferred by the noble family in which you preside, has been the great inducement for me to wish that I might be permitted to inscribe this work to your grace: the honours of that time were to me unexpected, they were unmerited, and they were transitory: but since I am thus allowed to make public my gratitude, I am in some degree restored to the honour of that period; I have again he happiness to find myself favoured, and my exertions stimulated, by the condescension of the Duke of Rutland.

It was my fortune, in a poem which yet circulates, to write of the virtues, talents, and heroic death of Lord Robert Manners, and to bear witness to the affection of a brother whose grief was poignant, and to be soothed only by remembrance of his worth whom he so deeply deplored. In a patron thus favourably predisposed, my Lord, I might look for much lenity, and could not fear the severity of critical examination: from your Grace, who, happily, have no such impediment to justice, I must not look for the same kind of indulgence. I am assured, by those whose situation gave them opportunity for knowledge, and whose abilities and attention guarded them from error, that I must not expect my failings will escape detection from want of discernment, neither am I to fear that any merit will be undistinguished through deficiency of taste. It is from this information, my Lord, and a consciousness of much which needs forgiveness, that I entreat your Grace to read my verses, with a wish, I had almost added, with a purpose to be pleased, and to make every possible allowance for subjects not always pleasing, for manners sometimes gross, and for language too frequently incorrect.

With the fullest confidence in your Grace's ability and favour, in the accuracy of your judgment and the lenity of your decision; with grateful remembrance of benefits received, and due consciousness of the little I could merit; with prayers that your Grace may long enjoy the dignities of the House of Rutland, and continue to dictate improvement for the surrounding country;—I terminate an address, in which a fear of offending your Grace has made me so cautious in my expressions, that I may justly fear to offend many of my readers, who will think that something more of animation should have been excited by the objects I view, the benevolence I honour, and the gratitude I profess.

I have the honour to be, my Lord,
Your Grace's
Most obliged and obedient humble servant,
GEORGE CRABBE.

PREFACE.

Whether, if I had not been encouraged by some proofs of public favour, I should have written the Poem now before the reader, is a question which I cannot positively determine; but I will venture to assert, that I should not, in that case, have committed the work to the press; I should not have allowed my own opinion of it to have led me into further disappointment, against the voice of judges impartial and indifferent, from whose sentence it had been fruitless to appeal: the success of a late publication, therefore, may be fairly assigned as the principal cause for the appearance of this.

When the ensuing Letters were so far written, that I could form an opinion of them, and when I began to conceive that they might not be unacceptable to the public, I felt myself prompted by duty, as well as interest, to put them to the press: I considered myself bound by gratitude for the favourable treatment I had already received, to show that I was not unmindful of it; and, however this might be mixed with other motives, it operated with considerable force upon my mind, acting as a stimulus to exertions naturally tardy, and to expectations easily checked.

It must nevertheless be acknowledged, that although such favourable opinion had been formed, I was not able, with the requisite impartiality, to determine the comparative value of an unpublished manuscript, and a work sent into the world. Books, like children, when established, have doubtless our parental affection and good wishes; we rejoice to hear that they are doing well, and are received and respected in good company: but it is to manuscripts in the study, as to children in the nursery, that our care, our anxiety, and our tenderness are principally directed: they are fondled as our endearing companions; their faults are corrected with the lenity of partial love, and their good parts are exaggerated by the strength of parental imagination; nor is it easy even for the more cool and reasonable among parents, thus circumstanced, to decide upon the comparative merits of their offspring, whether they be children of the bed or issue of the brain.

But, however favourable my own opinion may have been, or may still be, I could not venture to commit so long a Poem to the press without some endeavour to obtain the more valuable opinion of less partial judges: at the same time, I am willing to confess that I have lost some portion of the timidity once so painful, and that I am encouraged to take upon myself the decision of various points, which heretofore I entreated my friends to decide. Those friends were then my council, whose opinion I was implicitly to follow; they are now advisers, whose ideas I am at liberty to reject. This will not, I hope, seem like arrogance: it would be more safe, it would be more pleasant, still to have that reliance on the judgment of others; but it cannot always be obtained; nor are they, however friendly disposed, ever ready to lend a helping hand to him whom they consider as one who ought by this time to have cast away the timidity of inexperience, and to have acquired the courage that would enable him to decide for himself.

When it is confessed that I have less assistance from my friends, and that the appearance of this work is, in a great measure, occasioned by the success of a former, some readers will, I fear, entertain the opinion that the book before them was written in haste, and published without due examination and revisal: should this opinion be formed, there will doubtless occur many faults which may appear as originating in neglect: Now, readers are, I believe, disposed to treat with more than common severity those writers who have been led into presumption by the approbation bestowed on their diffidence, and into idleness and unconcern, by the praises given to their attention. I am therefore even anxious it should be generally known that sufficient time and application were bestowed upon this work, and by this I mean that no material alteration would be effected by delay: it is true that this confession removes one plea for the errors of the book, want of time; but in my opinion, there is not much consolation to be drawn by reasonable minds from this resource: if a work fails, it appears to be poor satisfaction when it is observed, that if the author had taken more care the event had been less disgraceful.

When the reader enters into the Poem, he will find the author retired from view, and an imaginary personage brought forward to describe his Borough for him: to him it seemed convenient to speak in the first person: but the inhabitant of a village, in the centre of the kingdom, could not appear in the character of a residing burgess in a large sea-port; and when, with this point, was considered what relations were to be given, what manners delineated, and what situations described, no method appeared to be so convenient as that of borrowing the assistance of an ideal friend: by this means the reader is in some degree kept from view of any particular place, nor will he perhaps be so likely to determine where those persons reside, and what their connexions, who are so intimately known to this man of straw.

From the title of this Poem, some persons will, I fear, expect a political satire,—an attack upon corrupt principles in a general view, or upon the customs and manners of some particular place; of these they will find nothing satirized, nothing related. It may be that graver readers would have preferred a more historical account of so considerable a Borough—its charter, privileges, trade, public structures, and subjects of this kind; but I have an apology for the omission of these things, in the difficulty of describing them, and in the utter repugnancy which subsists between the studies and objects of topography and poetry. What I thought I could best describe, that I attempted:—the sea, and the country in the immediate vicinity; the dwellings, and the inhabitants; some incidents and characters, with an exhibition of morals and manners, offensive perhaps to those of extremely delicate feelings, but sometimes, I hope, neither unamiable nor unaffecting: an Election indeed forms a part of one Letter, but the evil there described is not one greatly nor generally deplored, and there are probably many places of this kind where it is not felt.

From the variety of relations, characters, and descriptions which a BOROUGH affords, several were rejected which a reader might reasonably expect to have met with: in this case he is entreated to believe that these, if they occurred to the author, were considered by him as beyond his ability, as subjects which he could not treat in a manner satisfactory to himself. Possibly the admission of some will be thought to require more apology than the rejection of others: in such variety, it is to be apprehended, that almost every reader will find something not according with his ideas of propriety, or something repulsive to the tone of his feelings; nor could this be avoided but by the sacrifice of every event, opinion, and even expression, which could be thought liable to produce such effect; and this casting away so largely of our cargo, through fears of danger, though it might help us to clear it, would render our vessel of little worth when she came into port. I may likewise entertain a hope, that this very variety, which gives scope to objection and censure, will also afford a better chance for approval and satisfaction.

Of these objectionable parts many must be to me unknown; of others some opinion may be formed, and for their admission some plea may be stated.

In the first Letter is nothing which particularly calls for remark, except possibly the last line—giving a promise to the reader that he should both smile and sigh in the perusal of the following Letters. This may appear vain, and more than an author ought to promise; but let it be considered that the character assumed is that of a friend, who gives an account of objects, persons, and events to his correspondent, and who was therefore at liberty, without any imputation of this kind, to suppose in what manner he would be affected by such descriptions.

Nothing, I trust, in the second Letter, which relates to the imitation of what are called weather-stains on buildings, will seem to any invidious or offensive. I wished to make a comparison between those minute and curious bodies which cover the surface of some edifices, and those kinds of stain which are formed of boles and ochres, and laid on with a brush. Now, as the work of time cannot be anticipated in such cases, it may be very judicious to have recourse to such expedients as will give to a recent structure the venerable appearance of antiquity; and in this case, though I might still observe the vast difference between the living varieties of nature, and the distant imitation of the artist, yet I would not forbear to make use of his dexterity, because he could not clothe my freestone with *mucor*, *lichen*, and *byssus*.

The wants and mortifications of a poor Clergyman are the subjects of one portion of the third Letter; and he being represented as a stranger in the Borough, it may be necessary to make some apology for his appearance in the Poem. Previous to a late meeting of a literary society, whose benevolent purpose is well known to the public, I was induced by a friend to compose a few verses, in which, with the general commendation of the design, should be introduced a hint that the bounty might be farther extended; these verses a gentleman did me the honour to recite at the meeting, and they were printed as an extract from the Poem, to which in fact they may be called an appendage.

I am now arrived at that part of my work, which I may expect will bring upon me some animadversion. Religion is a subject deeply interesting to the minds of many, and when these minds are weak, they are often led by a warmth of feeling into the violence of causeless resentment: I am therefore anxious that my purpose should be understood; and I wish to point out what things they are which an author may hold up to ridicule and be blameless. In referring to the two principal divisions of enthusiastical teachers, I have denominated them, as I conceive they are generally called, *Calvinistic* and *Arminian* Methodists. The *Arminians*, though divided and perhaps subdivided, are still, when particular accuracy is not intended, considered as one body, having had, for many years, one head, who is yet held in high respect by the varying members of the present day: but the Calvinistic societies are to be looked upon rather as separate and independent congregations; and it is to one of these (unconnected, as is supposed, with any other) I more particularly allude. But while I am making use of this division, I must entreat that I may not be considered as one who takes upon him to censure the religious opinions of any society or individual: the reader will find that the spirit of the enthusiast, and not his opinions, his manners, and not his creed, have engaged my attention. I have nothing to observe of the Calvinist and Arminian, considered as such; but my remarks are pointed at the enthusiast and the bigot, at their folly and their craft.

To those readers who have seen the journals of the first Methodists, or the extracts quoted from them by their opposers* in the early times of this spiritual influenza, are sufficiently known all their leading notions and peculiarities; so that I have no need to enter into such unpleasant inquiries in this place: I have only to observe that their tenets remain the same, and have still the former effect on the minds of the converted: There is yet that ima-

* Methodists and Papists compared, Treatise on Grace, by Bishop Warburton, etc.

gined contention with the powers of darkness, that is at once so lamentable and so ludicrous:, there is the same offensive familiarity with the Deity, with a full trust and confidence both in the immediate efficacy of their miserably delivered supplications, and in the reality of numberless small miracles wrought at their request and for their convenience; there still exists, that delusion, by which some of the most common diseases of the body are regarded as proofs of the malignity of Satan contending for dominion over the soul: and there still remains the same wretched jargon, composed of scriptural language, debased by vulgar expressions, which has a kind of mystic influence on the minds of the ignorant. It will be recollected that it is the abuse of those scriptural terms which I conceive to be improper: they are doubtless most significant and efficacious when used with propriety; but it is painful to the mind of a soberly devout person, when he hears every rise and fall of the animal spirits, every whim and notion of enthusiastic ignorance, expressed in the venerable language of the Apostles and Evangelists.

The success of these people is great, but not surprising; as the powers they claim are given, and come not of education, many may, and therefore do, fancy they are endowed with them; so that they who do not venture to become preachers, yet exert the minor gifts, and gain reputation for the faculty of prayer, as soon as they can address the Creator in daring flights of unpremeditated absurdity. The less indigent gain the praise of hospitality, and the more harmonious become distinguished in their choirs: curiosity is kept alive by succession of ministers, and self-love is flattered by the consideration that they are the persons at whom the world wonders; add to this, that, in many of them, pride is gratified by their consequence as new members of a sect whom their conversion pleases, and by the liberty, which, as seceders they take, of speaking contemptuously of the Church and ministers whom they have relinquished.

Of those denominated *Calvinistic Methodists*, I had principally one sect in view, or, to adopt the term of its founder, *a church*. This *church* consists of several congregations in town and country, unknown perhaps in many parts of the kingdom, but, where known, the cause of much curiosity and some amusement. To such of my readers as may judge an enthusiastic teacher and his peculiarities to be unworthy any serious attention, I would observe that there is something unusually daring in the boast of this man, who claims the authority of a messenger, sent from God, and declares without hesitation that his call was immediate; that he is assisted by the sensible influence of the Spirit, and that miracles are perpetually wrought in his favour and for his convenience.

As it was and continues to be my desire to give proof that I had advanced nothing respecting this extraordinary person, his operations or assertions, which might not be readily, justified by quotations from his own writings, I had collected several of these and disposed them under certain heads; but I found that by this means a very disproportioned share of attention must be given to the subject, and after some consideration, I have determined to relinquish the design; and should any have curiosity to search whether my representation of the temper and disposition, the spirit and manners, the knowledge and capacity, of a very popular teacher be correct, he is referred to about fourscore pamphlets, whose titles will be found on the covers of the late editions of the *Bank of Faith*, itself a wonderful performance, which (according to the turn of mind in the reader) will either highly excite, or totally extinguish, curiosity. In these works will be abundantly seen, abuse and contempt of the Church of England and its ministers; vengeance and virulent denunciation against all offenders; scorn for morality and heathen virtue, with that kind of learning which the author possesses, and his peculiar style of composition. A few of the titles placed below will give some information to the reader respecting the merit and design of those performances.*

As many of the preacher's subjects are controverted and nice questions in divinity, he has sometimes allowed himself relaxation from the severity of study, and favoured his admirers with the effects of an humbler kind of inspiration, viz. that of the Muse. It must be confessed that these flights of fancy are very humble, and have nothing of that daring and mysterious nature which the prose of the author leads us to expect. *The Dimensions of eternal* Love is a title of one of his more learned productions, with which might have been expected (as a fit companion), *The Bounds of infinite Grace*; but no such work appears, and possibly the author considered one attempt of this kind was sufficient to prove the extent and direction of his abilities.

Of the whole of this mass of inquiry and decision, of denunciation and instruction (could we suppose it read by intelligent persons), different opinions would probably be formed; the more indignant and severe would condemn the whole as the produce of craft and hypocrisy, while the more lenient would allow that such things might originate in the wandering imagination of a dreaming enthusiast.

None of my readers will, I trust, do me so much injustice as to suppose I have here any other motive than a vindication of what I have advanced in the verses which describe this kind of character, or that I had there any other purpose than to express (what I conceive to be) justifiable indignation against the assurance, the malignity, and (what is of more importance) the pernicious influence of such sentiments on the minds of the simple and ignorant, who, if they give credit to his relations, must be no more than tools and instruments under the control and management of one *called to be their Apostle.*

Nothing would be more easy for me, as I have observed, than to bring forward quotations such as would justify all I have advanced; but even had I room, I cannot tell whether there be not something

* Barbar, in two parts: Bond-Child; Cry of Little Faith; Satan's Lawsuit; Forty Stripes for Satan; Myrrh and Odour of Saints; the Naked Bow of God; Rule and Riddle; Way and Fare for Wayfaring Men; Utility of the Books and Excellency of the Parchments; Correspondence between *Noctua, Aurita,* (the words so separated) and *Philomela* etc.

degrading in such kind of attack: the reader might smile at those miraculous accounts, but he would consider them and the language of the author as beneath his further attention: I therefore once more refer him to those pamphlets, which will afford matter for pity and for contempt, by which some would be amused and others astonished—not without sorrow, when they reflect that thousands look up to the writer as a man literally inspired, to whose wants they administer with their substance, and to whose guidance they prostrate their spirit and understanding.

Having been so long detained by this Letter, I must not permit my desire of elucidating what may seem obscure, or of defending what is liable to misconstruction, any further to prevail over a wish for brevity, and the fear of giving an air of importance to subjects which have perhaps little in themselves.

The circumstance recorded in the fifth Letter is a fact; although it may appear to many almost incredible, that, in this country, and but few years since, a close and successful man should be a stranger to the method of increasing money by the loan of it. The Minister of the place where the honest Fisherman resided has related to me the apprehension and suspicion he witnessed: With trembling hand and dubious look, the careful man received and surveyed the bond given to him; and, after a sigh or two of lingering mistrust, he placed it in the coffer whence he had just before taken his cash; for which, and for whose increase, he now indulged a belief, that it was indeed both promise and security.

If the Letter which treats of Inns should be found to contain nothing interesting or uncommon; if it describe things which we behold every day, and some which we do not wish to behold at any time; let it be considered that this Letter is one of the shortest, and that from a Poem whose subject was a Borough, populous and wealthy, these places of public accommodation could not, without some impropriety, be excluded.

I entertain the strongest, because the most reasonable hope, that no liberal practitioner in the Law will be offended by the notice taken of dishonourable and crafty attorneys. The increased difficulty of entering into the profession will in time render it much more free than it now is, from those who disgrace it: at present such persons remain; and it would not be difficult to give instances of neglect, ignorance, cruelty, oppression, and chicanery; nor are they by any means confined to one part of the country: quacks and impostors are indeed in every profession, as well with a license as without one. The character and actions of *Swallow* might doubtless be contrasted by the delineation of an able and upright Solicitor; but this Letter is of sufficient length, and such persons, without question, are already known to my readers.

When I observe, under the article Physic, that the young and less experienced physician will write rather with a view of making himself known, than to investigate and publish some useful fact, I would not be thought to extend this remark to all the publications of such men. I could point out a work, containing experiments the most judicious, and conclusions the most interesting, made by a gentleman, then young, which would have given just celebrity to a man after long practice. The observation is nevertheless generally true: many opinions have been adopted and many books written, not that the theory might be well defended, but that a young physician might be better known.

If I have in one Letter praised the good-humour of a man confessedly too inattentive to business, and, in another, if I have written somewhat sarcastically of "the brick-floored parlour which the butcher lets;" be credit given to me, that in the one case I had no intention to apologize for idleness, nor any design in the other to treat with contempt the resources of the poor. The good-humour is considered as the consolation of disappointment, and the room is so mentioned because the lodger is vain. Most of my readers will perceive this; but I shall be sorry if by any I am supposed to make pleas for the vices of men, or treat their wants and infirmities with derision or with disdain.

It is probable, that really polite people, with cultivated minds and harmonious tempers, may judge my description of a Card-club conversation to be highly exaggerated, if not totally fictitious; and I acknowledge that the club must admit a particular kind of members to afford such specimens of acrimony and objurgation: yet that such language is spoken, and such manners exhibited, is most certain, chiefly among those who, being successful in life, without previous education, not very nice in their feelings, or very attentive to improprieties, sit down to game with no other view than that of adding the gain of the evening to the profits of the day; whom therefore disappointment itself makes angry, and, when caused by another, resentful and vindictive.

The Letter on Itinerant Players will to some appear too harshly written, their profligacy exaggerated, and their distresses magnified; but though the respectability of a part of these people may give us a more favourable view of the whole body; though some actors be sober, and some managers prudent; still there is vice and misery left, more than sufficient to justify my description. But if I could find only one woman who (passing forty years on many stages, and sustaining many principal characters) laments, in her unrespected old age, that there was no workhouse to which she could legally sue for admission; if I could produce only one female, seduced upon the boards, and starved in her lodging, compelled by her poverty to sing, and by her sufferings to weep, without any prospect but misery, or any consolation but death; if I could exhibit only one youth who sought refuge from parental authority in the licentious freedom of a wandering company; yet, with three such examples, I should feel myself justified in the account I have given:—but such characters and sufferings are common, and there are few of these societies which could not show members of this description. To some, indeed, the life has its satisfactions: they never expected to be free from labour, and their present kind they think is light: they have no delicate ideas of shame, and therefore duns and hisses give them no other pain than what arises from the fear of not being trusted, joined with the apprehension that they may have nothing to subsist upon except their credit.

For the Alms-House itself, its Governors and Inhabitants, I have not much to offer, in favour of the subject or of the characters. One of these, *Sir Denys Brand*, may be considered as too highly placed for an author (who seldom ventures above middle-life) to delineate; and indeed I had some idea of reserving him for another occasion, where he might have appeared with those in his own rank; but then it is most uncertain whether he would ever appear, and he has been so many years prepared for the public whenever opportunity might offer, that I have at length given him place, and though with his inferiors, yet as a ruler over them. Of these, one (*Benbow*) may be thought too low and despicable to be admitted here; but he is a Borough-character, and, however disgusting in some respects a picture may be, it will please some, and be tolerated by many, if it can boast that one merit of being a faithful likeness.

Blaney and *Clelia*, a male and female inhabitant of this mansion, are drawn at some length; and I may be thought to have given them attention which they do not merit. I plead not for the originality, but for the truth of the character; and though it may not be very pleasing, it may be useful to delineate (for certain minds) these mixtures of levity and vice; people who are thus incurably vain and determinately worldly; thus devoted to enjoyment and insensible of shame, and so miserably fond of their pleasures, that they court even the remembrance with eager solicitation, by conjuring up the ghosts of departed indulgences with all the aid that memory can afford them. These characters demand some attention, because they hold out a warning to that numerous class of young people, who are too lively to be discreet; to whom the purpose of life is amusement, and who are always in danger of falling into vicious habits, because they have too much activity to be quiet, and too little strength to be steady.

The characters of the Hospital-Directors were written many years since, and, so far as I was capable of judging, are drawn with *fidelity*. I mention this circumstance, that, if any reader should find a difference in the versification or expression, he will be thus enabled to account for it.

The Poor are here almost of necessity introduced, for they must be considered, in every place, as a large and interesting portion of its inhabitants. I am aware of the great difficulty of acquiring just notions on the maintenance and management of this class of our fellow-subjects, and I forbear to express any opinion of the various modes which have been discussed or adopted: of one method only I venture to give my sentiments, that of collecting the poor of a hundred into one building.—This admission of a vast number of persons, of all ages and both sexes, of very different inclinations, habits, and capacities, into a society, must, at a first view, I conceive, be looked upon as a cause of both vice and misery; nor does any thing which I have heard or read invalidate the opinion; happily, it is not a prevailing one, as these houses are, I believe, still confined to that part of the kingdom where they originated.

To this subject follow several Letters describing the follies and crimes of persons in lower life, with one relation of a happier and more consolatory kind. It has been a subject of greater vexation to me than such a trifle ought to be, that I could not, without destroying all appearance of arrangement, separate these melancholy narratives, and place the fallen Clerk in Office at a greater distance from the Clerk of the Parish, especially as they resembled each other in several particulars; both being tempted, seduced, and wretched. Yet are there, I conceive, considerable marks of distinction: their guilt is of different kind; nor would either have committed the offence of the other. The Clerk of the Parish could break the commandment, but he could not have been induced to have disowned an article of that creed for which he had so bravely contended, and on which he fully relied; and the upright mind of the Clerk in Office would have secured him from being guilty of wrong and robbery, though his weak and vacillating intellect could not preserve him from infidelity and profaneness. Their melancholy is nearly alike, but not its consequences. *Jachin* retained his belief, and though he hated life, he could never be induced to quit it voluntarily; but *Abel* was driven to terminate his misery in a way which the unfixedness of his religious opinions rather accelerated than retarded. I am therefore not without hope that the more observant of my readers will perceive many marks of discrimination in these characters.

The Life of *Ellen Orford*, though sufficiently burthened with error and misfortune, has in it little besides, which resembles those of the above unhappy men, and is still more unlike that of *Grimes*, in a subsequent Letter. There is in this character cheerfulness and resignation, a more uniform piety, and an immovable trust in the aid of religion: this, with the light texture of the introductory part, will, I hope, take off from that idea of sameness which the repetition of crimes and distresses is likely to create. The character of *Grimes*, his obduracy and apparent want of feeling, his gloomy kind of misanthropy, the progress of his madness, and the horrors of his imagination, I must leave to the judgment and observation of my readers. The mind here exhibited is one untouched by pity, unstung by remorse, and uncorrected by shame: yet is this hardihood of temper and spirit broken by want, disease, solitude, and disappointment; and he becomes the victim of a distempered and horror-stricken fancy. It is evident, therefore, that no feeble vision, no half-visible ghost, not the momentary glance of an unbodied being, nor the half-audible voice of an invisible one, would be created by the continual workings of distress on a mind so depraved and flinty. The ruffian of Mr. *Scott**, has a mind of this nature: he has no shame or remorse: but the corrosion of hopeless want, the wastings of unabating disease, and the gloom of unvaried solitude, will have their effect on every nature; and the harder that nature is, and the longer time required to work upon it, so much the more strong and indelible is the impression. This is all the reason I am able to give,

*Marmion.

why a man of feeling so dull should yet become insane, or that his insanity should be of so horrible a nature.

That a Letter on Prisons should follow those narratives is unfortunate, but not to be easily avoided. I confess it is not pleasant to be detained so long by subjects so repulsive to the feelings of many, as the sufferings of mankind: but though I assuredly would have altered this arrangement, had I been able to have done it by substituting a better, yet am I not of opinion that my verses, or indeed the verses of any other person, can so represent the evils and distresses of life as to make any material impression on the mind, and much less any of injurious nature. Alas! sufferings real, evident, continually before us, have not effects very serious or lasting, even in the minds of the more reflecting and compassionate; nor indeed does it seem right that the pain caused by sympathy should serve for more than a stimulus to benevolence. If then the strength and solidity of truth placed before our eyes have effect so feeble and transitory, I need not be very apprehensive that my representations of Poorhouses and Prisons, of wants and sufferings, however faithfully taken, will excite any feelings which can be seriously lamented. It has always been held as a salutary exercise of the mind, to contemplate the evils and miseries of our nature: I am not therefore without hope, that even this gloomy subject of Imprisonment, and more especially the Dream of the condemned Highwayman, will excite in some minds that mingled pity and abhorrence, which, while it is not unpleasant to the feelings, is useful in its operation: it ties and binds us to all mankind by sensations common to us all, and in some degree connects us, without degradation, even to the most miserable and guilty of our fellow-men.

Our concluding subject is Education; and some attempt is made to describe its various seminaries, from that of the Poor Widow, who pronounces the alphabet for infants, to seats whence the light of learning is shed abroad on the world. If, in this Letter, I describe the lives of literary men as embittered by much evil; if they be often disappointed, and sometimes unfitted for the world they improve; let it be considered that they are described as men who possess that great pleasure, the exercise of their own talents, and the delight which flows from their own exertions: they have joy in their pursuits, and glory in their acquirements of knowledge. Their victory over difficulties affords the most rational cause of triumph, and the attainment of new ideas leads to incalculable riches, such as gratify the glorious avarice of aspiring and comprehensive minds. Here then I place the reward of learning.—Our Universities produce men of the first scholastic attainments, who are heirs to large possessions, or descendants from noble families. Now, to those so favoured, talents and acquirements are, unquestionably, means of arriving at the most elevated and important situations; but these must be the lot of a few: in general, the diligence, acuteness, and perseverance of a youth at the University, have no other reward than some College honours and emoluments, which they desire to exchange, many of them for very moderate incomes, in the obscurity of some distant village: so that, in stating the reward of an ardent and powerful mind to consist principally (I might have said entirely) in its own views, efforts, and excursions, I place it upon a sure foundation, though not so elevated as the more ambitious aspire to. It is surely some encouragement to a studious man to reflect, that if he be disappointed, he cannot be without gratification; and that if he gets but a very humble portion of what the world can give, he has a continual fruition of unwearying enjoyment, of which it has not power to deprive him.

Long as I have detained the reader, I take leave to add a few words on the subject of imitation, or, more plainly speaking, borrowing. In the course of a long Poem, and more especially of two long ones, it is very difficult to avoid a recurrence of the same thoughts, and of similar expressions; and, however careful I have been myself in detecting and removing these kinds of repetitions, my readers, I question not, would, if disposed to seek them, find many remaining. For these I can only plead that common excuse—they are the offences of a bad memory, and not of a voluntary inattention; to which I must add the difficulty (I have already mentioned) of avoiding the error: this kind of plagiarism will therefore, I conceive, be treated with lenity: and of the more criminal kind, borrowing from others, I plead, with much confidence, "not guilty." But while I claim exemption from guilt, I do not affirm that much of sentiment and much of expression may not be detected in the vast collection of English poetry: it is sufficient for an author that he uses not the words or ideas of another without acknowledgment, and this, and no more than this, I mean, by disclaiming debts of the kind; yet resemblances are sometimes so very striking, that it requires faith in a reader to admit they were undesigned. A line in the second Letter,

> And monuments themselves memorials need,

was written long before the author, in an accidental recourse to Juvenal, read—

> Quandoquidem data eunt ipsis quoque fata sepulchris.
> Sat. x. l. 146.

and for this I believe the reader will readily give me credit. But there is another apparent imitation in the life of *Blaney* (Letter xiv,) a simile of so particular a kind, that its occurrence to two writers at the same time must appear as an extraordinary event; for this reason I once determined to exclude it from the relation; but, as it was truly unborrowed, and suited the place in which it stood, this seemed, on after-consideration, to be an act of cowardice, and the lines are therefore printed as they were written about two months before the very same thought (prosaically drest) appeared in a periodical work of the last summer. It is highly probable, in these cases, that both may derive the idea from a forgotten but common source; and in this way I must entreat the reader to do me justice, by accounting for other such resemblances, should any be detected.

I know not whether to some readers the placing two or three Latin quotations to a Letter may no appear pedantic and ostentatious, while both they and the English ones may be thought unnecessary.

For the necessity I have not much to advance; but if they be allowable (and certainly the best writers have adopted them,) then, where two or three different subjects occur, so many of these mottoes seem to be required: nor will a charge of pedantry remain, when it is considered that these things are generally taken from some books familiar to the school-boy, and the selecting them is facilitated by the use of a book of common-place: yet, with this help, the task of motto-hunting has been so unpleasant to me, that I have in various instances given up the quotation I was in pursuit of, and substituted such English verse or prose as I could find or invent for my purpose.

THE BOROUGH.

LETTER I.

GENERAL DESCRIPTION.

These did the ruler of the deep ordain,
To build proud navies, and to rule the main.
POPE'S *Homer's Iliad*, book vi, line 45.

Such scenes has Deptford, navy-building town,
Woolwich and Wapping, smelling strong of pitch;
Such Lambeth, envy of each band and gown,
And Twickenham such, which fairer scenes enrich.
POPE'S *Imitation of Spenser.*

————Et cum cœlestibus undis
Æquoreæ miscentur aquæ: caret ignibus æther,
Cæcaque nox premitur tenebris hiemisque suisque;
Discutient tamen has, præbentque micantia lumen
Fulmina: fulmineis ardescunt ignibus undæ.
OVID. *Metamorph.* lib. xi, ver. 520.

The Difficulty of describing Town Scenery—A Comparison with certain views in the Country—The river and Quay—The Shipping and Business—Ship-Building—Sea-Boys and Port Views—Village and Town Scenery again compared—Walks from Town—Cottage and adjoining Heath, etc.—House of Sunday Entertainment—The Sea: a Summer and Winter View—A Shipwreck at Night, and its Effects on shore—Evening Amusements in the Borough—An Apology for the imperfect View which can be given of these Subjects.

"Describe the Borough"—though our idle tribe
May love description, can we so describe,
That you shall fairly streets and buildings trace,
And all that gives distinction to a place?
This cannot be; yet, moved by your request,
A part I paint—let fancy form the rest.

Cities and towns, the various haunts of men,
Require the pencil; they defy the pen:
Could he, who sang so well the Grecian fleet,
So well have sung of alley, lane, or street?
Can measured lines these various buildings show,
The Town-Hall Turning, or the Prospect Row?
Can I the seats of wealth and want explore,
And lengthen out my lays from door to door?

Then let thy fancy aid me—I repair
From this tall mansion of our last-year's mayor,
Till we the outskirts of the Borough reach,
And these half-buried buildings next the beach;
Where hang at open doors the net and cork,
While squalid sea-dames mend the meshy work;
Till comes the hour, when fishing through the tide,
The weary husband throws his freight aside;
A living mass, which now demands the wife,
Th' alternate labours of their humble life.

Can scenes like these withdraw thee from thy wood,
Thy upland forest or thy valley's flood?
Seek then thy garden's shrubby bound, and look,
As it steals by, upon the bordering brook;
That winding streamlet, limping, lingering, slow,
Where the reeds whisper when the zephyrs blow;
Where in the midst, upon her throne of green,
Sits the large lily* as the water's queen;
And makes the current, forced awhile to stay,
Murmur and bubble as it shoots away;
Draw then the strongest contrast to that stream,
And our broad river will before thee seem.

With ceaseless motion comes and goes the tide,
Flowing, it fills the channel vast and wide;
Then back to sea, with strong majestic sweep
It rolls, in ebb yet terrible and deep;
Here sampire-banks† and salt-wort‡ bound the flood,
There stakes and sea-weeds withering on the mud;
And higher up, a ridge of all things base,
Which some strong tide has roll'd upon the place.

Thy gentle river boasts its pigmy boat,
Urged on by pains, half grounded, half afloat;
While at her stern an angler takes his stand,
And marks the fish he purposes to land;
From that clear space, where, in the cheerful ray
Of the warm sun, the scaly people play.

Far other craft our prouder river shows,
Hoys, pinks, and sloops; brigs, brigantines, and snows:
Nor angler we on our wide stream descry,
But one poor dredger where his oysters lie:
He, cold and wet, and driving with the tide,
Beats his weak arms against his tarry side,
Then drains the remnant of diluted gin,
To aid the warmth that languishes within;
Renewing oft his poor attempts to beat
His tingling fingers into gathering heat.

He shall again be seen when evening comes,
And social parties crowd their favourite rooms:
Where on the table pipes and papers lie,
The steaming bowl or foaming tankard by;
'T is then, with all these comforts spread around,
They hear the painful dredger's welcome sound;
And few themselves the savoury boon deny,
The food that feeds, the living luxury.

Yon is our quay! those smaller hoys from town,
Its various wares, for country-use, bring down;
Those laden wagons, in return, impart
The country produce to the city mart;

* The white water-lily. Nymphæa alba.

† The jointed glasswort. *Salicornia* is here meant, not the true sampire, the *crithmum maritimum.*

‡ The salsola of botanists.

Hark! to the clamour in that miry road,
Bounded and narrow'd by yon vessel's load;
The lumbering wealth she empties round the place,
Package, and parcel, hogshead, chest, and case:
While the loud seaman and the angry hind,
Mingling in business, bellow to the wind.

Near these a crew amphibious, in the docks,
Rear, for the sea, those castles on the stocks:
See! the long keel, which soon the waves must hide;
See! the strong ribs which form the roomy side;
Bolts yielding slowly to the sturdiest stroke,
And planks* which curve and crackle in the smoke.
Around the whole rise cloudy wreaths, and far
Bear the warm pungence of o'er-boiling tar.

Dabbling on shore half-naked sea-boys crowd,
Swim round a ship, or swing upon the shroud;
Or in a boat purloin'd, with paddles play,
And grow familiar with the watery way:
Young though they be, they feel whose sons they are,
They know what British seamen do and dare;
Proud of that fame, they rise and they enjoy
The rustic wonder of the village-boy.

Before you bid these busy scenes adieu,
Behold the wealth that lies in public view,
Those far-extended heaps of coal and coke,
Where fresh-fill'd lime-kilns breathe their stifling smoke.
This shall pass off, and you behold, instead,
The night-fire gleaming on its chalky bed;
When from the light-house brighter beams will rise,
To show the shipman where the shallow lies.

Thy walks are ever pleasant; every scene
Is rich in beauty, lively, or serene——
Rich—is that varied view with woods around,
Seen from the seat, within the shrubb'ry bound;
Where shines the distant lake, and where appear
From ruins bolting, unmolested deer;
Lively—the village-green, the inn, the place,
Where the good widow schools her infant race.
Shops, whence are heard the hammer and the saw,
And village-pleasures unreproved by law;
Then how serene! when in your favourite room,
Gales from your jasmines soothe the evening gloom;
When from your upland paddock you look down,
And just perceive the smoke which hides the town;
When weary peasants at the close of day
Walk to their cots, and part upon the way;
When cattle slowly cross the shallow brook,
And shepherds pen their folds, and rest upon their crook.

We prune our hedges, prime our slender trees,
And nothing looks untutor'd and at ease;
On the wide heath, or in the flow'ry vale,
We scent the vapours of the sea-born gale;
Broad-beaten paths lead on from stile to stile,
And sewers from streets, the road-side banks defile;
Our guarded fields a sense of danger show,
Where garden-crops with corn and clover grow;
Fences are form'd of wreck and placed around,
(With tenters tipp'd) a strong repulsive bound;
Wide and deep ditches by the gardens run,
And there in ambush lie the trap and gun;
Or yon broad board, which guards each tempting prize,
"Like a tall bully, lifts its head and lies."

There stands a cottage with an open door,
Its garden undefended blooms before:
Her wheel is still, and overturn'd her stool,
While the lone widow seeks the neighb'ring pool:
This gives us hope, all views of town to shun—
No! here are tokens of the sailor son;
That old blue jacket, and that shirt of check,
And silken kerchief for the seaman's neck;
Sea-spoils and shells from many a distant shore,
And furry robe from frozen Labrador.

Our busy streets and sylvan walks between,
Fen, marshes, bog and heath all intervene;
Here pits of crag, with spongy, plashy base,
To some enrich th' uncultivated space:
For there are blossoms rare, and curious rush,
The gale's rich balm, and sun-dew's crimson blush,
Whose velvet leaf with radiant beauty dress'd,
Forms a gay pillow for the plover's breast.

Not distant far, a house commodious made,
(Lonely yet public stands) for Sunday trade;
Thither, for this day free, gay parties go,
Their tea-house walk, their tippling rendezvous;
There humble couples sit in corner-bowers,
Or gaily ramble for th' allotted hours!
Sailors and lasses from the town attend,
The servant lover, the apprentice-friend;
With all the idle social tribes who seek,
And find their humble pleasures once a week.

Turn to the watery world!—but who to thee
(A wonder yet unview'd) shall paint—the sea!
Various and vast, sublime in all its forms,
When lull'd by zephyrs, or when roused by storms,
In colours changing, when from clouds and sun
Shades after shades upon the surface run;
Embrown'd and horrid now, and now serene,
In limpid blue, and evanescent green;
And oft the foggy banks on ocean lie,
Lift the fair sail, and cheat th' experienced eye.*

Be it the summer-noon: a sandy space
The ebbing tide has left upon its place;
Then just the hot and stony beach above,
Light twinkling streams in bright confusion move;
(For heated thus, the warmer air ascends,
And with the cooler in its fall contends)—
Then the broad bosom of the ocean keeps
An equal motion; swelling as it sleeps,
Then slowly sinking; curling to the strand,
Faint, lazy waves o'ercreep the ridgy sand,
Or tap the tarry boat with gentle blow,
And back return in silence, smooth and slow.
Ships in the calm seem anchor'd; for they glide
On the still sea, urged solely by the tide;

* The curvature of planks for the sides of a ship, etc. is, I am informed, now generally made by the power of steam. Fire is nevertheless still used for boats and vessels of the smaller kind.

* Of the effect of these mists, known by the name of fog banks, wonderful and indeed incredible relations are given; but their property of appearing to elevate ships at sea, and to bring them in view, is, I believe, generally acknowledged.

Art thou not present this calm scene before,
Where all beside is pebbly length of shore,
And far as eye can reach, it can discern no more!

Yet sometimes comes a ruffling cloud to make
The quiet surface of the ocean shake;
As an awaken'd giant with a frown
Might show his wrath, and then to sleep sink down.

View now the winter-storm! above, one cloud,
Black and unbroken, all the skies o'ershroud;
Th' unwieldy porpoise through the day before
Had roll'd in view of boding men on shore;
And sometimes hid and sometimes show'd his form
Dark as the cloud, and furious as the storm.

All where the eye delights, yet dreads to roam,
The breaking billows cast the flying foam
Upon the billows rising—all the deep
Is restless change; the waves so swell'd and steep,
Breaking and sinking, and the sunken swells,
Nor one, one moment, in its station dwells:
But nearer land you may the billows trace,
As if contending in their watery chase;
May watch the mightiest till the shoal they reach,
Then break and hurry to their utmost stretch;
Curl'd as they come, they strike with furious force,
And then re-flowing, take their grating course,
Raking the rounded flints, which ages past
Roll'd by their rage, and shall to ages last.

Far off the petrel in the troubled way
Swims with her brood, or flutters in the spray;
She rises often, often drops again,
And sports at ease on the tempestuous main.

High o'er the restless deep, above the reach
Of gunner's hope, vast flights of wild-ducks stretch;
Far as the eye can glance on either side,
In a broad space and level line they glide;
All in their wedge-like figures from the north,
Day after day, flight after flight, go forth.

In-shore their passage tribes of sea-gulls urge,
And drop for prey within the sweeping surge;
Oft in the rough opposing blast they fly
Far back, then turn, and all their force apply,
While to the storm they give their weak complaining cry;
Or clap the sleek white pinion to the breast,
And in the restless ocean dip for rest.

Darkness begins to reign; the louder wind
Appals the weak and awes the firmer mind;
But frights not him, whom evening and the spray
In part conceal—yon prowler on his way:
Lo! he has something seen; he runs apace,
As if he fear'd companion in the chase;
He sees his prize, and now he turns again,
Slowly and sorrowing—"Was your search in vain?"
Gruffly he answers, "'T is a sorry sight!
A seaman's body: there'll be more to-night!"

Hark! to those sounds! they 're from distress at sea:
How quick they come! What terrors may there be!
Yes, 't is a driven vessel: I discern
Lights, signs of terror, gleaming from the stern;
Others behold them too, and from the town
In various parties seamen hurry down;
Their wives pursue, and damsels urged by dread,
Lest men so dear be into danger led;
Their head the gown has hooded, and their call
In this sad night is piercing like the squall;
They feel their kinds of power, and when they meet,
Chide, fondle, weep, dare, threaten, or entreat.

See one poor girl, all terror and alarm,
Has fondly seized upon her lover's arm;
"Thou shalt not venture;" and he answers "No!
I will not"—still she cries, "Thou shalt not go."

No need of this; not here the stoutest boat
Can through such breakers, o'er such billows float:
Yet may they view these lights upon the beach,
Which yield them hope, whom help can never reach.

From parted clouds the moon her radiance throws
On the wild waves, and all the danger shows;
But shows them beaming in her shining vest,
Terrific splendour! gloom in glory dress'd!
This for a moment, and then clouds again
Hide every beam, and fear and darkness reign.

But hear we now those sounds? Do lights appear?
I see them not! the storm alone I hear.
And lo! the sailors homeward take their way;
Man must endure—let us submit and pray.

Such are our winter-views; but night comes on—
Now business sleeps, and daily cares are gone;
Now parties form, and some their friends assist
To waste the idle hours at sober whist;
The tavern's pleasure or the concert's charm
Unnumber'd moments of their sting disarm;
Play-bills and open doors a crowd invite,
To pass off one dread portion of the night;
And show and song and luxury combined,
Lift off from man this burthen of mankind.

Others advent'rous walk abroad and meet
Returning parties pacing through the street;
When various voices, in the dying day,
Hum in our walks, and greet us in our way;
When tavern-lights flit on from room to room,
And guide the tippling sailor staggering home:
There as we pass, the jingling bells betray
How business rises with the closing day:
Now walking silent, by the river's side,
The ear perceives the rippling of the tide;
Or measured cadence of the lads who tow
Some enter'd hoy, to fix her in her row;
Or hollow sound, which from the parish-bell
To some departed spirit bids farewell!

Thus shall you something of our Borough know
Far as a verse, with Fancy's aid, can show;
Of sea or river, of a quay or street,
The best description must be incomplete;
But when a happier theme succeeds, and when
Men are our subjects and the deeds of men;
Then may we find the Muse in happier style,
And we may sometimes sigh and sometimes smile

LETTER II.

THE CHURCH.

——— Festinat enim decurrere velox
Flosculus angustæ miseræque brevissima vitæ
Portio! dum bibimus, dum serta, unguenta, puellas
Poscimus, obrepit non intellecta senectus.
JUVENAL. Satir. ix. lin. 126.

And when at last thy love shall die,
Wilt thou receive his parting breath?
Wilt thou repress each struggling sigh,
And cheer with smiles the bed of death?
PERCY.

Several Meanings of the word *Church*—The Building so called, here intended—Its Antiquity and Grandeur—Columns and Aisles—The Tower: the Stains made by Time compared with the mock Antiquity of the Artist—Progress of Vegetation on such Buildings—Bells—Tombs: one in decay—Mural Monuments, and the Nature of their Inscriptions—An Instance in a departed Burgess—Churchyard Graves—Mourners for the Dead—A Story of a betrothed Pair in humble Life, and Effects of Grief in the Survivor.

"What is a Church?"—Let Truth and Reason speak,
They would reply, "The faithful, pure, and meek,
From Christian folds, the once selected race,
Of all professions, and in every place."

"What is a Church?"—"A flock," our vicar cries,
"Whom bishops govern and whom priests advise;
Wherein are various states and due degrees,
The bench for honour, and the stall for ease;
That ease be mine, which, after all his cares,
The pious, peaceful prebendary shares."

"What is a Church?"—Our honest sexton tells,
"'T is a tall building, with a tower and bells;
Where priest and clerk with joint exertion strive
To keep the ardour of their flock alive;
That, by his periods eloquent and grave;
This, by responses, and a well-set stave:
These for the living; but when life be fled,
I toll myself the requiem for the dead."

'T is to this Church I call thee, and that place
Where slept our fathers when they'd run their race:
We too shall rest, and then our children keep
Their road in life, and then, forgotten, sleep;
Meanwhile the building slowly falls away,
And, like the builders, will in time decay.

The old foundation—but it is not clear
When it was laid—you care not for the year;
On this, as parts decay'd by time and storms,
Arose these various disproportion'd forms;
Yet Gothic, all the learn'd who visit us
(And our small wonders) have decided thus;
"Yon noble gothic arch," "That gothic door;"
So have they said; of proof you 'll need no more.

Here large plain columns rise in solemn style,
You'd love the gloom they make in either aisle;
When the sun's rays, enfeebled as they pass,
(And shorn of splendour) through the storied glass,
Faintly display the figures on the floor,
Which pleased distinctly in their place before.

But ere you enter, yon bold tower survey,
Tall and entire, and venerably grey,
For time has soften'd what was harsh when new,
And now the stains are all of sober hue;
The living stains which Nature's hand alone,
Profuse of life, pours forth upon the stone;
For ever growing; where the common eye
Can but the bare and rocky bed descry;
There Science loves to trace her tribes minute,
The juiceless foliage, and the tasteless fruit;
There she perceives them round the surface creep,
And while they meet, their due distinction keep;
Mix'd but not blended; each its name retains,
And these are nature's ever-during stains.

And wouldst thou, artist! with thy tints and brush,
Form shades like these? Pretender, where thy blush?
In three short hours shall thy presuming hand
Th' effect of three slow centuries command?*
Thou mayst thy various greens and greys contrive,
They are not lichens, nor like aught alive;—
But yet proceed, and when thy tints are lost,
Fled in the shower, or crumbled by the frost;
When all thy work is done away as clean
As if thou never spread'st thy grey and green;
Then mayst thou see how Nature's work is done,
How slowly true she lays her colours on;
When her least speck upon the hardest flint,
Has mark and form and is a living tint;
And so embodied with the rock, that few
Can the small germ upon the substance view.†

Seeds, to our eye invisible, will find
On the rude rock the bed that fits their kind;
There, in the rugged soil, they safely dwell,
Till showers and snows the subtle atoms swell,
And spread th' enduring foliage;—then we trace
The freckled flower upon the flinty base;
These all increase, till in unnoticed years
The stony tower as grey with age appears;
With coats of vegetation, thinly spread,
Coat above coat, the living on the dead;
These then dissolve to dust, and make a way
For bolder foliage, nursed by their decay:
The long-enduring ferns in time will all
Die and depose their dust upon the wall;

* If it should be objected, that centuries are not slower than hours, because the speed of time must be uniform, I would answer, that I understand so much, and mean that they are slower in no other sense, than because they are not finished so soon.

† This kind of vegetation, as it begins upon siliceous stones, is very thin, and frequently not to be distinguished from the surface of the flint. The byssus jolithus of Linnæus (lepraria jolithus of the present system), an adhesive carmine crust on rocks and old buildings, was, even by scientific persons, taken for the substance on which it spread. A great variety of these minute vegetables are to be found on some parts of the coast, where the beach, formed of stones of various kinds, is undisturbed, and exposed to every change of weather; in this situation, the different species of lichen, in their different stages of growth, have an appearance interesting and agreeable even to those who are ignorant of, and indifferent to the cause.

Where the wing'd seed may rest, till many a flower
Show Flora's triumph o'er the falling tower.

But ours yet stands, and has its bells renown'd,
For size magnificent and solemn sound;
Each has its motto: some contrived to tell,
In monkish rhyme, the uses of a bell;*
Such wondrous good, as few conceive could spring
From ten loud coppers when their clappers swing.
Enter'd the Church; we to a tomb proceed,
Whose names and titles few attempt to read;
Old English letters, and those half pick'd out,
Leave us, unskilful readers, much in doubt:
Our sons shall see its more degraded state;
The tomb of grandeur hastens to its fate:
That marble arch, our sexton's favourite show,
With all those ruff'd and painted pairs below;
The noble lady and the lord who rest
Supine, as courtly dame and warrior dress'd;
All are departed from their state sublime,
Mangled and wounded in their war with time,
Colleagued with mischief: here a leg is fled,
And lo! the baron with but half a head;
Midway is cleft the arch; the very base
Is batter'd round and shifted from its place.

Wonder not, mortal, at thy quick decay—
See! men of marble piece-meal melt away;
When whose the image we no longer read,
But monuments themselves memorials need.†

With few such stately proofs of grief or pride
By wealth erected, is our Church supplied;
But we have mural tablets, every size,
That woe could wish, or vanity devise.

Death levels man,—the wicked and the just,
The wise, the weak, lie blended in the dust;
And by the honours dealt to every name,
The king of terrors seems to level fame.
—See!—here lamented wives, and every wife
The pride and comfort of her husband's life;
Here, to her spouse, with every virtue graced,
His mournful widow has a trophy placed;
And here 't is doubtful if the duteous son,
Or the good father, be in praise outdone.

This may be nature; when our friends we lose,
Our alter'd feelings alter too our views;
What in their tempers teased us or distress'd,
Is, with our anger and the dead, at rest;
And much we grieve, no longer trial made,
For that impatience which we then display'd;
Now to their love and worth of every kind
A soft compunction turns th' afflicted mind;
Virtues neglected then, adored become,
And graces slighted, blossom on the tomb.

'T is well; but let not love nor grief believe
That we assent (who neither loved nor grieve)
To all that praise which on the tomb is read,
To all that passion dictates for the dead;
But more indignant, we the tomb deride,
Whose bold inscription flattery sells to pride.

Read of this Burgess—on the stone appear
How worthy he! how virtuous! and how dear!
What wailing was there when his spirit fled,
How mourn'd his lady for her lord when dead,
And tears abundant through the town were shed;
See! he was liberal, kind, religious, wise,
And free from all disgrace and all disguise;
His sterling worth, which words cannot express,
Lives with his friends, their pride and their distress.

All this of Jacob Holmes? for his the name;
He thus kind, liberal, just, religious?—shame!
What is the truth? Old Jacob married thrice;
He dealt in coals, and av'rice was his vice;
He ruled the Borough when his year came on,
And some forget, and some are glad he 's gone;
For never yet with shilling could he part,
But when it left his hand, it struck his heart.

Yet, here will love its last attentions pay,
And place memorials on these beds of clay.
Large level stones lie flat upon the grave,
And half a century's sun and tempest brave;
But many an honest tear and heartfelt sigh
Have follow'd those who now unnoticed lie;
Of these what numbers rest on every side!
Without one token left by grief or pride;
Their graves soon levell'd to the earth, and then
With other hillocks rise o'er other men;
Daily the dead on the decay'd are thrust,
And generations follow "dust to dust."

Yes! there are real mourners—I have seen
A fair, sad girl, mild, suffering, and serene;
Attention (through the day) her duties claim'd,
And to be useful as resign'd she aim'd:
Neatly she dress'd, nor vainly seem'd t' expect
Pity for grief, or pardon for neglect;
But when her wearied parents sunk to sleep,
She sought her place to meditate and weep:
Then to her mind was all the past display'd,
That faithful memory brings to sorrow's aid:
For then she thought on one regretted youth,
Her tender trust, and his unquestion'd truth;
In ev'ry place she wander'd, where they'd been,
And sadly-sacred held the parting-scene;
Where last for sea he took his leave—that place
With double interest would she nightly trace;
For long the courtship was, and he would say,
Each time he sail'd,—"This once, and then the day:"
Yet prudence tarried, but when last he went,
He drew from pitying love a full consent.

Happy he sail'd, and great the care she took,
That he should softly sleep, and smartly look;
White was his better linen, and his check
Was made more trim than any on the deck;
And every comfort men at sea can know
Was hers to buy, to make, and to bestow:
For he to Greenland sail'd, and much she told,
How he should guard against the climate's cold;
Yet saw not danger; dangers he 'd withstood,
Nor could she trace the fever in his blood:
His messmates smiled at flushings in his cheek,
And he too smiled, but seldom would he speak;
For now he found the danger, felt the pain,
With grievous symptoms he could not explain;

* The several purposes for which bells are used are expressed in two Latin verses of this kind.

† Quandoquidem data sunt ipsis quoque fata sepulchris.
JUVENAL. Sat. x, l. 146.

Hope was awaken'd, as for home he sail'd,
But quickly sank, and never more prevail'd.

He call'd his friend, and prefaced with a sigh
A lover's message—"Thomas, I must die:
Would I could see my Sally, and could rest
My throbbing temples on her faithful breast,
And gazing go!—if not, this trifle take,
And say, till death I wore it for her sake;
Yes! I must die—blow on, sweet breeze, blow on!
Give me one look, before my life be gone,
Oh! give me that, and let me not despair,
One last fond look—and now repeat the prayer."

He had his wish, had more; I will not paint
The lovers' meeting: she beheld him faint,—
With tender fears, she took a nearer view,
Her terrors doubling as her hopes withdrew;
He tried to smile, and, half succeeding, said,
"Yes! I must die;" and hope for ever fled.

Still long she nursed him: tender thoughts meantime
Were interchanged, and hopes and views sublime.
To her he came to die, and every day
She took some portion of the dread away;
With him she pray'd, to him his Bible read,
Soothed the faint heart, and held the aching head:
She came with smiles the hour of pain to cheer;
Apart she sigh'd; alone, she shed the tear;
Then, as if breaking from a cloud, she gave
Fresh light, and gilt the prospect of the grave.
One day he lighter seem'd, and they forgot
The care, the dread, the anguish of their lot;
They spoke with cheerfulness, and seem'd to think,
Yet said not so—"Perhaps he will not sink:"
A sudden brightness in his look appear'd,
A sudden vigour in his voice was heard;—
She had been reading in the Book of Prayer,
And led him forth, and placed him in his chair;
Lively he seem'd, and spoke of all he knew,
The friendly many, and the favourite few;
Nor one that day did he to mind recall
But she has treasured, and she loves them all;
When in her way she meets them, they appear
Peculiar people—death has made them dear.
He named his friend, but then his hand she press'd,
And fondly whisper'd, "Thou must go to rest;"
"I go," he said; but as he spoke, she found
His hand more cold, and fluttering was the sound!
Then gazed affrighten'd; but she caught a last,
A dying look of love,—and all was past!

She placed a decent stone his grave above,
Neatly engraved—an offering of her love;
For that she wrought, for that forsook her bed,
Awake alike to duty and the dead;
She would have grieved, had friends presumed to spare
The least assistance—'t was her proper care.

Here will she come, and on the grave will sit,
Folding her arms, in long abstracted fit;
But if observer pass, will take her round,
And careless seem, for she would not be found;
Then go again, and thus her hour employ,
While visions please her, and while woes destroy.

Forbear, sweet maid! nor be by fancy led,
To hold mysterious converse with the dead;
For sure at length thy thoughts, thy spirits pain,
In this sad conflict will disturb thy brain:
All have their tasks and trials; thine are hard,
But short the time, and glorious the reward;
Thy patient spirit to thy duties give,
Regard the dead, but to the living live.*

LETTER III.

THE VICAR—THE CURATE, ETC.

And telling me the sov'reign'st thing on earth
Was parmacity for an inward bruise.
SHAKSPEARE, *Henry IV*, Part I, Act I.

So gentle, yet so brisk, so wondrous sweet,
So fit to prattle at a lady's feet.
CHURCHILL.

Much are the precious hours of youth mispent
In climbing learning's rugged, steep ascent:
When to the top the bold adventurer's got,
He reigns vain monarch of a barren spot;
While in the vale of ignorance below,
Folly and vice to rank luxuriance grow;
Honours and wealth pour in on every side,
And proud preferment rolls her golden tide.
CHURCHILL.

VICAR.

The lately-departed Minister of the Borough—His soothing and supplicatory Manners—His cool and timid Affections—No Praise due to such negative Virtue—Address to Characters of this Kind—The Vicar's Employments—His Talents and moderate Ambition—His Dislike of Innovation—His mild but ineffectual Benevolence—A Summary of his Character.

CURATE.

Mode of paying the Borough-minister—The Curate has no such Resources—His Learning and Poverty—Erroneous ideas of his Parent—His Feelings as a Husband and Father—The dutiful Regard of his numerous family—His Pleasures as a Writer, how interrupted—No Resource in the Press—Vulgar Insult—His Account of a Literary Society, and a Fund for the Relief of Indigent Authors, etc.

WHERE ends our chancel in a vaulted space,
Sleep the departed vicars of the place;
Of most, all mention, memory, thought are past—
But take a slight memorial of the last.

To what famed college we our Vicar owe,
To what fair country, let historians show;
Few now remember when the mild young man,
Ruddy and fair, his Sunday-task began;

* It has been observed to me, that in the first part of the story I have represented this young woman as resigned and attentive to her duties; from which it should appear that the concluding advice is unnecessary; but if the reader will construe the expression "to the living live," into the sense—live entirely for them, attend to duties only which are real, and not those imposed by the imagination, I shall have no need to alter the line which terminates the story.

Few live to speak of that soft soothing look
He cast around, as he prepared his book;
It was a kind of supplicating smile,
But nothing hopeless of applause, the while;
And when he finish'd, his corrected pride
Felt the desert, and yet the praise denied.
Thus he his race began, and to the end
His constant care was, no man to offend;
No haughty virtues stirr'd his peaceful mind,
Nor urged the priest to leave the flock behind;
He was his Master's soldier, but not one
To lead an army of his martyrs on:
Fear was his ruling passion; yet was love,
Of timid kind, once known his heart to move;
It led his patient spirit where it paid
Its languid offering to a listening maid;
She, with her widow'd mother, heard him speak,
And sought awhile to find what he would seek:
Smiling he came, he smiled when he withdrew,
And paid the same attention to the two;
Meeting and parting without joy or pain,
He seem'd to come that he might go again.
The wondering girl, no prude, but something nice,
At length was chill'd by his unmelting ice;
She found her tortoise held such sluggish pace,
That she must turn and meet him in the chase:
This not approving, she withdrew till one
Came who appear'd with livelier hope to run;
Who sought a readier way the heart to move,
Than by faint dalliance of unfixing love.

Accuse me not that I approving paint
Impatient hope or love without restraint;
Or think the passions, a tumultuous throng,
Strong as they are, ungovernably strong:
But is the laurel to the soldier due,
Who cautious comes not into danger's view?
What worth has virtue by desire untried,
When Nature's self enlists on duty's side?

The married dame in vain assail'd the truth
And guarded bosom of the Hebrew youth;
But with the daughter of the Priest of On
The love was lawful, and the guard was gone;
But Joseph's fame had lessen'd in our view,
Had he, refusing, fled the maiden too.

Yet our good priest to Joseph's praise aspired,
At once rejecting what his heart desired;

"I am escaped," he said, when none pursued;
When none attack'd him, "I am unsubdued;"
"Oh pleasing pangs of love," he sang again,
Cold to the joy, and stranger to the pain.
Ev'n in his age would he address the young,
"I too have felt these fires, and they are strong;"
But from the time he left his favourite maid,
To ancient females his devoirs were paid;
And still they miss him after morning prayer;
Nor yet successor fills the Vicar's chair,
Where kindred spirits in his praise agree,
A happy few, as mild and cool as he;
The easy followers in the female train,
Led without love, and captives without chain.

Ye lilies male! think (as your tea you sip,
While the town small-talk flows from lip to lip;
Intrigues half-gather'd, conversation-scraps,
Kitchen-cabals, and nursery-mishaps,)
If the vast world may not some scene produce,
Some state where your small talents might have use;
Within seraglios you might harmless move,
'Mid ranks of beauty, and in haunts of love;
There from too daring man the treasures guard,
An easy duty, and its own reward;
Nature's soft substitutes, you there might save
From crime the tyrant, and from wrong the slave

But let applause be dealt in all we may,
Our priest was cheerful, and in season gay;
His frequent visits seldom fail'd to please;
Easy himself, he sought his neighbour's ease:
To a small garden with delight he came,
And gave successive flowers a summer's fame;
These he presented with a grace his own
To his fair friends, and made their beauties known,
Not without moral compliment; how they
"Like flowers were sweet, and must like flowers decay."

Simple he was, and loved the simple truth,
Yet had some useful cunning from his youth;
A cunning never to dishonour lent,
And rather for defence than conquest meant;
'Twas fear of power, with some desire to rise,
But not enough to make him enemies.
He ever aim'd to please; and to offend
Was ever cautious; for he sought a friend;
Yet for the friendship never much would pay,
Content to bow, be silent, and obey,
And by a soothing suff'rance find his way.
Fiddling and fishing were his arts: at times
He alter'd sermons, and he aim'd at rhymes;
And his fair friends, not yet intent on cards
Oft he amused with riddles and charades.

Mild were his doctrines, and not one discourse
But gain'd in softness what it lost in force:
Kind his opinions; he would not receive
An ill report, nor evil act believe;
"If true, 'twas wrong; but blemish great or small
Have all mankind; yea, sinners are we all."

If ever fretful thought disturb'd his breast,
If aught of gloom that cheerful mind oppress'd,
It sprang from innovation; it was then
He spake of mischief made by restless men;
Not by new doctrines: never in his life
Would he attend to controversial strife;
For sects he cared not: "They are not of us,
Nor need we, brethren, their concerns discuss;
But 'tis the change, the schism at home I feel;
Ills few perceive, and none have skill to heal:
Not at the altar our young brethren read
(Facing their flock) the decalogue and creed;
But at their duty, in their desks they stand,
With naked surplice, lacking hood, and band:
Churches are now of holy song bereft,
And half our ancient customs changed or left;
Few sprigs of ivy are at Christmas seen,
Nor crimson berry tips the holly's green;
Mistaken choirs refuse the solemn strain
Of ancient Sternhold, which from ours amain
Comes flying forth from aisle to aisle about,
Sweet links of harmony and long drawn out."

These were to him essentials; all things new
He deem'd superfluous, useless, or untrue;

To all beside indifferent, easy, cold,
Here the fire kindled, and the woe was told.

Habit with him was all the test of truth,
"It must be right: I've done it from my youth."
Questions he answer'd in as brief a way,
"It must be wrong—it was of yesterday."

Though mild benevolence our priest possess'd,
'T was but by wishes or by words express'd:
Circles in water, as they wider flow,
The less conspicuous in their progress grow;
And when at last they touch upon the shore,
Distinction ceases, and they're view'd no more.
His love, like that last circle, all embraced,
But with effect that never could be traced.

Now rests our Vicar. They who knew him best
Proclaim his life 't have been entirely rest;
Free from all evils which disturb his mind
Whom studies vex and controversies blind.
The rich approved,—of them in awe he stood;
The poor admired,—they all believed him good:
The old and serious of his habits spoke;
The frank and youthful loved his pleasant joke;
Mothers approved a safe contented guest,
And daughters one who back'd each small request:
In him his flock found nothing to condemn;
Him sectaries liked,—he never troubled them;
No trifles fail'd his yielding mind to please,
And all his passions sunk in early ease;
Nor one so old has left this world of sin
More like the being that he enter'd in.

THE CURATE.

Ask you what lands our pastor tithes?—Alas!
But few our acres, and but short our grass:
In some fat pastures of the rich, indeed,
May roll the single cow or favourite steed;
Who, stable-fed, is here for pleasure seen,
His sleek sides bathing in the dewy green;
But these, our hilly heath and common wide
Yield a slight portion for the parish-guide;
No crops luxuriant in our borders stand,
For here we plough the ocean, not the land;
Still reason wills that we our pastor pay,
And custom does it on a certain day:
Much is the duty, small the legal due,
And this with grateful minds we keep in view;
Each makes his off'ring, some by habit led,
Some by the thought, that all men must be fed;
Duty and love, and piety and pride,
Have each their force, and for the priest provide.

Not thus our Curate, one whom all believe
Pious and just, and for whose fate they grieve;
All see him poor, but ev'n the vulgar know
He merits love, and their respect bestow.
A man so learn'd you shall but seldom see,
Nor one so honour'd, so aggrieved as he;—
Not grieved by years alone; though this appear
Dark and more dark; severer on severe:
Not in his need,—and yet we all must grant
How painful 't is for feeling age to want:
Nor in his body's sufferings; yet we know
Where time has plough'd, there misery loves to sow;
But in the wearied mind, that all in vain
Wars with distress, and struggles with its pain.

His father saw his powers—"I'll give," quoth he,
"My first-born learning; 't will a portion be:"
Unhappy gift! a portion for a son!
But all he had:—he learn'd, and was undone!

Better, apprenticed to an humble trade,
Had he the cassock for the priesthood made,
Or thrown the shuttle, or the saddle shaped,
And all these pangs of feeling souls escaped.

He once had hope—hope, ardent, lively, light,
His feelings pleasant, and his prospects bright:
Eager of fame, he read, he thought, he wrote,
Weigh'd the Greek page, and added note on note;
At morn, at evening at his work was he,
And dream'd what his Euripides would be.

Then care began;—he loved, he woo'd, he wed;
Hope cheer'd him still, and Hymen bless'd his bed—
A Curate's bed! then came the woful years;
The husband's terrors, and the father's tears;
A wife grown feeble, mourning, pining, vex'd,
With wants and woes—by daily cares perplex'd;
No more a help, a smiling, soothing aid,
But boding, drooping, sickly, and afraid.

A kind physician, and without a fee,
Gave his opinion—"Send her to the sea."
"Alas!" the good man answer'd, "can I send
A friendless woman? Can I find a friend?
No; I must with her, in her need, repair
To that new place; the poor lie every where;—
Some priest will pay me for my pious pains:"
He said, he came, and here he yet remains.

Behold his dwelling; this poor hut he hires,
Where he from view, though not from want, retires
Where four fair daughters, and five sorrowing sons,
Partake his sufferings, and dismiss his duns,
All join their efforts, and in patience learn
To want the comforts they aspire to earn;
For the sick mother something they'd obtain,
To soothe her grief and mitigate her pain;
For the sad father something they'd procure,
To ease the burden they themselves endure.

Virtues like these at once delight and press
On the fond father with a proud distress;
On all around he looks with care and love,
Grieved to behold, but happy to approve.

Then from his care, his love, his grief he steals,
And by himself an author's pleasure feels:
Each line detains him; he omits not one,
And all the sorrows of his state are gone,—
Alas! even then, in that delicious hour,
He feels his fortune, and laments its power.

Some tradesman's bill his wandering eyes engage,
Some scrawl for payment thrust 'twixt page and page;
Some bold, loud rapping at his humble door,
Some surly message he has heard before,
Awake, alarm, and tell him he is poor.

An angry dealer, vulgar, rich, and proud,
Thinks of his bill, and passing, raps aloud;
The elder daughter meekly makes him way—
"I want my money, and I cannot stay:

My mill is stopp'd; what, Miss! I cannot grind;
Go tell your father he must raise the wind:"
Still trembling, troubled, the dejected maid
Says, "Sir! my father!—" and then stops afraid:
Ev'n his hard heart is soften'd, and he hears
Her voice with pity; he respects her tears;
His stubborn features half admit a smile,
And his tone softens—"Well! I'll wait awhile."

Pity! a man so good, so mild, so meek,
At such an age, should have his bread to seek;
And all those rude and fierce attacks to dread,
That are more harrowing than the want of bread;
Ah! who shall whisper to that misery peace!
And say that want and insolence shall cease?

"But why not publish?"—those who know too well,
Dealers in Greek, are fearful 't will not sell;
Then he himself is timid, troubled, slow,
Nor likes his labours nor his griefs to show;
The hope of fame may in his heart have place,
But he has dread and horror of disgrace;
Nor has he that confiding, easy way,
That might his learning and himself display;
But to his work he from the world retreats,
And frets and glories o'er the favourite sheets.

But see! the man himself; and sure I trace
Signs of new joy exulting in that face
O'er care that sleeps—we err, or we discern
Life in thy looks—the reason may we learn?

"Yes," he replied, "I'm happy, I confess,
To learn that some are pleased with happiness
Which others feel—there are who now combine
The worthiest natures in the best design,
To aid the letter'd poor, and soothe such ills as mine:
We who more keenly feel the world's contempt,
And from its miseries are the least exempt;
Now hope shall whisper to the wounded breast,
And grief, in soothing expectation, rest.

"Yes, I am taught that men who think, who feel,
Unite the pains of thoughtful men to heal;
Not with disdainful pride, whose bounties make
The needy curse the benefits they take;
Not with the idle vanity that knows
Only a selfish joy when it bestows;
Not with o'erbearing wealth, that, in disdain,
Hurls the superfluous bliss at groaning pain;
But these are men who yield such bless'd relief,
That with the grievance they destroy the grief;
Their timely aid the needy sufferers find,
Their generous manner soothes the suffering mind;
Theirs is a gracious bounty, form'd to raise
Him whom it aids; their charity is praise;
A common bounty may relieve distress,
But whom the vulgar succour, they oppress;
This though a favour, is an honour too,
Though mercy's duty, yet 't is merit's due;
When our relief from such resources rise,
All painful sense of obligation dies;
And grateful feelings in the bosom wake,
For 't is their offerings, not their alms, we take.

"Long may these founts of charity remain,
And never shrink, but to be fill'd again;
True! to the author they are now confined,
To him who gave the treasure of his mind,
His time, his health, and thankless found mankind
But there is hope that from these founts may flow
A sideway stream, and equal good bestow;
Good that may reach us, whom the day's distress
Keeps from the fame and perils of the press;
Whom study beckons from the ills of life,
And they from study; melancholy strife!
Who then can say, but bounty now so free,
And so diffused, may find its way to me?

"Yes! I may see my decent table yet
Cheer'd with the meal that adds not to my debt;
May talk of those to whom so much we owe,
And guess their names whom yet we may not know;
Bless'd we shall say are those who thus can give,
And next who thus upon the bounty live;
Then shall I close with thanks my humble meal,
And feel so well—Oh! God! how I shall feel!"

LETTER IV.

SECTS AND PROFESSIONS IN RELIGION.

——————But cast your eyes again,
And view those errors which new sects maintain,
Or which of old disturb'd the Churches' peaceful reign:
And we can point each period of the time
When they began and who begat the crime;
Can calculate how long th' eclipse endured;
Who interposed; what digits were obscured;
Of all which are already pass'd away,
We knew the rise, the progress, and decay.

DRYDEN, *Hind and Panther*, Part II.

Oh! said the Hind, how many sons have you
Who call you mother, whom you never knew?
But most of them who that relation plead
Are such ungracious youths as wish you dead;
They gape at rich revenues which you hold,
And fain would nibble at your grandame gold.

Hind and Panther.

Sects and Professions in Religion are numerous and successive—General Effect of false Zeal—Deists—Fanatical Idea of Church Reformers—The Church of Rome—Baptists—Swedenborgians—Universalists—Jews.

Methodists of two kinds; Calvinistic and Arminian.

The Preaching of a Calvinistic Enthusiast—His Contempt of Learning—Dislike to sound Morality: why—His Idea of Conversion—His Success and Pretensions to Humility.

The Arminian Teacher of the older Flock—Their Notions of the Operations and Power of Satan—Description of his Devices—Their Opinion of regular Ministers—Comparison of these with the Preacher himself—A Rebuke to his Hearers; introduces a Description of the powerful Effects of the Words in the early and awaken ing days of Methodism.

"Sects in Religion?"—Yes, of every race
We nurse some portion in our favour'd place;
Not one warm preacher of one growing sect
Can say our Borough treats him with neglect:
Frequent as fashions, they with us appear,
And you might ask, "How think we for the year!"
They come to us as riders in a trade,
And with much art exhibit and persuade.

Minds are for sects of various kinds decreed,
As diff'rent soils are form'd for diff'rent seed;
Some when converted sigh in sore amaze,
And some are wrapt in joy's ecstatic blaze;
Others again will change to each extreme,
They know not why—as hurried in a dream;
Unstable they, like water, take all forms,
Are quick and stagnant, have their calms and storms;
High on the hills, they in the sunbeams glow,
Then muddily they move, debased and slow;
Or cold and frozen rest, and neither rise nor flow.

Yet none the cool and prudent teacher prize,
On him they dote who wakes their ecstasies;
With passions ready primed such guide they meet,
And warm and kindle with th' imparted heat;
'T is he who wakes the nameless strong desire,
The melting rapture, and the glowing fire;
'T is he who pierces deep the tortured breast,
And stirs the terrors, never more to rest.

Opposed to these we have a prouder kind,
Rash without heat, and without raptures blind;
These our *Glad Tidings* unconcern'd peruse,
Search without awe, and without fear refuse;
The truths, the blessings found in Sacred Writ,
Call forth their spleen, and exercise their wit;
Respect from these nor saints nor martyrs gain,
The zeal they scorn, and they deride the pain;
And take their transient, cool, contemptuous view,
Of that which must be tried, and doubtless—*may be true.*

Friends of our faith we have, whom doubts like these,
And keen remarks, and bold objections please;
They grant such doubts have weaker minds oppress'd,
Till sound conviction gave the troubled rest.

"But still," they cry, "let none their censures spare,
They but confirm the glorious hopes we share;
From doubt, disdain, derision, scorn, and lies,
With five-fold triumph sacred truth shall rise."

Yes! I allow, so truth shall stand at last,
And gain fresh glory by the conflict past:—
As Solway-Moss (a barren mass and cold,
Death to the seed, and poison to the fold,)
The smiling plain and fertile vale o'erlaid,
Choked the green sod, and kill'd the springing blade;
That, changed by culture, may in time be seen,
Enrich'd by golden grain, and pasture green;
And these fair acres rented and enjoy'd,
May those excel by Solway-Moss destroy'd.*

Still must have mourn'd the tenant of the day
For hopes destroy'd and harvests swept away;
To him the gain of future years unknown,
The instant grief and suffering were his own:
So must I grieve for many a wounded heart,
Chill'd by those doubts which bolder minds impart:
Truth in the end shall shine divinely clear,
But sad the darkness till those times appear;
Contests for truth, as wars for freedom, yield
Glory and joy to those who gain the field:
But still the Christian must in pity sigh
For all who suffer, and uncertain die.

Here are, who all the Church maintains approve,
But yet the Church herself they will not love;
In angry speech, they blame the carnal tie,
Which pure Religion lost her spirit by;
What time from prisons, flames, and tortures led,
She slumber'd careless in a royal bed;
To make, they add, the Churches' glory shine,
Should Diocletian reign, not Constantine.

"In pomp," they cry, "is England's Church array'd,
Her cool reformers wrought like men afraid,
We would have pull'd her gorgeous temples down,
And spurn'd her mitre, and defiled her gown;
We would have trodden low both bench and stall,
Nor left a tythe remaining, great or small."

Let us be serious—Should such trials come,
Are they themselves prepared for martyrdom?
It seems to us that our reformers knew
Th' important work they undertook to do;
An equal priesthood they were loth to try,
Lest zeal and care should with ambition die;
To them it seem'd that, take the tenth away,
Yet priests must eat, and you must feed or pay:
Would they indeed, who hold such pay in scorn,
Put on the muzzle when they tread the corn?
Would they all, gratis, watch and tend the fold,
Nor take one fleece to keep them from the cold?

Men are not equal, and 't is meet and right
That robes and titles our respect excite;
Order requires it; 't is by vulgar pride
That such regard is censured and denied;
Or by that false enthusiastic zeal
That thinks the spirit will the priest reveal,
And show to all men, by their powerful speech,
Who are appointed and inspired to teach;
Alas! could we the dangerous rule believe,
Whom for their teacher should the crowd receive?
Since all the varying kinds demand respect,
All press you on to join their chosen sect,
Although but in this single point agreed,
"Desert your churches and adopt our creed."

We know full well how much our forms offend
The burthen'd papist and the simple friend;
Him, who new robes for every service takes,
And who in drab and beaver sighs and shakes;
He on the priest, whom hood and band adorn,
Looks with the sleepy eye of silent scorn,
But him I would not for my friend and guide,
Who views such things with spleen, or wears with pride.

* For an account of this extraordinary and interesting event, I refer my readers to the Journals of the year 1772.

See next our several sects,—but first behold
The Church of Rome, who here is poor and old:
Use not triumphant rail'ry, or at least,
Let not thy mother be a whore and beast;
Great was her pride indeed in ancient times,
Yet shall we think of nothing but her crimes?
Exalted high above all earthly things,
She placed her foot upon the neck of kings;
But some have deeply since avenged the crown,
And thrown her glory and her honours down;
Nor neck nor ear can she of kings command,
Nor place a foot upon her own fair land.

Among her sons, with us a quiet few,
Obscure themselves, her ancient state review;
And fond and melancholy glances cast
On power insulted, and on triumph pass'd:
They look, they can but look, with many a sigh,
On sacred buildings doom'd in dust to lie;
"On seats," they tell, "where priests 'mid tapers dim
Breathed the warm prayer, or tuned the midnight hymn;
Where trembling penitents their guilt confess'd,
Where want had succour, and contrition rest;
There weary men from trouble found relief,
There men in sorrow found repose from grief:
To scenes like these the fainting soul retired;
Revenge and anger in these cells expired;
By pity soothed, remorse lost half her fears,
And soften'd pride dropp'd penitential tears.

"Then convent-walls and nunnery-spires arose,
In pleasant spots which monk or abbot chose;
When counts and barons saints devoted fed,
And, making cheap exchange, had pray'r for bread.

"Now all is lost—the earth where abbeys stood
Is layman's land, the glebe, the stream, the wood;
His oxen low where monks retired to eat,
His cows repose upon the prior's seat;
And wanton doves within the cloisters bill,
Where the chaste votary warr'd with wanton will."

Such is the change they mourn; but they restrain
The rage of grief, and passively complain.

We've Baptists old and new; forbear to ask
What the distinction—I decline the task;
This I perceive, that when a sect grows old,
Converts are few, and the converted cold:
First comes the hot-bed heat, and while it glows
The plants spring up, and each with vigour grows;
Then comes the cooler day, and though awhile
The verdure prospers and the blossoms smile,
Yet poor the fruit, and form'd by long delay,
Nor will the profits for the culture pay;
The skilful gard'ner then no longer stops,
But turns to other beds for bearing crops.

Some Swedenborgians in our streets are found,
Those wandering walkers on enchanted ground;
Who in our world can other worlds survey,
And speak with spirits though confined in clay:
Of Bible-mysteries they the keys possess,
Assured themselves, where wiser men but guess:
'T is theirs to see around, about, above,—
How spirits mingle thoughts, and angels move;
Those whom our grosser views from us exclude,
To them appear—a heavenly multitude;
While the dark sayings, seal'd to men like us,
Their priests interpret, and their flocks discuss.

But while these gifted men, a favour'd fold,
New powers exhibit and new worlds behold;
Is there not danger lest their minds confound
The pure above them with the gross around?
May not these Phaëtons, who thus contrive
'Twixt heaven above and earth beneath to drive,
When from their flaming chariots they descend,
The worlds they visit in their fancies blend?
Alas! too sure on both they bring disgrace,
Their earth is crazy, and their heav'n is base.

We have, it seems, who treat, and doubtless well
Of a chastising, not awarding hell;
Who are assured that an offended God
Will cease to use the thunder and the rod;
A soul on earth, by crime and folly stain'd
When here corrected has improvement gain'd;
In other state still more improved to grow,
And nobler powers in happier world to know;
New strength to use in each divine employ,
And, more enjoying, looking to more joy.

A pleasing vision! could we thus be sure
Polluted souls would be at length so pure;
The view is happy; we may think it just,
It may be true—but who shall add it must?
To the plain words and sense of sacred writ,
With all my heart I reverently submit:
But where it leaves me doubtful, I'm afraid
To call conjecture to my reason's aid;
Thy thoughts, thy ways, great God! are not as mine,
And to thy mercy I my soul resign.

Jews are with us, but far unlike to those,
Who, led by David, warr'd with Israel's foes;
Unlike to those whom his imperial son
Taught truths divine—the preacher Solomon:
Nor war nor wisdom yield our Jews delight;
They will not study, and they dare not fight.*

These are, with us, a slavish, knavish crew,
Shame and dishonour to the name of Jew;
The poorest masters of the meanest arts,
With cunning head, and cold and cautious hearts
They grope their dirty way to petty gains,
While poorly paid for their nefarious pains.

Amazing race! deprived of land and laws,
A general language, and a public cause;
With a religion none can now obey,
With a reproach that none can take away:
A people still, whose common ties are gone;
Who, mix'd with every race, are lost in none.

What said their prophet?—"Shouldst thou disobey,
The Lord shall take thee from thy land away;
Thou shalt a by-word and a proverb be,
And all shall wonder at thy woes and thee;
Daughter and son shalt thou, while captive have,
And see them made the bond-maid and the slave;

* Some may object to this assertion: to whom I beg leave to answer, that I do not use the word *fight* in the sense of the Jew Mendoza.

He, whom thou leavest, the Lord thy God, shall bring
War to thy country on an eagle-wing:
A people strong and dreadful to behold,
Stern to the young, remorseless to the old;
Masters whose speech thou canst not understand,
By cruel signs shall give the harsh command;
Doubtful of life shalt thou by night, by day,
For grief, and dread, and trouble pine away;
Thy evening wish,—Would God! I saw the sun;
Thy morning sigh,—Would God! the day were done.
Thus shalt thou suffer, and to distant times
Regret thy misery, and lament thy crimes."*

A part there are, whom doubtless man might trust,
Worthy as wealthy, pure, religious, just;
They who with patience, yet with rapture look
On the strong promise of the sacred book:
As unfulfill'd th' endearing words they view,
And blind to truth, yet own their prophets true:
Well pleased they look for Sion's coming state,
Nor think of Julian's boast and Julian's fate.†

More might I add; I might describe the flocks
Made by seceders from the ancient stocks;
Those who will not to any guide submit,
Nor find one creed to their conceptions fit—
Each sect, they judge, in something goes astray,
And every church has lost the certain way;
Then for themselves they carve out creed and laws,
And weigh their atoms, and divide their straws.

A sect remains which, though divided long
In hostile parties, both are fierce and strong,
And into each enlists a warm and zealous throng.
Soon as they rose in fame, the strife arose,
The Calvinistic these, th' Arminian those;
With Wesley some remain'd, the remnant Whitfield chose.
Now various leaders both the parties take,
And the divided hosts their new divisions make.

See yonder preacher! to his people pass,
Borne up and swell'd by tabernacle-gas;
Much he discourses, and of various points,
All unconnected, void of limbs and joints;
He rails, persuades, explains, and moves the will,
By fierce bold words, and strong mechanic skill.

"That Gospel, Paul with zeal and love maintain'd,
To others lost, to you is now explain'd;
No worldly learning can these points discuss,
Books teach them not as they are taught to us;
Illiterate call us! let their wisest man
Draw forth his thousands as your teacher can:
They give their moral precepts; so, they say,
Did Epictetus once, and Seneca;
One was a slave, and slaves we all must be,
Until the Spirit comes and sets us free.
Yet hear you nothing from such men but works;
They make the christian service like the Turks'.

"Hark to the churchman: day by day he cries,
'Children of men, be virtuous and be wise;
Seek patience, justice, temp'rance, meekness, truth;
In age be courteous, be sedate in youth.'—
So they advise, and when such things be read,
How can we wonder that their flocks are dead?

"The heathens wrote of virtue, they could dwell
On such light points; in them it might be well,
They might for virtue strive; but I maintain,
Our strife for virtue would be proud and vain.
When Samson carried Gaza's gates so far,
Lack'd he a helping hand to bear the bar?
Thus the most virtuous must in bondage groan:
Samson is grace, and carries all alone.*

"Hear you not priests their feeble spirits spend,
In bidding sinners turn to God, and mend;
To check their passions and to walk aright,
To run the race, and fight the glorious fight?
Nay more—to pray, to study, to improve,
To grow in goodness, to advance in love?

"Oh! babes and sucklings, dull of heart and slow,
Can grace be gradual?—Can conversion grow?
The work is done by instantaneous call;
Converts at once are made, or not at all;
Nothing is left to grow, reform, amend;
The first emotion is the movement's end:
If once forgiven, debt can be no more;
If once adopted, will the heir be poor?
The man who gains the twenty-thousand prize,
Does he by little and by little rise?
There can no fortune for the soul be made,
By peddling cares and savings in her trade.

"Why are our sins forgiven?—Priests reply,
—'Because by faith on mercy we rely;
Because, believing, we repent and pray.'—
Is this their doctrine?—then they go astray:
We're pardon'd neither for belief nor deed,
For faith nor practice, principle nor creed;
Nor for our sorrow for our former sin,
Nor for our fears when better thoughts begin;
Nor prayers nor penance in the cause avail,
All strong remorse, all soft contrition fail;—
It is the *call!* till that proclaims us free,
In darkness, doubt, and bondage we must be;
Till that *assures* us, we've in vain endured,
And all is over when we're once assured.

"This is conversion:—First there comes a cry
Which utters, 'Sinner, thou 'rt condemn'd to die;'
Then the struck soul to every aid repairs,
To church and altar, ministers and prayers;
In vain she strives,—involved, ingulf'd in sin,
She looks for hell, and seems already in:
When in this travail, the new birth comes on,
And in an instant every pang is gone;
The mighty work is done without our pains,—
Claim but a part, and not a part remains.

"All this experience tells the soul, and yet
These moral men their pence and farthings set
Against the terrors of the countless debt:

* See the Book of Deuteronomy, chapter xxvii. and various other places.

† His boast, that he would rebuild the Temple of Jerusalem: his fate (whatever becomes of the miraculous part of the story,) that he died before the foundation was laid.

* Whoever has attended to the books or preaching of these enthusiastic people, must have observed much of this kind of absurd and foolish application of scripture history: it seems to them as reasoning.

But such compounders when they come to jail,
Will find that virtues never serve as bail.

'So much to duties: now to learning look,
And see their priesthood piling book on book;
Yea, books of infidels, we 're told, and plays,
Put out by heathens in the wink'd-on days;
The very letters are of crooked kind,
And show the strange perverseness of their mind.
Have I this learning? When the Lord would speak,
Think ye he needs the Latin or the Greek?
And lo! with all their learning, when they rise
To preach, in view the ready sermon lies;
Some low-prized stuff they purchased at the stalls,
And more like Seneca's than mine or Paul's:
Children of bondage, how should they explain
The spirit's freedom, while they wear a chain?
They study words, for meanings grow perplex'd,
And slowly hunt for truth from text to text,
Through Greek and Hebrew:—we the meaning seek
Of that within, who every tongue can speak:
This all can witness; yet the more I know,
The more a meek and humble mind I show.

"No; let the pope, the high and mighty priest,
Lord to the poor, and servant to the beast;
Let bishops, deans, and prebendaries swell
With pride and fatness till their hearts rebel:
I 'm meek and modest—If I could be proud,
This crowded meeting, lo! th' amazing crowd!
Your mute attention, and your meek respect,
My spirit's fervour, and my words' effect,
Might stir th' unguarded soul; and oft to me
The tempter speaks, whom I compel to flee;
He goes in fear, for he my force has tried,—
Such is my power! but can you call it pride?

"No, fellow-pilgrims! of the things I've shown
I might be proud, were they indeed my own!
But they are lent; and well you know the source
Of all that's mine, and must confide of course;
Mine! no, I err; 't is but consign'd to me,
And I am nought but steward and trustee."

Far other doctrines yon Arminian speaks:
"Seek grace," he cries, "for he shall find who seeks."
This is the ancient stock by Wesley led;
They the pure body, he the reverend head:
All innovation they with dread decline,
Their John the elder, was the John divine.
Hence, still their moving prayer, the melting hymn,
The varied accent, and the active limb;
Hence that implicit faith in Satan's might,
And their own matchless prowess in the fight.
In every act they see that lurking foe,
Let loose awhile about the world to go;
A dragon flying round the earth, to kill
The heavenly hope, and prompt the carnal will;
Whom sainted knights attack in sinners' cause,
And force the wounded victim from his paws;
Who but for them would man's whole race subdue,
For not a hireling will the foe pursue.

"Show me one churchman who will rise and pray
Through half the night, though lab'ring all the day,
Always abounding—show me him, I say:"—
Thus cries the preacher, and he adds, "their sheep
Satan devours at leisure as they sleep.
Not so with us; we drive him from the fold,
For ever barking and for ever bold:
While they securely slumber, all his schemes
Take full effect,—the devil never dreams:
Watchful and changeful through the world he goes,
And few can trace this deadliest of their foes;
But I detect, and at his work surprise
The subtle serpent under all disguise.

"Thus to man's soul the foe of souls will speak,
—'A saint elect, you can have nought to seek;
Why all this labour in so plain a case,
Such care to run, when certain of the race?'
All this he urges to the carnal will,
He knows you 're slothful, and would have you still:
Be this your answer,—'Satan, I will keep
'Still on the watch till you are laid asleep.'
Thus too the Christian's progress he 'll retard:—
'The gates of mercy are for ever barr'd;
And that with bolts so driven and so stout,
Ten thousand workmen cannot wrench them out.'
To this deceit you have but one reply,—
Give to the father of all lies, the lie.

"A sister's weakness he 'll by fits surprise,
His her wild laughter, his her piteous cries;
And should a pastor at her side attend,
He 'll use her organs to abuse her friend:
These are possessions—unbelieving wits
Impute them all to nature: 'They 're her fits,
'Caused by commotions in the nerves and brains;'—
Vain talk! but they 'll be fitted for their pains.

"These are in part the ills the foe has wrought,
And these the churchman thinks not worth his thought;
They bid the troubled try for peace and rest,
Compose their minds, and be no more distress'd;
As well might they command the passive shore
To keep secure, and be o'erflow'd no more;
To the wrong subject is their skill applied,—
To act like workmen, they should stem the tide.

"These are the church-physicians; they are paid
With noble fees for their advice and aid;
Yet know they not the inward pulse to feel,
To ease the anguish, or the wound to heal.
With the sick sinner, thus their work begins,
'Do you repent you of your former sins?
Will you amend if you revive and live?
And, pardon seeking, will you pardon give?
Have you belief in what your Lord has done,
And are you thankful?—all is well, my son.'

"A way far different ours—we thus surprise
A soul with questions, and demand replies;

"'How dropp'd you first,' I ask, 'the legal yoke?
What the first word the living Witness spoke?
Perceived you thunders roar and lightnings shine,
And tempests gathering ere the birth divine!
Did fire, and storm, and earthquake all appear
Before that still small voice, *What dost thou here?*
Hast thou by day and night, and soon and late,
Waited and watch'd before Admission-gate;

And so a pilgrim and a soldier pass'd
To Sion's hill through battle and through blast?
Then in thy way didst thou thy foe attack,
And madest thou proud Apollyon turn his back?'

"Heart-searching things are these, and shake the mind,
Yea, like the rustling of a mighty wind.

"Thus would I ask:—'Nay, let me question now,
How sink my sayings in your bosom? how?
Feel you a quickening? drops the subject deep?
Stupid and stony, no? you 're all asleep;
Listless and lazy, waiting for a close,
As if at church—Do I allow repose?
Am I a legal minister? do I
With form or rubrick, rule or rite comply?
Then whence this quiet, tell me, I beseech?
One might believe you heard your rector preach,
Or his assistant dreamer:—Oh! return,
Ye times of burning, when the heart would burn!
Now hearts are ice, and you, my freezing fold,
Have spirits sunk and sad, and bosoms stony cold.'

"Oh! now again for those prevailing powers,
Which once began this mighty work of ours;
When the wide field, God's temple, was the place,
And birds flew by to catch a breath of grace;
When 'mid his timid friends and threatening foes,
Our zealous chief like Paul at Athens rose:
When with infernal spite and knotty clubs,
The ill-one arm'd his scoundrels and his scrubs;
And there were flying all around the spot
Brands at the preacher, but they touch'd him not;
Stakes brought to smite him, threaten'd in his cause,
And tongues, attuned to curses, roar'd applause;
Louder and louder grew his awful tones,
Sobbings and sighs were heard, and rueful groans;
Soft women fainted, prouder man express'd
Wonder and wo, and butchers smote the breast;
Eyes wept, ears tingled; stiffening on each head,
The hair drew back, and Satan howl'd and fled.

"In that soft season when the gentle breeze
Rises all round, and swells by slow degrees;
Till tempests gather, when through all the sky
The thunders rattle, and the lightnings fly;
When rain in torrents wood and vale deform,
And all is horror, hurricane, and storm:

"So, when the preacher in that glorious time,
Than clouds more melting, more than storm sublime,
Dropp'd the new word, there came a charm around;
Tremors and terrors rose upon the sound;
The stubborn spirits by his force he broke,
As the fork'd lightning rives the knotted oak:
Fear, hope, dismay, all signs of shame or grace,
Chain'd every foot, or featured every face;
Then took his sacred trump a louder swell,
And now they groan'd, they sicken'd and they fell;
Again he sounded, and we heard the cry
Of the word-wounded, as about to die;
Further and further spread the conquering word,
As loud he cried,—'the battle of the Lord!'
Ev'n those apart who were the sound denied,
Fell down instinctive, and in spirit died.
Nor staid ye yet—his eye, his frown, his speech,
His very gesture had a power to teach;
With outstretch'd arms, strong voice, and piercing call,
He won the field, and made the Dagons fall;
And thus in triumph took his glorious way,
Through scenes of horror, terror, and dismay."

LETTER V.

ELECTIONS.

Say then which class to greater folly stoop,
The great in promise, or the poor in hope?

Be brave, for your leader is brave, and vows reformation; there shall be in England seven halfpenny loaves sold for a penny: and the three-hooped pot shall have ten hoops. I will make it felony to drink small beer: all shall eat and drink on my score, and I will apparel them all in one livery, that they may agree like brothers; and they shall all worship me as their lord.

SHAKSPEARE'S *Henry VI.*

The Evils of the Contest, and how in part to be avoided—The Miseries endured by a Friend of the Candidate—The various Liberties taken with him, who has no personal interest in the Success—The unreasonable Expectations of Voters—The censures of the opposing Party—The Vices as well as Follies shown in such Time of Contest—Plans and Cunning of Electors—Evils which remain after the Decision, opposed in vain by the efforts of the Friendly, and of the Successful; among whom is the Mayor—Story of his Advancement till he was raised to the Government of the Borough—These Evils not to be placed in Balance with the Liberty of the People, but are yet Subjects of just Complaint.

Yes, our Election 's past, and we 've been free,
Somewhat as madmen without keepers be;
And such desire of freedom has been shown,
That both the parties wish'd her all their own:
All our free smiths and cobblers in the town
Were loth to lay such pleasant freedom down;
To put the bludgeon and cockade aside,
And let us pass unhurt and undefied.

True! you might then your party's sign produce,
And so escape with only half the abuse;
With half the danger as you walk'd along,
With rage and threatening but from half the throng:
This you might do, and not your fortune mend,
For where you lost a foe, you gain'd a friend:
And to distress you, vex you, and expose,
Election-friends are worse than any foes;
The party-curse is with the canvass past,
But party-friendship, for your grief, will last.

Friends of all kinds, the civil and the rude,
Who humbly wish, or boldly dare to intrude,
These beg or take a liberty to come
(Friends should be free,) and make your house their home;
They know that warmly you their cause espouse,
And come to make their boastings and their bows:
You scorn their manners, you their words mistrust,
But you must hear them, and they know you must

One plainly sees a friendship firm and true,
Between the noble candidate and you;
So humbly begs (and states at large the case,)
"You 'll think of Bobby and the little place."

Stifling his shame by drink, a wretch will come,
And prate your wife and daughter from the room:
In pain you hear him, and at heart despise,
Yet with heroic mind your pangs disguise!
And still in patience to the sot attend,
To show what man can bear to serve a friend.

One enters hungry—not to be denied,
And takes his place and jokes—"We 're of a side."
Yet worse, the proser who, upon the strength
Of his one vote, has tales of three hours' length;
This sorry rogue you hear, yet with surprise
Start at his oaths, and sicken at his lies.

Then comes there one, and tells in friendly way,
What the opponents in their anger say;
All that through life has vex'd you, all abuse,
Will this kind friend in pure regard produce;
And having through your own offences run,
Adds (as appendage) what your friends have done.

Has any female cousin made a trip
To Gretna-Green, or more vexatious slip?
Has your wife's brother, or your uncle's son
Done aught amiss, or is he thought t' have done?
Is there of all your kindred some who lack
Vision direct, or have a gibbous back?
From your unlucky name may quips and puns
Be made by these upbraiding Goths and Huns?
To some great public character have you
Assign'd the fame to worth and talents due,
Proud of your praise?—In this, in any case,
Where the brute-spirit may affix disgrace,
These friends will smiling bring it, and the while
You silent sit, and practise for a smile.

Vain of their power, and of their value sure,
They nearly guess the tortures you endure;
Nor spare one pang—for they perceive your heart
Goes with the cause; you 'd die before you 'd start;
Do what they may, they 're sure you 'll not offend
Men who have pledged their honours to your friend.

Those friends indeed, who start as in a race,
May love the sport, and laugh at this disgrace;
They have in view the glory and the prize,
Nor heed the dirty steps by which they rise:
But we their poor associates lose the fame,
Though more than partners in the toil and shame.

Were this the whole; and did the time produce
But shame and toil, but riot and abuse;
We might be then from serious griefs exempt,
And view the whole with pity and contempt.
Alas! but here the vilest passions rule;
It is Seduction's, is Temptation's school;
Where vices mingle in the oddest ways,
The grossest slander and the dirtiest praise:
Flattery enough to make the vainest sick,
And clumsy stratagem, and scoundrel trick;
Nay more, your anger and contempt to cause,
These, while they fish for profit, claim applause;
Bribed, bought, and bound, they banish shame and fear;
Tell you they 're staunch, and have a soul sincere;
Then talk of honour, and if doubt 's express'd,
Show where it lies, and smite upon the breast.

Among these worthies, some at first declare
For whom they vote; he then has most to spare;
Others hang off—when coming to the post
Is spurring time, and then he 'll spare the most:
While some demurring, wait, and find at last
The bidding languish, and the market pass'd;
These will affect all bribery to condemn,
And be it Satan laughs, he laughs at them.

Some too are pious—One desired the Lord
To teach him where "to drop his little word;
To lend his vote, where it will profit best;
Promotion came not from the east or west;
But as their freedom had promoted some,
He should be glad to know which way 't would come.
It was a naughty world, and where to sell
His precious charge, was more than he could tell."

"But you succeeded?"—true, at mighty cost,
And our good friend, I fear, will think he 's lost:
Inns, horses, chaises, dinners, balls, and notes;
What fill'd their purses, and what drench'd their throats;
The private pension, and indulgent lease,—
Have all been granted to these friends who fleece;
Friends who will hang like burs upon his coat,
And boundless judge the value of a vote.

And though the terrors of the time be pass'd,
There still remain the scatterings of the blast;
The boughs are parted that entwined before,
And ancient harmony exists no more;
The gusts of wrath our peaceful seats deform,
And sadly flows the sighing of the storm:
Those who have gain'd are sorry for the gloom,
But they who lost, unwilling peace should come;
There open envy, here suppress'd delight,
Yet live till time shall better thoughts excite,
And so prepare us, by a six-years' truce,
Again for riot, insult, and abuse.

Our worthy mayor, on the victorious part,
Cries out for peace, and cries with all his heart;
He, civil creature! ever does his best,
To banish wrath from every voter's breast;
"For where," says he, with reason strong and plain,
"Where is the profit? what will anger gain?"
His short stout person he is wont to brace
In good brown broad-cloth, edged with two-inch lace,
When in his seat; and still the coat seems new,
Preserved by common use of seaman's blue.

He was a fisher from his earliest day,
And placed his nets within the Borough's bay;
Where by his skates, his herrings, and his soles,
He lived, nor dream'd of corporation-doles;*

* I am informed that some explanation is here necessary, though I am ignorant for what class of my readers it can be required. Some corporate bodies have actual property, as appears by their receiving rents; and they obtain money on the admission of members into their society: this they may lawfully share perhaps. There are, moreover, other doles, of still greater value, of which it is not necessary for me to explain the nature, or to inquire into the legality.

But toiling saved, and saving, never ceased
Till he had box'd up twelve score pounds at least:
He knew not money's power, but judged it best
Safe in his trunk to let his treasure rest;
Yet to a friend complain'd: "Sad charge, to keep
So many pounds, and then I cannot sleep:"
"Then put it out," replied the friend:—"What! give
My money up? why then I could not live."
"Nay, but for interest place it in his hands,
Who'll give you mortgage on his house or lands."
"Oh but," said Daniel, "that 's a dangerous plan;
He may be robb'd like any other man:"
"Still he is bound, and you may be at rest,
More safe the money than within your chest;
And you'll receive, from all deductions clear,
Five pounds for every hundred, every year."
"What good in that?" quoth Daniel, "for 't is plain,
If part I take, there can but part remain:"
"What! you, my friend, so skill'd in gainful things,
Have you to learn what interest money brings?"
"Not so," said Daniel, "perfectly I know,
He 's the most interest who has most to show."
"True! and he'll show the more, the more he lends;
Thus he his weight and consequence extends;
For they who borrow must restore each sum,
And pay for use—What, Daniel, art thou dumb?"
For much amazed was that good man—"Indeed!"
Said he with gladd'ning eye, "will money breed?
How have I lived! I grieve, with all my heart,
For my late knowledge in this precious art:—
Five pounds for every hundred will he give?
And then the hundred?—I begin to live."
So he began, and other means he found,
As he went on, to multiply a pound:
Though blind so long to interest, all allow
That no man better understands it now:
Him in our body-corporate we chose,
And once among us, he above us rose;
Stepping from post to post, he reach'd the chair,
And there he now reposes—that 's the mayor.

But 't is not he, 't is not the kinder few,
The mild, the good, who can our peace renew;
A peevish humour swells in every eye,
The warm are angry, and the cool are shy;
There is no more the social board at whist,
The good old partners are with scorn dismiss'd;
No more with dog and lantern comes the maid,
To guide the mistress when the rubber 's play'd;
Sad shifts are made lest ribands blue and green
Should at one table, at one time be seen:
On care and merit none will now rely,
'T is party sells, what party-friends must buy;
The warmest burgess wears a bodger's coat,
And fashion gains less int'rest than a vote;
Uncheck'd the vintner still his poison vends,
For he too votes, and can command his friends.

But this admitted; be it still agreed,
These ill effects from noble cause proceed;
Though like some vile excrescences they be,
The tree they spring from is a sacred tree,
And its true produce, strength and liberty.

Yet if we could th' attendant ills suppress,
If we could make the sum of mischief less;
If we could warm and angry men persuade
No more man's common comforts to invade;
And that old ease and harmony re-seat
In all our meetings, so in joy to meet;
Much would of glory to the Muse ensue,
And our good Vicar would have less to do.

LETTER VI.

PROFESSIONS—LAW.

Quid leges sine moribus
Vanæ proficiunt? HORACE.

Væ! misero mihi, mea nunc facinora
Aperiuntur, clam quæ speravi fore.
MANILIUS.

Trades and Professions of every Kind to be found in the Borough—Its Seamen and Soldiers—Law, the Danger of the Subject—Coddrington's Offence—Attorneys increased; their splendid Appearance, how supported—Some worthy Exceptions—Spirit of Litigation, how stirred up—A Boy articled as a Clerk; his Ideas—How this Profession perverts the Judgment—Actions appear through this Medium in a false Light—Success from honest Application—Archer, a worthy Character—Swallow, a Character of different Kind—His Origin, Progress, Success, etc.

"Trades and Professions"—these are themes the Muse,
Left to her freedom, would forbear to choose;
But to our Borough they in truth belong,
And we, perforce, must take them in our song.

Be it then known that we can boast of these
In all denominations, ranks, degrees;
All whom our numerous wants through life supply,
Who soothe us sick, attend us when we die,
Or for the dead their various talents try.
Then have we those who live by secret arts,
By hunting fortunes, and by stealing hearts;
Or who by nobler means themselves advance;
Or who subsist by charity and chance.

Say, of our native heroes shall I boast,
Born in our streets, to thunder on our coast,
Our Borough-seamen? Could the timid Muse
More patriot-ardour in their breasts infuse;
Or could she paint their merit or their skill,
She wants not love, alacrity, or will;
But needless all, that ardour is their own,
And for their deeds, themselves have made them known.

Soldiers in arms! Defenders of our soil!
Who from destruction save us; who from spoil
Protect the sons of peace, who traffic, or who toil,
Would I could duly praise you; that each deed
Your foes might honour, and your friends might read:
This too is needless; you've imprinted well
Your powers, and told what I should feebly tell.

Beside, a Muse like mine, to satire prone,
Would fail in themes where there is praise alone.
—Law shall I sing, or what to Law belongs?
Alas! there may be danger in such songs;
A foolish rhyme, 't is said, a trifling thing,
The law found treason, for it touch'd the king.
But kings have mercy, in these happy times,
Or surely *one* had suffer'd for his rhymes;
Our glorious Edwards and our Henrys bold,
So touch'd, had kept the reprobate in hold;
But he escaped,—nor fear, thank Heav'n, have I,
Who love my king, for such offence to die.
But I am taught the danger would be much,
If these poor lines should one attorney touch—
(One of those *limbs* of law who 're always here;
The *heads* come down to guide them twice a year.)
I might not swing indeed, but he in sport
Would whip a rhymer on from court to court;
Stop him in each, and make him pay for all
The long proceedings in that dreaded Hall:—
Then let my numbers flow discreetly on,
Warn'd by the fate of luckless Coddrington,*
Lest some *attorney* (pardon me the name)
Should wound a poor *solicitor* for fame.

One man of law in George the Second's reign
Was all our frugal fathers would maintain;
He too was kept for forms; a man of peace,
To frame a contract, or to draw a lease:
He had a clerk, with whom he used to write
All the day long, with whom he drank at night;
Spare was his visage, moderate his bill,
And he so kind, men doubted of his skill.

Who thinks of this, with some amazement sees,
For one so poor, three flourishing at ease;
Nay, one in splendour!—see that mansion tall,
That lofty door, the far-resounding hall;
Well-furnish'd rooms, plate shining on the board,
Gay liveried lads, and cellar proudly stored:
Then say how comes it that such fortunes crown
These sons of strife, these terrors of the town?

Lo! that small office! there th' incautious guest
Goes blindfold in, and that maintains the rest;
There in his web, th' observant spider lies,
And peers about for fat intruding flies;
Doubtful at first, he hears the distant hum,
And feels them flutt'ring as they nearer come;
They buzz and blink, and doubtfully they tread
On the strong birdlime of the utmost thread;
But when they 're once entangled by the gin,
With what an eager clasp he draws them in!
Nor shall they 'scape, till after long delay,
And all that sweetens life is drawn away.

"Nay, this," you cry, "is common-place, the tale
Of petty tradesmen o'er their evening-ale;
There are who, living by the legal pen,
Are held in honour—'honourable men.'"

Doubtless—there are who hold manorial courts,
Or whom the trust of powerful friends supports;
Or who, by labouring through a length of time,
Have pick'd their way, unsullied by a crime.
These are the few—in this, in every place,
Fix the litigious rupture-stirring race;
Who to contention as to trade are led,
To whom dispute and strife are bliss and bread.

There is a doubtful pauper, and we think
'T is not with us to give him meat and drink;
There is a child, and 't is not mighty clear
Whether the mother lived with us a year:
A road 's indicted, and our seniors doubt
If in our proper boundary or without:
But what says our attorney? He our friend
Tells us 't is just and manly to contend.

"What! to a neighbouring parish yield your cause,
While you have money, and the nation laws?
What! lose without a trial, that which tried,
May—nay it must—be given on our side?
All men of spirit would contend; such men
Than lose a pound would rather hazard ten.
What, be imposed on? No! a British soul
Despises imposition, hates control;
The law is open; let them, if they dare,
Support their cause; the Borough need not spare:
All I advise is vigour and good-will:
Is it agreed then?—Shall I file a bill?"

The trader, grazier, merchant, priest and all,
Whose sons aspiring, to professions call,
Choose from their lads some bold and subtle boy,
And judge him fitted for this grave employ:
Him a keen old practitioner admits,
To write five years and exercise his wits:
The youth has heard—it is in fact his creed—
Mankind dispute, that lawyers may be fee'd:
Jails, bailiffs, writs, all terms and threats of law,
Grow now familiar as once top and taw;
Rage, hatred, fear, the mind's severer ills,
All bring employment, all augment his bills:
As feels the surgeon for the mangled limb,
The mangled mind is but a job for him;
Thus taught to think, these legal reasoners draw
Morals and maxims from their views of law;
They cease to judge by precepts taught in schools,
By man's plain sense, or by religious rules;
No! nor by law itself, in truth discern'd,
But as its statutes may be warp'd and turn'd:
How they should judge of man, his word and deed,
They in their books and not their bosoms read:
Of some good act you speak with just applause,
"No! no!" says he, "'t would be a losing cause:"
Blame you some tyrant's deed?—he answers "Nay,
He 'll get a verdict; heed you what you say."
Thus to conclusions from examples led,
The heart resigns all judgment to the head;
Law, law alone for ever kept in view,
His measures guides, and rules his conscience too;
Of ten commandments, he confesses three
Are yet in force, and tells you which they be,
As law instructs him, thus: "Your neighbour's wife
You must not take, his chattels, nor his life;
Break these decrees, for damage you must pay;
These you must reverence, and the rest—you may."

Law was design'd to keep a state in peace;
To punish robbery, that wrong might cease;
To be impregnable; a constant fort,
To which the weak and injured might resort:

---

* The account of Coddrington occurs in "*The Mirrour for Magistrates*:" he suffered in the reign of Richard III

But these perverted minds its force employ,
Not to protect mankind, but to annoy;
And long as ammunition can be found,
Its lightning flashes and its thunders sound.

Or law with lawyers is an ample still,
Wrought by the passions' heat with chymic skill:
While the fire burns, the gains are quickly made,
And freely flow the profits of the trade;
Nay, when the fierceness fails, these artists blow
The dying fire, and make the embers glow,
As long as they can make the smaller profits flow;
At length the process of itself will stop,
When they perceive they 've drawn out every drop.

Yet I repeat, there are, who nobly strive
To keep the sense of moral worth alive;
Men who would starve, ere meanly deign to live
On what deception and chican'ry give.
And these at length succeed; they have their strife,
Their apprehensions, stops, and rubs in life;
But honour, application, care and skill,
Shall bend opposing fortune to their will.

Of such is Archer, he who keeps in awe
Contending parties by his threats of law:
He, roughly honest, has been long a guide
In Borough-business, on the conquering side;
And seen so much of both sides, and so long,
He thinks the bias of man's mind goes wrong:
Thus, though he 's friendly, he is still severe,
Surly though kind, suspiciously sincere:
So much he 's seen of baseness in the mind,
That, while a friend to man, he scorns mankind:
He knows the human heart, and sees with dread,
By slight temptation, how the strong are led;
He knows how interest can asunder rend,
The bond of parent, master, guardian, friend,
To form a new and a degrading tie
'Twixt needy vice and tempting villany.
Sound in himself, yet when such flaws appear,
He doubts of all, and learns that self to fear:
For where so dark the moral view is grown,
A timid conscience trembles for her own;
The pitchy taint of general vice is such
As daubs the fancy, and you dread the touch.

Far unlike him was one in former times,
Famed for the spoil he gather'd by his crimes;
Who, while his brethren nibbling held their prey,
He like an eagle seized and bore the whole away.

Swallow, a poor attorney, brought his boy
Up at his desk, and gave him his employ;
He would have bound him to an honest trade,
Could preparations have been duly made.
The clerkship ended, both the sire and son
Together did what business could be done;
Sometimes they 'd luck to stir up small disputes
Among their friends, and raise them into suits:
Though close and hard, the father was content
With this resource, now old and indolent:
But his young Swallow, gaping and alive
To fiercer feelings, was resolved to thrive:—
"Father," he said, "but little can they win,
Who hunt in couples where the game is thin;
Let 's part in peace, and each pursue his gain
Where it may start—our love may yet remain."

The parent growl'd, he couldn't think that love
Made the young cockatrice his den remove;
But, taught by habit, he the truth suppress'd,
Forced a frank look, and said he "thought it best."
Not long they 'd parted ere dispute arose;
The game they hunted quickly made them foes:
Some house, the father by his art had won,
Seem'd a fit cause of contest to the son,
Who raised a claimant, and then found a way
By a staunch witness to secure his prey.
The people cursed him, but in times of need
Trusted in one so certain to succeed:
By law's dark by-ways he had stored his mind
With wicked knowledge, how to cheat mankind.
Few are the freeholds in our ancient town;
A copy-right from heir to heir came down,
From whence some heat arose, when there was doubt,
In point of heirship; but the fire went out,
Till our attorney had the art to raise
The dying spark, and blow it to a blaze:
For this he now began his friends to treat;
His way to starve them was to make them eat,
And drink oblivious draughts—to his applause
It must be said, he never starved a cause;
He 'd roast and boil'd upon his board; the boast
Of half his victims was his boil'd and roast;
And these at every hour—he seldom took
Aside his client, till he 'd praised his cook;
Nor to an office led him, there in pain
To give his story and go out again;
But first the brandy and the chine were seen,
And then the business came by starts between.

"Well, if 't is so, the house to you belongs;
But have you money to redress these wrongs?
Nay, look not sad, my friend; if you 're correct,
You 'll find the friendship that you 'd not expect."

If right the man, the house was Swallow's own;
If wrong, his kindness and good-will were shown;
"Rogue!" "Villain!" "Scoundrel!" cried the losers all;
He let them cry, for what would that recall?
At length he left us, took a village seat,
And like a vulture look'd abroad for meat;
The Borough-booty, give it all its praise,
Had only served the appetite to raise;
But if from simple heirs he drew their land,
He might a noble feast at will command;
Still he proceeded by his former rules,
His bait, their pleasures, when he fish'd for fools;—
Flagons and haunches on his board were placed,
And subtle avarice look'd like thoughtless waste:
Most of his friends, though youth from him had fled,
Were young, were minors, of their sires in dread;
Or those whom widow'd mothers kept in bounds,
And check'd their generous rage for steeds and hounds;
Or such as travell'd 'cross the land to view
A Christian's conflict with a boxing Jew:
Some too had run upon Newmarket heath
With so much speed that they were out of breath,
Others had tasted claret, till they now
To humbler port would turn, and knew not how.
All these for favours would to Swallow run,
Who never sought their thanks for all he 'd done,

He kindly took them by the hand, then bow'd
Politely low, and thus his love avow'd—
(For he 'd a way that many judged polite,
A cunning dog—he 'd fawn before he 'd bite)—

"Observe, my friends, the frailty of our race
When age unmans us—let me state a case:
There 's our friend Rupert—we shall soon redress
His present evil—drink to our success—
I flatter not; but did you ever see
Limbs better turn'd? a prettier boy than he?
His senses all acute, his passions such
As nature gave—she never does too much;
His the bold wish the cup of joy to drain,
And strength to bear it without qualm or pain.

"Now view his father as he dozing lies,
Whose senses wake not when he opes his eyes;
Who slips and shuffles when he means to walk,
And lisps and gabbles if he tries to talk;
Feeling he 's none, he could as soon destroy
The earth itself, as aught it holds enjoy;
A nurse attends him to lay straight his limbs,
Present his gruel, and respect his whims:
Now shall this dotard from our hero hold
His lands and lordships? Shall he hide his gold?
That which he cannot use, and dare not show,
And will not give—why longer should he owe?
Yet, 't would be murder should we snap the locks,
And take the thing he worships from the box;
So let him dote and dream: but, till he die,
Shall not our generous heir receive supply?
For ever sitting on the river's brink,
And ever thirsty, shall he fear to drink?
The means are simple, let him only wish,
Then say he 's willing, and I 'll fill his dish."

They all applauded, and not least the boy,
Who now replied, "It fill'd his heart with joy
To find he needed not deliv'rance crave
Of death, or wish the justice in the grave;
Who, while he spent, would every art retain
Of luring home the scatter'd gold again:
Just as a fountain gaily spirts and plays
With what returns in still and secret ways."

Short was the dream of bliss; he quickly found,
His father's acres all were Swallow's ground.
Yet to those arts would other heroes lend
A willing ear, and Swallow was their friend:
Ever successful, some began to think
That Satan help'd him to his pen and ink;
And shrewd suspicions ran about the place,
"There was a compact"—I must leave the case.
But of the parties, had the fiend been one,
The business could not have been speedier done:
Still when a man has angled day and night,
The silliest gudgeons will refuse to bite:
So Swallow tried no more; but if they came
To seek his friendship, that remain'd the same:
Thus he retired in peace, and some would say
He 'd balk'd his partner, and had learn'd to pray.
To this some zealots lent an ear, and sought
How Swallow felt, then said "a change is wrought:"
'T was true there wanted all the signs of grace;
But there were strong professions in their place:
Then, too, the less that men from him expect,
The more the praise to the converting sect;
He had not yet subscribed to all their creed,
Nor own'd a call, but he confess'd the need:
His acquiescent speech, his gracious look,
That pure attention, when the brethren spoke,
Was all contrition,—he had felt the wound,
And with confession would again be sound.

True, Swallow's board had still the sumptuous treat:
But could they blame? the warmest zealots eat.
He drank—'t was needful his poor nerves to brace:
He swore—'t was habit; he was grieved—'t was grace.
What could they do a new-born zeal to nurse?
"His wealth 's undoubted—let him hold our purse;
He 'll add his bounty, and the house we 'll raise
Hard by the church, and gather all her strays;
We 'll watch her sinners as they home retire,
And pluck the brands from the devouring fire."

Alas! such speech was but an empty boast;
The good men reckon'd, but without their host:
Swallow, delighted, took the trusted store,
And own'd the sum—they did not ask for more,
Till more was needed; when they call'd for aid—
And had it?—No, their agent was afraid!
"Could he but know to whom he should refund,
He would most gladly—nay, he 'd go beyond;
But when such numbers claim'd, when some were gone,
And others going—he must hold it on.
The Lord would help them."—Loud their anger grew,
And while they threat'ning from his door withdrew,
He bow'd politely low, and bade them all adieu.

But lives the man by whom such deeds are done?
Yes, many such—but Swallow's race is run;
His name is lost,—for though his sons have name,
It is not his, they all escape the shame;
Nor is there vestige now of all he had,
His means are wasted, for his heir was mad:
Still we of Swallow as a monster speak,
A hard bad man, who prey'd upon the weak.

LETTER VII.

PROFESSIONS—PHYSIC.

Finirent multi letho mala; credula vitam
Spes alit, et melius cras fore semper ait.
TIBULLUS.

He fell to juggle, cant, and cheat—
For as those fowls that live in water
Are never wet, he did but smatter;
Whate'er he labour'd to appear,
His understanding still was clear.
A paltry wretch he had, half-starved,
That him in place of zany served.
BUTLER'S *Hudibras.*

The Worth and Excellence of the true Physician—Merit, not the sole Cause of Success—Modes of advancing Reputation—Motives of Medical Men for publishing their Works—The great Evil of Quackery—Present State of advertising Quacks

—Their Hazard—Some fail, and why—Causes of Success—How Men of Understanding are prevailed upon to have recourse to Empirics, and to permit their Names to be advertised—Evils of Quackery; to nervous Females; to Youth; to Infants—History of an advertising Empiric, etc.

Next, to a graver tribe we turn our view,
And yield the praise to worth and science due;
But this with serious words and sober style,
For these are friends with whom we seldom smile,
Helpers of men* they 're call'd, and we confess
Theirs the deep study, theirs the lucky guess.
We own that numbers join with care and skill,
A temperate judgment, a devoted will;
Men who suppress their feelings, but who feel
The painful symptoms they delight to heal:
Patient in all their trials, they sustain
The starts of passion, the reproach of pain;
With hearts affected, but with looks serene,
Intent they wait through all the solemn scene,
Glad if a hope should rise from nature's strife,
To aid their skill and save the lingering life;
But this must virtue's generous effort be,
And spring from nobler motives than a fee:
To the physicians of the soul, and these,
Turn the distress'd for safety, hope, and ease.

But as physicians of that nobler kind
Have their warm zealots, and their sectaries blind,
So among these for knowledge most renown'd,
Are dreamers strange, and stubborn bigots found.
Some, too, admitted to this honour'd name,
Have, without learning, found a way to fame;
And some by learning—young physicians write,
To set their merit in the fairest light;
With them a treatise is a bait that draws
Approving voices—'t is to gain applause,
And to exalt them in the public view,
More than a life of worthy toil could do.
When 't is proposed to make the man renown'd,
In every age, convenient doubts abound;
Convenient themes in every period start,
Which he may treat with all the pomp of art;
Curious conjectures he may always make,
And either side of dubious questions take:
He may a system broach, or, if he please,
Start new opinions of an old disease;
Or may some simple in the woodland trace,
And be its patron, till it runs its race;
As rustic damsels from their woods are won,
And live in splendour till their race be run;
It weighs not much on what their powers be shown,
When all his purpose is to make them known.

To show the world what long experience gains,
Requires not courage, though it calls for pains;
But at life's outset to inform mankind
Is a bold effort of a valiant mind.

The great good man, for noblest cause, displays
What many labours taught, and many days;
These sound instruction from experience give,
The others show us how they mean to live;

That they have genius, and they hope mankind
Will to its efforts be no longer blind.

There are beside, whom powerful friends advance,
Whom fashion favours, person, patrons, chance;
And merit sighs to see a fortune made
By daring rashness or by dull parade.

But these are trifling evils; there is one
Which walks uncheck'd, and triumphs in the sun.
There was a time, when we beheld the quack,
On public stage, the licensed trade attack;
He made his labour'd speech with poor parade,
And then a laughing zany lent him aid:
Smiling we pass'd him, but we felt the while
Pity so much, that soon we ceased to smile;
Assured that fluent speech and flow'ry vest
Disguised the troubles of a man distress'd.

But now our quacks are gamesters, and they play
With craft and skill to ruin and betray;
With monstrous promise they delude the mind,
And thrive on all that tortures human-kind.

Void of all honour, avaricious, rash,
The daring tribe compound their boasted trash—
Tincture or syrup, lotion, drop or pill:
All tempt the sick to trust the lying bill;
And twenty names of cobblers turn'd to squires,
Aid the bold language of these blushless liars.
There are among them those who cannot read,
And yet they 'll buy a patent, and succeed;
Will dare to promise dying sufferers aid,
For who, when dead, can threaten or upbraid?
With cruel avarice still they recommend
More draughts, more syrup to the journey's end,
"I feel it not;"—"Then take it every hour:"
"It makes me worse;"—"Why then it shows its power:"
"I fear to die;"—"Let not your spirits sink,
You're always safe, while you believe and drink."

How strange to add, in this nefarious trade,
That men of parts are dupes by dunces made!
That creatures, nature meant should clean our streets,
Have purchased lands and mansions, parks and seats;
Wretches with conscience so obtuse, they leave
Their untaught sons their parents to deceive;
And, when they 're laid upon their dying-bed,
No thought of murder comes into their head,
Nor one revengeful ghost to them appears,
To fill the soul with penitential fears.

Yet not the whole of this imposing train
Their gardens, seats, and carriages obtain;
Chiefly, indeed, they to the robbers fall,
Who are most fitted to disgrace them all:
But there is hazard—patents must be bought,
Venders and puffers for the poison sought;
And then in many a paper through the year,
Must cures and cases, oaths and proofs appear,
Men snatch'd from graves, as they were dropping in,
Their lungs cough'd up, their bones pierced through the skin;
Their liver all one scirrhus, and the frame
Poison'd with evils which they dare not name;

* Opiferque per orbem dicor.

Men who spent all upon physicians' fees,
Who never slept, nor had a moment's ease,
Are now as roaches sound, and all as brisk as bees.

If the sick gudgeons to the bait attend,
And come in shoals, the angler gains his end;
But should the advertising cash be spent,
Ere yet the town has due attention lent,
Then bursts the bubble, and the hungry cheat
Pines for the bread he ill deserves to eat;
It is a lottery, and he shares perhaps
The rich man's feast, or begs the pauper's scraps.

From powerful causes spring th' empiric's gains,
Man's love of life, his weakness, and his pains;
These first induce him the vile trash to try,
Then lend his name, that other men may buy:
This love of life, which in our nature rules,
To vile imposture makes us dupes and tools;
Then pain compels th' impatient soul to seize
On promised hopes of instantaneous ease;
And weakness too with every wish complies,
Worn out and won by importunities.

Troubled with something in your bile or blood,
You think your doctor does you little good;
And, grown impatient, you require in haste
The nervous cordial, nor dislike the taste;
It comforts, heals, and strengthens; nay, you think
It makes you better every time you drink:
"Then lend your name"—you 're loth, but yet confess
Its powers are great, and so you acquiesce;
Yet think a moment, ere your name you lend,
With whose 't is placed, and what you recommend;
Who tipples brandy will some comfort feel,
But will he to the med'cine set his seal?
Wait, and you 'll find the cordial you admire
Has added fuel to your fever's fire:
Say, should a robber chance your purse to spare,
Would you the honour of the man declare?
Would you assist his purpose? swell his crime?
Besides, he might not spare a second time.

Compassion sometimes sets the fatal sign;
The man was poor, and humbly begg'd a line;
Else how should noble names and titles back
The spreading praise of some advent'rous quack?
But he the moment watches, and entreats
Your honour's name,—your honour joins the cheats;
You judged the med'cine harmless, and you lent
What help you could, and with the best intent;
But can it please you, thus to league with all
Whom he can beg or bribe to swell the scrawl?
Would you these wrappers with your name adorn,
Which hold the poison for the yet unborn?

No class escapes them—from the poor man's pay
The nostrum takes no trifling part away;
See! those square patent bottles from the shop,
Now decoration to the cupboard's top;
And there a favourite hoard you 'll find within,
Companions meet! the julep and the gin.

Time too with cash is wasted; 't is the fate
Of real helpers to be call'd too late;
This find the sick, when (time and patience gone)
Death with a tenfold terror hurries on.

Suppose the case surpasses human skill,
There comes a quack to flatter weakness still;
What greater evil can a flatterer do,
Than from himself to take the sufferer's view?
To turn from sacred thoughts his reasoning powers,
And rob a sinner of his dying hours?
Yet this they dare, and craving to the last,
In hope's strong bondage hold their victim fast:
For soul or body no concern have they,
All their inquiry, "Can the patient pay?
And will he swallow draughts until his dying day?"

Observe what ills to nervous females flow,
When the heart flutters, and the pulse is low;
If once induced these cordial sips to try,
All feel the ease, and few the dangers fly;
For while obtain'd, of drams they 've all the force
And when denied, then drams are the resource.

Nor these the only evils—there are those
Who for the troubled mind prepare repose;
They write: the young are tenderly address'd,
Much danger hinted, much concern express'd;
They dwell on freedoms lads are prone to take,
Which makes the doctor tremble for their sake
Still if the youthful patient will but trust
In one so kind, so pitiful, and just;
If he will take the tonic all the time,
And hold but moderate intercourse with crime,
The sage will gravely give his honest word,
That strength and spirits shall be both restored;
In plainer English—if you mean to sin,
Fly to the drops, and instantly begin.

Who would not lend a sympathizing sigh,
To hear yon infant's pity-moving cry?
That feeble sob, unlike the new-born note,
Which came with vigour from the opening throat
When air and light first rush'd on lungs and eyes,
And there was life and spirit in the cries;
Now an abortive, faint attempt to weep,
Is all we hear; sensation is asleep:
The boy was healthy, and at first express'd
His feelings loudly, when he fail'd to rest;
When cramm'd with food, and tighten'd every limb,
To cry aloud was what pertain'd to him;
Then the good nurse (who, had she borne a brain,
Had sought the cause that made her babe complain,)
Has all her efforts, loving soul! applied,
To set the cry, and not the cause, aside;
She gave her powerful sweet without remorse,
The sleeping cordial—she had tried its force,
Repeating oft: the infant freed from pain,
Rejected food, but took the dose again.
Sinking to sleep; while she her joy express'd,
That her dear charge could sweetly take his rest:
Soon may she spare her cordial; not a doubt
Remains but quickly he will rest without.

This moves our grief and pity, and we sigh
To think what numbers from these causes die;
But what contempt and anger should we show,
Did we the lives of these impostors know!

Ere for the world's I left the cares of school,
One I remember who assumed the fool:
A part well suited—when the idler boys
Would shout around him, and he loved the noise;

They call'd him Neddy;—Neddy had the art
To play with skill his ignominious part;
When he his trifles would for sale display,
And act the mimic for a school-boy's pay.
For many years he plied his humble trade,
And used his tricks and talents to persuade;
The fellow barely read, but chanced to look
Among the fragments of a tatter'd book;
Where after many efforts made to spell
One puzzling word, be found it *oxymel*;
A potent thing, 't was said, to cure the ills
Of ailing lungs—the *oxymel of squills*:
Squills he procured, but found the bitter strong,
And most unpleasant; none would take it long;
But the pure acid and the sweet would make
A medicine numbers would for pleasure take.

There was a fellow near, an artful knave,
Who knew the plan, and much assistance gave;
He wrote the puffs, and every talent plied
To make it sell: it sold, and then he died.

Now all the profit fell to Ned's control,
And Pride and Avarice quarrell'd for his soul;
When mighty profits by the trash were made,
Pride built a palace, Avarice groan'd and paid;
Pride placed the signs of grandeur all about,
And Avarice barr'd his friends and children out.

Now see him doctor! yes, the idle fool,
The butt, the robber of the lads at school;
Who then knew nothing, nothing since acquired,
Became a doctor, honour'd and admired;
His dress, his frown, his dignity, were such,
Some who had known him thought his knowledge much;
Nay, men of skill, of apprehension quick,
Spite of their knowledge, trusted him when sick:
Though he could neither reason, write, nor spell,
They yet had hope his trash would make them well:
And while they scorn'd his parts, they took his oxymel.
Oh! when his nerves had once received a shock,
Sir Isaac Newton might have gone to Rock:*
Hence impositions of the grossest kind,
Hence thought is feeble, understanding blind;
Hence sums enormous by those cheats are made,
And deaths unnumbered by their dreadful trade.

Alas! in vain is my contempt express'd,
To stronger passions are my words address'd;
To pain, to fear, to terror, their appeal:
To those who, weakly reasoning, strongly feel.

What then our hopes?—perhaps there may by law
Be method found, these pests to curb and awe;
Yet in this land of freedom, law is slack
With any being to commence attack;
Then let us trust to science—there are those
Who can their falsehoods and their frauds disclose,
All their vile trash detect, and their low tricks expose:
Perhaps their numbers may in time confound
Their arts—as scorpions give themselves the wound:
For when these curers dwell in every place,
While of the cured we not a man can trace,
Strong truth may then the public mind persuade,
And spoil the fruits of this nefarious trade.

* An empiric who *flourished* at the same time with this great man.

LETTER VIII.

TRADES.

Non possidentem multa vocaveris
Recte beatum: rectius occupat
Nomen Beati, qui Deorum
Muneribus sapienter uti,
Duramque callet pauperiem pati.
HOR. lib. iv, od. 9.

Non uxor salvum te vult, non filius: omnes
Vicini oderunt; noti, pueri atque puellæ.
Miraris, cum tu argento post omnia ponas,
Si nemo præstet, quem non merearis, amorem?
HOR. Sat. lib. i.

Non propter vitam faciunt patrimonia quidam,
Sed vitio cæci propter patrimonia vivunt.
JUVENAL. Sat. 12.

No extensive Manufactories in the Borough: yet considerable fortunes made there—Ill Judgment of Parents in disposing of their Sons—The best educated not the most likely to succeed—Instance—Want of Success compensated by the lenient Power of some Avocations—The Naturalist—The Weaver an Entomologist, etc.—A Prize-Flower—Story of Walter and William.

Of manufactures, trade, inventions rare,
Steam-towers and looms, you 'd know our Borough's share—
'T is small: we boast not these rich subjects here,
Who hazard thrice ten thousand pounds a-year;
We've no huge buildings, where incessant noise
Is made by springs and spindles, girls and boys;
Where 'mid such thundering sounds, the maiden's song
Is "Harmony in uproar"* all day long.

Still common minds with us, in common trade,
Have gain'd more wealth than ever student made;
And yet a merchant, when he gives his son
His college-learning, thinks his duty done;
A way to wealth he leaves his boy to find,
Just when he 's made for the discovery blind.

Jones and his wife perceived their elder boy
Took to his learning, and it gave them joy;
This they encouraged, and were bless'd to see
Their son a fellow with a high degree;
A living fell, he married, and his sire
Declared 't was all a father could require;
Children then bless'd them, and when letters came,
The parents proudly told each grandchild's name.

Meantime the sons at home in trade were placed,
Money their object—just the father's taste;
Saving he lived and long, and when he died,
He gave them all his fortune to divide:

"Martin," said he, "at vast expense was taught;
He gain'd his wish, and has the ease he sought."

* The title of a short piece of humour by Arbuthnot.

Thus the good priest (the Christian scholar!) finds
What estimate is made by vulgar minds;
He sees his brothers, who had every gift
Of thriving now assisted in their thrift;
While he whom learning, habits, all prevent,
Is largely mulct for each impediment.

Yet let us own that trade has much of chance,
Not all the careful by their care advance;
With the same parts and prospects, one a seat
Builds for himself; one finds it in the Fleet.
Then to the wealthy you will see denied
Comforts and joys that with the poor abide:
There are who labour through the year, and yet
No more have gain'd than—not to be in debt;
Who still maintain the same laborious course,
Yet pleasure hails them from some favourite source;
And health, amusements, children, wife or friend,
With life's dull views their consolations blend.

Nor these alone possess the lenient power
Of soothing life in the desponding hour;
Some favourite studies, some delightful care,
The mind, with trouble and distresses, share;
And by a coin, a flower, a verse, a boat,
The stagnant spirits have been set afloat;
They pleased at first, and then the habit grew,
Till the fond heart no higher pleasure knew;
Till, from all cares and other comforts freed,
Th' important nothing took in life the lead.

With all his phlegm, it broke a Dutchman's heart,
At a vast price, with one loved root to part;
And toys like these fill many a British mind,
Although their hearts are found of firmer kind.

Oft have I smiled the happy pride to see
Of humble tradesmen, in their evening glee;
When of some pleasing, fancied good possess'd,
Each grew alert, was busy, and was bless'd;
Whether the call-bird yield the hour's delight,
Or, magnified in microscope, the mite;
Or whether tumblers, croppers, carriers seize
The gentle mind, they rule it and they please.

There is my friend the Weaver; strong desires
Reign in his breast; 't is beauty he admires:
See! to the shady grove he wings his way,
And feels in hope the raptures of the day—
Eager he looks; and soon, to glad his eyes,
From the sweet bower, by nature form'd, arise
Bright troops of virgin moths and fresh-born butterflies;
Who broke that morning from their half-year's sleep,
To fly o'er flow'rs where they were wont to creep.

Above the sovereign oak, a sovereign skims,
The purple Emp'ror, strong in wing and limbs:
There fair Camilla takes her flight serene,
Adonis blue, and Paphia silver-queen;
With every filmy fly from mead or bower,
And hungry Sphinx who threads the honey'd flower;
She o'er the Larkspur's bed, where sweets abound,
Views ev'ry bell, and hums th' approving sound;
Poised on her busy plumes, with feeling nice
She draws from every flower, nor tries a floret twice.

He fears no bailiff's wrath, no baron's blame,
His is untax'd and undisputed game;
Nor less the place of curious plant he knows;*
He both his Flora and his Fauna shows;
For him is blooming in its rich array
The glorious flower which bore the palm away;
In vain a rival tried his utmost art,
His was the prize, and joy o'erflow'd his heart.

"This, this! is beauty; cast, I pray, your eyes
On this my glory! see the grace! the size!
Was ever stem so tall, so stout, so strong,
Exact in breadth, in just proportion long!
These brilliant hues are all distinct and clean,
No kindred tint, no blending streaks between;
This is no shaded, run off,† pin-eyed‡ thing,
A king of flowers, a flower for England's king:
I own my pride, and thank the favouring star
Which shed such beauty on my fair Bizarre."§

Thus may the poor the cheap indulgence seize,
While the most wealthy pine and pray for ease;
Content not always waits upon success,
And more may he enjoy who profits less.

Walter and William took (their father dead)
Jointly the trade to which they both were bred;
When fix'd they married, and they quickly found
With due success their honest labours crown'd:
Few were their losses, but although a few,
Walter was vex'd, and somewhat peevish grew:
"You put your trust in every pleading fool,"
Said he to William, and grew strange and cool.
"Brother, forbear," he answered; "take your due,
Nor let my lack of caution injure you;"
Half friends they parted,—better so to close,
Than longer wait to part entirely foes.

Walter had knowledge, prudence, jealous care;
He let no idle views his bosom share;
He never thought nor felt for other men—
"Let one mind one, and all are minded then."
Friends he respected, and believed them just,
But they were men, and he would no man trust;
He tried and watch'd his people day and night,—
The good it harm'd not; for the bad 't was right:
He could their humours bear; nay disrespect,
But he could yield no pardon to neglect;

* In botanical language "*the habitat*," the favourite soil or situation of the more scarce species.

† This, it must be acknowledged, is contrary to the opinion of Thomson, and I believe of some other poets, who, in describing the varying hues of our most beautiful flowers, have considered them as lost and blended with each other; whereas their beauty, in the eye of a florist (and I conceive in that of the uninitiated also) depends upon the distinctness of their colours; the stronger the bounding line, and the less they break into the neighbouring tint, so much the richer and more valuable is the flower esteemed.

‡ An auricula, or any other single flower, is so called when the *stigma* (the part which arises from the seed-vessel) is protruded beyond the tube of the flower, and becomes visible.

§ This word, so far as it relates to flowers, means those variegated with three or more colours irregularly and indeterminately

That all about him were of him afraid,
'Was right," he said—"so should we be obey'd."

These merchant-maxims, much good-fortune too,
And ever keeping one grand point in view,
To vast amount his once small portion drew.

William was kind and easy; he complied
With all requests, or grieved when he denied;
To please his wife he made a costly trip,
To please his child he let a bargain slip;
Prone to compassion, mild with the distress'd,
He bore with all who poverty profess'd,
And some would he assist, nor one would he arrest.
He had some loss at sea, bad debts at land,
His clerk absconded with some bills in hand,
And plans so often fail'd that he no longer plann'd.
To a small house (his brother's) he withdrew,
At easy rent—the man was not a Jew;
And there his losses and his cares he bore,
Nor found that want of wealth could make him poor.

No, he in fact was rich; nor could he move,
But he was follow'd by the looks of love;
All he had suffer'd, every former grief,
Made those around more studious in relief;
He saw a cheerful smile in every face,
And lost all thoughts of error and disgrace.

Pleasant it was to see them in their walk
Round their small garden, and to hear them talk;
Free are their children, but their love refrains
From all offence—none murmurs, none complains;
Whether a book amused them, speech or play,
Their looks were lively, and their hearts were gay;
There no forced efforts for delight were made,
Joy came with prudence, and without parade;
Their common comforts they had all in view,
Light were their troubles, and their wishes few:
Thrift made them easy for the coming day,
Religion took the dread of death away;
A cheerful spirit still insured content,
And love smiled round them wheresoe'er they went.

Walter, meantime, with all his wealth's increase,
Gain'd many points, but could not purchase peace;
When he withdrew from business for an hour,
Some fled his presence, all confess'd his power;
He sought affection, but received instead
Fear undisguised, and love-repelling dread;
He look'd around him—"Harriet, dost thou love?"
"I do my duty," said the timid dove;
"Good Heav'n, your duty! prithee, tell me now—
To love and honour—was not that your vow?
Come, my good Harriet, I would gladly seek
Your inmost thought—Why can't the woman speak?
Have you not all things?"—"Sir, do I complain?"—
"No, that 's my part, which I perform in vain;
I want a simple answer, and direct—
But you evade; yes! 't is as I suspect.
Come then, my children! Watt! upon your knees
Vow that you love me."—"Yes, sir, if you please."—
"Again! by Heav'n, it mads me; I require
Love, and they 'll do whatever I desire:
Thus too my people shun me; I would spend
A thousand pounds to get a single friend;
I would be happy—I have means to pay
For love and friendship, and you run away;
Ungrateful creatures! why, you seem to dread
My very looks; I know you wish me dead.
Come hither, Nancy! you must hold me dear;
Hither, I say; why! what have you to fear?
You see I 'm gentle—Come, you trifler, come;
My God! she trembles! Idiot, leave the room!
Madam! your children hate me; I suppose
They know their cue: you make them all my foes
I 've not a friend in all the world—not one:
I 'd be a bankrupt sooner; nay, 't is done;
In every better hope of life I fail,
You 're all tormentors, and my house a jail;
Out of my sight! I 'll sit and make my will—
What, glad to go? stay, devils, and be still;
'T is to your uncle's cot you wish to run,
To learn to live at ease and be undone;
Him you can love, who lost his whole estate,
And I, who gain you fortunes, have your hate;
'T is in my absence, you yourselves enjoy:
Tom! are you glad to lose me? tell me, boy:
Yes! does he answer?"—"Yes! upon my soul;"
"No awe, no fear, no duty, no control!
Away! away! ten thousand devils seize
All I possess, and plunder where they please!
What 's wealth to me?—yes, yes! it gives me sway,
And you shall feel it—Go! begone, I say."

LETTER IX.

AMUSEMENTS.

Interpone tuis interdum gaudia curis,
Ut possis animo quemvis sufferre laborem.
CATULL. lib. 3.

——— Nostra fatiscat
Laxaturque chelys, vires instigat alitque
Tempestiva quies, major post otia virtus.
STATIUS SYLV. lib. iv.

Jamque mare et tellus nullum discrimen habebant;
Omnia pontus erant, deerant quoque littora ponto.
OVID. *Metamorph.* lib. i.

Common Amusements of a Bathing-place—Morning Rides, Walks, etc.—Company resorting to the Town—Different Choice of Lodgings—Cheap Indulgences—Sea-side Walks—Wealthy Invalid—Summer-Evening on the Sands—Sea Productions—"Water parted from the Sea"—Winter Views serene—In what Cases to be avoided—Sailing upon the River—A small Islet of Sand off the Coast—Visited by Company—Covered by the Flowing of the Tide—Adventure in that Place.

Of our amusements ask you?—We amuse
Ourselves and friends with sea-side walks and views,
Or take a morning ride, a novel, or the news;
Or, seeking nothing, glide about the street,
And so engaged, with various parties meet;
Awhile we stop, discourse of wind and tide,
Bathing and books, the raffle, and the ride:
Thus, with the aid which shops and sailing give,
Life passes on; 't is labour, but we live.

When evening comes, our invalids awake,
Nerves cease to tremble, heads forbear to ache;
Then cheerful meals the sunken spirits raise,
Cards or the dance, wine, visiting, or plays.

Soon as the season comes, and crowds arrive,
To their superior rooms the wealthy drive;
Others look round for lodging snug and small,
Such is their taste—they 've hatred to a hall;
Hence one his fav'rite habitation gets,
The brick-floor'd parlour which the butcher lets;
Where, through his single light, he may regard
The various business of a common yard,
Bounded by backs of buildings form'd of clay,
By stable, sties, and coops, et-cætera.

The needy-vain, themselves awhile to shun,
For dissipation to these dog-holes run;
Where each (assuming petty pomp) appears,
And quite forgets the shopboard and the shears.

For them are cheap amusements: they may slip
Beyond the town, and take a private dip;
When they may urge that, to be safe they mean,
They 've heard there 's danger in a light machine;
They too can gratis move the quays about,
And gather kind replies to every doubt;
There they a pacing, lounging tribe may view,
The stranger's guides, who 've little else to do;
The Borough's placemen, where no more they gain
Than keeps them idle, civil, poor, and vain.
Then may the poorest with the wealthy look
On ocean, glorious page of Nature's book!
May see its varying views in every hour,
All softness now, then rising with all power,
As sleeping to invite, or threat'ning to devour:
'T is this which gives us all our choicest views;
Its waters heal us, and its shores amuse.

See! those fair nymphs upon that rising strand,
Yon long salt lake has parted from the land;
Well pleased to press that path, so clean, so pure,
To seem in danger, yet to feel secure;
Trifling with terror, while they strive to shun
The curling billows; laughing as they run;
They know the neck that joins the shore and sea,
Or, ah! how changed that fearless laugh would be.

Observe how various parties take their way,
By sea-side walks, or make the sand-hills gay;
There group'd are laughing maids and sighing swains,
And some apart who feel unpitied pains;
Pains from diseases, pains which those who feel,
To the physician, not the fair, reveal:
For nymphs (propitious to the lover's sigh)
Leave these poor patients to complain and die.
Lo! where on that huge anchor sadly leans
That sick tall figure, lost in other scenes;
He late from India's clime impatient sail'd,
There, as his fortune grew, his spirits fail'd;
For each delight, in search of wealth he went,
For ease alone, the wealth acquired is spent—
And spent in vain; enrich'd, aggrieved, he sees
The envied poor possess'd of joy and ease:
And now he flies from place to place, to gain
Strength for enjoyment, and still flies in vain;
Mark! with what sadness, of that pleasant crew,
Boist'rous in mirth, he takes a transient view;
And fixing then his eye upon the sea,
Thinks what has been and what must shortly be:
Is it not strange that man should health destroy,
For joys that come when he is dead to joy?

Now is it pleasant in the summer-eve,
When a broad shore retiring waters leave,
Awhile to wait upon the firm fair sand,
When all is calm at sea, all still at land;
And there the ocean's produce to explore,
As floating by, or rolling on the shore:
Those living jellies,* which the flesh inflame,
Fierce as a nettle, and from that its name;
Some in huge masses, some that you may bring,
In the small compass of a lady's ring;
Figured by hand divine—there 's not a gem
Wrought by man's art to be compared to them;
Soft, brilliant, tender, through the wave they glow,
And make the moon-beam brighter where they flow
Involved in sea-wrack, here you find a race,
Which science doubting, knows not where to place;
On shell or stone is dropp'd the embryo-seed,
And quickly vegetates a vital breed.†

While thus with pleasing wonder you inspect
Treasures the vulgar in their scorn reject,
See as they float along th' entangled weeds
Slowly approach, upborne on bladdery beads;
Wait till they land, and you shall then behold
The fiery sparks those tangled frons infold,
Myriads of living points;‡ th' unaided eye
Can but the fire and not the form descry.
And now your view upon the ocean turn,
And there the splendour of the waves discern;
Cast but a stone, or strike them with an oar,
And you shall flames within the deep explore;
Or scoop the stream phosphoric as you stand,
And the cold flames shall flash along your hand;
When, lost in wonder, you shall walk and gaze
On weeds that sparkle, and on waves that blaze.§

The ocean too has winter-views serene,
When all you see through densest fog is seen;
When you can hear the fishers near at hand
Distinctly speak, yet see not where they stand;
Or sometimes them and not their boat discern,
Or half-conceal'd some figure at the stern;

* Some of the smaller species of the Medusa (sea-nettle) are exquisitely beautiful: their form is nearly oval, varied with serrated longitudinal lines; they are extremely tender, and by no means which I am acquainted with can be preserved, for they soon dissolve in either spirit of wine or water, and lose every vestige of their shape, and indeed of their substance: the larger species are found in mis-shapen masses of many pounds weight; these, when handled, have the effect of the nettle, and the stinging is often accompanied or succeeded by the more unpleasant feeling, perhaps in a slight degree resembling that caused by the torpedo.

† Various tribes and species of marine vermes are here meant: that which so nearly resembles a vegetable in its form, and perhaps, in some degree, manner of growth, is the coralline called by naturalists Sertularia, of which there are many species, in almost every part of the coast. The animal protrudes its many claws (apparently in search of prey) from certain pellucid vesicles which proceed from a horny, tenacious, branchy stem.

‡ These are said to be a minute kind of animal of the same class; when it does not shine, it is invisible to the naked eye.

§ For the cause or causes of this phenomenon, which is sometimes, though rarely, observed on our coasts, I must refer the reader to the writers on natural philosophy and natural history.

The view 's all bounded, and from side to side
Your utmost prospect but a few ells wide;
Boys who, on shore, to sea the pebble cast,
Will hear it strike against the viewless mast;
While the stern boatman growls his fierce disdain,
At whom he knows not, whom he threats in vain.

'T is pleasant then to view the nets float past,
Net after net till you have seen the last;
And as you wait till all beyond you slip,
A boat comes gliding from an anchor'd ship,
Breaking the silence with the dipping oar,
And their own tones, as labouring for the shore;
Those measured tones which with the scene agree,
And give a sadness to serenity.

All scenes like these the tender maid should shun,
Nor to a misty beach in autumn run;
Much should she guard against the evening cold,
And her slight shape with fleecy warmth infold;
This she admits, but not with so much ease
Gives up the night-walk when th' attendants please:
Her have I seen, pale, vapour'd through the day,
With crowded parties at the midnight play;
Faint in the morn, no powers could she exert;
At night with Pam delighted and alert;
In a small shop she's raffled with a crowd,
Breathed the thick air, and cough'd and laugh'd aloud;
She who will tremble if her eye explore
"The smallest monstrous mouse that creeps on floor;"
Whom the kind doctor charged with shaking head,
At early hour to quit the beaux for bed:
She has, contemning fear, gone down the dance,
Till she perceived the rosy morn advance;
Then has she wonder'd, fainting o'er her tea,
Her drops and julep should so useless be:
Ah! sure her joys must ravish every sense,
Who buys a portion at such vast expense.

Among those joys, 't is one at eve to sail
On the broad river with a favourite gale;
When no rough waves upon the bosom ride,
But the keel cuts, nor rises on the tide;
Safe from the stream the nearer gunwale stands,
Where playful children trail their idle hands:
Or strive to catch long grassy leaves that float
On either side of the impeded boat;
What time the moon arising shows the mud,
A shining border to the silver flood:
When, by her dubious light, the meanest views,
Chalk, stones, and stakes, obtain the richest hues;
And when the cattle, as they gazing stand,
Seem nobler objects than when view'd from land:
Then anchor'd vessels in the way appear,
And sea-boys greet them as they pass,—"What cheer?"
The sleeping shell-ducks at the sound arise
And utter loud their unharmonious cries;
Fluttering they move their weedy beds among,
Or instant diving, hide their plumeless young.

Along the wall, returning from the town,
The weary rustic homeward wanders down;
Who stops and gazes at such joyous crew,
And feels his envy rising at the view;
He the light speech and laugh indignant hears,
And feels more press'd by want, more vex'd by fears.

Ah! go in peace, good fellow, to thine home,
Nor fancy these escape the general doom;
Gay as they seem, be sure with them are hearts
With sorrow tried; there's sadness in their parts.
If thou couldst see them, when they think alone,
Mirth, music, friends, and these amusements gone;
Couldst thou discover every secret ill
That paints their spirit, or resists their will;
Couldst thou behold forsaken Love's distress,
Or Envy's pang at glory and success,
Or Beauty, conscious of the spoils of Time,
Or Guilt alarm'd when Memory shows the crime;
All that gives sorrow, terror, grief, and gloom;
Content would cheer thee trudging to thine home.*

There are, 't is true, who lay their cares aside,
And bid some hours in calm enjoyment glide;
Perchance some fair one to the sober night
Adds (by the very sweetness of her song) delight;
And, as the music on the water floats,
Some bolder shore returns the soften'd notes;
Then, youth, beware, for all around conspire
To banish caution and to wake desire:
The day's amusement, feasting, beauty, wine,
These accents sweet and this soft hour combine,
When most unguarded, then to win that heart of thine:
But see, they land! the fond enchantment flies,
And in its place life's common views arise.

Sometimes a party, row'd from town, will land
On a small islet form'd of shelly sand,
Left by the water when the tides are low,
But which the floods in their return o'erflow:
There will they anchor, pleased awhile to view
The watery waste, a prospect wild and new;
The now receding billows give them space,
On either side the growing shores to pace;
And then returning, they contract the scene,
Till small and smaller grows the walk between;
As sea to sea approaches, shore to shores,
Till the next ebb the sandy isle restores.

Then what alarm! what danger and dismay,
If all their trust, their boat should drift away;
And once it happen'd—gay the friends advanced,
They walk'd, they ran, they play'd, they sang, they danced;
The urns were boiling, and the cups went round,
And not a grave or thoughtful face was found.
On the bright sand they trod with nimble feet,
Dry shelly sand that made the summer seat;
The wondering mews flew fluttering o'er the head,
And waves ran softly up their shining bed.

Some form'd a party from the rest to stray,
Pleased to collect the trifles in their way.
These to behold they call their friends around,
No friends can hear, or hear another sound:
Alarm'd they hasten, yet perceive not why
But catch the fear that quickens as they fly.

---

* This is not offered as a reasonable source of contentment but as one motive for resignation: there would not be so much envy if there were more discernment.

For lo! a lady sage, who paced the sand
With her fair children one in either hand,
Intent on home, had turn'd, and saw the boat
Slipp'd from her moorings, and now far afloat;
She gazed, she trembled, and though faint her call,
It seem'd, like thunder, to confound them all.
Their sailor-guides, the boatman and his mate,
Had drunk, and slept regardless of their state.
"Awake!" they cried aloud: "Alarm the shore!
Shout all, or never shall we reach it more!"
Alas! no shout the distant land can reach,
Nor eye behold them from the foggy beach.
Again they join in one loud powerful cry,
Then cease, and eager listen for reply;
None came—the rising wind blew sadly by:
They shout once more, and then they turn aside,
To see how quickly flow'd the coming tide,
Between each cry they find the waters steal
On their strange prison, and new horrors feel;
Foot after foot on the contracted ground
The billows fall, and dreadful is the sound.
Less and yet less the sinking isle became,
And there was wailing, weeping, wrath, and blame.

Had one been there, with spirit strong and high,
Who could observe, as he prepared to die,
He might have seen of hearts the varying kind,
And traced the movement of each different mind:
He might have seen, that not the gentle maid
Was more than stern and haughty man afraid;
Such, calmly grieving, will their fears suppress,
And silent prayers to Mercy's throne address;
While fiercer minds, impatient, angry, loud,
Force their vain grief on the reluctant crowd:
The party's patron, sorely sighing, cried,
"Why would you urge me? I at first denied."
Fiercely they answer'd, "Why will you complain,
Who saw no danger, or was warn'd in vain?"
A few essay'd the troubled soul to calm,
But dread prevail'd, and anguish and alarm.

Now rose the water through the lessening sand,
And they seem'd sinking while they yet could stand;
The sun went down, they look'd from side to side,
Nor aught except the gathering sea descried;
Dark and more dark, more wet, more cold it grew,
And the most lively bade to hope adieu;
Children, by love then lifted from the seas,
Felt not the waters at the parents' knees,
But wept aloud; the wind increased the sound,
And the cold billows as they broke around.

"Once more, yet once again, with all our strength,
Cry to the land—we may be heard at length."
Vain hope, if yet unseen! but hark! an oar,
That sound of bliss! comes dashing to their shore;
Still, still the water rises, "Haste!" they cry,
"Oh! hurry, seamen; in delay we die:"
(Seamen were these, who in their ship perceived
The drifted boat, and thus her crew relieved.)
And now the keel just cuts the cover'd sand,
Now to the gunwale stretches every hand:
With trembling pleasure all confused embark,
And kiss the tackling of their welcome ark;
While the most giddy, as they reach the shore,
Think of their danger, and their God adore.

LETTER X.

CLUBS AND SOCIAL MEETINGS.

Non inter lances mensasque nitentes,
Cum stupet insanis acies fulgoribus, et cum
Acclinis falsis animus meliora recusat;
Verum hic impransi mecum disquirite.
HOR. Sat. 2, lib. 2.

O prodiga rerum
Luxuries, nunquam parvo contenta paratu,
Et quæsitorum terra pelagoque ciborum
Ambitiosa fames et lautæ gloria mensæ.
LUCAN. lib. 4.

Et quæ non prosunt singula, juncta juvant.

Rusticus agricolam, miles fera bella gerentem,
Rectorem dubiæ navita puppis amat.
OVID. *Pont.* lib. 2.

Desire of Country Gentlemen for Town Associations—Book-Clubs—Too much of literary Character expected from them—Literary Conversation prevented: by Feasting: by Cards—Good, notwithstanding, results—Card-club with Eagerness resorted to—Players—Umpires at the Whist Table—Petulances of Temper there discovered—Free-and-easy Club: not perfectly easy or free—Freedom, how interrupted—The superior Member—Termination of the Evening—Drinking and Smoking Clubs—The Midnight Conversation of the delaying Members—Society of the poorer Inhabitants: its Use: gives Pride and Consequence to the humble Character—Pleasant Habitations of the frugal Poor—Sailor returning to his Family—Freemasons' Club—The Mystery—What its origin—Its professed Advantages—Griggs and Gregorians—A Kind of Masons—Reflections on these various Societies.

You say you envy in your calm retreat
Our social meetings;—'t is with joy we meet:
In these our parties you are pleased to find
Good sense and wit, with intercourse of mind;
Composed of men, who read, reflect and write,
Who, when they meet, must yield and share delight:
To you our Book-club has peculiar charm,
For which you sicken in your quiet farm;
Here you suppose us at our leisure placed,
Enjoying freedom, and displaying taste;
With wisdom cheerful, temperately gay,
Pleased to enjoy, and willing to display.

If thus your envy gives your ease its gloom,
Give wings to fancy, and among us come.
We're now assembled; you may soon attend—
I'll introduce you—"Gentlemen, my friend."

"Now are you happy? you have pass'd a night
In gay discourse, and rational delight."

"Alas! not so: for how can mortals think,
Or thoughts exchange, if thus they eat and drink?
No! I confess, when we had fairly dined,
That was no time for intercourse of mind;

There was each dish prepared with skill t' invite,
And to detain the struggling appetite;
On such occasions minds with one consent
Are to the comforts of the body lent;
There was no pause — the wine went quickly
round,
Till struggling Fancy was by Bacchus bound;
Wine is to wit as water thrown on fire,
By duly sprinkling both are raised the higher;
Thus largely dealt, the vivid blaze they choke,
And all the genial flame goes off in smoke."

"But when no more your boards these loads
contain,
When wine no more o'erwhelms the labouring
brain,
But serves, a gentle stimulus; we know
How wit must sparkle, and how fancy flow."

It might be so, but no such club-days come:
We always find these dampers in the room:
If to converse were all that brought us here,
A few odd members would in turn appear;
Who dwelling nigh, would saunter in and out,
O'erlook the list and toss the books about;
Or yawning read them, walking up and down,
Just as the loungers in the shops in town;
Till fancying nothing would their minds amuse,
They 'd push them by, and go in search of news.

But our attractions are a stronger sort,
The earliest dainties and the oldest port;
All enter then with glee in every look,
And not a member thinks about a book.

Still let me own, there are some vacant hours,
When minds might work, and men exert their
powers:
Ere wine to folly spurs the giddy guest,
But gives to wit its vigour and its zest;
Then might we reason, might in turn display
Our several talents, and be wisely gay;
We might—but who a tame discourse regards,
When whist is named, and we behold the cards?

We from that time are neither grave nor gay;
Our thought, our care, our business is to play;
Fix'd on these spots and figures, each attends
Much to his partners, nothing to his friends.

Our public cares, the long, the warm debate,
That kept our patriots from their beds so late;
War, peace, invasion, all we hope or dread
Vanish like dreams when men forsake their bed;
And groaning nations and contending kings
Are all forgotten for these painted things:
Paper and paste, vile figures and poor spots,
Level all minds, philosophers and sots;
And give an equal spirit, pause, and force,
Join'd with peculiar diction, to discourse:
"Who deals?—you led—we 're three by cards—
had you
Honour in hand?"—"Upon my honour, two."
Hour after hour, men thus contending sit,
Grave without sense, and pointed without wit.

Thus it appears these envied clubs possess
No certain means for social happiness;
Yet there 's a good that flows from scenes like
these—
Man meets with man at leisure and at ease;
We to our neighbours and our equals come,
And rub off pride that man contracts at home;
For there, admired master, he is prone
To claim attention and to talk alone:
But here he meets with neither son nor spouse;
No humble cousin to his bidding bows;
To his raised voice his neighbours' voices rise,
To his high look as lofty look replies;
When much he speaks, he finds that ears are closed,
And certain signs inform him when he 's prosed;
Here all the value of a listener know,
And claim, in turn, the favour they bestow.

No pleasure gives the speech, when all would
speak
And all in vain a civil hearer seek.
To chance alone we owe the free discourse,
In vain you purpose what you cannot force;
'T is when the favourite themes unbidden spring
That fancy soars with such unwearied wing;
Then may you call in aid the moderate glass,
But let it slowly and unprompted pass;
So shall there all things for the end unite,
And give that hour of rational delight.

Men to their clubs repair, themselves to please,
To care for nothing, and to take their ease;
In fact, for play, for wine, for news they come:
Discourse is shared with friends or found at home.

But cards with books are incidental things;
We 've nights devoted to these queens and kings:
Then if we choose the social game, we may;
Now 't is a duty, and we 're bound to play;
Nor ever meeting of the social kind
Was more engaging, yet had less of mind.

Our eager parties, when the lunar light
Throws its full radiance on the festive night,
Of either sex, with punctual hurry come,
And fill, with one accord, an ample room;
Pleased, the fresh packs on cloth of green they see,
And seizing, handle with preluding glee;
They draw, they sit, they shuffle, cut and deal;
Like friends assembled, but like foes to feel:
But yet not all,—a happier few have joys
Of mere amusement, and their cards are toys;
No skill nor art, nor fretful hopes have they,
But while their friends are gaming, laugh and play.

Others there are, the veterans of the game,
Who owe their pleasure to their envied fame;
Through many a year, with hard-contested strife,
Have they attain'd this glory of their life:
Such is that ancient burgess, whom in vain
Would gout and fever on his couch detain;
And that large lady, who resolves to come,
Though a first fit has warn'd her of her doom!
These are as oracles: in every cause
They settle doubts, and their decrees are laws;
But all are troubled, when, with dubious look,
Diana questions what Apollo spoke.

Here avarice first, the keen desire of gain,
Rules in each heart, and works in every brain.
Alike the veteran-dames and virgins feel,
Nor care what grey-beards or what striplings deal,
Sex, age, and station, vanish from their view,
And gold, their sov'reign good, the mingled crowd
pursue.

Hence they are jealous, and as rivals, keep
A watchful eye on the beloved heap;
Meantime discretion bids the tongue be still,
And mild good-humour strives with strong ill-will;
Till prudence fails; when, all impatient grown,
They make their grief, by their suspicions, known.

"Sir, I protest, were Job himself at play,
He'd rave to see you throw your cards away;
Not that I care a button—not a pin
For what I lose; but we had cards to win:
A saint in heaven would grieve to see such hand
Cut up by one who will not understand."

"Complain of me! and so you might indeed,
If I had ventured on that foolish lead,
That fatal heart—but I forgot your play—
Some folk have ever thrown their hearts away."

"Yes, and their diamonds; I have heard of one
Who made a beggar of an only son."

"Better a beggar, than to see him tied
To art and spite, to insolence and pride."
"Sir, were I you, I'd strive to be polite,
Against my nature, for a single night."
"So did you strive, and, madam! with success;
I knew no being we could censure less!"

Is this too much? alas! my peaceful muse
Cannot with half their virulence abuse.
And hark! at other tables discord reigns,
With feign'd contempt for losses and for gains;
Passions awhile are bridled; then they rage,
In waspish youth, and in resentful age;
With scraps of insult—"Sir, when next you play,
Reflect whose money 't is you throw away.
No one on earth can less such things regard,
But when one's partner doesn't know a card——"

"I scorn suspicion, ma'am, but while you stand
Behind that lady, pray keep down your hand."

"Good heav'n, revoke! remember, if the set
Be lost, in honour you should pay the debt."

"There, there 's your money; but, while I have life,
I 'll never more sit down with man and wife;
They snap and snarl indeed, but in the heat
Of all their spleen, their understandings meet;
They are Freemasons, and have many a sign,
That we, poor devils! never can divine;
May it be told, do ye divide th' amount,
Or goes it all to family account?"

Next is the club, where to their friends in town
Our country neighbours once a month come down;
We term it Free-and-easy, and yet we
Find it no easy matter to be free;
Ev'n in our small assembly, friends among,
Are minds perverse, there 's something will be wrong,
Men are not equal; some will claim a right
To be the kings and heroes of the night;
Will their own favourite themes and notions start,
And you must hear, offend them, or depart.

There comes Sir Thomas from his village-seat,
Happy, he tells us, all his friends to meet;
He brings the ruin'd brother of his wife,
Whom he supports, and makes him sick of life;
A ready witness whom he can produce
Of all his deeds—a butt for his abuse;
Soon as he enters, has the guests espied,
Drawn to the fire, and to the glass applied—
"Well, what's the subject?—what are you about?
The news, I take it—come, I'll help you out;"
And then, without one answer, he bestows
Freely upon us all he hears and knows;
Gives us opinions, tells us how he votes,
Recites the speeches, adds to them his notes,
And gives old ill-told tales for new-born anecdotes;
Yet cares he nothing what we judge or think,
Our only duty's to attend and drink:
At length, admonish'd by his gout, he ends
The various speech, and leaves at peace his friends;
But now, alas! we 've lost the pleasant hour,
And wisdom flies from wine's superior power.

Wine, like the rising sun, possession gains,
And drives the mist of dullness from the brains;
The gloomy vapour from the spirit flies,
And views of gaiety and gladness rise:
Still it proceeds; till from the glowing heat,
The prudent calmly to their shades retreat;—
Then is the mind o'ercast—in wordy rage
And loud contention angry men engage;
Then spleen and pique, like fire-works thrown in spite,
To mischief turn the pleasures of the night;
Anger abuses, Malice loudly rails,
Revenge awakes, and Anarchy prevails:
Till wine, that raised the tempest, makes it cease,
And maudlin Love insists on instant peace;
He noisy mirth and roaring song commands,
Gives idle toasts, and joins unfriendly hands;
Till fuddled Friendship vows esteem and weeps,
And jovial Folly drinks and sings and sleeps.

A club there is of Smokers—Dare you come
To that close, clouded, hot, narcotic room?
When, midnight past, the very candles seem
Dying for air, and give a ghastly gleam;
When curling fumes in lazy wreaths arise,
And prosing topers rub their winking eyes;
When the long tale, renew'd when last they met,
Is spliced anew, and is unfinish'd yet;
When but a few are left the house to tire,
And they half-sleeping by the sleepy fire;
Ev'n the poor ventilating vane, that flew
Of late so fast, is now grown drowsy too;
When sweet, cold, clammy punch its aid bestows,
Then thus the midnight conversation flows:—

"Then, as I said, and—mind me—as I say,
At our last meeting—you remember"—"Ay;"
"Well, very well—then freely as I drink
I spoke my thought—you take me—what I think
And sir, said I, if I a freeman be,
It is my bounden duty to be free."

"Ay, there you posed him: I respect the chair
But man is man, although the man 's a mayor:
If Muggins live—no, no!—if Muggins die,
He 'll quit his office—neighbour, shall I try?"

"I'll speak my mind, for here are none but friends:
They're all contending for their private ends;
No public spirit—once a vote would bring,
I say a vote—was then a pretty thing;
It made a man to serve his country and his king:
But for that place, that Muggins must resign,
You've my advice—'t is no affair of mine."

The poor man has his club; he comes and spends
His hoarded pittance with his chosen friends;
Nor this alone,—a monthly dole he pays,
To be assisted when his health decays;
Some part his prudence, from the day's supply,
For cares and troubles in his age, lays by;
The printed rules he guards with painted frame,
And shows his children where to read his name:
Those simple words his honest nature move,
That bond of union tied by laws of love;
This is his pride, it gives to his employ
New value, to his home another joy;
While a religious hope its balm applies
For all his fate inflicts and all his state denies.

Much would it please you, sometimes to explore
The peaceful dwellings of our borough poor;
To view a sailor just return'd from sea,
His wife beside; a child on either knee,
And others crowding near, that none may lose
The smallest portion of the welcome news;
What dangers pass'd, "when seas ran mountains high,
When tempests raved, and horrors veil'd the sky;
When prudence fail'd, when courage grew dismay'd,
When the strong fainted, and the wicked pray'd,—
Then in the yawning gulf far down we drove,
And gazed upon the billowy mount above;
Till up that mountain, swinging with the gale,
We view'd the horrors of the watery vale."

The trembling children look with stedfast eyes,
And panting, sob involuntary sighs:
Soft sleep awhile his torpid touch delays,
And all is joy and piety and praise.

Masons are ours, Freemasons—but, alas!
To their own bards I leave the mystic class;
In vain shall one, and not a gifted man,
Attempt to sing of this enlighten'd clan:
I know no word, boast no directing sign,
And not one token of the race is mine;
Whether with Hiram, that wise widow's son,
They came from Tyre to royal Solomon,
Two pillars raising by their skill profound,
Boaz and Jachin through the East renown'd:
Whether the sacred books their rise express,
Or books profane, 't is vain for me to guess;
It may be, lost in date remote and high,
They know not what their own antiquity:
It may be too, derived from cause so low,
They have no wish their origin to show:
If, as crusaders, they combined to wrest
From heathen lords the land they long possess'd;
Or were at first some harmless club, who made
Their idle meetings solemn by parade;
Is but conjecture—for the task unfit,
Awe-struck and mute, the puzzling theme I quit:
Yet, if such blessings from their order flow,
We should be glad their moral code to know;
Trowels of silver are but simple things,
And aprons worthless as their apron-strings;
But if indeed you have the skill to teach
A social spirit, now beyond our reach;
If man's warm passions you can guide and bind,
And plant the virtues in the wayward mind;
If you can wake to christian-love the heart,—
In mercy, something of your powers impart.

But as it seems, we Masons must become
To know the secret, and must then be dumb;
And as we venture for uncertain gains,
Perhaps the profit is not worth the pains.

When Bruce, that dauntless traveller, thought he stood
On Nile's first rise! the fountain of the flood,
And drank exulting in the sacred spring,
The critics told him it was no such thing;
That springs unnumber'd round the country ran,
But none could show him where they first began:
So might we feel, should we our time bestow,
To gain these secrets and these signs to know;
Might question still if all the truth we found,
And firmly stood upon the certain ground;
We might our title to the mystery dread,
And fear we drank not at the river-head.

Griggs and Gregorians here their meetings hold,
Convivial sects, and Bucks alert and bold;
A kind of Masons, but without their sign;
The bonds of union—pleasure, song, and wine:
Man, a gregarious creature, loves to fly
Where he the trackings of the herd can spy;
Still to be one with many he desires,
Although it leads him through the thorns and briers.

A few! but few there are, who in the mind
Perpetual source of consolation find;
The weaker many to the world will come,
For comforts seldom to be found from home.

When the faint hands no more a brimmer hold,
When flannel-wreaths the useless limbs infold,
The breath impeded, and the bosom cold;
When half the pillow'd man the palsy chains,
And the blood falters in the bloated veins,
Then, as our friends no further aid supply
Than hope's cold phrase and courtesy's soft sigh,
We should that comfort for ourselves ensure,
Which friends could not, if we could friends, procure.

Early in life, when we can laugh aloud,
There's something pleasant in a social crowd,
Who laugh with us—but will such joy remain,
When we lie struggling on the bed of pain?
When our physician tells us with a sigh,
No more on hope and science to rely,
Life's staff is useless then; with labouring breath
We pray for hope divine—the staff of death—
This is a scene which few companions grace,
And where the heart's first favourites yield their place.

Here all the aid of man to man must end,
Here mounts the soul to her eternal Friend;
The tenderest love must here its tie resign,
And give th' aspiring heart to love divine.

Men feel their weakness, and to numbers run,
Themselves to strengthen, or themselves to shun;
And though to this our weakness may be prone,
Let 's learn to live, for we must die, alone.

LETTER XI.

INNS.

All the comforts of life in a tavern are known,
'T is his home who possesses not one of his own;
And to him who has rather too much of that one,
'T is the house of a friend where he 's welcome to run:
The instant you enter my door you 're my lord,
With whose taste and whose pleasure I 'm proud to accord;
And the louder you call and the longer you stay,
The more I am happy to serve and obey.

To the house of a friend if you 're pleased to retire,
You must all things admit, you must all things admire;
You must pay with observance the price of your treat,
You must eat what is praised, and must praise what you eat:
But here you may come, and no tax we require,
You may loudly condemn what you greatly admire;
You may growl at our wishes and pains to excel,
And may snarl at the rascals who please you so well.

At your wish we attend, and confess that your speech
On the nation's affairs might the minister teach;
His views you may blame, and his measures oppose,
There's no tavern-treason—you 're under the Rose;
Should rebellions arise in your own little state,
With me you may safely their consequence wait;
To recruit your lost spirits 't is prudent to come,
And to fly to a friend when the devil 's at home.

That I've faults is confess'd: but it won't be denied,
'T is my interest the faults of my neighbours to hide;
If I've sometimes lent Scandal occasion to prate,
I 've often conceal'd what she 'd love to relate;
If to Justice's bar some have wander'd from mine,
'T was because the dull rogues wouldn't stay by their wine;
And for brawls at my house, well the poet explains,
That men drink *shallow draughts*, and so madden their brains.

A difficult Subject for Poetry—Invocation of the Muse—Description of the principal Inn and those of the first Class—The large deserted Tavern—Those of a second Order—Their Company—One of particular Description—A lower Kind of Public-Houses: yet distinguished among themselves—Houses on the Quays for Sailors—The Green-Man: its Landlord, and the Adventure of his Marriage, etc.

Much do I need, and therefore will I ask,
A Muse to aid me in my present task;
For then with special cause we beg for aid,
When of our subject we are most afraid:
Inns are this subject—'t is an ill-drawn lot,
So, thou who gravely triflest, fail me not.
Fail not, but haste, and to my memory bring
Scenes yet unsung, which few would choose to sing;
Thou mad'st a Shilling splendid; thou hast thrown
On humble themes the graces all thine own;
By thee the Mistress of a village-school
Became a queen, enthroned upon her stool;
And far beyond the rest thou gavest to shine
Belinda's Lock—that deathless work was thine.

Come, lend thy cheerful light, and give to please,
These seats of revelry, these scenes of ease;
Who sings of Inns much danger has to dread,
And needs assistance from the fountain-head.

High in the street, o'erlooking all the place,
The rampant Lion shows his kingly face;
His ample jaws extend from side to side,
His eyes are glaring, and his nostrils wide;
In silver shag the sovereign form is dress'd,
A mane horrific sweeps his ample chest;
Elate with pride, he seems t' assert his reign,
And stands the glory of his wide domain.

Yet nothing dreadful to his friends the sight,
But sign and pledge of welcome and delight:
To him the noblest guest the town detains
Flies for repast, and in his court remains;
Him too the crowd with longing looks admire,
Sigh for his joys, and modestly retire;
Here not a comfort shall to them be lost
Who never ask or never feel the cost.

The ample yards on either side contain
Buildings where order and distinction reign;—
The splendid carriage of the wealthier guest,
The ready chaise and driver smartly dress'd;
Whiskeys and gigs and curricles are there,
And high-fed prancers many a raw-boned pair.
On all without a lordly host sustains
The care of empire, and observant reigns;
The parting guest beholds him at his side,
With pomp obsequious, bending in his pride;
Round all the place his eyes all objects meet,
Attentive, silent, civil, and discreet.
O'er all within the lady-hostess rules,
Her bar she governs, and her kitchen schools;
To every guest the appropriate speech is made,
And every duty with distinction paid;
Respectful, easy, pleasant, or polite—
"Your honour's servant — Mister Smith, good night."

Next, but not near, yet honour'd through the town,
There swing, incongruous pair! the Bear and Crown;
That Crown suspended gems and ribands deck,
A golden chain hangs o'er that furry neck:
Unlike the nobler beast, the Bear is bound,
And with the Crown so near him, scowls uncrown'd;
Less his dominion, but alert are all
Without, within, and ready for the call;
Smart lads and light run nimbly here and there,
Nor for neglected duties mourns the Bear.

To his retreats, on the election-day,
The losing party found their silent way;
There they partook of each consoling good,
Like him uncrown'd, like him in sullen mood—
Threatening, but bound.—Here meet a social kind,
Our various clubs for various cause combined;
Nor has he pride, but thankful takes as gain
The dew-drops shaken from the Lion's mane:

A thriving couple here their skill display,
And share the profits of no vulgar sway.

Third in our Borough's list appears the sign
Of a fair queen—the gracious Caroline;
But in decay—each feature in the face
Has stain of Time, and token of disgrace.
The storm of winter, and the summer-sun,
Have on that form their equal mischief done;
The features now are all disfigured seen,
And not one charm adorns the insulted queen:
To this poor face was never paint applied,
The unseemly work of cruel time to hide;
Here we may rightly such neglect upbraid,
Paint on such faces is by prudence laid.
Large the domain, but all within combine
To correspond with the dishonour'd sign;
And all around dilapidates: you call—
But none replies—they 're inattentive all:
At length a ruin'd stable holds your steed,
While you through large and dirty rooms proceed,
Spacious and cold; a proof they once had been
In honour—now magnificently mean;
Till in some small half-furnish'd room you rest,
Whose dying fire denotes it had a guest.
In those you pass'd where former splendour reign'd,
You saw the carpets torn, the paper stain'd;
Squares of discordant glass in windows fix'd,
And paper oil'd in many a space betwixt;
A soil'd and broken sconce, a mirror crack'd,
With table underpropp'd, and chairs new-back'd;
A marble side-slab with ten thousand stains,
And all an ancient tavern's poor remains.

With much entreaty, they your food prepare,
And acid wine afford, with meagre fare;
Heartless you sup; and when a dozen times
You 've read the fractured window's senseless rhymes;
Have been assured that Phœbe Green was fair,
And Peter Jackson took his supper there;
You reach a chilling chamber, where you dread
Damps hot or cold, from a tremendous bed;
Late comes your sleep, and you are waken'd soon
By rustling tatters of the old festoon.

O'er this large building, thus by time defaced,
A servile couple has its owner placed,
Who, not unmindful that its style is large,
To lost magnificence adapt their charge:
Thus an old beauty, who has long declined,
Keeps former dues and dignity in mind;
And wills that all attention should be paid
For graces vanish'd and for charms decay'd.

Few years have pass'd, since brightly 'cross the way,
Lights from each window shot the lengthen'd ray,
And busy looks in every face were seen,
Through the warm precincts of the reigning Queen:
There fires inviting blazed, and all around
Was heard the tinkling bells' seducing sound;
The nimble waiters to that sound from far
Sprang to the call, then hasten'd to the bar;
Where a glad priestess of the temple sway'd,
The most obedient, and the most obey'd;
Rosy and round, adorn'd in crimson vest,
And flaming ribands at her ample breast:
She, skill'd like Circe, tried her guests to move,
With looks of welcome and with words of love;
And such her potent charms, that men unwise
Were soon transform'd and fitted for the sties.

Her port in bottles stood, a well-stain'd row,
Drawn for the evening from the pipe below;
Three powerful spirits fill'd a parted case,
Some cordial-bottles stood in secret place;
Fair acid fruits in nets above were seen,
Her plate was splendid, and her glasses clean;
Basins and bowls were ready on the stand,
And measures clatter'd in her powerful hand.

Inferior houses now our notice claim,
But who shall deal them their appropriate fame?
Who shall the nice yet known distinction tell,
Between the peal complete and single bell?

Determine, ye, who on your shining nags
Wear oil-skin beavers and bear seal-skin bags;
Or ye, grave topers, who with coy delight
Snugly enjoy the sweetness of the night;
Ye travellers all, superior inns denied
By moderate purse, the low by decent pride;
Come and determine—will ye take your place
At the *full* orb, or *half* the lunar face?
With the Black Boy or Angel will you dine?
Will ye approve the Fountain or the Vine:
Horses the *white* or *black* will ye prefer?
The Silver-Swan, or swan opposed to her—
Rare bird! whose form the raven-plumage decks,
And graceful curve her three alluring necks?

All these a decent entertainment give,
And by their comforts comfortably live.

Shall I pass by the Boar?—there are who cry,
"Beware the Boar," and pass determined by:
Those dreadful tusks, those little peering eyes
And churning chaps, are tokens to the wise.
There dwells a kind old aunt, and there you see
Some kind young nieces in her company;
Poor village nieces, whom the tender dame
Invites to town, and gives their beauty fame;
The grateful sisters feel the important aid,
And the good aunt is flatter'd and repaid.

What though it may some cool observers strike
That such fair sisters should be so unlike;
That still another and another comes,
And at the matron's table smiles and blooms;
That all appear as if they meant to stay
Time undefined, nor name a parting day;
And yet, though all are valued, all are dear,
Causeless they go, and seldom more appear!

Yet let Suspicion hide her odious head,
And Scandal vengeance from a burgess dread:
A pious friend, who with the ancient dame
At sober cribbage takes an evening game;
His cup beside him, through their play he quaffs,
And oft renews, and innocently laughs;
Or, growing serious, to the text resorts,
And from the Sunday-sermon makes reports;
While all, with grateful glee, his wish attend,
A grave protector and a powerful friend:
But Slander says, who indistinctly sees,
Once he was caught with Silvia on his knees;—

A cautious burgess with a careful wife
To be so caught!—'t is false, upon my life.

Next are a lower kind, yet not so low
But they, among them, their distinctions know;
And when a thriving landlord aims so high
As to exchange the Chequer for the Pye,
Or from Duke William to the Dog repairs,
He takes a finer coat and fiercer airs.

Pleased with his power, the poor man loves to say
What favourite inn shall share his evening's pay,
Where he shall sit the social hour, and lose
His past day's labours and his next day's views.
Our seamen too have choice: one takes a trip
In the warm cabin of his favourite Ship;
And on the morrow in the humbler Boat
He rows, till fancy feels herself afloat;
Can he the sign—Three Jolly Sailors pass,
Who hears a fiddle and who sees a lass?
The Anchor too affords the seaman joys,
In small smoked room, all clamour, crowd, and noise;
Where a curved settle half surrounds the fire,
Where fifty voices purl and punch require;
They come for pleasure in their leisure hour,
And they enjoy it to their utmost power;
Standing they drink, they swearing smoke, while all
Call, or make ready for a second call:
There is no time for trifling—"Do ye see?
We drink and drub the French extempore."

See! round the room, on every beam and balk,
Are mingled scrolls of hieroglyphic chalk;
Yet nothing heeded—would one stroke suffice
To blot out all, here honour is too nice,—
"Let knavish landsmen think such dirty things,
We 're British tars, and British tars are kings."

But the Green-Man shall I pass by unsung,
Which mine own James upon his sign-post hung?
His sign, his image,—for he once was seen
A squire's attendant, clad in keeper's green;
Ere yet with wages more, and honour less,
He stood behind me in a graver dress.

James in an evil hour went forth to woo
Young Juliet Hart, and was her Romeo;
They 'd seen the play, and thought it vastly sweet
For two young lovers by the moon to meet;
The nymph was gentle, of her favours free,
Ev'n at a word—no Rosalind was she:
Nor, like that other Juliet, tried his truth
With—"Be thy purpose marriage, gentle youth?"
But him received, and heard his tender tale
When sang the lark, and when the nightingale:
So in few months the generous lass was seen
I' the way that all the Capulets had been.

Then first repentance seized the amorous man,
And—shame on love—he reason'd and he ran;
The thoughtful Romeo trembled for his purse,
And the sad sounds, "for better and for worse."

Yet could the lover not so far withdraw,
But he was haunted both by love and law:
Now law dismay'd him as he view'd its fangs,
Now pity seized him for his Juliet's pangs;
Then thoughts of justice and some dread of jail,
Where all would blame him and where none might bail;
These drew him back, till Juliet's hut appear'd
Where love had drawn him when he should have fear'd.

There sat the father in his wicker throne,
Uttering his curses in tremendous tone;
With foulest names his daughter he reviled,
And look'd a very Herod at the child:
Nor was she patient, but with equal scorn,
Bade him remember when his Joe was born:
Then rose the mother, eager to begin
Her plea for frailty, when the swain came in.

To him she turn'd and other theme began,
Show'd him his boy, and bade him be a man;
"An honest man, who, when he breaks the laws,
Will make a woman honest if there 's cause."
With lengthen'd speech she proved what came to pass
Was no reflection on a loving lass:
"If she your love as wife and mother claim,
What can it matter which was first the name?
But 't is most base, 't is perjury and theft,
When a lost girl is like a widow left;
The rogue who ruins"—here the father found
His spouse was treading on forbidden ground.

"That 's not the point," quoth he,—"I don' suppose
My good friend Fletcher to be one of those;
What 's done amiss he 'll mend in proper time—
I hate to hear of villany and crime:
'T was my misfortune, in the days of youth,
To find two lasses pleading for my truth;
The case was hard, I would with all my soul
Have wedded both, but law is our control;
So one I took, and when we gain'd a home,
Her friend agreed—what could she more?—to come;
And when she found that I 'd a widow'd bed,
Me she desired—what could I less?—to wed.
An easier case is yours: you 've not the smart
That two fond pleaders cause in one man's heart;
You 've not to wait from year to year distress'd,
Before your conscience can be laid at rest;
There smiles your bride, there sprawls your new-born son
—A ring, a license, and the thing is done."

"My loving James,"—the lass began her plea,
"I 'll make thy reason take a part with me:
Had I been froward, skittish, or unkind,
Or to thy person or thy passion blind;
Had I refused, when 't was thy part to pray,
Or put thee off with promise and delay;
Thou might'st in justice and in conscience fly,
Denying her who taught thee to deny:
But, James, with me thou hadst an easier task,
Bonds and conditions I forbore to ask;
I laid no traps for thee, no plots or plans,
Nor marriage named by license or by banns;
Nor would I now the parson's aid employ,
But for this cause,"—and up she held her boy.

Motives like these could heart of flesh resist?
James took the infant and in triumph kiss'd;
Then to his mother's arms the child restored,
Made his proud speech, and pledged his worthy word.

"Three times at church our banns shall publish'd be,
Thy health be drunk in bumpers three times three;
And thou shalt grace (bedeck'd in garments gay)
The christening-dinner on the wedding day."

James at my door then made his parting bow,
Took the Green-Man, and is a master now.

LETTER XII.

PLAYERS.

These are monarchs none respect,
Heroes, yet an humbled crew,
Nobles whom the crowd correct,
Wealthy men, whom duns pursue;
Beauties, shrinking from the view
Of the day's detecting eye;
Lovers, who with much ado
Long-forsaken damsels woo,
And heave the ill-feign'd sigh.

These are misers, craving means
Of existence through the day,
Famous scholars, conning scenes
Of a dull bewildering play;
Ragged beaux and misses grey
Whom the rabble praise and blame;
Proud and mean, and sad and gay,
Toiling after ease, are they,
Infamous,* and boasting fame.

Players arrive in the Borough—Welcomed by their former Friends—Are better fitted for Comic than Tragic Scenes: yet better approved in the latter by one Part of their Audience—Their general Character and Pleasantry—Particular Distresses and Labours—Their Fortitude and Patience—A private Rehearsal—The Vanity of the aged Actress—A Heroine from the Milliner's Shop—A deluded Tradesman—Of what Persons the Company is composed—Character and Adventures of Frederick Thompson.

Drawn by the annual call, we now behold
Our troop dramatic, heroes known of old,
And those, since last they march'd, inlisted and enroll'd:
Mounted on hacks or borne in wagons some,
The rest on foot (the humbler brethren) come.
Three favour'd places, an unequal time,
Join to support this company sublime:
Ours for the longer period—see how light
Yon parties move, their former friends in sight,
Whose claims are all allow'd, and friendship glads the night.
Now public rooms shall sound with words divine,
And private lodgings hear how heroes shine;
No talk of pay shall yet on pleasure steal,
But kindest welcome bless the friendly meal;
While o'er the social jug and decent cheer,
Shall be described the fortunes of the year.

Peruse these bills, and see what each can do,—
Behold! the prince, the slave, the monk, the Jew;
Change but the garment, and they 'll all engage
To take each part, and act in every age:
Cull'd from all houses, what a house are they!
Swept from all barns, our borough-critics say;
But with some portion of a critic's ire,
We all endure them; there are some admire:
They might have praise, confined to farce alone;
Full well they grin, they should not try to groan;
But then our servants' and our seamen's wives
Love all that rant and rapture as their lives;
He who 'Squire Richard's part could well sustain,
Finds as King Richard he must roar amain—
"My horse! my horse!"—Lo! now to their abodes,
Come lords and lovers, empresses and gods.
The master-mover of these scenes has made
No trifling gain in this adventurous trade;
Trade we may term it, for he duly buys
Arms out of use and undirected eyes;
These he instructs, and guides them as he can,
And vends each night the manufactured man:
Long as our custom lasts, they gladly stay,
Then strike their tents, like Tartars! and away!
The place grows bare where they too long remain,
But grass will rise ere they return again.

Children of Thespis, welcome! knights and queens!
Counts! barons! beauties! when before your scenes,
And mighty monarchs thund'ring from your throne;
Then step behind, and all your glory 's gone:
Of crown and palace, throne and guards bereft,
The pomp is vanish'd, and the care is left.
Yet strong and lively is the joy they feel
When the full house secures the plenteous meal;
Flatt'ring and flatter'd, each attempts to raise
A brother's merits for a brother's praise:
For never hero shows a prouder heart,
Than he who proudly acts a hero's part;
Nor without cause; the boards, we know, can yield
Place for fierce contest, like the tented field.

Graceful to tread the stage, to be in turn
The prince we honour, and the knave we spurn;
Bravely to bear the tumult of the crowd,
The hiss tremendous, and the censure loud:
These are their parts,—and he who these sustains
Deserves some praise and profit for his pains.
Heroes at least of gentler kind are they,
Against whose swords no weeping widows pray,
No blood their fury sheds, nor havoc marks their way.

Sad happy race! soon raised and soon depress'd,
Your days all pass'd in jeopardy and jest;
Poor without prudence, with afflictions vain,
Not warn'd by misery, not enrich'd by gain,
Whom justice pitying, chides from place to place,
A wandering, careless, wretched, merry race,
Who cheerful looks assume, and play the parts
Of happy rovers with repining hearts;
Then cast off care, and in the mimic pain
Of tragic wo, feel spirits light and vain,
Distress and hope—the mind's, the body's wear,
The man's affliction and the actor's tear:
Alternate times of fasting and excess
Are yours, ye smiling children of distress.

---

* Strolling players are thus held in a legal sense.

Slaves though ye be, your wandering freedom seems,
And with your varying views and restless schemes
Your griefs are transient, as your joys are dreams.

Yet keen those griefs—ah! what avail thy charms,
Fair Juliet! what that infant in thine arms;
What those heroic lines thy patience learns,
What all the aid thy present Romeo earns,
Whilst thou art crowded in that lumbering wain,
With all thy plaintive sisters to complain?

Nor is there lack of labour—To rehearse,
Day after day, poor scraps of prose and verse;
To bear each other's spirit, pride, and spite;
To hide in rant the heart-ache of the night;
To dress in gaudy patch-work, and to force
The mind to think on the appointed course;
This is laborious, and may be defined
The bootless labour of the thriftless mind.

There is a veteran dame; I see her stand
Intent and pensive with her book in hand;
Awhile her thoughts she forces on her part,
Then dwells on objects nearer to the heart;
Across the room she paces, gets her tone,
And fits her features for the Danish throne;
To-night a queen—I mark her motion slow,
I hear her speech, and Hamlet's mother know.

Methinks 't is pitiful to see her try
For strength of arms and energy of eye;
With vigour lost, and spirits worn away,
Her pomp and pride she labours to display;
And when awhile she 's tried her part to act,
To find her thoughts arrested by some fact;
When struggles more and more severe are seen
In the plain actress than the Danish queen,—
At length she feels her part, she finds delight,
And fancies all the plaudits of the night:
Old as she is, she smiles at every speech,
And thinks no youthful part beyond her reach;
But as the mist of vanity again
Is blown away, by press of present pain,
Sad and in doubt she to her purse applies
For cause of comfort, where no comfort lies;
Then to her task she sighing turns again,—
"Oh! Hamlet, thou hast cleft my heart in twain!"

And who that poor, consumptive, wither'd thing,
Who strains her slender throat and strives to sing?
Panting for breath, and forced her voice to drop,
And far unlike the inmate of the shop,
Where she, in youth and health, alert and gay,
Laugh'd off at night the labours of the day;
With novels, verses, fancy's fertile powers,
And sister-converse pass'd the evening-hours;
But Cynthia's soul was soft, her wishes strong,
Her judgment weak, and her conclusions wrong:
The morning-call and counter were her dread,
And her contempt the needle and the thread:
But when she read a gentle damsel's part,
Her wo, her wish!—she had them all by heart.

At length the hero of the boards drew nigh,
Who spake of love till sigh re-echo'd sigh;
He told in honey'd words his deathless flame,
And she his own by tender vows became;
Nor ring nor license needed souls so fond,
Alphonso's passion was his Cynthia's bond:
And thus the simple girl, to shame betray'd,
Sinks to the grave forsaken and dismay'd.

Sick without pity, sorrowing without hope,
See her! the grief and scandal of the troop;
A wretched martyr to a childish pride,
Her wo insulted, and her praise denied:
Her humble talents, though derided, used,
Her prospects lost, her confidence abused;
All that remains—for she not long can brave
Increase of evils—is an early grave.

Ye gentle Cynthias of the shop, take heed
What dreams ye cherish, and what books ye read.

A decent sum had Peter Nottage made,
By joining bricks—to him a thriving trade:
Of his employment master and his wife,
This humble tradesman led a lordly life;
The house of kings and heroes lack'd repairs,
And Peter, though reluctant, served the players:
Connected thus, he heard in way polite,—
"Come, Master Nottage, see us play to-night."
At first 't was folly, nonsense, idle stuff,
But seen for nothing it grew well enough;
And better now—now best, and every night,
In this fool's paradise he drank delight;
And as he felt the bliss, he wish'd to know
Whence all this rapture and these joys could flow;
For if the seeing could such pleasure bring,
What must the feeling?—feeling like a king?

In vain his wife, his uncle, and his friend,
Cried—"Peter! Peter! let such follies end;
'T is well enough these vagabonds to see,
But would you partner with a showman be?"
"Showman!" said Peter, "did not Quin and Clive,
And Roscius-Garrick, by the science thrive?
Showman!—'t is scandal; I 'm by genius led
To join a class who 've Shakspeare at their head."

Poor Peter thus by easy steps became
A dreaming candidate for scenic fame,
And, after years consumed, infirm and poor,
He sits and takes the tickets at the door.

Of various men these marching troops are made—
Pen-spurning clerks, and lads contemning trade;
Waiters and servants by confinement teased,
And youths of wealth by dissipation eased;
With feeling nymphs, who, such resource at hand,
Scorn to obey the rigour of command;
Some, who from higher views by vice are won,
And some of either sex by love undone;
The greater part lamenting as their fall,
What some an honour and advancement call.

There are who names in shame or fear assume,
And hence our Bevilles and our Savilles come;
It honours him, from tailor's board kick'd down,
As Mister Dormer to amuse the town;
Falling, he rises: but a kind there are
Who dwell on former prospects, and despair;
Justly but vainly they their fate deplore,
And mourn their fall who fell to rise no more.

Our merchant Thompson, with his sons around,
Most mind and talent in his Frederick found:

He was so lively, that his mother knew
If he were taught, that honour must ensue;
The father's views were in a different line,
But if at college he were sure to shine,
Then should he go—to prosper who could doubt?
When school-boy stigmas would be all wash'd out:
For there were marks upon his youthful face,
'Twixt vice and error—a neglected case—
These would submit to skill; a little time,
And none could trace the error or the crime;
Then let him go, and once at college, he
Might choose his station—what would Frederick be?
'T was soon determined—He could not descend
To pedant-laws and lectures without end;
And then the chapel—night and morn to pray,
Or mulct and threaten'd if he kept away;
No! not to be a bishop—so he swore,
And at his college he was seen no more.

His debts all paid, the father with a sigh,
Placed him in office—"Do, my Frederick, try;
Confine thyself a few short months, and then——"
He tried a fortnight, and threw down the pen.

Again demands were hush'd: "My son, you 're free,
But you 're unsettled; take your chance at sea:"
So in few days the midshipman equipp'd,
Received the mother's blessing and was shipp'd.

Hard was her fortune! soon compell'd to meet
The wretched stripling staggering through the street;
For, rash, impetuous, insolent and vain,
The captain sent him to his friends again:
About the borough roved th' unhappy boy,
And ate the bread of every chance-employ;
Of friends he borrow'd, and the parents yet
In secret fondness authorised the debt;
The younger sister, still a child, was taught
To give with feign'd affright the pittance sought;
For now the father cried—"It is too late
For trial more—I leave him to his fate,"—
Yet left him not; and with a kind of joy
The mother heard of her desponding boy:
At length he sicken'd, and he found, when sick,
All aid was ready, all attendance quick;
A fever seized him, and at once was lost
The thought of trespass, error, crime and cost;
Th' indulgent parents knelt beside the youth,
They heard his promise and believed his truth;
And when the danger lessen'd on their view,
They cast off doubt, and hope assurance grew;—
Nursed by his sisters, cherish'd by his sire,
Begg'd to be glad, encouraged to aspire,
His life, they said, would now all care repay,
And he might date his prospects from that day;
A son, a brother to his home received,
They hoped for all things, and in all believed.

And now will pardon, comfort, kindness, draw
The youth from vice? will honour, duty, law?
Alas! not all: the more the trials lent,
The less he seem'd to ponder and repent;
Headstrong, determined in his own career,
He thought reproof unjust and truth severe;
The soul's disease was to its crisis come,
He first abused and then abjured his home;
And when he chose a vagabond to be,
He made his shame his glory—"I 'll be free."

Friends, parents, relatives, hope, reason, love,
With anxious ardour for that empire strove;
In vain their strife, in vain the means applied,
They had no comfort, but that all were tried;
One strong vain trial made, the mind to move,
Was the last effort of parental love.

Ev'n then he watch'd his father from his home,
And to his mother would for pity come,
Where, as he made her tender terrors rise,
He talk'd of death, and threaten'd for supplies.
Against a youth so vicious and undone
All hearts were closed, and every door but one:
The players received him, they with open heart
Gave him his portion and assign'd his part;
And ere three days were added to his life,
He found a home, a duty, and a wife.

His present friends, though they were nothing nice,
Nor ask'd how vicious he, or what his vice,
Still they expected he should now attend
To the joint duty as an useful friend;
The leader too declared, with frown severe,
That none should pawn a robe that kings might wear;
And much it moved him, when he Hamlet play'd,
To see his Father's Ghost so drunken made:
Then too the temper, the unbending pride
Of this ally would no reproof abide:—
So leaving these, he march'd away and join'd
Another troop, and other goods purloin'd;
And other characters, both gay and sage,
Sober and sad, made stagger on the stage;
Then to rebuke, with arrogant disdain,
He gave abuse, and sought a home again.

Thus changing scenes, but with unchanging vice,
Engaged by many, but with no one twice:
Of this, a last and poor resource, bereft,
He to himself, unhappy guide! was left—
And who shall say where guided? to what seats
Of starving villany? of thieves and cheats?

In that sad time of many a dismal scene
Had he a witness (not inactive) been;
Had leagued with petty pilferers, and had crept
Where of each sex degraded numbers slept;
With such associates he was long allied,
Where his capacity for ill was tried,
And that once lost, the wretch was cast aside:
For now, though willing with the worst to act,
He wanted power for an important fact;
And while he felt as lawless spirits feel,
His hand was palsied, and he couldn't steal.

By these rejected, is there lot so strange,
So low! that he could suffer by the change?
Yes! the new station as a fall we judge,—
He now became the harlots' humble drudge,
Their drudge in common: they combined to save
Awhile from starving their submissive slave;
For now his spirit left him, and his pride,
His scorn, his rancour, and resentment died;
Few were his feelings—but the keenest these,
The rage of hunger, and the sigh for ease;

He who abused indulgence, now became
By want subservient and by misery tame;
A slave, he begg'd forbearance; bent with pain,
He shunn'd the blow,—"Ah! strike me not again."

Thus was he found: the master of a hoy
Saw the sad wretch, whom he had known a boy;
At first in doubt, but Frederick laid aside
All shame, and humbly for his aid applied:
He, tamed and smitten with the storms gone by,
Look'd for compassion through one living eye,
And stretch'd th' unpalsied hand: the seaman felt
His honest heart with gentle pity melt,
And his small boon with cheerful frankness dealt;
Then made inquiries of th' unhappy youth,
Who told, nor shame forbade him, all the truth.

"Young Frederick Thompson to a chandler's shop
By harlots order'd and afraid to stop!—
What! our good merchant's favourite to be seen
In state so loathsome and in dress so mean?"—

So thought the seaman as he bade adieu,
And, when in port, related all he knew.

But time was lost, inquiry came too late,
Those whom he served knew nothing of his fate;
No! they had seized on what the sailor gave,
Nor bore resistance from their abject slave;
The spoil obtain'd, they cast him from the door,
Robb'd, beaten, hungry, pain'd, diseased, and poor.

Then nature (pointing to the only spot
Which still had comfort for so dire a lot,)
Although so feeble, led him on the way,
And hope look'd forward to a happier day:
He thought, poor prodigal! a father yet
His woes would pity and his crimes forget;
Nor had he brother who with speech severe
Would check the pity or refrain the tear:
A lighter spirit in his bosom rose,
As near the road he sought an hour's repose.

And there he found it: he had left the town,
But buildings yet were scatter'd up and down;
To one of these, half-ruin'd and half-built,
Was traced this child of wretchedness and guilt;
There on the remnant of a beggar's vest,
Thrown by in scorn! the sufferer sought for rest;
There was this scene of vice and wo to close,
And there the wretched body found repose.

LETTER XIII.

THE ALMS-HOUSE AND TRUSTEES.

Do good by stealth, and blush to find it fame.

There are a sort of men whose visages
Do cream and mantle like a standing pool,
And do a wilful stillness entertain,
With purpose to be dress'd in an opinion;
As who would say, "I am Sir Oracle,
And when I ope my lips let no dog bark."
Merchant of Venice.

Sum felix; quis enim neget? felixque manebo;
Hoc quoque quis dubitet? Tutum me copia fecit.

The frugal Merchant—Rivalship in Modes of Frugality—Private Exceptions to the general Manners—Alms-House built—Its Description—Founder dies—Six Trustees—Sir Denys Brand, a Principal—His Eulogium in the Chronicles of the Day—Truth reckoned invidious on these Occasions—An Explanation of the Magnanimity and Wisdom of Sir Denys—His Kinds of Moderation and Humility—Laughton, his Successor, a planning, ambitious, wealthy Man—Advancement in Life his perpetual Object, and all Things made the Means of it—His Idea of Falsehood—His Resentment dangerous: how removed—Success produces Love of Flattery: his daily Gratification—His Merits and Acts of Kindness—His proper Choice of Alms-Men—In this Respect meritorious—His Predecessor not so cautious.

Leave now our streets, and in yon plain behold
Those pleasant seats for the reduced and old;
A merchant's gift, whose wife and children died,
When he to saving all his powers applied;
He wore his coat till bare was every thread,
And with the meanest fare his body fed.
He had a female cousin, who with care
Walk'd in his steps, and learn'd of him to spare;
With emulation and success they strove,
Improving still, still seeking to improve,
As if that useful knowledge they would gain—
How little food would human life sustain:
No pauper came their table's crums to crave;
Scraping they lived, but not a scrap they gave:
When beggars saw the frugal merchant pass,
It moved their pity, and they said, "Alas!
Hard is thy fate, my brother," and they felt
A beggar's pride as they that pity dealt:
The dogs, who learn of man to scorn the poor,
Bark'd him away from ev'ry decent door;
While they who saw him bare, but thought him rich
To show respect or scorn, they knew not which.

But while our merchant seem'd so base and mean
He had his wanderings, sometimes "not unseen;
To give in secret was a favourite act,
Yet more than once they took him in the fact:
To scenes of various wo he nightly went,
And serious sums in healing misery spent;
Oft has he cheer'd the wretched, at a rate
For which he daily might have dined on plate;
He has been seen—his hair all silver-white,
Shaking and shining—as he stole by night,
To feed unenvied on his still delight.
A two-fold taste he had; to give and spare,
Both were his duties, and had equal care;
It was his joy, to sit alone and fast,
Then send a widow and her boys repast:
Tears in his eyes would, spite of him, appear,
But he from other eyes has kept the tear:
All in a wint'ry night from far he came,
To soothe the sorrows of a suff'ring dame;
Whose husband robb'd him, and to whom he meant
A ling'ring, but reforming punishment:
Home then he walk'd, and found his anger rise,
When fire and rush-light met his troubled eyes
But these extinguish'd, and his prayer address'd
To Heaven in hope, he calmly sank to rest.

His seventieth year was pass'd, and then was seen
A building rising on the northern green;
There was no blinding all his neighbours' eyes,
Or surely no one would have seen it rise:
Twelve rooms contiguous stood, and six were near,
There men were placed, and sober matrons here;
There were behind small useful gardens made,
Benches before, and trees to give them shade;
In the first room were seen, above, below,
Some marks of taste, a few attempts at show;
The founder's picture and his arms were there,
(Not till he left us,) and an elbow'd chair;
There, 'mid these signs of his superior place,
Sat the mild ruler of this humble race.

Within the row are men who strove in vain,
Through years of trouble, wealth and ease to gain;
Less must they have than an appointed sum,
And freemen been, or hither must not come;
They should be decent and command respect
(Though needing fortune,) whom these doors protect,
And should for thirty dismal years have tried
For peace unfelt and competence denied.

Strange! that o'er men thus train'd in sorrow's school,
Power must be held, and they must live by rule;
Infirm, corrected by misfortunes, old,
Their habits settled and their passions cold;
Of health, wealth, power, and worldly cares, bereft,
Still must they not at liberty be left;
There must be one to rule them, to restrain
And guide the movements of his erring train.

If then control imperious, check severe,
Be needed where such reverend men appear;
To what would youth, without such checks, aspire,
Free the wild wish, uncurb'd the strong desire?
And where (in college or in camp) they found
The heart ungovern'd and the hand unbound?

His house endow'd, the generous man resign'd
All power to rule, nay power of choice declined;
He and the female saint survived to view
Their work complete, and bade the world adieu!

Six are the guardians of this happy seat,
And one presides when they on business meet;
As each expires, the five a brother choose;
Nor would Sir Denys Brand the charge refuse;
True, 'twas beneath him, "but to do men good
Was motive never by his heart withstood:"
He too is gone, and they again must strive
To find a man in whom his gifts survive.

Now, in the various records of the dead,
Thy worth, Sir Denys, shall be weigh'd and read;
There we the glory of thy house shall trace,
With each alliance of thy noble race.

"Yes! here we have him!—"Came in William's reign,
The Norman brand; the blood without a stain;
From the fierce Dane and ruder Saxon clear,
Pict, Irish, Scot, or Cambrian mountaineer;
But the pure Norman was the sacred spring,
And he, Sir Denys, was in heart a king:
Erect in person and so firm in soul,
Fortune he seem'd to govern and control;
Generous as he who gives his all away,
Prudent as one who toils for weekly pay;
In him all merits were decreed to meet,
Sincere, though cautious, frank, and yet discreet,
Just all his dealings, faithful every word,
His passions' master, and his temper's lord."

Yet more, kind dealers in decaying fame?
His magnanimity you next proclaim;
You give him learning, join'd with sound good sense,
And match his wealth with his benevolence;
What hides the multitude of sins, you add,
Yet seem to doubt if sins he ever had.

Poor honest truth! thou writest of living men,
And art a railer and detracter then;
They die, again to be described, and now
A foe to merit and mankind art thou!

Why banish truth? it injures not the dead,
It aids not them with flattery to be fed;
And when mankind such perfect pictures view,
They copy less the more they think them true.
Let us a mortal as he was behold,
And see the dross adhering to the gold;
When we the errors of the virtuous state,
Then erring men their worth may emulate.

View then this picture of a noble mind,
Let him be wise, magnanimous, and kind;
What was the wisdom? Was it not the frown
That keeps all question, all inquiry down?
His words were powerful and decisive all,
But his slow reasons came for no man's call.
"'T is thus," he cried, no doubt with kind intent,
To give results and spare all argument:—

"Let it be spared—all men at least agree
Sir Denys Brand had magnanimity:
His were no vulgar charities; none saw
Him like the merchant to the hut withdraw;
He left to meaner minds the simple deed,
By which the houseless rest, the hungry feed;
His was a public bounty vast and grand,
'T was not in him to work with viewless hand;
He raised the room that towers above the street,
A public room where grateful parties meet;
He first the life-boat plann'd: to him the place
Is deep in debt—'t was he revived the race;
To every public act this hearty friend
Would give with freedom or with frankness lend
His money built the jail, nor prisoner yet
Sits at his ease, but he must feel the debt;
To these let candour add his vast display,
Around his mansion all is grand and gay,
And this is bounty with the name of pay."

I grant the whole, nor from one deed retract,
But wish recorded too the private act;
All these were great, but still our hearts approve
Those simpler tokens of the christian love;
'T would give me joy some gracious deed to meet,
That has not call'd for glory through the street.
Who felt for many, could not always shun,
In some soft moment, to be kind to one;
And yet they tell us, when Sir Denys died,
That not a widow in the Borough sigh'd;
Great were his gifts, his mighty heart I own,
But why describe what all the world has known?

The rest is petty pride, the useless art
Of a vain mind to hide a swelling heart.
Small was his private room; men found him there
By a plain table, on a paltry chair;
A wretched floor-cloth, and some prints around,
The easy purchase of a single pound:
These humble trifles and that study small
Make a strong contrast with the servants' hall;
There barely comfort, here a proud excess,
The pompous seat of pamper'd idleness,
Where the sleek rogues with one consent declare,
They would not live upon his honour's fare;
He daily took but one half-hour to dine,
On one poor dish and some three sips of wine;
Then he'd abuse them for their sumptuous feasts,
And say, "My friends! you make yourselves like beasts;
One dish suffices any man to dine,
But you are greedy as a herd of swine;
Learn to be temperate."—Had they dared t' obey,
He would have praised and turn'd them all away.

Friends met Sir Denys riding in his ground,
And there the meekness of his spirit found:
For that grey coat, not new for many a year,
Hides all that would like decent dress appear:
An old brown pony 't was his will to ride,
Who shuffled onward, and from side to side;
A five-pound purchase, but so fat and sleek,
His very plenty made the creature weak.

"Sir Denys Brand! and on so poor a steed!"
"Poor! it may be—such things I never heed:"
And who that youth behind, of pleasant mien,
Equipp'd as one who wishes to be seen,
Upon a horse, twice victor for a plate,
A noble hunter, bought at dearest rate?—
Him the lad fearing, yet resolved to guide,
He curbs his spirit, while he strokes his pride.

"A handsome youth, Sir Denys; and a horse
Of finer figure never trod the course,—
Yours, without question?"—"Yes! I think a groom
Bought me the beast; I cannot say the sum:
I ride him not, it is a foolish pride
Men have in cattle—but my people ride;
The boy is—hark ye, sirrah! what's your name?
Ay, Jacob, yes! I recollect—the same;
As I bethink me now, a tenant's son—
I think a tenant—is your father one?"

There was an idle boy who ran about,
And found his master's humble spirit out;
He would at awful distance snatch a look,
Then run away and hide him in some nook;
"For oh!" quoth he, "I dare not fix my sight
On him, his grandeur puts me in a fright;
Oh! Mister Jacob, when you wait on him,
Do you not quake and tremble every limb?"

The steward soon had orders—"Summers, see
That Sam be clothed, and let him wait on me."

Sir Denys died, bequeathing all affairs
In trust to Laughton's long experienced cares;
Before a guardian, and Sir Denys dead,
All rule and power devolved upon his head:
Numbers are call'd to govern, but in fact
Only the powerful and assuming act.

Laughton, too wise to be a dupe to fame,
Cared not a whit of what descent he came,
Till he was rich; he then conceived the thought
To fish for pedigree, but never caught:
All his desire, when he was young and poor,
Was to advance; he never cared for more:
"Let me buy, sell, be factor, take a wife,
Take any road to get along in life."

Was he a miser then? a robber? foe
To those who trusted? a deceiver?—No!
He was ambitious; all his powers of mind
Were to one end controll'd, improved, combined;
Wit, learning, judgment, were, by his account,
Steps for the ladder he design'd to mount:
Such step was money: wealth was but his slave,
For power he gain'd it, and for power he gave;
Full well the Borough knows that he'd the art
Of bringing money to the surest mart;
Friends too were aids, they led to certain ends,
Increase of power and claim on other friends.
A favourite step was marriage: then he gain'd
Seat in our hall, and o'er his party reign'd;
Houses and lands he bought, and long'd to buy,
But never drew the springs of purchase dry,
And thus at last they answer'd every call,
The failing found him ready for their fall:
He walks along the street, the mart, the quay,
And looks and mutters, "This belongs to me."
His passions all partook the general bent;
Interest inform'd him when he should resent,
How long resist, and on what terms relent;
In points where he determined to succeed,
In vain might reason or compassion plead;
But gain'd his point, he was the best of men,
'T was loss of time to be vexatious then:
Hence he was mild to all men whom he led,
Of all who dared resist the scourge and dread.

Falsehood in him was not the useless lie
Of boasting pride or laughing vanity;
It was the gainful, the persuading art,
That made its way and won the doubting heart,
Which argued, soften'd, humbled, and prevail'd;
Nor was it tried till ev'ry truth had fail'd;
No sage on earth could more than he despise
Degrading, poor, unprofitable lies.

Though fond of gain, and grieved by wanton waste,
To social parties he had no distaste;
With one presiding purpose in his view,
He sometimes could descend to trifle too!
Yet, in these moments, he had still the art
To ope the looks and close the guarded heart;
And, like the public host, has sometimes made
A grand repast, for which the guests have paid.

At length, with power endued and wealthy grown,
Frailties and passions, long suppress'd, were shown;
Then to provoke him was a dangerous thing,
His pride would punish, and his temper sting;
His powerful hatred sought th' avenging hour,
And his proud vengeance struck with all his power,
Save when th' offender took a prudent way
The rising storm of fury to allay:
This might he do, and so in safety sleep
By largely casting to the angry deep;

Or, better yet (its swelling force t' assuage,)
By pouring oil of flattery on its rage.

And now, of all the heart approved, possess'd,
Fear'd, favour'd, follow'd, dreaded, and caress'd,
He gently yields to one mellifluous joy,
The only sweet that is not found to cloy,
Bland adulation! other pleasures pall
On the sick taste, and transient are they all;
But this one sweet has such enchanting power,
The more we take, the faster we devour;
Nauseous to those who must the dose apply,
And most disgusting to the standers-by;
Yet in all companies will Laughton feed,
Nor care how grossly men perform the deed.

As gapes the nursling, or, what comes more near,
Some Friendly-island chief, for hourly cheer;
When wives and slaves, attending round his seat,
Prepare by turns the masticated meat:
So for this master, husband, parent, friend,
His ready slaves their various efforts blend,
And, to their lord still eagerly inclined,
Pour the crude trash of a dependent mind.

But let the muse assign the man his due:
Worth he possess'd, nor were his virtues few;—
He sometimes help'd the injured in their cause;
His power and purse have back'd the failing laws;
He for religion has a due respect,
And all his serious notions are correct;
Although he pray'd and languish'd for a son,
He grew resign'd when Heaven denied him one;
He never to this quiet mansion sends
Subject unfit, in compliment to friends:
Not so Sir Denys, who would yet protest
He always chose the worthiest and the best:
Not men in trade by various loss brought down,
But those whose glory once amazed the town,
Who their last guinea in their pleasures spent,
Yet never fell so low as to repent;
To these his pity he could largely deal,
Wealth they had known, and therefore want could feel.

Three seats were vacant while Sir Denys reign'd,
And three such favourites their admission gain'd;
These let us view, still more to understand
The moral feelings of Sir Denys Brand.

LETTER XIV.

INHABITANTS OF THE ALMS-HOUSE.—BLANEY.

Sed quia cæcus inest vitiis amor, omne futurum
Despicitur; suadent brevem præsentia fructum,
Et ruit in vetitum damni secura libido.
CLAUDIAN, *in Eutrop.*

Nunquam parvo contenta peracta
Et quæsitorum terra pelagoque ciborum
Ambitiosa fames et lautæ gloria mensæ.

Et Luxus, populator Opum, tibi semper adhærens,
Infelix humili gressu comitatur Egestas.
CLAUDIAN, *in Rufinum.*

Behold what blessing wealth to life can lend!
POPE.

Blaney, a wealthy Heir, dissipated, and reduced to Poverty — His Fortune restored by Marriage: again consumed—His Manner of living in the West Indies—Recalled to a larger Inheritance —His more refined and expensive Luxuries—His Method of quieting Conscience—Death of his Wife—Again become poor—His Method of supporting Existence—His Ideas of Religion—His Habits and Connexions when old—Admitted into the Alms-House.

Observe that tall pale veteran! what a look
Of shame and guilt! who cannot read that book?
Misery and mirth are blended in his face,
Much innate vileness and some outward grace;
There wishes strong and stronger griefs are seen,
Looks ever changed, and never one serene:
Show not that manner, and these features all,
The serpent's cunning and the sinner's fall?

Hark to that laughter!—'t is the way he takes
To force applause for each vile jest he makes.
Such is yon man, by partial favour sent
To these calm seats to ponder and repent.

Blaney, a wealthy heir at twenty-one,
At twenty-five was ruin'd and undone:
These years with grievous crimes we need not load,
He found his ruin in the common road.—
Gamed without skill, without inquiry bought,
Lent without love, and borrow'd without thought.
But, gay and handsome, he had soon the dower
Of a kind wealthy widow in his power.
Then he aspired to loftier flights of vice,
To singing harlots of enormous price:
He took a jockey in his gig to buy
A horse, so valued, that a duke was shy.
To gain the plaudits of the knowing few,
Gamblers and grooms, what would not Blaney do?
His dearest friend, at that improving age,
Was Hounslow Dick, who drove the western stage.

Cruel he was not—If he left his wife,
He left her to her own pursuits in life;
Deaf to reports, to all expenses blind,
Profuse, not just, and careless, but not kind.

Yet thus assisted, ten long winters pass'd
In wasting guineas ere he saw his last;
Then he began to reason, and to feel
He could not dig, nor had he learn'd to steal.
And should he beg as long as he might live,
He justly fear'd that nobody would give:
But he could charge a pistol, and at will,
All that was mortal, by a bullet kill.
And he was taught, by those whom he would call
Man's surest guides—that he was mortal all.

While thus he thought, still waiting for the day,
When he should dare to blow his brains away,
A place for him a kind relation found,
Where England's monarch ruled, but far from English ground.
He gave employ that might for bread suffice,
Correct his habits and restrain his vice.

Here Blaney tried (what such man's miseries teach)
To find what pleasures were within his reach.
These he enjoy'd, though not in just the style
He once possess'd them in his native isle.

Congenial souls he found in every place,
Vice in all soils, and charms in every race:
His lady took the same amusing way,
And laugh'd at Time till he had turn'd them grey.
At length for England once again they steer'd,
By ancient views and new designs endear'd;
His kindred died, and Blaney now became
An heir to one who never heard his name.

What could he now?—The man had tried before
The joys of youth, and they were joys no more.
To vicious pleasure he was still inclined,
But vice must now be season'd and refined;
Then as a swine he would on pleasure seize,
Now common pleasures had no power to please.
Beauty alone has for the vulgar charms,
He wanted beauty trembling with alarms.
His was no more a youthful dream of joy,
The wretch desired to ruin and destroy.
He bought indulgence with a boundless price,
Most pleased when decency bow'd down to vice,
When a fair dame her husband's honour sold,
And a frail countess play'd for Blaney's gold.

"But did not conscience in her anger rise?"
Yes! and he learn'd her terrors to despise:
When stung by thought, to soothing books he fled,
And grew composed and harden'd as he read.
Tales of Voltaire, and essays gay and slight,
Pleased him and shone with their phosphoric light:
Which, though it rose from objects vile and base,
Where'er it came threw splendour on the place,
And was that light which the deluded youth,
And this grey sinner, deem'd the light of truth.

He different works for different cause admired,
Some fix'd his judgment, some his passions fired.
To cheer the mind and raise a dormant flame,
He had the books, decreed to lasting shame,
Which those who read are careful not to name.
These won to vicious act the yielding heart,
And then the cooler reasoners soothed the smart.

He heard of Blount, and Mandeville, and Chubb,
How they the doctors of their day would drub;
How Hume had dwelt on miracles so well,
That none would now believe a miracle.
And though he cared not works so grave to read,
He caught their faith, and sign'd the sinner's creed.

Thus was he pleased to join the laughing side,
Nor ceased the laughter when his lady died;
Yet was he kind and careful of her fame,
And on her tomb inscribed a virtuous name;
"A tender wife, respected, and so forth,"
The marble still bears witness to the worth.

He has some children, but he knows not where;
Something they cost, but neither love nor care:
A father's feelings he has never known,
His joys, his sorrows, have been all his own.

He now would build—and lofty seat he built,
And sought, in various ways, relief from guilt.
Restless, for ever anxious to obtain
Ease for the heart by ramblings of the brain,
He would have pictures, and of course a taste,
And found a thousand means his wealth to waste.
Newmarket steeds he bought at mighty cost;
They sometimes won, but Blaney always lost.

Quick came his ruin, came when he had still
For life a relish, and in pleasure skill.
By his own idle reckoning he supposed
His wealth would last him till his life was closed
But no! he found his final hoard was spent,
While he had years to suffer and repent.
Yet at the last, his noble mind to show,
And in his misery how he bore the blow,
He view'd his only guinea, then suppress'd,
For a short time, the tumults in his breast,
And, moved by pride, by habit and despair,
Gave it an opera-bird to hum an air.

Come ye! who live for pleasure, come, behold
A man of pleasure when he's poor and old;
When he looks back through life, and cannot find
A single action to relieve his mind;
When he looks forward, striving still to keep
A steady prospect of eternal sleep;
When not one friend is left, of all the train
Whom 'twas his pride and boast to entertain,—
Friends now employ'd from house to house to run
And say, "Alas! poor Blaney is undone!"—
Those whom he shook with ardour by the hand,
By whom he stood as long as he could stand,
Who seem'd to him from all deception clear,
And who, more strange! might think themselves sincere.

Lo! now the hero shuffling through the town
To hunt a dinner and to beg a crown.
To tell an idle tale, that boys may smile;
To bear a strumpet's billet-doux a mile;
To cull a wanton for a youth of wealth
(With reverend view to both his taste and health);
To be a useful, needy thing between
Fear and desire—the pander and the screen;
To flatter pictures, houses, horses, dress,
The wildest fashion or the worst excess;
To be the grey seducer, and entice
Unbearded folly into acts of vice:
And then, to level every fence which law
And virtue fix to keep the mind in awe,
He first inveigles youth to walk astray,
Next prompts and soothes them in their fatal way,
Then vindicates the deed, and makes the mind his prey.

Unhappy man! what pains he takes to state—
(Proof of his fear!) that all below is fate;
That all proceed in one appointed track,
Where none can stop, or take their journey back.
Then what is vice or virtue?—Yet he'll rail
At priests till memory and quotation fail;
He reads, to learn the various ills they've done,
And calls them vipers, every mother's son.

He is the harlot's aid, who wheedling tries
To move her friend for vanity's supplies.
To weak indulgence he allures the mind,
Loth to be duped, but willing to be kind.
And if successful—what the labour pays?
He gets the friend's contempt and Chloe's praise,
Who, in her triumph, condescends to say,
"What a good creature Blaney was to-day!"

Hear the poor demon when the young attend,
And willing ear to vile experience lend;

When he relates (with laughing, leering eye)
The tale licentious, mix'd with blasphemy.
No genuine gladness his narrations cause,
The frailest heart denies sincere applause:
And many a youth has turn'd him half aside,
And laugh'd aloud, the sign of shame to hide.

Blaney, no aid in his vile cause to lose,
Buys pictures, prints, and a licentious muse;
He borrows every help from every art,
To stir the passions and mislead the heart.
But from the subject let us soon escape,
Nor give this feature all its ugly shape:
Some to their crimes escape from satire owe,
Who shall describe what Blaney dares to show?

While thus the man, to vice and passion slave,
Was, with his follies, moving to the grave,
The ancient ruler of this mansion died,
And Blaney boldly for the seat applied.
Sir Denys Brand, then guardian, join'd his suit;
"'T is true," said he, "the fellow's quite a brute—
"A very beast; but yet, with all his sin,
"He has a manner—let the devil in."

They half complied, they gave the wish'd retreat,
But raised a worthier to the vacant seat.

Thus forced on ways unlike each former way,
Thus led to prayer without a heart to pray,
He quits the gay and rich, the young and free,
Among the badge-men with a badge to be:
He sees an humble tradesman raised to rule
The grey-beard pupils of this moral school;
Where he himself, an old licentious boy,
Will nothing learn, and nothing can enjoy;
In temp'rate measures he must eat and drink,
And, pain of pains! must live alone and think.

In vain, by fortune's smiles, thrice affluent made,
Still has he debts of ancient date unpaid;
Thrice into penury by error thrown,
Not one right maxim has he made his own;
The old men shun him,—some his vices hate,
And all abhor his principles and prate;
Nor love nor care for him will mortal show,
Save a frail sister in the female row.

LETTER XV.

INHABITANTS OF THE ALMS-HOUSE.—CLELIA.

She early found herself mistress of herself. All she did was right: all she said was admired. Early, very early, did she dismiss blushes from her cheek: she could not blush, because she could not doubt; and silence, whatever was the subject, was as much a stranger to her as diffidence.

RICHARDSON.

Quo fugit Venus? heu! Quove color? decens
Quo motus? Quid habes illius, illius,
Quæ spirabat amores,
Quæ me surpuerat mihi?

HORAT. lib. iv. od. 13.

Her lively and pleasant Manners—Her Reading and Decision—Her intercourse with different Classes of Society—Her Kind of Character—The favoured Lover—Her Management of him: his of her—After one Period, Clelia with an Attorney: her Manner and Situation there—Another such Period, when her Fortune still declines—Mistress of an Inn—A Widow—Another such Interval: she becomes poor and infirm, but still vain and frivolous—The fallen Vanity—Admitted into the House: meets Blaney.

We had a sprightly nymph—in every town
Are some such sprites, who wander up and down;
She had her useful arts, and could contrive,
In time's despite, to stay at twenty-five;—
"Here will I rest; move on, thou lying year,
This is mine age, and I will rest me here."

Arch was her look, and she had pleasant ways
Your good opinion of her heart to raise;
Her speech was lively, and with ease express'd,
And well she judged the tempers she address'd:
If some soft stripling had her keenness felt,
She knew the way to make his anger melt;
Wit was allow'd her, though but few could bring
Direct example of a witty thing;
'T was that gay, pleasant, smart, engaging speech,
Her beaux admired, and just within their reach;
Not indiscreet perhaps, but yet more free
Than prudish nymphs allow their wit to be.

Novels and plays, with poems, old and new,
Were all the books our nymph attended to;
Yet from the press no treatise issued forth,
But she would speak precisely of its worth.

She with the London stage familiar grew
And every actor's name and merit knew;
She told how this or that their part mistook,
And of the rival Romeos gave the look;
Of either house 't was hers the strength to see,
Then judge with candour—"Drury-Lane for me."

What made this knowledge, what this skill complete?
A fortnight's visit in Whitechapel-street.

Her place in life was rich and poor between,
With those a favourite, and with these a queen;
She could her parts assume, and condescend
To friends more humble while an humble friend;
And thus a welcome, lively guest could pass,
Threading her pleasant way from class to class.

"Her reputation?"—That was like her wit,
And seem'd her manner and her state to fit;
Something there was, what, none presumed to say,
Clouds lightly passing on a smiling day,—
Whispers and hints which went from ear to ear,
And mix'd reports no judge on earth could clear.

But of each sex a friendly number press'd
To joyous banquets this alluring guest:
There, if indulging mirth, and freed from awe,
If pleasing all, and pleased with all she saw,
Her speech were free, and such as freely dwelt
On the same feelings all around her felt;
Or if some fond presuming favourite tried
To come so near as once to be denied;

Yet not with brow so stern or speech so nice,
But that he ventured on denial twice:—
If these have been, and so has scandal taught,
Yet malice never found the proof she sought.

But then came one, the Lovelace of his day,
Rich, proud, and crafty, handsome, brave, and gay;
Yet loved he not those labour'd plans and arts,
But left the business to the ladies' hearts,
And when he found them in a proper train,
He thought all else superfluous and vain:
But in that training he was deeply taught,
And rarely fail'd of gaining all he sought;
He knew how far directly on to go,
How to recede and dally to and fro;
How to make all the passions his allies,
And, when he saw them in contention rise,
To watch the wrought-up heart, and conquer by surprise.

Our heroine fear'd him not; it was her part,
To make sure conquest of such gentle heart—
Of one so mild and humble; for she saw
In Henry's eye a love chastised by awe.
Her thoughts of virtue were not all sublime,
Nor virtuous all her thoughts; 't was now her time
To bait each hook, in every way to please,
And the rich prize with dext'rous hand to seize.
She had no virgin-terrors; she could stray
In all love's maze, nor fear to lose her way;
Nay, could go near the precipice, nor dread
A failing caution or a giddy head;
She'd fix her eyes upon the roaring flood,
And dance upon the brink where danger stood.

'T was nature all, she judged, in one so young,
To drop the eye and falter in the tongue;
To be about to take, and then command
His daring wish, and only view the hand:
Yes! all was nature; it became a maid
Of gentle soul t' encourage love afraid;—
He, so unlike the confident and bold,
Would fly in mute despair to find her cold:
The young and tender germ requires the sun
To make it spread: it must be smiled upon.
Thus the kind virgin gentle means devised,
To gain a heart so fond, a hand so prized;
More gentle still she grew, to change her way,
Would cause confusion, danger, and delay:
Thus (an increase of gentleness her mode,)
She took a plain, unvaried, certain road,
And every hour believed success was near,
Till there was nothing left to hope or fear.

It must be own'd that in this strife of hearts,
Man has advantage—has superior arts:
The lover's aim is to the nymph unknown,
Nor is she always certain of her own;
Or has her fears, nor these can so disguise,
But he who searches, reads them in her eyes,
In the avenging frown, in the regretting sighs:
These are his signals, and he learns to steer
The straighter course whenever they appear.

"Pass we ten years, and what was Clelia's fate?"
At an attorney's board alert she sate,
Not legal mistress: he with other men
Once sought her hand, but other views were then;
And when he knew he might the bliss command,
He other blessing sought, without the hand;
For still he felt alive the lambent flame,
And offer'd her a home,—and home she came.

There, though her higher friendships lived no more,
She loved to speak of what she shared before—
"Of the dear Lucy, heiress of the hall,—
Of good Sir Peter,—of their annual ball,
And the fair countess!—Oh! she loved them all!"
The humbler clients of her friend would stare,
The knowing smile,—but neither caused her care
She brought her spirits to her humble state,
And soothed with idle dreams her frowning fate.

"Ten summers pass'd, and how was Clelia then?"
Alas! she suffer'd in this trying ten;
The pair had parted; who to him attend,
Must judge the nymph unfaithful to her friend;
But who on her would equal faith bestow,
Would think him rash,—and surely she must know.

Then as a matron Clelia taught a school,
But nature gave no talents fit for rule:
Yet now, though marks of wasting years were seen,
Some touch of sorrow, some attack of spleen;
Still there was life, a spirit quick and gay,
And lively speech and elegant array.

The Griffin's landlord these allured so far,
He made her mistress of his heart and bar;
He had no idle retrospective whim,
Till she was his, her deeds concern'd not him.
So far was well,—but Clelia thought not fit
(In all the Griffin needed) to submit:
Gaily to dress and in the bar preside,
Soothed the poor spirit of degraded pride;
But cooking, waiting, welcoming a crew
Of noisy guests, were arts she never knew:
Hence daily wars, with temporary truce,
His vulgar insult and her keen abuse;
And as their spirits wasted in the strife,
Both took the Griffin's ready aid of life;
But she with greater prudence—Harry tried
More powerful aid, and in the trial died;
Yet drew down vengeance: in no distant time,
Th' insolvent Griffin struck his wings sublime;—
Forth from her palace walk'd th' ejected queen,
And show'd to frowning fate a look serene;
Gay spite of time, though poor, yet well attired,
Kind without love, and vain if not admired.

Another term is past; ten other years
In various trials, troubles, views, and fears:
Of these some pass'd in small attempts at trade;
Houses she kept for widowers lately made;
For now she said, "They'll miss th' endearin friend,
And I'll be there the soften'd heart to bend:"
And true, a part was done as Clelia plann'd—
The heart was soften'd but she miss'd the hand.
She wrote a novel, and Sir Denys said,
The dedication was the best he read;
But Edgeworths, Smiths, and Radcliffes so engross'd
The public ear, that all her pains were lost.

To keep a toy-shop was attempt the last,
There too she fail'd, and schemes and hopes were past.

Now friendless, sick and old, and wanting bread,
The first-born tears of fallen pride were shed—
True, bitter tears; and yet that wounded pride,
Among the poor, for poor distinctions sigh'd.
Though now her tales were to her audience fit;
Though loud her tones and vulgar grown her wit;
Though now her dress—(but let me not explain
The piteous patch-work of the needy-vain,
The flirtish form to coarse materials lent,
And one poor robe through fifty fashions sent;)
Though all within was sad, without was mean,—
Still 't was her wish, her comfort to be seen:
She would to plays on lowest terms resort,
Where once her box was to the beaux a court;
And, strange delight! to that same house where she
Join'd in the dance, all gaiety and glee,
Now with the menials crowding to the wall,
She 'd see, not share, the pleasures of the ball,
And with degraded vanity unfold,
How she too triumph'd in the years of old.
To her poor friends 't is now her pride to tell
On what a height she stood before she fell;
At church she points to one tall seat, and "There
We sat," she cries, "when my papa was mayor."
Not quite correct in what she now relates,
She alters persons, and she forges dates;
And finding memory's weaker help decay'd,
She boldly calls invention to her aid.

Touch'd by the pity he had felt before,
For her Sir Denys oped the alms-house door:
"With all her faults," he said, "the woman knew
How to distinguish—had a manner too;
And, as they say, she is allied to some
In decent station—let the creature come."

Here she and Blaney meet, and take their view
Of all the pleasures they would still pursue:
Hour after hour they sit, and nothing hide
Of vices past; their follies are their pride;
What to the sober and the cool are crimes,
They boast—exulting in those happy times;
The darkest deeds no indignation raise,
The purest virtue never wins their praise;
But still they on their ancient joys dilate,
Still with regret departed glories state,
And mourn their grievous fall, and curse their rigorous fate.

LETTER XVI.

INHABITANTS OF THE ALMS-HOUSE—BENBOW.

Thou art the Knight of the Burning Lamp—if thou wast any way given to virtue, I would swear by thy face; my oath should be by this fire. Oh! thou 'rt a perpetual triumph, thou hast saved me a thousand marks in links and torches, walking in a night betwixt tavern and tavern. SHAKSPEARE.

Ebrietas tibi fida comes, tibi Luxus, et atris
Circa te semper volitans Infamia pennis.
SILIUS ITALICUS.

Benbow, an improper Companion for the Badgemen of the Alms-house—He resembles Bardolph—Left in Trade by his Father—Contracts useless Friendships—His Friends drink with him, and employ others—Called worthy and honest! Why—Effect of Wine on the Mind of Man—Benbow's common Subject—the Praise of departed Friends and Patrons—'Squire Asgill, at the Grange: his Manners, Servants, Friends—True to his Church: ought therefore to be spared—His Son's different Conduct—Vexation of the Father's Spirit if admitted to see the Alteration—Captain Dowling, a boon Companion, ready to drink at all times, and with any Company: famous in his Club-room—His easy Departure—Dolley Murrey, a maiden advanced in Years: abides by Ratafia and Cards—Her free Manners Her Skill in the Game—Her Preparation and Death—Benbow, how interrupted: his Submission.

SEE! yonder badgeman, with that glowing face,
A meteor shining in this sober place;
Vast sums were paid, and many years were past,
Ere gems so rich around their radiance cast!
Such was the fiery front that Bardolph wore,
Guiding his master to the tavern-door;
There first that meteor rose, and there alone,
In its due place, the rich effulgence shone:
But this strange fire the seat of peace invades,
And shines portentous in these solemn shades.

Benbow, a boon companion, long approved
By jovial sets, and (as he thought) beloved,
Was judged as one to joy and friendship prone,
And deem'd injurious to himself alone.
Gen'rous and free, he paid but small regard
To trade, and fail'd; and some declared "'t was hard:"
These were his friends—his foes conceived the case
Of common kind; he sought and found disgrace:
The reasoning few, who neither scorn'd nor loved,
His feelings pitied and his faults reproved.

Benbow, the father, left possessions fair,
A worthy name and business to his heir;
Benbow, the son, those fair possessions sold,
And lost his credit, while he spent the gold.
He was a jovial trader: men enjoy'd
The night with him; his day was unemploy'd;
So when his credit and his cash were spent,
Here, by mistaken pity, he was sent;
Of late he came, with passions unsubdued,
And shared and cursed the hated solitude,
Where gloomy thoughts arise, where grievous cares intrude.

Known but in drink—he found an easy friend,
Well pleased his worth and honour to commend;
And thus inform'd, the guardian of the trust
Heard the applause and said the claim was just;
A worthy soul! unfitted for the strife,
Care and contention of a busy life;—
Worthy, and why?—that o'er the midnight bowl
He made his friend the partner of his soul,
And any man his friend:—then thus in glee,
"I speak my mind, I love the truth," quoth he,

Till 't was his fate that useful truth to find,
'T is sometimes prudent not to speak the mind.

With wine inflated, man is all upblown,
And feels a power which he believes his own;
With fancy soaring to the skies, he thinks
His all the virtues all the while he drinks;
But when the gas from the balloon is gone,
When sober thoughts and serious cares come on,
Where then the worth that in himself he found?—
Vanish'd—and he sank grov'ling on the ground.

Still some conceit will Benbow's mind inflate,
Poor as he is,—'t is pleasant to relate
The joys he once possess'd—it soothes his present state.

Seated with some grey beadsman, he regrets
His former feasting, though it swell'd his debts;
Topers once famed, his friends in earlier days,
Well he describes, and thinks description praise;
Each hero's worth with much delight he paints;
Martyrs they were, and he would make them saints.

"Alas! alas!" Old England now may say,
"My glory withers; it has had its day:
We 're fallen on evil times; men read and think;
Our bold forefathers loved to fight and drink.

"Then lived the good 'Squire Asgill — what a change
Has death and fashion shown us at the Grange!
He bravely thought it best became his rank,
That all his tenants and his tradesmen drank;
He was delighted from his favourite room
To see them 'cross the park go daily home,
Praising aloud the liquor and the host,
And striving who should venerate him most.

"No pride had he, and there was difference small
Between the master's and the servants' hall;
And here or there the guests were welcome all.
Of Heaven's free gifts he took no special care,
He never quarrell'd for a simple hare;
But sought, by giving sport, a sportsman's name,
Himself a poacher though at other game:
He never planted nor inclosed—his trees
Grew like himself, untroubled and at ease.
Bounds of all kinds he hated, and had felt
Choked and imprison'd in a modern belt,
Which some rare genius now has twined about
The good old house, to keep old neighbours out:
Along his valleys, in the evening hours,
The borough-damsels stray'd to gather flowers,
Or by the brakes and brushwood of the park,
To take their pleasant rambles in the dark.

"Some prudes, of rigid kind, forbore to call
On the kind females—favourites at the hall;
But better natures saw, with much delight,
The different orders of mankind unite;
'T was schooling pride to see the footman wait,
Smile on his sister and receive her plate.

"His worship ever was a churchman true,
He held in scorn the methodistic crew;
May God defend the Church and save the King,
He 'd pray devoutly and divinely sing.
Admit that he the holy day would spend
As priests approve not, still he was a friend:
Much then I blame the preacher, as too nice,
To call such trifles by the name of vice;
Hinting, though gently and with cautious speech,
Of good example—'t is their trade to preach:
But still 't was pity, when the worthy 'squire
Stuck to the church, what more could they require?
'T was almost joining that fanatic crew,
To throw such morals at his honour's pew;
A weaker man, had he been so reviled,
Had left the place—he only swore and smiled.

"But think, ye rectors and ye curates, think,
Who are your friends, and at their frailties wink,
Conceive not—mounted on your Sunday-throne,
Your fire-brands fall upon your foes alone;
They strike your patrons—and, should all withdraw,
In whom your wisdoms may discern a flaw,
You would the flower of all your audienee lose,
And spend your crackers on their empty pews.

"The father dead, the son has found a wife,
And lives a formal, proud, unsocial life;—
The lands are now enclosed; the tenants all,
Save at a rent-day, never see the hall:
No lass is suffer'd o'er the walks to come,
And if there's love, they have it all at home.

"Oh! could the ghost of our good 'squire arise,
And see such change; would it believe its eyes?
Would it not glide about from place to place,
And mourn the manners of a feebler race?
At that long table, where the servants found
Mirth and abundance while the year went round;
Where a huge pollard on the winter-fire,
At a huge distance made them all retire;
Where not a measure in the room was kept,
And but one rule—they tippled till they slept,—
There would it see a pale old hag preside,
A thing made up of stinginess and pride;
Who carves the meat, as if the flesh could feel,
Careless whose flesh must miss the plenteous meal.
Here would the ghost a small coal-fire behold,
Not fit to keep one body from the cold;
Then would it flit to higher rooms, and stay
To view a dull, dress'd company at play;
All the old comfort, all the genial fare
For ever gone! how sternly would it stare!
And though it might not to their view appear,
'T would cause among them lassitude and fear:
Then wait to see—where he delight has seen—
The dire effect of fretfulness and spleen.

"Such were the worthies of these better days;
We had their blessings—they shall have our praise

"Of Captain Dowling would you hear me speak
I 'd sit and sing his praises for a week:
He was a man, and manlike all his joy,—
I'm led to question was he ever boy?
Beef was his breakfast; if from sea and salt,
It relish'd better with his wine of malt;
Then, till he dined, if walking in or out,
Whether the gravel teased him or the gout,
Though short in wind and flannel'd every limb,
He drank with all who had concerns with him:
Whatever trader, agent, merchant, came,
They found him ready, every hour the same,

Whatever liquors might between them pass,
He took them all, and never balk'd his glass:
Nay, with the seamen working in the ship,
At their request he'd share the grog and flip:
But in the club-room was his chief delight,
And punch the favourite liquor of the night;
Man after man they from the trial shrank,
And Dowling ever was the last who drank:
Arrived at home, he, ere he sought his bed,
With pipe and brandy would compose his head;
Then half an hour was o'er the news beguiled,
When he retired as harmless as a child.
Set but aside the gravel and the gout,
And breathing short—his sand ran fairly out.

"At fifty-five we lost him—after that
Life grows insipid and its pleasures flat;
He had indulged in all that man can have,
He did not drop a dotard to his grave;
Still to the last, his feet upon the chair,
With rattling lungs now gone beyond repair;
When on each feature death had fix'd his stamp,
And not a doctor could the body vamp;
Still at the last, to his beloved bowl
He clung, and cheer'd the sadness of his soul;
For though a man may not have much to fear,
Yet death looks ugly, when the view is near:
—'I go,' he said, 'but still my friends shall say,
'T was as a man—I did not sneak away;
An honest life with worthy souls I've spent,—
Come, fill my glass;'—he took it and he went.

"Poor Dolly Murrey!—I might live to see
My hundredth year, but no such lass as she.
Easy by nature, in her humour gay,
She chose her comforts, ratafia and play:
She loved the social game, the decent glass;
And was a jovial, friendly, laughing lass;
We sat not then at Whist demure and still,
But pass'd the pleasant hours at gay quadrille:
Lame in her side, we placed her in her seat,
Her hands were free, she cared not for her feet;
As the game ended, came the glass around
(So was the loser cheer'd, the winner crown'd.)
Mistress of secrets, both the young and old
In her confided—not a tale she told;
Love never made impression on her mind,
She held him weak, and all his captives blind;
She suffer'd no man her free soul to vex,
Free from the weakness of her gentle sex;
One with whom ours unmoved conversing sate,
In cool discussion or in free debate.

"Once in her chair we'd placed the good old lass,
Where first she took her preparation-glass:
By lucky thought she'd been that day at prayers,
And long before had fix'd her small affairs;
So all was easy—on her cards she cast
A smiling look; I saw the thought that pass'd;
'A king,' she call'd—though conscious of her skill,
'Do more,' I answer'd—'More,' she said, 'I will;'
And more she did—cards answer'd to her call,
She saw the mighty to her mightier fall:
'A vole! a vole!' she cried, ''tis fairly won,
'My game is ended and my work is done;'—
This said, she gently, with a single sigh,
Died as one taught and practised how to die.

"Such were the dead-departed; I survive,
To breathe in pain among the dead-alive."
The bell then call'd these ancient men to pray,
"Again?" said Benbow,—"tolls it every day?
Where is the life I led?"—He sigh'd, and walk'd
his way.

LETTER XVII.

THE HOSPITAL AND GOVERNORS.

Blessed be the man who provideth for the sick and needy: the Lord shall deliver him in time of trouble.

Quas dederis, solas semper haberis opes.
MARTIAL.

Nil negat, et sese vel non poscentibus offert.
CLAUDIAN.

Decipias alios verbis voltuque benigno;
Nam mihi jam notus dissimulator eris.
MARTIAL.

Christian Charity anxious to provide for future as well as present Miseries—Hence the Hospital for the Diseased—Description of a recovered Patient—The Building: how erected—The Patrons and Governors—Eusebius—The more active Manager of Business a moral and correct Contributor—One of different Description—Good, the Result, however intermixed with Imperfection.

An ardent spirit dwells with christian love,
The eagle's vigour in the pitying dove;
'T is not enough that we with sorrow sigh,
That we the wants of pleading man supply;
That we in sympathy with sufferers feel,
Nor hear a grief without a wish to heal;
Not these suffice—to sickness, pain, and wo,
The christian spirit loves with aid to go;
Will not be sought, waits not for want to plead,
But seeks the duty—nay, prevents the need;
Her utmost aid to every ill applies,
And plans relief for coming miseries.

Hence yonder building rose: on either side
Far stretch'd the wards, all airy, warm, and wide,
And every ward has beds by comfort spread,
And smooth'd for him who suffers on the bed:
There have all kindness, most relief,—for some
Is cure complete,—it is the sufferer's home:
Fevers and chronic ills, corroding pains,
Each accidental mischief man sustains;
Fractures and wounds, and wither'd limbs and lame,
With all that, slow or sudden, vex our frame,
Have here attendance—here the sufferers lie,
(Where love and science every aid apply),
And heal'd with rapture live, or soothed by com-
fort die.

See! one relieved from anguish, and to-day
Allow'd to walk and look an hour away;
Two months confined by fever, frenzy, pain,
He comes abroad and is himself again:
'T was in the spring, when carried to the place,
The snow fell down and melted in his face.

'T is summer now; all objects gay and new,
Smiling alike the viewer and the view:
He stops as one unwilling to advance,
Without another and another glance.
With what a pure and simple joy he sees
Those sheep and cattle browzing at their ease!
Easy himself, there 's nothing breathes or moves
But he would cherish—all that lives he loves;
Observing every ward as round he goes,
He thinks what pain, what danger they enclose;
Warm in his wish for all who suffer there,
At every view he meditates a prayer:
No evil counsels in his breast abide,
There joy, and love, and gratitude reside.

The wish that Roman necks in one were found,
That he who form'd the wish might deal the wound,
This man had never heard; but of the kind,
Is that desire which rises in his mind;
He 'd have all English hands (for further he
Cannot conceive extends our charity),
All but his own, in one right-hand to grow,
And then what hearty shake would he bestow!

"How rose the building?"—Piety first laid
A strong foundation, but she wanted aid;
To Wealth unwieldy was her prayer address'd,
Who largely gave, and she the donor bless'd:
Unwieldy Wealth then to his couch withdrew,
And took the sweetest sleep he ever knew.

Then busy Vanity sustain'd her part,
"And much," she said "it moved her tender heart;
To her all kinds of man's distress were known,
And all her heart adopted as its own."

Then Science came—his talents he display'd,
And Charity with joy the dome survey'd;
Skill, Wealth, and Vanity, obtain the fame,
And Piety, the joy that makes no claim.

Patrons there are, and governors, from whom
The greater aid and guiding orders come;
Who voluntary cares and labours take,
The sufferers' servants for the service' sake;
Of these a part I give you—but a part,—
Some hearts are hidden, some have not a heart.

First let me praise—for so I best shall paint
That pious moralist, that reasoning saint!
Can I of worth like thine, Eusebius, speak?
The man is willing, but the muse is weak;
'T is thine to wait on wo! to soothe! to heal!
With learning social, and polite with zeal:
In thy pure breast although the passions dwell,
They 're train'd by virtue and no more rebel;
But have so long been active on her side,
That passion now might be itself the guide.

Law, conscience, honour, all obey'd; all give
Th' approving voice, and make it bliss to live;
While faith, when life can nothing more supply,
Shall strengthen hope, and make it bliss to die.

He preaches, speaks, and writes with manly sense,
No weak neglect, no labour'd eloquence;
Goodness and wisdom are in all his ways,
The rude revere him and the wicked praise.

Upon humility his virtues grow,
And tower so high because so fix'd below;
As wider spreads the oak his boughs around,
When deeper with his roots he digs the solid ground.

By him, from ward to ward, is every aid
The sufferer needs, with every care convey'd:
Like the good tree he brings his treasure forth,
And, like the tree, unconscious of his worth:
Meek as the poorest Publican is he,
And strict as lives the straitest Pharisee;
Of both, in him unite the better part,
The blameless conduct and the humble heart.

Yet he escapes not; he, with some, is wise
In carnal things, and loves to moralize:
Others can doubt, if all that christian care
Has not its price—there 's something he may share:
But this and ill severer he sustains,
As gold the fire, and as unhurt remains;
When most reviled, although he feels the smart,
It wakes to nobler deeds the wounded heart,
As the rich olive, beaten for its fruit,
Puts forth at every bruise a bearing shoot.

A second friend we have, whose care and zeal
But few can equal—few indeed can feel;
He lived a life obscure, and profits made
In the coarse habits of a vulgar trade.
His brother, master of a hoy, he loved
So well, that he the calling disapproved:
"Alas! poor Tom!" the landman oft would sigh,
When the gale freshen'd and the waves ran high;
And when they parted, with a tear he 'd say,
"No more adventure!—here in safety stay."
Nor did he feign; with more than half he had,
He would have kept the seaman, and been glad.

Alas! how few resist, when strongly tried—
A rich relation's nearer kinsman died;
He sicken'd, and to him the landman went,
And all his hours with cousin Ephraim spent.
This, Thomas heard, and cared not: "I," quoth he,
"Have one in port upon the watch for me."
So Ephraim died, and when the will was shown,
Isaac, the landman, had the whole his own:
Who to his brother sent a moderate purse,
Which he return'd, in anger, with his curse;
Then went to sea, and made his grog so strong,
He died before he could forgive the wrong.

The rich man built a house, both large and high,
He enter'd in and set him down to sigh;
He planted ample woods and gardens fair,
And walk'd with anguish and compunction there:
The rich man's pines, to every friend a treat,
He saw with pain, and he refused to eat;
His daintiest food, his richest wines were all
Turn'd by remorse to vinegar and gall:
The softest down, by living body press'd,
The rich man bought, and tried to take his rest;
But care had thorns upon his pillow spread,
And scatter'd sand and nettles in his bed:
Nervous he grew,—would often sigh and groan,
He talk'd but little, and he walk'd alone;
Till by his priest convinced, that from one deed
Of genuine love would joy and health proceed;
He from that time with care and zeal began
To seek and soothe the grievous ills of man,
And as his hands their aid to grief apply,
He learns to smile and he forgets to sigh.

Now he can drink his wine and taste his food,
And feel the blessings, Heav'n has dealt, are good;
And, since the suffering seek the rich man's door,
He sleeps as soundly as when young and poor.

Here much he gives—is urgent more to gain;
He begs—rich beggars seldom sue in vain:
Preachers most famed he moves, the crowd to move,
And never wearies in the work of love:
He rules all business, settles all affairs,
He makes collections, he directs repairs;
And if he wrong'd one brother,—Heav'n forgive
The man by whom so many brethren live!

Then, 'mid our signatures, a name appears
Of one for wisdom famed above his years;
And these were forty: he was from his youth
A patient searcher after useful truth:
To language little of his time he gave,
To science less, nor was the muse's slave;
Sober and grave, his college sent him down,
A fair example for his native town.

Slowly he speaks, and with such solemn air,
You 'd think a Socrates or Solon there;
For though a Christian, he 's disposed to draw
His rules from reason's and from nature's law.
"Know," he exclaims, "my fellow mortals, know,
Virtue alone is happiness below;
And what is virtue? prudence first to choose
Life's real good,—the evil to refuse;
Add justice then, the eager hand to hold,
To curb the lust of power, and thirst of gold;
Join temp'rance next, that cheerful health insures,
And fortitude unmoved, that conquers or endures."

He speaks, and lo!—the very man you see,
Prudent and temperate, just and patient he,
By prudence taught his worldly wealth to keep,
No folly wastes, no avarice swells the heap:
He no man's debtor, no man's patron lives;
Save sound advice, he neither asks nor gives;
By no vain thoughts or erring fancy sway'd,
His words are weighty, or at least are weigh'd,
Temp'rate in every place—abroad, at home,
Thence will applause, and hence will profit come;
And health from either he in time prepares
For sickness, age, and their attendant cares,
But not for fancy's ills;—he never grieves
For love that wounds or friendship that deceives;
His patient soul endures what Heav'n ordains,
But neither feels nor fears ideal pains.

"Is aught then wanted in a man so wise?"—
Alas!—I think he wants infirmities;
He wants the ties that knit us to our kind—
The cheerful, tender, soft, complacent mind,
That would the feelings, which he dreads, excite,
And make the virtues he approves delight;
What dying martyrs, saints, and patriots feel,
The strength of action and the warmth of zeal.

Again attend!—and see a man whose cares
Are nicely placed on either world's affairs,—
Merchant and saint; 't is doubtful if he knows
To which account he most regard bestows:
Of both he keeps his ledger:—there he reads
Of gainful ventures and of godly deeds;
There all he gets or loses find a place,
A lucky bargain and a lack of grace.

The joys above this prudent man invite
To pay his tax—devotion!—day and night;
The pains of hell his timid bosom awe,
And force obedience to the church's law:
Hence that continual thought,—that solemn air,—
Those sad good works, and that laborious prayer.

All these (when conscience, waken'd and afraid,
To think how avarice calls and is obey'd)
He in his journal finds, and for his grief
Obtains the transient opium of relief.

"Sink not, my soul!—my spirit, rise and look
O'er the fair entries of this precious book:
Here are the sins, our debts;—this fairer side
Has what to carnal wish our strength denied;
Has those religious duties every day
Paid,—which so few upon the sabbath pay;
Here too are conquests over frail desires,
Attendance due on all the church requires;
Then alms I give—for I believe the word
Of holy writ, and lend unto the Lord,
And if not all th' importunate demand,
The fear of want restrains my ready hand;
—Behold! what sums I to the poor resign,
Sums placed in Heaven's own book, as well as mine.
Rest then, my spirit!—fastings, prayers, and alms
Will soon suppress these idly-raised alarms,
And weigh'd against our frailties, set in view
A noble balance in our favour due:
Add that I yearly here affix my name,
Pledge for large payment—not from love of fame,
But to make peace within;—that peace to make,
What sums I lavish! and what gains forsake!
Cheer up, my heart!—let's cast off every doubt,
Pray without dread, and place our money out."

Such the religion of a mind that steers
Its way to bliss, between its hopes and fears;
Whose passions in due bounds each other keep,
And thus subdued, they murmur till they sleep;
Whose virtues all their certain limits know,
Like well-dried herbs that neither fade nor grow;
Who for success and safety ever tries,
And with both worlds alternately complies.

Such are the guardians of this bless'd estate,
Whate'er without, they 're praised within the gate
That they are men, and have their faults, is true,
But here their worth alone appears in view:
The Muse indeed, who reads the very breast,
Has something of the secrets there express'd,
But yet in charity;—and when she sees
Such means for joy or comfort, health or ease,
And knows how much united minds effect,
She almost dreads their failings to detect;
But truth commands:—in man's erroneous kind,
Virtues and frailties mingle in the mind;
Happy!—when fears to public spirit move,
And even vices to the work of love.

LETTER XVIII.

THE POOR AND THEIR DWELLINGS.

Bene paupertas
Humili tecto contenta latot.
SENECA.

Omnes quibu' res sunt minu' secundæ, magi' sunt, nescio quo modo,
Suspiciosi; ad contumeliam omnia accipiunt magis;
Propter suam impotentiam se semper credunt negligi.
TERENT, *in Adelph.* Act 4, Scene 3.

Show not to the poor thy pride,
Let their home a cottage be;
Nor the feeble body hide
In a palace fit for thee;
Let him not about him see
Lofty ceilings, ample halls,
Or a gate his boundary be,
Where nor friend or kinsman calls.

Let him not one walk behold,
That only one which he must tread,
Nor a chamber large and cold,
Where the aged and sick are led;
Better far his humble shed,
Humble sheds of neighbours by,
And the old and tatter'd bed,
Where he sleeps and hopes to die.

To quit of torpid sluggishness the cave,
And from the pow'rful arms of sloth be free,
'T is rising from the dead—Alas! it cannot be.
THOMSON'S *Castle of Indolence.*

The method of treating the Borough Paupers—Many maintained at their own Dwellings—Some Characters of the Poor—The School-mistress, when aged—The Idiot—The poor Sailor—The declined Tradesman and his Companion—This contrasted with the Maintenance of the Poor in a common Mansion erected by the Hundred—The Objections to this Method: not Want, nor Cruelty, but the necessary Evils of this Mode—What they are—Instances of the Evil—A Return to the Borough Poor—The dwellings of these—The Lanes and By-ways—No Attention here paid to Convenience—The Pools in the Path-ways—Amusements of Sea-port Children—The Town-Flora—Herbs on Walls and vacant Spaces—A Female inhabitant of an Alley—A large Building let to several poor Inhabitants—Their Manners and Habits.

YES! we 've our Borough-vices, and I know
How far they spread, how rapidly they grow;
Yet think not virtue quits the busy place,
Nor charity, the virtues' crown and grace.

"Our poor, how feed we!"—To the most we give
A weekly dole, and at their homes they live;—
Others together dwell,—but when they come
To the low roof, they see a kind of home,
A social people whom they 've ever known,
With their own thoughts and manners like their own.

At her old house, her dress, her air the same,
I see mine ancient letter-loving dame:
"Learning, my child," said she, "shall fame command;
Learning is better worth than house or land
For houses perish, lands are gone and spent;
In learning then excel, for that 's most excellent"

"And what her learning?"—'T is with awe to look
In every verse throughout one sacred book;
From this her joy, her hope, her peace is sought;
This she has learn'd, and she is nobly taught.

If aught of mine have gain'd the public ear;
If RUTLAND deigns these humble Tales to hear;
If critics pardon, what my friends approved;
Can I mine ancient widow pass unmoved?
Shall I not think what pains the matron took,
When first I trembled o'er the gilded book?
How she, all patient, both at eve and morn,
Her needle pointed at the guarding horn;
And how she soothed me, when, with study sad,
I labour'd on to reach the final zad?
Shall I not grateful still the dame survey,
And ask the muse the poet's debt to pay?

Nor I alone, who hold a trifler's pen,
But half our bench of wealthy, weighty men,
Who rule our Borough, who enforce our laws;
They own the matron as the leading cause,
And feel the pleasing debt, and pay the just applause:
To her own house is borne the week's supply;
There she in credit lives, there hopes in peace to die.

With her a harmless idiot we behold,
Who hoards up silver shells for shining gold;
These he preserves, with unremitted care,
To buy a seat, and reign the Borough's mayor:
Alas!—who could the ambitious changeling tell,
That what he sought our rulers dared to sell?

Near these a sailor, in that hut of thatch
(A fish-boat's cabin is its nearest match),
Dwells, and the dungeon is to him a seat,
Large as he wishes—in his view complete:
A lockless coffer and a lidless hutch
That hold his stores, have room for twice as much:
His one spare shirt, long glass, and iron box,
Lie all in view; no need has he for locks:
Here he abides, and as our strangers pass,
He shows the shipping, he presents the glass;
He makes (unask'd) their ports and business known,
And (kindly heard) turns quickly to his own,
Of noble captains, heroes every one,—
You might as soon have made the steeple run:
And then his messmates, if you 're pleased to stay,
He 'll one by one the gallant souls display,
And as the story verges to an end,
He 'll wind from deed to deed, from friend to friend;
He 'll speak of those long lost, the brave of old,
As princes generous and as heroes bold;
Then will his feelings rise, till you may trace
Gloom, like a cloud, frown o'er his manly face,—
And then a tear or two, which sting his pride;
These he will dash indignantly aside,
And splice his tale;—now take him from his cot,
And for some cleaner birth exchange his lot,

How will he all that cruel aid deplore?
His heart will break, and he will fight no more.

Here is the poor old merchant: he declined,
And, as they say, is not in perfect mind;
In his poor-house, with one poor maiden friend,
Quiet he paces to his journey's end.

Rich in his youth, he traded and he fail'd;
Again he tried; again his fate prevail'd;
His spirits low and his exertions small,
He fell perforce, he seem'd decreed to fall:
Like the gay knight, unapt to rise was he,
But downward sank with sad alacrity.
A borough-place we gain'd him—in disgrace
For gross neglect, he quickly lost the place;
But still he kept a kind of sullen pride,
Striving his wants to hinder or to hide:
At length, compell'd by very need, in grief
He wrote a proud petition for relief.

"He did suppose a fall, like his, would prove
Of force to wake their sympathy and love;
Would make them feel the changes all may know,
And stir them up a new regard to show."

His suit was granted;—to an ancient maid,
Relieved herself, relief for him was paid:
Here they together (meet companions) dwell,
And dismal tales of man's misfortunes tell:
"'T was not a world for them, God help them! they
Could not deceive, nor flatter, nor betray;
But there's a happy change, a scene to come,
And they, God help them! shall be soon at home."

If these no pleasures nor enjoyments gain,
Still none their spirits nor their speech restrain;
They sigh at ease, 'mid comforts they complain.
The poor will grieve, the poor will weep and sigh,
Both when they know, and when they know not why;
But we our bounty with such care bestow,
That cause for grieving they shall seldom know.

Your plan I love not;—with a number you
Have placed your poor, your pitiable few;
There, in one house, throughout their lives to be,
The pauper-palace which they hate to see:
That giant building, that high-bounding wall,
Those bare-worn walks, that lofty thundering hall!
That large loud clock, which tolls each dreaded hour,
Those gates and locks, and all those signs of power:
It is a prison, with a milder name,
Which few inhabit without dread or shame.

Be it agreed—the poor who hither come
Partake of plenty, seldom found at home;
That airy rooms and decent beds are meant
To give the poor by day, by night, content;
That none are frighten'd, once admitted here,
By the stern looks of lordly overseer:
Grant that the guardians of the place attend,
And ready ear to each petition lend;
That they desire the grieving poor to show
What ills they feel, what partial acts they know,
Not without promise, nay desire to heal
Each wrong they suffer and each wo they feel.

Alas! their sorrows in their bosom dwell;
They've much to suffer, but have nought to tell;
They have no evil in the place to state,
And dare not say, it is the house they hate:
They own there's granted all such place can give,
But live repining, for 't is there they live.

Grandsires are there, who now no more must see,
No more must nurse upon the trembling knee
The lost loved daughter's infant progeny:
Like death's dread mansion, this allows not place
For joyful meetings of a kindred race.

Is not the matron there, to whom the son
Was wont at each declining day to run;
He (when his toil was over) gave delight,
By lifting up the latch, and one "good night?"
Yes, she is here; but nightly to her door
The son, still lab'ring, can return no more.
Widows are here, who in their huts were left,
Of husbands, children, plenty, ease bereft;
Yet all that grief within the humble shed
Was soften'd, soften'd in the humble bed:
But here, in all its force, remains the grief,
And not one soft'ning object for relief.

Who can, when here, the social neighbour meet?
Who learn the story current in the street?
Who to the long-known intimate impart
Facts they have learn'd or feelings of the heart?—
They talk indeed, but who can choose a friend,
Or seek companions at their journey's end?
Here are not those whom they, when infants, knew;
Who, with like fortune, up to manhood grew;
Who, with like troubles, at old age arrived;
Who, like themselves, the joy of life survived;
Whom time and custom so familiar made,
That looks the meaning in the mind convey'd:
But here to strangers, words nor looks impart
The various movements of the suffering heart;
Nor will that heart with those alliance own,
To whom its views and hopes are all unknown.

What, if no grievous fears their lives annoy,
Is it not worse no prospects to enjoy?
'T is cheerless living in such bounded view,
With nothing dreadful, but with nothing new;
Nothing to bring them joy, to make them weep,—
The day itself is, like the night, asleep:
Or on the sameness if a break be made,
'T is by some pauper to his grave convey'd;
By smuggled news from neighb'ring village told,
News never true, or truth a twelvemonth old;
By some new inmate doom'd with them to dwell,
Or justice come to see that all goes well;
Or change of room, or hour of leave to crawl
On the black footway winding with the wall,
Till the stern bell forbids, or master's sterner call.

Here too the mother sees her children train'd,
Her voice excluded and her feelings pain'd:
Who govern here, by general rules must move,
Where ruthless custom rends the bond of love.
Nations we know have nature's law transgress'd,
And snatch'd the infant from the parent's breast
But still for public good the boy was train'd,
The mother suffer'd, but the matron gain'd:
Here nature's outrage serves no cause to aid;
The ill is felt, but not the Spartan made.

Then too I own, it grieves me to behold
Those ever virtuous, helpless now and old,
By all for care and industry approved,
For truth respected, and for temper loved;
And who, by sickness and misfortune tried,
Gave want its worth and poverty its pride:
I own it grieves me to behold them sent
From their old home; 't is pain, 't is punishment,
To leave each scene familiar, every face,
For a new people and a stranger race;
For those who, sunk in sloth and dead to shame,
From scenes of guilt with daring spirits came;
Men, just and guileless, at such manners start,
And bless their God that time has fenced their heart,
Confirm'd their virtue, and expell'd the fear
Of vice in minds so simple and sincere.

Here the good pauper, losing all the praise
By worthy deeds acquired in better days,
Breathes a few months, then, to his chamber led,
Expires, while strangers prattle round his bed.

The grateful hunter, when his horse is old,
Wills not the useless favourite to be sold;
He knows his former worth, and gives him place
In some fair pasture, till he runs his race:
But has the labourer, has the seaman done
Less worthy service, though not dealt to one?
Shall we not then contribute to their ease,
In their old haunts, where ancient objects please?
That, till their sight shall fail them, they may trace
The well-known prospect and the long-loved face.

The noble oak, in distant ages seen,
With far-stretch'd boughs and foliage fresh and green,
Though now its bare and forky branches show
How much it lacks the vital warmth below,
The stately ruin yet our wonder gains,
Nay, moves our pity, without thought of pains:
Much more shall real wants and cares of age
Our gentler passions in their cause engage;—
Drooping and burthen'd with a weight of years,
What venerable ruin man appears!
How worthy pity, love, respect, and grief—
He claims protection—he compels relief;—
And shall we send him from our view, to brave
The storms abroad, whom we at home might save,
And let a stranger dig our ancient brother's grave?
No!—we will shield him from the storm he fears,
And when he falls, embalm him with our tears.

Farewell to these; but all our poor to know,
Let's seek the winding lane, the narrow row,
Suburban prospects, where the traveller stops
To see the sloping tenement on props,
With building yards inmix'd, and humble sheds and shops;
Where the Cross-Keys and Plumber's-Arms invite
Laborious men to taste their coarse delight;
Where the low porches, stretching from the door,
Gave some distinction in the days of yore,
Yet now neglected, more offend the eye,
By gloom and ruin, than the cottage by;
Places like these the noblest town endures,
The gayest palace has its sinks and sewers.

Here is no pavement, no inviting shop,
To give us shelter, when compelled to stop;
But plashy puddles stand along the way,
Fill'd by the rain of one tempestuous day;
And these so closely to the buildings run,
That you must ford them, for you cannot shun;
Though here and there convenient bricks are laid,
And door-side heaps afford their dubious aid.

Lo! yonder shed; observe its garden-ground,
With the low paling, form'd of wreck, around;
There dwells a fisher; if you view his boat,
With bed and barrel—'t is his house afloat;
Look at his house, where ropes, nets, blocks, abound,
Tar, pitch, and oakum—'t is his boat aground:
That space enclosed, but little he regards,
Spread o'er with relics of masts, sails, and yards:
Fish by the wall, on spit of elder, rest,
Of all his food, the cheapest and the best,
By his own labour caught, for his own hunger dress'd.

Here our reformers come not; none object
To paths polluted, or upbraid neglect;
None care that ashy heaps at doors are cast,
That coal-dust flies along the blinding blast:
None heed the stagnant pools on either side,
Where new-launch'd ships of infant sailors ride:
Rodneys in rags here British valour boast,
And lisping Nelsons fright the Gallic coast.
They fix the rudder, set the swelling sail,
They point the bowsprit, and they blow the gale
True to her port, the frigate scuds away,
And o'er that frowning ocean finds her bay:
Her owner rigg'd her, and he knows her worth,
And sees her, fearless, gunwale-deep go forth;
Dreadless he views his sea, by breezes curl'd,
When inch-high billows vex the watery world.

There, fed by food they love, to rankest size,
Around the dwellings docks and wormwood rise;
Here the strong mallow strikes her slimy root,
Here the dull night-shade hangs her deadly fruit;
On hills of dust the henbane's faded green,
And pencil'd flower of sickly scent is seen;
At the wall's base the fiery nettle springs,
With fruit globose and fierce with poison'd stings;
Above (the growth of many a year) is spread
The yellow level of the stone-crop's bed;
In every chink delights the fern to grow,
With glossy leaf and tawny bloom below:*
These, with our sea-weeds, rolling up and down,
Form the contracted Flora† of the town.

Say, wilt thou more of scenes so sordid know?
Then will I lead thee down the dusty row;
By the warm alley and the long close lane,—
There mark the fractured door and paper'd pane,
Where flags the noon-tide air, and, as we pass,
We fear to breathe the putrefying mass:

---

* This scenery is, I must acknowledge, in a certain degree like that heretofore described in the Village; but that also was a maritime country:—if the objects be similar, the pictures must (in their principal features) be alike, or be bad pictures. I have varied them as much as I could, consistently with my wish to be accurate.

† The reader unacquainted with the language of botany is informed, that the Flora of a place means the vegetable species it contains, and is the title of a book which describes them.

But fearless yonder matron; she disdains
To sigh for zephyrs from ambrosial plains;
But mends her meshes torn, and pours her lay
All in the stifling fervour of the day.

Her naked children round the alley run,
And roll'd in dust, are bronzed beneath the sun;
Or gambol round the dame, who, loosely dress'd,
Woos the coy breeze, to fan the open breast:
She, once a handmaid, strove by decent art
To charm her sailor's eye and touch his heart;
Her bosom then was veil'd in kerchief clean,
And fancy left to form the charms unseen.

But when a wife, she lost her former care,
Nor thought on charms, nor time for dress could spare;
Careless she found her friends who dwelt beside,
No rival beauty kept alive her pride;
Still in her bosom virtue keeps her place,
But decency is gone, the virtues' guard and grace.

See that long boarded building!—By these stairs
Each humble tenant to that home repairs—
By one large window lighted—it was made
For some bold project, some design in trade:
This fail'd,—and one, a humourist in his way
(Ill was the humour,) bought it in decay;
Nor will he sell, repair, or take it down;
'T is his,—what cares he for the talk of town?
"No! he will let it to the poor;—a home
Where he delights to see the creatures come:"
"They may be thieves;"—"Well, so are richer men;"
"Or idlers, cheats, or prostitutes:"—"What then?"
"Outcasts pursued by justice, vile and base;"—
"They need the more his pity and the place:"
Convert to system his vain mind has built,
He gives asylum to deceit and guilt.

In this vast room, each place by habit fix'd,
Are sexes, families, and ages mix'd,—
To union forced by crime, by fear, by need,
And all in morals and in modes agreed;
Some ruin'd men, who from mankind remove;
Some ruin'd females, who yet talk of love;
And some grown old in idleness—the prey
To vicious spleen, still railing through the day;
And need and misery, vice and danger bind
In sad alliance each degraded mind.

That window view!—oil'd paper and old glass
Stain the strong rays, which, though impeded, pass,
And give a dusty warmth to that huge room,
The conquer'd sunshine's melancholy gloom;
When all those western rays, without so bright,
Within become a ghastly glimmering light,
As pale and faint upon the floor they fall,
Or feebly gleam on the opposing wall:
That floor, once oak, now pieced with fir unplaned,
Or, where not pieced, in places bored and stain'd;
That wall once whiten'd, now an odious sight,
Stain'd with all hues, except its ancient white;
The only door is fasten'd by a pin,
Or stubborn bar, that none may hurry in:
For this poor room, like rooms of greater pride,
At times contains what prudent men would hide.

Where'er the floor allows an even space,
Chalking and marks of various games have place;
Boys without foresight, pleased in halters swing;
On a fix'd hook men cast a flying ring;
While gin and snuff their female neighbours share,
And the black beverage in the fractured ware.

On swinging shelf are things incongruous stored,—
Scraps of their food,—the cards and cribbage-board,—
With pipes and pouches; while on peg below,
Hang a lost member's fiddle and its bow:
That still reminds them how he'd dance and play,
Ere sent untimely to the convicts' Bay.

Here by a curtain, by a blanket there,
Are various beds conceal'd, but none with care;
Where some by day and some by night, as best
Suit their employments, seek uncertain rest;
The drowsy children at their pleasure creep
To the known crib, and there securely sleep.

Each end contains a grate, and these beside
Are hung utensils for their boil'd and fried—
All used at any hour, by night, by day,
As suit the purse, the person, or the prey.

Above the fire, the mantel-shelf contains
Of china-ware some poor unmatch'd remains;
There many a tea-cup's gaudy fragment stands,
All placed by vanity's unwearied hands;
For here she lives, e'en here she looks about,
To find some small consoling objects out:
Nor heed these Spartan dames their house, nor sit
'Mid cares domestic,—they nor sew nor knit;
But of their fate discourse, their ways, their wars,
With arm'd authorities, their 'scapes and scars;
These lead to present evils, and a cup,
If fortune grants it, winds description up.

High hung on either end, and next the wall,
Two ancient mirrors show the forms of all,
In all their force;—these aid them in their dress,
But with the good, the evils too express,
Doubling each look of care, each token of distress

LETTER XIX.

THE POOR OF THE BOROUGH—THE PARISH-CLERK.

Nam dives qui fieri vult,
Et citò vult fieri; sed quæ reverentia legum,
Quis metus, aut pudor est unquam properantis aveni?
JUVENAL, Sat. 14

Nocté brevem si forte indulsit cura soporem,
Et toto versata thoro jam membra quiescunt,
Continuo templum et violati Numinis aras,
Et quod præcipius mentem sudoribus urget,
Te videt in somnis; tuá sacra et majora imago
Humana turbat pavidum, cogitque fateri.
JUVENAL, Sat. 13.

The Parish-Clerk began his Duties with the late Vicar, a grave and austere Man; one fully orthodox; a Detector and Opposer of the Wiles of Satan—His Opinion of his own Fortitude—The more frail offended by these Professions—His good Advice gives further Provocation—They invent Stratagems to overcome his Virtue—His Triumph—He is yet not invulnerable: is assaulted by Fear of Want, and Avarice—He gradually yields to the Seduction—He reasons with himself and is persuaded—He offends, but with Terror; repeats his Offence; grows familiar with Crime; is detected—His Sufferings and Death.

WITH our late vicar, and his age the same,
His clerk, hight Jachin, to his office came;
The like slow speech was his, the like tall slender frame:
But Jachin was the gravest man on ground,
And heard his master's jokes with look profound;
For worldly wealth this man of letters sigh'd,
And had a sprinkling of the spirit's pride:
But he was sober, chaste, devout, and just,
One whom his neighbours could believe and trust:
Of none suspected, neither man nor maid
By him were wrong'd, or were of him afraid.

There was indeed a frown, a trick of state
In Jachin;—formal was his air and gait;
But if he seem'd more solemn and less kind
Than some light men to light affairs confined,
Still 't was allow'd that he should so behave
As in high seat, and be severely grave.

This book-taught man, to man's first foe profess'd
Defiance stern, and hate that knew not rest;
He held that Satan, since the world began,
In every act, had strife with every man;
That never evil deed on earth was done,
But of the acting parties he was one;
The flattering guide to make ill prospects clear;
To smooth rough ways the constant pioneer;
The ever-tempting, soothing, softening power,
Ready to cheat, seduce, deceive, devour.

"Me has the sly seducer oft withstood,"
Said pious Jachin,—"but he gets no good;
I pass the house where swings the tempting sign,
And pointing, tell him, 'Satan, that is thine:'
I pass the damsels passing down the street,
And look more grave and solemn when we meet;
Nor doth it irk me to rebuke their smiles,
Their wanton ambling and their watchful wiles:
Nay, like the good John Bunyan, when I view
Those forms, I 'm angry at the ills they do;
That I could pinch and spoil, in sin's despite,
Beauties! which frail and evil thoughts excite.*

"At feasts and banquets seldom am I found,
And (save at church) abhor a tuneful sound;
To plays and shows I run not to and fro,
And where my master goes forbear to go."

No wonder Satan took the thing amiss,
To be opposed by such a man as this—
A man so grave, important, cautious, wise,
Who dared not trust his feeling or his eyes;
No wonder he should lurk and lie in wait,
Should fit his hooks and ponder on his bait;
Should on his movements keep a watchful eye,
For he pursued a fish who led the fry.

With his own peace our clerk was not content,
He tried, good man! to make his friends repent.

"Nay, nay, my friends, from inns and taverns fly;
You may suppress your thirst, but not supply;
A foolish proverb says, 'the devil 's at home;'
But he is there, and tempts in every room:
Men feel, they know not why, such places please;
His are the spells—they 're idleness and ease;
Magic of fatal kind he throws around,
Where care is banish'd but the heart is bound.

"Think not of beauty; when a maid you meet,
Turn from her view and step across the street;
Dread all the sex: their looks create a charm,
A smile should fright you and a word alarm:
E'en I myself, with all my watchful care,
Have for an instant felt th' insidious snare,
And caught my sinful eyes at th' endangering stare;
Till I was forced to smite my bounding breast
With forceful blow, and bid the bold one rest.

"Go not with crowds when they to pleasure run,
But public joy in private safety shun:
When bells, diverted from their true intent,
Ring loud for some deluded mortal sent
To hear or make long speech in parliament;
What time the many, that unruly beast,
Roars its rough joy and shares the final feast:
Then heed my counsel, shut thine ears and eyes;
A few will hear me—for the few are wise."

Not Satan's friends, nor Satan's self could bear
The cautious man who took of souls such care;
An interloper,—one who, out of place,
Had volunteer'd upon the side of grace:
There was his master ready once a week
To give advice; what further need he seek?
"Amen, so be it:"—what had he to do
With more than this?—'t was insolent and new;
And some determined on a way to see
How frail he was, that so it might not be.

First they essay'd to tempt our saint to sin,
By points of doctrine argued at an inn;
Where he might warmly reason, deeply drink,
Then lose all power to argue and to think.

In vain they tried; he took the question up,
Clear'd every doubt, and barely touch'd the cup:
By many a text he proved his doctrine sound,
And look'd in triumph on the tempters round.

Next 't was their care an artful lass to find,
Who might consult him, as perplex'd in mind:
She they conceived might put her case with fears,
With tender tremblings and seducing tears;
She might such charms of various kind display,
That he would feel their force and melt away:
For why of nymphs such caution and such dread,
Unless he felt and fear'd to be misled?

She came, she spake: he calmly heard her case,
And plainly told her 't was a want of grace;
Bade her "such fancies and affections check,
And wear a thicker muslin on her neck."
Abased, his human foes the combat fled,
And the stern clerk yet higher held his head.

* John Bunyan, in one of the many productions of his zeal, has ventured to make public this extraordinary sentiment, which the frigid piety of our clerk so readily adopted.

They were indeed a weak, impatient set,
But their shrewd prompter had his engines yet;
Had various means to make a mortal trip,
Who shunn'd a flowing bowl and rosy lip;
And knew a thousand ways his heart to move,
Who flies from banquets and who laughs at love.

Thus far the playful Muse has lent her aid,
But now departs, of graver theme afraid;
Her may we seek in more appropriate time,—
There is no jesting with distress and crime.

Our worthy clerk had now arrived at fame,
Such as but few in his degree might claim;
But he was poor, and wanted not the sense
That lowly rates the praise without the pence:
He saw the common herd with reverence treat
The weakest burgess whom they chanced to meet;
While few respected his exalted views,
And all beheld his doublet and his shoes:
None, when they meet, would to his parts allow
(Save his poor boys) a hearing or a bow:
To this false judgment of the vulgar mind,
He was not fully, as a saint, resign'd;
He found it much his jealous soul affect,
To fear derision and to find neglect.

The year was bad, the christening-fees were small,
The weddings few, the parties paupers all:
Desire of gain with fear of want combined,
Raised sad commotion in his wounded mind;
Wealth was in all his thoughts, his views, his dreams,
And prompted base desires and baseless schemes.

Alas! how often erring mortals keep
The strongest watch against the foes who sleep;
While the more wakeful, bold, and artful foe
Is suffer'd guardless and unmark'd to go.

Once in a month the sacramental bread
Our clerk with wine upon the table spread;
The custom this, that, as the vicar reads,
He for our off'rings round the church proceeds:
Tall spacious seats the wealthier people hid,
And none had view of what his neighbour did;
Laid on the box and mingled when they fell,
Who should the worth of each oblation tell?
Now as poor Jachin took the usual round,
And saw the alms and heard the metal sound,
He had a thought;—at first it was no more
Than—"these have cash and give it to the poor:"
A second thought from this to work began—
"And can they give it to a poorer man?"
Proceeding thus,—"My merit could they know,
And knew my need, how freely they'd bestow!
But though they know not, these remain the same;
And are a strong, although a secret claim:
To me, alas! the want and worth are known,
Why then, in fact, 't is but to take my own."

Thought after thought pour'd in, a tempting train,—
"Suppose it done,—who is it could complain?
How could the poor? for they such trifles share,
As add no comfort, as suppress no care;
But many a pittance makes a worthy heap,—
What says the law? that silence puts to sleep:—
Nought then forbids, the danger could we shun,
And sure the business may be safely done.

"But am I earnest?—earnest? No.—I say,
If such my mind, that I could plan a way;
Let me reflect;—I 've not allow'd me time
To purse the pieces, and if dropp'd they'd chime:"
Fertile is evil in the soul of man,—
He paused,—said Jachin, "They may drop on bran.
Why then 't is safe and (all consider'd) just,
The poor receive it,—'t is no breach of trust:
The old and widows may their trifles miss,
There must be evil in a good like this:
But I 'll be kind—the sick I 'll visit twice,
When now but once, and freely give advice.
Yet let me think again."—Again he tried,
For stronger reasons on his passion's side,
And quickly these were found, yet slowly he complied.

The morning came: the common service done,—
Shut every door,—the solemn rite begun,—
And, as the priest the sacred sayings read,
The clerk went forward, trembling as he tread;
O'er the tall pew he held the box, and heard
The offer'd piece, rejoicing as he fear'd:
Just by the pillar, as he cautious tripp'd,
And turn'd the aisle, he then a portion slipp'd
From the full store, and to the pocket sent,
But held a moment—and then down it went.

The priest read on, on walk'd the man afraid,
Till a gold offering in the plate was laid;
Trembling he took it, for a moment stopp'd,
Then down it fell, and sounded as it dropp'd;
Amazed he started, for th' affrighted man,
Lost and bewilder'd, thought not of the bran;
But all were silent, all on things intent
Of high concern, none ear to money lent;
So on he walk'd, more cautious than before,
And gain'd the purposed sum and one piece more.

Practice makes perfect;—when the month came round,
He dropp'd the cash, nor listen'd for a sound;
But yet, when last of all th' assembled flock,
He ate and drank—it gave th' electric shock:
Oft was he forced his reasons to repeat,
Ere he could kneel in quiet at his seat;
But custom soothed him—ere a single year
All this was done without restraint or fear:
Cool and collected, easy and composed,
He was correct till all the service closed;
Then to his home, without a groan or sigh,
Gravely he went, and laid his treasure by.

Want will complain: some widows had express'd
A doubt if they were favour'd like the rest;
The rest described with like regret their dole,
And thus from parts they reason'd to the whole;
When all agreed some evil must be done,
Or rich men's hearts grew harder than a stone

Our easy vicar cut the matter short;
He would not listen to such vile report.

All were not thus—there govern'd in that year
A stern stout churl, an angry overseer;
A tyrant fond of power, loud, lewd, and most severe.
Him the mild vicar, him the graver clerk,
Advised, reproved, but nothing would he mark,

Save the disgrace, "and that, my friends," said he,
"Will I avenge, whenever time may be."
And now, alas! 't was time;—from man to man
Doubt and alarm and shrewd suspicions ran.

With angry spirit and with sly intent,
This parish-ruler to the altar went;
A private mark he fix'd on shillings three,
And but one mark could in the money see;
Besides, in peering round, he chanced to note
A sprinkling slight on Jachin's Sunday-coat:
All doubt was over:—when the flock were bless'd,
In wrath he rose, and thus his mind express'd.

"Foul deeds are here!" and saying this, he took
The clerk, whose conscience, in her cold-fit, shook:
His pocket then was emptied on the place;
All saw his guilt; all witness'd his disgrace;
He fell, he fainted, not a groan, a look,
Escaped the culprit; 't was a final stroke—
A death-wound never to be heal'd—a fall
That all had witness'd, and amazed were all.

As he recover'd, to his mind it came,
"I owe to Satan this disgrace and shame:"
All the seduction now appear'd in view;
"Let me withdraw," he said, and he withdrew;
No one withheld him, all in union cried,
E'en the avenger,—"We are satisfied:"
For what has death in any form to give,
Equal to that man's terrors, if he live?

He lived in freedom, but he hourly saw
How much more fatal justice is than law;
He saw another in his office reign,
And his mild master treat him with disdain;
He saw that all men shunn'd him, some reviled,
The harsh pass'd frowning, and the simple smiled;
The town maintain'd him, but with some reproof,
"And clerks and scholars proudly kept aloof."

In each lone place, dejected and dismay'd,
Shrinking from view, his wasting form he laid;
Or to the restless sea and roaring wind
Gave the strong yearnings of a ruin'd mind:
On the broad beach, the silent summer-day,
Stretch'd on some wreck, he wore his life away;
Or where the river mingles with the sea,
Or on the mud-bank by the elder-tree,
Or by the bounding marsh-dyke, there was he:
And when unable to forsake the town,
In the blind courts he sate desponding down—
Always alone; then feebly would he crawl
The church-way walk, and lean upon the wall:
Too ill for this, he lay beside the door,
Compell'd to hear the reasoning of the poor:
He look'd so pale, so weak, the pitying crowd
Their firm belief of his repentance vow'd;
They saw him then so ghastly and so thin,
That they exclaim'd, "Is this the work of sin?"

"Yes," in his better moments, he replied,
"Of sinful avarice and the spirit's pride;
While yet untempted, I was safe and well;
Temptation came; I reason'd, and I fell:
To be man's guide and glory I design'd,
A rare example for our sinful kind;
But now my weakness and my guilt I see,
And am a warning—man, be warn'd by me!"

He said, and saw no more the human face;
To a lone loft he went, his dying place,
And, as the vicar of his state inquired,
Turn'd to the wall and silently expired!

LETTER XX.

THE POOR OF THE BOROUGH.—ELLEN ORFORD.

Patience and sorrow strove
Who should express her goodliest.
SHAKSPEARE, *Lear.*

"No charms she now can boast,"—'t is true.
But other charmers wither too:
"And she is old,"—the fact I know,
And old will other heroines grow;
But not like them has she been laid,
In ruin'd castle, sore dismay'd;
Where naughty man and ghostly sprite
Fill'd her pure mind with awe and dread,
Stalk'd round the room, put out the light,
And shook the curtains round her bed.
No cruel uncle kept her land,
No tyrant father forced her hand;
She had no vixen virgin-aunt,
Without whose aid she could not eat,
And yet who poison'd all her meat
With gibe and sneer and taunt.
Yet of the heroine she'd a share,
She saved a lover from despair,
And granted all his wish in spite
Of what she knew and felt was right:
But heroine then no more,
She own'd the fault, and wept and pray'd,
And humbly took the parish aid,
And dwelt among the poor.

The Widow's Cottage—Blind Ellen one—Hers not the Sorrows or Adventures of Heroines—What these are, first described—Deserted Wives; rash lovers; courageous Damsels; in desolated Mansions; in grievous Perplexity—These Evils, however severe, of short Duration—Ellen's Story—Her Employment in Childhood—First Love; first Adventure; its miserable Termination—An idiot Daughter—A Husband—Care in Business without Success—The Man's Despondency and its Effect—Their Children: how disposed of—One particularly unfortunate—Fate of the Daughter—Ellen keeps a School and is happy—Becomes blind: loses her School—Her Consolations.

Observe yon tenement, apart and small,
Where the wet pebbles shine upon the wall;
Where the low benches lean beside the door,
And the red paling bounds the space before;
Where thrift and lavender, and lad's-love* bloom,—
That humble dwelling is the widow's home.
There live a pair, for various fortunes known,
But the blind Ellen will relate her own:—
Yet ere we hear the story she can tell,
On prouder sorrows let us briefly dwell.

* The lad's or boy's-love of some counties is the plant southernwood, the *artemisia abrotanum* of botanists.

I 've often marvel'd, when by night, by day,
I 've mark'd the manners moving in my way,
And heard the language and beheld the lives
Of lass and lover, goddesses and wives,
That books, which promise much of life to give,
Should show so little how we truly live.

To me it seems, their females and their men
Are but the creatures of the author's pen;
Nay, creatures borrow'd, and again convey'd
From book to book—the shadows of a shade:
Life, if they 'd search, would show them many a change;
The ruin sudden and the misery strange!
With more of grievous, base, and dreadful things,
Than novelist relates, or poet sings:
But they, who ought to look the world around,
Spy out a single spot in fairy-ground;
Where all, in turn, ideal forms behold,
And plots are laid and histories are told.

Time have I lent—I would their debt were less—
To flow'ry pages of sublime distress;
And to the heroine's soul-distracting fears
I early gave my sixpences and tears.
Oft have I travell'd in these tender vales,
To Darnley-Cottages and Maple-Vales,
And watch'd the fair-one from the first-born sigh,
When Henry pass'd and gazed in passing by;
Till I beheld them pacing in the park,
Close by a coppice where 't was cold and dark.
When such affection with such fate appear'd,
Want and a father to be shunn'd and fear'd,
Without employment, prospect, cot, or cash,
That I have judged th' heroic souls were rash.

Now shifts the scene,—the fair in tower confined,
In all things suffers but in change of mind;
Now woo'd by greatness to a bed of state,
Now deeply threaten'd with a dungeon's grate;
Till suffering much and being tried enough,
She shines, triumphant maid!—temptation-proof.

Then was I led to vengeful monks, who mix
With nymphs and swains, and play unpriestly tricks;
Then view'd banditti who in forest wide,
And cavern vast, indignant virgins hide,
Who, hemm'd with bands of sturdiest rogues about,
Find some strange succour, and come virgins out.

I 've watch'd a wint'ry night on castle-walls,
I 've stalk'd by moonlight through deserted halls,
And when the weary world was sunk to rest,
I 've had such sights as—may not be express'd.

Lo! that chateau, the western tower decay'd,
The peasants shun it,—they are all afraid;
For there was done a deed!—could walls reveal,
Or timbers tell it, how the heart would feel!
Most horrid was it:—for, behold, the floor
Has stain of blood, and will be clean no more.
Hark to the winds! which through the wide saloon
And the long passage send a dismal tune,—
Music that ghosts delight in;—and now heed
Yon beauteous nymph, who must unmask the deed.
See! with majestic sweep she swims alone
Through rooms, all dreary, guided by a groan:
Though windows rattle, and though tap'stries shake,
And the feet falter every step they take,

'Mid moans and gibing sprites she silent goes,
To find a something, which will soon expose
The villanies and wiles of her determined foes:
And, having thus adventured, thus endured,
Fame, wealth, and lover, are for life secured.

Much have I fear'd, but am no more afraid,
When some chaste beauty, by some wretch betray'd,
Is drawn away with such distracted speed,
That she anticipates a dreadful deed:
Not so do I—Let solid walls impound
The captive fair, and dig a moat around;
Let there be brazen locks and bars of steel,
And keepers cruel, such as never feel;
With not a single note the purse supply,
And when she begs, let men and maids deny:
Be windows those from which she dares not fall,
And help so distant, 't is in vain to call;
Still means of freedom will some power devise,
And from the baffled ruffian snatch his prize.

To Northern Wales, in some sequester'd spot,
I 've follow'd fair Louisa to her cot:
Where, then a wretched and deserted bride,
The injured fair-one wish'd from man to hide:
Till by her fond repenting Belville found,
By some kind chance—the straying of a hound,
He at her feet craved mercy, nor in vain,
For the relenting dove flew back again.

There 's something rapturous in distress, or, oh!
Could Clementina bear her lot of wo?
Or what she underwent could maiden undergo!
The day was fix'd; for so the lover sigh'd,
So knelt and craved, he could n't be denied;
When, tale most dreadful! every hope adieu,—
For the fond lover is the brother too:
All other griefs abate; this monstrous grief
Has no remission, comfort, or relief;
Four ample volumes, through each page disclose,—
Good Heaven protect us! only woes on woes;
Till some strange means afford a sudden view
Of some vile plot, and every woe adieu! *

Now should we grant these beauties all endure
Severest pangs, they 've still the speediest cure;
Before one charm be wither'd from the face,
Except the bloom, which shall again have place,
In wedlock ends each wish, in triumph all disgrace;
And life to come, we fairly may suppose,
One light, bright contrast to these wild dark woes.

These let us leave, and at her sorrows look,
Too often seen, but seldom in a book;
Let her who felt, relate them:—on her chair
The heroine sits—in former years the fair,

* As this incident points out the work alluded to, I wish it to be remembered, that the gloomy tenour, the querulous melancholy of the story, is all I censure. The language of the writer is often animated, and is, I believe, correct: the characters well drawn, and the manners described from real life; but the perpetual occurrence of sad events, the protracted list of teasing and perplexing mischances, joined with much waspish invective, unallayed by pleasantry or sprightliness, and these continued through many hundred pages, render publications, intended for amusement and executed with ability, heavy and displeasing:—you find your favourite persons happy in the end; but they have teased you so much with their perplexities by the way, that you were frequently disposed to quit them in their distresses.

Now aged and poor; but Ellen Orford knows,
That we should humbly take what Heav'n bestows.

"My father died—again my mother wed,
And found the comforts of her life were fled;
Her angry husband vex'd, through half his years
By loss and troubles, fill'd her soul with fears:
Their children many, and 't was my poor place
To nurse and wait on all the infant-race;
Labour and hunger were indeed my part,
And should have strengthen'd an erroneous heart.

"Sore was the grief to see him angry come,
And, teased with business, make distress at home:
The father's fury and the children's cries
I soon could bear, but not my mother's sighs;
For she look'd back on comforts, and would say,
'I wrong'd thee, Ellen,' and then turn away:
Thus for my age's good, my youth was tried,
And this my fortune till my mother died.

"So, amid sorrow much and little cheer—
A common case, I pass'd my twentieth year;
For these are frequent evils; thousands share
An equal grief—the like domestic care.

"Then in my days of bloom, of health and youth,
One, much above me, vow'd his love and truth:
We often met, he dreading to be seen,
And much I question'd what such dread might mean;
Yet I believed him true; my simple heart
And undirected reason took his part.

"Can he who loves me, whom I love, deceive?
Can I such wrong of one so kind believe,
Who lives but in my smile, who trembles, when I grieve?

"He dared not marry, but we met to prove
What sad encroachments and deceits has love;
Weak that I was, when he, rebuked, withdrew,
I let him see that I was wretched too;
When less my caution, I had still the pain
Of his or mine own weakness to complain.

"Happy the lovers class'd alike in life,
Or happier yet the rich endowing wife;
But most aggrieved the fond believing maid,
Of her rich lover tenderly afraid:
You judge th' event; for grievous was my fate,
Painful to feel, and shameful to relate:
Ah! sad it was my burthen to sustain,
When the last misery was the dread of pain;
When I have grieving told him my disgrace,
And plainly mark'd indifference in his face.

"Hard! with these fears and terrors to behold
The cause of all, the faithless lover cold;
Impatient grown at every wish denied,
And barely civil, soothed and gratified;
Peevish when urged to think of vows so strong,
And angry when I spake of crime and wrong.

"All this I felt, and still the sorrow grew
Because I felt that I deserved it too,
And begg'd my infant stranger to forgive
The mother's shame, which in herself must live.

"When known that same, I, soon expell'd from home,
With a frail sister shared a hovel's gloom;
There barely fed—(what could I more request?)
My infant slumberer sleeping at my breast,
I from my window saw his blooming bride,
And my seducer smiling at her side:
Hope lived till then; I sank upon the floor,
And grief and thought and feeling were no more:
Although revived, I judged that life would close,
And went to rest, to wonder that I rose:
My dreams were dismal, wheresoe'er I stray'd,
I seem'd ashamed, alarm'd, despised, betray'd;
Always in grief, in guilt, disgraced, forlorn,
Mourning that one so weak, so vile, was born;
The earth a desert, tumult in the sea,
The birds affrighted fled from tree to tree,
Obscured the setting sun, and every thing like me
But Heav'n had mercy, and my need at length
Urged me to labour, and renew'd my strength.

"I strove for patience as a sinner must,
Yet felt th' opinion of the world unjust:
There was my lover, in his joy, esteem'd,
And I, in my distress, as guilty deem'd;
Yet sure, not all the guilt and shame belong
To her who feels and suffers for the wrong:
The cheat at play may use the wealth he 's won,
But is not honour'd for the mischief done;
The cheat in love may use each villain-art,
And boast the deed that breaks the victim's heart.

"Four years were past; I might again have found
Some erring wish, but for another wound:
Lovely my daughter grew, her face was fair,
But no expression ever brighten'd there;
I doubted long, and vainly strove to make
Some certain meaning of the words she spake;
But meaning there was none, and I survey'd
With dread the beauties of my idiot-maid.

"Still I submitted;—Oh! 't is meet and fit
In all we feel to make the heart submit;
Gloomy and calm my days, but I had then,
It seem'd, attractions for the eyes of men:
The sober master of a decent trade
O'erlook'd my errors, and his offer made;
Reason assented:—true, my heart denied,
'But thou,' I said, 'shalt be no more my guide.'

"When wed, our toil and trouble, pains and care,
Of means to live procured us humble share;
Five were our sons,—and we, though careful, found
Our hopes declining as the year came round:
For I perceived, yet would not soon perceive,
My husband stealing from my view to grieve;
Silent he grew, and when he spoke he sigh'd,
And surly look'd, and peevishly replied:
Pensive by nature, he had gone of late
To those who preach'd of destiny and fate,
Of things fore-doom'd, and of election-grace,
And how in vain we strive to run our race:
That all by works and moral worth we gain
Is to perceive our care and labour vain;
That still the more we pay, our debts the more remain:
That he who feels not the mysterious call,
Lies bound in sin, still grov'ling from the fall.
My husband felt not:—our persuasion, prayer,
And our best reason darken'd his despair;

His very nature changed; he now reviled
My former conduct,—he reproach'd my child:
He talk'd of bastard slips, and cursed his bed,
And from our kindness to concealment fled;
For ever to some evil change inclined,
To every gloomy thought he lent his mind,
Nor rest would give to us, nor rest himself could find;
His son suspended saw him, long bereft
Of life, nor prospect of revival left.

"With him died all our prospects, and once more
I shared th' allotments of the parish poor;
They took my children too, and this I know
Was just and lawful, but I felt the blow:
My idiot-maid and one unhealthy boy
Were left, a mother's misery and her joy.

"Three sons I follow'd to the grave, and one—
Oh! can I speak of that unhappy son?
Would all the memory of that time were fled,
And all those horrors, with my child, were dead!
Before the world seduced him, what a grace
And smile of gladness shone upon his face!
Then he had knowledge; finely would he write;
Study to him was pleasure and delight;
Great was his courage, and but few could stand
Against the sleight and vigour of his hand;
The maidens loved him;—when he came to die,
No, not the coldest could suppress a sigh:
Here I must cease—how can I say, my child
Was by the bad of either sex beguiled?
Worst of the bad—they taught him that the laws
Made wrong and right; there was no other cause;
That all religion was the trade of priests,
And men, when dead, must perish like the beasts:—
And he, so lively and so gay before——
Ah! spare a mother—I can tell no more.

"Int'rest was made that they should not destroy
The comely form of my deluded boy—
But pardon came not; damp the place and deep
Where he was kept, as they'd a tiger keep;
For he, unhappy! had before them all
Vow'd he'd escape, whatever might befall.

"He'd means of dress, and dress'd beyond his means,
And so to see him in such dismal scenes,
I cannot speak it—cannot bear to tell
Of that sad hour—I heard the passing-bell!

"Slowly they went; he smiled and look'd so smart,
Yet sure he shudder'd when he saw the cart,
And gave a look—until my dying-day,
That look will never from my mind away:
Oft as I sit, and ever in my dreams,
I see that look, and they have heard my screams.

"Now let me speak no more—yet all declared
That one so young, in pity should be spared,
And one so manly;—on his graceful neck,
That chains of jewels may be proud to deck,
To a small mole a mother's lips have press'd,—
And there the cord—my breath is sore oppress'd.

"I now can speak again;—my elder boy
Was that year drown'd—a seaman in a hoy:
He left a numerous race; of these would some
In their young troubles to my cottage come,
And these I taught—an humble teacher I—
Upon their heavenly Parent to rely.

"Alas! I needed such reliance more:
My idiot-girl, so simply gay before,
Now wept in pain; some wretch had found a time
Depraved and wicked, for that coward-crime;
I had indeed my doubt, but I suppress'd
The thought that day and night disturb'd my rest
She and that sick-pale brother—but why strive
To keep the terrors of that time alive?

"The hour arrived, the new, th' undreaded pain,
That came with violence and yet came in vain.
I saw her die: her brother too is dead;
Nor own'd such crime—what is it that I dread?

"The parish-aid withdrawn, I look'd around,
And in my school a bless'd subsistence found—
My winter-calm of life: to be of use
Would pleasant thoughts and heavenly hopes produce;
I loved them all; it soothed me to presage
The various trials of their riper age,
Then dwell on mine, and bless the Power who gave
Pains to correct us, and remorse to save.

"Yes! these were days of peace, but they are past,—
A trial came, I will believe, a last;
I lost my sight, and my employment gone,
Useless I live, but to the day live on;
Those eyes, which long the light of heaven enjoy'd
Were not by pain, by agony destroy'd:
My senses fail not all; I speak, I pray;
By night my rest, my food I take by day;
And as my mind looks cheerful to my end,
I love mankind, and call my God my friend."

LETTER XXI.

THE POOR OF THE BOROUGH—ABEL KEENE.

Cœpis melius quam desines: ultima primis
Cedunt. Dissimiles: hic vir et ille puer.
OVID. *Deianira Herculi.*

Now the Spirit speaketh expressly, that, in the latter times, some shall depart from the faith, giving heed to seducing spirits and doctrines of devils.
Epistle to Timothy.

Abel, a poor Man, Teacher of a School of the lower Order: is placed in the Office of a Merchant; is alarmed by Discourses of the Clerks; unable to reply; becomes a Convert; dresses, drinks, and ridicules his former Conduct — The Remonstrance of his Sister, a devout Maiden—Its Effect—The Merchant dies—Abel returns to Poverty unpitied; but relieved—His abject Condition—His Melancholy—He wanders about: is found — His own Account of himself, and the Revolutions in his Mind.

A quiet simple man was Abel Keene,
He meant no harm, nor did he often mean:
He kept a school of loud rebellious boys,
And growing old, grew nervous with the noise;
When a kind merchant hired his useful pen,
And made him happiest of accompting men;
With glee he rose to every easy day,
When half the labour brought him twice the pay.

There were young clerks, and there the merchant's son,
Choice spirits all, who wish'd him to be one;
It must, no question, give them lively joy,
Hopes long indulged, to combat and destroy;
At these they level'd all their skill and strength,—
He fell not quickly, but he fell at length:
They quoted books, to him both bold and new,
And scorn'd as fables all he held as true;
" Such monkish stories and such nursery lies,"
That he was struck with terror and surprise.

" What! all his life had he the laws obey'd,
Which they broke through, and were not once afraid?
Had he so long his evil passions check'd,
And yet at last had nothing to expect?
While they their lives in joy and pleasure led,
And then had nothing, at the end, to dread?
Was all his priest with so much zeal convey'd,
A part! a speech! for which the man was paid?
And were his pious books, his solemn prayers,
Not worth one tale of the admired Voltaire's?
Then was it time, while yet some years remain'd,
To drink untroubled and to think unchain'd,
And on all pleasures, which his purse could give,
Freely to seize, and while he lived, to live."
Much time he pass'd in this important strife,
The bliss or bane of his remaining life;
For converts all are made with care and grief,
And pangs attend the birth of unbelief;
Nor pass they soon;—with awe and fear he took
The flow'ry way, and cast back many a look.

The youths applauded much his wise design,
With weighty reasoning o'er their evening wine;
And much in private 't would their mirth improve,
To hear how Abel spake of life and love;
To hear him own what grievous pains it cost,
Ere the old saint was in the sinner lost,
Ere his poor mind, with every deed alarm'd,
By wit was settled, and by vice was charm'd.

For Abel enter'd in his bold career,
Like boys on ice, with pleasure and with fear;
Lingering, yet longing for the joy, he went,
Repenting now, now dreading to repent:
With awkward pace, and with himself at war,
Far gone, yet frighten'd that he went so far;
Oft for his efforts he'd solicit praise,
And then proceed with blunders and delays:
The young more aptly passion's call pursue,
But age and weakness start at scenes so new,
And tremble when they've done, for all they dared to do.

At length example Abel's dread removed,
With small concern he sought the joys he loved;
Not resting here, he claim'd his share of fame,
And first their votary, then their wit became;
His jest was bitter and his satire bold,
When he his tales of formal brethren told;
What time with pious neighbours he discuss'd,
Their boasted treasure and their boundless trust:
" Such were our dreams," the jovial elder cried;
" Awake and live," his youthful friends replied.

Now the gay clerk a modest drab despised,
And clad him smartly as his friends advised;
So fine a coat upon his back he threw,
That not an alley-boy old Abel knew;
Broad polish'd buttons blazed that coat upon,
And just beneath the watch's trinkets shone,—
A splendid watch, that pointed out the time,
To fly from business and make free with crime:
The crimson waistcoat and the silken hose
Rank'd the lean man among the Borough beaux;
His raven hair he cropp'd with fierce disdain,
And light elastic locks encased his brain:
More pliant pupil who could hope to find,
So deck'd in person and so changed in mind?

When Abel walk'd the streets, with pleasant mien
He met his friends, delighted to be seen;
And when he rode along the public way,
No beau so gaudy, and no youth so gay.

His pious sister, now an ancient maid,
For Abel fearing, first in secret pray'd;
Then thus in love and scorn her notions she convey'd:

" Alas! my brother! can I see thee pace
Hoodwink'd to hell, and not lament thy case,
Nor stretch my feeble hand to stop thy headlong race?
Lo! thou art bound; a slave in Satan's chain,
The righteous Abel turn'd the wretched Cain;
His brother's blood against the murderer cried,
Against thee thine, unhappy suicide!
Are all our pious nights and peaceful days,
Our evening readings and our morning praise,
Our spirits' comfort in the trials sent,
Our hearts' rejoicings in the blessings lent,
All that o'er grief a cheering influence shed,
Are these for ever and for ever fled?

" When in the years gone by, the trying years,
When faith and hope had strife with wants and fears,
Thy nerves have trembled till thou couldst not eat
(Dress'd by this hand) thy mess of simple meat;
When, grieved by fastings, gall'd by fates severe,
Slow pass'd the days of the successless year;
Still in these gloomy hours, my brother then
Had glorious views, unseen by prosperous men:
And when thy heart has felt its wish denied,
What gracious texts hast thou to grief applied;
Till thou hast enter'd in thine humble bed,
By lofty hopes and heavenly musings fed;
Then I have seen thy lively looks express
The spirit's comforts in the man's distress.

" Then didst thou cry, exulting, 'Yes, 't is fit,'
'T is meet and right, my heart! that we submit:
And wilt thou, Abel, thy new pleasures weigh
Against such triumphs?—Oh! repent and pray.

" What are thy pleasures?—with the gay to sit,
And thy poor brain torment for awkward wit;

All thy good thoughts (thou hatest them) to restrain,
And give a wicked pleasure to the vain;
Thy long lean frame by fashion to attire,
That lads may laugh and wantons may admire;
To raise the mirth of boys, and not to see,
Unhappy maniac! that they laugh at thee.

"These boyish follies, which alone the boy
Can idly act or gracefully enjoy,
Add new reproaches to thy fallen state,
And make men scorn what they would only hate.

"What pains, my brother, dost thou take to prove
A taste for follies which thou canst not love?
Why do thy stiffening limbs the steed bestride—
That lads may laugh to see thou canst not ride?
And why (I feel the crimson tinge my cheek)
Dost thou by night in Diamond-Alley sneak?

"Farewell! the parish will thy sister keep,
Where she in peace shall pray and sing and sleep,
Save when for thee she mourns, thou wicked, wandering sheep!
When youth is fall'n, there's hope the young may rise,
But fallen age for ever hopeless lies:
Torn up by storms and placed in earth once more,
The younger tree may sun and soil restore;
But when the old and sapless trunk lies low,
No care or soil can former life bestow;
Reserved for burning is the worthless tree;
And what, O Abel! is reserved for thee?"

These angry words our hero deeply felt,
Though hard his heart, and indisposed to melt!
To gain relief he took a glass the more,
And then went on as careless as before;
Thenceforth, uncheck'd, amusements he partook,
And (save his ledger) saw no decent book;
Him found the merchant punctual at his task,
And that perform'd, he'd nothing more to ask;
He cared not how old Abel play'd the fool,
No master he, beyond the hours of school:
Thus they proceeding, had their wine and joke,
Till merchant Dixon felt a warning stroke,
And, after struggling half a gloomy week,
Left his poor clerk another friend to seek.

Alas! the son, who led the saint astray,
Forgot the man whose follies made him gay;
He cared no more for Abel in his need,
Than Abel cared about his hackney steed;
He now, alas! had all his earnings spent,
And thus was left to languish and repent;
No school nor clerkship found he in the place,
Now lost to fortune, as before to grace.

For town-relief the grieving man applied,
And begg'd with tears what some with scorn denied;
Others look'd down upon the glowing vest,
And frowning, ask'd him at what price he dress'd?
Happy for him his country's laws are mild,
They must support him, though they still reviled;
Grieved, abject, scorn'd, insulted, and betray'd,
Of God unmindful, and of man afraid;—
No more he talk'd; 't was pain, 't was shame to speak,
His heart was sinking and his frame was weak.

His sister died with such serene delight,
He once again began to think her right;
Poor like himself, the happy spinster lay,
And sweet assurance bless'd her dying-day:
Poor like the spinster, he, when death was nigh,
Assured of nothing, felt afraid to die.
The cheerful clerks who sometimes pass'd the door,
Just mention'd "Abel!" and then thought no more.
So Abel, pondering on his state forlorn,
Look'd round for comfort, and was chased by scorn.
And now we saw him on the bench reclined,
Or causeless walking in the wint'ry wind;
And when it raised a loud and angry sea,
He stood and gazed, in wretched reverie:
He heeded not the frost, the rain, the snow;
Close by the sea he walk'd alone and slow:
Sometimes his frame through many an hour he spread
Upon a tombstone, moveless as the dead;
And was there found a sad and silent place,
There would he creep with slow and measured pace:
Then would he wander by the river's side,
And fix his eyes upon the falling tide;
The deep dry ditch, the rushes in the fen,
And mossy crag-pits were his lodgings then:
There, to his discontented thoughts a prey,
The melancholy mortal pined away.

The neighb'ring poor at length began to speak
Of Abel's ramblings—he'd been gone a week;
They knew not where, and little care they took
For one so friendless and so poor to look.
At last a stranger, in a pedler's shed,
Beheld him hanging—he had long been dead.
He left a paper, penn'd at sundry times,
Intitled this—"My Groanings and my Crimes!"

"I was a christian man, and none could lay
Aught to my charge; I walk'd the narrow way.
All then was simple faith, serene and pure,
My hope was steadfast and my prospects sure.
Then was I tried by want and sickness sore,
But these I clapp'd my shield of faith before,
And cares and wants and man's rebukes I bore.
Alas! new foes assail'd me; I was vain,
They stung my pride and they confused my brain
Oh! these deluders! with what glee they saw
Their simple dupe transgress the righteous law;
'Twas joy to them to view that dreadful strife,
When faith and frailty warr'd for more than life.
So with their pleasures they beguiled the heart,
Then with their logic they allay'd the smart;
They proved, (so thought I then,) with reasons strong,
That no man's feelings ever led him wrong:
And thus I went, as on the varnish'd ice,
The smooth career of unbelief and vice.
Oft would the youths, with sprightly speech and bold,
Their witty tales of naughty priests unfold;
''T was all a craft,' they said, 'a cunning trade,
Not she the priests, but priests religion made:'
So I believed:"—No, Abel! to thy grief,
So thou relinquish'dst all that was belief:—
"I grew as very flint, and when the rest
Laugh'd at devotion, I enjoy'd the jest;
But this all vanish'd like the morning dew,
When unemploy'd, and poor again I grew,
Yea! I was doubly poor, for I was wicked too

"The mouse that trespass'd and the treasure stole,
Found his lean body fitted to the hole;
Till having fatted, he was forced to stay,
And, fasting, starve his stolen bulk away:
Ah! worse for me—grown poor, I yet remain
In sinful bonds, and pray and fast in vain."

"At length I thought, although these friends of sin
Have spread their net and caught their prey therein;
Though my hard heart could not for mercy call,
Because, though great my grief, my faith was small;
Yet, as the sick on skilful men rely,
The soul diseased may to a doctor fly.

"A famous one there was, whose skill had wrought
Cures past belief, and him the sinners sought;
Numbers there were defiled by mire and filth,
Whom he recover'd by his goodly tilth:—
'Come, then,' I said, 'let me the man behold,
And tell my case'—I saw him and I told.

"With trembling voice, 'Oh! reverend sir,' I said,
I once believed, and I was then misled;
And now such doubts my sinful soul beset,
I dare not say that I'm a Christian yet.
Canst thou, good sir, by thy superior skill,
Inform my judgment and direct my will?
Ah! give thy cordial; let my soul have rest,
And be the outward man alone distress'd;
For at my state I tremble.'—'Tremble more,'
Said the good man, 'and then rejoice therefore;
'T is good to tremble; prospects then are fair,
When the lost soul is plunged in deep despair.
Once thou wert simply honest, just and pure,
Whole, as thou thought'st, and never wish'd a cure:
Now thou hast plunged in folly, shame, disgrace;
Now thou 'rt an object meet for healing grace;
No merit thine, no virtue, hope, belief,
Nothing hast thou, but misery, sin, and grief,
The best, the only titles to relief.'

"'What must I do,' I said, 'my soul to free?
'—Do nothing, man, it will be done for thee.'
'But must I not, my reverend guide, believe?'
'—If thou art call'd, thou wilt the faith receive:'—
'But I repent not.'—Angry he replied,
'If thou art call'd, thou needest nought beside:
Attend on us, and if 't is Heaven's decree,
The call will come,—if not, ah! wo for thee.'

"There then I waited, ever on the watch,
A spark of hope, a ray of light to catch;
His words fell softly like the flakes of snow,
But I could never find my heart o'erflow:
He cried aloud, till in the flock began
The sigh, the tear, as caught from man to man;
They wept and they rejoiced, and there was I,
Hard as a flint, and as the desert dry.
To me no tokens of the call would come,
I felt my sentence and received my doom;
But I complain'd—'Let thy repining cease,
Oh! man of sin, for they thy guilt increase;
It bloweth where it listeth;—die in peace.'
—'In peace, and perish?' I replied; 'impart
Some better comfort to a burthen'd heart.'—
'Alas!' the priest return'd, 'can I direct
The heavenly call?—Do I proclaim th' elect?
Raise not thy voice against th' Eternal will,
But take thy part with sinners, and be still.'*

"Alas! for me, no more the times of peace
Are mine on earth—in death my pains may cease.

"Foes to my soul! ye young seducers, know,
What serious ills from your amusements flow;
Opinions, you with so much ease profess,
O'erwhelm the simple and their minds oppress:
Let such be happy, nor with reasons strong,
That make them wretched, prove their notions wrong.
Let them proceed in that they deem the way,
Fast when they will, and at their pleasure pray,
Yes, I have pity for my brethren's lot,
And so had Dives, but it help'd him not:
And is it thus?—I 'm full of doubts:—Adieu!
Perhaps his reverence is mistaken too."

LETTER XXII.

THE POOR OF THE BOROUGH.—PETER GRIMES.

——— Was a sordid soul,
Such as does murder for a meed:
Who but for fear knows no control,
Because his conscience, sear'd and foul,
Feels not the import of the deed;
One whose brute feeling ne'er aspires
Beyond his own more brute desires.

SCOTT. *Marmion.*

* In a periodical work for the month of June last, the preceding dialogue is pronounced to be a most abominable caricature, if meant to be applied to Calvinists in general, and greatly distorted, if designed for an individual: now the author in his preface has declared, that he takes not upon him the censure of any sect or society for their opinions; and the lines themselves evidently point to an individual, whose sentiments they very fairly represent, without any distortion whatsoever. In a pamphlet intitled "A Cordial for a Sin-despairing Soul," originally written by a teacher of religion, and lately republished by another teacher of greater notoriety, the reader is informed that after he had full assurance of his salvation, the Spirit entered particularly into the subject with him; and, among many other matters of like nature, assured him that "his sins were fully and freely forgiven, as if they had never been committed; not for any act done by him, whether believing in Christ, or repenting of sin; nor yet for the sorrows and miseries he endured, nor for any service he should be called upon in his militant state, but for his own name and for his glory's sake,"* etc. And the whole drift and tenour of the book is to the same purpose, viz: the uselessness of all religious duties, such as prayer, contrition, fasting, and good works: he shows the evil done by reading such books as the Whole Duty of Man and the Practice of Piety: and complains heavily of his relation, an Irish bishop, who wanted him to join with the household in family prayer: in fact, the whole work inculcates that sort of quietism which this dialogue alludes to, and that without any recommendation of attendance on the teachers of the Gospel, but rather holding forth encouragement to the supineness of man's nature; by the information that he in vain looks for acceptance by the employment of his talents; and that his hopes of glory are rather extinguished than raised by any application to the means of grace.

* Cordial, etc. page 87.

Methought the souls of all that I had murder'd
Came to my tent, and every one did threat——
SHAKSPEARE. *Richard III.*

The times have been,
That when the brains were out, the man would die,
And there an end; but now they rise again,
With twenty mortal murders on their crowns,
And push us from our stools.
Macbeth.

The Father of Peter a Fisherman—Peter's early Conduct—His Grief for the old Man—He takes an Apprentice—The Boy's Suffering and Fate—A second Boy: how he died—Peter acquitted—A third Apprentice—A Voyage by Sea: the Boy does not return—Evil Report on Peter: he is tried and threatened—Lives alone—His Melancholy and incipient Madness—Is observed and visited—He escapes and is taken; is lodged in a Parish-house; Women attend and watch him—He speaks in a Delirium; grows more collected—His Account of his Feelings and visionary Terrors previous to his Death.

Old Peter Grimes made fishing his employ,
His wife he cabin'd with him and his boy,
And seem'd that life laborious to enjoy:
To town came quiet Peter with his fish,
And had of all a civil word and wish.
He left his trade upon the sabbath-day,
And took young Peter in his hand to pray:
But soon the stubborn boy from care broke loose,
At first refused, then added his abuse:
His father's love he scorn'd, his power defied,
But being drunk, wept sorely when he died.

Yes! then he wept, and to his mind there came
Much of his conduct, and he felt the shame,—
How he had oft the good old man reviled,
And never paid the duty of a child;
How, when the father in his Bible read,
He in contempt and anger left the shed:
"It is the word of life," the parent cried;
—"This is the life itself," the boy replied;
And while old Peter in amazement stood,
Gave the hot spirit to his boiling blood:—
How he, with oath and furious speech, began
To prove his freedom and assert the man;
And when the parent check'd his impious rage,
How he had cursed the tyranny of age,—
Nay, once had dealt the sacrilegious blow
On his bare head, and laid his parent low;
The father groan'd—"If thou art old," said he,
"And hast a son—thou wilt remember me:
Thy mother left me in a happy time,
Thou kill'dst not her.—Heav'n spares the double crime."

On an inn-settle, in his maudlin grief,
This he revolved, and drank for his relief.

Now lived the youth in freedom, but debarr'd
From constant pleasure, and he thought it hard;
Hard that he could not every wish obey,
But must awhile relinquish ale and play;
Hard! that he could not to his cards attend,
But must acquire the money he would spend.

With greedy eye he look'd on all he saw,
He knew not justice, and he laugh'd at law;
On all he mark'd he stretch'd his ready hand;
He fish'd by water, and he filch'd by land:
Oft in the night has Peter dropp'd his oar,
Fled from his boat and sought for prey on shore
Oft up the hedge-row glided, on his back
Bearing the orchard's produce in a sack,
Or farm-yard load, tugg'd fiercely from the stack
And as these wrongs to greater numbers rose,
The more he look'd on all men as his foes.

He built a mud-wall'd hovel, where he kept
His various wealth, and there he oft-times slept;
But no success could please his cruel soul,
He wish'd for one to trouble and control;
He wanted some obedient boy to stand
And bear the blow of his outrageous hand;
And hoped to find in some propitious hour
A feeling creature subject to his power.

Peter had heard there were in London then,—
Still have they being!—workhouse-clearing men,
Who, undisturb'd by feelings just or kind,
Would parish-boys to needy tradesmen bind:
They in their want a trifling sum would take,
And toiling slaves of piteous orphans make.

Such Peter sought, and when a lad was found,
The sum was dealt him, and the slave was bound.
Some few in town observed in Peter's trap
A boy, with jacket blue and woollen cap;
But none inquired how Peter used the rope,
Or what the bruise, that made the stripling stoop
None could the ridges on his back behold,
None sought him shiv'ring in the winter's cold;
None put the question,—"Peter, dost thou give
The boy his food?—What, man! the lad must live,
Consider, Peter, let the child have bread,
He'll serve thee better if he's stroked and fed."
None reason'd thus—and some, on hearing cries,
Said calmly, "Grimes is at his exercise."

Pinn'd, beaten, cold, pinch'd, threaten'd, and abused—
His efforts punish'd and his food refused,—
Awake tormented,—soon aroused from sleep,—
Struck if he wept, and yet compell'd to weep,
The trembling boy dropp'd down and strove to pray,
Received a blow, and trembling turn'd away,
Or sobb'd and hid his piteous face;—while he,
The savage master, grinn'd in horrid glee:
He'd now the power he ever loved to show,
A feeling being subject to his blow.

Thus lived the lad, in hunger, peril, pain,
His tears despised, his supplications vain:
Compell'd by fear to lie, by need to steal,
His bed uneasy and unbless'd his meal,
For three sad years the boy his tortures bore,
And then his pains and trials were no more.

"How died he, Peter?" when the people said,
He growl'd—"I found him lifeless in his bed;"
Then tried for softer tone, and sigh'd, "Poor Sam is dead."
Yet murmurs were there, and some questions ask'd,—
How he was fed, how punish'd, and how task'd?

Much they suspected, but they little proved,
And Peter pass'd untroubled and unmoved.

Another boy with equal ease was found,
The money granted, and the victim bound;
And what his fate?—One night it chanced he fell
From the boat's mast and perish'd in her well.
Where fish were living kept, and where the boy
(So reason'd men) could not himself destroy;—

"Yes! so it was," said Peter, "in his play
(For he was idle both by night and day),
He climb'd the main-mast and then fell below;"—
Then show'd his corpse and pointed to the blow:
"What said the jury?"—they were long in doubt,
But sturdy Peter faced the matter out:
So they dismiss'd him, saying at the time,
"Keep fast your hatchway when you 've boys who climb."
This hit the conscience, and he colour'd more
Than for the closest questions put before.

Thus all his fears the verdict set aside,
And at the slave-shop Peter still applied.

Then came a boy, of manners soft and mild,—
Our seamen's wives with grief beheld the child;
All thought (the poor themselves) that he was one
Of gentle blood, some noble sinner's son,
Who had, belike, deceived some humble maid,
Whom he had first seduced and then betray'd:—
However this, he seem'd a gracious lad,
In grief submissive and with patience sad.

Passive he labour'd, till his slender frame
Bent with his loads, and he at length was lame:
Strange that a frame so weak could bear so long
The grossest insult and the foulest wrong!
But there were causes—in the town they gave
Fire, food, and comfort, to the gentle slave;
And though stern Peter, with a cruel hand,
And knotted rope, enforced the rude command,
Yet he consider'd what he 'd lately felt,
And his vile blows with selfish pity dealt.

One day such draughts the cruel fisher made,
He could not vend them in his borough-trade,
But sail'd for London-mart: the boy was ill,
But ever humbled to his master's will;
And on the river, where they smoothly sail'd,
He strove with terror and awhile prevail'd;
But new to danger on the angry sea,
He clung affrighten'd to his master's knee:
The boat grew leaky and the wind was strong,
Rough was the passage and the time was long;
His liquor fail'd, and Peter's wrath arose,—
No more is known—the rest we must suppose,
Or learn of Peter;—Peter says, "he spied
The stripling's danger and for harbour tried;
Meantime the fish, and then th' apprentice died."

The pitying women raised a clamour round,
And weeping said, "Thou hast thy 'prentice drown'd."

Now the stern man was summon'd to the hall,
To tell his tale before the burghers all:
He gave th' account; profess'd the lad he loved,
And kept his brazen features all unmoved.

The mayor himself with tone severe replied,—
"Henceforth with thee shall never boy abide;
Hire thee a freeman, whom thou durst not beat,
But who, in thy despite, will sleep and eat:
Free thou art now!—again shouldst thou appear,
Thou 'lt find thy sentence, like thy soul, severe."

Alas! for Peter, not a helping hand,
So was he hated, could he now command;
Alone he row'd his boat, alone he cast
His nets beside, or made his anchor fast;
To hold a rope or hear a curse was none,—
He toil'd and rail'd, he groan'd and swore alone.

Thus by himself compell'd to live each day,
To wait for certain hours the tide's delay;
At the same times the same dull views to see,
The bounding marsh-bank and the blighted tree;
The water only, when the tides were high,
When low, the mud half-cover'd and half-dry;
The sun-burnt tar that blisters on the planks,
And bank-side stakes in their uneven ranks;
Heaps of entangled weeds that slowly float,
As the tide rolls by the impeded boat.

When tides were neap, and, in the sultry day,
Through the tall bounding mud-banks made their way,
Which on each side rose swelling, and below
The dark warm flood ran silently and slow;
There anchoring, Peter chose from man to hide,
There hang his head, and view the lazy tide
In its hot slimy channel slowly glide;
Where the small eels that left the deeper way
For the warm shore, within the shallows play;
Where gaping muscles, left upon the mud,
Slope their slow passage to the fallen flood;—
Here dull and hopeless he 'd lie down and trace
How sidelong crabs had scrawl'd their crooked race;
Or sadly listen to the tuneless cry
Of fishing gull or clanging golden-eye;
What time the sea-birds to the marsh would come,
And the loud bittern, from the bull-rush home,
Gave from the salt-ditch side the bellowing boom:
He nursed the feelings these dull scenes produce,
And loved to stop beside the opening sluice;
Where the small stream, confined in narrow bound
Ran with a dull, unvaried, sadd'ning sound;
Where all, presented to the eye or ear,
Oppress'd the soul with misery, grief, and fear.

Besides these objects, there were places three,
Which Peter seem'd with certain dread to see;
When he drew near them he would turn from each,
And loudly whistle till he pass'd the reach.*

A change of scene to him brought no relief;
In town, 't was plain, men took him for a thief:
The sailors' wives would stop him in the street,
And say, "Now, Peter, thou 'st no boy to beat:"
Infants at play, when they perceived him, ran,
Warning each other—"That 's the wicked man:"
He growl'd an oath, and in an angry tone
Cursed the whole place, and wish'd to be alone.

* The reaches in a river are those parts which extend from point to point. Johnson has not the word precisely in this sense; but it is very common, and I believe used wheresoever a navigable river can be found in this country

Alone he was, the same dull scenes in view,
And still more gloomy in his sight they grew:
Though man he hated, yet employ'd alone
At bootless labour, he would swear and groan,
Cursing the shoals that glided by the spot,
And gulls that caught them when his arts could not.

Cold nervous tremblings shook his sturdy frame,
And strange disease, he couldn't say the name;
Wild were his dreams, and oft he rose in fright
Waked by his view of horrors in the night,—
Horrors that would the sternest minds amaze,
Horrors that demons might be proud to raise:
And though he felt forsaken, grieved at heart,
To think he lived from all mankind apart;
Yet, if a man approach'd, in terrors he would start.

A winter pass'd since Peter saw the town,
And summer-lodgers were again come down;
These, idly curious, with their glasses spied
The ships in bay as anchor'd for the tide,—
The river's craft,—the bustle of the quay,—
And sea-port views, which landmen love to see.

One, up the river, had a man and boat
Seen day by day, now anchor'd, now afloat;
Fisher he seem'd, yet used no net nor hook;
Of sea-fowl swimming by no heed he took,
But on the gliding waves still fix'd his lazy look:
At certain stations he would view the stream,
As if he stood bewilder'd in a dream,
Or that some power had chain'd him for a time,
To feel a curse or meditate on crime.

This known, some curious, some in pity went,
And others question'd—"Wretch, dost thou repent?"
He heard, he trembled, and in fear resign'd
His boat: new terror fill'd his restless mind;
Furious he grew, and up the country ran,
And there they seized him—a distemper'd man:—
Him we received, and to a parish-bed,
Follow'd and cursed, the groaning man was led.

Here when they saw him, whom they used to shun,
A lost, lone man, so harass'd and undone;
Our gentle females, ever prompt to feel,
Perceived compassion on their anger steal;
His crimes they could not from their memories blot,
But they were grieved and trembled at his lot.

A priest too came, to whom his words are told;
And all the signs they shudder'd to behold.

"Look! look!" they cried; "his limbs with horror shake,
And as he grinds his teeth, what noise they make!
How glare his angry eyes, and yet he 's not awake:
See! what cold drops upon his forehead stand,
And how he clenches that broad bony hand."

The priest attending, found he spoke at times
As one alluding to his fears and crimes:
"It was the fall," he mutter'd, "I can show
The manner how—I never struck a blow:"—
And then aloud—"Unhand me, free my chain;
On oath, he fell—it struck him to the brain:—
Why ask my father?—that old man will swear
Against my life; besides, he wasn't there:—

R

What, all agreed?—Am I to die to-day?—
My Lord, in mercy, give me time to pray."

Then, as they watch'd him, calmer he became,
And grew so weak he couldn't move his frame,
But murmuring spake,—while they could see and hear
The start of terror and the groan of fear;
See the large dew-beads on his forehead rise,
And the cold death-drop glaze his sunken eyes;
Nor yet he died, but with unwonted force
Seem'd with some fancied being to discourse:
He knew not us, or with accustom'd art
He hid the knowledge, yet exposed his heart;
'T was part confession and the rest defence,
A madman's tale, with gleams of waking sense.

"I'll tell you all," he said, "the very day
When the old man first placed them in my way:
My father's spirit—he who always tried
To give me trouble, when he lived and died—
When he was gone, he could not be content
To see my days in painful labour spent,
But would appoint his meetings, and he made
Me watch at these, and so neglect my trade.

"'T was one hot noon, all silent, still, serene,
No living being had I lately seen;
I paddled up and down and dipp'd my net,
But (such his pleasure) I could nothing get,—
A father's pleasure, when his toil was done,
To plague and torture thus an only son!
And so I sat and look'd upon the stream,
How it ran on, and felt as in a dream:
But dream it was not; no!—I fix'd my eyes
On the mid stream and saw the spirits rise;
I saw my father on the water stand,
And hold a thin pale boy in either hand;
And there they glided ghastly on the top
Of the salt flood, and never touch'd a drop:
I would have struck them, but they knew th' intent,
And smiled upon the oar, and down they went.

"Now, from that day, whenever I began
To dip my net, there stood the hard old man—
He and those boys: I humbled me and pray'd
They would be gone;—they heeded not but stay'd:
Nor could I turn, nor would the boat go by,
But gazing on the spirits, there was I:
They bade me leap to death, but I was loth to die:
And every day, as sure as day arose,
Would these three spirits meet me ere the close;
To hear and mark them daily was my doom,
And 'Come,' they said, with weak, sad voices 'come.'
To row away with all my strength I tried,
But there were they, hard by me in the tide,
The three unbodied forms—and 'Come,' still 'come,' they cried.

"Fathers should pity—but this old man shook
His hoary locks, and froze me by a look:
Thrice, when I struck them, through the water came
A hollow groan, that weaken'd all my frame:
'Father!' said I, 'have mercy:'—He replied,
I know not what—the angry spirit lied,

Didst thou not draw thy knife?' said he:—'T was true,
But I had pity and my arm withdrew:
He cried for mercy which I kindly gave,
But he has no compassion in his grave.

"There were three places, where they ever rose,—
The whole long river has not such as those,—
Places accursed, where, if a man remain,
He 'll see the things which strike him to the brain;
And there they made me on my paddle lean,
And look at them for hours;—accursed scene!
When they would glide to that smooth eddy-space,
Then bid me leap and join them in the place;
And at my groans each little villain sprite
Enjoy'd my pains and vanish'd in delight.
In one fierce summer-day, when my poor brain
Was burning hot and cruel was my pain,
Then came this father-foe, and there he stood
With his two boys again upon the flood;
There was more mischief in their eyes, more glee
In their pale faces when they glared at me:
Still did they force me on the oar to rest,
And when they saw me fainting and oppress'd,
He, with his hand, the old man, scoop'd the flood,
And there came flame about him mix'd with blood;
He bade me stoop and look upon the place,
Then flung the hot-red liquor in my face;
Burning it blazed, and then I roar'd for pain,
I thought the demons would have turn'd my brain.

"Still there they stood, and forced me to behold
A place of horrors—they can not be told—
Where the flood open'd, there I heard the shriek
Of tortured guilt—no earthly tongue can speak:
'All days alike! for ever!' did they say,
'And unremitted torments every day'—
Yes, so they said:"—But here he ceased and gazed
On all around, affrighten'd and amazed;
And still he tried to speak, and look'd in dread
Of frighten'd females gathering round his bed;
Then dropp'd exhausted and appear'd at rest,
Till the strong foe the vital powers possess'd;
Then with an inward, broken voice he cried,
"Again they come," and mutter'd as he died.

LETTER XXIII.

PRISONS.

Pœna autem vehemens ac multo sævior illis,
Quas et Cæditius gravis invenit aut Rhadamanthus,
Nocte dieque suum gestare in pectore testem.
JUVENAL. Sat. 13, l. 197.

Think my former state a happy dream,
From which awaked, the truth of what we are
Shows us but this,—I am sworn brother now
To grim Necessity, and he and I
Will keep a league till death.
Richard II.

The Mind of Man accommodates itself to all Situations; Prisons otherwise would be intolerable—Debtors: their different Kinds: three particularly described; others more briefly—An arrested Prisoner: his Account of his Feelings and his Situation—The Alleviations of a Prison—Prisoners for Crimes—Two condemned: a vindictive Female: a Highwayman—The Interval between Condemnation and Execution—His Feelings as the Time approaches—His Dream.

'T is well—that man to all the varying states
Of good and ill his mind accommodates;
He not alone progressive grief sustains,
But soon submits to unexperienced pains:
Change after change, all climes his body bears;
His mind repeated shocks of changing cares:
Faith and fair virtue arm the nobler breast;
Hope and mere want of feeling aid the rest.

Or who could bear to lose the balmy air
Of summer's breath, from all things fresh and fair,
With all that man admires or loves below;
All earth and water, wood and vale bestow,
Where rosy pleasures smile, whence real blessings flow;
With sight and sound of every kind that lives,
And crowning all with joy that freedom gives?

Who could from these, in some unhappy day,
Bear to be drawn by ruthless arms away,
To the vile nuisance of a noisome room,
Where only insolence and misery come?
(Save that the curious will by chance appear,
Or some in pity drop a fruitless tear;)
To a damp prison, where the very sight
Of the warm sun is favour and not right;
Where all we hear or see the feelings shock,
The oath and groan, the fetter and the lock?

Who could bear this and live?—Oh! many a year
All this is borne, and miseries more severe;
And some there are, familiar with the scene,
Who live in mirth, though few become serene.

Far as I might the inward man perceive,
There was a constant effort—not to grieve;
Not to despair, for better days would come,
And the freed debtor smile again at home:
Subdued his habits, he may peace regain,
And bless the woes that were not sent in vain.

Thus might we class the debtors here confined,
The more deceived, the more deceitful kind;
Here are the guilty race, who mean to live
On credit, that credulity will give;
Who purchase, conscious they can never pay;
Who know their fate, and traffic to betray;
On whom no pity, fear, remorse, prevail,
Their aim a statute, their resource a jail:—
These as the public spoilers we regard,
No dun so harsh, no creditor so hard.

A second kind are they, who truly strive
To keep their sinking credit long alive;
Success, nay prudence, they may want, but yet
They would be solvent, and deplore a debt;
All means they use, to all expedients run,
And are by slow, sad steps, at last undone:
Justly, perhaps, you blame their want of skill,
But mourn their feelings and absolve their will.

There is a debtor, who his trifling *all*
Spreads in a shop; it would not fill a stall:
There at one window his temptation lays,
And in new modes disposes and displays:
Above the door you shall his name behold,
And what he vends in ample letters told,
The words *repository*, *warehouse*, all
He uses to enlarge concerns so small:
He to his goods assigns some beauty's name,
Then in her reign, and hopes they 'll share her fame;
And talks of credit, commerce, traffic, trade,
As one important by their profit made;
But who can paint the vacancy, the gloom,
And spare dimensions of one backward room?
Wherein he dines, if so 't is fit to speak,
Of one day's herring and the morrow's steak;
An anchorite in diet, all his care
Is to display his stock and vend his ware.

Long waiting hopeless, then he tries to meet
A kinder fortune in a distant street;
There he again displays, increasing yet
Corroding sorrow and consuming debt:
Alas! he wants the requisites to rise—
The true connexions, the availing ties;
They who proceed on certainties advance,
These are not times when men prevail by chance:
But still he tries, till, after years of pain,
He finds, with anguish, he has tried in vain.
Debtors are these on whom 't is hard to press,
'T is base, impolitic, and merciless.

To these we add a miscellaneous kind,
By pleasure, pride, and indolence confined;
Those whom no calls, no warnings could divert,
The unexperienced, the and inexpert;
The builder, idler, schemer, gamester, sot,—
The follies different, but the same their lot;
Victims of horses, lasses, drinking, dice,
Of every passion, humour, whim, and vice.

See! that sad merchant, who but yesterday
Had a vast household in command and pay;
He now entreats permission to employ
A boy he needs, and then entreats the boy.

And there sits one, improvident but kind,
Bound for a friend, whom honour could not bind;
Sighing, he speaks to any who appear,
"A treach'rous friend—'t was that which sent me here:
I was too kind,—I thought I could depend
On his bare word—he was a treach'rous friend."

A female too!—it is to her a home,
She came before—and she again will come:
Her friends have pity; when their anger drops,
They take her home;—she 's tried her schools and shops—
Plan after plan;—but fortune would not mend,
She to herself was still the treach'rous friend;
And wheresoe'er began, all here was sure to end:
And there she sits as thoughtless and as gay,
As if she'd means, or not a debt to pay—
Or knew to-morrow she 'd be call'd away—
Or felt a shilling and could dine to-day.

While thus observing, I began to trace
The sober'd features of a well-known face—
Looks once familiar, manners form'd to please,
And all illumined by a heart at ease:
But fraud and flattery ever claim'd a part
(Still unresisted) of that easy heart;
But he at length beholds me—"Ah! my friend!
And have thy pleasures this unlucky end?"

"Too sure," he said, and smiling as he sigh'd;
"I went astray, though prudence seem'd my guide;
All she proposed I in my heart approved,
And she was honour'd, but my pleasure loved—
Pleasure, the mistress to whose arms I fled,
From wife-like lectures angry prudence read.

"Why speak the madness of a life like mine,
The powers of beauty, novelty, and wine?
Why paint the wanton smile, the venal vow,
Or friends whose worth I can appreciate now?

"Oft I perceived my fate, and then would say,
I'll think to-morrow, I must live to-day;
So am I here—I own the laws are just—
And here, where thought is painful, think I must:
But speech is pleasant, this discourse with thee
Brings to my mind the sweets of liberty,
Breaks on the sameness of the place, and gives
The doubtful heart conviction that it lives.

"Let me describe my anguish, in the hour
When law detain'd me and I felt its power.

"When in that shipwreck, this I found my shore,
And join'd the wretched, who were wreck'd before;
When I perceived each feature in the face,
Pinch'd through neglect or turbid by disgrace;
When in these wasting forms affliction stood
In my afflicted view, it chill'd my blood,—
And forth I rush'd, a quick retreat to make,
Till a loud laugh proclaim'd the dire mistake:
But when the groan had settled to a sigh,
When gloom became familiar to the eye,
When I perceive how others seem to rest,
With every evil rankling in my breast,—
Led by example, I put on the man,
Sing off my sighs, and trifle as I can.

Homer! nay Pope! (for never will I seek
Applause for learning—nought have I with Greek)
Give us the secrets of his pagan hell,
Where ghost with ghost in sad communion dwell;
Where shade meets shade, and round the gloomy meads
They glide and speak of old heroic deeds,—
What fields they conquer'd, and what foes they slew
And sent to join the melancholy crew.

"When a new spirit in that world was found,
A thousand shadowy forms came flitting round;
Those who had known him, fond inquiries made,—
'Of all we left, inform us, gentle shade,
Now as we lead thee in our realms to dwell,
Our twilight groves, and meads of asphodel.'

"What paints the poet, is our station here,
Where we like ghosts and flitting shades appear
This is the hell he sings, and here me meet,
And former deeds to new-made friends repeat:
Heroic deeds, which here obtain us fame,
And are, in fact the causes why we came:
Yes! this dim region is old Homer's hell,
Abate but groves and meads of asphodel

"Here, when a stranger from your world we spy,
We gather round him and for news apply;
He hears unheeding, nor can speech endure,
But shivering gazes on the vast obscure:
We smiling pity, and by kindness show
We felt his feelings and his terrors know;
Then speak of comfort—time will give him sight,
Where now 't is dark; where now 't is wo—delight.

"'Have hope,' we say, 'and soon the place to thee
Shall not a prison but a castle be;
When to the wretch whom care and guilt confound,
The world 's a prison with a wider bound;
Go where he may, he feels himself confined,
And wears the fetters of an abject mind.'

"But now adieu! those giant keys appear,
Thou art not worthy to be inmate here:
Go to thy world, and to the young declare
What we, our spirits and employments, are;
Tell them how we the ills of life endure,
Our empire stable, and our state secure;
Our dress, our diet, for their use describe,
And bid them haste to join the gen'rous tribe:
Go to thy world, and leave us here to dwell,
Who to its joys and comforts bid farewell."

Farewell to these; but other scenes I view,
And other griefs, and guilt of deeper hue;
Where conscience gives to outward ills her pain,
Gloom to the night, and pressure to the chain:
Here separate cells awhile in misery keep
Two doom'd to suffer: there they strive for sleep;
By day indulged, in larger space they range,
Their bondage certain, but their bounds have change.

One was a female, who had grievous ill
Wrought in revenge, and she enjoy'd it still:
With death before her, and her fate in view,
Unsated vengeance in her bosom grew:
Sullen she was and threat'ning; in her eye
Glared the stern triumph that she dared to die:
But first a being in the world must leave—
'T was once reproach; 't was now a short reprieve.

She was a pauper bound, who early gave
Her mind to vice, and doubly was a slave;
Upbraided, beaten, held by rough control,
Revenge sustain'd, inspired, and fill'd her soul:
She fired a full-stored barn, confess'd the fact,
And laugh'd at law and justified the act:
Our gentle vicar tried his powers in vain,
She answer'd not, or answer'd with disdain;
Th' approaching fate she heard without a sigh,
And neither cared to live nor fear'd to die.

Not so he felt, who with her was to pay
The forfeit, life—with dread he view'd the day,
And that short space which yet for him remain'd,
Till with his limbs his faculties were chain'd:
He paced his narrow bounds some ease to find,
But found it not,—no comfort reach'd his mind:
Each sense was palsied; when he tasted food,
He sigh'd and said, "Enough—'t is very good."
Since his dread sentence, nothing seem'd to be
As once it was—he seeing could not see,
Nor hearing, hear aright;—when first I came
Within his view, I fancied there was shame,
I judged resentment; I mistook the air,—
These fainter passions live not with despair;
Or but exist and die:—Hope, fear, and love,
Joy, doubt, and hate, may other spirits move,
But touch not his, who every waking hour
Has one fix'd dread, and always feels its power.

"But will not mercy?"—No! she cannot plead
For such an outrage;—'t was a cruel deed;
He stopp'd a timid traveller;—to his breast,
With oaths and curses, was the danger press'd:—
No! he must suffer; pity we may find
For one man's pangs, but must not rob mankind

Still I behold him, every thought employ'd
On one dire view!—all others are destroy'd;
This makes his features ghastly, gives the tone
Of his few words resemblance to a groan:
He takes his tasteless food, and when 't is done,
Counts up his meals, now lessen'd by that one;
For expectation is on time intent,
Whether he brings us joy or punishment.

Yes! e'en in sleep the impressions all remain,
He hears the sentence and he feels the chain;
He sees the judge and jury, when he shakes,
And loudly cries, "Not guilty," and awakes:
Then chilling tremblings o'er his body creep,
Till worn-out nature is compell'd to sleep.

Now comes the dream again; it shows each scene,
With each small circumstance that comes between—
The call to suffering and the very deed—
There crowds go with him, follow, and precede;
Some heartless shout, some pity, all condemn,
While he in fancied envy looks at them;
He seems the place for that sad act to see,
And dreams the very thirst which then will be:
A priest attends—it seems, the one he knew
In his best days, beneath whose care he grew.

At this his terrors take a sudden flight,
He sees his native village with delight;
The house, the chamber, where he once array'd
His youthful person; where he knelt and pray'd:
Then too the comforts he enjoy'd at home,
The days of joy; the joys themselves are come;—
The hours of innocence;—the timid look
Of his loved maid, when first her hand he took
And told his hope; her trembling joy appears,
Her forced reserve, and his retreating fears.

All now is present;—'t is a moment's gleam
Of former sunshine—stay, delightful dream!
Let him within his pleasant garden walk,
Give him her arm, of blessings let them talk.

Yes! all are with him now, and all the while
Life's early prospects and his Fanny's smile:
Then come his sister and his village-friend,
And he will now the sweetest moments spend
Life has to yield;—No! never will he find
Again on earth such pleasure in his mind:
He goes through shrubby walks these friends among,
Love in their looks and honour on the tongue:
Nay, there 's a charm beyond what nature shows,
The bloom is softer and more sweetly glows;-
Pierced by no crime, and urged by no desire
For more than true and honest hearts require

They feel the calm delight, and thus proceed
Through the green lane—then linger in the mead—
Stray o'er the heath in all its purple bloom,—
And pluck the blossom where the wild bees hum;
Then through the broomy bound with ease they pass,
And press the sandy sheep-walk's slender grass,
Where dwarfish flowers among the gorse are spread,
And the lamb browses by the linnet's bed;
Then 'cross the bounding brook they make their way
O'er its rough bridge—and there behold the bay!—
The ocean smiling to the fervid sun—
The waves that faintly fall and slowly run—
The ships at distance and the boats at hand;
And now they walk upon the sea-side sand,
Counting the number and what kind they be,
Ships softly sinking in the sleepy sea:
Now arm in arm, now parted, they behold
The glitt'ring waters on the shingles roll'd:
The timid girls, half dreading their design,
Dip the small foot in the retarded brine,
And search for crimson weeds, which spreading flow,
Or lie like pictures on the sand below;
With all those bright red pebbles that the sun
Through the small waves so softly shines upon;
And those live lucid jellies which the eye
Delights to trace as they swim glitt'ring by:
Pearl-shells and rubied star-fish they admire,
And will arrange above the parlour-fire,—
Tokens of bliss!—"Oh! horrible! a wave
Roars as it rises—save me, Edward! save!"
She cries:—Alas! the watchman on his way
Calls and lets in—truth, terror, and the day!

LETTER XXIV.

SCHOOLS.

Tu quoque ne metuas, quamvis schola verbere multo
Increpet et truculenta senex geret ora magister;
Degeneres animos timor arguit: at tibi consta
Intrepidus, nec te clamor plagæque sonantes,
Nec matutinis agitet formido sub horis,
Quod sceptrum vibrat ferulæ, quod multa supellex
Virgea, quod molis scuticam prætexit aluta,
Quod fervent trepido subsellia vestra tumultu,
Pompa loci, et vani fugiatur scena timoris.

AUSONIUS *in Protreptico ad Nepotem.*

Be it a weakness, it deserves some praise,—
We love the play-place of our early days;
The scene is touching, and the heart is stone
That feels not at that sight—and feels at none.
The wall on which we tried our graving skill;
The very name we carved subsisting still;
The bench on which we sat while deep employ'd,
Though mangled, hack'd, and hew'd, yet not destroy'd.
The little ones unbutton'd, glowing hot,
Playing our games, and on the very spot;
As happy as we once to kneel and draw
The chalky ring and knuckle down at taw.
This fond attachment to the well-known place,
When first we started into life's long race,
Maintains its hold with such unfailing sway,
We feel it e'en in age and at our latest day.

COWPER.

Schools of every Kind to be found in the Borough—The School for Infants—The School Preparatory; the Sagacity of the Mistress in foreseeing Character—Day-Schools of the lower Kind—A Master with Talents adapted to such Pupils: one of superior Qualifications—Boarding-Schools: that for young Ladies: one going first to the Governess, one finally returning Home—School for Youth: Master and Teacher; various Dispositions and Capacities—The Miser-Boy—The Boy-Bully—Sons of Farmers: how amused—What Study will effect, examined—A College Life: one sent from his College to a Benefice; one retained there in Dignity—The Advantages in either Case not considerable—Where then the Good of a Literary Life?—Answered—Conclusion.

To every class we have a school assign'd,
Rules for all ranks and food for every mind:
Yet one there is, that small regard to rule
Or study pays, and still is deem'd a school;
That, where a deaf, poor, patient widow sits,
And awes some thirty infants as she knits;
Infants of humble, busy wives, who pay
Some trifling price for freedom through the day.
At this good matron's hut the children meet,
Who thus becomes the mother of the street:
Her room is small, they cannot widely stray,—
Her threshold high, they cannot run away:
Though deaf, she sees the rebel-heroes shout,—
Though lame, her white rod nimbly walks about;
With band of yarn she keeps offenders in,
And to her gown the sturdiest rogue can pin:
Aided by these, and spells, and tell-tale birds,
Her power they dread and reverence her words.

To learning's second seats we now proceed,
Where humming students gilded primers read;
Or books with letters large and pictures gay,
To make their reading but a kind of play—
"Reading made Easy," so the titles tell;
But they who read must first begin to spell:
There may be profit in these arts, but still
Learning is labour, call it what you will;
Upon the youthful mind a heavy load,
Nor must we hope to find the royal road.
Some will their easy steps to science show,
And some to heav'n itself their by-way know;
Ah! trust them not,—who fame or bliss would share,
Must learn by labour, and must live by care.

Another matron, of superior kind,
For higher schools prepares the rising mind;
Preparatory she her learning calls,
The step first made to colleges and halls.

She early sees to what the mind will grow,
Nor abler judge of infant-powers I know;
She sees what soon the lively will impede,
And how the steadier will in turn succeed;
Observes the dawn of wisdom, fancy, taste,
And knows what parts will wear and what will waste:
She marks the mind too lively, and at once
Sees the gay coxcomb and the rattling dunce.

Long has she lived, and much she loves to trace
Her former pupils, now a lordly race;
Whom when she sees rich robes and furs bedeck,
She marks the pride which once she strove to check:
A burgess comes, and she remembers well
How hard her task to make his worship spell;
Cold, selfish, dull, inanimate, unkind,
'T was but by anger he display'd a mind:
Now civil, smiling, complaisant, and gay,
The world has worn th' unsocial crust away;
That sullen spirit now a softness wears,
And, save by fits, e'en dullness disappears:
But still the matron can the man behold,
Dull, selfish, hard, inanimate, and cold.
A merchant passes,—"probity and truth,
Prudence and patience, mark'd thee from thy youth."
Thus she observes, but oft retains her fears
For him, who now with name unstain'd appears;
Nor hope relinquishes, for one who yet
Is lost in error and involved in debt:
For latent evil in that heart she found,
More open here, but here the core was sound.

Various our day-schools: here behold we one
Empty and still:—the morning duties done,
Soil'd, tatter'd, worn, and thrown in various heaps,
Appear their books, and there confusion sleeps;
The workmen all are from the Babel fled,
And lost their tools, till the return they dread:
Meantime the master, with his wig awry,
Prepares his books for business by-and-by:
Now all th' insignia of the monarch laid
Beside him rest, and none stand by afraid;
He, while his troop light-hearted leap and play,
Is all intent on duties of the day;
No more the tyrant stern or judge severe,
He feels the father's and the husband's fear.

Ah! little think the timid trembling crowd,
That one so wise, so powerful, and so proud,
Should feel himself, and dread the humble ills
Of rent-day charges and of coalman's bills;
That while they mercy from their judge implore,
He fears himself—a knocking at the door;
And feels the burthen as his neighbour states
His humble portion to the parish-rates.

They sit th' allotted hours, then eager run,
Rushing to pleasure when the duty's done;
His hour of leisure is of different kind,
Then cares domestic rush upon his mind,
And half the ease and comfort he enjoys,
Is when surrounded by slates, books, and boys.

Poor Reuben Dixon has the noisiest school
Of ragged lads, who ever bow'd to rule;
Low in his price—the men who heave our coals,
And clean our causeways, send him boys in shoals:
To see poor Reuben, with his fry beside,—
Their half-check'd rudeness and his half-scorn'd pride,—
Their room, the sty in which th' assembly meet,
In the close lane behind the Northgate-street;
T' observe his vain attempts to keep the peace,
'Till tolls the bell, and strife and troubles cease,—
Calls for our praise; his labour praise deserves,
But not our pity; Reuben has no nerves:
'Mid noise and dirt, and stench, and play, and prate,
He calmly cuts the pen or views the slate.

But Leonard!—yes, for Leonard's fate I grieve,
Who loathes the station which he dares not leave;
He cannot dig, he will not beg his bread,
All his dependence rests upon his head;
And deeply skill'd in sciences and arts,
On vulgar lads he wastes superior parts.

Alas! what grief that feeling mind sustains,
In guiding hands and stirring torpid brains;
He whose proud mind from pole to pole will move,
And view the wonders of the worlds above;
Who thinks and reasons strongly:—hard his fate,
Confined for ever to the pen and slate:
True, he submits; and when the long dull day
Has slowly pass'd, in weary tasks, away,
To other worlds with cheerful view he looks,
And parts the night between repose and books.

Amid his labours, he has sometimes tried
To turn a little from his cares aside;
Pope, Milton, Dryden, with delight has seized,
His soul engaged and of his trouble eased:
When, with a heavy eye and ill-done sum,
No part conceived, a stupid boy will come,
Then Leonard first subdues the rising frown,
And bids the blockhead lay his blunders down;
O'er which disgusted he will turn his eye,
To his sad duty his sound mind apply,
And, vex'd in spirit, throw his pleasures by.

Turn we to schools which more than these afford—
The sound instruction and the wholesome board;
And first our school for ladies:—pity calls
For one soft sigh, when we behold these walls,
Placed near the town, and where, from window high
The fair, confined, may our free crowds espy,
With many a stranger gazing up and down,
And all the envied tumult of the town;
May, in the smiling summer-eve, when they
Are sent to sleep the pleasant hours away,
Behold the poor (whom they conceive the bless'd)
Employ'd for hours, and grieved they cannot rest.

Here the fond girl, whose days are sad and few
Since dear mamma pronounced the last adieu,
Looks to the road, and fondly thinks she hears
The carriage-wheels, and struggles with her tears:
All yet is new, the misses great and small,
Madam herself, and teachers, odious all;
From laughter, pity, nay command, she turns,
But melts in softness, or with anger burns;
Nauseates her food, and wonders who can sleep
On such mean beds, where she can only weep:
She scorns condolence—But to all she hates
Slowly at length her mind accommodates;
Then looks on bondage with the same concern
As others felt, and finds that she must learn
As others learn'd—the common lot to share,
To search for comfort and snbmit to care.

There are, 't is said, who on these seats attend,
And to these ductile minds destruction vend;
Wretches (to virtue, peace, and nature, foes)
To these soft minds, their wicked trash expose;
Seize on the soul, ere passions take the sway,
And lead the heart, ere yet it feels, astray:

Smugglers obscene!—and can there be who take
Infernal pains, the sleeping vice to wake?
Can there be those, by whom the thought defiled
Enters the spotless bosom of a child?
By whom the ill is to the heart convey'd,
Who lend the foe, not yet in arms, their aid,
And sap the city-walls before the siege be laid?

Oh! rather skulking in the by-ways steal,
And rob the poorest traveller of his meal;
Burst through the humblest trader's bolted door;
Bear from the widow's hut her winter-store!
With stolen steed, on highways take your stand,
Your lips with curses arm'd, with death your hand;—
Take all but life—the virtuous more would say,
Take life itself, dear as it is, away,
Rather than guilty thus the guileless soul betray.

Years pass away—let us suppose them past,
Th' accomplish'd nymph for freedom looks at last;
All hardships over, which a school contains,
The spirit's bondage and the body's pains;
Where teachers make the heartless, trembling set
Of pupils suffer for their own regret;
Where winter's cold, attack'd by one poor fire,
Chills the fair child, commanded to retire;
She felt it keenly in the morning air,
Keenly she felt it at the evening prayer.
More pleasant summer; but then walks were made,
Not a sweet ramble, but a slow parade;
They moved by pairs beside the hawthorn-hedge,
Only to set their feelings on an edge;
And now at eve, when all their spirits rise,
Are sent to rest, and all their pleasure dies;
Where yet they all the town alert can see,
And distant plough-boys pacing o'er the lea.

These and the tasks successive masters brought—
The French they conn'd, the curious works they wrought;
The hours they made their taper fingers strike,
Note after note, all dull to them alike;
Their drawings, dancings on appointed days,
Playing with globes, and getting parts of plays;
The tender friendships made 'twixt heart and heart,
When the dear friends had nothing to impart:—

All! all! are over;—now th' accomplish'd maid
Longs for the world, of nothing there afraid:
Dreams of delight invade her gentle breast,
And fancied lovers rob the heart of rest;
At the paternal door a carriage stands,
Love knits their hearts and Hymen joins their hands.

Ah!—world unknown! how charming is thy view,
Thy pleasures many, and each pleasure new:
Ah!—world experienced! what of thee is told?
How few thy pleasures, and those few how cold!

Within a silent street, and far apart
From noise of business, from a quay or mart,
Stands an old spacious building, and the din
You hear without, explains the work within;
Unlike the whispering of the nymphs, this noise
Loudly proclaims a "boarding-school for boys:"
The master heeds it not, for thirty years
Have render'd all familiar to his ears;
He sits in comfort, 'mid the various sound
Of mingled tones for ever flowing round;
Day after day he to his task attends,—
Unvaried toil, and care that never ends:
Boys in their works proceed; while his employ
Admits no change, or changes but the boy:
Yet time has made it easy;—he beside
Has power supreme, and power is sweet to pride:
But grant him pleasure;—what can teachers feel,
Dependent helpers always at the wheel?
Their power despised, their compensation small,
Their labour dull, their life laborious all;
Set after set the lower lads to make
Fit for the class which their superiors take;
The road of learning for a time to track
In roughest state, and then again go back:
Just the same way on other troops to wait,—
Attendants fix'd at learning's lower gate.

The day-tasks now are over,—to their ground
Rush the gay crowd with joy-compelling sound;
Glad to illude the burthens of the day,
The eager parties hurry to their play:
Then in these hours of liberty we find
The native bias of the opening mind;
They yet possess not skill the mask to place,
And hide the passions glowing in the face;
Yet some are found—the close, the sly, the mean,
Who know already all must not be seen.

Lo! one who walks apart, although so young,
He lays restraint upon his eye and tongue;
Nor will he into scrapes or danger get,
And half the school are in the stripling's debt:
Suspicious, timid, he is much afraid
Of trick and plot:—he dreads to be betray'd:
He shuns all friendship, for he finds they lend,
When lads begin to call each other friend:
Yet self with self has war; the tempting sight
Of fruit on sale provokes his appetite;
See! how he walks the sweet seduction by;
That he is tempted, costs him first a sigh,—
'T is dangerous to indulge, 't is grievous to deny!
This he will choose, and whispering asks the price,
The purchase dreadful, but the portion nice;
Within the pocket he explores the pence:
Without, temptation strikes on either sense,
The sight, the smell;—but then he thinks again
Of money gone! while fruit nor taste remain.
Meantime there comes an eager thoughtless boy,
Who gives the price and only feels the joy:
Example dire! the youthful miser stops,
And slowly back the treasured coinage drops:
Heroic deed! for should he now comply,
Can he to-morrow's appetite deny?
Beside, these spendthrifts who so friendly live,
Cloy'd with their purchase, will a portion give:—
Here ends debate, he buttons up his store,
And feels the comfort that it burns no more.

Unlike to him the tyrant-boy, whose sway
All hearts acknowledge; him the crowds obey
At his command they break through every rule,
Whoever governs, he controls the school:
'T is not the distant emperor moves their fear,
But the proud viceroy who is ever near.

Verres could do that mischief in a day,
For which not Rome, in all its power, could pay;
And these boy-tyrants will their slaves distress,
And do the wrongs no master can redress:
The mind they load with fear: it feels disdain
For its own baseness; yet it tries in vain
To shake th' admitted power;—the coward comes again:
'T is more than present pain these tyrants give,
Long as we 've life some strong impressions live;
And these young ruffians in the soul will sow
Seeds of all vices that on weakness grow.

Hark! at his word the trembling younglings flee,
Where he is walking none must walk but he;
See! from the winter-fire the weak retreat,
His the warm corner, his the favourite seat,
Save when he yields it to some slave to keep
Awhile, then back, at his return, to creep:
At his command his poor dependents fly,
And humbly bribe him as a proud ally;
Flatter'd by all, the notice he bestows,
Is gross abuse, and bantering and blows;
Yet he 's a dunce, and, spite of all his fame
Without the desk, within he feels his shame:
For there the weaker boy, who felt his scorn,
For him corrects the blunders of the morn;
And he is taught, unpleasant truth! to find
The trembling body has the prouder mind.

Hark! to that shout, that burst of empty noise,
From a rude set of bluff, obstreperous boys;
They who, like colts let loose, with vigour bound,
And thoughtless spirit, o'er the beaten ground;
Fearless they leap, and every youngster feels
His Alma active in his hands and heels.

These are the sons of farmers, and they come
With partial fondness for the joys of home;
Their minds are coursing in their fathers' fields,
And e'en the dream a lively pleasure yields;
They, much enduring, sit th' allotted hours,
And o'er a grammar waste their sprightly powers,
They dance; but them can measured steps delight,
Whom horse and hounds to daring deeds excite?
Nor could they bear to wait from meal to meal,
Did they not slyly to the chamber steal,
And there the produce of the basket seize,
The mother's gift! still studious of their ease.
Poor Alma, thus oppress'd, forbears to rise,
But rests or revels in the arms and thighs.*

"But is it sure that study will repay
The more attentive and forbearing?"—Nay!
The farm, the ship, the humble shop have each
Gains which severest studies seldom reach.

At college place a youth, who means to raise
His state by merit and his name by praise;
Still much he hazards; there is serious strife
In the contentions of a scholar's life:
Not all the mind's attention, care, distress,
Nor diligence itself, ensure success:
His jealous heart a rival's power may dread,
'Till its strong feelings have confused his head,
And, after days and months, nay, years of pain,
He finds just lost the object he would gain.

But grant him this and all such life can give,
For other prospects he begins to live;
Begins to feel that man was form'd to look
And long for other objects than a book:
In his mind's eye his house and glebe he sees,
And farms and talks with farmers at his ease;
And time is lost, till fortune sends him forth
To a rude world unconscious of his worth;
There in some petty parish to reside,
The college-boast, then turn'd the village-guide;
And though awhile his flock and dairy please,
He soon reverts to former joys and ease,
Glad when a friend shall come to break his rest,
And speak of all the pleasures they possess'd,
Of masters, fellows, tutors, all with whom
They shared those pleasures, never more to come;
Till both conceive the times by bliss endear'd,
Which once so dismal and so dull appear'd.

But fix our scholar, and suppose him crown'd
With all the glory gain'd on classic ground;
Suppose the world without a sigh resign'd,
And to his college all his care confined;
Give him all honours that such states allow,
The freshman's terror and the tradesman's bow;
Let his apartments with his taste agree,
And all his views be those he loves to see;
Let him each day behold the savoury treat,
For which he pays not, but is paid to eat;
These joys and glories soon delight no more,
Although withheld, the mind is vex'd and sore;
The honour too is to the place confined,
Abroad they know not each superior mind:
Strangers no *wranglers* in these figures see,
Nor give they worship to a high degree;
Unlike the prophet's is the scholar's case,
His honour all is in his dwelling-place:
And there such honours are familiar things;
What is a monarch in a crowd of kings?
Like other sovereigns he 's by forms address'd,
By statutes govern'd and with rules oppress'd.

When all these forms and duties die away,
And the day passes like the former day,
Then of exterior things at once bereft,
He's to himself and one attendant left:
Nay, John too goes; nor aught of service more
Remains for him; he gladly quits the door,
And, as he whistles to the college-gate,
He kindly pities his poor master's fate.

Books cannot always please, however good,
Minds are not ever craving for their food;
But sleep will soon the weary soul prepare
For cares to-morrow that were this day's care:
For forms, for feasts, that sundry times have past,
And formal feasts that will for ever last.

"But then from study will no comforts rise?"
Yes! such as studious minds alone can prize;
Comforts, yea!—joys ineffable they find,
Who seek the prouder pleasures of the mind:
The soul, collected in those happy hours,
Then makes her efforts, then enjoys her powers;
And in those seasons feels herself repaid,
For labours past and honours long delay'd.

* Should any of my readers find themselves at a loss in this place I beg leave to refer them to a poem of Prior, called Alma, or the Progress of the Mind.

No! 't is not worldly gain, although by chance
The sons of learning may to wealth advance;
Nor station high, though in some favouring hour
The sons of learning may arrive at power;
Nor is it glory, though the public voice
Of honest praise will make the heart rejoice:
But 't is the mind's own feelings give the joy,
Pleasures she gathers in her own employ—
Pleasures that gain or praise cannot bestow,
Yet can dilate and raise them when they flow.

For this the poet looks the world around,
Where form and life and reasoning man are found:
He loves the mind, in all its modes, to trace,
And all the manners of the changing race;
Silent he walks the road of life along,
And views the aims of its tumultuous throng:
He finds what shapes the Proteus-passions take,
And what strange waste of life and joy they make,
And loves to show them in their varied ways,
With honest blame or with unflattering praise:
'T is good to know, 't is pleasant to impart,
These turns and movements of the human heart;
The stronger features of the soul to paint,
And make distinct the latent and the faint;
Man as he is, to place in all men's view,
Yet none with rancour, none with scorn pursue:
Nor be it ever of my portraits told—
"Here the strong lines of malice we behold."—

This let me hope, that when in public view
I bring my pictures, men may feel them true;
"This is a likeness," may they all declare,
"And I have seen him, but I know not where:"
For I should mourn the mischief I had done,
If as the likeness all would fix on one.

Man's vice and crime I combat as I can,
But to his God and conscience leave the man;
I search (a Quixote!) all the land about,
To find its giants and enchanters out,
(The giant-folly, the enchanter-vice,
Whom doubtless I shall vanquish in a trice;)
But is there man whom I would injure?—no!
I am to him a fellow, not a foe,—
A fellow-sinner, who must rather dread
The bolt, than hurl it at another's head.

No! let the guiltless, if there such be found,
Launch forth the spear, and deal the deadly wound
How can I so the cause of virtue aid,
Who am myself attainted and afraid?
Yet as I can, I point the powers of rhyme,
And, sparing criminals, attack the crime.

Tales.

TO HER GRACE

ISABELLA DUCHESS DOWAGER OF RUTLAND.

Madam,

The dedication of works of literature to persons of superior worth and eminence appears to have been a measure early adopted, and continued to the present time; so that, whatever objections have been made to the language of dedicators, such addresses must be considered as perfectly consistent with reason and propriety: in fact, superior rank and elevated situation in life naturally and justly claim such respect; and it is the prerogative of greatness to give countenance and favour to all who appear to merit and to need them: it is likewise the prerogative of every kind of superiority and celebrity, of personal merit when peculiar or extraordinary, of dignity, elegance, wealth, and beauty; certainly of superior intellect and intellectual acquirements: every such kind of eminence has its privilege, and being itself an object of distinguished approbation, it gains attention for whomsoever its possessor distinguishes and approves.

Yet the causes and motives for an address of this kind rest not entirely with the merit of the patron, the feelings of the author himself having their weight and consideration in the choice he makes: he may have gratitude for benefits received; or pride, not illaudable, in aspiring to the favour of those whose notice confers honour; or he may entertain a secret but strong desire of seeing a name in the entrance of his work which he is accustomed to utter with peculiar satisfaction, and to hear mentioned with veneration and delight.

Such, madam, are the various kinds of eminence for which an author on these occasions would probably seek, and they meet in your grace; such too are the feelings by which he would be actuated, and they centre in me: let me therefore entreat your grace to take this book into your favour and protection, and to receive it as an offering of the utmost respect and duty, from,

May it please Your Grace,
Your Grace's most obedient, humble,
And devoted servant,

Geo. Crabbe.

Muston, July 31, 1812.

PREFACE.

That the appearance of the present work before the public is occasioned by a favourable reception of the former two, I hesitate not to acknowledge; because, while the confession may be regarded as some proof of gratitude, or at least of attention from an author to his readers, it ought not to be considered as an indication of vanity. It is unquestionably very pleasant to be assured that our labours are well received; but, nevertheless, this must not be taken for a just and full criterion of their merit: publications of great intrinsic value have been met with so much coolness, that a writer who succeeds in obtaining some degree of notice should look upon himself rather as one favoured than meritorious, as gaining a prize from Fortune, and not a recompense for desert: and, on the contrary, as it is well known tnat books of very inferior kind have been at once pushed into the strong current of popularity, and are there kept buoyant by the force of the stream, the writer who acquires not this adventitious help may be reckoned rather as unfortunate than undeserving; and from these opposite considerations it follows, that a man may speak of his success without incurring justly the odium of conceit, and may likewise acknowledge a disappointment without an adequate cause for humiliation or self-reproach.

But were it true that something of the complacency of self-approbation would insinuate itself into an author's mind with the idea of success, the sensation would not be that of unalloyed pleasure; it would perhaps assist him to bear, but it would not enable him to escape, the mortification he must encounter from censures, which, though he may be unwilling to admit, yet he finds himself unable to confute; as well as from advice, which, at the same time that he cannot but approve, he is compelled to reject.

Reproof and advice, it is probable, every author will receive, if we except those who merit so much of the former, that the latter is contemptuously denied them; now of these, reproof, though it may cause more temporary uneasiness, will in many cases create less difficulty, since errors may be corrected when opportunity occurs: but advice, I repeat, may be of such nature, that it will be painful to reject, and yet impossible to follow it; and in this predicament I conceive myself to be placed. There has been recommended to me, and from authority which neither inclination nor prudence leads me to resist, in any new work I might undertake, an unity of subject, and that arrangement of my materials which connects the whole and gives additional interest to every part; in fact, if not an Epic Poem, strictly so denominated, yet such composition as would possess a regular succession of events, and a catastrophe to which every incident should be subservient, and which every character, in a greater or less degree, should conspire to accomplish.

In a Poem of this nature, the principal and inferior characters in some degree resemble a general and his army, where no one pursues his peculiar objects and adventures, or pursues them in unison with the movements and grand purposes of the whole body; where there is a community of interests and a subordination of actors: and it was upon this view of the subject, and of the necessity for such distribution of persons and events, that I found myself obliged to relinquish an undertaking, for which the characters I could command, and the adventures I could describe, were altogether unfitted.

But if these characters which seemed to be at my disposal were not such as would coalesce into one body, nor were of a nature to be commanded by one mind, so neither on examination did they appear as an unconnected multitude, accidentally collected, to be suddenly dispersed; but rather beings of whom might be formed groups and smaller societies, the relations of whose adventures and pursuits might bear that kind of similitude to an Heroic Poem, which these minor associations of men (as pilgrims on the way to their saint, or parties in search of amusement, travellers excited by curiosity, or adventurers in pursuit of gain) have in points of connexion and importance with a regular and disciplined army.

Allowing this comparison, it is manifest that while much is lost for want of unity of subject and grandeur of design, something is gained by greater variety of incident and more minute display of character, by accuracy of description and diversity of scene: in these narratives we pass from gay to grave, from lively to severe, not only without impropriety, but with manifest advantage. In one continued and connected Poem, the reader is, in general, highly gratified or severely disappointed; by many independent narratives, he has the renovation of hope, although he has been dissatisfied, and a prospect of reiterated pleasure, should he find himself entertained.

I mean not, however, to compare these different modes of writing as if I were balancing their advantages and defects before I could give preference to either; with me the way I take is not a matter of choice, but of necessity; I present not my Tales to the reader as if I had chosen the best method of ensuring his approbation, but as using the only means I possessed of engaging his attention.

It may probably be remarked that Tales, however dissimilar, might have been connected by some associating circumstance to which the whole number might bear equal affinity, and that examples of such union are to be found in Chaucer, in Boccace, and other collectors and inventors of Tales, which, considered in themselves, are altogether independent; and to this idea I gave so much consideration as convinced me that I could not avail myself of the benefit of such artificial mode of affinity. To imitate the English poet, characters must be found adapted to their several relations, and this is a point of great difficulty and hazard: much allowance seems to be required even for Chaucer himself, since it is difficult to conceive that on any occasion the devout and delicate Prioress, the courtly and valiant Knight, and "the poure good Man the persone of a Towne," would be the voluntary companions of the drunken Miller, the licentious Sompnour, and "the Wanton Wife of Bath," and enter into that colloquial and travelling intimacy which, if a common pilgrimage to the shrine of St. Thomas may be said to excuse, I know nothing beside (and certainly nothing in these times) that would produce such effect. Boccace, it is true, avoids all difficulty of this kind, by not assigning to the ten relators of his hundred Tales any marked or peculiar characters; nor though there are male and female in company, can the sex of the narrator be distinguished in the narration. To have followed the method of Chaucer might have been of use, but could scarcely be adopted, from its difficulty; and to have taken that of the Italian writer would have been perfectly easy, but could be of no service: the attempt at union therefore has been relinquished, and these relations are submitted to the public, connected by no other circumstance than their being the productions of the same author, and devoted to the same purpose, the entertainment of his readers.

It has been already acknowledged, that these compositions have no pretensions to be estimated with the more lofty and heroic kind of poems, but I feel great reluctance in admitting that they have not a fair and legitimate claim to the poetic character. In vulgar estimation, indeed, all that is not prose passes for poetry; but I have not ambition of so humble a kind as to be satisfied with a concession which requires nothing in the poet, except his ability for counting syllables; and I trust something more of the poetic character will be allowed to the succeeding pages than what the heroes of the Dunciad might share with the author: nor was I aware that by describing, as faithfully as I could, men, manners, and things, I was forfeiting a just title to a name which has been freely granted to many whom to equal, and even to excel, is but very stinted commendation.

In this case it appears that the usual comparison between poetry and painting entirely fails. The artist who takes an accurate likeness of individuals, or a faithful representation of scenery, may not rank so high in the public estimation as one who paints an historical event, or an heroic action; but he is nevertheless a painter, and his accuracy is so far from diminishing his reputation, that it procures for him in general both fame and emolument. Nor is it perhaps with strict justice determined that the credit and reputation of those verses which strongly and faithfully delineate character and manners, should be lessened in the opinion of the public by the very accuracy which gives value and distinction to the productions of the pencil.

Nevertheless, it must be granted that the pretensions of any composition to be regarded as poetry will depend upon that definition of the poetic character which he who undertakes to determine the question has considered as decisive; and it is confessed also that one of great authority may be adopted, by which the verses now before the reader, and many others which have probably amused and delighted him, must be excluded. A definition like this will be found in the words which the greatest of poets, not divinely inspired, has given to the most noble and valiant Duke of Athens—

> The poet's eye, in a fine frenzy rolling,
> Doth glance from heaven to earth, from earth to heaven:
> And as Imagination bodies forth
> The forms of things unknown, the poet's pen
> Turns them to shapes, and gives to airy nothing
> A local habitation, and a name.*

Hence we observe the poet is one who, in the excursions of his fancy between heaven and earth, lights upon a kind of fairy-land, in which he places a creation of his own, where he embodies shapes, and gives action and adventure to his ideal offspring; taking captive the imagination of his readers, he elevates them above the grossness of actual being, into the soothing and pleasant atmosphere of supramundane existence: there he obtains for his visionary inhabitants the interest that engages a reader's attention without ruffling his feelings, and excites that moderate kind of sympathy which the realities of nature oftentimes fail to produce, either because they are so familiar and insignificant that they excite no determinate emotion, or are so harsh and powerful that the feelings excited are grating and distasteful.

Be it then granted that (as Duke Theseus observes) "such tricks have strong Imagination," and that such poets "are of imagination all compact;" let it be further conceded, that theirs is a higher and more dignified kind of composition, nay, the only kind that has pretensions to inspiration; still, that these poets should so entirely engross the title as to exclude those who address their productions to the plain sense and sober judgment of their readers, rather than to their fancy and imagination, I must repeat that I am unwilling to admit—because I conceive that, by granting such right of exclusion, a vast deal of what has been hitherto received as genuine poetry would no longer be entitled to that appellation.

All that kind of satire wherein character is skilfully delineated must (this criterion being allowed) no longer be esteemed as genuine poetry; and for the same reason many affecting narratives which are founded on real events, and borrow no aid whatever from the imagination of the writer, must likewise be rejected. A considerable part of the poems, as they have hitherto been denominated, of Chaucer, are of this naked and unveiled character: and there are in his Tales many pages of coarse, accurate, and minute, but very striking description. Many small poems in a subsequent age, of most impressive kind, are adapted and addressed to the common sense of the reader, and prevail by the strong language of truth and nature; they amused our ancestors, and they continue to engage our interest, and excite our feelings, by the same powerful appeals to the heart and affections. In times less remote, Dryden has given us much of this poetry, in which the force of expression and accuracy of description have neither needed nor obtained assistance from the fancy of the writer. The characters in his Absalom and Achitophel are instances of this, and more especially those of Doeg and Og in the second part; these, with all their grossness, and almost offensive

* Midsummer Night's Dream; act iv. scene 1.

accuracy, are found to possess that strength and spirit which has preserved from utter annihilation the dead bodies of Tate, to whom they were inhumanly bound, happily with a fate the reverse of that caused by the cruelty of Mezentius; for there the living perished in the putrefaction of the dead, and here the dead are preserved by the vitality of the living. And, to bring forward one other example, it will be found that Pope himself has no small portion of this actuality of relation, this nudity of description, and poetry without an atmosphere; the lines beginning, "In the worst inn's worst room," are an example, and many others may be seen in his Satires, Imitations, and above all in his Dunciad. The frequent absence of those "Sports of Fancy," and "Tricks of strong Imagination," have been so much observed, that some have ventured to question whether even this writer were a poet; and though, as Dr. Johnson has remarked, it would be difficult to form a definition of one in which Pope should not be admitted, yet they who doubted his claim, had, it is likely, provided for his exclusion by forming that kind of character for their poet, in which this elegant versifier, for so he must be then named, should not be comprehended.

These things considered, an author will find comfort in his expulsion from the rank and society of poets, by reflecting that men much his superiors were likewise shut out, and more especially when he finds also that men not much his superiors are entitled to admission.

But in whatever degree I may venture to differ from any others in my notion of the qualifications and character of the true poet, I most cordially assent to their opinion who assert that his principal exertions must be made to engage the attention of his readers. And further, I must allow that the effect of poetry should be to lift the mind from the painful realities of actual existence, from its every-day concerns, and its perpetually-occurring vexations, and to give it repose by substituting objects in their place which it may contemplate with some degree of interest and satisfaction. But what is there in all this, which may not be effected by a fair representation of existing character? nay, by a faithful delineation of those painful realities, those every-day concerns, and those perpetually-occuring vexations themselves, provided they be not (which is hardly to be supposed) the very concerns and distresses of the reader? for when it is admitted that they have no particular relation to him, but are the troubles and anxieties of other men, they excite and interest his feelings as the imaginary exploits, adventures, and perils of romance;—they soothe his mind, and keep his curiosity pleasantly awake; they appear to have enough of reality to engage his sympathy, but possess not interest sufficient to create painful sensations. Fiction itself, we know, and every work of fancy, must for a time have the effect of realities; nay, the very enchanters, spirits, and monsters of Ariosto and Spenser must be present in the mind of the reader while he is engaged by their operations, or they would be as the objects and incidents of a nursery tale to a rational understanding, altogether despised and neglected. In truth, I can but consider this pleasant effect upon the mind of a reader, as depending neither upon the events related (whether they be actual or imaginary,) nor upon the characters introduced (whether taken from life or fancy,) but upon the manner in which the poem itself is conducted; let that be judiciously managed, and the occurrences actually copied from life will have the same happy effect as the inventions of a creative fancy;—while, on the other hand, the imaginary persons and incidents to which the poet has given "a local habitation, and a name," will make upon the concurring feelings of the reader the same impressions with those taken from truth and nature, because they will appear to be derived from that source, and therefore of necessity will have a similar effect.

Having thus far presumed to claim for the ensuing pages the rank and title of poetry, I attempt no more, nor venture to class or compare them with any other kinds of poetical composition; their place will doubtless be found for them.

A principal view and wish of the poet must be to engage the mind of his readers, as, failing in that point, he will scarcely succeed in any other: I therefore willingly confess that much of my time and assiduity has been devoted to this purpose; but, to the ambition of pleasing, no other sacrifices have, I trust, been made, than of my own labour and care. Nothing will be found that militates against the rules of propriety and good manners, nothing that offends against the more important precepts of morality and religion; and with this negative kind of merit, I commit my book to the judgment and taste of the reader—not being willing to provoke his vigilance by professions of accuracy, nor to solicit his indulgence by apologies for mistakes.

TALE I.

THE DUMB ORATORS; OR, THE BENEFIT OF SOCIETY.

With fair round belly with good capon lined,
With eyes severe——
Full of wise saws and modern instances.
As you Like it, act ii, scene 7.

Deep shame hath struck me dumb.
King John, act iv, scene 2.

He gives the bastinado with his tongue,
Our ears are cudgell'd.
King John, act iv, scene 2.

Let 's kill all the lawyers;
Now show yourselves men: 't is for liberty:
We will not leave one lord or gentleman.
Henry VI, part 2, act ii, scene 7.

And thus the whirligig of time brings in his revenges.
Twelfth Night, act v, scene last.

That all men would be cowards if they dare,
Some men we know have courage to declare;
And this the life of many a hero shows,
That like the tide, man's courage ebbs and flows:
With friends and gay companions round them, then
Men boldly speak and have the hearts of men;

Who, with opponents seated, miss the aid
Of kind applauding looks, and grow afraid;
Like timid trav'llers in the night, they fear
Th' assault of foes, when not a friend is near.

In contest mighty and of conquest proud
Was Justice Bolt, impetuous, warm, and loud;
His fame, his prowess, all the country knew,
And disputants, with one so fierce, were few:
He was a younger son, for law design'd,
With dauntless look and persevering mind;
While yet a clerk, for disputation famed,
No efforts tired him, and no conflicts tamed.

Scarcely he bade his master's desk adieu,
When both his brothers from the world withdrew.
An ample fortune he from them possess'd,
And was with saving care and prudence bless'd.
Now would he go and to the country give
Example how an English 'squire should live;
How bounteous, yet how frugal man may be,
By a well-order'd hospitality;
He would the rights of all so well maintain,
That none should idle be, and none complain.

All this and more he purposed—and what man
Could do, he did to realize his plan:
But time convinced him that we cannot keep
A breed of reasoners like a flock of sheep;
For they, so far from following as we lead,
Make that a cause why they will not proceed.
Man will not follow where a rule is shown,
But loves to take a method of his own;
Explain the way with all your care and skill,
This will he quit, if but to prove he will.—
Yet had our Justice honour—and the crowd,
Awed by his presence, their respect avow'd.

In later years he found his heart incline,
More than in youth, to gen'rous food and wine;
But no indulgence check'd the powerful love
He felt to teach, to argue, and reprove.

Meetings, or public calls, he never miss'd—
To dictate often, always to assist.
Oft he the clergy join'd, and not a cause
Pertain'd to them but he could quote the laws;
He upon tithes and residence display'd
A fund of knowledge for the hearer's aid;
And could on glebe and farming, wool and grain,
A long discourse, without a pause, maintain.

To his experience and his native sense
He join'd a bold imperious eloquence;
The grave, stern look of men inform'd and wise,
A full command of feature, heart, and eyes,
An awe-compelling frown, and fear-inspiring size.
When at the table, not a guest was seen
With appetite so ling'ring, or so keen;
But when the outer man no more required,
The inner waked, and he was man inspired.
His subjects then were those, a subject true
Presents in fairest form to public view;
Of Church and State, of Law, with mighty strength
Of words he spoke, in speech of mighty length:
And now, into the vale of years declined,
He hides too little of the monarch-mind:
He kindles anger by untimely jokes,
And opposition by contempt provokes;
Mirth he suppresses by his awful frown,
And humble spirits, by disdain, keeps down;
Blamed by the mild, approved by the severe,
The prudent fly him, and the valiant fear.

For overbearing is his proud discourse,
And overwhelming of his voice the force;
And overpowering is he when he shows
What floats upon a mind that always overflows.

This ready man at every meeting rose,
Something to hint, determine, or propose;
And grew so fond of teaching, that he taught
Those who instruction needed not or sought:
Happy our hero, when he could excite
Some thoughtless talker to the wordy fight:
Let him a subject at his pleasure choose,
Physic or Law, Religion or the Muse;
On all such themes he was prepared to shine,
Physician, poet, lawyer, and divine.
Hemm'd in by some tough argument, borne down
By press of language and the awful frown,
In vain for mercy shall the culprit plead;
His crime is past and sentence must proceed:
Ah! suffering man, have patience, bear thy woes—
For lo! the clock—at ten the Justice goes.

This powerful man, on business or to please
A curious taste, or weary grown of ease,
On a long journey travell'd many a mile
Westward, and halted midway in our isle;
Content to view a city large and fair,
Though none had notice—what a man was there!

Silent two days, he then began to long
Again to try a voice so loud and strong;
To give his favourite topics some new grace,
And gain some glory in such distant place;
To reap some present pleasure, and to sow
Seeds of fair fame, in after-time to grow:
Here will men say, "We heard, at such an hour,
The best of speakers—wonderful his power."

Inquiry made, he found that day would meet
A learned club, and in the very street;
Knowledge to gain and give, was the design;
To speak, to hearken, to debate, and dine:
This pleased our traveller, for he felt his force
In either way, to eat or to discourse.

Nothing more easy than to gain access
To men like these, with his polite address:
So he succeeded, and first look'd around,
To view his objects and to take his ground;
And therefore silent chose awhile to sit,
Then enter boldly by some lucky hit;
Some observation keen or stroke severe,
To cause some wonder or excite some fear.

Now, dinner past, no longer he suppress'd
His strong dislike to be a silent guest;
Subjects and words were now at his command—
When disappointment frown'd on all he plann'd
For, hark!—he heard amazed, on every side,
His church insulted and her priests belied;
The laws reviled, the ruling power abused,
The land derided, and its foes excused:—
He heard and ponder'd.—What, to men so vile,
Should be his language? For his threat'ning style

They were too many:—if his speech were meek,
They would despise such poor attempts to speak;
At other times with every word at will,
He now sat lost, perplex'd, astonish'd, still.

Here were Socinians, Deists, and indeed
All who, as foes to England's church, agreed;
But still with creeds unlike, and some without a creed:
Here, too, fierce friends of liberty he saw,
Who own'd no prince and who obey no law;
There were Reformers of each different sort,
Foes to the laws, the priesthood, and the court;
Some on their favourite plans alone intent,
Some purely angry and malevolent:
The rash were proud to blame their country's laws;
The vain, to seem supporters of a cause;
One call'd for change that he would dread to see;
Another sigh'd for Gallic liberty!
And numbers joining with the forward crew,
For no one reason—but that numbers do.

"How," said the Justice, "can this trouble rise,
This shame and pain, from creatures I despise?"
And conscience answer'd—"The prevailing cause
Is thy delight in listening to applause;
Here, thou art seated with a tribe, who spurn
Thy favourite themes, and into laughter turn
Thy fears and wishes; silent and obscure,
Thyself, shalt thou the long harangue endure;
And learn, by feeling, what it is to force
On thy unwilling friends the long discourse:
What though thy thoughts be just, and these, it seems,
Are traitors' projects, idiots' empty schemes?
Yet, minds like bodies cramm'd, reject their food,
Nor will be forced and tortured for their good!"

At length, a sharp, shrewd, sallow man arose,
And begg'd he briefly might his mind disclose;
"It was his duty, in these worst of times,
T' inform the govern'd of their rulers' crimes:"
This pleasant subject to attend, they each
Prepared to listen, and forbore to teach.

Then voluble and fierce the wordy man
Through a long chain of favourite horrors ran:—
First, of the church, from whose enslaving power
He was deliver'd, and he bless'd the hour;
"Bishops and deans, and prebendaries all,"
He said, "were cattle fatt'ning in the stall;
Slothful and pursy, insolent and mean,
Were every bishop, prebendary, dean,
And wealthy rector: curates, poorly paid,
Were only dull;—he would not them upbraid."

From priests he turn'd to canons, creeds, and prayers,
Rubrics and rules, and all our church affairs;
Churches themselves, desk, pulpit, altar, all
The Justice reverenced—and pronounced their fall.

Then from religion Hammond turn'd his view,
To give our rulers the correction due;
Not one wise action had these triflers plann'd;
There was it seem'd, no wisdom in the land;
Save in this patriot tribe, who meet at times
To show the statesman's errors and his crimes.

Now here was Justice Bolt compell'd to sit,
To hear the deist's scorn, the rebel's wit;
The fact mis-stated, the envenom'd lie,
And staring, spell-bound, made not one reply.

Then were our laws abused—and with the laws
All who prepare, defend, or judge a cause:
"We have no lawyer whom a man can trust,"
Proceeded Hammond—"If the laws were just;
But they are evil; 't is the savage state
Is only good, and ours sophisticate!
See! the free creatures in their woods and plains,
Where without laws each happy monarch reigns,
King of himself—while we a number dread,
By slaves commanded and by dunces led;
Oh, let the name with either state agree—
Savage our own we 'll name, and civil theirs shall be."

The silent Justice still astonish'd sate,
And wonder'd much whom he was gazing at;
Twice he essay'd to speak—but in a cough
The faint, indignant, dying speech went off:
"But who is this?" thought he—"a demon vile,
With wicked meaning and a vulgar style:
Hammond they call him; they can give the name
Of man to devils.—Why am I so tame?
Why crush I not the viper?"—Fear replied,
"Watch him awhile, and let his strength be tried;
He will be foil'd, if man; but if his aid
Be from beneath, 't is well to be afraid."

"We are call'd free!" said Hammond—"doleful times
When rulers add their insult to their crimes;
For should our scorn expose each powerful vice,
It would be libel, and we pay the price."

Thus with licentious words the man went on,
Proving that liberty of speech was gone;
That all were slaves—nor had we better chance
For better times than as allies to France.
Loud groan'd the stranger—Why, he must relate;
And own'd, "In sorrow for his country's fate;"
"Nay, she were safe," the ready man replied,
"Might patriots rule her, and could reasoners guide;
When all to vote, to speak, to teach, are free,
Whate'er their creeds or their opinions be;
When books of statutes are consumed in flames,
And courts and copyholds are empty names;
Then will be times of joy—but ere they come,
Havock, and war, and blood must be our doom."

The man here paused—then loudly for reform
He call'd, and hail'd the prospect of the storm;
The wholesome blast, the fertilizing flood—
Peace gain'd by tumult, plenty bought with blood:
Sharp means, he own'd; but when the land's disease
Asks cure complete, no med'cines are like these.

Our Justice now, more led by fear than rage,
Saw it in vain with madness to engage;
With imps of darkness no man seeks to fight,
Knaves to instruct, or set deceivers right:
Then as the daring speech denounced these woes,
Sick at the soul, the grieving guest arose;
Quick on the board his ready cash he threw,
And from the demons to his closet flew:

There when secured, he pray'd with earnest zeal,
That all they wish'd these patriot-souls might feel;
"Let them to France, their darling country, haste,
And all the comforts of a Frenchman taste;
Let them his safety, freedom, pleasure know,
Feel all their rulers on the land bestow;
And be at length dismiss'd by one unerring blow;
Not hack'd and hew'd by one afraid to strike,
But shorn by that which shears all men alike;
Nor, as in Britain, let them curse delay
Of law, but borne without a form away—
Suspected, tried, condemn'd, and carted in a day;
Oh! let them taste what they so much approve,
These strong fierce freedoms of the land they love."*

Home came our hero, to forget no more
The fear he felt and ever must deplore:
For though he quickly join'd his friends again,
And could with decent force his themes maintain,
Still it occurr'd that, in a luckless time,
He fail'd to fight with heresy and crime;
It was observed his words were not so strong,
His tones so powerful, his harangues so long,
As in old times—for he would often drop
The lofty look, and of a sudden stop;
When conscience whisper'd, that he once was still,
And let the wicked triumph at their will;
And therefore now, when not a foe was near,
He had no right so valiant to appear.

Some years had pass'd, and he perceived his fears
Yield to the spirit of his earlier years—
When at a meeting, with his friends beside,
He saw an object that awaked his pride;
His shame, wrath, vengeance, indignation—all
Man's harsher feelings did that sight recall.

For lo! beneath him fix'd, our man of law
That lawless man the foe of order saw;
Once fear'd, now scorn'd: once dreaded, now abhorr'd;
A wordy man, and evil every word:
Again he gazed—"It is," said he, "the same;
Caught and secure: his master owes him shame:"
So thought our hero, who each instant found
His courage rising, from the numbers round.

As when a felon has escaped and fled,
So long, that law conceives the culprit dead;
And back recall'd her myrmidons, intent
On some new game, and with a stronger scent;
Till she beholds him in a place, where none
Could have conceived the culprit would have gone;
There he sits upright in his seat, secure,
As one whose conscience is correct and pure;
This rouses anger for the old offence,
And scorn for all such seeming and pretence;
So on this Hammond look'd our hero bold,
Rememb'ring well that vile offence of old;
And now he saw the rebel dared t' intrude
Among the pure, the loyal, and the good;
The crime provoked his wrath, the folly stirr'd his blood:

* The reader will perceive in these and the preceding verses allusions to the state of France, as that country was circumstanced some years since, rather than as it appears to be in the present date,—several years elapsing between the alarm of the loyal magistrate on the occasion now related, and a subsequent event that farther illustrates the remark with which the narrative commences.

Nor wonder was it if so strange a sight
Caused joy with vengeance, terror with delight;
Terror like this a tiger might create,
A joy like that to see his captive state,
At once to know his force and then decree his fate.

Hammond, much praised by numerous friends, was come
To read his lectures, so admired at home;
Historic lectures, where he loved to mix
His free plain hints on modern politics;
Here, he had heard, that numbers had design,
Their business finish'd, to sit down and dine;
This gave him pleasure, for he judged it right
To show by day, that he could speak by night.
Rash the design—for he perceived, too late,
Not one approving friend beside him sate;
The greater number, whom he traced around,
Were men in black, and he conceived they frown'd.
"I will not speak," he thought; "no pearls of mine
Shall be presented to this herd of swine!"
Not this avail'd him, when he cast his eye
On Justice Bolt; he could not fight, nor fly:
He saw a man to whom he gave the pain,
Which now he felt must be return'd again;
His conscience told him with what keen delight
He, at that time, enjoy'd a stranger's fright;
That stranger now befriended—he alone,
For all his insult, friendless, to atone;
Now he could feel it cruel that a heart
Should be distress'd, and none to take its part;
"Though one by one," said Pride, "I would defy
Much greater men, yet meeting every eye,
I do confess a fear—but he will pass me by."

Vain hope! the Justice saw the foe's distress,
With exultation he could not suppress;
He felt the fish was hook'd—and so forbore,
In playful spite, to draw it to the shore.
Hammond look'd round again; but none were near
With friendly smile, to still his growing fear;
But all above him seem'd a solemn row
Of priests and deacons, so they seem'd below:
He wonder'd who his right-hand man might be—
Vicar of Holt cum Uppingham was he;
And who the man of that dark frown possess'd—
Rector of Bradley and of Barton-west;
"A pluralist," he growl'd—but check'd the word,
That warfare might not, by his zeal, be stirr'd.

But now began the man above to show
Fierce looks and threat'nings to the man below;
Who had some thoughts his peace by flight to seek-
But how then lecture, if he dared not speak!—

Now as the Justice for the war prepared,
He seem'd just then to question if he dared:
"He may resist, although his power be small,
And growing desperate may defy us all;
One dog attack, and he prepares for flight—
Resist another, and he strives to bite;
Nor can I say, if this rebellious cur
Will fly for safety, or will scorn to stir."
Alarm'd by this, he lash'd his soul to rage,
Burn'd with strong shame and hurried to engage.

As a male turkey straggling on the green,
When by fierce harriers, terriers, mongrels seen,

He feels the insult of the noisy train,
And skulks aside, though moved by much disdain;
But when that turkey, at his own barn-door,
Sees one poor straying puppy and no more,
(A foolish puppy who had left the pack,
Thoughtless what foe was threat'ning at his back,)
He moves about, as ship prepared to sail,
He hoists his proud rotundity of tail,
The half-seal'd eyes and changeful neck he shows,
Where, in its quick'ning colours, vengeance glows;
From red to blue the pendent wattles turn,
Blue mix'd with red, as matches when they burn;
And thus th' intruding snarler to oppose,
Urged by enkindling wrath, he gobbling goes.

So look'd our hero in his wrath, his cheeks
Flush'd with fresh fires and glow'd in tingling streaks;
His breath by passion's force awhile restrain'd,
Like a stopp'd current, greater force regain'd;
So spoke, so look'd he, every eye and ear
Were fix'd to view him, or were turn'd to hear.

"My friends, you know me, you can witness all,
How urged by passion, I restrain my gall;
And every motive to revenge withstand—
Save when I hear abused my native land.

"Is it not known, agreed, confirm'd, confess'd,
That of all people, we are govern'd best?
We have the force of monarchies; are free,
As the most proud republicans can be;
And have those prudent counsels that arise
In grave and cautious aristocracies;
And live there those, in such all-glorious state,
Traitors protected in the land they hate?
Rebels, still warring with the laws that give
To them subsistence?—Yes, such wretches live.

"Ours is a church reform'd, and now no more
Is aught for man to mend or to restore;
'T is pure in doctrines, 't is correct in creeds,
Has nought redundant, and it nothing needs;
No evil is therein—no wrinkle, spot,
Stain, blame, or blemish:—I affirm there 's not.

"All this you know—now mark what once befell,
With grief I bore it, and with shame I tell;
I was entrapp'd—yes, so it came to pass,
'Mid heathen rebels, a tumultuous class;
Each to his country bore a hellish mind,
Each like his neighbour was of cursed kind;
The land that nursed them they blasphemed; the laws,
Their sovereign's glory, and their country's cause;
And who their mouths, their master-fiend, and who
Rebellion's oracle?——You, caitiff, you!"

He spoke, and standing stretch'd his mighty arm,
And fix'd the man of words, as by a charm.

"How raved that railer! Sure some hellish power
Restrain'd my tongue in that delirious hour,
Or I had hurl'd the shame and vengeance due
On him, the guide of that infuriate crew;
But to mine eyes such dreadful looks appear'd,
Such mingled yell of lying words I heard,
That I conceived around were demons all,
And till I fled the house, I fear'd its fall.

"Oh! could our country from our coasts expel
Such foes! to nourish those who wish her well:
This her mild laws forbid, but we may still
From us eject them by our sovereign will;
This let us do."—He said, and then began
A gentler feeling for the silent man;
Ev'n in our hero's mighty soul arose
A touch of pity for experienced woes;
But this was transient, and with angry eye
He sternly look'd, and paused for a reply.

'T was then the man of many words would speak—
But, in his trial, had them all to seek:
To find a friend he look'd the circle round,
But joy or scorn in every feature found;
He sipp'd his wine, but in those times of dread
Wine only adds confusion to the head;
In doubt he reason'd with himself—"And how
Harangue at night, if I be silent now?
From pride and praise received, he sought to draw
Courage to speak, but still remain'd the awe;
One moment rose he with a forced disdain,
And then abash'd, sunk sadly down again;
While in our hero's glance he seem'd to read,
"Slave and insurgent! what hast thou to plead?"—

By desperation urged, he now began:
"I seek no favour—I—the Rights of Man!
Claim; and I—nay!—but give me leave—and I
Insist—a man—that is—and in reply,
I speak."——Alas! each new attempt was vain:
Confused he stood, he sate, he rose again;
At length he growl'd defiance, sought the door,
Cursed the whole synod, and was seen no more.

"Laud we," said Justice Bolt, "the Powers above
Thus could our speech the sturdiest foe remove."
Exulting now he gain'd new strength of fame,
And lost all feelings of defeat and shame.

"He dared not strive, you witness'd—dared not lift
His voice, nor drive at his accursed drift:
So all shall tremble, wretches who oppose
Our church or state—thus be it to our foes."

He spoke, and, seated with his former air,
Look'd his full self, and fill'd his ample chair;
Took one full bumper to each favourite cause,
And dwelt all night on politics and laws,
With high applauding voice, that gain'd him high applause.

TALE II.

THE PARTING HOUR.

I did not take my leave of him, but had
Most pretty things to say: ere I could tell him
How I would think of him, at certain hours,
Such thoughts and such:—or ere I could
Give him that parting kiss, which I had set
Betwixt two charming words—comes in my father—
Cymbeline, act i, scene 4.

Grief hath changed me since you saw me last,
And careful hours with Time's deformed hand
Have written strange defeatures o'er my face.
Comedy of Errors, act v, scene 1.

> Oh! if thou be the same Egean, speak,
> And speak unto the same Emilia.
>
> *Comedy of Errors*, act v, scene 5.

> I ran it through, ev'n from my boyish days
> To the very moment that she bade me tell it:
> Wherein I spake of most disastrous chances,
> Of moving accidents, by flood, and field;
> Of being taken by th' insolent foe
> And sold to slavery.
>
> *Othello*, act i, scene 3.

> An old man, broken with the storms of fate,
> Is come to lay his weary bones among you;
> Give him a little earth for charity.
>
> *Henry VIII*, act iv, scene 2.

Minutely trace man's life; year after year,
Through all his days let all his deeds appear,
And then, though some may in that life be strange,
Yet there appears no vast nor sudden change:
The links that bind those various deeds are seen,
And no mysterious void is left between.

But let these binding links be all destroy'd,
All that through years he suffer'd or enjoy'd;
Let that vast gap be made, and then behold—
This was the youth, and he is thus, when old;
Then we at once the work of Time survey,
And in an instant see a life's decay;
Pain mix'd with pity in our bosoms rise,
And sorrow takes new sadness from surprise.

Beneath yon tree, observe an ancient pair—
A sleeping man; a woman in her chair,
Watching his looks with kind and pensive air;
No wife, nor sister she, nor is the name
Nor kindred of this friendly pair the same;
Yet so allied are they, that few can feel
Her constant, warm, unwearied, anxious zeal;
Their years and woes, although they long have loved,
Keep their good name and conduct unreproved;
Thus life's small comforts they together share,
And while life lingers for the grave prepare.

No other subjects on their spirits press,
Nor gain such int'rest as the past distress;
Grievous events that from the mem'ry drive
Life's common cares, and those alone survive,
Mix with each thought, in every action share,
Darken each dream, and blend with every prayer.

To David Booth, his fourth and last-born boy,
Allen his name, was more than common joy;
And as the child grew up, there seem'd in him
A more than common life in every limb;
A strong and handsome stripling he became,
And the gay spirit answer'd to the frame;
A lighter, happier lad was never seen,
For ever easy, cheerful, or serene;
His early love he fix'd upon a fair
And gentle maid—they were a handsome pair.

They at an infant-school together play'd,
Where the foundation of their love was laid;
The boyish champion would his choice attend
In every sport, in every fray defend.
As prospects open'd and as life advanced,
They walk'd together, they together danced;
On all occasions, from their early years,
They mix'd their joys and sorrows, hopes and fears;
Each heart was anxious, till it could impart
Its daily feelings to its kindred heart;
As years increased, unnumber'd petty wars
Broke out between them; jealousies and jars;
Causeless indeed, and follow'd by a peace,
That gave to love—growth, vigour, and increase.
Whilst yet a boy, when other minds are void,
Domestic thoughts young Allen's hours employ'd;
Judith in gaining hearts had no concern,
Rather intent the matron's part to learn;
Thus early prudent and sedate they grew,
While lovers, thoughtful—and though children, true.
To either parents not a day appear'd,
When with this love they might have interfered:
Childish at first, they cared not to restrain;
And strong at last, they saw restriction vain;
Nor knew they when that passion to reprove—
Now idle fondness, now resistless love.

So while the waters rise, the children tread
On the broad estuary's sandy bed;
But soon the channel fills, from side to side
Comes danger rolling with the deep'ning tide;
Yet none who saw the rapid current flow
Could the first instant of that danger know.

The lovers waited till the time should come
When they together could possess a home:
In either house were men and maids unwed,
Hopes to be soothed, and tempers to be led.
Then Allen's mother of his favourite maid
Spoke from the feelings of a mind afraid:
"Dress and amusements were her sole employ,"
She said—"entangling her deluded boy;"
And yet, in truth, a mother's jealous love
Had much imagined and could little prove;
Judith had beauty—and if vain, was kind,
Discreet, and mild, and had a serious mind.

Dull was their prospect—when the lovers met,
They said, we must not—dare not venture yet;
"Oh! could I labour for thee," Allen cried,
"Why should our friends be thus dissatisfied?
On my own arm I could depend, but they
Still urge obedience—must I yet obey?"
Poor Judith felt the grief, but grieving begg'd delay

At length a prospect came that seem'd to smile,
And faintly woo them, from a Western Isle;
A kinsman there a widow's hand had gain'd,
"Was old, was rich, and childless yet remain'd;
Would some young Booth to his affairs attend,
And wait awhile, he might expect a friend."
The elder brothers, who were not in love,
Fear'd the false seas, unwilling to remove;
But the young Allen, an enamour'd boy,
Eager an independence to enjoy,
Would through all perils seek it,—by the sea,—
Through labour, danger, pain, or slavery.
The faithful Judith his design approved,
For both were sanguine, they were young and loved
The mother's slow consent was then obtain'd;
The time arrived, to part alone remain'd:
All things prepared, on the expected day
Was seen the vessel anchor'd in the bay.
From her would seamen in the evening come
To take th' advent'rous Allen from his home;

With his own friends the final day he pass'd,
And every painful hour, except the last.
The grieving father urged the cheerful glass,
To make the moments with less sorrow pass;
Intent the mother look'd upon her son,
And wish'd th' assent withdrawn, the deed undone;
The younger sister, as he took his way,
Hung on his coat, and begg'd for more delay:
But his own Judith call'd him to the shore,
Whom he must meet, for they might meet no more:—
And there he found her—faithful, mournful, true,
Weeping and waiting for a last adieu!
The ebbing tide had left the sand, and there
Moved with slow steps the melancholy pair:
Sweet were the painful moments—but how sweet,
And without pain, when they again should meet!
Now either spoke, as hope and fear impress'd
Each their alternate triumph in the breast.

Distance alarm'd the maid—she cried, "'T is far!"
And danger too—"it is a time of war:
Then in those countries are diseases strange,
And women gay, and men are prone to change;
What then may happen in a year, when things
Of vast importance every moment brings!
But hark! an oar!" she cried, yet none appear'd—
'T was love's mistake, who fancied what it fear'd;
And she continued—"Do, my Allen, keep
Thy heart from evil, let thy passions sleep;
Believe it good, nay glorious, to prevail,
And stand in safety where so many fail;
And do not, Allen, or for shame, or pride,
Thy faith abjure, or thy professions hide;
Can I believe *his* love will lasting prove,
Who has no rev'rence for the God I love?
I know thee well! how good thou art and kind;
But strong the passions that invade thy mind.—
Now, what to me hath Allen to commend?"—
"Upon my mother," said the youth, "attend;
Forget her spleen, and in my place appear;
Her love to me will make my Judith dear:
Oft I shall think (such comfort lovers seek),
Who speaks of me, and fancy what they speak;
Then write on all occasions, always dwell
On hope's fair prospects, and be kind and well,
And ever choose the fondest, tenderest style."
She answer'd, "No," but answer'd with a smile.
"And now, my Judith, at so sad a time,
Forgive my fear, and call it not my crime;
When with our youthful neighbours 't is thy chance
To meet in walks, the visit, or the dance,
When every lad would on my lass attend,
Choose not a smooth designer for a friend;
That fawning Philip!—nay be not severe,
A rival's hope must cause a lover's fear."

Displeased she felt, and might in her reply
Have mix'd some anger, but the boat was nigh,
Now truly heard!—it soon was full in sight;—
Now the sad farewell, and the long good-night;
For, see!—his friends come hast'ning to the beach,
And now the gunwale is within the reach;
"Adieu!—farewell!—remember!"—and what more
Affection taught, was utter'd from the shore!
But Judith left them with a heavy heart,
Took a last view, and went to weep apart!
And now his friends went slowly from the place,
Where she stood still the dashing oar to trace,
Till all were silent!—for the youth she pray'd,
And softly then return'd the weeping maid.

They parted, thus by hope and fortune led,
And Judith's hours in pensive pleasure fled;
But when return'd the youth!—the youth no more
Return'd exulting to his native shore;
But forty years were past, and then there came
A worn-out man with wither'd limbs and lame,
His mind oppress'd with woes, and bent with age his frame:
Yes! old and grieved, and trembling with decay,
Was Allen landing in his native bay,
Willing his breathless form should blend with kindred clay.
In an autumnal eve he left the beach,
In such an eve he chanced the port to reach:
He was alone; he press'd the very place
Of the sad parting, of the last embrace:
There stood his parents, there retired the maid,
So fond, so tender, and so much afraid;
And on that spot, through many a year, his mind
Turn'd mournful back, half sinking, half resign'd

No one was present; of its crew bereft,
A single boat was in the billows left;
Sent from some anchor'd vessel in the bay,
At the returning tide to sail away:
O'er the black stern the moonlight softly play'd,
The loosen'd foresail flapping in the shade;
All silent else on shore; but from the town
A drowsy peal of distant bells came down:
From the tall houses here and there, a light
Served some confused remembrance to excite:
"There," he observed, and new emotions felt,
"Was my first home—and yonder Judith dwelt;
Dead! dead are all! I long—I fear to know,"
He said, and walk'd impatient, and yet slow.

Sudden there broke upon his grief a noise
Of merry tumult and of vulgar joys:
Seamen returning to their ship, were come,
With idle numbers straying from their home;
Allen among them mix'd, and in the old
Strove some familiar features to behold;
While fancy aided memory:—"Man! what cheer?"
A sailor cried; "Art thou at anchor here?"
Faintly he answer'd, and then tried to trace
Some youthful features in some aged face:
A swarthy matron he beheld, and thought
She might unfold the very truths he sought:
Confused and trembling, he the dame address'd:
"The Booths! yet live they?" pausing and oppress'd;
Then spake again:—"Is there no ancient man,
David his name?—assist me, if you can.—
Flemmings there were—and Judith, doth she live?"
The woman gazed, nor could an answer give;
Yet wond'ring stood, and all were silent by,
Feeling a strange and solemn sympathy.
The woman musing said—"She knew full well
Where the old people came at last to dwell;
They had a married daughter and a son,
But they were dead, and now remain'd not one."

"Yes," said an elder, who had paused intent
On days long past, "there was a sad event;—

One of these Booths—it was my mother's tale—
Here left his lass, I know not where to sail:
She saw their parting, and observed the pain;
But never came th' unhappy man again:"
"The ship was captured"—Allen meekly said,
'And what became of the forsaken maid?"
The woman answer'd: "I remember now,
She used to tell the lasses of her vow,
And of her lover's loss, and I have seen
The gayest hearts grow sad where she has been;
Yet in her grief she married, and was made
Slave to a wretch, whom meekly she obey'd
And early buried—but I know no more.
And hark! our friends are hast'ning to the shore."

Allen soon found a lodging in the town,
And walk'd a man unnoticed up and down.
This house, and this he knew, and thought a face
He sometimes could among a number trace:
Of names remember'd there remain'd a few,
But of no favourites, and the rest were new:
A merchant's wealth, when Allen went to sea,
Was reckon'd boundless.—Could he living be?
Or lived his son? for one he had, the heir
To a vast business, and a fortune fair.
No! but that heir's poor widow, from her shed,
With crutches went to take her dole of bread:
There was a friend whom he had left a boy,
With hope to sail the master of a hoy;
Him, after many a stormy day, he found
With his great wish, his life's whole purpose crown'd.
This hoy's proud captain look'd in Allen's face,—
"Yours is, my friend," said he, "a woful case;
We cannot all succeed; I now command
The Betsy sloop, and am not much at land;
But when we meet, you shall your story tell
Of foreign parts—I bid you now farewell!"

Allen so long had left his native shore,
He saw but few whom he had seen before:
The older people, as they met him, cast
A pitying look, oft speaking as they pass'd—
"The man is Allen Booth, and it appears
He dwelt among us in his early years;
We see the name engraved upon the stones,
Where this poor wanderer means to lay his bones."
Thus where he lived and loved—unhappy change!—
He seems a stranger, and finds all are strange.

But now a widow, in a village near,
Chanced of the melancholy man to hear;
Old as she was, to Judith's bosom came
Some strong emotions at the well-known name;
He was her much-loved Allen, she had stay'd
Ten troubled years, a sad afflicted maid;
Then was she wedded, of his death assured,
And much of mis'ry in her lot endured:
Her husband died; her children sought their bread
In various places, and to her were dead.
The once fond lovers met; not grief nor age,
Sickness or pain, their hearts could disengage;
Each had immediate confidence; a friend
Both now beheld, on whom they might depend:
"Now is there one to whom I can express
My nature's weakness and my soul's distress."
Allen look'd up, and with impatient heart—
"Let me not lose thee—never let us part:
So Heaven this comfort to my sufferings give,
It is not all distress to think and live."
Thus Allen spoke—for time had not removed
The charms attach'd to one so fondly loved;
Who with more health, the mistress of their cot,
Labours to soothe the evils of his lot.
To her, to her alone, his various fate,
At various times, 'tis comfort to relate;
And yet his sorrow—she too loves to hear
What wrings her bosom, and compels the tear.

First he related how he left the shore,
Alarm'd with fears that they should meet no more:
Then, ere the ship had reach'd her purposed course,
They met and yielded to the Spanish force;
Then cross th' Atlantic seas they bore their prey,
Who grieving landed from their sultry bay;
And marching many a burning league, he found
Himself a slave upon a miner's ground:
There a good priest his native language spoke,
And gave some ease to his tormenting yoke;
Kindly advanced him in his master's grace,
And he was station'd in an easier place:
There, hopeless ever to escape the land,
He to a Spanish maiden gave his hand;
In cottage shelter'd from the blaze of day
He saw his happy infants round him play;
Where summer shadows, made by lofty trees,
Waved o'er his seat, and soothed his reveries;
E'en then he thought of England, nor could sigh,
But his fond Isabel demanded, "Why?"
Grieved by the story, she the sigh repaid,
And wept in pity for the English maid:
Thus twenty years were pass'd, and pass'd his views
Of future bliss, for he had wealth to lose:
His friend now dead, some foe had dared to paint
"His faith as tainted: he his spouse would taint;
Make all his children infidels, and found
An English heresy on Christian ground."

"Whilst I was poor," said Allen, "none would care
What my poor notions of religion were;
None ask'd me whom I worshipp'd, how I pray'd,
If due obedience to the laws were paid:
My good adviser taught me to be still,
Nor to make converts had I power or will.
I preach'd no foreign doctrine to my wife,
And never mention'd Luther in my life;
I, all they said, say what they would, allow'd,
And when the fathers bade me bow, I bow'd:
Their forms I follow'd, whether well or sick,
And was a most obedient Catholic.
But I had money, and these pastors found
My notions vague, heretical, unsound:
A wicked book they seized; the very Turk
Could not have read a more pernicious work
To me pernicious, who if it were good
Or evil question'd not, nor understood:
Oh! had I little but the book possess'd,
I might have read it, and enjoy'd my rest."

Alas! poor Allen, through his wealth was seen
Crimes that by poverty conceal'd had been:
Faults that in dusty pictures rest unknown
Are in an instant through the varnish shown.

He told their cruel mercy; how at last,
In Christian kindness for the merits past,

They spared his forfeit life, but bade him fly,
Or for his crime and contumacy die;
Fly from all scenes, all objects of delight:
His wife, his children, weeping in his sight,
All urging him to flee, he fled, and cursed his flight.

He next related, how he found a way,
Guileless and grieving, to Campeachy Bay:
There in the woods he wrought, and there, among
Some lab'ring seamen, heard his native tongue:
The sound, one moment, broke upon his pain
With joyful force; he long'd to hear again:
Again he heard; he seized an offer'd hand,
"And when beheld you last our native land?"
He cried, "and in what county? quickly say"—
The seamen answer'd—strangers all were they;
One only at his native port had been;
He, landing once, the quay and church had seen,
For that esteem'd; but nothing more he knew.
Still more to know, would Allen join the crew,
Sail where they sail'd, and, many a peril past,
They at his kinsman's isle their anchor cast;
But him they found not, nor could one relate
Aught of his will, his wish, or his estate.
This grieved not Allen; then again he sail'd
For England's coast, again his fate prevail'd:
War raged, and he, an active man and strong,
Was soon impress'd, and, served his country long.
By various shores he pass'd, on various seas,
Never so happy as when void of ease.—
And then he told how in a calm distress'd,
Day after day his soul was sick of rest;
When, as a log upon the deep they stood,
Then roved his spirit to the inland wood;
Till, while awake, he dream'd, that on the seas
Were his loved home, the hill, the stream, the trees:
He gazed, he pointed to the scenes:—"There stand
My wife, my children, 't is my lovely land;
See! there my dwelling—oh! delicious scene
Of my best life—unhand me—are ye men?"

And thus the frenzy ruled him, till the wind
Brush'd the fond pictures from the stagnant mind.

He told of bloody fights, and how at length
The rage of battle gave his spirits strength:
'T was in the Indian seas his limb he lost,
And he was left half-dead upon the coast;
But living gain'd 'mid rich aspiring men,
A fair subsistence by his ready pen.
"Thus," he continued, "pass'd unvaried years,
Without events producing hopes or fears."
Augmented pay procured him decent wealth,
But years advancing undermined his health;
Then oft-times in delightful dream he flew
To England's shore, and scenes his childhood knew:
He saw his parents, saw his fav'rite maid,
No feature wrinkled, not a charm decay'd;
And thus excited, in his bosom rose
A wish so strong, it baffled his repose;
Anxious he felt on English earth to lie;
To view his native soil, and there to die.

He then described the gloom, the dread he found,
When first he landed on the chosen ground,
Where undefined was all he hoped and fear'd,
And how confused and troubled all appear'd;
His thoughts in past and present scenes employ'd,
All views in future blighted and destroy'd:
His were a medley of bewild'ring themes,
Sad as realities, and wild as dreams.

Here his relation closes, but his mind
Flies back again some resting-place to find;
Thus silent, musing through the day, he sees
His children sporting by those lofty trees,
Their mother singing in the shady scene,
Where the fresh springs burst o'er the lively green;—
So strong his eager fancy, he affrights
The faithful widow by its powerful flights;
For what disturbs him he aloud will tell,
And cry—"'T is she, my wife! my Isabel!
Where are my children?"—Judith grieves to hear
How the soul works in sorrows so severe;
Assiduous all his wishes to attend,
Deprived of much, he yet may boast a friend;
Watch'd by her care, in sleep, his spirit takes
Its flight, and watchful finds her when he wakes.

'T is now her office; her attention see!
While her friend sleeps beneath that shading tree,
Careful she guards him from the glowing heat,
And pensive muses at her Allen's feet.

And where is he? Ah! doubtless in those scenes
Of his best days, amid the vivid greens,
Fresh with unnumber'd rills, where ev'ry gale
Breathes the rich fragrance of the neighb'ring vale;
Smiles not his wife, and listens as there comes
The night-bird's music from the thick'ning glooms?
And as he sits with all these treasures nigh,
Blaze not with fairy light the phosphor-fly,
When like a sparkling gem it wheels illumined by?
This is the joy that now so plainly speaks
In the warm transient flushing of his cheeks;
For he is list'ning to the fancied noise
Of his own children, eager in their joys:
All this he feels, a dream's delusive bliss
Gives the expression, and the glow like this.
And now his Judith lays her knitting by,
These strong emotions in her friend to spy;
For she can fully of their nature deem——
But see! he breaks the long-protracted theme,
And wakes and cries—"My God! 't was but a dream."

TALE III.

THE GENTLEMAN FARMER.

Pause then,
And weigh thy value with an even hand:
If thou beest rated by thy estimation,
Thou dost deserve enough.
Merchant of Venice, act ii, scene 7.

Because I will not do them wrong to mistrust any, I will do myself the right to trust none: and the fine is (for which I may go the finer), I will live a bachelor.
Much Ado about Nothing, act i, scene 3.

Throw physic to the dogs, I 'll none of it.
Macbeth, act v, scene 3.

His promises are, as he then was, mighty;
And his performance, as he now is, nothing.
Henry VIII, act iv, scene 2.

GWYN was a farmer, whom the farmers all,
Who dwelt around, the Gentleman would call;
Whether in pure humility or pride,
They only knew, and they would not decide.

Far diff'rent he from that dull plodding tribe,
Whom it was his amusement to describe;
Creatures no more enliven'd than a clod,
But treading still as their dull fathers trod;
Who lived in times when not a man had seen
Corn sown by drill, or thresh'd by a machine:
He was of those whose skill assigns the prize
For creatures fed in pens, and stalls, and sties;
And who, in places where improvers meet,
To fill the land with fatness, had a seat;
Who in large mansions live like petty kings,
And speak of farms but as amusing things;
Who plans encourage, and who journals keep,
And talk with lords about a breed of sheep.

Two are the species in this genus known;
One, who is rich in his profession grown,
Who yearly finds his ample stores increase,
From fortune's favours and a favouring lease;
Who rides his hunter, who his house adorns;
Who drinks his wine, and his disbursements scorns;
Who freely lives, and loves to show he can—
This is the farmer made the gentleman.

The second species from the world is sent,
Tired with its strife, or with his wealth content;
In books and men beyond the former read,
To farming solely by a passion led,
Or by a fashion: curious in his land;
Now planning much, now changing what he plann'd;
Pleased by each trial, not by failures vex'd,
And ever certain to succeed the next;
Quick to resolve, and easy to persuade—
This is the gentleman a farmer made.

Gwyn was of these; he from the world withdrew
Early in life, his reasons known to few;
Some disappointment said, some pure good sense,
The love of land, the press of indolence;
His fortune known, and coming to retire,
If not a farmer, men had call'd him 'squire.

Forty and five his years, no child or wife
Cross'd the still tenour of his chosen life;
Much land he purchased, planted far around,
And let some portions of superfluous ground
To farmers near him, not displeased to say,
"My tenants," nor "our worthy landlord," they.

Fix'd in his farm, he soon display'd his skill
In small-boned lambs, the horse-hoe, and the drill;
From these he rose to themes of nobler kind,
And show'd the riches of a fertile mind;
To all around their visits he repaid,
And thus his mansion and himself display'd.
His rooms were stately, rather fine than neat,
And guests politely call'd his house a seat;
At much expense was each apartment graced,
His taste was gorgeous, but it still was taste;
In full festoons the crimson curtains fell,
The sofas rose in bold elastic swell;
Mirrors in gilded frames display'd the tints
Of glowing carpets and of colour'd prints;
The weary eye saw every object shine,
And all was costly, fanciful, and fine.

As with his friends he pass'd the social hours,
His generous spirit scorn'd to hide its powers;
Powers unexpected, for his eye and air
Gave no sure signs that eloquence was there;
Oft he began with sudden fire and force,
As loth to lose occasion for discourse;
Some, 't is observed, who feel a wish to speak,
Will a due place for introduction seek;
On to their purpose step by step they steal,
And all their way, by certain signals, feel;
Others plunge in at once, and never heed
Whose turn they take, whose purpose they impede;
Resolved to shine, they hasten to begin,
Of ending thoughtless—and of these was Gwyn.
And thus he spake—

"It grieves me to the soul
To see how man submits to man's control;
How overpower'd and shackled minds are led
In vulgar tracks, and to submission bred;
The coward never on himself relies,
But to an equal for assistance flies;
Man yields to custom as he bows to fate,
In all things ruled—mind, body, and estate;
In pain, in sickness, we for cure apply
To them we know not, and we know not why;
But that the creature has some jargon read,
And got some Scotchman's system in his head;
Some grave impostor, who will health insure,
Long as your patience or your wealth endure;
But mark them well, the pale and sickly crew,
They have not health, and can they give it you?
These solemn cheats their various methods choose;
A system fires them, as a bard his muse:
Hence wordy wars arise: the learn'd divide,
And groaning patients curse each erring guide.

"Next, our affairs are govern'd, buy or sell,
Upon the deed the law must fix its spell;
Whether we hire or let, we must have still
The dubious aid of an attorney's skill;
They take a part in every man's affairs,
And in all business some concern is theirs;
Because mankind in ways prescribed are found,
Like flocks that follow on a beaten ground,
Each abject nature in the way proceeds,
That now to shearing, now to slaughter leads.

"Should you offend, though meaning no offence,
You have no safety in your innocence;
The statute broken then is placed in view,
And men must pay for crimes they never knew:
Who would by law regain his plunder'd store,
Would pick up fallen merc'ry from the floor;
If he pursue it, here and there it slides;
He would collect it, but it more divides;
This part and this he stops, but still in vain,
It slips aside, and breaks in parts again;
Till, after time and pains, and care and cost,
He finds his labour and his object lost.

"But most it grieves me (friends alone are round)
To see a man in priestly fetters bound:

Guides to the soul, these friends of Heaven contrive,
Long as man lives, to keep his fears alive;
Soon as an infant breathes, their rites begin;
Who knows not sinning, must be freed from sin;
Who needs no bond, must yet engage in vows;
Who has no judgment, must a creed espouse:
Advanced in life, our boys are bound by rules,
Are catechised in churches, cloisters, schools,
And train'd in thraldom to be fit for tools:
The youth grown up, he now a partner needs,
And lo! a priest, as soon as he succeeds.
What man of sense can marriage-rites approve?
What man of spirit can be bound to love?
Forced to be kind! compell'd to be sincere!
Do chains and fetters make companions dear?
Pris'ners indeed we bind; but though the bond
May keep them safe, it does not make them fond:
The ring, the vow, the witness, license, prayers,
All parties known! made public all affairs!
Such forms men suffer, and from these they date
A deed of love begun with all they hate:
Absurd! that none the beaten road should shun,
But love to do what other dupes have done.

"Well, now your priest has made you one of twain,
Look you for rest? Alas! you look in vain.
If sick, he comes; you cannot die in peace,
Till he attends to witness your release;
To vex your soul, and urge you to confess
The sins you feel, remember, or can guess:
Nay, when departed, to your grave he goes,
But there indeed he hurts not your repose.

"Such are our burthens; part we must sustain,
But need not link new grievance to the chain:
Yet men like idiots will their frames surround
With these vile shackles, nor confess they're bound:
In all that most confines them they confide,
Their slavery boast, and make their bonds their pride;
E'en as the pressure galls them, they declare,
(Good souls!) how happy and how free they are!
As madmen, pointing round their wretched cells,
Cry, 'Lo! the palace where our honour dwells.'

"Such is our state: but I resolve to live
By rules my reason and my feelings give;
No legal guards shall keep enthrall'd my mind,
No slaves command me, and no teachers blind.

"Tempted by sins, let me their strength defy,
But have no second in a surplice by;
No bottle-holder, with officious aid,
To comfort conscience, weaken'd and afraid:
Then if I yield, my frailty is not known;
And, if I stand, the glory is my own.

"When Truth and Reason are our friends, we seem
Alive! awake!—the superstitious dream.

"Oh! then, fair Truth, for thee alone I seek,
Friend to the wise, supporter of the weak;
From thee we learn whate'er is right and just;
Forms to despise, professions to distrust;
Creeds to reject, pretensions to deride,
And following thee, to follow none beside."

Such was the speech; it struck upon the ear
Like sudden thunder, none expect to hear.
He saw men's wonder with a manly pride,
And gravely smiled at guest electrified:
"A farmer this!" they said, "Oh! let him seek
That place where he may for his country speak;
On some great question to harangue for hours,
While speakers hearing, envy nobler powers!"

Wisdom like this, as all things rich and rare,
Must be acquired with pains, and kept with care;
In books he sought it, which his friends might view,
When their kind host the guarding curtain drew.
There were historic works for graver hours,
And lighter verse, to spur the languid powers;
There metaphysics, logic there had place;
But of devotion not a single trace—
Save what is taught in Gibbon's florid page,
And other guides of this inquiring age;
There Hume appear'd, and near, a splendid book
Composed by Gay's good Lord of Bolingbroke:
With these were mix'd the light, the free, the vain,
And from a corner peep'd the sage Tom Paine:
Here four neat volumes Chesterfield were named,
For manners much and easy morals famed;
With chaste Memoirs of Females, to be read
When deeper studies had confused the head.

Such his resources, treasures where he sought
For daily knowledge till his mind was fraught:
Then when his friends were present, for their use
He would the riches he had stored produce;
He found his lamp burn clearer, when each day
He drew for all he purposed to display:
For these occasions, forth his knowledge sprung,
As mustard quickens on a bed of dung;
All was prepared, and guests allow'd the praise,
For what they saw he could so quickly raise.

Such this new friend; and when the year came round,
The same impressive, reasoning sage was found;
Then, too, was seen the pleasant mansion graced
With a fair damsel—his no vulgar taste;
The neat Rebecca—sly, observant, still,
Watching his eye, and waiting on his will;
Simple yet smart her dress, her manners meek,
Her smiles spoke for her, she would seldom speak:
But watch'd each look, each meaning to detect,
And (pleased with notice) felt for all neglect.

With her lived Gwyn a sweet harmonious life,
Who, forms excepted, was a charming wife:
The wives indeed, so made by vulgar law,
Affected scorn, and censured what they saw;
And what they saw not, fancied; said 'twas sin,
And took no notice of the wife of Gwyn:
But he despised their rudeness, and would prove
Theirs was compulsion and distrust, not love;
"Fools as they were! could they conceive that rings
And parsons' blessings were substantial things?"
They answer'd "Yes;" while he contemptuous spoke
Of the low notions held by simple folk;
Yet, strange that anger in a man so wise
Should from the notions of these fools arise;
Can they so vex us, whom we so despise?

Brave as he was, our hero felt a dread
Lest those who saw him kind should think him led;
If to his bosom fear a visit paid,
It was, lest he should be supposed afraid;
Hence sprang his orders; not that he desired
The things when done: obedience he required;
And thus, to prove his absolute command,
Ruled every heart, and moved each subject hand;
Assent he ask'd for every word and whim,
To prove that *he alone was king of him.*

The still Rebecca, who her station knew,
With ease resign'd the honours not her due;
Well pleased, she saw that men her board would grace,
And wish'd not there to see a female face;
When by her lover she his spouse was styled,
Polite she thought it, and demurely smiled;
But when he wanted wives and maidens round
So to regard her, she grew grave, and frown'd;
And sometimes whisper'd—"Why should you respect
These people's notions, yet their forms reject?"

Gwyn, though from marriage bond and fetter free,
Still felt abridgment in his liberty;
Something of hesitation he betray'd,
And in her presence thought of what he said.
Thus fair Rebecca, though she walk'd astray,
His creed rejecting, judged it right to pray;
To be at church, to sit with serious looks,
To read her Bible and her Sunday-books:
She hated all those new and daring themes,
And call'd his free conjectures, "devil's dreams:"
She honour'd still the priesthood in her fall,
And claim'd respect and reverence for them all;
Call'd them "of sin's destructive power the foes,
And not such blockheads as he might suppose."
Gwyn to his friends would smile, and sometimes say,
"'T is a kind fool, why vex her in her way?"
Her way she took, and still had more in view,
For she contrived that he should take it too.
The daring freedom of his soul, 't was plain,
In part was lost in a divided reign;
A king and queen, who yet in prudence sway'd
Their peaceful state, and were in turn obey'd.

Yet such our fate, that when we plan the best,
Something arises to disturb our rest:
For though in spirits high, in body strong,
Gwyn something felt—he knew not what—was wrong;
He wish'd to know, for he believed the thing,
If unremoved, would other evil bring:
"She must perceive, of late he could not eat,
And when he walk'd, he trembled on his feet:
He had forebodings, and he seem'd as one
Stopp'd on the road, or threaten'd by a dun;
He could not live, and yet, should he apply
To those physicians—he must sooner die."

The mild Rebecca heard with some disdain,
And some distress, her friend and lord complain:
His death she fear'd not, but had painful doubt
What his distemper'd nerves might bring about;
With power like hers she dreaded an ally,
And yet there was a person in her eye;—
She thought, debated, fix'd—"Alas!" she said,
"A case like yours must be no more delay'd:
You hate these doctors: well! but were a friend
And doctor one, your fears would have an end:
My cousin Mollet—Scotland holds him now—
Is above all men skilful, all allow;
Of late a doctor, and within a while
He means to settle in this favour'd isle;
Should he attend you, with his skill profound,
You must be safe, and shortly would be sound."

When men in health against physicians rail,
They should consider that their nerves may fail;
Who calls a lawyer rogue, may find, too late,
On one of these depends his whole estate:
Nay, when the world can nothing more produce,
The priest, th' insulted priest, may have his use;
Ease, health, and comfort, lift a man so high,
These powers are dwarfs that he can scarcely spy;
Pain, sickness, languor, keep a man so low,
That these neglected dwarfs to giants grow.
Happy is he who through the medium sees
Of clear good sense—but Gwyn was not of these.

He heard and he rejoiced: "Ah! let him come,
And till he fixes, make my house his home."
Home came the doctor—he was much admired;
He told the patient what his case required;
His hours for sleep, his time to eat and drink;
When he should ride, read, rest, compose, or think.
Thus join'd peculiar skill and art profound,
To make the fancy-sick no more than fancy-sound

With such attention, who could long be ill?
Returning health proclaim'd the doctor's skill.
Presents and praises from a grateful heart
Were freely offer'd on the patient's part;
In high repute the doctor seem'd to stand,
But still had got no footing in the land;
And, as he saw the seat was rich and fair,
He felt disposed to fix his station there:
To gain his purpose he perform'd the part
Of a good actor, and prepared to start;
Not like a traveller in a day serene,
When the sun shone and when the roads were clean:
Not like the pilgrim, when the morning grey,
The ruddy eve succeeding, sends his way;
But in a season when the sharp east wind
Had all its influence on a nervous mind;
When past the parlour's front it fiercely blew,
And Gwyn sat pitying every bird that flew,
This strange physician said—"Adieu! adieu!
Farewell!—Heaven bless you!—if you should—but no,
You need not fear—farewell! 't is time to go."

The doctor spoke; and as the patient heard,
His old disorders (dreadful train!) appear'd;
"He felt the tingling tremor, and the stress
Upon his nerves that he could not express;
Should his good friend forsake him, he perhaps
Might meet his death, and surely a relapse."

So, as the doctor seem'd intent to part,
He cried in terror—"Oh! be where thou art:
Come, thou art young, and unengaged; oh! come
Make me thy friend, give comfort to mine home;
I have now symptoms that require thine aid,
Do, doctor, stay"—th' obliging doctor stay'd.

Thus Gwyn was happy; he had now a friend,
And a meek spouse on whom he could depend:
But now possess'd of male and female guide,
Divided power he thus must subdivide:
In earlier days he rode, or sat at ease
Reclined, and having but himself to please;
Now if he would a fav'rite nag bestride
He sought permission—"Doctor, may I ride?"
(Rebecca's eye her sovereign pleasure told)—
"I think you may, but guarded from the cold,
Ride forty minutes."—Free and happy soul!
He scorn'd submission, and a man's control;
But where such friends in every care unite
All for his good, obedience is delight.

Now Gwyn a sultan bade affairs adieu,
Led and assisted by the faithful two;
The favourite fair, Rebecca, near him sat,
And whisper'd whom to love, assist, or hate;
While the chief vizier eased his lord of cares,
And bore himself the burden of affairs:
No dangers could from such alliance flow,
But from that law, that changes all below.

When wint'ry winds with leaves bestrew'd the ground,
And men were coughing all the village round;
When public papers of invasion told,
Diseases, famines, perils new and old;
When philosophic writers fail'd to clear
The mind of gloom, and lighter works to cheer;
Then came fresh terrors on our hero's mind—
Fears unforeseen, and feelings undefined.

"In outward ills," he cried, "I rest assured
Of my friend's aid; they will in time be cured:
But can his art subdue, resist, control
These inward griefs and troubles of the soul?
Oh! my Rebecca! my disorder'd mind,
No help in study, none in thought can find;
What must I do, Rebecca?" She proposed
The parish-guide; but what could be disclosed
To a proud priest?—"No! him have I defied,
Insulted, slighted—shall he be my guide?
But one there is, and if report be just,
A wise good man, whom I may safely trust;
Who goes from house to house, from ear to ear,
To make his truths, his Gospel truths, appear;
True if indeed they be, 't is time that I should hear:
Send for that man; and if report be just,
I, like Cornelius, will the teacher trust;
But if deceiver, I the vile deceit
Shall soon discover, and discharge the cheat."

To Doctor Mollet was the grief confess'd,
While Gwyn the freedom of his mind express'd;
Yet own'd it was to ills and errors prone,
And he for guilt and frailty must atone.
"My books, perhaps," the wav'ring mortal cried,
"Like men deceive—I would be satisfied;
And to my soul the pious man may bring
Comfort and light—do let me try the thing."

The cousins met, what pass'd with Gwyn was told:
"Alas!" the doctor said, "how hard to hold
These easy minds, where all impressions made
At first sink deeply, and then quickly fade;
For while so strong these new-born fancies reign,
We must divert them, to oppose is vain:
You see him valiant now, he scorns to heed
The bigot's threat'nings or the zealot's creed;
Shook by a dream, he next for truth receives
What frenzy teaches, and what fear believes;
And this will place him in the power of one
Whom we must seek, because we cannot shun."

Wisp had been ostler at a busy inn,
Where he beheld and grew in dread of sin;
Then to a Baptists' meeting found his way,
Became a convert, and was taught to pray;
Then preach'd; and being earnest and sincere,
Brought other sinners to religious fear:
Together grew his influence and his fame,
Till our dejected hero heard his name:
His little failings were, a grain of pride,
Raised by the numbers he presumed to guide:
A love of presents, and of lofty praise
For his meek spirit and his humble ways;
But though this spirit would on flattery feed,
No praise could blind him and no arts mislead:—
To him the doctor made the wishes known
Of his good patron, but conceal'd his own;
He of all teachers had distrust and doubt,
And was reserved in what he came about;
Though on a plain and simple message sent,
He had a secret and a bold intent:
Their minds at first were deeply veil'd; disguise
Form'd the slow speech, and oped the eager eyes
Till by degrees sufficient light was thrown
On every view, and all the business shown.
Wisp, or a skilful guide who led the blind,
Had powers to rule and awe the vapourish mind;
But not the changeful will, the wavering fear to bind:
And should his conscience give him leave to dwell
With Gwyn, and every rival power expel
(A dubious point), yet he, with every care,
Might soon the lot of the rejected share;
And other Wisps be found like him to reign,
And then be thrown upon the world again:
He thought it prudent then, and felt it just,
The present guides of his new friend to trust;
True, he conceived, to touch the harder heart
Of the cool doctor, was beyond his art;
But mild Rebecca he could surely sway,
While Gwyn would follow where she led the way:
So to do good, (and why a duty shun,
Because rewarded for the good when done?)
He with his friends would join in all they plann'd,
Save when his faith or feelings should withstand;
There he must rest, sole judge of his affairs,
While they might rule exclusively in theirs.

When Gwyn his message to the teacher sent,
He fear'd his friends would show their discontent;
And prudent seem'd it to th' attendant pair,
Not all at once to show an aspect fair:
On Wisp they seem'd to look with jealous eye,
And fair Rebecca was demure and shy;
But by degrees the teacher's worth they knew,
And were so kind, they seem'd converted too.

Wisp took occasion to the nymph to say,
"You must be married: will you name the day?"
She smiled,—"'T is well; but should he not comply,
Is it quite safe th' experiment to try?"—

"My child," the teacher said, "who feels remorse,
(And feels not he?) must wish relief of course;
And can he find it, while he fears the crime?—
You must be married; will you name the time?"

Glad was the patron as a man could be,
Yet marvell'd too, to find his guides agree;
"But what the cause?" he cried; "'tis genuine love for me."

Each found his part, and let one act describe
The powers and honours of th' accordant tribe:—
A man for favour to the mansion speeds,
And cons his threefold task as he proceeds;
To teacher Wisp he bows with humble air,
And begs his interest for a barn's repair:
Then for the doctor he inquires, who loves
To hear applause for what his skill improves,
And gives for praise, assent,—and to the fair
He brings of pullets a delicious pair;
Thus sees a peasant with discernment nice,
And love of power, conceit, and avarice.

Lo! now the change complete: the convert Gwyn
Has sold his books, and has renounced his sin;
Mollet his body orders, Wisp his soul,
And o'er his purse the lady takes control;
No friends beside he needs, and none attend—
Soul, body, and estate, has each a friend;
And fair Rebecca leads a virtuous life—
She rules a mistress, and she reigns a wife.

TALE IV.

PROCRASTINATION.

Heaven witness
I have been to you ever true and humble.
Henry VIII. act iv. scene 4.

Gentle lady,
When first I did impart my love to you,
I freely told you all the wealth I had.
Merchant of Venice, act iii. scene 2.

The fatal time
Cuts off all ceremonies and vows of love,
And ample interchange of sweet discourse,
Which so long sunder'd friends should dwell upon.
Richard III. act v. scene 3.

I know thee not, old man; fall to thy prayers.
Henry IV. Part 2, act v. scene 5.

Farewell,
Thou pure impiety, thou impious purity,
For thee I'll lock up all the gates of love.
Much Ado about Nothing, act iv. scene 2.

Love will expire, the gay, the happy dream
Will turn to scorn, indiff'rence, or esteem:
Some favour'd pairs, in this exchange, are bless'd,
Nor sigh for raptures in a state of rest;
Others, ill-match'd, with minds unpair'd, repent
At once the deed, and know no more content;
From joy to anguish they, in haste, decline,
And with their fondness, their esteem resign:
More luckless still their fate, who are the prey
Of long-protracted hope and dull delay;

'Mid plans of bliss the heavy hours pass on,
Till love is wither'd, and till joy is gone.

This gentle flame two youthful hearts possess'd,
The sweet disturber of unenvied rest:
The prudent Dinah was the maid beloved,
And the kind Rupert was the swain approved:
A wealthy aunt her gentle niece sustain'd,
He with a father, at his desk remain'd;
The youthful couple, to their vows sincere,
Thus loved expectant; year succeeding year,
With pleasant views and hopes, but not a prospect near.
Rupert some comfort in his station saw,
But the poor virgin lived in dread and awe;
Upon her anxious looks the widow smiled,
And bade her wait, "for she was yet a child."
She for her neighbour had a due respect,
Nor would his son encourage or reject;
And thus the pair, with expectations vain,
Beheld the seasons change and change again:
Meantime the nymph her tender tales perused,
Where cruel aunts impatient girls refused;
While hers, though teasing, boasted to be kind,
And she, resenting, to be all resign'd.

The dame was sick, and when the youth applied
For her consent, she groan'd, and cough'd, and cried:
Talk'd of departing, and again her breath
Drew hard, and cough'd, and talk'd again of death:
"Here you may live, my Dinah! here the boy
And you together my estate enjoy;"
Thus to the lovers was her mind express'd,
Till they forbore to urge the fond request.

Servant, and nurse, and comforter, and friend,
Dinah had still some duty to attend;
But yet their walk, when Rupert's evening call
Obtain'd an hour, made sweet amends for all;
So long they now each other's thoughts had known,
That nothing seem'd exclusively their own;
But with the common wish, the mutual fear,
They now had travell'd to their thirtieth year.

At length a prospect open'd—but, alas!
Long time must yet, before the union, pass;
Rupert was call'd in other climes t' increase
Another's wealth, and toil for future peace;
Loth were the lovers, but the aunt declared
'T was fortune's call, and they must be prepared;
"You now are young, and for this brief delay,
And Dinah's care, what I bequeath will pay;
All will be yours; nay, love, suppress that sigh;
The kind must suffer, and the best must die:"
Then came the cough, and strong the signs it gave
Of holding long contention with the grave.

The lovers parted with a gloomy view,
And little comfort but that both were true;
He for uncertain duties doom'd to steer,
While hers remain'd too certain and severe.

Letters arrived, and Rupert fairly told
"His cares were many, and his hopes were cold,
The view more clouded, that was never fair,
And love alone preserved him from despair:"
In other letters brighter hopes he drew,
"His friends were kind, and he believed them true

When the sage widow Dinah's grief descried,
She wonder'd much why one so happy sigh'd:
Then bade her see how her poor aunt sustain'd
The ills of life, nor murmur'd nor complain'd.
To vary pleasures, from the lady's chest
Were drawn the pearly string and tabby vest;
Beads, jewels, laces, all their value shown,
With the kind notice—"They will be your own."

This hope, these comforts, cherish'd day by day,
To Dinah's bosom made a gradual way;
Till love of treasure had as large a part,
As love of Rupert, in the virgin's heart.
Whether it be that tender passions fail,
From their own nature, while the strong prevail;
Or whether av'rice, like the poison-tree,*
Kills all beside it, and alone will be;
Whatever cause prevail'd, the pleasure grew
In Dinah's soul,—she loved the hoards to view;
With lively joy those comforts she survey'd,
And love grew languid in the careful maid.

Now the grave niece partook the widow's cares,
Look'd to the great and ruled the small affairs;
Saw clean'd the plate, arranged the china show,
And felt her passion for a shilling grow:
Th' indulgent aunt increased the maid's delight,
By placing tokens of her wealth in sight;
She loved the value of her bonds to tell,
And spake of stocks, and how they rose and fell.

This passion grew, and gain'd at length such sway,
That other passions shrank to make it way;
Romantic notions now the heart forsook,
She read but seldom, and she changed her book;
And for the verses she was wont to send,
Short was her prose, and she was Rupert's friend.
Seldom she wrote, and then the widow's cough,
And constant call, excused her breaking off;
Who, now oppress'd, no longer took the air,
But sate and dozed upon an easy chair.
The cautious doctor saw the case was clear,
But judged it best to have companions near;
They came, they reason'd, they prescribed—at last,
Like honest men, they said their hopes were past;
Then came a priest—'tis comfort to reflect,
When all is over, there was no neglect;
And all was over—by her husband's bones,
The widow rests beneath the sculptured stones,
That yet record their fondness and their fame,
While all they left the virgin's care became;
Stock, bonds, and buildings;—it disturb'd her rest,
To think what load of troubles she possess'd:
Yet, if a trouble, she resolved to take
Th' important duty, for the donor's sake;
She too was heiress to the widow's taste,
Her love of hoarding, and her dread of waste.

Sometimes the past would on her mind intrude,
And then a conflict full of care ensued;
The thoughts of Rupert on her mind would press,
His worth she knew, but doubted his success;
Of old she saw him heedless; what the boy
Forbore to save, the man would not enjoy;
Oft had he lost the chance that care would seize,
Willing to live, but more to live at ease:
Yet could she not a broken vow defend,
And Heav'n, perhaps, might yet enrich her friend.

Month after month was pass'd, and all were spent
In quiet comfort and in rich content:
Miseries there were, and woes the world around,
But these had not her pleasant dwelling found;
She knew that mothers grieved, and widows wept,
And she was sorry, said her prayers, and slept:
Thus pass'd the seasons, and to Dinah's board
Gave what the seasons to the rich afford;
For she indulged, nor was her heart so small,
That one strong passion should engross it all.

A love of splendour now with av'rice strove,
And oft appear'd to be the stronger love:
A secret pleasure fill'd the widow's breast,
When she reflected on the hoards possess'd;
But livelier joy inspired th' ambitious maid,
When she the purchase of those hoards display'd:
In small but splendid room she loved to see
That all was placed in view and harmony;
There, as with eager glance she look'd around,
She much delight in every object found;
While books devout were near her—to destroy,
Should it arise, an overflow of joy.

Within that fair apartment, guests might see
The comforts cull'd for wealth by vanity:
Around the room an Indian paper blazed,
With lively tint and figures boldly raised;
Silky and soft upon the floor below,
Th' elastic carpet rose with crimson glow;
All things around implied both cost and care,
What met the eye was elegant or rare:
Some curious trifles round the room were laid,
By hope presented to the wealthy maid:
Within a costly case of varnish'd wood,
In level rows, her polish'd volumes stood;
Shown as a favour to a chosen few,
To prove what beauty for a book could do;
A silver urn with curious work was fraught;
A silver lamp from Grecian pattern wrought:
Above her head, all gorgeous to behold,
A time-piece stood on feet of burnish'd gold;
A stag's-head crest adorn'd the pictured case,
Through the pure crystal shone th' enamell'd face;
And while on brilliants moved the hands of steel,
It click'd from pray'r to pray'r, from meal to meal.

Here as the lady sate, a friendly pair
Stept in t' admire the view, and took their chair:
They then related how the young and gay
Were thoughtless wandering in the broad highway;
How tender damsels sail'd in tilted boats,
And laugh'd with wicked men in scarlet coats;
And how we live in such degen'rate times,
That men conceal their wants, and show their crimes;
While vicious deeds are screen'd by fashion's name,
And what was once our pride is now our shame.

Dinah was musing, as her friends discoursed,
When these last words a sudden entrance forced
Upon her mind, and what was once her pride
And now her shame, some painful views supplied.

---

* Allusion is here made, not to the well-known species of *sumach*, called the poison-oak, or *toxicodendron*, but to the *upas*, or poison-tree of Java: whether it be real or imaginary, this is no proper place for inquiry.

Thoughts of the past within her bosom press'd
And there a change was felt, and was confess'd:
While thus the virgin strove with secret pain,
Her mind was wandering o'er the troubled main;
Still she was silent, nothing seem'd to see,
But sate and sigh'd in pensive reverie.

The friends prepared new subjects to begin,
When tall Susannah, maiden starch, stalk'd in;
Not in her ancient mode, sedate and slow,
As when she came, the mind she knew, to know;
Nor as, when list'ning half an hour before,
She twice or thrice tapp'd gently at the door;
But, all decorum cast in wrath aside,
"I think the devil's in the man!" she cried;
"A huge tall sailor, with his tawny cheek,
And pitted face, will with my lady speak;
He grinn'd an ugly smile, and said he knew,
Please you, my lady, 't would be joy to you;
What must I answer?"—Trembling and distress'd,
Sank the pale Dinah, by her fears oppress'd;
When thus alarm'd, and brooking no delay,
Swift to her room the stranger made his way.

"Revive, my love!" said he, "I've done thee harm,
Give me thy pardon," and he look'd alarm:
Meantime the prudent Dinah had contrived
Her soul to question, and she then revived.

"See! my good friend," and then she raised her head,
"The bloom of life, the strength of youth is fled;
Living we die; to us the world is dead;
We parted bless'd with health, and I am now
Age-struck and feeble, so I find art thou;
Thine eye is sunken, furrow'd is thy face,
And downward look'st thou—so we run our race;
And happier they, whose race is nearly run,
Their troubles over, and their duties done."

"True, lady, true, we are not girl and boy;
But time has left us something to enjoy."

"What! thou hast learn'd my fortune?—yes, I live
To feel how poor the comforts wealth can give;
Thou too perhaps art wealthy; but our fate
Still mocks our wishes, wealth is come too late."

"To me nor late nor early; I am come
Poor as I left thee to my native home:
Nor yet," said Rupert, "will I grieve; 't is mine
To share thy comforts, and the glory thine;
For thou wilt gladly take that generous part
That both exalts and gratifies the heart;
While mine rejoices."—"Heavens!" return'd the maid,
"This talk to one so wither'd and decay'd?
No! all my care is now to fit my mind
For other spousal, and to die resign'd:
As friend and neighbour, I shall hope to see
These noble views, this pious love in thee;
That we together may the change await,
Guides and spectators in each other's fate;
When fellow-pilgrims, we shall daily crave
The mutual prayer that arms us for the grave."

Half angry, half in doubt, the lover gazed
On the meek maiden, by her speech amazed:
"Dinah," said he, "dost thou respect thy vows?
What spousal mean'st thou?—thou art Rupert's spouse;
The chance is mine to take, and thine to give;
But, trifling this, if we together live:
Can I believe, that, after all the past,
Our vows, our loves, thou wilt be false at last?
Something thou hast—I know not, what—in view;
I find thee pious—let me find thee true."

"Ah! cruel this; but do, my friend, depart;
And to its feelings leave my wounded heart."

"Nay, speak at once; and, Dinah, let me know,
Mean'st thou to take me, now I 'm wreck'd, in tow?
Be fair; nor longer keep me in the dark;
Am I forsaken for a trimmer spark?
Heav'n's spouse thou art not; nor can I believe
That God accepts her who will man deceive:
True I am shatter'd, I have service seen,
And service done, and have in trouble been;
My cheek (it shames me not) has lost its red,
And the brown buff is o'er my features spread;
Perchance my speech is rude; for I among
Th' untamed have been, in temper and in tongue,
Have been trepann'd, have lived in toil and care,
And wrought for wealth I was not doom'd to share;
It touch'd me deeply, for I felt a pride
In gaining riches for my destined bride:
Speak then my fate; for these my sorrows past,
Time lost, youth fled, hope wearied, and at last
This doubt of thee—a childish thing to tell,
But certain truth—my very throat they swell;
They stop the breath, and but for shame could I
Give way to weakness, and with passion cry;
These are unmanly struggles, but I feel
This hour must end them, and perhaps will heal."—

Here Dinah sigh'd as if afraid to speak—
And then repeated—"They were frail and weak,
His soul she loved, and hoped he had the grace
To fix his thoughts upon a better place."

She ceased;—with steady glance, as if to see
The very root of this hypocrisy,—
He her small fingers moulded in his hard
And bronzed broad hand; then told her his regard,
His best respect were gone, but love had still
Hold in his heart, and govern'd yet the will—
Or he would curse her:—saying this, he threw
The hand in scorn away, and bade adieu
To every lingering hope, with every care in view.

Proud and indignant, suffering, sick, and poor,
He grieved unseen; and spoke of love no more—
Till all he felt in indignation died,
As hers had sunk in avarice and pride.

In health declining, as in mind distress'd,
To some in power his troubles he confess'd,
And shares a parish-gift;—at prayers he sees
The pious Dinah dropp'd upon her knees;
Thence as she walks the street with stately air
As chance directs, oft meet the parted pair:
When he, with thickset coat of badge-man's blue
Moves near her shaded silk of changeful hue;
When his thin locks of grey approach her braid,
A costly purchase made in beauty's aid;

When his frank air, and his unstudied pace,
Are seen with her soft manner, air, and grace,
And his plain artless look with her sharp meaning face;
It might some wonder in a stranger move,
How these together could have talk'd of love.

Behold them now!—see there a tradesman stands,
And humbly hearkens to some fresh commands;
He moves to speak, she interrupts him—"Stay,"
Her air expresses—"Hark! to what I say:"
Ten paces off, poor Rupert on a seat
Has taken refuge from the noonday-heat,
His eyes on her intent, as if to find
What were the movements of that subtle mind:
How still!—how earnest is he!—it appears
His thoughts are wand'ring through his earlier years;
Through years of fruitless labour, to the day
When all his earthly prospects died away:
"Had I," he thinks, "been wealthier of the two,
Would she have found me so unkind, untrue?
Or knows not man when poor, what man when rich will do?
Yes, yes! I feel that I had faithful proved,
And should have soothed and raised her, bless'd and loved."

But Dinah moves—she had observed before
The pensive Rupert at an humble door:
Some thoughts of pity raised by his distress,
Some feeling touch of ancient tenderness;
Religion, duty urged the maid to speak
In terms of kindness to a man so weak:
But pride forbad, and to return would prove
She felt the shame of his neglected love;
Nor wrapp'd in silence could she pass, afraid
Each eye should see her, and each heart upbraid;
One way remain'd—the way the Levite took,
Who without mercy could on misery look;
(A way perceived by craft, approved by pride),
She cross'd, and pass'd him on the other side.

TALE V.

THE PATRON.

> It were all one,
> That I should love a bright peculiar star,
> And think to wed it; she is so much above me:
> In her bright radiance and collateral heat
> Must I be comforted, not in her sphere.
>
> *All's Well that Ends Well*, act i, scene 1.

> Poor wretches, that depend
> On greatness' favours, dream as I have done,—
> Wake and find nothing.
>
> *Cymbeline*, act v, scene 4.

> And since—
> Th' affliction of my mind amends, with which
> I fear a madness held me.
>
> *Tempest*, act v.

A BOROUGH-BAILIFF, who to law was train'd,
A wife and sons in decent state maintain'd;
He had his way in life's rough ocean steer'd,
And many a rock and coast of danger clear'd;
He saw where others fail'd, and care had he
Others in him should not such failings see;
His sons in various busy states were placed,
And all began the sweets of gain to taste,
Save John, the younger; who, of sprightly parts,
Felt not a love for money-making arts:
In childhood feeble, he, for country air,
Had long resided with a rustic pair;
All round whose room were doleful ballads, songs,
Of lovers' sufferings and of ladies' wrongs;
Of peevish ghosts who came at dark midnight,
For breach of promise, guilty men to fright;
Love, marriage, murder, were the themes, with these
All that on idle, ardent spirits seize;
Robbers at land and pirates on the main,
Enchanters foil'd, spells broken, giants slain;
Legends of love, with tales of halls and bowers,
Choice of rare songs, and garlands of choice flowers
And all the hungry mind without a choice devours.

From village-children kept apart by pride,
With such enjoyments, and without a guide,
Inspired by feelings all such works infused,
John snatch'd a pen, and wrote as he perused:
With the like fancy he could make his knight
Slay half an host and put the rest to flight;
With the like knowledge, he could make him ride
From isle to isle at Parthenissa's side;
And with a heart yet free, no busy brain
Form'd wilder notions of delight and pain,
The raptures smiles create, the anguish of disdain.

Such were the fruits of John's poetic toil,
Weeds, but still proof of vigour in the soil:
He nothing purposed but with vast delight,
Let Fancy loose, and wonder'd at her flight:
His notions of poetic worth were high,
And of his own still-hoarded poetry;—
These to his father's house he bore with pride,
A miser's treasure, in his room to hide;
Till spurr'd by glory, to a reading friend
He kindly show'd the sonnets he had penn'd:
With erring judgment, though with heart sincere,
That friend exclaim'd, "These beauties must appear."
In Magazines they claim'd their share of fame,
Though undistinguish'd by their author's name;
And with delight the young enthusiast found
The muse of Marcus with applauses crown'd;
This heard the father, and with some alarm:
"The boy," said he, "will neither trade nor farm;
He for both law and physic is unfit;
Wit he may have, but cannot live on wit:
Let him his talents then to learning give,
Where verse is honour'd, and where poets live."

John kept his terms at college unreproved,
Took his degree, and left the life he loved;
Not yet ordain'd, his leisure he employ'd
In the light labours he so much enjoy'd;
His favourite notions and his daring views
Were cherish'd still; and he adored the Muse.

"A little time, and he should burst to light,
And admiration of the world excite;
And every friend, now cool and apt to blame
His fond pursuit, would wonder at his fame."
When led by fancy, and from view retired,
He call'd before him all his heart desired;

'Fame shall be mine, then wealth shall I possess,
And beauty next an ardent lover bless;
For me the maid shall leave her nobler state,
Happy to raise and share her poet's fate."
He saw each day his father's frugal board,
With simple fare by cautious prudence stored;
Where each indulgence was foreweigh'd with care,
And the grand maxims were to save and spare:
Yet in his walks, his closet, and his bed,
All frugal cares and prudent counsels fled;
And bounteous Fancy, for his glowing mind,
Wrought various scenes, and all of glorious kind;
Slaves of the *ring* and *lamp!* what need of you,
When Fancy's self such magic deeds can do?

Though rapt in visions of no vulgar kind,
To common subjects stoop'd our poet's mind;
And oft, when wearied with more ardent flight,
He felt a spur satiric song to write;
A rival burgess his bold muse attack'd,
And whipp'd severely for a well-known fact;
For while he seem'd to all demure and shy,
Our poet gazed at what was passing by;
And ev'n his father smiled when playful wit
From his young bard, some haughty object hit.

From ancient times the borough where they dwelt
Had mighty contest at elections felt;
Sir Godfrey Ball, 't is true, had held in pay
Electors many for the trying day;
But in such golden chains to bind them all
Required too much for e'en Sir Godfrey Ball.
A member died, and to supply his place,
Two heroes enter'd for th' important race;
Sir Godfrey's friend and Earl Fitzdonnel's son,
Lord Frederick Damer, both prepared to run;
And partial numbers saw with vast delight
Their good young lord oppose the proud old knight.

Our poet's father, at a first request,
Gave the young lord his vote and interest;
And what he could our poet, for he stung
The foe by verse satiric, said and sung.
Lord Frederick heard of all this youthful zeal,
And felt as lords upon a canvass feel;
He read the satire, and he saw the use
That such cool insult, and such keen abuse,
Might on the wavering minds of voting men produce;
Then too his praises were in contrast seen,
"A lord as noble as the knight was mean."

"I much rejoice," he cried, "such worth to find;
To this the world must be no longer blind:
His glory will descend from sire to son,
The Burns of English race, the happier Chatterton."
Our poet's mind, now hurried and elate,
Alarm'd the anxious parent for his fate;
Who saw with sorrow, should their friend succeed,
That much discretion would their poet need.

Their friends succeeded, and repaid the zeal
The poet felt, and made opposers feel,
By praise (from lords how soothing and how sweet!)
And invitation to his noble seat.
The father ponder'd, doubtful if the brain
Of his proud boy such honour could sustain;
Pleased with the favours offer'd to a son,
But seeing dangers few so ardent shun.

Thus, when they parted, to the youthful breast
The father's fears were by his love impress'd:
"There will you find, my son, the courteous ease
That must subdue the soul it means to please;
That soft attention which ev'n beauty pays
To wake our passions, or provoke our praise;
There all the eye beholds will give delight,
Where every sense is flatter'd like the sight:
This is your peril; can you from such scene
Of splendour part, and feel your mind serene,
And in the father's humble state resume
The frugal diet and the narrow room?"
To this the youth with cheerful heart replied,
Pleased with the trial, but as yet untried;
And while professing patience, should he fail,
He suffer'd hope o'er reason to prevail.

Impatient, by the morning mail convey'd,
The happy guest his promised visit paid;
And now arriving at the hall, he tried
For air composed, serene and satisfied;
As he had practised in his room alone,
And there acquired a free and easy tone:
There he had said, "Whatever the degree
A man obtains, what more than man is he?"
And when arrived—"This room is but a room;
Can aught we see the steady soul o'ercome?
Let me in all a manly firmness show,
Upheld by talents, and their value know."

This reason urged; but it surpass'd his skill
To be in act as manly as in will:
When he his lordship and the lady saw,
Brave as he was, he felt oppress'd with awe;
And spite of verse, that so much praise had won,
The poet found he was the bailiff's son.

But dinner came, and the succeeding hours
Fix'd his weak nerves, and raised his failing powers
Praised and assured, he ventured once or twice
On some remark, and bravely broke the ice;
So that at night, reflecting on his words,
He found, in time, he might converse with lords.

Now was the sister of his patron seen—
A lovely creature, with majestic mien;
Who, softly smiling while she look'd so fair,
Praised the young poet with such friendly air;
Such winning frankness in her looks express'd,
And such attention to her brother's guest,
That so much beauty, join'd with speech so kind,
Raised strong emotions in the poet's mind;
Till reason fail'd his bosom to defend
From the sweet power of this enchanting friend.—
Rash boy! what hope thy frantic mind invades?
What love confuses, and what pride persuades?
Awake to truth! shouldst thou deluded feed
On hopes so groundless, thou art mad indeed.

What say'st thou, wise one? "that all powerful love
Can fortune's strong impediments remove;
Nor is it strange that worth should wed to worth,
The pride of genius with the pride of birth."
While thou art dreaming thus, the beauty spies
Love in thy tremor, passion in thine eyes;

And with th' amusement pleased, of conquest vain,
She seeks her pleasure, careless of thy pain;
She gives thee praise to humble and confound,
Smiles to ensnare, and flatters thee to wound.

Why has she said that in the lowest state
The noble mind insures a noble fate?
And why thy daring mind to glory call?
That thou mayst dare and suffer, soar and fall.
Beauties are tyrants, and if they can reign,
They have no feeling for their subjects' pain;
Their victim's anguish gives their charms applause,
And their chief glory is the woe they cause:
Something of this was felt, in spite of love,
Which hope, in spite of reason, would remove.

Thus lived our youth, with conversation, books,
And Lady Emma's soul-subduing looks;
Lost in delight, astonish'd at his lot,
All prudence banish'd, all advice forgot—
Hopes, fears, and every thought, were fix'd upon the spot.

'T was autumn yet, and many a day must frown
On Brandon-Hall, ere went my lord to town;
Meantime the father, who had heard his boy
Lived in a round of luxury and joy,
And justly thinking that the youth was one
Who, meeting danger, was unskill'd to shun;
Knowing his temper, virtue, spirit, zeal,
How prone to hope and trust, believe and feel;
These on the parent's soul their weight impress'd,
And thus he wrote the counsels of his breast.

"John, thou 'rt a genius; thou hast some pretence,
I think, to wit, but hast thou sterling sense?
That which, like gold, may through the world go forth,
And always pass for what 't is truly worth?
Whereas this genius, like a bill, must take
Only the value our opinions make.

"Men famed for wit, of dangerous talents vain,
Treat those of common parts with proud disdain;
The powers that wisdom would, improving, hide,
They blaze abroad with inconsid'rate pride;
While yet but mere probationers for fame,
They seize the honour they should then disclaim:
Honour so hurried to the light must fade,
The lasting laurels flourish in the shade.

"Genius is jealous; I have heard of some
Who, if unnoticed, grew perversely dumb;
Nay, different talents would their envy raise;
Poets have sicken'd at a dancer's praise;
And one, the happiest writer of his time,
Grew pale at hearing Reynolds was sublime;
That Rutland's duchess wore a heavenly smile—
And I, said he, neglected all the while!

"A waspish tribe are these, on gilded wings,
Humming their lays, and brandishing their stings;
And thus they move their friends and foes among,
Prepared for soothing or satiric song.

"Hear me, my boy; thou hast a virtuous mind—
But be thy virtues of the sober kind;
Be not a Quixote, ever up in arms
To give the guilty and the great alarms:
If never heeded, thy attack is vain;
And if they heed thee, they 'll attack again;
Then too in striking at that heedless rate,
Thou in an instant mayst decide thy fate.

"Leave admonition—let the vicar give
Rules how the nobles of his flock should live;
Nor take that simple fancy to thy brain,
That thou canst cure the wicked and the vain.

"Our Pope, they say, once entertain'd the whim
Who fear'd not God should be afraid of him;
But grant they fear'd him, was it further said,
That he reform'd the hearts he made afraid?
Did Chartres mend? Ward, Waters, and a score
Of flagrant felons, with his floggings sore?
Was Cibber silenced? No; with vigour bless'd,
And brazen front, half earnest, half in jest,
He dared the bard to battle, and was seen
In all his glory match'd with Pope and spleen;
Himself he stripp'd, the harder blow to hit,
Then boldly match'd his ribaldry with wit;
The poet's conquest Truth and Time proclaim,
But yet the battle hurt his peace and fame.

"Strive not too much for favour; seem at ease,
And rather pleased thyself, than bent to please:
Upon thy lord with decent care attend,
But not too near; thou canst not be a friend;
And favourite be not, 't is a dangerous post—
Is gain'd by labour, and by fortune lost:
Talents like thine may make a man approved,
But other talents trusted and beloved.
Look round, my son, and thou wilt early see
The kind of man thou art not form'd to be.

"The real favourites of the great are they
Who to their views and wants attention pay,
And pay it ever; who, with all their skill,
Dive to the heart, and learn the secret will;
If that be vicious, soon can they provide
The favourite ill, and o'er the soul preside;
For vice is weakness, and the artful know
Their power increases as the passions grow;
If indolent the pupil, hard their task;
Such minds will ever for amusement ask;
And great the labour! for a man to choose
Objects for one whom nothing can amuse;
For ere those objects can the soul delight,
They must to joy the soul herself excite;
Therefore it is, this patient, watchful kind
With gentle friction stir the drowsy mind:
Fix'd on their end, with caution they proceed,
And sometimes give, and sometimes take the lead;
Will now a hint convey, and then retire,
And let the spark awake the lingering fire;
Or seek new joys and livelier pleasures bring,
To give the jaded sense a quick'ning spring.

"These arts, indeed, my son must not pursue;
Nor must he quarrel with the tribe that do:
It is not safe another's crimes to know,
Nor is it wise our proper worth to show:—
'My lord,' you say, 'engaged me for that worth;'—
True, and preserve it ready to come forth:
If question'd, fairly answer—and that done,
Shrink back, be silent, and thy father's son;
For they who doubt thy talents scorn thy boast,
But they who grant them will dislike thee most;

Observe the prudent; they in silence sit,
Display no learning, and affect no wit;
They hazard nothing, nothing they assume,
But know the useful art of *acting dumb.*
Yet to their eyes each varying look appears,
And every word finds entrance at their ears.

"Thou art religion's advocate—take heed,
Hurt not the cause, thy pleasure 't is to plead;
With wine before thee, and with wits beside,
Do not in strength of reas'ning powers confide;
What seems to thee convincing, certain, plain,
They will deny, and dare thee to maintain;
And thus will triumph o'er the eager youth,
While thou wilt grieve for so disgracing truth.

"With pain I've seen, these wrangling wits among,
Faith's weak defenders, passionate and young;
Weak thou art not, yet not enough on guard,
Where wit and humour keep their watch and ward:
Men gay and noisy will o'erwhelm thy sense,
Then loudly laugh at Truth's and thy expense;
While the kind ladies will do all they can
To check their mirth, and cry, '*The good young man!*'

"Prudence, my boy, forbids thee to commend
The cause or party of thy noble friend;
What are his praises worth, who must be known
To take a patron's maxims for his own?
When ladies sing, or in thy presence play,
Do not, dear John, in rapture melt away;
'T is not thy part, there will be list'ners round,
To cry *divine!* and dote upon the sound;
Remember too, that though the poor have ears,
They take not in the music of the spheres:
They must not feel the warble and the thrill,
Or be dissolved in ecstasy at will;
Beside, 't is freedom in a youth like thee
To drop his awe, and deal in ecstasy!

"In silent ease, at least in silence, dine,
Nor one opinion start of food or wine:
Thou know'st that all the science thou canst boast
Is of thy father's simple boil'd and roast;
Nor always these; he sometimes saved his cash,
By interlinear days of frugal hash:
Wine hadst thou seldom; wilt thou be so vain
As to decide on claret or champagne?
Dost thou from me derive this taste sublime,
Who order port the dozen at a time?
When (every glass held precious in our eyes)
We judged the value by the bottle's size:
Then never merit for thy praise assume,
Its worth well knows each servant in the room.

"Hard, boy, thy task, to steer thy way among
That servile, supple, shrewd, insidious throng;
Who look upon thee as of doubtful race,
An interloper, one who wants a place:
Freedom with these let thy free soul contemn,
Nor with thy heart's concerns associate them.

"Of all be cautious—but be most afraid
Of the pale charms that grace my lady's maid;
Of those sweet dimples, of that fraudful eye,
The frequent glance design'd for thee to spy;
The soft bewitching look, the fond bewailing sigh:
Let others frown and envy! she the while
(Insidious syren!) will demurely smile;
And for her gentle purpose, every day
Inquire thy wants, and meet thee in thy way;
She has her blandishments, and though so weak,
Her person pleases, and her actions speak:
At first her folly may her aim defeat;
But kindness shown at length will kindness meet.
Have some offended? them will she disdain,
And, for thy sake, contempt and pity feign;
She hates the vulgar, she admires to look
On woods and groves, and dotes upon a book;
Let her once see thee on her features dwell,
And hear one sigh, then liberty farewell.

"But, John, remember we cannot maintain
A poor, proud girl, extravagant and vain.

"Doubt much of friendship: shouldst thou find a friend
Pleased to advise thee, anxious to commend;
Should he the praises he has heard report,
And confidence (in thee confiding) court;
Much of neglectful patrons should he say,
And then exclaim—'How long must merit stay!'
Then show how high thy modest hopes may stretch,
And point to stations far beyond thy reach;
Let such designer, by thy conduct, see
(Civil and cool) he makes no dupe of thee;
And he will quit thee, as a man too wise
For him to ruin first, and then despise.

"Such are thy dangers;—yet, if thou canst steer
Past all the perils, all the quicksands clear,
Then mayst thou profit; but if storms prevail,
If foes beset thee, if thy spirits fail,—
No more of winds or waters be the sport,
But in thy father's mansion find a port."
Our poet read.—"It is in truth," said he,
"Correct in part, but what is *this* to me?
I love a foolish Abigail! in base
And sordid office! fear not such disgrace:
Am I so blind?" "Or thou wouldst surely see
That lady's fall, if she should stoop to thee!"
"The cases differ." "True! for what surprise
Could from thy marriage with the maid arise?
But through the island would the shame be spread,
Should the fair mistress deign with thee to wed."

John saw not this; and many a week had pass'd
While the vain beauty held her victim fast;
The noble friend still condescension show'd,
And, as before, with praises overflow'd;
But his grave lady took a silent view
Of all that pass'd, and smiling, pitied too.

Cold grew the foggy morn, the day was brief,
Loose on the cherry hung the crimson leaf;
The dew dwelt ever on the herb; the woods
Roar'd with strong blasts, with mighty showers the floods;
All green was vanish'd, save of pine and yew,
That still display'd their melancholy hue,
Save the green holly with its berries red,
And the green moss that o'er the gravel spread.

To public views my lord must soon attend;
And soon the ladies—would they leave their friend?

The time was fix'd—approach'd—was near—was come;
The trying time that fill'd his soul with gloom:
Thoughtful our poet in the morning rose,
And cried, "One hour my fortune will disclose;
Terrific hour! from thee have I to date
Life's loftier views, or my degraded state;
For now to be what I have been before
Is so to fall, that I can rise no more."

The morning meal was past, and all around
The mansion rang with each discordant sound;
Haste was in every foot, and every look
The trav'llers' joy for London-journey spoke:
Not so our youth; whose feelings, at the noise
Of preparation, had no touch of joys;
He pensive stood, and saw each carriage drawn,
With lackeys mounted, ready on the lawn:
The ladies came; and John in terror threw
One painful glance, and then his eyes withdrew;
Not with such speed, but he in other eyes
With anguish read—"I pity but despise—
Unhappy boy! presumptuous scribbler!—you
To dream such dreams!—be sober, and adieu!"

Then came the noble friend—"And will my lord
Vouchsafe no comfort? drop no soothing word?
Yes, he must speak:" he speaks, "My good young friend,
You know my views; upon my care depend;
My hearty thanks to your good father pay,
And be a student.—Harry, drive away."

Stillness reign'd all around; of late so full
The busy scene, deserted now and dull:
Stern is his nature who forbears to feel
Gloom o'er his spirits on such trials steal;
Most keenly felt our poet as he went
From room to room without a fix'd intent.
"And here," he thought, "I was caress'd; admired
Were here my songs; she smiled, and I aspired:
The change how grievous!" As he mused, a dame
Busy and peevish to her duties came;
Aside the tables and the chairs she drew,
And sang and mutter'd in the poet's view:—
"This was her fortune; here they leave the poor;
Enjoy themselves, and think of us no more:
I had a promise—" here his pride and shame
Urged him to fly from this familiar dame;
He gave one farewell look, and by a coach
Reach'd his own mansion at the night's approach.

His father met him with an anxious air,
Heard his sad tale, and check'd what seem'd despair.
Hope was in him corrected, but alive;
My lord would something for a friend contrive;
His word was pledged; our hero's feverish mind
Admitted this, and half his grief resign'd:
But when three months had fled, and every day
Drew from the sickening hopes their strength away,
The youth became abstracted, pensive, dull;
He utter'd nothing, though his heart was full:
Teased by inquiring words and anxious looks,
And all forgetful of his muse and books;
Awake he mourn'd, but in his sleep perceived
A lovely vision that his pain relieved;
His soul, transported, hail'd the happy seat,
Where once his pleasure was so pure and sweet;
Where joys departed came in blissful view,
Till reason waked, and not a joy he knew

Questions now vex'd his spirit, most from those
Who are called friends, because they are not foes:
"John!" they would say; he, starting, turn'd around;
"John!" there was something shocking in the sound;
Ill brook'd he then the pert familiar phrase,
The untaught freedom, and th' inquiring gaze:
Much was his temper touch'd, his spleen provoked,
When ask'd how ladies talk'd, or walk'd, or look'd?
"What said my lord of politics? how spent
He there his time? and was he glad he went?"

At length a letter came, both cool and brief,
But still it gave the burthen'd heart relief:
Though not inspired by lofty hopes, the youth
Placed much reliance on Lord Frederick's truth;
Summon'd to town, he thought the visit one
Where something fair and friendly would be done.
Although he judged not, as before his fall,
When all was love and promise at the hall.

Arrived in town, he early sought to know
The fate such dubious friendship would bestow.
At a tall building trembling he appear'd,
And his low rap was indistinctly heard;
A well-known servant came—"Awhile," said he,
"Be pleased to wait, my lord has company."

Alone our hero sate; the news in hand,
Which though he read, he could not understand:
Cold was the day: in days so cold as these
There needs a fire, where minds and bodies freeze.
The vast and echoing room, the polish'd grate,
The crimson chairs, the sideboard with its plate;
The splendid sofa, which, though made for rest,
He then had thought it freedom to have press'd;
The shining tables curiously inlaid,
Were all in comfortless proud style display'd,
And to the troubled feelings terror gave,
That made the once-dear friend, the sick'ning slave.

"Was he forgotten?" Thrice upon his ear
Struck the loud clock, yet no relief was near.
Each rattling carriage, and each thundering stroke
On the loud door, the dream of fancy broke:
Oft as a servant chanced the way to come,
"Brings he a message?" no! he pass'd the room:
At length 't is certain: "Sir, you will attend
"At twelve on Thursday!" Thus the day had end.

Vex'd by these tedious hours of needless pain,
John left the noble mansion with disdain:
For there was something in that still, cold place,
That seem'd to threaten and portend disgrace.

Punctual again the modest rap declared
The youth attended; then was all prepared:
For the same servant, by his lord's command,
A paper offer'd to his trembling hand:
"No more!" he cried, "disdains he to afford
One kind expression, one consoling word?"

With troubled spirit he began to read
That "In the church my lord could not succeed;"
Who had "to peers of either kind applied,
And was with dignity and grace denied·

While his own livings were by men possess'd,
Not likely in their chancels yet to rest.
And therefore, all things weigh'd (as he, my lord,
Had done maturely, and he pledged his word,)
Wisdom it seem'd for John to turn his view
To busier scenes, and bid the church adieu!"

Here grieved the youth; he felt his father's pride
Must with his own be shock'd and mortified:
But when he found his future comforts placed
Where he, alas! conceived himself disgraced—
In some appointment on the London quays,
He bade farewell to honour and to ease;
His spirit fell, and, from that hour assured
How vain his dreams, he suffer'd and was cured.

Our poet hurried on, with wish to fly
From all mankind, to be conceal'd, and die.
Alas! what hopes, what high romantic views
Did that one visit to the soul infuse,
Which, cherish'd with such love, 't was worse than
death to lose!
Still he would strive, though painful was the strife,
To walk in this appointed road of life;
On these low duties duteous he would wait,
And patient bear the anguish of his fate.
Thanks to the patron, but of coldest kind,
Express'd the sadness of the poet's mind;
Whose heavy hours were pass'd with busy men,
In the dull practice of th' official pen;
Who to superiors must in time impart
(The custom this) his progress in their art:
But so had grief on his perception wrought,
That all unheeded were the duties taught;
No answers gave he when his trial came,
Silent he stood, but suffering without shame;
And they observed that words severe or kind
Made no impression on his wounded mind;
For all perceived from whence the failure rose,
Some grief whose cause he deign'd not to disclose.
A soul averse from scenes and works so new,
Fear ever shrinking from the vulgar crew;
Distaste for each mechanic law and rule,
Thoughts of past honour and a patron cool;
A grieving parent, and a feeling mind,
Timid and ardent, tender and refined:
These all with mighty force the youth assail'd,
Till his soul fainted, and his reason fail'd:
When this was known, and some debate arose
How they who saw it should the fact disclose,
He found their purpose, and in terror fled
From unseen kindness, with mistaken dread.

Meantime the parent was distress'd to find
His son no longer for a priest design'd;
But still he gain'd some comfort by the news
Of John's promotion, though with humbler views:
For he conceived that in no distant time
The boy would learn to scramble and to climb:
He little thought a son, his hope and pride,
His favour'd boy, was now a home denied:
Yes! while the parent was intent to trace
How men in office climb from place to place,
By day, by night, o'er moor and heath and hill,
Roved the sad youth, with ever-changing will,
Of every aid bereft, exposed to every ill.

Thus as he sate, absorb'd in all the care
And all the hope that anxious fathers share,
A friend abruptly to his presence brought,
With trembling hand the subject of his thought;
Whom he had found afflicted and subdued
By hunger, sorrow, cold, and solitude.

Silent he enter'd the forgotten room,
As ghostly forms may be conceived to come;
With sorrow-shrunken face and hair upright,
He look'd dismay, neglect, despair, affright;
But dead to comfort, and on misery thrown,
His parent's loss he felt not, nor his own.

The good man, struck with horror, cried aloud,
And drew around him an astonish'd crowd;
The sons and servants to the father ran,
To share the feelings of the grieved old man.

"Our brother, speak!" they all exclaim'd; "explain
Thy grief, thy suffering:"—but they ask'd in vain:
The friend told all he knew; and all was known,
Save the sad causes whence the ills had grown:
But, if obscure the cause, they all agreed
From rest and kindness must the cure proceed:
And he was cured; for quiet, love, and care,
Strove with the gloom, and broke on the despair;
Yet slow their progress, and, as vapours move
Dense and reluctant from the wintry grove;
All is confusion till the morning light
Gives the dim scene obscurely to the sight;
More and yet more defined the trunks appear,
Till the wild prospect stands distinct and clear;—
So the dark mind of our young poet grew
Clear and sedate; the dreadful mist withdrew:
And he resembled that bleak wintry scene,
Sad, though unclouded; dismal, though serene.

At times he utter'd, "What a dream was mine!
And what a prospect! glorious and divine!
Oh! in that room, and on that night, to see
These looks, that sweetness beaming all on me;
Thy syren-flattery—and to send me then,
Hope-raised and soften'd, to those heartless men,
That dark-brow'd stern director, pleased to show
Knowledge of subjects, I disdain'd to know;
Cold and controlling—but 't is gone, 't is past;
I had my trial, and have peace at last."

Now grew the youth resign'd; he bade adieu
To all that hope, to all that fancy drew;
His frame was languid, and the hectic heat
Flush'd on his pallid face, and countless beat
The quick'ning pulse, and faint the limbs that bore
The slender form that soon would breathe no more.

Then hope of holy kind the soul sustain'd,
And not a lingering thought of earth remain'd.
Now Heaven had all, and he could smile at love,
And the wild sallies of his youth reprove;
Then could he dwell upon the tempting days,
The proud aspiring thought, the partial praise
Victorious now, his worldly views were closed,
And on the bed of death the youth reposed.

The father grieved—but as the poet's heart
Was all unfitted for his earthly part;
As, he conceived, some other haughty fair
Would, had he lived, have led him to despair;
As, with this fear, the silent grave shut out
All feverish hope, and all tormenting doubt;

While the strong faith the pious youth possess'd,
His hope enlivening, gave his sorrows rest;
Soothed by these thoughts, he felt a mournful joy
For his aspiring and devoted boy.

Meantime the news through various channels spread,
The youth, once favour'd with such praise, was dead:
"Emma," the lady cried, "my words attend,
Your syren-smiles have kill'd your humble friend;
The hope you raised can now delude no more,
Nor charms, that once inspired, can now restore."

Faint was the flush of anger and of shame,
That o'er the cheek of conscious beauty came:
"You censure not," said she, "the sun's bright rays,
When fools imprudent dare the dangerous gaze;
And should a stripling look till he were blind,
You would not justly call the light unkind:
But is he dead? and am I to suppose
The power of poison in such looks as those?"
She spoke, and, pointing to the mirror, cast
A pleased gay glance, and curtsied as she pass'd.

My lord, to whom the poet's fate was told,
Was much affected, for a man so cold:
"Dead!" said his lordship, "run distracted, mad!
Upon my soul I'm sorry for the lad;
And now, no doubt, th' obliging world will say
That my harsh usage help'd him on his way:
What! I suppose, I should have nursed his muse,
And with champagne have brighten'd up his views;
Then had he made me famed my whole life long,
And stunn'd my ears with gratitude and song.
Still should the father hear that I regret
Our joint misfortune—Yes! I 'll not forget."—

Thus they:—The father to his grave convey'd
The son he loved, and his last duties paid.

"There lies my boy," he cried, "of care bereft,
And Heav'n be praised, I 've not a genius left:
No one among ye, sons! is doom'd to live
On high-raised hopes of what the great may give;
None, with exalted views and fortunes mean,
To die in anguish, or to live in spleen:
Your pious brother soon escaped the strife
Of such contention, but it cost his life;
You then, my sons, upon yourselves depend,
And in your own exertions find the friend."

TALE VI.

THE FRANK COURTSHIP.

Yes, faith, it is my cousin's duty to make a curtsy, and say, "Father, as it please you;" but for all that, cousin, let him be a handsome fellow, or else make another curtsy, and say, "Father, as it pleases me."

Much Ado about Nothing, act ii, scene i.

He cannot flatter, he!
An honest mind and plain—he must speak truth.

King Lear, act ii, scene 2.

God hath given you one face, and you make yourselves another: you jig, you amble, you nick-name God's creatures, and make your wantonness your ignorance.

Hamlet, act iii, scene i.

What fire is in my ears? Can this be true?
Am I contemn'd for pride and scorn so much!

Much Ado about Nothing, act ii, scene i.

Grave Jonas Kindred, Sybil Kindred's sire,
Was six feet high, and look'd six inches higher;
Erect, morose, determined, solemn, slow,
Who knew the man, could never cease to know;
His faithful spouse, when Jonas was not by,
Had a firm presence and a steady eye;
But with her husband dropp'd her look and tone,
And Jonas ruled unquestion'd and alone.

He read, and oft would quote the sacred words,
How pious husbands of their wives were lords;
Sarah called Abraham lord! and who could be,
So Jonas thought, a greater man than he?
Himself he view'd with undisguised respect,
And never pardon'd freedom or neglect.

They had one daughter, and this favourite child
Had oft the father of his spleen beguiled;
Soothed by attention from her early years,
She gain'd all wishes by her smiles or tears:
But Sybil then was in that playful time,
When contradiction is not held a crime;
When parents yield their children idle praise
For faults corrected in their after days.

Peace in the sober house of Jonas dwelt,
Where each his duty and his station felt:
Yet not that peace some favour'd mortals find,
In equal views and harmony of mind;
Not the soft peace that blesses those who love,
Where all with one consent in union move;
But it was that which one superior will
Commands, by making all inferiors still;
Who bids all murmurs, all objections cease,
And with imperious voice announces—Peace!

They were, to wit, a remnant of that crew,
Who, as their foes maintain, their sovereign slew;
An independent race, precise, correct,
Who ever married in the kindred sect:
No son or daughter of their order wed
A friend to England's king who lost his head;
Cromwell was still their saint, and when they met,
They mourn'd that saints* were not our rulers yet.

Fix'd were their habits: they arose betimes,
Then pray'd their hour, and sang their party-rhymes:
Their meals were plenteous, regular, and plain;
The trade of Jonas brought him constant gain:
Vender of hops and malt, of coals and corn—
And, like his father, he was merchant born:
Neat was their house; each table, chair, and stool,
Stood in its place, or moving moved by rule;
No lively print or picture graced the room;
A plain brown paper lent its decent gloom;
But here the eye, in glancing round, survey'd
A small recess that seem'd for china made;
Such pleasing pictures seem'd this pencill'd ware,
That few would search for nobler objects there—

* This appellation is here used not ironically, nor with malignity; but it is taken merely to designate a morosely devout people, with peculiar austerity of manners.

Yet, turn'd by chosen friends, and there appear'd
His stern, strong features, whom they all revered;
For there in lofty air was seen to stand
The bold protector of the conquer'd land;
Drawn in that look with which he wept and swore,
Turn'd out the members, and made fast the door,
Ridding the house of every knave and drone,
Forced, though it grieved his soul, to rule alone.
The stern still smile each friend approving gave,
Then turn'd the view, and all again were grave.

There stood a clock, though small the owner's need,
For habit told when all things should proceed;
Few their amusements, but when friends appear'd,
They with the world's distress their spirits cheer'd;
The nation's guilt, that would not long endure
The reign of men so modest and so pure:
Their town was large, and seldom pass'd a day
But some had fail'd, and others gone astray;
Clerks had absconded, wives eloped, girls flown
To Gretna-Green, or sons rebellious grown;
Quarrels and fires arose;—and it was plain
The times were bad; the saints had ceased to reign!
A few yet lived to languish and to mourn
For good old manners never to return.

Jonas had sisters, and of these was one
Who lost a husband and an only son:
Twelve months her sables she in sorrow wore,
And mourn'd so long that she could mourn no more.
Distant from Jonas, and from all her race,
She now resided in a lively place;
There, by the sect unseen, at whist she play'd,
Nor was of churchmen or their church afraid:
If much of this the graver brother heard,
He something censured, but he little fear'd;
He knew her rich and frugal; for the rest,
He felt no care, or, if he felt, suppress'd:
Nor for companion when she ask'd her niece,
Had he suspicions that disturb'd his peace;
Frugal and rich, these virtues as a charm
Preserved the thoughtful man from all alarm;
An infant yet, she soon would home return,
Nor stay the manners of the world to learn;
Meantime his boys would all his care engross,
And he his comforts if he felt the loss.

The sprightly Sybil, pleased and unconfined,
Felt the pure pleasure of the op'ning mind:
All here was gay and cheerful—all at home
Unvaried quiet and unruffled gloom:
There were no changes, and amusements few;
Here, all was varied, wonderful, and new;
There were plain meals, plain dresses, and grave looks—
Here, gay companions and amusing books;
And the young beauty soon began to taste
The light vocations of the scene she graced.

A man of business feels it as a crime
On calls domestic to consume his time;
Yet this grave man had not so cold a heart,
But with his daughter he was grieved to part:
And he demanded that in every year
The aunt and niece should at his house appear.

"Yes! we must go, my child, and by our dress
A grave conformity of mind express;
Must sing at meeting, and from cards refrain,
The more t' enjoy when we return again."

Thus spake the aunt, and the discerning child
Was pleased to learn how fathers are beguiled.
Her artful part the young dissembler took,
And from the matron caught th' approving look:
When thrice the friends had met, excuse was sent
For more delay, and Jonas was content;
Till a tall maiden by her sire was seen,
In all the bloom and beauty of sixteen;
He gazed admiring;—she, with visage prim,
Glanced an arch look of gravity on him;
For she was gay at heart, but wore disguise,
And stood a vestal in her father's eyes:
Pure, pensive, simple, sad; the damsel's heart,
When Jonas praised, reproved her for the part;
For Sybil, fond of pleasure, gay and light,
Had still a secret bias to the right;
Vain as she was—and flattery made her vain—
Her simulation gave her bosom pain.

Again return'd, the matron and the niece
Found the late quiet gave their joy increase;
The aunt infirm, no more her visits paid,
But still with her sojourn'd the favourite maid.
Letters were sent when franks could be procured,
And when they could not, silence was endured;
All were in health, and if they older grew,
It seem'd a fact that none among them knew;
The aunt and niece still led a pleasant life,
And quiet days had Jonas and his wife.

Near him a widow dwelt of worthy fame,
Like his her manners, and her creed the same;
The wealth her husband left, her care retain'd
For one tall youth, and widow she remain'd;
His love respectful all her care repaid,
Her wishes watch'd, and her commands obey'd.

Sober he was and grave from early youth,
Mindful of forms, but more intent on truth;
In a light drab he uniformly dress'd,
And look serene th' unruffled mind express'd;
A hat with ample verge his brows o'erspread,
And his brown locks curl'd graceful on his head,
Yet might observers in his speaking eye
Some observation, some acuteness spy;
The friendly thought it keen, the treacherous deem'd it sly;
Yet not a crime could foe or friend detect,
His actions all were, like his speech, correct;
And they who jested on a mind so sound,
Upon his virtues must their laughter found;
Chaste, sober, solemn, and devout they named
Him who was thus, and not of *this* ashamed.

Such were the virtues Jonas found in one
In whom he warmly wish'd to find a son:
Three years had pass'd since he had Sybil seen;
But she was doubtless what she once had been,
Lovely and mild, obedient and discreet;
The pair must love whenever they should meet;
Then ere the widow or her son should choose
Some happier maid, he would explain his views.
Now she, like him, was politic and shrewd,
With strong desire of lawful gain embued;
To all he said, she bow'd with much respect,
Pleased to comply, yet seeming to reject;

Cool and yet eager, each admired the strength
Of the opponent, and agreed at length:
As a drawn battle shows to each a force,
Powerful as his, he honours it of course;
So in these neighbours, each the power discern'd,
And gave the praise that was to each return'd.

Jonas now ask'd his daughter—and the aunt,
Though loth to lose her, was obliged to grant:—
But would not Sybil to the matron cling,
And fear to leave the shelter of her wing?
No! in the young there lives a love of change,
And to the easy they prefer the strange!
Then too the joys she once pursued with zeal,
From whist and visits sprung, she ceased to feel;
When with the matrons Sybil first sat down,
To cut for partners and to stake her crown,
This to the youthful maid preferment seem'd,
Who thought that woman she was then esteem'd;
But in few years, when she perceived, indeed,
The real woman to the girl succeed,
No longer tricks and honours fill'd her mind,
But other feelings, not so well defined;
She then reluctant grew, and thought it hard,
To sit and ponder o'er an ugly card;
Rather the nut-tree shade the nymph preferr'd,
Pleased with the pensive gloom and evening bird;
Thither, from company retired, she took
The silent walk, or read the fav'rite book.

The father's letter, sudden, short, and kind,
Awaked her wonder, and disturb'd her mind;
She found new dreams upon her fancy seize,
Wild roving thoughts and endless reveries:
The parting came;—and, when the aunt perceived
The tears of Sybil, and how much she grieved—
To love for her that tender grief she laid,
That various, soft, contending passions made.

When Sybil rested in her father's arms,
His pride exulted in a daughter's charms,
A maid accomplish'd he was pleased to find,
Nor seem'd the form more lovely than the mind:
But when the fit of pride and fondness fled,
He saw his judgment by his hopes misled;
High were the lady's spirits, far more free
Her mode of speaking than a maid's should be;
Too much, as Jonas thought, she seem'd to know,
And all her knowledge was disposed to show;
"Too gay her dress, like theirs who idly dote
On a young coxcomb, or a coxcomb's coat;
In foolish spirits when our friends appear,
And vainly grave when not a man is near."

Thus Jonas, adding to his sorrow blame,
And terms disdainful to his sister's name:—
"The sinful wretch has by her arts defiled
The ductile spirit of my darling child."

"The maid is virtuous," said the dame—Quoth he,
"Let her give proof, by acting virtuously.
Is it in gaping when the elders pray?
In reading nonsense half a summer's day?
In those mock forms that she delights to trace,
Or her loud laughs in Hezekiah's face?
She—O Susannah!—to the world belongs;
She loves the follies of its idle throngs,
And reads soft tales of love, and sings love's soft'-
ning songs.

But, as our friend is yet delay'd in town,
We must prepare her till the youth comes down;
You shall advise the maiden; I will threat;
Her fears and hopes may yield us comfort yet."

Now the grave father took the lass aside,
Demanding sternly, "Wilt thou be a bride?"
She answer'd, calling up an air sedate,
"I have not vow'd against the holy state."

"No folly, Sybil," said the parent; "know
What to their parents virtuous maidens owe:
A worthy, wealthy youth, whom I approve,
Must thou prepare to honour and to love.
Formal to thee his air and dress may seem,
But the good youth is worthy of esteem;
Shouldst thou with rudeness treat him; of disdain
Should he with justice or of slight complain,
Or of one taunting speech give certain proof,
Girl! I reject thee from my sober roof."

"My aunt," said Sybil, "will with pride protect
One whom a father can for this reject;
Nor shall a formal, rigid, soulless boy
My manners alter, or my views destroy!"

Jonas then lifted up his hands on high,
And utt'ring something 'twixt a groan and sigh,
Left the determined maid, her doubtful mother by.

"Hear me," she said; "incline thy heart, my
child,
And fix thy fancy on a man so mild:
Thy father, Sybil, never could be moved
By one who loved him, or by one he loved.
Union like ours is but a bargain made
By slave and tyrant—he will be obey'd;
Then calls the quiet, comfort—but thy youth
Is mild by nature, and as frank as truth."

"But will he love?" said Sybil; "I am told
That these mild creatures are by nature cold."

"Alas!" the matron answer'd, "much I dread
That dangerous love by which the young are led
That love is earthy; you the creature prize,
And trust your feelings and believe your eyes:
Can eyes and feelings inward worth descry?
No! my fair daughter, on our choice rely!
Your love, like that display'd upon the stage,
Indulged is folly, and opposed is rage;—
More prudent love our sober couples show,
All that to mortal beings, mortals owe;—
All flesh is grass—before you give a heart,
Remember, Sybil, that in death you part;
And should your husband die before your love,
What needless anguish must a widow prove!
No! my fair child, let all such visions cease;
Yield but esteem, and only try for peace."

"I must be loved," said Sybil; "I must see
The man in terrors who aspires to me;
At my forbidding frown, his heart must ache,
His tongue must falter, and his frame must shake:
And if I grant him at my feet to kneel,
What trembling, fearful pleasure must he feel!
Nay, such the raptures that my smiles inspire,
That reason's self must for a time retire."

"Alas! for good Josiah," said the dame,
These wicked thoughts would fill his soul with
shame;"

He kneel and tremble at a thing of dust!
He cannot, child:"—the child replied, "He must."

They ceased: the matron left her with a frown;
So Jonas met her when the youth came down:
"Behold," said he, "thy future spouse attends;
Receive him, daughter, as the best of friends;
Observe, respect him—humble be each word
That welcomes home thy husband and thy lord."

Forewarn'd, thought Sybil, with a bitter smile,
I shall prepare my manner and my style.

Ere yet Josiah enter'd on his task,
The father met him—"Deign to wear a mask
A few dull days, Josiah—but a few—
It is our duty, and the sex's due;
I wore it once, and every grateful wife
Repays it with obedience through her life:
Have no regard to Sybil's dress, have none
To her pert language, to her flippant tone:
Henceforward thou shalt rule unquestion'd and alone;
And she thy pleasure in thy looks shall seek—
How she shall dress, and whether she may speak."

A sober smile return'd the youth, and said,
"Can I cause fear, who am myself afraid?"

Sybil, meantime, sat thoughtful in her room,
And often wonder'd—"Will the creature come?
Nothing shall tempt, shall force me to bestow
My hand upon him, yet I wish to know."

The door unclosed, and she beheld her sire
Lead in the youth, then hasten to retire;
"Daughter, my friend—my daughter, friend"—he cried,
And gave a meaning look, and stepp'd aside;
That look contain'd a mingled threat and prayer,
"Do take him child—offend him, if you dare."

The couple gazed—were silent, and the maid
Look'd in his face, to make the man afraid;
The man, unmoved, upon the maiden cast
A steady view—so salutation pass'd:
But in this instant Sybil's eye had seen
The tall fair person, and the still staid mien;
The glow that temp'rance o'er the cheek had spread,
Where the soft down half veil'd the purest red;
And the serene deportment that proclaim'd
A heart unspotted, and a life unblamed:
But then with these she saw attire too plain,
The pale brown coat, though worn without a stain;
The formal air, and something of the pride
That indicates the wealth it seems to hide:
And looks that were not, she conceived, exempt
From a proud pity, or a sly contempt.

Josiah's eyes had their employment too,
Engaged and soften'd by so bright a view;
A fair and meaning face, an eye of fire,
That check'd the bold, and made the free retire:
But then with these he mark'd the studied dress
And lofty air, that scorn or pride express;
With that insidious look, that seem'd to hide
In an affected smile the scorn and pride;
And if his mind the virgin's meaning caught,
He saw a foe with treacherous purpose fraught—
Captive the heart to take, and to reject it caught.

Silent they sate—thought Sybil, that he seeks
Something, no doubt; I wonder if he speaks:
Scarcely she wonder'd, when these accents fell
Slow in her ear—"Fair maiden, art thou well?"
"Art thou physician?" she replied; "my hand,
My pulse, at least, shall be at thy command."

She said—and saw, surprised, Josiah kneel,
And gave his lips the offer'd pulse to feel;
The rosy colour rising in her cheek,
Seem'd that surprise unmix'd with wrath to speak.
Then sternness she assumed, and—"Doctor, tell,
Thy words cannot alarm me—am I well?"
"Thou art," said he; "and yet thy dress so light,
I do conceive, some danger must excite:"
"In whom?" said Sybil, with a look demure:
"In more," said he, "than I expect to cure.
I, in thy light luxuriant robe, behold
Want and excess, abounding and yet cold;
Here needed, there display'd, in many a wanton fold:
Both health and beauty, learned authors show,
From a just medium in our clothing flow."

"Proceed, good doctor; if so great my need,
What is thy fee? Good doctor! Pray proceed."

"Large is my fee, fair lady, but I take
None till some progress in my cure I make:
Thou hast disease, fair maiden; thou art vain;
Within that face sit insult and disdain;
Thou art enamour'd of thyself; my art
Can see the naughty malice of thy heart:
With a strong pleasure would thy bosom move,
Were I to own thy power, and ask thy love;
And such thy beauty, damsel, that I might,
But for thy pride feel danger in thy sight,
And lose my present peace in dreams of vain delight."

"And can thy patients," said the nymph, "endure
Physic like this? and will it work a cure?"

"Such is my hope, fair damsel; thou, I find,
Hast the true tokens of a noble mind;
But the world wins thee, Sybil, and thy joys
Are placed in trifles, fashions, follies, toys:
Thou hast sought pleasure in the world around,
That in thine own pure bosom should be found:
Did all that world admire thee, praise and love,
Could it the least of nature's pains remove?
Could it for errors, follies, sins atone,
Or give thee comfort, thoughtful and alone?
It has, believe me, maid, no power to charm
Thy soul from sorrow, or thy flesh from harm:
Turn, then, fair creature, from a world of sin,
And seek the jewel happiness within."

"Speak'st thou at meeting?" said the nymph; "thy speech
Is that of mortal very prone to teach;
But wouldst thou, doctor, from the patient learn
Thine own disease?—The cure is thy concern."

"Yea, with good will."—"Then know, 't is thy complaint,
That, for a sinner, thou 'rt too much a saint;
Hast too much show of the sedate and pure,
And without cause art formal and demure.

This makes a man unsocial, unpolite;
Odious when wrong, and insolent if right.
Thou mayst be good, but why should goodness be
Wrapt in a garb of such formality?
Thy person well might please a damsel's eye,
In decent habit with a scarlet dye;
But, jest apart—what virtue canst thou trace
In that broad brim that hides thy sober face?
Does that long-skirted drab, that over-nice
And formal clothing, prove a scorn of vice?
Then for thine accent—what in sound can be
So void of grace as dull monotony!
Love has a thousand varied notes to move
The human heart;—thou mayst not speak of love
Till thou hast cast thy formal ways aside,
And those becoming youth and nature tried:
Not till exterior freedom, spirit, ease,
Prove it thy study and delight to please;
Not till these follies meet thy just disdain,
While yet thy virtues and thy worth remain."

"This is severe!—Oh, maiden, wilt not thou
Something for habits, manners, modes, allow?"—

"Yes! but allowing much, I much require,
In my behalf, for manners, modes, attire!"

"True, lovely Sybil; and, this point agreed,
Let me to those of greater weight proceed:
Thy father!"—"Nay," she quickly interposed,
"Good doctor, here our conference is closed!"

Then left the youth, who, lost in his retreat,
Pass'd the good matron on her garden-seat;
His looks were troubled, and his air, once mild
And calm, was hurried:—"My audacious child!"
Exclaim'd the dame, "I read what she has done
In thy displeasure—Ah! the thoughtless one!
But yet, Josiah, to my stern good man
Speak of the maid as mildly as you can:
Can you not seem to woo a little while
The daughter's will, the father to beguile!
So that his wrath in time may wear away;
Will you preserve our peace, Josiah? say."

"Yes! my good neighbour," said the gentle youth,
"Rely securely on my care and truth;
And should thy comfort with my efforts cease,
And only then—perpetual is thy peace."

The dame had doubts: she well his virtues knew,
His deeds were friendly, and his words were true;
"But to address this vixen is a task
He is ashamed to take, and I to ask."
Soon as the father from Josiah learn'd
What pass'd with Sybil, he the truth discern'd.
"He loves," the man exclaim'd, "he loves, 't is plain,
The thoughtless girl, and shall he love in vain?
She may be stubborn, but she shall be tried,
Born as she is of wilfulness and pride."

With anger fraught, but willing to persuade,
The wrathful father met the smiling maid:
"Sybil," said he, "I long, and yet I dread
To know thy conduct—hath Josiah fled?
And, grieved and fretted by thy scornful air,
For his lost peace, betaken him to prayer?
Couldst thou his pure and modest mind distress,
By vile remarks upon his speech, address,
Attire, and voice?"—"All this I must confess."—
"Unhappy child! what labour will it cost
To win him back!"—"I do not think him lost."
"Courts he then, trifler! insult and disdain?"—
"No: but from these he courts me to refrain."
"Then hear me, Sybil—should Josiah leave
Thy father's house?"—"My father's child would grieve:"
"That is of grace, and if he come again
To speak of love?"—"I might from grief refrain."—
"Then wilt thou, daughter, our design embrace?"—
"Can I resist it, if it be of grace?"
"Dear child! in three plain words thy mind express—
Wilt thou have this good youth?"—"Dear father! yes."

TALE VII.

THE WIDOW'S TALE.

Ah me! for aught that I could ever read,
Or ever hear by tale or history,
The course of true love never did run smooth;
But either it was different in blood,
Or else misgrafted in respect of years,
Or else it stood upon the choice of friends;
Or if there were a sympathy in choice,
War, death, or sickness did lay siege to it.
Midsummer Night's Dream, act i, scene 1.

Oh! thou didst then ne'er love so heartily,
If thou rememberest not the slightest folly
That ever love did make thee run into.
As You Like It, act ii, scene 4.

Cry the man mercy; love him, take his offer.
As You Like It, act iii, scene 5.

To farmer Moss, in Langar Vale, came down
His only daughter, from her school in town;
A tender, timid maid! who knew not how
To pass a pig-sty, or to face a cow:
Smiling she came, with petty talents graced,
A fair complexion, and a slender waist.

Used to spare meals, disposed in manner pure,
Her father's kitchen she could ill endure;
Where by the steaming beef he hungry sat,
And laid at once a pound upon his plate;
Hot from the field, her eager brother seized
An equal part, and hunger's rage appeased;
The air, surcharged with moisture, flagg'd around,
And the offended damsel sigh'd and frown'd;
The swelling fat in lumps conglomerate laid,
And fancy's sickness seized the loathing maid;
But when the men beside their station took,
The maidens with them, and with these the cook
When one huge wooden bowl before them stood,
Fill'd with huge balls of farinaceous food;
With bacon, mass saline, where never lean
Between the brown and bristly rind was seen:
When from a single horn the party drew
Their copious draughts of heavy ale and new;

When the coarse cloth she saw, with many a stain,
Soil'd by rude hinds who cut and came again—
She could not breathe, but, with a heavy sigh,
Rein'd the fair neck, and shut th' offended eye;
She minced the sanguine flesh in frustums fine,
And wonder'd much to see the creatures dine:
When she resolved her father's heart to move,
If hearts of farmers were alive to love.

She now entreated by herself to sit
In the small parlour, if papa thought fit,
And there to dine, to read, to work alone:—
"No!" said the farmer, in an angry tone;
"These are your-school-taught airs; your mother's pride
Would send you there; but I am now your guide.—
Arise betimes, our early meals prepare,
And this despatch'd, let business be your care;
Look to the lasses, let there not be one
Who lacks attention, till her tasks be done;
In every household work your portion take,
And what you make not, see that others make:
At leisure times attend the wheel, and see
The whitening web be sprinkled on the lea;
When thus employ'd, should our young neighbour view
A useful lass, you may have more to do."

Dreadful were these commands; but worse than these
The parting hint—a farmer could not please:
'T is true she had without abhorrence seen
Young Harry Carr, when he was smart and clean;
But to be married—be a farmer's wife—
A slave! a drudge!—she could not, for her life.

With swimming eyes the fretful nymph withdrew,
And, deeply sighing, to her chamber flew;
Then on her knees, to Heav'n she grieving pray'd
For change of prospect to a tortured maid.

Harry, a youth whose late-departed sire
Had left him all industrious men require,
Saw the pale beauty—and her shape and air
Engaged him much, and yet he must forbear;
"For my small farm what can the damsel do?"
He said—then stopp'd to take another view:
"Pity so sweet a lass will nothing learn
Of household cares—for what can beauty earn
By those small arts which they at school attain,
That keep them useless, and yet make them vain?"

This luckless damsel look'd the village round,
To find a friend, and one was quickly found;
A pensive widow—whose mild air and dress
Pleased the sad nymph, who wish'd her soul's distress
To one so seeming kind, confiding, to confess.—

"What lady that?" the anxious lass inquired,
Who then beheld the one she most admired:
"Here," said the brother, "are no ladies seen—
That is a widow dwelling on the green;
A dainty dame, who can but barely live
On her poor pittance, yet contrives to give:
She happier days has known, but seems at ease,
And you may call her lady, if you please:
But if you wish, good sister, to improve,
You shall see twenty better worth your love."

These Nancy met; but, spite of all they taught,
This useless widow was the one she sought:
The father growl'd; but said he knew no harm
In such connexion that could give alarm:
"And if we thwart the trifler in her course,
'T is odds against us she will take a worse."

Then met the friends; the widow heard the sigh
That ask'd at once compassion and reply:—
"Would you, my child, converse with one so poor,
Yours were the kindness—yonder is my door;
And, save the time that we in public pray,
From that poor cottage I but rarely stray."

There went the nymph, and made her strong complaints,
Painting her wo as injured feeling paints.

"Oh, dearest friend! do think how one must feel,
Shock'd all day long, and sicken'd every meal!
Could you behold our kitchen (and to you
A scene so shocking must indeed be new),
A mind like yours, with true refinement graced
Would let no vulgar scenes pollute your taste;
And yet, in truth, from such a polish'd mind
All base ideas must resistance find,
And sordid pictures from the fancy pass,
As the breath startles from the polish'd glass.

"Here you enjoy a sweet romantic scene,
Without so pleasant, and within so clean;
These twining jess'mines, what delicious gloom
And soothing fragrance yield they to the room!
What lovely garden! there you oft retire,
And tales of wo and tenderness admire:
In that neat case your books, in order placed,
Soothe the full soul, and charm the cultured taste;
And thus, while all about you wears a charm,
How must you scorn the farmer and the farm!"

The widow smiled, and "Know you not," said she,
"How much these farmers scorn or pity me;
Who see what you admire, and laugh at all they see?
True, their opinion alters not my fate,
By falsely judging of an humble state:
This garden, you with such delight behold,
Tempts not a feeble dame who dreads the cold;
These plants, which please so well your livelier sense,
To mine but little of their sweets dispense;
Books soon are painful to my failing sight,
And oftener read from duty than delight;
(Yet let me own, that I can sometimes find
Both joy and duty in the act combined);
But view me rightly, you will see no more
Than a poor female, willing to be poor;
Happy indeed, but not in books nor flowers,
Not in fair dreams, indulged in earlier hours,
Of never-tasted joys;—such visions shun,
My youthful friend, nor scorn the farmer's son.'

"Nay," said the damsel, nothing pleased to see
A friend's advice could like a father's be,
"Bless'd in your cottage, you must surely smile
At those who live in our detested style:

To my Lucinda's sympathizing heart
Could I my prospects and my griefs impart,
She would console me; but I dare not show
Ills that would wound her tender soul to know:
And I confess, it shocks my pride to tell
The secrets of the prison where I dwell;
For that dear maiden would be shock'd to feel
The secrets I should shudder to reveal;
When told her friend was by a parent ask'd,
Fed you the swine?—Good heav'n! how I am task'd!
What! can you smile? Ah! smile not at the grief
That woos your pity and demands relief."

"Trifles, my love; you take a false alarm;
Think, I beseech you, better of the farm:
Duties in every state demand your care,
And light are those that will require it there:
Fix on the youth a favouring eye, and these,
To him pertaining, or as his, will please."

"What words," the lass replied, "offend my ear!
Try you my patience? Can you be sincere?
And am I told a willing hand to give
To a rude farmer, and with rustic live?
Far other fate was yours:—some gentle youth
Admired your beauty, and avow'd his truth;
The power of love prevail'd, and freely both
Gave the fond heart, and pledged the binding oath;
And then the rivals' plot, the parent's power,
And jealous fears, drew on the happy hour:
Ah! let not memory lose the blissful view,
But fairly show what love has done for you."

"Agreed, my daughter; what my heart has known
Of love's strange power shall be with frankness shown:
But let me warn you, that experience finds
Few of the scenes that lively hope designs."—

"Mysterious all," said Nancy; "you, I know,
Have suffer'd much; now deign the grief to show;—
I am your friend, and so prepare my heart
In all your sorrows to receive a part."

The widow answer'd: "I had once, like you,
Such thoughts of love; no dream is more untrue:
You judge it fated and decreed to dwell
In youthful hearts, which nothing can expel,
A passion doom'd to reign, and irresistible.
The struggling mind, when once subdued, in vain
Rejects the fury or defies the pain;
The strongest reason fails the flame t' allay,
And resolution droops and faints away:
Hence, when the destined lovers meet, they prove
At once the force of this all-powerful love:
Each from that period feels the mutual smart,
Nor seeks to cure it—heart is changed for heart;
Nor is there peace till they delighted stand,
And, at the altar—hand is join'd in hand.

"Alas! my child, there are who, dreaming so,
Waste their fresh youth, and waking feel the wo;
There is no spirit sent the heart to move
With such prevailing and alarming love;
Passion to reason will submit—or why
Should wealthy maids the poorest swains deny?
Or how could classes and degrees create
The slightest bar to such resistless fate?
Yet high and low, you see, forbear to mix;
No beggars' eyes the heart of kings transfix,
And who but am'rous peers or nobles sigh
When titled beauties pass triumphant by?
For reason wakes, proud wishes to reprove;
You cannot hope, and therefore dare not love:
All would be safe, did we at first inquire—
'Does reason sanction what our hearts desire?'
But quitting precept, let example show
What joys from love uncheck'd by prudence flow.

"A youth my father in his office placed,
Of humble fortune, but with sense and taste;
But he was thin and pale, had downcast looks;
He studied much, and pored upon his books:
Confused he was when seen, and, when he saw
Me or my sisters, would in haste withdraw;
And had this youth departed with the year,
His loss had cost us neither sigh nor tear.

"But with my father still the youth remain'd,
And more reward and kinder notice gain'd:
He often, reading, to the garden stray'd,
Where I by books or musing was delay'd;
This to discourse in summer evenings led,
Of these same evenings, or of what we read:
On such occasions we were much alone;
But, save the look, the manner, and the tone,
(These might have meaning), all that we discuss'd
We could with pleasure to a parent trust.

"At length 'twas friendship—and my friend and I
Said we were happy, and began to sigh:
My sisters first, and then my father, found
That we were wandering o'er enchanted ground;
But he had troubles in his own affairs,
And would not bear addition to his cares:
With pity moved, yet angry, 'Child,' said he,
'Will you embrace contempt and beggary?
Can you endure to see each other cursed
By want, of every human wo the worst?
Warring for ever with distress, in dread
Either of begging or of wanting bread;
While poverty, with unrelenting force,
Will your own offspring from your love divorce;
They, through your folly, must be doom'd to pine,
And you deplore your passion, or resign;
For, if it die, what good will then remain?
And if it live, it doubles every pain.'"

"But you were true," exclaim'd the lass, "and fled
The tyrant's power who fill'd your soul with dread?"
"But," said the smiling friend, "he fill'd my mouth with bread:
And in what other place that bread to gain
We long consider'd, and we sought in vain:
This was my twentieth year—at thirty-five
Our hope was fainter, yet our love alive;
So many years in anxious doubt had pass'd."
"Then," said the damsel, "you were bless'd at last?"
A smile again adorn'd the widow's face,
But soon a starting tear usurp'd its place.

"Slow pass'd the heavy years, and each had more
Pains and vexations than the years before.
My father fail'd; his family was rent,
And to new states his grieving daughters sent:

Each to more thriving kindred found a way,
Guests without welcome—servants without pay;
Our parting hour was grievous; still I feel
The sad, sweet converse at our final meal;
Our father then reveal'd his former fears,
Cause of his sternness, and then join'd our tears;
Kindly he strove our feelings to repress,
But died, and left us heirs to his distress.
The rich, as humble friends, my sisters chose,
I with a wealthy widow sought repose;
Who with a chilling frown her friend received,
Bade me rejoice, and wonder'd that I grieved:
In vain my anxious lover tried his skill
To rise in life, he was dependent still;
We met in grief, nor can I paint the fears
Of these unhappy, troubled, trying years:
Our dying hopes and stronger fears between,
We felt no season peaceful or serene;
Our fleeting joys, like meteors in the night,
Shone on our gloom with inauspicious light;
And then domestic sorrows, till the mind,
Worn with distresses, to despair inclined;
Add too the ill that from the passion flows,
When its contemptuous frown the world bestows,
The peevish spirit caused by long delay,
When being gloomy we contemn the gay,
When, being wretched, we incline to hate
And censure others in a happier state;
Yet loving still, and still compell'd to move
In the sad labyrinth of ling'ring love:
While you, exempt from want, despair, alarm,
May wed—oh! take the farmer and the farm."

"Nay," said the nymph, "joy smiled on you at last?"
"Smiled for a moment," she replied, "and pass'd:
My lover still the same dull means pursued,
Assistant call'd, but kept in servitude;
His spirits wearied in the prime of life,
By fears and wishes in eternal strife;
At length he urged impatient—'Now consent;
With thee united, fortune may relent.'
I paused, consenting; but a friend arose,
Pleased a fair view, though distant, to disclose;
From the rough ocean we beheld a gleam
Of joy, as transient as the joys we dream;
By lying hopes deceived, my friend retired,
And sail'd—was wounded—reach'd us—and expired!
You shall behold his grave, and when I die,
There—but 't is folly—I request to lie.

"Thus," said the lass, "to joy you bade adieu!
But how a widow?—that cannot be true:
Or was it force, in some unhappy hour,
That placed you, grieving, in a tyrant's power?

"Force, my young friend, when forty years are fled,
Is what a woman seldom has to dread;
She needs no brazen locks nor guarding walls,
And seldom comes a lover though she calls:
Yet moved by fancy, one approved my face,
Though time and tears had wrought it much disgrace.

"The man I married was sedate and meek,
And spoke of love as men in earnest speak;
Poor as I was, he ceaseless sought, for years,
A heart in sorrow and a face in tears;
That heart I gave not; and 't was long before
I gave attention, and then nothing more;
But in my breast some grateful feeling rose
For one whose love so sad a subject chose;
Till long delaying, fearing to repent,
But grateful still, I gave a cold assent.

"Thus we were wed; no fault had I to find,
And he but one; my heart could not be kind:
Alas! of every early hope bereft,
There was no fondness in my bosom left;
So had I told him, but had told in vain,
He lived but to indulge me and complain:
His was this cottage, he inclosed this ground,
And planted all these blooming shrubs around;
He to my room these curious trifles brought,
And with assiduous love my pleasure sought:
He lived to please me, and I ofttimes strove
Smiling, to thank his unrequited love:
'Teach me,' he cried, 'that pensive mind to ease,
For all my pleasure is the hope to please.'

"Serene, though heavy, were the days we spent,
Yet kind each word, and gen'rous each intent;
But his dejection lessen'd every day,
And to a placid kindness died away:
In tranquil ease we pass'd our latter years,
By griefs untroubled, unassail'd by fears.

"Let not romantic views your bosom sway,
Yield to your duties, and their call obey:
Fly not a youth, frank, honest, and sincere;
Observe his merits, and his passion hear!
'T is true, no hero, but a farmer sues—
Slow in his speech, but worthy in his views;
With him you cannot that affliction prove
That rends the bosom of the poor in love:
Health, comfort, competence, and cheerful days,
Your friends' approval, and your father's praise,
Will crown the deed, and you escape *their* fate
Who plan so wildly, and are wise too late."

The damsel heard; at first th' advice was strange,
Yet wrought a happy, nay, a speedy change:
"I have no care," she said, when next they met,
"But one may wonder he is silent yet;
He looks around him with his usual stare,
And utters nothing—not that I shall care."

This pettish humour pleased th' experienced friend—
None need despair, whose silence can offend;
"Should I," resumed the thoughtful lass, "consent
To hear the man, the man may now repent:
Think you my sighs shall call him from the plough,
Or give one hint, that 'You may woo me now?'"

"Persist, my love," replied the friend, "and gain
A parent's praise, *that* cannot be in vain."

The father saw the change, but not the cause,
And gave the alter'd maid his fond applause:
The coarser manners she in part removed,
In part endured, improving and improved;
She spoke of household works, she rose betimes,
And said neglect and indolence were crimes,
The various duties of their life she weigh'd,
And strict attention to her dairy paid;

The names of servants now familiar grew,
And fair Lucinda's from her mind withdrew:
As prudent travellers for their ease assume
Their modes and language to whose lands they come:
So to the farmer this fair lass inclined,
Gave to the business of the farm her mind;
To useful arts she turn'd her hand and eye;
And by her manners told him—"You may try."

Th' observing lover more attention paid,
With growing pleasure, to the alter'd maid;
He fear'd to lose her, and began to see
That a slim beauty might a helpmate be:
'Twixt hope and fear he now the lass address'd,
And in his Sunday robe his love express'd:
She felt no chilling dread, no thrilling joy,
Nor was too quickly kind, too slowly coy;
But still she lent an unreluctant ear
To all the rural business of the year;
Till love's strong hopes endured no more delay,
And Harry ask'd, and Nancy named the day.

"A happy change! my boy," the father cried:
"How lost your sister all her school-day pride?"
The youth replied, "It is the widow's deed:
The cure is perfect, and was wrought with speed."—
"And comes there, boy, this benefit of books,
Of that smart dress, and of those dainty looks?
We must be kind—some offerings from the farm
To the white cot will speak our feelings warm;
Will show that people, when they know the fact,
Where they have judged severely, can retract.
Oft have I smiled, when I beheld her pass
With cautious step, as if she hurt the grass;
Where if a snail's retreat she chanced to storm,
She look'd as begging pardon of the worm;
And what, said I, still laughing at the view,
Have these weak creatures in the world to do?
But some are made for action, some to speak;
And, while she looks so pitiful and meek,
Her words are weighty, though her nerves are weak."

Soon told the village-bells the rite was done,
That join'd the school-bred miss and farmer's son;
Her former habits some slight scandal raised,
But real worth was soon perceived and praised;
She, her neat taste imparted to the farm,
And he, th' improving skill and vigorous arm.

TALE VIII.

THE MOTHER.

What though you have beauty,
Must you be therefore proud and pitiless?
As You Like It, act iii. scene 5.

I would not marry her, though she were endow'd with all that Adam had left him before he transgress'd.
As You Like It.

Wilt thou love such a woman? What! to make thee an instrument, and play false strains upon thee!—Not to be endured.
As You Like It.

Your son,
As mad in folly, lack'd the sense to know
Her estimation hence.
All's Well that Ends Well, act v, scene 3.

Be this sweet Helen's knell;
He left a wife whose words all ears took captive,
Whose dear perfection, hearts that scorn'd to serve
Humbly call'd mistress.
All's Well that Ends Well, act v, scene 3.

There was a worthy, but a simple pair,
Who nursed a daughter, fairest of the fair:
Sons they had lost, and she alone remain'd,
Heir to the kindness they had all obtain'd;
Heir to the fortune they design'd for all,
Nor had th' allotted portion then been small;
But now, by fate enrich'd with beauty rare,
They watch'd their treasure with peculiar care:
The fairest features they could early trace,
And, blind with love, saw merit in her face—
Saw virtue, wisdom, dignity, and grace:
And Dorothea, from her infant years,
Gain'd all her wishes from their pride or fears:
She wrote a billet, and a novel read,
And with her fame her vanity was fed;
Each word, each look, each action was a cause
For flattering wonder, and for fond applause;
She rode or danced, and ever glanced around,
Seeking for praise, and smiling when she found.
The yielding pair to her petitions gave
An humble friend to be a civil slave;
Who for a poor support herself resign'd
To the base toil of a dependent mind:
By nature cold, our heiress stoop'd to art,
To gain the credit of a tender heart.
Hence at her door must suppliant paupers stand,
To bless the bounty of her beauteous hand:
And now, her education all complete,
She talk'd of virtuous love and union sweet;
She was indeed by no soft passions moved,
But wish'd, with all her soul, to be beloved.
Here on the favour'd beauty fortune smiled;
Her chosen husband was a man so mild,
So humbly temper'd, so intent to please,
It quite distress'd her to remain at ease,
Without a cause to sigh, without pretence to tease:
She tried his patience in a thousand modes,
And tired it not upon the roughest roads.
Pleasure she sought, and, disappointed, sigh'd
For joys, she said, "to her alone denied;"
And she was "sure her parents, if alive,
Would many comforts for their child contrive:"
The gentle husband bade her name him one;
"No—that," she answer'd, "should for her be done;
How could she say what pleasures were around?
But she was certain many might be found."—
"Would she some sea-port, Weymouth, Scarborough, grace?"—
"He knew she hated every watering-place;"—
"The town?"—"What! now 't was empty, joyless, dull?"
—"In winter?"—"No; she liked it worse when full."
She talk'd of building—"Would she plan a room?"
"No! she could live, as he desired, in gloom:"
"Call then our friends and neighbours:"—"He might call,
And they might come and fill his ugly hall;
A noisy vulgar set, he knew she scorn'd them all:"
"Then might their two dear girls the time employ,
And their improvement yield a solid joy:"—

"Solid indeed! and heavy—oh! the bliss
Of teaching letters to a lisping Miss!"—
"My dear, my gentle Dorothea, say,
Can I oblige you?"—"You may go away."

Twelve heavy years this patient soul sustain'd
This wasp's attacks, and then her praise obtain'd,
Graved on a marble tomb, where he at peace remain'd.

Two daughters wept their loss; the one a child
With a plain face, strong sense, and temper mild,
Who keenly felt the mother's angry taunt,
"Thou art the image of thy pious aunt:"
Long time had Lucy wept her slighted face,
And then began to smile at her disgrace.
Her father's sister, who the world had seen
Near sixty years when Lucy saw sixteen,
Begg'd the plain girl: the gracious mother smiled,
And freely gave her grieved but passive child;
And with her elder-born, the beauty bless'd,
This parent rested, if such maids can rest:
No miss her waxen babe could so admire,
Nurse with such care, or with such pride attire;
They were companions meet, with equal mind,
Bless'd with one love, and to one point inclined;
Beauty to keep, adorn, increase, and guard,
Was their sole care, and had its full reward:
In rising splendour with the one it reign'd,
And in the other was by care sustain'd,
The daughter's charms increased, the parent's yet remain'd.

Leave we those ladies to their daily care,
To see how meekness and discretion fare:—
A village-maid, unvex'd by want or love,
Could not with more delight than Lucy move;
The village-lark, high-mounted in the spring,
Could not with purer joy than Lucy sing;
Her cares all light, her pleasures all sincere,
Her duty joy, and her companion dear;
In tender friendship and in true respect
Lived aunt and niece, no flattery, no neglect—
They read, walk'd, visited—together pray'd,
Together slept the matron and the maid:
There was such goodness, such pure nature seen
In Lucy's looks, a manner so serene;
Such harmony in motion, speech, and air,
That without fairness she was more than fair:
Had more than beauty in each speaking grace,
That lent their cloudless glory to the face;
Where mild good sense in placid looks was shown,
And felt in every bosom but her own.
The one presiding feature in her mind,
Was the pure meekness of a will resign'd;
A tender spirit, freed from all pretence
Of wit, and pleased in mild benevolence;
Bless'd in protecting fondness she reposed,
With every wish indulged though undisclosed;
But love, like zephyr on the limpid lake,
Was now the bosom of the maid to shake,
And in that gentle mind a gentle strife to make.

Among their chosen friends, a favour'd few,
The aunt and niece a youthful rector knew;
Who, though a younger brother, might address
A younger sister, fearless of success:
His friends, a lofty race, their native pride
At first display'd, and their assent denied;
But, pleased such virtues and such love to trace,
They own'd she would adorn the loftiest race.
The aunt a mother's caution to supply,
Had watch'd the youthful priest with jealous eye;
And, anxious for her charge, had view'd unseen
The cautious life that keeps the conscience clean:
In all she found him all she wish'd to find,
With slight exception of a lofty mind;
A certain manner that express'd desire
To be received as brother to the 'squire.
Lucy's meek eye had beam'd with many a tear,
Lucy's soft heart had beat with many a fear,
Before he told (although his looks, she thought,
Had oft confess'd) that he her favour sought:
But when he kneel'd (she wish'd him not to kneel,)
And spoke the fears and hopes that lovers feel;
When too the prudent aunt herself confess'd,
Her wishes on the gentle youth would rest;
The maiden's eye with tender passion beam'd,
She dwelt with fondness on the life she schemed;
The household cares, the soft and lasting ties
Of love, with all his binding charities;
Their village taught, consoled, assisted, fed,
Till the young zealot tears of pleasure shed.

But would her mother? Ah! she fear'd it wrong
To have indulged these forward hopes so long;
Her mother loved, but was not used to grant
Favours so freely as her gentle aunt.—
Her gentle aunt, with smiles that angels wear,
Dispell'd her Lucy's apprehensive tear;
Her prudent foresight the request had made
To one whom none could govern, few persuade;
She doubted much if one in earnest woo'd
A girl with not a single charm endued;
The sister's nobler views she then declared,
And what small sum for Lucy could be spared;
"If more than this the foolish priest requires,
Tell him," she wrote, "to check his vain desires."
At length, with many a cold expression mix'd,
With many a sneer on girls so fondly fix'd,
There came a promise—should they not repent,
But take with grateful minds the portion meant,
And wait the sister's day—the mother might consent.

And here, might pitying hope o'er truth prevail,
Or love o'er fortune, we would end our tale:
For who more bless'd than youthful pair removed
From fear of want—by mutual friends approved;
Short time to wait, and in that time to live
With all the pleasures hope and fancy give;
Their equal passion raised on just esteem,
When reason sanctions all that love can dream?

Yes! reason sanctions what stern fate denies:
The early prospect in the glory dies,
As the soft smiles on dying infants play
In their mild features, and then pass away.

The beauty died, ere she could yield her hand
In the high marriage by the mother plann'd:
Who grieved indeed, but found a vast relief
In a cold heart, that ever warr'd with grief.

Lucy was present when her sister died,
Heiress to duty that she ill supplied:
There were no mutual feelings, sister arts,
No kindred taste, nor intercourse of hearts.

When in the mirror play'd the matron's smile,
The maiden's thoughts were trav'lling all the while;
And when desired to speak, she sigh'd to find
Her pause offended; "Envy made her blind:
Tasteless she was, nor had a claim in life
Above the station of a rector's wife;
Yet as an heiress, she must shun disgrace,
Although no heiress to her mother's face:
It is your duty," said th' imperious dame,
"(Advanced your fortune) to advance your name,
And with superior rank, superior offers claim:
Your sister's lover, when his sorrows die,
May look upon you, and for favour sigh;
Nor can you offer a reluctant hand;
His birth is noble, and his seat is grand."

Alarm'd was Lucy, was in tears—"A fool!
Was she a child in love?—a miss at school?
Doubts any mortal, if a change of state
Dissolves all claims and ties of earlier date?"

The rector doubted, for he came to mourn
A sister dead, and with a wife return:
Lucy with heart unchanged received the youth,
True in herself, confiding in his truth;
But own'd her mother's change: the haughty dame
Pour'd strong contempt upon the youthful flame;
She firmly vow'd her purpose to pursue,
Judged her own cause, and bade the youth adieu!
The lover begg'd, insisted, urged his pain,
His brother wrote to threaten and complain,
Her sister reasoning proved the promise made,
Lucy appealing to a parent pray'd;
And all opposed th' event that she design'd,
But all in vain—she never changed her mind;
And coldly answer'd in her wonted way,
That she "would rule, and Lucy must obey."

With peevish fear, she saw her health decline,
And cried, "Oh! monstrous, for a man to pine;
But if your foolish heart must yield to love,
Let him possess it whom I now approve;
This is my pleasure:"—Still the rector came
With larger offers and with bolder claim;
But the stern lady would attend no more—
She frown'd, and rudely pointed to the door;
Whate'er he wrote, he saw unread return'd,
And he, indignant, the dishonour spurn'd;
Nay, fix'd suspicion where he might confide,
And sacrificed his passion to his pride.

Lucy, meantime, though threaten'd and distress'd,
Against her marriage made a strong protest:
All was domestic war: the aunt rebell'd
Against the sovereign will, and was expell'd;
And every power was tried and every art,
To bend to falsehood one determined heart;
Assail'd, in patience it received the shock,
Soft as the wave, unshaken as the rock:
But while th' unconquer'd soul endures the storm
Of angry fate, it preys upon the form;
With conscious virtue she resisted still,
And conscious love gave vigour to her will:
But Lucy's trial was at hand; with joy
The mother cried—"Behold your constant boy—
Thursday—was married:—take the paper, sweet,
And read the conduct of your reverend cheat;
See with what pomp of coaches, in what crowd
The creature married—of his falsehood proud!
False, did I say?—at least no whining fool;
And thus will hopeless passions ever cool:
But shall his bride your single state reproach?
No! give him crowd for crowd, and coach for coach.
Oh! you retire; reflect then, gentle miss,
And gain some spirit in a cause like this."

Some spirit Lucy gain'd; a steady soul,
Defying all persuasion, all control:
In vain reproach, derision, threats were tried;
The constant mind all outward force defied,
By vengeance vainly urged, in vain assail'd by pride:
Fix'd in her purpose, perfect in her part,
She felt the courage of a wounded heart;
The world receded from her rising view,
When Heaven approach'd as earthly things withdrew;
Not strange before, for in the days of love,
Joy, hope, and pleasure, she had thoughts above;
Pious when most of worldly prospects fond,
When they best pleased her she could look beyond;
Had the young priest a faithful lover died,
Something had been her bosom to divide;
Now Heaven had all, for in her holiest views
She saw the matron whom she fear'd to lose;
While from her parent, the dejected maid
Forced the unpleasant thought, or thinking pray'd.

Surprised, the mother saw the languid frame,
And felt indignant, yet forbore to blame:
Once with a frown she cried, "And do you mean
To die of love—the folly of fifteen?"
But as her anger met with no reply,
She let the gentle girl in quiet die;
And to her sister wrote, impell'd by pain,
"Come quickly, Martha, or you come in vain."
Lucy meantime profess'd with joy sincere,
That nothing held, employ'd, engaged her here.

"I am an humble actor, doom'd to play
A part obscure, and then to glide away;
Incurious how the great or happy shine,
Or who have parts obscure and sad as mine;
In its best prospect I but wish'd, for life,
To be th' assiduous, gentle, useful wife;
That lost, with wearied mind, and spirit poor,
I drop my efforts, and can act no more;
With growing joy I feel my spirits tend
To that last scene where all my duties end."

Hope, ease, delight, the thoughts of dying gave
Till Lucy spoke with fondness of the grave;
She smiled with wasted form, but spirit firm,
And said, "She left but little for the worm:"
As toll'd the bell, "There's one," she said, "hath press'd
A while before me to the bed of rest;"
And she beside her with attention spread
The decorations of the maiden dead.

While quickly thus the mortal part declined,
The happiest visions fill'd the active mind;
A soft, religious melancholy gain'd
Entire possession, and for ever reign'd:
On holy writ her mind reposing dwelt,
She saw the wonders, she the mercies felt

Till in a bless'd and glorious reverie,
She seem'd the Saviour as on earth to see,
And, fill'd with love divine, th' attending friend to be;
Or she who trembling, yet confiding, stole
Near to the garment, touch'd it, and was whole,
When, such th' intenseness of the working thought,
On her it seem'd the very deed was wrought;
She the glad patient's fear and rapture found,
The holy transport, and the healing wound;
This was so fix'd, so grafted in the heart,
That she adopted, nay became the part:
But one chief scene was present to her sight,
Her Saviour resting in the tomb by night;
Her fever rose, and still her wedded mind
Was to that scene, that hallow'd cave, confined—
Where in the shade of death the body laid,
There watch'd the spirit of the wandering maid,
Her looks were fix'd, entranced, illumed, serene,
In the still glory of the midnight scene:
There at her Saviour's feet, in visions bless'd,
Th' enraptured maid a sacred joy possess'd;
In patience waiting for the first-born ray
Of that all-glorious and triumphant day:
To this idea all her soul she gave,
Her mind reposing by the sacred grave;
Then sleep would seal the eye, the vision close,
And steep the solemn thoughts in brief repose.

Then grew the soul serene, and all its powers
Again restored illumed the dying hours;
But reason dwelt where fancy stray'd before,
And the mind wander'd from its views no more;
Till death approach'd, when every look express'd
A sense of bliss, till every sense had rest.

The mother lives, and has enough to buy
Th' attentive ear and the submissive eye
Of abject natures—these are daily told,
How triumph'd beauty in the days of old;
How, by her window seated, crowds have cast
Admiring glances, wondering as they pass'd:
How from her carriage as she stepp'd to pray,
Divided ranks would humbly make her way;
And how each voice in the astonish'd throng
Pronounced her peerless as she moved along.

Her picture then the greedy dame displays;
Touch'd by no shame, she now demands its praise;
In her tall mirror then she shows a face,
Still coldly fair with unaffecting grace;
These she compares, "It has the form," she cries,
"But wants the air, the spirit, and the eyes;
This, as a likeness, is correct and true,
But there alone the living grace we view."
This said, th' applauding voice the dame required,
And, gazing, slowly from the glass retired.

TALE IX.

ARABELLA.

> Thrice blessed they that master so their blood—
> But earthly happier is the rose distill'd,
> Than that which, withering on the virgin thorn,
> Grows, lives, and dies in single blessedness.
> *Midsummer Night's Dream*, act 1, scene 1.

> I sometimes do excuse the thing I hate,
> For his advantage whom I dearly love.
> *Measure for Measure*, act ii, scene 4.

> Contempt, farewell! and maiden pride, adieu!
> *Measure for Measure*, act ii, scene 4.

Of a fair town where Doctor Rack was guide,
His only daughter was the boast and pride;
Wise Arabella, yet not wise alone,
She like a bright and polish'd brilliant shone;
Her father own'd her for his prop and stay,
Able to guide, yet willing to obey;
Pleased with her learning while discourse could please,
And with her love in languor and disease:
To every mother were her virtues known,
And to their daughters as a pattern shown;
Who in her youth had all that age requires,
And with her prudence, all that youth admires.
These odious praises made the damsels try
Not to obtain such merits, but deny;
For, whatsoever wise mammas might say,
To guide a daughter, this was not the way;
From such applause disdain and anger rise,
And envy lives where emulation dies.
In all his strength, contends the noble horse,
With one who just precedes him on the course,
But when the rival flies too far before,
His spirit fails, and he attempts no more.

This reasoning maid, above her sex's dread!
Had dared to read, and dared to say she read;
Not the last novel, not the new-born play;
Not the mere trash and scandal of the day;
But (though her young companions felt the shock)
She studied Berkeley, Bacon, Hobbes, and Locke:
Her mind within the maze of history dwelt,
And of the moral muse the beauty felt!
The merits of the Roman page she knew,
And could converse with More and Montagu:
Thus she became the wonder of the town,
From that she reap'd, to that she gave renown,
And strangers coming, all were taught t' admire
The learned lady, and the lofty spire.

Thus fame in public fix'd the maid, where all
Might threw their darts, and see the idol fall;
A hundred arrows came with vengeance keen,
From tongues envenom'd, and from arms unseen;
A thousand eyes were fix'd upon the place,
That, if she fell, she might not fly disgrace:
But malice vainly throws the poison'd dart,
Unless our frailty shows the peccant part;
And Arabella still preserved her name
Untouch'd, and shone with undisputed fame;
Her very notice some respect would cause,
And her esteem was honour and applause.

Men she avoided; not in childish fear,
As if she thought some savage foe was near;
Not as a prude, who hides that man should seek,
Or who by silence hints that they should speak;
But with discretion all the sex she view'd,
Ere yet engaged, pursuing, or pursued;
Ere love had made her to his vices blind
Or hid the favourite's failings from her mind

Thus was the picture of the man portray'd,
By merit destined for so rare a maid;
At whose request she might exchange her state,
Or still be happy in a virgin's fate.

He must be one with manners like her own,
His life unquestion'd, his opinions known;
His stainless virtue must all tests endure,
His honour spotless, and his bosom pure;
She no allowance made for sex or times,
Of lax opinion—crimes were ever crimes;
No wretch forsaken must his frailty curse,
No spurious offspring drain his private purse:
He at all times his passions must command,
And yet possess—or be refused her hand.

All this without reserve the maiden told,
And some began to weigh the rector's gold;
To ask what sum a prudent man might gain,
Who had such store of virtues to maintain?

A Doctor Campbell, north of Tweed, came forth,
Declared his passion, and proclaim'd his worth;
Not unapproved, for he had much to say
On every cause, and in a pleasant way;
Not all his trust was in a pliant tongue,
His form was good, and ruddy he, and young:
But though the Doctor was a man of parts,
He read not deeply male or female hearts;
But judged that all whom he esteem'd as wise
Must think alike, though some assumed disguise;
That every reasoning Bramin, Christian, Jew,
Of all religions took their liberal view;
And of her own, no doubt, this learned maid
Denied the substance, and the forms obey'd;
And thus persuaded, he his thoughts express'd
Of her opinions, and his own profess'd:
"All states demand this aid, the vulgar need
Their priests and pray'rs, their sermons and their creed;
And those of stronger minds should never speak
(In his opinion) what might hurt the weak:
A man may smile, but still he should attend
His hour at church, and be the church's friend,
What there he thinks conceal, and what he hears commend."

Frank was the speech, but heard with high disdain,
Nor had the Doctor leave to speak again;
A man who own'd, nay gloried in deceit,
"He might despise her, but he should not cheat."

Then Vicar Holmes appear'd; he heard it said
That ancient men best pleased the prudent maid;
And true it was her ancient friends she loved,
Servants when old she favour'd and approved;
Age in her pious parents she revered,
And neighbours were by length of days endear'd;
But, if her husband too must ancient be,
The good old Vicar found it was not he.

On Captain Bligh her mind in balance hung—
Though valiant, modest; and reserved, though young:
Against these merits must defects be set—
Though poor, imprudent; and though proud, in debt:
In vain the Captain close attention paid;
She found him wanting, whom she fairly weigh'd.

Then came a youth, and all their friends agreed,
That Edward Huntly was the man indeed;
Respectful duty he had paid awhile,
Then ask'd her hand, and had a gracious smile.
A lover now declared, he led the fair
To woods and fields, to visits and to pray'r;
Then whisper'd softly—"Will you name the day?"
She softly whisper'd—"If you love me, stay:"
"Oh! try me not beyond my strength," he cried:
"Oh! be not weak," the prudent maid replied;
"But by some trial your affection prove—
Respect and not impatience argues love:
And love no more is by impatience known,
Than Ocean's depth is by its tempests shown:
He whom a weak and fond impatience sways,
But for himself with all his fervour prays,
And not the maid he woos, but his own will obeys,
And will she love the being who prefers,
With so much ardour, his desire to hers?"

Young Edward grieved, but let not grief be seen;
He knew obedience pleased his fancy's queen:
Awhile he waited, and then cried—"Behold!
The year advancing, be no longer cold!"
For she had promised—"Let the flowers appear,
And I will pass with thee the smiling year."
Then pressing grew the youth; the more he press'd,
The less inclined the maid to his request:
"Let June arrive."—Alas! when April came,
It brought a stranger, and the stranger shame;
Nor could the lover from his house persuade
A stubborn lass whom he had mournful made;
Angry and weak, by thoughtless vengeance moved,
She told her story to the fair beloved;
In strongest words th' unwelcome truth was shown,
To blight his prospects, careless of her own.

Our heroine grieved, but had too firm a heart
For him to soften, when she swore to part;
In vain his seeming penitence and pray'r,
His vows, his tears; she left him in despair:
His mother fondly laid her grief aside,
And to the reason of the nymph applied—

"It well becomes thee, lady, to appear,
But not to be, in very truth, severe;
Although the crime be odious in thy sight,
That daring sex is taught such things to slight,
His heart is thine, although it once was frail;
Think of his grief, and let his love prevail!—"

"Plead thou no more," the lofty lass return'd;
"Forgiving woman is deceived and spurn'd:
Say that the crime is common—shall I take
A common man my wedded lord to make?
See! a weak woman by his arts betray'd,
An infant born his father to upbraid;
Shall I forgive his vileness, take his name,
Sanction his error, and partake his shame?
No! this assent would kindred frailty prove,
A love for him would be a vicious love:
Can a chaste maiden secret counsel hold
With one whose crime by every mouth is told?
Forbid it spirit, prudence, virtuous pride;
He must despise me, were he not denied:
The way from vice the erring mind to win
Is with presuming sinners to begin,
And show, by scorning them, a just contempt for sin."

The youth repulsed, to one more mild convey'd
His heart, and smiled on the remorseless maid;
The maid, remorseless in her pride, the while
Despised the insult, and return'd the smile.

First to admire, to praise her, and defend,
Was (now in years advanced) a virgin friend:
Much she preferr'd, she cried, a single state,
"It was her choice"—it surely was her fate;
And much it pleased her in the train to view
A maiden vot'ress, wise and lovely too.

Time to the yielding mind his change imparts,
He varies notions, and he alters hearts;
'T is right, 't is just to feel contempt for vice,
But he that shows it may be over-nice:
There are who feel, when young, the false sublime,
And proudly love to show disdain for crime;
To whom the future will new thoughts supply,
The pride will soften, and the scorn will die;
Nay, where they still the vice itself condemn,
They bear the vicious, and consort with them:
Young Captain Grove, when one had changed his side,
Despised the venal turn-coat, and defied;
Old Colonel Grove now shakes him by the hand,
Though he who bribes may still his vote command:
Why would not Ellen to Belinda speak,
When she had flown to London for a week;
And then return'd, to every friend's surprise,
With twice the spirit, and with half the size?
She spoke not then—but after years had flown,
A better friend had Ellen never known:
Was it the lady her mistake had seen?
Or had she also such a journey been?
No: 't was the gradual change in human hearts,
That time, in commerce with the world, imparts;
That on the roughest temper throws disguise,
And steals from virtue her asperities.
The young and ardent, who with glowing zeal
Felt wrath for trifles, and were proud to feel,
Now find those trifles all the mind engage,
To soothe dull hours, and cheat the cares of age;
As young Zelinda, in her quaker-dress,
Disdain'd each varying fashion's vile excess,
And now her friends on old Zelinda gaze,
Pleased in rich silks and orient gems to blaze:
Changes like these 't is folly to condemn,
So virtue yields not, nor is changed with them.

Let us proceed:—Twelve brilliant years were past,
Yet each with less of glory than the last;
Whether these years to this fair virgin gave
A softer mind—effect they often have;
Whether the virgin-state was not so bless'd
As that good maiden in her zeal profess'd;
Or whether lovers falling from her train,
Gave greater price to those she could retain,
Is all unknown;—but Arabella now
Was kindly listening to a merchant's vow;
Who offer'd terms so fair, against his love
To strive was folly, so she never strove.—
Man in his earlier days we often find
With a too easy and unguarded mind;
But by increasing years and prudence taught,
He grows reserved, and locks up every thought:
Not thus the maiden, for in blooming youth
She hides her thought, and guards the tender truth:
This, when no longer young, no more she hides
But frankly in the favour'd swain confides:
Man, stubborn man, is like the growing tree,
That longer standing, still will harder be;
And like its fruit, the virgin, first austere,
Then kindly softening with the ripening year.

Now was the lover urgent, and the kind
And yielding lady to his sui inclined:
"A little time, my friend, is just, is right;
We must be decent in our neighbours' sight:"
Still she allow'd him of his hopes to speak,
And in compassion took off week by week;
Till few remain'd, when, wearied with delay,
She kindly meant to take off day by day.

That female friend who gave our virgin praise
For flying man and all his treacherous ways,
Now heard with mingled anger, shame and fear,
Of one accepted, and a wedding near;
But she resolved again with friendly zeal
To make the maid her scorn of wedlock feel;
For she was grieved to find her work undone,
And like a sister mourn'd the failing nun.

Why are these gentle maidens prone to make
Their sister-doves the tempting world forsake?
Why all their triumph when a maid disdains
The tyrant-sex, and scorns to wear its chains?
Is it pure joy to see a sister flown
From the false pleasures they themselves have known?
Or do they, as the call-birds in the cage,
Try, in pure envy, others to engage;
And therefore paint their native woods and groves,
As scenes of dangerous joys and naughty loves?

Strong was the maiden's hope; her friend was proud,
And had her notions to the world avow'd;
And, could she find the Merchant weak and frail,
With power to prove it, then she must prevail;
For she aloud would publish his disgrace,
And save his victim from a man so base.

When all inquiries had been duly made,
Came the kind friend her burden to unlade—
"Alas! my dear! not all our care and art
Can tread the maze of man's deceitful heart:
Look not surprise—nor let resentment swell
Those lovely features, all will yet be well;
And thou, from love's and man's deceptions free,
Wilt dwell in virgin-state, and walk to heav'n with me."

The maiden frown'd, and then conceived "that wives
Could walk as well, and lead as holy lives
As angry prudes who scorn'd the marriage-chain,
Or luckless maids who sought it still ir vain."

The friend was vex'd—she paused, at length she cried:
"Know your own danger, then your lot decide,
That traitor Beswell, while he seeks your hand,
Has, I affirm, a wanton at command;
A slave, a creature from a foreign place,
The nurse and mother of a spurious race;

Brown, ugly bastards—(Heaven the word forgive,
And the deed punish!)—in his cottage live;
To town if business calls him, there he stays
In sinful pleasures wasting countless days;
Nor doubt the facts, for I can witness call
For every crime, and prove them one and all."

Here ceased th' informer; Arabella's look
Was like a school-boy's puzzled by his book;
Intent she cast her eyes upon the floor,
Paused—then replied—
"I wish to know no more:
I question not your motive, zeal, or love,
But must decline such dubious points to prove—
All is not true, I judge, for who can guess
Those deeds of darkness men with care suppress?
He brought a slave perhaps to England's coast,
And made her free; it is our country's boast!
And she perchance too grateful—good and ill
Were sown at first, and grow together still;
The colour'd infants on the village-green,
What are they more than we have often seen?
Children half-clothed who round their village stray,
In sun or rain, now starved, now beaten, they
Will the dark colour of their fate betray:
Let us in Christian love for all account,
And then behold to what such tales amount."

"His heart is evil," said th' impatient friend:
"My duty bids me try that heart to mend,"
Replied the virgin—"We may be too nice,
And lose a soul in our contempt of vice;
If false the charge, I then shall show regard
For a good man, and be his just reward:
And what for virtue can I better do
Than to reclaim him, if the charge be true?"

She spoke, nor more her holy work delay'd;
'T was time to lend an erring mortal aid:
"The noblest way," she judged, "a soul to win,
Was with an act of kindness to begin,
To make the sinner sure, and then t' attack the sin."*

TALE X.

THE LOVER'S JOURNEY.

The sun is in the heavens, and the proud day,
Attended with the pleasures of the world,
Is all too wanton.
King John, act iii, scene 3.

The lunatic, the lover, and the poet,
Are of imagination all compact.
Midsummer Night's Dream.

Oh! how the spring of love resembleth
Th' uncertain glory of an April day,
Which now shows all her beauty to the sun,
And by and by a cloud bears all away.

And happily I have arrived at last
Unto the wished haven of my bliss.
Taming of the Shrew, act v scene i.

It is the soul that sees; the outward eyes
Present the object, but the mind descries;
And thence delight, disgust, or cool indiff'rence rise:
When minds are joyful, then we look around,
And what is seen is all on fairy ground;
Again they sicken, and on every view
Cast their own dull and melancholy hue;
Or, if absorb'd by their peculiar cares,
The vacant eye on viewless matter glares,
Our feelings still upon our views attend,
And their own natures to the objects lend;
Sorrow and joy are in their influence sure,
Long as the passion reigns th' effects endure;
But love in minds his various changes makes,
And clothes each object with the change he takes;
His light and shade on every view he throws,
And on each object, what he feels, bestows.

Fair was the morning, and the month was June,
When rose a lover; love awakens soon;
Brief his repose, yet much he dreamt the while
Of that day's meeting, and his Laura's smile;
Fancy and love that name assign'd to her,
Call'd Susan in the parish-register;
And he no more was John—his Laura gave
The name Orlando to her faithful slave.

Bright shone the glory of the rising day,
When the fond traveller took his favourite way;
He mounted gaily, felt his bosom light,
And all he saw was pleasing in his sight.

"Ye hours of expectation, quickly fly,
And bring on hours of blest reality;
When I shall Laura see, beside her stand,
Hear her sweet voice, and press her yielded hand."

First o'er a barren heath beside the coast
Orlando rode, and joy began to boast.

"This neat low gorse," said he, "with golden bloom,
Delights each sense, is beauty, is perfume;
And this gay ling, with all its purple flowers,
A man at leisure might admire for hours;
This green-fringed cup-moss has a scarlet tip,
That yields to nothing but my Laura's lip;
And then how fine this herbage! men may say
A heath is barren; nothing is so gay:
Barren or bare to call such charming scene
Argues a mind possess'd by care and spleen."

Onward he went, and fiercer grew the heat,
Dust rose in clouds before the horse's feet;
For now he pass'd through lanes of burning sand,
Bounds to thin crops or yet uncultured land;
Where the dark poppy flourish'd on the dry
And sterile soil, and mock'd the thin-set rye.

"How lovely this!" the rapt Orlando said;
"With what delight is labouring man repaid!
The very lane has sweets that all admire,
The rambling suckling and the vigorous brier:
See! wholesome wormwood grows beside the way,
Where dew-press'd yet the dog-rose bends the spray

---

* As the author's purpose in this Tale may be mistaken, he wishes to observe, that conduct like that of the lady's here described must be meritorious or censurable just as the motives to it are pure or selfish; that these motives may in a great measure be concealed from the mind of the agent; and that we often take credit to our virtue for actions which spring originally from our tempers, inclinations, or our indifference. It cannot therefore be improper, much less immoral, to give an instance of such self-deception.

Fresh herbs the fields, fair shrubs the banks adorn,
And snow-white bloom falls flaky from the thorn;
No fostering hand they need, no sheltering wall,
They spring uncultured and they bloom for all."

The lover rode as hasty lovers ride,
And reach'd a common pasture wild and wide;
Small black-legg'd sheep devour with hunger keen
The meagre herbage, fleshless, lank, and lean;
Such o'er thy level turf, Newmarket! stray,
And there, with other *black-legs*, find their prey:
He saw some scatter'd hovels; turf was piled
In square brown stacks; a prospect bleak and wild!
A mill, indeed, was in the centre found,
With short sear herbage withering all around;
A smith's black shed opposed a wright's long shop,
And join'd an inn where humble travellers stop.

"Ay, this is nature," said the gentle squire;
"This ease, peace, pleasure—who would not admire?
With what delight these sturdy children play,
And joyful rustics at the close of day;
Sport follows labour, on this even space
Will soon commence the wrestling and the race;
Then will the village-maidens leave their home,
And to the dance with buoyant spirits come;
No affectation in their looks is seen,
Nor know they what disguise or flattery mean;
Nor aught to move an envious pang they see,
Easy their service, and their love is free;
Hence early springs that love, it long endures,
And life's first comfort, while they live, ensures:
They the low roof and rustic comforts prize,
Nor cast on prouder mansions envying eyes:
Sometimes the news at yonder town they hear,
And learn what busier mortals feel and fear;
Secure themselves, although by tales amazed,
Of towns bombarded and of cities razed;
As if they doubted, in their still retreat,
The very news that makes their quiet sweet,
And their days happy—happier only knows
He on whom Laura her regard bestows."

On rode Orlando, counting all the while
The miles he pass'd and every coming mile;
Like all attracted things, he quicker flies,
The place approaching where th' attraction lies;
When next appear'd a *dam*—so call the place—
Where lies a road confined in narrow space;
A work of labour, for on either side
Is level fen, a prospect wild and wide,
With dikes on either hand by ocean's self supplied:
Far on the right the distant sea is seen,
And salt the springs that feed the marsh between;
Beneath an ancient bridge, the straiten'd flood
Rolls through its sloping banks of slimy mud;
Near it a sunken boat resists the tide,
That frets and hurries to the opposing side;
The rushes sharp, that on the borders grow,
Bend their brown flow'rets to the stream below,
Impure in all its course, in all its progress slow:
Here a grave Flora* scarcely deigns to bloom,
Nor wears a rosy blush, nor sheds perfume;
The few dull flowers that o'er the place are spread
Partake the nature of their fenny bed;
Here on its wiry stem, in rigid bloom,
Grows the salt lavender that lacks perfume;
Here the dwarf sallows creep, the septfoil harsh,
And the soft slimy mallow of the marsh;
Low on the ear the distant billows sound,
And just in view appears their stony bound;
No hedge nor tree conceals the glowing sun,
Birds, save a wat'ry tribe, the district shun,
Nor chirp among the reeds where bitter waters run.

"Various as beauteous, Nature, is thy face,"
Exclaim'd Orlando: "all that grows has grace;
All are appropriate—bog, and marsh, and fen,
Are only poor to undiscerning men;
Here may the nice and curious eye explore
How Nature's hand adorns the rushy moor;
Here the rare moss in secret shade is found,
Here the sweet myrtle of the shaking ground;
Beauties are these that from the view retire,
But well repay th' attention they require;
For these my Laura will her home forsake,
And all the pleasures they afford partake."

Again the country was enclosed, a wide
And sandy road has banks on either side;
Where, lo! a hollow on the left appear'd,
And there a gipsy-tribe their tent had rear'd;
'T was open spread, to catch the morning sun,
And they had now their early meal begun,
When two brown boys just left their grassy seat,
The early trav'ller with their pray'rs to greet:
While yet Orlando held his pence in hand,
He saw their sister on her duty stand;
Some twelve years old, demure, affected, sly,
Prepared the force of early powers to try;
Sudden a look of languor he descries,
And well-feign'd apprehension in her eyes;
Train'd but yet savage, in her speaking face
He mark'd the features of her vagrant race;
When a light laugh and roguish leer express'd
The vice implanted in her youthful breast:
Forth from the tent her elder brother came,
Who seem'd offended, yet forbore to blame
The young designer, but could only trace
The looks of pity in the trav'ller's face:
Within, the father, who from fences nigh
Had brought the fuel for the fire's supply,
Watch'd now the feeble blaze, and stood dejected by:
On ragged rug, just borrow'd from the bed,
And by the hand of coarse indulgence fed,

* The ditches of a fen so near the ocean are lined with irregular patches of a coarse and stained lava; a muddy sediment rests on the horse-tail and other perennial herbs, which in part conceal the shallowness of the stream; a fat-leaved pale-flowering scurvy-grass appears early in the year, and the razor-edged bull-rush in the summer and autumn. The fen itself has a dark and saline herbage; there are rushes and *arrow-head*, and in a few patches the flakes of the cotton-grass are seen, but more commonly the *sea-aster*, the dullest of that numerous and hardy genus; a *thrift*, blue in flower, but withering and remaining withered till the winter scatters it; the *saltwort*, both simple and shrubby; a few kinds of grass changed by their soil and atmosphere, and low plants of two or three denominations undistinguished in a general view of the scenery; such is the vegetation of the fen when it is at a small distance from the ocean; and in this case there arise from it effluvia strong and peculiar, half-saline, half-putrid, which would be considered by most people as offensive, and by some as dangerous; but there are others to whom singularity of taste or association of ideas has rendered it agreeable and pleasant.

In dirty patchwork negligently dress'd,
Reclined the wife, an infant at her breast;
In her wild face some touch of grace remain'd,
Of vigour palsied and of beauty stain'd;
Her blood-shot eyes on her unheeding mate
Were wrathful turn'd, and seem'd her wants to state,
Cursing his tardy aid—her mother there
With gipsy-state engross'd the only chair;
Solemn and dull her look; with such she stands,
And reads the milk-maid's fortune in her hands,
Tracing the lines of life; assumed through years,
Each feature now the steady falsehood wears;
With hard and savage eye she views the food,
And grudging pinches their intruding brood;
Last in the group, the worn-out grandsire sits,
Neglected, lost, and living but by fits;
Useless, despised, his worthless labours done,
And half protected by the vicious son,
Who half supports him; he with heavy glance
Views the young ruffians who around him dance;
And, by the sadness in his face, appears
To trace the progress of their future years:
Through what strange course of misery, vice, deceit,
Must wildly wander each unpractised cheat!
What shame and grief, what punishment and pain,
Sport of fierce passions, must each child sustain—
Ere they like him approach their latter end,
Without a hope, a comfort, or a friend!

But this Orlando felt not; "Rogues," said he,
"Doubtless they are, but merry rogues they be;
They wander round the land, and be it true,
They break the laws—then let the laws pursue
The wanton idlers; for the life they live,
Acquit I cannot, but I can forgive."
This said, a portion from his purse was thrown,
And every heart seem'd happy like his own.

He hurried forth, for now the town was nigh—
"The happiest man of mortal men am I."
Thou art! but change in every state is near,
(So while the wretched hope, the blest may fear;)
"Say, where is Laura?"—"That her words must show,"
A lass replied; "read this, and thou shalt know!"

"What, gone!"—her friend insisted—forced to go:—
"Is vex'd, was teased, could not refuse her!—No?"
"But you can follow:" "Yes:" "The miles are few,
The way is pleasant; will you come?—Adieu!
Thy Laura!" "No! I feel I must resign
The pleasing hope, thou hadst been here, if mine:
A lady was it?—Was no brother there?
But why should I afflict me if there were?"
"The way is pleasant:" "What to me the way?
I cannot reach her till the close of day.
My dumb companion! is it thus we speed?
Not I from grief nor thou from toil art freed;
Still art thou doom'd to travel and to pine,
For my vexation—What a fate is mine!

"Gone to a friend, she tells me; I commend
Her purpose; means she to a female friend?
By Heaven, I wish she suffer'd half the pain
Of hope protracted through the day in vain:
Shall I persist to see th' ungrateful maid?
Yes, I will see her, slight her, and upbraid:
What! in the very hour? she knew the time,
And doubtless chose it to increase her crime."

Forth rode Orlando by a river's side,
Inland and winding, smooth, and full and wide,
That roll'd majestic on, in one soft-flowing tide
The bottom gravel, flow'ry were the banks,
Tall willows, waving in their broken ranks;
The road, now near, now distant, winding led
By lovely meadows which the waters fed;
He pass'd the way-side inn, the village spire,
Nor stopp'd to gaze, to question, or admire;
On either side the rural mansions stood,
With hedge-row trees, and hills high-crown'd with wood,
And many a devious stream that reach'd the nobler flood.

"I hate these scenes," Orlando angry cried,
"And these proud farmers! yes, I hate their pride:
See! that sleek fellow, how he strides along,
Strong as an ox, and ignorant as strong;
Can yon close crops a single eye detain
But his who counts the profits of the grain?
And these vile beans with deleterious smell,
Where is their beauty? can a mortal tell?
These deep fat meadows I detest; it shocks
One's feelings there to see the grazing ox;—
For slaughter fatted, as a lady's smile
Rejoices man, and means his death the while.
Lo! now the sons of labour! every day
Employ'd in toil, and vex'd in every way;
Theirs is but mirth assumed, and they conceal,
In their affected joys, the ills they feel:
I hate these long green lanes; there 's nothing seen
In this vile country but eternal green;
Woods! waters! meadows! Will they never end?
'T is a vile prospect:—Gone to see a friend!"—

Still on he rode! a mansion fair and tall
Rose on his view—the pride of Loddon-Hall:
Spread o'er the park he saw the grazing steer,
The full-fed steed, the herds of bounding deer:
On a clear stream the vivid sunbeams play'd,
Through noble elms, and on the surface made
That moving picture, checker'd light and shade;
Th' attended children, there indulged to stray,
Enjoy'd and gave new beauty to the day;
Whose happy parents from their room were seen
Pleased with the sportive idlers on the green.

"Well!" said Orlando, "and for one so bless'd,
A thousand reasoning wretches are distress'd;
Nay, these so seeming glad, are grieving like the rest:
Man is a cheat—and all but strive to hide
Their inward misery by their outward pride.
What do yon lofty gates and walls contain,
But fruitless means to soothe unconquer'd pain?
The parents read each infant daughter's smile,
Form'd to seduce, encouraged to beguile;
They view the boys unconscious of their fate,
Sure to be tempted, sure to take the bait;
These will be Lauras, sad Orlandos these—
There 's guilt and grief in all one bears and sees"

Our trav'ller, lab'ring up a hill, look'd down
Upon a lively, busy, pleasant town;
All he beheld were there alert, alive,
The busiest bees that ever stock'd a hive:
A pair were married, and the bells aloud
Proclaim'd their joy, and joyful seem'd the crowd;
And now proceeding on his way, he spied,
Bound by strong ties, the bridegroom and the bride:
Each by some friends attended, near they drew,
And spleen beheld them with prophetic view.

"Married! nay, mad!" Orlando cried in scorn;
"Another wretch on this unlucky morn:
What are this foolish mirth, these idle joys?
Attempts to stifle doubt and fear by noise:
To me these robes, expressive of delight,
Foreshow distress, and only grief excite;
And for these cheerful friends, will they behold
Their wailing brood in sickness, want, and cold;
And his proud look, and her soft languid air
Will—but I spare you—go, unhappy pair!"

And now approaching to the journey's end,
His anger fails, his thoughts to kindness tend,
He less offended feels, and rather fears t' offend:
Now gently rising, hope contends with doubt,
And casts a sunshine on the views without;
And still reviving joy and lingering gloom
Alternate empire o'er his soul assume;
Till, long perplex'd, he now began to find
The softer thoughts engross the settling mind:
He saw the mansion, and should quickly see
His Laura's self—and angry could he be?
No! the resentment melted all away——
"For this my grief a single smile will pay,"
Our trav'ller cried;—"And why should it offend,
That one so good should have a pressing friend?
Grieve not, my heart! to find a favourite guest
Thy pride and boast—ye selfish sorrows, rest;
She will be kind, and I again be blest."

While gentler passions thus his bosom sway'd,
He reach'd the mansion, and he saw the maid;
"My Laura!"—"My Orlando!—this is kind;
In truth I came persuaded, not inclined:
Our friends' amusement let us now pursue,
And I to-morrow will return with you."

Like man entranced, the happy lover stood—
"As Laura wills, for she is kind and good;
Ever the truest, gentlest, fairest, best—
As Laura wills, I see her and am blest."

Home went the lovers through that busy place,
By Loddon-Hall, the country's pride and grace;
By the rich meadows where the oxen fed,
Through the green vale that form'd the river's bed;
And by unnumber'd cottages and farms,
That have for musing minds unnumber'd charms;
And how affected by the view of these
Was then Orlando—did they pain or please?

Nor pain nor pleasure could they yield—and why?
The mind was fill'd, was happy, and the eye
Roved o'er the fleeting views, that but appear'd to die.

Alone Orlando on the morrow paced
The well-known road; the gypsy-tent he traced;
The dam high-raised, the reedy dikes between,
The scatter'd hovels on the barren green,
The burning sand, the fields of thin-set rye,
Mock'd by the useless Flora, blooming by;
And last the heath with all its various bloom,
And the close lanes that led the trav'ller home.

Then could these scenes the former joys renew?
Or was there now dejection in the view?—
Nor one or other would they yield—and why?
The mind was absent, and the vacant eye
Wander'd o'er viewless scenes, that but appear'd to die.

TALE XI.

EDWARD SHORE.

> Seem they grave or learned?
> Why, so didst thou—Seem they religious?
> Why, so didst thou; or are they spare in diet,
> Free from gross passion, or of mirth or anger,
> Constant in spirit, not swerving with the blood,
> Garnish'd and deck'd in modest compliment,
> Not working with the eye without the ear,
> And but with purged judgment trusting neither?
> Such and so finely bolted didst thou seem.
> *Henry V*, act ii, scene 2.

> Better I were distract,
> So should my thoughts be sever'd from my griefs,
> And woes by strong imagination lose
> The knowledge of themselves.
> *Lear*, act iv, scene 6.

GENIUS! thou gift of Heav'n! thou light divine!
Amid what dangers art thou doom'd to shine!
Oft will the body's weakness check thy force,
Oft damp thy vigour, and impede thy course;
And trembling nerves compel thee to restrain
Thy nobler efforts, to contend with pain;
Or Want (sad guest!) will in thy presence come,
And breathe around a melancholy gloom;
To life's low cares will thy proud thought confine,
And make her sufferings, her impatience, thine.

Evil and strong, seducing passions prey
On soaring minds, and win them from their way;
Who then to vice the subject spirits give,
And in the service of the conqu'ror live;
Like captive Samson making sport for all,
Who fear'd their strength, and glory in their fall.

Genius, with virtue, still may lack the aid
Implored by humble minds and hearts afraid;
May leave to timid souls the shield and sword
Of the tried faith, and the resistless word;
Amid a world of dangers venturing forth,
Frail, but yet fearless, proud in conscious worth,
Till strong temptation, in some fatal time,
Assails the heart, and wins the soul to crime;
When left by honour, and by sorrow spent,
Unused to pray, unable to repent,
The nobler powers that once exalted high
Th' aspiring man, shall then degraded lie:
Reason, through anguish, shall her throne forsake,
And strength of mind but stronger madness make

When Edward Shore had reach'd his twentieth year,
He felt his bosom light, his conscience clear;
Applause at school the youthful hero gain'd,
And trials there with manly strength sustain'd:
With prospect bright upon the world he came,
Pure love of virtue, strong desire of fame:
Men watch'd the way his lofty mind would take,
And all foretold the progress he would make.

Boast of these friends, to older men a guide,
Proud of his parts, but gracious in his pride;
He bore a gay good-nature in his face,
And in his air were dignity and grace;
Dress that became his state and years he wore,
And sense and spirit shone in Edward Shore.

Thus while admiring friends the youth beheld,
His own disgust their forward hopes repell'd;
For he unfix'd, unfixing, look'd around,
And no employment but in seeking found;
He gave his restless thoughts to views refined,
And shrank from worldly cares with wounded mind.

Rejecting trade, awhile he dwelt on laws,
"But who could plead, if unapproved the cause?"
A doubting, dismal tribe physicians seem'd;
Divines o'er texts and disputations dream'd;
War and its glory he perhaps could love,
But there again he must the cause approve.

Our hero thought no deed should gain applause,
Where timid virtue found support in laws;
He to all good would soar, would fly all sin,
By the pure prompting of the will within;
"Who needs a law that binds him not to steal,"
Ask'd the young teacher, "can he rightly feel?
To curb the will, or arm in honour's cause,
Or aid the weak—are these enforced by laws?
Should we a foul, ungenerous action dread,
Because a law condemns th' adulterous bed?
Or fly pollution, not for fear of stain,
But that some statute tells us to refrain?
The grosser herd in ties like these we bind,
In virtue's freedom moves th' enlighten'd mind."
"Man's heart deceives him," said a friend: "Of course,"
Replied the youth, "but, has it power to force?
Unless it forces, call it as you will,
It is but wish, and proneness to the ill."

"Art thou not tempted?" "Do I fall?" said Shore:
"The pure have fallen."—"Then are pure no more:
While reason guides me, I shall walk aright,
Nor need a steadier hand, or stronger light;
Nor this in dread of awful threats, design'd
For the weak spirit and the grov'ling mind;
But that, engaged by thoughts and views sublime,
I wage free war with grossness and with crime."
Thus look'd he proudly on the vulgar crew,
Whom statutes govern, and whom fears subdue.

Faith, with his virtue, he indeed profess'd,
But doubts deprived his ardent mind of rest;
Reason, his sovereign mistress, fail'd to show
Light through the mazes of the world below;
Questions arose, and they surpass'd the skill
Of his sole aid, and would be dubious still;
These to discuss he sought no common guide,
But to the doubters in his doubts applied;
When all together might in freedom speak,
And their loved truth with mutual ardour seek.
Alas! though men who feel their eyes decay
Take more than common pains to find their way,
Yet, when for this they ask each other's aid,
Their mutual purpose is the more delay'd:
Of all their doubts, their reasoning clear'd not one,
Still the same spots were present in the sun;
Still the same scruples haunted Edward's mind,
Who found no rest, nor took the means to find.

But though with shaken faith, and slave to fame,
Vain and aspiring on the world he came;
Yet was he studious, serious, moral, grave,
No passion's victim, and no system's slave;
Vice he opposed, indulgence he disdain'd,
And o'er each sense in conscious triumph reign'd

Who often reads, will sometimes wish to write,
And Shore would yield instruction and delight:
A serious drama he design'd, but found
'T was tedious travelling in that gloomy ground;
A deep and solemn story he would try,
But grew ashamed of ghosts, and laid it by;
Sermons he wrote, but they who knew his creed,
Or knew it not, were ill disposed to read;
And he would lastly be the nation's guide,
But, studying, fail'd to fix upon a side;
Fame he desired, and talents he possess'd,
But loved not labour, though he could not rest,
Nor firmly fix the vacillating mind,
That, ever working, could no centre find.

'T is thus a sanguine reader loves to trace
The Nile forth rushing on his glorious race;
Calm and secure the fancied traveller goes
Through sterile deserts and by threat'ning foes;
He thinks not then of Afric's scorching sands,
Th' Arabian sea, the Abyssinian bands,
Fasils* and Michaels, and the robbers all,
Whom we politely chiefs and heroes call:
He of success alone delights to think,
He views that fount, he stands upon the brink,
And drinks a fancied draught, exulting so to drink

In his own room, and with his books around,
His lively mind its chief employment found,
Then idly busied, quietly employ'd,
And, lost to life, his visions were enjoy'd:
Yet still he took a keen inquiring view
Of all that crowds neglect, desire, pursue;
And thus abstracted, curious, still serene,
He, unemploy'd, beheld life's shifting scene;
Still more averse from vulgar joys and cares,
Still more unfitted for the world's affairs.

There was a house where Edward ofttimes went,
And social hours in pleasant trifling spent;

* Fasil was a rebel chief, and Michael the general of the royal army in Abyssinia, when Mr. Bruce visited that country. In all other respects their characters were nearly similar.—They are both represented as cruel and treacherous; and even the apparently strong distinction of loyal and rebellious is in a great measure set aside, when we are informed that Fasil was an open enemy, and Michael an insolent and ambitious controller of the royal person and family.

He read, conversed and reason'd, sang and play'd,
And all were happy while the idler stay'd;
Too happy one, for thence arose the pain,
Till this engaging trifler came again.

But did he love? We answer, day by day,
The loving feet would take th' accustom'd way,
The amorous eye would rove as if in quest
Of something rare, and on the mansion rest;
The same soft passion touch'd the gentle tongue,
And Anna's charms in tender notes were sung;
The ear too seem'd to feel the common flame,
Soothed and delighted with the fair one's name:
And thus as love each other part possess'd,
The heart, no doubt, its sovereign power confess'd.

Pleased in her sight, the youth required no more;
Nor rich himself, he saw the damsel poor;
And he too wisely, nay, too kindly loved,
To pain the being whom his soul approved.

A serious friend our cautious youth possess'd,
And at his table sat a welcome guest;
Both unemploy'd, it was their chief delight
To read what free and daring authors write;
Authors who loved from common views to soar,
And seek the fountains never traced before;
Truth they profess'd, yet often left the true
And beaten prospect, for the wild and new.
His chosen friend his fiftieth year had seen,
His fortune easy, and his air serene;
Deist and atheist call'd; for few agreed
What were his notions, principles, or creed;
His mind reposed not, for he hated rest,
But all things made a query or a jest;
Perplex'd himself, he ever sought to prove
That man is doom'd in endless doubt to rove;
Himself in darkness he profess'd to be,
And would maintain that not a man could see.

The youthful friend, dissentient, reason'd still
Of the soul's prowess, and the subject will;
Of virtue's beauty, and of honour's force,
And a warm zeal gave life to his discourse:
Since from his feelings all his fire arose,
And he had interest in the themes he chose.

The friend, indulging a sarcastic smile,
Said—"Dear enthusiast! thou wilt change thy style,
When man's delusions, errors, crimes, deceit,
No more distress thee, and no longer cheat."

Yet lo! this cautious man, so coolly wise,
On a young beauty fix'd unguarded eyes;
And her he married: Edward at the view
Bade to his cheerful visits long adieu;
But haply err'd, for this engaging bride
No mirth suppress'd, but rather cause supplied:
And when she saw the friends, by reasoning long,
Confused if right, and positive if wrong,
With playful speech and smile, that spoke delight,
She made them careless both of wrong or right.

This gentle damsel gave consent to wed,
With school, and school-day dinners in her head:
She now was promised choice of daintiest food,
And costly dress, that made her sovereign good;
With walks on hilly heath to banish spleen,
And summer-visits when the roads were clean.

All these she loved, to these she gave consent,
And she was married to her heart's content.

Their manner this—the friends together read,
Till books a cause for disputation bred;
Debate then follow'd, and the vapour'd child
Declared they argued till her head was wild;
And strange to her it was that mortal brain
Could seek the trial, or endure the pain.

Then as the friend reposed, the younger pair
Sat down to cards, and play'd beside his chair;
Till he awaking, to his books applied,
Or heard the music of th' obedient bride:
If mild the evening, in the fields they stray'd,
And their own flock with partial eye survey'd,
But oft the husband, to indulgence prone,
Resumed his book, and bade them walk alone.

"Do, my kind Edward! I must take mine ease,
Name the dear girl the planets and the trees;
Tell her what warblers pour their evening song,
What insects flutter, as you walk along;
Teach her to fix the roving thoughts, to bind
The wandering sense, and methodize the mind."

This was obey'd; and oft when this was done,
They calmly gazed on the declining sun;
In silence saw the glowing landscape fade,
Or, sitting, sang beneath the arbour's shade:
Till rose the moon, and on each youthful face
Shed a soft beauty, and a dangerous grace.

When the young wife beheld in long debate
The friends, all careless as she seeming sate;
It soon appear'd, there was in one combined
The nobler person and the richer mind:
He wore no wig, no grisly beard was seen,
And none beheld him careless or unclean;
Or watch'd him sleeping:—we indeed have heard
Of sleeping beauty, and it has appear'd;
'T is seen in infants—there indeed we find
The features soften'd by the slumbering mind;
But other beauties, when disposed to sleep,
Should from the eye of keen inspector keep:
The lovely nymph who would her swain surprise,
May close her mouth, but not conceal her eyes;
Sleep from the fairest face some beauty takes,
And all the homely features homelier makes;
So thought our wife, beholding with a sigh
Her sleeping spouse, and Edward smiling by.

A sick relation for the husband sent,
Without delay the friendly sceptic went;
Nor fear'd the youthful pair, for he had seen
The wife untroubled, and the friend serene:
No selfish purpose in his roving eyes,
No vile deception in her fond replies:
So judged the husband, and with judgment true,
For neither yet the guilt or danger knew.

What now remain'd? but they again should play
Th' accustom'd game, and walk th' accustom'd way;
With careless freedom should converse or read,
And the friend's absence neither fear nor heed:
But rather now they seem'd confused, constrain'd;
Within their room still restless they remain'd,
And painfully they felt, and knew each other pain'd.—

Ah! foolish men! how could ye thus depend,
One on himself, the other on his friend?

The youth with troubled eye the lady saw,
Yet felt too brave, too daring to withdraw;
While she, with tuneless hand the jarring keys
Touching, was not one moment at her ease:
Now would she walk, and call her friendly guide,
Now speak of rain, and cast her cloak aside;
Seize on a book, unconscious what she read,
And, restless still, to new resources fled;
Then laugh'd aloud, then tried to look serene,
And ever changed, and every change was seen.

Painful it is to dwell on deeds of shame—
The trying day was past, another came;
The third was all remorse, confusion, dread;
And (all too late!) the fallen hero fled.

Then felt the youth, in that seducing time,
How feebly honour guards the heart from crime:
Small is his native strength; man needs the stay,
The strength imparted in the trying day;
For all that honour brings against the force
Of headlong passion, aids its rapid course;
Its slight resistance but provokes the fire,
As wood-work stops the flame, and then conveys it higher.

The husband came; a wife by guilt made bold
Had, meeting, soothed him, as in days of old;
But soon this fact transpired; her strong distress,
And his friend's absence, left him nought to guess.

Still cool, though grieved, thus prudence bade him write—
"I cannot pardon, and I will not fight;
Thou art too poor a culprit for the laws,
And I too faulty to support my cause:
All must be punish'd; I must sigh alone,
At home thy victim for her guilt atone;
And thou, unhappy! virtuous now no more,
Must loss of fame, peace, purity deplore;
Sinners with praise will pierce thee to the heart,
And saints deriding, tell thee what thou art."

Such was his fall; and Edward, from that time,
Felt in full force the censure and the crime—
Despised, ashamed; his noble views before,
And his proud thoughts, degraded him the more:
Should he repent—would that conceal his shame?
Could peace be his? It perish'd with his fame:
Himself he scorn'd, nor could his crime forgive;
He fear'd to die, yet felt ashamed to live:
Grieved, but not contrite was his heart; oppress'd,
Not broken; not converted, but distress'd;
He wanted will to bend the stubborn knee,
He wanted light the cause of ill to see,
To learn how frail is man, how humble then should be;
For faith he had not, or a faith too weak
To gain the help that humbled sinners seek;
Else had he pray'd—to an offended God
His tears had flown a penitential flood;
Though far astray, he would have heard the call
Of mercy—"Come! return, thou prodigal;"
Then, though confused, distress'd, ashamed, afraid,
Still had the trembling penitent obey'd;
Though faith had fainted, when assail'd by fear,
Hope to the soul had whisper'd, "Persevere!"
Till in his Father's house an humbled guest,
He would have found forgiveness, comfort, rest.

But all this joy was to our youth denied
By his fierce passions and his daring pride;
And shame and doubt impell'd him in a course,
Once so abhorr'd, with unresisted force.
Proud minds and guilty, whom their crimes oppress,
Fly to new crimes for comfort and redress;
So found our fallen youth a short relief
In wine, the opiate guilt applies to grief,—
From fleeting mirth that o'er the bottle lives,
From the false joy its inspiration gives;
And from associates pleased to find a friend,
With powers to lead them, gladden, and defend,
In all those scenes where transient ease is found,
For minds whom sins oppress, and sorrows wound.

Wine is like anger; for it makes us strong,
Blind and impatient, and it leads us wrong;
The strength is quickly lost, we feel the error long:
Thus led, thus strengthen'd in an evil cause,
For folly pleading, sought the youth applause;
Sad for a time, then eloquently wild,
He gaily spoke as his companions smiled;
Lightly he rose, and with his former grace
Proposed some doubt, and argued on the case;
Fate and fore-knowledge were his favourite themes—
How vain man's purpose, how absurd his schemes:
"Whatever is, was ere our birth decreed;
We think our actions from ourselves proceed,
And idly we lament th' inevitable deed;
It seems our own, but there 's a power above
Directs the motion, nay, that makes us move,
Nor good nor evil can you beings name,
Who are but rooks and castles in the game;
Superior natures with their puppets play,
Till, bagg'd or buried, all are swept away."

Such were the notions of a mind to ill
Now prone, but ardent, and determined still:
Of joy now eager, as before of fame,
And screen'd by folly when assail'd by shame,
Deeply he sank; obey'd each passion's call,
And used his reason to defend them all.

Shall I proceed, and step by step relate
The odious progress of a sinner's fate?
No—let me rather hasten to the time
(Sure to arrive) when misery waits on crime.

With virtue, prudence fled; what Shore possess'd
Was sold, was spent, and he was now distress'd:
And Want, unwelcome stranger, pale and wan,
Met with her haggard looks the hurried man;
His pride felt keenly what he must expect
From useless pity and from cold neglect.

Struck by new terrors, from his friends he fled,
And wept his woes upon a restless bed;
Retiring late, at early hour to rise,
With shrunken features, and with bloodshot eyes.
If sleep one moment closed the dismal view,
Fancy her terrors built upon the true;
And night and day had their alternate woes,
That baffled pleasure, and that mock'd repose;
Till to despair and anguish was consign'd
The wreck and ruin of a noble mind.

Now seized for debt, and lodged within a jail,
He tried his friendships, and he found them fail;

Then fail'd his spirits, and his thoughts were all
Fix'd on his sins, his sufferings, and his fall:
His ruffled mind was pictured in his face,
Once the fair seat of dignity and grace:
Great was the danger of a man so prone
To think of madness, and to think alone;
Yet pride still lived, and struggled to sustain
The drooping spirit and the roving brain;
But this too fail'd: a friend his freedom gave,
And sent him help the threat'ning world to brave;
Gave solid counsel what to seek or flee,
But still would stranger to his person be:
In vain! the truth determined to explore,
He traced the friend whom he had wrong'd before.

This was too much; both aided and advised
By one who shunn'd him, pitied, and despised:
He bore it not: 't was a deciding stroke,
And on his reason like a torrent broke:
In dreadful stillness he appear'd awhile,
With vacant horror and a ghastly smile;
Then rose at once into the frantic rage,
That force controll'd not, nor could love assuage.

Friends now appear'd, but in the man was seen
The angry maniac, with vindictive mien;
Too late their pity gave to care and skill
The hurried mind and ever-wandering will;
Unnoticed pass'd all time, and not a ray
Of reason broke on his benighted way;
But now he spurn'd the straw in pure disdain,
And now laugh'd loudly at the clinking chain.

Then as its wrath subsided, by degrees
The mind sank slowly to infantine ease;
To playful folly, and to causeless joy,
Speech without aim, and without end, employ;
He drew fantastic figures on the wall,
And gave some wild relation of them all;
With brutal shape he join'd the human face,
And idiot smiles approved the motley race.

Harmless at length th' unhappy man was found,
The spirit settled, but the reason drown'd;
And all the dreadful tempest died away,
To the dull stilness of the misty day.

And now his freedom he attain'd—if free,
The lost to reason, truth, and hope, can be;
His friends, or wearied with the charge, or sure
The harmless wretch was now beyond a cure,
Gave him to wander where he pleased, and find
His own resources for the eager mind;
The playful children of the place he meets,
Playful with them he rambles through the streets;
In all they need, his stronger arm he lends,
And his lost mind to these approving friends.

That gentle maid, whom once the youth had loved,
Is now with mild religious pity moved;
Kindly she chides his boyish flights, while he
Will for a moment fix'd and pensive be;
And as she trembling speaks, his lively eyes
Explore her looks, he listens to her sighs;
Charm'd by her voice, th' harmonious sounds invade
His clouded mind, and for a time persuade:
Like a pleased infant, who has newly caught
From the maternal glance a gleam of thought;
He stands enrapt, the half-known voice to hear,
And starts, half-conscious, at the falling tear.

Rarely from town, nor then unwatch'd, he goes,
In darker mood, as if to hide his woes;
Returning soon, he with impatience seeks
His youthful friends, and shouts, and sings, and speaks;
Speaks a wild speech with action all as wild—
The children's leader, and himself a child;
He spins their top, or at their bidding, bends
His back, while o'er it leap his laughing friends;
Simple and weak, he acts the boy once more,
And heedless children call him Silly Shore.

TALE XII.

'SQUIRE THOMAS; OR, THE PRECIPITATE CHOICE.

Such smiling rogues as these,
Like rats, oft bite the holy cords in twain,
Too intrinsicate t' unloose——
Lear, act i, scene 2.

My other self, my counsel's consistory,
My oracle, my prophet,——
I as a child will go by thy direction.
Richard III, act ii, scene 2.

If I do not have pity upon her, I 'm a villain: if I do not love her, I 'm a Jew.
Much Ado about Nothing, act ii, scene 3.

Women are soft, mild, pitiable, flexible;
But thou art obdurate, flinty, rough, remorseless.
Henry VI, part 3, act ii, scene 4.

He must be told of it, and he shall: the office
Becomes a woman best; I 'll take it upon me;
If I prove honey-mouth'd, let my tongue blister.
Winter's Tale, act ii, scene 2.

Disguise—I see thou art a wickedness.
Twelfth Night, act ii, scene 2.

'Squire Thomas flatter'd long a wealthy aunt,
Who left him all that she could give or grant:
Ten years he tried, with all his craft and skill,
To fix the sovereign lady's varying will;
Ten years enduring at her board to sit,
He meekly listen'd to her tales and wit;
He took the meanest office man can take,
And his aunt's vices for her money's sake:
By many a threat'ning hint she waked his fear,
And he was pain'd to see a rival near;
Yet all the taunts of her contemptuous pride
He bore, nor found his grov'ling spirit tried:
Nay, when she wish'd his parents to traduce,
Fawning he smiled, and justice call'd th' abuse;
"They taught you nothing; are you not, at best,"
Said the proud dame, "a trifler, and a jest?
Confess you are a fool!"—he bow'd, and he confess'd.

This vex'd him much, but could not always last
The dame is buried, and the trial past.

There was a female, who had courted long
Her cousin's gifts, and deeply felt the wrong;

By a vain boy forbidden to attend
The private councils of her wealthy friend,
She vow'd revenge, nor should that crafty boy
In triumph undisturb'd his spoils enjoy;
He heard, he smiled, and when the will was read,
Kindly dismiss'd the kindred of the dead;
"The dear deceased," he call'd her, and the crowd
Moved off with curses deep and threat'nings loud.

The youth retired, and, with a mind at ease,
Found he was rich, and fancied he must please:
He might have pleased, and to his comfort found
The wife he wish'd, if he had sought around;
For there were lasses of his own degree,
With no more hatred to the state than he:
But he had courted spleen and age so long,
His heart refused to woo the fair and young;
So long attended on caprice and whim,
He thought attention now was due to him;
And as his flattery pleased the wealthy dame,
Heir to the wealth he might the flattery claim;
But this the fair, with one accord, denied,
Nor waived for man's caprice the sex's pride:
There is a season when to them is due
Worship and awe, and they will claim it too:
"Fathers," they cry, "long hold us in their chain;
Nay, tyrant brothers claim a right to reign;
Uncles and guardians we in turn obey,
And husbands rule with ever-during sway;
Short is the time when lovers at the feet
Of beauty kneel, and own the slavery sweet;
And shall we this our triumph, this the aim
And boast of female power, forbear to claim?
No! we demand that homage, that respect,
Or the proud rebel punish and reject."

Our hero, still too indolent, too nice
To pay for beauty the accustom'd price,
No less forbore t' address the humbler maid,
Who might have yielded with the price unpaid;
But lived, himself to humour and to please,
To count his money, and enjoy his ease.

It pleased a neighbouring 'squire to recommend
A faithful youth, as servant to his friend;
Nay, more than servant, whom he praised for parts
Ductile yet strong, and for the best of hearts;
One who might ease him in his small affairs,
With tenants, tradesmen, taxes, and repairs;
Answer his letters, look to all his dues,
And entertain him with discourse and news.

The 'squire believed, and found the trusted youth
A very pattern for his care and truth;
Not for his virtues to be praised alone,
But for a modest mien and humble tone;
Assenting always, but as if he meant
Only to strength of reasons to assent:
For was he stubborn, and retain'd his doubt,
Till the more subtle 'squire had forced it out;
"Nay, still was right, but he perceived that strong
And powerful minds could make the right the wrong."

When the 'squire's thoughts on some fair damsel dwelt,
The faithful friend his apprehensions felt;
It would rejoice his faithful heart to find
A lady suited to his master's mind;
But who deserved that master? who would prove
That hers was pure, uninterested love?
Although a servant, he would scorn to take
A countess, till she suffer'd for his sake;
Some tender spirit, humble, faithful, true,
Such, my dear master! must be sought for you.

Six months had pass'd, and not a lady seen,
With just this love, 'twixt fifty and fifteen;
All seem'd his doctrine or his pride to shun,
All would be woo'd, before they would be won;
When the chance naming of a race and fair,
Our 'squire disposed to take his pleasure there:
The friend profess'd, "although he first began
To hint the thing, it seem'd a thoughtless plan:
The roads, he fear'd, were foul, the days were short,
The village far, and yet there might be sport."

"What! you of roads and starless nights afraid?
You think to govern! you to be obey'd!"
Smiling he spoke, the humble friend declared
His soul's obedience, and to go prepared.

The place was distant, but with great delight
They saw a race, and hail'd the glorious sight:
The 'squire exulted, and declared the ride
Had amply paid, and he was satisfied.
They gazed, they feasted, and, in happy mood,
Homeward return'd, and hastening as they rode;
For short the day, and sudden was the change
From light to darkness, and the way was strange;
Our hero soon grew peevish, then distress'd;
He dreaded darkness, and he sigh'd for rest:
Going, they pass'd a village; but, alas!
Returning saw no village to repass;
The 'squire remember'd too a noble hall,
Large as a church, and whiter than its wall:
This he had noticed as they rode along,
And justly reason'd that their road was wrong.
George, full of awe, was modest in reply—
"The fault was his, 't was folly to deny;
And of his master's safety were he sure,
There was no grievance he would not endure."
This made his peace with the relenting 'squire,
Whose thoughts yet dwelt on supper and a fire;
When, as they a reach'd a long and pleasant green,
Dwellings of men, and next a man, were seen.

"My friend," said George, "to travellers astray
Point out an inn, and guide us on the way."

The man look'd up; "Surprising! can it be
My master's son? as I 'm alive, 't is he."

"How! Robin," George replied, "and are we near
My father's house? how strangely things appear!—
Dear sir, though wanderers, we at last are right:
Let us proceed, and glad my father's sight;
We shall at least be fairly lodged and fed,
I can ensure a supper and a bed;
Let us this night, as one of pleasure date,
And of surprise: it is an act of fate."
"Go on," the 'squire in happy temper cried;
"I like such blunder! I approve such guide."

They ride, they halt, the farmer comes in haste,
Then tells his wife how much their house is graced
They bless the chance, they praise the lucky son,
That caused the error—Nay! it was not one

But their good fortune—Cheerful grew the 'squire,
Who found dependants, flattery, wine, and fire;
He heard the jack turn round; the busy dame
Produced her damask; and with supper came
The daughter, dress'd with care, and full of maiden-shame.

Surprised, our hero saw the air and dress,
And strove his admiration to express;
Nay! felt it too—for Harriet was, in truth,
A tall fair beauty in the bloom of youth;
And from the pleasure and surprise, a grace
Adorn'd the blooming damsel's form and face;
Then too, such high respect and duty paid
By all—such silent reverence in the maid;
Vent'ring with caution, yet with haste, a glance;
Loth to retire, yet trembling to advance,
Appear'd the nymph, and in her gentle guest
Stirr'd soft emotions till the hour of rest:
Sweet was his sleep, and in the morn again
He felt a mixture of delight and pain:
"How fair, how gentle," said the 'squire, "how meek,
And yet how sprightly, when disposed to speak!
Nature has bless'd her form, and Heaven her mind,
But in her favours Fortune is unkind;
Poor is the maid—nay, poor she cannot prove
Who is enrich'd with beauty, worth, and love."

The 'squire arose, with no precise intent
To go or stay—uncertain what he meant:
He moved to part—they begg'd him first to dine;
And who could then escape from love and wine?
As came the night, more charming grew the fair,
And seem'd to watch him with a two-fold care:
On the third morn, resolving not to stay
Though urged by love, he bravely rode away.

Arrived at home, three pensive days he gave
To feelings fond and meditations grave;
Lovely she was, and, if he did not err,
As fond of him as his fond heart of her;
Still he delay'd, unable to decide
Which was the master-passion, love or pride:
He sometimes wonder'd how his friend could make,
And then exulted in, the night's mistake;
Had she but fortune, "doubtless then," he cried,
"Some happier man had won the wealthy bride."

While thus he hung in balance, now inclined
To change his state, and then to change his mind—
That careless George dropp'd idly on the ground
A letter, which his crafty master found;
The stupid youth confess'd his fault, and pray'd
The generous 'squire to spare a gentle maid;
Of whom her tender mother, full of fears,
Had written much—"She caught her oft in tears,
For ever thinking on a youth above
Her humble fortune—still she own'd not love;
Nor can define, dear girl! the cherish'd pain,
But would rejoice to see the cause again:
That neighbouring youth, whom she endured before,
She now rejects, and will behold no more:
Raised by her passion, she no longer stoops
To her own equals, but she pines and droops,
Like to a lily, on whose sweets the sun
Has withering gazed—she saw and was undone:

His wealth allured her not—nor was she moved
By his superior state, himself she loved;
So mild, so good, so gracious, so genteel—
But spare your sister, and her love conceal;
We must the fault forgive, since she the pain must feel."
"Fault!" said the 'squire, "there's coarseness in the mind
That thus conceives of feelings so refined;
Here end my doubts, nor blame yourself, my friend,
Fate made you careless—here my doubts have end."

The way is plain before us—there is now
The lover's visit first, and then the vow
Mutual and fond, the marriage-rite, the bride
Brought to her home with all a husband's pride;
The 'squire receives the prize his merits won,
And the glad parents leave the patron-son.

But in short time he saw with much surprise,
First gloom, then grief, and then resentment rise,
From proud, commanding frowns, and anger-darting eyes:
"Is there in Harriet's humble mind this fire,
This fierce impatience?" ask'd the puzzled 'squire:
"Has marriage changed her? or the mask she wore
Has she thrown by, and is herself once more?"

Hour after hour, when clouds on clouds appear,
Dark and more dark, we know the tempest near;
And thus the frowning brow, the restless form,
And threat'ning glance, forerun domestic storm:
So read the husband, and, with troubled mind,
Reveal'd his fears—"My love, I hope you find
All here is pleasant—but I must confess
You seem offended, or in some distress;
Explain the grief you feel, and leave me to redress."

"Leave it to you?" replied the nymph—"indeed!
What—to the cause from whence the ills proceed?
Good Heaven! to take me from a place, where I
Had every comfort underneath the sky;
And then immure me in a gloomy place,
With the grim monsters of your ugly race,
That from their canvas staring, make me dread
Through the dark chambers where they hang to tread!
No friend nor neighbour comes to give that joy,
Which all things here must banish or destroy:
Where is the promised coach? the pleasant ride?
Oh! what a fortune has a farmer's bride!
Your sordid pride has placed me just above
Your hired domestics—and what pays me? love!
A selfish fondness I endure each hour,
And share unwitness'd pomp, unenvied power;
I hear your folly, smile at your parade,
And see your favourite dishes duly made;
Then am I richly dress'd for you t' admire,
Such is my duty and my lord's desire;
Is this a life for youth, for health, for joy?
Are these my duties—this my base employ?
No! to my father's house will I repair,
And make your idle wealth support me there;
Was it your wish to have an humble bride
For bondage thankful? Curse upon your pride.
Was it a slave you wanted? You shall see,
That if not happy, I at least am free.

Well, sir, your answer:"—Silent stood the 'squire,
As looks a miser at his house on fire;
Where all he deems is vanish'd in that flame,
Swept from the earth his substance and his name;
So, lost to every promised joy of life,
Our 'squire stood gaping at his angry wife;—
His fate, his ruin, where he saw it vain
To hope for peace, pray, threaten, or complain;
And thus, betwixt his wonder at the ill
And his despair—there stood he gaping still.

"Your answer, sir—shall I depart a spot
I thus detest?"—"Oh, miserable lot!"
Exclaim'd the man. "Go, serpent! nor remain
To sharpen wo by insult and disdain:
A nest of harpies was I doom'd to meet;
What plots, what combinations of deceit!
I see it now—all plann'd, design'd, contrived;
Served by that villain—by this fury wived—
What fate is mine! What wisdom, virtue, truth
Can stand, if demons set their traps for youth?
He lose his way! vile dog! he cannot lose
The way a villain through his life pursues;
And thou, deceiver! thou afraid to move,
And hiding close the serpent in the dove!
I saw—but, fated to endure disgrace—
Unheeding saw, the fury in thy face;
And call'd it spirit—Oh! I might have found
Fraud and imposture—all the kindred round!
A nest of vipers"—

—"Sir, I 'll not admit
These wild effusions of your angry wit:
Have you that value, that we all should use
Such mighty arts for such important views?
Are you such prize—and is my state so fair
That they should sell their souls to get me there!
Think you that we alone our thoughts disguise?
When in pursuit of some contended prize,
Mask we alone the heart, and soothe whom we despise!
Speak you of craft and subtle schemes, who know
That all your wealth you to deception owe;
Who play'd for ten dull years a scoundrel-part,
To worm yourself into a widow's heart?
Now, when you guarded, with superior skill,
That lady's closet, and preserved her will,
Blind in your craft, you saw not one of those
Opposed by you might you in turn oppose;
Or watch your motions, and by art obtain
Share of that wealth you gave your peace to gain?
Did conscience never"—

—"Cease, Tormentor, cease—
Or reach me poison——let me rest in peace!"

"Agreed—but hear me—let the truth appear;"
"Then state your purpose—I 'll be calm and hear."
"Know then, this wealth, sole object of your care,
I had some right, without your hand, to share;
My mother's claim was just—but soon she saw
Your power, compell'd, insulted, to withdraw:
'T was then my father, in his anger, swore
You should divide the fortune, or restore;
Long we debated—and you find me now
Heroic victim to a father's vow;
Like Jephtha's daughter, but in different state,
And both decreed to mourn our early fate;
Hence was my brother servant to your pride,
Vengeance made him your slave—and me your bride:
Now all is known—a dreadful price I pay
For our revenge—but still we have our day;
All that you love you must with others share,
Or all you dread from their resentment dare!
Yet terms I offer—let contention cease:
Divide the spoil, and let us part in peace."

Our hero trembling heard—he sat—he rose—
Nor could his motions nor his mind compose;
He paced the room—and, stalking to her side,
Gazed on the face of his undaunted bride;
And nothing there but scorn and calm aversion spied.
He would have vengeance, yet he fear'd the law:
Her friends would threaten, and their power he saw;
"Then let her go:"—but oh! a mighty sum
Would that demand, since he had let her come;
Nor from his sorrows could he find redress,
Save that which led him to a like distress,
And all his ease was in his wife to see
A wretch as anxious and distress'd as he:
Her strongest wish, the fortune to divide
And part in peace, his avarice denied;
And thus it happen'd, as in all deceit,
The cheater found the evil of the cheat;
The husband grieved—nor was the wife at rest;
Him she could vex, and he could her molest;
She could his passions into frenzy raise,
But when the fire was kindled, fear'd the blaze:
As much they studied, so in time they found
The easiest way to give the deepest wound;
But then, like fencers, they were equal still,
Both lost in danger what they gain'd in skill;
Each heart a keener kind of rancour gain'd,
And paining more, was more severely pain'd;
And thus by both were equal vengeance dealt,
And both the anguish they inflicted felt.

TALE XIII.

JESSE AND COLIN.

Then she plots. then she ruminates, then she devises; and what they think in their hearts they may effect, they will break their hearts but they will effect.

Merry Wives of Windsor, act ii, scene 2.

She hath spoken that she should not, I am sure of that; Heaven knows what she hath known.

Macbeth, act v, scene 1.

Our house is hell, and thou a merry devil.

Merchant of Venice, act ii, scene 3.

And yet, for aught I see, they are as sick that surfeit of too much, as they that starve with nothing; it is no mean happiness, therefore, to be seated in the mean.

Merchant of Venice, act i, scene 2.

A VICAR died, and left his daughter poor—
It hurt her not, she was not rich before:
Her humble share of worldly goods she sold,
Paid every debt, and then her fortune told;
And found, with youth and beauty, hope and health,
Two hundred guineas was her worldly wealth;

It then remain'd to choose her path in life,
And first, said Jesse, "Shall I be a wife?—
Colin is mild and civil, kind and just,
I know his love, his temper I can trust;
But small his farm, it asks perpetual care,
And we must toil as well as trouble share:
True, he was taught in all the gentle arts
That raise the soul, and soften human hearts;
And boasts a parent, who deserves to shine
In higher class, and I could wish her mine;
Nor wants he will his station to improve,
A just ambition waked by faithful love;—
Still is he poor—and here my father's friend
Deigns for his daughter, as her own, to send;
A worthy lady, who it seems has known
A world of griefs and troubles of her own:
I was an infant, when she came, a guest
Beneath my father's humble roof to rest;
Her kindred all unfeeling, vast her woes,
Such her complaint, and there she found repose;
Enrich'd by fortune, now she nobly lives,
And nobly, from the blest abundance, gives;
The grief, the want of human life, she knows,
And comfort there and here relief bestows;
But are they not dependants?—Foolish pride!
Am I not honour'd by such friend and guide?
Have I a home," (here Jesse dropp'd a tear),
"Or friend beside?"—A faithful friend was near.

Now Colin came, at length resolved to lay
His heart before her and to urge her stay;
True, his own plough the gentle Colin drove,
An humble farmer with aspiring love;
Who, urged by passion, never dared till now,
Thus urged by fears, his trembling hopes avow:
Her father's glebe he managed; every year
The grateful vicar held the youth more dear;
He saw indeed the prize in Colin's view,
And wish'd his Jesse with a man so true;
Timid as true, he urged with anxious air
His tender hope, and made the trembling prayer;
When Jesse saw, nor could with coldness see,
Such fond respect, such tried sincerity:
Grateful for favours to her father dealt,
She more than grateful for his passion felt;
Nor could she frown on one so good and kind,
Yet fear'd to smile, and was unfix'd in mind;
But prudence placed the female friend in view—
What might not one so rich and grateful do?
So lately, too, the good old vicar died,
His faithful daughter must not cast aside
The signs of filial grief, and be a ready bride:
Thus, led by prudence, to the lady's seat
The village-beauty purposed to retreat;
But, as in hard-fought fields the victor knows
What to the vanquish'd he in honour owes,
So in this conquest over powerful love,
Prudence resolved a generous foe to prove;
And Jesse felt a mingled fear and pain
In her dismission of a faithful swain,
Gave her kind thanks, and when she saw his wo,
Kindly betray'd that she was loth to go;
"But would she promise, if abroad she met
A frowning world, she would remember yet
Where dwelt a friend?"—"That could she not forget."
And thus they parted; but each faithful heart
Felt the compulsion and refused to part.

Now by the morning mail the timid maid
Was to that kind and wealthy dame convey'd;
Whose invitation, when her father died,
Jesse as comfort to her heart applied;
She knew the days her generous friend had seen—
As wife and widow, evil days had been;
She married early, and for half her life
Was an insulted and forsaken wife;
Widow'd and poor, her angry father gave,
Mix'd with reproach, the pittance of a slave;
Forgetful brothers pass'd her, but she knew
Her humbler friends, and to their home withdrew:
The good old vicar to her sire applied
For help, and help'd her when her sire denied;
When in few years death stalk'd through bower and hall,
Sires, sons, and sons of sons, were buried all:
She then abounded, and had wealth to spare
For softening grief she once was doom'd to share;
Thus train'd in misery's school, and taught to feel,
She would rejoice an orphan's woes to heal:
So Jesse thought, who look'd within her breast,
And thence conceived how bounteous minds are bless'd.

From her vast mansion look'd the lady down
On humbler buildings of a busy town;
Thence came her friends of either sex, and all
With whom she lived on terms reciprocal:
They pass'd the hours with their accustom'd ease,
As guests inclined, but not compell'd to please;
But there were others in the mansion found,
For office chosen, and by duties bound;
Three female rivals, each of power possess'd,
Th' attendant-maid, poor friend, and kindred-guest.

To these came Jesse, as a seaman thrown
By the rude storm upon a coast unknown:
The view was flattering, civil seem'd the race,
But all unknown the dangers of the place.

Few hours had pass'd, when, from attendants freed,
The lady utter'd—"This is kind indeed:
Believe me, love! that I for one like you
Have daily pray'd, a friend discreet and true;
Oh! wonder not that I on you depend,
You are mine own hereditary friend:
Hearken, my Jesse, never can I trust
Beings ungrateful, selfish, and unjust;
But you are present, and my load of care
Your love will serve to lighten and to share:
Come near me, Jesse—let not those below
Of my reliance on your friendship know;
Look as they look, be in their freedoms free—
But all they say do you convey to me."

Here Jesse's thoughts to Colin's cottage flew,
And with such speed she scarce their absence knew.

"Jane loves her mistress, and should she depart,
I lose her service, and she breaks her heart;
My ways and wishes, looks and thoughts she knows,
And duteous care by close attention shows:
But is she faithful? in temptation strong?
Will she not wrong me? ah! I fear the wrong:
Your father loved me; now, in time of need,
Watch for my good, and to his place succeed.

"Blood doesn't bind—that girl, who every day
Eats of my bread, would wish my life away;

I am her *dear relation*, and she thinks
To make her fortune, an ambitious minx!
She only courts me for the prospect's sake,
Because she knows I have a will to make;
Yes, love! my will delay'd, I know not how—
But you are here, and I will make it now.

"That idle creature, keep her in your view,
See what she does, what she desires to do;
On her young mind may artful villains prey,
And to my plate and jewels find a way;
A pleasant humour has the girl: her smile
And cheerful manner tedious hours beguile:
But well observe her, ever near her be,
Close in your thoughts, in your professions free.

"Again, my Jesse, hear what I advise,
And watch a woman ever in disguise;
Issop, that widow, serious, subtle, sly—
But what of this—I must have company:
She markets for me, and although she makes
Profit, no doubt, of all she undertakes,
Yet she is one I can to all produce,
And all her talents are in daily use;
Deprived of her, I may another find
As sly and selfish, with a weaker mind
But never trust her, she is full of art,
And worms herself into the closest heart;
Seem then, I pray you, careless in her sight,
Nor let her know, my love, how we unite.

"Do, my good Jesse, cast a view around,
And let no wrong within my house be found;
That girl associates with——I know not who
Are her companions, nor what ill they do;
'T is then the widow plans, 't is then she tries
Her various arts and schemes for fresh supplies;
'T is then, if ever, Jane her duty quits,
And, whom I know not, favours and admits:
Oh! watch their movements all; for me 't is hard,
Indeed is vain, but you may keep a guard;
And I, when none your watchful glance deceive,
May make my will, and think what I shall leave."

Jesse, with fear, disgust, alarm, surprise,
Heard of these duties for her ears and eyes;
Heard by what service she must gain her bread,
And went with scorn and sorrow to her bed.

Jane was a servant fitted for her place,
Experienced, cunning, fraudful, selfish, base;
Skill'd in those mean humiliating arts
That make their way to proud and selfish hearts;
By instinct taught, she felt an awe, a fear,
For Jesse's upright, simple character;
Whom with gross flattery she awhile assail'd,
And then beheld with hatred when it fail'd;
Yet trying still upon her mind for hold,
She all the secrets of the mansion told;
And to invite an equal trust, she drew
Of every mind a bold and rapid view;
But on the widow'd friend with deep disdain,
And rancorous envy, dwelt the treacherous Jane:—
In vain such arts, without deceit or pride,
With a just taste and feeling for her guide,
From all contagion Jesse kept apart,
Free in her manners, guarded in her heart.

Jesse one morn was thoughtful, and her sigh
The widow heard as she was passing by;
And—"Well!" she said, "is that some distant swain,
Or aught with us, that gives your bosom pain?
Come, we are fellow-sufferers, slaves in thrall,
And tasks and griefs are common to us all;
Think not my frankness strange: they love to paint
Their state with freedom, who endure restraint;
And there is something in that speaking eye
And sober mien, that prove I may rely:
You came a stranger; to my words attend,
Accept my offer, and you find a friend;
It is a labyrinth in which you stray,
Come, hold my clue, and I will lead the way.

"Good Heav'n! that one so jealous, envious, base,
Should be the mistress of so sweet a place;
She, who so long herself was low and poor,
Now broods suspicious on her useless store;
She loves to see us abject, loves to deal
Her insult round, and then pretends to feel:
Prepare to cast all dignity aside,
For know your talents will be quickly tried;
Nor think, from favours past, a friend to gain,
'T is but by duties we our posts maintain:
I read her novels, gossip through the town,
And daily go, for idle stories, down;
I cheapen all she buys, and bear the curse
Of honest tradesmen for my niggard purse;
And, when for her this meanness I display,
She cries, "I heed not what I throw away;'
Of secret bargains I endure the shame,
And stake my credit for our fish and game;
Oft has she smiled to hear 'her generous soul
Would gladly give, but stoops to my control:'
Nay! I have heard her, when she chanced to come
Where I contended for a petty sum,
Affirm 't was painful to behold such care,
"But Issop's nature is to pinch and spare:"
Thus all the meanness of the house is mine,
And my reward—to scorn her, and to dine.

"See next that giddy thing, with neither pride
To keep her safe, nor principle to guide:
Poor, idle, simple flirt! as sure as fate
Her maiden-fame will have an early date:
Of her beware; for all who live below
Have faults they wish not all the world to know:
And she is fond of listening, full of doubt,
And stoops to guilt to find an error out.

"And now once more observe the artful maid,
A lying, prying, jilting, thievish jade;
I think, my love, you will not condescend
To call a low, illiterate girl your friend:
But in our troubles we are apt, you know,
To lean on all who some compassion show;
And she has flexile features, acting eyes,
And seems with every look to sympathise:
No mirror can a mortal's grief express
With more precision, or can feel it less;
That proud, mean spirit, she by fawning courts,
By vulgar flattery, and by vile reports;
And, by that proof she every instant gives
To one so mean, that yet a meaner lives.—

"Come, I have drawn the curtain, and you see
Your fellow-actors, all your company,

Should you incline to throw reserve aside,
And in my judgment and my love confide,
I could some prospects open to your view,
That ask attention—and till then, adieu."

"Farewell!" said Jesse, hastening to her room,
Where all she saw within, without, was gloom:
Confused, perplex'd, she pass'd a dreary hour,
Before her reason could exert its power;
To her all seem'd mysterious, all allied
To avarice, meanness, folly, craft, and pride;
Wearied with thought, she breathed the garden's air,
Then came the laughing lass, and join'd her there.

"My sweetest friend has dwelt with us a week,
And does she love us? be sincere and speak;
My aunt you cannot—Lord! how I should hate
To be like her, all misery and state;
Proud, and yet envious, she disgusted sees
All who are happy, and who look at ease.
Let friendship bind us, I will quickly show
Some favourites near us, you'll be bless'd to know;
My aunt forbids it—but, can she expect
To soothe her spleen, we shall ourselves neglect?
Jane and the widow were to watch and stay
My free-born feet; I watch'd as well as they;
Lo! what is this? this simple key explores
The dark recess that holds the spinster's stores;
And led by her ill star, I chanced to see
Where Issop keeps her stock of ratafie;
Used in the hours of anger and alarm,
It makes her civil, and it keeps her warm;
Thus bless'd with secrets, both would choose to hide,
Their fears now grant me what their scorn denied.

"My freedom thus by their assent secured,
Bad as it is, the place may be endured;
And bad it is, but her estates, you know,
And her beloved hoards, she must bestow;
So we can slyly our amusements take,
And friends of demons, if they help us, make."

"Strange creatures these," thought Jessy, half inclined
To smile at one malicious and yet kind;
Frank and yet cunning, with a heart to love
And malice prompt—the serpent and the dove.
Here could she dwell? or could she yet depart?
Could she be artful? could she bear with art?—
This splendid mansion gave the cottage grace,
She thought a dungeon was a happier place;
And Colin pleading, when he pleaded best,
Wrought not such sudden change in Jesse's breast.

The wondering maiden, who had only read
Of such vile beings, saw them now with dread;
Safe in themselves—for nature has design'd
The creature's poison harmless to the kind;
But all beside who in the haunts are found
Must dread the poison, and must feel the wound.

Days full of care, slow weary weeks pass'd on,
Eager to go, still Jesse was not gone;
Her time in trifling or in tears she spent,
She never gave, she never felt content:
The lady wonder'd that her humble guest
Strove not to please, would neither lie nor jest;
She sought no news, no scandal would convey,
But walk'd for health, and was at church to pray;
All this displeased, and soon the widow cried:
"Let me be frank—I am not satisfied;
You know my wishes, I your judgment trust;
You can be useful, Jesse, and you must;
Let me be plainer, child—I want an ear,
When I am deaf, instead of mine to hear;
When mine is sleeping, let your eye awake;
When I observe not, observation take;
Alas! I rest not on my pillow laid,
Then threat'ning whispers make my soul afraid;
The tread of strangers to my ear ascends,
Fed at my cost, the minions of my friends;
While you, without a care, a wish to please,
Eat the vile bread of idleness and ease."

Th' indignant girl astonish'd answer'd—"Nay!
This instant, madam, let me haste away;
Thus speaks my father's, thus an orphan's friend?
This instant, lady, let your bounty end."

The lady frown'd indignant—"What!" she cried,
"A vicar's daughter with a princess' pride!
And pauper's lot! but pitying I forgive;
How, simple Jessy, do you think to live?
Have I not power to help you, foolish maid?
To my concerns be your attention paid;
With cheerful mind th' allotted duties take,
And recollect I have a will to make."

Jessy, who felt as liberal natures feel,
When thus the baser their designs reveal,
Replied—"Those duties were to her unfit,
Nor would her spirit to her tasks submit.'
In silent scorn the lady sate awhile,
And then replied with stern contemptuous smile—

"Think you, fair madam, that you came to share
Fortunes like mine without a thought or care?
A guest, indeed! from every trouble free,
Dress'd by my help, with not a care for me;
When I a visit to your father made,
I for the poor assistance largely paid;
To his domestics I their tasks assign'd,
I fix'd the portion for his hungry hind;
And had your father (simple man!) obey'd
My good advice, and watch'd as well as pray'd,
He might have left you something with his prayers,
And lent some colour for these lofty airs.—

"In tears! my love! Oh, then my soften'd heart
Cannot resist—we never more will part;
I need your friendship—I will be your friend,
And thus determined, to my will attend."

Jesse went forth, but with determined soul
To fly such love, to break from such control;
"I hear enough," the trembling damsel cried;
"Flight be my care, and Providence my guide:
Ere yet a prisoner, I escape will make;
Will, thus display'd, th' insidious arts forsake,
And, as the rattle sounds, will fly the fatal snake."

Jesse her thanks upon the morrow paid,
Prepared to go, determined though afraid.

"Ungrateful creature," said the lady, "this
Could I imagine?—are you frantic, miss?
What! leave your friend, your prospects—is it true?"
This Jesse answer'd by a mild 'Adieu'!"

The dame replied, "Then houseless may you rove,
The starving victim to a guilty love;
Branded with shame, in sickness doom'd to nurse
An ill-form'd cub, your scandal and your curse;
Spurn'd by its scoundrel father, and ill fed
By surly rustics with the parish-bread!—
Relent you not?—speak—yet I can forgive;
Still live with me"—"With you," said Jesse, "live?
No! I would first endure what you describe,
Rather than breathe with your detested tribe;
Who long have feign'd, till now their very hearts
Are firmly fix'd in their accursed parts;
Who all profess esteem, and feel disdain,
And all, with justice, of deceit complain;
Whom I could pity, but that, while I stay,
My terror drives all kinder thoughts away;
Grateful for this, that when I think of you,
I little fear what poverty can do."

The angry matron her attendant Jane
Summon'd in haste to soothe the fierce disdain:

"A vile detested wretch!" the lady cried,
"Yet shall she be, by many an effort, tried,
And, clogg'd with debt and fear, against her will abide;
And once secured, she never shall depart
Till I have proved the firmness of her heart;
Then when she dares not, would not, cannot go,
I'll make her feel what 't is to use me so."

The pensive Colin in his garden stray'd,
But felt not then the beauties it display'd;
There many a pleasant object met his view,
A rising wood of oaks behind it grew;
A stream ran by it, and the village-green
And public road were from the gardens seen;
Save where the pine and larch the bound'ry made,
And on the rose-beds threw a softening shade.

The mother sat beside the garden-door,
Dress'd as in times ere she and hers were poor;
The broad-laced cap was known in ancient days,
When madam's dress compell'd the village praise;
And still she look'd as in the times of old,
Ere his last farm the erring husband sold;
While yet the mansion stood in decent state,
And paupers waited at the well-known gate.

"Alas! my son!" the mother cried, "and why
That silent grief and oft-repeated sigh?
True we are poor, but thou hast never felt
Pangs to thy father for his error dealt;
Pangs from strong hopes of visionary gain,
For ever raised, and ever found in vain.
He rose unhappy! from his fruitless schemes,
As guilty wretches from their blissful dreams;
But thou wert then, my son, a playful child,
Wondering at grief, gay, innocent, and wild;
Listening at times to thy poor mother's sighs,
With curious looks and innocent surprise;
Thy father dying, thou, my virtuous boy,
My comfort always, waked my soul to joy;
With the poor remnant of our fortune left,
Thou hast our station of its gloom bereft:
Thy lively temper, and thy cheerful air,
Have cast a smile on sadness and despair;
Thy active hand has dealt to this poor space
The bliss of plenty and the charm of grace;
And all around us wonder when they find
Such taste and strength, such skill and power combined;
There is no mother, Colin, no not one,
But envies me so kind, so good a son;
By thee supported on this failing side,
Weakness itself awakes a parent's pride:
I bless the stroke that was my grief before,
And feel such joy that 't is disease no more;
Shielded by thee, my want becomes my wealth—
And soothed by Colin, sickness smiles at health;
The old men love thee, they repeat thy praise,
And say, like thee were youth in earlier days;
While every village-maiden cries, 'How gay,
How smart, how brave, how good is Colin Grey!'

"Yet thou art sad; alas! my son, I know
Thy heart is wounded, and the cure is slow:
Fain would I think that Jesse still may come
To share the comforts of our rustic home:
She surely loved thee: I have seen the maid,
When thou hast kindly brought the vicar aid—
When thou hast eased his bosom of its pain,
Oh! I have seen her—she will come again."

The matron ceased; and Colin stood the while
Silent, but striving for a grateful smile;
He then replied—"Ah! sure, had Jesse stay'd,
And shared the comforts of our sylvan shade,
The tenderest duty and the fondest love
Would not have fail'd that generous heart to move;
A grateful pity would have ruled her breast,
And my distresses would have made me blest.

"But she is gone, and ever has in view
Grandeur and state—and what will then ensue?
Surprise and then delight, in scenes so fair and new;
For many a day, perhaps for many a week,
Home will have charms, and to her bosom speak;
But thoughtless ease, and affluence and pride,
Seen day by day, will draw the heart aside:
And she at length, though gentle and sincere,
Will think no more of our enjoyments here."

Sighing he spake—but hark! he hears th' approach
Of rattling wheels! and lo! the evening coach
Once more the movement of the horses' feet
Makes the fond heart with strong emotion beat;
Faint were his hopes, but never had the sight
Drawn him to gaze beside his gate at night;
And when with rapid wheels it hurried by,
He grieved his parent with a hopeless sigh;
And could the blessing have been bought—what sum
Had he not offer'd, to have Jesse come!
She came—he saw her bending from the door,
Her face, her smile, and he beheld no more;
Lost in his joy—the mother lent her aid
T' assist and to detain the willing maid;
Who thought her late, her present home to make,
Sure of a welcome for the vicar's sake:
But the good parent was so pleased, so kind,
So pressing Colin, she so much inclined,
That night advanced; and then so long detain'd,
No wishes to depart she felt, or feign'd;
Yet long in doubt she stood, and then perforce remain'd.

Here was a lover fond, a friend sincere;
Here was content and joy, for she was here:
In the mild evening, in the scene around,
The maid, now free, peculiar beauties found;
Blended with village-tones, the evening-gale
Gave the sweet night-bird's warblings to the vale;
The youth embolden'd, yet abash'd, now told
His fondest wish, nor found the maiden cold;
The mother smiling whisper'd—"Let him go
And seek the license!" Jesse answer'd, "No:"
But Colin went. I know not if they live
With all the comforts wealth and plenty give:
But with pure joy to envious souls denied,
To suppliant meanness and suspicious pride;
And village-maids of happy couples say,
"They live like Jesse Bourn and Colin Grey."

TALE XIV.

THE STRUGGLES OF CONSCIENCE.

> I am a villain: yet I lie, I am not:
> Fool! of thyself speak well:—Fool! do not flatter.
> My Conscience hath a thousand several tongues,
> And every tongue brings in a several tale.
> *Richard III,* act v, scene 3.

> My Conscience is but a kind of hard Conscience. . . . The fiend gives the more friendly counsel.
> *Merchant of Venice,* act ii, scene 2.

> Thou hast it now—and I fear
> Thou play'dst most foully for it.
> *Macbeth,* act iii, scene 1.

> Canst thou not minister to a mind diseased,
> Pluck from the memory a rooted sorrow,
> Rase out the written troubles of the brain,
> And with some sweet oblivious antidote
> Cleanse the foul bosom of that perilous stuff
> Which weighs upon the heart?
> *Macbeth,* act v, scene 3.

> Soft! I did but dream—
> Oh! coward Conscience, how dost thou afflict me!
> *Richard III,* act v, scene 3.

A SERIOUS toyman in the city dwelt,
Who much concern for his religion felt;
Reading, he changed his tenets, read again,
And various questions could with skill maintain;
Papist and quaker if we set aside,
He had the road of every traveller tried;
There walk'd awhile, and on a sudden turn'd
Into some by-way he had just discern'd:
He had a nephew, Fulham—Fulham went
His uncle's way, with every turn content;
He saw his pious kinsman's watchful care,
And thought such anxious pains his own might spare,
And he, the truth obtain'd, without the toil, might share.
In fact, young Fulham, though he little read,
Perceived his uncle was by fancy led;
And smiled to see the constant care he took,
Collating creed with creed, and book with book.

At length the senior fix'd; I pass the sect
He call'd a church, 't was precious and elect;
Yet the seed fell not in the richest soil,
For few disciples paid the preacher's toil;
All in an attic-room were wont to meet,
These few disciples at their pastor's feet;
With these went Fulham, who, discreet and grave,
Follow'd the light his worthy uncle gave;
Till a warm preacher found a way t' impart
Awakening feelings to his torpid heart:
Some weighty truths, and of unpleasant kind,
Sank, though resisted, in his struggling mind;
He wish'd to fly them, but compell'd to stay,
Truth to the waking Conscience found her way;
For though the youth was call'd a prudent lad,
And prudent was, yet serious faults he had;
Who now reflected—"Much am I surprised,
I find these notions cannot be despised;
No! there is something I perceive at last,
Although my uncle cannot hold it fast;
Though I the strictness of these men reject,
Yet I determine to be circumspect:
This man alarms me, and I must begin
To look more closely to the things within;
These sons of zeal have I derided long,
But now begin to think the laughers wrong;
Nay, my good uncle, by all teachers moved,
Will be preferr'd to him who none approved;
Better to love amiss than nothing to have loved."

Such were his thoughts, when Conscience first began
To hold close converse with th' awaken'd man:
He from that time reserved and cautious grew,
And for his duties felt obedience due;
Pious he was not, but he fear'd the pain
Of sins committed, nor would sin again.
Whene'er he stray'd, he found his Conscience rose,
Like one determined what was ill t' oppose,
What wrong to accuse, what secret to disclose:
To drag forth every latent act to light,
And fix them fully in the actor's sight:
This gave him trouble, but he still confess'd
The labour useful, for it brought him rest.

The uncle died, and when the nephew read
The will, and saw the substance of the dead—
Five hundred guineas, with a stock in trade—
He much rejoiced, and thought his fortune made;
Yet felt aspiring pleasure at the sight,
And for increase, increasing appetite:
Desire of profit, idle habits check'd,
(For Fulham's virtue was to be correct);
He and his Conscience had their compact made—
"Urge me with truth, and you will soon persuade;
But not," he cried, "for mere ideal things
Give me to feel those terror-breeding stings."

"Let not such thoughts," she said, "your mind confound;
Trifles may wake me, but they never wound;
In them indeed there is a wrong and right,
But you will find me pliant and polite;
Not like a Conscience of the dotard kind,
Awake to dreams, to dire offences blind:
Let all within be pure, in all beside
Be your own master, governor, and guide;
Alive to danger, in temptation strong,
And I shall sleep our whole existence long."

"Sweet be thy sleep," said Fulham; "strong must be
The tempting ill that gains access to me:

Never will I to evil deed consent,
Or, if surprised, oh! how will I repent!
Should gain be doubtful, soon would I restore
The dangerous good, or give it to the poor,
Repose for them my growing wealth shall buy—
Or build—who knows?—an hospital like Guy?—
Yet why such means to soothe the smart within,
While firmly purposed to renounce the sin?"

Thus our young Trader and his Conscience dwelt
In mutual love, and great the joy they felt;
But yet in small concerns, in trivial things,
"She was," he said, "too ready with the stings;
And he too apt, in search of growing gains,
To lose the fear of penalties and pains:
Yet these were trifling bickerings, petty jars,
Domestic strifes, preliminary wars;"
He ventured little, little she express'd
Of indignation, and they both had rest.

Thus was he fix'd to walk the worthy way,
When profit urged him to a bold essay:—
A time was that when all at pleasure gamed
In lottery-chances, yet of law unblamed;
This Fulham tried: who would to him advance
A pound or crown, he gave in turn a chance
For weighty prize—and should they nothing share,
They had their crown or pound in Fulham's ware;
Thus the old stores within the shop were sold
For that which none refuses, new or old.
Was this unjust? yet Conscience could not rest,
But made a mighty struggle in the breast;
And gave th' aspiring man an early proof,
That should they war he would have work enough:
"Suppose," said she, "your vended numbers rise
The same with those which gain each real prize,
(Such your proposal), can you ruin shun?"
"A hundred thousand," he replied, "to one."
"Still it may happen:" "I the sum must pay."
"You know you cannot:" "I can run away."
"That is dishonest:"—"Nay, but you must wink
At a chance-hit; it cannot be, I think:
Upon my conduct as a whole decide,
Such trifling errors let my virtues hide;
Fail I at meeting? am I sleepy there?
My purse refuse I with the priest to share?
Do I deny the poor a helping hand?
Or stop the wicked women in the Strand?
Or drink at club beyond a certain pitch?
Which are your charges? Conscience, tell me which?"

"'T is well," said she, "but—" "Nay, I pray have done:
Trust me, I will not into danger run."

The lottery drawn, not one demand was made;
Fulham gain'd profit and increase of trade.
"See now," said he—for Conscience yet arose—
"How foolish 't is such measures to oppose:
Have I not blameless thus my state advanced?"—
"Still," mutter'd Conscience, "still it might have chanced."
'Might!" said our hero, "who is so exact
As to inquire what might have been a fact?"

Now Fulham's shop contains a curious view
Of costly trifles elegant and new:
The papers told where kind mammas might buy
The gayest toys to charm an infant's eye;
Where generous beaux might gentle damsels please
And travellers call who cross the land or seas,
And find the curious art, the neat device
Of precious value and of trifling price.

Here Conscience rested, she was pleased to find
No less an active than an honest mind;
But when he named the price, and when he swore
His conscience check'd him, that he ask'd no more
When half he sought had been a large increase
On fair demand, she could not rest in peace:
(Beside th' affront to call th' adviser in,
Who would prevent, to justify the sin?)
She therefore told him, that "he vainly tried
To soothe her anger, conscious that he lied;
If thus he grasp'd at such usurious gains,
He must deserve, and should expect her pains."

The charge was strong; he would in part confess
Offence there was—But, who offended less?
"What! is a mere assertion call'd a lie?
And if it be, are men compell'd to buy?
'T was strange that Conscience on such points should dwell,
While he was acting (he would call it) well:
He bought as others buy, he sold as others sell:
There was no fraud, and he demanded cause
Why he was troubled, when he kept the laws?"

"My laws?" said Conscience: "What," said he, "are thine?
"Oral or written, human or divine?
Show me the chapter, let me see the text;
By laws uncertain subjects are perplex'd:
Let me my finger on the statute lay,
And I shall feel it duty to obey."

"Reflect," said Conscience, "'t was your own desire
That I should warn you—does the compact tire?
Repent you this? then bid me not advise,
And rather hear your passions as they rise;
So you may counsel and remonstrance shun,
But then remember it was war begun;
And you may judge from some attacks, my friend,
What serious conflicts will on war attend."

"Nay, but," at length the thoughtful man replied,
"I say not that; I wish you for my guide;
Wish for your checks and your reproofs—but then
Be like a Conscience of my fellow-men;
Worthy I mean, and men of good report,
And not the wretches who with conscience sport:
There 's Bice, my friend, who passes off his grease
Of pigs for bears', in pots a crown a-piece;
His Conscience never checks him when he swears
The fat he sells is honest fat of bears;
And so it is, for he contrives to give
A drachm to each—'t is thus that tradesmen live:
Now why should you and I be over-nice;
What man is held in more repute than Bice?"

Here ended the dispute; but yet 't was plain
The parties both expected strife again:
Their friendship cool'd, he look'd about and saw
Numbers who seem'd unshackled by his awe;
While like a school-boy he was threaten'd still,
Now for the deed, now only for the will;

Here Conscience answer'd, "To thy neighbour's guide
Thy neighbour leave, and in thine own confide."

Such were each day the charges and replies,
When a new object caught the trader's eyes;
A vestry-patriot, could he gain the name,
Would famous make him, and would pay the fame:
He knew full well the sums bequeath'd in charge
For schools, for alms-men, for the poor, were large;
Report had told, and he could feel it true,
That most unfairly dealt the trusted few;
No partners would they in their office take,
Nor clear accounts at annual meetings make;
Aloud our hero in the vestry spoke
Of hidden deeds, and vow'd to draw the cloak;
It was the poor man's cause, and he for one
Was quite determined to see justice done:
His foes affected laughter, then disdain,
They too were loud and threat'ning, but in vain;
The pauper's friend, their foe, arose and spoke again:
Fiercely he cried, "Your garbled statements show
That you determine we shall nothing know;
But we shall bring your hidden crimes to light,
Give you to shame, and to the poor their right."

Virtue like this might some approval ask—
But Conscience sternly said, "You wear a mask!"
"At least," said Fulham, "If I have a view
To serve myself, I serve the public too."

Fulham, though check'd, retain'd his former zeal,
And this the cautious rogues began to feel:
"Thus will he ever bark," in peevish tone,
An elder cried—"the cur must have a bone:"
They then began to hint, and to begin
Was all they needed—it was felt within;
In terms less veil'd an offer then was made,
Though distant still, it fail'd not to persuade:
More plainly then was every point proposed,
Approved, accepted, and the bargain closed.
"Th' exulting paupers hail'd their friend's success,
And bade adieu to murmurs and distress."

Alas! their friend had now superior light,
And, view'd by that, he found that all was right;
"There were no errors, the disbursements small;
This was the truth, and truth was due to all."

And rested Conscience? No! she would not rest,
Yet was content with making a protest:
Some acts she now with less resistance bore,
Nor took alarm so quickly as before:
Like those in towns besieged, who every ball
At first with terror view, and dread them all,
But, grown familiar with the scenes, they fear
The danger less, as it approaches near;
So Conscience, more familiar with the view
Of growing evils, less attentive grew:
Yet he who felt some pain, and dreaded more,
Gave a peace-offering to the angry poor.

Thus had he quiet—but the time was brief,
From his new triumph sprang a cause of grief;
In office join'd, and acting with the rest,
He must admit the sacramental test:
Now, as a sectary, who had all his life,
As he supposed, been with the church at strife,
(No rules of hers, no laws had he perused,
Nor knew the tenets he by rote abused;)
Yet Conscience here arose more fierce and strong,
Than when she told of robbery and wrong;
"Change his religion! No! he must be sure
That was a blow no conscience could endure."

Though friend to virtue, yet she oft abides
In early notions, fix'd by erring guides;
And is more startled by a call from those,
Than when the foulest cries her rest oppose;
By error taught, by prejudice misled,
She yields her rights, and fancy rules instead;
When Conscience all her stings and terror deals,
Not as truth dictates, but as fancy feels:
And thus within our hero's troubled breast,
Crime was less torture than the odious test.
New forms, new measures, he must now embrace,
With sad conviction that they warr'd with grace;
To his new church no former friend would come,
They scarce preferr'd her to the church of Rome:
But thinking much, and weighing guilt and gain,
Conscience and he commuted for her pain;
Then promised Fulham to retain his creed,
And their peculiar paupers still to feed;
Their attic-room (in secret) to attend,
And not forget he was the preacher's friend;
Thus he proposed, and Conscience, troubled, tried,
And wanting peace, reluctantly complied.

Now care subdued, and apprehensions gone,
In peace our hero was aspiring on;
But short the period—soon a quarrel rose,
Fierce in the birth, and fatal in the close;
With times of truce between, which rather proved
That both were weary, than that either loved.

Fulham e'en now disliked the heavy thrall,
And for her death would in his anguish call,
As Rome's mistaken friend exclaim'd, *Let Carthage fall!*
So felt our hero, so his wish express'd,
Against this powerful sprite—*delenda est;*
Rome in her conquest saw not danger near,
Freed from her rival, and without a fear;
So, Conscience conquer'd, men perceive how free,
But not how fatal such a state must be.
Fatal not free our hero's; foe or friend,
Conscience on him was destined to attend:
She dozed indeed, grew dull, nor seem'd to spy
Crime following crime, and each of deeper dye;
But all were noticed, and the reckoning time
With her account came on—crime following crime.

This, once a foe, now brother in the trust,
Whom Fulham late described as fair and just,
Was the sole guardian of a wealthy maid,
Placed in his power, and of his frown afraid:
Not quite an idiot, for her busy brain
Sought, by poor cunning, trifling points to gain;
Success in childish projects her delight,
She took no heed of each important right.
The friendly parties met—the guardian cried,
"I am too old; my sons have each a bride:
Martha, my ward, would make an easy wife;
On easy terms I'll make her yours for life;
And then the creature is so weak and mild,
She may be soothed and threaten'd as a child:"—

"Yet not obey," said Fulham, "for your fools,
Female and male, are obstinate as mules."

Some points adjusted, these new friends agreed,
Proposed the day, and hurried on the deed.

"'T is a vile act," said Conscience:—"It will prove,"
Replied the bolder man, "an act of love;
Her wicked guardian might the girl have sold
To endless misery for a tyrant's gold;
Now may her life be happy—for I mean
To keep my temper even and serene."
"I cannot thus compound," the spirit cried,
"Nor have my laws thus broken and defied:
This is a fraud, a bargain for a wife;
Expect my vengeance, or amend your life."

The wife was pretty, trifling, childish, weak;
She could not think, but would not cease to speak:
This he forbad—she took the caution ill,
And boldly rose against his sovereign will;
With idiot-cunning she would watch the hour,
When friends were present, to dispute his power:
With tyrant-craft, he then was still and calm,
But raised in private terror and alarm:
By many trials, she perceived how far
To vex and tease, without an open war;
And he discover'd that so weak a mind
No art could lead, and no compulsion bind;
The rudest force would fail such mind to tame,
And she was callous to rebuke and shame;
Proud of her wealth, the power of law she knew,
And would assist him in the spending too:
His threat'ning words with insult she defied,
To all his reasoning with a stare replied;
And when he begg'd her to attend, would say,
"Attend I will—but let me have my way."

Nor rest had Conscience: "While you merit pain
From me," she said, "you seek redress in vain."
His thoughts were grievous: "All that I possess
From this wild bargain adds to my distress;
To pass a life with one who will not mend,
Who cannot love, nor save, nor wisely spend,
Is a vile prospect, and I see no end;
For if we part, I must of course restore
Much of her money, and must wed no more.

"Is there no way?"—here Conscience rose in power,
"Oh! fly the danger of this fatal hour;
I am thy Conscience, faithful, fond, and true,
Ah, fly this thought, or evil must ensue;
Fall on thy knees, and pray with all thy soul,
Thy purpose banish, thy design control;
Let every hope of such advantage cease,
Or never more expect a moment's peace."

Th' affrighten'd man a due attention paid,
Felt the rebuke, and the command obey'd.

Again the wife rebell'd, again express'd
A love for pleasure—a contempt of rest;
"She, whom she pleased, would visit, would receive
Those who pleased her, nor deign to ask for leave."

"One way there is," said he; "I might contrive
Into a trap this foolish thing to drive:
Who pleased her, said she?—I'll be certain who—"
"Take heed," said Conscience, "what thou mean'st to do:
Ensnare thy wife?"—"Why yes," he must confess,
"It might be wrong—but there was no redress;
Beside, to think," said he, "is not to sin."
"Mistaken man!" replied the power within.
No guest unnoticed to the lady came,
He judged th' event with mingled joy and shame;
Oft he withdrew, and seem'd to leave her free,
But still as watchful as a lynx was he;
Meanwhile the wife was thoughtless, cool, and gay,
And, without virtue, had no wish to stray.

Though thus opposed, his plans were not resign'd;
"Revenge," said he, "will prompt that daring mind:
Refused supplies, insulted and distress'd,
Enraged with me, and near a favourite guest—
Then will her vengeance prompt the daring deed,
And I shall watch, detect her, and be freed."

There was a youth—but let me hide the name,
With all the progress of this deed of shame;
He had his views—on him the husband cast
His net, and saw him in his trammels fast.

"Pause but a moment—think what you intend,"
Said the roused sleeper: "I am yet a friend:
Must all our days in enmity be spent?"
"No!" and he paused—"I surely shall repent:"
Then hurried on—the evil plan was laid,
The wife was guilty, and her friend betray'd,
And Fulham gain'd his wish, and for his will was paid.

Had crimes less weighty on the spirit press'd,
This troubled Conscience might have sunk to rest;
And, like a foolish guard, been bribed to peace,
By a false promise, that offence should cease;
Past faults had seem'd familiar to the view,
Confused if many, and obscure though true;
And Conscience, troubled with the dull account,
Had dropp'd her tale, and slumber'd o'er th' amount:
But, struck by daring guilt, alert she rose,
Disturb'd, alarm'd, and could no more repose;
All hopes of friendship, and of peace, were past,
And every view with gloom was overcast.
Hence from that day, that day of shame and sin,
Arose the restless enmity within;
On no resource could Fulham now rely,
Doom'd all expedients, and in vain, to try;
For Conscience, roused, sat boldly on her throne,
Watch'd every thought, attack'd the foe alone,
And with envenom'd sting drew forth the inward groan:
Expedients fail'd that brought relief before,
In vain his alms gave comfort to the poor,
Give what he would, to him the comfort came no more:
Not prayer avail'd, and when (his crimes confess'd)
He felt some ease—she said—"are they redress'd?
You still retain the profit, and be sure,
Long as it lasts, this anguish shall endure."

Fulham still tried to soothe her, cheat, mislead;
But Conscience laid her finger on the deed,
And read the crime with power, and all that must succeed:

He tried t' expel her, but was sure to find
Her strength increased by all that he design'd;
Nor ever was his groan more loud and deep,
Than when refresh'd she rose from momentary sleep.

Now desperate grown, weak, harass'd, and afraid,
From new allies he sought for doubtful aid;
To thought itself he strove to bid adieu,
And from devotion to diversions flew;
He took a poor domestic for a slave,
(Though Avarice grieved to see the price he gave;)
Upon his board, once frugal, press'd a load
Of viands rich, the appetite to goad;
The long-protracted meal, the sparkling cup,
Fought with his gloom, and kept his courage up:
Soon as the morning came, there met his eyes
Accounts of wealth, that he might reading rise;
To profit then he gave some active hours,
Till food and wine again should renovate his powers:
Yet, spite of all defence, of every aid,
The watchful foe her close attention paid:
In every thoughtful moment, on she press'd,
And gave at once her dagger to his breast;
He waked at midnight, and the fears of sin,
As waters, through a bursten dam, broke in;
Nay, in the banquet, with his friends around,
When all their cares and half their crimes were drown'd,
Would some chance act awake the slumbering fear,
And care and crime in all their strength appear:
The news is read, a guilty victim swings,
And troubled looks proclaim the bosom-stings;
Some pair are wed; this brings the wife in view,
And some divorced: this shows the parting too;
Nor can he hear of evil word or deed,
But they to thought, and thought to sufferings lead.

Such was his life—no other changes came,
The hurrying day, the conscious night the same;
The night of horror—when he starting cried,
To the poor startled sinner at his side;
"Is it in law? am I condemn'd to die?
Let me escape!——I'll give—oh! let me fly—
How! but a dream—no judges! dungeon! chain!
Or these grim men!—I will not sleep again.—
Wilt thou, dread being! thus thy promise keep?
Day is thy time—and wilt thou murder sleep?
Sorrow and want repose, and wilt thou come,
Nor give one hour of pure untroubled gloom?

"Oh! Conscience! Conscience! man's most faithful friend,
Him canst thou comfort, ease, relieve, defend;
But if he will thy friendly checks forego,
Thou art, oh! woe for me, his deadliest foe!"

TALE XV.

ADVICE; OR, THE 'SQUIRE AND THE PRIEST.

His hours fill'd up with riots, banquets, sports,——
And never noted him in any study,
Any retirement, any sequestration.
Henry V, act i, scene 1.

I will converse with iron-witted fools,
With unrespective boys; none are for me,
Who look into me with considerate eyes.
Richard III, act iv, scene 2.

You cram these words into mine ears, against
The stomach of my sense.
Tempest, act ii, scene 1.

A wealthy lord of far-extended land
Had all that pleased him placed at his command;
Widow'd of late, but finding much relief
In the world's comforts, he dismiss'd his grief;
He was by marriage of his daughters eased,
And knew his sons could marry if they pleased;
Meantime in travel he indulged the boys,
And kept no spy nor partner of his joys.

These joys, indeed, were of the grosser kind,
That fed the cravings of an earthly mind;
A mind that, conscious of its own excess,
Felt the reproach his neighbours would express.
Long at th' indulgent board he loved to sit,
Where joy was laughter, and profaneness wit;
And such the guest and manners of the hall,
No wedded lady on the 'squire would call:
Here reign'd a favourite, and her triumph gain'd
O'er other favourites who before had reign'd;
Reserved and modest seem'd the nymph to be,
Knowing her lord was charm'd with modesty;
For he, a sportsman keen, the more enjoy'd,
The greater value had the thing destroy'd.

Our 'squire declared, that, from a wife released,
He would no more give trouble to a priest;
Seem'd it not, then, ungrateful and unkind,
That he should trouble from the priesthood find?
The church he honour'd, and he gave the due
And full respect to every son he knew:
But envied those who had the luck to meet
A gentle pastor, civil and discreet;
Who never bold and hostile sermon penn'd,
To wound a sinner, or to shame a friend;
One whom no being either shunn'd or fear'd,
Such must be loved wherever they appear'd.

Not such the stern old rector of the time,
Who soothed no culprit, and who spared no crime;
Who would his fears and his contempt express
For irreligion and licentiousness;
Of him our village lord, his guests among,
By speech vindictive proved his feelings stung.

"Were he a bigot," said the 'squire, "whose zeal
Condemn'd us all, I should disdain to feel:
But when a man of parts, in college train'd,
Prates of our conduct—who would not be pain'd?
While he declaims (where no one dares reply)
On men abandon'd, grov'ling in the sty
(Like beasts in human shape) of shameless luxury
Yet with a patriot's zeal I stand the shock
Of vile rebuke, example to his flock:
But let this rector, thus severe and proud,
Change his wide surplice for a narrow shroud,
And I will place within his seat a youth,
Train'd by the Graces, to explain the truth;
Then shall the flock with gentle hand be led,
By wisdom won, and by compassion fed."

This purposed teacher was a sister's son,
Who of her children gave the priesthood one,

And she had early train'd for this employ
The pliant talents of her college-boy:
At various times her letters painted all
Her brother's views—the manners of the hall;
The rector's harshness, and the mischief made
By chiding those whom preachers should persuade:
This led the youth to views of easy life,
A friendly patron, an obliging wife;
His tithe, his glebe, the garden and the steed,
With books as many as he wish'd to read.

All this accorded with the uncle's will;
He loved a priest compliant, easy, still;
Sums he had often to his favourite sent,
"To be," he wrote, "in manly freedom spent;
For well it pleased his spirit to assist
An honest lad, who scorn'd a Methodist:"
His mother too, in her maternal care,
Bade him of canting hypocrites beware;
Who from his duties would his heart seduce,
And make his talents of no earthly use.

Soon must a trial of his worth be made—
The ancient priest is to the tomb convey'd;
And the youth summon'd from a serious friend
His guide and host, new duties to attend.

Three months before, the nephew and the 'squire
Saw mutual worth to praise and to admire;
And though the one too early left his wine,
The other still exclaim'd—"My boy will shine:
Yes, I perceive that he will soon improve,
And I shall form the very guide I love;
Decent abroad, he will my name defend,
And, when at home, be social and unbend."

The plan was specious, for the mind of James
Accorded duly with his uncle's schemes:
He then aspired not to a higher name
Than sober clerks of moderate talents claim;
Gravely to pray, and rev'rendly to preach,
Was all he saw, good youth! within his reach:
Thus may a mass of sulphur long abide,
Cold and inert, but to the flame applied,
Kindling it blazes, and consuming turns
To smoke and poison, as it boils and burns.

James, leaving college, to a preacher stray'd;
What call'd, he knew not—but the call obey'd:
Mild, idle, pensive, ever led by those
Who could some specious novelty propose;
Humbly he listen'd, while the preacher dwelt
On touching themes, and strong emotions felt;
And in this night was fix'd that pliant will
To one sole point, and he retains it still.

At first his care was to himself confined;
Himself assured, he gave it to mankind:
His zeal grew active—honest, earnest zeal,
And comfort dealt to him, he long'd to deal;
He to his favourite preacher now withdrew,
Was taught to teach, instructed to subdue;
And train'd for ghostly warfare, when the call
Of his new duties reach'd him from the hall.

Now to the 'squire, although alert and stout,
Came unexpected an attack of gout;
And the grieved patron felt such serious pain,
He never thought to see a church again:
Thrice had the youthful rector taught the crowd,
Whose growing numbers spoke his powers aloud,
Before the patron could himself rejoice
(His pain still lingering) in the general voice;
For he imputed all this early fame
To graceful manner, and the well-known name;
And to himself assumed a share of praise,
For worth and talents he was pleased to raise.

A month had flown, and with it fled disease;
What pleased before, began again to please;
Emerging daily from his chamber's gloom,
He found his old sensations hurrying home;
Then call'd his nephew, and exclaim'd, "My boy,
Let us again the balm of life enjoy;
The foe has left me, and I deem it right,
Should he return, to arm me for the fight."

Thus spoke the 'squire, the favourite nymph stood by,
And view'd the priest with insult in her eye:
She thrice had heard him when he boldly spoke
On dangerous points, and fear'd he would revoke:
For James she loved not—and her manner told,
"This warm affection will be quickly cold:"
And still she feared impression might be made
Upon a subject, nervous and decay'd;
She knew her danger, and had no desire
Of reformation in the gallant 'squire;
And felt an envious pleasure in her breast
To see the rector daunted and distress'd.

Again the uncle to the youth applied—
"Cast, my dear lad, that cursed gloom aside:
There are for all things time and place; appear
Grave in your pulpit, and be merry here:
Now take your wine—for woes a sure resource,
And the best prelude to a long discourse."

James half obey'd, but cast an angry eye
On the fair lass, who still stood watchful by;
Resolving thus, "I have my fears—but still
I must perform my duties, and I will:
No love, no interest, shall my mind control;
Better to lose my comforts than my soul;
Better my uncle's favour to abjure,
Than the upbraidings of my heart endure."

He took his glass, and then address'd the 'squire
"I feel not well, permit me to retire."
The 'squire conceived that the ensuing day
Gave him these terrors for the grand essay,
When he himself should this young preacher try,
And stand before him with observant eye;
This raised compassion in his manly breast,
And he would send the rector to his rest:
Yet first, in soothing voice—"A moment stay,
And these suggestions of a friend obey;
Treasure these hints, if fame or peace you prize—
The bottle emptied, I shall close my eyes.

"On every priest a two-fold care attends,
To prove his talents, and insure his friends;
First, of the first—your stores at once produce,
And bring your reading to its proper use:
On doctrines dwell, and every point enforce
By quoting much, the scholar's sure resource;
For he alone can show us on each head
What ancient schoolmen and sage fathers said.
No worth has knowedge, if you fail to show
How well you studied, and how much you know:

Is faith your subject, and you judge it right
On theme so dark to cast a ray of light?
Be it that faith the orthodox maintain,
Found in the rubrick, what the creeds explain;
Fail not to show us on this ancient faith
(And quote the passage) what some martyr saith:
Dwell not one moment on a faith that shocks
The minds of men sincere and orthodox;
That gloomy faith, that robs the wounded mind
Of all the comfort it was wont to find
From virtuous acts, and to the soul denies
Its proper due for alms and charities;
That partial faith, that, weighing sins alone,
Lets not a virtue for a fault atone;
That starving faith, that would our tables clear,
And make one dreadful Lent of all the year;
And cruel too, for this is faith that rends
Confiding beauties from protecting friends;
A faith that all embracing, what a gloom
Deep and terrific o'er the land would come!
What scenes of horror would that time disclose!
No sight but misery, and no sound but woes;
Your noble faith, in loftier style convey'd,
Shall be with praise and admiration paid:
On points like these your hearers all admire
A preacher's depth, and nothing more require;
Shall we a studious youth to college send,
That every clown his words may comprehend?
'T is for your glory, when your hearers own
Your learning matchless, but the sense unknown.

"Thus honour gain'd, learn now to gain a friend,
And the sure way is—never to offend;
For, James, consider—what your neighbours do
Is their own business, and concerns not you:
Shun all resemblance to that forward race
Who preach of sins before a sinner's face;
And seem as if they overlook'd a pew,
Only to drag a failing man in view:
Much should I feel, when groaning in disease,
If a rough hand upon my limb should seize;
But great my anger, if this hand were found
The very doctor's, who should make it sound:
So feel our minds, young priest, so doubly feel,
When hurt by those whose office is to heal.

"Yet of our duties you must something tell,
And must at times on sin and frailty dwell;
Here you may preach in easy, flowing style,
How errors cloud us, and how sins defile:
Here bring persuasive tropes and figures forth,
To show the poor that wealth is nothing worth;
That they, in fact, possess an ample share
Of the world's good, and feel not half its care;
Give them this comfort, and, indeed, my gout
In its full vigour causes me some doubt;
And let it always, for your zeal, suffice,
That vice you combat, in the abstract—vice:
The very captious will be quiet then;
We all confess we are offending men:
In lashing sin, of every stroke beware,
For sinners feel, and sinners you must spare;
In general satire, every man perceives
A slight attack, yet neither fears nor grieves;
But name th' offence, and you absolve the rest,
And point the dagger at a single breast.

"Yet are there sinners of a class so low,
That you with safety may the lash bestow;
Poachers, and drunkards, idle rogues, who feed
At others' cost, a mark'd correction need:
And all the better sort, who see your zeal,
Will love and reverence for their pastor feel;
Reverence for one who can inflict the smart,
And love, because he deals them not a part.

"Remember well what love and age advise;
A quiet rector is a parish prize,
Who in his learning has a decent pride;
Who to his people is a gentle guide;
Who only hints at failings that he sees;
Who loves his glebe, his patron, and his ease,
And finds the way to fame and profit is to please."

The nephew answer'd not, except a sigh
And look of sorrow might be term'd reply;
He saw the fearful hazard of his state,
And held with truth and safety strong debate;
Nor long he reason'd, for the zealous youth
Resolved, though timid, to profess the truth;
And though his friend should like a lion roar,
Truth would he preach, and neither less nor more.

The bells had toll'd—arrived the time of prayer,
The flock assembled, and the 'squire was there:
And now can poet sing, or proseman say,
The disappointment of that trying day?

As he who long had train'd a favourite steed
(Whose blood and bone gave promise of his speed),
Sanguine with hope, he runs with partial eye
O'er every feature, and his bets are high;
Of triumph sure, he sees the rivals start,
And waits their coming with exulting heart;
Forestalling glory, with impatient glance,
And sure to see his conquering steed advance;
The conquering steed advances—luckless day!
A rival's Herod bears the prize away.
Nor second his, nor third, but lagging last,
With hanging head he comes, by all surpass'd:
Surprise and wrath the owner's mind inflame,
Love turns to scorn, and glory ends in shame;—
Thus waited, high in hope, the partial 'squire,
Eager to hear, impatient to admire:
When the young preacher in the tones that find
A certain passage to the kindling mind,
With air and accent strange, impressive, sad,
Alarm'd the judge—he trembled for the lad;
But when the text announced the power of grace,
Amazement scowl'd upon his clouded face,
At this degenerate son of his illustrious race;
Staring he stood, till hope again arose,
That James might well define the words he chose.
For this he listen'd—but, alas! he found
The preacher always on forbidden ground.

And now the uncle left the hated pew,
With James, and James's conduct in his view.
A long farewell to all his favourite schemes!
For now no crazed fanatic's frantic dreams
Seem'd vile as James's conduct, or as James:
All he had long derided, hated, fear'd,
This from the chosen youth the uncle heard,
The needless pause, the fierce disorder'd air,
The groan for sin, the vehemence of prayer,
Gave birth to wrath, that, in a long discourse
Of grace triumphant, rose to four-fold force,

He found his thoughts despised, his rules transgress'd,
And while the anger kindled in his breast,
The pain must be endured that could not be express'd:
Each new idea more inflamed his ire,
As fuel thrown upon a rising fire:
A hearer yet, he sought by threatening sign
To ease his heart, and awe the young divine;
But James refused those angry looks to meet,
Till he dismiss'd his flock, and left his seat:
Exhausted then he felt his trembling frame,
But fix'd his soul—his sentiments the same;
And therefore wise it seem'd to fly from rage,
And seek for shelter in his parsonage:
There, if forsaken, yet consoled to find
Some comforts left though not a few resign'd;
There, if he lost an erring parent's love,
An honest conscience must the cause approve;
If the nice palate were no longer fed,
The mind enjoy'd delicious thoughts instead;
And if some part of earthly good was flown,
Still was the tithe of ten good farms his own.

Fear now, and discord, in the village reign,
The cool remonstrate, and the meek complain;
But there is war within, and wisdom pleads in vain:
Now dreads the uncle, and proclaims his dread,
Lest the boy-priest should turn each rustic head;
The certain converts cost him certain wo,
The doubtful fear lest they should join the foe:
Matrons of old, with whom he used to joke,
Now pass his Honour with a pious look;
Lasses, who met him once with lively airs,
Now cross his way, and gravely walk to prayers:
An old companion, whom he long has loved,
By coward fears confess'd his conscience moved;
As the third bottle gave its spirit forth,
And they bore witness to departed worth,
The friend arose, and he too would depart:—
"Man," said the 'squire, "thou wert not wont to start;
Hast thou attended to that foolish boy,
Who would abridge all comforts, or destroy?"

Yes, he had listen'd, who had slumber'd long,
And was convinced that something must be wrong:
But, though affected, still his yielding heart,
And craving palate, took the uncle's part;
Wine now oppress'd him, who, when free from wine,
Could seldom clearly utter his design;
But though by nature and indulgence weak,
Yet, half converted, he resolved to speak;
And, speaking, own'd, "that in his mind the youth
Had gifts and learning, and that truth was truth:
The 'squire he honour'd, and, for his poor part,
He hated nothing like a hollow heart:
But 't was a maxim he had often tried,
That right was right, and there he would abide;
He honour'd learning, and he would confess
The preacher had his talents—more or less:
Why not agree? he thought the young divine
Had no such strictness—they might drink and dine;
For them sufficient—but he said before,—
That truth was truth, and he would drink no more."

This heard the 'squire with mix'd contempt and pain;
He fear'd the priest this recreant sot would gain.
The favourite nymph, though not a convert made,
Conceived the man she scorn'd her cause would aid;
And when the spirits of her lord were low,
The lass presumed the wicked cause to show:
"It was the wretched life his honour led,
And would draw vengeance on his guilty head;
Their loves (Heav'n knew how dreadfully distress'd
The thought had made her!) were as yet unbless'd:
And till the church had sanction'd"—Here she saw
The wrath that forced her trembling to withdraw.

Add to these outward ills, some inward light,
That show'd him all was not correct and right:
Though now he less indulged—and to the poor,
From day to day, sent alms from door to door;
Though he some ease from easy virtues found,
Yet conscience told him he could not compound;
But must himself the darling sin deny,
Change the whole heart—but here a heavy sigh
Proclaim'd, "How vast the toil! and ah! how weak am I!"

James too has trouble—he divided sees
A parish, once harmonious and at ease:
With him united are the simply meek,
The warm, the sad, the nervous, and the weak;
The rest his uncle's save the few beside
Who own no doctrine, and obey no guide;
With stragglers of each adverse camp, who lend
Their aid to both, but each in turn offend.

Though zealous still, yet he begins to feel
The heat too fierce, that glows in vulgar zeal;
With pain he hears his simple friends relate
Their week's experience, and their woful state:
With small temptation struggling every hour,
And bravely battling with the tempting power;
His native sense is hurt by strange complaints
Of inward motions in these warring saints;
Who never cast on sinful bait a look
But they perceive the devil at the hook:
Grieved, yet compell'd to smile, he finds it hard
Against the blunders of conceit to guard;
He sighs to hear the jests his converts cause,
He cannot give their erring zeal applause;
But finds it inconsistent to condemn
The flights and follies he has nursed in them:
These, in opposing minds, contempt produce,
Or mirth occasion, or provoke abuse;
On each momentous theme disgrace they bring,
And give to Scorn her poison and her sting.

TALE XVI.

THE CONFIDANT.

Think'st thou I'd make a life of jealousy,
To follow still the changes of the moon,
With fresh suspicion?

Othello, act iii, scene 3

Why hast thou lost the fresh blood in thy cheeks,
And given my treasure and my rights in thee
To thick-eyed musing and cursed melancholy?

Henry IV, Part 1, act ii, scene 3.

It is excellent
To have a giant's strength, but tyrannous
To use it as a giant.

Measure for Measure, act ii, scene 2.

Anna was young and lovely—in her eye
The glance of beauty, in her cheek the dye;
Her shape was slender, and her features small,
But graceful, easy, unaffected all:
The liveliest tints her youthful face disclosed;
There beauty sparkled, and there health reposed;
For the pure blood that flush'd that rosy cheek
Spoke what the heart forbad the tongue to speak;
And told the feelings of that heart as well,
Nay, with more candour than the tongue could tell:
Though this fair lass had with the wealthy dwelt,
Yet like the damsel of the cot she felt;
And, at the distant hint or dark surmise,
The blood into the mantling cheek would rise.

Now Anna's station frequent terrors wrought
In one whose looks were with such meaning fraught;
For on a lady, as an humble friend,
It was her painful office to attend.

Her duties here were of the usual kind—
And some the body harass'd, some the mind:
Billets she wrote, and tender stories read,
To make the lady sleepy in her bed;
She play'd at whist, but with inferior skill,
And heard the summons as a call to drill;
Music was ever pleasant till she play'd
At a request that no request convey'd;
The lady's tales with anxious looks she heard,
For she must witness what her friend averr'd;
The lady's taste she must in all approve,
Hate whom she hated, whom she loved must love:
These with the various duties of her place,
With care she studied, and perform'd with grace;
She veil'd her troubles in a mask of ease,
And show'd her pleasure was a power to please.

Such were the damsel's duties; she was poor—
Above a servant, but with service more:
Men on her face with careless freedom gazed,
Nor thought how painful was the glow they raised;
A wealthy few to gain her favour tried,
But not the favour of a grateful bride:
They spoke their purpose with an easy air,
That shamed and frighten'd the dependent fair;
Past time she view'd, the passing time to cheat,
But nothing found to make the present sweet;
With pensive soul she read life's future page,
And saw dependent, poor, repining age.

But who shall dare t' assert what *years* may bring,
When wonders from the passing *hour* may spring?
There dwelt a yeoman in the place, whose mind
Was gentle, generous, cultivated, kind;
For thirty years he labour'd; fortune then
Placed the mild rustic with superior men:
A richer Stafford who had lived to save,
What he had treasured to the poorer gave;
Who with a sober mind that treasure view'd,
And the slight studies of his youth renew'd:
He not profoundly, but discreetly read,
And a fair mind with useful culture fed;
Then thought of marriage—"But the great," said he,
"I shall not suit, nor will the meaner me;"
Anna he saw, admired her modest air;
He thought her virtuous, and he knew her fair;
Love raised his pity for her humble state,
And prompted wishes for her happier fate;
No pride in money would his feelings wound,
Nor vulgar manners hurt him and confound:
He then the lady at the hall address'd,
Sought her consent, and his regard express'd;
Yet if some cause his earnest wish denied,
He begg'd to know it, and he bow'd and sigh'd.

The lady own'd that she was loth to part,
But praised the damsel for her gentle heart,
Her pleasing person, and her blooming health;
But ended thus, "Her virtue is her wealth."

"Then is she rich!" he cried, with lively air;
"But whence, so please you, came a lass so fair?"

"A placeman's child was Anna, one who died
And left a widow by afflictions tried;
She to support her infant daughter strove,
But early left the object of her love;
Her youth, her beauty, and her orphan-state
Gave a kind countess interest in her fate;
With her she dwelt, and still might dwelling be,
When the earl's folly caused the lass to flee;
A second friend was she compell'd to shun
By the rude offers of an uncheck'd son;
I found her then, and with a mother's love
Regard the gentle girl whom you approve;
Yet, e'en with me protection is not peace,
Nor man's designs, nor beauty's trial, cease;
Like sordid boys by costly fruit they feel,
They will not purchase, but they try to steal."

Now this good lady, like a witness true,
Told but the truth, and all the truth she knew;
And 't is our duty and our pain to show
Truth this good lady had not means to know.
Yes, there was lock'd within the damsel's breast
A fact important to be now confess'd;
Gently, my muse, th' afflicting tale relate,
And have some feeling for a sister's fate.

Where Anna dwelt, a conquering hero came,—
An Irish captain, Sedley was his name;
And he too had that same prevailing art,
That gave soft wishes to the virgin's heart;
In years they differ'd; he had thirty seen
When this young beauty counted just fifteen;
But still they were a lovely lively pair,
And trod on earth as if they trod on air.

On love, delightful theme! the captain dwelt,
With force still growing with the hopes he felt,
But with some caution and reluctance told,
He had a father crafty, harsh, and old;
Who, as possessing much, would much expect,
Or both, for ever, from his love reject:
Why then offence to one so powerful give,
Who (for their comfort) had not long to live?

With this poor prospect the deluded maid,
In words confiding, was indeed betray'd;
And, soon as terrors in her bosom rose,
The hero fled; they hinder'd his repose.
Deprived of him, she to a parent's breast
Her secrets trusted, and her pains express'd:
Let her to town (so prudence urged) repair,
To shun disgrace, at least to hide it there,

But ere she went, the luckless damsel pray'd
A chosen friend might lend her kindly aid:
"Yes; my soul's sister, my Eliza, come,
Hear her last sigh, and ease thy Anna's doom:"
"'T is a fool's wish," the angry father cried,
But, lost in troubles of his own, complied:
And dear Eliza to her friend was sent,
T' indulge that wish, and be her punishment;
The time arrived, and brought a tenfold dread;
The time was past, and all the terror fled;
The infant died; the face resumed each charm,
And reason now brought trouble and alarm:
"Should her Eliza—no! she was too just,
Too good and kind—but ah! too young to trust."
Anna return'd, her former place resumed,
And faded beauty with new grace re-bloom'd,
And if some whispers of the past were heard,
They died innoxious, as no cause appear'd;
But other cares on Anna's bosom press'd,
She saw her father gloomy and distress'd;
He died o'erwhelm'd with debt, and soon was shed
The filial sorrow o'er a mother dead:
She sought Eliza's arms, that faithful friend was
wed;
Then was compassion by the countess shown,
And all th' adventures of her life are known.

And now beyond her hopes—no longer tried
By slavish awe—she lived a yeoman's bride;
Then bless'd her lot, and with a grateful mind
Was careful, cheerful, vigilant, and kind:
The gentle husband felt supreme delight,
Bless'd by her joy, and happy in her sight;
He saw with pride in every friend and guest
High admiration and regard express'd:
With greater pride, and with superior joy,
He look'd exulting on his first-born boy:
To her fond breast the wife her infant strain'd,
Some feelings utter'd, some were not explain'd;
And she enraptured with her treasure grew,
The sight familiar, but the pleasure new.

Yet there appear'd within that tranquil state
Some threat'ning prospect of uncertain fate;
Between the married when a secret lies,
It wakes suspicion from enforced disguise;
Still thought the wife upon her absent friend,
With all that must upon her truth depend;
"There is no being in the world beside,
Who can discover what that friend will hide;
Who knew the fact, knew not my name or state,
Who these can tell can not the fact relate;
But thou, Eliza, canst the whole impart,
And all my safety is thy generous heart."

Mix'd with these fears—but light and transient
these—
Fled years of peace, prosperity, and ease:
So tranquil all that scarce a gloomy day
For days of gloom unmix'd prepared the way;
One eve, the wife, still happy in her state,
Sang gaily, thoughtless of approaching fate:
Then came a letter, that (received in dread
Not unobserved) she in confusion read;
The substance this—"Her friend rejoiced to find
That she had riches with a grateful mind;
While poor Eliza had from place to place
Been lured by hope to labour for disgrace;
That every scheme her wandering husband tried,
Pain'd while he lived, and perish'd when he died."
She then of want in angry style complain'd,
Her child a burden to her life remain'd,
Her kindred shunn'd her prayers, no friend her
soul sustain'd.

"Yet why neglected? Dearest Anna knew
Her worth once tried, her friendship ever true;
She hoped, she trusted, though by wants oppress'd,
To lock the treasured secret in her breast;
Yet, vex'd by trouble, must apply to one,
For kindness due to her for kindness done."

In Anna's mind was tumult, in her face
Flushings of dread had momentary place:
"I must," she judged, "these cruel lines expose,
Or fears, or worse than fears, my crime disclose."

The letter shown, he said, with sober smile—
"Anna, your friend has not a friendly style:
Say, where could you with this fair lady dwell,
Who boasts of secrets that she scorns to tell?"
"At school," she answer'd: he "at school!" replied;
"Nay, then I know the secrets you would hide:
Some longings these, without dispute,
Some youthful gaspings for forbidden fruit;
Why so disorder'd, love? are such the crimes
That give us sorrow in our graver times?
Come, take a present for your friend, and rest
In perfect peace—you find you are confess'd."

This cloud, though past, alarm'd the conscious
wife,
Presaging gloom and sorrow for her life;
Who to her answer join'd a fervent prayer,
That her Eliza would a sister spare:
If she again—but was there cause?—should send,
Let her direct—and then she named a friend:
A sad expedient untried friends to trust,
And still to fear the tried may be unjust:
Such is his pain, who, by his debt oppress'd,
Seeks by new bonds a temporary rest.

Few were her peaceful days till Anna read
The words she dreaded, and had cause to dread:—

"Did she believe, did she, unkind, suppose
That thus Eliza's friendship was to close?
No! though she tried, and her desire was plain,
To break the friendly bond, she strove in vain:
Ask'd she for silence? why so loud the call,
And yet the token of her love so small?
By means like these will you attempt to bind
And check the movements of an injured mind?
Poor as I am, I shall be proud to show
What dangerous secrets I may safely know:
Secrets to men of jealous minds convey'd,
Have many a noble house in ruins laid:
Anna, I trust, although with wrongs beset,
And urged by want, I shall be faithful yet;
But what temptation may from these arise,
To take a slighted woman by surprise,
Becomes a subject for your serious care—
For who offends, must for offence prepare."

Perplex'd, dismay'd, the wife foresaw her doom
A day deferr'd was yet a day to come;
But still, though painful her suspended state,
She dreaded more the crisis of her fate;

Better to die than Stafford's scorn to meet,
And her strange friend perhaps would be discreet:
Presents she sent, and made a strong appeal
To woman's feelings, begging her to feel;
With too much force she wrote of jealous men,
And her tears falling spoke beyond her pen;
Eliza's silence she again implored,
And promised all that prudence could afford.

For looks composed and careless Anna tried;
She seem'd in trouble, and unconscious sigh'd:
The faithful husband, who devoutly loved
His silent partner, with concern reproved:
"What secret sorrows on my Anna press,
That love may not partake, nor care redress?"
"None, none," she answer'd, with a look so kind,
That the fond man determined to be blind.

A few succeeding weeks of brief repose
In Anna's cheek revived the faded rose;
A hue like this the western sky displays,
That glows awhile, and withers as we gaze.

Again the friend's tormenting letter came—
"The wants she suffer'd were affection's shame;
She with her child a life of terrors led,
Unhappy fruit! but of a lawful bed:
Her friend was tasting every bliss in life,
The joyful mother, and the wealthy wife;
While she was placed in doubt, in fear, in want,
To starve on trifles that the happy grant;
Poorly for all her faithful silence paid,
And tantalized by ineffectual aid:
She could not thus a beggar's lot endure;
She wanted something permanent and sure:
If they were friends, then equal be their lot,
And she was free to speak if they were not."

Despair and terror seized the wife, to find
The artful workings of a vulgar mind:
Money she had not, but the hint of dress
Taught her new bribes, new terrors to redress:
She with such feeling then described her woes,
That envy's self might on the view repose;
Then to a mother's pains she made appeal,
And painted grief like one compell'd to feel.

Yes! so she felt, that in her air, her face,
In every purpose, and in every place;
In her slow motion, in her languid mien,
The grief, the sickness of her soul were seen.

Of some mysterious ill the husband sure,
Desired to trace it, for he hoped to cure;
Something he knew obscurely, and had seen
His wife attend a cottage on the green;
Love, loth to wound, endured conjecture long,
Till fear would speak, and spoke in language strong.

"All I must know, my Anna—truly know
Whence these emotions, terrors, troubles flow;
Give me thy grief, and I will fairly prove
Mine is no selfish, no ungenerous love."

Now Anna's soul the seat of strife became,
Fear with respect contended, love with shame;
But fear prevailing was the ruling guide,
Prescribing what to show and what to hide.

"It is my friend," she said—"But why disclose
A woman's weakness struggling with her woes?
Yes, she has grieved me by her fond complaints,
The wrongs she suffers, the distress she paints:
Something we do—but she afflicts me still,
And says, with power to help, I want the will;
This plaintive style I pity and excuse,
Help when I can, and grieve when I refuse;
But here my useless sorrows I resign,
And will be happy in a love like thine."
The husband doubted; he was kind but cool:—
"'T is a strong friendship to arise at school;
Once more then, love, once more the sufferer aid,—
I too can pity, but I must upbraid;
Of these vain feelings then thy bosom free,
Nor be o'erwhelm'd by useless sympathy."

The wife again despatch'd the useless bribe,
Again essay'd her terrors to describe;
Again with kindest words entreated peace,
And begg'd her offerings for a time might cease.

A calm succeeded, but too like the one
That causes terror ere the storm comes on:
A secret sorrow lived in Anna's heart,
In Stafford's mind a secret fear of art;
Not long they lasted—this determined foe
Knew all her claims, and nothing would forego;
Again her letter came, where Anna read,
"My child, one cause of my distress, is dead:
Heav'n has my infant:" "Heartless wretch!" she cried,
"Is this thy joy?" "I am no longer tied;
Now will I, hast'ning to my friend, partake
Her cares and comforts, and no more forsake;
Now shall we both in equal station move,
Save that my friend enjoys a husband's love."

Complaint and threats so strong the wife amazed,
Who wildly on her cottage-neighbour gazed;
Her tones, her trembling, first betray'd her grief;
When floods of tears gave anguish its relief.

She fear'd that Stafford would refuse assent,
And knew her selfish friend would not relent;
She must petition, yet delay'd the task,
Ashamed, afraid, and yet compell'd to ask;
Unknown to him some object fill'd her mind,
And, once suspicious, he became unkind:
They sate one evening, each absorb'd in gloom,
When, hark! a noise, and, rushing to the room,
The friend tripp'd lightly in, and laughing said,
"I come."

Anna received her with an anxious mind,
And meeting whisper'd, "Is Eliza kind?"
Reserved and cool, the husband sought to prove
The depth and force of this mysterious love.
To nought that pass'd between the stranger-friend
And his meek partner seem'd he to attend;
But, anxious, listen'd to the lightest word
That might some knowledge of his guest afford;
And learn the reason one to him so dear
Should feel such fondness, yet betray such fear.

Soon he perceived this uninvited guest,
Unwelcome too, a sovereign power possess'd;
Lofty she was and careless, while the meek
And humbled Anna was afraid to speak:
As mute she listen'd with a painful smile,
Her friend sate laughing and at ease the while,

Telling her idle tales with all the glee
Of careless and unfeeling levity.
With calm good sense he knew his wife endued,
And now with wounded pride her conduct view'd;
Her speech was low, her every look convey'd—
"I am a slave, subservient and afraid."
All trace of comfort vanish'd if she spoke,
The noisy friend upon her purpose broke;
To her remarks with insolence replied,
And her assertions doubted or denied;
While the meek Anna like an infant shook,
Woe-struck and trembling at the serpent's look.

"There is," said Stafford, "yes, there is a cause—
This creature frights her, overpowers and awes."
Six weeks had pass'd—"In truth, my love, this friend
Has liberal notions; what does she intend?
Without a hint she came, and will she stay
Till she receives the hint to go away?"

Confused the wife replied, in spite of truth,
"I love the dear companion of my youth."
"'T is well," said Stafford; "then your loves renew;
Trust me, your rivals, Anna, will be few."

Though playful this, she felt too much distress'd
T' admit the consolation of a jest;
Ill she reposed, and in her dreams would sigh,
And, murmuring forth her anguish, beg to die;
With sunken eye, slow pace, and pallid cheek,
She look'd confusion, and she fear'd to speak.

All this the friend beheld, for, quick of sight,
She knew the husband eager for her flight;
And that by force alone she could retain
The lasting comforts she had hope to gain:
She now perceived, to win her post for life,
She must infuse fresh terrors in the wife;
Must bid to friendship's feebler ties adieu,
And boldly claim the object in her view:
She saw the husband's love, and knew the power
Her friend might use in some propitious hour.

Meantime the anxious wife, from pure distress
Assuming courage, said, "I will confess;"
But with her children felt a parent's pride,
And sought once more the hated truth to hide.

Offended, grieved, impatient, Stafford bore
The odious change till he could bear no more;
A friend to truth, in speech and action plain,
He held all fraud and cunning in disdain;
But, fraud to find, and falsehood to detect,
For once he fled to measures indirect.

One day the friends were seated in that room
The guest with care adorn'd, and named her home:
To please the eye, there curious prints were placed,
And some light volumes to amuse the taste;
Letters and music, on a table laid,
The favourite studies of the fair betray'd;
Beneath the window was the toilet spread,
And the fire gleam'd upon a crimson bed.

In Anna's looks and falling tears were seen
How interesting had their subjects been:
"Oh! then," resumed the friend, "I plainly find
That you and Stafford know each other's mind;
I must depart, must on the world be thrown,
Like one discarded, worthless and unknown;
But shall I carry, and to please a foe,
A painful secret in my bosom? No!
Think not your friend a reptile you may tread
Beneath your feet, and say, the worm is dead;
I have some feeling, and will not be made
The scorn of her whom love cannot persuade:
Would not your word, your slightest wish, effect
All that I hope, petition, or expect?
The power you have, but you the use decline—
Proof that you feel not, or you fear not mine.
There was a time, when I, a tender maid,
Flew at a call, and your desires obey'd;
A very mother to the child became,
Consoled your sorrow, and conceal'd your shame;
But now, grown rich and happy, from the door
You thrust a bosom friend, despised and poor;
That child alive, its mother might have known
The hard ungrateful spirit she has shown."

Here paused the guest, and Anna cried at length—
"You try me, cruel friend! beyond my strength;
Would I had been beside my infant laid,
Where none would vex me, threaten, or upbraid."

In Anna's looks the friend beheld despair;
Her speech she soften'd, and composed her air:
Yet while professing love, she answered still—
"You can befriend me, but you want the will."
They parted thus, and Anna went her way,
To shed her secret sorrows, and to pray.

Stafford, amused with books, and fond of home,
By reading oft dispell'd the evening gloom;
History or tale—all heard him with delight,
And thus was pass'd this memorable night.

The listening friend bestow'd a flattering smile
A sleeping boy the mother held the while;
And ere she fondly bore him to his bed,
On his fair face the tear of anguish shed.

And now his task resumed, "My tale," said he,
"Is short and sad, short may our sadness be!"

"The Caliph Harun,* as historians tell,
Ruled, for a tyrant, admirably well;
Where his own pleasures were not touch'd, to men
He was humane, and sometimes even then;
Harun was fond of fruits, and gardens fair,
And woe to all whom he found poaching there!
Among his pages was a lively boy,
Eager in search of every trifling joy;
His feelings vivid, and his fancy strong,
He sigh'd for pleasure while he shrank from wrong;
When by the caliph in the garden placed
He saw the treasures which he long'd to taste;
And oft alone he ventured to behold
Rich hanging fruits with rind of glowing gold;
Too long he staid forbidden bliss to view,
His virtue failing, as his longings grew;
Athirst and wearied with the noon-tide heat,
Fate to the garden led his luckless feet;
With eager eyes and open mouth he stood,
Smelt the sweet breath, and touch'd the fragrant food;

* The sovereign here meant is the Haroun Alraschid, or Harun al Rashid who died early in the ninth century: he is often the hearer, and sometimes the hero, of a tale in the Arabian Nights' Entertainments.

The tempting beauty sparkling in the sun
Charm'd his young sense—he ate, and was undone:
When the fond glutton paused, his eyes around
He turn'd, and eyes upon him turning found;
Pleased he beheld the spy, a brother-page,
A friend allied in office and in age;
Who promised much that secret he would be,
But high the price he fix'd on secrecy.

"'Were you suspected, my unhappy friend,'
Began the boy, 'where would your sorrows end?
In all the palace there is not a page
The caliph would not torture in his rage:
I think I see thee now impaled alive,
Writhing in pangs—but come, my friend! revive;
Had some beheld you, all your purse contains
Could not have saved you from terrific pains;
I scorn such meanness; and, if not in debt,
Would not an asper on your folly set.'

"The hint was strong; young Osmyn search'd his store
For bribes, and found he soon could bribe no more;
That time arrived, for Osmyn's stock was small,
And the young tyrant now possess'd it all;
The cruel youth, with his companions near,
Gave the broad hint that raised the sudden fear;
Th' ungenerous insult now was daily shown,
And Osmyn's peace and honest pride were flown;
Then came augmenting woes, and fancy strong
Drew forms of suffering, a tormenting throng;
He felt degraded, and the struggling mind
Dared not be free, and could not be resign'd;
And all his pains and fervent prayers obtain'd
Was truce from insult, while the fears remain'd.

"One day it chanced that this degraded boy
And tyrant-friend were fix'd at their employ;
Who now had thrown restraint and form aside,
And for his bribe in plainer speech applied:
'Long have I waited, and the last supply
Was but a pittance, yet how patient I!
But give me now what thy first terrors gave,
My speech shall praise thee, and my silence save.'

"Osmyn had found, in many a dreadful day,
The tyrant fiercer when he seem'd in play:
He begg'd forbearance; 'I have not to give;
Spare me awhile, although 't is pain to live:
Oh! had that stolen fruit the power possess'd
To war with life, I now had been at rest.'

"'So fond of death,' replied the boy, ''t is plain
Thou hast no certain notion of the pain;
But to the caliph were a secret shown,
Death has no pain that would be then unknown.'

"Now, says the story, in a closet near,
The monarch seated, chanced the boys to hear;
There oft he came, when wearied on his throne,
To read, sleep, listen, pray, or be alone.

"The tale proceeds, when first the caliph found
That he was robb'd, although alone, he frown'd;
And swore in wrath, that he would send the boy
Far from his notice, favour, or employ;
But gentler movements soothed his ruffled mind,
And his own failings taught him to be kind.

"Relenting thoughts then painted Osmyn young,
His passion urgent, and temptation strong;
And that he suffer'd from their villain-spy
Pains worse than death till he desired to die;
Then if his morals had received a stain,
His bitter sorrows made him pure again:
To Reason, Pity lent her generous aid,
For one so tempted, troubled, and betray'd;
And a free pardon the glad boy restored
To the kind presence of a gentle lord;
Who from his office and his country drove
That traitor-friend, whom pains nor pray'rs could move;
Who raised the fears no mortal could endure,
And then with cruel av'rice sold the cure.

"My tale is ended; but, to be applied,
I must describe the place where caliphs hide."

Here both the females look'd alarm'd, distress'd,
With hurried passions hard to be express'd.

"It was a closet by a chamber placed,
Where slept a lady of no vulgar taste;
Her friend attended in that chosen room
That she had honour'd and proclaim'd her home;
To please the eye were chosen pictures placed,
And some light volumes to amuse the taste;
Letters and music on a table laid,
For much the lady wrote, and often play'd;
Beneath the window was a toilet spread,
And a fire gleam'd upon a crimson bed."

He paused, he rose; with troubled joy the wife
Felt the new era of her changeful life;
Frankness and love appear'd in Stafford's face,
And all her trouble to delight gave place.

Twice made the guest an effort to sustain
Her feelings, twice resumed her seat in vain,
Nor could suppress her shame, nor could support her pain:
Quick she retired, and all the dismal night
Thought of her guilt, her folly, and her flight;
Then sought unseen her miserable home,
To think of comforts lost, and brood on wants to come.

TALE XVII.

RESENTMENT.

> She hath a tear for pity, and a hand
> Open as day for melting charity;
> Yet, notwithstanding, being incensed, is flint——
> Her temper, therefore, must be well observ'd.
>
> *Henry IV*, Part i, act iv, scene 4.

> Three or four wenches where I stood cried—" Alas! good soul!" and forgave him with all their hearts: but there is no heed to be taken of them; if Cæsar had stabb'd their mothers, they would have done no less.
>
> *Julius Cæsar*, act i, scene 2.

> How dost? Art cold?
> I'm cold myself—Where is the straw, my fellow?
> The art of our necessities is strange,
> That can make vile things precious.
>
> *King Lear*, act iii, scene 2

Females there are of unsuspicious mind,
Easy and soft, and credulous and kind;

Who, when offended for the twentieth time,
Will hear th' offender and forgive the crime:
And there are others whom, like these to cheat,
Asks but the humblest efforts of deceit;
But they, once injured, feel a strong disdain,
And, seldom pardoning, never trust again;
Urged by religion, they forgive—but yet
Guard the warm heart, they never more forget:
Those are like wax—apply them to the fire,
Melting, they take th' impressions you desire;
Easy to mould, and fashion as you please,
And again moulded with an equal ease:
Like smelted iron these the forms retain,
But once impress'd will never melt again.

A busy port a serious merchant made
His chosen place to recommence his trade;
And brought his lady, who, their children dead,
Their native seat of recent sorrow fled:
The husband duly on the quay was seen,
The wife at home became at length serene;
There in short time the social couple grew
With all acquainted, friendly with a few;
When the good lady, by disease assail'd,
In vain resisted—hope and science fail'd:
Then spake the female friends, by pity led,
"Poor merchant Paul! what think ye? will he wed?
A quiet, easy, kind, religious man,
Thus can he rest?—I wonder if he can."

He too, as grief subsided in his mind,
Gave place to notions of congenial kind:
Grave was the man, as we have told before;
His years were forty—he might pass for more;
Composed his features were, his stature low,
His air important, and his motion slow;
His dress became him, it was neat and plain,
The colour purple, and without a stain;
His words were few, and special was his care
In simplest terms his purpose to declare;
A man more civil, sober, and discreet,
More grave and courteous, you could seldom meet:
Though frugal he, yet sumptuous was his board,
As if to prove how much he could afford;
For though reserved himself, he loved to see
His table plenteous, and his neighbours free:
Among these friends he sat in solemn style,
And rarely soften'd to a sober smile;
For this observant friends their reasons gave—
"Concerns so vast would make the idlest grave;
And for such men to be of language free,
Would seem incongruous as a singing-tree:
Trees have their music, but the birds they shield
The pleasing tribute for protection yield;
Each ample tree the tuneful choir defends,
As this rich merchant cheers his happy friends!"

In the same town it was his chance to meet
A gentle lady, with a mind discreet;
Neither in life's decline, nor bloom of youth,
One famed for maiden modesty and truth:
By nature cool, in pious habits bred,
She look'd on lovers with a virgin's dread:
Deceivers, rakes, and libertines were they,
And harmless beauty their pursuit and prey;
As bad as giants in the ancient times
Were modern lovers, and the same their crimes:

Soon as she heard of her all-conquering charms,
At once she fled to her defensive arms;
Conn'd o'er the tales her maiden aunt had told,
And, statue-like, was motionless and cold;
From prayer of love, like that Pygmalion pray'd,
Ere the hard stone became the yielding maid—
A different change in this chaste nymph ensued,
And turn'd to stone the breathing flesh and blood:
Whatever youth described his wounded heart,
"He came to rob her, and she scorn'd his art;
And who of raptures once presumed to speak,
Told listening maids he thought them fond and weak:
But should a worthy man his hopes display
In few plain words, and beg a *yes* or *nay*,
He would deserve an answer just and plain,
Since adulation only moved disdain—
Sir, if my friends object not, come again."

Hence, our grave lover, though he liked the face,
Praised not a feature—dwelt not on a grace;
But in the simplest terms declared his state,
"A widow'd man, who wish'd a virtuous mate;
Who fear'd neglect, and was compell'd to trust
Dependants wasteful, idle, or unjust;
Or should they not the trusted stores destroy,
At best, they could not help him to enjoy;
But with her person and her prudence blest,
His acts would prosper, and his soul have rest:
Would she be his?"—"Why that was much to say;
She would consider: he a while might stay;
She liked his manners, and believed his word;
He did not flatter, flattery she abhorr'd:
It was her happy lot in peace to dwell—
Would change make better what was now so well?
But she would ponder."—"This," he said, "was kind,"
And begg'd to know "when she had fix'd her mind."

Romantic maidens would have scorn'd the air,
And the cool prudence of a mind so fair;
But well it pleased this wiser maid to find
Her own mild virtues in her lover's mind.

His worldly wealth she sought, and quickly grew
Pleased with her search, and happy in the view
Of vessels freighted with abundant stores,
Of rooms whose treasures press'd the groaning floors;
And he of clerks and servants could display
A little army on a public day.
Was this a man like needy bard to speak
Of balmy lip, bright eye, or rosy cheek?

The sum appointed for her widow'd state,
Fix'd by her friend, excited no debate;
Then the kind lady gave her hand and heart,
And, never finding, never dealt with art:
In his engagements she had no concern;
He taught her not, nor did she wish to learn:
On him in all occasions she relied,
His word her surety, and his worth her pride.

When ship was launch'd, and merchant Paul had share,
A bounteous feast became the lady's care;
Who then her entry to the dinner made,
In costly raiment, and with kind parade.

Call'd by this duty on a certain day,
And robed to grace it in a rich array,

Forth from her room with measured step she came,
Proud of th' event, and stately look'd the dame:
The husband met her at his study-door—
"This way, my love—one moment and no more:
A trifling business—you will understand,
The law requires that you affix your hand;
But first attend, and you shall learn the cause
Why forms like these have been prescribed by laws."
Then from his chair a man in black arose,
And with much quickness hurried off his prose:
That "Ellen Paul the wife, and so forth, freed
From all control, her own the act and deed,
And forasmuch"——said she, "I 've no distrust,
For he that asks it is discreet and just;
Our friends are waiting—where am I to sign?—
There!——Now be ready when we meet to dine."

This said, she hurried off in great delight,
The ship was launch'd, and joyful was the night.

Now, says the reader, and in much disdain,
This serious merchant was a rogue in grain;
A treacherous wretch, an artful, sober knave,
And ten times worse for manners cool and grave,
And she devoid of sense, to set her hand
To scoundrel deeds she could not understand.

Alas! 't is true; and I in vain had tried
To soften crime, that cannot be denied;
And might have labour'd many a tedious verse
The latent cause of mischief to rehearse:
Be it confess'd, that long, with troubled look,
This trader view'd a huge accompting book
(His former marriage for a time delay'd
The dreaded hour, the present lent its aid:)
But he too clearly saw the evil day,
And put the terror, by deceit, away;
Thus by connecting with his sorrows crime,
He gain'd a portion of uneasy time.—
All this too late the injured lady saw,
What law had given, again she gave to law;
His guilt, her folly—these at once impress'd
Their lasting feelings on her guileless breast.

"Shame I can bear," she cried, "and want sustain,
But will not see this guilty wretch again;"
For all was lost, and he, with many a tear,
Confess'd the fault—she turning scorn'd to hear.
To legal claims he yielded all his worth,
But small the portion, and the wrong'd were wroth,
Nor to their debtor would a part allow;
And where to live he knew not—knew not how.

The wife a cottage found, and thither went
The suppliant man, but she would not relent:
Thenceforth she utter'd with indignant tone,
"I feel the misery, and will feel alone:"
He would turn servant for her sake, would keep
The poorest school; the very streets would sweep,
To show his love—"It was already shown:
And her affliction should be all her own.
His wants and weakness might have touch'd her heart,
But from his meanness she resolved to part."

In a small alley was she lodged, beside
Its humblest poor, and at the view she cried:
"Welcome—yes! let me welcome, if I can,
The fortune dealt me by this cruel man;
Welcome this low-thatch'd roof, this shatter'd door
These walls of clay, this miserable floor;
Welcome my envied neighbours; this, to you,
Is all familiar—all to me is new:
You have no hatred to the loathsome meal;
Your firmer nerves no trembling terrors feel,
Nor, what you must expose, desire you to conceal
What your coarse feelings bear without offence,
Disgusts my taste, and poisons every sense:
Daily shall I your sad relations hear,
Of wanton women, and of men severe;
There will dire curses, dreadful oaths abound,
And vile expressions shock me and confound;
Noise of dull wheels, and songs with horrid words
Will be the music that this lane affords;
Mirth that disgusts, and quarrels that degrade
The human mind, must my retreat invade:
Hard is my fate! yet easier to sustain,
Than to abide with guilt and fraud again;
A grave impostor! who expects to meet,
In such grey locks and gravity, deceit?
Where the sea rages, and the billows roar,
Men know the danger, and they quit the shore;
But, be there nothing in the way descried,
When o'er the rocks smooth runs the wicked tide—
Sinking unwarn'd, they execrate the shock,
And the dread peril of the sunken rock."

A frowning world had now the man to dread,
Taught in no arts, to no profession bred:
Pining in grief, beset with constant care,
Wandering he went, to rest he knew not where.

Meantime the wife—but she abjured the name—
Endured her lot, and struggled with the shame;
When lo! an uncle on the mother's side,
In nature something, as in blood allied,
Admired her firmness, his protection gave,
And show'd a kindness she disdain'd to crave.

Frugal and rich the man, and frugal grew
The sister-mind, without a selfish view;
And further still—the temp'rate pair agreed
With what they saved the patient poor to feed.
His whole estate, when to the grave consign'd,
Left the good kinsman to the kindred mind;
Assured that law, with spell secure and tight,
Had fix'd it as her own peculiar right.

Now to her ancient residence removed,
She lived as widow, well endow'd and loved;
Decent her table was, and to her door
Came daily welcomed the neglected poor:
The absent sick were soothed by her relief,
As her free bounty sought the haunts of grief,
A plain and homely charity had she,
And loved the objects of her alms to see;
With her own hands she dress'd the savoury meat,
With her own fingers wrote the choice receipt;
She heard all tales that injured wives relate,
And took a double interest in their fate;
But of all husbands not a wretch was known
So vile, so mean, so cruel, as her own.

This bounteous lady kept an active spy,
To search th' abodes of want, and to supply;
The gentle Susan served the liberal dame—
Unlike their notions, yet their deeds the same:

No practised villain could a victim find
Than this stern lady more completely blind;
Nor (if detected in his fraud) could meet
One less disposed to pardon a deceit;
The wrong she treasured, and on no pretence
Received th' offender, or forgot th' offence:
But the kind servant, to the thrice-proved knave
A fourth time listen'd, and the past forgave.
First in her youth, when she was blithe and gay,
Came a smooth rogue, and stole her love away;
Then to another and another flew,
To boast the wanton mischief he could do:
Yet she forgave him, though so great her pain,
That she was never blithe or gay again.

Then came a spoiler, who, with villain-art,
Implored her hand, and agonized her heart;
He seized her purse, in idle waste to spend
With a vile wanton, whom she call'd her friend;
Five years she suffer'd—he had revell'd five—
Then came to show her he was just alive;
Alone he came, his vile companion dead;
And he, a wand'ring pauper, wanting bread;
His body wasted, wither'd life and limb;
When this kind soul became a slave to him:
Nay, she was sure that, should he now survive,
No better husband would be left alive;
For him she mourn'd, and then alone and poor,
Sought and found comfort at her lady's door:
Ten years she served, and, mercy her employ,
Her tasks were pleasure, and her duty joy.

Thus lived the mistress and the maid, design'd
Each other's aid—one cautious, and both kind;
Oft at their window, working, they would sigh
To see the aged and the sick go by:
Like wounded bees, that at their home arrive,
Slowly and weak, but labouring for the hive.

The busy people of a mason's yard
The curious lady view'd with much regard;
With steady motion she perceived them draw
Through blocks of stone the slowly-working saw;
It gave her pleasure and surprise to see
Among these men the signs of revelry:
Cold was the season, and confined their view,
Tedious their tasks, but merry were the crew:
There she beheld an aged pauper wait,
Patient and still, to take an humble freight;
Within the panniers on an ass he laid
The ponderous grit, and for the portion paid;
This he re-sold, and, with each trifling gift,
Made shift to live, and wretched was the shift.

Now will it be by every reader told
Who was this humble trader, poor and old.—
In vain an author would a name suppress,
From the least hint a reader learns to guess;
Of children lost, our novels sometimes treat,
We never care—assured again to meet:
In vain the writer for concealment tries,
We trace his purpose under all disguise;
Nay, though he tells us they are dead and gone,
Of whom we wot—they will appear anon;
Our favourites fight, are wounded, hopeless lie,
Survive they cannot—nay, they cannot die;
Now, as these tricks and stratagems are known,
'T is best, at once, the simple truth to own.

This was the husband—in an humble shed
He nightly slept, and daily sought his bread:
Once for relief the weary man applied;
"Your wife is rich," the angry vestry cried;
Alas! he dared not to his wife complain,
Feeling her wrongs, and fearing her disdain:
By various methods he had tried to live,
But not one effort would subsistence give:
He was an usher in a school, till noise
Made him less able than the weaker boys;
On messages he went, till he in vain
Strove names, or words, or meanings to retain;
Each small employment in each neighbouring town
By turn he took, to lay as quickly down:
For, such his fate, he fail'd in all he plann'd,
And nothing prosper'd in his luckless hand.

At his old home, his motive half suppress'd,
He sought no more for riches, but for rest:
There lived the bounteous wife, and at her gate
He saw in cheerful groups the needy wait;
"Had he a right with bolder hope t' apply?"
He ask'd—was answer'd, and went groaning by:
For some remains of spirit, temper, pride,
Forbade a prayer he knew would be denied.

Thus was the grieving man, with burthen'd ass,
Seen day by day along the street to pass:
"Who is he, Susan? who the poor old man?
He never calls—do make him, if you can."—
The conscious damsel still delay'd to speak,
She stopp'd confused, and had her words to seek;
From Susan's fears the fact her mistress knew,
And cried—"The wretch! what scheme has he in view?
Is this his lot?—but let him, let him feel—
Who wants the courage, not the will to steal."

A dreadful winter came, each day severe,
Misty when mild, and icy cold when clear;
And still the humble dealer took his load,
Returning slow, and shivering on the road:
The lady, still relentless, saw him come,
And said—"I wonder, has the wretch a home?"
"A hut! a hovel!"—"Then his fate appears
To suit his crime;"—"Yes, lady, not his years;—
No! nor his sufferings—nor that form decay'd."
"Well! let the parish give its paupers aid;
You must the vileness of his acts allow;"
"And you, dear lady, that he feels it now."
"When such dissemblers on their deeds reflect,
Can they the pity they refused expect?
He that doth evil, evil shall he dread."
"The snow," quoth Susan, "falls upon his bed—
It blows beside the thatch—it melts upon his head."—
"'T is weakness, child, for grieving guilt to feel:"
"Yes, but he never sees a wholesome meal;
Through his bare dress appears his shrivell'd skin,
And ill he fares without, and worse within!
With that weak body, lame, diseased, and slow,
What cold, pain, peril, must the sufferer know!"
"Think on his crime."—"Yes, sure 't was very wrong;
But look, (God bless him!) how he gropes along."—
"Brought me to shame."—"Oh! yes, I know it all—
What cutting blast! and he can scarcely crawl;
He freezes as he moves—he dies! if he should fall:

With cruel fierceness drives this icy sleet,
And must a Christian perish in the street,
In sight of Christians?—There! at last, he lies;—
Nor unsupported can he ever rise:
He cannot live."—"But is he fit to die?"—
Here Susan softly mutter'd a reply,
Look'd round the room—said something of its state,
Dives the rich, and Lazarus at his gate;
And then aloud—"In pity do behold
The man affrighten'd, weeping, trembling, cold:
Oh! how those flakes of snow their entrance win
Through the poor rags, and keep the frost within;
His very heart seems frozen as he goes,
Leading that starved companion of his woes:
He tried to pray—his lips, I saw them move,
And he so turn'd his piteous looks above;
But the fierce wind the willing heart opposed,
And, ere he spoke, the lips in misery closed:
Poor suffering object! yes, for ease you pray'd,
And God will hear—he only, I'm afraid."

"Peace! Susan, peace! Pain ever follows sin."—
'Ah! then," thought Susan, "when will ours begin?
When reach'd his home, to what a cheerless fire
And chilling bed will those cold limbs retire!
Yet ragged, wretched as it is, that bed
Takes half the space of his contracted shed;
I saw the thorns beside the narrow grate,
With straw collected in a putrid state:
There will he, kneeling, strive the fire to raise,
And that will warm him, rather than the blaze;
The sullen, smoky blaze, that cannot last
One moment after his attempt is past:
And I so warmly and so purely laid,
To sink to rest—indeed, I am afraid."
"Know you his conduct?"—"Yes, indeed, I know—
And how he wanders in the wind and snow:
Safe in our rooms the threat'ning storm we hear,
But he feels strongly what we faintly fear."
"Wilful was rich, and he the storm defied;
Wilful is poor, and must the storm abide;"
Said the stern lady—"'T is in vain to feel;
Go and prepare the chicken for our meal."

Susan her task reluctantly began,
And utter'd as she went—"The poor old man!"
But while her soft and ever-yielding heart
Made strong protest against her lady's part,
The lady's self began to think it wrong,
To feel so wrathful and resent so long.

"No more the wretch would she receive again,
No more behold him—but she would sustain;
Great his offence, and evil was his mind—
But he had suffer'd; and she would be kind:
She spurn'd such baseness, and she found within
A fair acquittal from so foul a sin;
Yet she too err'd, and must of Heaven expect
To be rejected, him should she reject."

Susan was summon'd—"I'm about to do
A foolish act, in part seduced by you;
Go to the creature—say that I intend,
Foe to his sins, to be his sorrow's friend;
Take, for his present comforts, food and wine,
And mark his feelings at this act of mine:
Observe if shame be o'er his features spread,
By his own victim to be soothed and fed;
But, this inform him, that it is not love
That prompts my heart, that duties only move:
Say, that no merits in his favour plead,
But miseries only, and his abject need;
Nor bring me grov'ling thanks, nor high-flown praise;
I would his spirits, not his fancy raise:
Give him no hope that I shall ever more
A man so vile to my esteem restore;
But warn him rather, that, in time of rest,
His crimes be all remember'd and confess'd:
I know not all that form the sinner's debt,
But there is one that he must not forget."

The mind of Susan prompted her with speed
To act her part in every courteous deed:
All that was kind she was prepared to say,
And keep the lecture for a future day;
When he had all life's comforts by his side,
Pity might sleep, and good advice be tried.

This done, the mistress felt disposed to look,
As self-approving, on a pious book:
Yet, to her native bias still inclined,
She felt her act too merciful and kind;
But when, long musing on the chilling scene
So lately past—the frost and sleet so keen—
The man's whole misery in a single view—
Yes! she could think some pity was his due.

Thus fix'd, she heard not her attendant glide
With soft slow step—till, standing by her side,
The trembling servant gasp'd for breath, and shed
Relieving tears, then utter'd—"He is dead!"

"Dead!" said the startled lady; "Yes, he fell
Close at the door where he was wont to dwell;
There his sole friend, the ass, was standing by,
Half dead himself, to see his master die."

"Expired he then, good Heaven! for want of food?"
"No! crusts and water in a corner stood;—
To have this plenty, and to wait so long,
And to be right too late, is doubly wrong:
Then, every day to see him totter by,
And to forbear—Oh! what a heart had I!"

"Blame me not, child; I tremble at the news."
"'Tis my own heart," said Susan, "I accuse:
To have this money in my purse—to know
What grief was his, and what to grief we owe;
To see him often, always to conceive
How he must pine and languish, groan and grieve;
And every day in ease and peace to dine,
And rest in comfort!—what a heart is mine!"—

TALE XVIII.

THE WAGER.

'Tis thought your deer doth hold you at a bay.
Taming of the Shrew, act v, scene 2.

I choose her for myself:
If she and I are pleased, what's that to you?
———, act v, scene 2

Let's send each one to his wife,
And he whose wife is most obedient
Shall win the wager.
Taming of the Shrew, act v, scene 2.

Now by the world it is a lusty wench,
I love her ten times more than e'er I did.
———, act ii, scene v.

COUNTER and CLUBB were men in trade, whose pains,
Credit, and prudence brought them constant gains;
Partners and punctual, every friend agreed
Counter and Clubb were men who must succeed.
When they had fix'd some little time in life,
Each thought of taking to himself a wife:
As men in trade alike, as men in love
They seem'd with no according views to move;
As certain ores in outward view the same,
They show'd their difference when the magnet came.
Counter was vain: with spirit strong and high,
'T was not in him like suppliant swain to sigh:
"His wife might o'er his men and maids preside,
And in her province be a judge and guide;
But what he thought, or did, or wish'd to do,
She must not know, or censure if she knew;
At home, abroad, by day, by night, if he
On aught determined, so it was to be:
How is a man," he ask'd, "for business fit,
Who to a female can his will submit?
Absent awhile, let no inquiring eye
Or plainer speech presume to question why,
But all be silent; and, when seen again,
Let all be cheerful—shall a wife complain?
Friends I invite, and who shall dare t' object,
Or look on them with coolness or neglect?
No! I must ever of my house be head,
And, thus obey'd, I condescend to wed."

Clubb heard the speech—"My friend is nice," said he;
"A wife with less respect will do for me:
How is he certain such a prize to gain?
What he approves, a lass may learn to feign,
And so affect t' obey till she begins to reign;
Awhile complying, she may vary then,
And be as wives of more unwary men;
Beside, to him who plays such lordly part,
How shall a tender creature yield her heart?
Should he the promised confidence refuse,
She may another more confiding choose;
May show her anger, yet her purpose hide,
And wake his jealousy, and wound his pride.
In one so humbled, who can trace the friend?
I on an equal, not a slave, depend;
If true, my confidence is wisely placed,
And being false, she only is disgraced."

Clubb, with these notions, cast his eye around,
And one so easy soon a partner found.
The lady chosen was of good repute;
Meekness she had not, and was seldom mute;
Though quick to anger, still she loved to smile;
And would be calm if men would wait awhile:
She knew her duty, and she loved her way,
More pleased in truth to govern than obey;
She heard her priest with reverence, and her spouse
As one who felt the pressure of her vows:
Useful and civil, all her friends confess'd—
Give her her way, and she would choose the best;
Though some indeed a sly remark would make—
Give it her not, and she would choose to take.

All this, when Clubb some cheerful months had spent,
He saw, confess'd, and said he was content.

Counter meantime selected, doubted, weigh'd,
And then brought home a young complying maid;—
A tender creature, full of fears as charms,
A beauteous nursling from its mother's arms;
A soft, sweet blossom, such as men must love,
But to preserve must keep it in the stove:
She had a mild, subdued, expiring look—
Raise but the voice, and this fair creature shook;
Leave her alone, she felt a thousand fears—
Chide, and she melted into floods of tears;
Fondly she pleaded and would gently sigh,
For very pity, or she knew not why;
One whom to govern none could be afraid—
Hold up the finger, this meek thing obey'd;
Her happy husband had the easiest task—
Say but his will, no question would she ask;
She sought no reasons, no affairs she knew,
Of business spoke not, and had nought to do.

Oft he exclaim'd, "How meek! how mild! how kind!
With her 't were cruel but to seem unkind;
Though ever silent when I take my leave,
It pains my heart to think how hers will grieve;
'T is heaven on earth with such a wife to dwell,
I am in raptures to have sped so well;
But let me not, my friend, your envy raise,
No! on my life, your patience has my praise."

His friend, though silent, felt the scorn implied—
"What need of patience? to himself he cried:
"Better a woman o'er her house to rule,
Than a poor child just hurried from her school;
Who has no care, yet never lives at ease;
Unfit to rule, and indisposed to please;
What if he govern? there his boast should end,
No husband's power can make a slave his friend."

It was the custom of these friends to meet
With a few neighbours in a neighbouring street;
Where Counter ofttimes would occasion seize
To move his silent friend by words like these:
"A man," said he, "if govern'd by his wife,
Gives up his rank and dignity in life;
Now better fate befalls my friend and me"—
He spoke, and look'd th' approving smile to see.

The quiet partner, when he chose to speak,
Desired his friend, "another theme to seek;
When thus they met, he judged that state-affairs
And such important subjects should be theirs:"
But still the partner, in his lighter vein,
Would cause in Clubb affliction or disdain;
It made him anxious to detect the cause
Of all that boasting—"Wants my friend applause?
This plainly proves him not at perfect ease,
For, felt he pleasure, he would wish to please.—
These triumphs here for some regrets atone—
Men who are blest let other men alone."
Thus made suspicious, he observed and saw
His friend each night at early hour withdraw

He sometimes mention'd Juliet's tender nerves,
And what attention such a wife deserves:
"In this," thought Clubb, "full sure some mystery lies—
He laughs at me, yet he with much complies,
And all his vaunts of bliss are proud apologies."

With such ideas treasured in his breast,
He grew composed, and let his anger rest;
Till Counter once (when wine so long went round
That friendship and discretion both were drown'd)
Began in teasing and triumphant mood
His evening banter.—"Of all earthly good,
The best," he said, "was an obedient spouse,
Such as my friend's—that every one allows:
What if she wishes his designs to know?
It is because she would her praise bestow;
What if she wills that he remains at home?
She knows that mischief may from travel come.
I, who am free to venture where I please,
Have no such kind preventing checks as these;
But mine is double duty, first to guide
Myself aright, then rule a house beside;
While this our friend, more happy than the free,
Resigns all power, and laughs at liberty."

"By Heaven," said Clubb, "excuse me if I swear,
I 'll bet a hundred guineas, if he dare,
That uncontroll'd I will such freedom take,
That he will fear to equal—there 's my stake."

"A match!" said Counter, much by wine inflamed;
"But we are friends—let smaller stake be named:
Wine for our future meeting, that will I
Take and no more—what peril shall we try?"
"Let 's to Newmarket," Clubb replied; "or choose
Yourself the place, and what you like to lose;
And he who first returns, or fears to go,
Forfeits his cash.—" Said Counter, "Be it so."

The friends around them saw with much delight
The social war, and hail'd the pleasant night;
Nor would they further hear the cause discuss'd,
Afraid the recreant heart of Clubb to trust.

Now sober thoughts return'd as each withdrew,
And of the subject took a serious view;
"'T was wrong," thought Counter, "and will grieve my love;"
"'T was wrong," thought Clubb, "my wife will not approve,
But friends were present; I must try the thing,
Or with my folly half the town will ring."

He sought his lady—"Madam, I 'm to blame,
But was reproach'd, and could not bear the shame;
Herein my folly—for 't is best to say
The very truth—I 've sworn to have my way:
To that Newmarket—(though I hate the place,
And have no taste or talents for a race,
Yet so it is—well, now prepare to chide—)
I laid a wager that I dared to ride;
And I must go: by Heaven, if you resist
I shall be scorn'd, and ridiculed, and hiss'd;
Let me with grace before my friends appear,
You know the truth, and must not be severe;
He too must go, but that he will of course;
Do you consent?—I never think of force."

"You never need," the worthy dame replied;
"The husband's honour is the woman's pride;
If I in trifles be the wilful wife,
Still for your credit I would lose my life;
Go! and when fix'd the day of your return,
Stay longer yet, and let the blockheads learn,
That though a wife may sometimes wish to rule
She would not make th' indulgent man a fool;
I would at times advise—but idle they
Who think th' assenting husband *must* obey."

The happy man, who thought his lady right
In other cases, was assured to-night;
Then for the day with proud delight prepared,
To show his doubting friends how much he dared.

Counter—who grieving sought his bed, his rest
Broken by pictures of his love distress'd—
With soft and winning speech the fair prepared;
"She all his councils, comforts, pleasures shared:
She was assured he loved her from his soul,
She never knew and need not fear control;
But so it happen'd—he was grieved at heart,
It happen'd so, that they awhile must part—
A little time—the distance was but short,
And business call'd him—he despised the sport—
But to Newmarket he engaged to ride,
With his friend Clubb," and there he stopp'd and sigh'd.

Awhile the tender creature look'd dismay'd,
Then floods of tears the call of grief obey'd:—

"She an objection! No!" she sobb'd, "not one,
Her work was finish'd, and her race was run;
For die she must, indeed she would not live
A week alone, for all the world could give;
He too must die in that same wicked place;
It always happen'd—was a common case;
Among those horrid horses, jockeys, crowds,
'T was certain death—they might bespeak their shrouds;
He would attempt a race, be sure to fall—
And she expire with terror—that was all;
With love like hers she was indeed unfit
To bear such horrors, but she must submit."

"But for three days, my love! three days at most—"
"Enough for me; I then shall be a ghost—"
"My honour 's pledged!"—"Oh! yes, my dearest life,
I know your honour must outweigh your wife;
But ere this absence, have you sought a friend?
I shall be dead—on whom can you depend?
Let me one favour of your kindness crave,
Grant me the stone I mention'd for my grave.—"

"Nay, love, attend—why, bless my soul—I say
I will return—there—weep no longer—nay!—"
"Well! I obey, and to the last am true,
But spirits fail me; I must die; adieu!"

"What, madam! must?—'t is wrong—I 'm angry—zounds!
Can I remain and lose a thousand pounds?"

"Go then, my love! it is a monstrous sum,
Worth twenty wives—go, love! and I am dumb
Nor be displeased—had I the power to live,
You might be angry, now you must forgive;

Alas! I faint—ah! cruel—there's no need
Of wounds or fevers—this had done the deed."

The lady fainted, and the husband sent
For every aid, for every comfort went;
Strong terror seized him; "Oh! she loved so well,
And who th' effect of tenderness could tell?"

She now recover'd, and again began
With accent querulous—"Ah! cruel man—"
Till the sad husband, conscience-struck, confess'd,
'T was very wicked with his friend to jest;
For now he saw that those who were obey'd,
Could like the most subservient feel afraid;
And though a wife might not dispute the will
Of her liege lord, she could prevent it still.

The morning came, and Clubb prepared to ride
With a smart boy, his servant and his guide;
When, ere he mounted on the ready steed,
Arrived a letter, and he stopp'd to read.

"My friend," he read—"our journey I decline,
A heart too tender for such strife is mine;
Yours is the triumph, be you so inclined;
But you are too considerate and kind:
In tender pity to my Juliet's fears
I thus relent, o'ercome by love and tears;
She knows your kindness; I have heard her say,
A man like you 't is pleasure to obey:
Each faithful wife, like ours, must disapprove
Such dangerous trifling with connubial love;
What has the idle world, my friend, to do
With our affairs? they envy me and you:
What if I could my gentle spouse command—
Is that a cause I should her tears withstand?
And what if you, a friend of peace, submit
To one you love—is that a theme for wit?
'T was wrong, and I shall henceforth judge it weak
Both of submission and control to speak:
Be it agreed that all contention cease,
And no such follies vex our future peace;
Let each keep guard against domestic strife,
And find nor slave nor tyrant in his wife."

"Agreed," said Clubb, "with all my soul agreed;"
And to the boy, delighted, gave his steed;
"I think my friend has well his mind express'd,
And I assent; such things are not a jest."

"True," said the wife, "no longer he can hide
The truth that pains him by his wounded pride:
Your friend has found it not an easy thing,
Beneath his yoke, this yielding soul to bring;
These weeping willows, though they seem inclined
By every breeze, yet not the strongest wind
Can from their bent divert this weak but stubborn
kind;
Drooping they seek your pity to excite,
But 't is at once their nature and delight;
Such women feel not; while they sigh and weep,
'T is but their habit—their affections sleep;
They are like ice that in the hand we hold,
So very melting, yet so very cold;
On such affection let not man rely,
The husbands suffer, and the ladies sigh:
But your friend's offer let us kindly take,
And spare his pride for his vexation's sake;
For he has found, and through his wife will find,
'T is easiest dealing with the firmest mind—
More just when it resists, and, when it yields, more
kind."

TALE XIX.

THE CONVERT.

A tapster is a good trade, and an old cloak makes a new jerkin; a wither'd serving-man, a fresh tapster.
Merry Wives of Windsor, act i, scene 3.

A fellow, sir, that I have known go about with my troll-my-dames.
Winter's Tale, act iv, scene 2.

I myself, sometimes leaving the fear of Heaven on the left hand, and holding mine honour in my necessity, am forced to shuffle, to hedge, and to lurch.
Merry Wives of Windsor, act ii, scene 2.

Yea, and at that very moment,
Consideration like an angel came,
And whipp'd th' offending Adam out of him.
Henry V, act i, scene 1.

I have lived long enough: My May of life
Is fallen into the sere, the yellow leaf;
And that which should accompany old age,
As honour, love, obedience, troops of friends,
I must not look to have.
Macbeth, act v, scene 3.

Some to our hero have a hero's name
Denied, because no father's he could claim;
Nor could his mother with precision state
A full fair claim to her certificate;
On her own word the marriage must depend—
A point she was not eager to defend:
But who, without a father's name, can raise,
His own so high, deserves the greater praise:
The less advantage to the strife he brought,
The greater wonders has his prowess wrought;
He who depends upon his wind and limbs,
Needs neither cork nor bladder when he swims;
Nor will by empty breath be puff'd along,
As not himself—but in his helpers—strong.

Suffice it then, our hero's name was clear,
For, call John Dighton, and he answer'd, "Here!"
But who that name in early life assign'd
He never found, he never tried to find;
Whether his kindred were to John digrace,
Or John to them, is a disputed case;
His infant-state owed nothing to their care—
His mind neglected, and his body bare;
All his success must on himself depend,
He had no money, counsel, guide or friend;
But in a market-town an active boy
Appear'd, and sought in various ways employ;
Who soon, thus cast upon the world, began
To show the talents of a thriving man.

With spirit high John learn'd the world to brave,
And in both senses was a ready knave;
Knave as of old, obedient, keen, and quick,
Knave as at present, skill'd to shift and trick;
Some humble part of many trades he caught,
He for the builder and the painter wrought;

For serving-maids on secret errands ran,
The waiter's helper, and the hostler's man;
And when he chanced (oft chanced he) place to lose,
His varying genius shone in blacking shoes:
A midnight fisher by the pond he stood,
Assistant poacher, he o'erlook'd the wood;
At an election John's impartial mind
Was to no cause or candidate confined;
To all in turn he full allegiance swore,
And in his hat the various badges bore:
His liberal soul with every sect agreed,
Unheard their reasons, he received their creed;
At church he deign'd the organ-pipes to fill,
And at the meeting sang both loud and shrill:
But the full purse these different merits gain'd,
By strong demands his lively passions drain'd;
Liquors he loved of each inflaming kind,
To midnight revels flew with ardent mind;
Too warm at cards, a losing game he play'd,
To fleecing beauty his attention paid;
His boiling passions were by oaths express'd,
And lies he made his profit and his jest.

Such was the boy, and such the man had been,
But fate or happier fortune changed the scene:
A fever seized him, "He should surely die—"
He fear'd, and lo! a friend was praying by;
With terror moved, this teacher he address'd,
And all the errors of his youth confess'd:
The good man kindly clear'd the sinner's way
To lively hope, and counsell'd him to pray;
Who then resolved, should he from sickness rise,
To quit cards, liquors, poaching, oaths, and lies:
His health restored, he yet resolved, and grew
True to his masters, to their meeting true:
His old companions at his sober face
Laugh'd loud, while he, attesting it was grace,
With tears besought them all his calling to embrace:
To his new friends such convert gave applause,
Life to their zeal, and glory to their cause:
Though terror wrought the mighty change, yet strong
Was the impression, and it lasted long;
John at the lectures due attendance paid,
A convert meek, obedient, and afraid.
His manners strict, though form'd on fear alone,
Pleased the grave friends, nor less his solemn tone,
The lengthen'd face of care, the low and inward groan:
The stern good men exulted, when they saw
Those timid looks of penitence and awe;
Nor thought that one so passive, humble, meek,
Had yet a creed and principles to seek.

The faith that reason finds, confirms, avows,
The hopes, the views, the comforts she allows—
These were not his, who by his feelings found,
And by them only, that his faith was sound;
Feelings of terror these, for evil past,
Feelings of hope, to be received at last;
Now weak, now lively, changing with the day,
These were his feelings, and he felt his way.

Sprung from such sources, will this faith remain
While these supporters can their strength retain:
As heaviest weights the deepest rivers pass,
While icy chains fast bind the solid mass;
So, born of feelings, faith remains secure,
Long as their firmness and their strength endure:
But when the waters in their channel glide,
A bridge must bear us o'er the threat'ning tide:
Such bridge is reason, and there faith relies,
Whether the varying spirits fall or rise.

His patrons, still disposed their aid to lend,
Behind a counter placed their humble friend;
Where pens and paper were on shelves display'd,
And pious pamphlets on the windows laid;
By nature active and from vice restrain'd,
Increasing trade his bolder views sustain'd;
His friends and teachers, finding so much zeal
In that young convert whom they taught to feel,
His trade encouraged, and were pleased to find
A hand so ready, with such humble mind.

And now, his health restored, his spirits eased,
He wish'd to marry, if the teachers pleased.
They, not unwilling, from the virgin-class
Took him a comely and a courteous lass;
Simple and civil, loving and beloved,
She long a fond and faithful partner proved;
In every year the elders and the priest
Were duly summon'd to a christening feast;
Nor came a babe, but by his growing trade,
John had provision for the coming made;
For friends and strangers all were pleased to deal
With one whose care was equal to his zeal.

In human friendship, it compels a sigh,
To think what trifles will dissolve the tie.
John, now become a master of his trade,
Perceived how much improvement might be made
And as this prospect open'd to his view,
A certain portion of his zeal withdrew;
His fear abated—"What had he to fear—
His profits certain, and his conscience clear?"
Above his door a board was placed by John,
And, "Dighton, stationer," was gilt thereon;
His window next, enlarged to twice the size,
Shone with such trinkets as the simple prize;
While in the shop with pious works were seen
The last new play, review, or magazine;
In orders punctual, he observed—"The books
He never read, and could he judge their looks?
Readers and critics should their merits try,
He had no office but to sell and buy;
Like other traders, profit was his care;
Of what they print, the authors must beware."
He held his patrons and his teachers dear,
But with his trade—they must not interfere.

'T was certain now that John had lost the dread
And pious thoughts that once such terrors bred;
His habits varied, and he more inclined
To the vain world, which he had half resign'd:
He had moreover in his brethren seen,
Or he imagined, craft, conceit, and spleen;
"They are but men," said John, "and shall I then
Fear man's control, or stand in awe of men?
'T is their advice (their convert's rule and law,)
And good it is—I will not stand in awe."

Moreover Dighton, though he thought of books
As one who chiefly on the title looks,
Yet sometimes ponder'd o'er a page to find,
When vex'd with cares, amusement for his mind.

And by degrees that mind had treasured much
From works his teachers were afraid to touch:
Satiric novels, poets bold and free,
And what their writers term philosophy;
All these were read, and he began to feel
Some self-approval on his bosom steal.
Wisdom creates humility, but he
Who thus collects it, will not humble be:
No longer John was fill'd with pure delight
And humble reverence in a pastor's sight;
Who, like a grateful zealot, listening stood,
To hear a man so friendly and so good;
But felt the dignity of one who made
Himself important by a thriving trade;
And growing pride in Dighton's mind was bred
By the strange food on which it coarsely fed.

Their brother's fall the grieving brethren heard,
The pride indeed to all around appear'd;
The world his friends agreed had won the soul
From its best hopes, the man from their control:
To make him humble, and confine his views
Within their bounds, and books which they peruse;
A deputation from these friends select,
Might reason with him to some good effect;
Arm'd with authority, and led by love,
They might those follies from his mind remove;
Deciding thus, and with this kind intent,
A chosen body with its speaker went.

"John," said the teacher, "John," with great concern,
"We see thy frailty, and thy fate discern—
Satan with toils thy simple soul beset,
And thou art careless, slumbering in the net;
Unmindful art thou of thy early vow;
Who at the morning-meeting sees thee now?
Who at the evening? where is brother John?
We ask—are answer'd, To the tavern gone:
Thee on the sabbath seldom we behold;
Thou canst not sing, thou 'rt nursing for a cold:
This from the churchmen thou hast learn'd, for they
Have colds and fevers on the sabbath-day;
When in some snug warm room they sit and pen
Bills from their ledgers, (world-entangled men!)

"See with what pride thou hast enlarged thy shop;
To view thy tempting stores the heedless stop;
By what strange names dost thou these baubles know,
Which wantons wear, to make a sinful show?
Hast thou in view these idle volumes placed
To be the pander of a vicious taste?
What's here? a book of dances!—you advance
In goodly knowledge—John, wilt learn to dance?
How! 'Go—' it says, and 'to the devil go!
And shake thyself!' I tremble—but 't is so——
Wretch as thou art, what answer canst thou make?
Oh! without question thou wilt go and shake.
What's here? the 'School for Scandal'—pretty schools?
Well, and art thou proficient in the rules?
Art thou a pupil, is it thy design
To make our names contemptible as thine?
Old Nick, a Novel!' oh! 't is mighty well—
A fool has courage when he laughs at hell;
'Frolic and Fun,' the humours of 'Tim Grin;'
Why, John, thou grow'st facetious in thy sin;
And what? 'the Archdeacon's Charge'—'t is mighty well—
If Satan publish'd, thou wouldst doubtless sell;
Jests, novels, dances, and this precious stuff,
To crown thy folly we have seen enough;
We find thee fitted for each evil work—
Do print the Koran, and become a Turk.

"John, thou art lost; success and worldly pride
O'er all thy thoughts and purposes preside,
Have bound thee fast, and drawn thee far aside:
Yet turn; these sin-traps from thy shop expel,
Repent and pray, and all may yet be well.

"And here thy wife, thy Dorothy, behold,
How fashion's wanton robes her form infold!
Can grace, can goodness with such trappings dwell?
John, thou hast made thy wife a Jezebel:
See! on her bosom rests the sign of sin,
The glaring proof of naughty thoughts within;
What? 't is a cross; come hither—as a friend,
Thus from thy neck the shameful badge I rend."

"Rend, if you dare," said Dighton; "you shall find
A man of spirit, though to peace inclined;
Call me ungrateful! have I not my pay
At all times ready for the expected day?—
To share my plenteous board you deign to come,
Myself your pupil, and my house your home;
And shall the persons who my meat enjoy
Talk of my faults, and treat me as a boy?
Have you not told how Rome's insulting priests
Led their meek laymen like a herd of beasts;
And by their fleecing and their forgery made
Their holy calling an accursed trade?
Can you such acts and insolence condemn,
Who to your utmost power resemble them?

"Concerns it you what books I set for sale?
The tale perchance may be a virtuous tale;
And for the rest, 't is neither wise nor just,
In you, who read not, to condemn on trust;
Why should th' Archdeacon's Charge your spleen excite?
He, or perchance th' archbishop, may be right.

"That from your meetings I refrain, is true;
I meet with nothing pleasant—nothing new;
But the same proofs, that not one text explain,
And the same lights, where all things dark remain
I thought you saints on earth—but I have found
Some sins among you, and the best unsound;
You have your failings, like the crowds below,
And at your pleasure hot and cold can blow.
When I at first your grave deportment saw,
(I own my folly), I was fill'd with awe;
You spoke so warmly, and it seems so well,
I should have thought it treason to rebel;
Is it a wonder that a man like me
Should such perfection in such teachers see?
Nay, should conceive you sent from heav'n to brave
The host of sin, and sinful souls to save?
But as our reason wakes, our prospects clear,
And failings, flaws, and blemishes appear.

"When you were mounted in your rostrum high,
We shrank beneath your tone, your frown, your eye;

Then you beheld us abject, fallen, low,
And felt your glory from your baseness grow;
Touch'd by your words, I trembled like the rest,
And my own vileness and your power confess'd:
These, I exclaim'd, are men divine, and gazed
On him who taught, delighted and amazed;
Glad when he finish'd, if by chance he cast
One look on such a sinner, as he pass'd.

"But when I view'd you in a clearer light,
And saw the frail and carnal appetite;
When, at his humble pray'r, you deign'd to eat,
Saints as you are, a civil sinner's meat;
When as you sat contented and at ease,
Nibbling at leisure on the ducks and pease,
And, pleased some comforts in your place to find,
You could descend to be a little kind;
And gave us hope, in heaven there might be room
For a few souls beside your own to come;
While this world's good engaged your carnal view,
And like a sinner you enjoy'd it too;
All this perceiving, can you think it strange
That change in you should work an equal change?"

"Wretch that thou art," an elder cried, "and gone
For everlasting."——"Go thyself," said John;
"Depart this instant, let me hear no more;
My house my castle is, and that my door."

The hint they took, and from the door withdrew,
And John to meeting bade a long adieu;
Attach'd to business, he in time became
A wealthy man of no inferior name.
It seem'd, alas! in John's deluded sight,
That all was wrong because not all was right;
And when he found his teachers had their stains,
Resentment and not reason broke his chains:
Thus on his feelings he again relied,
And never look'd to reason for his guide:
Could he have wisely view'd the frailty shown,
And rightly weigh'd their wanderings and his own,
He might have known that men may be sincere,
Though gay and feasting on the savoury cheer;
That doctrines sound and sober they may teach,
Who love to eat with all the glee they preach;
Nay, who believe the duck, the grape, the pine,
Were not intended for the dog and swine:
But Dighton's hasty mind on every theme
Ran from the truth, and rested in th' extreme:
Flaws in his friends he found, and then withdrew
(Vain of his knowledge) from their virtues too.
Best of his books he loved the liberal kind,
That, if they improve not, still enlarge the mind;
And found himself, with such advisers, free
From a fix'd creed, as mind enlarged could be.
His humble wife at these opinions sigh'd,
But her he never heeded till she died;
He then assented to a last request,
And by the meeting-window let her rest;
And on her stone the sacred text was seen,
Which had her comfort in departing been.

Dighton with joy beheld his trade advance,
Yet seldom publish'd, loth to trust to chance;
Then wed a doctor's sister—poor indeed,
But skill'd in works her husband could not read;
Who, if he wish'd new ways of wealth to seek,
Could make her half-crown pamphlet in a week:
This she rejected, though without disdain,
And chose the old and certain way to gain.

Thus he proceeded; trade increased the while,
And fortune woo'd him with perpetual smile:
On early scenes he sometimes cast a thought,
When on his heart the mighty change was wrought
And all the ease and comfort converts find
Was magnified in his reflecting mind:
Then on the teacher's priestly pride he dwelt,
That caused his freedom, but with this he felt
The danger of the free—for since that day,
No guide had shown, no brethren join'd his way;
Forsaking one, he found no second creed,
But reading doubted, doubting what he read.

Still, though reproof had brought some present pain,
The gain he made was fair and honest gain;
He laid his wares indeed in public view,
But that all traders claim a right to do:
By means like these, he saw his wealth increase,
And felt his consequence, and dwelt in peace.

Our hero's age was threescore years and five,
When he exclaim'd, "Why longer should I strive?
Why more amass, who never must behold
A young John Dighton to make glad the old?"
(The sons he had to early graves were gone,
And girls were burdens to the mind of John.)
"Had I a boy, he would our name sustain,
That now to nothing must return again;
But what are all my profits, credit, trade,
And parish-honours?—folly and parade."

Thus Dighton thought, and in his looks appear'd
Sadness increased by much he saw and heard:
The brethren often at the shop would stay,
And make their comments ere they walk'd away:
They mark'd the window, fill'd in every pane
With lawless prints of reputation slain;
Distorted forms of men with honours graced,
And our chief rulers in derision placed:
Amazed they stood, remembering well the days,
When to be humble was their brother's praise;
When at the dwelling of their friend they stopp'd
To drop a word, or to receive it dropp'd;
Where they beheld the prints of men renown'd,
And far-famed preachers pasted all around;
(Such mouths! eyes! hair! so prim! so fierce! so sleek!
They look'd as speaking what is wo to speak:)
On these the passing brethren loved to dwell—
How long they spake! how strongly! warmly! well!
What power had each to dive in mysteries deep,
To warm the cold, to make the harden'd weep;
To lure, to fright, to soothe, to awe the soul,
And list'ning flocks to lead and to control!

But now discoursing, as they linger'd near
They tempted John (whom they accused) to hear
Their weighty charge—"And can the lost-one feel,
As in the time of duty, love, and zeal;

When all were summon'd at the rising sun,
And he was ready with his friends to run;
When he, partaking with a chosen few,
Felt the great change, sensation rich and new?
No! all is lost, her favours fortune shower'd
Upon the man, and he is overpower'd;
The world has won him with its tempting store
Of needless wealth, and that has made him poor:
Success undoes him; he has risen to fall,
Has gain'd a fortune, and has lost his all;
Gone back from Sion, he will find his age
Loth to commence a second pilgrimage;
He has retreated from the chosen track;
And now must ever bear the burden on his back."

Hurt by such censure, John began to find
Fresh revolutions working in his mind;
He sought for comfort in his books, but read
Without a plan or method in his head;
What once amused, now rather made him sad,
What should inform, increased the doubts he had;
Shame would not let him seek at church a guide,
And from his meeting he was held by pride;
His wife derided fears she never felt,
And passing brethren daily censures dealt;
Hope for a son was now for ever past,
He was the first John Dighton, and the last;
His stomach fail'd, his case the doctor knew,
But said, "he still might hold a year or two:"
"No more!" he said, "but why should I complain?
A life of doubt must be a life of pain:
Could I be sure—but why should I despair?
I 'm sure my conduct has been just and fair;
In youth indeed I had a wicked will,
But I repented, and have sorrow still:
I had my comforts, and a growing trade
Gave greater pleasure than a fortune made;
And as I more possess'd and reason'd more,
I lost those comforts I enjoy'd before,
When reverend guides I saw my table round;
And in my guardian guest my safety found:
Now sick and sad, no appetite, no ease,
Nor pleasure have I, nor a wish to please;
Nor views, nor hopes, nor plans, nor taste have I,
Yet sick of life, have no desire to die."

He said, and died; his trade, his name is gone,
And all that once gave consequence to John.

Unhappy Dighton! had he found a friend,
When conscience told him it was time to mend!
A friend discreet, considerate, kind, sincere,
Who would have shown the grounds of hope and fear;
And proved that spirits, whether high or low,
No certain tokens of man's safety show;
Had reason ruled him in her proper place,
And virtue led him while he lean'd on grace;
Had he while zealous been discreet and pure,
His knowledge humble, and his hope secure;—
These guides had placed him on the solid rock,
Where faith had rested, nor received a shock;
But his, alas! was placed upon the sand,
Where long it stood not, and where none can stand.

TALE XX.

THE BROTHERS.

A brother noble,
Whose nature is so far from doing harms,
That he suspects none; on whose foolish honesty
My practice may ride easy.
King Lear, act i, scene 2.

He lets me feed with hinds,
Bars me the place of brother.
As You Like It, act i, scene 1.

'T was I, but 't is not I: I do not shame
To tell you what I was, being what I am.
As You Like It, act iv, scene 3.

Than old George Fletcher, on the British coast,
Dwelt not a seaman who had more to boast;
Kind, simple, and sincere—he seldom spoke,
But sometimes sang and chorus'd—"*Hearts of Oak;*"
In dangers steady, with his lot content,
His days in labour and in love were spent.

He left a son so like him, that the old
With joy exclaim'd, "'T is Fletcher we behold;"
But to his brother when the kinsmen came,
And view'd his form, they grudged the father's name.

George was a bold, intrepid, careless lad,
With just the failings that his father had;
Isaac was weak, attentive, slow, exact,
With just the virtues that his father lack'd.

George lived at sea: upon the land a guest—
He sought for recreation, not for rest—
While, far unlike, his brother's feebler form
Shrank from the cold, and shudder'd at the storm;
Still with the seaman's to connect his trade,
The boy was bound where blocks and ropes were made.

George, strong and sturdy, had a tender mind,
And was to Isaac pitiful and kind;
A very father, till his art was gain'd,
And then a friend unwearied he remain'd:
He saw his brother was of spirit low,
His temper peevish, and his motions slow;
Not fit to bustle in a world, or make
Friends to his fortune for his merit's sake:
But the kind sailor could not boast the art
Of looking deeply in the human heart;
Else had he seen that this weak brother knew
What men to court—what objects to pursue;
That he to distant gain the way discern'd,
And none so crooked but his genius learn'd.

Isaac was poor, and this the brother felt;
He hired a house, and there the landman dwelt;
Wrought at his trade, and had an easy home,
For there would George with cash and comforts come;
And when they parted, Isaac look'd around,
Where other friends and helpers might be found.

He wish'd for some port-place, and one might fall,
He wisely thought, if he should try for all;
He had a vote—and, were it well applied,
Might have its worth—and he had views beside;
Old Burgess Steel was able to promote
An humble man who served him with a vote;
For Isaac felt not what some tempers feel,
But bow'd and bent the neck to Burgess Steel;
And great attention to a lady gave,
His ancient friend, a maiden spare and grave:
One whom the visage long and look demure
Of Isaac pleased—he seem'd sedate and pure;
And his soft heart conceived a gentle flame
For her who waited on this virtuous dame:
Not an outrageous love, a scorching fire,
But friendly liking and chastised desire;
And thus he waited, patient in delay,
In present favour and in fortune's way.

George then was coasting—war was yet delay'd,
And what he gain'd was to his brother paid;
Nor ask'd the seaman what he saved or spent:
But took his grog, wrought hard, and was content;
Till war awaked the land, and George began
To think what part became a useful man:
"Press'd, I must go; why, then, 't is better far
At once to enter like a British tar,
Than a brave captain and the foe to shun
As if I fear'd the music of a gun."
"Go not!" said Isaac—"You shall wear disguise."
"What!" said the seaman, "clothe myself with lies?"—
"Oh! but there 's danger."—"Danger in the fleet?
You cannot mean, good brother, of defeat;
And other dangers I at land must share—
So now adieu! and trust a brother's care."

Isaac awhile demurr'd—but, in his heart,
So might he share, he was disposed to part:
The better mind will sometimes feel the pain
Of benefactions—favour is a chain;
But they the feeling scorn, and what they wish disdain;—
While beings form'd in coarser mould will hate
The helping hand they ought to venerate;
No wonder George should in this cause prevail,
With one contending who was glad to fail:
"Isaac, farewell! do wipe that doleful eye;
Crying we came, and groaning we may die.
Let us do something 'twixt the groan and cry:
And hear me, brother, whether pay or prize,
One half to thee I give and I devise;
For thou hast oft occasion for the aid
Of learn'd physicians, and they will be paid:
Their wives and children men support, at sea,
And thou, my lad, art wife and child to me:
Farewell!—I go where hope and honour call,
Nor does it follow that who fights must fall."

Isaac here made a poor attempt to speak,
And a huge tear moved slowly down his cheek;
Like Pluto's iron drop, hard sign of grace,
It slowly roll'd upon the rueful face,
Forced by the striving will alone its way to trace.

Years fled—war lasted—George at sea remain'd,
While the slow landman still his profits gain'd:
A humble place was vacant—he besought
His patron's interest, and the office caught;
For still the virgin was his faithful friend,
And one so sober could with truth commend,
Who of his own defects most humbly thought,
And their advice with zeal and reverence sought:
Whom thus the mistress praised, the maid approved,
And her he wedded whom he wisely loved.

No more he needs assistance—but, alas!
He fears the money will for liquor pass;
Or that the seaman might to flatterers lend,
Or give support to some pretended friend:
Still he must write—he wrote, and he confess'd
That, till absolved, he should be sore distress'd;
But one so friendly would, he thought, forgive
The hasty deed—Heav'n knew how he should live;
"But you," he added, "as a man of sense,
Have well consider'd danger and expense:
I ran, alas! into the fatal snare,
And now for trouble must my mind prepare;
And how, with children, I shall pick my way,
Through a hard world, is more than I can say:
Then change not, brother, your more happy state,
Or on the hazard long deliberate."

George answer'd gravely, "It is right and fit,
In all our crosses, humbly to submit:
Your apprehensions are unwise, unjust;
Forbear repining, and expel distrust."—
He added, "Marriage was the joy of life,"
And gave his service to his brother's wife;
Then vow'd to bear in all expense a part,
And thus concluded, "Have a cheerful heart."

Had the glad Isaac been his brother's guide,
In these same terms the seaman had replied;
At such reproofs the crafty landman smiled,
And softly said—"This creature is a child."

Twice had the gallant ship a capture made—
And when in port the happy crew were paid,
Home went the sailor, with his pocket stored,
Ease to enjoy, and pleasure to afford;
His time was short, joy shone in every face,
Isaac half fainted in the fond embrace:
The wife resolved her honour'd guest to please,
The children clung upon their uncle's knees;
The grog went round, the neighbours drank his health,
And George exclaim'd—"Ah! what to this is wealth?
Better," said he, "to bear a loving heart,
Than roll in riches——but we now must part!"

All yet is still—but hark! the winds o'ersweep
The rising waves, and howl upon the deep;
Ships late becalm'd on mountain-billows ride—
So life is threaten'd and so man is tried.

Ill were the tidings that arrived from sea,
The worthy George must now a cripple be;
His leg was lopp'd; and though his heart wa sound,
Though his brave captain was with glory crown'd—
Yet much it vex'd him to repose on shore,
An idle log, and be of use no more:
True, he was sure that Isaac would receive
All of his brother that the foe might leave;
To whom the seaman his design had sent,
Ere from the port the wounded hero went:

His wealth and expectations told, he "knew
Wherein they fail'd, what Isaac's love would do;
That he the grog and cabin would supply,
Where George at anchor during life would lie."

The landman read—and, reading, grew distress'd:—
"Could he resolve t' admit so poor a guest?
Better at Greenwich might the sailor stay,
Unless his purse could for his comforts pay;"
So Isaac judged, and to his wife appeal'd,
But yet acknowledged it was best to yield:
"Perhaps his pension, with what sums remain
Due or unsquander'd, may the man maintain;
Refuse we must not."—With a heavy sigh
The lady heard, and made her kind reply:
"Nor would I wish it, Isaac, were we sure
How long his crazy building will endure;
Like an old house, that every day appears
About to fall—he may be propp'd for years;
For a few months, indeed, we might comply,
But these old batter'd fellows never die."

The hand of Isaac, George on entering took,
With love and resignation in his look;
Declared his comfort in the fortune past,
And joy to find his anchor safely cast;
Call then my nephews, let the grog be brought,
And I will tell them how the ship was fought."

Alas! our simple seaman should have known,
That all the care, the kindness, he had shown,
Were from his brother's heart, if not his memory, flown:
All swept away to be perceived no more,
Like idle structures on the sandy shore;
The chance amusement of the playful boy,
That the rude billows in their rage destroy.

Poor George confess'd, though loth the truth to find,
Slight was his knowledge of a brother's mind:
The vulgar pipe was to the wife offence,
The frequent grog to Isaac an expense;
Would friends like hers, she question'd, "choose to come,
Where clouds of poison'd fume defiled a room?
This could their lady-friend, and Burgess Steel,
(Teased with his worship's asthma) bear to feel?
Could they associate or converse with him—
A loud rough sailor with a timber limb?"

Cold as he grew, still Isaac strove to show,
By well-feign'd care, that cold he could not grow;
And when he saw his brother look distress'd,
He strove some petty comforts to suggest;
On his wife solely their neglect to lay,
And then t' excuse it, is a woman's way;
He too was chidden when her rules he broke,
And then she sicken'd at the scent of smoke.

George, though in doubt, was still consoled to find
His brother wishing to be reckon'd kind:
That Isaac seem'd concern'd by his distress
Gave to his injured feelings some redress:
But none he found disposed to lend an ear
To stories, all were once intent to hear:
Except his nephew, seated on his knee,
He found no creature cared about the sea;

But George indeed—for George they call'd the boy,
When his good uncle was their boast and joy—
Would listen long, and would contend with sleep,
To hear the woes and wonders of the deep;
Till the fond mother cried—"That man will teach
The foolish boy his loud and boisterous speech."
So judged the father—and the boy was taught
To shun the uncle, whom his love had sought.

The mask of kindness now but seldom worn,
George felt each evil harder to be borne;
And cried (vexation growing day by day,)
"Ah! brother Isaac!—What! I'm in the way!"
"No! on my credit, look ye, No! but I
Am fond of peace, and my repose would buy
On any terms—in short, we must comply:
My spouse had money—she must have her will—
Ah! brother—marriage is a bitter pill."—

George tried the lady—"Sister, I offend."
"Me?" she replied—"Oh no!—you may depend
On my regard—but watch your brother's way,
Whom I, like you, must study and obey."

"Ah!" thought the seaman, "what a head was mine,
That easy berth at Greenwich to resign!
I'll to the parish"——but a little pride,
And some affection, put the thought aside.

Now gross neglect and open scorn he bore
In silent sorrow—but he felt the more:
The odious pipe he to the kitchen took,
Or strove to profit by some pious book.

When the mind stoops to this degraded state,
New griefs will darken the dependant's fate;
"Brother!" said Isaac, "you will sure excuse
The little freedom I'm compell'd to use:
My wife's relations—(curse the haughty crew)—
Affect such niceness, and such dread of you:
You speak so loud—and they have natures soft—
Brother——I wish——do go upon the loft!"

Poor George obey'd, and to the garret fled,
Where not a being saw the tears he shed:
But more was yet required, for guests were come
Who could not dine if he disgraced the room.
It shock'd his spirit to be esteem'd unfit
With an own brother and his wife to sit;
He grew rebellious—at the vestry spoke
For weekly aid——they heard it as a joke:
"So kind a brother, and so wealthy——you
Apply to us?——No! this will never do:
Good neighbour Fletcher," said the overseer,
"We are engaged—you can have nothing here!"

George mutter'd something in despairing tone,
Then sought his loft, to think and grieve alone;
Neglected, slighted, restless on his bed,
With heart half broken, and with scraps ill fed;
Yet was he pleased, that hours for play design'd
Were given to ease his ever-troubled mind;
The child still listen'd with increasing joy,
And he was soothed by the attentive boy.

At length he sicken'd, and this duteous child
Watch'd o'er his sickness, and his pains beguiled;
The mother bade him from the loft refrain,
But, though with caution, yet he went again;

And now his tales the sailor feebly told,
His heart was heavy, and his limbs were cold:
The tender boy came often to entreat
His good kind friend would of his presents eat;
Purloin'd or purchased, for he saw, with shame,
The food untouch'd that to his uncle came;
Who, sick in body and in mind, received
The boy's indulgence, gratified and grieved.

"Uncle will die!" said George—the piteous wife
Exclaim'd, "she saw no value in his life;
But sick or well, to my commands attend,
And go no more to your complaining friend."
The boy was vex'd; he felt his heart reprove
The stern decree.—What! punish'd for his love!
No! he would go, but softly to the room,
Stealing in silence—for he knew his doom.

Once in a week the father came to say,
"George, are you ill?"—and hurried him away;
Yet to his wife would on their duties dwell,
And often cry, "Do use my brother well:"
And something kind, no question, Isaac meant,
Who took vast credit for the vague intent.
But truly kind, the gentle boy essay'd
To cheer his uncle, firm, although afraid;
But now the father caught him at the door,
And, swearing—yes, the man in office swore,
And cried, "Away! How! brother, I'm surprised,
That one so old can be so ill advised:
Let him not dare to visit you again,
Your cursed stories will disturb his brain;
Is it not vile to court a foolish boy,
Your own absurd narrations to enjoy?
What! sullen!—ha! George Fletcher! you shall see,
Proud as you are, your bread depends on me!"

He spoke, and, frowning, to his dinner went,
Then cool'd and felt some qualms of discontent;
And thought on times when he compell'd his son
To hear these stories, nay, to beg for one:
But the wife's wrath o'ercame the brother's pain,
And shame was felt, and conscience rose in vain.

George yet stole up, he saw his uncle lie
Sick on the bed, and heard his heavy sigh:
So he resolved, before he went to rest,
To comfort one so dear and so distress'd;
Then watch'd his time, but with a child-like art,
Betray'd a something treasured at his heart:
Th' observant wife remark'd, "the boy is grown
So like your brother, that he seems his own;
So close and sullen! and I still suspect
They often meet—do watch them and detect."

George now remark'd that all was still as night,
And hasten'd up with terror and delight;
"Uncle!" he cried, and softly tapp'd the door;
"Do let me in"—but he could add no more;
The careful father caught him in the fact,
And cried,—"You serpent! is it thus you act?
Back to your mother!"—and with hasty blow,
He sent th' indignant boy to grieve below;
Then at the door an angry speech began—
"Is this your conduct?—is it thus you plan?
Seduce my child, and make my house a scene
Of vile dispute——What is it that you mean?—
George, are you dumb? do learn to know your friends,
And think awhile on whom your bread depends:
What? not a word? be thankful I am cool—
But, sir, beware, nor longer play the fool;
Come! Brother, come! what is it that you seek
By this rebellion?—Speak, you villain, speak!—
Weeping! I warrant—sorrow makes you dumb:
I'll ope your mouth, impostor! if I come:
Let me approach—I'll shake you from the bed,
You stubborn dog——Oh God! my brother's dead!—"

Timid was Isaac, and in all the past
He felt a purpose to be kind at last;
Nor did he mean his brother to depart,
Till he had shown this kindness of his heart:
But day by day he put the cause aside,
Induced by av'rice, peevishness, or pride.
But now awaken'd from this fatal time
His conscience Isaac felt, and found his crime:
He raised to George a monumental stone,
And there retired to sigh and think alone;
An ague seized him, he grew pale, and shook—
"So," said his son, "would my poor uncle look."
"And so, my child, shall I like him expire."
"No! you have physic and a cheerful fire."
"Unhappy sinner! yes, I'm well supplied
With every comfort my cold heart denied."
He view'd his brother now, but not as one
Who vex'd his wife by fondness for her son;
Not as with wooden limb, and seaman's tale,
The odious pipe, vile grog, or humbler ale:
He now the worth and grief alone can view
Of one so mild, so generous, and so true;
"The frank, kind brother, with such open heart,
And I to break it—'t was a demon's part!"

So Isaac now, as led by conscience, feels,
Nor his unkindness palliates or conceals.
"This is your folly," said his heartless wife:
"Alas! my folly cost my brother's life;
It suffer'd him to languish and decay,
My gentle brother, whom I could not pay,
And therefore left to pine, and fret his life away."

He takes his son, and bids the boy unfold
All the good uncle of his feelings told,
All he lamented—and the ready tear
Falls as he listens, soothed, and grieved to hear.

"Did he not curse me, child?"—"He never cursed,
But could not breathe, and said his heart would burst:"
"And so will mine:"—"Then, father, you must pray;
My uncle said it took his pains away."

Repeating thus his sorrows, Isaac shows
That he, repenting, feels the debt he owes,
And from this source alone his every comfort flows.
He takes no joy in office, honours, gain;
They make him humble, nay, they give him pain;
"These from my heart," he cries, "all feeling drove,
They made me cold to nature, dead to love:"
He takes no joy in home, but sighing, sees
A son in sorrow, and a wife at ease:
He takes no joy in office—see him now,
And Burgess Steel has but a passing bow;
Of one sad train of gloomy thoughts possess'd,
He takes no joy in friends, in food, in rest—
Dark are the evil days, and void of peace the best

As thus he lives, if living be to sigh,
And from all comforts of the world to fly,
Without a hope in life—without a wish to die.

TALE XXI.

THE LEARNED BOY.

Like one well studied in a sad ostent,
To please his grandam.
Merchant of Venice, act ii, scene 2.

And then the whining school-boy, with his satchel
And shining morning face, creeping like snail,
Unwillingly to school.
As You Like It, act ii, scene 7.

He is a better scholar than I thought he was—
He has a good sprag memory.
Merry Wives of Windsor, act iv, scene 1.

One that feeds
On objects, arts, and imitations,
Which out of use, and stal'd by other men,
Begin his fashion.
Julius Cæsar, act iv, scene 1.

Oh! torture me no more—I will confess.
Henry VI, Part 2. act iii, scene 3.

An honest man was Farmer Jones, and true,
He did by all as all by him should do;
Grave, cautious, careful, fond of gain was he,
Yet famed for rustic hospitality:
Left with his children in a widow'd state,
The quiet man submitted to his fate;
Though prudent matrons waited for his call,
With cool forbearance he avoided all;
Though each profess'd a pure maternal joy,
By kind attention to his feeble boy:
And though a friendly widow knew no rest,
Whilst neighbour Jones was lonely and distress'd;
Nay, though the maidens spoke in tender tone
Their hearts' concern to see him left alone—
Jones still persisted in that cheerless life,
As if 't were sin to take a second wife.

Oh! 't is a precious thing, when wives are dead,
To find such numbers who will serve instead:
And in whatever state a man be thrown,
'T is that precisely they would wish their own;
Left the departed infants—then their joy
Is to sustain each lovely girl and boy:
Whatever calling his, whatever trade,
To that their chief attention has been paid;
His happy taste in all things they approve,
His friends they honour, and his food they love;
His wish for order, prudence in affairs,
And equal temper, (thank their stars!) are theirs;
In fact, it seem'd to be a thing decreed,
And fix'd as fate, that marriage must succeed;
Yet some like Jones, with stubborn hearts and hard,
Can hear such claims, and show them no regard.

Soon as our farmer, like a general, found
By what strong foes he was encompass'd round—
Engage he dared not, and he could not fly,
But saw his hope in gentle parley lie;
With looks of kindness then, and trembling heart,
He met the foe, and art opposed to art.

Now spoke that foe insidious—gentle tones,
And gentle looks, assumed for Farmer Jones:
"Three girls," the widow cried, "a lively three
To govern well—indeed it cannot be."
"Yes," he replied, "it calls for pains and care;
But I must bear it:"—"Sir, you cannot bear;
Your son is weak, and asks a mother's eye:"
"That, my kind friend, a father's may supply:"
"Such growing griefs your very soul will tease:"
"To grieve another would not give me ease—
I have a mother"—"She, poor ancient soul!
Can she the spirits of the young control?
Can she thy peace promote, partake thy care,
Procure thy comforts, and thy sorrows share?
Age is itself impatient, uncontroll'd:"
"But wives like mothers must at length be old."
"Thou hast shrewd servants—they are evils sore:"
"Yet a shrewd mistress might afflict me more."
"Wilt thou not be a weary wailing man?"
"Alas! and I must bear it as I can."

Resisted thus, the widow soon withdrew,
That in his pride the hero might pursue;
And off his wonted guard, in some retreat,
Find from a foe prepared entire defeat:
But he was prudent, for he knew in flight
These Parthian warriors turn again and fight:
He but at freedom, not at glory aim'd,
And only safety by his caution claim'd.

Thus, when a great and powerful state decrees,
Upon a small one, in its love, to seize—
It vows in kindness to protect, defend,
And be the fond ally, the faithful friend;
It therefore wills that humbler state to place
Its hopes of safety in a fond embrace;
Then must that humbler state its wisdom prove,
By kind rejection of such pressing love;
Must dread such dangerous friendship to commence,
And stand collected in its own defence:—
Our farmer thus the proffer'd kindness fled,
And shunn'd the love that into bondage led.

The widow failing, fresh besiegers came,
To share the fate of this retiring dame:
And each foresaw a thousand ills attend
The man, that fled from so discreet a friend;
And pray'd, kind soul! that no event might make
The harden'd heart of Farmer Jones to ache.

But still he govern'd with resistless hand,
And where he could not guide he would command:
With steady view in course direct he steer'd,
And his fair daughters loved him, though they fear'd;
Each had her school, and as his wealth was known,
Each had in time a household of her own.

The boy indeed was, at the grandam's side,
Humour'd and train'd, her trouble and her pride:
Companions dear, with speech and spirits mild,
The childish widow and the vapourish child;
This nature prompts; minds uninform'd and weak
In such alliance ease and comfort seek;
Push'd by the levity of youth aside,
The cares of man, his humour, or his pride,
They feel, in their defenceless state, allied:
The child is pleased to meet regard from age,
The old are pleased ev'n children to engage;

And all their wisdom, scorn'd by proud mankind,
They love to pour into the ductile mind;
By its own weakness into error led,
And by fond age with prejudices fed.

The father, thankful for the good he had,
Yet saw with pain a whining timid lad;
Whom he instructing led through cultured fields,
To show what man performs, what nature yields:
But Stephen, listless, wander'd from the view,
From beasts he fled, for butterflies he flew,
And idly gazed about, in search of something new.
The lambs indeed he loved, and wish'd to play
With things so mild, so harmless, and so gay;
Best pleased the weakest of the flock to see,
With whom he felt a sickly sympathy.

Meantime, the dame was anxious, day and night,
To guide the notions of her babe aright,
And on the favourite mind to throw her glimmering light;
Her Bible-stories she impress'd betimes,
And fill'd his head with hymns and holy rhymes;
On powers unseen, the good and ill, she dwelt,
And the poor boy mysterious terrors felt;
From frightful dreams, he waking sobb'd in dread,
Till the good lady came to guard his bed.

The father wish'd such errors to correct,
But let them pass in duty and respect:
But more it grieved his worthy mind to see
That Stephen never would a farmer be;
In vain he tried the shiftless lad to guide,
And yet 't was time that something should be tried:
He at the village-school perchance might gain
All that such mind could gather and retain;
Yet the good dame affirm'd her favourite child
Was apt and studious, though sedate and mild;
"That he on many a learned point could speak,
And that his body, not his mind, was weak."

The father doubted—but to school was sent
The timid Stephen, weeping as he went:
There the rude lads compell'd the child to fight,
And sent him bleeding to his home at night;
At this the grandam more indulgent grew,
And bade her darling "shun the beastly crew;
Whom Satan ruled, and who were sure to lie,
Howling in torments, when they came to die:"
This was such comfort, that in high disdain
He told their fate, and felt their blows again:
Yet if the boy had not a hero's heart,
Within the school he play'd a better part;
He wrote a clean fine hand, and at his slate,
With more success than many a hero, sate;
He thought not much indeed—but what depends
On pains and care, was at his fingers' ends.

This had his father's praise, who now espied
A spark of merit, with a blaze of pride:
And though a farmer he would never make,
He might a pen with some advantage take;
And as a clerk that instrument employ,
So well adapted to a timid boy.

A London cousin soon a place obtain'd,
Easy but humble—little could be gain'd:
The time arrived when youth and age must part,
Tears in each eye, and sorrow in each heart;
The careful father bade his son attend
To all his duties, and obey his friend;
To keep his church and there behave aright,
As one existing in his Maker's sight,
Till acts to habits led, and duty to delight;
"Then try, my boy, as quickly as you can,
T' assume the looks and spirit of a man;
I say, be honest, faithful, civil, true,
And this you may, and yet have courage too:
Heroic men, their country's boast and pride,
Have fear'd their God, and nothing fear'd beside;
While others daring, yet imbecile, fly
The power of man, and that of God defy:
Be manly then, though mild, for sure as fate,
Thou art, my Stephen, too effeminate;
Here, take my purse, and make a worthy use
('T is fairly stock'd) of what it will produce:
And now my blessing, not as any charm,
Or conjuration; but 't will do no harm."

Stephen, whose thoughts were wandering up and down,
Now charm'd with promis'd sights in London-town,
Now loth to leave his grandam—lost the force,
The drift, and tenor of this grave discourse;
But, in a general way, he understood
'T was good advice, and meant, "My son, be good;"
And Stephen knew that all such precepts mean
That lads should read their Bible, and be clean.

The good old lady, though in some distress,
Begg'd her dear Stephen would his grief suppress;
"Nay, dry those eyes, my child, and first of all,
Hold fast thy faith, whatever may befall:
Hear the best preacher, and preserve the text
For meditation, till you hear the next;
Within your Bible night and morning look—
There is your duty, read no other book;
Be not in crowds, in broils, in riots seen,
And keep your conscience and your linen clean:
Be you a Joseph, and the time may be,
When kings and rulers will be ruled by thee."

"Nay," said the father—"Hush, my son," replied
The dame—"The Scriptures must not be denied."

The lad, still weeping, heard the wheels approach,
And took his place within the evening coach,
With heart quite rent asunder: On one side
Was love, and grief, and fear, for scenes untried;
Wild-beasts and wax-work fill'd the happier part
Of Stephen's varying and divided heart:
This he betray'd by sighs and questions strange,
Of famous shows, the Tower, and the Exchange.

Soon at his desk was placed the curious boy,
Demure and silent at his new employ:
Yet as he could, he much attention paid
To all around him, cautious and afraid;
On older clerks his eager eyes were fix'd,
But Stephen never in their council mix'd:
Much their contempt he fear'd, for if like them,
He felt assured he should himself contemn;
Oh! they were all so eloquent, so free,
No! he was nothing—nothing could he be:
They dress so smartly, and so boldly look,
And talk as if they read it from a book;
"But I," said Stephen, "will forbear to speak,
And they will think me prudent and not weak

They talk, the instant they have dropp'd the pen,
Of singing-women and of acting-men;
Of plays and places where at night they walk
Beneath the lamps, and with the ladies talk;
While other ladies for their pleasure sing,
Oh! 't is a glorious and a happy thing:
They would despise me, did they understand
I dare not look upon a scene so grand;
Or see the plays when critics rise and roar,
And hiss and groan, and cry—Encore! encore!—
There 's one among them looks a little kind;
If more encouraged, I would ope my mind."

Alas! poor Stephen, happier had he kept
His purpose secret, while his envy slept;
Virtue, perhaps, had conquer'd, or his shame
At least preserved him simple as he came.
A year elapsed before this clerk began
To treat the rustic something like a man;
He then in trifling points the youth advised,
Talk'd of his coat, and had it modernized;
Or with the lad a Sunday-walk would take,
And kindly strive his passions to awake;
Meanwhile explaining all they heard and saw,
Till Stephen stood in wonderment and awe:
To a neat garden near the town they stray'd,
Where the lad felt delighted and afraid;
There all he saw was smart, and fine, and fair—
He could but marvel how he ventured there:
Soon he observed, with terror and alarm,
His friend enlock'd within a lady's arm,
And freely talking—"But it is," said he,
"A near relation, and that makes him free;"
And much amazed was Stephen, when he knew
This was the first and only interview:
Nay, had that lovely arm by him been seized,
The lovely owner had been highly pleased:
"Alas!" he sigh'd, "I never can contrive,
At such bold, blessed freedoms to arrive;
Never shall I such happy courage boast,
I dare as soon encounter with a ghost."

Now to a play the friendly couple went,
But the boy murmur'd at the money spent;
"He loved," he said, "to buy, but not to spend—
They only talk awhile, and there 's an end."

"Come, you shall purchase books," the friend replied;
"You are bewilder'd, and you want a guide;
To me refer the choice, and you shall find
The light break in upon your stagnant mind!"

The cooler clerks exclaim'd, "In vain your art
T' improve a cub without a head or heart;
Rustics though coarse, and savages though wild,
Our cares may render liberal and mild;
But what, my friend, can flow from all these pains!
There is no dealing with a lack of brains."—

"True, I am hopeless to behold him man,
But let me make the booby what I can:
Though the rude stone no polish will display,
Yet you may strip the rugged coat away."

Stephen beheld his books—"I love to know
How money goes—now here is that to show:
And now," he cried, "I shall be pleased to get
Beyond the Bible—there I puzzle yet."

He spoke abash'd—"Nay, nay!" the friend replied,
"You need not lay the good old book aside;
Antique and curious, I myself indeed
Read it at times, but as a man should read;
A fine old work it is, and I protest
I hate to hear it treated as a jest;
The book has wisdom in it, if you look
Wisely upon it, as another book:
For superstition (as our priests of sin
Are pleased to tell us) makes us blind within:
Of this hereafter—we will now select
Some works to please you, others to direct:
Tales and romances shall your fancy feed,
And reasoners form your morals and your creed."

The books were view'd, the price was fairly paid,
And Stephen read undaunted, undismay'd:
But not till first he paper'd all the row,
And placed in order, to enjoy the show;
Next letter'd all the backs with care and speed,
Set them in ranks, and then began to read.

The love of order,—I the thing receive
From reverend men, and I in part believe,—
Shows a clear mind and clean, and whoso needs
This love, but seldom in the world succeeds;
And yet with this some other love must be,
Ere I can fully to the fact agree:
Valour and study may by order gain,
By order sovereigns hold more steady reign:
Through all the tribes of nature order runs,
And rules around in systems and in suns:
Still has the love of order found a place,
With all that 's low, degrading, mean, and base,
With all that merits scorn, and all that meets disgrace:
In the cold miser, of all change afraid,
In pompous men in public seats obey'd;
In humble placemen, heralds, solemn drones,
Fanciers of flowers, and lads like Stephen Jones;
Order to these is armour and defence,
And love of method serves in lack of sense.

For rustic youth could I a list produce
Of Stephen's books, how great might be the use,
But evil fate was theirs—survey'd, enjoy'd
Some happy months, and then by force destroy'd:
So will'd the fates—but these, with patience read,
Had vast effect on Stephen's heart and head.

This soon appear'd—within a single week
He oped his lips, and made attempt to speak;
He fail'd indeed—but still his friend confess'd
The best have fail'd, and he had done his best:
The first of swimmers, when at first he swims,
Has little use or freedom in his limbs;
Nay, when at length he strikes with manly force,
The cramp may seize him, and impede his course
Encouraged thus, our clerk again essay'd
The daring act, though daunted and afraid;
Succeeding now, though partial his success,
And pertness mark'd his manner and address,
Yet such improvement issued from his books,
That all discern'd it in his speech and looks;
He ventured then on every theme to speak,
And felt no feverish tingling in his cheek;
His friend approving, hail'd the happy change,
The clerks exclaim'd—"'T is famous, and 't is strange!"

Two years had pass'd; the youth attended still,
(Though thus accomplish'd) with a ready quill;
He sat th' allotted hours, though hard the case,
While timid prudence ruled in virtue's place;
By promise bound, the son his letters penn'd
To his good parent, at the quarter's end.
At first he sent those lines, the state to tell
Of his own health, and hoped his friends were well;
He kept their virtuous precepts in his mind,
And needed nothing—then his name was sign'd:
But now he wrote of Sunday walks and views,
Of actors' names, choice novels, and strange news;
How coats were cut, and of his urgent need
For fresh supply, which he desired with speed.
The father doubted, when these letters came,
To what they tended, yet was loth to blame:
"Stephen was once *my duteous son*, and now
My most obedient—this can I allow?
Can I with pleasure or with patience see
A boy at once so heartless, and so free?"

But soon the kinsman heavy tidings told,
That love and prudence could no more withhold:
"Stephen, though steady at his desk, was grown
A rake and coxcomb—this he grieved to own;
His cousin left his church, and spent the day
Lounging about in quite a heathen way;
Sometimes he swore, but had indeed the grace
To show the shame imprinted on his face:
I search'd his room, and in his absence read
Books that I knew would turn a stronger head;
The works of atheists half the number made,
The rest were lives of harlots leaving trade;
Which neither man or boy would deign to read,
If from the scandal and pollution freed:
I sometimes threaten'd, and would fairly state
My sense of things so vile and profligate;
But I'm a cit, such works are lost on me—
They're knowledge, and (good Lord!) philosophy."

"Oh, send him down," the father soon replied;
"Let me behold him, and my skill be tried:
If care and kindness lose their wonted use,
Some rougher medicine will the end produce."

Stephen with grief and anger heard his doom—
"Go to the farmer? to the rustic's home?
Curse the base threat'ning—" "Nay, child, never curse;
Corrupted long, your case is growing worse."—
"I!" quoth the youth, "I challenge all mankind
To find a fault; what fault have you to find?
Improve I not in manner, speech, and grace?
Inquire—my friends will tell it to your face;
Have I been taught to guard his kine and sheep?
A man like me has other things to keep;
This let him know."—"It would his wrath excite:
But come, prepare, you must away to-night."
"What! leave my studies, my improvements leave,
My faithful friends and intimates to grieve!"—
"Go to your father, Stephen, let him see
All these improvements: they are lost on me."

The youth, though loth, obey'd, and soon he saw
The farmer-father, with some signs of awe;
Who kind, yet silent, waited to behold
How one would act, so daring, yet so cold:

And soon he found, between the friendly pair
That secrets pass'd which he was not to share;
But he resolved those secrets to obtain,
And quash rebellion in his lawful reign.

Stephen, though vain, was with his father mute,
He fear'd a crisis, and he shunn'd dispute;
And yet he long'd with youthful pride to show
He knew such things as farmers could not know,
These to the grandam he with freedom spoke,
Saw her amazement, and enjoy'd the joke;
But on the father when he cast his eye,
Something he found that made his valour shy;
And thus there seem'd to be a hollow truce,
Still threat'ning something dismal to produce.

Ere this the father at his leisure read
The son's choice volumes, and his wonder fled:
He saw how wrought the works of either kind
On so presuming, yet so weak a mind;
These in a chosen hour he made his prey,
Condemn'd, and bore with vengeful thoughts away,
Then in a close recess the couple near
He sat unseen to see, unheard to hear.

There soon a trial for his patience came;
Beneath were placed the youth and ancient dame,
Each on a purpose fix'd—but neither thought
How near a foe, with power and vengeance fraught.

And now the matron told, as tidings sad,
What she had heard of her beloved lad;
How he to graceless, wicked men gave heed,
And wicked books would night and morning read;
Some former lectures she again began,
And begg'd attention of her little man;
She brought, with many a pious boast, in view
His former studies, and condemn'd the new:
Once he the names of saints and patriarchs old,
Judges and kings, and chiefs and prophets, told;
Then he in winter-nights the Bible took,
To count how often in the sacred book
The sacred name appear'd, and could rehearse
Which were the middle chapter, word, and verse,
The very letter in the middle placed,
And so employ'd the hours that others waste.

"Such wert thou once; and now, my child, they say
Thy faith like water runneth fast away;
The prince of devils hath, I fear, beguiled
The ready wit of my backsliding child."

On this, with lofty looks, our clerk began
His grave rebuke, as he assumed the man—

"There is no devil," said the hopeful youth,
"Nor prince of devils; that I know for truth:
Have I not told you how my books describe
The arts of priests and all the canting tribe?
Your Bible mentions Egypt, where it seems
Was Joseph found when Pharaoh dream'd his dreams:
Now in that place, in some bewilder'd head,
(The learned write) religious dreams were bred;
Whence through the earth, with various forms combined,
They came to frighten and afflict mankind,
Prone (so I read) to let a priest invade
Their souls with awe, and by his craft be made
Slave to his will, and profit to his trade:

So say my books, and how the rogues agreed
To blind the victims, to defraud and lead;
When joys above to ready dupes were sold,
And hell was threaten'd to the shy and cold.

"Why so amazed, and so prepared to pray?
As if a Being heard a word we say:
This may surprise you; I myself began
To feel disturb'd, and to my Bible ran;
I now am wiser—yet agree in this,
The book has things that are not much amiss;
It is a fine old work, and I protest
I hate to hear it treated as a jest:
The book has wisdom in it, if you look
Wisely upon it as another book."—

"Oh! wicked! wicked! my unhappy child,
How hast thou been by evil men beguiled!"

"How! wicked, say you? you can little guess
The gain of that which you call wickedness:
Why, sins you think it sinful but to name
Have gain'd both wives and widows wealth and fame;
And this because such people never dread
Those threaten'd pains; hell comes not in their head:
Love is our nature, wealth we all desire,
And what we wish 't is lawful to acquire;
So say my books—and what beside they show
'T is time to let this honest farmer know.
Nay, look not grave; am I commanded down
To feed his cattle and become his clown?
Is such his purpose? then he shall be told
The vulgar insult—"

—"Hold, in mercy hold—"
"Father, oh! father! throw the whip away;
I was but jesting, on my knees I pray—
There, hold his arm—oh! leave us not alone:
In pity cease, and I will yet atone
For all my sin—" In vain; stroke after stroke,
On side and shoulder, quick as mill-wheels broke;
Quick as the patient's pulse, who trembling cried,
And still the parent with a stroke replied;
Till all the medicine he prepared was dealt,
And every bone the precious influence felt;
Till all the panting flesh was red and raw,
And every thought was turn'd to fear and awe;
Till every doubt to due respect gave place—
Such cures are done when doctors know the case.

"Oh! I shall die—my father! do receive
My dying words; indeed I do believe;
The books are lying books, I know it well,
There is a devil, oh! there is a hell;
And I 'm a sinner: spare me, I am young,
My sinful words were only on my tongue;
My heart consented not; 't is all a lie;
Oh! spare me then, I 'm not prepared to die."

"Vain, worthless, stupid wretch!" the father cried,
"Dost thou presume to teach? art thou a guide?
Driveller and dog, it gave the mind distress
To hear thy thoughts in their religious dress;
Thy pious folly moved my strong disdain,
Yet I forgave thee for thy want of brain:
But Job in patience must the man exceed
Who could endure thee in thy present creed;
Is it for thee, thou idiot, to pretend
The wicked cause a helping hand to lend?
Canst thou a judge in any question be?
Atheists themselves would scorn a friend like thee.—

"Lo! yonder blaze thy worthies; in one heap
Thy scoundrel-favourites must for ever sleep:
Each yields its poison to the flame in turn,
Where whores and infidels are doom'd to burn;
Two noble faggots made the flame you see,
Reserving only two fair twigs for thee;
That in thy view the instruments may stand,
And be in future ready for my hand:
The just mementos that, though silent, show
Whence thy correction and improvements flow;
Beholding these, thou wilt confess their power,
And feel the shame of this important hour.

"Hadst thou been humble, I had first design'd
By care from folly to have freed thy mind;
And when a clean foundation had been laid,
Our priest, more able, would have lent his aid:
But thou art weak, and force must folly guide,
And thou art vain, and pain must humble pride:
Teachers men honour, learners they allure;
But learners teaching, of contempt are sure;
Scorn is their certain meed, and smart their only cure!"

Tales of the Hall.

TO HER GRACE THE DUCHESS OF RUTLAND.

MADAM,

IT is the privilege of those who are placed in that elevated situation to which your Grace is an ornament, that they give honour to the person upon whom they confer a favour. When I dedicate to your Grace the fruits of many years, and speak of my debt to the House of Rutland, I feel that I am not without pride in the confession, nor insensible to the honour which such gratitude implies. Forty years have elapsed since this debt commenced. On my entrance into the cares of life, and while contending with its difficulties, a Duke and Duchess of Rutland observed and protected me—in my progress a Duke and Duchess of Rutland favoured and assisted me—and, when I am retiring from the world, a Duke and Duchess of Rutland receive my thanks, and accept my offering. All, even in this world of mutability, is not change: I have experienced unvaried favour—I have felt undiminished respect.

With the most grateful remembrance of what I owe, and the most sincere conviction of the little I can return, I present these pages to your Grace's acceptance, and beg leave to subscribe myself,

May it please your Grace,
With respect and gratitude,
Your Grace's most obedient and devoted Servant,
GEORGE CRABBE.

Trowbridge, June, 1819.

PREFACE.

If I did not fear that it would appear to my readers like arrogancy, or if it did not seem to myself indecorous to send two volumes of considerable magnitude from the press without preface or apology, without one petition for the reader's attention, or one plea for the writer's defects, I would most willingly spare myself an address of this kind, and more especially for these reasons; first, because a preface is a part of a book seldom honoured by a reader's perusal; secondly, because it is both difficult and distressing to write that which we think will be disregarded; and thirdly, because I do not conceive that I am called upon for such introductory matter by any of the motives which usually influence an author when he composes his prefatory address.

When a writer, whether of poetry or prose, first addresses the public, he has generally something to offer which relates to himself or to his work, and which he considers as a necessary prelude to the work itself, to prepare his readers for the entertainment or the instruction they may expect to receive, for one of these every man who publishes must suppose he affords—this the act itself implies; and in proportion to his conviction of this fact must be his feeling of the difficulty in which he has placed himself: the difficulty consists in reconciling the implied presumption of the undertaking, whether to please or to instruct mankind, with the diffidence and modesty of an untried candidate for fame or favour. Hence originate the many reasons an author assigns for his appearance in that character, whether they actually exist, or are merely offered to hide the motives which cannot be openly avowed; namely, the want or the vanity of the man, as his wishes for profit or reputation may most prevail with him.

Now, reasons of this kind, whatever they may be, cannot be availing beyond their first appearance. An author, it is true, may again feel his former apprehensions, may again be elevated or depressed by the suggestions of vanity and diffidence, and may be again subject to the cold and hot fit of aguish expectation; but he is no more a stranger to the press, nor has the motives or privileges of one who is. With respect to myself, it is certain they belong not to me. Many years have elapsed since I became a candidate for indulgence as an inexperienced writer; and to assume the language of such writer now, and to plead for his indulgences, would be proof of my ignorance of the place assigned to me, and the degree of favour which I have experienced; but of that place I am not uninformed, and with that degree of favour I have no reason to be dissatisfied.

It was the remark of the pious, but on some occasions the querulous author of the *Night Thoughts*, that he had "been so long remembered, he was forgotten;" an expression in which there is more appearance of discontent than of submission: if he had patience, it was not the patience that *smiles at grief*. It is not therefore entirely in the sense of the good Doctor that I apply these words to myself, or to my more early publications. So many years indeed have passed since their first appearance, that I have no reason to complain, on that account, if they be now slumbering with other poems of decent reputation in their day—not dead indeed, nor entirely forgotten, but certainly not the subjects of discussion or conversation as when first introduced to the notice of the public, by those whom the public will not forget, whose protection was credit to their author, and whose approbation was fame to them. Still these early publications had so long preceded any other, that, if not altogether unknown, I was, when I came again before the public, in a situation which excused, and perhaps rendered necessary some explanation; but this also has passed away, and none of my readers will now take the trouble of making any inquiries respecting my motives for writing or for publishing these Tales or verses of any description: known to each other as readers and authors are known, they will require no preface to bespeak their good will, nor shall I be under the necessity of soliciting the kindness which experience has taught me, endeavouring to merit, I shall not fail to receive.

There is one motive—and it is a powerful one—which sometimes induces an author, and more particularly a poet, to ask the attention of his readers to his prefatory addresses. This is when he has some favourite and peculiar style or manner which he would explain and defend, and chiefly if he should have adopted a mode of versification of which an uninitiated reader was not likely to perceive either the merit or the beauty. In such case it is natural, and surely pardonable, to assert and to prove, as far as reason will bear us on, that such method of writing has both; to show in what the beauty consists, and what peculiar difficulty there is, which, when conquered, creates the merit. How far any particular poet has or has not succeeded in such attempt is not my business nor my purpose to inquire: I have no peculiar notion to defend, no poetical heterodoxy to support, nor theory of any kind to vindicate or oppose—that which I have used is probably the most common measure in our language; and therefore, whatever be its advantages or defects, they are too well known to require from me a description of the one, or an apology for the other.

Perhaps still more frequent than any explanation

of the work is an account of the author himself, the situation in which he is placed, or some circumstances of peculiar kind in his life, education, or employment. How often has youth been pleaded for deficiencies or redundancies, for the existence of which youth may be an excuse, and yet be none for their exposure! Age too has been pleaded for the errors and failings in a work which the octogenarian had the discernment to perceive, and yet had not the fortitude to suppress. Many other circumstances are made apologies for a writer's infirmities; his much employment, and many avocations, adversity, necessity, and the good of mankind. These, or any of them, however availing in themselves, avail not me. I am neither so young nor so old, so much engaged by one pursuit, or by many,—I am not so urged by want, or so stimulated by a desire of public benefit,—that I can borrow one apology from the many which I have named. How far they prevail with our readers, or with our judges, I cannot tell; and it is unnecessary for me to inquire into the validity of arguments which I have not to produce.

If there be any combination of circumstances which may be supposed to affect the mind of a reader, and in some degree to influence his judgment, the junction of youth, beauty, and merit in a female writer may be allowed to do this; and yet one of the most forbidding of titles is "Poems by a very young Lady," and this although beauty and merit were largely insinuated. Ladies, it is true, have of late little need of any indulgence as authors, and names may readily be found which rather excite the envy of man than plead for his lenity. Our estimation of title also in a writer has materially varied from that of our predecessors; "Poems by a Nobleman" would create a very different sensation in our minds from that which was formerly excited when they were so announced. A noble author had then no pretensions to a seat so secure on the "sacred hill," that authors not noble, and critics not gentle, dared not attack; and they delighted to take revenge by their contempt and derision of the poet, for the pain which their submission and respect to the man had cost them. But in our times we find that a nobleman writes, not merely as well, but better than other men; insomuch that readers in general begin to fancy that the Muses have relinquished their old partiality for rags and a garret, and are become altogether aristocratical in their choice. A conceit so well supported by fact would be readily admitted, did it not appear at the same time, that there were in the higher ranks of society men, who could write as tamely, or as absurdly, as they had ever been accused of doing. We may, therefore, regard the works of any noble author as extraordinary productions; but must not found any theory upon them; and, notwithstanding their appearance, must look on genius and talent as we are wont to do on time and chance, that happen indifferently to all mankind.

But whatever influence any peculiar situation of a writer might have, it cannot be a benefit to me, who have no such peculiarity. I must rely upon the willingness of my readers to be pleased with that which was designed to give them pleasure, and upon the cordiality which naturally springs from a remembrance of our having before parted without any feelings of disgust on the one side, or of mortification on the other.

With this hope I would conclude the present subject; but I am called upon by duty to acknowledge my obligations, and more especially for two of the following Tales:—the Story of Lady Barbara, in Book XVI, and that of Ellen, in Book XVIII. The first of these I owe to the kindness of a fair friend, who will, I hope, accept the thanks which I very gratefully pay, and pardon me if I have not given to her relation the advantages which she had so much reason to expect. The other story, that of Ellen, could I give it in the language of him who related it to me, would please and affect my readers. It is by no means my only debt, though the one I now more particularly acknowledge; for who shall describe all that he gains in the social, the unrestrained, and the frequent conversations with a friend, who is at once communicative and judicious?—whose opinions, on all subjects of literary kind, are founded on good taste, and exquisite feeling? It is one of the greatest "pleasures of my memory" to recall in absence those conversations; and if I do not in direct terms mention with whom I conversed, it is both because I have no permission, and my readers will have no doubt.

The first intention of the poet must be to please; for, if he means to instruct, he must render the instruction which he hopes to convey palatable and pleasant. I will not assume the tone of a moralist, nor promise that my relations shall be beneficial to mankind; but I have endeavoured, not unsuccessfully I trust, that, in whatsoever I have related or described, there should be nothing introduced which has a tendency to excuse the vices of man, by associating with them sentiments that demand our respect, and talents that compel our admiration.—There is nothing in these pages which has the mischievous effect of confounding truth and error, or confusing our ideas of right and wrong. I know not which is most injurious to the yielding minds of the young, to render virtue less respectable by making its possessors ridiculous, or by describing vice with so many fascinating qualities, that it is either lost in the assemblage, or pardoned by the association. Man's heart is sufficiently prone to make excuse for man's infirmity; and needs not the aid of poetry, or eloquence, to take from vice its native deformity. A character may be respectable with all its faults, but it must not be made respectable by them. It is grievous when genius will condescend to place strong and evil spirits in a commanding view, or excite our pity and admiration for men of talents, degraded by crime, when struggling with misfortune. It is but too true that great and wicked men may be so presented to us, as to demand our applause, when they should excite our abhorrence; but it is surely for the interest of mankind, and our own self-direction, that we should ever keep at unapproachable distance our respect and our reproach.

I have one observation more to offer. It may appear to some that a minister of religion, in the decline of life, should have no leisure for such amusements as these; and for them I have no reply;—but to those who are more indulgent to the propensities, the studies, and the habits of mankind, I offer some apology when I produce these volumes, not as the occupations of my life, but the fruits of my leisure, the employment of that time which, if not given to them, had passed in the vacuity of unrecorded idleness; or had been lost in the indulgence of unregistered thoughts and fancies, that melt away in the instant they are conceived, and "*leave not a wreck behind.*"

TALES OF THE HALL.

BOOK I.

THE HALL.

The Meeting of the Brothers, George and Richard —The Retirement of the elder to his native Village—Objects and Persons whom he found there —The Brother described in various Particulars —The Invitation and Journey of the younger— His Soliloquy and Arrival.

The Brothers met who many a year had past
Since their last meeting, and that seem'd their last;
They had no parent then or common friend
Who might their hearts to mutual kindness bend;
Who, touching both in their divided state,
Might generous thoughts and warm desires create;
For there are minds whom we must first excite
And urge to feeling, ere they can unite;
As we may hard and stubborn metals beat
And blend together, if we duly heat.

The elder, George, had past his threescore years,
A busy actor, sway'd by hopes and fears
Of powerful kind; and he had fill'd the parts
That try our strength and agitate our hearts.
He married not, and yet he well approved
The social state; but then he rashly loved;
Gave to a strong delusion all his youth,
Led by a vision till alarm'd by truth:
That vision past, and of that truth possest,
His passions wearied and disposed to rest,
George yet had will and power a place to choose,
Where Hope might sleep, and terminate her views.

He chose his native village, and the hill
He climb'd a boy had its attraction still;
With that small brook beneath, where he would stand,
And stooping fill the hollow of his hand
To quench th' impatient thirst—then stop awhile
To see the sun upon the waters smile,
In that sweet weariness, when, long denied,
We drink and view the fountain that supplied
The sparkling bliss—and feel, if not express,
Our perfect ease in that sweet weariness.

The oaks yet flourish'd in that fertile ground,
Where still the church with lofty tower was found;

And still that Hall, a first, a favourite view,
But not the elms that form'd its avenue;
They fell ere George arrived, or yet had stood,
For he in reverence held the living wood,
That widely spreads in earth the deepening root,
And lifts to heaven the still aspiring shoot;
From age to age they fill'd a growing space,
But hid the mansion they were meant to grace.

It was an ancient, venerable hall,
And once surrounded by a moat and wall;
A part was added by a squire of taste,
Who, while unvalued acres ran to waste,
Made spacious rooms, whence he could look about,
And mark improvements as they rose without:
He fill'd the moat, he took the wall away,
He thinn'd the park, and bade the view be gay:
The scene was rich, but he who should behold
Its worth was poor, and so the whole was sold.

Just then our merchant from his desk retired,
And made the purchase that his heart desired;
The Hall of Binning, his delight a boy,
That gave his fancy in her flight employ;
Here, from his father's modest home, he gazed,
Its grandeur charm'd him, and its height amazed:
Work of past ages; and the brick-built place
Where he resided was in much disgrace;
But never in his fancy's proudest dream
Did he the master of that mansion seem:
Young was he then, and little did he know
What years on care and diligence bestow;
Now young no more, retired to views well known,
He finds that object of his awe his own;
The Hall at Binning!—how he loves the gloom
That sun-excluding window gives the room;
Those broad brown stairs on which he loves to tread;
Those beams within; without, that length of lead,
On which the names of wanton boys appear,
Who died old men, and left memorials here,
Carvings of feet and hands, and knots and flowers,
The fruits of busy minds in idle hours.

Here, while our squire the modern part possess'd,
His partial eye upon the old would rest;
That best his comforts gave—this sooth'd his feelings best.

Here day by day, withdrawn from busy life,
No child t' awake him, to engage no wife,
When friends were absent, not to books inclined,
He found a sadness steal upon his mind;
Sighing, the works of former lords to see,
"I follow them," he cried, "but who will follow me?"

Some ancient men whom he a boy had known
He knew again, their changes were his own;
Comparing now he view'd them, and he felt
That time with him in lenient mood had dealt;
While some the half-distinguish'd features bore
That he was doubtful if he saw before,
And some in memory lived, whom he must see no more.

Here George had found, yet scarcely hoped to find,
Companions meet, minds fitted to his mind;

Here, late and loth, the worthy rector came,
From college dinners and a fellow's fame;
Yet, here when fix'd, was happy to behold
So near a neighbour in a friend so old:
Boys on one form they parted, now to meet
In equal state, their worships on one seat.

Here were a sister-pair, who seem'd to live
With more respect than affluence can give;
Although not affluent, they, by nature graced,
Had sense and virtue, dignity and taste;
Their minds by sorrows, by misfortunes tried,
Were vex'd and heal'd, were pain'd and purified.

Hither a sage physician came, and plann'd,
With Books his guides, improvements on his land;
Nor less to mind than matter would he give
His noble thoughts, to know how spirits live
And what is spirit; him his friends advised
To think with fear, but caution he despised,
And hints of fear provoked him till he dared
Beyond himself, nor bold assertion spared,
But fiercely spoke, like those who strongly feel,
"Priests and their craft, enthusiasts and their zeal."

More yet appear'd, of whom as we proceed—
Ah! yield not yet to languor—you shall read.

But ere the events that from this meeting rose,
Be they of pain or pleasure, we disclose,
It is of custom, doubtless is of use,
That we our heroes first should introduce.
Come, then, fair Truth! and let me clearly see
The minds I paint, as they are seen in thee;
To me their merits and their faults impart;
Give me to say, "frail being! such thou art,"
And closely let me view the naked human heart.

George loved to think: but as he late began
To muse on all the grander thoughts of man,
He took a solemn and a serious view
Of his religion, and he found it true;
Firmly, yet meekly, he his mind applied
To this great subject, and was satisfied.

He then proceeded, not so much intent,
But still in earnest, and to church he went.
Although they found some difference in their creed,
He and his pastor cordially agreed;
Convinced that they who would the truth obtain
By disputation, find their efforts vain;
The church he view'd as liberal minds will view,
And there he fix'd his principles and pew.

He saw, he thought he saw, how weakness, pride,
And habit, draw seceding crowds aside:
Weakness that loves on trifling points to dwell,
Pride that at first from Heaven's own worship fell,
And habit, going where it went before,
Or to the meeting or the tavern-door.

George loved the cause of freedom, but reproved
All who with wild and boyish ardour loved;
Those who believed they never could be free,
Except when fighting for their liberty;
Who by their very clamour and complaint
Invite coercion or enforce restraint:
He thought a trust so great, so good a cause,
Was only to be kept by guarding laws;
For public blessings firmly to secure,
We must a lessening of the good endure.
The public waters are to none denied,
All drink the stream, but only few must guide;
There must be reservoirs to hold supply,
And channels form'd to send the blessing by;
The public good must be a private care,
None all they would may have, but all a share;
So we must freedom with restraint enjoy,
What crowds possess they will, uncheck'd, destroy;
And hence, that freedom may to all be dealt,
Guards must be fix'd, and safety must be felt.
So thought our squire, nor wish'd the guards t' appear
So strong, that safety might be bought too dear.
The constitution was the ark that he
Join'd to support with zeal and sanctity,
Nor would expose it, as th' accursed son
His father's weakness, to be gazed upon.

I for that freedom make, said he, my prayer,
That suits with all, like atmospheric air;
That is to mortal man by heaven assign'd,
Who cannot bear a pure and perfect kind:
The lighter gas, that, taken in the frame,
The spirit heats, and sets the blood in flame,
Such is the freedom which when men approve,
They know not what a dangerous thing they love

George chose the company of men of sense,
But could with wit in moderate share dispense;
He wish'd in social ease his friends to meet,
When still he thought the female accent sweet;
Well from the ancient, better from the young,
He loved the lispings of the mother tongue.

He ate and drank, as much as men who think
Of life's best pleasures, ought to eat or drink;
Men purely temperate might have taken less,
But still he loved indulgence, not excess;
Nor would alone the grants of fortune taste,
But shared the wealth he judged it crime to waste,
And thus obtain'd the sure reward of care;
For none can spend like him who learns to spare.

Time, thought, and trouble made the man appear—
By nature shrewd—sarcastic and severe;
Still he was one whom those who fully knew
Esteem'd and trusted, one correct and true;
All on his word with surety might depend,
Kind as a man, and faithful as a friend:
But him the many know not, knew not cause
In their new squire for censure or applause;
Ask them, "Who dwelt within that lofty wall?"
And they would say, "the gentleman was tall;
Look'd old when follow'd, but alert when met,
And had some vigour in his movements yet;
He stoops, but not as one infirm; and wears
Dress that becomes his station and his years."

Such was the man who from the world return'd,
Nor friend nor foe; he prized it not, nor spurn'd,
But came and sat him in his village down,
Safe from its smile, and careless of its frown:
He, fairly looking into life's account,
Saw frowns and favours were of like amount;
And viewing all—his perils, prospects, purse,
He said, "Content! 't is well it is no worse."

Through ways more rough had fortune RICHARD led,
The world he traversed was the book he read;
Hence clashing notions and opinions strange
Lodged in his mind; all liable to change.

By nature generous, open, daring, free,
The vice he hated was hypocrisy:
Religious notions, in her latter years,
His mother gave, admonish'd by her fears;
To these he added, as he chanced to read
A pious work or learn a christian creed:
He heard the preacher by the highway side,
The church's teacher, and the meeting's guide;
And mixing all their matters in his brain,
Distill'd a something he could ill explain;
But still it served him for his daily use,
And kept his lively passions from abuse;
For he believed, and held in reverence high,
The truth so dear to man—" not all shall die."
The minor portions of his creed hung loose,
For time to shapen and a whole produce;
This love effected, and a favourite maid,
With clearer views, his honest flame repaid;
Hers was the thought correct, the hope sublime,
She shaped his creed, and did the work of time.

He spake of freedom as a nation's cause,
And loved, like George, our liberty and laws;
But had more youthful ardour to be free,
And stronger fears for injured liberty:
With him, on various questions that arose,
The monarch's servants were the people's foes;
And though he fought with all a Briton's zeal,
He felt for France as Freedom's children feel;
Went far with her in what she thought reform,
And hail'd the revolutionary storm;
Yet would not here, where there was least to win,
And most to love, the doubtful work begin;
But look'd on change with some religious fear,
And cried, with filial dread, "Ah! come not here."

His friends he did not as the thoughtful choose;
Long to deliberate was, he judged, to lose:
Frankly he join'd the free, nor suffer'd pride
Or doubt to part them, whom their fate allied;
Men with such minds at once each other aid,
" Frankness," they cry, " with frankness is repaid;
If honest, why suspect? if poor, of what afraid?
Wealth's timid votaries may with caution move,
Be it our wisdom to confide and love."

So pleasures came (not purchased first or plann'd),
But the chance pleasures that the poor command;
They came but seldom, they remain'd not long,
Nor gave him time to question " are they wrong?"
These he enjoy'd, and left to after time
To judge the folly or decide the crime;
Sure had he been, he had perhaps been pure
From this reproach—but Richard was not sure—
Yet from the sordid vice, the mean, the base,
He stood aloof—death frown'd not like disgrace.

With handsome figure, and with manly air,
He pleased the sex, who all to him were fair;
With filial love he look'd on forms decay'd,
And admiration's debt to beauty paid;
On sea or land, wherever Richard went,
He felt affection, and he found content;
There was in him a strong presiding hope
In fortune's tempests, and it bore him up:
But when that mystic vine his mansion graced,
When numerous branches round his board were placed,
When sighs of apprehensive love were heard,
Then first the spirit of the hero fear'd;
Then he reflected on the father's part,
And all an husband's sorrow touch'd his heart;
Then thought he, " Who will their assistance lend?
And be the children's guide, the parent's friend?
Who shall their guardian, their protector be?
I have a brother—Well!—and so has he."

And now they met: a message—kind, 't is true,
But verbal only—ask'd an interview;
And many a mile, perplex'd by doubt and fear,
Had Richard past, unwilling to appear—
" How shall I now my unknown way explore,
He proud and rich—I very proud and poor?
Perhaps my friend a dubious speech mistook,
And George may meet me with a stranger's look;
Then to my home when I return again,
How shall I bear this business to explain,
And tell of hopes raised high, and feelings hurt, in vain?

How stands the case? My brother's friend and mine
Met at an inn, and set them down to dine:
When having settled all their own affairs,
And kindly canvass'd such as were not theirs,
Just as my friend was going to retire,
'Stay!—you will see the brother of our squire,'
Said his companion; 'be his friend, and tell
The captain that his brother loves him well,
And when he has no better things in view,
Will be rejoiced to see him—Now, adieu!'

Well! here I am; and, brother, take you heed,
I am not come to flatter you and feed;
You shall no soother, fawner, hearer find,
I will not brush your coat, nor smooth your mind;
I will not hear your tales the whole day long,
Nor swear you 're right if I believe you wrong;
Nor be a witness of the facts you state,
Nor as my own adopt your love or hate:
I will not earn my dinner when I dine,
By taking all your sentiments for mine;
Nor watch the guiding motions of your eye,
Before I venture question or reply:
Nor when you speak, affect an awe profound,
Sinking my voice, as if I fear'd the sound;
Nor to your looks obediently attend,
The poor, the humble, the dependent friend:
Yet son of that dear mother could I meet—
But lo! the mansion—'t is a fine old seat!"

The Brothers met, with both too much at heart
To be observant of each other's part;
" Brother, I 'm glad," was all that George could say
Then stretch'd his hand, and turn'd his head away;
For he in tender tears had no delight,
But scorn'd the thought, and ridiculed the sight,
Yet now with pleasure, though with some surprise,
He felt his heart o'erflowing at his eyes.

Richard, meantime, made some attempts to speak,
Strong in his purpose, in his trial weak;

We cannot nature by our wishes rule,
Nor at our will her warm emotions cool;—
At length affection, like a risen tide,
Stood still, and then seem'd slowly to subside;
Each on the other's looks had power to dwell,
And Brother Brother greeted passing well.

BOOK II.

THE BROTHERS.

Further Account of the Meeting—Of the Men—The Mother—The Uncle—The private Tutor—The second Husband—Dinner Conversation—School of the Rector and Squire—The Master.

At length the Brothers met, no longer tried
By those strong feelings that in time subside:
Not fluent yet their language, but the eye
And action spoke both question and reply;
Till the heart rested, and could calmly feel,
Till the shook compass felt the settling steel;
Till playful smiles on graver converse broke,
And either speaker less abruptly spoke:
Still was there ofttimes silence, silence blest,
Expressive, thoughtful—their emotions' rest;
Pauses that came not from a want of thought,
But want of ease, by wearied passion sought;
For souls, when hurried by such powerful force,
Rest, and retrace the pleasure of the course.

They differ'd much; yet might observers trace
Likeness of features both in mind and face;
Pride they possess'd, that neither strove to hide,
But not offensive, not obtrusive pride:
Unlike had been their life, unlike the fruits,
Of different tempers, studies, and pursuits;
Nay, in such varying scenes the men had moved,
'T was passing strange that aught alike they loved:
But all distinction now was thrown apart,
While these strong feelings ruled in either heart.
As various colours in a painted ball,
While it has rest, are seen distinctly all;
Till, whirl'd around by some exterior force,
They all are blended in the rapid course:
So in repose, and not by passion sway'd,
We saw the difference by their habits made;
But, tried by strong emotions, they became
Fill'd with one love, and were in heart the same;
Joy to the face its own expression sent,
And gave a likeness in the looks it lent.

All now was sober certainty; the joy
That no strong passions swell till they destroy:
For they, like wine, our pleasures raise so high,
That they subdue our strength, and then they die.
George in his brother felt a growing pride,
He wonder'd who that fertile mind supplied—
"Where could the wanderer gather on his road
Knowledge so various? how the mind this food?
No college train'd him, guideless through his life,
Without a friend—not so! he has a wife.
Ah! had I married, I might now have seen
My——No! it never, never could have been:
That long enchantment, that pernicious state!—
True, I recover'd, but alas! too late—
And here is Richard, poor indeed—but—nay!
This is self-torment—foolish thoughts, away!"

Ease leads to habit, as success to ease,
He lives by rule who lives himself to please;
For change in trouble, and a man of wealth
Consults his quiet as he guards his health:
And habit now on George had sovereign power,
His actions all had their accustom'd hour:
At the fix'd time he slept, he walk'd, he read,
Or sought his grounds, his gruel, and his bed;
For every season he with caution dress'd,
And morn and eve had the appropriate vest;
He talk'd of early mists, and night's cold air,
And in one spot was fix'd his worship's chair.

But not a custom yet on Richard's mind
Had force, or him to certain modes confined;
To him no joy such frequent visits paid,
That habit by its beaten track was made:
He was not one who at his ease could say,
"We 'll live to-morrow as we lived to-day;"
But he and his were as the ravens fed,
As the day came it brought the daily bread.

George, born to fortune, though of moderate kind,
Was not in haste his road through life to find:
His father early lost, his mother tried
To live without him, liked it not, and—sigh'd,
When, for her widow'd hand, an amorous youth applied:
She still was young, and felt that she could share
A lover's passion, and an husband's care;
Yet past twelve years before her son was told,
To his surprise, "your father you behold."
But he beheld not with his mother's eye
The new relation, and would not comply;
But all obedience, all connexion spurn'd,
And fled their home, where he no more return'd.

His father's brother was a man whose mind
Was to his business and his bank confined;
His guardian care the captious nephew sought,
And was received, caress'd, advised, and taught.

"That Irish beggar, whom your mother took,
Does you this good, he sends you to your book;
Yet love not books beyond their proper worth,
But when they fit you for the world, go forth:
They are like beauties, and may blessings prove,
When we with caution study them, or love;
But when to either we our souls devote,
We grow unfitted for that world, and dote."

George to a school of higher class was sent,
But he was ever grieving that he went:
A still, retiring, musing, dreaming boy,
He relish'd not their sudden bursts of joy;
Nor the tumultuous pleasures of a rude,
A noisy, careless, fearless multitude:
He had his own delights, as one who flies
From every pleasure that a crowd supplies:
Thrice he return'd, but then was weary grown,
And was indulged with studies of his own.
Still could the rector and his friend relate
The small adventures of that distant date;

And Richard listen'd as they spake of time
Past in that world of misery and crime.

Freed from his school, a priest of gentle kind
The uncle found to guide the nephew's mind;
Pleased with his teacher, George so long remain'd,
The mind was weaken'd by the store it gain'd.

His guardian uncle, then on foreign ground,
No time to think of his improvements found;
Nor had the nephew, now to manhood grown,
Talents or tastes for trade or commerce shown,
But shunn'd a world of which he little knew,
Nor of that little did he like the view.

His mother chose, nor I the choice upbraid,
An Irish soldier of a house decay'd,
And passing poor, but precious in her eyes
As she in his; they both obtain'd a prize.
To do the captain justice, she might share
What of her jointure his affairs could spare:
Irish he was in his profusion—true,
But he was Irish in affection too;
And though he spent her wealth and made her grieve,
He always said "my dear," and "with your leave."
Him she survived: she saw his boy possess'd
Of manly spirit, and then sank to rest.

Her sons thus left, some legal cause required
That they should meet, but neither this desired:
George, a recluse, with mind engaged, was one
Who did no business, with whom none was done;
Whose heart, engross'd by its peculiar care,
Shared no one's counsel—no one his might share.

Richard, a boy, a lively boy, was told
Of his half-brother, haughty, stern, and cold;
And his boy folly, or his manly pride
Made him on measures cool and harsh decide:
So, when they met, a distant cold salute
Was of a long-expected day the fruit;
The rest by proxies managed, each withdrew,
Vex'd by the business and the brother too;
But now they met when time had calm'd the mind,
Both wish'd for kindness, and it made them kind:
George had no wife or child, and was disposed
To love the man on whom his hope reposed:
Richard had both; and those so well beloved,
Husband and father were to kindness moved;
And thus th' affections check'd, subdued, restrain'd,
Rose in their force, and in their fulness reign'd.

The bell now bids to dine; the friendly priest,
Social and shrewd, the day's delight increased:
Brief and abrupt their speeches while they dined,
Nor were their themes of intellectual kind;
Nor, dinner past, did they to these advance,
But left the subjects they discuss'd to chance.

Richard, whose boyhood in the place was spent,
Profound attention to the speakers lent
Who spake of men; and, as he heard a name,
Actors and actions to his memory came:
Then, too, the scenes he could distinctly trace,
Here he had fought, and there had gain'd a race,
In that church-walk he had affrighted been,
In that old tower he had a something seen;
What time, dismiss'd from school, he upward cast
A fearful look, and trembled as he past.

No private tutor Richard's parents sought,
Made keen by hardship, and by trouble taught;
They might have sent him (some the counsel gave)
Seven gloomy winters of the North to brave,
Where a few pounds would pay for board and bed
While the poor frozen boy was taught and fed;
When, say he lives, fair, freckled, lank and lean,
The lad returns shrewd, subtle, close and keen;
With all the northern virtues and the rules
Taught to the thrifty in these thriving schools:
There had he gone, and borne this trying part,
But Richard's mother had a mother's heart.

Now squire and rector were return'd to school,
And spoke of him who there had sovereign rule:
He was, it seem'd, a tyrant of the sort
Who make the cries of tortured boys his sport;
One of a race, if not extinguish'd, tamed,
The flogger now is of the act ashamed;
But this great mind all mercy's calls withstood,
This Holofernes was a man of blood.

"Students," he said, "like horses on the road,
Must well be lash'd before they take the load;
They may be willing for a time to run,
But you must whip them ere the work be done:
To tell a boy, that, if he will improve,
His friends will praise him, and his parents love,
Is doing nothing—he has not a doubt
But they will love him, nay, applaud, without:
Let no fond sire a boy's ambition trust,
To make him study, let him see he must."

Such his opinion; and to prove it true,
At least sincere, it was his practice too;
Pluto they call'd him, and they named him well,
'T was not an heaven where he was pleased to dwell;
From him a smile was like the Greenland sun,
Surprising, nay portentous, when it shone;
Or like the lightning, for the sudden flash
Prepared the children for the thunder's crash.

O! had Narcissa, when she fondly kiss'd
The weeping boy whom she to school dismiss'd,
Had she beheld him shrinking from the arm
Uplifted high to do the greater harm,
Then seen her darling stript, and that pure white,
And—O! her soul had fainted at the sight;
And with those looks that love could not withstand,
She would have cried, "Barbarian, hold thy hand!"
In vain! no grief to this stern soul could speak,
No iron-tear roll down this Pluto's cheek.

Thus far they went, half earnest, half in jest,
Then turn'd to themes of deeper interest;
While Richard's mind that for awhile had stray'd,
Call'd home its powers, and due attention paid.

BOOK III.

BOYS AT SCHOOL.

The School—Schoolboys—The Boy-Tyrant—Sir Hector Blane—Schoolboys in after life how changed—how the same—The patronized Boy, his Life and Death—Reflections—Story of Harry Bland.

We name the world a school, for day by day
We something learn, till we are call'd away;
The school we name a world,—for vice and pain,—
Fraud and contention, there begin to reign;
And much, in fact, this lesser world can show
Of grief and crime that in the greater grow.
"You saw," said George, "in that still-hated school
How the meek suffer, how the haughty rule;
There soft, ingenuous, gentle minds endure
Ills that ease, time, and friendship fail to cure;
There the best hearts, and those, who shrink from sin,
Find some seducing imp to draw them in;
Who takes infernal pleasure to impart
The strongest poison to the purest heart.
Call to your mind this scene—Yon boy behold:
How hot the vengeance of a heart so cold!
See how he beats, whom he had just reviled
And made rebellious—that imploring child:
How fierce his eye, how merciless his blows,
And how his anger on his insult grows;
You saw this Hector and his patient slave,
Th' insulting speech, the cruel blows he gave.

Mix'd with mankind, his interest in his sight,
We found this Nimrod civil and polite;
There was no triumph in his manner seen,
He was so humble you might think him mean:
Those angry passions slept till he attain'd
His purposed wealth, and waked when that was gain'd;
He then resumed the native wrath and pride,
The more indulged, as longer laid aside;
Wife, children, servants, all obedience pay,
The slaves at school no greater slaves than they.
No more dependent, he resumes the rein,
And shows the schoolboy turbulence again.

Were I a poet, I would say he brings
To recollection some impetuous springs;
See! one that issues from its humble source,
To gain new powers, and run its noisy course;
Frothy and fierce among the rocks it goes,
And threatens all that bound it or oppose:
Till wider grown, and finding large increase,
Though bounded still, it moves along in peace;
And as its waters to the ocean glide,
They bear a busy people on its tide;
But there arrived, and from its channel free,
Those swelling waters meet the mighty sea;
With threat'ning force the new-form'd billows swell,
And now affright the crowd they bore so well."

"Yet," said the rector, "all these early signs
Of vice are lost, and vice itself declines;
Religion counsels, troubles, sorrows rise,
And the vile spirit in the conflict dies.

Sir Hector Blane, the champion of the school,
Was very blockhead, but was form'd for rule:
Learn he could not; he said he could not learn,
But he profess'd it gave him no concern.
Books were his horror, dinner his delight,
And his amusement to shake hands and fight;
Argue he could not, but in case of doubt,
Or disputation, fairly boxed it out:
This was his logic, and his arm so strong,
His cause prevail'd, and he was never wrong;
But so obtuse—you must have seen his look,
Desponding, angry, puzzled o'er his book.

Can you not see him on the morn that proved
His skill in figures? Pluto's self was moved—
'Come, six times five?' th' impatient teacher cried
In vain, the pupil shut his eyes, and sigh'd.
'Try, six times count your fingers; how he stands!—
Your fingers, idiot!'—'What, of both my hands?'

With parts like these his father felt assured,
In busy times, a ship might be procured;
He too was pleased to be so early freed,
He now could fight, and he in time might read.
So he has fought, and in his country's cause
Has gain'd him glory, and our hearts' applause.
No more the blustering boy a school defies,
We see the hero from the tyrant rise,
And in the captain's worth the student's dulness dies."

"Be all allow'd;" replied the squire, "I give
Praise to his actions; may their glory live!
Nay, I will hear him in his riper age
Fight his good ship, and with the foe engage;
Nor will I quit him when the cowards fly,
Although, like them, I dread his energy.

But still, my friend, that ancient spirit reigns:
His powers support the credit of his brains,
Insisting ever that he must be right,
And for his reasons still prepared to fight.
Let him a judge of England's prowess be,
And all her floating terrors on the sea;
But this contents not, this is not denied,
He claims a right on all things to decide—
A kind of patent-wisdom, and he cries,
''T is so!' and bold the hero that denies.
Thus the boy-spirit still the bosom rules,
And the world's maxims were at first the school's."

"No doubt," said Jacques, "there are in minds the seeds
Of good and ill, the virtues and the weeds;
But is it not of study the intent
This growth of evil nature to prevent?
To check the progress of each idle shoot
That might retard the ripening of the fruit?"

"Our purpose certain! and we much effect,
We something cure, and something we correct;
But do your utmost, when the man you see,
You find him what you saw the boy would be,

Disguised a little; but we still behold
What pleased and what offended us of old.
Years from the mind no native stain remove,
But lay the varnish of the world above.
Still, when he can, he loves to step aside
And be the boy, without a check or guide;
In the old wanderings he with pleasure strays,
And reassumes the bliss of earlier days.

I left at school the boy with pensive look,
Whom some great patron order'd to his book,
Who from his mother's cot reluctant came,
And gave *my lord*, for this compassion, fame;
Who, told of all his patron's merit, sigh'd,
I know not why, in sorrow or in pride;
And would, with vex'd and troubled spirit, cry,
'I am not happy; let your envy die.'
Him left I with you; who, perhaps, can tell
If fortune bless'd him, or what fate befell:
I yet remember how the idlers ran
To see the carriage of the godlike man,
When pride restrain'd me; yet I thought the deed
Was noble, too,—and how did it succeed?"

Jacques answer'd not till he had backward cast
His view, and dwelt upon the evil past;
Then, as he sigh'd, he smiled;—from folly rise
Such smiles, and misery will create such sighs.
And Richard now from his abstraction broke,
Listening attentive as the rector spoke.

"This noble lord was one disposed to try
And weigh the worth of each new luxury;
Now, at a certain time, in pleasant mood,
He tried the luxury of doing good;
For this he chose a widow's handsome boy,
Whom he would first improve, and then employ.
The boy was gentle, modest, civil, kind,
But not for bustling through the world design'd;
Reserved in manner, with a little gloom,
Apt to retire, but never to assume;
Possess'd of pride that he could not subdue,
Although he kept his origin in view.
Him sent my lord to school, and this became
A theme for praise, and gave his lordship fame;
But when the boy was told how great his debt,
He proudly ask'd, 'is it contracted yet?'

With care he studied, and with some success;
His patience great, but his acquirements less:
Yet when he heard that Charles would not excel,
His lordship answer'd, with a smile, ''t is well;
Let him proceed, and do the best he can,
I want no pedant, but a useful man.'

The speech was heard, and praise was amply dealt,
His lordship felt it, and he said he felt—
'It is delightful,' he observed, 'to raise
And foster merit,—it is more than praise.'

Five years at school th' industrious boy had past,
'And what,' was whisper'd, 'will be done at last?'
My lord was troubled, for he did not mean
To have his bounty watch'd and overseen;
Bounty that sleeps when men applaud no more,
The generous act that waked their praise before;
The deed was pleasant while the praise was new,
But none the progress would with wonder view:
It was a debt contracted; he who pays
A debt is just, but must not look for praise:
The deed that once had fame must still proceed,
Though fame no more proclaims 'how great the deed!'
The boy is taken from his mother's side,
And he who took him must be now his guide.
But this, alas! instead of bringing fame,
A tax, a trouble, to my lord became.

'The boy is dull, you say,—why then by trade,
By law, by physic, nothing can be made;
If a small living—mine are both too large,
And then the college is a cursed charge:
The sea is open; should he there display
Signs of dislike, he cannot run away.'

Now Charles, who acted no heroic part,
And felt no seaman's glory warm his heart,
Refused the offer.—Anger touch'd my lord:—
'He does not like it—Good, upon my word—
If I at college place him, he will need
Supplies for ever, and will not succeed;—
Doubtless in me 't is duty to provide
Not for his comfort only, but his pride—
Let him to sea!'—He heard the words again,
With promise join'd—with threat'ning; all in vain:
Charles had his own pursuits; for aid to these
He had been thankful, and had tried to please;
But urged again, as meekly as a saint,
He humbly begg'd to stay at home, and paint.
'Yes, pay some dauber, that this stubborn fool
May grind his colours, and may boast his school'

As both persisted, 'Choose, good sir, your way,
The peer exclaim'd, 'I have no more to say.
I seek your good, but I have no command
Upon your will, nor your desire withstand.'

Resolved and firm, yet dreading to offend,
Charles pleaded *genius* with his noble friend:
'Genius!' he cried, 'the name that triflers give
To their strong wishes without pains to live;
Genius! the plea of all who feel desire
Of fame, yet grudge the labours that acquire:
But say 't is true; how poor, how late the gain,
And certain ruin if the hope be vain!'
Then to the world appeal'd my lord, and cried,
'Whatever happens, I am justified.'
Nay, it was trouble to his soul to find
There was such hardness in the human mind:
He wash'd his hands before the world, and swore
That he 'such minds would patronize no more.'

Now Charles his bread by daily labours sought,
And this his solace, 'so Corregio wrought.'
Alas, poor youth! however great his name,
And humble thine, thy fortune was the same:
Charles drew and painted, and some praise obtain'd
For care and pains; but little more was gain'd:
Fame was his hope, and he contempt display'd
For approbation, when 't was coolly paid:
His daily tasks he call'd a waste of mind,
Vex'd at his fate, and angry with mankind:
'Thus have the blind to merit ever done,
And Genius mourn'd for each neglected son.'

Charles murmur'd thus, and angry and alone
Half breathed the curse, and half suppress'd the groan;

Then still more sullen grew, and still more proud,
Fame so refused he to himself allow'd,
Crowds in contempt he held, and all to him was crowd.

If aught on earth, the youth his mother loved,
And, at her death, to distant scenes removed.

Years past away, and where he lived, and how,
Was then unknown—indeed we know not now;
But once at twilight walking up and down,
In a poor alley of the mighty town,
Where, in her narrow courts and garrets, hide
The grieving sons of genius, want, and pride,
I met him musing: sadness I could trace,
And conquer'd hope's meek anguish, in his face.
See him I must: but I with ease address'd,
And neither pity nor surprise express'd;
I strove both grief and pleasure to restrain,
But yet I saw that I was giving pain.
He said, with quick'ning pace, as loth to hold
A longer converse, that 'the day was cold,
That he was well, that I had scarcely light
To aid my steps,' and bade me then good night!

I saw him next where he had lately come,
A silent pauper in a crowded room;
I heard his name, but he conceal'd his face,
To his sad mind his misery was disgrace:
In vain I strove to combat his disdain
Of my compassion——'Sir, I pray refrain;'
For I had left my friends and stepp'd aside,
Because I fear'd his unrelenting pride.

He then was sitting on a workhouse-bed,
And on the naked boards reclined his head,
Around were children with incessant cry,
And near was one, like him, about to die;
A broken chair's deal bottom held the store
That he required—he soon would need no more;
A yellow tea-pot, standing at his side,
From its half spout the cold black tea supplied.

Hither, it seem'd, the fainting man was brought,
Found without food,—it was no longer sought:
For his employers knew not whom they paid,
Nor where to seek him whom they wish'd to aid:
Here brought, some kind attendant he address'd,
And sought some trifles which he yet possess'd;
Then named a lightless closet, in a room
Hired at small rate, a garret's deepest gloom.
They sought the region, and they brought him all
That he his own, his proper wealth could call:
A better coat, less pieced; some linen neat,
Not whole; and papers many a valued sheet;
Designs and drawings; these, at his desire,
Were placed before him at the chamber fire,
And while th' admiring people stood to gaze,
He, one by one, committed to the blaze,
Smiling in spleen; but one he held a while,
And gave it to the flames, and could not smile.

The sickening man—for such appear'd the fact—
Just in his need, would not a debt contract;
But left his poor apartment for the bed
That earth might yield him, or some way-side shed;
Here he was found, and to this place convey'd,
Where he might rest, and his last debt be paid:
Fame was his wish, but he so far from fame,
That no one knew his kindred, or his name,
Or by what means he lived, or from what place he came.

Poor Charles! unnoticed by thy titled friend,
Thy days had calmly past, in peace thine end:
Led by thy patron's vanity astray,
Thy own misled thee in thy trackless way,
Urging thee on by hopes absurd and vain,
Where never peace or comfort smiled again!

Once more I saw him, when his spirits fail'd,
And my desire to aid him then prevail'd;
He show'd a softer feeling in his eye,
And watch'd my looks, and own'd the sympathy:
'T was now the calm of wearied pride; so long
As he had strength was his resentment strong,
But in such place, with strangers all around,
And they such strangers, to have something found
Allied to his own heart, an early friend,
One, only one, who would on him attend,
To give and take a look! at this his journey's end;
One link, however slender, of the chain
That held him where he could not long remain;
The one sole interest!—No, he could not now
Retain his anger; Nature knew not how;
And so there came a softness to his mind,
And he forgave the usage of mankind.
His cold long fingers now were press'd to mine,
And his faint smile of kinder thoughts gave sign;
His lips moved often as he tried to lend
His words their sound, and softly whisper'd, 'friend!'
Not without comfort in the thought express'd
By that calm look with which he sank to rest."

"The man," said George, "you see, through life retain'd
The boy's defects: his virtues too remain'd.

But where are now those minds so light and gay,
So forced on study, so intent on play,
Swept by the world's rude blasts, from hope's dear views away?
Some grieved for long neglect in earlier times,
Some sad from frailties, some lamenting crimes;
Thinking, with sorrow, on the season lent
For noble purpose, and in trifling spent;
And now, at last, when they in earnest view
The nothing done—what work they find to do?
Where is that virtue that the generous boy
Felt, and resolved that nothing should destroy?
He who with noble indignation glow'd
When vice had triumph? who his tear bestow'd
On injured merit? he who would possess
Power, but to aid the children of distress!
Who has such joy in generous actions shown,
And so sincere, they might be call'd his own;
Knight, hero, patriot, martyr! on whose tongue,
And potent arm, a nation's welfare hung;
He who to public misery brought relief,
And soothed the anguish of domestic grief,
Where now his virtue's fervour, spirit, zeal?
Who felt so warmly, has he ceased to feel?
The boy's emotions of that noble kind,
Ah! sure th' experienced man has not resign'd;

Or are these feelings varied? has the knight,
Virtue's own champion, now refused to fight?
Is the deliverer turn'd th' oppressor now?
Has the reformer dropt the dangerous vow?
Or has the patriot's bosom lost its heat,
And forced him, shivering, to a snug retreat?
Is such the grievous lapse of human pride?
Is such the victory of the youth untried?
Here will I pause, and then review the shame
Of Harry Bland, to hear his parent's name;
That mild, that modest boy, whom well we knew,
In him long time the secret sorrow grew;
He wept alone; then to his friend confess'd
The grievous fears that his pure mind oppress'd;
And thus, when terror o'er his shame obtain'd
A painful conquest, he his case explain'd:
And first his favourite question'd—'Willie, tell,
Do all the wicked people go to hell?'

Willie with caution answer'd, 'Yes, they do,
Or else repent; but what is this to you?'
'O! yes, dear friend:' he then his tale began—
'He fear'd his father was a wicked man,
Nor had repented of his naughty life;
The wife he had indeed was not a wife,
Not as my mother was; the servants all
Call her a name—I 'll whisper what they call.
She saw me weep, and ask'd, in high disdain,
If tears could bring my mother back again?
This I could bear, but not when she pretends
Such fond regard, and what I speak commends;
Talks of my learning, fawning wretch! and tries
To make me love her,—love! when I despise.
Indeed I had it in my heart to say
Words of reproach, before I came away;
And then my father's look is not the same,
He puts his anger on to hide his shame.'

With all these feelings delicate and nice,
This dread of infamy, this scorn of vice,
He left the school, accepting, though with pride,
His father's aid—but there would not reside;
He married then a lovely maid, approved
Of every heart as worthy to be loved;
Mild as the morn in summer, firm as truth,
And graced with wisdom in the bloom of youth.

How is it, men, when they in judgment sit,
On the same fault, now censure, now acquit?
Is it not thus, that *here* we view the sin,
And *there* the powerful cause that drew us in?
'T is not that men are to the evil blind,
But that a different object fills the mind.
In judging others we can see too well
Their grievous fall, but not how grieved they fell;
Judging ourselves, we to our minds recall,
Not how we fell, but how we grieved to fall.
Or could this man, so vex'd in early time,
By this strong feeling for his father's crime,
Who to the parent's sin was barely just,
And mix'd with filial fear the man's disgust;
Could he, without some strong delusion, quit
The path of duty, and to shame submit?
Cast off the virtue he so highly prized,
'And be the very creature he despised?'

A tenant's wife, half forward, half afraid,
Features, it seem'd, of powerful cast display'd,
That bore down faith and duty; common fame
Speaks of a contract that augments the shame.

There goes he, not unseen, so strong the will,
And blind the wish, that bear him to the mill;
There he degraded sits, and strives to please
The miller's children, laughing at his knees;
And little Dorcas, now familiar grown,
Talks of her rich papa, and of her own.
He woos the mother's now precarious smile
By costly gifts, that tempers reconcile;
While the rough husband, yielding to the pay
That buys his absence, growling stalks away.
'T is said th' offending man will sometimes sigh,
And say, 'My God, in what a dream am I?
I will awake:' but, as the day proceeds,
The weaken'd mind the day's indulgence needs;
Hating himself at every step he takes,
His mind approves the virtue he forsakes,
And yet forsakes her. O! how sharp the pain,
Our vice, ourselves, our habits to disdain;
To go where never yet in peace we went,
To feel our hearts can bleed, yet not relent;
To sigh, yet not recede; to grieve, yet not repent!"

BOOK IV.

ADVENTURES OF RICHARD.

Meeting of the Brothers in the Morning—Pictures, Music, Books—The Autumnal Walk—The Farm—The Flock—Effect of Retirement upon the Mind—Dinner—Richard's Adventure at Sea—George inquires into the Education of his Brother—Richard's Account of his Occupations in his early Life; his Pursuits, Associations, Partialities, Affections and Feelings—His Love of Freedom—The Society he chose—The Friendships he engaged in—and the Habits he contracted.

Eight days had past; the Brothers now could meet
With ease, and take the customary seat.
"These," said the host, for he perceived where stray'd
His brother's eye, and what he now survey'd;
"These are the costly trifles that we buy,
Urged by the strong demands of vanity,
The thirst and hunger of a mind diseased,
That must with purchased flattery be appeased;
But yet, 't is true, the things that you behold
Serve to amuse us as we 're getting old:
These pictures, as I heard our artists say,
Are genuine all, and I believe they may;
They cost the genuine sums, and I should grieve
If, being willing, I could not believe.

And there is music; when the ladies come,
With their keen looks they scrutinize the room
To see what pleases, and I must expect
To yield them pleasure, or to find neglect:
For, as attractions from our person fly,
Our purses, Richard, must the want supply;

Yet would it vex me could the triflers know
That they can shut out comfort or bestow.

But see this room: here, Richard, you will find
Books for all palates, food for every mind;
This readers term the ever-new delight,
And so it is, if minds have appetite:
Mine once was craving; great my joy, indeed,
Had I possess'd such food when I could feed;
When at the call of every new-born wish
I could have keenly relish'd every dish—
Now, Richard, now, I stalk around and look
Upon the dress and title of a book,
Try half a page, and then can taste no more,
But the dull volume to its place restore;
Begin a second slowly to peruse,
Then cast it by, and look about for news;
The news itself grows dull in long debates,—
I skip, and see what the conclusion states;
And many a speech, with zeal and study made
Cold and resisting spirits to persuade,
Is lost on mine; alone, we cease to feel
What crowds admire, and wonder at their zeal.

But how the day? No fairer will it be?
Walk you? Alas! 't is requisite for me—
Nay, let me not prescribe—my friends and guests
are free."

It was a fair and mild autumnal sky,
And earth's ripe treasures met th' admiring eye,
As a rich beauty, when her bloom is lost,
Appears with more magnificence and cost:
The wet and heavy grass, where feet had stray'd,
Not yet erect, the wanderer's way betray'd:
Showers of the night had swell'd the deep'ning rill,
The morning breeze had urged the quick'ning mill;
Assembled rooks had wing'd their sea-ward flight,
By the same passage to return at night.
While proudly o'er them hung the steady kite,
Then turn'd him back and left the noisy throng,
Nor deign'd to know them as he sail'd along.
Long yellow leaves, from osiers, strew'd around,
Choked the small stream, and hush'd the feeble
sound;
While the dead foliage dropt from loftier trees
Our squire beheld not with his wonted ease,
But to his own reflections made reply,
And said aloud, "Yes! doubtless we must die."

"We must," said Richard, "and we would not live
To feel what dotage and decay will give;
But we yet taste whatever we behold,
The morn is lovely, though the air is cold:
There is delicious quiet in this scene,
At once so rich, so varied, so serene;
Sounds to delight us,—each discordant tone
Thus mingled please, that fail to please alone;
This hollow wind, this rustling of the brook,
The farm-yard noise, the woodman at yon oak—
See, the axe falls!—now listen to the stroke!
That gun itself, that murders all this peace,
Adds to the charm, because it soon must cease."

"No doubt," said George, "the country has its
charms!
My farm behold! the model for all farms!
Look at the land—you find not there a weed,
We grub the roots, and suffer none to seed.
To land like this no botanist will come,
To seek the precious ware he hides at home;
Pressing the leaves and flowers with effort nice,
As if they came from herbs in Paradise;
Let them their favourites with my neighbours see,
They have no—what? no *habitat* with me.

Now see my flock, and hear its glory;—none
Have that vast body and that slender bone;
They are the village boast, the dealer's theme,
Fleece of such staple! flesh in such esteem!"

"Brother," said Richard, "do I hear aright?
Does the land truly give so much delight?"

"So says my bailiff: sometimes I have tried
To catch the joy, but nature has denied;
It will not be—the mind has had a store
Laid up for life, and will admit no more;
Worn out in trials, and about to die,
In vain to these we for amusement fly;
We farm, we garden, we our poor employ,
And much command, though little we enjoy;
Or, if ambitious, we employ our pen,
We plant a desert, or we drain a fen:
And—here, behold my medal!—this will show
What men may merit when they nothing know."

"Yet reason here," said Richard, "joins with
pride:—"
"I did not ask th' alliance," George replied—
I grant it true, such trifle may induce
A dull, proud man, to wake and be of use;
And there are purer pleasures, that a mind
Calm and uninjured may in villas find;
But where th' affections have been deeply tried,
With other food that mind must be supplied:
'T is not in trees or medals to impart
The powerful medicine for an aching heart;
The agitation dies, but there is still
The backward spirit, the resisting will.
Man takes his body to a country-seat,
But minds, dear Richard, have their own retreat;
Oft when the feet are pacing o'er the green,
The mind is gone where never grass was seen,
And never thinks of hill, or vale, or plain,
Till want of rest creates a sense of pain,
That calls that wandering mind, and brings it
home again.
No more of farms: but here I boast of minds
That make a friend the richer when he finds;
These shalt thou see;—but, Richard, be it known,
Who thinks to see must in his turn be shown:—
But now farewell! to thee will I resign
Woods, walks, and valleys! take them till we dine."

The Brothers dined, and with that plenteous fare
That seldom fails to dissipate our care,
At least the lighter kind; and oft prevails
When reason, duty, nay, when kindness fails.
Yet food and wine, and all that mortals bless,
Lead them to think of peril and distress;
Cold, hunger, danger, solitude, and pain,
That men in life's adventurous ways sustain.

"Thou hast sail'd far, dear brother," said the squire—
Permit me of those unknown lands t' inquire,
Lands never till'd, where thou hast wondering been,
And all the marvels thou hast heard and seen:
Do tell me something of the miseries felt
In climes where travellers freeze, and where they melt;
And be not nice,—we know 't is not in men,
Who travel far, to hold a steady pen:
Some will, 't is true, a bolder freedom take,
And keep our wonder always wide awake;
We know of those whose dangers far exceed
Our frail belief, that trembles as we read;
Such as in deserts burn, and thirst, and die,
Save a last gasp that they recover by;
Then, too, their hazard from a tyrant's arms,
A tiger's fury, or a lady's charms;
Beside th' accumulated evils borne
From the bold outset to the safe return.
These men abuse; but thou hast fair pretence
To modest dealing, and to mild good sense;
Then let me hear thy struggles and escapes
In the far lands of crocodiles and apes:
Say, hast thou, Bruce-like, knelt upon the bed
Where the young Nile uplifts his branchy head?
Or been partaker of th' unhallow'd feast,
Where beast-like man devours his fellow beast,
And churn'd the bleeding life; while each great dame
And sovereign beauty bade adieu to shame?
Or did the storm, that thy wreck'd pinnace bore,
Impel thee gasping on some unknown shore;
Where, when thy beard and nails were savage grown,
Some swarthy princess took thee for her own,
Some danger-dreading Yarico, who, kind,
Sent thee away, and, prudent, staid behind?

Come—I am ready wonders to receive,
Prone to assent, and willing to believe."

Richard replied: "It must be known to you,
That tales improbable may yet be true;
And yet it is a foolish thing to tell
A tale that shall be judged improbable;
While some impossibilities appear
So like the truth, that we assenting hear:
Yet, with your leave, I venture to relate
A chance-affair, and fact alone will state;
Though, I confess, it may suspicion breed,
And you may cry, 'improbable, indeed!'

When first I tried the sea, I took a trip,
But duty none, in a relation's ship;
Thus, unengaged, I felt my spirits light,
Kept care at distance, and put fear to flight;
Oft this same spirit in my friends prevail'd,
Buoyant in dangers, rising when assail'd;
When, as the gale at evening died away,
And die it will with the retiring day,
Impatient then, and sick of very ease,
We loudly whistled for the slumbering breeze.

One eve it came; and, frantic in my joy,
I rose and danced, as idle as a boy;
The cabin-lights were down, that we might learn
A trifling something from the ship astern;
The stiffening gale bore up the growing wave,
And wilder motion to my madness gave:
Oft have I since, when thoughtful and at rest,
Believed some maddening power my mind possess'd;
For, in an instant, as the stern sank low,
(How moved I knew not—What can madness know?)
Chance that direction to my motion gave,
And plunged me headlong in the roaring wave:
Swift flew the parting ship,—the fainter light
Withdrew,—or horror took them from my sight

All was confused above, beneath, around;
All sounds of terror; no distinguish'd sound
Could reach me, now on sweeping surges tost,
And then between the rising billows lost;
An undefined sensation stopp'd my breath;
Disorder'd views and threat'ning signs of death
Met in one moment, and a terror gave—
I cannot paint it—to the moving grave.
My thoughts were all distressing, hurried, mix'd,
On all things fixing, not a moment fix'd:
Vague thoughts of instant danger brought their pain,
New hopes of safety banish'd them again;
Then the swoln billow all these hopes destroy'd,
And left me sinking in the mighty void:
Weaker I grew, and grew the more dismay'd,
Of aid all hopeless, yet in search of aid;
Struggling awhile upon the wave to keep,
Then, languid, sinking in the yawning deep:
So tost, so lost, so sinking in despair,
I pray'd in heart an undirected prayer,
And then once more I gave my eyes to view
The ship now lost, and bade the light adieu!
From my chill'd frame th' enfeebled spirit fled,
Rose the tall billows round my deep'ning bed,
Cold seized my heart, thought ceased, and I was dead.

Brother, I have not,—man has not the power
To paint the horrors of that life-long hour;
Hour!—but of time I knew not—when I found
Hope, youth, life, love, and all they promised, drown'd;
When all so indistinct, so undefined,
So dark and dreadful, overcame the mind;
When such confusion on the spirit dwelt,
That, feeling much, it knew not what it felt.

Can I, my brother—ought I to forget
That night of terror? No! it threatens yet.
Shall I days, months—nay, years, indeed, neglect,
Who then could feel what moments must effect
Were aught effected? who, in that wild storm,
Found there was nothing I could well perform;
For what to us are moments, what are hours,
If lost our judgment, and confused our powers!

Oft in the times when passion strives to reign,
When duty feebly holds the slacken'd chain,
When reason slumbers, then remembrance draws
This view of death, and folly makes a pause—
The view o'ercomes the vice, the fear the frenzy awes.

I know there wants not this to make it true,
What danger bids be done, in safety do;
Yet such escapes may make our purpose sure,
Who slights such warning may be too secure."

"But the escape!"—"Whate'er they judged might save
Their sinking friend they cast upon the wave;
Something of these my heaven-directed arm
Unconscious seized, and held as by a charm:
The crew astern beheld me as I swam,
And I am saved—O! let me say I am."

"Brother," said George, "I have neglected long
To think of all thy perils:—it was wrong;
But do forgive me; for I could not be
Than of myself more negligent of thee.
Now tell me, Richard, from the boyish years
Of thy young mind, that now so rich appears,
How was it stored? 't was told me, thou wert wild,
A truant urchin,—a neglected child.
I heard of this escape, and sat supine
Amid the danger that exceeded thine;
Thou couldst but die—the waves could but unfold
Thy warm gay heart, and make that bosom cold—
While I——but no! Proceed, and give me truth;
How past the years of thy unguided youth?
Thy father left thee to the care of one
Who could not teach, could ill support a son;
Yet time and trouble feeble minds have stay'd,
And fit for long-neglected duties made:
I see thee struggling in the world, as late
Within the waves, and with an equal fate,
By Heaven preserved—but tell me, whence and how
Thy gleaning came?—a dexterous gleaner thou!"

"Left by that father, who was known to few,
And to that mother, who has not her due
Of honest fame," said Richard, "our retreat
Was a small cottage, for our station meet,
On Barford Downs: that mother, fond and poor,
There taught some truths, and bade me seek for more,
Such as our village-school and books a few
Supplied; but such I cared not to pursue;
I sought the town, and to the ocean gave
My mind and thoughts, as restless as the wave:
Where crowds assembled, I was sure to run,
Hear what was said, and mused on what was done;
Attentive listening in the moving scene,
And often wondering what the men could mean.

When ships at sea made signals of their need,
I watch'd on shore the sailors, and their speed:
Mix'd in their act, nor rested till I knew
Why they were call'd, and what they were to do.

Whatever business in the port was done,
I, without call, was with the busy one;
Not daring question, but with open ear
And greedy spirit, ever bent to hear.

To me the wives of seamen loved to tell
What storms endanger'd men esteem'd so well;
What wond'rous things in foreign parts they saw,
Lands without bounds, and people without law.

No ships were wreck'd upon that fatal beach,
But I could give the luckless tale of each;
Eager I look'd, till I beheld a face
Of one disposed to paint their dismal case;
Who gave the sad survivors' doleful tale,
From the first brushing of the mighty gale
Until they struck; and, suffering in their fate,
I long'd the more they should its horrors state;
While some, the fond of pity, would enjoy
The earnest sorrows of the feeling boy.

I sought the men return'd from regions cold,
The frozen straits, where icy mountains roll'd;
Some I could win to tell me serious tales
Of boats uplifted by enormous whales,
Or, when harpoon'd, how swiftly through the sea
The wounded monsters with the cordage flee;
Yet some uneasy thoughts assail'd me then,
The monsters warr'd not with, nor wounded men
The smaller fry we take, with scales and fins,
Who gasp and die—this adds not to our sins;
But so much blood! warm life, and frames so large
To strike, to murder—seem'd an heavy charge.

They told of days, where many goes to one—
Such days as ours; and how a larger sun,
Red, but not flaming, roll'd, with motion slow,
On the world's edge, and never dropt below.

There were fond girls, who took me to their side
To tell the story how their lovers died;
They praised my tender heart, and bade me prove
Both kind and constant when I came to love.
In fact, I lived for many an idle year
In fond pursuit of agitations dear;
For ever seeking, ever pleased to find,
The food I loved, I thought not of its kind:
It gave affliction while it brought delight,
And joy and anguish could at once excite.

One gusty day, now stormy and now still,
I stood apart upon the western hill,
And saw a race at sea: a gun was heard,
And two contending boats in sail appear'd;
Equal awhile; then one was left behind,
And for a moment had her chance resign'd,
When, in a moment, up a sail they drew—
Not used before—their rivals to pursue.
Strong was the gale! in hurry now there came
Men from the town, their thoughts, their fears the same;
And women too! affrighted maids and wives,
All deeply feeling for their sailors' lives.

The strife continued; in a glass we saw
The desperate efforts, and we stood in awe,
When the last boat shot suddenly before,
Then fill'd, and sank—and could be seen no more!

Then were those piercing shrieks, that frantic flight,
All hurried! all in tumult and affright!
A gathering crowd from different streets drew near
All ask, all answer—none attend, none hear!

One boat is safe; and see! she backs her sail
To save the sinking—Will her care avail?

O! how impatient on the sands we tread,
And the winds roaring, and the women led,

As up and down they pace with frantic air,
And scorn a comforter, and will despair;
They know not who in either boat is gone,
But think the father, husband, lover, one.

And who is she apart? She dares not come
To join the crowd, yet cannot rest at home:
With what strong interest looks she at the waves,
Meeting and clashing o'er the seamen's graves:
'T is a poor girl betroth'd—a few hours more,
And *he* will lie a corpse upon the shore.

Strange, that a boy could love these scenes, and cry
In very pity—but that boy was I.
With pain my mother would my tales receive,
And say, 'my Richard, do not learn to grieve.'

One wretched hour had past before we knew
Whom they had saved! Alas! they were but two,
An orphan'd lad and widow'd man—no more!
And they unnoticed stood upon the shore,
With scarce a friend to greet them—widows view'd
This man and boy, and then their cries renew'd:—
'T was long before the signs of wo gave place
To joy again; grief sat on every face.

Sure of my mother's kindness, and the joy
She felt in meeting her rebellious boy,
I at my pleasure our new seat forsook,
And, undirected, these excursions took:
I often rambled to the noisy quay,
Strange sounds to hear, and business strange to me:
Seamen and carmen, and I know not who,
A lewd, amphibious, rude, contentious crew—
Confused as bees appear about their hive,
Yet all alert to keep their work alive.

Here, unobserved as weed upon the wave,
My whole attention to the scene I gave;
I saw their tasks, their toil, their care, their skill,
Led by their own and by a master-will;
And though contending, toiling, tugging on,
The purposed business of the day was done.

The open shops of craftsmen caught my eye,
And there my questions met the kind reply:
Men, when alone, will teach; but in a crowd,
The child is silent, or the man is proud;
But, by themselves, there is attention paid
To a mild boy, so forward, yet afraid.

I made me interest at the inn's fire-side,
Amid the scenes to bolder boys denied;
For I had patrons there, and I was one,
They judged, who noticed nothing that was done.
'A quiet lad!' would my protector say:
'To him, now, this is better than his play:
Boys are as men; some active, shrewd, and keen,
They look about if aught is to be seen;
And some, like Richard here, have not a mind
That takes a notice—but the lad is kind.'

I loved in summer on the heath to walk,
And seek the shepherd—shepherds love to talk:
His superstition was of ranker kind,
And he with tales of wonder stored my mind;
Wonders that he in many a lonely eve
Had seen, himself, and therefore must believe.

His boy, his Joe, he said, from duty ran,
Took to the sea, and grew a fearless man:
'On yonder knoll—the sheep were in the fold—
His spirit past me, shivering-like and cold!
I felt a fluttering, but I knew not how,
And heard him utter, like a whisper, 'now!'
Soon came a letter from a friend—to tell
That he had fallen, and the time he fell.'

Even to the smugglers' hut the rocks between,
I have, adventurous in my wandering, been:
Poor, pious Martha served the lawless tribe,
And could their merits and their faults describe
Adding her thoughts; 'I talk, my child, to you,
Who little think of what such wretches do.'

I loved to walk where none had walk'd before,
About the rock that ran along the shore;
Or far beyond the sight of men to stray,
And take my pleasure when I lost my way;
For then 'twas mine to trace the hilly heath,
And all the mossy moor that lies beneath:
Here had I favourite stations, where I stood
And heard the murmurs of the ocean flood,
With not a sound beside, except when flew
Aloft the lapwing, or the gray curlew,
Who with wild notes my fancied power defied,
And mock'd the dreams of solitary pride.

I loved to stop at every creek and bay
Made by the river in its winding way,
And call to memory—not by marks they bare,
But by the thoughts that were created there.

Pleasant it was to view the sea-gulls strive
Against the storm, or in the ocean dive,
With eager scream, or when they dropping gave
Their closing wings to sail upon the wave:
Then as the winds and waters raged around,
And breaking billows mix'd their deafening sound
They on the rolling deep securely hung,
And calmly rode the restless waves among.
Nor pleased it less around me to behold,
Far up the beach, the yesty sea-foam roll'd;
Or from the shore upborne, to see on high,
Its frothy flakes in wild confusion fly:
While the salt spray that clashing billows form,
Gave to the taste a feeling of the storm.

Thus, with the favourite views, for many an hour
Have I indulged the dreams of princely power;
When the mind, wearied by excursions bold,
The fancy jaded, and the bosom cold,
Or when these wants, that will on kings intrude,
Or evening-fears, broke in on solitude;
When I no more my fancy could employ,
I left in haste what I could not enjoy,
And was my gentle mother's welcome boy.

But now thy walk,—this soft autumnal gloom
Bids no delay—at night I will resume
My subject, showing, not how I improved
In my strange school, but what the things I loved,
My first-born friendships, ties by forms uncheck'd
And all that boys acquire whom men neglect."

BOOK V.

RUTH.

Richard resumes his Narrative—Visits a Family in a Seaport—The Man and his Wife—Their Dwelling—Books, Number and Kind—The Friendship contracted—Employment there—Hannah, the Wife, her Manner; open Mirth and latent Grief—She gives the Story of Ruth, her Daughter—Of Thomas, a Sailor—Their Affection—A Press-gang—Reflections—Ruth disturbed in Mind—A Teacher sent to comfort her—His Fondness—Her reception of him—Her Supplication—Is refused—She deliberates—Is decided.

Richard would wait till George the tale should ask,
Nor waited long—He then resumed the task.

"South in the port, and eastward in the street,
Rose a small dwelling, my beloved retreat,
Where lived a pair, then old; the sons had fled
The home they fill'd: a part of them were dead;
Married a part; while some at sea remain'd,
And stillness in the seaman's mansion reign'd;
Lord of some petty craft, by night and day,
The man had fish'd each fathom of the bay.

My friend the matron woo'd me, quickly won,
To fill the station of an absent son;
(Him whom at school I knew, and Peter known,
I took his home and mother for my own:)
I read, and doubly was *I* paid to hear
Events that fell upon no listless ear:
She grieved to say her parents could neglect
Her education!—'t was a sore defect;
She, who had ever such a vast delight
To learn, and now could neither read nor write:
But hear she could, and from our stores I took,
Librarian meet! at her desire, our book.
Full twenty volumes—I would not exceed
The modest truth—were there for me to read;
These a long shelf contain'd, and they were found
Books truly speaking, volumes fairly bound;
The rest,—for some of other kinds remain'd,
And these a board beneath the shelf contain'd,—
Had their deficiencies in part; they lack'd
One side or both, or were no longer back'd;
But now became degraded from their place,
And were but pamphlets of a bulkier race.
Yet had we pamphlets, an inviting store,
From sixpence downwards—nay, a part were more;
Learning abundance, and the various kinds
For relaxation—food for different minds;
A piece of Wingate—thanks for all we have—
What we of figures needed, fully gave;
Culpepper, new in numbers, cost but thrice
The ancient volume's unassuming price,
But told what planet o'er each herb had power,
And how to take it in the lucky hour.

History we had—wars, treasons, treaties, crimes,
From Julius Cæsar to the present times;
Questions and answers, teaching what to ask
And what reply,—a kind, laborious task;
A scholar's book it was, who, giving, swore
It held the whole he wish'd to know, and more.

And we had poets, hymns and songs divine;
The most we read not, but allow'd them fine.

Our tracts were many, on the boldest themes—
We had our metaphysics, spirits, dreams,
Visions and warnings, and portentous sights
Seen, though but dimly, in the doleful nights,
When the good wife her wintry vigil keeps,
And thinks alone of him at sea, and weeps.

Add to all these our works in single sheets,
That our Cassandras sing about the streets:
These, as I read, the grave good man would say,
'Nay, Hannah!' and she answer'd 'What is Nay!
What is there, pray, so hurtful in a song?
It is our fancy only makes it wrong;
His purer mind no evil thoughts alarm,
And innocence protects him like a charm.'
Then would the matron, when the song had past,
And her laugh over, ask an hymn at last;
To the coarse jest she would attention lend,
And to the pious psalm in reverence bend:
She gave her every power and all her mind
As chance directed, or as taste inclined.

More of our learning I will now omit,
We had our Cyclopædias of Wit,
And all our works, rare fate! were to our genius fit.

When I had read, and we were weary grown
Of other minds, the dame disclosed her own;
And long have I in pleasing terror stay'd
To hear of boys trepann'd, and girls betray'd;
Ashamed so long to stay, and yet to go afraid.

I could perceive, though Hannah bore full well
The ills of life, that few with her would dwell,
But pass away, like shadows o'er the plain
From flying clouds, and leave it fair again;
Still every evil, be it great or small,
Would one past sorrow to the mind recall,
The grand disease of life, to which she turns,
And common cares and lighter suffering spurns.
'O! these are nothing,—they will never heed
Such idle contests who have fought indeed,
And have the wounds unclosed.'—I understood
My hint to speak, and my design pursued,
Curious the secret of that heart to find,
To mirth, to song, to laughter loud inclined,
And yet to bear and feel a weight of grief behind
How does she thus her little sunshine throw
Always before her?—I should like to know.
My friend perceived, and would no longer hide
The bosom's sorrow—Could she not confide
In one who wept, unhurt—in one who felt, untried?

'Dear child, I show you sins and sufferings strange
But you, like Adam, must for knowledge change
That blissful ignorance: remember, then,
What now you feel should be a check on men;
For then your passions no debate allow,
And therefore lay up resolution now.

'T is not enough, that when you can persuade
A maid to love, you know there 's promise made;
'T is not enough that you design to keep
That promise made, nor leave your lass to weep:
But you must guard yourself against the sin,
And think it such to draw the party in;
Nay, the more weak and easy to be won,
The viler you who have the mischief done.

I am not angry, love; but men should know
They cannot always pay the debt they owe
Their plighted honour; they may cause the ill
They cannot lessen, though they feel a will;
For *he* had truth with love, but love in youth
Does wrong, that cannot be repair'd by truth.

Ruth—I may tell, too oft had she been told—
Was tall and fair, and comely to behold;
Gentle and simple, in her native place
Not one compared with her in form or face;
She was not merry, but she gave our hearth
A cheerful spirit that was more than mirth.

There was a sailor boy, and people said
He was, as man, a likeness of the maid;
But not in this—for he was ever glad,
While Ruth was apprehensive, mild, and sad;
A quiet spirit hers, and peace would seek
In meditation: tender, mild, and meek!
Her loved the lad most truly; and, in truth,
She took an early liking to the youth:
To her alone were his attentions paid,
And they became the bachelor and maid.
He wish'd to marry, but so prudent we
And worldly wise, we said it could not be:
They took the counsel,—may be they approved,—
But still they grieved and waited, hoped and loved.

Now, my young friend, when of such state I speak
As one of danger, you will be to seek;
You know not, Richard, where the danger lies
In loving hearts, kind words, and speaking eyes;
For lovers speak their wishes with their looks
As plainly, love, as you can read your books.
Then, too, the meetings and the partings, all
The playful quarrels in which lovers fall,
Serve to one end—each lover is a child,
Quick to resent and to be reconciled;
And then their peace brings kindness that remains,
And so the lover from the quarrel gains:
When he has fault that she reproves, his fear
And grief assure her she was too severe,
And that brings kindness—when he bears an ill,
Or disappointment, and is calm and still,
She feels his own obedient to her will,
And that brings kindness—and what kindness brings
I cannot tell you:—these were trying things.
They were as children, and they fell at length;
The trial, doubtless, is beyond their strength
Whom grace supports not; and will grace support
The too confiding, who their danger court?
Then they would marry,—but were now too late,—
All could their fault in sport or malice state;
And though the day was fix'd, and now drew on,
I could perceive my daughter's peace was gone;
She could not bear the bold and laughing eye
That gazed on her—reproach she could not fly;
Her grief she would not show, her shame could not deny.
For some with many virtues come to shame,
And some that lose them all preserve their name.

Fix'd was the day; but ere that day appear'd,
A frightful rumour through the place was heard;
War, who had slept awhile, awaked once more,
And gangs came pressing till they swept the shore:
Our youth was seized and quickly sent away,
Nor would the wretches for his marriage stay,
But bore him off, in barbarous triumph bore,
And left us all our miseries to deplore:
There were wives, maids, and mothers on the beach,
And some sad story appertain'd to each;
Most sad to Ruth—to neither could she go!
But sad apart, and suffer'd matchless wo!
On the vile ship they turn'd their earnest view,
Not one last look allow'd,—not one adieu!
They saw the men on deck, but none distinctly knew.
And there she staid, regardless of each eye,
With but one hope, a fervent hope to die:
Nor cared she now for kindness—all beheld
Her, who invited none, and none repell'd;
For there are griefs, my child, that sufferers hide,
And there are griefs that men display with pride;
But there are other griefs that, so we feel,
We care not to display them nor conceal:
Such were our sorrows on that fatal day,
More than our lives the spoilers tore away;
Nor did we heed their insult—some distress
No form or manner can make more or less,
And this is of that kind—this misery of a press!
They say such things must be—perhaps they must
But, sure, they need not fright us and disgust:
They need not soulless crews of ruffians send
At once the ties of humble love to rend:
A single day had Thomas stay'd on shore
He might have wedded, and we ask'd no more;
And that stern man, who forced the lad away,
Might have attended, and have graced the day,
His pride and honour might have been at rest,
It is no stain to make a couple blest!
Blest!—no, alas! it was to ease the heart
Of one sore pang, and then to weep and part!
But this he would not.—English seamen fight
For England's gain and glory—it is right
But will that public spirit be so strong,
Fill'd, as it must be, with their private wrong?
Forbid it, honour! one in all the fleet
Should hide in war, or from the foe retreat;
But is it just, that he who so defends
His country's cause, should hide him from her friends?
Sure, if they must upon our children seize,
They might prevent such injuries as these;
Might hours—nay, days—in many a case allow
And soften all the griefs we suffer now.
Some laws, some orders might in part redress
The licensed insults of a British press,
That keeps the honest and the brave in awe,
Where might is right, and violence is law.

Be not alarm'd, my child; there 's none regard
What you and I conceive so cruel-hard:

There is compassion, I believe; but still
One wants the power to help, and one the will,
And so from war to war the wrongs remain,
While Reason pleads, and Misery sighs in vain.

Thus my poor Ruth was wretched and undone,
Nor had an husband for her only son,
Nor had he father; hope she did awhile,
And would not weep, although she could not smile;
Till news was brought us that the youth was slain,
And then, I think, she never smiled again;
Or if she did, it was but to express
A feeling far, indeed, from happiness!
Something that her bewilder'd mind conceived:
When she inform'd us that she never grieved,
But was right merry, then her head was wild,
And grief had gain'd possession of my child:
Yet, though bewilder'd for a time, and prone
To ramble much and speak aloud, alone;
Yet did she all that duty ever ask'd
And more, her will self-govern'd and untask'd:
With meekness, bearing all reproach, all joy
To her was lost; she wept upon her boy,
Wish'd for his death, in fear that he might live
New sorrow to a burthen'd heart to give.

There was a teacher, where my husband went—
Sent, as he told the people—what he meant
You cannot understand, but—he was sent:
This man from meeting came, and strove to win
Her mind to peace by drawing off the sin,
Or what it was, that, working in her breast,
Robb'd it of comfort, confidence, and rest:
He came and reason'd, and she seem'd to feel
The pains he took—her griefs began to heal;
She ever answer'd kindly when he spoke,
And always thank'd him for the pains he took;
So, after three long years, and all the while
Wrapt up in grief, she blest us with a smile,
And spoke in comfort; but she mix'd no more
With younger persons, as she did before.
Still Ruth was pretty; in her person neat;
So thought the teacher, when they chanced to meet:
He was a weaver by his worldly trade,
But powerful work in the assemblies made;
People came leagues to town to hear him sift
The holy text,—he had the grace and gift;
Widows and maidens flock'd to hear his voice;
Of either kind he might have had his choice;—
But he had chosen—we had seen how shy
The girl was getting, my good man and I;
That when the weaver came, she kept with us,
Where he his points and doctrines might discuss;
But in our bit of garden, or the room
We call our parlour, there he must not come.
She loved him not, and though she could attend
To his discourses, as her guide and friend,
Yet now to these she gave a listless ear,
As if a friend she would no longer hear;
This might he take for woman's art, and cried,
Spouse of my heart, I must not be denied!'—
Fearless he spoke, and I had hope to see
My girl a wife—but this was not to be.

My husband, thinking of his worldly store,
And not, frail man, enduring to be poor,
Seeing his friend would for his child provide
And hers, he grieved to have the man denied,
For Ruth, when press'd, rejected him, and grew
To her old sorrow, as if that were new.
'Who shall support her?' said her father, 'how
Can I, infirm and weak as I am now?
And here a loving fool,'——this gave her pain,
Severe, indeed, but she would not complain;
Nor would consent, although the weaver grew
More fond, and would the frighten'd girl pursue.

O! much she begg'd him to forbear, to stand
Her soul's kind friend, and not to ask her hand:
She could not love him.—'Love me!' he replied,
"'The love you mean is love unsanctified,
An earthly, wicked, sensual, sinful kind,
A creature-love, the passion of the blind.'
"'He did not court her, he would have her know,
For that poor love that will on beauty grow;
No! he would take her as the prophet took
One of the harlots in the holy book;
And then he look'd so ugly and severe!
And yet so fond—she could not hide her fear.

"'This fondness grew her torment; she would fly,
In woman's terror, if he came but nigh;
Nor could I wonder he should odious prove,
So like a ghost that left a grave for love.

But still her father lent his cruel aid
To the man's hope, and she was more afraid:
He said, no more she should his table share,
But be the parish or the teacher's care.
'Three days I give you: see that all be right
On Monday-morning—this is Thursday-night—
Fulfil my wishes, girl! or else forsake my sight!'

I see her now; and she that was so meek,
It was a chance that she had power to speak,
Now spoke in earnest—'Father! I obey,
And will remember the appointed day!'

Then came the man: she talk'd with him apart,
And, I believe, laid open all her heart;
But all in vain—she said to me, in tears,
'Mother! that man is not what he appears;
He talks of heaven, and let him, if he will,
But he has earthly purpose to fulfil;
Upon my knees I begg'd him to resign
The hand he asks—he said, it shall be mine:
What! did the holy men of Scripture deign
To hear a woman when she said 'refrain?'
Of whom they chose they took them wives, and these
Made it their study and their wish to please;
The women then were faithful and afraid,
As Sarah Abraham, they their lords obey'd,
And so she styled him; 't is in later days
Of foolish love that we our women praise,
Fall on the knee, and raise the suppliant hand,
And court the favour that we might command.'

O! my dear mother, when this man has power,
How will he treat me—first may beasts devour!
Or death in every form that I could prove,
Except this selfish being's hateful love.'

'I gently blamed her, for I knew how hard
It is to force affection and regard.

Ah! my dear lad, I talk to you as one
Who knew the misery of an heart undone;
You know it not; but, dearest boy, when man,
Do not an ill because you find you can:
Where is the triumph? when such things men seek
They only drive to wickedness the weak.

Weak was poor Ruth, and this good man so hard,
That to her weakness he had no regard:
But we had two days' peace; he came, and then
My daughter whisper'd, 'Would there were no men!
None to admire or scorn us, none to vex
A simple, trusting, fond, believing sex;
Who truly love the worth that men profess,
And think too kindly for their happiness.'

Poor Ruth! few heroines in the tragic page
Felt more than thee in thy contracted stage;
Fair, fond, and virtuous, they our pity move,
Impell'd by duty, agonised by love;
But no Mandane, who in dread has knelt
On the bare boards, has greater terrors felt,
Nor been by warring passions more subdued
Than thou, by this man's grovelling wish pursued;
Doom'd to a parent's judgment, all unjust,
Doom'd the chance mercy of the world to trust,
Or to wed grossness and conceal disgust.

If Ruth was frail, she had a mind too nice
To wed with that which she beheld as vice;
To take a reptile, who, beneath a show
Of peevish zeal, let carnal wishes grow;
Proud and yet mean, forbidding and yet full
Of eager appetites, devout and dull,
Waiting a legal right that he might seize
His own, and his impatient spirit ease;
Who would at once his pride and love indulge,
His temper humour, and his spite divulge.

This the poor victim saw—a second time,
Sighing, she said, 'Shall I commit the crime,
And now untempted? Can the form or rite
Make me a wife in my Creator's sight?
Can I the words without a meaning say?
Can I pronounce love, honour, or obey?
And if I cannot, shall I dare to wed,
And go an harlot to a loathed bed!
Never, dear mother! my poor boy and I
Will at the mercy of a parish lie;
Reproved for wants that vices would remove,
Reproach'd for vice that I could never love,
Mix'd with a crew long wedded to disgrace,
A vulgar, forward, equalizing race,—
And am I doom'd to beg a dwelling in that place?'

Such was her reasoning: many times she weigh'd
The evils all, and was of each afraid;
She loath'd the common board, the vulgar seat,
Where shame, and want, and vice, and sorrow meet,
Where frailty finds allies, where guilt insures retreat.

But peace again is fled: the teacher comes,
And new importance, haughtier air assumes.
No hapless victim of a tyrant's love
More keenly felt, or more resisting strove
Against her fate; she look'd on every side,
But there were none to help her, none to guide:—
And he, the man who should have taught the soul,
Wish'd but the body in his base control.

She left her infant on the Sunday morn,
A creature doom'd to shame! in sorrow born;
A thing that languish'd, nor arrived at age
When the man's thoughts with sin and pain engage—
She came not home to share our humble meal,
Her father thinking what his child would feel
From his hard sentence—still she came not home
The night grew dark, and yet she was not come;
The east-wind roar'd, the sea return'd the sound,
And the rain fell as if the world were drown'd:
There were no lights without, and my good man,
To kindness frighten'd, with a groan began
To talk of Ruth, and pray; and then he took
The Bible down, and read the holy book;
For he had learning: and when that was done,
We sat in silence—whither could we run?
We said, and then rush'd frighten'd from the door,
For we could bear our own conceit no more:
We call'd on neighbours—there she had not been:
We met some wanderers—ours they had not seen;
We hurried o'er the beach, both north and south,
Then join'd, and wander'd to our haven's mouth:
Where rush'd the falling waters wildly out,
I scarcely heard the good man's fearful shout,
Who saw a something on the billow ride,
And—Heaven have mercy on our sins! he cried,
It is my child!—and to the present hour
So he believes—and spirits have the power.

And she was gone! the waters wide and deep
Roll'd o'er her body as she lay asleep.
She heard no more the angry waves and wind,
She heard no more the threat'ning of mankind;
Wrapt in dark weeds, the refuse of the storm,
To the hard rock was borne her comely form!

But O! what storm was in that mind? what strife,
That could compel her to lay down her life?
For she was seen within the sea to wade,
By one at distance, when she first had pray'd;
Then to a rock within the hither shoal
Softly and with a fearful step she stole;
Then, when she gain'd it, on the top she stood
A moment still—and dropt into the flood!
The man cried loudly, but he cried in vain,—
She heard not then—she never heard again!
She had—pray, Heav'n!—she had that world in sight,
Where frailty mercy finds, and wrong has right,
But, sure, in this her portion such has been,
Well had it still remain'd a world unseen!'

Thus far the dame: the passions will dispense
To such a wild and rapid eloquence—
Will to the weakest mind their strength impart,
And give the tongue the language of the heart."

BOOK VI.

ADVENTURES OF RICHARD CONCLUDED.

Richard relates his Illness and Retirement—A Village Priest and his two Daughters—His peculiar Studies—His Simplicity of Character—Arrival of a third Daughter—Her Zeal in his Conversion—Their Friendship—How terminated—An happy Day—Its Commencement and Progress—A Journey along the Coast—Arrival as a Guest—Company—A Lover's Jealousy—it increases—dies away—An Evening Walk—Suspense—Apprehension—Resolution—Certainty.

"This then, dear Richard, was the way you took
To gain instruction—thine a curious book,
Containing much of both the false and true;
But thou hast read it, and with profit too.

Come, then, my Brother, now thy tale complete—
I know thy first embarking in the fleet,
Thy entrance in the army, and thy gain
Of plenteous laurels in the wars in Spain,
And what then follow'd; but I wish to know
When thou that heart hadst courage to bestow,
When to declare it gain'd, and when to stand
Before the priest, and give the plighted hand;
So shall I boldness from thy frankness gain
To paint the frenzy that possess'd my brain;
For rather there than in my heart I found
Was my disease; a poison, not a wound,
A madness, Richard—but, I pray thee, tell
Whom hast thou loved so dearly and so well?"

The younger man his gentle host obey'd,
For some respect, though not required, was paid,
Perhaps with all that independent pride
Their different states would to the memory glide;
Yet was his manner unconstrain'd and free,
And nothing in it like servility.

Then he began:—"When first I reach'd the land,
I was so ill that death appear'd at hand;
And though the fever left me, yet I grew
So weak 't was judged that life would leave me too.
I sought a village-priest, my mother's friend,
And I believed with him my days would end:
The man was kind, intelligent, and mild,
Careless and shrewd, yet simple as the child;
For of the wisdom of the world his share
And mine were equal—neither had to spare;
Else—with his daughters, beautiful and poor—
He would have kept a sailor from his door:
Two then were present, who adorn'd his home,
But ever speaking of a third to come;
Cheerful they were, not too reserved or free,
I loved them both, and never wished them three.

The vicar's self, still further to describe,
Was of a simple, but a studious tribe;
He from the world was distant, not retired,
Nor of it much possess'd, nor much desired:
Grave in his purpose, cheerful in his eye,
And with a look of frank benignity.
He lost his wife when they together past
Years of calm love that triumph'd to the last.
He much of nature, not of man had seen;
Yet his remarks were often shrewd and keen;
Taught not by books t' approve or to condemn,
He gain'd but little that he knew from them;
He read with reverence and respect the few,
Whence he his rules and consolations drew;
But men and beasts, and all that lived and moved,
Were books to him; he studied them and loved.

He knew the plants in mountain, wood, or mead;
He knew the worms that on the foliage feed;
Knew the small tribes that 'scape the careless eye,
The plant's disease that breeds the embryo-fly;
And the small creatures who on bark or bough
Enjoy their changes, changed we know not how:
But now th' imperfect being scarcely moves,
And now takes wing and seeks the sky it loves.

He had no system, and forbore to read
The learned labours of th' immortal Swede;
But smiled to hear the creatures he had known
So long, were now in class and order shown,
Genus and species—'is it meet,' said he,
'This creature's name should one so sounding be?
'T is but a fly, though first-born of the spring—
Bombilius majus, dost thou call the thing?
Majus, indeed! and yet, in fact, 't is true,
We all are majors, all are minors too,
Except the first and last,—th' immensely distant two.
And here again,—what call the learned this?
Both Hippobosca and Hirundinis?
Methinks the creature should be proud to find
That he employs the talents of mankind;
And that his sovereign master shrewdly looks,
Counts all his parts, and puts them in his books.
Well! go thy way, for I do feel it shame
To stay a being with so proud a name."

Such were his daughters, such my quiet friend,
And pleasant was it thus my days to spend;
And when Matilda at her home I saw,
Whom I beheld with anxiousness and awe,
The ease and quiet that I found before
At once departed, and return'd no more.
No more their music soothed me as they play'd,
But soon her words a strong impression made:
The sweet enthusiast, as I deem'd her, took
My mind, and fix'd it to her speech and look;
My soul, dear girl! she made her constant care,
But never whisper'd to my heart 'beware!'
In love no dangers rise till we are in the snare.
Her father sometimes question'd of my creed,
And seem'd to think it might amendment need;
But great the difference when the pious maid
To the same errors her attention paid;
Her sole design that I should think aright,
And my conversion her supreme delight:
Pure was her mind, and simple her intent,
Good all she sought, and kindness all she meant.
Next to religion friendship was our theme,
Related souls and their refined esteem:
We talk'd of scenes where this is real found,
And love subsists without a dart or wound;
But there intruded thoughts not all serene,
And wishes not so calm would intervene."

"Saw not her father?"
"Yes; but saw no more
Than he had seen without a fear before:
He had subsisted by the church and plough,
And saw no cause for apprehension now.
We, too, could live: he thought not passion wrong,
But only wonder'd we delay'd so long.
More had he wonder'd had he known esteem
Was all we mention'd, friendship was our theme.—
Laugh, if you please, I must my tale pursue—
This sacred friendship thus in secret grew
An intellectual love, most tender, chaste, and true:
Unstain'd, we said, nor knew we how it chanced
To gain some earthly soil as it advanced;
But yet my friend, and she alone, could prove
How much it differ'd from romantic love—
But this and more I pass—No doubt, at length,
We could perceive the weakness of our strength.
O! days remember'd well! remember'd all!
The bitter-sweet, the honey and the gall;
Those garden rambles in the silent night,
Those trees so shady, and that moon so bright;
That thickset alley by the arbour closed,
That woodbine seat where we at last reposed;
And then the hopes that came and then were gone,
Quick as the clouds beneath the moon past on:
Now, in this instant, shall my love be shown,
I said—O! no, the happy time is flown!

You smile; remember, I was weak and low,
And fear'd the passion as I felt it grow:
Will she, I said, to one so poor attend,
Without a prospect, and without a friend?
I dared not ask her—till a rival came,
But hid the secret, slow-consuming flame.

I once had seen him; then familiar, free,
More than became a common guest to be;
And sure, I said, he has a look of pride
And inward joy—a lover satisfied.

Can you not, Brother, on adventures past
A thought, as on a lively prospect, cast?
On days of dear remembrance! days that seem,
When past—nay, even when present, like a dream—
These white and blessed days, that softly shine
On few, nor oft on them—have they been thine?"

George answer'd, "Yes! dear Richard, through the years
Long past, a day so white and mark'd appears:
As in the storm that pours destruction round,
Is here and there a ship in safety found;
So in the storms of life some days appear
More blest and bright for the preceding fear;
These times of pleasure that in life arise,
Like spots in deserts, that delight, surprise,
And to our wearied senses give the more,
For all the waste behind us and before;
And thou, dear Richard, hast then had thy share
Of those enchanting times that baffle care?"

"Yes, I have felt this life-refreshing gale
That bears us onward when our spirits fail;
That gives those spirits vigour and delight—
I would describe it, could I do it right.

Such days have been—a day of days was one
When, rising gaily with the rising sun,
I took my way to join a happy few,
Known not to me, but whom Matilda knew,
To whom she went a guest, and message sent,
'Come thou to us,' and as a guest I went.

There are two ways to Brandon—by the heath
Above the cliff, or on the sand beneath,
Where the small pebbles, wetted by the wave,
To the new day reflected lustre gave:
At first above the rocks I made my way,
Delighted looking at the spacious bay,
And the large fleet that to the northward steer'd
Full sail, that glorious in my view appear'd;
For where does man evince his full control
O'er subject matter, where displays the soul
Its mighty energies with more effect
Than when her powers that moving mass direct?
Than when man guides the ship man's art has made,
And makes the winds and waters yield him aid?

Much as I long'd to see the maid I loved,
Through scenes so glorious I at leisure moved;
For there are times when we do not obey
The master-passion—when we yet delay—
When absence, soon to end, we yet prolong,
And dally with our wish although so strong.

High were my joys, but they were sober too,
Nor reason spoil'd the pictures fancy drew;
I felt—rare feeling in a world like this—
The sober certainty of waking bliss;
Add too the smaller aids to happy men,
Convenient helps—these too were present then.

But what are spirits? light indeed and gay
They are, like winter flowers, nor last a day;
Comes a rude icy wind,—they feel, and fade away

High beat my heart when to the house I came,
And when the ready servant gave my name;
But when I enter'd that pernicious room,
Gloomy it look'd, and painful was the gloom;
And jealous was the pain, and deep the sigh
Caused by this gloom, and pain, and jealousy:
For there Matilda sat, and her beside
That rival soldier, with a soldier's pride;
With self-approval in his laughing face,
His seem'd the leading spirit of the place:
She was all coldness—yet I thought a look,
But that corrected, tender welcome spoke:
It was as lightning which you think you see,
But doubt, and ask if lightning it could be.

Confused and quick my introduction pass'd,
When I, a stranger and on strangers cast,
Beheld the gallant man as he display'd
Uncheck'd attention to the guilty maid:
O! how it grieved me that she dared t' excite
Those looks in him that show'd so much delight,
Egregious coxcomb! there—he smiled again,
As if he sought to aggravate my pain:
Still she attends—I must approach- -and find,
Or make, a quarrel, to relieve my mind.

In vain I try—politeness as a shield
The angry strokes of my contempt repell'd,
Nor must I violate the social law
That keeps the rash and insolent in awe.

Once I observed, on hearing my replies,
The woman's terror fix'd on me the eyes
That look'd entreaty; but the guideless rage
Of jealous minds no softness can assuage.
But, lo! they rise, and all prepare to take
The promised pleasure on the neighbouring lake.

Good heaven! they whisper! Is it come to this?
Already!—then may I my doubt dismiss:
Could he so soon a timid girl persuade?
What rapid progress has the coxcomb made!
And yet how cool her looks, and how demure!
The falling snow nor lily's flower so pure:
What can I do? I must the pair attend,
And watch this horrid business to its end.

There, forth they go! He leads her to the shore—
Nay, I must follow,—I can bear no more:
What can the handsome gipsy have in view
In trifling thus, as she appears to do?
I, who for months have labour'd to succeed,
Have only lived her vanity to feed.

O! you will make me room—'t is very kind,
And meant for him—it tells him he must mind;
Must not be careless:—I can serve to draw
The soldier on, and keep the man in awe.
O! I did think she had a guileless heart,
Without deceit, capriciousness, or art;
And yet a stranger, with a coat of red,
Has, by an hour's attention, turn'd her head.

Ah! how delicious was the morning drive,
The soul awaken'd and its hopes alive:
How dull this scene by trifling minds enjoy'd,
The heart in trouble and its hope destroy'd.

Well, now we land—And will he yet support
This part? What favour has he now to court?
Favour! O, no! He means to quit the fair;
How strange! how cruel! Will she not despair?

Well! take her hand—no further if you please,
I cannot suffer fooleries like these:
How? 'Love to Julia!' to his wife?—O! dear
And injured creature, how must I appear,
Thus haughty in my looks, and in my words severe?
Her love to Julia, to the school-day friend
To whom these letters she has lately penn'd!
Can she forgive? And now I think again,
The man was neither insolent nor vain;
Good humour chiefly would a stranger trace,
Were he impartial, in the air or face;
And I so splenetic the whole way long,
And she so patient—it was very wrong.

The boat had landed in a shady scene;
The grove was in its glory, fresh and green;
The showers of late had swell'd the branch and bough,
And the sun's fervour made them pleasant now,
Hard by an oak arose in all its pride,
And threw its arms along the water's side;
Its leafy limbs, that on the glassy lake
Stretch far, and all those dancing shadows make.

And now we walk—now smaller parties seek
Or sun or shade as pleases—Shall I speak?
Shall I forgiveness ask, and then apply
For——O! that vile and intercepting cry.
Alas! what mighty ills can trifles make,—
A hat! the idiot's—fallen in the lake!
What serious mischief can such idlers do?
I almost wish the head had fallen too.

No more they leave us, but will hover round,
As if amusement at our cost they found;
Vex'd and unhappy I indeed had been,
Had I not something in my charmer seen
Like discontent, that, though corrected, dwelt
On that dear face, and told me what she felt.

Now must we cross the lake, and as we cross'd
Was my whole soul in sweet emotion lost;
Clouds in white volumes roll'd beneath the moon,
Softening her light that on the waters shone:
This was such bliss! even then it seem'd relief
To veil the gladness in a show of grief:
We sigh'd as we conversed, and said, how deep
This lake on which those broad dark shadows sleep;
There is between us and a watery grave
But a thin plank, and yet our fate we brave.
'What if it burst?' Matilda, then my care
Would be for thee: all danger I would dare,
And, should my efforts fail, thy fortune would I share.
'The love of life,' she said, 'would powerful prove!'
O! not so powerful as the strength of love:
A look of kindness gave the grateful maid,
That had the real effort more than paid.

But here we land, and haply now may choose
Companions home—our way, too, we may lose
In these drear, dark, inosculating lanes,
The very native of his doubt complains;
No wonder then that in such lonely ways
A stranger, heedless of the country, strays;
A stranger, too, whose many thoughts all meet
In one design, and none regard his feet.

'Is this the path?' the cautious fair one cries;
I answer, Yes!—'We shall our friends surprise,'
She added, sighing—I return the sighs.

'Will they not wonder?' O! they would, indeed,
Could they the secrets of this bosom read,
These chilling doubts, these trembling hopes I feel!
The faint, fond hopes I can no more conceal—
I love thee, dear Matilda!—to confess
The fact is dangerous, fatal to suppress.

And now in terror I approach the home
Where I may wretched but not doubtful come,
Where I must be all ecstasy, or all,—
O! what will you a wretch rejected call?
Not man, for I shall lose myself, and be
A creature lost to reason, losing thee.

Speak, my Matilda! on the rack of fear
Suspend me not—I would my sentence hear,
Would learn my fate——Good Heaven! and what portend
These tears?—and fall they for thy wretched friend?
Or——but I cease; I cannot paint the bliss,
From a confession soft and kind as this;

Nor where we walk'd, nor how our friends we met,
Or what their wonder—I am wondering yet;
For he who nothing heeds has nothing to forget.

All thought, yet thinking nothing—all delight
In every thing, but nothing in my sight!
Nothing I mark or learn, but am possess'd
Of joys I cannot paint, and I am bless'd
In all that I conceive—whatever is, is best.
Ready to aid all beings, I would go
The world around to succour human wo;
Yet am so largely happy, that it seems
There are no woes, and sorrows are but dreams.

There is a college joy, to scholars known,
When the first honours are proclaim'd their own;
There is ambition's joy, when in their race
A man surpassing rivals gains his place;
There is a beauty's joy, amid a crowd
To have that beauty her first fame allow'd;
And there 's the conqueror's joy, when, dubious held
And long the fight, he sees the foe repell'd:

But what are these, or what are other joys,
That charm kings, conquerors, beauteous nymphs,
and boys,
Or greater yet, if greater yet be found,
To that delight when love's dear hope is crown'd?
To the first beating of a lover's heart,
When the loved maid endeavours to impart,
Frankly yet faintly, fondly yet in fear,
The kind confession that he holds so dear.
Now in the morn of our return how strange
Was this new feeling, this delicious change:
That sweet delirium, when I gazed in fear,
That all would yet be lost and disappear.

Such was the blessing that I sought for pain,
In some degree to be myself again;
And when we met a shepherd old and lame,
Cold and diseased, it seem'd my blood to tame;
And I was thankful for the moral sight,
That soberized the vast and wild delight."

BOOK VII.

THE ELDER BROTHER.

Conversation—Story of the elder Brother—His romantic Views and Habits—The Scene of his Meditations—Their Nature—Interrupted by an Adventure—The Consequences of it—A strong and permanent Passion—Search of its Object—Long ineffectual—How found—The first Interview—The second—End of the Adventure—Retirement.

"Thanks, my dear Richard; and, I pray thee, deign
To speak the truth—does all this love remain,
And all this joy? for views and flights sublime,
Ardent and tender, are subdued by time.
Speak'st thou of her to whom thou madest thy vows,
Of my fair sister, of thy lawful spouse?
Or art thou talking some frail love about,
The rambling fit, before th' abiding gout?"

"Nay, spare me, Brother, an adorer spare:
Love and the gout! thou wouldst not these compare?"

"Yea, and correctly; teasing ere they come,
They then confine their victim to his home:
In both are previous feints and false attacks,
Both place the grieving patient on their racks:
They both are ours, with all they bring, for life,
'T is not in us t' expel or gout or wife;
On man a kind of dignity they shed,
A sort of gloomy pomp about his bed:
Then if he leaves them, go where'er he will,
They have a claim upon his body still;
Nay, when they quit him, as they sometimes do,
What is there left t' enjoy or to pursue?—
But dost thou love this woman?"
"O! beyond
What I can tell thee of the true and fond:
Hath she not soothed me, sick, enrich'd me, poor,
And banish'd death and misery from my door?
Has she not cherish'd every moment's bliss,
And made an Eden of a world like this?
When Care would strive with us his watch to keep,
Has she not sung the snarling fiend to sleep?
And when Distress has look'd us in the face,
Has she not told him, 'thou art not Disgrace?'"

"I must behold her, Richard; I must see
This patient spouse who sweetens misery—
But didst thou need, and wouldst thou not apply?—
Nay thou wert right—but then how wrong was I!"
"My indiscretion was—"
"No more repeat;
Would I were nothing worse than indiscreet;—
But still there is a plea that I could bring,
Had I the courage to describe the thing."

"Then thou too, Brother, couldst of weakness tell,
Thou, too, hast found the wishes that rebel
Against the sovereign reason; at some time
Thou hast been fond, heroic, and sublime;
Wrote verse, it may be, and for one dear maid
The sober purposes of life delay'd;
From year to year the fruitless chase pursued,
And hung enamour'd o'er the flying good:
Then be thy weakness to a Brother shown,
And give him comfort who displays his own."

"Ungenerous youth! dost thou presuming ask
A man so grave his failings to unmask?
What if I tell thee of a waste of time,
That on my spirit presses as a crime,
Wilt thou despise me?—I, who, soaring, fell
So late to rise—Hear then the tale I tell;
Who tells what thou shalt hear, esteems his hearer
well.

"Yes, my dear Richard, thou shalt hear me own
Follies and frailties thou hast never known;
Thine was a frailty,—folly, if you please,—
But mine a flight, a madness, a disease.

Turn with me to my twentieth year, for then
The lover's frenzy ruled the poet's pen;
When virgin reams were soil'd with lays of love,
The flinty hearts of fancied nymphs to move:
Then was I pleased in lonely ways to tread,
And muse on tragic tales of lovers dead;
For all the merit I could then descry
In man or woman was for love to die.

I mused on charmers chaste, who pledged their truth,
And left no more the once-accepted youth;
Though he disloyal, lost, diseased, became,
The widow'd turtle's was a deathless flame;
This faith, this feeling, gave my soul delight,
Truth in the lady, ardour in the knight.

I built me castles wondrous rich and rare,
Few castle-builders could with me compare;
The hall, the palace, rose at my command,
And these I fill'd with objects great and grand.
Virtues sublime, that nowhere else would live,
Glory and pomp, that I alone could give;
Trophies and thrones by matchless valour gain'd,
Faith unreproved, and chastity unstain'd;
With all that soothes the sense and charms the soul,
Came at my call, and were in my control.

And who was I? a slender youth and tall,
In manner awkward, and with fortune small;
With visage pale, my motions quick and slow,
That fall and rising in the spirits show;
For none could more by outward signs express
What wise men lock within the mind's recess;
Had I a mirror set before my view,
I might have seen what such a form could do;
Had I within the mirror truth beheld,
I should have such presuming thoughts repell'd:
But awkward as I was, without the grace
That gives new beauty to a form or face;
Still I expected friends most true to prove,
And grateful, tender, warm, assiduous love.

Assured of this, that love's delicious bond
Would hold me ever faithful, ever fond;
It seem'd but just that I in love should find
A kindred heart as constant and as kind.
Give me, I cried, a beauty; none on earth
Of higher rank or nobler in her birth;
Pride of her race, her father's hope and care,
Yet meek as children of the cottage are;
Nursed in the court, and there by love pursued,
But fond of peace, and blest in solitude;
By rivals honour'd, and by beauties praised,
Yet all unconscious of the envy raised;
Suppose her this, and from attendants freed,
To want my prowess in a time of need,
When safe and grateful she desires to show
She feels the debt that she delights to owe,
And loves the man who saved her in distress—
So fancy will'd, nor would compound for less.

This was my dream.—In some auspicious hour,
In some sweet solitude, in some green bower,
Whither my fate should lead me, there, unseen,
I should behold my fancy's gracious queen,
Singing sweet song! that I should hear awhile,
Then catch the transient glory of a smile;
Then at her feet with trembling hope should kneel,
Such as rapt saints and raptured lovers feel;
To watch the chaste unfoldings of her heart,
In joy to meet, in agony to part,
And then in tender song to soothe my grief,
And hail, in glorious rhyme, my *Lady of the Leaf*

To dream these dreams I chose a woody scene,
My guardian-shade, the world and me between;
A green inclosure, where beside its bound
A thorny fence beset its beauties round,
Save where some creature's force had made a way
For me to pass, and in my kingdom stray:
Here then I stray'd, then sat me down to call,
Just as I will'd, my shadowy subjects all!
Fruits of all minds conceived on every coast,
Fay, witch, enchanter, devil, demon, ghost;
And thus with knights and nymphs, in halls and bowers,
In war and love, I pass'd unnumber'd hours:
Gross and substantial beings all forgot,
Ideal glories beam'd around the spot,
And all that was, with me, of this poor world was not.

Yet in this world there was a single scene,
That I allow'd with mine to intervene;
This house, where never yet my feet had stray'd,
I with respect and timid awe survey'd;
With pleasing wonder I have oft-times stood,
To view these turrets rising o'er the wood;
When fancy to the halls and chambers flew,
Large, solemn, silent, that I must not view;
The moat was then, and then o'er all the ground
Tall elms and ancient oaks stretch'd far around;
And where the soil forbad the nobler race,
Dwarf trees and humbler shrubs had found their place,
Forbidding man in their close hold to go,
Haw, gatter, holm, the service and the sloe;
With tangling weeds that at the bottom grew,
And climbers all above their feathery branches threw.
Nor path of man or beast was there espied,
But there the birds of darkness loved to hide,
The loathed toad to lodge, and speckled snake to glide.
To me this hall, thus view'd in part, appear'd
A mansion vast—I wonder'd, and I fear'd;
There as I wander'd, fancy's forming eye
Could gloomy cells and dungeons dark espy;
Winding through these, I caught th' appalling sound
Of troubled souls, that guilty minds confound,
Where murder made its way, and mischief stalk'd around.
Above the roof were raised the midnight storms,
And the wild lights betray'd the shadowy forms.

With all these flights and fancies, then so dear,
I reach'd the birth-day of my twentieth year;
And in the evening of a day in June
Was singing—as I sang—some heavenly tune;
My native tone, indeed, was harsh and hoarse,
But he who feels such powers can sing of course—

Is there a good on earth, or gift divine,
That fancy cannot say, behold! 't is mine?

So was I singing, when I saw descend
From this old seat a lady and her friend;
Downward they came with steady pace and slow,
Arm link'd in arm, to bless my world below.
I knew not yet if they escaped, or chose
Their own free way,—if they had friends or foes,—
But near to my dominion drew the pair,
Link'd arm in arm, and walk'd, conversing, there.

I saw them ere they came, myself unseen,
My lofty fence and thorny bound between—
And one alone, one matchless face I saw,
And, though at distance, felt delight and awe:
Fancy and truth adorn'd her; fancy gave
Much, but not all; truth help'd to make their slave;
For she was lovely, all was not the vain
Or sickly homage of a fever'd brain;
No! she had beauty, such as they admire
Whose hope is earthly, and whose love desire;
Imagination might her aid bestow,
But she had charms that only truth could show.

Their dress was such as well became the place,
But one superior; hers the air, the grace,
The condescending looks, that spoke the nobler race.
Slender she was and tall: her fairy-feet
Bore her right onward to my shady seat;
And O! I sigh'd that she would nobly dare
To come, nor let her friend th' adventure share;
But see how I in my dominion reign,
And never wish to view the world again.

Thus was I musing, seeing with my eyes
These objects, with my mind her fantasies,
And chiefly thinking—is this maid, divine
As she appears, to be this queen of mine?
Have I from henceforth beauty in my view,
Not airy all, but tangible and true?
Here then I fix, here bound my vagrant views,
And here devote my heart, my time, my muse.

She saw not this, though ladies early trace
Their beauty's power, the glories of their face;
Yet knew not this fair creature—could not know—
That new-born love! that I too soon must show:
And I was musing—how shall I begin?
How make approach my unknown way to win,
And to that heart, as yet untouch'd, make known
The wound, the wish, the weakness of my own?
Such is my part, but——Mercy! what alarm?
Dare aught on earth that sovereign beauty harm?
Again—the shrieking charmers—how they rend
The gentle air——The shriekers lack a friend—
They are my princess and th' attendant maid
In so much danger, and so much afraid!—
But whence the terror?—Let me haste and see
What has befallen them who cannot flee—
Whence can the peril rise? What can that peril be?

It soon appear'd, that while this nymph divine
Moved on, there met the rude uncivil kine,
Who knew her not—the damsel was not there
Who kept them—all obedient—in her care;
Strangers they thus defied and held in scorn,
And stood in threat'ning posture, hoof and horn:
While Susan—pail in hand—could stand the while
And prate with Daniel at a distant stile.

As feeling prompted, to the place I ran,
Resolved to save the maids and show the man:
Was each a cow like that which challenged Guy,
I had resolved t' attack it, and defy
In mortal combat! to repel or die.
That was no time to parley—or to say,
I will protect you—fly in peace away!
Lo! yonder stile—but with an air of grace,
As I supposed, I pointed to the place.

The fair ones took me at my sign, and flew,
Each like a dove, and to the stile withdrew;
Where safe, at distance, and from terrors free,
They turn'd to view my beastly foes and me.

I now had time my business to behold,
And did not like it—let the truth be told:
The cows, though cowards, yet in numbers strong
Like other mobs, by might defended wrong;
In man's own pathway fix'd, they seem'd disposed
For hostile measure, and in order closed,
Then halted near me, as I judged, to treat,
Before we came to triumph or defeat.

I was in doubt: 't was sore disgrace, I knew,
To turn my back, and let the cows pursue;
And should I rashly mortal strife begin,
'T was all unknown who might the battle win;
And yet to wait, and neither fight nor fly,
Would mirth create,—I could not that deny;
It look'd as if for safety I would treat,
Nay, sue for peace—No! rather come defeat!
'Look to me, loveliest of thy sex! and give
One cheering glance, and not a cow shall live,
For lo! this iron bar, this strenuous arm,
And those dear eyes to aid me as a charm.'

Say, goddess! Victory! say, on man or cow
Meanest thou now to perch?—On neither now—
For, as I ponder'd, on their way appear'd
The Amazonian milker of the herd;
These, at the wonted signals, made a stand,
And woo'd the nymph of the relieving hand;
Nor heeded now the man, who felt relief
Of other kind, and not unmix'd with grief;
For now he neither should his courage prove,
Nor in his dying moments boast his love.
My sovereign beauty with amazement saw—
So she declared—the horrid things in awe;
Well pleased, she witness'd what respect was paid
By such brute natures—Every cow afraid,
And kept at distance by the powers of one,
Who had to her a dangerous service done,
That prudence had declined, that valour's self might shun.

So thought the maid, who now, beyond the stile,
Received her champion with a gracious smile;
Who now had leisure on those charms to dwell,
That he could never from his thought expel;
There are, I know, to whom a lover seems,
Praising his mistress, to relate his dreams;

But, Richard, looks like those, that angel-face
Coula I no more in sister-angel trace;
O! it was more than fancy! it was more
Than in my darling views I saw before,
When I my idol made, and my allegiance swore.

Henceforth 't was bliss upon that face to dwell,
Till every trace became indelible;
I bless'd the cause of that alarm, her fright,
And all that gave me favour in her sight,
Who then was kind and grateful, till my mind,
Pleased and exulting, awe awhile resign'd.
For in the moment when she feels afraid,
How kindly speaks the condescending maid;
She sees her danger near, she wants her lover's aid.
As fire electric, when discharged, will strike
All who receive it, and they feel alike,
So in the shock of danger and surprise
Our minds are struck, and mix, and sympathise.
But danger dies, and distance comes between
My state and that of my all-glorious queen;
Yet much was done—upon my mind a chain
Was strongly fix'd, and likely to remain;
Listening, I grew enamour'd of the sound,
And felt to her my very being bound;
I bless'd the scene, nor felt a power to move,
Lost in the ecstasies of infant-love.

She saw and smiled; the smile delight convey'd,
My love encouraged, and my act repaid:
In that same smile I read the charmer meant
To give her hero chaste encouragement;
It spoke, as plainly as a smile can speak,
'Seek whom you love, love freely whom you seek.'

Thus, when the lovely witch had wrought her charm,
She took th' attendant maiden by the arm,
And left me fondly gazing, till no more
I could the shade of that dear form explore;
Then to my secret haunt I turn'd again,
Fire in my heart, and fever in my brain;
That face of her for ever in my view,
Whom I was henceforth fated to pursue,
To hope I know not what, small hope in what I knew.

O! my dear Richard, what a waste of time
Gave I not thus to lunacy sublime;
What days, months, years, (to useful purpose lost)
Has not this dire infatuation cost?
To this fair vision I, a bonded slave,
Time, duty, credit, honour, comfort, gave;
Gave all—and waited for the glorious things
That hope expects, but fortune never brings.

Yet let me own, while I my fault reprove,
There is one blessing still affix'd to love—
To love like mine—for, as my soul it drew
From reason's path, it shunn'd dishonour's too;
It made my taste refined, my feelings nice,
And placed an angel in the way of vice.

This angel now, whom I no longer view'd,
Far from this scene her destined way pursued;
No more that mansion held a form so fair,
She was away, and beauty was not there.

Such, my dear Richard, was my early flame,
My youthful frenzy—give it either name;
It was the withering bane of many a year,
That past away in causeless hope and fear;
The hopes, the fears, that every dream could kill,
Or make alive, and lead my passive will.

At length I learnt one name my angel bore,
And Rosabella I must now adore:
Yet knew but this—and not the favour'd place
That held the angel or th' angelic race;
Nor where, admired, the sweet enchantress dwelt,
But I had lost her—that, indeed, I felt.

Yet, would I say, she will at length be mine!
Did ever hero hope or love resign?
Though men oppose, and fortune bids despair,
She will in time her mischief well repair,
And I, at last, shall wed this fairest of the fair!
My thrifty uncle, now return'd, began
To stir within me what remain'd of man;
My powerful frenzy painted to the life,
And ask'd me if I took a dream to wife?
Debate ensued, and though not well content,
Upon a visit to his house I went:
He, the most saving of mankind, had still
Some kindred feeling; he would guide my will,
And teach me wisdom—so affection wrought,
That he to save me from destruction sought:
To him destruction, the most awful curse
Of misery's children, was—an empty purse!
He his own books approved, and thought the pen
An useful instrument for trading men;
But judged a quill was never to be slit
Except to make it for a merchant fit:
He, when inform'd how men of taste could write,
Look'd on his ledger with supreme delight;
Then would he laugh, and, with insulting joy,
Tell me aloud, 'that 's poetry, my boy;
These are your golden numbers—them repeat,
The more you have, the more you 'll find them sweet—
Their numbers move all hearts—no matter for their feet.
Sir, when a man composes in this style,
What is to him a critic's frown or smile?
What is the puppy's censure or applause
To the good man who on his banker draws,
Buys an estate, and writes upon the grounds,
Pay to A. B. an hundred thousand pounds?
Thus, my dear nephew, thus your talents prove;
Leave verse to poets, and the poor to love.'

Some months I suffered thus; compell'd to sit
And hear a wealthy kinsman aim at wit;
Yet there was something in his nature good,
And he had feeling for the tie of blood:
So while I languish'd for my absent maid
I some observance to my uncle paid."

"Had you inquired?" said Richard.

"I had placed
Inquirers round, but nothing could be traced;
Of every reasoning creature at this Hall,
And tenant near it, I applied to all—
Tell me if she—and I described her well—
Dwelt long a guest, or where retired to dwell?

But no! such lady they remember'd not—
They saw that face, strange beings! and forgot.
Nor was inquiry all; but I pursued
My soul's first wish, with hope's vast strength endued:
I cross'd the seas, I went where strangers go,
And gazed on crowds as one who dreads a foe,
Or seeks a friend; and, when I sought in vain,
Fled to fresh crowds, and hoped, and gazed again."

"It was a strong possession."—"Strong and strange,
I felt the evil, yet desired not change:
Years now had flown, nor was the passion cured,
But hope had life, and so was life endured;
The mind's disease, with all its strength, stole on,
Till youth, and health, and all but love were gone.
And there were seasons, Richard, horrid hours
Of mental suffering! they o'erthrew my powers,
And made my mind unsteady—I have still,
At times, a feeling of that nameless ill,
That is not madness—I could always tell
My mind was wandering—knew it was not well;
Felt all my loss of time, the shameful waste
Of talents perish'd, and of parts disgraced:
But though my mind was sane, there was a void—
My understanding seem'd in part destroy'd;
I thought I was not of my species one,
But unconnected! injured and undone.

While in this state, once more my uncle pray'd
That I would hear—I heard, and I obey'd;
For I was thankful that a being broke
On this my sadness, or an interest took
In my poor life—but, at his mansion, rest
Came with its halcyon stillness to my breast:
Slowly there enter'd in my mind concern
For things about me—I would something learn,
And to my uncle listen; who, with joy,
Found that ev'n yet I could my powers employ,
Till I could feel new hopes my mind possess,
Of ease at least, if not of happiness:
Till, not contented, not in discontent,
As my good uncle counsell'd, on I went;
Conscious of youth's great error—nay, the crime
Of manhood now—a dreary waste of time!
Conscious of that account which I must give
How life had past with me—I strove to live.

Had I, like others, my first hope attain'd,
I must, at least, a certainty have gain'd;
Had I, like others, lost the hope of youth,
Another hope had promised greater truth;
But I in baseless hopes, and groundless views,
Was fated time, and peace, and health to lose,
Impell'd to seek, for ever doom'd to fail,
Is—I distress you—let me end my tale.

Something one day occurr'd about a bill
That was not drawn with true mercantile skill,
And I was ask'd and authorized to go
To seek the firm of Clutterbuck and Co.;
Their hour was past—but when I urged the case,
There was a youth who named a second place:
Where, on occasions of important kind,
I might the man of occupation find
In his retirement, where he found repose
From the vexations that in business rose.

I found, though not with ease, this private seat
Of soothing quiet, wisdom's still retreat.

The house was good, but not so pure and clean
As I had houses of retirement seen;
Yet men, I knew, of meditation deep,
Love not their maidens should their studies sweep;
His room I saw, and must acknowledge, there
Were not the signs of cleanliness or care:
A female servant, void of female grace,
Loose in attire, proceeded to the place:
She stared intrusive on my slender frame,
And boldly ask'd my business and my name.

I gave them both; and, left to be amused,
Well as I might, the parlour I perused.
The shutters half unclosed, the curtains fell
Half down, and rested on the window-sill,
And thus, confusedly, made the room half visible:
Late as it was, the little parlour bore
Some tell-tale tokens of the night before;
There were strange sights and scents about the room,
Of food high season'd, and of strong perfume;
Two unmatch'd sofas ample rents display'd,
Carpet and curtains were alike decay'd;
A large old mirror, with once-gilded frame,
Reflected prints that I forbear to name,
Such as a youth might purchase—but, in truth,
Not a sedate or sober-minded youth:
The cinders yet were sleeping in the grate,
Warm from the fire, continued large and late,
As left by careless folk, in their neglected state;
The chairs in haste seem'd whirl'd about the room,
As when the sons of riot hurry home,
And leave the troubled place to solitude and gloom.

All this, for I had ample time, I saw,
And prudence question'd—should we not withdraw?
For he who makes me thus on business wait,
Is not for business in a proper state;
But man there was not, was not he for whom
To this convenient lodging I was come;
No! but a lady's voice was heard to call
On my attention—and she had it all;
For lo! she enters, speaking ere in sight,
'Monsieur! I shall not want the chair to-night—
Where shall I see him?'—This dear hour atones
For all affection's hopeless sighs and groans—
Then turning to me—'Art thou come at last?
A thousand welcomes—be forgot the past:
Forgotten all the grief that absence brings,
Fear that torments, and jealousy that stings—
All that is cold, injurious, and unkind,
Be it for ever banish'd from the mind;
And in that mind, and in that heart, be now
The soft endearment, and the binding vow."

She spoke—and o'er the practised features threw
The looks that reason charm, and strength subdue.

Will you not ask, how I beheld that face,
Or read the mind, and read it in that place?
I have tried, Richard, oft-times, and in vain,
To trace my thoughts, and to review that train—
If train there were—that meadow, grove, and stile,
The fright, th' escape, her sweetness and her smile;
Years since elapsed, and hope, from year to year,
To find her free—and then to find her here!

But is it she?—O! yes; the rose is dead,
All beauty, fragrance, freshness, glory fled:
But yet 't is she—the same and not the same—
Who to my bower an heavenly being came;
Who waked my soul's first thought of real bliss,
Whom long I sought, and now I find her—this.

I cannot paint her—something I had seen
So pale and slim, and tawdry and unclean;
With haggard looks, of vice and wo the prey,
Laughing in languor, miserably gay:
Her face, where face appear'd, was amply spread,
By art's coarse pencil, with ill-chosen red,
The flower's fictitious bloom, the blushing of the dead:
But still the features were the same, and strange
My view of both—the sameness and the change,
That fix'd me gazing and my eye enchain'd,
Although so little of herself remain'd;
It is the creature whom I loved, and yet
Is far unlike her—Would I could forget
The angel or her fall! the once adored
Or now despised! the worshipp'd or deplored!

'O! Rosabella!' I prepared to say,
'Whom I have loved,' but prudence whisper'd nay,
And folly grew ashamed—discretion had her day.
She gave her hand; which, as I lightly press'd,
The cold but ardent grasp my soul oppress'd;
The ruin'd girl disturb'd me, and my eyes
Look'd, I conceive, both sorrow and surprise.

I spoke my business—'He,' she answer'd, 'comes
And lodges here—he has the backward rooms—
He now is absent, and I chanced to hear
Will not before to-morrow eve appear,
And may be longer absent——O! the night
When you preserved me in that horrid fright;
A thousand, thousand times, asleep, awake,
I thought of what you ventured for my sake—
Now have you thought—yet tell me so—deceive
Your Rosabella, willing to believe?
O! there is something in love's first-born pain
Sweeter than bliss—it never comes again—
But has your heart been faithful?'—Here my pride
To anger rising, her attempt defied—
'My faith must childish in your sight appear,
Who have been faithful—to how many, dear?'

If words had fail'd, a look explain'd their style,
She could not blush assent, but she could smile:
Good heaven! I thought, have I rejected fame,
Credit, and wealth, for one who smiles at shame?

She saw me thoughtful—saw it, as I guess'd,
With some concern, though nothing she express'd.

Come, my dear friend, discard that look of care,
All things were made to be, as all things are;
All to seek pleasure as the end design'd
The only good in matter or in mind;
So was I taught by one, who gave me all
That my experienced heart can wisdom call.

I saw thee young, love's soft obedient slave,
And many a sigh to my young lover gave;
And I had, spite of cowardice or cow,
Return'd thy passion, and exchanged my vow;
But while I thought to bait the amorous hook,
One set for me my eager fancy took;
There was a crafty eye, that far could see,
And through my failings fascinated me:
Mine was a childish wish, to please my boy;
His a design, his wishes to enjoy.
O! we have both about the world been tost,
Thy gain I know not—I, they cry, am lost;
So let the wise ones talk; they talk in vain,
And are mistaken both in loss and gain:
'T is gain to get whatever life affords,
'T is loss to spend our time in empty words.

I was a girl, and thou a boy wert then,
Nor aught of women knew, nor I of men;
But I have traffick'd in the world, and thou,
Doubtless, canst boast of thy experience now;
Let us the knowledge we have gain'd produce,
And kindly turn it to our common use.'

Thus spoke the syren in voluptuous style,
While I stood gazing and perplex'd the while,
Chain'd by that voice, confounded by that smile.
And then she sang, and changed from grave to gay,
Till all reproach and anger died away.

'My Damon was the first to wake,
  The gentle flame that cannot die;
My Damon is the last to take
  The faithful bosom's softest sigh:
The life between is nothing worth,
  O! cast it from thy thought away;
Think of the day that gave it birth,
  And this its sweet returning day.

Buried be all that has been done,
  Or say that nought is done amiss;
For who the dangerous path can shun
  In such bewildering world as this?
But love can every fault forgive,
  Or with a tender look reprove;
And now let naught in memory live,
  But that we meet, and that we love.'

And then she moved my pity; for she wept,
And told her miseries till resentment slept;
For when she saw she could not reason blind,
She pour'd her heart's whole sorrows on my mind,
With features graven on my soul, with sighs
Seen but not heard, with soft imploring eyes,
And voice that needed not, but had the aid
Of powerful words to soften and persuade.

'O! I repent me of the past; and sure
Grief and repentance make the bosom pure:
Yet meet thee not with clean and single heart,
As on the day we met!—and but to part,
Ere I had drunk the cup that to my lip
Was held and press'd till I was forced to sip:
I drank indeed, but never ceased to hate,—
It poison'd, but could not intoxicate:
T' excuse my fall I plead not love's excess,
But a weak orphan's need and loneliness.
I had no parent upon earth—no door
Was oped to me—young, innocent, and poor,

Vain, tender and resentful—and my friend
Jealous of one who must on her depend,
Making life misery—You could witness then
That I was precious in the eyes of men;
So, made by them a goddess, and denied
Respect and notice by the women's pride;
Here scorn'd, there worshipp'd—will it strange appear,
Allured and driven, that I settled here?
Yet loved it not; and never have I pass'd
One day, and wish'd another like the last.
There was a fallen angel, I have read,
For whom their tears the sister-angels shed,
Because, although she ventured to rebel,
She was not minded like a child of hell.—
Such is my lot! and will it not be given
To grief like mine, that I may think of heaven?
Behold how there the glorious creatures shine,
And all my soul to grief and hope resign?'

I wonder'd, doubting—and is this a fact,
I thought; or part thou art disposed to act?

'Is it not written, He, who came to save
Sinners, the sins of deepest dye forgave?
That he his mercy to the sufferers dealt,
And pardon'd error when the ill was felt?
Yes! I would hope, there is an eye that reads
What is within, and sees the heart that bleeds——
But who on earth will one so lost deplore,
And who will help that lost one to restore?
Who will on trust the sigh of grief receive;
And—all things warring with belief—believe?'

Soften'd, I said—'Be mine the hand and heart,
If with your world you will consent to part.'
She would—she tried—Alas! she did not know
How deeply rooted evil habits grow;
She felt the truth upon her spirits press,
But wanted ease, indulgence, show, excess,
Voluptuous banquets, pleasures—not refined,
But such as soothe to sleep th' opposing mind—
She look'd for idle vice, the time to kill,
And subtle, strong apologies for ill;
And thus her yielding, unresisting soul
Sank, and let sin confuse her and control:
Pleasures that brought disgust yet brought relief,
And minds she hated help'd to war with grief."

"Thus then she perish'd?"—
"Nay—but thus she proved
Slave to the vices that she never loved:
But while she thus her better thoughts opposed,
And woo'd the world, the world's deceptions closed:—
I had long lost her; but I sought in vain
To banish pity:—still she gave me pain,
Still I desired to aid her—to direct,
And wish'd the world, that won her, to reject:
Nor wish'd in vain—there came, at length, request
That I would see a wretch with grief oppress'd,
By guilt affrighted—and I went to trace
Once more the vice-worn features of that face,
That sin-wreck'd being! and I saw her laid
Where never worldly joy a visit paid:
That world receding fast! the world to come
Conceal'd in terror, ignorance, and gloom;
Sins, sorrow, and neglect: with not a spark
Of vital hope,—all horrible and dark—
It frighten'd me!—I thought, and shall not I
Thus feel? thus fear?—this danger can I fly?
Do I so wisely live that I can calmly die?

The wants I saw I could supply with ease,
But there were wants of other kind than these;
Th' awakening thought, the hope-inspiring view—
The doctrines awful, grand, alarming, true—
Most painful to the soul, and yet most healing too:
Still I could something offer, and could send
For other aid—a more important friend,
Whose duty call'd him, and his love no less,
To help the grieving spirit in distress;
To save in that sad hour the drooping prey,
And from its victim drive despair away.
All decent comfort round the sick were seen;
The female helpers quiet, sober, clean;
Her kind physician with a smile appear'd,
And zealous love the pious friend endear'd:
While I, with mix'd sensations, could inquire,
Hast thou one wish, one unfulfill'd desire?
Speak every thought, nor unindulged depart,
If I can make thee happier than thou art.

Yes! there was yet a female friend, an old
And grieving nurse! to whom it should be told—
If I would tell—that she, her child, had fail'd,
And turn'd from truth! yet truth at length prevail'd.

'T was in that chamber, Richard, I began
To think more deeply of the end of man:
Was it to jostle all his fellows by,
To run before them, and say, 'here am I,
Fall down, and worship?'—Was it, life throughout,
With circumspection keen to hunt about
As spaniels for their game, where might be found
Abundance more for coffers that abound?
Or was it life's enjoyments to prefer,
Like this poor girl, and then to die like her?
No! He, who gave the faculties, design'd
Another use for the immortal mind:
There is a state in which it will appear
With all the good and ill contracted here;
With gain and loss, improvement and defect;
And then, my soul! what hast thou to expect
For talents laid aside, life's waste, and time's neglect?

Still as I went came other change—the frame
And features wasted, and yet slowly came
The end; and so inaudible the breath,
And still the breathing, we exclaim'd—'t is death!
But death it was not: when, indeed, she died,
I sat and his last gentle stroke espied:
When—as it came—or did my fancy trace
That lively, lovely flushing o'er the face?
Bringing back all that my young heart impress'd!
It came—and went!—She sigh'd, and was at rest.

Adieu, I said, fair Frailty! dearly cost
The love I bore thee—time and treasure lost;
And I have suffer'd many years in vain;
Now let me something in my sorrows gain
Heaven would not all this wo for man intend
If man's existence with his wo should end;

Heaven would not pain, and grief, and anguish give,
If man was not by discipline to live;
And for that brighter, better world prepare,
That souls with souls, when purified, shall share,
Those stains all done away that must not enter there.

Home I return'd, with spirits in that state
Of vacant wo, I strive not to relate,
Nor how, deprived of all her hope and strength,
My soul turn'd feebly to the world at length.
I travell'd then till health again resumed
Its former seat—I must not say re-bloom'd;
And then I fill'd, not loth, that favourite place
That has enrich'd some seniors of our race;
Patient and dull I grew; my uncle's praise
Was largely dealt me on my better days;
A love of money—other love at rest—
Came creeping on, and settled in my breast;
The force of habit held me to the oar,
Till I could relish what I scorn'd before:
I now could talk and scheme with *men of sense*,
Who deal for millions, and who sigh for pence;
And grew so like them, that I heard with joy
Old Blueskin said I was a pretty boy;
For I possess'd the caution with the zeal,
That all true lovers of their interest feel:
Exalted praise! and to the creature due,
Who loves that interest solely to pursue.

But I was sick, and sickness brought disgust;
My peace I could not to my profits trust:
Again some views of brighter kind appear'd,
My heart was humbled, and my mind was clear'd;
I felt those helps that souls diseased restore,
And that cold frenzy, avarice, raged no more.
From dreams of boundless wealth I then arose;
This place, the scene of infant bliss, I chose,
And here I find relief, and here I seek repose.

Yet much is lost, and not yet much is found,
But what remains, I would believe, is sound;
That first wild passion, that last mean desire,
Are felt no more; but holier hopes require
A mind prepared and steady—my reform
Has fears like his, who, suffering in a storm,
Is on a rich but unknown country cast,
The future fearing, while he feels the past;
But whose more cheerful mind, with hope imbued,
Sees through receding clouds the rising good."

BOOK VIII.

THE SISTERS.

Morning Walk and Conversation—Visit at a Cottage—Characters of the Sisters—Lucy and Jane—Their Lovers—Their Friend the Banker, and his Lady—Their intimacy—Its Consequence—Different Conduct of the Lovers—The Effect upon the Sisters—Their present State—The Influence of their Fortune upon the Minds of either.

The morning shone in cloudless beauty bright;
Richard his letters read with much delight;
George from his pillow rose in happy tone,
His bosom's lord sat lightly on his throne:
They read the morning news—they saw the sky
Inviting call'd them, and the earth was dry.

"The day invites us, brother," said the 'squire;
"Come, and I'll show thee something to admire:
We still may beauty in our prospects trace;
If not, we have them in both mind and face.

'T is but two miles—to let such women live
Unseen of him, what reason can I give?
Why should not Richard to the girls be known?
Would I have all their friendship for my own?
Brother, there dwell, yon northern hill below,
Two favourite maidens, whom 't is good to know;
Young, but experienced; dwellers in a cot,
Where they sustain and dignify their lot,
The best good girls in all our world below—
O! you must know them—Come! and you shall know.

But lo! the morning wastes—here, Jacob, stir—
If Phœbe comes, do you attend to her;
And let not Mary get a chattering press
Of idle girls to hear of her distress:
Ask her to wait till my return—and hide
From her meek mind your plenty and your pride;
Nor vex a creature, humble, sad, and still,
By your coarse bounty, and your rude good-will."

This said, the brothers hasten'd on their way,
With all the foretaste of a pleasant day;
The morning purpose in the mind had fix'd
The leading thought, and that with others mix'd.

"How well it is," said George, "when we possess
The strength that bears us up in our distress;
And need not the resources of our pride,
Our fall from greatness and our wants to hide;
But have the spirit and the wish to show,
We know our wants as well as others know.
'T is true, the rapid turns of fortune's wheel
Make even the virtuous and the humble feel:
They for a time must suffer, and but few
Can bear their sorrows and our pity too.

Hence all these small expedients, day by day,
Are used to hide the evils they betray:
When, if our pity chances to be seen,
The wounded pride retorts, with anger keen,
And man's insulted grief takes refuge in his spleen.

When Timon's board contains a single dish,
Timon talks much of market-men and fish,
Forgetful servants, and th' infernal cook,
Who always spoil'd whate'er she undertook.

But say, it tries us from our height to fall,
Yet is not life itself a trial all?
And not a virtue in the bosom lives,
That gives such ready pay as patience gives;
That pure submission to the ruling mind,
Fix'd, but not forced; obedient, but not blind;
The will of heaven to make her own she tries,
Or makes her own to heaven a sacrifice.

And is there aught on earth so rich or rare,
Whose pleasures may with virtue's pains compare?
This fruit of patience, this the pure delight,
That 't is a trial in her Judge's sight;
Her part still thriving duty to sustain,
Not spurning pleasure, not defying pain;
Never in triumph till her race be won,
And never fainting till her work be done.

With thoughts like these they reach'd the village brook,
And saw a lady sitting with her book;
And so engaged she heard not, till the men
Were at her side, nor was she frighten'd then;
But to her friend, the squire, his smile return'd,
Through which the latent sadness he discern'd.

The stranger-brother at the cottage door
Was now admitted, and was strange no more:
Then of an absent sister he was told,
Whom they were not at present to behold;
Something was said of nerves, and that disease,
Whose varying powers on mind and body seize,
Enfeebling both!—Here chose they to remain
One hour in peace, and then return'd again.

"I know not why," said Richard, "but I feel
The warmest pity on my bosom steal
For that dear maid! How well her looks express
For this world's good a cherish'd hopelessness!
A resignation that is so entire,
It feels not now the stirrings of desire;
What now to her is all the world esteems?
She is awake, and cares not for its dreams:
But moves while yet on earth, as one above
Its hopes and fears—its loathing and its love.

"But shall I learn," said he, "these sisters' fate?"—
And found his brother willing to relate.

"The girls were orphans early; yet I saw,
When young, their father—his profession law;
He left them but a competence, a store
That made his daughters neither rich nor poor;
Not rich, compared with some who dwelt around;
Not poor, for want they neither fear'd nor found;
Their guardian uncle was both kind and just,
One whom a parent might in dying trust;
Who, in their youth, the trusted store improved,
And, when he ceased to guide them, fondly loved.

These sister beauties were in fact the grace
Of yon small town,—it was their native place;
Like Saul's famed daughters were the lovely twain,
As Micah, Lucy, and as Merab, Jane:
For this was tall, with free commanding air,
And that was mild, and delicate, and fair.

Jane had an arch delusive smile, that charm'd
And threaten'd too; alluring, it alarm'd;
The smile of Lucy her approval told,
Cheerful, not changing, neither kind nor cold.

When children, Lucy love alone possess'd,
Jane was more punish'd and was more caress'd;
If told the childish wishes, one bespoke
A lamb, a bird, a garden, and a brook;
The other wish'd a joy unknown, a rout
Or crowded ball, and to be first led out.

Lucy loved all that grew upon the ground,
And loveliness in all things living found;
The gilded fly, the fern upon the wall,
Were nature's works, and admirable all;
Pleased with indulgence of so cheap a kind,
Its cheapness never discomposed her mind.

Jane had no liking for such things as these,
Things pleasing her must her superiors please
The costly flower was precious in her eyes,
That skill can vary, or that money buys;
Her taste was good, but she was still afraid,
Till fashion sanction'd the remarks she made.

The sisters read, and Jane with some delight,
The satires keen that fear or rage excite,
That men in power attack, and ladies high,
And give broad hints that we may know them by
She was amused when sent to haunted rooms,
Or some dark passage where the spirit comes
Of one once murder'd! then she laughing read,
And felt at once the folly and the dread:
As rustic girls to crafty gipsies fly,
And trust the liar though they fear the lie;
Or as a patient, urged by grievous pains,
Will fee the daring quack whom he disdains,
So Jane was pleased to see the beckoning hand,
And trust the magic of the Radcliffe-wand.

In her religion—for her mind, though light,
Was not disposed our better views to slight—
Her favourite authors were a solemn kind,
Who fill with dark mysterious thoughts the mind;
And who with such conceits her fancy plied,
Became her friend, philosopher, and guide.

She made the Progress of the Pilgrim one
To build a thousand pleasant views upon;
All that connects us with a world above
She loved to fancy, and she long'd to prove;
Well would the poet please her, who could lead
Her fancy forth, yet keep untouch'd her creed.

Led by an early custom, Lucy spied,
When she awaked, the Bible at her side;
That, ere she ventured on a world of care,
She might for trials, joys or pains prepare,
For every dart a shield, a guard for every snare.

She read not much of high heroic deeds,
Where man the measure of man's power exceeds;
But gave to luckless love and fate severe
Her tenderest pity and her softest tear.

She mix'd not faith with fable, but she trod
Right onward, cautious in the ways of God;
Nor did she dare to launch on seas unknown,
In search of truths by some adventurers shown,
But her own compass used, and kept a course her own.

The maidens both their loyalty declared,
And in the glory of their country shared;
But Jane that glory felt with proud delight,
When England's foes were vanquish'd in the fight
While Lucy's feelings for the brave who bled
Put all such glorious triumphs from her head.

They both were frugal; Lucy from the fear
Of wasting that which want esteems so dear,
But finds so scarce, her sister from the pain
That springs from want, when treated with disdain.

Jane borrow'd maxims from a doubting school,
And took for truth the test of ridicule;
Lucy saw no such virtue in a jest,
Truth was with her of ridicule a test.

They loved each other with the warmth of youth,
With ardour, candour, tenderness, and truth;
And though their pleasures were not just the same,
Yet both were pleased whenever one became;
Nay, each would rather in the act rejoice,
That was th' adopted, not the native choice.

Each had a friend, and friends to minds so fond
And good are soon united in the bond;
Each had a lover; but it seem'd that fate
Decreed that these should not approximate.
Now Lucy's lover was a prudent swain,
And thought, in all things, what would be his gain;
The younger sister first engaged his view,
But with her beauty he her spirit knew;
Her face he much admired, 'but, put the case,'
Said he, 'I marry, what is then a face?
At first it pleases to have drawn the lot;
He then forgets it, but his wife does not;
Jane too,' he judged, 'would be reserved and nice,
And many lovers had enhanced her price.'

Thus thinking much, but hiding what he thought,
The prudent lover Lucy's favour sought,
And he succeeded,—she was free from art,
And his appear'd a gentle guileless heart;
Such she respected; true, her sister found
His placid face too ruddy and too round,
Too cold and inexpressive; such a face
Where you could nothing mark'd or manly trace.

But Lucy found him to his mother kind,
And saw the Christian meekness of his mind;
His voice was soft, his temper mild and sweet,
His mind was easy, and his person neat.

Jane said he wanted courage; Lucy drew
No ill from that, though she believed it too;
'It is religious, Jane, be not severe;'
'Well, Lucy, then it is religious fear.'
Nor could the sister, great as was her love,
A man so lifeless and so cool approve.

Jane had a lover, whom a lady's pride
Might wish to see attending at her side,
Young, handsome, sprightly, and with good address,
Not mark'd for folly, error or excess;
Yet not entirely from their censure free,
Who judge our failings with severity;
The very care he took to keep his name
Stainless, with some was evidence of shame.

Jane heard of this, and she replied, 'Enough;
Prove but the facts, and I resist not proof;
Nor is my heart so easy as to love
The man my judgment bids me not approve.'
But yet that heart a secret joy confess'd,
To find no slander on the youth would rest;
His was, in fact, such conduct, that a maid
Might think of marriage, and be not afraid;
And she was pleased to find a spirit high,
Free from all fear, that spurn'd hypocrisy.

'What fears my sister?' said the partial fair,
For Lucy fear'd,—'Why tell me to beware?
No smooth deceitful varnish can I find;
His is a spirit generous, free, and kind;
And all his flaws are seen, all floating in his mind.
A little boldness in his speech. What then?
It is the failing of these generous men.
A little vanity, but—O! my dear,
They all would show it, were they all sincere.

But come, agreed; we'll lend each other eyes
To see our favourites, when they wear disguise;
And all those errors that will then be shown
Uninfluenced by the workings of our own.'

Thus lived the sisters, far from power removed,
And far from need, both loving and beloved.
Thus grew, as myrtles grow; I grieve at heart
That I have pain and sorrow to impart.
But so it is, the sweetest herbs that grow
In the lone vale, where sweetest waters flow,
Ere drops the blossom, or appears the fruit,
Feel the vile grub, and perish at the root;
And in a quick and premature decay,
Breathe the pure fragrance of their life away.

A town was near, in which the buildings all
Were large, but one pre-eminently tall—
An huge high house. Without there was an air
Of lavish cost; no littleness was there;
But room for servants, horses, whiskies, gigs,
And walls for pines and peaches, grapes and figs;
Bright on the sloping grass the sun-beams shone,
And brought the summer of all climates on.

Here wealth its prowess to the eye display'd,
And here advanced the seasons, there delay'd;
Bid the due heat each growing sweet refine,
Made the sun's light with grosser fire combine,
And to the Tropic gave the vigour of the Line.

Yet, in the master of this wealth, behold
A light vain coxcomb taken from his gold,
Whose busy brain was weak, whose boasting heart was cold.
Oh! how he talk'd to that believing town,
That he would give it riches and renown;
Cause a canal where treasures were to swim,
And they should owe their opulence to him!
In fact, of riches he insured a crop,
So they would give him but a seed to drop.
As used the alchymist his boasts to make,
'I give you millions for the mite I take;'
The mite they never could again behold,
The millions all were Eldorado gold.

By this professing man, the country round
Was search'd to see where money could be found.

The thriven farmer, who had lived to spare,
Became an object of especial care;
He took the frugal tradesman by the hand,
And wish'd him joy of what he might command·
And the industrious servant, who had laid
His saving by, it was his joy to aid;

Large talk, and hints of some productive plan,
Half named, won all his hearers to a man;
Uncertain projects drew them wondering on,
And avarice listen'd till distrust was gone.

But when to these dear girls he found his way,
All easy, artless, innocent were they;
When he compell'd his foolish wife to be
At once so great, so humble, and so free;
Whom others sought, nor always with success!
But they were both her pride and happiness;
And she esteem'd them, but attended still
To the vile purpose of her husband's will;
And when she fix'd his snares about their mind
Respected those whom she essay'd to blind;
Nay with esteem she some compassion gave
To the fair victims whom she would not save.

The Banker's wealth and kindness were her themes,
His generous plans, his patriotic schemes;
What he had done for some, a favourite few,
What for his favourites still he meant to do;
Not that he always listen'd—which was hard—
To her, when speaking of her great regard
For certain friends—'but you, as I may say,
Are his own choice—I am not jealous—nay!'

Then came the man himself, and came with speed,
As just from business of importance freed;
Or just escaping, came with looks of fire,
As if he'd just attain'd his full desire;
As if Prosperity and he for life
Were wed, and he was showing off his wife;
Pleased to display his influence, and to prove
Himself the object of her partial love:
Perhaps with this was join'd the latent fear,
The time would come when he would not be dear.

Jane laugh'd at all their visits and parade,
And call'd it friendship in an hot-house made;
A style of friendship suited to his taste,
Brought on, and ripen'd, like his grapes, in haste;
She saw the wants that wealth in vain would hide,
And all the tricks and littleness of pride;
On all the wealth would creep the vulgar stain,
And grandeur strove to look itself in vain.

Lucy perceived—but she replied, 'why heed
Such small defects?—they're very kind indeed!"
And kind they were, and ready to produce
Their easy friendship, ever fit for use;
Friendship that enters into all affairs,
And daily wants, and daily gets, repairs.

Hence at the cottage of the sisters stood
The Banker's steed—he was so very good;
Oft through the roads, in weather foul or fair,
Their friend's gay carriage bore the gentle pair;
His grapes and nectarines woo'd the virgins' hand,
His books and roses were at their command;
And costly flowers,—he took upon him shame
That he could purchase what he could not name.

Lucy was vex'd to have such favours shown,
And they returning nothing of their own;
Jane smiled, and begg'd her sister to believe,—
'We give at least as much as we receive.'

Alas! and more; they gave their ears and eyes,
His splendour oft-times took them by surprise;
And if in Jane appear'd a meaning smile,
She gazed, admired, and paid respect the while;
Would she had rested there! Deluded maid,
She saw not yet the fatal price she paid;
Saw not that wealth, though join'd with folly, grew
In her regard; she smiled, but listen'd too;
Nay would be grateful, she would trust her all,
Her funded source,—to him a matter small;
Taken for their sole use, and ever at their call:
To be improved—he knew not how indeed,
But he had methods—and they must succeed.

This was so good, that Jane, in very pride,
To spare him trouble, for a while denied;
And Lucy's prudence, though it was alarm'd,
Was by the splendour of the Banker charm'd;
What was her paltry thousand pounds to him,
Who would expend five thousand on a whim?
And then the portion of his wife was known;
But not that she reserved it for her own.

Lucy her lover trusted with the fact,
And frankly ask'd, 'if he approved the act?'
'It promised well,' he said; 'he could not tell
How it might end, but sure it promised well;
He had himself a trifle in the Bank,
And should be sore uneasy if it sank.'

Jane from her lover had no wish to hide
Her deed; but was withheld by maiden pride,
To talk so early—as if one were sure
Of being his; she could not that endure.
But when the sisters were apart, and when
They freely spoke of their affairs and men,
They thought with pleasure of the sum improved,
And so presented to the men they loved.

Things now proceeded in a quiet train;
No cause appear'd to murmur or complain;
The moneyed man, his ever-smiling dame,
And their young darlings, in their carriage came;
Jane's sprightly lover smiled their pomp to see,
And ate their grapes with gratitude and glee,
But with the freedom there was nothing mean,
Humble, or forward, in his freedom seen;
His was the frankness of a mind that shows
It knows itself, nor fears for what it knows:
But Lucy's ever humble friend was awed
By the profusion he could not applaud;
He seem'd indeed reluctant to partake
Of the collation that he could not make;
And this was pleasant in the maiden's view,—
Was modesty—was moderation too;
Though Jane esteem'd it meanness; and she saw
Fear in that prudence, avarice in that awe.

But both the lovers now to town are gone,
By business one is call'd, by duty one;
While rumour rises,—whether false or true
The ladies knew not—it was known to few—
But fear there was, and on their guardian-friend
They for advice and comfort would depend
When rose the day; meantime from Belmont place
Came vile report, predicting quick disgrace.

'T was told—the servants, who had met to thank
Their lord for placing money in his Bank—
Their kind free master, who such wages gave,
And then increased whatever they could save—
They who had heard they should their savings lose,
Were weeping, swearing, drinking at the news;
And still the more they drank, the more they wept,
And swore, and rail'd, and threaten'd till they slept.

The morning truth confirm'd the evening dread;
The Bank was broken, and the Banker fled;
But left a promise that his friends should have,
To the last shilling—what his fortunes gave.

The evil tidings reach'd the sister-pair,
And one like Sorrow look'd, and one Despair;
They from each other turn'd th' afflicting look,
And loth and late the painful silence broke.

'The odious villain!' Jane in wrath began;
In pity Lucy, 'the unhappy man!
When time and reason our affliction heal,
How will the author of our sufferings feel!'

'And let him feel, my sister,—let the woes
That he creates be bane to his repose!
Let them be felt in his expiring hour,
When death brings all its dread, and sin its power:
Then let the busy foe of mortals state
The pangs he caused, his own to aggravate!

Wretch! when our life was glad, our prospects gay,
With savage hand to sweep them all away:
And he must know it—know when he beguiled
His easy victims—how the villain smiled!

Oh! my dear Lucy, could I see him crave
The food denied, a beggar and a slave,
To stony hearts he should with tears apply,
And Pity's self withhold the struggling sigh;
Or, if relenting weakness should extend
Th' extorted scrap that justice would not lend,
Let it be poison'd by the curses deep
Of every wretch whom he compels to weep!'

'Nay, my sweet sister, if you thought such pain
Were his, your pity would awake again;
Your generous heart the wretch's grief would feel,
And you would soothe the pangs you could not heal.'

'Oh! never, never,—I would still contrive
To keep the slave whom I abhorr'd alive;
His tortured mind with horrid fears to fill,
Disturb his reason, and misguide his will;
Heap coals of fire, to lie like melted lead,
Heavy and hot, on his accursed head;
Not coals that mercy kindles hearts to melt,
But he should feel them hot as fires are felt;
Corroding ever, and through life the same,
Strong self-contempt and ever-burning shame;
Let him so wretched feel that he may fly
To desperate thoughts, and be resolved to die—
And then let death such frightful visions give,
That he may dread the attempt, and beg to live!'

So spake th' indignant maid, when Lucy sigh'd,
And, waiting softer times, no more replied.

Barlow was then in town; and there he thought
Of bliss to come, and bargains to be bought;
And was returning homeward—when he found
The Bank was broken, and his venture drown'd.

'Ah! foolish maid,' he cried, 'and what wilt thou
Say for thy friends and their excesses now?
All now is brought completely to an end;
What can the spendthrift now afford to spend?
Had my advice been—true, I gave consent,
The thing was purposed; what could I prevent?

Who will her idle taste for flowers supply,—
Who send her grapes and peaches! let her try;—
There's none will give her, and she cannot buy.

Yet would she not be grateful if she knew
What to my faith and generous love was due?
Daily to see the man who took her hand,
When she had not a sixpence at command;
Could I be sure that such a quiet mind
Would be for ever grateful, mild, and kind,
I might comply—but how will Bloomer act,
When he becomes acquainted with the fact?
The loss to him is trifling—but the fall
From independence, that to her is all;
Now should he marry, 't will be shame to me
To hold myself from my engagement free;
And should he not, it will be double grace
To stand alone in such a trying case.

Come then, my Lucy, to thy faithful heart
And humble love I will my views impart,
Will see the grateful tear that softly steals
Down the fair face and all thy joy reveals;
And when I say it is a blow severe,
Then will I add—restrain, my love, the tear,
And take this heart, so faithful and so fond,
Still bound to thine; and fear not for that bond.'

He said; and went, with purpose he believed
Of generous nature—so is man deceived.

Lucy determined that her lover's eye
Should not distress nor supplication spy;
That in her manner he should nothing find,
To indicate the weakness of her mind.
He saw no eye that wept, no frame that shook,
No fond appeal was made by word or look;
Kindness there was, but join'd with some restraint;
And traces of the late event were faint.

He look'd for grief deploring, but perceives
No outward token that she longer grieves;
He had expected for his efforts praise,
For he resolved the drooping mind to raise;
She would, he judged, be humble, and afraid
That he might blame her rashness and upbraid;
And lo! he finds her in a quiet state,
Her spirit easy and her air sedate;
As if her loss was not a cause for pain,
As if assured that he would make it gain.—

Silent awhile, he told the morning news,
And what he judged they might expect to lose;
He thought himself, whatever some might boast,
The composition would be small at most;
Some shabby matter, she would see no more
The tithe of what she held in hand before.

How did her sister feel? and did she think
Bloomer was honest, and would never shrink?
'But why that smile? is loss like yours so light
That it can aught like merriment excite?
Well, he is rich, we know, and can afford
To please his fancy, and to keep his word;
To him 't is nothing; had he now a fear,
He must the meanest of his sex appear:
But the true honour, as I judge the case,
Is, both to feel the evil, and embrace.'

Here Barlow stopp'd, a little vex'd to see
No fear or hope, no dread or ecstasy:
Calmly she spoke—'Your prospects, sir, and mine
Are not the same,—their union I decline;
Could I believe the hand for which you strove
Had yet its value, did you truly love,
I had with thanks address'd you, and replied,
Wait till your feelings and my own subside,
Watch your affections, and, if still they live,
What pride denies, my gratitude shall give;
Ev'n then, in yielding, I had first believed
That I conferr'd the favour, not received.

You I release—nay, hear me—I impart
Joy to your soul,—I judge not of your heart.
Think'st thou a being, to whom God has lent
A feeling mind, will have her bosom rent
By man's reproaches? Sorrow will be thine,
For all thy pity prompts thee to resign!
Think'st thou that meekness' self would condescend
To take the husband when she scorns the friend?
Forgive the frankness, and rejoice for life,
Thou art not burden'd with so poor a wife.

Go! and be happy—tell, for the applause
Of hearts like thine, we parted, and the cause
Give, as it pleases.' With a foolish look
That a dull school-boy fixes on his book
That he resigns, with mingled shame and joy;
So Barlow went, confounded like the boy.

Jane, while she wept to think her sister's pain
Was thus increased, felt infinite disdain;
Bound as she was, and wedded by the ties
Of love and hope, that care and craft despise;
She could but wonder that a man, whose taste
And zeal for money had a Jew disgraced,
Should love her sister; yet with this surprise,
She felt a little exultation rise;
Hers was a lover who had always held
This man as base, by generous scorn impell'd;
And yet, as one, of whom for Lucy's sake
He would a civil distant notice take.

Lucy, with sadden'd heart and temper mild,
Bow'd to correction, like an humbled child,
Who feels the parent's kindness, and who knows
Such the correction he, who loves, bestows.

Attending always, but attending more
When sorrow ask'd his presence, than before,
Tender and ardent, with the kindest air
Came Bloomer, fortune's error to repair;
Words sweetly soothing spoke the happy youth,
With all the tender earnestness of truth.
There was no doubt of his intention now—
He will his purpose with his love avow:

So judged the maid; yet, waiting, she admired
His still delaying what he most desired;
Till, from her spirit's agitation free,
She might determine when the day should be.
With such facility the partial mind
Can the best motives for its favourites find.
Of this he spake not, but he stay'd beyond
His usual hour;—attentive still and fond;—
The hand yet firmer to the hand he prest,
And the eye rested where it loved to rest;
Then took he certain freedoms, yet so small
That it was prudish so the things to call;
Things they were not—'Describe'—that none can do,
They had been nothing had they not been new;
It was the manner and the look; a maid,
Afraid of such, is foolishly afraid;
For what could she explain? The piercing eye
Of jealous fear could nought amiss descry.

But some concern now rose; the youth would seek
Jane by herself, and then would nothing speak,
Before not spoken; there was still delay,
Vexatious, wearying, wasting, day by day.

'He does not surely trifle!' Heaven forbid!
She now should doubly scorn him if he did.

Ah! more than this, unlucky girl! is thine;
Thou must the fondest views of life resign;
And in the very time resign them too,
When they were brightening on the eager view.
I will be brief,—nor have I heart to dwell
On crimes they almost share who paint them well.

There was a moment's softness, and it seem'd
Discretion slept, or so the lover dream'd;
And watching long the now confiding maid,
He thought her guardless, and grew less afraid;
Led to the theme that he had shunn'd before,
He used a language he must use no more—
For if it answers, there is no more need,
And no more trial, should it not succeed.

Then made he that attempt, in which to fail
Is shameful,—still more shameful to prevail.

Then was there lightning in that eye that shed
Its beams upon him,—and his frenzy fled;
Abject and trembling at her feet he laid,
Despised and scorn'd by the indignant maid,
Whose spirits in their agitation rose,
Him, and her own weak pity, to oppose:
As liquid silver in the tube mounts high,
Then shakes and settles as the storm goes by.

While yet the lover stay'd, the maid was strong,
But when he fled, she droop'd and felt the wrong—
Felt the alarming chill, th' enfeebled breath,
Closed the quick eye, and sank in transient death.
So Lucy found her; and then first that breast
Knew anger's power, and own'd the stranger guest.

'And is this love? Ungenerous! Has he too
Been mean and abject? Is no being true?'
For Lucy judged that, like her prudent swain,
Bloomer had talk'd of what a man might gain;
She did not think a man on earth was found,
A wounded bosom, while it bleeds, to wound;

Thought not that mortal could be so unjust,
As to deprive affliction of its trust;
Thought not a lover could the hope enjoy,
That must the peace, he should promote, destroy;
Thought not, in fact, that in the world were those,
Who, to their tenderest friends, are worse than foes,
Who win the heart, deprive it of its care,
Then plant remorse and desolation there.

Ah! cruel he, who can that heart deprive
Of all that keeps its energy alive;
Can see consign'd to shame the trusting fair,
And turn confiding fondness to despair;
To watch that time—a name is not assign'd
For crime so odious, nor shall learning find.
Now, from that day has Lucy laid aside
Her proper cares, to be her sister's guide,
Guard, and protector. At their uncle's farm
They past the period of their first alarm,
But soon retired, nor was he grieved to learn
They made their own affairs their own concern.

I knew not then their worth; and, had I known,
Could not the kindness of a friend have shown;
For men they dreaded; they a dwelling sought,
And there the children of the village taught;
There, firm and patient, Lucy still depends
Upon her efforts, not upon her friends;
She is with persevering strength endued,
And can be cheerful—for she will be good.
Jane too will strive the daily tasks to share,
That so employment may contend with care;
Not power, but will, she shows, and looks about
On her small people, who come in and out;
And seems of what they need, or she can do, in doubt.

There sits the chubby crew on seats around,
While she, all rueful at the sight and sound,
Shrinks from the free approaches of the tribe,
Whom she attempts lamenting to describe,
With stains the idlers gather'd in their way,
The simple stains of mud, and mould, and clay,
And compound of the streets, of what we dare not say;
With hair uncomb'd, grimed face, and piteous look,
Each heavy student takes the odious book,
And on the lady casts a glance of fear,
Who draws the garment close as he comes near;
She then for Lucy's mild forbearance tries,
And from her pupils turns her brilliant eyes,
Making new efforts, and with some success,
To pay attention while the students guess;
Who to the gentler mistress fain would glide,
And dread their station at the lady's side.

Such is their fate:—there is a friendly few
Whom they receive, and there is chance for you;
Their school, and something gather'd from the wreck
Of that bad Bank, keeps poverty in check;
And true respect, and high regard, are theirs,
The children's profit, and the parent's prayers.

With Lucy rests the one peculiar care,
That few must see, and none with her may share;
More dear than hope can be, more sweet than pleasures are.

For her sad sister needs the care of love
That will direct her, that will not reprove,
But waits to warn: for Jane will walk alone,
Will sing in low and melancholy tone;
Will read or write, or to her plants will run
To shun her friends,—alas! her thoughts to shun.

It is not love alone disturbs her rest,
But loss of all that ever hope possess'd;
Friends ever kind, life's lively pleasures, ease,
When her enjoyments could no longer please;
These were her comforts then! she has no more of these.

Wrapt in such thoughts, she feels her mind astray,
But knows 't is true, that she has lost her way;
For Lucy's smile will check the sudden flight,
And one kind look let in the wonted light.

Fits of long silence she endures, then talks
Too much—with too much ardour, as she walks;
But still the shrubs that she admires dispense
Their balmy freshness to the hurried sense,
And she will watch their progress, and attend
Her flowering favourites as a guardian friend;
To sun or shade she will her sweets remove,
And here, she says, I may with safety love.

But there are hours when on that bosom steals
A rising terror,—then indeed she feels;—
Feels how she loved the promised good, and how
She feels the failure of the promise now.

That other spoiler did as robbers do,
Made poor our state, but not disgraceful too.
This spoiler shames me, and I look within
To find some cause that drew him on to sin;
He and the wretch who could thy worth forsake
Are the fork'd adder and the loathesome snake:
Thy snake could slip in villain-fear away,
But had no fang to fasten on his prey.

Oh! my dear Lucy, I had thought to live
With all the comforts easy fortunes give;
A wife caressing, and caress'd,—a friend,
Whom he would guide, advise, consult, defend,
And make his equal;—then I fondly thought
Among superior creatures to be brought:
And while with them, delighted to behold
No eye averted, and no bosom cold;—
Then at my home, a mother, to embrace
My————Oh! my sister, it was surely base!
I might forget the wrong, I cannot the disgrace.

Oh! when I saw that triumph in his eyes,
I felt my spirits with his own arise;
I call'd it joy, and said, the generous youth
Laughs at my loss—no trial for his truth;
It is a trifle he can not lament,
A sum not equal to his annual rent;
And yet that loss, the cause of every ill,
Has made me poor, and him—'

'O! poorer still;
Poorer, my Jane, and far below thee now:
The injurer he, the injured sufferer thou;
And shall such loss afflict thee?'—

'Lose I not
With him what fortune could in life allot?

Lose I not hope, life's cordial, and the views
Of an aspiring spirit?—O! I lose
Whate'er the happy feel, whate'er the sanguine
choose.

Would I could lose this bitter sense of wrong,
And sleep in peace—but it will not be long!
And here is something, Lucy, in my brain,
I know not what—it is a cure for pain;
But is not death!—no beckoning hand I see,
No voice I hear that comes alone to me:
It is not death, but change; I am not now
As I was once,—nor can I tell you how;
Nor is it madness,—ask, and you shall find
In my replies the soundness of my mind:
Oh! I should be a trouble all day long,
A very torment, if my head were wrong.'

At times there is upon her features seen,
What moves suspicion—she is too serene.
Such is the motion of a drunken man,
Who steps sedately, just to show he can.
Absent at times she will her mother call,
And cry at mid-day, 'then good night to all.'

But most she thinks there will some good ensue
From something done, or what she is to do;
Long wrapt in silence, she will then assume
An air of business, and shake off her gloom;
Then cry exulting, 'Oh! it must succeed,
There are ten thousand readers—all men read:
There are my writings,—you shall never spend
Your precious moments to so poor an end;
Our peasants' children may be taught by those
Who have no powers such wonders to compose;
So let me call them,—what the world allows,
Surely a poet without shame avows;
Come, let us count what numbers we believe
Will buy our work—Ah! sister, do you grieve?
You weep; there's something I have said amiss,
And vex'd my sister—What a world is this!
And how I wander!—Where has fancy run?
Is there no poem? Have I nothing done?
Forgive me, Lucy, I had fix'd my eye,
And so my mind, on works that cannot die:
Marmion and *Lara* yonder in the case,
And so I put me in the poet's place.

Still, be not frighten'd; it is but a dream:
I am not lost, bewilder'd though I seem.
I will obey thee—but suppress thy fear—
I am at ease,—then why that silly tear?'
Jane, as these melancholy fits invade
The busy fancy, seeks the deepest shade;
She walks in ceaseless hurry, till her mind
Will short repose in verse and music find:
Then her own songs to some soft tune she sings,
And laughs, and calls them melancholy things.
Not frenzy all: in some her erring Muse
Will sad, afflicting, tender strains infuse:
Sometimes on death she will her lines compose,
Or give her serious page of solemn prose;
And still those favourite plants her fancy please,
And give to care and anguish rest and ease.

'Let me not have this gloomy view,
About my room, around my bed;
But morning roses, wet with dew,
To cool my burning brows instead.
As flow'rs that once in Eden grew,
Let them their fragrant spirits shed,
And every day the sweets renew,
Till I, a fading flower, am dead.

Oh! let the herbs I loved to rear
Give to my sense their perfumed breath
Let them be placed about my bier,
And grace the gloomy house of death.
I'll have my grave beneath an hill,
Where only Lucy's self shall know;
Where runs the pure pellucid rill
Upon its gravelly bed below:
There violets on the borders blow,
And insects their soft light display,
Till, as the morning sun-beams glow,
The cold phosphoric fires decay.

That is the grave to Lucy shown,
The soil a pure and silver sand,
The green cold moss above it grown,
Unpluck'd of all but maiden hand:
In virgin earth, till then unturn'd,
There let my maiden form be laid,
Nor let my changed clay be spurn'd,
Nor for new guest that bed be made.

There will the lark,—the lamb, in sport,
In air,—on earth,—securely play,
And Lucy to my grave resort,
As innocent, but not so gay.
I will not have the churchyard ground,
With bones all black and ugly grown,
To press my shivering body round,
Or on my wasted limbs be thrown.

With ribs and skulls I will not sleep,
In clammy beds of cold blue clay,
Through which the ringed earth-worms creep,
And on the shrouded bosom prey;
I will not have the bell proclaim
When those sad marriage-rites begin,
And boys, without regard or shame,
Press the vile mouldering masses in.

Say not, it is beneath my care;
I cannot these cold truths allow;
These thoughts may not afflict me there,
But, oh! they vex and tease me now.
Raise not a turf, nor set a stone,
That man a maiden's grave may trace,
But thou, my Lucy, come alone,
And let affection find the place.

O! take me from a world I hate,
Men cruel, selfish, sensual, cold;
And, in some pure and blessed state,
Let me my sister minds behold:
From gross and sordid views refined,
Our heaven of spotless love to share,
For only generous souls design'd,
And not a man to meet us there.'

BOOK IX.

THE PRECEPTOR HUSBAND.

The Morning Ride—Conversation—Character of one whom they meet—His early Habits and Mode of Thinking—The Wife whom he would choose—The one chosen—His Attempts to teach—In History—In Botany—The Lady's Proficiency—His Complaint—Her Defence and Triumph—The Trial ends.

"Whom pass'd we musing near the woodman's shed,
Whose horse not only carried him but led,
That his grave rider might have slept the time,
Or solved a problem, or composed a rhyme?
A more abstracted man within my view
Has never come—He recollected you."

"Yes,—he was thoughtful—thinks the whole day long,
Deeply, and chiefly that he once thought wrong;
He thought a strong and kindred mind to trace
In the soft outlines of a trifler's face.

Poor Finch! I knew him when at school,—a boy
Who might be said his labours to enjoy;
So young a pedant that he always took
The girl to dance who most admired her book;
And would the butler and the cook surprise,
Who listen'd to his Latin exercise;
The matron's self the praise of Finch avow'd,
He was so serious, and he read so loud:
But yet, with all this folly and conceit,
The lines he wrote were elegant and neat;
And early promise in his mind appear'd
Of noble efforts when by reason clear'd.

And when he spoke of wives, the boy would say,
His should be skill'd in Greek and algebra;
For who would talk with one to whom his themes,
And favourite studies, were no more than dreams?
For this, though courteous, gentle, and humane,
The boys contemn'd and hated him as vain,
Stiff and pedantic—"

"Did the man enjoy,
In after life, the visions of the boy?"

"At least they form'd his wishes, they were yet
The favourite views on which his mind was set:
He quaintly said, how happy must they prove,
Who, loving, study—or who, studious, love;
Who feel their minds with sciences imbued,
And their warm hearts by beauty's force subdued.

His widow'd mother, who the world had seen,
And better judge of either sex had been,
Told him that just as their affairs were placed,
In some respects, he must forego his taste;
That every beauty, both of form and mind,
Must be by him, if unendow'd, resign'd;
That wealth was wanted for their joint affairs;
His sisters' portions, and the Hall's repairs.
The son assented—and the wife must bring
Wealth, learning, beauty, ere he gave the ring;
But as these merits, when they all unite,
Are not produced in every soil and site;
And when produced are not the certain gain
Of him who would these precious things obtain;
Our patient student waited many a year,
Nor saw this phœnix in his walks appear.
But as views mended in the joint estate,
He would a something in his points abate;
Give him but learning, beauty, temper, sense,
And he would then the happy state commence.
The mother sigh'd, but she at last agreed,
And now the son was likely to succeed;
Wealth is substantial good the fates allot,
We know we have it, or we have it not;
But all those graces, which men highly rate,
Their minds themselves imagine and create;
And therefore Finch was in a way to find
A good that much depended on his mind.

He look'd around, observing, till he saw
Augusta Dallas! when he felt an awe
Of so much beauty and commanding grace,
That well became the honours of her race:

This lady never boasted of the trash
That commerce brings: she never spoke of cash,
The gentle blood that ran in every vein
At all such notions blush'd in pure disdain.—

Wealth once relinquish'd, there was all beside,
As Finch believed, that could adorn a bride;
He could not gaze upon the form and air,
Without concluding all was right and fair;
Her mild but dignified reserve supprest
All free inquiry—but his mind could rest,
Assured that all was well, and in that view was blest.

And now he asked, 'am I the happy man
Who can deserve her? is there one who can?'
His mother told him, he possess'd the land
That puts a man in heart to ask a hand;
All who possess it feel they bear about
A spell that puts a speedy end to doubt:
But Finch was modest—'May it then be thought
That she can so be gained?'—'She may be sought:'
'Can love with land be won?' 'By land is beauty bought.
Do not, dear Charles, with indignation glow,
All value that the want of which they know;
Nor do I blame her; none that worth denies:
But can my son be sure of what he buys?
Beauty she has, but with it can you find
The inquiring spirit, or the studious mind?
This wilt thou need who art to thinking prone,
And minds unpair'd had better think alone;
Then how unhappy will the husband be,
Whose sole associate spoils his company?'
This he would try; but all such trials prove
Too mighty for a man disposed to love;
He whom the magic of a face enchains
But little knowledge of the mind obtains;
If by his tender heart the man is led,
He finds how erring is the soundest head.

The lady saw his purpose; she could meet
The man's inquiry, and his aim defeat;

She had a studied flattery in her look,
She could be seen retiring with a book;
She by attending to his speech could prove,
That she for learning had a fervent love;
Yet love alone she modestly declared,
She must be spared inquiry, and was spared;
Of her poor studies she was not so weak,
As in his presence, or at all, to speak;
But to discourse with him—who all agreed,
Has read so much, would be absurd indeed;
Ask what he might, she was so much a dunce
She would confess her ignorance at once.

All this the man believed not,—doom'd to grieve
For this belief, he this would not believe:
No! he was quite in raptures to discern
That love, and that avidity to learn.
'Could she have found,' she said, 'a friend, a guide,
Like him, to study had been all her pride;
But, doom'd so long to frivolous employ,
How could she those superior views enjoy?
The day might come—a happy day for her,
When she might choose the ways she would prefer.'

Then too he learn d, in accidental way,
How much she grieved to lose the given day
In dissipation wild, in visitation gay.
Happy, most happy, must the woman prove
Who proudly looks on him she vows to love;
Who can her humble acquisitions state,
That he will praise, at least will tolerate.

Still the cool mother sundry doubts express'd,—
'How! is Augusta graver than the rest?
There are three others: they are not inclined
To feed with precious food the empty mind:
Whence this strong relish?' 'It is very strong,'
Replied the son, 'aud has possess'd her long,
Increased indeed, I may presume, by views,—
We may suppose—ah! may she not refuse?'

'Fear not!—I see the question must be tried,
Nay, is determined—let us to your bride.'

They soon were wedded, and the nymph appear'd
By all her promised excellence endear'd:
Her words were kind, were cautious, and were few,
And she was proud—of what her husband knew.

Weeks pass'd away, some five or six, before,
Bless'd in the present, Finch could think of more:
A month was next upon a journey spent,
When to the Lakes the fond companions went;
Then the gay town received them, and, at last,
Home to their mansion, man and wife, they pass'd.

And now in quiet way they came to live
On what their fortune, love, and hopes would give.
The honeyed moon had nought but silver rays,
And shone benignly on their early days;
The second moon a light less vivid shed,
And now the silver rays were tinged with lead.
They now began to look beyond the Hall,
And think what friends would make a morning-call;
Their former appetites return'd, and now
Both could their wishes and their tastes avow;
'T was now no longer 'just what you approve,'
But 'let the wild fowl be to-day, my love.'
In fact the senses, drawn aside by force
Of a strong passion, sought their usual course.

Now to her music would the wife repair,
To which he listen'd once with eager air;
When there was so much harmony within,
That any note was sure its way to win;
But now the sweet melodious tones were sent
From the struck chords, and none cared where they went.
Full well we know that many a favourite air,
That charms a party, fails to charm a pair;
And as Augusta play'd she look'd around,
To see if one was dying at the sound:
But all were gone—a husband, wrapt in gloom,
Stalk'd careless, listless, up and down the room.

And now 't is time to fill that ductile mind
With knowledge, from his stores of various kind:
His mother, in a peevish mood, had ask'd,
'Does your Augusta profit? is she task'd?'

'Madam!' he cried, offended with her looks,
'There 's time for all things, and not all for books
Just on one's marriage to sit down, and prate
On points of learning, is a thing I hate—'

''T is right, my son, and it appears to me
If deep your hatred, you must well agree.'

Finch was too angry for a man so wise,
And said, 'Insinuation I despise!
Nor do I wish to have a mind so full
Of learned trash—it makes a woman dull:
Let it suffice, that I in her discern
An aptitude, and a desire to learn.—'

The matron smiled, but she observed a frown
On her son's brow, and calmly sat her down;
Leaving the truth to Time, who solves our doubt,
By bringing his all-glorious daughter out—
Truth! for whose beauty all their love profess,
And yet how many think it ugliness!

'Augusta, love,' said Finch, 'while you engage
In that embroidery, let me read a page;
Suppose it Hume's; indeed he takes a side,
But still an author need not be our guide;
And as he writes with elegance and ease,
Do now attend—he will be sure to please.
Here at the Revolution we commence,—
We date, you know, our liberties from hence.'

'Yes, sure,' Augusta answer'd with a smile,
'Our teacher always talk'd about his style;
When we about the Revolution read,
And how the martyrs to the flames were led;
The good old bishops, I forget their names.
But they were all committed to the flames;
Maidens and widows, bachelors and wives,
The very babes and sucklings lost their lives.
I read it all in Guthrie at the school,—
What now!—I know you took me for a fool;
There were five bishops taken from the stall,
And twenty widows, I remember all;

And by this token, that our teacher tried
To cry for pity, till she howl'd and cried.'

True, true, my love, but you mistake the thing,—
The Revolution that made William king
Is what I mean; the Reformation you,
In Edward and Elizabeth.'—''T is true:
But the nice reading is the love between
The brave lord Essex and the cruel queen;
And how he sent the ring to save his head,
Which the false lady kept till he was dead.

This is all true: now read, and I 'll attend:
But was not she a most deceitful friend?
It was a monstrous, vile, and treacherous thing,
To show no pity, and to keep the ring;
But the queen shook her in her dying bed,
And 'God forgive you!' was the word she said;
'Not I for certain:'——Come, I will attend,
So read the Revolutions to an end.'

Finch, with a timid, strange, inquiring look,
Softly and slowly laid aside the book
With sigh inaudible——'Come, never heed,'
Said he, recovering, 'now I cannot read.'

They walk'd at leisure through their wood and groves,
In fields and lanes, and talk'd of plants and loves,
And loves of plants.—Said Finch, 'Augusta, dear,
You said you loved to learn,—were you sincere?
Do you remember that you told me once
How much you grieved, and said you were a dunce?
That is, you wanted information. Say
What would you learn? I will direct your way.'

'Goodness!' said she, 'what meanings you discern
In a few words! I said I wish'd to learn,
And so I think I did; and you replied,
The wish was good: what would you now beside?
Did not you say it show'd an ardent mind;
And pray what more do you expect to find?'

'My dear Augusta, could you wish indeed
For any knowledge, and not then proceed?
That is not wishing——'

'Mercy! how you tease!
You knew I said it with a view to please;
A compliment to you, and quite enough,—
You would not kill me with that puzzling stuff!
Sure I might say I wish'd; but that is still
Far from a promise: it is not,—'I will.'

'But come, to show you that I will not hide
My proper talents, you shall be my guide;
And lady Boothby, when we meet, shall cry,
She 's quite as good a botanist as I.'

'Right, my Augusta;' and, in manner grave,
Finch his first lecture on the science gave;
An introduction,—and he said, 'My dear,
Your thought was happy,—let us persevere;
And let no trifling cause our work retard,—'
Agreed the lady, but she fear'd it hard.

Now o'er the grounds they rambled many a mile;
He show'd the flowers, the stamina, the style,
Calix and corol, pericarp and fruit,
And all the plant produces, branch and root;
Of these he treated, every varying shape,
Till poor Augusta panted to escape:
He show'd the various foliage plants produce,
Lunate and lyrate, runcinate, retuse;
Long were the learned words, and urged with force,
Panduriform, pinnatifid, premorse,
Latent, and patent, papulous, and plane,—
'Oh!' said the pupil, 'it will turn my brain.'
'Fear not,' he answer'd, and again, intent
To fill that mind, o'er class and order went;
And stopping, 'Now,' said he, 'my love, attend.'
'I do,' said she, 'but when will be an end?'
'When we have made some progress,—now begin,
Which is the stigma, show me with the pin:
Come, I have told you, dearest, let me see,
Times very many [illegible]-tell it now to me.'

'Stig[illegible]ow,—the things with yellow heads,
That shed [illegible] dust, and grow upon the threads;
You call them wives and husbands, but you know
That is a joke—here, look, and I will show
All I remember.'—Doleful was the look
Of the preceptor, when he shut his book,
(The system brought to aid them in their view,)
And now with sighs return'd—'It will not do.'

A handsome face first led him to suppose,
There must be talent with such looks as those;
The want of talent taught him now to find
The face less handsome with so poor a mind;
And half the beauty faded, when he found
His cherish'd hopes were falling to the ground.

Finch lost his spirit; but e'en then he sought
For fancied powers: she might in time be taught.
Sure there was nothing in that mind to fear;
The favourite study did not yet appear.—

Once he express'd a doubt if she could look
For five succeeding minutes on a book;
When, with awaken'd spirit, she replied,
He was mistaken, and she would be tried.'

With this delighted, he new hopes express'd,—
'How do I know?—She may abide the test?
Men I have known, and famous in their day,
Who were by chance directed in their way:
I have been hasty.—Well, Augusta, well,
What is your favourite reading? prithee tell;
Our different tastes may different books require,—
Yours I may not peruse, and yet admire:
Do then explain'—'Good Heaven!' said she, in haste,
How do I hate these lectures upon taste!'

'I lecture not, my love; but do declare,—
You read you say—what your attainments are.'
'Oh! you believe,' said she, 'that other things
Are read as well as histories of kings,
And loves of plants, with all that simple stuff
About their sex, of which I know enough.
Well, if I must, I will my studies name,
Blame if you please—I know you love to blame.
When all our childish books were set apart,
The first I read was 'Wanderings of the heart:'
It was a story, where was done a deed
So dreadful, that alone I fear'd to read.

The next was 'The Confessions of a Nun,—'
'T was quite a shame such evil should be done;
Nun of—no matter for the creature's name,
For there are girls no nunnery can tame:
Then was the story of the Haunted Hall,
Where the huge picture nodded from the wall
When the old lord look'd up with trembling dread,
And I grew pale, and shudder'd, as I read:
Then came the tales of Winters, Summers, Springs,
At Bath and Brighton,—they were pretty things!
No ghosts nor spectres there were heard or seen,
But all was love and flight to Gretna-green.
Perhaps your greater learning may despise
What others like, and there your wisdom lies,—
Well! do not frown,—I read the tender tales
Of lonely cots, retreats in silent vales
For maids forsaken, and suspected wives,
Against whose peace some foe his plot contrives;
With all the hidden schemes that none can clear
Till the last book, and then the ghosts appear.

I read all plays that on the boards succeed,
And all the works, that ladies ever read,—
Shakspeare, and all the rest,—I did, indeed,—
Ay! you may stare; but, sir, believe it true
That we can read and learn, as well as you.

I would not boast,—but I could act a scene
In any play, before I was fifteen.

Nor is this all; for many are the times
I read in Pope and Milton, prose and rhymes;
They were our lessons, and, at ten years old,
I could repeat——but now enough is told.
Sir, I can tell you I my mind applied
To all my studies, and was not denied
Praise for my progress——are you satisfied?'

'Entirely, madam! else were I possess'd
By a strong spirit who could never rest.
Yes! yes, no more I question,—here I close
The theme for ever—let us to repose.'"

BOOK X.

THE OLD BACHELOR.

A Friend arrives at the Hall—Old Bachelors and Maids—Relation of one—His Parents—The first Courtship—The second—The third—Long Interval—Travel—Decline of Life—the fourth Lady—Conclusion.

Save their kind friend the rector, Richard yet
Had not a favourite of his brother met;
Now at the Hall that welcome guest appear'd,
By trust, by trials, and by time endear'd;
Of him the grateful squire his love profess'd,
And full regard—he was of friends the best;
"Yet not to him alone this good I owe,
This social pleasure that our friends bestow;
The sex, that wrought in earlier life my woes,
With loss of time, who murder'd my repose,
They to my joys administer, nor vex
Me more; and now I venerate the sex;
And boast the friendship of a spinster kind,
Cheerful and pleasant, to her fate resign'd:
Then by her side my bachelor I place,
And hold them honours to the human race.
Yet these are they in tale and song display'd,
The peevish man, and the repining maid;
Creatures made up of misery and spite,
Who taste no pleasures, except those they blight,
From whom th' affrighten'd niece and nephew fly,—
Fear'd while they live, and useless till they die.

Not such these friends of mine; they never meant
That youth should so be lost, or life be spent.
They had warm passions, tender hopes, desires
That youth indulges, and that love inspires;
But fortune frown'd on their designs, displaced
The views of hope, and love's gay dreams disgraced;
Took from the soul her sunny views, and spread
A cloud of dark but varying gloom instead:
And shall we these with ridicule pursue,
Because they did not what they could not do?
If they their lot preferr'd, still why the jest
On those who took the way they judged the best?
But if they sought a change, and sought in vain,
'T is worse than brutal to deride their pain—
But you will see them; see the man I praise,
The kind protector in my troubled days,
Himself in trouble; you shall see him now,
And learn his worth! and my applause allow."

This friend appear'd, with talents form'd to please,
And with some looks of sprightliness and ease;
To him indeed the ills of life were known,
But misery had not made him all her own.

They spoke on various themes, and George design'd
To show his brother this, the favourite mind;
To lead the friend, by subjects he could choose
To paint himself, his life, and earlier views
What he was bless'd to hope what he was doom'd to lose.

They spoke of marriage, and he understood
Their call on him, and said, "It is not good
To be alone, although alone to be
Is freedom; so are men in deserts free.
Men who unyoked and unattended groan,
Condemn'd and grieved to walk their way alone:
Whatever ills a married pair betide,
Each feels a stay, a comfort, or a guide;
'Not always comfort,' will our wits reply.—
Wits are not judges, nor the cause shall try.

Have I not seen, when grief his visits paid,
That they were easier by communion made?
True, with the quiet times and days serene,
There have been flying clouds of care and spleen,
But is not man, the solitary, sick
Of his existence, sad and splenetic?
And who will help him, when such evils come,
To bear the pressure or to clear the gloom?

Do you not find, that joy within the breast
Of the unwedded man is soon suppress'd?

While, to the bosom of a wife convey'd,
Increase is by participation made?
The lighted lamp that gives another light,
Say, is it by th' imparted blaze less bright?
Are not both gainers when the heart's distress
Is so divided, that the pain is less?
And when the tear has stood in either eye,
Love's sun shines out, and they are quickly dry."

He ended here,—but would he not confess,
How came these feelings on his mind to press?
He would! nor fear'd his weakness to display
To men like them; their weakness too had they.

Bright shone the fire, wine sparkled, sordid care
Was banish'd far, at least appear'd not there;
A kind and social spirit each possess'd,
And thus began his tale the friendly guest.

"Near to my father's mansion,—but apart,
I must acknowledge, from my father's heart—
Dwelt a keen sportsman, in a pleasant seat;
Nor met the neighbours as should neighbours meet;
To them revenge appear'd a kind of right,
A lawful pleasure, an avow'd delight;
Their neighbours too blew up their passion's fire,
And urged the anger of each rival-squire;
More still their waspish tempers to inflame,
A party-spirit, friend of anger, came:
Oft would my father cry, 'that tory-knave,
That villain-placeman, would the land enslave.'
Not that his neighbour had indeed a place,
But would accept one—that was his disgrace;
Who, in his turn, was sure my father plann'd
To revolutionize his native land.
He dared the most destructive things advance,
And even pray'd for liberty to France;
Had still good hope that Heaven would grant his prayer,
That he might see a revolution there.
At this the tory-squire was much perplex'd,
'Freedom in France!—what will he utter next?
Sooner should I in Paris look to see
An English army sent their guard to be.'

My poor mamma, who had her mind subdued
By whig-control, and hated every feud,
Would have her neighbour met with mind serene;
But fiercer spirit fired the tory-queen:
My parents both had given her high disgust,
Which she resenting said, Revenge is just;
And till th' offending parties chose to stoop,
She judged it right to keep resentment up;
Could she in friendship with a woman live
Who could the insult of a man forgive?
Did not her husband in a crowded room
Once call her idiot, and the thing was dumb?
The man's attack was brutal to be sure,
But she no less an idiot to endure.

This lofty dame, with unrelenting soul,
Had a fair girl to govern and control;
The dear Maria!—whom, when first I met,—
Shame on this weakness! do I feel it yet?

The parent's anger, you will oft-times see,
Prepares the children's minds for amity;
Youth will not enter into such debate,
'T is not in them to cherish groundless hate:
Nor can they feel men's quarrels or their cares,
Of whig or tory, partridges or hares.

Long ere we loved, this gentle girl and I
Gave to our parents' discord many a sigh;
It was not ours,—and when the meeting came,
It pleased us much to find our thoughts the same;
But grief and trouble in our minds arose
From the fierce spirits we could not compose;
And much it vex'd us that the friends so dear
To us should foes among themselves appear.

Such was this maid, the angel of her race,
Whom I had loved in any time and place,
But in a time and place which chance assign'd;
When it was almost treason to be kind;
When we had vast impediments in view,
Then wonder not that love in terror grew
With double speed—we look'd, and strove to find
A kindred spirit in the hostile mind;
But is it hostile! there appears no sign
In those dear looks of warfare—none have mine.
At length I whisper'd—'Would that war might cease
Between our houses, and that all was peace!'
A sweet confusion on her features rose,
'She could not bear to think of having foes,
When we might all as friends and neighbours live,
And for that blessing, O! what would she give?'—
'Then let us try and our endeavours blend,'
I said, 'to bring these quarrels to an end;
Thus, with one purpose in our hearts, we strove,
And, if no more, increased our secret love;
Love that with such impediments in view
To meet the growing danger stronger grew;
And from that time each heart, resolved and sure,
Grew firm in hope, and patient to endure.

To those who know this season of delight
I need not strive their feelings to excite;
To those who know not the delight or pain,
The best description would be lent in vain:
And to the grieving, who will no more find
The bower of bliss, to paint it were unkind;
I pass it by, to tell that long we tried
To bring our fathers over to our side;
'T was bootless on their wives our skill to try,
For one would not, and one in vain comply.

First I began my father's heart to move,
By boldly saying, 'We are born to love;'
My father answer'd, with an air of ease,
'Well! very well! be loving if you please!
Except a man insults us or offends,
In my opinion we should all be friends.'

This gain'd me nothing; little would accrue
From clearing points so useless though so true;
But with some pains I brought him to confess,
That to forgive our wrongs is to redress:

'It might be so,' he answer'd, yet with doubt
That it might not,' but what is this about?'
I dared not speak directly, but I strove
To keep my subjects, harmony and love.

Coolly my father look'd, and much enjoy'd
The broken eloquence his eye destroy'd;
Yet less confused, and more resolved at last,
With bolder effort to my point I past;
And fondly speaking of my peerless maid,
I call'd her worth and beauty to my aid,
'Then make her mine!' I said, and for his favour pray'd

My father's look was one I seldom saw,
It gave no pleasure, nor created awe;
It was the kind of cool contemptuous smile
Of witty persons, overcharged with bile;
At first he spoke not, nor at last to me—

'Well now, and what if such a thing could be?
What if the boy should his addresses pay
To the tall girl, would that old tory say?
I have no hatred to the dog,—but, still,
It was some pleasure when I used him ill;
This I must lose if we should brethren be,
Yet may be not, for brethren disagree;
The fool is right,—there is no bar in life
Against their marriage,—let her be his wife.
Well, sir, you hear me!'—Never man complied,
And left a beggar so dissatisfied;
Though all was granted, yet was grace refused:
I felt as one indulged, and yet abused,
And yet, although provoked, I was not unamused.

In a reply like this appear'd to meet
All that encourage hope, and that defeat;
Consent, though cool, had been for me enough,
But this consent had something of reproof;
I had prepared my answer to his rage,
With his contempt I thought not to engage:
I, like a hero, would my castle storm,
And meet the giant in his proper form;
Then, conquering him, would set my princess free,
This would a trial and a triumph be:
When lo! a sneering menial brings the keys,
And cries in scorn, 'Come, enter, if you please;
You 'll find the lady sitting on her bed,
And 't is expected that you woo and wed.'

Yet not so easy was my conquest found;
I met with trouble ere with triumph crown'd.
Triumph, alas!—My father little thought,
A king at home, how other minds are wrought;
True, his meek neighbour was a gentle squire,
And had a soul averse from wrath and ire;
He answer'd frankly, when to him I went,
'I give you little, sir, in my consent:'
He and my mother were to us inclined,
The powerless party with the peaceful mind;
But that meek man was destined to obey
A sovereign lady's unremitted sway;
Who bore no partial, no divided rule,
All were obedient pupils in her school.
She had religious zeal, both strong and sour,
That gave an active sternness to her power;
But few could please her, she herself was one
By whom that deed was very seldom done;
With such a being, so disposed to feed
Contempt and scorn—how was I to succeed?
But love commanded, and I made my prayer
To the stern lady, with an humble air;
Said all that lovers hope, all measures tried
That love suggested, and bow'd down to pride.

Yes! I have now the tigress in my eye—
When I had ceased and waited her reply,
A pause ensued, and then she slowly rose,
With bitter smile predictive of my woes;
A look she saw was plainly understood——

'Admire my daughter! Sir, you 're very good,
The girl is decent, take her all in all,—
Genteel, we hope—perhaps a thought too tall;
A daughter's portion hers—you 'll think her fortune small,
Perhaps her uncles, in a cause so good,
Would do a little for their flesh and blood;
We are not ill allied,—and say we make
Her portion decent—whither would you take?
Is there some cottage on your father's ground,
Where may a dwelling for the girl be found?
Or a small farm, your mother understands
How to make useful such a pair of hands.

But this we drop at present, if you please,
We shall have leisure for such things as these;
They will be proper ere you fix the day
For the poor girl to honour and obey;
At present therefore we may put an end
To our discourse—Good morrow to you, friend!'

Then with a solemn curtsey and profound,
Her laughing eye she lifted from the ground,
And left me lost in thought, and gazing idly round.

Still we had hope, and, growing bold in time,
I would engage the father in our crime;
But he refused, for though he wish'd us well,
He said, 'he must not make his house a hell;—'
And sure the meaning look that I convey'd
Did not inform him that the hell was made.

Still hope existed that a mother's heart
Would in a daughter's feelings take a part;
Nor was it vain,—for there is found access
To a hard heart, in time of its distress:

The mother sicken'd, and the daughter sigh'd,
And we petition'd till our queen complied;
She thought of dying, and if power must cease
Better to make, than cause th' expected peace;
And sure this kindness, mixing with the blood,
Its balmy influence caused the body's good;
For as a charm, it work'd upon the frame
Of the reviving and relenting dame;
For when recover'd, she no more opposed
Her daughter's wishes.—Here contention closed.

Then bliss ensued, so exquisitely sweet,
That with it once, once only, we can meet;
For though we love again, and though once more
We feel th' enlivening hope we felt before,
Still the pure freshness of the joy that cast
Its sweet around us is for ever past.
O! time to memory precious,—ever dear,
Though ever painful this eventful year;
What bliss is now in view! and now what woes appear!
Sweet hours of expectation!—I was gone
To the vile town to press our business on;

To urge its formal instruments,—and lo!
Comes with dire looks a messenger of wo,
With tidings sad as death!—With all my speed
I reach'd her home!—but that pure soul was freed—
She was no more—for ever shut that eye,
That look'd all soul, as if it could not die;
It could not see me—O! the strange distress
Of these new feelings!—misery's excess;
What can describe it? words will not express.
When I look back upon that dreadful scene,
I feel renew'd the anguish that has been;
And reason trembles——Yes! you bid me cease,
Nor try to think; but I will think in peace.—
Unbid and unforbidden, to the room
I went, a gloomy wretch amid that gloom;
And there the lovely being on her bed
Shrouded and cold was laid—Maria dead!
There was I left,—and I have now no thought
Remains with me, how fear or fancy wrought;
I know I gazed upon the marble cheek,
And pray'd the dear departed girl to speak—
Further I know not, for, till years were fled,
All was extinguish'd—all with her was dead.
I had a general terror, dread of all
That could a thinking, feeling man befall;
I was desirous from myself to run,
And something, but I knew not what, to shun:
There was a blank from this I cannot fill,
It is a puzzle and a terror still.
Yet did I feel some intervals of bliss,
Ev'n with the horrors of a fate like this;
And dreams of wonderful construction paid
For waking horror—dear angelic maid!

When peace return'd, unfelt for many a year,
And hope, discarded flatterer, dar'd t' appear;
I heard of my estate, how free from debt,
And of the comforts life afforded yet;
Beside the best of comforts in a life
So sad as mine—a fond and faithful wife.
My gentle mother, now a widow, made
These strong attempts to guide me or persuade.

'Much time is lost,' she said, 'but yet my son
May, in the race of life, have much to run;
When I am gone, thy life to thee will seem
Lonely and sad, a melancholy dream;
Get thee a wife—I will not say to love,
But one, a friend in thy distress to prove;
One who will kindly help thee to sustain
Thy spirit's burden in its hours of pain;
Say, will you marry?—I in haste replied,
'And who would be the self-devoted bride?
There is a melancholy power that reigns
Tyrant within me—who would bear his chains,
And hear them clicking every wretched hour,
With will to aid me, but without the power?
But if such one were found with easy mind,
Who would not ask for raptures——I 'm resign'd.

'T is quite enough,' my gentle mother cried,
We leave the raptures, and will find the bride.'

There was a lady near us, quite discreet,
Whom in our visits 't was our chance to meet,
One grave and civil, who had no desire
That men should praise her beauties or admire;
She in our walks would sometimes take my arm,
But had no foolish fluttering or alarm;
She wish'd no heart to wound, no truth to prove,
And seem'd, like me, as one estranged from love;
My mother praised her, and with so much skill,
She gave a certain bias to my will;
But calm indeed our courtship; I profess'd
A due regard—My mother did the rest;
Who soon declared that we should love, and grow
As fond a couple as the world could show;
And talk'd of boys and girls with so much glee,
That I began to wish the thing could be.

Still when the day that soon would come was named,
I felt a cold fit, and was half ashamed;
But we too far proceeded to revoke,
And had been much too serious for a joke.
I shook away the fear that man annoys,
And thought a little of the girls and boys.

A week remain'd,—for seven succeeding days
Nor man nor woman might control my ways;
For seven dear nights I might to rest retire
At my own time, and none the cause require;
For seven blest days I might go in and out,
And none demand, 'Sir, what are you about?'
For one whole week I might at will discourse
On any subject, with a freeman's force.

Thus while I thought, I utter'd, as men sing
In under-voice, reciting 'With this ring,'
That when the hour should come, I might not dread
These, or the words that follow'd, 'I thee wed.

Such was my state of mind, exulting now
And then depress'd—I cannot tell you how—
When a poor lady, whom her friends could send
On any message, a convenient friend,
Who had all feelings of her own o'ercome,
And could pronounce to any man his doom;
Whose heart indeed was marble, but whose face
Assumed the look adapted to the case;
Enter'd my room, commission'd to assuage
What was foreseen, my sorrow and my rage.

It seem'd the lady whom I could prefer,
And could my much-loved freedom lose for her
Had bold attempts, but not successful, made,
The heart of some rich cousin to invade;
Who, half resisting, half complying, kept
A cautious distance, and the business slept.

This prudent swain his own importance knew
And swore to part the now affianced two:
Fill'd with insidious purpose, forth he went,
Profess'd his love, and woo'd her to consent:
'Ah! were it true!' she sigh'd; he boldly swore
His love sincere, and mine was sought no more.

All this the witch at dreadful length reveal'd,
And begg'd me calmly to my fate to yield:
Much pains she took engagements old to state,
And hoped to hear me curse my cruel fate,
Threat'ning my luckless life; and thought it strange
In me to bear the unexpected change:
In my calm feelings she beheld disguise,
And told of some strange wildness in my eyes.

But there was nothing in the eye amiss,
And the heart calmly bore a stroke like this;
Not so my mother; though of gentle kind,
She could no mercy for the creature find.

'Vile plot!' she said.—'But, madam, if they plot,
And you would have revenge, disturb them not.'

'What can we do, my son?'—'Consult our ease,
And do just nothing, madam, if you please.'

'What will be said?'—'We need not that discuss;
Our friends and neighbours will do that for us.'

'Do you so lightly, son, your loss sustain?—'
'Nay, my dear madam, but I count it gain.'

'The world will blame us sure, if we be still.'—
'And, if we stir, you may be sure it will.'

Not to such loss your father had agreed.'—
'No, for my father's had been loss indeed.'

With gracious smile my mother gave assent,
And let th' affair slip by with much content.

Some old dispute, the lover meant should rise,
Some point of strife they could not compromise,
Displeased the squire—he from the field withdrew,
Not quite conceal'd, not fully placed in view;
But half advancing, half retreating, kept
At his old distance, and the business slept.

Six years had past, and forty ere the six,
When Time began to play his usual tricks:
The locks, once comely in a virgin's sight,
Locks of pure brown display'd th' encroaching white;
The blood, once fervid, now to cool began,
And Time's strong pressure to subdue the man:
I rode or walk'd as I was wont before,
But now the bounding spirit was no more;
A moderate pace would now my body heat,
A walk of moderate length distress my feet.
I show'd my stranger-guest those hills sublime,
But said, 'the view is poor, we need not climb.'
At a friend's mansion I began to dread
The cold neat parlour, and the gay glazed bed;
At home I felt a more decided taste,
And must have all things in my order placed;
I ceased to hunt, my horses pleased me less,
My dinner more; I learn'd to play at chess;
I took my dog and gun, but saw the brute
Was disappointed that I did not shoot;
My morning walks I now could bear to lose,
And bless'd the shower that gave me not to choose:
In fact, I felt a languor stealing on;
The active arm, the agile hand were gone;
Small daily actions into habits grew,
And new dislike to forms and fashion new;
I loved my trees in order to dispose,
I number'd peaches, look'd how stocks arose,
Told the same story oft—in short, began to prose.

My books were changed; I now preferr'd the truth
To the light reading of unsettled youth;
Novels grew tedious, but by choice or chance,
I still had interest in the wild romance:
There is an age, we know, when tales of love
Form the sweet pabulum our hearts approve;
Then as we read we feel, and are indeed,
We judge th' heroic men of whom we read;
But in our after life these fancies fail,
We cannot be the heroes of the tale;
The parts that Cliffords, Mordaunts, Bevilles play
We cannot,—cannot be so smart and gay.

But all the mighty deeds and matchless powers
Of errant knights we never fancied ours,
And thus the prowess of each gifted knight
Must at all times create the same delight;
Lovelace a forward youth might hope to seem,
But Lancelot never,—that he could not dream;
Nothing reminds us in the magic page
Of old romance, of our declining age:
If once our fancy mighty dragons slew,
This is no more than fancy now can do;
But when the heroes of a novel come,
Conquer'd and conquering, to a drawing-room,
We no more feel the vanity that sees
Within ourselves what we admire in these,
And so we leave the modern tale, to fly
From realm to realm with Tristram or Sir Guy.

Not quite a Quixote, I could not suppose
That queens would call me to subdue their foes;
But, by a voluntary weakness sway'd,
When fancy call'd, I willingly obey'd.

Such I became, and I believed my heart
Might yet be pierced by some peculiar dart
Of right heroic kind, and I could prove
Fond of some peerless nymph that deign'd to love,
Some high-soul'd virgin, who had spent her time
In studies grave, heroic and sublime;
Who would not like me less that I had spent
Years eight and forty, just the age of Kent;
But not with Kent's discretion, for I grew
Fond of a creature whom my fancy drew;
A kind of beings who are never found
On middle-earth, but grow on fairy-ground.

These found I not; but I had luck to find
A mortal woman of this fairy kind;
A thin, tall, upright, serious, slender maid,
Who in my own romantic regions stray'd;
From the world's glare to this sweet vale retired,
To dwell unseen, unsullied, unadmired;
In all her virgin excellence, above
The gaze of crowds, and hopes of vulgar love.

We spoke of noble deeds in happier times,
Of glorious virtues, of debasing crimes:
Warm was the season, and the subject too,
And therefore warm in our discourse we grew.
Love made such haste, that ere a month was flown
Since first we met, he had us for his own:
Riches are trifles in a hero's sight,
And lead to questions low and unpolite;
I nothing said of money or of land,
But bent my knee, and fondly ask'd her hand,
And the dear lady, with a grace divine,
Gave it, and frankly answer'd, 'it is thine.'

Our reading was not to romance confined,
But still it gave its colour to the mind;

Gave to our studies something of its force,
And made profound and tender our discourse;
Our subjects all, and our religion, took
The grave and solemn spirit of our book:
And who had seen us walk, or heard us read,
Would say, 'these lovers are sublime indeed.'

I knew not why, but when the day was named
My ardent wishes felt a little tamed;
My mother's sickness then awaked my grief,
And yet, to own the truth, was some relief;
It left uncertain that decisive time
That made my feelings nervous and sublime.

Still all was kindness, and at morn and eve
I made a visit, talk'd, and took my leave:
Kind were the lady's looks, her eyes were bright,
And swam, I thought, in exquisite delight;
A lovely red suffused the virgin cheek,
And spoke more plainly than the tongue could speak;
Plainly all seem'd to promise love and joy,
Nor fear'd we aught that might our bliss destroy.

Engaged by business, I one morn delay'd
My usual call on the accomplish'd maid;
But soon, that small impediment removed,
I paid the visit that decisive proved;
For the fair lady had, with grieving heart,
So I believed, retired to sigh apart;
I saw her friend, and begg'd her to entreat
My gentle nymph her sighing swain to meet.

The gossip gone—What demon, in his spite
To love and man, could my frail mind excite,
And lead me curious on, against all sense of right?
There met my eye, unclosed, a closet's door—
Shame! how could I the secrets there explore?
Pride, honour, friendship, love, condemn'd the deed,
And yet, in spite of all, I could proceed!
I went, I saw—Shall I describe the hoard
Of precious worth in seal'd deposits stored
Of sparkling hues? Enough—enough is told,
'T is not for man such mysteries to unfold.

Thus far I dare—Whene'er those orbits swam
In that blue liquid that restrain'd their flame,
As showers the sunbeams—when the crimson glow
Of the red rose o'erspread those cheeks of snow,
I saw, but not the cause—'t was not the red
Of transient blush that o'er her face was spread;
'T was not the lighter red, that partly streaks
The Catherine pear, that brighten'd o'er her cheeks,
Nor scarlet blush of shame—but such disclose
The velvet petals of the Austrian rose
When first unfolded, warm the glowing hue,
Nor cold as rouge, but deepening on the view:
Such were those cheeks—the causes unexplored
Were now detected in that secret hoard;
And ever to that rich recess would turn
My mind, and cause for such effect discern.
Such was my fortune, O! my friends, and such
The end of lofty hopes that grasp'd too much.
This was, indeed, a trying time in life,
I lost at once a mother and a wife;
Yet compensation came in time for these.
And what I lost in joy, I gain'd in ease."—

"But," said the squire, "did thus your courtship cease?
Resign'd your mistress her betroth'd in peace?"—
"Yes; and had sense her feelings to restrain,
Nor ask'd me once my conduct to explain;
But me she saw those swimming eyes explore,
And explanation she required no more:
Friend to the last, I left her with regret—
Nay, leave her not, for we are neighbours yet.

These views extinct, I travell'd, not with taste,
But so that time ran wickedly to waste;
I penn'd some notes, and might a book have made,
But I had no connexion with the trade;
Bridges and churches, towers and halls, I saw,
Maids and madonnas, and could sketch and draw:
Yes, I had made a book, but that my pride
In the not making was more gratified.

There was one feeling upon foreign ground,
That more distressing than the rest was found;
That though with joy I should my country see,
There none had pleasure in expecting me.

I now was sixty, but could walk and eat;
My food was pleasant, and my slumbers sweet;
But what could urge me at a day so late
To think of women?—my unlucky fate.
It was not sudden; I had no alarms,
But was attack'd when resting on my arms;
Like the poor soldier; when the battle raged
The man escaped, though twice or thrice engaged,
But when it ended, in a quiet spot
He fell, the victim of a random-shot.

With my good friend the vicar oft I spent
The evening hours in quiet, as I meant;
He was a friend in whom, although untried
By aught severe, I found I could confide;
A pleasant, sturdy disputant was he,
Who had a daughter—such the Fates decree,
To prove how weak is man—poor yielding man, like me.

Time after time the maid went out and in,
Ere love was yet beginning to begin;
The first awakening proof the early doubt,
Rose from observing she went in and out.
My friend, though careless, seem'd my mind to explore,
'Why do you look so often at the door?'
I then was cautious, but it did no good,
For she, at least, my meanings understood;
But to the vicar nothing she convey'd
Of what she thought—she did not feel afraid.

I must confess, this creature in her mind
Nor face had beauty that a man would blind;
No poet of her matchless charms would write,
Yet sober praise they fairly would excite:
She was a creature form'd man's heart to make
Serenely happy, not to pierce and shake;
If she were tried for breaking human hearts,
Men would acquit her—she had not the arts;
Yet without art, at first without design,
She soon became the arbitress of mine;
Without pretensions—nay, without pretence,
But by a native strange intelligence

Women possess when they behold a man
Whom they can tease, and are assured they can;
Then 't is their soul's delight and pride to reign
O'er the fond slave, to give him ease or pain,
And stretch and loose by turns the weighty view-
less chain.

Though much she knew, yet nothing could she
prove;
I had not yet confess'd the crime of love;
But in an hour when guardian-angels sleep,
I fail'd the secret of my soul to keep;
And then I saw the triumph in those eyes
That spoke—'Ay, now you are indeed my prize.'
I almost thought I saw compassion, too,
For all the cruel things she meant to do.
Well I can call to mind the managed air
That gave no comfort, that brought no despair,
That in a dubious balance held the mind,
To each side turning, never much inclined.

She spoke with kindness—thought the honour high,
And knew not how to give a fit reply;
She could not, would not, dared not, must not deem
Such language proof of aught but my esteem;
It made her proud—she never could forget
My partial thoughts,—she felt her much in debt:
She who had never in her life indulged
The thought of hearing what I now divulged,
I who had seen so many and so much,—
It was an honour—she would deem it such:
Our different years, indeed, would put an end
To other views, but still her father's friend
To her, she humbly hoped, would his regard extend.

Thus saying nothing, all she meant to say,
She play'd the part the sex delights to play;
Now by some act of kindness giving scope
To the new workings of excited hope,
Then by an air of something like disdain,
But scarcely seen, repelling it again;
Then for a season, neither cold nor kind,
She kept a sort of balance in the mind,
And, as his pole a dancer on the rope,
The equal poise on both sides kept me up.

Is it not strange that man can fairly view
Pursuit like this, and yet his point pursue?
While he the folly fairly will confess,
And even feel the danger of success?
But so it is, and nought the Circes care
How ill their victims with their poison fare,
When thus they trifle, and with quiet soul
Mix their ingredients in the maddening bowl,
Their high regard, the softness of their air,
The pitying grief that saddens at a prayer,
Their grave petitions for the peace of mind
That they determine you shall never find,
And all their vain amazement that a man
Like you should love—they wonder how you can.

For months the idler play'd her wicked part,
Then fairly gave the secret of her heart.
'She hoped'—I now the smiling gipsy view—
'Her father's friend would be her lover's too,
Young Henry Gale'—But why delay so long?
She could not tell—she fear'd it might be wrong,

'But I was good'—I knew not, I was weak,
And spoke as love directed me to speak.

When in my arms their boy and girl I take,
I feel a fondness for the mother's sake;
But though the dears some softening thoughts ex-
cite,
I have no wishes for the father's right.

Now all is quiet, and the mind sustains
Its proper comforts, its befitting pains;
The heart reposes; it has had its share
Of love, as much as it could fairly bear,
And what is left in life, that now demands its care?

For O! my friends, if this were all indeed,
Could we believe that nothing would succeed;
If all were but this daily dose of life,
Without a care or comfort, child or wife;
These walks for health with nothing more in view,
This doing nothing, and with labour too;
This frequent asking when 't is time to dine,
This daily dozing o'er the news and wine;
This age's riddle, when each day appears
So very long, so very short the years;
If this were all—but let me not suppose—
What then were life! whose virtues, trials, woes,
Would sleep th' eternal sleep, and there the scene
would close.

This cannot be—but why has Time a pace
That seems unequal in our mortal race?
Quick is that pace in early life, but slow,
Tedious, and heavy, as we older grow;
But yet, though slow, the movements are alike,
And with no force upon the memory strike,
And therefore tedious as we find them all,
They leave us nothing we in view recall;
But days that we so dull and heavy knew
Are now as moments passing in review,
And hence arises ancient men's report,
That days are tedious, and yet years are short."

BOOK XI.

THE MAID'S STORY.

A Mother's Advice—Trials for a young Lady—Ancient Lovers—The Mother a Wife—Grandmamma—Genteel Economy—Frederick, a young Collegian—Grandmamma dies—Retreat with Biddy—Comforts of the Poor—Return Home—Death of the Husband—Nervous Disorders—Conversion—Frederick a Teacher—Retreat to Sidmouth—Self-examination—The Mother dies—Frederick a Soldier—Retirement with a Friend—Their Happiness how interrupted—Frederick an Actor—Is dismissed and supported—A last Adventure.

Three days remain'd their friend, and then again
The Brothers left, themselves to entertain;
When spake the younger—"It would please me
well
To hear thy spinster-friend her story tell,

And our attention would be nobly paid
Thus to compare the Bachelor and Maid."

"Frank as she is," replied the squire, "nor one
Is more disposed to show what she has done
With time, or time with her; yet all her care
And every trial she might not declare
To one a stranger; but to me, her friend,
She has the story of these trials penn'd;
These shalt thou hear, for well the maid I know,
And will her efforts and her conquests show.
Jacques is abroad, and we alone shall dine,
And then to give this lady's tale be mine;
Thou wilt attend to this good spinster's life,
And grieve and wonder she is not a wife;
But if we judge by either words or looks,
Her mode of life, her morals, or her books,
Her pure devotion, unaffected sense,
Her placid aid, her mild benevolence,
Her gay good humour, and her manners free,
She is as happy as a maid can be;
If as a wife, I know not, and decline
Question like this, till I can judge of thine."

Then from a secret hoard drew forth the squire
His tale, and said, "Attention I require—
My verse you may condemn, my theme you must admire."

I to your kindness speak, let that prevail,
And of my frailty judge as beings frail.——

My father dying, to my mother left
An infant charge, of all things else bereft;
Poor, but experienced in the world, she knew
What others did, and judged what she could do;
Beauty she justly weigh'd, was never blind
To her own interest, and she read mankind:
She view'd my person with approving glance,
And judged the way my fortune to advance;
Taught me betimes that person to improve,
And made a lawful merchandize of love;
Bade me my temper in subjection keep,
And not permit my vigilance to sleep;
I was not one, a miss, who might presume
Now to be crazed by mirth, now sunk in gloom;
Nor to be fretful, vapourish, or give way
To spleen and anger, as the wealthy may;
But I must please, and all I felt of pride,
Contempt, and hatred, I must cast aside.

"Have not one friend," my mother cried, "not one;
That bane of our romantic triflers shun;
Suppose her true, can she afford you aid?
Suppose her false, your purpose is betray'd;
And then in dubious points, and matters nice,
How can you profit by a child's advice?
While you are writing on from post to post,
Your hour is over, and a man is lost;
Girls of their hearts are scribbling; their desires,
And what the folly of the heart requires,
Dupes to their dreams—but I the truth impart,
You cannot, child, afford to have a heart;
Think nothing of it; to yourself be true,
And keep life's first great business in your view;—
Take it, dear Martha, for a useful rule,
She who is poor is ugly or a fool;
Or, worse than either, has a bosom fill'd
With soft emotions, and with raptures thrill'd.

Read not too much, nor write in verse or prose,
For then you make the dull and foolish foes;
Yet those who do, deride not nor condemn,
It is not safe to raise up foes in them;
For though they harm you not, as blockheads do,
There is some malice in the scribbling crew."

Such her advice; full hard with her had dealt
The world, and she the usage keenly felt.

"Keep your good name," she said, "and that to keep
You must not suffer vigilance to sleep:
Some have, perhaps, the name of chaste retain'd,
When nought of chastity itself remain'd;
But there is danger—few have means to blind
The keen-eyed world, and none to make it kind.

And one thing more—to free yourself from foes
Never a secret to your friend disclose;
Secrets with girls, like loaded guns with boys,
Are never valued till they make a noise;
To show how trusted, they their power display;
To show how worthy, they the trust betray;
Like pence in children's pockets secrets lie
In female bosoms—they must burn or fly.

Let not your heart be soften'd; if it be,
Let not the man his softening influence see;
For the most fond will sometimes tyrants prove,
And wound the bosom where they trace the love.
But to your fortune look, on that depend
For your life's comfort, comforts that attend
On wealth alone—wealth gone, they have their end."

Such were my mother's cares to mend my lot,
And such her pupil they succeeded not.

It was conceived the person I had then
Might lead to serious thought some wealthy men,
Who having none their purpose to oppose
Would soon be won their wishes to disclose:
My mother thought I was the very child
By whom the old and amorous are beguiled;
So mildly gay, so ignorantly fair,
And pure, no doubt, as sleeping infants are:
Then I had lessons how to look and move,
And, I repeat, make merchandize of love.

Thrice it was tried if one so young could bring
Old wary men to buy the binding ring;
And on the taper finger, to whose tip
The fond old swain would press his withering lip,
Place the strong charm:—and one would win my heart
By re-assuming youth—a trying part;
Girls, he supposed, all knew the young were bold,
And he would show that spirit in the old;
In boys they loved to hear the rattling tongue,
And he would talk as idly as the young;
He knew the vices our Lotharios boast,
And he would show of every vice the ghost,
The evil's self, without disguise or dress,
Vice in its own pure native ugliness;

Not as the drunkenness of slaves to prove
Vice hateful, but that seeing, I might love.
He drove me out, and I was pleased to see
Care of himself, it served as care for me;
For he would tell me, that he should not spare
Man, horse, or carriage, if I were not there:
Provoked at last, my malice I obey'd,
And smiling said, "Sir, I am not afraid."

This check'd his spirit; but he said, "Could you
Have charge so rich, you would be careful too."

And he, indeed, so very slowly drove,
That we dismiss'd the over-cautious love.

My next admirer was of equal age,
And wish'd the child's affection to engage,
And keep the fluttering bird a victim in his cage:
He had no portion of his rival's glee,
But gravely praised the gravity in me;
Religious, moral, both in word and deed,
But warmly disputatious in his creed:
Wild in his younger time, as we were told,
And therefore like a penitent when old.
Strange! he should wish a lively girl to look
Upon the methods his repentance took.

Then he would say, he was no more a rake
To squander money for his passions' sake;
Yet, upon proper terms, as man discreet,
He with my mother was disposed to treat,
To whom he told, "the price of beauty fell
In every market, and but few could sell;
That trade in India, once alive and brisk,
Was overdone, and scarcely worth the risk."
Then stopp'd to speak of board, and what for life
A wife would cost——if he should take a wife.

Hardly he bargain'd, and so much desired,
That we demurr'd; and he, displeased, retired.

And now I hoped to rest, nor act again
The paltry part for which I felt disdain,
When a third lover came within our view,
And somewhat differing from the former two;
He had been much abroad, and he had seen
The world's weak side, and read the hearts of men;
But all, it seem'd, this study could produce,
Was food for spleen, derision, and abuse;
He levell'd all, as one who had intent
To clear the vile and spot the innocent;
He praised my sense, and said I ought to be
From girl's restraint and nursery maxims free;
He praised my mother; but he judged her wrong
To keep us from th' admiring world so long;
He praised himself; and then his vices named,
And call'd them follies, and was not ashamed.
He more than hinted that the lessons taught
By priests were all with superstition fraught;
And I must think them for the crowd design'd,
Not to alarm the free and liberal mind.

Wisdom with him was virtue. They were wrong
And weak, he said, who went not with the throng;
Man must his passions order and restrain
In all that gives his fellow-subjects pain;
But yet of guilt he would in pity speak,
And as he judged, the wicked were the weak.

Such was the lover of a simple maid,
Who seem'd to call his logic to his aid,
And to mean something: I will not pretend
To judge the purpose of my reasoning friend,
Who was dismiss'd, in quiet to complain
That so much labo r was bestow'd in vain.

And now my mother seem'd disposed to try
A life of reason and tranquillity;
Ere this, her health and spirits were the best,
Hers the day's trifling, and the nightly rest;
But something new was in her mind instill'd;
Unquiet thoughts the matron bosom fill'd;
For five-and-forty peaceful years she bore
Her placid looks, and dress becoming wore:
She could a compliment with pleasure take,
But no absurd impression could it make.
Now were her nerves disorder'd; she was weak,
And must the help of a physician seek;
A Scotch physician, who had just began
To settle near us, quite a graceful man,
And very clever, with a soft address,
That would his meaning tenderly express.

Sick as my mother seem'd, when he inquired
If she was ill, he found her well attired;
She purchased wares so showy and so fine,
The venders all believed th' indulgence mine:
But I, who thrice was woo'd, had lovers three,
Must now again a very infant be;
While the good lady, twenty years a wife,
Was to decide the colour of his life:
And she decided. She was wont t' appear
To these unequal marriages severe;
Her thoughts of such with energy she told,
And was repulsive, dignified, and cold;
But now, like monarchs weary of a throne,
She would no longer reign—at least alone.

She gave her pulse, and, with a manner sweet,
Wish'd him to feel how kindly they could beat;
And 't is a thing quite wonderful to tell,
How soon he understood them, and how well.

Now, when she married, I from home was sent,
With grandmamma to keep perpetual Lent;
For she would take me on conditions cheap,
For what we scarcely could a parrot keep:
A trifle added to the daily fare
Would feed a maiden who must learn to spare.

With grandmamma I lived in perfect ease;
Consent to starve, and I was sure to please.
Full well I knew the painful shifts we made
Expenses all to lessen or evade,
And tradesmen's flinty hearts to soften and persuade.

Poor grandmamma among the gentry dwelt
Of a small town, and all the honour felt;
Shrinking from all approaches to disgrace
That might be mark'd in so genteel a place;
Where every daily deed, as soon as done,
Ran through the town as fast as it could run:—
At dinners what appear'd—at cards who lost or won.

Our good appearance through the town was known;
Hunger and thirst were matters of our own;

And you would judge that she in scandal dealt
Who told on what we fed, or how we felt.

We had a little maid, some four feet high,
Who was employ'd our household stores to buy;
For she would weary every man in trade
And tease t' assent whom she could not persuade.

Methinks I see her, with her pigmy light,
Precede her mistress in a moonless night;
From the small lantern throwing through the street
The dimm'd effulgence at her lady's feet;
What time she went to prove her well-known skill
With rival friends at their beloved quadrille.

"And how 's your pain?" inquired the gentle maid,
For that was asking if with luck she play'd;
And this she answer'd as the cards decreed,
"O Biddy! ask not—very bad indeed;"
Or, in more cheerful tone, from spirit light,
"Why, thank you, Biddy, pretty well to-night."

The good old lady often thought me vain,
And of my dress would tenderly complain;
But liked my taste in food of every kind,
As from all grossness, like her own, refined:
Yet when she hinted that on herbs and bread
Girls of my age and spirit should be fed,
Whate'er my age had borne, my flesh and blood,
Spirit and strength, the interdict withstood;
But though I might the frugal soul offend
Of the good matron, now my only friend,
And though her purse suggested rules so strict,
Her love could not the punishment inflict:
She sometimes watch'd the morsel with a frown,
And sigh'd to see, but let it still go down.

Our butcher's bill, to me a monstrous sum,
Was such, that summon'd, he forbore to come:
Proud man was he, and when the bill was paid,
He put the money in his bag and play'd,
Jerking it up, and catching it again,
And poising in his hand in pure disdain;
While the good lady, awed by man so proud,
And yet disposed to have her claims allow'd,
Balanced between humility and pride,
Stood a fall'n empress at the butcher's side,
Praising his meat as delicate and nice——
"Yes, madam, yes! if people pay the price."

So lived the lady, and so murmur'd I,
In all the grief of pride and poverty:
Twice in the year there came a note to tell
How well mamma, who hoped the child was well;
It was not then a pleasure to be styled,
By a mamma of such experience, Child!
But I suppress'd the feelings of my pride,
Or other feelings set them all aside.

There was a youth from college, just the one
I judged mamma would value as a son;
He was to me good, handsome, learn'd, genteel,
I cannot now what then I thought reveal;
But, in a word, he was the very youth
Who told me what I judged the very truth,
That love like his and charms like mine agreed,
For all description they must both exceed:
Yet scarcely can I throw a smile on things
So painful, but that Time his comfort brings,
Or rather throws oblivion on the mind,
For we are more forgetful than resign'd.

We both were young, had heard of love and read,
And could see nothing in the thing to dread,
But like a simple pair our time employ'd
In pleasant views to be in time enjoy'd;
When Frederick came, the kind old lady smiled
To see the youth so taken with her child;
A nice young man, who came with unsoil'd feet
In her best room, and neither drank nor eat:
Alas! he planted in a vacant breast
The hopes and fears that robb'd it of its rest.

All now appear'd so right, so fair, so just,
We surely might the lovely prospect trust;
Alas! poor Frederick and his charmer found
That they were standing on fallacious ground:
All that the father of the youth could do
Was done—and now he must himself pursue
Success in life; and, honest truth to state,
He was not fitted for a candidate:
I, too, had nothing in this world below,
Save what a Scotch physician could bestow,
Who for a pittance took my mother's hand,
And if disposed, what had they to command?

But these were after fears, nor came t' annoy
The tender children in their dreams of joy;
Who talk'd of glebe and garden, tithe and rent,
And how a fancied income should be spent;
What friends, what social parties we should see,
And live with what genteel economy;
In fact, we gave our hearts as children give,
And thought of living as our neighbours live.

Now when assured ourselves that all was well,
'T was right our friends of these designs to tell;
For this we parted.—Grandmamma, amazed,
Upon her child with fond compassion gazed;
Then pious tears appear'd, but not a word
In aid of weeping till she cried, "Good Lord!"
She then, with hurried motion, sought the stairs,
And calling Biddy, bade her come to prayers.

Yet the good lady early in her life
Was call'd to vow the duties of a wife;
She sought the altar by her friends' advice,
No free-will offering, but a sacrifice:
But here a forward girl and eager boy
Dared talk of life, and turn their heads with joy.

To my mamma I wrote in just the way
I felt, and said what dreaming lasses say;
How handsome Frederick was, by all confess'd,
How well he look'd, how very well he dress'd;
With learning much, that would for both provide,
His mother's darling, and his father's pride;
And then he loves me more than mind can guess,
Than heart conceive, or eloquence express

No letter came a doubtful mind to ease,
And, what was worse, no Frederick came to please,
To college gone—so thought our little maid—
But not to see me! I was much afraid;
I walk'd the garden round, and deeply sigh'd,
When grandmamma grew faint! and dropt, and died:

A fate so awful and so sudden drove
All else away, and half extinguish'd love.

Strange people came; they search'd the house around,
And, vulgar wretches! sold whate'er they found:
The secret hoards that in the drawers were kept,
The silver toys that with the tokens slept,
The precious beads, the corals with their bells,
That laid secure, lock'd up in secret cells,
The costly silk, the tabby, the brocade,
The very garment for the wedding made,
Were brought to sale, with many a jest thereon;
"Going—a bridal dress—for—Going!—Gone."
That ring, dear pledge of early love and true,
That to the wedded finger almost grew,
Was sold for six and ten-pence to a Jew!

Great was the fancied worth; but ah! how small
The sum thus made, and yet how valued all!
But all that to the shameful service went
Just paid the bills, the burial, and the rent;
And I and Biddy, poor deserted maids!
Were turn'd adrift to seek for other aids.

Now left by all the world, as I believed,
I wonder'd much that I so little grieved;
Yet I was frighten'd at the painful view
Of shiftless want, and saw not what to do:
In times like this the poor have little dread,
They can but work, and they shall then be fed;
And Biddy cheer'd me with such thoughts as this,
"You'll find the poor have their enjoyments, Miss!"
Indeed I saw, for Biddy took me home
To a forsaken hovel's cold and gloom;
And while my tears in plenteous flow were shed,
With her own hands she placed her proper bed,
Reserved for need—A fire was quickly made,
And food, the purchase for the day, display'd:
She let in air to make the damps retire,
Then placed her sad companion at her fire;
She then began her wonted peace to feel,
She bought her wool, and sought her favourite wheel,
That as she turn'd, she sang with sober glee,
"Begone, dull Care! I'll have no more with thee;"
Then turn'd to me, and bade me weep no more,
But try and taste the pleasures of the poor.

When dinner came, on table brown and bare
Were placed the humblest forms of earthen ware,
With one blue dish, on which our food was placed,
For appetite provided, not for taste:
I look'd disgusted, having lately seen
All so minutely delicate and clean;
Yet, as I sate, I found to my surprise
A vulgar kind of inclination rise,
And near my humble friend, and nearer drew,
Tried the strange food, and was partaker too.

I walk'd at eve, but not where I was seen,
And thought, with sorrow, what can Frederick mean?
I must not write, I said, for I am poor;
And then I wept till I could weep no more.

Kind-hearted Biddy tried my griefs to heal,
"This is a nothing to what others feel;
Life has a thousand sorrows worse than this,
A lover lost is not a fortune, Miss!
One goes, another comes, and which is best
There is no telling—set your heart at rest."

At night we pray'd—I dare not say a word
Of our devotion, it was so absurd;
And very pious upon Biddy's part,
But mine were all effusions of the heart;
While she her angels call'd their peace to shed,
And bless the corners of our little bed.
All was a dream! I said, is this indeed
To be my life? and thus to lodge and feed,
To pay for what I have, and work for what I need?
Must I be poor? and Frederick, if we meet,
Would not so much as know me in the street?
Or, as he walk'd with ladies, he would try
To be engaged as we were passing by—
And then I wept to think that I should grow
Like them whom he would be ashamed to know

On the third day, while striving with my fate,
And hearing Biddy all its comforts state,
Talking of all her neighbours, all her schemes,
Her stories, merry jests, and warning dreams;
With tales of mirth and murder! O! the nights
Past, said the maiden, in such dear delights,
And I was thinking, can the time arrive
When I shall thus be humbled, and survive?
Then I beheld a horse and handsome gig,
With the good air, tall form, and comely wig
Of Doctor Mackey—I in fear began
To say, Good heaven preserve me from the man!
But fears ill reason,—heaven to such a mind
Had lent a heart compassionate and kind.

From him I learnt that one had call'd to know
What with my hand my parents could bestow;
And when he learn'd the truth, in high disdain
He told my fate, and home return'd again.

"Nay, be not grieved, my lovely girl; but few
Wed the first love, however kind and true;
Something there comes to break the strongest vow,
Or mine had been my gentle Mattie now.
When the good lady died—but let me leave
All gloomy subjects—'t is not good to grieve."

Thus the kind Scotchman soothed me: he sustain'd
A father's part, and my submission gain'd:
Then my affection; and he often told
My sterner parent that her heart was cold;
He grew in honour—he obtain'd a name—
And now a favourite with the place became;
To me most gentle, he would condescend
To read and reason, be the guide and friend;
He taught me knowledge of the wholesome kind,
And fill'd with many a useful truth my mind:
Life's common burden daily lighter grew,
And even Frederick lessen'd in my view:
Cold and repulsive as he once appear'd,
He was by every generous act endear'd;
And, above all, that he with ardour fill'd
My soul for truth—a love by him instill'd;
Till my mamma grew jealous of a maid
To whom an husband such attention paid:
Not grossly jealous; but it gave her pain,
And she observed, "He made her daughter vain

And what his help to one who must not look
To gain her bread by poring on a book?"

This was distress; but this, and all beside,
Was lost in grief—my kinder parent died,
When praised and loved, when joy and health he gave,
He sank lamented to an early grave:
Then love and wo—the parent and the child,
Lost in one grief, allied and reconciled.

Yet soon a will, that left me half his worth,
To the same spirit gave a second birth:
But 't was a mother's spleen; and she indeed
Was sick, and sad, and had of comfort need;
I watch'd the way her anxious spirit took,
And often found her musing o'er a book;
She changed her dress, her church, her priest, her prayer,
Join'd a new sect, and sought her comforts there;
Some strange coarse people came, and were so free
In their addresses, they offended me;
But my mamma threw all her pride away—
More humble she as more assuming they.

"And what," they said, as having power, "are now
The inward conflicts? do you strive? and how?"
Themselves confessing thoughts so new and wild,
I thought them like the visions of a child.
"Could we," they ask, "our best good deeds condemn?
And did we long to touch the garment's hem?
And was it so with us? for so it was with them."

A younger few assumed a softer part,
And tried to shake the fortress of my heart;
To this my pliant mother lent her aid,
And wish'd the winning of her erring maid:
I was constrain'd her female friends to hear;
But suffer'd not a bearded convert near:
Though more than one attempted, with their whine,
And "Sister! sister! how that heart of thine?"
But this was freedom I for ever check'd:
Mine was a heart no brother could affect.

But "would I hear the preacher, and receive
The dropping dew of his discourse at eve?
The soft, sweet words?" I gave two precious hours
To hear of gifts and graces; helps and powers;
When a pale youth, who should dismiss the flock,
Gave to my bosom an electric shock.
While in that act he look'd upon my face
As one in that all-equalizing place:
Nor, though he sought me, would he lay aside
Their cold, dead freedom, or their dull, sad pride.

Of his conversion he with triumph spoke,
Before he orders from a bishop took:
Then how his father's anger he had braved,
And, safe himself, his erring neighbours saved.
Me he rejoiced a sister to behold
Among the members of his favourite fold;
He had not sought me, the availing call
Demanded all his love, and had it all;
But, now thus met, it must be heaven's design.
Indeed! I thought, it never shall be mine;
Yes, we must wed. He was not rich: and I
Had of the earthly good a mean supply;
But it sufficed. Of his conversion then
He told, and labours in converting men;
For he was chosen all their bands among—
Another Daniel! honour'd, though so young.

He call'd me sister: show'd me that he knew
What I possess'd; and told what it would do.
My looks, I judge, express'd my full disdain,
But it was given to the man in vain:
They preach till they are proud, and pride disturbs the brain.

Is this the youth once timid, mild, polite?
How odious now, and sick'ning to the sight!
Proud that he sees, and yet so truly blind,
With all this blight and mildew on the mind!

Amazed, the solemn creature heard me vow
That I was not disposed to take him now.

"Then, art thou changed, fair maiden? changed thy heart?"
I answered, "No; but I perceive thou art."

Still was my mother sad, her nerves relax'd,
And our small income for advice was tax'd.
When I, who long'd for change and freedom, cried,
Let sea and Sidmouth's balmy air be tried;
And so they were, and every neighbouring scene,
That make the bosom, like the clime, serene,
Yet were her teachers loth to yield assent;
And not without the warning voice we went;
And there was secret counsel all unknown
To me—but I had counsel of my own.

And now there pass'd a portion of my time
In ease delicious, and in joy sublime—
With friends endear'd by kindness—with delight,—
In all that could the feeling mind excite,
Or please, excited, walks in every place
Where we could pleasure find and beauty trace,
Or views at night, where on the rocky steep
Shines the full moon, or glitters on the deep.

Yes, they were happy days; but they are fled!
All now are parted—part are with the dead!
Still it is pleasure, though 't is mix'd with pain,
To think of joys that cannot live again!
Here cannot live; but they excite desire
Of purer kind, and heavenly thoughts inspire!

And now my mother, weaken'd in her mind,
Her will, subdued before, to me resign'd.
Wean'd from her late directors, by degrees
She sank resign'd, and only sought for ease:
In a small town upon the coast we fix'd,
Nor in amusement with associates mix'd.
My years—but other mode will I pursue,
And count my time by what I sought to do.

And was that mind at ease? could I avow
That no once leading thoughts engaged me now?
Was I convinced th' enthusiastic man
Had ruin'd what the loving boy began?

I answer doubting—I could still detect
Feelings too soft—yet him I could reject—
Feelings that came when I had least employ,
When common pleasures I could least enjoy—

When I was pacing lonely in the rays
Of a full moon, in lonely walks and ways—
When I was sighing o'er a tale's distress,
And paid attention to my Bible less.

These found, I sought my remedies for these;
I suffer'd common things my mind to please,
And common pleasures: seldom walk'd alone,
Nor when the moon upon the waters shone;
But then my candles lit, my window closed,
My needle took, and with my neighbours prosed:
And in one year—nay, ere the end of one,
My labour ended, and my love was done.

My heart at rest, I boldly look'd within,
And dared to ask it of its secret sin;
Alas! with pride it answer'd, "Look around,
And tell me where a better heart is found."
And then I traced my virtues: O! how few,
In fact, they were, and yet how vain I grew!
Thought of my kindness, condescension, ease,
My will, my wishes, nay, my power to please.
I judged me prudent, rational, discreet,
And void of folly, falsehood and deceit.
I read, not lightly, as I some had known,
But made an author's meaning all my own:
In short, what lady could a poet choose
As a superior subject for his muse?

So said my heart, and Conscience straight replied—
"I say the matter is not fairly tried:
I am offended, hurt, dissatisfied:
First of the Christian graces, let me see
What thy pretensions to humility?
Art thou prepared for trial? Wilt thou say
I am this being, and for judgment pray?
And with the gallant Frenchman, wilt thou cry,
When to thy judge presented, thus am I—
Thus was I form'd—these talents I possess'd—
So I employ'd them—and thou know'st the rest."

Thus Conscience; and she then a picture drew,
And bade me think and tremble at the view.
One I beheld—a wife, a mother—go
To gloomy scenes of wickedness and wo;
She sought her way through all things vile and base,
And made a prison a religious place:
Fighting her way—the way that angels fight
With powers of darkness—to let in the light;
Tell me, my heart, hast thou such victory won
As this, a sinner of thy sex, has done,
And calls herself a sinner? What art thou?
And where thy praise and exaltation now?
Yet is she tender, delicate, and nice,
And shrinks from all depravity and vice;
Shrinks from the ruffian gaze, the savage gloom,
That reign where guilt and misery find an home:
Guilt chain'd, and misery purchased; and with them
All we abhor, abominate, condemn—
The look of scorn, the scowl, th' insulting leer
Of shame, all fix'd on her who ventures here:
Yet all she braved! she kept her stedfast eye
On the dear cause, and brush'd the baseness by.

So would a mother press her darling child
Close to her breast, with tainted rags defiled.
But thou hast talents truly! say the ten:
Come, let us look at their improvement then.

What hast thou done to aid thy suffering kind,
To help the sick, the deaf, the lame, the blind?
Hast thou not spent thy intellectual force
On books abstruse, in critical discourse?
Wasting in useless energy thy days,
And idly listening to their common praise,
Who can a kind of transient fame dispense,
And say—"a woman of exceeding sense."

Thus tried, and failing, the suggestions fled,
And a corrected spirit reign'd instead.

My mother yet was living; but the flame
Of life now flash'd, and fainter then became;
I made it pleasant, and was pleased to see
A parent looking as a child to me.

And now our humble place grew wond'rous gay;
Came gallant persons in their red array:
All strangers welcome there, extremely welcome they.
When in the church I saw inquiring eyes
Fix'd on my face with pleasure and surprise;
And soon a knocking at my door was heard;
And soon the lover of my youth appear'd—
Frederick, in all his glory, glad to meet,
And say, "his happiness was now complete."

He told his flight from superstitious zeal;
But first what torments he was doom'd to feel:—
"The tender tears he saw from women fall—
The strong persuasions of the brethren all—
The threats of crazed enthusiasts, bound to keep
The struggling mind, and awe the straying sheep—
From these, their love, their curses, and their creed,
Was I by reason and exertion freed."

Then, like a man who often had been told
And was convinced success attends the bold,
His former purpose he renew'd, and swore
He never loved me half so well before:
Before he felt a something to divide
The heart, that now had not a love beside.

In earlier times had I myself amused,
And first my swain perplex'd, and then refused;
Cure for conceit;—but now in purpose grave,
Strong and decisive the reply I gave.
Still he would come, and talk as idlers do,
Both of his old associates and his new;
Those who their dreams and reveries receive
For facts, and those who would not facts believe.

He now conceived that truth was hidden, placed
He knew not where, she never could be traced;
"But that in every place, the world around,
Might some resemblance of the nymph be found:
Yet wise men knew these shadows to be vain,
Such as our true philosophers disdain,—
They laugh to see what vulgar minds pursue—
Truth, as a mistress, never in their view—
But there the shadow flies, and that, they cry, is true."

Thus, at the college and the meeting train'd,
My lover seem'd his acmè to have gain'd;
With some compassion I essay'd a cure:
"If truth be hidden, why art thou so sure?"

This he mistook for tenderness, and cried,
"If sure of thee, I care not what beside!"
Compell'd to silence, I, in pure disdain,
Withdrew from one so insolent and vain;
He then retired, and, I was kindly told,
"In pure compassion grew estranged and cold."

My mother died; but, in my grief, drew near
A bosom friend, who dried the useless tear.
We lived together: we combined our shares
Of the world's good, and learn'd to brave its cares:
We were the ladies of the place, and found
Protection and respect the country round;
We gave, and largely, for we wish'd to live
In good repute—for this 't is good to give;
Our annual present to the priest convey'd
Was kindly taken:—we in comfort pray'd;
There none molested in the crimson pew
The worthy ladies, whom the vicar knew:
And we began to think that life might be,
Not happy all, but innocently free.

My friend in early life was bound to one
Of gentle kindred, but a younger son.
He fortune's smile with perseverance woo'd,
And wealth beneath the burning sun pursued:
There, urged by love and youthful hope, he went,
Loth; but 't was all his fortune could present.
From hence he wrote; and, with a lover's fears,
And gloomy fondness, talk'd of future years;
To her devoted, his Priscilla found
His faithful heart still suffering with its wound,
That would not heal. A second time she heard;
And then no more: nor lover since appear'd.
Year after year the country's fleet arrived,
Confirm'd her fear, and yet her love survived;
It still was living; yet her hope was dead,
And youthful dreams, nay, youth itself, was fled;
And he was lost: so urged her friends, so she
At length believed, and thus retired with me;
She would a dedicated vestal prove,
And give her virgin vows to heaven and love;
She dwelt with fond regret on pleasures past,
With ardent hope on those that ever last;
Pious and tender, every day she view'd
With solemn joy our perfect solitude;
Her reading, that which most delighted her,
That soothed the passions, yet would gently stir;
The tender, softening, melancholy strain,
That caused not pleasure, but that vanquish'd pain,
In tears she read, and wept, and long'd to read again.

But other worlds were her supreme delight,
And there, it seem'd, she long'd to take her flight;
Yet patient, pensive, arm'd by thoughts sublime,
She watch'd the tardy step of lingering time.

My friend, with face that most would handsome call,
Possess'd the charm that wins the heart of all;
And, thrice entreated by a lover's prayer,
She thrice refused him with determined air.

"No! had the world one monarch, and was he
All that the heart could wish its lord to be,—
Lovely and loving, generous, brave, and true,—
Vain were his hopes to waken hers anew!"
For she was wedded to ideal views,
And fancy's prospects, that she would not lose,
Would not forego, to be a mortal's wife,
And wed the poor realities of life.

There was a day, ere yet the autumn closed,
When, ere her wintry wars, the earth reposed,
When from the yellow weed the feathery crown,
Light as the curling smoke, fell slowly down;
When the wing'd insect settled in our sight,
And waited wind to recommence her flight;
When the wide river was a silver sheet,
And on the ocean slept th' unanchor'd fleet;
When from our garden, as we look'd above,
There was no cloud, and nothing seem'd to move;
Then was my friend in ecstasies—she cried,
"There is, I feel there is, a world beside!
Martha, dear Martha! we shall hear not then
Of hearts distress'd by good or evil men,
But all will constant, tender, faithful be—
So had I been, and so had one with me;
But in this world the fondest and the best
Are the most tried, most troubled, and distress'd:
This is the place for trial, here we prove,
And there enjoy, the faithfulness of love.

Nay, were he here in all the pride of youth,
With honour, valour, tenderness, and truth,
Entirely mine, yet what could I secure,
Or who one day of comfort could insure?

No! all is closed on earth, and there is now
Nothing to break th' indissoluble vow;
But in that world will be th' abiding bliss,
That pays for every tear and sigh in this."

Such her discourse, and more refined it grew,
Till she had all her glorious dream in view;
And she would further in that dream proceed
Than I dare go, who doubtfully agreed:
Smiling I ask'd, again to draw the soul
From flight so high, and fancy to control,
"If this be truth, the lover's happier way
Is distant still to keep the purposed day;
The real bliss would mar the fancied joy,
And marriage all the dream of love destroy."

She softly smiled, and as we gravely talk'd,
We saw a man who up the gravel walk'd,
Not quite erect, nor quite by age depress'd,
A travell'd man, and as a merchant dress'd;
Large chain of gold upon his watch he wore,
Small golden buckles on his feet he bore;
A head of gold his costly cane display'd,
And all about him love of gold betray'd.

This comely man moved onward, and a pair,
Of comely maidens met with serious air;
Till one exclaim'd, and wildly look'd around,
"O heav'n, 't is Paul!" and dropt upon the ground
But she recover'd soon, and you must guess
What then ensued, and how much happiness.

They parted lovers, both distress'd to part!
They met as neighbours, heal'd, and whole of heart
She in his absence look'd to heaven for bliss,
He was contented with a world like this;

And she prepared in some new state to meet
The man now seeking for some snug retreat.
He kindly told her he was firm and true,
Nor doubted her, and bade her then adieu!

"What shall I do?" the sighing maid began,
'How lost the lover! O, how gross the man."

For the plain dealer had his wish declared,
Nor she, devoted victim! could be spared:
He spoke as one decided; she as one
Who fear'd the love, and would the lover shun.

"O Martha, sister of my soul! how dies
Each lovely view! for can I truth disguise,
That this is he? No! nothing shall persuade;
This is a man the naughty world has made,
An eating, drinking, buying, bargaining man—
And can I love him? No! I never can,
What once he was, what fancy gave beside,
Full well I know, my love was then my pride;
What time has done, what trade and travel wrought,
You see! and yet your sorrowing friend is sought;
But can I take him?"—"Take him not," I cried,
"If so averse—but why so soon decide!"

Meantime a daily guest the man appear'd,
Set all his sail, and for his purpose steer'd;
Loud and familiar, loving, fierce and free,
He overpower'd her soft timidity;
Who, weak and vain, and grateful to behold
The man was hers, and hers would be the gold;
Thus sundry motives, more than I can name,
Leagued on his part, and she a wife became.

A home was offer'd, but I knew too well
What comfort was with married friends to dwell;
I was resign'd, and had I felt distress,
Again a lover offer'd some redress;
Behold, a hero of the buskin hears
My loss, and with consoling love appears;
Frederick was now a hero on the stage,
In all its glories, rhapsody, and rage;
Again himself he offer'd, offer'd all
That his an hero of the kind can call.

He for my sake would hope of fame resign,
And leave the applause of all the world for mine.
Hard fate was Frederick's never to succeed,
Yet ever try—but so it was decreed:
His mind was weaken'd; he would laugh and weep,
And swore profusely I had murder'd sleep,
Had quite unmann'd him, cleft his heart in twain,
And he should never be himself again.

He *was* himself; weak, nervous, kind, and poor,
Ill dress'd and idle, he besieged my door,
Borrow'd,—or, worse, made verses on my charms,
And did his best to fill me with alarms;
I had some pity, and I sought the price
Of my repose—my hero was not nice;
There was a loan, and promise I should be
From all the efforts of his fondness free,
From hunger's future claims, or those of vanity.
"Yet," said he, bowing, "do to study take!
O! what a Desdemona wouldst thou make!"

Thus was my lover lost; yet even now
He claims one thought, and this we will allow.

His father lived to an extreme old age,
But never kind!—his son had left the stage,
And gain'd some office, but an humble place,
And that he lost! Want sharpen'd his disgrace,
Urged him to seek his father—but too late,
His jealous brothers watch'd and barr'd the gate.

The old man died; but there is one who pays
A moderate pension for his latter days,
Who, though assured inquiries will offend,
Is ever asking for this unknown friend;
Some partial lady, whom he hopes to find
As to his wants so to his wishes kind.

"Be still," a cool adviser sometimes writes—
"Nay, but," says he, "the gentle maid invites—
Do, let me know the young! the soft! the fair!"

"Old man," 't is answer'd, "take thyself to prayer;
Be clean, be sober, to thy priest apply,
And—dead to all around thee—learn to die!"

Now had I rest from life's strong hopes and fears,
And no disturbance mark'd the flying years;
So on in quiet might those years have past,
But for a light adventure, and a last.

A handsome boy, from school-day bondage free,
Came with mamma to gaze upon the sea;
With soft blue eye he look'd upon the waves,
And talk'd of treacherous rocks, and seamen's graves;
There was much sweetness in his boyish smile,
And signs of feelings frank, that knew not guile.

The partial mother, of her darling proud,
Besought my friendship, and her own avow'd;
She praised her Rupert's person, spirit, ease,
How fond of study, yet how form'd to please;
In our discourse he often bore a part,
And talk'd, heaven bless him! of his feeling heart;
He spoke of pleasures souls like his enjoy,
And hated Lovelace like a virtuous boy;
He felt for Clementina's holy strife,
And was Sir Charles as large and true as life:
For Virtue's heroines was his soul distress'd;
True love and guileless honour fill'd his breast,
When, as the subjects drew the frequent sigh,
The tear stood trembling in his large blue eye,
And softly he exclaim'd, "Sweet, sweetest sympathy!"

When thus I heard the handsome stripling speak,
I smiled assent, and thought to pat his cheek;
But when I saw the feelings blushing there,
Signs of emotion strong, they said, forbear!

The youth would speak of his intent to live
On that estate which heaven was pleased to give,
There with the partner of his joys to dwell,
And nurse the virtues that he loved so well;
The humble good of happy swains to share,
And from the cottage drive distress and care;
To the dear infants make some pleasures known,
And teach, he gravely said, the virtues to his own.

He loved to read in verse, and verse-like prose,
The softest tales of love-inflicted woes;
When, looking fondly, he would smile and cry,
"Is there not bliss in sensibility?"

We walk'd together, and it seem'd not harm
In linking thought with thought, and arm with arm,
Till the dear boy would talk too much of bliss,
And indistinctly murmur—"such as this."

When no maternal wish her heart beguiled,
The lady call'd her son "the darling child;"
When with some nearer view her speech began,
She changed her phrase, and said, "the good young man!"
And lost, when hinting of some future bride,
The woman's prudence in the mother's pride.

Still decent fear and conscious folly strove
With fond presumption and aspiring love,
But now too plain to me the strife appear'd,
And what he sought I knew, and what he fear'd;
The trembling hand and frequent sigh disclosed
The wish that prudence, care, and time opposed.

Was I not pleased, will you demand?—Amused
By boyish love, that woman's pride refused?
This I acknowledge, and from day to day
Resolved no longer at such game to play;
Yet I forbore, though to my purpose true,
And firmly fix'd to bid the youth adieu.

There was a moonlight eve, serenely cool,
When the vast ocean seem'd a mighty pool;
Save the small rippling waves that gently beat,
We scarcely heard them falling, at our feet:
His mother absent, absent every sound
And every sight that could the youth confound;
The arm, fast lock'd in mine, his fear betray'd,
And when he spoke not, his designs convey'd;
He oft-times gasp'd for breath, he tried to speak,
And studying words, at last had words to seek.

Silent the boy, by silence more betray'd,
And fearing lest he should appear afraid,
He knelt abruptly, and his speech began—
"Pity the pangs of an unhappy man."

"Be sure," I answer'd, "and relieve them too—
But why that posture? What the woes to you?
To feel for others' sorrows is humane,
But too much feeling is our virtue's bane.

Come, my dear Rupert! now your tale disclose,
That I may know the sufferer and his woes,
Know there is pain that wilful man endures,
That our reproof and not our pity cures;
For though for such assumed distress we grieve,
Since they themselves as well as us deceive,
Yet we assist not."——The unhappy youth,
Unhappy then, beheld not all the truth.

"O! what is this?" exclaim'd the dubious boy,
"Words that confuse the being they destroy?
So have I read the gods to madness drive
The man condemn'd with adverse fate to strive;
O! make thy victim though by misery sure,
And let me know the pangs I must endure;
For, like the Grecian warrior, I can pray
Falling, to perish in the face of day."

"Pretty, my Rupert; and it proves the use
Of all that learning which the schools produce:
But come, your arm—no trembling, but attend
To sober truth, and a maternal friend.

You ask for pity?"—"O! indeed I do."
"Well then, you have it, and assistance too:
Suppose us married!"—"O! the heavenly thought!"
"Nay—nay, my friend, be you by wisdom taught;
For wisdom tells you, love would soon subside,
Fall, and make room for penitence and pride;
Then would you meet the public eye, and blame
Your private taste, and be o'erwhelm'd with shame;
How must it then your bosom's peace destroy
To hear it said, 'The mother and her boy!'
And then to show the sneering world it lies,
You would assume the man, and tyrannize;
Ev'n Time, Care's general soother, would augment
Your self-reproaching, growing discontent.

Add twenty years to my precarious life,
And lo! your aged, feeble, wailing wife;
Displeased, displeasing, discontented, blamed;
Both, and with cause, ashaming and ashamed;
When I shall bend beneath a press of time,
Thou wilt be all erect in manhood's prime:
Then wilt thou fly to younger minds t' assuage
Thy bosom's pain, and I in jealous age
Shall move contempt, if still—if active, rage:
And though in anguish all my days are past,
Yet far beyond thy wishes they may last;
May last till thou, thy better prospects fled,
Shall have no comfort when thy wife is dead.

Then thou in turn, though none will call thee old,
Will feel thy spirit fled, thy bosom cold;
No strong or eager wish to make the will,
Life will appear to stagnate and be still,
As now with me it slumbers; O! rejoice
That I attend not to that pleading voice;
So will new hopes this troubled dream succeed,
And one will gladly hear my Rupert plead."

Ask you, while thus I could the youth deny
Was I unmoved?—Inexorable I,
Fix'd and determined: thrice he made his prayer,
With looks of sadness first, and then despair;
Thrice doom'd to bear refusal, not exempt,
At the last effort, from a slight contempt.

Did his distress, his pains, your joy excite?—
No; but I fear'd his perseverance might.
Was there no danger in the moon's soft rays,
To hear the handsome stripling's earnest praise
Was there no fear that while my words reproved
The eager youth, I might myself be moved?
Not for his sake alone I cried persist
No more, and with a frown the cause dismiss'd

Seek you th' event?—I scarcely need reply,
Love, unreturn'd, will languish, pine, and die:
We lived awhile in friendship, and with joy
I saw depart in peace the amorous boy.
We met some ten years after, and he then
Was married, and as cool as married men;

He talk'd of war and taxes, trade and farms,
And thought no more of me, or of my charms.

We spoke; and when, alluding to the past,
Something of meaning in my look I cast,
He, who could never thought or wish disguise,
Look'd in my face with trouble and surprise;
To kill reserve, I seized his arm, and cried,
"Know me, my lord!" when laughing, he replied,
Wonder'd again, and look'd upon my face,
And seem'd unwilling marks of time to trace;
But soon I brought him fairly to confess,
That boys in love judge ill of happiness.

Love had his day—to graver subjects led,
My will is govern'd, and my mind is fed;
And to more vacant bosoms I resign
The hopes and fears that once affected mine.

BOOK XII.

SIR OWEN DALE.

The Rector at the Hall—Why absent—He relates the story of Sir Owen—His Marriage—Death of his Lady—His Mind acquires new Energy—His Passions awake—His Taste and Sensibility—Admires a Lady—Camilla—Her Purpose—Sir Owen's Disappointment—His Spirit of Revenge—How gratified—The Dilemma of Love—An Example of Forgiveness—Its Effect.

Again the Brothers saw their friend the priest,
Who shared the comforts he so much increased;
Absent of late—and thus the squire address'd,
With welcome smile, his ancient friend and guest.

"What has detain'd thee? some parochial case?
Some man's desertion, or some maid's disgrace?
Or wert thou call'd, as parish priest, to give
Name to a new-born thing that would not live,
That its weak glance upon the world had thrown,
And shrank in terror from the prospect shown?
Or hast thou heard some dying wretch deplore,
That of his pleasures he could taste no more?
Who wish'd thy aid his spirits to sustain,
And drive away the fears that gave him pain?
For priests are thought to have a patent charm
To ease the dying sinner of alarm:
Or was thy business of the carnal sort,
And thou wert gone a patron's smile to court,
And Croft or Cresswell wouldst to Binning add,
Or take, kind soul! whatever could be had?
Once more I guess: th' election now is near;
My friend, perhaps, is sway'd, by hope or fear,
And all a patriot's wishes, forth to ride,
And hunt for votes to prop the fav'rite side?"

"More private duty call'd me hence, to pay
My friends respect on a rejoicing day,"
Replied the Rector: "there is born a son,
Pride of an ancient race, who pray'd for one,
And long desponded. Would you hear the tale—
Ask, and 't is granted—of Sir Owen Dale?"

"Grant," said the Brothers, "for we humbly ask;
Ours be the gratitude, and thine the task:
Yet dine we first: then to this tale of thine,
As to thy sermon, seriously incline:
In neither case our rector shall complain,
Of this recited, that composed in vain.

Something we heard of vengeance, who appall'd
Like an infernal spirit, him who call'd;
And, ere he vanish'd, would perform his part,
Inflicting tortures on the wounded heart;
Of this but little from report we know;
If you the progress of revenge can show,
Give it, and all its horrors, if you please,
We hear our neighbour's sufferings much at ease.

Is it not so? For do not men delight—
We call them men—our bruisers to excite,
And urge with bribing gold, and feed them for the fight?
Men beyond common strength, of giant size,
And threat'ning terrors in each other's eyes;
When in their naked, native force display'd,
Look answers look, affrighting and afraid;
While skill, like spurs and feeding, gives the arm
The wicked power to do the greater harm:
Maim'd in the strife, the falling man sustains
Th' insulting shout, that aggravates his pains:
Man can bear this; and shall thy hearers heed
A tale of human sufferings? Come! proceed."

Thus urged, the worthy rector thought it meet
Some moral truth, as preface, to repeat;
Reflection serious,—common-place, 't is true,—
But he would act as he was wont to do,
And bring his morals in his neighbour's view.

"O! how the passions, insolent and strong,
Bear our weak minds their rapid course along
Make us the madness of their will obey;
Then die, and leave us to our griefs a prey!"

Sir Owen Dale his fortieth year had seen,
With temper placid, and with mind serene;
Rich; early married to an easy wife,
They led in comfort a domestic life:
He took of his affairs a prudent care,
And was by early habit led to spare;
Not as a miser, but in pure good taste,
That scorn'd the idle wantonness of waste.

In fact, the lessons he from prudence took
Were written in his mind, as in a book:
There what to do he read, and what to shun;
And all commanded was with promptness done;
He seem'd without a passion to proceed,
Or one whose passion no correction need;
Yet some believed those passions only slept,
And were in bounds by early habits kept:
Curb'd as they were by fetters worn so long,
There were who judged them a rebellious throng

To these he stood, not as a hero true,
Who fought his foes, and in the combat slew,
But one who all those foes, when sleeping found,
And, unresisted, at his pleasure bound.

We thought—for I was one—that we espied
Some indications strong of dormant pride;
It was his wish in peace with all to live;
And he could pardon, but could not forgive:
Nay, there were times when stern defiance shook
The moral man, and threaten'd in his look.

Should these fierce passions—so we reason'd—break
Their long-worn chain, what ravage will they make!
In vain will prudence then contend with pride,
And reason vainly bid revenge subside;
Anger will not to meek persuasion bend,
Nor to the pleas of hope or fear attend:
What curb shall, then, in their disorder'd race,
Check the wild passions? what the calm replace?
Virtue shall strive in vain; and has he help in grace?

While yet the wife with pure discretion ruled,
The man was guided, and the mind was school'd;
But then that mind unaided ran to waste:
He had some learning, but he wanted taste;
Placid, not pleased—contented, not employ'd,—
He neither time improved, nor life enjoy'd.

That wife expired, and great the loss sustain'd,
Though much distress he neither felt nor feign'd;
He loved not warmly; but the sudden stroke
Deeply and strongly on his habits broke.

He had no child to soothe him, and his farm,
His sports, his speculations, lost their charm;
Then would he read and travel, would frequent
Life's busy scenes, and forth Sir Owen went:
The mind, that now was free, unfix'd, uncheck'd,
Read and observed with wonderful effect;
And still the more he gain'd, the more he long'd
To pay that mind his negligence had wrong'd;
He felt his pleasures rise as he improved;
And, first enduring, then the labour loved.

But, by the light let in, Sir Owen found
Some of those passions had their chain unbound;
As from a trance they rose to act their part,
And seize, as due to them, a feeling heart.

His very person now appear'd refined,
And took some graces from th' improving mind;
He grew polite without a fix'd intent,
And to the world a willing pupil went.

Restore him twenty years,—restore him ten,—
And bright had been his earthly prospect then:
But much refinement, when it late arrives,
May be the grace, not comfort, of our lives.

Now had Sir Owen feeling; things of late
Indifferent, he began to love or hate;
What once could neither good nor ill impart
Now pleased the senses, and now touch'd the heart;
Prospects and pictures struck th' awaken'd sight,
And each new object gave a new delight.

He, like th' imperfect creature who had shaped
A shroud to hide him, had at length escaped,
Changed from his grub-like state, to crawl no more,
But a wing'd being, pleased and form'd to soar.

Now, said his friends, while thus his views improve,
And his mind softens, what if he should love?
True; life with him has yet serene appear'd,
And therefore love in wisdom should be fear'd:
Forty and five his years, and then to sigh
For beauty's favour!—Son of frailty, fly!

Alas! he loved; it was our fear, but ours,
His friends alone. He doubted not his pow'rs
To win the prize, or to repel the charm,
To gain the battle, or escape the harm;
For he had never yet resistance proved,
Nor fear'd that friends should say—'Alas! he loved.'

Younger by twenty years, Camilla found
Her face unrivall'd when she smiled or frown'd:
Of all approved; in manner, form, and air,
Made to attract; gay, elegant, and fair:
She had, in beauty's aid, a fair pretence
To cultivated, strong intelligence;
For she a clear and ready mind had fed
With wholesome food; unhurt by what she read:
She loved to please; but, like her dangerous sex,
To please the more whom she design'd to vex.

This heard Sir Owen, and he saw it true;
It promised pleasure, promised danger too;
But this he knew not then, or slighted if he knew.

Yet he delay'd, and would by trials prove
That he was safe; would see the signs of love;
Would not address her while a fear remain'd;
But win his way, assured of what he gain'd.

This saw the lady, not displeased to find
A man at once so cautious and so blind;
She saw his hopes that she would kindly show
Proofs of her passion—that she his should know.

"So, when my heart is bleeding in his sight,
His love acknowledged will the pains requite;
It is, when conquer'd, he the heart regards;
Well, good Sir Owen! let us play our cards."

He spake her praise in terms that love affords,
By words select, and looks surpassing words;
Kindly she listen'd, and in turn essay'd
To pay th' applauses—and she amply paid:
A Beauty flattering!—beauteous flatterers feel
The ill you cause, when thus in praise you deal;
For surely he is more than man, or less,
When praised by lips that he would die to press,
And yet his senses undisturb'd can keep,
Can calmly reason, or can soundly sleep.

Not so Sir Owen; him Camilla praised,
And lofty hopes and strong emotions raised;
This had alone the strength of man subdued:
But this enchantress various arts pursued.

Let others pray for music—others pray'd
In vain;—Sir Owen ask'd, and was obey'd:
Let others, walking, sue that arm to take,
Unmoved she kept it for Sir Owen's sake;
Each small request she granted, and though small
He thought them pledges of her granting all.

And now the lover, casting doubt aside,
Urged the fond suit that—could not be denied;
Joy more than reverence moved him when he said,
"Now banish all my fears, angelic maid?"
And as she paused for words, he gaily cried,
"I must not, cannot, will not be denied."

Ah! good Sir Owen, think not favours, such
As artful maids allow, amount to much;
The sweet, small, poison'd baits, that take the eye
And win the soul of all who venture nigh.

Camilla listen'd, paused, and look'd surprise,
Fair witch! exulting in her witcheries!
She turn'd aside her face, withdrew her hand,
And softly said, "Sir, let me understand."

"Nay my dear lady! what can words explain,
If all my looks and actions plead in vain?
I love"—She show'd a cool respectful air,
And he began to falter in his prayer,
Yet urged her kindness—Kindness she confess'd,
It was esteem, she felt it, and express'd,
For her dear father's friend; and was it right
That friend of his—she thought of hers—to slight?

This to the wond'ring lover strange and new,
And false appear'd—he would not think it true;
Still he pursued the lovely prize, and still
Heard the cold words, design'd his hopes to kill;
He felt dismay'd, as he perceived success
Had inverse ratio, more obtaining less;
And still she grew more cool in her replies,
And talk'd of age and improprieties.

Then to his friends, although it hurt his pride,
And to the lady's, he for aid applied;
Who kindly woo'd for him, but strongly were denied.

And now it was those fiercer passions rose,
Urged by his love to murder his repose;
Shame took his soul to be deceived so long,
And fierce revenge for such contemptuous wrong:
Jealous he grew, and jealousy supplied
His mind with rage, unsooth'd, unsatisfied;
And grievous were the pangs of deeply wounded pride.
His generous soul had not the grief sustain'd,
Had he not thought, 'revenge may be obtain'd.'

Camilla grieved, but grief was now too late;
She hush'd her fears, and left th' event to fate;
Four years elapsed, nor knew Sir Owen yet
How to repay the meditated debt;
The lovely foe was in her thirtieth year,
Nor saw the favourite of the heart appear;
'T is sure less sprightly the fair nymph became,
And spoke of former levities with shame:
But this, alas! was not in time confess'd,
And vengeance waited in Sir Owen's breast.

But now the time arrives—the maid must feel
And grieve for wounds that she refused to heal.
Sir Owen, childless, in his love had rear'd
A sister's son, and now the youth appear'd
In all the pride of manhood, and, beside,
With all a soldier's spirit and his pride:
Valiant and poor, with all that arms bestow,
And wants that captains in their quarters know;
Yet to his uncle's generous heart was due
The praise, that wants of any kinds were few.

When he appear'd, Sir Owen felt a joy
Unknown before, his vengeance bless'd the boy—
"To him I dare confide a cause so just;
Love him she may—O! could I say, she must."

Thus fix'd, he more than usual kindness show'd,
Nor let the captain name the debt he owed;
But when he spoke of gratitude, exclaim'd,
"My dearest Morden! make me not ashamed;
Each for a friend should do the best he can,
The most obliged is the obliging man;
But if you wish to give as well as take,
You may a debtor of your uncle make."

Morden was earnest in his wish to know
How he could best his grateful spirit show.

Now the third dinner had their powers renew'd,
And fruit and wine upon the table stood;
The fire brought comfort, and the warmth it lent
A cheerful spirit to the feelings sent,
When thus the uncle—"Morden, I depend
On you for aid—assist me as a friend:
Full well I know that you would much forego
And much endure, to wreak me on my foe.
Charles, I am wrong'd, insulted—nay, be still,
Nor look so fiercely,—there are none to kill.

I loved a lady, somewhat late in life,
Perhaps too late, and would have made a wife;
Nay, she consented; for consent I call
The mark'd distinction that was seen of all,
And long was seen; but when she knew my pain,
Saw my first wish her favour to obtain,
And ask her hand—no sooner was it ask'd,
Than she the lovely Jezebel unmask'd;
And by her haughty airs, and scornful pride,
My peace was wounded—nay, my reason tried;
I felt despised and fallen when we met,
And she, O folly! looks too lovely yet;
Yet love no longer in my bosom glows,
But my heart warms at the revenge it owes.

O! that I saw her with her soul on fire,
Desperate from love, and sickening with desire;
While all beheld her just, unpitied pain,
Grown in neglect, and sharpen'd by disdain!
Let her be jealous of each maid she sees,
Striving by every fruitless art to please,
And when she fondly looks, let looks and fondness tease!
So, lost on passion's never-resting sea,
Hopeless and helpless, let her think of me.

Charles, thou art handsome, nor canst want the art
To warm a cold or win a wanton heart;
Be my avenger"——
Charles, with smile, not vain,
Nor quite unmix'd with pity and disdain,
Sate mute with wonder; but he sat not long
Without reflection:—Was Sir Owen wrong?
"So must I think; for can I judge it right
To treat a lovely lady with despite?

Because she play'd too roughly with the love
Of a fond man whom she could not approve,
And yet to vex him for the love he bore
Is cause enough for his revenge, and more.

But, thoughts, to council!—Do I wear a charm
That will preserve my citadel from harm?
Like the good knight, I have a heart that feels
The wounds that beauty makes and kindness heals:
Beauty she has, it seems, but is not kind—
So found Sir Owen, and so I may find.

Yet why, O heart of tinder! why afraid?
Comes so much danger from so fair a maid?
Wilt thou be made a voluntary prize
To the fierce firing of two wicked eyes?
Think her a foe, and on the danger rush,
Nor let thy kindred for a coward blush.

But how if this fair creature should incline
To think too highly of this love of mine,
And, taking all my counterfeit address
For sterling passion, should the like profess?

Nay, this is folly; or if I perceive
Aught of the kind, I can but take my leave;
And if the heart should feel a little sore,
Contempt and anger will its ease restore.

Then, too, to his all-bounteous hand I owe
All I possess, and almost all I know;
And shall I for my friend no hazard run,
Who seeks no more for all his love has done?

'T is but to meet and bow, to talk and smile,
To act a part, and put on love awhile;
And the good knight shall see, this trial made,
That I have just his talents to persuade;
For why the lady should her heart bestow
On me, or I of her enamour'd grow,
There's none can reason give, there's none can danger show."

These were his rapid thoughts, and then he spoke.
"I make a promise, and will not revoke;
You are my judge in what is fit and right,
And I obey you—bid me love or fight;
Yet had I rather, so the act could meet
With your concurrence,—not to play the cheat;
In a fair cause"——"Charles, fighting for your king,
Did you e'er judge the merits of the thing?
Show me a monarch who has cause like mine,
And yet what soldier would his cause decline?"

Poor Charles or saw not, or refused to see,
How weak the reasoning of our hopes may be,
And said—"Dear uncle, I my king obey'd,
And for his glory's sake the soldier play'd;
Now a like duty shall your nephew rule,
And for your vengeance I will play the fool."

'T was well; but ere they parted for repose,
A solemn oath must the engagement close.
'Swear to me, nephew, from the day you meet
This cruel girl, there shall be no deceit;
That by all means approved and used by man
You win this dangerous woman, if you can;
That being won, you my commands obey,
Leave her lamenting, and pursue your way;
And that, as in my business, you will take
My will as guide, and no resistance make:
Take now an oath—within the volume look,
There is the Gospel—swear, and kiss the book."

"It cannot be," thought Charles, "he cannot rest
In this strange humour,—it is all a jest,
All but dissimulation——Well, sir, there;
Now I have sworn as you would have me swear."

"T is well," the uncle said in solemn tone:
"Now send me vengeance, Fate, and groan for groan!"

The time is come: the soldier now must meet
Th' unconscious object of the sworn deceit.
They meet; each other's looks the pair explore,
And, such their fortune, wish'd to part no more.

Whether a man is thus disposed to break
An evil compact he was forced to make,
Or whether some contention in the breast
Will not permit a feeling heart to rest;
Or was it nature, who in every case
Has made such mind subjected to such face;
Whate'er the cause, no sooner met the pair
Than both began to love, and one to feel despair.

But the fair damsel saw with strong delight
Th' impression made, and gloried in the sight:
No chilling doubt alarm'd her tender breast,
But she rejoiced in all his looks profess'd;
Long ere his words her lover's hopes convey'd,
They warm'd the bosom of the conscious maid;
The spirit seem'd each nature to inspire,
And the two hearts were fix'd in one desire.

"Now," thought the courteous maid, "my father's friend
Will ready pardon to my fault extend;
He shall no longer lead that hermit's life,
But love his mistress in his nephew's wife;
My humble duty shall his anger kill,
And I who fled his love will meet his will,
Prevent his least desire, and every wish fulfil."

Hail, happy power! that to the present lends
Such views; not all on Fortune's wheel depends.
Hope, fair enchantress, drives each cloud away,
And now enjoys the glad, but distant day.

Still fears ensued; for love produces fear.—
"To this dear maid can I indeed be dear?
My fatal oath, alas! I now repent;
Stern in his purpose, he will not relent;
Would, ere that oath, I had Camilla seen!
I had not then my honour's victim been;
I must be honest, yet I know not how,
'T is crime to break, and death to keep my vow."

Sir Owen closely watch'd both maid and man,
And saw with joy proceed his cruel plan;
Then gave his praise—"She has it—has it deep
In her capricious heart,—it murders sleep;
You see the looks that grieve, you see the eyes that weep;

Now breathe again, dear youth, the kindling fire,
And let her feel what she could once inspire."

Alas! obedience was an easy task,
So might he cherish what he meant to ask;
He ventured soon, for Love prepared his way,
He sought occasion, he forbad delay;
In spite of vow foregone he taught the youth
The looks of passion, and the words of truth;
In spite of woman's caution, doubt, and fear,
He bade her credit all she wish'd to hear;
An honest passion ruled in either breast,
And both believed the truth that both profess'd.

But now, 'mid all her new-born hopes, the eyes
Of fair Camilla saw through all disguise,
Reserve, and apprehension——Charles, who now
Grieved for his duty, and abhorr'd his vow,
Told the full fact, and it endear'd him more;
She felt her power, and pardon'd all he swore,
Since to his vow he could his wish prefer,
And loved the man who gave his world for her.

What must they do, and how their work begin,
Can they that temper to their wishes win?
They tried, they fail'd; and all they did t' assuage
The tempest of his soul provoked his rage;
The uncle met the youth with angry look,
And cried, "Remember, sir, the oath you took;
And have my pity, Charles, but nothing more,
Death, and death only, shall her peace restore;
And am I dying?—I shall live to view
The harlot's sorrow, and enjoy it too.

How! words offend you! I have borne for years
Unheeded anguish, shed derided tears,
Felt scorn in every look, endured the stare
Of wondering fools, who never felt a care;
On me all eyes were fix'd, and I the while
Sustain'd the insult of a rival's smile.

And shall I now—entangled thus my foe
My honest vengeance for a boy forego?
A boy forewarn'd, forearm'd? Shall this be borne,
And I be cheated, Charles, and thou forsworn?
Hope not, I say, for thou mayst change as well
The sentence graven on the gates of hell—
'Here bid adieu to hope,—here hopeless beings dwell.'

But does she love thee, Charles? I cannot live
Dishonour'd, unrevenged—I may forgive,
But to thy oath I bind thee; on thy soul—
Seek not my injured spirit to control;
Seek not to soften, I am hard of heart,
Harden'd by insult:—leave her now, and part,
And let me know she grieves while I enjoy her smart.'

Charles first in anger to the knight replied,
Then felt the clog upon his soul, and sigh'd:
To his obedience made his wishes stoop,
And now admitted, now excluded hope;
As lovers do, he saw a prospect fair,
And then so dark, he sank into despair.

The uncle grieved; he even told the youth
That he was sorry, and it seem'd a truth;
But though it vex'd, it varied not his mind,
He bound himself, and would his nephew bind.

"I told him this, placed danger in his view,
Bade him be certain, bound him to be true:
And shall I now my purposes reject,
Because my warnings were of no effect?"

Thus felt Sir Owen as a man whose cause
Is very good—it has his own applause.

Our knight a tenant had in high esteem,
His constant boast, when justice was his theme:
He praised the farmer's sense, his shrewd discourse,
Free without rudeness, manly, and not coarse;
As farmer, tenant, nay, as man, the knight
Thought Ellis all that is approved and right;
Then he was happy; and some envy drew,
For knowing more than other farmers knew;
They call'd him learned, and it soothed their pride,
While he in his was pleased and gratified.

Still more t' offend, he to the altar led
The vicar's niece, to early reading bred;
Who, though she freely ventured on the life,
Could never fully be the farmer's wife;
She had a softness, gentleness, and ease,
Sure a coarse mind to humble and displease:
O! had she never known a fault beside,
How vain their spite, how impotent their pride!

Three darling girls the happy couple bless'd,
Who now the sweetest lot of life possess'd;
For what can more a grateful spirit move
Than health with competence, and peace with love!

Ellis would sometimes, thriving man! retire
To the town inn, and quit the parlour fire;
But he was ever kind where'er he went,
And trifling sums in his amusements spent;
He bought, he thought for her—she should have been content:
Oft, when he cash received at Smithfield mart,
At Cranbourn-alley he would leave a part;
And, if to town he follow'd what he sold,
Sure was his wife a present to behold.

Still, when his evenings at the inn were spent,
She mused at home in sullen discontent;
And, sighing, yielded to a wish that some
With social spirit to the farm would come:
There was a farmer in the place, whose name,
And skill in rural arts, was known to fame;
He had a pupil, by his landlord sent,
On terms that gave the parties much content;
The youth those arts, and those alone, should learn,
With aught beside his guide had no concern:
He might to neighb'ring towns or distant ride,
And there amusements seek without a guide:
With handsome prints his private room was graced,
His music there, and there his books were placed:
Men knew not if he farm'd, but they allow'd him taste.

Books, prints, and music, cease, at times, to charm,
And sometimes men can neither ride nor farm;
They look for kindred minds, and Cecil found,
In farmer Ellis, one inform'd and sound;

But in his wife—I hate the fact I tell—
A lovely being, who could please too well:
And he was one who never would deny
Himself a pleasure, or indeed would try.

Early and well the wife of Ellis knew
Where danger was, and trembled at the view;
So evil spirits tremble, but are still
Evil, and lose not the rebellious will:
She sought not safety from the fancied crime,
"And why retreat before the dangerous time?"

Oft came the student of the farm and read,
And found his mind with more than reading fed:
This Ellis seeing, left them, or he staid,
As pleased him, not offended nor afraid;
He came in spirits with his girls to play,
Then ask excuse, and, laughing, walk away:
When, as he enter'd, Cecil ceased to read,
He would exclaim, "Proceed, my friend, proceed!"
Or, sometimes weary, would to bed retire,
And fear and anger by his ease inspire.

"My conversation does he then despise?
Leaves he this slighted face for other eyes?"
So said Alicia; and she dwelt so long
Upon that thought, to leave her was to wrong.

Alas! the woman loved the soothing tongue,
That yet pronounced her beautiful and young;
The tongue that, seeming careless, ever praised;
The eye that, roving, on her person gazed;
The ready service, on the watch to please;
And all such sweet, small courtesies as these.

Still there was virtue, but a rolling stone
On a hill's brow is not more quickly gone;
The slightest motion,—ceasing from our care,—
A moment's absence,—when we're not aware,
When down it rolls, and at the bottom lies,
Sunk, lost, degraded, never more to rise!
Far off the glorious height from whence it fell,
With all things base and infamous to dwell.

Friendship with woman is a dangerous thing—
Thence hopes avow'd and bold confessions spring:
Frailties confess'd to other frailties lead,
And new confessions new desires succeed;
And, when the friends have thus their hearts disclosed,
They find how little is to guilt opposed.

The foe's attack will on the fort begin,
When he is certain of a friend within.

When all was lost,—or, in the lover's sight,
When all was won,—the lady thought of flight.

"What! sink a slave?" she said, "and with deceit
The rigid virtue of a husband meet?
No! arm'd with death, I would his fury brave,
And own the justice of the blow he gave!
But thus to see him easy, careless, cold,
And his confiding folly to behold;
To feel incessant fears that he should read,
In looks assumed, the cause whence they proceed,
I cannot brook; nor will I here abide
Till chance betrays the crime that shame would hide:
Fly with me, Henry!" Henry sought in vain
To soothe her terrors and her griefs restrain:
He saw the lengths that women dared to go,
And fear'd the husband both as friend and foe.
Of farming weary—for the guilty mind
Can no resource in guiltless studies find,
Left to himself, his mother all unknown,
His titled father, loth the boy to own,
Had him to decent expectations bred,
A favour'd offspring of a lawless bed;
And would he censure one who should pursue
The way he took? Alicia yet was new:
Her passion pleased him: he agreed on flight:
They fix'd the method, and they chose the night.

Then, while the farmer read of public crimes,
Collating coolly Chronicles and Times,
The flight was taken by the guilty pair,
That made one passage in the columns there.

The heart of Ellis bled; the comfort, pride,
The hope and stay of his existence, died;
Rage from the ruin of his peace arose,
And he would follow and destroy his foes;
Would with wild haste the guilty pair pursue,
And when he found—Good heaven! what would he do?

That wretched woman he would wildly seize,
And agonize her heart, his own to ease.
That guilty man would grasp, and in her sight
Insult his pangs, and her despair excite;
Bring death in view, and then the stroke suspend,
And draw out tortures till his life should end:
O! it should stand recorded in all time,
How they transgress'd, and he avenged the crime!

In this bad world should all his business cease,
He would not seek—he would not taste of peace;
But wrath should live till vengeance had her due,
And with his wrath his life should perish too.

His girls—not his—he would not be so weak—
Child was a word he never more must speak!
How did he know what villains had defiled
His honest bed?—He spurn'd the name of child:
Keep them he must; but he would coarsely hide
Their forms, and nip the growth of woman's pride;
He would consume their flesh, abridge their food,
And kill the mother-vices in their blood.

All this Sir Owen heard, and grieved for all,
He with the husband mourn'd Alicia's fall;
But urged the vengeance with a spirit strong,
As one whose own rose high against the wrong.
He saw his tenant by this passion moved,
Shared in his wrath, and his revenge approved.

Years now unseen, he mourn'd this tenant's fate,
And wonder'd how he bore his widow'd state;
Still he would mention Ellis with the pride
Of one who felt himself to worth allied:
Such were his notions—had been long, but now
He wish'd to see if vengeance lived, and how.
He doubted not a mind so strong must feel
Most righteously, and righteous measures deal.
Then would he go, and haply he might find
Some new excitement for a weary mind;

Might learn the miseries of a pair undone,
One scorn'd and hated, lost and perish'd one:
Yes, he would praise to virtuous anger give,
And so his vengeance should be nursed and live.

Ellis was glad to see his landlord come,
A transient joy broke in upon his gloom,
And pleased he led the knight to a superior room;
Where she was wont in happier days to sit,
Who paid with smiles his condescending wit.

There the sad husband, who had seldom been
Where prints acquired in happier days were seen,
Now struck by these, and carried to the past,
A painful look on every object cast:
Sir Owen saw his tenant's troubled state,
But still he wish'd to know the offenders' fate.

"Know you they suffer, Ellis?"—Ellis knew;—
"'T is well! 't is just! but have they all their due?
Have they in mind and body, head and heart,
Sustain'd the pangs of their accursed part?"

"They have!"—"'T is well!"—"And wants enough to shake
The firmest mind, the stoutest heart to break."

"But have you seen them in such misery dwell?"
"In misery past description."—"That is well."

"Alas! Sir Owen, it perhaps is just,—
Yet I began my purpose to distrust;
For they to justice have discharged a debt,
That vengeance surely may her claim forget."

"Man, can you pity?"
"As a man I feel
Miseries like theirs."
"But never would you heal?"

"Hear me, Sir Owen:—I had sought them long,
Urged by the pain of ever-present wrong;
Yet had not seen; and twice the year came round—
Years hateful now—ere I my victims found:
But I did find them, in the dungeon's gloom
Of a small garret—a precarious home,
For that depended on the weekly pay,
And they were sorely frighten'd on the day;
But there they linger'd on from week to week,
Haunted by ills of which 't is hard to speak,
For they are many and vexatious all,
The very smallest—but they none were small.

The roof, unceil'd in patches, gave the snow
Entrance within, and there were heaps below;
I pass'd a narrow region dark and cold,
The strait of stairs to that infectious hold;
And, when I enter'd, misery met my view
In every shape she wears, in every hue,
And the bleak icy blast across the dungeon flew;
There frown'd the ruin'd walls that once were white;
There gleam'd the panes that once admitted light;
There lay unsavoury scraps of wretched food;
And there a measure, void of fuel, stood;
But who shall part by part describe the state
Of these, thus follow'd by relentless fate?
All, too, in winter, when the icy air
Breathed its bleak venom on the guilty pair.

That man, that Cecil!—he was left, it seems,
Unnamed, unnoticed: farewell to his dreams!
Heirs made by law rejected him of course,
And left him neither refuge nor resource:—
Their father's? No: he was the harlot's son
Who wrong'd them, whom their duty bade them shun;
And they were duteous all, and he was all undone.

Now the lost pair, whom better times had led
To part disputing, shared their sorrow's bed:
Their bed!—I shudder as I speak—and shared
Scraps to their hunger by the hungry spared."

"Man! my good Ellis! can you sigh?"—"I can:
In short, Sir Owen, I must feel as man;
And could you know the miseries they endured,
The poor uncertain pittance they procured;
When laid aside the needle and the pen,
Their sickness won their neighbours of their den,
Poor as they are, and they are passing poor,
To lend some aid to those who needed more:
Then, too, an ague with the winter came,
And in this state—that wife I cannot name
Brought forth a famish'd child of suffering and of shame.
This had you known, and traced them to this scene,
Where all was desolate, defiled, unclean,
A fireless room, and where a fire had place,
The blast loud howling down the empty space,
You must have felt a part of the distress,
Forgot your wrongs, and made their suffering less!"

"Sought you them, Ellis, from the mean intent
To give them succour?"
"What indeed I meant
At first was vengeance; but I long pursued
The pair, and I at last their misery view'd
In that vile garret, which I cannot paint—
The sight was loathsome, and the smell was faint;
And there that wife,—whom I had loved so well,
And thought so happy, was condemn'd to dwell;
The gay, the grateful wife, whom I was glad
To see in dress beyond our station clad,
And to behold among our neighbours fine,
More than perhaps became a wife of mine;
And now among her neighbours to explore,
And see her poorest of the very poor!—
I would describe it, but I bore a part,
Nor can explain the feelings of the heart;
Yet memory since has aided me to trace
The horrid features of that dismal place.

There she reclined unmoved, her bosom bare
To her companion's unimpassion'd stare,
And my wild wonder:—Seat of virtue! chaste
As lovely once! O! how wert thou disgraced!
Upon that breast, by sordid rags defiled,
Lay the wan features of a famish'd child;—
That sin-born babe in utter misery laid,
Too feebly wretched even to cry for aid;
The ragged sheeting, o'er her person drawn,
Served for the dress that hunger placed in pawn.

At the bed's feet the man reclined his frame.
Their chairs were perish'd to support the flame
That warm'd his agued limbs; and, sad to see
That shook him fiercely as he gazed on me.

I was confused in this unhappy view:
My wife! my friend! I could not think it true;
My children's mother,—my Alicia,—laid
On such a bed! so wretched,—so afraid!
And her gay, young seducer, in the guise
Of all we dread, abjure, defy, despise,
And all the fear and terror in his look,
Still more my mind to its foundation shook.

At last he spoke:—'Long since I would have died,
But could not leave her, though for death I sigh'd,
And tried the poison'd cup, and dropt it as I tried.

She is a woman, and that famish'd thing
Makes her to life, with all its evils, cling:
Feed her, and let her breathe her last in peace,
And all my sufferings with your promise cease!'

Ghastly he smiled:—I knew not what I felt,
But my heart melted—hearts of flint would melt,
To see their anguish, penury, and shame,
How base, how low, how groveling they became:
I could not speak my purpose, but my eyes
And my expression bade the creature rise.

Yet, O! that woman's look! my words are vain
Her mix'd and troubled feelings to explain;
True, there was shame and consciousness of fall,
But yet remembrance of my love withal,
And knowledge of that power which she would now recall.

But still the more that she to memory brought,
The greater anguish in my mind was wrought;
The more she tried to bring the past in view,
She greater horror on the present threw;
So that, for love or pity, terror thrill'd
My blood, and vile and odious thoughts instill'd.

This war within, these passions in their strife,
If thus protracted, had exhausted life;
But the strong view of these departed years
Caused a full burst of salutary tears,
And as I wept at large, and thought alone,
I felt my reason re-ascend her throne."

"My friend!" Sir Owen answer'd, "what became
Of your just anger?—when you saw their shame,
It was your triumph, and you should have shown
Strength, if not joy—their sufferings were their own."

"Alas, for them! their own in very deed!
And they of mercy had the greater need;
Their own by purchase, for their frailty paid,—
And wanted Heaven's own justice human aid?
And seeing this, could I beseech my God
For deeper misery, and a heavier rod?"

"But could you help them?"—"Think, Sir Owen, how
I saw them then—methinks I see them now!
She had not food, nor aught a mother needs,
Who for another life and dearer feeds:
I saw her speechless; on her wither'd breast
The wither'd child extended, but not prest,
Who sought, with moving lip and feeble cry,
Vain instinct! for the fount without supply.

Sure it was all a grievous, odious scene,
Where all was dismal, melancholy, mean,
Foul with compell'd neglect, unwholesome and unclean;
That arm,—that eye,—the cold, the sunken cheek,—
Spoke all, Sir Owen—fiercely miseries speak!"

"And you relieved?"
"If hell's seducing crew
Had seen that sight, they must have pitied too."

"Revenge was thine—thou hadst the power, the right;
To give it up was Heaven's own act to slight."

"Tell me not, sir, of rights, and wrongs, or powers!
I felt it written—Vengeance is not ours!"

"Well, Ellis, well!—I find these female foes,
Or good or ill, will murder our repose;
And we, when Satan tempts them, take the cup,
The fruit of their foul sin, and drink it up:
But shall our pity all our claims remit,
And we the sinners of their guilt acquit?"

"And what, Sir Owen, will our vengeance do?
It follows us when we our foe pursue,
And, as we strike the blow, it smites the smiters too."

"What didst thou, man?"
"I brought them to a cot
Behind your larches,—a sequester'd spot,
Where dwells the woman: I believe her mind
Is now enlighten'd—I am sure resign'd:
She gave her infant, though with aching heart
And faltering spirit, to be nursed apart."

"And that vile scoundrel"——
"Nay, his name restore,
And call him Cecil,—for he is no more:
When my vain help was offer'd, he was past
All human aid, and shortly breathed his last;
But his heart open'd, and he lived to see
Guilt in himself, and find a friend in me.

Strange was their parting, parting on the day
I offer'd help, and took the man away,
Sure not to meet again, and not to live
And taste of joy—He feebly cried, 'Forgive!
I have thy guilt, thou mine, but now adieu!
Tempters and tempted! what will thence ensue
I know not, dare not think!'—He said, and he withdrew."

"But, Ellis, tell me, didst thou thus desire
To heap upon their heads those coals of fire?"

"If fire to melt, that feeling is confest,—
If fire to shame, I let that question rest;
But if aught more the sacred words imply,
I know it not—no commentator I."

"Then did you freely from your soul forgive?"—

"Sure as I hope before my Judge to live,
Sure as I trust his mercy to receive,
Sure as his word I honour and believe,

Sure as the Saviour died upon the tree
For all who sin,—for that dear wretch and me,—
Whom never more on earth will I forsake or see."

Sir Owen softly to his bed adjourn'd,
Sir Owen quickly to his home return'd;
And all the way he meditating dwelt
On what this man in his affliction felt;
How he, resenting first, forbore, forgave,
His passion's lord, and not his anger's slave:
And as he rode he seem'd to fear the deed
Should not be done, and urged unwonted speed.

Arrived at home, he scorn'd the change to hide,
Nor would indulge a mean and selfish pride,
That would some little at a time recal
Th' avenging vow; he now was frankness all:
He saw his nephew, and with kindness spoke—
"Charles, I repent my purpose, and revoke;
Take her—I 'm taught, and would I could repay
The generous teacher; hear me, and obey:
Bring me the dear coquette, and let me vow
On lips half perjured to be passive now:
Take her, and let me thank the powers divine
She was not stolen when her hand was mine,
Or when her heart—Her smiles I must forget,
She may revenge, and cancel either debt."

Here ends our tale, for who will doubt the bliss
Of ardent lovers in a case like this?
And if Sir Owen's was not half so strong,
It may, perchance, continue twice as long.

BOOK XIII.

DELAY HAS DANGER.

Morning Excursion—Lady at Silford, who?—Reflections on Delay—Cecilia and Henry—The Lovers contracted—Visit to the Patron—Whom he finds there—Fanny described—The yielding of Vanity—Delay—Resentment—Want of Resolution — Further Entanglement — Danger — How met—Conclusion.

Three weeks had past, and Richard rambles now
Far as the dinners of the day allow;
He rode to Farley Grange and Finley Mere,
That house so ancient, and that lake so clear:
He rode to Ripley through that river gay,
Where in the shallow stream the loaches play,
And stony fragments stay the winding stream,
And gilded pebbles at the bottom gleam,
Giving their yellow surface to the sun,
And making proud the waters as they run:
It is a lovely place, and at the side
Rises a mountain-rock in rugged pride;
And in that rock are shapes of shells, and forms
Of creatures in old worlds, of nameless worms,
Whose generations lived and died ere man,
A worm of other class, to crawl began.

There is a town call'd Silford, where his steed
Our traveller rested—He the while would feed
His mind by walking to and fro, to meet,
He knew not what adventure, in the street:
A stranger there, but yet a window-view
Gave him a face that he conceived he knew;
He saw a tall, fair, lovely lady, dress'd
As one whom taste and wealth had jointly bless'd
He gazed, but soon a footman at the door
Thundering, alarm'd her, who was seen no more

"This was the lady whom her lover bound
In solemn contract, and then proved unsound:
Of this affair I have a clouded view,
And should be glad to have it clear'd by you."

So Richard spake, and instant George replied,
"I had the story from the injured side,
But when resentment and regret were gone,
And pity (shaded by contempt) came on.
Frail was the hero of my tale, but still
Was rather drawn by accident than will;
Some without meaning into guilt advance,
From want of guard, from vanity, from chance:
Man's weakness flies his more immediate pain,
A little respite from his fears to gain;
And takes the part that he would gladly fly,
If he had strength and courage to deny.

But now my tale, and let the moral say,
When hope can sleep, there 's danger in delay.
Not that for rashness, Richard, I would plead,
For unadvised alliance: No, indeed:
Think ere the contract—but, contracted, stand
No more debating, take the ready hand:
When hearts are willing, and when fears subside,
Trust not to time, but let the knot be tied;
For when a lover has no more to do,
He thinks in leisure, what shall I pursue?
And then who knows what objects come in view?
For when, assured, the man has nought to keep
His wishes warm and active, then they sleep:
Hopes die with fears; and then a man must lose
All the gay visions, and delicious views,
Once his mind's wealth! He travels at his ease,
Nor horrors now nor fairy-beauty sees;
When the kind goddess gives the wish'd assent,
No mortal business should the deed prevent;
But the blest youth should legal sanction seek
Ere yet th' assenting blush has fled the cheek.

And—hear me, Richard,—man has reptile-pride
That often rises when his fears subside;
When, like a trader feeling rich, he now
Neglects his former smile, his humble bow,
And, conscious of his hoarded wealth, assumes
New airs, nor thinks how odious he becomes.

There is a wandering, wavering train of thought
That something seeks where nothing should be sought,
And will a self-delighted spirit move
To dare the danger of pernicious love.

"First be it granted all was duly said
By the fond youth to the believing maid,

Let us suppose with many a sigh there came
The declaration of the deathless flame;—
And so her answer—'She was happy then,
Blest in herself, and did not think of men;
And with such comforts in her present state,
A wish to change it was to tempt her fate:
That she would not; but yet she would confess
With him she thought her hazard would be less;
Nay, more, she would esteem, she would regard express:
But to be brief—if he could wait and see
In a few years what his desires would be.'"—

Henry for years read months, then weeks, nor found
The lady thought his judgment was unsound;
"For months read weeks," she read it to his praise,
And had some thoughts of changing it to *days*.

And here a short excursion let me make,
A lover tried, I think, for lovers' sake;
And teach the meaning in a lady's mind
When you can none in her expressions find:
Words are design'd that meaning to convey,
But often *Yea* is hidden in a *Nay!*
And what the charmer wills, some gentle hints betray.

Then, too, when ladies mean to yield at length,
They match their reasons with the lover's strength,
And, kindly cautious, will no force employ
But such as he can baffle or destroy.

As when heroic lovers beauty woo'd,
And were by magic's mighty art withstood,
The kind historian, for the dame afraid,
Gave to the faithful knight the stronger aid.

A downright *No!* would make a man despair,
Or leave for kinder nymph the cruel fair;
But "*No!* because I 'm very happy now,
Because I dread th' irrevocable vow,
Because I fear papa will not approve,
Because I love not—No, I cannot love;
Because you men of Cupid make a jest,
Because——in short, a single life is best."
A *No!* when back'd by reasons of such force,
Invites approach, and will recede of course.

Ladies, like towns besieged, for honour's sake,
Will some defence or its appearance make;
On first approach there 's much resistance made,
And conscious weakness hides in bold parade;
With lofty looks, and threat'nings stern and proud,
"Come, if you dare," is said in language loud,
But if th' attack be made with care and skill,
"Come," says the yielding party, "if you will;"
Then each the other's valiant acts approve,
And twine their laurels in a wreath of love.—

We now retrace our tale, and forward go,—
Thus Henry rightly read Cecilia's No!
His prudent father, who had duly weigh'd,
And well approved the fortune of the maid,
Not much resisted, just enough to show
He knew his power, and would his son should know.

"Harry, I will, while I your bargain make,
That you a journey to our patron take:
I know her guardian; care will not become
A lad when courting; as you must be dumb,
You may be absent; I for you will speak,
And ask what you are not supposed to seek."

Then came the parting hour, and what arise
When lovers part! expressive looks and eyes,
Tender and tearful,—many a fond adieu,
And many a call the sorrow to renew;
Sighs such as lovers only can explain,
And words that they might undertake in vain.

Cecilia liked it not; she had, in truth,
No mind to part with her enamour'd youth;
But thought it foolish thus themselves to cheat,
And part for nothing but again to meet.

Now Henry's father was a man whose heart
Took with his interest a decided part;
He knew his lordship, and was known for acts
That I omit,—they were acknowledged facts;
An interest somewhere; I the place forget,
And the good deed—no matter—'t was a debt:
Thither must Henry, and in vain the maid
Express'd dissent—the father was obey'd.

But though the maid was by her fears assail'd,
Her reason rose against them, and prevail'd;
Fear saw him hunting, leaping, falling—led,
Maim'd and disfigured, groaning to his bed;
Saw him in perils, duels,—dying,—dead.

But Prudence answer'd, "Is not every maid
With equal cause for him she loves afraid?"
And from her guarded mind Cecilia threw
The groundless terrors that will love pursue.

She had no doubts, and her reliance strong
Upon the honour that she would not wrong:
Firm in herself, she doubted not the truth
Of him, the chosen, the selected youth;
Trust of herself a trust in him supplied,
And she believed him faithful, though untried:
On her he might depend, in him she would confide.

If some fond girl express'd a tender pain
Lest some fair rival should allure her swain,
To such she answer'd, with a look severe,
"Can one you doubt be worthy of your fear?"

My lord was kind,—a month had pass'd away,
And Henry stay'd—he sometimes named a day;
But still my lord was kind, and Henry still must stay:
His father's words to him were words of fate—
"Wait, 't is your duty; 't is my pleasure, wait!"

In all his walks, in hilly heath or wood,
Cecilia's form the pensive youth pursued;
In the gray morning, in the silent noon,
In the soft twilight, by the sober moon,
In those forsaken rooms, in that immense saloon;
And he, now fond of that seclusion grown,
There reads her letters, and there writes his own.

"Here none approach," said he, "to interfere,
But I can think of my Cecilia here!"

But there did come—and how it came to pass
Who shall explain?—a mild and blue-eyed lass;—

It was the work of accident, no doubt—
The cause unknown—we say "as things fall out;"
The damsel enter'd there, in wand'ring round about:
At first she saw not Henry; and she ran,
As from a ghost, when she beheld a man.

She was esteem'd a beauty through the hall,
And so admitted, with consent of all;
And, like a treasure, was her beauty kept
From every guest who in the mansion slept;
Whether as friends who join'd the noble pair,
Or those invited by the steward there.

She was the daughter of a priest, whose life
Was brief and sad: he lost a darling wife,
And Fanny then her father, who could save
But a small portion; but his all he gave,
With the fair orphan, to a sister's care,
And her good spouse: they were the ruling pair—
Steward and steward's lady—o'er a tribe,
Each under each, whom I shall not describe.

This grave old couple, childless and alone,
Would, by their care, for Fanny's loss atone:
She had been taught in schools of honest fame;
And to the hall, as to a home, she came,
My lord assenting: yet, as meet and right,
Fanny was held from every hero's sight,
Who might in youthful error cast his eyes
On one so gentle as a lawful prize,
On border land, whom as their right or prey,
A youth from either side might bear away.
Some handsome lover of th' inferior class
Might as a wife approve the lovely lass;
Or some invader from the class above,
Who, more presuming, would his passion prove
By asking less, love only for his love.

This much experienced aunt her fear express'd,
And dread of old and young, of host and guest.

"Go not, my Fanny, in their way," she cried,
"It is not right that virtue should be tried;
So, to be safe, be ever at my side."

She was not ever at that side; but still
Observed her precepts, and obey'd her will.

But in the morning's dawn and evening's gloom
She could not lock the damsel in her room;
And Fanny thought, "I will ascend these stairs
To see the chapel,—there are none at prayers;
None," she believed, "had yet to dress return'd,
By whom a timid girl might be discern'd:"
In her slow motion, looking, as she glides,
On pictures, busts, and what she met besides,
And speaking softly to herself alone,
Or singing low in melancholy tone;
And thus she rambled through the still domain,
Room after room, again, and yet again.

But, to retrace our story, still we say,
To this saloon the maiden took her way;
Where she beheld our youth, and frighten'd ran,
And so their friendship in her fear began.

But dare she thither once again advance,
And still suppose the man will think it chance?
Nay, yet again, and what has chance to do
With this?—I know not: doubtless Fanny knew.

Now, of the meeting of a modest maid
And sober youth why need we be afraid?
And when a girl's amusements are so few
As Fanny's were, what would you have her do?
Reserved herself, a decent youth to find,
And just be civil, sociable, and kind,
And look together at the setting sun,
Then at each other—What the evil done?

Then Fanny took my little lord to play,
And bade him not intrude on Henry's way:

"O, he intrudes not!" said the youth, and grew
Fond of the child, and would amuse him too;
Would make such faces, and assume such looks—
He loved it better than his gayest books.

When man with man would an acquaintance seek,
He will his thoughts in chosen language speak;
And they converse on divers themes, to find
If they possess a corresponding mind;
But man with woman has foundation laid,
And built up friendship ere a word is said:
'T is not with words that they their wishes tell,
But with a language answering quite as well;
And thus they find, when they begin t' explore
Their way by speech, they knew it all before.

And now it chanced again the pair, when dark,
Met in their way, when wandering in the park;
Not in the common path, for so they might,
Without a wonder, wander day or night;
But, when in pathless ways their chance will bring
A musing pair, we do admire the thing.

The youth in meeting read the damsel's face,
As if he meant her inmost thoughts to trace;
On which her colour changed, as if she meant
To give her aid, and help his kind intent.

Both smiled and parted, but they did not speak—
The smile implied, "Do tell me what you seek:"
They took their different ways with erring feet,
And met again, surprised that they could meet;
Then must they speak—and something of the air
Is always ready—"'T is extremely fair!"

"It was so pleasant!" Henry said; "the beam
Of that sweet light so brilliant on the stream;
And chiefly yonder, where that old cascade
Has for an age its simple music made;
All so delightful, soothing, and serene!
Do you not feel it? not enjoy the scene?
Something it has that words will not express,
But rather hide, and make th' enjoyment less:
'T is what our souls conceive, 't is what our hearts confess."

Poor Fanny's heart at these same words confess'd
How well he painted, and how rightly guess'd;
And, while they stood admiring their retreat,
Henry found something like a mossy seat;
But Fanny sat not; no, she rather pray'd
That she might leave him, she was so afraid.

"Not, sir, of you; your goodness I can trust,
But folks are so censorious and unjust,

They make no difference, they pay no regard
To our true meaning, which is very hard
And very cruel; great the pain it cost
To lose such pleasure, but it must be lost:
Did people know how free from thought of ill
One's meaning is, their malice would be still."

At this she wept; at least a glittering gem
Shone in each eye, and there was fire in them,
For as they fell, the sparkles, at his feet,
He felt emotions very warm and sweet.

"A lovely creature! not more fair than good,
By all admired, by some, it seems, pursued,
Yet self-protected by her virtue's force
And conscious truth—What evil in discourse
With one so guarded, who is pleased to trust
Herself with me, reliance strong and just?"

Our lover then believed he must not seem
Cold to the maid who gave him her esteem;
Not manly this; Cecilia had his heart,
But it was lawful with his time to part;
It would be wrong in her to take amiss
A virtuous friendship for a girl like this;
False or disloyal he would never prove,
But kindness here took nothing from his love:
Soldiers to serve a foreign prince are known,
When not on present duty to their own;
So, though our bosom's queen we still prefer,
We are not always on our knees to her.
"Cecilia present, witness yon fair moon,
And yon bright orbs, that fate would change as soon
As my devotion; but the absent sun
Cheers us no longer when his course is run;
And then those starry twinklers may obtain
A little worship till he shines again."

The father still commanded "Wait awhile,"
And the son answer'd in submissive style,
Grieved, but obedient; and obedience teased
His lady's spirit more than grieving pleased:
That he should grieve in absence was most fit,
But not that he to absence should submit;
And in her letters might be traced reproof,
Distant indeed, but visible enough;
This should the wandering of his heart have stay'd;
Alas! the wanderer was the vainer made.

The parties daily met, as by consent,
And yet it always seem'd by accident;
Till in the nymph the shepherd had been blind
If he had fail'd to see a manner kind,
With that expressive look, that seem'd to say,
"You do not speak, and yet you see you may."

O! yes, he saw, and he resolved to fly,
And blamed his heart, unwilling to comply:
He sometimes wonder'd how it came to pass,
That he had all this freedom with the lass;
Reserved herself, with strict attention kept,
And care and vigilance that never slept:
"How is it thus that they a beauty trust
With me, who feel the confidence is just?
And they, too, feel it; yes, they may confide,"—
He said in folly, and he smiled in pride.

'T is thus our secret passions work their way,
And the poor victims know not they obey.

Familiar now became the wandering pair,
And there was pride and joy in Fanny's air;
For though his silence did not please the maid,
She judged him only modest and afraid;
The gentle dames are ever pleased to find
Their lovers dreading they should prove unkind,
So, blind by hope, and pleased with prospects gay,
The generous beauty gave her heart away
Before he said, "I love!"—alas! he dared not say.

Cecilia yet was mistress of his mind,
But oft he wish'd her, like his Fanny, kind;
Her fondness soothed him, for the man was vain,
And he perceived that he could give her pain:
Cecilia liked not to profess her love,
But Fanny ever was the yielding dove;
Tender and trusting, waiting for the word,
And then prepared to hail her bosom's lord.

Cecilia once her honest love avow'd,
To make him happy, not to make him proud;
But she would not, for every asking sigh,
Confess the flame that waked his vanity;
But this poor maiden, every day and hour,
Would, by fresh kindness, feed the growing power,
And he indulged, vain being! in the joy,
That he alone could raise it, or destroy;
A present good, from which he dared not fly,
Cecila absent, and his Fanny by.

O! vain desire of youth, that in the hour
Of strong temptation, when he feels the power,
And knows how daily his desires increase,
Yet will he wait, and sacrifice his peace,
Will trust to chance to free him from the snare,
Of which, long since, his conscience said, beware!
Or look for strange deliverance from that ill,
That he might fly, could he command the will!
How can he freedom from the future seek,
Who feels already that he grows too weak?
And thus refuses to resist, till time
Removes the power, and makes the way for crime:
Yet thoughts he had, and he would think, "Forego
My dear Cecilia? not for kingdoms! No!
But may I, ought I not the friend to be
Of one who feels this fond regard for me?
I wrong no creature by a kindness lent
To one so gentle, mild, and innocent;
And for that fair one, whom I still adore,
By feeling thus I think of her the more;"
And not unlikely, for our thoughts will tend
To those whom we are conscious we offend.

Had Reason whisper'd, "Has Cecilia leave
Some gentle youth in friendship to receive,
And be to him the friend that you appear
To this soft girl?—would not some jealous fear
Proclaim your thoughts, that he approach'd too near?"

But Henry, blinded still, presumed to write
Of one in whom Cecilia would delight;
A mild and modest girl, a gentle friend,
If, as he hoped, her kindness would descend—
But what he fear'd to lose or hoped to gain
By writing thus, he had been ask'd in vain.

It was his purpose, every morn he rose,
The dangerous friendship he had made to close;

It was his torment nightly, ere he slept,
To feel his prudent purpose was not kept.

True, he has wonder'd why the timid maid
Meets him so often, and is not afraid;
And why that female dragon, fierce and keen,
Has never in their private walks been seen;
And often he has thought, "What can their silence mean?

They can have no design, or plot, or plan,—
In fact I know not how the thing began,—
'T is their dependence on my credit here,
And fear not, nor, in fact, have cause to fear."

But did that pair, who seem'd to think that all
Unwatch'd will wander and unguarded fall,
Did they permit a youth and maid to meet
Both unreproved? were they so indiscreet?

This sometimes enter'd Henry's mind, and then,
"Who shall account for women or for men?"
He said, "or who their secret thoughts explore?
Why do I vex me? I will think no more."

My lord of late had said, in manner kind,
"My good friend Harry, do not think us blind!"
Letters had past, though he had nothing seen,
His careful father and my lord between;
But to what purpose was to him unknown—
It might be borough business, or their own.

Fanny, it seem'd, was now no more in dread,
If one approach'd, she neither fear'd nor fled:
He mused on this,—"But wherefore her alarm?
She knows me better, and she dreads no harm."

Something his father wrote that gave him pain:
"I know not, son, if you should yet remain;—
Be cautious, Harry; favours to procure
We strain a point, but we must first be sure:
Love is a folly,—that, indeed, is true,—
But something still is to our honour due,
So I must leave the thing to my good lord and you."

But from Cecilia came remonstrance strong:
"You write too darkly, and you stay too long;
We hear reports; and, Henry,—mark me well,—
I heed not every tale that triflers tell;—
Be you no trifler; dare not to believe
That I am one whom words and vows deceive;
You know your heart, your hazard you will learn,
And this your trial—instantly return."

"Unjust, injurious, jealous, cruel maid!
Am I a slave, of haughty words afraid?
Can she who thus commands expect to be obey'd?
O! how unlike this dear assenting soul,
Whose heart a man might at his will control!"

Uneasy, anxious, fill'd with self-reproof,
He now resolved to quit his patron's roof;
And then again his vacillating mind
To stay resolved, and that her pride should find:
Debating thus, his pen the lover took,
And chose the words of anger and rebuke.

Again, yet once again, the conscious pair
Met, and "O, speak!" was Fanny's silent prayer;
And, "I must speak," said the embarrass'd youth,
"Must save my honour, must confess the truth:
Then I must lose her; but, by slow degrees,
She will regain her peace, and I my ease."

Ah! foolish man! to virtue true nor vice,
He buys distress, and self-esteem the price;
And what his gain?—a tender smile and sigh
From a fond girl to feed his vanity.

Thus, every day they lived, and every time
They met, increased his anguish and his crime.

Still in their meetings they were oft-times nigh
The darling theme, and then past trembling by;
On those occasions Henry often tried
For the sad truth—and then his heart denied
The utterance due: thus daily he became
The prey of weakness, vanity, and shame.

But soon a day, that was their doubts to close,
On the fond maid and thoughtless youth arose.
Within the park, beside the bounding brook,
The social pair their usual ramble took;
And there the steward found them: they could trace
News in his look, and gladness in his face.

He was a man of riches, bluff and big,
With clean brown broad-cloth, and with white cut wig:
He bore a cane of price, with riband tied,
And a fat spaniel waddled at his side:
To every being whom he met he gave
His looks expressive; civil, gay, or grave,
But condescending all; and each declared
How much he govern'd, and how well he fared.

This great man bow'd, not humbly, but his bow
Appear'd familiar converse to allow:
The trembling Fanny, as he came in view,
Within the chestnut grove in fear withdrew;
While Henry wonder'd, not without a fear,
Of that which brought th' important man so near:
Doubt was dispersed by—"My esteem'd young man!"
As he with condescending grace began——

"Though you with youthful frankness nobly trust
Your Fanny's friends, and doubtless think them just;
Though you have not, with craving soul, applied
To us, and ask'd the fortune of your bride,
Be it our care that you shall not lament
That love has made you so improvident.

An orphan maid——Your patience! you shall have
Your time to speak, I now attention crave;—
Fanny, dear girl! has in my spouse and me
Friends of a kind we wish our friends to be,
None of the poorest——nay, sir, no reply,
You shall not need——and we are born to die·
And one yet crawls on earth, of whom, I say,
That what he has he cannot take away;
Her mother's father, one who has a store
Of this world's good, and always looks for more,
But, next his money, loves the girl at heart,
And she will have it when they come to part."

"Sir," said the youth, his terrors all awake,
"Hear me, I pray, I beg,—for mercy's sake!

Sir, were the secrets of my soul confess'd,
Would you admit the truths that I protest
Are such——your pardon"——

"Pardon! good, my friend,
I not alone will pardon, I commend:
Think you that I have no remembrance left
Of youthful love, and Cupid's cunning theft?
How nymphs will listen when their swains persuade,
How hearts are gain'd, and how exchange is made?—
Come, sir, your hand"——

"In mercy, hear me now!"
"I cannot hear you, time will not allow:
You know my station, what on me depends,
For ever needed—but we part as friends;
And here comes one who will the whole explain,
My better self—and we shall meet again."

"Sir, I entreat"——

"Then be entreaty made
To her, a woman, one you may persuade;
A little teasing, but she will comply,
And loves her niece too fondly to deny."

"O! he is mad, and miserable I!"
Exclaim'd the youth; "But let me now collect
My scatter'd thoughts, I something must effect."

Hurrying she came—"Now, what has he confess'd,
Ere I could come to set your heart at rest?
What! he has grieved you! Yet he, too, approves
The thing! but man will tease you, if he loves.

But now for business: tell me, did you think
That we should always at your meetings wink?
Think you, you walk'd unseen? There are who bring
To me all secrets—O, you wicked thing!

Poor Fanny! now I think I see her blush,
All red and rosy when I beat the bush;
And hide your secret, said I, if you dare!
So out it came, like an affrighted hare.

Miss! said I, gravely; and the trembling maid
Pleased me at heart to see her so afraid;
And then she wept;—now, do remember this,
Never to chide her when she does amiss;
For she is tender as the callow bird,
And cannot bear to have her temper stirr'd;—
Fanny, I said. then whisper'd her the name,
And caused such looks—Yes, yours are just the same;
But hear my story—When your love was known
For this our child—she is, in fact, our own—
Then, first debating, we agreed at last
To seek my lord, and tell him what had past."

"To tell the earl?"

"Yes, truly, and why not?
And then together we contrived our plot."

"Eternal God!"

"Nay, be not so surprised,—
In all the matter we were well advised;
We saw my Lord, and Lady Jane was there,
And said to Johnson, 'Johnson, take a chair:'
True, we are servants in a certain way,
But in the higher places so are they;
We are obey'd in ours, and they in theirs obey—
So Johnson bow'd, for that was right and fit,
And had no scruple with the earl to sit—
Why look you so impatient while I tell
What they debated?—you must like it well.

'Let them go on,' our gracious earl began;
'They will go off,' said, joking, my good man:
'Well!' said the countess,—she's a lover's friend,—
'What if they do, they make the speedier end'——
But be you more composed, for that dear child
Is with her joy and apprehension wild:
O! we have watch'd you on from day to day,
'There go the lovers!' we were wont to say—
"But why that look?"

"Dear madam, I implore
A single moment!"

"I can give no more:
Here are your letters—that's a female pen,
Said I to Fanny—''t is his sister's, then,'
Replied the maid.—No! never must you stray;
Or hide your wanderings, if you should, I pray;
I know, at least I fear, the best may err,
But keep the by-walks of your life from her:
That youth should stray is nothing to be told,
When they have sanction in the grave and old,
Who have no call to wander and transgress,
But very love of change and wantonness.

I prattle idly, while your letters wait,
And then my lord has much that he would state
All good to you—do clear that clouded face,
And with good looks your lucky lot embrace.

Now mind that none with hers divide your heart,
For she would die ere lose the smallest part;
And I rejoice that all has gone so well,
For who th' effect of Johnson's rage can tell?
He had his fears when you began to meet,
But I assured him there was no deceit:
He is a man who kindness will requite,
But injured once, revenge is his delight;
And he would spend the best of his estates
To ruin, goods and body, them he hates;
While he is kind enough when he approves
A deed that 's done, and serves the man he loves:
Come, read your letters—I must now be gone,
And think of matters that are coming on."

Henry was lost,—his brain confused, his soul
Dismay'd and sunk, his thoughts beyond control.
Borne on by terror, he foreboding read
Cecilia's letter! and his courage fled;
All was a gloomy, dark, and dreadful view,
He felt him guilty, but indignant too:
And as he read, he felt the high disdain
Of injured men—"She may repent, in vain."

Cecilia much had heard, and told him all
That scandal taught—"A servant at the hall,
Or servant's daughter, in the kitchen bred,
Whose father would not with her mother wed,
Was now his choice! a blushing fool, the toy,
Or the attempted both of man and boy;
More than suspected, but without the wit
Or the allurements for such creatures fit;

Not virtuous though unfeeling, cold as ice
And yet not chaste, the weeping fool of vice;
Yielding, not tender; feeble, not refined;
Her form insipid, and without a mind.

Rival! she spurn'd the word; but let him stay,
Warn'd as he was! beyond the present day,
Whate'er his patron might object to this,
The uncle-butler, or the weeping miss—
Let him from this one single day remain,
And then return! he would to her, in vain:
There let him then abide, to earn, or crave
Food undeserved! and be with slaves a slave."

Had reason guided anger, govern'd zeal,
Or chosen words to make a lover feel,
She might have saved him—anger and abuse
Will but defiance and revenge produce.

"Unjust and cruel, insolent and proud!"
He said, indignant, and he spoke aloud.
"Butler! and servant! Gentlest of thy sex,
Thou wouldst not thus a man who loved thee vex;
Thou wouldst not thus to vile report give ear,
Nor thus enraged for fancied crimes appear;
I know not what, dear maid!—if thy soft smiles
were here."

And then, that instant, there appear'd the maid,
By his sad looks in her approach dismay'd;
Such timid sweetness, and so wrong'd, did more
Than all her pleading tenderness before.

In that weak moment, when disdain and pride,
And fear and fondness, drew the man aside,
In this weak moment—"Wilt thou," he began,
"Be mine?" and joy o'er all her features ran;
"I will!" she softly whisper'd; but the roar
Of cannon would not strike his spirit more;
Ev'n as his lips the lawless contract seal'd
He felt that conscience lost her seven-fold shield,
And honour fled; but still he spoke of love,
And all was joy in the consenting dove.

That evening all in fond discourse was spent,
When the sad lover to his chamber went,
To think on what had past, to grieve and to repent:
Early he rose, and look'd with many a sigh
On the red light that fill'd the eastern sky;
Oft had he stood before, alert and gay,
To hail the glories of the new-born day:
But now dejected, languid, listless, low,
He saw the wind upon the water blow,
And the cold stream curl'd onward as the gale
From the pine-hill blew harshly down the dale;
On the right side the youth a wood survey'd,
With all its dark intensity of shade;
Where the rough wind alone was heard to move,
In this, the pause of nature and of love,
When now the young are rear'd, and when the old,
Lost to the tie, grow negligent and cold—
Far to the left he saw the huts of men,
Half hid in mist, that hung upon the fen;
Before him swallows, gathering for the sea,
Took their short flights, and twitter'd on the lea;
And near the bean-sheaf stood, the harvest done,
And slowly blacken'd in the sickly sun;

All these were sad in nature, or they took
Sadness from him, the likeness of his look,
And of his mind—he ponder'd for a while,
Then met his Fanny with a borrow'd smile.

Not much remain'd; for money and my lord
Soon made the father of the youth accord;
His prudence half resisted, half obey'd,
And scorn kept still the guardians of the maid
Cecilia never on the subject spoke,
She seem'd as one who from a dream awoke;
So all was peace, and soon the married pair
Fix'd with fair fortune in a mansion fair.

Five years had past, and what was Henry then?
The most repining of repenting men;
With a fond, teasing, anxious wife, afraid
Of all attention to another paid;
Yet powerless she her husband to amuse,
Lives but t' entreat, implore, resent, accuse;
Jealous and tender, conscious of defects,
She merits little, and yet much expects;
She looks for love that now she cannot see,
And sighs for joy that never more can be;
On his retirements her complaints intrude,
And fond reproof endears his solitude:
While he her weakness (once her kindness) sees,
And his affections in her languor freeze;
Regret, uncheck'd by hope, devours his mind,
He feels unhappy, and he grows unkind.

"Fool! to be taken by a rosy cheek,
And eyes that cease to sparkle or to speak;
Fool! for this child my freedom to resign,
When one the glory of her sex was mine;
While from this burthen to my soul I hide,
To think what Fate has dealt, and what denied.

What fiend possess'd me when I tamely gave
My forced assent to be an idiot's slave?
Her beauty vanish'd, what for me remains?
Th' eternal clicking of the galling chains:
Her person truly I may think my own,
Seen without pleasure, without triumph shown:
Doleful she sits, her children at her knees,
And gives up all her feeble powers to please;
Whom I, unmoved, or moved with scorn, behold,
Melting as ice, as vapid and as cold."

Such was his fate, and he must yet endure
The self-contempt that no self-love can cure:
Some business call'd him to a wealthy town
When unprepared for more than Fortune's frown
There at a house he gave his luckless name,
The master absent, and Cecilia came:
Unhappy man! he could not, dared not speak,
But look'd around, as if retreat to seek:
This she allow'd not; but, with brow severe,
Ask'd him his business, sternly bent to hear;
He had no courage, but he view'd that face
As if he sought for sympathy and grace;
As if some kind returning thought to trace:
In vain; not long he waited, but with air,
That of all grace compell'd him to despair,
She rang the bell, and, when a servant came,
Left the repentant traitor to his shame;
But, going, spoke, "Attend this person out,
And if he speaks, hear what he comes about!"

Then, with cool curtsey, from the room withdrew,
That seem'd to say, "Unhappy man, adieu!"

Thus will it be when man permits a vice
First to invade his heart, and then entice;
When wishes vain and undefined arise,
And that weak heart deceive, seduce, surprise;
When evil Fortune works on Folly's side,
And rash Resentment adds a spur to Pride;
Then Life's long troubles from those actions come,
In which a moment may decide our doom.

THE NATURAL DEATH OF LOVE.

The Rector of the Parish—His Manner of teaching—Of living—Richard's Correspondence—The Letters received—Love that survives Marriage—That dies in consequence—That is permitted to die for want of Care—Henry and Emma, a Dialogue—Complaints on either Side—And Replies—Mutual Accusation—Defence of acknowledged Error—Means of restoring Happiness—The one to be adopted.

Richard one month had with his brother been,
And had his guests, his friends, his favourites seen;
Had heard the rector, who with decent force,
But not of action, aided his discourse:
"A moral teacher!" some, contemptuous, cried;
He smiled, but nothing of the fact denied,
Nor, save by his fair life, to charge so strong replied.
Still, though he bade them not on aught rely,
That was their own, but all their worth deny,
They call'd his pure advice his cold morality;
And though he felt that earnestness and zeal,
That made some portion of his hearers feel,
Nay, though he loved the minds of men to lead
To the great points that form the Christian's creed,
Still he offended, for he would discuss
Points that to him seem'd requisite for us;
And urge his flock to virtue, though he knew
The very heathen taught the virtues too:
Nor was this moral minister afraid
To ask of inspiration's self the aid
Of truths by him so sturdily maintain'd,
That some confusion in the parish reign'd;
"Heathens," they said, "can tell us right from wrong,
But to a Christian higher points belong."
Yet Jacques proceeded, void of fear and shame,
In his old method, and obtain'd the name
Of *Moral Preacher*—yet they all agreed,
Whatever error had defiled his creed,
His life was pure, and him they could commend,
Not as their guide, indeed, but as their friend:
Truth, justice, pity, and a love of peace,
Were his—but there must approbation cease;
He either did not, or he would not see,
That if he meant a favourite priest to be,
He must not show, but learn of them, the way
To truth—he must not dictate, but obey:
They wished him not to bring them further light
But to convince them that they now were right,
And to assert that justice will condemn
All who presumed to disagree with them:
In this he fail'd; and his the greater blame,
For he persisted, void of fear or shame.

Him Richard heard, and by his friendly aid
Were pleasant views observed and visits paid;
He to peculiar people found his way,
And had his question answer'd, "Who are they?"

Twice in the week came letters, and delight
Beam'd in the eye of Richard at the sight;
Letters of love, all full and running o'er,
The paper fill'd till it could hold no more;
Cross'd with discolour'd ink, the doublings full,
No fear that love should find abundance dull;
Love reads unsated all that love inspires,
When most indulged, indulgence still requires;
Looks what the corners, what the crossings tell,
And lifts each folding for a fond farewell.
George saw and smiled—"To lovers we allow
All this o'erflowing, but a husband thou!
A father too: can time create no change?
Married, and still so foolish?—very strange!
What of this wife or mistress is the art?"—
"The simple truth, my brother, to impart,
Her heart, whene'er she writes, feels writing to a heart."

"Fortune, dear Richard, is thy friend—a wife
Like thine must soften every care of life,
And all its woes—I know a pair, whose lives
Run in the common track of men and wives;
And half their worth, at least, this pair would give
Could they like thee and thy Matilda live.

They were, as lovers, of the fondest kind,
With no defects in manner or in mind;
In habit, temper, prudence, they were those
Whom, as examples, I could once propose;
Now this, when married, you no longer trace,
But discontent and sorrow in the place:
Their pictures, taken as the pair I saw
In a late contest, I have tried to draw;
'T is but a sketch, and at my idle time
I put my couple in the garb of rhyme:
Thou art a critic of the milder sort,
And thou wilt judge with favour my report.

Let me premise, twelve months have flown away,
Swiftly or sadly, since the happy day.

Let us suppose the couple left to spend
Some hours without engagement or a friend;
And be it likewise on our mind impress'd,
They pass for persons happy and at rest;
Their love by Hymen crown'd, and all their prospects bless'd.

Love has slow death and sudden: wretches prove
That fate severe—the sudden death of love;
It is as if, on day serenely bright,
Came with its horrors instantaneous night;
Others there are with whom love dies away
In gradual waste and unperceived decay;
Such is that death of love that nature finds
Most fitted for the use of common minds,

The natural death; but doubtless there are some
Who struggle hard when they perceive it come;
Loth to be loved no longer, loth to prove
To the once dear that they no longer love;
And some with not successless arts will strive
To keep the weak'ning, fluttering flame alive.
But see my verse: in this I try to paint
The passion failing, fading to complaint,
The gathering grief for joys remember'd yet,
The vain remonstrance, and the weak regret:
First speaks the wife in sorrow, she is grieved
T' admit the truth, and would be still deceived."

HENRY AND EMMA.

E. Well, my good sir, I shall contend no more;
But, O! the vows you made, the oaths you swore—

H. To love you always:—I confess it true;
And do I not? If not, what can I do?
Moreover think what you yourself profess'd,
And then the subject may for ever rest.

E. Yes, sir, obedience I profess'd; I know
My debt, and wish to pay you all I owe,
Pay without murmur; but that vow was made
To you, who said it never should be paid;—
Now truly tell me why you took such care
To make me err? I ask'd you not to swear,
But rather hoped you would my mind direct,
And say, when married, what you would expect.

You may remember—it is not so long
Since you affirm'd that I could not be wrong;
I told you then—you recollect, I told
The very truth—that humour would not hold;
Not that I thought, or ever could suppose,
The mighty raptures were so soon to close—
Poetic flights of love all sunk in sullen prose.

Do you remember how you used to hang
Upon my looks? your transports when I sang?
I play'd—you melted into tears; I moved—
Voice, words, and motion, how you all approved;
A time when Emma reign'd, a time when Henry loved:
You recollect?

H. Yes, surely; and then why
The needless truths? do I the facts deny?
For this remonstrance I can see no need,
Or this impatience—if you do, proceed.

E. O! that is now so cool, and with a smile
That sharpens insult—I detest the style;
And, now I talk of styles, with what delight
You read my lines—I then, it seems, could write:
In short, when I was present you could see
But one dear object, and you lived for me;
And now, sir, what your pleasure? Let me dress,
Sing, speak, or write, and you your sense express
Of my poor taste—my words are not correct;
In all I do is failing or defect—
Some error you will seek, some blunder will detect;
And what can such dissatisfaction prove?
I tell you, Henry, you have ceased to love.

H. I own it not; but if a truth it be,
It is the fault of nature, not of me.
Remember you, my love, the fairy tale,
Where the young pairs were spell-bound in the vale?
When all around them gay or glorious seem'd,
And of bright views and ceaseless joys they dream'd;
Young love and infant life no more could give—
They said but half, when they exclaim'd, "We live!"
All was so light, so lovely, so serene,
And not a trouble to be heard or seen;
Till, melting into truth, the vision fled,
And there came miry roads and thorny ways instead.

Such was our fate, my charmer! we were found
A wandering pair, by roguish Cupid bound;
All that I saw was gifted to inspire
Grand views of bliss, and wake intense desire
Of joys that never pall, of flights that never tire;
There was that purple light of love, that bloom,
That ardent passions in their growth assume,
That pure enjoyment of the soul—O! weak
Are words such loves and glowing thoughts to speak!
I sought to praise thee, and I felt disdain
Of my own effort; all attempts were vain.

Nor they alone were charming; by that light
All loved of thee grew lovely in my sight;
Sweet influence not its own in every place
Was found, and there was found in all things grace;
Thy shrubs and plants were seen new bloom to bear,
Not the Arabian sweets so fragrant were,
Nor Eden's self, if aught with Eden might compare.

You went the church-way walk, you reach'd the farm,
And gave the grass and babbling springs a charm;
Crop, whom you rode,—sad rider though you be,—
Thenceforth was more than Pegasus to me:
Have I not woo'd your snarling cur to bend
To me the paw and greeting of a friend?
And all his surly ugliness forgave,
Because, like me, he was my Emma's slave?
Think you, thus charm'd, I would the spell revoke?
Alas! my love, we married, and it broke!

Yet no deceit or falsehood stain'd my breast,
What I asserted might a saint attest;
Fair, dear, and good thou wert, nay, fairest, dearest, best:
Nor shame, nor guilt, nor falsehood I avow,
But 't is by heaven's own light I see thee now;
And if that light will all those glories chase,
'T is not my wish that will the good replace.

E. O! sir, this boyish tale is mighty well,
But 't was your falsehood that destroy'd the spell:
Speak not of nature, 't is an evil mind
That makes you to accustom'd beauties blind;
You seek the faults yourself, and then complain you find.

H. I sought them not; but, madam, 't is in vain
The course of love and nature to restrain;
Lo! when the buds expand, the leaves are green,
Then the first opening of the flower is seen,

Then comes the honeyed breath and rosy smile,
That with their sweets the willing sense beguile;
But, as we look, and love, and taste, and praise,
And the fruit grows, the charming flower decays;
Till all is gather'd, and the wintry blast
Moans o'er the place of love and pleasure past.

So 't is with beauty,—such the opening grace
And dawn of glory in the youthful face;
Then are the charms unfolded to the sight,
Then all is loveliness and all delight;
The nuptial tie succeeds, the genial hour,
And, lo! the falling off of beauty's flower;
So, through all nature is the progress made,—
The bud, the bloom, the fruit,—and then we fade.

Then sigh no more,—we might as well retain
The year's gay prime as bid that love remain,
That fond, delusive, happy, transient spell,
That hides us from a world wherein we dwell,
And forms and fits us for that fairy ground,
Where charming dreams and gay conceits abound;
Till comes at length th' awakening strife and care,
That we, as tried and toiling men, must share.

E. O! sir, I must not think that heaven approves
Ungrateful man or unrequited loves;
Nor that we less are fitted for our parts
By having tender souls and feeling hearts.

H. Come, my dear friend, and let us not refuse
The good we have, by grief for that we lose;
But let us both the very truth confess;
This must relieve the ill, and may redress.

E. O! much I fear! I practised no deceit,
Such as I am I saw you at my feet;
If for a goddess you a girl would take,
'T is you yourself the disappointment make.

H. And I alone?—O! Emma, when I pray'd
For grace from thee, transported and afraid,
Now raised to rapture, now to terror doom'd,
Was not the goddess by the girl assumed?
Did not my Emma use her skill to hide—
Let us be frank—her weakness and her pride?
Did she not all her sex's arts pursue,
To bring the angel forward to my view?
Was not the rising anger oft suppress'd?
Was not the waking passion hush'd to rest?
And when so mildly sweet you look'd and spoke,
Did not the woman deign to wear a cloak?
A cloak she wore, or, though not clear my sight,
I might have seen her—Think you not I might?

E. O! this is glorious!—while your passion lives,
To the loved maid a robe of grace it gives;
And then, unjust! beholds her with surprise,
Unrobed, ungracious, when the passion dies.

H. For this, my Emma, I to heaven appeal,
I felt entirely what I seem'd to feel;
Thou wert all precious in my sight, to me
The being angels are supposed to be;
And am I now of my deception told,
Because I 'm doom'd a woman to behold?

E. Sir! in few words I would a question ask—
Mean these reproaches that I wore a mask?
Mean you that I by art or caution tried
To show a virtue, or a fault to hide?

H. I will obey you—When you seem'd to feel
Those books we read, and praised them with such zeal,
Approving all that certain friends approved,
Was it the pages, or the praise you loved!
Nay, do not frown—I much rejoiced to find
Such early judgment in such gentle mind;
But, since we married, have you deign'd to look
On the grave subjects of one favourite book?
Or have the once-applauded pages power
T' engage their warm approver for an hour!

Nay, hear me further—When we view'd that dell,
Where lie those ruins—you must know it well—
When that worn pediment your walk delay'd,
And the stream gushing through the arch decay'd;
When at the venerable pile you stood,
Till the does ventured on our solitude,
We were so still! before the growing day
Call'd us reluctant from our seat away—
Tell me, was all the feeling you express'd
The genuine feeling of my Emma's breast?
Or was it borrow'd, that her faithful slave
The higher notion of her taste might have?
So may I judge, for of that lovely scene
The married Emma has no witness been;
No more beheld that water, falling, flow
Through the green fern that there delights to grow.

Once more permit me—Well, I know, you feel
For suffering men, and would their sufferings heal,
But when at certain huts you chose to call,
At certain seasons, was compassion all?
I there beheld thee, to the wretched dear
As angels to expiring saints appear
When whispering hope—I saw an infant press'd
And hush'd to slumber on my Emma's breast!
Hush'd be each rude suggestion!—Well I know,
With a free hand your bounty you bestow;
And to these objects frequent comforts send,
But still they see not now their pitying friend.

A merchant, Emma, when his wealth he states,
Though rich, is faulty if he over-rates
His real store; and, gaining greater trust
For the deception, should we deem him just?

If in your singleness of heart you hide
No flaw or frailty, when your truth is tried,
And time has drawn aside the veil of love,
We may be sorry, but we must approve;
The fancied charms no more our praise compel,
But doubly shines the worth that stands so well.

E. O! precious are you all, and prizes too,
Or could we take such guilty pains for you?
Believe it not—As long as passion lasts,
A charm about the chosen maid it casts;
And the poor girl has little more to do
Than just to keep in sight as you pursue:
Chance to a ruin leads her; you behold,
And straight the angel of her taste is told;
Chance to a cottage leads you, and you trace
A virtuous pity in the angel's face;

She reads a work you chance to recommend,
And likes it well—at least, she likes the friend;
But when it chances this no more is done,
She has not left one virtue—No! not one!

But be it said, good sir, we use such art,
Is it not done to hold a fickle heart,
And fix a roving eye?—Is that design
Shameful or wicked that would keep you mine?
If I confess the art, I would proceed
To say of such that every maid has need.
Then when you flatter—in your language—praise,
In our own view you must our value raise;
And must we not, to this mistaken man,
Appear as like his picture as we can?
If you will call—nay, treat us as divine,
Must we not something to your thoughts incline?
If men of sense will worship whom they love,
Think you the idol will the error prove?
What! show him all her glory is pretence,
And make an idiot of this man of sense?

Then, too, suppose we should his praise refuse,
And clear his mind, we may our lover lose;
In fact, you make us more than nature makes,
And we, no doubt, consent to your mistakes;
You will, we know, until the frenzy cools,
Enjoy the transient paradise of fools;
But fancy fled, you quit the blissful state,
And truth for ever bars the golden gate.

H. True! but how ill each other to upbraid,
'T is not our fault that we no longer staid;
No sudden fate our lingering love suppress,
It died an easy death, and calmly sank to rest:
To either sex is the delusion lent,
And when it fails us, we should rest content,
'T is cruel to reproach, when bootless to repent.

E. Then wise the lovers who consent to wait,
And always lingering, never try the state;
But hurried on, by what they call their pain
And I their bliss, no longer they refrain;
To ease that pain, to lose that bliss, they run
To the church magi, and the thing is done;
A spell is utter'd, and a ring applied,
And forth they walk a bridegroom and a bride,
To find this counter-charm, this marriage rite,
Has put their pleasant fallacies to flight!
But tell me, Henry, should we truly strive,
May we not bid the happy dream revive?

H. Alas! they say when weakness or when vice
Expels a foolish pair from Paradise,
The guardian power to prayer has no regard,
The knowledge once obtain'd, the gate is barr'd;
Or could we enter we should still repine,
Unless we could the knowledge too resign.
And let us calmly view our present fate,
And make a humble Eden of our state;
With this advantage, that what now we gain,
Experience gives, and prudence will retain.

E. Ah! much I doubt—when you in fury broke
That lovely vase by one impassion'd stroke,
And thousand china-fragments met my sight,
Till rising anger put my grief to flight;
As well might you the beauteous jar repiece,
As joy renew and bid vexation cease.

H. Why then 't is wisdom, Emma, not to keep
These griefs in memory; they had better sleep.

There was a time when this heaven-guarded isle,
Whose valleys flourish—nay, whose mountains smile,
Was sterile, wild, deform'd, and beings rude
Creatures scarce wilder than themselves pursued;
The sea was heard around a waste to howl,
The night-wolf answer'd to the whooting owl,
And all was wretched—Yet who now surveys
The land, withholds his wonder and his praise?
Come, let us try and make our moral view
Improve like this—this have we power to do.

E. O! I'll be all forgetful, deaf and dumb,
And all you wish, to have these changes come.

H. And come they may, if not as heretofore,
We cannot all the lovely vase restore;
What we beheld in Love's perspective glass
Has pass'd away—one sigh! and let it pass—
It was a blissful vision, and it fled,
And we must get some actual good instead:
Of good and evil that we daily find,
That we must hoard, *this* banish from the mind;
The food of Love, that food on which he thrives,
To find must be the business of our lives;
And when we know what Love delights to see,
We must his guardians and providers be.

As careful peasants, with incessant toil,
Bring earth to vines in bare and rocky soil,
And, as they raise with care each scanty heap,
Think of the purple clusters they shall reap;
So those accretions to the mind we'll bring,
Whence fond regard and just esteem will spring,
Then, though we backward look with some regret
On those first joys, we shall be happy yet.

Each on the other must in all depend,
The kind adviser, the unfailing friend;
Through the rough world we must each other aid,
Leading and led, obeying and obey'd;
Favour'd and favouring, eager to believe
What should be truth—unwilling to perceive
What might offend—determined to remove
What has offended; wisely to improve
What pleases yet, and guard returning love.

Nor doubt, my Emma, but in many an hour
Fancy, who sleeps, shall wake with all her power;
And we shall pass—though not perhaps remain—
To fairy-land, and feel its charm again.

BOOK XV.

GRETNA GREEN.

Richard meets an Acquaintance of his Youth—The Kind of Meeting—His School—The Doctor Sidmere and his Family—Belwood, a Pupil—The Doctor's Opinion of him—The Opinion of his Wife--and of his Daughter—Consultation—The Lovers—Flight to Gretna Green—Return no more—The Doctor and his Lady—Belwood and his Wife—The Doctor reflects—Goes to his Son-in-law—His Reception and Return.

"I met," said Richard, when return'd to dine,
"In my excursion, with a friend of mine;
Friend! I mistake,—but yet I knew him well,
Ours was the village where he came to dwell;
He was an orphan born to wealth, and then
Placed in the guardian-care of cautious men;
When our good parent, who was kindness all,
Fed and caress'd him when he chose to call;
And this he loved, for he was always one
For whom some pleasant service must be done,
Or he was sullen—He would come and play
At his own time, and at his pleasure stay;
But our kind parent soothed him as a boy
Without a friend; she loved he should enjoy
A day of ease, and strove to give his mind employ:
She had but seldom the desired success,
And therefore parting troubled her the less;
Two years he there remain'd, then went his way,
I think to school, and him I met to-day.

I heard his name, or he had past unknown,
And, without scruple, I divulged my own:
His words were civil, but not much express'd,
'Yes! he had heard I was my brother's guest;'
Then would explain, what was not plain to me,
Why he could not a social neighbour be.
He envied you, he said, your quiet life,
And me a loving and contented wife;
You, as unfetter'd by domestic bond,
Me, as a husband and a father fond:
I was about to speak, when to the right
The road then turn'd, and lo! his house in sight.

'Adieu!' he said, nor gave a word or sign
Of invitation—'Yonder house is mine;
Your brother's I prefer, if I might choose—
But, my dear sir, I have no time to lose.'

Say, is he poor? or has he fits of spleen?
Or is he melancholy, moped, or mean?
So cold, so distant——I bestow'd some pains
Upon the fever in my Irish veins."

"Well, Richard, let your native wrath be tamed,
The man has half the evils you have named;
He is not poor, indeed, nor is he free
From all the gloom and care of poverty."

"But is he married?"—"Hush! the bell, my friend;
That business done, we will to this attend;
And, o'er our wine engaged, and at our ease,
We may discourse of Belwood's miseries;
Not that his sufferings please me—No, indeed;
But I from such am happy to be freed."

Their speech, of course, to this misfortune led,
A weak young man improvidently wed.

"Weak," answer'd Richard; "but we do him wrong
To say that his affection was not strong."

"That we may doubt," said George; "in men so weak
You may in vain the strong affections seek;
They have strong appetites; a fool will eat
As long as food is to his palate sweet;
His rule is not what sober nature needs,
But what the palate covets as he feeds:
He has the passions, anger, envy, fear,
As storm is angry, and as frost severe;
Uncheck'd, he still retains what nature gave,
And has what creatures of the forest have.

Weak boys, indulged by parents just as weak,
Will with much force of their affection speak;
But let mamma the accustom'd sweets withhold,
And the fond boys grow insolent and cold.

Weak men profess to love, and while untried
May woo with warmth, and grieve to be denied;
But this is selfish ardour,—all the zeal
Of their pursuit is from the wish they feel
For self-indulgence—When do they deny
Themselves? and when the favourite object fly?
Or, for that object's sake, with her requests comply?
Their sickly love is fed with hopes of joy,
Repulses damp it, and delays destroy;
Love, that to virtuous acts will some excite,
In others but provokes an appetite;
In better minds, when love possession takes
And meets with peril, he the reason shakes;
But these weak natures, when they love profess,
Never regard their small concerns the less.

That true and genuine love has Quixote-flights
May be allow'd—in vision it delights;
But in its loftiest flight, its wildest dream,
Has something in it that commands esteem:
But this poor love to no such region soars,
But, Sancho-like, its selfish loss deplores;
Of its own merits and its service speaks,
And full reward for all its duty seeks."

—"When a rich boy, with all the pride of youth,
Weds a poor beauty, will you doubt his truth;
Such love is tried—it indiscreet may be,
But must be generous"—

"That I do not see;
Just at this time the balance of the mind
Is this or that way by the weights inclined;
In this scale beauty, wealth in that abides,
In dubious balance, till the last subsides;
Things are not poised in just the equal state,
That the ass stands stock-still in the debate;
Though when deciding he may slowly pass
And long for both—the nature of the ass;
'T is but an impulse that he must obey
When he resigns one bundle of the hay."

Take your friend Belwood, whom his guardians sent
To Doctor Sidmere—full of dread he went;
Doctor they call'd him—he was not of us,
And where he was—we need not now discuss:
He kept a school, he had a daughter fair,
He said, as angels,—say, as women are.

Clara, this beauty, had a figure light,
Her face was handsome, and her eyes were bright;
Her voice was music, not by anger raised;
And sweet her dimple, either pleased or praised;
All round the village was her fame allow'd,
She was its pride, and not a little proud.
The ruling thought that sway'd her father's mind
Was this—I am for dignity design'd:
Riches he rather as a mean approved,
Yet sought them early, and in seeking loved;
For this he early made the marriage vow,
But fail'd to gain—I recollect not how;
For this his lady had his wrath incurr'd,
But that her feelings seldom could be stirr'd;
To his fair daughter, famed as well as fair,
He look'd, and found his consolation there.

The Doctor taught of youth some half a score,
Well-born and wealthy—He would take no more;
His wife, when peevish, told him, "Yes! and glad"—
It might be so—no more were to be had:
Belwood, it seems, for college was design'd,
But for more study he was not inclined:
He thought of labouring there with much dismay,
And motives mix'd here urged the long delay.

He now on manhood verged, at least began
To talk as he supposed became a man.

"Whether he chose the college or the school
Was his own act, and that should no man rule;
He had his reasons for the step he took,
Did they suppose he stay'd to read his book?"

Hopeless, the Doctor said, "This boy is one
With whom I fear there 's nothing to be done."

His wife replied, who more had guess'd or knew,
"You only mean there 's nothing he can do;
Ev'n there you err, unless you mean indeed
That the poor lad can neither think nor read."

—"What credit can I by such dunce obtain?"—
"Credit? I know not—you may something gain;
'T is true he has no passion for his books,
But none can closer study Clara's looks;
And who controls him? now his father 's gone,
There 's not a creature cares about the son.
If he be brought to ask your daughter's hand,
All that he has will be at her command;
And who is she? and whom does she obey?
Where is the wrong, and what the danger, pray?
Becoming guide to one whom guidance needs
Is merit surely—If the thing succeeds,
Cannot you always keep him at your side,
And be his honour'd guardian and his guide?
And cannot I my pretty Clara rule?
Is not this better than a noisy school?"

The Doctor thought and mused, he felt and fear'd,
Wish'd it to be—then wish'd he had not heard;
But he was angry—that at least was right,
And gave him credit in his lady's sight;—
Then, milder grown, yet something still severe,
He said, "Consider, Madam, think and fear;"
But, ere they parted, softening to a smile,
"Farewell!" said he—"I 'll think myself awhile."

James and his Clara had, with many a pause
And many a doubt, infringed the Doctor's laws
At first with terror, and with eyes turn'd round
On every side for fear they should be found;
In the long passage, and without the gate,
They met, and talk'd of love and his estate;
Sweet little notes, and full of hope, were laid
Where they were found by the attentive maid;
And these she answer'd kindly as she could,
But still 'I dare not' waited on 'I would;'
Her fears and wishes she in part confess'd,
Her thoughts and views she carefully suppress'd,
Her Jemmy said at length, "He did not heed
His guardian's anger—What was he, indeed?
A tradesman once, and had his fortune gain'd
In that low way,—such anger he disdain'd—
He loved her pretty looks, her eyes of blue,
Her auburn-braid, and lips that shone like dew;
And did she think her Jemmy stay'd at school
To study Greek?—What, take him for a fool?
Not he, by Jove! for what he had to seek
He would in English ask her, not in Greek;
Will you be mine? are all your scruples gone?
Then let's be off—I've that will take us on."
'T was true; the clerk of an attorney there
Had found a Jew,—the Jew supplied the heir.

Yet had he fears—"My guardians may condemn
The choice I make—but what is that to them?
The more they strive my pleasure to restrain,
The less they 'll find they 're likely to obtain;
For when they work one to a proper cue,
What they forbid one takes delight to do."

Clara exulted—now the day would come
Belwood must take her in her carriage home;
"Then I shall hear what envy will remark
When I shall sport the ponies in the park;
When my friend Jane will meet me at the ball,
And see me taken out the first of all:
I see her looks when she beholds the men
All crowd about me—she will simper then,
And cry with her affected air and voice,
'O! my sweet Clara, how do I rejoice
At your good fortune!'—'Thank you, dear,' say I
'But some there are that could for envy die.'"

Mamma look'd on with thoughts to these allied,
She felt the pleasure of reflected pride;
She should respect in Clara's honour find—
But she to Clara's secret thoughts was blind;
O! when we thus design, we do but spread
Nets for our feet, and to our toils are led:
Those whom we think we rule their views attain,
And we partake the guilt without the gain.

The Doctor long had thought, till he became
A victim both to avarice and shame;
From his importance, every eye was placed
On his designs—How dreadful it disgraced!

"O! that unknown to him the pair had flown
To that same Green, the project all their own!
And should they now be guilty of the act,
Am not I free from knowledge of the fact?
Will they not, if they will?"—'T is thus we meet
The check of conscience, and our guide defeat.

This friend, this spy, this counsellor at rest,
More pleasing views were to the mind address'd.

The mischief done, he would be much displeased,
For weeks, nay, months, and slowly be appeased;—
Yet of this anger if they felt the dread,
Perhaps they dare not steal away to wed;
And if on hints of mercy they should go,
He stood committed—it must not be so.

In this dilemma either horn was hard,—
Best to seem careless, then, and off one's guard;
And, lest their terror should their flight prevent,
His wife might argue—fathers will relent
On such occasions—and that she should share
The guilt and censure was her proper care.

"Suppose them wed," said he, "and at my feet,
I must exclaim that instant—Vile deceit!
Then will my daughter, weeping, while they kneel,
For its own Clara beg my heart may feel:
At last, but slowly, I may all forgive,
And their adviser and director live."

When wishes only weak the heart surprise,
Heaven, in its mercy, the fond prayer denies;
But when our wishes are both base and weak,
Heaven, in its justice, gives us what we seek.

All pass'd that was expected, all prepared
To share the comfort—What the comfort shared?

The married pair, on their return, agreed
That they from school were now completely freed;
Were man and wife, and to their mansion now
Should boldly drive, and their intents avow:
The acting guardian in the mansion reign'd,
And, thither driving, they their will explain'd:
The man awhile discoursed in language high,
The ward was sullen, and made brief reply;
Till, when he saw th' opposing strength decline,
He bravely utter'd—"Sir, the house is mine!"
And, like a lion, lash'd by self-rebuke,
His own defence he bravely undertook.

"Well! be it right or wrong, the thing is past:
You cannot hinder what is tight and fast:
The church has tied us; we are hither come
To our own place, and you must make us room."

The man reflected—"You deserve, I know,
Foolish young man! what fortune will bestow:
No punishment from me your actions need,
Whose pains will shortly to your fault succeed."

James was quite angry, wondering what was meant
By such expressions—Why should he repent?

New trial came—The wife conceived it right
To see her parents; "So," he said, "she might,
If she had any fancy for a jail,
But upon him no creature should prevail;
No! he would never be again the fool
To go and starve, or study at a school!"

"O! but to see her parents!"—"Well! the sight
Might give her pleasure—very like it might,
And she might go; but to his house restored,
He would not now be catechised and bored."

It was her duty;—"Well!" said he again,
"There you may go—and there you may remain!"

Already this?—Even so: he heard it said
How rash and heedless was the part he play'd;
For love of money in his spirit dwelt,
And there repentance was intensely felt:
His guardian told him he had bought a toy
At tenfold price, and bargain'd like a boy:
Angry at truth, and wrought to fierce disdain,
He swore his loss should be no woman's gain;
His table she might share, his name she must,
But if aught more—she gets it upon trust.

For a few weeks his pride her face display'd—
He then began to thwart her, and upbraid;
He grew imperious, insolent, and loud—
His blinded weakness made his folly proud;
He would be master,—she had no pretence
To counsel him, as if he wanted sense;
He must inform her, she already cost
More than her worth, and more should not be lost
But still concluding, "if your will be so
That you must see the old ones, do it—go!"

Some weeks the Doctor waited, and the while
His lady preach'd in no consoling style:
At last she fear'd that rustic had convey'd
Their child to prison—yes, she was afraid,—
There to remain in that old hall alone
With the vile heads of stags, and floors of stone.

"Why did you, sir, who know such things so well,
And teach us good, permit them to rebel?
Had you o'erawed and check'd them when in sight,
They would not then have ventured upon flight—
Had you"——"Out, serpent! did not you begin?
What! introduce, and then upbraid the sin!
For sin it is, as I too well perceive:
But leave me, woman, to reflection leave;
Then to your closet fly, and on your knees
Beg for forgiveness for such sins as these."

"A moody morning!" with a careless air
Replied the wife—"Why counsel me to prayer?
I think the lord and teacher of a school
Should pray himself, and keep his temper cool."

Calm grew the husband when the wife was gone—
"The game," said he, "is never lost till won:
'T is true, the rebels fly their proper home,
They come not nigh, because they fear to come;
And for my purpose fear will doubtless prove
Of more importance and effect than love;—
Suppose me there—suppose the carriage stops,
Down on her knees my trembling daughter drops;
Slowly I raise her, in my arms to fall,
And call for mercy as she used to call;
And shall that boy, who dreaded to appear
Before me, cast away at once his fear!
'T is not in nature! He who once would cower
Beneath my frown, and sob for half an hour;
He who would kneel with motion prompt and quick
If I but look'd—as dogs that do a trick;
He still his knee-joints flexible must feel,
And have a slavish promptitude to kneel;—
Soon as he sees me he will drop his lip,
And bend like one made ready for the whip:

O! come, I trifle, let me haste away—
What! throw it up, when I have cards to play?"

The Doctor went, a self-invited guest;
He met his pupil, and his frown repress'd,
For in those lowering looks he could discern
Resistance sullen and defiance stern;
Yet was it painful to put off his style
Of awful distance, and assume a smile:
So between these, the gracious and the grand,
Succeeded nothing that the Doctor plann'd.

The sullen youth, with some reviving dread,
Bow'd and then hang'd disconsolate his head;
And, muttering welcome in a muffled tone,
Stalk'd 'cross the park to meditate alone,
Saying, or rather seeming to have said,
"Go! seek your daughter, and be there obey'd."

He went—The daughter her distresses told,
But found her father to her interests cold;
He kindness and complacency advised;
She answer'd, "these were sure to be despised;
That of the love her husband once possess'd
Not the least spark was living in his breast;
The boy repented and grew savage soon;
There never shone for her a honey-moon.
Soon as he came, his cares all fix'd on one,
Himself, and all his passion was a gun;
And though he shot as he did all beside,
It still remain'd his only joy and pride:
He left her there,—she knew not where he went,—
But knew full well he should the slight repent;
She was not one his daily taunts to bear,
He made the house a hell that he should share;
For, till he gave her power herself to please,
Never for him should be a moment's ease."

"He loves you, child!" the softening father cried:
—"He loves himself, and not a soul beside:
Loves me! why, yes, and so he did the pears
You caught him stealing—would he had the fears!
Would you could make him tremble for his life,
And then to you return the stolen wife,
Richly endow'd—but, O! the idiot knows
The worth of every penny he bestows.

Were he but fool alone, I'd find a way
To govern him, at least to have my day;
Or were he only brute, I'd watch the hour,
And make the brute-affection yield me power;
But silly both and savage—O! my heart;
It is too great a trial!—we must part."

"Oblige the savage by some act!"—"The debt,
You find, the fool will instantly forget;
Oblige the fool with kindness or with praise,
And you the passions of the savage raise."

"Time will do much."—"Can time my name restore?"
"Have patience, child."—"I am a child no more;
Nor more dependent; but, at woman's age,
I feel that wrongs provoke me and enrage:
Sir, could you bring me comfort, I were cool;
But keep your counsel for your boys at school."

26

The Doctor then departed—Why remain
To hear complaints, who could himself complain,
Who felt his actions wrong, and knew his efforts vain?

The sullen youth, contending with his fate,
Began the darling of his heart to hate;
Her pretty looks, her auburn braid, her face,
All now remain'd the proofs of his disgrace;
While, more than hateful in his vixen's eyes,
He saw her comforts from his griefs arise;
Who felt a joy she strove not to conceal,
When their expenses made her miser feel.

War was perpetual: on a first attack
She gain'd advantage, he would turn his back;
And when her small-shot whistled in his ears,
He felt a portion of his early fears;
But if he turn'd him in the battle's heat,
And fought in earnest, hers was then defeat;
His strength of oath and curse brought little harm
But there was no resisting strength of arm.

Yet wearied both with war, and vex'd at heart,
The slaves of passion judged it best to part:
Long they debated, nor could fix a rate
For a man's peace with his contending mate;
But mutual hatred, scorn, and fear, assign'd
That price—that peace it was not theirs to find.

The watchful husband lived in constant hope
To hear the wife had ventured to elope;
But though not virtuous, nor in much discreet,
He found her coldness would such views defeat;
And thus, by self-reproof and avarice scourged,
He wore the galling chains his folly forged.

The wife her pleasures, few and humble, sought,
And with anticipated stipend bought;
Without a home, at fashion's call she fled
To a hired lodging and a widow'd bed;
Husband and parents banish'd from her mind,
She seeks for pleasures that she cannot find;
And grieves that so much treachery was employ'd
To gain a man who has her peace destroy'd.

Yet more the grieving father feels distress,
His error greater, and his motives less;
He finds too late, by stooping to deceit,
It is ourselves and not the world we cheat;
For, though we blind it, yet we can but feel
That we have something evil to conceal;
Nor can we by our utmost care be sure
That we can hide the sufferings we endure.

BOOK XVI.

LADY BARBARA; OR, THE GHOST.

Introductory Discourse—For what Purpose would a Ghost appear?—How the Purpose would be answered—The Fact admitted, would not Doubts return?—Family Stories of Apparitions—Story of Lady Barbara—Her Widowhood—Resides with a Priest—His Family—A favourite Boy—

His Education—His Fondness for the Lady—It becomes Love—His Reflections—His Declaration—Her Reply—Her Relation—Why she must not marry a second Time—How warned—Tokens of the Appearance—The Lover argues with the Lady—His Success—The Consequences of it.

The Brothers spoke of Ghosts,—a favourite theme
With those who love to reason or to dream;
Why they, as greater men were wont to do,
Felt strong desire to think the stories true;
Stories of spirits freed, who came to prove
To spirits bound in flesh that yet they love,
To give them notice of the things below,
Which we must wonder how they came to know,
Or known, would think of coming to relate
To creatures who are tried by unknown fate.

"Warning," said Richard, "seems the only thing
That would a spirit on an errand bring;
To turn a guilty mind from wrong to right
A ghost might come, at least I think it might."

"But," said the Brother, "if we here are tried,
A spirit sent would put that law aside;
It gives to some advantage others need,
Or hurts the sinner should it not succeed:
If from the dead, said Dives, one were sent
To warn my brethren, sure they would repent;
But Abraham answer'd, if they now reject
The guides they have, no more would that effect;
Their doubts too obstinate for grace would prove,
For wonder hardens hearts it fails to move.

Suppose a sinner in an hour of gloom,
And let a ghost with all its horrors come;
From lips unmoved let solemn accents flow,
Solemn his gesture be, his motion slow;
Let the waved hand and threatening look impart
Truth to the mind and terror to the heart;
And, when the form is fading to the view,
Let the convicted man cry, 'this is true!'

Alas! how soon would doubts again invade
The willing mind, and sins again persuade!
I saw it—What?—I was awake, but how?
Not as I am, or I should see it now:
It spoke, I think,—I thought, at least, it spoke,—
And look'd alarming—yes, I felt the look.

But then in sleep those horrid forms arise,
That the soul sees,—and, we suppose, the eyes,—
And the soul hears,—the senses then thrown by,
She is herself the ear, herself the eye;
A mistress so will free her servile race
For their own tasks, and take herself the place:
In sleep what forms will ductile fancy take,
And what so common as to dream awake?
On others thus do ghostly guests intrude?
Or why am I by such advice pursued?
One out of millions who exist, and why
They know not—cannot know—and such am I;
And shall two beings of two worlds, to meet,
The laws of one, perhaps of both, defeat?
It cannot be—But if some being lives
Who such kind warning to a favourite gives,
Let him these doubts from my dull spirit clear,
And once again, expected guest! appear.

And if a second time the power complied,
Why is a third, and why a fourth denied?
Why not a warning ghost for ever at our side?
Ah, foolish being! thou hast truth enough,
Augmented guilt would rise on greater proof;
Blind and imperious passion disbelieves,
Or madly scorns the warning it receives,
Or looks for pardon ere the ill be done,
Because 't is vain to strive our fate to shun;
In spite of ghosts, predestined woes would come,
And warning add new terrors to our doom.

Yet there are tales that would remove our doubt,
The whisper'd tales that circulate about,
That in some noble mansion take their rise,
And told with secresy and awe, surprise:
It seems not likely people should advance,
For Falsehood's sake, such train of circumstance;
Then the ghosts bear them with a ghost-like grace,
That suits the person, character, and place.

But let us something of the kind recite:
What think you, now, of Lady Barbara's sprite?"

"I know not what to think; but I have heard
A ghost, to warn her or advise, appear'd;
And that she sought a friend before she died
To whom she might the awful fact confide,
Who seal'd and secret should the story keep
Till Lady Barbara slept her final sleep,
In that close bed, that never spirit shakes,
Nor ghostly visiter the sleeper wakes."

"Yes, I can give that story, not so well
As your old woman would the legend tell,
But as the facts are stated: and now hear
How ghosts advise, and widows persevere."

When her lord died, who had so kind a heart,
That any woman would have grieved to part,
It had such influence on his widow's mind,
That she the pleasures of the world resign'd,
Young as she was, and from the busy town
Came to the quiet of a village down;
Not as insensible to joys, but still
With a subdued but half-rebellious will;
For she had passions warm, and feeling strong,
With a right mind, that dreaded to be wrong;—
Yet she had wealth to tie her to the place
Where it procures delight and veils disgrace;
Yet she had beauty to engage the eye,
A widow still in her minority;
Yet she had merit worthy men to gain,
And yet her hand no merit could obtain;
For, though secluded, there were trials made,
When he who soften'd most could not persuade,
Awhile she hearken'd as her swain proposed,
And then his suit with strong refusal closed.

"Thanks and farewell!—give credit to my word,
That I shall die the widow of my lord;
'T is my own will, I now prefer the state,—
If mine should change, it is the will of fate."

Such things were spoken, and the hearers cried,
"'T is very strange,—perhaps she may be tried."

The lady past her time in taking air,
In working, reading, charities, and prayer;
In the last duties she received the aid
Of an old friend, a priest, with whom she pray'd;
And to his mansion with a purpose went,
That there should life be innocently spent;
Yet no cold vot'ress of the cloister she,
Warm her devotion, warm her charity;
The face the index of a feeling mind,
And her whole conduct rational and kind.

Though rich and noble, she was pleased to slide
Into the habits of her reverend guide,
And so attended to his girls and boys,
She seem'd a mother in her fears and joys;
On her they look'd with fondness, something check'd
By her appearance, that engaged respect;
For still she dress'd as one of higher race,
And her sweet smiles had dignity and grace.

George was her favourite, and it gave her joy
To indulge and to instruct the darling boy;
To watch, to soothe, to check the forward child,
Who was at once affectionate and wild;
Happy and grateful for her tender care,
And pleased her thoughts and company to share.

George was a boy with spirit strong and high,
With handsome face, and penetrating eye;
O'er his broad forehead hung his locks of brown,
That gave a spirit to his boyish frown;
"My little man," were words that she applied
To him, and he received with growing pride;
Her darling, even from his infant years,
Had something touching in his smiles and tears;
And in his boyish manners he began
To show the pride that was not made for man;
And it became the child, the mother cried,
And the kind lady said it was not pride.

George, to his cost, though sometimes to his praise,
Was quite a hero in these early days,
And would return from heroes just as stout,
Blood in his crimson cheek, and blood without.

"What! he submit to vulgar boys and low,
He bear an insult, he forget a blow!
They call'd him Parson—let his father bear
His own reproach, it was his proper care;
He was no parson, but he still would teach
The boys their manners, and yet would not preach."

The father, thoughtful of the time foregone,
Was loth to damp the spirit of his son;
Rememb'ring he himself had early laurels won;
The mother, frighten'd, begg'd him to refrain,
And not his credit or his linen stain:
While the kind friend so gently blamed the deed,
He smiled in tears, and wish'd her to proceed;
For the boy pleased her, and that roguish eye
And darling look were cause of many a sigh,
When she had thought how much would such quick temper try:
And oft she felt a kind of gathering gloom,
Sad, and prophetic of the ills to come.

Years fled unmark'd; the lady taught no more
Th' adopted tribe, as she was wont before;
But by her help the school the lasses sought,
And by the vicar's self the boy was taught;
Not unresisting when that cursed Greek
Ask'd so much time for words that none will speak.

"What can men worse for mortal brain contrive
Than thus a hard dead language to revive!
Heav'ns, if a language once be fairly dead,
Let it be buried, not preserved and read,
The bane of every boy to decent station bred.
If any good these crabbed books contain,
Translate them well, and let them then remain;
To one huge vault convey the useless store,
Then lose the key, and never find it more."

Something like this the lively boy express'd,
When Homer was his torment and his jest.

"George," said the father, "can at pleasure seize
The point he wishes, and with too much ease;
And hence, depending on his powers and vain,
He wastes the time that he will sigh to gain."

The partial widow thought the wasted days
He would recover, urged by love and praise;
And thus absolved, the boy, with grateful mind,
Repaid a love so useful and so blind;
Her angry words he loved, although he fear'd,
And words not angry doubly kind appear'd.

George, then on manhood verging, felt the charms
Of war, and kindled at the world's alarms;
Yet war was then, though spreading wide and far
A state of peace to what has since been war:
'T was then some dubious claim at sea or land,
That placed a weapon in a warrior's hand;
But in these times the causes of our strife
Are hearth and altar, liberty and life.

George, when from college he return'd, and heard
His father's questions, cold and shy appear'd.

"Who had the honours?"—"Honours!" said the youth,
"Honour at college!—very good, in truth!"

"What hours to study did he give?"—He gave
Enough to feel they made him like a slave—
And the good vicar found, if George should rise,
It would not be by college exercise.

"At least the time for your degree abide,
And be ordain'd," the man of peace replied;
"Then you may come and aid me while I keep,
And watch, and shear the hereditary sheep;
Choose then your spouse."—That heard the youth and sigh'd,
Nor to aught else attended or replied.

George had of late indulged unusual fears
And dangerous hopes: he wept unconscious tears;—
Whether for camp or college, well he knew
He must at present bid his friends adieu;
His father, mother, sisters,—could he part
With these, and feel no sorrow at his heart?

But from that lovely lady could he go?
That fonder, fairer, dearer mother?—No!
For while his father spoke, he fix'd his eyes
On that dear face, and felt a warmth arise,
A trembling flush of joy, that he could ill disguise—
Then ask'd himself from whence this growing bliss,
This new-found joy, and all that waits on this?
Why sinks that voice so sweetly in mine ear?
What makes it now a livelier joy to hear?
Why gives that touch—Still, still do I retain
The fierce delight that tingled through each vein—
Why at her presence with such quickness flows
The vital current?—Well a lover knows.

O! tell me not of years,—can she be old?
Those eyes, those lips, can man unmoved behold?
Has time that bosom chill'd? are cheeks so rosy cold?
No, she is young, or I her love t' engage
Will grow discreet, and that will seem like age:
But speak it not; Death's equalizing arm
Levels not surer than Love's stronger charm,
That bids all inequalities be gone,
That laughs at rank, that mocks comparison.

There is not young or old, if Love decrees,
He levels orders, he confounds degrees;
There is not fair, or dark, or short, or tall,
Or grave, or sprightly—Love reduces all;
From each abundant good a portion takes,
And for each want a compensation makes;
Then tell me not of years—Love, power divine,
Takes, as he wills, from hers, and gives to mine.

And she, in truth, was lovely—Time had strown
No snows on her, though he so long had flown;
The purest damask blossom'd in her cheek,
The eyes said all that eyes are wont to speak;
Her pleasing person she with care adorn'd,
Nor arts that stay the flying graces scorn'd;
Nor held it wrong these graces to renew,
Or give the fading rose its opening hue:
Yet few there were who needed less the art
To hide an error, or a grace impart.

George, yet a child, her faultless form admired,
And call'd his fondness love, as truth required;
But now, when conscious of the secret flame,
His bosom's pain, he dared not give the name;
In her the mother's milder passion grew,
Tender she was, but she was placid too;
From him the mild and filial love was gone,
And a strong passion came in triumph on.

"Will she," he cried, "this impious love allow?
And, once my mother, be my mistress now?
The parent-spouse? how far the thought from her,
And how can I the daring wish aver?
When first I speak it, how will those dear eyes
Gleam with awaken'd horror and surprise;
Will she not, angry and indignant, fly
From my imploring call, and bid me die?
Will she not shudder at the thought, and say,
My son! and lift her eyes to heaven and pray?
Alas! I fear—and yet my soul she won
While she with fond endearments call'd me son!
Then first I felt—yet knew that I was wrong—
This hope, at once so guilty and so strong:
She gave—I feel it now—a mother's kiss,
And quickly fancy took a bolder bliss;
But hid the burning blush, for fear that eye
Should see the transport, and the bliss deny:
O! when she knows the purpose I conceal,
When my fond wishes to her bosom steal,
How will the angel fear? How will the woman feel?

And yet perhaps this instant, while I speak,
She knows the pain I feel, the cure I seek;
Better than I she may my feelings know,
And nurse the passion that she dares not show:
She reads the look,—and sure my eyes have shown
To her the power and triumph of her own,—
And in maternal love she veils the flame
That she will heal with joy, yet hear with shame.

Come, let me then—no more a son—reveal
The daring hope, and for her favour kneel;
Let me in ardent speech my meanings dress,
And, while I mourn the fault, my love confess;
And, once confess'd, no more that hope resign,
For she or misery henceforth must be mine.

O! what confusion shall I see advance
On that dear face, responsive to my glance!
Sure she can love!"

In fact, the youth was right;
She could, but love was dreadful in her sight;
Love like a spectre in her view appear'd,
The nearer he approach'd the more she fear'd.

But knew she, then, this dreaded love? She guess'd
That he had guilt—she knew he had not rest:
She saw a fear that she could ill define,
And nameless terrors in his looks combine;
It is a state that cannot long endure,
And yet both parties dreaded to be sure.

All views were past of priesthood and a gown,
George, fix'd on glory, now prepared for town;
But first this mighty hazard must be run,
And more than glory either lost or won:
Yet, what was glory? Could he win that heart
And gain that hand, what cause was there to part?
Her love afforded all that life affords—
Honour and fame were phantasies and words!

But he must see her—She alone was seen
In the still evening of a day serene:
In the deep shade beyond the garden walk
They met, and talking, ceased and fear'd to talk;
At length she spoke of parent's love,—and now
He hazards all—"No parent, lady, thou!
None, none to me! but looks so fond and mild
Would well become the parent of my child"

She gasp'd for breath—then sat as one resolved
On some high act, and then the means revolved.

"It cannot be, my George, my child, my son!
The thought is misery!—Guilt and misery shun:
Far from us both be such design, O, far!
Let it not pain us at the awful bar,
Where souls are tried, where known the mother's part
That I sustain, and all of either heart.

To wed with thee I must all shame efface,
And part with female dignity and grace:
Was I not told, by one who knew so well
This rebel heart, that it must not rebel?
Were I not warn'd, yet Reason's voice would cry,
'Retreat, resolve, and from the danger fly!'
If Reason spoke not, yet would woman's pride
A woman's will by better counsel guide;
And should both Pride and Prudence plead in vain,
There is a warning that must still remain,
And, though the heart rebell'd, would ever cry 'Refrain.'"

He heard, he grieved—so check'd, the eager youth
Dared not again repeat th' offensive truth,
But stopp'd and fix'd on that loved face an eye
Of pleasing passion, trembling to reply;
And that reply was hurried, was express'd
With bursts of sorrow from a troubled breast;
He could not yet forbear the tender suit,
Yet dared not speak—his eloquence was mute.
But though awhile in silence he suppresst
The pleading voice, and bade his passion rest,
Yet in each motion, in each varying look,
In every tender glance, that passion spoke.—
Words find, ere long, a passage; and once more
He warmly urges what he urged before;
He feels acutely, and he thinks, of course,
That what he feels his language will enforce;
Flame will to flame give birth, and fire to fire,
And so from heart to heart is caught desire;
He wonders how a gentle mind so long
Resists the pleading of a love so strong—
"And can that heart," he cries, "that face belie,
And know no softness? Will it yet deny?"—

"I tell thee, George, as I have told before,
I feel a mother's love, and feel no more;
A child I bore thee in my arms, and how
Could I—did prudence yield—receive thee now?"

At her remonstrance hope revived, for oft
He found her words severe, her accents soft;
In eyes that threaten'd tears of pity stood,
And truth she made as gracious as she could;—
But, when she found the dangerous youth would seek
His peace alone, and still his wishes speak,
Fearful she grew, that, opening thus his heart,
He might to hers a dangerous warmth impart:
All her objections slight to him appear'd,—
But one she had, and now it must be heard.

"Yes, it must be! and he shall understand
What powers, that are not of the world, command;
So shall he cease, and I in peace shall live—"
Sighing she spoke—"that widowhood can give!"
Then to her lover turn'd, and gravely said,
"Let due attention to my words be paid:
Meet me to-morrow, and resolve t' obey;"
Then named the hour and place, and went her way.

Before that hour, or moved by spirit vain
Of woman's wish to triumph and complain,
She had his parents summon'd, and had shown
Their son's strong wishes, nor conceal'd her own:
"And do you give," she said, "a parent's aid
To make the youth of his strange love afraid;
And, be it sin or not, be all the shame display'd."

The good old pastor wonder'd, seem'd to grieve,
And look'd suspicious on this child of Eve:
He judged his boy, though wild, had never dared
To talk of love, had not rebuke been spared;
But he replied, in mild and tender tone,
"It is not sin, and therefore shame has none."
The different ages of the pair he knew,
And quite as well their different fortunes too:
A meek, just man; but difference in his sight
That made the match unequal made it right:
"His son, his friend united, and become
Of his own hearth—the comforts of his home—
Was it so wrong? Perhaps it was her pride
That felt the distance, and the youth denied?"

The blushing widow heard, and she retired,
Musing on what her ancient friend desired;
She could not, therefore, to the youth complain,
That his good father wish'd him to refrain;
She could not add, your parents, George, obey,
They will your absence—no such will had they.

Now, in th' appointed minute met the pair,
Foredoom'd to meet: George made the lover's prayer,—
That was heard kindly; then the lady tried
For a calm spirit, felt it, and replied.

"George, that I love thee why should I suppress?
For 't is a love that virtue may profess—
Parental,—frown not,—tender, fix'd, sincere;
Thou art for dearer ties by much too dear,
And nearer must not be, thou art so very near:
Nay, do not reason, prudence, pride agree,
Our very feelings, that it must not be.
Nay, look not so, I shun the task no more,
But will to thee thy better self restore.

Then hear, and hope not; to the tale I tell
Attend! obey me, and let all be well.
Love is forbad to me, and thou wilt find
All thy too ardent views must be resign'd;
Then from thy bosom all such thoughts remove,
And spare the curse of interdicted love.

If doubts at first assail thee, wait awhile,
Nor mock my sadness with satiric smile;
For, if not much of other worlds we know,
Nor how a spirit speaks in this below,
Still there is speech and intercourse; and now
The truth of what I tell I first avow,
True will I be in all, and be attentive thou.

"I was a Ratcliffe, taught and train'd to live
In all the pride that ancestry can give;
My only brother, when our mother died,
Fill'd the dear offices of friend and guide;
My father early taught us all he dared,
And for his bolder flights our minds prepared.
He read the works of deists, every book
From crabbed Hobbes to courtly Bolingbroke,
And when we understood not, he would cry,
Let the expressions in your memory lie,

The light will soon break in, and you will find
Rest for your spirits, and be strong of mind!

Alas! however strong, however weak,
The rest was something we had still to seek!

He taught us duties of no arduous kind,
The easy morals of the doubtful mind;
He bade us all our childish fears control,
And drive the nurse and grandam from the soul;
Told us the word of God was all we saw,
And that the law of nature was his law;
This law of nature we might find abstruse,
But gain sufficient for our common use.

Thus, by persuasion, we our duties learn'd,
And were but little in the cause concern'd.
We lived in peace, in intellectual ease,
And thought that virtue was the way to please,
And pure morality the keeping free
From all the stains of vulgar villany.

But Richard, dear enthusiast! shunn'd reproach,
He let no stain upon his name encroach;
But fled the hated vice, was kind and just,
That all must love him, and that all might trust.

Free, sad discourse was ours; we often sigh'd
To think we could not in some truths confide:
Our father's final words gave no content,
We found not what his self-reliance meant:
To fix our faith some grave relations sought,
Doctrines and creeds of various kind they brought,
And we as children heard what they as doctors
taught.

Some to the priest referr'd us, in whose book
No unbeliever could resisting look;
Others to some great preacher's, who could tame
The fiercest mind, and set the cold on flame;
For him no rival in dispute was found
Whom he could not confute or not confound.
Some mystics told us of the sign and seal,
And what the spirit would in time reveal,
If we had grace to wait, if we had hearts to feel:
Others, to reason trusting, said, believe
As she directs, and what she proves receive;
While many told us, it is all but guess,
Stick to your church, and calmly acquiesce.

Thus, doubting, wearied, hurried, and perplex'd,
This world was lost in thinking of the next:
When spoke my brother—'From my soul I hate
This clash of thought, this ever-doubting state;
For ever seeking certainty, yet blind
In our research, and puzzled when we find.

Could not some spirit, in its kindness, steal
Back to our world, and some dear truth reveal?
Say there is danger,—if it could be done,
Sure one would venture,—I would be the one;
And when a spirit—much as spirits might—
I would to thee communicate my light!'

I sought my daring brother to oppose,
But awful gladness in my bosom rose:
I fear'd my wishes; but through all my frame
A bold and elevating terror came:

Yet with dissembling prudence I replied,
'Know we the laws that may be thus defied?
Should the free spirit to th' embodied tell
The precious secret, would it not rebel?'
Yet while I spoke I felt a pleasing glow
Suffuse my cheek at what I long'd to know;
And I, like Eve transgressing, grew more bold
And wish'd to hear a spirit and behold.

'I have no friend,' said he, 'to not one man
Can I appear; but, love! to thee I can:
Who first shall die'——I wept, but—'I agree
To all thou say'st, dear Richard! and would be
The first to wing my way, and bring my news to
thee.'

Long we conversed, but not till we perceived
A gathering gloom—Our freedom gain'd, we
grieved;
Above the vulgar, as we judged, in mind,
Below in peace, more sad as more refined;
'T was joy, 't was sin—Offenders at the time,
We felt the hurried pleasure of our crime
With pain that time creates, and this in both—
Our mind united as the strongest oath.
O, my dear George! in ceasing to obey,
Misery and trouble meet us in our way!
I felt as one intruding in a scene
Where none should be, where none had ever been;
Like our first parent, I was new to sin,
But plainly felt its sufferings begin:
In nightly dreams I walk'd on soil unsound,
And in my day-dreams endless error found.

With this dear brother I was doom'd to part,
Who, with a husband, shared a troubled heart:
My lord I honour'd; but I never proved
The madd'ning joy, the boast of some who loved:
It was a marriage that our friends profess'd
Would be most happy, and I acquiesced;
And we were happy, for our love was calm,
Not life's delicious essence, but its balm.

My brother left us,—dear, unhappy boy!
He never seem'd to taste of earthly joy,
Never to live on earth, but ever strove
To gain some tidings of a world above.

Parted from him, I found no more to please,
Ease was my object, and I dwelt in ease;
And thus in quiet, not perhaps content,
A year in wedlock, lingering time! was spent.

One night I slept not, but I courted sleep,
And forced my thoughts on tracks they could not
keep;
Till nature, wearied in the strife, reposed,
And deep forgetfulness my wanderings closed.

My lord was absent—distant from the bed
A pendent lamp its soften'd lustre shed;
But there was light that chased away the gloom,
And brought to view each object in the room:
These I observed ere yet I sunk in sleep,
That, if disturb'd not, had been long and deep.
I was awaken'd by some being nigh,
It seem'd some voice, and gave a timid cry,—
When sounds, that I describe not, slowly broke
On my attention——'Be composed, and look!'-

I strove, and I succeeded; look'd with awe,
But yet with firmness, and my brother saw.

George, why that smile!—By all that God has done,
By the great Spirit, by the blessed Son,
By the one holy Three, by the thrice holy One,
I saw my brother,—saw him by my bed,
And every doubt in full conviction fled!—
It was his own mild spirit—He awhile
Waited my calmness with benignant smile;
So softly shines the veiled sun, till past
The cloud, and light upon the world is cast;
That look composed and soften'd I survey'd,
And met the glance fraternal less afraid;
Though in those looks was something of command,
And traits of what I fear'd to understand.

Then spoke the spirit—George, I pray, attend—
'First let all doubts of thy religion end—
The word reveal'd is true: inquire no more,
Believe in meekness, and with thanks adore:
Thy priest attend, but not in all rely,
And to objectors seek for no reply:
Truth, doubt, and error, will be mix'd below—
Be thou content the greater truths to know,
And in obedience rest thee——For thy life
Thou needest counsel—now a happy wife,
A widow soon! and then, my sister, then
Think not of marriage, think no more of men;—
Life will have comforts; thou wilt much enjoy
Of moderate good, then do not this destroy;
Fear much, and wed no more; by passion led,
Shouldst thou again'—Art thou attending?—'wed,
Care in thy ways will growl, and anguish haunt thy bed:
A brother's warning on thy heart engrave:
Thou art a mistress—then be not a slave!
Shouldst thou again that hand in fondness give,
What life of misery art thou doom'd to live!
How wilt thou weep, lament, implore, complain!
How wilt thou meet derision and disdain!
And pray to heaven in doubt, and kneel to man in vain!
Thou read'st of woes to tender bosoms sent—
Thine shall with tenfold agony be rent;
Increase of anguish shall new years bestow,
Pain shall on thought and grief on reason grow,
And this th' advice I give increase the ill I show.'

'A second marriage!—No!—by all that's dear!'
I cried aloud—The spirit bade me hear.

'There will be trial,—how I must not say,
Perhaps I cannot—listen, and obey!—
Free is thy will—th' event I cannot see,
Distinctly cannot, but thy will is free:
Come, weep not, sister—spirits can but guess,
And not ordain—but do not wed distress;
For who would rashly venture on a snare?'
'I swear!' I answer'd.—'No, thou must not swear,'
He said, or I had sworn; but still the vow
Was past, was in my mind, and there is now:
Never! O, never!—Why that sullen air?
Think'st thou—ungenerous!—I would wed despair?

Was it not told me thus?—and then I cried,
'Art thou in bliss?'—but nothing he replied,
Save of my fate, for that he came to show,
Nor of aught else permitted me to know.

'Forewarn'd, forearm thee, and thy way pursue,
Safe, if thou wilt, not flow'ry—now, adieu!'
'Nay, go not thus,' I cried, 'for this will seem
The work of sleep, a mere impressive dream;
Give me some token, that I may indeed
From the suggestions of my doubts be freed!'

'Be this a token—ere the week be fled
Shall tidings greet thee from the newly dead.'

'Nay, but,' I said, with courage not my own,
'O! be some signal of thy presence shown;
Let not this visit with the rising day
Pass, and be melted like a dream away.'

'O, woman! woman! ever anxious still
To gain the knowledge, not to curb the will!
Have I not promised?—Child of sin, attend—
Make not a lying spirit of thy friend:
Give me thy hand!'——I gave it, for my soul
Was now grown ardent, and above control;
Eager I stretch'd it forth, and felt the hold
Of shadowy fingers, more than icy cold:
A nameless pressure on my wrist was made,
And instant vanish'd the beloved shade!
Strange it will seem, but, ere the morning came,
I slept, nor felt disorder in my frame:
Then came a dream—I saw my father's shade,
But not with awe like that my brother's made;
And he began—'What! made a convert, child!
Have they my favourite by their creed beguiled?
Thy brother's weakness I could well foresee,
But had, my girl, more confidence in thee:
Art thou, indeed, before their ark to bow?
I smiled before, but I am angry now:
Thee will they bind by threats, and thou wilt shake
At tales of terror that the miscreants make:
Between the bigot and enthusiast led,
Thou hast a world of miseries to dread:
Think for thyself, nor let the knaves or fools
Rob thee of reason, and prescribe thee rules.'

Soon as I woke, and could my thoughts collect,
What can I think, I cried, or what reject?
Was it my brother? Aid me, power divine!
Have I not seen him, left he not a sign!
Did I not then the placid features trace
That now remain—the air, the eye, the face?
And then my father—but how different seem
These visitations—this, indeed, a dream!

Then for that token on my wrist—'t is here,
And very slight to you it must appear;
Here, I'll withdraw the bracelet—'t is a speck!
No more! but 't is upon my life a check."

O! lovely all, and like its sister arm!
Call this a check, dear lady? 't is a charm—
A slight, an accidental mark—no more"——
Slight as it is, it was not there before:
Then was there weakness, and I bound it——Nay!
This is infringement—take those lips away!

On the fourth day came letters, and I cried,
Richard is dead, and named the day he died:
A proof of knowledge, true! but one, alas! of pride
The signs to me were brought, and not my lord,
But I impatient waited not the word;
And much he marvell'd, reading of the night
In which th' immortal spirit took its flight.

Yes! I beheld my brother at my bed,
The hour he died! the instant he was dead—
His presence now I see! now trace him as he fled.

Ah! fly me, George, in very pity, fly;
Thee I reject, but yield thee reasons why;
Our fate forbids,—the counsel heaven has sent
We must adopt, or grievously repent;
And I adopt"——George humbly bow'd, and sigh'd,
But, lost in thought, he look'd not nor replied;
Yet feebly utter'd in his sad adieu,
"I must not doubt thy truth, but perish if thou 'rt true."

But when he thought alone, his terror gone
Of the strange story, better views came on.

"Nay, my enfeebled heart, be not dismay'd!
A boy again, am I of ghosts afraid!
Does she believe it? Say she does believe,
Is she not born of error and of Eve?
O! there is lively hope I may the cause retrieve."

"'If you re-wed,' exclaim'd the Ghost—For what
Puts he the case, if marry she will not!
He knows her fate—but what am I about?
Do I believe?—'t is certain I have doubt,
And so has she,—what therefore will she do?
She the predicted fortune will pursue,
And by th' event will judge if her strange dream was true;
The strong temptation, to her thought applied
Will gain new strength, and will not be denied;
The very threat against the thing we love
Will the vex'd spirit to resistance move;
With vows to virtue weakness will begin,
And fears of sinning let in thoughts of sin."

Strong in her sense of weakness, now withdrew
The cautious lady from the lover's view;
But she perceived the looks of all were changed,—
Her kind old friends grew peevish and estranged;
A fretful spirit reign'd, and discontent
From room to room in sullen silence went;
And the kind widow was distress'd at heart
To think that she no comfort could impart:
"But he will go," she said, "and he will strive
In fields of glorious energy to drive
Love from his bosom—Yes, I then may stay,
And all will thank me on a future day."

So judged the lady, nor appear'd to grieve,
Till the young soldier came to take his leave;
But not of all assembled—No! he found
His gentle sisters all in sorrows drown'd;
With many a shaken hand, and many a kiss,
He cried, "Farewell! a solemn business this;
Nay, Susan, Sophie!—heaven and earth, my dears!
I am a soldier—What do I with tears?

He sought his parents;—they together walk'd,
And of their son, his views and dangers, talk'd;
They knew not how to blame their friend, but still
They murmur'd, "She may save us if she will:
Were not these visions working in her mind
Strange things—'t is in her nature to be kind."

Their son appear'd—He soothed them, and was bless'd,
But still the fondness of his soul confess'd—
And where the lady?—To her room retired!
Now show, dear son, the courage she required.

George bow'd in silence, trying for assent
To his hard fate, and to his trial went:
Fond, but yet fix'd, he found her in her room;
Firm, and yet fearful, she beheld him come:
Nor sought he favour now—No! he would meet his doom.

"Farewell! and, Madam, I beseech you pray
That this sad spirit soon may pass away;
That sword or ball would to the dust restore
This body, that the soul may grieve no more
For love rejected——O! that I could quit
The life I loathe, who am for nothing fit,
No, not to die!"——"Unhappy, wilt thou make
The house all wretched for thy passion's sake?
And most its grieving object?"

"Grieving?—No!
Or as a conqueror mourns a dying foe,
That makes his triumph sure——Couldst thou deplore
The evil done, the pain would be no more;
But an accursed dream has steel'd thy breast,
And all the woman in thy soul suppress'd."—

"O! it was vision, George; a vision true
As ever seer or holy prophet knew."—

"Can spirits, lady, though they might alarm,
Make an impression on that lovely arm?
A little cold the cause, a little heat,
Or vein minute, or artery's morbid beat,
Even beauty these admit."—

"I did behold
My brother's form."—

"Yes, so thy Fancy told,
When in the morning she her work survey'd,
And call'd the doubtful Memory to her aid."—

"Nay, think! the night he died—the very night!"
"—'T is very true, and so perchance he might,
But in thy mind—not, lady, in thy sight!
Thou wert not well; forms delicately made
These dreams and fancies easily invade;
The mind and body feel the slow disease,
And dreams are what the troubled fancy sees."—

"O! but how strange that all should be combined!"
"True; but such combinations we may find;
A dream's predicted number gain'd a prize,
Yet dreams make no impression on the wise,
Though some chance good, some lucky gain may rise."

"O! but those words, that voice so truly known!"—
No doubt, dear lady, they were all thine own;
Memory for thee thy brother's form portray'd;
It was thy fear the awful warning made:
Thy former doubts of a religious kind
Account for all these wanderings of the mind."

"But then, how different when my father came!
These could not in their nature be the same!"—

"Yes, all are dreams; but some as we awake
Fly off at once, and no impression make:
Others are felt, and ere they quit the brain
Make such impression that they come again,
As half familiar thoughts, and half unknown,
And scarcely recollected as our own;
For half a day abide some vulgar dreams,
And give our grandams and our nurses themes;
Others, more strong, abiding figures draw
Upon the brain, and we assert 'I saw;'
And then the fancy on the organs place
A powerful likeness of a form and face.

Yet more—in some strong passion's troubled reign,
Or when the fever'd blood inflames the brain,
At once the outward and the inward eye
The real object and the fancied spy;
The eye is open and the sense is true,
And therefore they the outward object view;
But while the real sense is fix'd on these,
The power within its own creation sees;
And these, when mingled in the mind, create
Those striking visions which our dreamers state;
For knowing that is true that met the sight,
They think the judgment of the fancy right;——
Your frequent talk of dreams has made me turn
My mind on them, and these the facts I learn.
Or should you say, 't is not in us to take
Heed in both ways, to sleep and be awake,
Perhaps the things by eye and mind survey'd
Are in their quick alternate efforts made;
For by this mixture of the truth, the dream
Will in the morning fresh and vivid seem.

Dreams are like portraits, and we find they please
Because they are confess'd resemblances;
But those strange night-mare visions we compare
To waxen figures—they too real are,
Too much a very truth, and are so just
To life and death, they pain us or disgust.

Hence from your mind these idle visions shake,
And O! my love, to happiness awake!"—

"It *was* a warning, tempter! from the dead;
And, wedding thee, I should to misery wed!"—

"False and injurious! What! unjust to thee?
O! hear the vows of Love—it cannot be;
What, I forbear to bless thee?—I forego
That first great blessing of existence? Nö!
Did every ghost that terror saw arise
With such prediction, I should say it lies;
But none there are—a mighty gulf between
Hides the ideal world from objects seen;
We know not where unbodied spirits dwell,
But this we know, they are invisible;—
Yet I have one that fain would dwell with thee,
And always with thy purer spirit be."

"O! leave me, George!"
"To take the field, and die,
So leave thee, lady? Yes, I will comply;
Thou art too far above me—Ghosts withstand
My hopes in vain, but riches guard thy hand,
For I am poor—affection and a heart
To thee devoted, I but these impart:
Then bid me go, I will thy words obey,
But let not visions drive thy friend away."—

"Hear me, Oh! hear me—Shall I wed my son?"—
"I am in fondness and obedience one;
And I will reverence, honour, love, adore,
Be all that fondest sons can be—and more;
And shall thy son, if such he be, proceed
To fierce encounters, and in battle bleed?
No; thou canst weep!"—
"O! leave me, I entreat;
Leave me a moment—we shall quickly meet."—

"No! here I kneel, a beggar at thy feet."—
He said, and knelt—with accents, softer still,
He woo'd the weakness of a failing will,
And erring judgment—took her hand, and cried,
"Withdraw it not!—O! let it thus abide,
Pledge of thy love—upon thy act depend
My joy, my hope,—thus they begin or end!
Withdraw it not."——He saw her looks express'd
Favour and grace—the hand was firmer press'd;—
Signs of opposing fear no more were shown,
And, as he press'd, he felt it was his own.

Soon through the house was known the glad assent,
The night so dreaded was in comfort spent;
War was no more, the destined knot was tied,
And the fond widow made a fearful bride.

Let mortal frailty judge how mortals frail
Thus in their strongest resolutions fail,
And though we blame, our pity will prevail.

Yet, with that Ghost—for so she thought—in view,
When she believed that all he told was true;
When every threat was to her mind recall'd,
Till it became affrighten'd and appall'd;
When Reason pleaded, think! forbear! refrain!
And when, though trifling, stood that mystic stain,
Predictions, warnings, threats, were present all in
vain.

Th' exulting youth a mighty conqueror rose,
And who hereafter shall his will oppose?

Such is our tale; but we must yet attend
Our weak, kind widow to her journey's end;
Upon her death-bed laid, confessing to a friend
Her full belief, for to the hour she died
This she profess'd——"The truth I must not hide
It was my brother's form, and in the night he died
In sorrow and in shame has pass'd my time,
All I have suffer'd follow from my crime;
I sinn'd with warning—when I gave my hand
A power within said, urgently,—Withstand!
And I resisted—O! my God, what shame,
What years of torment from that frailty came

That husband-son!—I will my fault review;
What did he not that men or monsters do?
His day of love, a brief autumnal day,
Ev'n in its dawning hasten'd to decay;
Doom'd from our odious union to behold
How cold he grew, and then how worse than cold;
Eager he sought me, eagerly to shun,
Kneeling he woo'd me, but he scorn'd me, won;
The tears he caused served only to provoke
His wicked insult o'er the heart he broke;
My fond compliance served him for a jest,
And sharpen'd scorn——'I ought to be distress'd;
Why did I not with my chaste ghost comply!'
And with upbraiding scorn he told me why;—
O! there was grossness in his soul; his mind
Could not be raised, nor soften'd, nor refined.

Twice he departed in his rage, and went
I know not where, nor how his days were spent;
Twice he return'd a suppliant wretch, and craved,
Mean as profuse, the trifle I had saved.

I have had wounds, and some that never heal,
What bodies suffer, and what spirits feel;
But he is gone who gave them, he is fled
To his account! and my revenge is dead—
Yet is it duty, though with shame, to give
My sex a lesson—let my story live;
For if no ghost the promised visit paid,
Still was a deep and strong impression made,
That wisdom had approved, and prudence had obey'd;
But from another world that warning came,
And O! in this be ended all my shame!

Like the first being of my sex I fell,
Tempted, and with the tempter doom'd to dwell—
He was the master-fiend, and where he reign'd was hell."

This was her last, for she described no more
The rankling feelings of a mind so sore,
But died in peace.—One moral let us draw—
Be it a ghost or not the lady saw—

If our discretion tells us how to live,
We need no ghost a helping hand to give;
But if discretion cannot us restrain,
It then appears a ghost would come in vain.

BOOK XVII.

THE WIDOW.

The Morning Walk—Village Scenery—The Widow's Dwelling—Her Story related—The first Husband—His Indulgence—Its Consequence—Dies—The second—His Authority—Its Effects—His Death—A third Husband—Determinately indulgent—He dies also—The Widow's Retirement.

Richard one morning—it was custom now—
Walk'd and conversed with labourers at the plough,
With thrashers hastening to their daily task,
With woodmen resting o'er the enlivening flask,
And with the shepherd, watchful of his fold
Beneath the hill, and pacing in the cold:
Further afield he sometimes would proceed,
And take a path wherever it might lead.

It led him far about to Wickham Green,
Where stood the mansion of the village queen;
Her garden yet its wintry blossoms bore,
And roses graced the windows and the door—
That lasting kind that through the varying year
Or in the bud or in the bloom appear;
All flowers that now the gloomy days adorn
Rose on the view, and smiled upon that morn:
Richard a damsel at the window spied,
Who kindly drew a useless veil aside,
And show'd a lady who was sitting by,
So pensive, that he almost heard her sigh:
Full many years she could, no question, tell,
But in her mourning look'd extremely well.

"In truth," said Richard, when he told at night
His tale to George, "it was a pleasant sight;
She look'd like one who could, in tender tone,
Say, 'Will you let a lady sigh alone?
See! Time has touch'd me gently in his race,
And left no odious furrows in my face:
See, too, this house and garden, neat and trim,
Kept for its master—Will you stand for him?'

Say this is vain and foolish if you please,
But I believe her thoughts resembled these:
'Come!' said her looks, 'and we will kindly take
The visit kindness prompted you to make.'
And I was sorry that so much good play
Of eye and attitude was thrown away
On one who has his lot, on one who had his day.'

"Your pity, brother," George, with smile, replied,
"You may dismiss, and with it send your pride:
No need of pity, when the gentle dame
Has thrice resign'd and reassumed her name;
And be not proud—for, though it might be thine,
She would that hand to humbler men resign.

Young she is not,—it would be passing strange
If a young beauty thrice her name should change,
Yes! she has years beyond your reckoning seen—
Smiles and a window years and wrinkles screen;
But she, in fact, has that which may command
The warm admirer and the willing hand:
What is her fortune we are left to guess,
But good the sign—she does not much profess;
Poor she is not,—and there is that in her
That easy men to strength of mind prefer;
She may be made, with little care and skill,
Yielding her own, t' adopt a husband's will:
Women there are, who of a man will take
The helm, and steer—will no resistance make:
Who, if neglected, will the power assume,
And then what wonder if the shipwreck come?

Queens they will be if man allow the means,
And give the power to these domestic queens;
Whom, if he rightly trains, he may create
And make obedient members of his state."

Harriet at school was very much the same
As other misses, and so home she came,
Like other ladies, there to live and learn,
To wait her season, and to take her turn.

Their husbands maids as priests their livings gain,
The best, they find, are hardest to obtain:
On those that offer both awhile debate—
"I need not take it, it is not so late;
Better will come if we will longer stay,
And strive to put ourselves in fortune's way:"
And thus they wait, till many years are past,
For what comes slowly—*but it comes at last.*

Harriet was wedded,—but it must be said,
The vow'd obedience was not duly paid:
Hers was an easy man,—it gave him pain
To hear a lady murmur and complain:
He was a merchant, whom his father made
Rich in the gains of a successful trade:
A lot more pleasant, or a view more fair,
Has seldom fallen to a youthful pair.

But what is faultless in a world like this?
In every station something seems amiss:
The lady, married, found the house too small—
"Two shabby parlours, and that ugly hall!
Had we a cottage somewhere, and could meet
One's friends and favourites in one's snug retreat;
Or only join a single room to these,
It would be living something at our ease,
And have one's self, at home, the comfort that one
sees."

Such powers of reason, and of mind such strength,
Fought with man's fear, and they prevail'd at length;
The room was built,—and Harriet did not know
A prettier dwelling, either high or low;
But Harriet loved such conquests, loved to plead
With her reluctant man, and to succeed;
It was such pleasure to prevail o'er one
Who would oppose the thing that still was done,
Who never gain'd the race, but yet would groan
and run.

But there were times when love and pity gave
Whatever thoughtless vanity could crave:
She now the carriage chose with freshest name,
And was in quite a fever till it came;
But can a carriage be alone enjoy'd?
The pleasure not partaken is destroy'd;
"I must have some good creature to attend
On morning visits as a kind of friend."

A courteous maiden then was found to sit
Beside the lady, for her purpose fit,
Who had been train'd in all the soothing ways
And servile duties from her early days;
One who had never from her childhood known
A wish fulfill'd, a purpose of her own:
Her part it was to sit beside the dame,
And give relief in every want that came;
To soothe the pride, to watch the varying look,
And bow in silence to the dumb rebuke.

This supple being strove with all her skill
To draw her master's to her lady's will;
For they were like the magnet and the steel,
At times so distant that they could not feel;
Then would she gently move them, till she saw
That to each other they began to draw;
And then would leave them, sure on her return
In Harriet's joy her conquest to discern.

She was a mother now, and grieved to find
The nursery window caught the eastern wind;
What could she do with fears like these oppress'd?
She built a room all window'd to the west;
For sure in one so dull, so bleak, so old,
She and her children must expire with cold:
Meantime the husband murmur'd—"So he might;
She would be judged by Cousins—Was it right?"

Water was near them, and, her mind afloat,
The lady saw a cottage and a boat,
And thought what sweet excursions they might
make,
How they might sail, what neighbours they might
take,
And nicely would she deck the lodge upon the lake.

She now prevail'd by habit; had her will,
And found her patient husband sad and still:
Yet this displeased; she gain'd, indeed, the prize,
But not the pleasure of her victories;
Was she a child to be indulged? He knew
She would have right, but would have reason too.

Now came the time, when in her husband's face
Care, and concern, and caution she could trace;
His troubled features gloom and sadness bore,
Less he resisted, but he suffer'd more;
His nerves were shook like hers; in him her grief
Had much of sympathy, but no relief.

She could no longer read, and therefore kept
A girl to give her stories while she wept;
Better for Lady Julia's woes to cry,
Than have her own for ever in her eye:
Her husband grieved and o'er his spirits came
Gloom, and disease attack'd his slender frame;
He felt a loathing for the wretched state
Of his concerns, so sad, so complicate;
Grief and confusion seized him in the day,
And the night pass'd in agony away:
"My ruin comes!" was his awakening thought,
And vainly through the day was comfort sought;
"There, take my all!" he said, and in his dream
Heard the door bolted, and his children scream.
And he was right, for not a day arose
That he exclaim'd not, "Will it never close?"
"Would it were come!"—but still he shifted on,
Till health, and hope, and life's fair views were
gone.

Fretful herself, he of his wife in vain
For comfort sought——"He would be well again;
Time would disorders of such nature heal!
O! if he felt what she was doom'd to feel,
Such sleepless nights! such broken rest! her frame
Rack'd with diseases that she could not name!
With pangs like hers no other was oppress'd!"
Weeping, she said, and sigh'd herself to rest.

The suffering husband look'd the world around,
And saw no friend: on him misfortune frown'd,

Him self-reproach tormented; sorely tried,
By threats he mourn'd, and by disease he died.

As weak as wailing infancy or age,
How could the widow with the world engage?
Fortune not now the means of comfort gave,
Yet all her comforts Harriet wept to have.

"My helpless babes," she said, "will nothing know,"
Yet not a single lesson would bestow;
Her debts would overwhelm her, that was sure,
But one privation would she not endure;
"We shall want bread! the thing is past a doubt."—
"Then part with Cousins!"—"Can I do without?"—
"Dismiss your servants!"—"Spare me them, I pray!"—
"At least your carriage!"—"What will people say?"—
"That useless boat, that folly on the lake!"—
"O! but what cry and scandal will it make!"
It was so hard on her, who not a thing
Had done such mischief on their heads to bring;
This was her comfort, this she would declare,
And then slept soundly on her pillow'd chair:
When not asleep, how restless was the soul
Above advice, exempted from control!
For ever begging all to be sincere,
And never willing any truth to hear;
A yellow paleness o'er her visage spread,
Her fears augmented as her comforts fled;
Views dark and dismal to her mind appear'd,
And death she sometimes woo'd, and always fear'd.

Among the clerks there was a thoughtful one,
Who still believed that something might be done;
All in his view was not so sunk and lost,
But of a trial things would pay the cost:
He judged the widow, and he saw the way
In which her husband suffer'd her to stray;
He saw entangled and perplex'd affairs,
And Time's sure hand at work on their repairs;
Children he saw, but nothing could he see
Why he might not their careful father be;
And looking keenly round him, he believed
That what was lost might quickly be retrieved.

Now thought our clerk—"I must not mention love,
That she at least must seem to disapprove;
But I must fear of poverty enforce,
And then consent will be a thing of course.

"Madam!" said he, "with sorrow I relate
That our affairs are in a dreadful state;
I call'd on all our friends, and they declared
They dared not meddle—not a creature dared;
But still our perseverance chance may aid,
And though I'm puzzled, I am not afraid;
If you, dear lady, will attention give
To me, the credit of the house shall live;
Do not, I pray you, my proposal blame,
It is my wish to guard your husband's fame,
And ease your trouble: then your cares resign
To my discretion—and, in short, be mine."

'Yours! O! my stars!—Your goodness, sir, deserves
My grateful thanks—take pity on my nerves;
I shake and tremble at a thing so new,
And fear 't is what a lady should not do;
And then to marry upon ruin's brink
In all this hurry—What will people think?"

"Nay, there 's against us neither rule nor law,
And people's thinking is not worth a straw:
Those who are prudent have too much to do
With their own cares to think of me and you;
And those who are not are so poor a race,
That what they utter can be no disgrace:—
Come! let us now embark, when time and tide
Invite to sea, in happy hour decide;
If yet we linger, both are sure to fail,
The turning waters and the varying gale;
Trust me, our vessel shall be ably steer'd,
Nor will I quit her, till the rocks are clear'd."

Allured and frighten'd, soften'd and afraid,
The widow doubted, ponder'd, and obey'd:
So were they wedded, and the careful man
His reformation instantly began;
Began his state with vigour to reform,
And made a calm by laughing at the storm.

Th' attendant-maiden he dismiss'd—for why?
She might on him and love like his rely;
She needed none to form her children's mind,
That duty nature to her care assign'd;
In vain she mourn'd, it was her health he prized,
And hence enforced the measures he advised:
She wanted air; and walking, she was told,
Was safe, was pleasant!—he the carriage sold;
He found a tenant who agreed to take
The boat and cottage on the useless lake;
The house itself had now superfluous room,
And a rich lodger was induced to come.

The lady wonder'd at the sudden change,
That yet was pleasant, that was very strange;
When every deed by her desire was done,
She had no day of comfort—no, not one;
When nothing moved or stopp'd at her request,
Her heart had comfort, and her temper rest;
For all was done with kindness,—most polite
Was her new lord, and she confess'd it right;
For now she found that she could gaily live
On what the chance of common life could give:
And her sick mind was cured of every ill,
By finding no compliance with her will;
For when she saw that her desires were vain,
She wisely thought it foolish to complain.

Born for her man, she gave a gentle sigh
To her lost power, and grieved not to comply;
Within, without, the face of things improved,
And all in order and subjection moved.

As wealth increased, ambition now began
To swell the soul of the aspiring man;
In some few years he thought to purchase land,
And build a seat that Hope and Fancy plann'd;
To this a name his youthful bride should give!
Harriet, of course, not many years would live;
Then he would farm, and every soil should show
The tree that best upon the place would grow:
He would, moreover, on the bench debate
On sundry questions—when a magistrate;

It was a vast concern, including all
That we can happiness or comfort call:
And yet she found that those who waited long
Before their choice, had often chosen wrong;
Nothing, indeed, could for her loss atone,
But 't was the greater that she lived alone;
She, too, had means, and therefore what the use
Of more, that still more trouble would produce?
And pleasure too she own'd, as well as care,
Of which, at present, she had not her share.

The things he offer'd, she must needs confess,
They were all women's wishes, more or less;
But were expensive; though a man of sense
Would by his prudence lighten the expense:
Prudent he was, but made a sad mistake
When he proposed her faded face to take;
And yet 't is said there's beauty that will last
When the rose withers and the bloom be past.

One thing displeased her,—that he could suppose
He might so soon his purposes disclose;
Yet had she hints of such intent before,
And would excuse him if he wrote no more;
What would the world?—and yet she judged them fools
Who let the world's suggestions be their rules;
What would her friends?—Yet in her own affairs
It was her business to decide, not theirs:
Adieu! then, sir," she added; "thus you find
The changeless purpose of a steady mind,
In one now left alone, but to her fate resign'd."

The marriage follow'd; and th' experienced dame
Consider'd what the conduct that became
A thrice-devoted lady—She confess'd
That when indulged she was but more distress'd;
And by her second husband when controll'd,
Her life was pleasant, though her love was cold;
"Then let me yield," she said, and with a sigh,
"Let me to wrong submit, with right comply."

Alas! obedience may mistake, and they
Who reason not will err when they obey;
And fated was the gentle dame to find
Her duty wrong, and her obedience blind.

The man was kind, but would have no dispute,
His love and kindness both were absolute;
She needed not her wishes to express
To one who urged her on to happiness;
For this he took her to the lakes and seas,
To mines and mountains, nor allow'd her ease,
She must be pleased, he said, and he must live to please.

He hurried north and south, and east and west;
When age required, they would have time to rest:
He in the richest dress her form array'd,
And cared not what he promised, what he paid;
She should share all his pleasures as her own,
And see whatever could be sought or shown.

This run of pleasure for a time she bore,
And then affirm'd that she could taste no more;
She loved it while its nature it retain'd,
But made a duty, it displeased and pain'd:
"Have we not means?" the joyous husband cried,
"But I am wearied out," the wife replied;
"Wearied with pleasure! Thing till now unheard—
Are all that sweeten trouble to be fear'd?
'T is but the sameness tires you,—cross the seas,
And let us taste the world's varieties.

'T is said, in Paris that a man may live
In all the luxuries a world can give,
And in a space confined to narrow bound
All the enjoyments of our life are found;
There we may eat and drink, may dance and dress,
And in its very essence joy possess;
May see a moving crowd of lovely dames,
May win a fortune at your favourite games;
May hear the sounds that ravish human sense,
And all without receding foot from thence."

The conquer'd wife, resistless and afraid,
To the strong call a sad obedience paid.

As we an infant in its pain, with sweets
Loved once, now loath'd, torment him till he eats,
Who on the authors of his new distress
Looks trembling with disgusted weariness,
So Harriet felt, so look'd, and seem'd to say,
"O! for a day of rest, a holiday!"

At length her courage rising with her fear,
She said, "our pleasures may be bought too dear!"

To this he answer'd—"Dearest! from thy heart
Bid every fear of evil times depart;
I ever trusted in the trying hour
To my good stars, and felt the ruling power;
When want drew nigh, his threat'ning speed was stopp'd,
Some virgin aunt, some childless uncle dropp'd;
In all his threats I sought expedients new,
And my last, best resource was found in you."

Silent and sad the wife beheld her doom,
And sat her down to see the ruin come;
And meet the ills that rise where money fails,
Debts, threats and duns, bills, bailiffs, writs and jails.

These was she spared; ere yet by want oppress'd,
Came one more fierce than bailiff in arrest;
Amid a scene where Pleasure never came,
Though never ceased the mention of his name,
The husband's heated blood received the breath
Of strong disease, that bore him to his death.

Her all collected,—whether great or small
The sum, I know not, but collected all;—
The widow'd lady to her cot retired,
And there she lives delighted and admired:
Civil to all, compliant and polite,
Disposed to think, "whatever is, is right;"
She wears the widow's weeds, she gives the widow's mite.
At home awhile, she in the autumn finds
The sea an object for reflecting minds,
And change for tender spirits; there she reads,
And weeps in comfort in her graceful weeds.

What gives our tale its moral? Here we find
That wives like these are not for rule design'd,

Nor yet for blind submission; happy they,
Who while they feel it pleasant to obey,
Have yet a kind companion at their side
Who in their journey will his power divide,
Or yield the reins, and bid the lady guide;
Then points the wonders of the way, and makes
The duty pleasant that she undertakes;
He shows her objects as they move along,
And gently rules the movements that are wrong:
He tells her all the skilful diver's art,
And smiles to see how well she acts her part;
Nor praise denies to courage or to skill,
In using power that he resumes at will.

BOOK XVIII.

ELLEN.

A Morning Ride—A Purchase of the Squire—The Way to it described—The former Proprietor—Richard's Return—Inquiries respecting a Lady whom he had seen—Her History related—Her Attachment to a Tutor—They are parted—Impediments removed—How removed in vain—Fate of the Lover—Of Ellen.

Bleak was the morn—said Richard, with a sigh,
"I must depart!"—"That, Brother, I deny,"
Said George—"You may; but I perceive not why."

This point before had been discuss'd, but still
The guest submitted to the ruling will;
But every day gave rise to doubt and fear,—
He heard not now, as he was wont to hear,
That all was well;—though little was express'd,
It seem'd to him the writer was distress'd;
Restrain'd! there was attempt and strife to please,
Pains and endeavour—not Matilda's ease;—
Not the pure lines of love! the guileless friend
In all her freedom—What could this portend!

"Fancy!" said George, "the self-tormentor's pain"—
And Richard still consented to remain.

"Ride you this fair cool morning?" said the squire:
"Do—for a purchase I have made inquire,
And with you take a will complacently t' admire:
Southward at first, dear Richard, make your way,
Cross Hilton Bridge, move on through Breken Clay,
At Dunham wood turn duly to the east,
And there your eyes upon the ocean feast;
Then ride above the cliff, or ride below,
You'll be enraptured, for your taste I know;
It is a prospect that a man might stay
To his bride hastening on his wedding-day;
At Tilburn Sluice once more ascend and view
A decent house; an ample garden too,
And planted well behind—a lively scene, and new;
A little taste, a little pomp display'd,
By a dull man, who had retired from trade
To enjoy his leisure—Here he came prepared
To farm, nor cost in preparation spared;
But many works he purchased, some he read,
And often rose with projects in his head,
Of crops in courses raised, of herds by matching bred.

We had just found these little humours out,
Just saw—he saw not—what he was about;
Just met as neighbours, still disposed to meet,
Just learn'd the current tales of Dowling Street,
And were just thinking of our female friends,
Saying,—'You know not what the man intends,
A rich, kind, hearty'—and it might be true
Something he wish'd, but had no time to do;
A cold ere yet the falling leaf! of small
Effect till then, was fatal in the fall;
And of that house was his possession brief—
Go; and guard well against the falling leaf.

But hear me, Richard, looking to my ease,
Try if you can find something that will please;
Faults if you see, and such as must abide,
Say they are small, or say that I can hide;
But faults that I can change, remove, or mend,
These like a foe detect—or like a friend.

Mark well the rooms, and their proportions learn,
In each some use, some elegance discern;
Observe the garden, its productive wall,
And find a something to commend in all;
Then should you praise them in a knowing way,
I'll take it kindly—that is well—be gay.

Nor pass the pebbled cottage as you rise
Above the sluice, till you have fix'd your eyes
On the low woodbined window, and have seen,
So fortune favour you, the ghost within;
Take but one look, and then your way pursue,
It flies all strangers, and it knows not you."

Richard return'd, and by his Brother stood,
Not in a pensive, not in pleasant mood;
But by strong feeling into stillness wrought,
As nothing thinking, or with too much thought;
Or like a man who means indeed to speak,
But would his hearer should his purpose seek.

When George—"What is it, Brother, you would hide?
Or what confess?"—"Who is she?" he replied,
"That angel whom I saw, to whom is she allied?
Of this fair being let me understand,
And I will praise your purpose, house and land.

Hers was that cottage on the rising ground,
West of the waves, and just beyond their sound;
'T is larger than the rest, and whence, indeed,
You might expect a lady to proceed;
But O! this creature, far as I could trace,
Will soon be carried to another place.

Fair, fragile thing! I said, when first my eye
Caught hers, wilt thou expand thy wings and fly
Or wilt thou vanish? beauteous spirit, stay!—
For will it not (I question'd) melt away?
No! it was mortal—I unseen was near,
And saw the bosom's sigh, the standing tear!
She thought profoundly, for I stay'd to look,
And first she read, then laid aside her book

Then on her hand reclined her lovely head,
And seem'd unconscious of the tear she shed.

'Art thou so much,' I said, 'to grief a prey?'
Till pity pain'd me, and I rode away.

Tell me, my Brother, is that sorrow dread
For the great change that bears her to the dead?
Has she connexions? does she love?—I feel
Pity and grief; wilt thou her woes reveal?"

"They are not lasting, Richard, they are woes
Chastised and meek! she sings them to repose;
If not, she reasons; if they still remain,
She finds resource, that none shall find in vain.

Whether disease first grew upon regret,
Or nature gave it, is uncertain yet,
And must remain; the frame was slightly made,
That grief assail'd, and all is now decay'd!

But though so willing from the world to part,
I must not call her case a broken heart;
Nor dare I take upon me to maintain
That hearts once broken never heal again."

She was an only daughter, one whose sire
Loved not that girls to knowledge should aspire;
But he had sons, and Ellen quickly caught
Whatever they were by their masters taught;
This, when the father saw—"It is the turn
Of her strange mind," said he, "but let her learn;
'T is almost pity with that shape and face—
But is a fashion, and brings no disgrace;
Women of old wrote verse, or for the stage
Brought forth their works! they now are reasoners sage,
And with severe pursuits dare grapple and engage.
If such her mind, I shall in vain oppose,
If not, her labours of themselves will close."

Ellen, 't was found, had skill without pretence,
And silenced envy by her meek good sense;
That Ellen learnt, her various knowledge proved;
Soft words and tender looks, that Ellen loved;
For he who taught her brothers found in her
A constant, ready, eager auditor;
This he perceived, nor could his joy disguise,
It tuned his voice, it sparkled in his eyes.

Not very young, nor very handsome he,
But very fit an Abelard to be;
His manner and his meekness hush'd alarm
In all but Ellen—Ellen felt the charm;
Hers was fond "filial love," she found delight
To have her mind's dear father in her sight;
But soon the borrow'd notion she resign'd!
He was no father—even to the mind.

But Ellen had her comforts—"He will speak,"
She said, "for he beholds me fond and weak;
Fond, and he therefore may securely plead,—
Weak, I have therefore of his firmness need;
With whom my father will his Ellen trust,
Because he knows him to be kind and just."

Alas! too well the conscious lover knew
The parent's mind, and well the daughter's too;
He felt of duty the imperious call,
Beheld his danger, and must fly or fall.
What would the parent, what his pupils think?
O! he was standing on perdition's brink:
In his dilemma flight alone remain'd,
And could he fly whose very soul was chain'd?
He knew she loved; she tried not to conceal
A hope she thought that virtue's self might feel.

Ever of her and her frank heart afraid,
Doubting himself, he sought in absence, aid,
And had resolved on flight, but still the act delay'd;
At last so high his apprehension rose,
That he would both his love and labour close.

"While undisclosed my fear each instant grows,
And I lament the guilt that no one knows,
Success undoes me, and the view that cheers
All other men, all dark to me appears!"

Thus as he thought, his Ellen at his side
Her soothing softness to his grief applied;
With like effect as water cast on flame,
For he more heated and confused became,
And broke in sorrow from the wondering maid,
Who was at once offended and afraid;
Yet "Do not go!" she cried, and was awhile obey'd.

"Art thou then ill, dear friend?" she ask'd and took
His passive hand—"How very pale thy look!
And thou art cold, and tremblest—pray thee tell
Thy friend, thy Ellen, is her master well?
And let her with her loving care attend
To all that vexes and disturbs her friend."

"Nay, my dear lady! we have all our cares,
And I am troubled with my poor affairs:
Thou canst not aid me, Ellen; could it be
And might it, doubtless, I would fly to thee;
But we have sundry duties, and must all,
Hard as it may be, go where duties call—
Suppose the trial were this instant thine,
Couldst thou the happiest of thy views resign
At duty's strong command?"—"If thou wert by,"
Said the unconscious maiden, "I would try!"—
And as she sigh'd she heard the soft responsive sigh.

And then assuming steadiness, "Adieu!"
He cried, and from the grieving Ellen flew;
And to her father with a bleeding heart
He went, his grief and purpose to impart;
Told of his health, and did in part confess
That he should love the noble maiden less.

The parent's pride to sudden rage gave way—
"And the girl loves! that plainly you would say—
And you with honour, in your pride, retire!—
Sir, I your prudence envy and admire."
But here the father saw the rising frown,
And quickly let his lofty spirit down.

"Forgive a parent!—I may well excuse
A girl who could perceive such worth, and choose
To make it hers: we must not look to meet
All we might wish;—Is age itself discreet?
Where conquest may not be, 't is prudence to retreat."

Then with the kindness worldly minds assume,
He praised the self-pronounced and rigorous doom;
He wonder'd not that one so young should love,
And much he wish'd he could the choice approve;
Much he lamented such a mind to lose,
And begg'd to learn if he could aid his views,
If such were form'd—then closed the short account,
And to a shilling paid the full amount.

So Cecil left the mansion, and so flew
To foreign shores, without an interview;
He must not say, I love—he could not say, Adieu!

Long was he absent; as a guide to youth,
With grief contending, and in search of truth;
In courting peace, and trying to forget
What was so deeply interesting yet.

A friend in England gave him all the news,
A sad indulgence that he would not lose;
He told how Ellen suffer'd, how they sent
The maid from home in sullen discontent,
With some relation on the Lakes to live,
In all the sorrow such retirements give;
And there she roved among the rocks, and took
Moss from the stone, and pebbles from the brook;
Gazed on the flies that settled on the flowers,
And so consumed her melancholy hours.

Again he wrote—The father then was dead,
And Ellen to her native village fled,
With native feeling—there she oped her door,
Her heart, her purse, and comforted the poor,
The sick, the sad,—and there she pass'd her days,
Deserving much, but never seeking praise,
Her task to guide herself, her joy the fallen to raise.
Nor would she nicely faults and merits weigh,
But loved the impulse of her soul t' obey;
The prayers of all she heard, their sufferings view'd,
Nor turn'd from any, save when Love pursued;
For though to love disposed, to kindness prone,
She thought of Cecil, and she lived alone.

Thus heard the lover of the life she past
Till his return,—and he return'd at last;
For he had saved, and was a richer man
Than when to teach and study he began;
Something his father left, and he could fly
To the loved country where he wish'd to die.

"And now," he said, "this maid with gentle mind
May I not hope to meet, as good, as kind,
As in the days when first her friend she knew
And then could trust—and he indeed is true?
She knew my motives, and she must approve
The man who dared to sacrifice his love
And fondest hopes to virtue: virtuous she,
Nor can resent that sacrifice in me."

He reason'd thus, but fear'd, and sought the friend
In his own country, where his doubts must end;
They then together to her dwelling came,
And by a servant sent her lover's name,
A modest youth, whom she before had known,
His favourite then, and doubtless *then* her own.
They in the carriage heard the servants speak
At Ellen's door—"A maid so heavenly meek,
Who would all pain extinguish! Yet will she
Pronounce my doom, I feel the certainty!"—
"Courage!" the friend exclaim'd, "the lover's fear
Grows without ground;" but Cecil would not hear:
He seem'd some dreadful object to explore,
And fix'd his fearful eye upon the door,
Intensely longing for reply—the thing
That must to him his future fortune bring;
And now it brought! like Death's cold hand it came—
"The lady was a stranger to the name!"

Backward the lover in the carriage fell,
Weak, but not fainting—"All," said he, "is well!
Return with me—I have no more to seek!"
And this was all the woful man would speak.

Quickly he settled all his worldly views,
And sail'd from home, his fiercer pains to lose
And nurse the milder—now with labour less
He might his solitary world possess,
And taste the bitter-sweet of love in idleness.

Greece was the land he chose; a mind decay'd
And ruin'd there through glorious ruin stray'd;
There read, and walk'd, and mused,—there loved and wept, and pray'd.
Nor would he write, nor suffer hope to live,
But gave to study all his mind could give;
Till, with the dead conversing, he began
To lose the habits of a living man,
Save that he saw some wretched, them he tried
To soothe,—some doubtful, them he strove to guide;
Nor did he lose the mind's ennobling joy
Of that new state that death must not destroy;
What Time had done we know not,—Death was nigh,
To his first hopes the lover gave a sigh,
But hopes more new and strong confirm'd his wish to die.

Meantime poor Ellen in her cottage thought
"That he would seek her—sure she should be sought
She did not mean—It was an evil hour,
Her thoughts were guardless, and beyond her power;
And for one speech, and that in rashness made!
Have I no friend to soothe him and persuade?
He must not leave me—He again will come,
And we shall have one hope, one heart, one home!"

But when she heard that he on foreign ground
Sought his lost peace, hers never more was found·
But still she felt a varying hope that love
Would all these slight impediments remove;—
"Has he no friend to tell him that our pride
Resents a moment and is satisfied?
Soon as the hasty sacrifice is made,
A look will soothe us, and a tear persuade;
Have I no friend to say 'Return again,
Reveal your wishes, and relieve her pain?'"

With suffering mind the maid her prospects view'd,
That hourly varied with the varying mood;

As past the day, the week, the month, the year,
The faint hope sicken'd, and gave place to fear.

No Cecil came!—"Come, peevish and unjust!"
Sad Ellen cried, "why cherish this disgust?
Thy Ellen's voice could charm thee once, but thou
Canst nothing see or hear of Ellen now!"

Yes! she was right; the grave on him was closed,
And there the lover and the friend reposed.
The news soon reach'd her, and she then replied
In his own manner—"I am satisfied!"

To her a lover's legacy is paid,
The darling wealth of the devoted maid;
From this her best and favourite books she buys,
From this are doled the favourite charities;
And when a tale or face affects her heart,
This is the fund that must relief impart.

Such have the ten last years of Ellen been!
Her very last that sunken eye has seen!
That half angelic being still must fade
Till all the angel in the mind be made;—
And now the closing scene will shortly come—
She cannot visit sorrow at her home;
But still she feeds the hungry, still prepares
The usual softeners of the peasant's cares,
And though she prays not with the dying now,
She teaches them to die, and shows them how.

"Such is my tale, dear Richard, but that told
I must all comments on the text withhold;
What is the sin of grief I cannot tell,
Nor of the sinners who have loved too well;
But to the cause of mercy I incline,
Or, O! my Brother, what a fate is mine!"

BOOK XIX.

WILLIAM BAILEY.

Discourse on Jealousy—Of unsuspicious Men—Visit William and his Wife—His Dwelling—Story of William and Fanny—Character of both—Their Contract—Fanny's Visit to an Aunt—Its Consequences—Her Father's Expectation—His Death—William a Wanderer—His Mode of Living—The Acquaintance he forms—Travels across the Kingdom—Whom he finds—The Event of their Meeting.

The letters Richard in a morning read
To quiet and domestic comforts led;
And George, who thought the world could not supply
Comfort so pure, reflected with a sigh;
Then would pursue the subject, half in play,
Half earnest, till the sadness wore away.

They spoke of Passion's errors, Love's disease,
His pains, afflictions, wrongs, and jealousies;
Of Herod's vile commandment—that his wife
Should live no more, when he no more had life,
He could not bear that royal Herod's spouse
Should, as a widow, make her second vows;
Or that a mortal with his queen should wed,
Or be the rival of the mighty dead.

"Herods," said Richard, "doubtless may be found,
But haply do not in the world abound:
Ladies, indeed, a dreadful lot would have,
If jealousy could act beyond the grave:
No doubt Othellos every place supply,
Though every Desdemona does not die;
But there are lovers in the world, who live
Slaves to the sex, and every fault forgive."

"I know," said George, "a happy man and kind,
Who finds his wife is all he wish'd to find,
A mild, good man, who, if he nothing sees,
Will suffer nothing to disturb his ease;
Who, ever yielding both to smiles and sighs,
Admits no story that a wife denies,—
She guides his mind, and she directs his eyes.

Richard, there dwells within a mile a pair
Of good examples,—I will guide you there:
Such man is William Bailey,—but his spouse
Is virtue's self since she had made her vows:
I speak of ancient stories, long worn out,
That honest William would not talk about;
But he will sometimes check her starting tear
And call her self-correction too severe.

In their own inn the gentle pair are placed,
Where you behold the marks of William's taste;
They dwell in plenty, in respect, and peace,
Landlord and lady of the Golden Fleece:
Public indeed their calling,—but there come
No brawl, no revel to that decent room;
All there is still, and comely to behold,
Mild as the fleece, and pleasant as the gold;
But mild and pleasant as they now appear,
They first experienced many a troubled year;
And that, if known, might not command our praise,
Like the smooth tenor of their present days.

Our hostess, now so grave and steady grown,
Has had some awkward trials of her own:
She was not always so resign'd and meek,—
Yet can I little of her failings speak;
Those she herself will her misfortunes deem,
And slides discreetly from the dubious theme;
But you shall hear the tale that I will tell,
When we have seen the mansion where they dwell.

They saw the mansion,—and the couple made
Obeisance due, and not without parade:
"His honour, still obliging, took delight
To make them pleasant in each other's sight;
It was their duty—they were very sure
It was their pleasure."
This they could endure,
Nor turn'd impatient——in the room around
Were care and neatness: instruments were found
For sacred music, books with prints and notes
By learned men and good, whom William quotes
In mode familiar—Beveridge, Dodderidge, Hall,
Pyle, Whitby, Hammond—he refers to all.

Next they beheld his garden, fruitful, nice,
And, as he said, his little paradise.

In man and wife appear'd some signs of pride,
Which they perceiv'd not, or they would not hide,—
"Their honest saving, their good name, their skill,
His honour's land, which they had grace to till;
And more his favour shown, with all their friends good will."

This past, the visit was with kindness closed,
And George was ask'd to do as he proposed.

"Richard," said he, "though I myself explore
With no distaste the annals of the poor,
And may with safety to a brother show
What of my humble friends I chance to know,
Richard, there are who call the subjects low.

The host and hostess of the Fleece—'t is base—
Would I could cast some glory round the place!

The lively heroine once adorn'd a farm,—
And William's virtue has a kind of charm:
Nor shall we, in our apprehension, need
Riches or rank——I think I may proceed:
Virtue and worth there are who will not see
In humble dress, but low they cannot be."

The youth's addresses pleased his favourite maid,—
They wish'd for union, but were both afraid;
They saw the wedded poor,—and fear the bliss delay'd:
Yet they appear'd a happier lass and swain
Than those who will not reason or refrain.

William was honest, simple, gentle, kind,
Laborious, studious, and to thrift inclined;
More neat than youthful peasant in his dress,
And yet so careful, that it cost him less:
He kept from inns, though doom'd an inn to keep,
And all his pleasures and pursuits were cheap:
Yet would the youth perform a generous deed,
When reason saw or pity felt the need;
He of his labour and his skill would lend,
Nay, of his money, to a suffering friend.

William had manual arts,—his room was graced
With carving quaint, that spoke the master's taste;
But if that taste admitted some dispute,
He charm'd the nymphs with flageolet and flute.

Constant at church, and there a little proud,
He sang with boldness, and he read aloud;
Self-taught to write, he his example took
And form'd his letters from a printed book.

I've heard of ladies who profess'd to see
In a man's writing what his mind must be;
As Doctor Spurzheim's pupils, when they look
Upon a skull, will read it as a book—
Our talents, tendencies, and likings trace,
And find for all the measure and the place:
Strange times! when thus we are completely read
By man or woman, by the hand or head!
Believe who can,—but William's even mind
All who beheld might in his writing find;
His not the scratches where we try in vain
Meanings and words to construe or explain.

But with our village hero to proceed,—
He read as learned clerks are wont to read;
Solemn he was in tone, and slow in pace,
By nature gifted both with strength and grace.

Black parted locks his polish'd forehead press'd;
His placid looks an easy mind confess'd;
His smile content, and seldom more, convey'd;
Not like the smile of fair illusive maid,
When what she feels is hid, and what she wills betray'd.

The lighter damsels call'd his manner prim,
And laugh'd at virtue so array'd in him;
But they were wanton, as he well replied,
And hoped their own would not be strongly tried:
Yet was he full of glee, and had his strokes
Of rustic wit, his repartees and jokes;
Nor was averse, ere yet he pledged his love,
To stray with damsels in the shady grove;
When he would tell them, as they walk'd along,
How the birds sang, and imitate their song:
In fact, our rustic had his proper taste,
Was with peculiar arts and manners graced—
And Absalom had been, had Absalom been chaste

Frances, like William, felt her heart incline
To neat attire—but Frances would be fine:
Though small the farm, the farmer's daughter knew
Her rank in life, and she would have it too:
This, and this only, gave the lover pain,
He thought it needless, and he judged it vain:
Advice in hints he to the fault applied,
And talk'd of sin, of vanity, and pride.

"And what is proud," said Frances, "but to stand
Singing at church, and sawing thus your hand?
Looking at heaven above, as if to bring
The holy angels down to hear you sing?
And when you write, you try with all your skill,
And cry, no wonder that you wrote so ill!
For you were ever to yourself a rule,
And humbly add, you never were at school—
Is that not proud?—And I have heard beside,
The proudest creatures have the humblest pride:
If you had read the volumes I have hired,
You'd see your fault, nor try to be admired;
For they who read such books can always tell
The fault within, and read the mind as well."

William had heard of hiring books before,
He knew she read, and he inquired no more;
On him the subject was completely lost,
What he regarded was the time and cost:
Yet that was trifling—just a present whim,
'Novels and stories! what were they to him?"

With such slight quarrels, or with those as slight,
They lived in love, and dream'd of its delight.
Her duties Fanny knew, both great and small,
And she with diligence observed them all;
If e'er she fail'd a duty to fulfil,
'T was childish error, not rebellious will;
For her much reading, though it touch'd her heart,
Could neither vice nor indolence impart.

Yet, when from William and her friends retired,
She found her reading had her mind inspired
With hopes and thoughts of high mysterious things,
Such as the early dreams of kindness brings;
And then she wept, and wonder'd as she read,
And new emotions in her heart were bred:
She sometimes fancied that when love was true
'Twas more than she and William ever knew;
More than the shady lane in summer-eve,
More than the sighing when he took his leave;
More than his preference when the lads advance
And choose their partners for the evening dance:
Nay, more than midnight thoughts and morning dreams,
Or talk when love and marriage are the themes;
In fact, a something not to be defined,
Of all subduing, all commanding kind,
That fills the fondest heart, that rules the proudest mind.

But on her lover Fanny still relied,
Her best companion, her sincerest guide,
On whom she could rely, on whom she would confide.

All jealous fits were past; in either now
Were tender wishes for the binding vow;
There was no secret one alone possess'd,
There was no hope that warm'd a single breast;
Both felt the same concerns their thoughts employ,
And neither knew one solitary joy.

Then why so easy, William? why consent
To wait so long? thou wilt at last repent;
"Within a month," does Care and Prudence say,
If all be ready, linger not a day;
Ere yet the choice be made, on choice debate,
But having chosen, dally not with fate.

While yet to wait the pair were half content,
And half disposed their purpose to repent,
A spinster-aunt, in some great baron's place,
Would see a damsel, pride of all her race:
And Fanny, flatter'd by the matron's call,
Obey'd her aunt, and long'd to see the Hall;
For halls and castles in her fancy wrought,
And she accounts of love and wonder sought;
There she expected strange events to learn,
And take in tender secrets fond concern;
There she expected lovely nymphs to view,
Perhaps to hear and meet their lovers too;
The Julias, tender souls! the Henrys kind and true:
There she expected plottings to detect,
And—but I know not what she might expect—
All she was taught in books to be her guide,
And all that nature taught the nymph beside.

Now that good dame had in the castle dwelt
So long that she for all its people felt;
She kept her sundry keys, and ruled o'er all,
Female and male, domestics in the hall;
By her lord trusted, worthy of her trust,
Proud but obedient, bountiful but just.

She praised her lucky stars, that in her place
She never found neglect, nor felt disgrace;
To do her duty was her soul's delight,
This her inferiors would to theirs excite,
This her superiors notice and requite;
To either class she gave the praises due,
And still more grateful as more favour'd grew:
Her lord and lady were of peerless worth,
In power unmatch'd, in glory and in birth;
And such the virtue of the noble race,
It reach'd the meanest servant in the place;
All, from the chief attendant on my lord
To the groom's helper, had her civil word;
From Miss Montregor, who the ladies taught,
To the rude lad who in the garden wrought;
From the first favourite to the meanest drudge,
Were no such women, heaven should be her judge,
Whatever stains were theirs, let them reside
In that pure place, and they were mundified;
The sun of favour on their vileness shone,
And all their faults like morning mists were gone.

There was Lord Robert! could she have her choice,
From the world's masters he should have her voice;
So kind and gracious in his noble ways,
It was a pleasure speaking in his praise:
And Lady Catharine,—O! a prince's pride
Might by one smile of hers be gratified;
With her would monarchs all their glory share,
And in her presence banish all their care.

Such was the matron, and to her the maid
Was by her lover carefully convey'd.

When William first the invitation read
It some displeasure in his spirit bred,
Not that one jealous thought the man possess'd,
He was by fondness, not by fear distress'd;
But when his Fanny to his mind convey'd
The growing treasures of the ancient maid,
The thirty years, come June, of service past,
Her lasting love, her life that would not last;
Her power! her place! what interest! what respect
She had acquired—and shall we her neglect?

"No, Frances, no!" he answer'd, "you are right;
But things appear in such a different light!"

Her parents blest her, and as well became
Their love, advised her, that they might not blame
They said, "If she should earl or countess meet
She should be humble, cautious, and discreet:
Humble, but not abased, remembering all
Are kindred sinners,—children of the fall;
That from the earth our being we receive,
And all are equal when the earth we leave."

They then advised her in a modest way
To make replies to what the lord might say;
Her aunt would aid her, who was now become
With nobles noble, and with lords at home.

So went the pair; and William told at night
Of a reception gracious and polite;
He spake of galleries long and pictures tall,
The handsome parlours, the prodigious hall;
The busts, the statues, and the floors of stone,
The storied arras, and the vast saloon,
In which was placed an Indian chest and screen
With figures such as he had never seen:
He told of these as men enraptured tell,
And gave to all their praise, and all was well.

Left by the lover, the desponding maid
Was of the matron's ridicule afraid;
But when she heard a welcome frank and kind,
The wonted firmness repossess'd her mind;
Pleased by the looks of love her aunt display'd,
Her fond professions, and her kind parade.

In her own room, and with her niece apart,
She gave up all the secrets of her heart;
And, grown familiar, bid her Fanny come,
Partake her cheer, and make herself at home.

Shut in that room, upon its cheerful board
She laid the comforts of no vulgar hoard;
Then press'd the damsel both with love and pride,
For both she felt—and would not be denied.

Grace she pronounced before and after meat,
And bless'd her God that she could talk and eat;
Then with new glee she sang her patron's praise—
"He had no paltry arts, no pimping ways;
She had the roast and boil'd of every day,
That sent the poor with grateful hearts away;
And she was grateful—Come, my darling, think
Of them you love the best, and let us drink."

And now she drank the healths of those above,
Her noble friends, whom she must ever love;
But not together, not the young and old,
But one by one, the number duly told;
And told their merits too—there was not one
Who had not said a gracious thing or done;
Nor could she praise alone, but she would take
A cheerful glass for every favourite's sake,
And all were favourites—till the rosy cheek
Spoke for the tongue that nearly ceased to speak;
That rosy cheek that now began to shine,
And show the progress of the rosy wine:
But there she ended—felt the singing head,
Then pray'd as custom will'd, and so to bed.

The morn was pleasant, and the ancient maid
With her fair niece about the mansion stray'd;
There was no room without th' appropriate tale
Of blood and murder, female sprite or male;
There was no picture that th' historic dame
Pass'd by and gave not its peculiar fame;
The births, the visits, weddings, burials, all
That chanced for ages at the noble Hall.

These and each revolution she could state,
And give strange anecdotes of love and hate;
This was her first delight, her pride, her boast,
She told of many an heiress, many a toast,
Of Lady Ellen's flight, of Lord Orlando's ghost;
The maid turn'd pale, and what should then ensue
But wine and cake—then dame was frighten'd too.

The aunt and niece now walk'd about the grounds,
And sometimes met the gentry in their rounds;
"Do let us turn!" the timid girl exclaim'd—
"Turn!" said the aunt, "of what are you ashamed?
What is there frightful in such looks as those?
What is it, child, you fancy or suppose?
Look at Lord Robert, see if you can trace
More than true honour in that handsome face!
What! you must think, by blushing in that way,
My lord has something about love to say;

But I assure you that he never spoke
Such things to me in earnest or in joke,
And yet I meet him in all sorts of times,
When wicked men are thinking of their crimes.

There! let them pass——Why, yes, indeed 't is true
That was a look, and was design'd for you;
But what the wonder when the sight is new?
For my lord's virtue you may take my word,
He would not do a thing that was absurd."

A month had pass'd; "And when will Fanny come?"
The lover ask'd, and found the parents dumb;
They had not heard for more than half the space,
And the poor maiden was in much disgrace;
Silence so long they could not understand,
And this of one who wrote so neat a hand;
Their sister sure would send were aught amiss,
But youth is thoughtless—there is hope in this.

As time elapsed, their wonder changed to wo,
William would lose another day, and go;
Yet if she should be wilful and remain,
He had no power to take her home again:
But he would go:—He went, and he return'd,
And in his look the pair his tale discern'd;
Stupid in grief, it seem'd not that he knew
How he came home, or what he should pursue.
Fanny was gone!—her aunt was sick in bed,
Dying, she said—none cared if she were dead,
Her charge, his darling, was decoy'd, was fled!
But at what time, and whither, and with whom,
None seem'd to know—all surly, shy, or dumb.

Each blamed himself, all blamed the erring maid
They vow'd revenge; they cursed their fate, and pray'd.
Moved by his grief, the father sought the place,
Ask'd for his girl, and talk'd of her disgrace;
Spoke of the villain, on whose cursed head
He pray'd that vengeance might be amply shed;
Then sought his sister, and beheld her grief,
Her pain, her danger,—this was no relief.

"Where is my daughter? bring her to my sight!"—
"Brother, I'm rack'd and tortured day and night."—
"Talk not to me! What grief have you to tell,
Is your soul rack'd, or is your bosom hell?
Where is my daughter?"—"She would take her oath
For their right doing, for she knew them both,
And my young lord was honour."—"Woman, cease!
And give your guilty conscience no such peace—
You 've sold the wretched girl, and have betray'd your niece."—
"The Lord be good! and O! the pains that come
In limb and body—Brother, get you home!
Your voice runs through me,—every angry word,
If he should hear it, would offend my lord."

"Has he a daughter? let her run away
With a poor dog, and hear what he will say!
No matter what, I 'll ask him for his son."—
"And so offend? Now, brother, pray be gone!"

My lord appear'd, perhaps by pity moved,
And kindly said he no such things approved,

Nay, he was angry with the foolish boy,
Who might his pleasures at his ease enjoy;
The thing was wrong — he hoped the farm did well,—
The angry father doom'd the farm to hell;
He then desired to see the villain-son,
Though my lord warn'd him such excess to shun;
Told him he pardon'd, though he blamed such rage,
And bade him think upon his state and age.

"Think! yes, my lord! but thinking drives me mad—
Give me my child!—Where is she to be had?
I 'm old and poor, but I with both can feel,
And so shall he that could a daughter steal!
Think you, my lord, I can be so bereft
And feel no vengeance for the villain's theft?
Old if I am, could I the robber meet
I 'd lay his breathless body at my feet—
Was that a smile, my lord? think you your boy
Will both the father and the child destroy?"

My lord replied—"I 'm sorry from my soul!
But boys are boys, and there is no control."

'So, for your great ones Justice slumbers then!
If men are poor they must not feel as men—
Will your son marry?"—"Marry!" said my lord,
Your daughter?—marry—no, upon my word!"

"What, then, our stations differ!—but your son
Thought not of that—his crime has made them one,
In guilt united—She shall be his wife,
Or I th' avenger that will take his life!"

"Old man, I pity and forgive you; rest
In hope and comfort,—be not so distress'd,
Things that seem bad oft happen for the best;
The girl has done no more than thousands do,
Nor has the boy—they laugh at me and you."—
"And this my vengeance—curse him!"—"Nay, forbear;
I spare your frenzy; in compassion spare."

"Spare me, my lord! and what have I to dread!
O! spare not, heaven, the thunder o'er his head—
The bolt he merits!"——
Such was his redress;
And he return'd to brood upon distress.

And what of William?—William from the time
Appear'd partaker both of grief and crime;
He cared for nothing, nothing he pursued,
But walk'd about in melancholy mood;
He ceased to labour,—all he loved before
He now neglected, and would see no more;
He said his flute brought only to his mind
When he was happy, and his Fanny kind;
And his loved walks, and every object near,
And every evening-sound she loved to hear,
The shady lane, broad heath, and starry sky,
Brought home reflections, and he wish'd to die:
Yet there he stray'd, because he wish'd to shun
The world he hated, where his part was done;
As if, though lingering on the earth, he there
Had neither hope nor calling, tie nor care.

At length a letter from the daughter came,
'Frances' subscribed, and that the only name;
She "pitied much her parents, spoke of fate,
And begg'd them to forget her, not to hate;
Said she had with her all the world could give,
And only pray'd that they in peace should live,—
That which is done, is that we're born to do,
This she was taught, and she believed it true;
True, that she lived in pleasure and delight,
But often dream'd and saw the farm by night;
The boarded room that she had kept so neat,
And all her roses in the window-seat;
The pear-tree shade, the jasmine's lovely gloom,
With its long twigs that blossom'd in the room;
But she was happy, and the tears that fell
As she was writing had no grief to tell;
We weep when we are glad, we sigh when we are well."

A bill inclosed, that they beheld with pain
And indignation, they return'd again;
There was no mention made of William's name,
Check'd as she was by pity, love, and shame.

William who wrought for bread and never sought
More than the day demanded when he wrought,
Was to a sister call'd, of all his race
The last, and dying in a distant place;
In tender terror he approach'd her bed,
Beheld her sick, and buried her when dead:
He was her heir, and what she left was more
Than he required, who was content before.

With their minds' sufferings, and growing pain,
That ancient couple could not long remain,
Nor long remain'd; and in their dying groan
The suffering youth perceived himself alone;
For of his health or sickness, peace or care,
He knew not one in all the world to share;
Now every scene would sad reflections give,
And most his home, and there he could not live;
There every walk would now distressing prove,
And of his loss remind him, and his love.

With the small portion by his sister left
He roved about as one of peace bereft,
And by the body's movements hoped to find
A kind of wearied stillness in the mind,
And sooner bring it to a sleepy state,
As rocking infants will their pains abate.

Thus careless, lost, unheeding where he went,
Nine weary years the wandering lover spent.

His sole employment, all that could amuse,
Was his companions on the road to choose;
With such he travell'd through the passing day,
Friends of the hour, and walkers by the way;
And from the sick, the poor, the halt, the blind,
He learn'd the sorrows of his suffering kind.

He learn'd of many how unjust their fate,
For their connexions dwelt in better state;
They had relations famous, great or rich,
Learned or wise, they never scrupled which;
But while they cursed these kindred churls, would try
To build their fame, and for their glory lie.

Others delighted in misfortunes strange,
The sports of fortune in her love for change.

Some spoke of wonders they before had seen,
When on their travels they had wandering been;
How they had sail'd the world about, and found
The sailing plain, although the world was round;
How they beheld for months th' unsetting sun,
What deeds they saw! what they themselves had done!—
What leaps at Rhodes!—what glory then they won!

There were who spoke in terms of high disdain
Of their contending against power in vain,
Suffering from tyranny of law long borne,
And life's best spirits in contentions worn:
Happy in this, th' oppressors soon will die,
Each with the vex'd and suffering man to lie—
And thus consoled exclaim, 'And is not sorrow dry?"

But vice offended: when he met with those
Who could a deed of violence propose,
And cry, "Should they what we desire possess?
Should they deprive us, and their laws oppress?"
William would answer, "Ours is not redress:"—
"Would you oppression then for ever feel?"
"'T is not my choice; but yet I must not steal:"—
"So, first they cheat us, and then make their laws
To guard their treasures and to back their cause:
What call you then, my friend, the rights of man?"
"To get his bread," said William, "if he can;
And if he cannot, he must then depend
Upon a Being he may make his friend:"—
"Make!" they replied; and conference had end.

But female vagrants would at times express
A new-born pleasure at the mild address;
His modest wish, clothed in accent meek,
That they would comfort in religion seek.

"I am a sinful being!" William cried;
"Then what am I?" the conscious heart replied:
And oft-times ponder'd in a pensive way,
"He is not happy, yet he loves to pray."

But some would freely on his thoughts intrude,
And thrust themselves 'twixt him and solitude:
They would his faith and of its strength demand,
And all his soul's prime motions understand:
How! they would say, such wo and such belief,
Such trust in heaven, and yet on earth such grief!
Thou art almost, my friend,—thou art not all,
Thou hast not yet the self-destroying call;
Thou hast a carnal wish, perhaps a will
Not yet subdued,—the root is growing still:
There is the strong man yet that keeps his own,
Who by a stronger must be overthrown;
There is the burden that must yet be gone,
And then the pilgrim may go singing on.

William to this would seriously incline,
And to their comforts would his heart resign;
It soothed, it raised him,—he began to feel
Th' enlivening warmth of methodistic zeal;
He learn'd to know the brethren by their looks—
He sought their meetings, he perused their books;
But yet was not within the pale and yoke,
And as a novice of experience spoke;
But felt the comfort, and began to pray
For such companions on the king's highway.

William had now across the kingdom sped,
To th' Eastern ocean from St. David's head;
And wandering late, with various thoughts oppress'd,
'T was midnight ere he reach'd his place of rest,—
A village inn, that one wayfaring friend
Could from experience safely recommend,
Where the kind hostess would be more intent
On what he needed than on what he spent;
Her husband, once a heathen, she subdued,
And with religious fear his mind imbued;
Though his conviction came too late to save
An erring creature from an early grave.

Since that event, the cheerful widow grew
In size and substance,—her the brethren knew—
And many friends were hers, and lovers not a few;
But either love no more could warm her heart,
Or no man came who could the warmth impart.

William drew near, and saw the comely look
Of the good lady, bending o'er her book;
Hymns it appear'd—for now a pleasing sound
Seem'd as a welcome in his wanderings found.
He enter'd softly, not as they who think
That they may act the ruffian if they drink,
And who conceive, that for their paltry pence
They may with rules of decency dispense;
Far unlike these was William,—he was kind,
Exacting nothing, and to all resign'd.

He saw the hostess reading,—and their eyes
Met in good will, and something like surprise:
It was not beauty William saw, but more,
Something like that which he had loved before—
Something that brought his Fanny to his view,
In the dear time when she was good and true;
And his, it seem'd, were features that were seen
With some emotion—she was not serene:
And both were moved to ask what looks like those could mean.
At first she colour'd to the deepest red,
That hurried off, till all the rose was fled;
She call'd a servant, whom she sent to rest,
Then made excuse to her attentive guest;
She own'd the thoughts confused,—'t was very true,
He brought a dear departed friend in view:
Then, as he listen'd, bade him welcome there
With livelier looks and more engaging air,
And stirr'd the fire of ling, and brush'd the wicker chair,
Waiting his order with the cheerful look,
That proved how pleasant were the pains she took.

He was refresh'd —— They spake on various themes—
Our early pleasures, Reason's first-drawn schemes,
Youth's strong illusions, Love's delirious dreams:
Then from her book he would presume to ask
A song of praise, and she perform'd the task:
The clock struck twelve—He started—'must I go?
His looks spoke plainly, and the lady's 'No:'
So down he sat,—and when the clock struck one
There was no start, no effort to be gone:
Nor stay'd discourse——.

"And so your loves were cross'd,
And the loved object to your wishes lost?

But was she faithless, or were you to blame?
I wish I knew her—Will you tell her name?"

"Excuse me—that would hurt her if alive;
And, if no more, why should her fault survive?"

"But love you still?"—
"Alas! I feel I do,
When I behold her very looks in you!"

"Yet, if the frail one's name must not be known,
My friendly guest may trust me with his own."

This done, the lady paused, and then replied—
"It grieves me much to see your spirit tried;—
But she was like me,—how I came to know
The lamb that stray'd I will hereafter show;—
We were indeed as sisters——Should I state
Her quiet end, you would no longer hate:
I see your heart,—and I shall quickly prove,
Though she deserved not, yet she prized your love:
Long as she breathed was heard her William's name—
And such affection half absolves her shame.

Weep not, but hear me, how I came to know
Thee and thy Frances—this to heaven I owe;
And thou shalt view the pledge, the very ring,
The birth-day token—well you know the thing;
'This,' if I ever—thus I was to speak,
As she had spoken—but I see you weak:
She was not worthy——"
"O! you cannot tell
By what accursed means my Fanny fell!
What bane, compulsion, threats—for she was pure:
But from such toils what being is secure?
Force, not persuasion, robb'd me——"
"You are right;
So has she told me, in her Maker's sight:
She loved not vice——"
"O! no,—her heart approved
All that her God commanded to be loved;
And she is gone——"
"Consider! death alone
Could for the errors of her life atone."

"Speak not of them! I would she knew how dear
I hold her yet!—But dost thou give the tear
To my loved Frances?—No! I cannot part
With one who has her face, who has her heart;
With looks so pleasing, when I thee behold,
She lives—that bosom is no longer cold—
Then tell me—Art thou not—in pity speak—
One whom I sought, while living meant to seek—
Art thou my Fanny?—Let me not offend—
Be something to me—be a sufferer's friend—
Be more—Be all!——The precious truth confess—
Art thou not Frances?"——
"O, my William! yes!
But spare me, spare thyself, and suffer less:
In my best days, the spring-time of my life,
I was not worthy to be William's wife;
A widow now—not poor, indeed—not cast
In outer darkness—sorrowing for the past,
And for the future hoping—but no more—
Let me the pledges of thy love restore,
And give the ring thou gavest—let it be
A token still of my regard for thee,—
But only that,—and to a worthier now
Consign the gift."——
"The only worthy thou!"
Replied the lover; and what more express'd
May be omitted—here our tale shall rest.

This pair, our host and hostess of the Fleece,
Command some wealth, and smile at its increase;
Saving and civil, cautious and discreet,
All sects and parties in their mansion meet;
There from their chapels teachers go to share
The creature-comforts,—mockery grins not there;
There meet the wardens at their annual feast,
With annual pun—"the parish must be fleeced;"
There traders find a parlour cleanly swept
For their reception, and in order kept;
And there the sons of labour, poor, but free,
Sit and enjoy their hour of liberty.

So live the pair,—and life's disasters seem
In their unruffled calm a troubled dream;
In comfort runs the remnant of their life—
He the fond husband, she the faithful wife.

BOOK XX.

THE CATHEDRAL-WALK.

George in his hypochondriac State—A Family Mansion now a Farm-house—The Company there—Their Conversation—Subjects afforded by the Pictures—Doubts if Spirits can appear—Arguments—Facts—The Relation of an old Lady—Her Walks in a Cathedral—Appearance there.

In their discourse again the Brothers dwelt
On early subjects—what they once had felt,
Once thought of things mysterious;—themes that all
With some degree of reverence recall.
George then reverted to the days of old,
When his heart fainted, and his hope was cold;
When by the power of fancy he was sway'd,
And every impulse of the mind obey'd.

"Then, my dear Richard," said the 'Squire, "my case
Was call'd consumptive—I must seek a place
And soil salubrious, thither must repair
And live on asses' milk and milder air.
My uncle bought a farm, and on the land
The fine old mansion yet was left to stand,
Not in this state, but old and much decay'd;
Of this a part was habitable made;
The rest—who doubts?—was by the spirits seized,
Ghosts of all kinds, who used it as they pleased.

The worthy farmer tenant yet remain'd,
Of good report—he had a fortune gain'd;
And his three daughters at their school acquired
The air and manner that their swains admired;
The mother-gossip and these daughters three
Talk'd of genteel and social company,

And while the days were fine, and walks were clean,
A fresh assemblage day by day were seen.

There were the curate's gentle maids, and some
From all the neighbouring villages would come;
There, as I stole the yew-tree shades among,
I saw the parties walking, old and young,
Where I was nothing—if perceived, they said,
'The man is harmless, be not you afraid;
A poor young creature, who, they say, is cross'd
In love, and has in part his senses lost;
His health for certain, and he comes to spend
His time with us; we hope our air will mend
A frame so weaken'd, for the learned tribe
A change of air for stubborn ills prescribe;
And doing nothing often has prevail'd
When ten physicians have prescribed and fail'd;
Not that for air or change there's much to say,
But nature then has time to take her way;
And so we hope our village will restore
This man to health that he possess'd before.
He loves the garden avenues, the gloom
Of the old chambers, of the tap'stried room,
And we no notice take, we let him go and come.'

So spake a gay young damsel; but she knew
Not all the truth,—in part her tale was true.
Much it amused me in the place to be
This harmless cipher, seeming not to see,
Yet seeing all,—unnoticed to appear,
Yet noting all; and not disposed to hear,
But to go forth,—break in on no one's plan,
And hear them speak of the forsaken man.

In scenes like these, a mansion so decay'd,
With blighted trees in hoary moss array'd,
And ivied walls around, for many an hour
I walk'd alone, and felt their witching power;
So others felt;—the young of either sex
Would in these walks their timid minds perplex
By meeting terrors, and the old appear'd,
Their fears upbraiding, like the young who fear'd;
Among them all some sad discourse at night
Was sure to breed a terrified delight:
Some luckless one of the attentive dames
Had figures seen like those within the frames,
Figures of lords who once the land possess'd,
And who could never in their coffins rest;
Unhappy spirits! who could not abide
The loss of all their consequence and pride,
'T was death in all his power, their very names had died.

These tales of terror views terrific bred,
And sent the hearers trembling to their bed."

In an autumnal evening, cool and still,
The sun just dropp'd beneath a distant hill,
The children gazing on the quiet scene,
Then rose in glory Night's majestic queen;
And pleasant was the chequer'd light and shade
Her golden beams and maple shadows made;
An ancient tree that in the garden grew,
And that fair picture on the gravel threw.

Then all was silent, save the sounds that make
Silence more awful, while they faintly break;
The frighten'd bat's low shriek, the beetle's hum,
With nameless sounds we know not whence they come.

Such was the evening; and that ancient seat
The scene where then some neighbours chanced to meet;
Up to the door led broken steps of stone,
Whose dewy surface in the moonlight shone;
On vegetation, that with progress slow
Where man forbears to fix his foot, will grow;
The window's depth and dust repell'd the ray
Of the moon's light and of the setting day;
Pictures there were, and each display'd a face
And form that gave their sadness to the place;
The frame and canvas show'd that worms unseen,
Save in their works, for years had working been;
A fire of brushwood on the irons laid
All the dull room in fitful views display'd,
And with its own wild light in fearful forms array'd.
In this old Hall, in this departing day,
Assembled friends and neighbours, grave and gay,
When one good lady at a picture threw
A glance that caused inquiry—"Tell us who?"

"That was a famous warrior; one they said,
That by a spirit was awhile obey'd;
In all his dreadful battles he would say
'Or win or lose, I shall escape to-day;'
And though the shot as thick as hail came round,
On no occasion he received a wound;
He stood in safety, free from all alarm,
Protected, heaven forgive him, by his charm:
But he forgot the date, till came the hour
When he no more had the protecting power;
And then he bade his friends around farewell!
'I fall!' he cried, and in the instant fell.

Behold those infants in the frame beneath!
A witch offended wrought their early death;
She form'd an image, made as wax to melt,
And each the wasting of the figure felt;
The hag confess'd it when she came to die,
And no one living can the truth deny.

But see a beauty in King William's days,
With that long waist, and those enormous stays;
She had three lovers, and no creature knew
The one preferr'd, or the discarded two;
None could the secret of her bosom see;
Living, poor maid, th' attention of the three,
She kept such equal weight in either scale,
'T was hard to say who would at last prevail;
Thus you may think in either heart arose
A jealous anger, and the men were foes;
Each with himself concluded, two aside,
The third may make the lovely maid his bride:
This caused their fate—It was on Thursday night
The deed was done, and bloody was the fight;
Just as she went, poor thoughtless girl! to prayers,
Ran wild the maid with horror up the stairs;
Pale as a ghost, but not a word she said,
And then the lady utter'd, 'Coates is dead.'

Then the poor damsel found her voice and cried.
'Ran through the body, and that instant died!
But he pronounced your name, and so was satisfied.'
A second fell, and he who did survive
Was kept by skill and sovereign drugs alive;

'O! would she see me!' he was heard to say,
'No! I'll torment him to his dying day!'
The maid exclaim'd, and every Thursday night
Her spirit came his wretched soul to fright;
Once as she came he cried aloud 'Forgive!'
'Never!' she answer'd, 'never while you live,
Nor when you die, as long as time endures;
You have my torment been, and I'll be yours!'
That is the lady, and the man confess'd
Her vengeful spirit would not let him rest."

"But are there ghosts!" exclaim'd a timid maid;
"My father tells me not to be afraid;
He cries when buried we are safe enough,
And calls such stories execrable stuff."

"Your father, child," the former lady cried,
"Has learning much, but he has too much pride;
It is impossible for him to tell
What things in nature are impossible,
Or out of nature, or to prove to whom
Or for what purposes a ghost may come;
It may not be intelligence to bring,
But to keep up a notion of the thing;
And though from one such fact there may arise
An hundred wild improbabilities,
Yet had there never been the truth, I say,
The very lies themselves had died away."

"True," said a friend; "Heaven doubtless may dispense
A kind of dark and clouded evidence;
God has not promised that he will not send
A spirit freed to either foe or friend;
He may such proof, and only such bestow,
Though we the certain truth can never know;
And therefore though such floating stories bring
No strong or certain vouchers of the thing,
Still would I not, presuming, pass my word
That all such tales were groundless and absurd."

"But you will grant," said one who sate beside,
"That all appear so when with judgment tried?"

"For that concession, madam, you may call,
When we have sate in judgment upon all."

An ancient lady, who with pensive smile
Had heard the stories, and been mute the while,
Now said, "Our prudence had been better shown
By leaving uncontested things unknown;
Yet if our children must such stories hear,
Let us provide some antidotes to fear;
For all such errors in the minds of youth,
In any mind, the only cure is truth;
And truths collected may in time decide
Upon such facts, or prove, at least, a guide:
If then permitted, I will fairly state
One fact, nor doubt the story I relate;
I for your perfect acquiescence call,
'T is of myself I tell."——"O! tell us all!"
Said every being there: then silent was the Hall.

"Early in life, beneath my parent's roof,
Of man's true honour I had noble proof;
A generous lover who was worthy found,
Where half his sex are hollow and unsound.
My father fail'd in trade, and sorrowing died,
When all our loss a generous youth supplied;
And soon the time drew on when he could say,
'O! fix the happy, fix the early day!'
Nor meant I to oppose his wishes, or delay:
But then came fever, slight at first indeed,
Then hastening on and threatening in its speed;
It mock'd the powers of medicine; day by day
I saw those helpers sadly walk away;
So came the hand-like cloud, and with such power
And with such speed, that brought the mighty shower.

Him nursed I dying, and we freely spoke
Of what might follow the expected stroke;
We talk'd of spirits, of their unknown powers,
And dared to dwell on what the fate of ours;
But the dread promise, to appear again,
Could it be done, I sought not to obtain;
But yet we were presuming—'Could it be,'
He said, 'O Emma! I would come to thee!'

At his last hour his reason, late astray,
Again return'd t' illuminate his way.

In the last night my mother long had kept
Unwearied watch, and now reclined and slept;
The nurse was dreaming in a distant chair,
And I had knelt to soothe him with a prayer;
When, with a look of that peculiar kind
That gives its purpose to the fellow mind,
His manner spoke—'Confide—be not afraid—
I shall remember,'—this was all convey'd,—
'I know not what awaits departed man,
But this believe—I meet thee if I can.'

I wish'd to die,—and grief, they say, will kill,
But you perceive 't is slowly, if it will;
That I was wretched you may well believe—
I judged it right, and was resolved to grieve;
I lost my mother when there lived not one,
Man, woman, child, whom I would seek or shun.

The Dean, my uncle, with congenial gloom,
Said, 'Will you share a melancholy home?'
For he bewail'd a wife, as I deplored
My fate, and bliss that could not be restored.

In his cathedral's gloom I pass'd my time,
Much in devotion, much in thought sublime;
There oft I paced the aisles, and watch'd the glow
Of the sun setting on the stones below,
And saw the failing light, that strove to pass
Though the dim coating of the storied glass,
Nor fell within, but till the day was gone
The red faint fire upon the window shone.
I took the key, and oft-times chose to sta
Till all was vanish'd of the tedious day,
Till I perceived no light, nor heard a sound,
That gave me notice of a world around.

Then had I grief's proud thoughts, and said, in tone
Of exultation, 'World, I am alone!
I care not for thee, thou art vile and base,
And I shall leave thee for a nobler place.

So I the world abused,—in fact, to me
Urbane and civil as the world could be;

Nor should romantic grievers thus complain,
Although but little in the world they gain,
But let them think if they have nothing done
To make this odious world so sad a one,
Or what their worth and virtue that should make
This graceless world so pleasant for their sake.

But to my tale :—Behold me as I tread
The silent mansions of the favour'd dead,
Who sleep in vaulted chambers, till their clay
In quiet dissolution melts away
In this their bodies' home—The spirits, where are they ?

'And where *his* spirit ?—Doors and walls impede
The embodied spirit, not the spirit freed :'
And, saying this, I at the altar knelt,
And painful joys and rapturous anguish felt;
Till strong, bold hopes possess'd me, and I cried,
'Even at this instant is he at my side;'
Yes, now, dear spirit! art thou by to prove
That mine is lasting, mine the loyal love!

Thus have I thought, returning to the Dean,
As one who had some glorious vision seen :
He ask'd no question, but would sit and weep,
And cry, in doleful tone, 'I cannot sleep !'

In dreams the chosen of my heart I view'd,
And thus th' impression day by day renew'd;
I saw him always, always loved to see,
For when alone he was my company :
In company with him alone I seem'd,
And, if not dreaming, was as one who dream'd.

Thus, robb'd of sleep, I found, when evening came,
A pleasing torpor steal upon my frame;
But still the habit drew my languid feet
To the loved darkness of the favourite seat;
And there, by silence and by sadness press'd,
I felt a world my own, and was at rest.

One night, when urged with more than usual zeal,
And feeling all that such enthusiasts feel,
I paced the altar by, the pillars round,
And knew no terror in the sacred ground;
For mine were thoughts that banish'd all such fear,—
I wish'd, I long'd to have that form appear;
And, as I paced the sacred aisles, I cried,
'Let not thy Emma's spirit be denied
The sight of thine ; or, if I may not see,
Still by some token let her certain be !"

At length the anxious thoughts my strength subdued,
And sleep o'erpower'd me in my solitude ;
Then was I dreaming of unearthly race,
The glorious inmates of a blessed place;
Where lofty minds celestial views explore,
Heaven's bliss enjoy, and heaven's great King adore;
Him that I sought whom I had loved so well—
For sure he dwelt where happy spirits dwell!

While thus engaged, I started at a sound,
Of what I knew not, but I look'd around;
For I was borne on visionary wings,
And felt no dread of sublunary things;
But rising, walk'd—A distant window threw
A weak, soft light, that help'd me in my view;
Something with anxious heart I hoped to see,
And pray'd, 'O! God of all things, let it be!
For all are thine, were made by thee, and thou
Canst both the meeting and the means allow;
Thou canst make clear my sight, or thou canst make
More gross the form that his loved mind shall take,
Canst clothe his spirit for my fleshly sight,
Or make my earthly sense more pure and bright.'

So was I speaking, when without a sound
There was a movement in the sacred ground :
I saw a figure rising, but could trace
No certain features, no peculiar face;
But I prepared my mind that form to view,
Nor felt a doubt,—he promised, and was true!
I should embrace his angel, and my clay,
And what was mortal in me, melt away.

O! that ecstatic horror in my frame,
That o'er me thus, a favour'd mortal, came!
Bless'd beyond mortals,—and the body now
I judged would perish, though I knew not how;
The gracious power around me could translate
And make me pass to that immortal state :
Thus shall I pay the debt that must be paid,
And dying live, nor be by death delay'd;
And when so changed, I should with joy sustain
The heavenly converse, and with him remain.

I saw the distant shade, and went with awe,
But not with terror, to the form I saw;
Yet slowly went, for he I did believe
Would meet, and soul to soul his friend receive;
So on I drew, concluding in my mind,
I cannot judge what laws may spirits bind;
Though I dissolve, and mingle with the blest,
I am a new and uninstructed guest,
And ere my love can speak, he should be first address'd.

Thus I began to speak,—my new-born pride,
My love, and daring hope, the words supplied.

'Dear, happy shade! companion of the good,
The just, the pure, do I on thee intrude ?
Art thou not come my spirit to improve,
To form, instruct, and fit me for thy love,
And, as in love we parted, to restore
The blessing lost, and then to part no more?
Let me with thee in thy pure essence dwell,
Nor go to bid them of my house farewell,
But thine be ever !'——How shall I relate
Th' event that finish'd this ecstatic state ?
Yet let me try.—It turn'd, and I beheld
An hideous form, that hope and zeal expell'd :
In a dim light the horrid shape appear'd,
That wisdom would have fled, and courage fear'd,
Pale, and yet bloated, with distorted eyes
Distant and deep, a mouth of monstrous size,
That would in day's broad glare a simple maid surprise :
He heard my words, and cried, with savage shout,
'Bah !—bother !—blarney !—What is this about ?'
Love, lover, longing, in an instant fled,—
Now I had vice and impudence to dread;

And all my high-wrought fancies died away
To woman's trouble, terror, and dismay.

'What,' said the wretch, 'what is it you would have?
Would'st hang a man for peeping in a grave?
Search me yourself, and try if you can feel
Aught I have taken,—there was nought to steal:
'T was told they buried with the corpse enough
To pay the hazard,—I have made the proof,
Nor gain'd a tester—What I tell is true;
But I 'm no fool, to be betray'd by you,—
I 'll hazard nothing, curse me if I do!'

The light increased, and plainly now appear'd
A knavish fool whom I had often fear'd,
But hid the dread; and I resolved at least
Not to expose it to the powerful beast.

'Come, John,' I said, suppressing fear and doubt,
'Walk on before, and let a lady out!'—
'Lady!' the wretch replied, with savage grin,
'Apply to him that let the lady in:
What! you would go, I take it, to the Dean,
And tell him what your ladyship has seen?'

When thus the fool exposed the knave, I saw
The means of holding such a mind in awe,
And gain my safety by his dread of law.

'Alas!' I cried, 'I fear the Dean like you,
For I transgress, and am in trouble too:
If it be known that we are here, as sure
As here we are we must the law endure:
Each other's counsel therefore let us keep,
And each steal homeward to our beds and sleep.'

Steal!' said the ruffian's conscience—'Well, agreed;
Steal on, and let us to the door proceed:'—
Yet, ere he moved, he stood awhile, and took
Of my poor form a most alarming look;
But, hark!' I cried, and he to move began,—
Escape alone engaged the dreadful man:
With eager hand I oped the ponderous door—
The wretch rush'd by me, and was heard no more.

So I escaped,—and when my dreams came on,
I check'd the madness by the thoughts of John:
Yet say I not what can or cannot be,
But give the story of my ghost and me."

BOOK XXI.

SMUGGLERS AND POACHERS.

A Widow at the Hall—Inquiry of Richard—Relation of two Brothers—Their different Character—Disposition—Modes of thinking—James a Servant—Robert joins the Smugglers—Rachel at the Hall—James attached to her—Trade fails—Robert a Poacher—Is in Danger—How released—James and Rachel—Revenge excited—Association formed—Attack resolved—Preparation made for Resistance—A Night Adventure—Reflections.

There was a widow in the village known
To our good Squire, and he had favour shown
By frequent bounty—She as usual came,
And Richard saw the worn and weary frame,
Pale cheek, and eye subdued, of her whose mind
Was grateful still, and glad a friend to find,
Though to the world long since and all its hopes resign'd:
Her easy form, in rustic neatness clad,
Was pleasing still! but she for ever sad.

"Deep is her grief?" said Richard—"Truly deep,
And very still, and therefore seems to sleep;
To borrow simile, to paint her woes,
Theirs, like the river's motion, seems repose,
Making no petty murmuring,—settled, slow,
They never waste, they never overflow.
Rachel is one of those—for there are some
Who look for nothing in their days to come,
No good nor evil, neither hope nor fear,
Nothing remains or cheerful or severe;
One day is like the past, the year's sweet prime
Like the sad fall,—for Rachel heeds not time:
Nothing remains to agitate her breast,
Spent is the tempest, and the sky at rest;
But while it raged her peace its ruin met,
And now the sun is on her prospects set;—
Leave her, and let us her distress explore,
She heeds it not—she has been left before."

There were two lads call'd Shelley hither brought,
But whence we know not—it was never sought;
Their wandering mother left them, left her name,
And the boys throve and valiant men became:
Handsome, of more than common size, and tall,
And, no one's kindred, seem'd beloved of all;
All seem'd alliance by their deeds to prove,
And loved the youths who could not claim their love.

One was call'd James, the more sedate and grave,
The other Robert—names their neighbours gave;
They both were brave, but Robert loved to run
And meet his danger—James would rather shun
The dangerous trial, but whenever tried
He all his spirit to the act applied.

Robert would aid on any man bestow,
James would his man and the occasion know;
For that was quick and prompt—this temperate and slow.

Robert would all things he desired pursue,
James would consider what was best to do;
All spoke of Robert as a man they loved,
And most of James as valued and approved.

Both had some learning: Robert his acquired
By quicker parts, and was by praise inspired;
James, as he was in his acquirements slow,
Would learn the worth of what he tried to know.

In fact, this youth was generous—that was just;
The one you loved, the other you would trust:
Yet him you loved you would for truth approve,
And him you trusted you would likewise love.

Such were the brothers—James had found his way
To Nether Hall, and there inclined to stay;
He could himself command, and therefore could obey:
He with the keeper took his daily round,
A rival grew, and some unkindness found;
But his superior farm'd! the place was void,
And James guns, dogs, and dignity enjoy'd.

Robert had scorn of service; he would be
A slave to no man—happy were the free,
And only they;—by such opinions led,
Robert to sundry kinds of trade was bred;
Nor let us wonder if he sometimes made
An active partner in a lawless trade;
Fond of adventure, wanton as the wave,
He loved the danger and the law to brave;
But these were chance-adventures, known to few,—
Not that the hero cared what people knew.

The brothers met not often—When they met
James talk'd of honest gains and scorn of debt,
Of virtuous labour, of a sober life,
And what with credit would support a wife.

But Robert answer'd—"How can men advise
Who to a master let their tongue and eyes?
Whose words are not their own? whose foot and hand
Run at a nod, or act upon command?
Who cannot eat or drink, discourse or play,
Without requesting others that they may.

Debt you would shun; but what advice to give
Who owe your service every hour you live!
Let a bell sound, and from your friends you run,
Although the darling of your heart were one;
But if the bondage fits you, I resign
You to your lot—I am content with mine!"

Thus would the lads their sentiments express,
And part in earnest, part in playfulness;
Till love, controller of all hearts and eyes,
Breaker of bonds, of friendship's holy ties,
Awakener of new wills and slumbering sympathies,
Began his reign,—till Rachel, meek-eyed maid,
That form, those cheeks, that faultless face display'd,
That child of gracious nature, ever neat
And never fine; a flowret simply sweet,
Seeming at least unconscious she was fair;
Meek in her spirit, timid in her air,
And shrinking from his glance if one presumed
To come too near the beauty as it bloom'd.

Robert beheld her in her father's cot
Day after day, and blest his happy lot;
He look'd indeed, but he could not offend
By gentle looks—he was her father's friend:
She was accustom'd to that tender look,
And frankly gave the hand he fondly took;
She loved his stories, pleased she heard him play,
Pensive herself, she loved to see him gay,
And if they loved not yet, they were in Love's highway.

But Rachel now to womanhood was grown,
And would no more her faith and fondness own;
She called her latent prudence to her aid,
And grew observant cautious and afraid;
She heard relations of her lover's guile,
And could believe the danger of her smile·
With art insidious rival damsels strove
So show how false his speech, how feign'd his love;
And though her heart another story told,
Her speech grew cautious, and her manner cold.

Rachel had village fame, was fair and tall,
And gain'd a place of credit at the Hall;
Where James beheld her seated in that place,
With a child's meekness, and an angel's face;
Her temper soft, her spirit firm, her words
Simple and few as simple truth affords.

James could but love her,—he at church had seen
The tall, fair maid, had met her on the green,
Admiring always, nor surprised to find
Her figure often present to his mind;
But now he saw her daily, and the sight
Gave him new pleasure and increased delight

But James, still prudent and reserved, though sure
The love he felt was love that would endure,
Would wait awhile, observing what was fit,
And meet, and right, nor would himself commit:
Then was he flatter'd—James in time became
Rich, both as slayer of the Baron's game,
And as protector,—not a female dwelt
In that demesne who had not feign'd or felt
Regard for James; and he from all had praise
Enough a young man's vanity to raise;
With all these pleasures he of course must part
When Rachel reign'd sole empress of his heart.

Robert was now deprived of that delight
He once experienced in his mistress' sight;
For, though he now his frequent visits paid,
He saw but little of the cautious maid;
The simple common pleasures that he took
Grew dull, and he the wonted haunts forsook;
His flute and song he left, his book and pen,
And sought the meetings of adventurous men;
There was a love-born sadness in his breast,
That wanted stimulus to bring on rest;
These simple pleasures were no more of use,
And danger only could repose produce;
He join'd th' associates in their lawless trade,
And was at length of their profession made.

He saw connected with th' adventurous crew
Those whom he judged were sober men and true;
He found that some, who should the trade prevent,
Gave it by purchase their encouragement;
He found that contracts could be made with those
Who had their pay these dealers to oppose;
And the good ladies whom at church he saw
With looks devout, of reverence and awe,
Could change their feelings as they change their place,
And, whispering, deal for spicery and lace:
And thus the craft and avarice of these
Urged on the youth, and gave his conscience ease.

Him loved the maiden Rachel, fondly loved,
As many a sigh and tear in absence proved,

And many a fear for dangers that she knew,
And many a doubt what one so gay might do:
Of guilt she thought not,—she had often heard
They bought and sold, and nothing wrong appear'd;
Her father's maxim this: she understood
There was some ill,—but he, she knew, was good:
It was a traffic—but was done by night—
If wrong, how trade? why secrecy, if right?
But Robert's conscience, she believed, was pure—
And that he read his Bible she was sure.

James, better taught, in confidence declared
His grief for what his guilty brother dared:
He sigh'd to think how near he was akin
To one reduced by godless men to sin;
Who, being always of the law in dread,
To other crimes were by the danger led—
And crimes with like excuse——The smuggler cries,
"What guilt is his who pays for what he buys?"
The poacher questions, with perverted mind,
"Were not the gifts of heaven for all design'd?"
This cries, "I sin not—take not till I pay;"—
That, "My own hand brought down my proper prey:"—
And while to such fond arguments they cling,
How fear they God? how honour they the king?
Such men associate, and each other aid,
Till all are guilty, rash, and desperate made;
Till to some lawless deed the wretches fly,
And in the act, or for the acting, die.

The maid was frighten'd,—but, if this was true,
Robert for certain no such danger knew,
He always pray'd ere he a trip began,
And was too happy for a wicked man:
How could a creature, who was always gay,
So kind to all men, so disposed to pray,
How could he give his heart to such an evil way?
Yet she had fears,—for she could not believe
That James could lie, or purpose to deceive;
But still she found, though not without respect
For one so good, she must the man reject;
For, simple though she was, full well she knew
What this strong friendship led him to pursue;
And, let the man be honest as the light,
Love warps the mind a little from the right;
And she proposed, against the trying day,
What in the trial she should think and say.

And now, their love avow'd, in both arose
Fear and disdain—the orphan pair were foes.

Robert, more generous of the two, avow'd
His scorn, defiance, and contempt aloud.

James talk'd of pity in a softer tone,
To Rachel speaking, and with her alone:
He knew full well, he said, to what must come
His wretched brother, what would be his doom:
Thus he her bosom fenced with dread about;
But love he could not with his skill drive out.
Still he effected something,—and that skill
Made the love wretched, though it could not kill;
Had Robert fail'd, though much he tried, to prove
He had no guilt—She granted he had love.

Thus they proceeded, till a winter came,
When the stern keeper told of stolen game:
Throughout the woods the poaching dogs had been,
And from him nothing should the robbers screen,
From him and law,—he would all hazards run,
Nor spare a poacher, were his brother one—
Love, favour, interest, tie of blood should fail,
Till vengeance bore him bleeding to the jail.

Poor Rachel shudder'd,—smuggling she could name
Without confusion, for she felt not shame;
But poachers were her terror, and a wood
Which they frequented had been mark'd by blood;
And though she thought her Robert was secure
In better thoughts, yet could she not be sure.

James now was urgent,—it would break his heart
With hope, with her, and with such views to part,
When one so wicked would her hand possess,
And he a brother!—that was his distress,
And must be hers——She heard him, and she sigh'd,
Looking in doubt,—but nothing she replied.

There was a generous feeling in her mind,
That told her this was neither good nor kind:
James caused her terror, but he did no more—
Her love was now as it had been before.

Their traffic fail'd,—and the adventurous crew
No more their profitless attempts renew:
Dig they will not, and beg they might in vain—
Had they not pride, and what can then remain?

Now was the game destroy'd, and not a hare
Escaped at least the danger of the snare;
Woods of their feather'd beauty were bereft,
The beauteous victims of the silent theft;
The well-known shops received a large supply,
That they who could not kill at least might buy.

James was enraged, enraged his lord, and both
Confirm'd their threatening with a vengeful oath:
Fresh aid was sought,—and nightly on the lands
Walk'd on their watch the strong determined bands:
Pardon was offer'd, and a promised pay
To him who would the desperate gang betray.

Nor fail'd the measure,—on a certain night
A few were seized—the rest escaped by flight;
Yet they resisted boldly ere they fled,
And blows were dealt around, and blood was shed;
Two groaning helpers on the earth were laid,
When more arrived the lawful cause to aid:
Then four determined men were seized and bound,
And Robert in this desperate number found:
In prison fetter'd, he deplored his fate,
And cursed the folly he perceived too late.

James was a favourite with his lord,—the zeal
He show'd was such as masters ever feel;
If he for vengeance on a culprit cried,
Or if for mercy, still his lord complied:
And now, 't was said, he will for mercy plead,
For his own brother's was the guilty deed:
True, the hurt man is in a mending way,
But must be crippled to his dying day.

Now James had vow'd the law should take its course,
He would not stay it, if he did not force

He could his witness, if he pleased, withdraw,
Or he could arm with certain death the law:
This he attested to the maid, and true,
If this he could not, yet he much could do.

How suffer'd then that maid,—no thought she had,
No view of days to come, that was not sad;
As sad as life with all its hopes resign'd,
As sad as aught but guilt can make mankind.

With bitter grief the pleasures she review'd
Of early hope, with innocence pursued,
When she began to love, and he was fond and good:
He now must die, she heard from every tongue—
Die, and so thoughtless! perish, and so young!
Brave, kind, and generous, tender, constant, true,
And he must die—then will I perish too!

A thousand acts in every age will prove
Women are valiant in a cause they love;
If fate the favour'd swain in danger place,
They heed not danger—perils they embrace;
They dare the world's contempt, they brave their name's disgrace;
They on the ocean meet its wild alarms,
They search the dungeon with extended arms;
The utmost trial of their faith they prove,
And yield the lover to assert their love.

James knew his power—his feelings were not nice—
Mercy he sold, and she must pay the price:
If his good lord forbore to urge their fate,
And he the utmost of their guilt to state,
The felons might their forfeit lives redeem,
And in their country's cause regain esteem;
But never more that man, whom he had shame
To call his brother, must she see or name.

Rachel was meek, but she had firmness too,
And reason'd much on what she ought to do:
In Robert's place, she knew what she should choose—
But life was not the thing she fear'd to lose:
She knew that she could not their contract break,
Nor for her life a new engagement make,
But he was man, and guilty,—death so near
Might not to his as to her mind appear;
And he might wish, to spare that forfeit life,
The maid he loved might be his brother's wife,
Although that brother was his bitter foe,
And he must all the sweets of life forego.

This would she try,—Intent on this alone,
She could assume a calm and settled tone:
She spake with firmness—"I will Robert see,
Know what he wishes, and what I must be;"
For James had now discover'd to the maid
His inmost heart, and how he must be paid,
If he his lord would soften, and would hide
The facts that must the culprit's fate decide.
"Go not," he said,—for she her full intent
Proclaim'd——To go she purposed, and she went:
She took a guide, and went with purpose stern
The secret wishes of her friend to learn.

She saw him fetter'd, full of grief, alone,
Still as the dead, and he suppress'd a groan
At her appearance——Now she pray'd for strength;
And the sad couple could converse at length.

It was a scene that shook her to repeat,—
Life fought with love, both powerful, and both sweet.

"Wilt thou die, Robert, or preserve thy life!
Shall I be thine own maid, or James's wife?"

"His wife! No!—Never will I thee resign—
No, Rachel, no!"——"Then am I ever thine:
I know thee rash and guilty,—but to thee
I pledged my vow, and thine will ever be:
Yet think again,—the life that God has lent
Is thine, but not to cast away.—Consent,
If 't is thy wish; for this I made my way
To thy distress—Command, and I obey."

"Perhaps my brother may have gain'd thy heart!"—
"Then why this visit, if I wish'd to part?
Was it, ah, man ungrateful! wise to make
Effort like this, to hazard for thy sake
A spotless reputation, and to be
A suppliant to that stern man for thee?
But I forgive,—thy spirit has been tried,
And thou art weak, but still thou must decide.

I ask'd thy brother, James, wouldst thou command,
Without the loving heart, the obedient hand?
I ask thee, Robert, lover, canst thou part
With this poor hand, when master of the heart?
He answer'd, 'Yes?'—I tarry thy reply,
Resign'd with him to live, content with thee to die."

Assured of this, with spirits low and tame,
Here life so purchased—there a death of shame;
Death once his merriment, but now his dread,
And he with terror thought upon the dead:
"O! sure 't is better to endure the care
And pain of life, than go we know not where!—
And is there not the dreaded hell for sin,
Or is it only this I feel within?
That, if it lasted, no man would sustain,
But would by any change relieve the pain:
Forgive me, love! it is a loathsome thing
To live not thine; but still this dreaded sting
Of death torments me—I to nature cling——
Go, and be his—but love him not, be sure—
Go, love him not,—and I will life endure:
He, too, is mortal!"——Rachel deeply sigh'd,
But would no more converse: she had complied,
And was no longer free—she was his brother's bride.

"Farewell!" she said, with kindness, but not fond,
Feeling the pressure of the recent bond,
And put her tenderness apart to give
Advice to one who so desired to live:
She then departed, join'd the attending guide,
Reflected—wept—was sad—was satisfied.

James on her worth and virtue could depend,—
He listen'd gladly to her story's end:
Again he promised Robert's life to save,
And claim'd the hand that she in payment gave.

Robert, when death no longer was in view,
Scorn'd what was done, but could not this undo;
The day appointed for the trial near
He view'd with shame, and not unmix'd with fear,—

James might deceive him; and, if not, the schemes
Of men may fail——Can I depend on James?

He might; for now the grievous price was paid—
James to the altar led the victim maid,
And gave the trembling girl his faithful word
For Robert's safety, and so gave my lord.

But this, and all the promise hope could give,
Gilded not life—it was not joy to live;
There was no smile in Rachel, nothing gay;
The hours pass'd off, but never danced away.

When drew the gloomy day for trial near,
There came a note to Robert—"Banish fear!"
He knew whence safety came,—his terror fled,
But rage and vengeance fill'd his soul instead.

A stronger fear in his companions rose—
The day of trial on their hopes might close:
They had no brothers, none to intercede
For them, their friends suspected, and in need;
Scatter'd, they judged, and could unite no more,—
Not so, they then were at the prison door.

For some had met who sought the haunts they loved,
And were to pity and to vengeance moved:
Their fellows perish! and they see their fall,—
Why not attempt the steep but guardless wall?

Attempt was made, his part assign'd each man,
And they succeeded in the desperate plan;
In truth, a purposed mercy smoothed their way,
But that they knew not—all triumphant they.
Safe in their well-known haunts, they all prepared
To plan anew, and show how much they dared.

With joy the troubled heart of Robert beat,
For life was his, and liberty was sweet;
He look'd around in freedom——in delight?
O! no—his Rachel was another's right!
"Right!—has he then preserved me in the day
Of my distress?—He has the lovely pay!
But I no freedom at the slave's request,
The price I paid shall then be repossess'd!
Alas! her virtue and the law prevent,
Force cannot be, and she will not consent;
But were that brother gone!—A brother? No!
A circumventor!—and the wretch shall go!
Yet not this hand—How shifts about my mind,
Ungovern'd, guideless, drifting in the wind,
And I am all a tempest, whirl'd around
By dreadful thoughts, that fright me and confound;—
I would I saw him on the earth laid low!
I wish the fate, but must not give the blow!"

So thinks a man when thoughtful; he prefers
A life of peace till man his anger stirs,
Then all the efforts of his reason cease,
And he forgets how pleasant was that peace;
Till the wild passions what they seek obtain,
And then he sinks into his calm again.

Now met the lawless clan,—in secret met,
And down at their convivial board were set;
The plan in view to past adventures led,
And the past conflicts present anger bred;
They sigh'd for pleasures gone, they groan'd for heroes dead:
Their ancient stores were rifled,—strong desires
Awaked, and wine rekindled latent fires.

It was a night such bold desires to move;
Strong winds and wintry torrents fill'd the grove;
The crackling boughs that in the forest fell,
The cawing rooks, the cur's affrighten'd yell;
The scenes above the wood, the floods below,
Were mix'd, and none the single sound could know;
"Loud blow the blasts," they cried, "and call us as they blow."

In such a night—and then the heroes told
What had been done in better times of old;
How they had conquer'd all opposed to them,
By force in part, in part by stratagem;
And as the tales inflamed the fiery crew,
What had been done they then prepared to do;
"'T is a last night!" they said—the angry blast
And roaring floods seem'd answering "'t is a last!"

James knew they met, for he had spies about,
Grave, sober men, whom none presumed to doubt;
For if suspected, they had soon been tried
Where fears are evidence, and doubts decide:
But these escaped——Now James companions took,
Sturdy and bold, with terror-stirring look;
He had before, by informations led,
Left the afflicted partner of his bed;
Awaked his men, and through plantations wide,
Deep woods, and trackless ling, had been their guide;
And then return'd to wake the pitying wife,
And hear her tender terrors for his life.

But in this night a sure informer came,
They were assembled who attack'd his game;
Who more than once had through the park made way,
And slain the dappled breed, or vow'd to slay;
The trembling spy had heard the solemn vow,
And need and vengeance both inspired them now.

The keeper early had retired to rest
For brief repose;—sad thoughts his mind possess'd;
In his short sleep he started from his bed,
And ask'd in fancy's terror "Is he dead?"

There was a call below, when James awoke,
Rose from his bed, and arms to aid him took,
Not all defensive!—there his helpers stood,
Arm'd like himself, and hastening to the wood.

"Why this?" he said, for Rachel pour'd her tears
Profuse, that spoke involuntary fears:
"Sleep, that so early thou for us mayst wake,
And we our comforts in return may take;
Sleep, and farewell!" he said, and took his way,
And the sad wife in neither could obey;
She slept not nor well fared, but restless dwelt
On her past life, and past afflictions felt;
The man she loved the brother and the foe
Of him she married!—It had wrought her wo;

Not that she loved but pitied, and that now
Was, so she fear'd, infringement of her vow:
James too was civil, though she must confess
That his was not her kind of happiness;
That he would shoot the man who shot a hare
Was what her timid conscience could not bear;
But still she loved him—wonder'd where he stray'd
In this loud night! and if he were afraid.

More than one hour she thought, and dropping then
In sudden sleep, cried loudly "Spare him, men!
And do no murder!"—then awaked she rose,
And thought no more of trying for repose.

'T was past the dead of night, when every sound
That nature mingles might be heard around:
But none from man,—man's feeble voice was hush'd,
Where rivers swelling roar'd, and woods were crush'd;
Hurried by these, the wife could sit no more,
But must the terrors of the night explore.

Softly she left her door, her garden gate,
And seem'd as then committed to her fate;
To every horrid thought and doubt a prey,
She hurried on, already lost her way;
Oft as she glided on in that sad night,
She stopp'd to listen, and she look'd for light;
An hour she wander'd, and was still to learn
Aught of her husband's safety or return:
A sudden break of heavy clouds could show
A place she knew not, but she strove to know;
Still further on she crept with trembling feet,
With hope a friend, with fear a foe to meet:
And there was something fearful in the sight,
And in the sound of what appear'd to-night;
For now, of night and nervous terror bred,
Arose a strong and superstitious dread;
She heard strange noises, and the shapes she saw
Of fancied beings bound her soul in awe.

The moon was risen, and she sometimes shone
Through thick white clouds that flew tumultuous on,
Passing beneath her with an eagle's speed,
That her soft light imprison'd and then freed:
The fitful glimmering through the hedge-row green
Gave a strange beauty to the changing scene;
And roaring winds and rushing waters lent
Their mingled voice that to the spirit went.

To these she listen'd; but new sounds were heard;
And sight more startling to her soul appear'd;
There were low lengthen'd tones with sobs between,
And near at hand, but nothing yet was seen;
She hurried on, and "Who is there?" she cried,
"A dying wretch!"—was from the earth replied.

It was her lover, was the man she gave,
The price she paid, himself from death to save;
With whom, expiring, she must kneel and pray,
While the soul flitted from the shivering clay
That press'd the dewy ground, and bled its life away!

This was the part that duty bad her take,
Instant and ere her feelings were awake;
But now they waked to anguish; there came then,
Hurrying with lights, loud-speaking, eager men.
"And here, my lord, we met—And who is here
The keeper's wife—Ah! woman go not near!
There lies the man that was the head of all—
See, in his temples went the fatal ball!
And James that instant, who was then our guide,
Felt in his heart the adverse shot, and died!
It was a sudden meeting, and the light
Of a dull moon made indistinct our fight;
He foremost fell!—But see, the woman creeps
Like a lost thing, that wanders as she sleeps.
See, here her husband's body—but she knows
That other dead! and that her action shows.
Rachel! why look you at your mortal foe?
She does not hear us—Whither will she go?"

Now, more attentive, on the dead they gazed,
And they were brothers: sorrowing and amazed,
On all a momentary silence came,
A common softness, and a moral shame.

"Seized you the poachers?" said my lord—"They fled,
And we pursued not—one of them was dead,
And one of us; they hurried through the wood,
Two lives were gone, and we no more pursued.
Two lives of men, of valiant brothers lost!
Enough, my lord, do hares and pheasants cost!"

So many thought, and there is found a heart
To dwell upon the deaths of either part;
Since this their morals have been more correct,
The cruel spirit in the place is check'd;
His lordship holds not in such sacred care,
Nor takes such dreadful vengeance for a hare;
The smugglers fear, the poacher stands in awe
Of Heaven's own act, and reverence the law;
There was, there is a terror in the place
That operates on man's offending race;
Such acts will stamp their moral on the soul,
And while the bad they threaten and control,
Will to the pious and the humble say,
Yours is the right, the safe, the certain way,
'T is wisdom to be good, 't is virtue to obey.

So Rachel thinks, the pure, the good, the meek,
Whose outward acts the inward purpose speak
As men will children at their sports behold,
And smile to see them, though unmoved and cold,
Smile at the recollected games, and then
Depart and mix in the affairs of men;
So Rachel looks upon the world, and sees
It cannot longer pain her, longer please,
But just detain the passing thought, or cause
A gentle smile at pity or applause;
And then the recollected soul repairs
Her slumbering hope, and heeds her own affairs.

BOOK XXII.

THE VISIT CONCLUDED.

Richard prepares to depart—Visit to the Rector—His Reception—Visit to the Sisters—Their present Situation—The Morning of the last Day—The Conference of the Brothers—Their Excursion—Richard dissatisfied—The Brother expostulates—The End of their Ride, and of the Day's Business—Conclusion.

"No letters, Tom?" said Richard—"None to-day."
"Excuse me, Brother, I must now away;
Matilda never in her life so long
Deferr'd—Alas! there must be something wrong!"

"Comfort!" said George, and all he could he lent;
"Wait till your promised day, and I consent;
Two days, and those of hope, may cheerfully be spent.

And keep your purpose, to review the place,
My choice; and I beseech you do it grace:
Mark each apartment, their proportions learn,
And either use or elegance discern;
Look o'er the land, the gardens, and their wall,
Find out the something to admire in all;
And should you praise them in a knowing style,
I 'll take it kindly—it is well—a smile."

Richard must now his morning visits pay,
And bid farewell! for he must go away.

He sought the Rector first, not lately seen,
For he had absent from his parish been;
"Farewell!" the younger man with feeling cried,
"Farewell!" the cold but worthy priest replied;
"When do you leave us?"—"I have days but two:"
"'T is a short time—but, well—Adieu, adieu!"

"Now here is one," said Richard, as he went
To the next friend in pensive discontent,
"With whom I sate in social, friendly ease,
Whom I respected, whom I wish'd to please;
Whose love profess'd, I question'd not was true,
And now to hear his heartless, 'Well! adieu!'
But 't is not well—and he a man of sense,
Grave, but yet looking strong benevolence;
Whose slight acerbity and roughness told
To his advantage; yet the man is cold;
Nor will he know, when rising in the morn,
That such a being to the world was born.

Are such the friendships we contract in life?
O! give me then the friendship of a wife!
Adieus, nay, parting-pains to us are sweet,
They make so glad the moments when we meet.

For though we look not for regard intense,
Or warm professions in a man of sense,
Yet in the daily intercourse of mind
I thought that found which I desired to find,
Feeling and frankness—thus it seem'd to me,
And such farewell!—Well, Rector, let it be!"

Of the fair sisters then he took his leave,
Forget he could not, he must think and grieve,
Must the impression of their wrongs retain,
Their very patience adding to his pain;
And still the better they their sorrows bore,
His friendly nature made him feel them more.
He judged they must have many a heavy hour
When the mind suffers from a want of power;
When troubled long we find our strength decay'd,
And cannot then recall our better aid;
For to the mind, ere yet that aid has flown,
Grief has possess'd, and made it all his own;
And patience suffers, till, with gather'd might,
The scatter'd forces of the soul unite.

But few and short such times of suffering were
In Lucy's mind, and brief the reign of care.

Jane had, indeed, her flights, but had in them
What we could pity but must not condemn;
For they were always pure and oft sublime,
And such as triumph'd over earth and time,
Thoughts of eternal love that souls possess,
Foretaste divine of Heaven's own happiness.

Oft had he seen them, and esteem had sprung
In his free mind for maids so sad and young,
So good and grieving, and his place was high
In their esteem, his friendly brother's nigh,
But yet beneath; and when he said adieu!
Their tone was kind, and was responsive too.

Parting was painful; when adieu he cried,
"You will return?" the gentle girls replied;
"You must return! your Brother knows you now,
But to exist without you knows not how;
Has he not told us of the lively joy
He takes—forgive us—in the Brother-boy?
He is alone and pensive; you can give
Pleasure to one by whom a number live
In daily comfort—sure for this you met,
That for his debtors you might pay a debt—
The poor are call'd ungrateful, but you still
Will have their thanks for this—indeed you will."

Richard but little said, for he of late
Held with himself contention and debate.

"My brother loves me, his regard I know,
But will not such affection weary grow?
He kindly says, 'defer the parting day,'
But yet may wish me in his heart away;
Nothing but kindness I in him perceive,
In me 't is kindness then to take my leave;
Why should I grieve if he should weary be?
There have been visiters who wearied me;
He yet may love, and we may part in peace,
Nay, in affection—novelty must cease—
Man is but man; the thing he most desires
Pleases awhile—then pleases not—then tires;
George to his former habits and his friends
Will now return, and so my visit ends."

Thus Richard communes with his heart; but still
He found opposed his reason and his will,
Found that his thoughts were busy in this train,
And he was striving to be calm in vain.

These thoughts were passing while he yet forbore
To leave the friends whom he might see no more.

Then came a chubby child and sought relief,
Sobbing in all the impotence of grief;
A full fed girl she was, with ruddy cheek,
And features coarse, that grosser feelings speak,
To whom another miss, with passions strong,
And slender fist, had done some baby-wrong.
On Lucy's gentle mind had Barlow wrought
To teach this child, whom she had labouring taught
With unpaid love—this unproductive brain
Would little comprehend, and less retain.

A farmer's daughter, with redundant health,
And double Lucy's weight and Lucy's wealth,
Had won the man's regard, and he with her
Possess'd the treasure vulgar minds prefer;
A man of thrift, and thriving, he possess'd
What he esteem'd of earthly good the best;
And Lucy's well-stored mind had not a charm
For this true lover of the well-stock'd farm,
This slave to petty wealth and rustic toil,
This earth-devoted wooer of the soil:—
But she with meekness took the wayward child,
And sought to make the savage nature mild.

But Jane her judgment with decision gave—
"Train not an idiot to oblige a slave."

And where is Bloomer? Richard would have said,
But he was cautious, feeling, and afraid;
And little either of the hero knew,
And little sought—He might be married too.

Now to his home, the morning visits past,
Return'd the guest—that evening was his last.

He met his brother, and they spoke of those
From whom his comforts in the village rose;
Spoke of the favourites, whom so good and kind
It was peculiar happiness to find:
Then for the sisters in their griefs they felt,
And, sad themselves, on saddening subjects dwelt.

But George was willing all this wo to spare,
And let to-morrow be to-morrow's care:
He of his purchase talk'd—a thing of course,
As men will boldly praise a new-bought horse.

Richard was not to all its beauty blind,
And promised still to seek with hope to find:
"The price indeed——"
"Yes, that," said George, "is high;
But if I bought not, one was sure to buy,
Who might the social comforts we enjoy,
And every comfort lessen or destroy.

We must not always reckon what we give,
But think how precious 't is in peace to live;
Some neighbour Nimrod might in very pride
Have stirr'd my anger, and have then defied:
Or worse, have loved, and teased me to excess
By his kind care to give me happiness;
Or might his lady and her daughter bring
To raise my spirits, to converse, and sing:
'T was not the benefits alone I view'd,
But thought what horrid things I might exclude.

Some party man might here have sat him down,
Some country champion, railing at the crown,
Or some true courtier, both prepared to prove,
Who loved not them, could not their country love·
If we have value for our health and ease,
Should we not buy off enemies like these?"

So pass'd the evening in a quiet way,
When, lo! the morning of the parting day.

Each to the table went with clouded look,
And George in silence gazed upon a book;
Something that chance had offer'd to his view,—
He knew not what, or cared not, if he knew.

Richard his hand upon a paper laid,—
His vacant eye upon the carpet stray'd;
His tongue was talking something of the day,
And his vex'd mind was wandering on his way.

They spake by fits,—but neither had concern
In the replies,—they nothing wish'd to learn,
Nor to relate; each sat as one who tries
To baffle sadnesses and sympathies:
Each of his Brother took a steady view,—
As actor he, and as observer too.
Richard, whose heart was ever free and frank,
Had now a trial, and before it sank:
He thought his Brother—parting now so near—
Appear'd not as his Brother should appear;
He could as much of tenderness remark
When parting for a ramble in the park.

"Yet, is it just?" he thought; "and would I see
My Brother wretched but to part with me?
What can he further in my mind explore?
He saw enough, and he would see no more:
Happy himself, he wishes now to slide
Back to his habits——He is satisfied;
But I am not—this cannot be denied.

He has been kind,—so let me think him still;
Yet he expresses not a wish, a will,
To meet again!"——And thus Affection strove
With pride, and petulance made war on love:
He thought his Brother cool—he knew him kind-
And there was sore division in his mind.

"Hours yet remain,—'t is misery to sit
With minds for conversation all unfit;
No evil can from change of place arise,
And good will spring from air and exercise:
Suppose I take the purposed ride with you,
And guide your jaded praise to objects new,
That buyers see?"——
And Richard gave assent
Without resistance, and without intent:
He liked not nor declined,—and forth the Brothers went.

"Come, my dear Richard! let us cast away
All evil thoughts,—let us forget the day,
And fight like men with grief till we like boys are gay."

Thus George,—and even this in Richard's mind
Was judged an effort rather wise than kind;
This flow'd from something he observed of late,
And he could feel it, but he could not state;

He thought some change appear'd,—yet fail'd to prove,
Even as he tried, abatement in the love;
But in his Brother's manner was restraint
That he could feel, and yet he could not paint.

That they should part in peace full well he knew,
But much he fear'd to part with coolness too:
George had been peevish when the subject rose,
And never fail'd the parting to oppose;
Name it, and straight his features cloudy grew
To stop the journey as the clouds will do;—
And thus they rode along in pensive mood,
Their thoughts pursuing, by their cares pursued.

'Richard!" said George, "I see it is in vain
By love or prayer my Brother to retain;
And, truth to tell, it was a foolish thing
A man like thee from thy repose to bring.
Ours to disturb——Say, how am I to live
Without the comforts thou art wont to give?
How will the heavy hours my mind afflict,—
No one t' agree, no one to contradict,
None to awake, excite me, or prevent,
To hear a tale, or hold an argument,
To help my worship in a case of doubt,
And bring me in my blunders fairly out.

Who now by manners lively or serene
Comes between me and sorrow like a screen,
And giving, what I look'd not to have found,
A care, an interest in the world around?"

Silent was Richard, striving to adjust
His thoughts for speech,—for speak, he thought, he must:
Something like war within his bosom strove—
His mild, kind nature, and his proud self-love:
Grateful he was, and with his courage meek,—
But he was hurt, and he resolved to speak.

"Yes, my dear Brother! from my soul I grieve
Thee and the proofs of thy regard to leave:
Thou hast been all that I could wish,—my pride
Exults to find that I am thus allied:
Yet to express a feeling, how it came,
The pain it gives, its nature and its name,
I know not,—but of late I will confess,
Not that thy love is little, but is less.

Hadst thou received me in thy present mood,
Sure I had held thee to be kind and good;
But thou wert all the warmest heart could state,
Affection dream, or hope anticipate;
I must have wearied thee, yet, day by day,—
'Stay!' said my Brother, and 't was good to stay;
But now, forgive me, thinking I perceive
Change undefined, and as I think I grieve.

Have I offended?—Proud although I be,
I will be humble, and concede to thee:
Have I intruded on thee when thy mind
Was vex'd, and then to solitude inclined?
O! there are times when all things will molest
Minds so disposed, so heavy, so oppress'd;
And thine, I know, is delicate and nice,
Sickening at folly, and at war with vice:
Then, at a time when thou wert vex'd with these
I have intruded, let affection tease,
And so offended."——

"Richard, if thou hast,
'T is at this instant, nothing in the past:
No, thou art all a Brother's love would choose;
And, having lost thee, I shall interest lose
In all that I possess: I pray thee tell
Wherein thy host has fail'd to please thee well,—
Do I neglect thy comforts?"—

"O! not thou,
But art thyself uncomfortable now,
And 't is from thee and from thy looks I gain
This painful knowledge—'t is my Brother's pain;
And yet that something in my spirit lives,
Something that spleen excites and sorrow gives,
I may confess,—for not in thee I trace
Alone this change, it is in all the place:
Smile if thou wilt in scorn, for I am glad
A smile at any rate is to be had.

But there is Jacques, who ever seem'd to treat
Thy Brother kindly as we chanced to meet;
Nor with thee only pleased our worthy guide,
But in the hedge-row path and green-wood side,
There he would speak with that familiar ease
That makes a trifle, makes a nothing please.

But now to my farewell,—and that I spoke
With honest sorrow,—with a careless look,
Gazing unalter'd on some stupid prose—
His sermon for the Sunday I suppose,—
'Going?' said he: 'why then the 'Squire and you
Will part at last—You 're going?—Well, adieu!'

True, we were not in friendship bound like those,
Who will adopt each other's friends and foes,
Without esteem or hatred of their own,—
But still we were to intimacy grown;
And sure of Jacques when I had taken leave
It would have grieved me,—and it ought to grieve.
But I in him could not affection trace,—
Careless he put his sermons in their place,
With no more feeling than his sermon-case.

Not so those generous girls beyond the brook,—
It quite unmann'd me as my leave I took.

But, my dear Brother! when I take at night,
In my own home, and in their mother's sight,
By turns my children, or together see
A pair contending for the vacant knee,
When to Matilda I begin to tell
What in my visit first and last befell—
Of this your village, of her tower and spire,
And, above all, her Rector and her 'Squire,
How will the tale be marr'd when I shall end—
I left displeased the Brother and the friend?"

"Nay, Jacques is honest—Marry, he was then
Engaged—What! part an author and his pen?
Just in the fit, and when th' inspiring ray
Shot on his brain, t' arrest it in its way!
Come, thou shalt see him in an easier vein!
Nor of his looks nor of his words complain:

Art thou content?"—
If Richard had replied,
"I am," his manner had his words belied:
Even from his Brother's cheerfulness he drew
Something to vex him—what, he scarcely knew:
So he evading said, "My evil fate
Upon my comforts throws a gloom of late:
Matilda writes not; and, when last she wrote,
I read no letter—'t was a trader's note,—
'Yours I received,' and all that formal prate
That is so hateful, that she knows I hate.

Dejection reigns, I feel, but cannot tell
Why upon me the dire infection fell:
Madmen may say that they alone are sane,
And all beside have a distemper'd brain;
Something like this I feel,—and I include
Myself among the frantic multitude:
But, come, Matilda writes, although but ill,
And home has health, and that is comfort still."

George stopt his horse, and with the kindest look
Spoke to his Brother,—earnestly he spoke,
As one who to his friend his heart reveals,
And all the hazard with the comfort feels.

"Soon as I loved thee, Richard,—and I loved
Before my reason had the will approved,
Who yet right early had her sanction lent,
And with affection in her verdict went,—
So soon I felt, that thus a friend to gain,
And then to lose, is but to purchase pain:
Daily the pleasure grew, then sad the day
That takes it all in its increase away!

Patient thou wert, and kind,—but well I knew
The husband's wishes, and the father's too;
I saw how check'd they were, and yet in secret grew:
Once and again, I urged thee to delay
Thy purposed journey, still deferr'd the day,
And still on its approach the pain increased
Till my request and thy compliance ceased;
I could not further thy affection task,
No more of one so self-resisting ask;
But yet to lose thee, Richard, and with thee
All hope of social joys—it cannot be.
Nor could I bear to meet thee as a boy
From school, his parents, to obtain a joy,
That lessens day by day, and one will soon destroy.

No! I would have thee, Brother, all my own,
To grow beside me as my trees have grown;
For ever near me, pleasant in my sight,
And in my mind, my pride and my delight.

Yet will I tell thee, Richard; had I found
Thy mind dependent and thy heart unsound,
Hadst thou been poor, obsequious, and disposed
With any wish or measure to have closed,
Willing on me and gladly to attend,
The younger brother, the convenient friend;
Thy speculation its reward had made
Like other ventures—thou hadst gain'd in trade;
What reason urged, or Jacques esteem'd thy due,
Thine had it been, and I, a trader too,
Had paid my debt, and home my Brother sent,
Nor glad nor sorry that he came or went;
Who to his wife and children would have told,
They had an uncle, and the man was old;
Till every girl and boy had learn'd to prate
Of uncle George, his gout, and his estate.

Thus had we parted; but as now thou art,
I must not lose thee—No! I cannot part;
Is it in human nature to consent,
To give up all the good that heaven has lent,
All social ease and comfort to forego,
And live again the solitary? No!

We part no more, dear Richard! thou wilt need
Thy Brother's help to teach thy boys to read;
And I should love to hear Matilda's psalm,
To keep my spirit in a morning calm,
And feel the soft devotion that prepares
The soul to rise above its earthly cares;
Then thou and I, an independent two,
May have our parties and defend them too;
Thy liberal notions, and my loyal fears,
Will give us subjects for our future years;
We will for truth alone contend and read,
And our good Jacques shall oversee our creed.

Such were my views; and I had quickly made
Some bold attempts my Brother to persuade
To think as I did; but I knew too well
Whose now thou wert, with whom thou wert to dwell,
And why, I said, return him doubtful home,
Six months to argue if he then would come,
Some six months after? and, beside, I know
That all the happy are of course the slow;
And thou at home art happy, there wilt stay,
Dallying 'twixt will and will-not many a day,
And fret the gloss of hope, and hope itself away.

Jacques is my friend; to him I gave my heart,
You see my Brother, see I would not part;
Wilt thou an embassy of love disdain?
Go to this sister, and my views explain;
Gloss o'er my failings, paint me with a grace
That Love beholds, put meaning in my face;
Describe that dwelling; talk how well we live,
And all its glory to our village give;
Praise the kind sisters whom we love so much,
And thine own virtues like an artist touch.

Tell her, and here my secret purpose show,
That no dependence shall my sister know;
Hers all the freedom that she loves shall be,
And mine the debt,—then press her to agree;
Say, that my Brother's wishes wait on hers,
And his affection what she wills prefers.

Forgive me, Brother,—these my words and more
Our friendly Rector to Matilda bore;
At large, at length, were all my views explain'd,
And to my joy my wishes I obtain'd.

Dwell in that house, and we shall still be near,
Absence and parting I no more shall fear;
Dwell in thy home, and at thy will exclude
All who shall dare upon thee to intrude.

Again thy pardon,—'t was not my design
To give surprise; a better view was mine,

But let it pass—and yet I wish'd to see
That meeting too: and happy may it be!"

Thus George had spoken, and then look'd around,
And smiled as one who then his road had found;
"Follow!" he cried, and briskly urged his horse:
Richard was puzzled, but obey'd of course;
He was affected like a man astray,
Lost, but yet knowing something of the way;
Till a wood clear'd, and still conceal'd the view,
Richard the purchase of his Brother knew;
And something flash'd upon his mind not clear,
But much with pleasure mix'd, in part with fear;
As one who wandering through a stormy night
Sees his own home, and gladdens at the sight,
Yet feels some doubt if fortune had decreed
That lively pleasure in such time of need;
So Richard felt—but now the mansion came
In view direct—he knew it for the same;
There too the garden walk, the elms design'd
To guard the peaches from the eastern wind;
And there the sloping glass, that when he shines
Gives the sun's vigour to the ripening vines.—

"It is my Brother's!"—
"No!" he answers, "No!
'T is to thy own possession that we go;
It is thy wife's, and will thy children's be,
Earth, wood, and water!—and for thine and thee;
Bought in thy name—Alight, my friend, and come,
I do beseech thee, to thy proper home;
There wilt thou soon thy own Matilda view,
She knows our deed, and she approves it too;
Before her all our views and plans were laid,
And Jacques was there t' explain and to persuade.
Here, on this lawn, thy boys and girls shall run,
And play their gambols when their tasks are done;
There, from that window, shall their mother view
The happy tribe, and smile at all they do;
While thou, more gravely, hiding thy delight,
Shalt cry 'O! childish!' and enjoy the sight.

Well, my dear Richard, there 's no more to say—
Stay, as you will—do any thing—but stay;
Be, I dispute not, steward—what you will,
Take your own name, but be my Brother still.

And hear me, Richard! if I should offend,
Assume the patron, and forget the friend;
If aught in word or manner I express
That only touches on thy happiness;
If I be peevish, humoursome, unkind,
Spoil'd as I am by each subservient mind;
For I am humour'd by a tribe who make
Me more capricious for the pains they take
To make me quiet; shouldst thou ever feel
A wound from this, this leave not time to heal,
But let thy wife her cheerful smile withhold,
Let her be civil, distant, cautious, cold;
Then shall I woo forgiveness, and repent,
Nor bear to lose the blessings Heaven has lent.

But this was needless—there was joy of heart,
All felt the good that all desired t' impart;
Respect, affection, and esteem combined,
In sundry portions ruled in every mind;
And o'er the whole an unobtrusive air
Of pious joy, that urged the silent prayer,
And bless'd the new-born feelings——Here we close
Our Tale of Tales!—Health, reader, and repose!

Posthumous Poems of Mr. Crabbe,

RECENTLY PUBLISHED BY HIS SONS.

["There are, in my recess at home, where they have been long undisturbed, another series of Stories—in number and quantity sufficient for a volume; and as I suppose they are much like the former in execution, and sufficiently different in events and characters, they may hereafter, in peaceable times, be worth something to you; and the more, because I shall, whatever is mortal of me, be at rest in the chancel of Trowbridge church; for the works of authors departed are generally received with some favour, partly as they are old acquaintances, and in part because there can be no more of them."—*Mr. Crabbe to his Son George*, dated Clifton, October 29, 1831.]

TO

SAMUEL ROGERS, ESQ.

Sir,

It is our belief that, in respectfully inscribing to you these Tales, we select the name which, if our Father had himself superintended their publication, he would have been most ambitious to connect with them.

We have the honour to be, Sir,
Your grateful and faithful
humble Servants,
GEORGE CRABBE.
JOHN CRABBE.

ADVERTISEMENT.

Although, in a letter written shortly before his death, Mr. Crabbe mentioned the following pieces as fully prepared for the press; and to withhold from the Public what he had thus described, could not have been consistent with filial reverence; yet his executors must confess that, when they saw the first pages of his MS. reduced to type, they became very sensible that, had he himself lived to edit these compositions, he would have considered it necessary to bestow on them a good deal more of revision and correction, before finally submitting them to the eye of the world. They perceived that his language had not always effected the complete developement of his ideas; that images were here and there left imperfect—nay, trains of reflection rather hinted than expressed; and that, in many places, thoughts in themselves valuable could not have failed to derive much additional weight and point, from the last touches of his own pen.

Under such circumstances, it was a very great relief to their minds to learn, that several persons of the highest eminence in literature had read these poetical Remains before any part of them was committed to the printer; and that the verdict of such judges was, on the whole, more favourable than they themselves had begun to anticipate:—that, in the opinion of those whose esteem had formed the highest honour of their father's life, his fame would not be tarnished by their compliance with the terms of his literary bequest; that, though not so uniformly polished as some of his previous performances, these Posthumous Essays would still be found to preserve, in the main, the same characteristics on which his reputation had been established; much of the same quiet humour and keen observation; the same brief and vivid description; the same unobtrusive pathos; the same prevailing reverence for moral truth, and rational religion,—and, in a word, not a few "things which the world would not willingly let die."

The following verses are therefore at length submitted to the Public; not indeed without deep anxiety, but still with some considerable hope, that they may be received with a fair portion of favour now, and allowed to descend to posterity as not, on the whole, unworthy of a place in their Author's collective works.

TALE I.

SILFORD HALL; OR, THE HAPPY DAY.

Within a village, many a mile from town,
A place of small resort and no renown;—
Save that it form'd a way, and gave a name
To Silford Hall, it made no claim to fame;—
It was the gain of some, the pride of all,
That travellers stopt to ask for Silford Hall.

Small as it was, the place could boast a School,
In which *Nathaniel Perkin* bore the rule.
Not mark'd for learning deep, or talents rare,
But for his varying tasks and ceaseless care;
Some forty boys, the sons of thrifty men,
He taught to read, and part to use the pen;
While, by more studious care, a favourite few
Increased his pride—for if the Scholar knew
Enough for praise, say what the Teacher's due?—
These to his presence, slates in hand, moved on,
And a grim smile their feats in figures won.

This Man of Letters woo'd in early life
The Vicar's maiden, whom he made his wife.
She too can read, as by her song she proves—
The song Nathaniel made about their loves:
Five rosy girls, and one fair boy, increased
The Father's care, whose labours seldom ceased.
No day of rest was his. If, now and then,
His boys for play laid by the book and pen,
For Lawyer Slow there was some deed to write,
Or some young farmer's letter to indite,
Or land to measure, or, with legal skill,
To frame some yeoman's widow's peevish will;
And on the Sabbath,—when his neighbours drest,
To hear their duties, and to take their rest—
Then, when the Vicar's periods ceased to flow,
Was heard Nathaniel, in his seat below.

Such were his labours; but the time is come
When his son *Peter* clears the hours of gloom,
And brings him aid: though yet a boy, he shares
In staid Nathaniel's multifarious cares.
A king his father, he, a prince, has rule—
The first of subjects, viceroy of the school:
But though a prince within that realm he reigns,
Hard is the part his duteous soul sustains.
He with his Father, o'er the furrow'd land,
Draws the long chain in his uneasy hand,
And neatly forms at home, what there they rudely plann'd.
Content, for all his labour, if he gains
Some words of praise and sixpence for his pains.
Thus many a hungry day the Boy has fared,
And would have ask'd a dinner, had he dared.
When boys are playing, he, for hours of school,
Has sums to set, and copy-books to rule;
When all are met, for some sad dunce afraid,
He, by allowance, lends his timely aid—
Taught at the student's failings to connive,
Yet keep his Father's dignity alive:
For even Nathaniel fears, and might offend,
If too severe, the farmer, now his friend;
Or her, that farmer's lady, who well knows
Her boy is bright, and needs nor threats nor blows:
This seem'd to Peter hard; and he was loth,
T' obey and rule, and have the cares of both—
To miss the master's dignity, and yet
No portion of the school-boy's play to get.
To him the Fiend, as once to Launcelot, cried,
"Run from thy wrongs!"—"Run where?" his fear replied:
"Run!"—said the Tempter, "if but hard thy fare,
Hard is it now—it *may* be mended there."

But still, though tempted, he refused to part,
And felt the Mother clinging at his heart.
Nor this alone—he, in that weight of care,
Had help, and bore it as a man should bear.
A drop of comfort in his cup was thrown;
It was his treasure, and it was his own.
His Father's shelves contained a motley store
Of letter'd wealth; and this he might explore.
A part his mother in her youth had gain'd,
A part Nathaniel from his club obtain'd,
And part—a well-worn kind—from sire to son remain'd.

He sought his Mother's hoard, and there he found
Romance in sheets, and poetry unbound;
Soft Tales of Love, which never damsel read,
But tears of pity stain'd her virgin bed.
There were Jane Shore and Rosamond the Fair,
And humbler heroines frail as these were there,

There was a tale of one forsaken Maid,
Who till her death the work of vengeance stay'd;
Her Lover, then at sea, while round him stood
A dauntless crew, the angry ghost pursued;
In a small boat, without an oar or sail,
She came to call him, nor would force avail,
Nor prayer; but, conscience-stricken, down he leapt,
And o'er his corse the closing billows slept;
All vanish'd then! but of the crew were some,
Wondering whose ghost would on the morrow come.

A learned Book was there, and in it schemes
How to cast Fortunes and interpret Dreams;
Ballads were there of Lover's bliss or bale,
The Kitchen Story, and the Nursery Tale.
His hungry mind disdain'd not humble food,
And read with relish keen of Robin Hood;
Of him, all-powerful made by magic gift,
And Giants slain—of mighty Hickerthrift;
Through Crusoe's Isle delighted had he stray'd,
Nocturnal visits had to witches paid,
Gliding through haunted scenes, enraptured and afraid.

A loftier shelf with real books was graced,
Bound, or part bound, and ranged in comely taste;
Books of high mark, the mind's more solid food,
Which some might think the owner understood;
But Fluxions, Sections, Algebraic lore,
Our Peter left for others to explore,
And quickly turning to a favourite kind,
Found, what rejoiced him at his heart to find.

Sir Walter wrote not then, or He by whom
Such gain and glory to Sir Walter come—
That Fairy-Helper, by whose secret aid,
Such views of life are to the world convey'd—
As inspiration known in after-times,
The sole assistant in his prose or rhymes.
But there were fictions wild that please the boy,
Which men, too, read, condemn, reject, enjoy—
Arabian Nights, and Persian Tales were there,
One volume each, and both the worse for wear;
There by Quarles' Emblems, Esop's Fables stood,
The coats in tatters, and the cuts in wood.
There, too, "The English History," by the pen
Of Doctor Cooke, and other learned men,
In numbers, sixpence each; by these was seen,
And highly prized, the Monthly Magazine;—
Not such as now will men of taste engage,
But the cold gleanings of a former age,
Scraps cut from sermons, scenes removed from plays,
With heads of heroes famed in Tyburn's palmy days.

The rest we pass—though Peter pass'd them not,
But here his cares and labours all forgot:
Stain'd, torn, and blotted every noble page,
Stood the chief poets of a former age—
And of the present; not their works complete,
But in such portions as on bulks we meet,
The refuse of the shops, thrown down upon the street.
There Shakspeare, Spenser, Milton found a place,
With some a nameless, some a shameless race,
Which many a weary walker resting reads,
And, pondering o'er the short relief, proceeds,
While others lingering pay the written sum,
Half loth, but longing for delight to come.

Of the Youth's morals we would something speak;
Taught by his Mother what to shun or seek:
She show'd the heavenly way, and in his youth,
Press'd on his yielding mind the Gospel truth,
How weak is man, how much to ill inclined,
And where his help is placed, and how to find.
These words of weight sank deeply in his breast,
And awful Fear and holy Hope imprest.
He shrank from vice, and at the startling view,
As from an adder in his path, withdrew.
All else was cheerful. Peter's easy mind
To the gay scenes of village-life inclined.
The lark that soaring sings his notes of joy,
Was not more lively than th' awaken'd boy.
Yet oft with this a softening sadness dwelt,
While, feeling thus, he marvell'd why he felt.
"I am not sorry," said the Boy, "but still,
"The tear will drop—I wonder why it will!"

His books, his walks, his musing, morn and eve,
Gave such impressions as such minds receive;
And with his moral and religious views
Wove the wild fancies of an Infant-Muse,
Inspiring thoughts that he could not express,
Obscure sublime! his secret happiness.
Oft would he strive for words, and oft begin
To frame in verse the views he had within;
But ever fail'd: for how can words explain
The unform'd ideas of a teeming brain?

Such was my Hero, whom I would portray
In one exploit—the Hero of a Day.

At six miles' distance from his native town
Stood Silford Hall, a seat of much renown—
Computed miles, such weary travellers ride,
When they in chance wayfaring men confide.
Beauty and grandeur were within; around,
Lawn, wood, and water; the delicious ground
Had parks where deer disport, had fields where game abound.
Fruits of all tastes in spacious gardens grew;
And flowers of every scent and every hue,
That native in more favour'd climes arise,
Are here protected from th' inclement skies.

To this fair place, with mingled pride and shame,
This lad of learning without knowledge came—
Shame for his conscious ignorance—and pride
To this fair seat in this gay style to ride.

The cause that brought him was a small account,
His father's due, and he must take the amount,
And sign a stamp'd receipt! this done, he might
Look all around him, and enjoy the sight.

So far to walk was, in his mother's view,
More than her darling Peter ought to do;
Peter indeed knew more, but he would hide
His better knowledge, for he wish'd to ride;
So had his father's nag, a beast so small,
That if he fell, he had not far to fall.

His fond and anxious mother in his best,
Her darling child for the occasion drest:
All in his coat of green she clothed her boy,
And stood admiring with a mother's joy:
Large was it made and long, as meant to do
For Sunday-service, when he older grew—
Not brought in daily use in one year's wear or two.
White was his waistcoat, and what else he wore
Had clothed the lamb or parent ewe before.
In all the mother show'd her care or skill;
A riband black she tied beneath his frill;
Gave him his stockings, white as driven snow,
And bade him heed the miry way below;
On the black varnish of the comely shoe,
Shone the large buckle of a silvery hue.
Boots he had worn, had he such things possest—
But bootless grief!—he was full proudly drest;
Full proudly look'd, and light he was of heart,
When thus for Silford Hall prepared to start.

Nathaniel's self with joy the stripling eyed,
And gave a shilling with a father's pride;
Rules of politeness too with pomp he gave,
And show'd the lad how scholars should behave.

Ere yet he left her home, the Mother told—
For she had seen—what things he should behold.
There, she related, her young eyes had view'd
Stone figures shaped like naked flesh and blood,
Which, in the hall and up the gallery placed,
Were proofs, they told her, of a noble taste;
Nor she denied—but, in a public hall,
Her judgment taken, she had clothed them all.
There, too, were station'd, each upon its seat,
Half forms of men, without their hands and feet;
These and what more within that hall might be
She saw, and oh! how long'd her son to see!
Yet could he hope to view that noble place,
Who dared not look the porter in the face?

Forth went the pony, and the rider's knees
Cleaved to her sides—he did not ride with ease;
One hand a whip, and one a bridle held,
In case the pony falter'd or rebell'd.

The village boys beheld him as he pass'd,
And looks of envy on the hero cast;
But he was meek, nor let his pride appear,
Nay, truth to speak, he felt a sense of fear,
Lest the rude beast, unmindful of the rein,
Should take a fancy to turn back again.

He found, and wonder 't is he found, his way,
The orders many that he must obey:
Now to the right, then left, and now again,
Directly onward, through the winding lane;
Then, half-way o'er the common, by the mill,
Turn from the cottage and ascend the hill,
Then—spare the pony, boy!—as you ascend—
You see the Hall, and that's your journey's end."

Yes, he succeeded, not remembering aught
Of this advice, but by his pony taught.
Soon as he doubted, he the bridle threw
On the steed's neck, and said—"Remember you!"
For oft the creature had his father borne,
Sound on his way, and safe on his return.

29 *

So he succeeded, and the modest youth
Gave praise where praise had been assign'd by truth.

His business done,—for fortune led his way
To him whose office was such debts to pay,
The farmer-bailiff, but he saw no more
Than a small room, with bare and oaken floor,
A desk with books thereon—he'd seen such things before;
"Good day!" he said, but linger'd as he spoke
"Good day," and gazed about with serious look;
Then slowly moved, and then delay'd awhile,
In dumb dismay which raised a lordly smile
In those who eyed him, then again moved on,
As all might see, unwilling to be gone.

While puzzled thus, and puzzling all about,
Involved, absorb'd, in some bewildering doubt,
A lady enter'd, Madame Johnson call'd,
Within whose presence stood the lad appall'd.
A learned Lady this, who knew the names
Of all the pictures in the golden frames;
Could every subject, every painter, tell,
And on the merits and their failures dwell;
And if perchance there was a slight mistake—
These the most knowing on such matters make.

"And what dost mean, my pretty lad?" she cried,
"Dost stay or go?"—He first for courage tried,
Then for fit words,—then boldly he replied,
That he "would give a hundred pounds, if so
He had them, all about that house to go;
For he had heard that it contain'd such things
As never house could boast, except the king's."

The ruling Lady, smiling, said, "In truth
Thou shalt behold them all, my pretty youth.
Tom! first the creature to the stable lead,
Let it be fed; and you, my child, must feed;
For three good hours must pass ere dinner come,"—
"Supper," thought he, "she means, our time at home."

First was he feasted to his heart's content,
Then, all in rapture, with the Lady went;
Through rooms immense, and galleries wide and tall,
He walk'd entranced—he breathed in Silford Hall.

Now could he look on that delightful place,
The glorious dwelling of a princely race;
His vast delight was mix'd with equal awe,
There was such magic in the things he saw.
Oft standing still, with open mouth and eyes,
Turn'd here and there, alarm'd as one who tries
T' escape from something strange, that would before him rise.
The wall would part, and beings without name
Would come—for such to his adventures came.
Hence undefined and solemn terror press'd
Upon his mind, and all his powers possess'd
All he had read of magic, every charm,
Were he alone, might come and do him harm.
But his gaze rested on his friendly guide—
"I'm safe," he thought, "so long as you abide."

In one large room was found a bed of state—
"And can they soundly sleep beneath such weight,
Where they may figures in the night explore,
Form'd by the dim light dancing on the floor
From the far window; mirrors broad and high
Doubling each terror to the anxious eye?—
'T is strange," thought Peter, "that such things produce
No fear in *her;* but there is much in use."

On that reflecting brightness, passing by,
The Boy one instant fix'd his restless eye—
And saw himself: he had before descried
His face in one his mother's store supplied;
But here he could his whole dimensions view,
From the pale forehead to the jet-black shoe.
Passing he look'd, and looking, grieved to pass
From the fair figure smiling in the glass.
'T was so Narcissus saw the boy advance
In the dear fount, and met th' admiring glance
So loved—But no! our happier boy admired,
Not the slim form, but what the form attired,—
The riband, shirt, and frill, all pure and clean,
The white-ribb'd stockings, and the coat of green.

The Lady now appear'd to move away—
And this was threat'ning; for he dared not stay,
Lost and alone; but earnestly he pray'd—
"Oh! do not leave me—I am not afraid,
But 't is so lonesome; I shall never find
My way alone, no better than the blind."

The Matron kindly to the Boy replied,
"Trust in my promise, I will be thy guide."
Then to the Chapel moved the friendly pair,
And well for Peter that his guide was there!
Dim, silent, solemn was the scene—he felt
The cedar's power, that so unearthly smelt;
And then the stain'd, dark, narrow windows threw
Strange, partial beams on pulpit, desk, and pew:
Upon the altar, glorious to behold,
Stood a vast pair of candlesticks in gold!
With candles tall, and large, and firm, and white,
Such as the halls of giant-kings would light.
There was an organ, too, but now unseen;
A long black curtain served it for a screen;
Not so the clock, that both by night and day,
Click'd the short moments as they pass'd away.

"Is this a church? and does the parson read"—
Said Peter—"here?—I mean a church indeed."—
"Indeed it is, or as a church is used,"
Was the reply,—and Peter deeply mused,
Not without awe. His sadness to dispel,
They sought the gallery, and then all was well.

Yet enter'd there, although so clear his mind
From every fear substantial and defined,
Yet there remain'd some touch of native fear—
Of something awful to the eye and ear—
A ghostly voice might sound—a ghost itself appear.

There noble Pictures filled his mind with joy—
He gazed and thought, and was no more the boy;
And Madam heard him speak, with some surprise,
Of heroes known to him from histories.
He knew the actors in the deeds of old,—
He could the Roman marvels all unfold.
He to his guide a theme for wonder grew,
At once so little and so much he knew—
Little of what was passing every day,
And much of that which long had pass'd away;
So like a man, and yet so like a child,
That his good friend stood wond'ring as she smiled.

The Scripture Pieces caused a serious awe,
And he with reverence look'd on all he saw;
His pious wonder he express'd aloud,
And at the Saviour Form devoutly bow'd.

Portraits he pass'd admiring; but with pain
Turn'd from some objects, nor would look again.
He seem'd to think that something wrong was done,
When crimes were shown he blush'd to look upon.
Not so his guide—"What youth is that," she cried,
"That handsome stripling at the lady's side;
Can you inform me how the youth is named?"
He answered, "*Joseph;*" but he look'd ashamed.
"Well, and what then? Had you been Joseph, boy!
Would you have been so peevish and so coy?"
Our hero answer'd with a glowing face,
"His mother told him he should pray for grace."
A transient cloud o'ercast the matron's brow;
She seem'd disposed to laugh——but knew not how;
Silent awhile, then placid she appear'd—
"'T is but a child," she thought, and all was clear'd.

No—laugh she could not; still, the more she sought
To hide her thoughts, the more of his she caught.
A hundred times she had these pictures named,
And never felt perplex'd, disturb'd, ashamed;
Yet now the feelings of a lad so young
Call'd home her thoughts and paralysed her tongue.
She pass'd the offensive pictures silent by,
With one reflecting, self-reproving sigh;
Reasoning how habit will the mind entice
To approach and gaze upon the bounds of vice,
As men, by custom, from some cliff's vast height,
Look pleased, and make their danger their delight.

"Come, let us on!—see there a Flemish view,
A Country Fair, and all as Nature true.
See there the merry creatures, great and small,
Engaged in drinking, gaming, dancing all,
Fiddling or fighting—all in drunken joy!"
"But is this Nature?" said the wondering Boy.

"Be sure it is! and those Banditti there—
Observe the faces, forms, the eyes, the air:
See rage, revenge, remorse, disdain, despair!"

"And is that Nature, too?" the stripling cried.—
"Corrupted Nature," said the serious guide.

She then display'd her knowledge.—"That, my dear,
Is called a Titian, this a Guido here,
And yon a Claude—you see that lovely light,
So soft and solemn, neither day nor night.'

"Yes!" quoth the Boy, "and there is just the breeze,
That curls the water, and that fans the trees;
The ships that anchor in that pleasant bay
All look so safe and quiet—Claude you say?"

On a small picture Peter gazed and stood
In admiration—" 't was so dearly good."
" For how much money think you, then, my lad,
Is such a 'dear good picture' to be had?
'T is a famed master's work—a Gerard Dow,
At least the seller told the buyer so."

" I tell the price!" quoth Peter—" I as soon
Could tell the price of pictures in the moon;
But I have heard, when the great race was done,
How much was offered for the horse that won."—

" A thousand pounds: but, look the country round,
And, may be, ten such horses might be found;
While, ride or run where'er you choose to go,
You 'll nowhere find so fine a Gerard Dow."

" If this be true," says Peter, " then, of course,
You'd rate the picture higher than the horse."

" Why, thou 'rt a reasoner, Boy!" the lady cried;
" But see that infant on the other side;
'T is by Sir Joshua.* Did you ever see
A Babe so charming?"—" No, indeed," said he;
" I wonder how he could that look invent,
That seems so sly, and yet so innocent."

In this long room were various Statues seen,
And Peter gazed thereon with awe-struck mien.

" Why look so earnest, Boy?"—" Because they bring
To me a story of an awful thing."
" Tell then thy story."——He who never stay'd
For words or matter, instantly obey'd.—

" A holy pilgrim to a city sail'd,
Where every sin o'er sinful men prevail'd;
Who, when he landed, look'd in every street,
As he was wont, a busy crowd to meet;
But now of living beings found he none,
Death had been there, and turn'd them all to stone;
All in an instant, as they were employ'd,
Was life in every living man destroy'd—
The rich, the poor, the timid and the bold,
Made in a moment such as we behold."

" Come, my good lad, you 've yet a room to see.
Are you awake?"—" I am amazed," said he;
I know they 're figures form'd by human skill,
But 't is so awful, and this place so still?

" And what is this?" said Peter, who had seen
A long wide table, with its cloth of green,
Its net-work pockets, and its studs of gold—
For such they seem'd, and precious to behold.
There too were ivory balls, and one was red,
Laid with long sticks upon the soft green bed,
And printed tables on the wall beside—
" Oh! what are these?" the wondering Peter cried.

" This, my good lad, is call'd the Billiard-room,"
Answer'd his guide, " and here the gentry come,
And with these maces and these cues they play,
At their spare time, or in a rainy day."

" And what this chequer'd box?—for play, I guess?"—
" You judge it right; 't is for the game of Chess.
There! take your time, examine what you will,
There 's King, Queen, Knight,—it is a game of skill:
And these are Bishops; you the difference see."—
" What! do they make a game of *them?*" quoth he.—
" Bishops, like Kings," she said, " are here but names;
Not that I answer for their Honours' games."

All round the House did Peter go, and found
Food for his wonder all the house around.
There guns of various bore, and rods, and lines,
And all that man for deed of death designs,
In beast, or bird, or fish, or worm, or fly—
Life in these last must means of death supply;
The living bait is gorged, and both the victims die.
" God gives man leave his creatures to destroy."—
" What! for his sport?" replied the pitying Boy.—
" Nay," said the Lady, " why the sport condemn!
As die they must, 't is much the same to them."
Peter had doubts; but with so kind a friend,
He would not on a dubious point contend.

Much had he seen, and every thing he saw
Excited pleasure not unmix'd with awe.
Leaving each room, he turn'd as if once more
To enjoy the pleasure that he felt before—
" What then must their possessors feel? how grand
And happy they who can such joys command!
For they may pleasures all their lives pursue,
The winter pleasures, and the summer's too—
Pleasures for every hour in every day—
Oh! how their time must pass in joy away!"

So Peter said.—Replied the courteous Dame:
" What you call pleasure scarcely owns the name.
The very changes of amusement prove
There 's nothing that deserves a lasting love.
They hunt, they course, they shoot, they fish, they game;
The objects vary, though the end the same—
A search for that which flies them; no, my Boy!
'T is not enjoyment, 't is pursuit of joy."

Peter was thoughtful — thinking, 'What! not these,
Who can command, or purchase, what they please—
Whom many serve, who only speak the word,
And they have all that earth or seas afford—
All that can charm the mind and please the eye—
And *they* not happy!—but I 'll ask her why.'

So Peter ask'd—" 'T is not," she said, " for us,
Their Honours' inward feelings to discuss;
But if they 're happy, they would still confess
'T is not these things that make their happiness.

Look from this window! at his work behold
Yon gard'ner's helper—he is poor and old,
He not one thing of all you see can call
His own; but haply, he o'erlooks them all.

* In the year 1783, Mr. Crabbe very frequently passed his mornings at the easel of Sir Joshua Reynolds, conversing on a variety of subjects, while this distinguished artist was employed upon that celebrated painting, then preparing for the Empress Catharine of Russia."

Hear him! he whistles through his work, or stops
But to admire his labours and his crops:
To-day as every former day he fares,
And for the morrow has nor doubts nor cares;
Pious and cheerful, proud when he can please,
Judge if Joe Tompkin wants such things as these.

Come, let us forward!" and she walk'd in haste
To a large room, itself a work of taste,
But chiefly valued for the works that drew
The eyes of Peter—this indeed was new,
Was most imposing—Books of every kind
Were there disposed, the food for every mind.
With joy perplex'd, round cast he wondering eyes,
Still in his joy, and dumb in his surprise.

Above, beneath, around, on every side,
Of every form and size were Books descried;
Like Bishop Hatto,* when the rats drew near,
And war's new dangers waked his guilty fear,
When thousands came beside, behind, before,
And up and down came on ten thousand more;
A tail'd and whisker'd army, each with claws
As sharp as needles, and with teeth like saws,†—
So fill'd with awe, and wonder in his looks,
Stood Peter, 'midst this multitude of Books;
But guiltless he and fearless; yet he sigh'd
To think what treasures were to him denied.

But wonder ceases on continued view;
And the Boy sharp for close inspection grew.
Prints on the table he at first survey'd,
Then to the Books his full attention paid.
At first, from tome to tome, as fancy led,
He view'd the binding, and the titles read;
Lost in delight, and with his freedom pleased,
Then three huge folios from their shelf he seized;
Fixing on one, with prints of every race,
Of beast and bird most rare in every place,—
Serpents, the giants of their tribe, whose prey
Are giants too—a wild ox once a day;
Here the fierce tiger, and the desert's kings,
And all that move on feet, or fins, or wings—
Most rare and strange; a second volume told
Of battles dire, and dreadful to behold,
On sea or land, and fleets dispers'd in storms;
A third has all creative fancy forms,—
Hydra and dire chimera, deserts rude,
And ruins grand, enriching solitude:
Whatever was, or was supposed to be,
Saw Peter here, and still desired to see.

Again he look'd, but happier had he been,
That Book of Wonders he had never seen;

*[For the history of Hatto, Archbishop of Mentz, see Coryat's Crudities, p. 571. See also, among Mr. Southey's minor poems, "God's Judgment on a Bishop."]

†["And in at the windows, and in at the door,
And through the walls by thousands they pour,
And down through the ceiling and up through the floor,
From the right and the left, from behind and before,
From within and without, from above and below,
And all at once to the Bishop they go.
They have whetted their teeth against the stones,
And now they pick the Bishop's bones,
They gnawed the flesh from every limb,
For they were sent to do judgment on him!"—SOUTHEY.]

For there were tales of men of wicked mind,
And how the foe of man deludes mankind.
Magic and murder every leaf bespread—
Enchanted halls, and chambers of the dead,
And ghosts that haunt the scenes where once the victims bled.

Just at this time, when Peter's heart began
To admit the fear that shames the valiant man,
He paused—but why? "Here 's one my guard to be;
When thus protected, none can trouble me:"
Then rising look'd he round, and lo! alone was he.

Three ponderous doors, with locks of shining brass,
Seem'd to invite the trembling Boy to pass;
But fear forbade, till fear itself supplied
The place of courage, and at length he tried.
He grasp'd the key—Alas! though great his need,
The key turn'd not, the bolt would not recede.
Try then again; for what will not distress?
Again he tried, and with the same success.
Yet one remains, remains untried one door—
A failing hope, for two had fail'd before;
But a bold prince, with fifty doors in sight,
Tried forty-nine, before he found the right;
Before he mounted on the brazen horse,
And o'er the walls pursued his airy course.
So his cold hand on this last key he laid:
"Now turn," said he; the treacherous bolt obey'd—
The door receded—bringing full in view
The dim, dull chapel, pulpit, desk, and pew.

It was not right—it would have vex'd a saint;
And Peter's anger rose above restraint.
"Was this her love," he cried, "to bring me here,
Among the dead, to die myself with fear!"—
For Peter judged, with monuments around,
The dead must surely in the place be found:—
"With cold to shiver, and with hunger pine—
'We 'll see the rooms,' she said, 'before we dine;'
And spake so kind! That window gives no light:
Here is enough the boldest man to fright;
It hardly now is day, and soon it will be night."

Deeply he sigh'd, nor from his heart could chase
The dread of dying in that dismal place;
Anger and sorrow in his bosom strove,
And banish'd all that yet remained of love;
When soon despair had seiz'd the trembling Boy,
But hark, a voice! the sound of peace and joy.

"Where art thou, lad?"—"Oh! here am I, in doubt,
And sorely frighten'd—can you let me out?"
"Oh! yes, my child; it was indeed a sin,
Forgetful as I was, to bolt you in.
I left you reading, and from habit lock'd
The door behind me, but in truth am shock'd
To serve you thus; but we will make amends
For such mistake. Come, cheerly, we are friends."

"Oh! yes," said Peter, quite alive to be
So kindly used, and have so much to see,
And having so much seen; his way he spied,
Forgot his peril, and rejoin'd his guide.

Now all beheld his admiration rais'd,
The lady thank'd, her condescension prais'd,

And fix'd the hour for dinner, forth the Boy
Went in a tumult of o'erpowering joy,
To view the gardens, and what more was found
In the wide circuit of that spacious ground,
Till, with his thoughts bewilder'd, and oppress'd
With too much feeling, he inclined to rest.

Then in the park he sought its deepest shade,
By trees more aged than the mansion made,
That ages stood; and there unseen a brook
Ran not unheard, and thus our traveller spoke,—
"I am so happy, and have such delight,
I cannot bear to see another sight;
It wearies one like work;" and so, with deep
Unconscious sigh—he laid him down to sleep.

Thus he reclining slept, and, oh! the joy
That in his dreams possess'd the happy boy,—
Composed of all he knew, and all he read,
Heard, or conceived, the living and the dead.

The Caliph Haroun, walking forth by night
To see young David and Goliah fight,
Rose on his passive fancy—then appear'd
The fleshless forms of beings scorn'd or feared
By just or evil men—the baneful race
Of spirits restless, borne from place to place:
Rivers of blood from conquer'd armies ran,
The flying steed was by, the marble man;
Then danced the fairies round their pigmy queen,
And their feet twinkled on the dewy green,
All in the moon-beam's glory. As they fled,
The mountain loadstone rear'd its fatal head,
And drew the iron-bolted ships on shore,
Where he distinctly heard the billows roar,—
Mix'd with a living voice of—"Youngster, sleep no more,
But haste to dinner." Starting from the ground,
The waking boy obey'd that welcome sound.

He went and sat, with equal shame and pride,
A welcome guest at Madam Johnson's side.
At his right hand was Mistress Kitty placed,
And Lucy, maiden sly, the stripling faced.
Then each the proper seat at table took—
Groom, butler, footman, laundress, coachman, cook;
For all their station and their office knew,
Nor sat as rustics or the rabble do.

The youth to each the due attention paid,
And hob-or-nobb'd with Lady Charlotte's maid;
With much respect each other they address'd,
And all encouraged their enchanted guest.
Wine, fruit, and sweetmeats closed repast so long,
And Mistress Flora sang an opera song.

Such was the Day the happy Boy had spent,
And forth delighted from the Hall he went:
Bowing his thanks, he mounted on his steed,
More largely fed than he was wont to feed;
And well for Peter that his pony knew
From whence he came, the road he should pursue;
For the young rider had his mind estranged
From all around, disturb'd and disarranged,
In pleasing tumult, in a dream of bliss,
Enjoy'd but seldom in a world like this.

But though the pleasures of the day were past,—
For lively pleasures are not form'd to last,—

And though less vivid they became, less strong,
Through life they lived, and were enjoy'd as long;
So deep the impression of that happy Day,
Nor time nor cares could wear it all away;
Ev'n to the last, in his declining years,
He told of all his glories, all his fears.

How blithely forward in that morn he went,
How blest the hours in that fair palace spent,
How vast that Mansion, sure for monarch plann'd,
The rooms so many, and yet each so grand,—
Millions of books in one large hall were found,
And glorious pictures every room around;
Beside that strangest of the wonders there,
That house itself contain'd a house of prayer.

He told of park and wood, of sun and shade,
And how the lake below the lawn was made:
He spoke of feasting such as never boy,
Taught in his school, was fated to enjoy—
Of ladies' maids as ladies' selves were dress'd,
And her, his friend, distinguish'd from the rest,
By grandeur in her look, and state that she possess'd.
He pass'd not one; his grateful mind o'erflow'd
With scenes of all he felt, and they bestow'd.

He spake of every office, great or small,
Within, without, and spake with praise of all—
So pass'd the happy Boy, that Day at Silford Hall.

[*** In the first draft of "Silford Hall" the conclusion is different: and we think it right to preserve the following verses in a note, as they appear to leave little doubt that the story was in fact suggested by the Poet's recollection of his own boyish visits, when an apothecary's apprentice, to Chevely, a seat of the noble family with whom, in after-years, he was domesticated as Chaplain.

Dream on, dear Boy! let pass a few brief years,
Replete with troubles, comforts, hopes, and fears,
Bold expectations, efforts wild and strong,
And thou shalt find thy fond conjectures wrong.
Imagination rules thee: thine are dreams,
And every thing to thee is what it seems:
Thou seest the surfaces of things, that pass
Before thee, colour'd by thy fancy's glass.
The fact below is hidden! What is true
In that fair mansion comes not in thy view;
And thou wouldst feel a new and strange surprise,
Should all within upon thy mind arise.
Thou think'st the lords of all these glorious things
Are blest supremely! so they are,—like kings!
Envy them not their lofty state, my boy;
They but possess the things that you enjoy.

"Nay, but they're lords of all you see around——
Ring but a bell, and men obey the sound;
Make but a motion with the hand or eye,
And their attendants at the signal fly."

True, my fair lad! but this is contract all,
For James is paid to heed his Honour's call:
Let wages cease, and lay the livery by,
And James will heed no more than you or I.
Service has lawful bound, and that beyond
Is no obedience—'t is not in the bond.
Footman, or groom, or butler, still he knows,
So does his lord, the duty that he owes.

Labourers, you say, are grieved with daily toil—
True—but the sweater goes not with the soil;
He can change places, change his way of life,
Take new employments,—say can take a wife;

If he offend, he knows the law's decrée,
Nor can his judge in his accuser see;
And, more than all the rest—or young or old,
Useful or useless, he cannot be sold:
Sorrow and want may in his cot be found,
But not a Slave can live on British ground.

Nor have the lords of all this wealth you see,
Their perfect freedom: few are truly free:
Who rank the highest find the check of fate,
And kings themselves are subject to their state.

Riches, and all that we desire to gain,
Bind their possessors in a golden chain—
'T is kept in peril, and 't is lost with pain.

And thou too, Boy! wilt pass unheeding by
The scenes that now delight thine eager eye.
Dream on awhile! and there shall come a strange,
And, couldst thou see it, an amazing change.
Thou who wert late so happy, and so proud,
To be a seat with liveried men allow'd,
And would not, dared not, in thy very shame,
The titles of their noble masters name—
Titles that, scarcely known, upon thy tongue
With tremulous and erring accent hung——

Oh! had they told thee, when thou sat'st with pride,
And grateful joy, at Madam Johnson's side,
And heard the lisping Flora, blue-eyed maid,
Bid thee be neither bashful nor afraid,
When Mrs. Jane thy burning blush had raised,
Because thy modesty and sense she praised—
Couldst thou have seen that in that place a room
Should be thine own, thy house, thy hall, thy home,
With leave to wander as thou wouldst, to lead
Just as thy fancy was disposed to feed,
To live with those who were so far above
Thy reach, it seem'd to thee a crime to love,
Or even admire them!—Little didst thou know
How near approach the lofty and the low!
In all we dare, and all we dare not name,
How much the great and little are the same!

Well, thou hast tried it—thou hast closely seen
What greatness has without it, and within;
Where now the joyful expectation?—fled!
The strong anticipating spirit?—dead!]

TALE II.

THE FAMILY OF LOVE.

In a large town, a wealthy thriving place,
Where hopes of gain excite an anxious race;
Which dark dense wreaths of cloudy volumes cloak,
And mark, for leagues around, the place of smoke;
Where fire to water lends its powerful aid,
And steam produces—strong ally to trade:—
Arrived a Stranger, whom no merchant knew,
Nor could conjecture what he came to do:
He came not there a fortune to amend,
He came not there a fortune made to spend;
His age not that which men in trade employ:
The place not that where men their wealth enjoy;
Yet there was something in his air that told
Of competency gain'd, before the man was old.
He brought no servants with him: those he sought
Were soon his habits and his manners taught—
His manners easy, civil, kind, and free;
His habits such as aged men's will be;
To self indulgent; wealthy men like him
Plead for these failings—'t is their way, their whim.

His frank good-humour, his untroubled air,
His free address, and language bold but fair,
Soon made him friends—such friends as all may make,
Who take the way that he was pleased to take.
He gave his dinners in a handsome style,
And met his neighbours with a social smile;
The wealthy all their easy friend approved,
Whom the more liberal for his bounty loved;
And even the cautious and reserv'd began
To speak with kindness of the frank old man,
Who, though associate with the rich and grave,
Laugh'd with the gay, and to the needy gave
What need requires. At church a seat was shown,
That he was kindly ask'd to think his own:
Thither he went, and neither cold nor heat,
Pains nor pretences, kept him from his seat.
This to his credit in the town was told,
And ladies said, "'T is pity he is old:
Yet, for his years, the Stranger moves like one
Who, of his race, has no small part to run."
No envy he by ostentation raised,
And all his hospitable table praised.
His quiet life censorious talk suppress'd,
And numbers hail'd him as their welcome guest.

'T was thought a man so mild, and bounteous too,
A world of good within the town might do;
To vote him honours, therefore, they inclined;
But these he sought not, and with thanks resign'd;
His days of business he declared were past,
And he would wait in quiet for the last;
But for a dinner and a day of mirth
He was the readiest being upon earth.

Men call'd him Captain, and they found the name
By him accepted without pride or shame.
Not in the Navy—that did not appear:
Not in the Army—that at least was clear—
"But as he speaks of sea-affairs, he made,
No doubt, his fortune in the way of trade;
He might, perhaps, an India-ship command—
We 'll call him *Captain*, now he comes to land."

The Stranger much of various life had seen,
Been poor, been rich, and in the state between;
Had much of kindness met, and much deceit,
And all that man who deals with men must meet.
Not much he read; but from his youth had thought,
And been by care and observation taught:
'T is thus a man his own opinions makes;
He holds that fast, which he with trouble takes:
While one whose notions all from books arise,
Upon his authors, not himself, relies—
A borrow'd wisdom this, that does not make us wise.

Inured to scenes, where wealth and place command
Th' observant eye, and the obedient hand,
A tory-spirit his—he ever paid
Obedience due, and look'd to be obey'd.
"Man upon man depends, and, break the chain,
He soon returns to savage life again;
As of fair virgins dancing in a round,
Each binds another, and herself is bound,
On either hand a social tribe he sees,
By those assisted, and assisting these;

While to the general welfare all belong,
The high in power, the low in number strong."

Such was the Stranger's creed—if not profound,
He judged it useful, and proclaim'd it sound;
And many liked it: invitations went
To Captain Elliot, and from him were sent—
These last so often, that his friends confess'd,
The Captain's cook had not a place of rest.
Still were they something at a loss to guess
What his profession was from his address;
For much he knew, and too correct was he
For a man train'd and nurtured on the sea;
Yet well he knew the seaman's words and ways,—
Seaman's his look, and nautical his phrase:
In fact, all ended just where they began,
With many a doubt of this amphibious man.

Though kind to all, he look'd with special grace
On a few members of an ancient race,
Long known, and well respected in the place;
Dyson their name; but how regard for these
Rose in his mind, or why they seem'd to please,
Or by what ways, what virtues—not a cause
Can we assign, for Fancy has no laws;
But, as the Captain show'd them such respect,
We will not treat the Dysons with neglect.

Their father died while yet engaged by trade
To make a fortune, that was never made,
But to his children taught; for he would say
"I place them—all I can—in Fortune's way."

James was his first-born; when his father died,
He, in their large domain, the place supplied,
And found, as to the Dysons all appear'd,
Affairs less gloomy than their sire had fear'd;
But then if rich or poor, all now agree
Frugal and careful, James must wealthy be:
And wealth in wedlock sought, he married soon,
And ruled his Lady from the honey-moon:
Nor shall we wonder; for, his house beside,
He had a sturdy multitude to guide;
Who now his spirit vex'd, and now his temper tried;
Men who by labours live, and, day by day,
Work, weave, and spin their active lives away:
Like bees industrious, they for others strive,
With, now and then, some murmuring in the hive.

James was a churchman—'twas his pride and boast;
Loyal his heart, and "Church and King" his toast;
He for Religion might not warmly feel,
But for the Church he had abounding zeal.

Yet no dissenting sect would he condemn,
"They're naught to us," said he, "nor we to them;
'T is innovation of our own I hate,
Whims and inventions of a modern date.

Why send you Bibles all the world about,
That men may read amiss, and learn to doubt?
Why teach the children of the poor to read,
That a new race of doubters may succeed?
Now can you scarcely rule the stubborn crew,
And what if they should know as much as you?
Will a man labour when to learning bred,
Or use his hands who can employ his head?
Will he a clerk or master's self obey,
Who thinks himself as well inform'd as they?"

These were his favourite subjects—these he chose,
And where he ruled no creature durst oppose.

"We're rich," quoth James; "but if we thus proceed,
And give to all, we shall be poor indeed:
In war we subsidise the world—in peace
We christianise—our bounties never cease:
We learn each stranger's tongue, that they with ease
May read translated Scriptures, if they please;
We buy them presses, print them books, and then
Pay and export poor learned, pious men;
Vainly we strive a fortune now to get,
So tax'd by private claims, and public debt."

Still he proceeds—"You make your prisons light,
Airy and clean, your robbers to invite;
And in such ways your pity show to vice,
That you the rogues encourage, and entice."

For lenient measures James had no regard—
"Hardship," he said, "must work upon the hard;
Labour and chains such desperate men require;
To soften iron you must use the fire."

Active himself, he labour'd to express,
In his strong words, his scorn of idleness;
From him in vain the beggar sought relief—
"Who will not labour is an idle thief,
Stealing from those who will;" he knew not how
For the untaught and ill-taught to allow,
Children of want and vice, inured to ill,
Unchain'd the passions, and uncurb'd the will.

Alas! he look'd but to his own affairs,
Or to the rivals in his trade, and theirs:
Knew not the thousands who must all be fed,
Yet ne'er were taught to earn their daily bread;
Whom crimes, misfortunes, errors only teach,
To seek their food where'er within their reach,
Who for their parents' sins, or for their own,
Are now as vagrants, wanderers, beggars known,
Hunted and hunting through the world, to share
Alms and contempt, and shame and scorn to bear,
Whom Law condemns, and Justice, with a sigh,
Pursuing, shakes her sword and passes by.—
If to the prison we should these commit,
They for the gallows will be render'd fit.

But James had virtues—was esteem'd as one
Whom men look'd up to, and relied upon.
Kind to his equals, social when they met—
If out of spirits, always out of debt;
True to his promise, he a lie disdain'd,
And e'en when tempted in his trade, refrain d,
Frugal he was, and loved the cash to spare,
Gain'd by much skill, and nursed by constant care
Yet liked the social board, and when he spoke,
Some hail'd his wisdom, some enjoy'd his joke
To him a Brother look'd as one to whom,
If fortune frown'd, he might in trouble come;
His Sisters view'd the important man with awe
As if a parent in his place they saw.

All lived in Love; none sought their private ends;
The Dysons were a Family of Friends.

His brother David was a studious boy,
Yet could his sports as well as books enjoy.
E'en when a boy, he was not quickly read,
If by the heart you judged him, or the head.
His father thought he was decreed to shine,
And be in time an eminent Divine;
But if he ever to the Church inclined,
It is too certain that he changed his mind.
He spoke of scruples, but who knew him best
Affirm'd, no scruples broke on David's rest.
Physic and Law were each in turn proposed,
He weigh'd them nicely, and with Physic closed.

He had a serious air, a smooth address,
And a firm spirit that ensured success.
He watch'd his brethren of the time, how they
Rose into fame, that he might choose his way.

Some, he observed, a kind of roughness used,
And now their patients banter'd, now abused:
The awe-struck people were at once dismay'd,
As if they begg'd the advice for which they paid.

There are who hold that no disease is slight,
Who magnify the foe with whom they fight.
The sick was told that his was that disease
But rarely known on mortal frame to seize;
Which only skill profound, and full command
Of all the powers in nature could withstand.
Then, if he lived, what fame the conquest gave!
And if he died—"No human power could save!"

Mere fortune sometimes, and a lucky case,
Will make a man the idol of a place—
Who last, advice to some fair duchess gave,
Or snatch'd a widow's darling from the grave,
Him first she honours of the lucky tribe,
Fills him with praise, and wooes him to prescribe.
In his own chariot soon he rattles on,
And half believes the lies that built him one.

But not of these was David: care and pain,
And studious toil prepared his way to gain.
At first observed, then trusted, he became
At length respected, and acquired a name.
Keen, close, attentive, he could read mankind,
The feeble body, and the failing mind;
And if his heart remain'd untouch'd, his eyes,
His air, and tone, with all could sympathise.

This brought him fees, and not a man was he
In weak compassion to refuse a fee.
Yet though the Doctor's purse was well supplied,
Though patients came, and fees were multiplied,
Some secret drain, that none presumed to know,
And few e'en guess'd, for ever kept it low.
Some of a patient spake, a tender fair,
Of whom the doctor took peculiar care,
But not a fee: he rather largely gave,
Nor spared himself, 't was said, this gentle friend to save.
Her case consumptive, with perpetual need
Still to be fed, and still desire to feed;
An eager craving, seldom known to cease,
And gold alone brought temporary peace.—

So, rich he was not; James some fear express'd,
Dear Doctor David would be yet distress'd;
For if now poor, when so repaid his skill,
What fate were his, if he himself were ill!

In his religion, Doctor Dyson sought
To teach himself—"A man should not be taught,
Should not, by forms or creeds, his mind debase,
That keep in awe an unreflecting race."
He heeded not what Clarke and Paley say,
But thought himself as good a judge as they;
Yet to the Church profess'd himself a friend,
And would the rector for his hour attend;
Nay, praise the learn'd discourse, and learnedly defend.
For since the common herd of men are blind,
He judged it right that guides should be assign'd;
And that the few who could themselves direct
Should treat those guides with honour and respect.
He was from all contracted notions freed,
But gave his Brother credit for his creed;
And if in smaller matters he indulged,
'T was well, so long as they were not divulged.

Oft was the spirit of the Doctor tried,
When his grave Sister wish'd to be his guide.
She told him, "all his real friends were grieved
To hear it said, how little he believed:
Of all who bore the name she never knew
One to his pastor or his church untrue;
All have the truth with mutual zeal profess'd,
And why, dear Doctor, differ from the rest?"

"'T is my hard fate," with serious looks replied
The man of doubt, "to err with such a guide."
"Then why not turn from such a painful state?"—
The doubting man replied, "It is my fate."

Strong in her zeal, by texts and reasons back'd,
In his grave mood the Doctor she attack'd:
Cull'd words from Scripture to announce his doom,
And bade him "think of dreadful things to come."

"If such," he answer'd, "be that state untried,
In peace, dear Martha, let me here abide;
Forbear to insult a man whose fate is known,
And leave to Heaven a matter all his own."

In the same cause the Merchant, too, would strive;
He ask'd, "Did ever unbeliever thrive?
Had he respect? could he a fortune make?
And why not then such impious men forsake?"

"Thanks, my dear James, and be assured I feel,
If not your reason, yet at least your zeal;
And when those wicked thoughts, that keep me poor,
And bar respect, assail me as before
With force combined, you'll drive the fiend away,
For you shall reason, James, and Martha pray."

But though the Doctor could reply with ease,
To all such trivial arguments as these,—
Though he could reason, or at least deride,
There was a power that would not be defied;
A closer reasoner, whom he could not shun,
Could not refute, from whom he could not run;

For Conscience lived within; she slept, 't is true,
But when she waked, her pangs awaken'd too.
She bade him think; and as he thought, a sigh
Of deep remorse precluded all reply.
No soft insulting smile, no bitter jest,
Could this commanding power of strength divest,
But with reluctant fear her terrors he confess'd.
His weak advisers he could scorn or slight,
But not their cause; for, in their folly's spite,
They took the wiser part, and chose their way aright.

Such was the Doctor, upon whom for aid
Had some good ladies call'd, but were afraid—
Afraid of one who, if report were just,
The arm of flesh, and that alone would trust.
But these were few—the many took no care
Of what they judged to be his own affair:
And if he them from their diseases freed,
They neither cared nor thought about his creed:
They said his merits would for much atone,
And only wonder'd that he lived alone.

The widow'd Sister near the Merchant dwelt,
And her late loss with lingering sorrow felt.
Small was her jointure, and o'er this she sigh'd,
That to her heart its bounteous wish denied,
Which yet all common wants, but not her all, supplied.
Sorrows like showers descend, and as the heart
For them prepares, they good or ill impart;
Some on the mind, as on the ocean rain,
Fall and disturb, but soon are lost again—
Some, as to fertile lands, a boon bestow,
And seed, that else had perish'd, live and grow;
Some fall on barren soil, and thence proceed
The idle blossom, and the useless weed;
But how her griefs the Widow's heart impress'd,
Must from the tenor of her life be guess'd.

Rigid she was, persisting in her grief,
Fond of complaint, and adverse to relief.
In her religion she was all severe,
And as she was, was anxious to appear.
When sorrow died, restraint usurp'd the place,
And sate in solemn state upon her face,
Reading she loved not, nor would deign to waste
Her precious time on trifling works of taste;
Though what she did with all that precious time
We know not, but to waste it was a crime—
As oft she said, when with a serious friend
She spent the hours as duty bids us spend;
To read a novel was a kind of sin—
Albeit once Clarissa took her in;
And now of late she heard with much surprise,
Novels there were that made a compromise
Betwixt amusement and religion; these
Might charm the worldly, whom the stories please,
And please the serious, whom the sense would charm,
And thus indulging, be secured from harm—
A happy thought, when from the foe we take
His arms, and use them for religion's sake.

Her Bible she perused by day, by night;
It was her task—she said 't was her delight;
Found in her room, her chamber, and her pew,
For ever studied, yet for ever new—
All must be new that we cannot retain,
And new we find it when we read again.

The hardest texts she could with ease expound,
And meaning for the most mysterious found,
Knew which of dubious senses to prefer:
The want of Greek was not a want in her;—
Instinctive light no aid from Hebrew needs—
But full conviction without study breeds;
O'er mortal powers by inborn strength prevails,
Where Reason trembles, and where Learning fails.

To the Church strictly from her childhood bred,
She now her zeal with party-spirit fed:
For brother James she lively hopes express'd,
But for the Doctor's safety felt distress'd;
And her light Sister, poor, and deaf, and blind,
Fill'd her with fears of most tremendous kind.
But David mock'd her for the pains she took,
And Fanny gave resentment for rebuke;
While James approved the zeal, and praised the call,
"That brought," he said, "a blessing on them all:
Goodness like this to all the House extends,
For were they not a Family of Friends?"

Their sister Frances, though her prime was past
Had beauty still—nay, beauty form'd to last;
'T was not the lily and the rose combined,
Nor must we say the beauty of the mind;
But feature, form, and that engaging air,
That lives when ladies are no longer fair.
Lovers she had, and she remember'd yet,
For who the glories of their reign forget?
Some she rejected in her maiden pride,
And some in maiden hesitation tried,
Unwilling to renounce, unable to decide.
One lost, another would her grace implore,
Till all were lost, and lovers came no more:
Nor had she that, in beauty's failing state,
Which will recall a lover, or create;
Hers was the slender portion that supplied
Her real wants, but all beyond denied.

When Fanny Dyson reach'd her fortieth year,
She would no more of love or lovers hear;
But one dear Friend she chose, her guide, her stay;
And to each other all the world were they;
For all the world had grown to them unkind,
One sex censorious, and the other blind.
The Friend of Frances longer time had known
The world's deceits, and from its follies flown.
With her dear Friend, life's sober joys to share
Was all that now became her wish and care.
They walk'd together, they conversed and read,
And tender tears for well-feign'd sorrows shed:
And were so happy in their quiet lives,
They pitied sighing maids, and weeping wives.

But Fortune to our state such change imparts,
That Pity stays not long in human hearts;
When sad for others' woes our hearts are grown,
This soon gives place to sorrows of our own.

There was among our guardian Volunteers
A Major Bright—he reckon'd fifty years:
A reading man of peace, but call'd to take
His sword and musket for his country's sake

Not to go forth and fight, but here to stay,
Invaders, should they come, to chase or slay.

Him had the elder Lady long admired,
As one from vain and trivial things retired;
With him conversed; but to a Friend so dear,
Gave not that pleasure—Why? is not so clear;
But chance effected this: the Major now
Gave both the time his duties would allow;
In walks, in visits, when abroad, at home,
The friendly Major would to either come.
He never spoke—for he was not a boy—
Of ladies' charms, or lover's grief and joy.
All his discourses were of serious kind,
The heart they touch'd not, but they fill'd the mind.
Yet—oh, the pity! from this grave good man
The cause of coolness in the Friends began.
The sage Sophronia—that the chosen name—
Now more polite, and more estranged became.
She could but feel that she had longer known
This valued friend—he was indeed her own;
But Frances Dyson, to confess the truth,
Had more of softness—yes, and more of youth;
And though he said such things had ceased to please,
The worthy Major was not blind to these:
So without thought, without intent, he paid
More frequent visits to the younger Maid.

Such the offence; and though the Major tried
To tie again the knot he thus untied,
His utmost efforts no kind looks repaid,—
He moved no more the inexorable maid.
The Friends too parted, and the elder told
Tales of false hearts, and friendships waxing cold;
And wonder'd what a man of sense could see
In the light airs of wither'd vanity.

'T is said that Frances now the world reviews,
Unwilling all the little left to lose;
She and the Major on the walks are seen,
And all the world is wondering what they mean.

Such were the four whom Captain Elliot drew
To his own board, as the selected few.
For why? they seem'd each other to approve,
And call'd themselves a Family of Love.

These were not all: there was a youth beside,
Left to his uncles when his parents died:
A Girl, their sister, by a Boy was led
To Scotland, where a boy and girl may wed—
And they returned to seek for pardon, peace, and bread.
Five years they lived to labour, weep, and pray,
When Death, in Mercy, took them both away.

Uncles and aunts received this lively child,
Grieved at his fate, and at his follies smiled;
But when the child to boy's estate grew on,
The smile was vanish'd, and the pity gone.
Slight was the burden, but in time increased,
Until at length both love and pity ceased.
Then Tom was idle; he would find his way
To his aunt's stores, and make her sweets his prey:
By uncle Doctor on a message sent,
He stopp'd to play, and lost it as he went.
His grave aunt Martha, with a frown austere,
And a rough hand, produced a transient fear;
But Tom, to whom his rude companions taught
Language as rude, vindictive measures sought;
He used such words, that when she wish'd to speak
Of his offence, she had her words to seek.
The little wretch had call'd her—'t was a shame
To think such thought, and more to name such name.

Thus fed and beaten, Tom was taught to pray
For his true friends: "but who," said he, are they?"
By nature kind, when kindly used, the Boy
Hail'd the strange good with tears of love and joy;
But, roughly used, he felt his bosom burn
With wrath he dared not on his uncles turn;
So with indignant spirit, still and strong,
He nursed the vengeance, and endured the wrong.

To a cheap school, far north, the boy was sent:
Without a tear of love or grief he went;
Where, doom'd to fast and study, fight and play,
He staid five years, and wish'd five more to stay.
He loved o'er plains to run, up hills to climb,
Without a thought of kindred, home, or time;
Till from the cabin of a coasting hoy,
Landed at last the thin and freckled boy,
With sharp keen eye, but pale and hollow cheek,
All made more sad from sickness of a week.
His aunts and uncles felt—nor strove to hide
From the poor boy, their pity and their pride:
He had been taught that he had not a friend,
Save these on earth, on whom he might depend;
And such dependence upon these he had,
As made him sometimes desperate, always sad.

"Awkward and weak, where can the lad be placed,
And we not troubled, censured, or disgraced?
Do, Brother James, th' unhappy boy enrol
Among your set: you only can control."
James sigh'd, and Thomas to the Factory went,
Who there his days in sundry duties spent.
He ran, he wrought, he wrote—to read or play
He had no time, nor much to feed or pray.
What pass'd without he heard not—or he heard
Without concern, what he nor wish'd nor fear'd;
Told of the Captain and his wealth, he sigh'd,
And said, "how well his table is supplied:"
But with the sigh it caused the sorrow fled;
He was not feasted, but he must be fed,
And he could sleep full sound, though not full soft his bed.

But still, ambitious thoughts his mind possess'd,
And dreams of joy broke in upon his rest.
Improved in person, and enlarged in mind,
The good he found not he could hope to find.
Though now enslaved, he hail'd the approaching day,
When he should break his chains and flee away.

Such were the Dysons: they were first of those
Whom Captain Elliot as companions chose;
Them he invited, and the more approved,
As it appear'd that each the other loved.
Proud of their brothers were the sister pair,
And if not proud, yet kind the brothers were.

This pleased the Captain, who had never known,
Or he had loved, such kindred of his own:
Them he invited, save the Orphan lad,
Whose name was not the one his Uncles had;
No Dyson he, nor with the party came—
The worthy Captain never heard his name;
Uncles and Aunts forbore to name the boy,
For then, of course, must follow his employ.
Though all were silent, as with one consent,
None told another what his silence meant,
What hers; but each suppress'd the useless truth,
And not a word was mention'd of the youth.

Familiar grown, the Dysons saw their host,
With none beside them: it became their boast,
Their pride, their pleasure; but to some it seem'd
Beyond the worth their talents were esteem'd.
This wrought no change within the Captain's mind;
To all men courteous, he to them was kind.

One day with these he sat, and only these,
In a light humour, talking at his ease;
Familiar grown, he was disposed to tell
Of times long past, and what in them befell—
Not of his life their wonder to attract,
But the choice tale, or insulated fact.
Then, as it seem'd, he had acquired a right
To hear what they could from their stores recite.
Their lives, they said, were all of common kind;
He could no pleasure in such trifles find.

They had an uncle—'t is their father's tale—
Who in all seas had gone where ship can sail,
Who in all lands had been where men can live;
"He could indeed some strange relations give,
And many a bold adventure; but in vain
We look for him; he comes not home again."

"And is it so? why then, if so it be,"
Said Captain Elliot, "you must look to me:
"I knew John Dyson"——Instant every one
Was moved to wonder—"knew my Uncle John!
Can he be rich? be childless? he is old,
That is most certain—What! can more be told?
Will he return, who has so long been gone,
And lost to us? Oh! what of Uncle John?"

This was aside: their unobservant friend
Seem'd on their thoughts but little to attend;
A traveller speaking, he was more inclined
To tell his story than their thoughts to find.

"Although, my Friends, I love you well, 't is true,
'T was your relation turn'd my mind to you;
For we were friends of old, and friends like us are few;
And though from dearest friends a man will hide
His private vices in his native pride,
Yet such our friendship from its early rise,
We no reserve admitted, no disguise;
But 't is the story of my friend I tell,
And to all others let me bid farewell.

Take each your glass, and you shall hear how John,
My old companion, through the world has gone;
I can describe him to the very life,
Him and his ways, his ventures, and his wife."

"Wife!" whisper'd all; "then what his life to us,
His ways and ventures if he ventured thus?"
This, too, apart; yet were they all intent,
And, gravely listening, sigh'd with one consent.

"My friend, your Uncle, was design'd for trade,
To make a fortune as his father made;
But early he perceived the house declined,
And his domestic views at once resign'd;
While stout of heart, with life in every limb,
He would to sea, and either sink or swim.
No one forbad; his father shook his hand,
Within it leaving what he could command.

He left his home, but I will not relate
What storms he braved, and how he bore his fate,
Till his brave frigate was a Spanish prize,
And prison walls received his first-born sighs,
Sighs for the freedom that an English boy,
Or English man, is eager to enjoy.

Exchanged, he breathed in freedom, and aboard
An English ship, he found his peace restored;
War raged around, each British tar was press'd
To serve his king, and John among the rest;
Oft had he fought and bled, and 't was his fate
In that same ship to grow to man's estate.
Again 't was war: of France a ship appear'd
Of greater force, but neither shunn'd or fear'd;
'T was in the Indian Sea, the land was nigh,
When all prepared to fight, and some to die;
Man after man was in the ocean thrown,
Limb after limb was to the surgeon shown,
And John at length, poor John! held forth his own.—

A tedious case—the battle ceased with day,
And in the night the foe had slipp'd away.
Of many wounded were a part convey'd
To land, and he among the number laid;
Poor, suffering, friendless, who shall now impart
Life to his hope, or comfort to his heart?
A kind good priest among the English there
Selected him as his peculiar care;
And, when recover'd, to a powerful friend
Was pleased the lad he loved to recommend;
Who read your Uncle's mind, and, pleased to read,
Placed him where talents will in time succeed.

I will not tease you with details of trade,
But say he there a decent fortune made,—
Not such as gave him, if return'd, to buy
A Duke's estate, or principality,
But a fair fortune: years of peace he knew,
That were so happy, and that seem'd so few.

Then came a cloud; for who on earth has seen
A changeless fortune, and a life serene?
Ah! then how joyous were the hours we spent!
But joy is restless, joy is not content.

There one resided, who, to serve his friend,
Was pleased a gay fair lady to commend;
Was pleased t' invite the happy man to dine,
And introduced the subject o'er their wine;
Was pleased the lady his good friend should know
And as a secret his regard would show.

A modest man lacks courage; but, thus train'd,
Your Uncle sought her favour and obtain'd:
To me he spake, enraptured with her face,
Her angel smile, her unaffected grace;
Her fortune small indeed; but 'curse the pelf,
She is a glorious fortune in herself!'
'John!' answer'd I, 'friend John, to be sincere,
These are fine things, but may be bought too dear.
You are no stripling, and, it must be said,
Have not the form that charms a youthful maid.
What you possess, and what you leave behind,
When you depart, may captivate her mind;
And I suspect she will rejoice at heart,
Your will once made, if you should soon depart.'

Long our debate, and much we disagreed;
'You need no wife,' I said,—said he, 'I need;
I want a house, I want in all I see
To take an interest; what is mine to me?'
So spake the man, who to his word was just,
And took the words of others upon trust.
He could not think that friend in power so high,
So much esteem'd, could like a villain lie;
Nor, till the knot, the fatal knot was tied,
Had urged his wedding a dishonour'd bride.
The man he challenged, for his heart was rent
With rage and grief, and was to prison sent;
For men in power—and this, alas! was one—
Revenge on all, the wrongs themselves have done;
And he whose spirit bends not to the blow
The tyrants strike, shall no forgiveness know,
For 't is to slaves alone that tyrants favour show.

This cost him much; but that he did not heed;
The lady died, and my poor friend was freed.
'Enough of ladies!' then said he, and smiled;
'I 've now no longings for a neighbour's child.'
So patient he return'd, and not in vain,
To his late duties, and grew rich again.
He was no miser; but the man who takes
Care to be rich, will love the gain he makes:
Pursuing wealth, he soon forgot his woes,
No acts of his were bars to his repose.

Now John was rich, and old and weary grown,
Talk'd of the country that he calls his own,
And talk'd to me; for now, in fact, began
My better knowledge of the real man.
Though long estranged, he felt a strong desire,
That made him for his former friends inquire;
What Dysons yet remain'd, he long'd to know,
And doubtless meant some proofs of love to show.
His purpose known, our native land I sought,
And with the wishes of my Friend am fraught."

Fix'd were all eyes, suspense each bosom shook,
And expectation hung on every look.

"'Go to my kindred, seek them all around,
Find all you can, and tell me all that 's found;
Seek them if prosperous, seek them in distress,
Hear what they need, know what they all possess;
What minds, what hearts they have, how good they are,
How far from goodness—speak, and no one spare,
And no one slander: let me clearly see
What is in them, and what remains for me.'
Such is my charge, and haply I shall send
Tidings of joy and comfort to my Friend.
Oft would he say, 'If of our race survive
Some two or three, to keep the name alive,
I will not ask if rich or great they be,
But if they live in love, like you and me.'

'T was not my purpose yet awhile to speak
As I have spoken; but why further seek?
All that I heard I in my heart approve;
You are indeed a Family of Love:
And my old friend were happy in the sight
Of those, of whom I shall such tidings write."

The Captain wrote not: he perhaps was slow,
Perhaps he wish'd a little more to know.
He wrote not yet, and while he thus delay'd,
Frances alone an early visit paid.
The maiden Lady braved the morning cold,
To tell her Friend what duty bade be told,
Yet not abruptly—she has first to say,
"How cold the morning, but how fine the day!—
I fear you slept but ill, we kept you long,
You made us all so happy, but 't was wrong—
So entertain'd, no wonder we forgot
How the time pass'd; I fear me you did not."

In this fair way the Lady seldom fail'd
To steer her course, still sounding as she sail'd.

"Dear Captain Elliot, how your Friends you read!
We are a loving Family indeed;
Left in the world each other's aid to be,
And join to raise a fallen family.
Oh! little thought we there was one so near,
And one so distant, to us all so dear:
All, all alike; he cannot know, dear man!
Who needs him most, as one among us can—
One who can all our wants distinctly view,
And tell him fairly what were just to do:
But you, dear Captain Elliot, as his friend,
As ours, no doubt, will your assistance lend.
Not for the world would I my Brothers blame;
Good men they are: 't was not for that I came.
No! did they guess what shifts I make, the grief
That I sustain, they 'd fly to my relief;
But I am proud as poor; I cannot plead
My cause with them, nor show how much I need;
But to my Uncle's Friend it is no shame,
Nor have I fear to seem the thing I am;
My humble pittance life's mere need supplies,
But all indulgence, all beyond denies.
I aid no pauper, I myself am poor,
I cannot help the beggar at my door.
I from my scanty table send no meat;
Cook'd and recook'd is every joint I eat.
At Church a sermon begs our help,—I stop
And drop a tear; nought else have I to drop;
But pass the outstretch'd plate with sorrow by,
And my sad heart this kind relief deny.
My dress—I strive with all my maiden skill
To make it pass, but 't is disgraceful still;
Yet from all others I my wants conceal,
Oh! Captain Elliot, there are few that feel!
But did that rich and worthy Uncle know
What you, dear Sir, will in your kindness show,
He would his friendly aid with generous hand bestow.

Good men my Brothers both, and both are raised
Far above want—the Power that gave be praised!
My Sister's jointure, if not ample, gives
All she can need, who as a lady lives;
But I, unaided, may through all my years
Endure these ills—forgive these foolish tears.

Once, my dear Sir—I then was young and gay,
And men would talk—but I have had my day:
Now all I wish is so to live, that men
May not despise me whom they flatter'd then.
If you, kind Sir——"
Thus far the Captain heard,
Nor save by sign or look had interfered;
But now he spoke; to all she said agreed,
And she conceived it useless to proceed.
Something he promised, and the lady went
Half-pleased away, yet wondering what he meant;
Polite he was and kind, but she could trace
A smile, or something like it, in his face;
'T was not a look that gave her joy or pain—
She tried to read it, but she tried in vain.

Then call'd the Doctor—'t was his usual way—
To ask "How fares my worthy friend to-day?"
To feel his pulse, and as a friend to give
Unfee'd advice how such a man should live;
And thus, digressing, he could soon contrive,
At his own purpose smoothly to arrive.

"My brother! yes, he lives without a care,
And, though he needs not, yet he loves to spare:
James I respect, and yet it must be told,
His speech is friendly, but his heart is cold.
His smile assumed has not the real glow
Of love!—a sunbeam shining on the snow.
Children he has; but are they causes why
He should our pleas resist, our claims deny?
Our Father left the means by which he thrives,
While we are labouring to support our lives.
We, need I say? my widow'd sister lives
On a large jointure; nay, she largely gives;—
And Fanny sighs—for gold does Fanny sigh?
Or wants she that which money cannot buy—
Youth and young hopes?—Ah! could my kindred share
The liberal mind's distress, and daily care,
The painful toil to gain the petty fee,
They 'd bless their stars, and join to pity me.
Hard is his fate, who would, with eager joy,
To save mankind his every power employ;
Yet in his walk unnumber'd insults meets,
And gains 'mid scorn the food that chokes him as he eats.

Oh! Captain Elliot, you who know mankind,
With all the anguish of the feeling mind,
Bear to our kind relation these the woes
That e'en to you 'tis misery to disclose.
You can describe what I but faintly trace—
A man of learning cannot bear disgrace;
Refinement sharpens woes that wants create,
And 't is fresh grief such grievous things to state;
Yet those so near me let me not reprove—
I love them well, and they deserve my love:
But want they know not—Oh! that I could say
I am in this as ignorant as they."

The Doctor thus—the Captain grave and kind,
To the sad tale with serious looks inclined,
And promise made to keep th' important speech in mind.

James and the widow, how is yet unknown,
Heard of these visits, and would make their own.
All was not fair, they judged, and both agreed
To their good Friend together to proceed.
Forth then they went to see him, and persuade—
As warm a pair as ever Anger made.
The Widow lady must the speaker be:
So James agreed; for words at will had she;
And then her Brother, if she needed proof,
Should add, "'Tis truth:"—it was for him enough.

"Oh! Sir, it grieves me"—for we need not dwell
On introduction: all was kind and well—
"Oh! Sir, it grieves, it shocks us both to hear
What has, with selfish purpose gain'd your ear—
Our very flesh and blood, and, as you know, how dear.
Doubtless they came your noble mind t' impress
With strange descriptions of their own distress;
But I would to the Doctor's face declare,
That he has more to spend and more to spare,
With all his craft, than we with all our care.

And for our Sister, all she has she spends
Upon herself; herself alone befriends.
She has the portion that our Father left,
While me of mine a careless wretch bereft,
Save a small part; yet I could joyful live,
Had I my mite—the widow's mite—to give.
For this she cares not; Frances does not know
Their heartfelt joy, who largely can bestow.
You, Captain Elliot, feel the pure delight,
That our kind acts in tender hearts excite,
When to the poor we can our alms extend,
And make the Father of all Good our friend;
And, I repeat, I could with pleasure live,
Had I my mite—the widow's mite—to give.

We speak not thus, dear Sir, with vile intent,
Our nearest friends to wrong or circumvent;
But that our Uncle, worthy man! should know
How best his wealth, Heaven's blessing, to bestow•
What widows need, and chiefly those who feel
For all the sufferings which they cannot heal;
And men in trade, with numbers in their pay,
Who must be ready for the reckoning-day,
Or gain or lose!"—
—"Thank Heaven," said James, "as yet
I've not been troubled by a dun or debt."
—The Widow sigh'd, convinced that men so weak
Will ever hurt the cause for which they speak;
However tempted to deceive, still they
Are ever blundering to the broad high-way
Of very truth:—But Martha pass'd it by
With a slight frown, and half-distinguish'd sigh

"Say to our Uncle, sir, how much I long
To see him sit his kindred race among:
To hear his brave exploits, to nurse his age,
And cheer him in his evening's pilgrimage•
How were I blest to guide him in the way
Where the religious poor in secret pray.

To be the humble means by which his heart
And liberal hand might peace and joy impart!
But now, farewell!"—and slowly, softly, fell
The tender accents as she said "farewell!"

The Merchant stretch'd his hand, his leave to take,
And gave the Captain's a familiar shake,
Yet seem'd to doubt if this was not too free,
But, gaining courage, said, "Remember me."

Some days elapsed, the Captain did not write,
But still was pleased the party to invite;
And, as he walk'd, his custom every day,
A tall pale stripling met him on his way,
Who made some efforts, but they proved too weak,
And only show'd he was inclin'd to speak.
"What wouldst thou, lad?" the Captain ask'd, and gave
The youth a power his purposed boon to crave,
Yet not in terms direct—"My name,' quoth he,
Is Thomas Bethel; you have heard of me."—
Not good nor evil, Thomas—had I need
Of so much knowledge:—but pray now proceed."—

"Dyson my mother's name; but I have not
That interest with you, and the worse my lot.
I serve my Uncle James, and run and write,
And watch and work from morning until night;
Confin'd among the looms, and webs, and wheels,
You cannot think how like a slave one feels.
'T is said you have a ship at your command,—
An' please you, sir, I'm weary of the land,
And I have read of foreign parts such things,
As make me sick of Uncle's wheels and springs."

"But, Thomas, why to sea? you look too slim
For that rough work — and, Thomas, can you swim?"
That he could not, but still he scorn'd a lie,
And boldly answer'd, "No, but I can try."—
"Well, my good lad, but tell me, can you read?"
Now, with some pride he answer'd, "Yes, indeed!
I construe Virgil, and our Usher said,
I might have been in Homer had I staid,
And he was sorry when I came away,
And so was I, but Uncle would not pay;
He told the master I had read enough,
And Greek was all unprofitable stuff;
So all my learning now is thrown away,
And I've no time for study or for play;
I 'm order'd here and there, above, below,
And call'd a dunce for what I cannot know;
Oh, that I were but from this bondage free!
Do, please your honour, let me go to sea."

"But why to sea? they want no Latin there;
Hard is their work, and very hard their fare."

"But then," said Thomas, "if on land, I doubt
My Uncle Dyson soon would find me out;
And though he tells me what I yearly cost,
'T is my belief he 'd miss me were I lost.
For he has said, that I can act as well
As he himself—but this you must not tell."

"Tell, Thomas! no, I scorn the base design,
Give me your hand, I pledge my word with mine;
And if I cannot do thee good, my friend,
Thou may'st at least upon that word depend.
And hark ye, lad, thy worthy name retain
To the last hour, or I shall help in vain;
And then the more severe and hard thy part,
Thine the more praise, and thine the happier art.
We meet again—farewell!"—and Thomas went
Forth to his tasks, half hungry, half content.

"I never ask'd for help," thought he, "but twice,
And all they then would give me was advice;
My Uncle Doctor, when I begg'd his aid,
Bade me work on, and never be afraid,
But still be good; and I 've been good so long,
I 'm half persuaded that they tell me wrong.
And now this Captain still repeats the same,
But who can live upon a virtuous name,
Starving and praised?—'have patience—patience still!'
He said and smiled, "and, if I can, I will."

So Thomas rested with a mind intent
On what the Captain by his kindness meant.

Again the invited party all attend,
These dear relations, on this generous Friend.
They ate, they drank, each striving to appear
Fond, frank, forgiving—above all, sincere.
Such kindred souls could not admit disguise,
Or envious fears, or painful jealousies;
So each declared, and all in turn replied,
"'T is just indeed, and cannot be denied."

Now various subjects rose,—the country's cause,
The war, the allies, the lottery, and the laws.
The widow'd sister then advantage took
Of a short pause, and, smiling softly, spoke:
She judged what subject would his mind excite—
"Tell us, dear Captain, of that bloody fight,
When our brave Uncle, bleeding at his gun,
Gave a loud shout to see the Frenchmen run."

"Another day,"—replied the modest host;
"One cannot always of one's battles boast.
Look not surprise—behold the man in me!
Another Uncle shall you never see.
No other Dyson to this place shall come,
Here end my travels, here I place my home;
Here to repose my shatter'd frame I mean,
Until the last long journey close the scene."

The Ladies softly brush'd the tears away;
James look'd surprise, but knew not what to say;
But Doctor Dyson lifted up his voice,
And said, "Dear Uncle, how we all rejoice!"

"No question, Friends! and I your joy approve,
We are, you know, a Family of Love."

So said the wary Uncle, but the while
Wore on his face a questionable smile,
That vanish'd, as he spake in grave and solemn style—

"Friends and relations! let us henceforth seem
Just as we are, nor of our virtues dream,
That with our waking vanish.—What we are
Full well we know—t' improve it be our care.

Forgive the trial I have made.: 't is one
That has no more than I expected done.
If as frail mortals you, my Friends, appear,
I look'd for no angelic beings here,
For none that riches spurn'd as idle pelf,
Or served another as he served himself.
Deceived no longer, let us all forgive;
I 'm old, but yet a tedious time may live.
This dark complexion India's suns bestow,
These shrivell'd looks to years of care I owe;
But no disease ensures my early doom,—
And I may live—forgive me—years to come.
But while I live, there may some good be done,
Perchance to many, but at least to One."—

Here he arose, retired, return'd, and brought
The Orphan boy, whom he had train'd and taught
For this his purpose; and the happy boy,
Though bade to hide, could ill suppress, his joy.—

"This young relation, with your leave, I take,
That he his progress in the world may make—
Not in my house a slave or spy to be,
And first to flatter, then to govern me;—
He shall not nurse me when my senses sleep,
Nor shall the key of all my secrets keep,
And be so useful that a dread to part
Shall make him master of my easy heart;—
But to be placed where merit may be proved,
And all that now impedes his way removed.

And now no more on these affairs I dwell,
What I possess that I alone can tell,
And to that subject we will bid farewell.
As go I must, when Heaven is pleased to call,
What I shall leave will seem or large or small,
As you shall view it. When this pulse is still,
You may behold my wealth, and read my will.

And now, as Captain Elliot much has known,
That to your Uncle never had been shown,
From him one word of honest counsel hear—
And think it always gain to be sincere."

TALE III.

THE EQUAL MARRIAGE.

There are gay nymphs whom serious matrons blame,
And men adventurous treat as lawful game,—
Misses, who strive, with deep and practised arts,
To gain and torture inexperienced hearts;
The hearts entangled they in pride retain,
And at their pleasure make them feel their chain:
For this they learn to manage air and face,
To look a virtue, and to act a grace,
To be whatever men with warmth pursue—
Chaste, gay, retiring, tender, timid, true,
To-day approaching near, to-morrow just in view.

Maria Glossip was a thing like this—
A much observing, much experienced Miss;
Who on a stranger-youth would first decide
Th' important question—"Shall I be his bride?"
But if unworthy of a lot so bless'd,
'T was something yet to rob the man of rest;
The heart, when stricken, she with hope could feed,
Could court pursuit, and, when pursued, recede.
Hearts she had won, and with delusion fed,
With doubt bewilder'd, and with hope misled;
Mothers and rivals she had made afraid,
And wrung the breast of many a jealous maid;
Friendship, the snare of lovers, she profess'd,
And turn'd the heart's best feelings to a jest.

Yet seem'd the nymph as gentle as a dove,
Like one all guiltless of the game of love,—
Whose guileless innocence might well be gay;
Who had no selfish secrets to betray;
Sure, if she play'd, she knew not how to play.
Oh! she had looks so placid and demure,
Not Eve, ere fallen, seem'd more meek or pure;
And yet the Tempter of the falling Eve
Could not with deeper subtlety deceive.

A Sailor's heart the Lady's kindness moved,
And winning looks, to say how well he loved;
Then left her hopeful for the stormy main,
Assured of love when he return'd again.
Alas! the gay Lieutenant reach'd the shore,
To be rejected, and was gay no more;
Wine and strong drink the bosom's pain suppress'd,
Till Death procured, what love denied him—rest.
But men of more experience learn to treat
These fair enslavers with their own deceit.

Finch was a younger brother's youngest son,
Who pleased an Uncle with his song and gun;
Who call'd him 'Bob,' and 'Captain'—by that name
Anticipating future rank and fame:
Not but there was for this some fair pretence—
He was a cornet in the Home Defence.
The Youth was ever drest in dapper style,
Wore spotless linen, and a ceaseless smile;
His step was measured, and his air was nice—
They bought him high, who had him at the price
That his own judgment and becoming pride,
And all the merit he assumed, implied.
A life he loved of liberty and ease,
And all his pleasant labour was to please;
Not call'd at present hostile men to slay,
He made the hearts of gentle dames his prey.

Hence tales arose, and one of sad report—
A fond, fair girl became his folly's sport,—
A cottage lass, who "knew the youth would prove
For ever true, and give her love for love;
Sure when he could, and that would soon be known,
He would be proud to show her as his own."

But still she felt the village damsels' sneer,
And her sad soul was fill'd with secret fear;
His love excepted, earth was all a void,
And he, the excepted man, her peace destroy'd.
When the poor Jane was buried, we could hear
The threat of rustics whisper'd round her bier

Stories like this were told, but yet, in time
Fair ladies lost their horror at the crime;
They knew that cottage girls were forward things,
Who never heed a nettle till it stings;

Then, too, the Captain had his fault confess'd,
And scorn'd to turn a murder to a jest.

Away with murder!—This accomplish'd swain
Beheld Maria, and confess'd her reign—
She came, invited by the rector's wife,
Who "never saw such sweetness in her life."
Now, as the rector was the Uncle's friend,
It pleased the Nephew there his steps to bend,
Where the fair damsel then her visit paid,
And seem'd an unassuming rustic maid:
A face so fair, a look so meek, he found
Had pierced that heart, no other nymph could wound.

"Oh, sweet Maria"—so began the Youth
His meditations—"thine the simple truth!
Thou hast no wicked wisdom of thy sex,
No wish to gain a subject-heart—then vex.
That heavenly bosom no proud passion swells,
No serpent's wisdom with thy meekness dwells;
Oh! could I bind thee to my heart, and live
In love with thee, on what our fortunes give!
Far from the busy world, in some dear spot,
Where Love reigns king, we 'd find some peaceful cot.
To wed, indeed, no prudent man would choose;
But, such a maid will lighter bonds refuse!"

And was this youth a rake?—In very truth;
Yet, feeling love, he felt it as a youth;
If he had vices, they were laid aside;
He quite forgot the simple girl who died;
With dear Maria he in peace would live,
And what had pass'd—Maria would forgive.

The fair Coquette at first was pleased to find
A swain so knowing had become so blind;
And she determined, with her utmost skill,
To bind the rebel to her sovereign will.
She heard the story of the old deceit,
And now resolv'd he should with justice meet;—
"Soon as she saw him on her hook secure,
He should the pangs of perjur'd man endure."

These her first thoughts—but as, from time to time,
The Lover came, she dwelt not on his crime—
"Crime could she call it? prudes, indeed, condemn
These slips of youth—but she was not of them."
So gentler thoughts arose as, day by day,
The Captain came his passion to display.
When he display'd his passion, and she felt,
Not without fear, her heart begin to melt—
Joy came with terror at a state so new;
Glad of his truth; if he indeed were true!

This she decided as the heart decides,
Resolv'd to be the happiest of brides.
"Not great my fortune—hence," said she, "'tis plain,
Me, and not mine, dear Youth! he hopes to gain;
Nor has he much; but, as he sweetly talks,
We from our cot shall have delightful walks,
Love, lord within it! I shall smile to see
My little cherubs on the father's knee."
Then sigh'd the nymph, and in her fancied lot,
She all the mischiefs of the past forgot.

Such were their tender meditations; thus
Would they the visions of the day discuss:
Each, too, the old sad habits would no more
Indulge; both dare be virtuous and be poor.

They both had pass'd the year when law allows
Free-will to lover who would fain be spouse:
Yet the good youth his Uncle's sanction sought—
'Marry her, Bob! and are you really caught?
Then you've exchanged, I warrant, heart for heart—
'T is well! I meant to warn her of your art:
This Parson's Babe has made you quite a fool—
But are you sure your ardour will not cool?
Have you not habits, Boy? but take your chance!
How will you live? I cannot much advance.
But hear you not what through the village flies,
That this your dove is famed for her disguise?
Yet, say they not, she leads a gayish life?
Art sure she'll show the virtues of a wife?"—

"Oh, Sir, she's all that mortal man can love!"
"Then marry, Bob! and that the fact will prove—
Yet in a kind of lightness, folk agree,"—
"Lightness in her! indeed, it cannot be—
'T is Innocence alone that makes her manners free."

"Well, my good friend! then Innocence alone
Is to a something like Flirtation prone;
And I advise—but let me not offend—
That Prudence should on Innocence attend,
Lest some her sportive purity mistake,
And term your angel more than half a rake."

The nymph, now sure, could not entirely curb
The native wish her lover to disturb;
Oft he observ'd her, and could ill endure
The gentle coquetry of maid so pure:
Men he beheld press round her, and the Fair
Caught every sigh, and smiled at every prayer;
And grieved he was with jealous pains to see
The effects of all her wit and pleasantry.

"Yet why alarm'd?"—he said, "with so much sense,
She has no freedom, dashing, or pretence:
'T is her gay mind, and I should feel a pride
In her chaste levities"—he said, and sigh'd.
Yet when, apart from company, he chose
To talk a little of his bosom's woes—
But one sweet smile, and one soft speech, suppress'd
All pain, and set his feeling heart at rest.
Nay, in return, she felt, or feign'd, a fear,
"He was too lively to be quite sincere—
She knew a certain lady, and could name
A certain time"—So, even was the blame,
And thus the loving pair more deep in love became.

They married soon—for why delay the thing
That such amazing happiness would bring?—
Now of that blissful state, O Muse of Hymen! sing

Love dies all kinds of death: in some so quick
It comes—he is not previously sick;
But ere the sun has on the couple shed
The morning rays, the smile of Love is fled.

And what the cause? for Love should not expire,
And none the reason of such fate require.
Both had a mask, that with such pains they wore,
Each took it off when it avail'd no more.
They had no feeling of each other's pain;
To wear it longer had been crime in vain.

As in some pleasant eve we view the scene,
Though cool yet calm, if joyless yet serene,—
Who has not felt a quiet still delight
In the clear, silent, love-befriending night?
The moon so sweetly bright, so softly fair,
That all but happy lovers would be there,—
Thinking there must be in her still domain
Something that soothes the sting of mortal pain:
While earth itself is dress'd in light so clear,
That they might rest contented to be here!

Such is the night; but when the morn awakes,
The storm arises, and the forest shakes:
This mighty change the grieving travellers find,
The freezing snows fast drifting in the wind;
Firs deeply laden shake the snowy top,
Streams slowly freezing, fretting till they stop;
And void of stars the angry clouds look down
On the cold earth, exchanging frown with frown.

Such seem'd, at first, the cottage of our pair—
Fix'd in their fondness, in their prospects fair;
Youth, health, affection, all that life supplies,
Bright as the stars that gild the cloudless skies—
Were theirs, or seem'd to be: but soon the scene
Was black as if its light had never been.
Weary full soon, and restless then they grew,
Then off the painful mask of prudence threw,
For Time has told them all; and taught them what to rue.
They long again to tread the former round
Of dissipation—"Why should he be bound,
While his sweet inmate of the cottage sighs
For adulation, rout, and rhapsodies?
Not Love himself, did love exist, could lead
A heart like hers, that flutter'd to be freed."

But Love, or what seem'd like him, quickly died,
Nor Prudence, nor Esteem, his place supplied.
Disguise thrown off, each reads the other's heart,
And feels with horror that they cannot part.

Still they can speak—and 't is some comfort still,
That each can vex the other when they will:
Words half in jest to words in earnest led,
And these the earnest angry passions fed,
Till all was fierce reproach, and peace for ever fled.

"And so you own it! own it to my face,
Your love is vanish'd—infamous and base!"

"Madam, I loved you truly, while I deem'd
You were the truthful being that you seem'd;
But when I see your native temper rise
Above control, and break through all disguise,
Casting it off, as serpents do their skin,
And showing all the folds of vice within,—
What see I then to love? was I in love with Sin?"

"So I may think, and you may feel it too;
A loving couple, Sir, were Sin and you!
Whence all this anger? is it that you find
You cannot always make a woman blind?
You talk'd of falsehood and disguise—talk on
But all my trust and confidence are gone;
Remember you with what a serious air
You talk'd of love as if you were at prayer?
You spoke of home-born comforts, quiet, ease,
And the pure pleasure that must always please,
With an assumed and sentimental air,
Smiting your breast, and acting like a player.
Then your life's comfort! and your holy joys!
Holy, forsooth! and your sweet girls and boys,
How you would train them!—All this farce review,
And then, Sir, talk of being just and true!"—

"Madam! your sex expects that ours should lie.
The simple creatures know it, and comply—
You hate the truth; there 's nothing you despise
Like a plain man, who spurns your vanities.
Are you not early taught your prey to catch?
When your mammas pronounce—'A proper match!'
What said your own?—'Do, daughter! curb your tongue,
And you may win him, for the man is young;
But if he views you as ourselves, good bye
To speculation!—He will never try.'

Then is the mask assum'd, and then you bait
Your hook with kindness! and as anglers wait,
Now here, now there, with keen and eager glance,
Marking your victims as the shoals advance;
When, if the gaping wretch should make a snap,
You jerk him up, and have him in your trap,
Who gasping, panting, in your presence lies,
And you exulting view the imprison'd prize.

Such are your arts! while he did but intend,
In harmless play an idle hour to spend,
Lightly to talk of love! your fix'd intent
Is on to lure him where he never meant
To go, but going, must his speed repent.
If he of Cupid speaks, you watch your man,
And make a change for Hymen if you can;
Thus he, ingenuous, easy, fond, and weak,
Speaks the rash words he has been led to speak;
Puts the dire question that he meant to shun,
And by a moment's frenzy is undone."—

"Well!" said the Wife, "admit this nonsense true,—
A mighty prize she gains in catching you;
For my part, Sir, I most sincerely wish
My landing-net had miss'd my precious fish!"

"Would that it had! or I had wisely lent
An ear to those who said I should repent."

"Hold, Sir! at least my reputation spare,
And add another falsehood if you dare."—

"Your reputation, Madam!—rest secure,
That will all scandal and reproach endure,
And be the same in worth: it is like him
Who floats, but finds he cannot sink or swim·
Half rais'd above the storm, half sunk below
It just exists, and that is all we know.

Such the good name that you so much regard,
And yet to seek afloat find somewhat hard.
Nay, no reply! in future I decline
Dispute, and take my way."—
"And I, Sir, mine."

Oh! happy, happy, happy pair! both sought,
Both seeking—catching both, and caught.

TALE IV.

RACHEL.

It chanced we walk'd upon the heath, and met
A wandering woman; her thin clothing wet
With morning fog; the little care she took
Of things like these, was written in her look.
Not pain from pinching cold was in her face,
But hurrying grief, that knows no resting place,—
Appearing ever as on business sent,
The wandering victim of a fix'd intent;
Yet in her fancied consequence and speed,
Impell'd to beg assistance for her need.

When she beheld my friend and me, with eye
And pleading hand, she sought our charity;
More to engage our friendly thoughts the while,
She threw upon her miseries a smile,
That, like a varnish on a picture laid,
More prominent and bold the figures made:
Yet was there sign of joy that we complied,
The moment's wish indulged and gratified.

"Where art thou wandering, Rachel? whither stray,
From thy poor hearth in such unwholesome day?"
Ask'd my kind friend, who had familiar grown
With Rachel's grief, and oft compassion shown;
Oft to her hovel had in winter sent
The means of comfort—oft with comforts went.
Him well she knew, and with requests pursued,
Though too much lost and spent for gratitude.

"Where art thou wandering, Rachel? let me hear?"—
"The fleet! the fleet!" she answer'd, "will appear
Within the bay, and I shall surely know
The news to-night!—turn tide, and breezes blow!
For if I lose my time, I must remain
Till the next year before they come again!"

"What can they tell thee, Rachel?"—
"Should I say,
I must repent me to my dying day.
Then should I lose the pension that they give;
For who would trust their secrets to a sieve?
I must be gone!"—And with her wild, but keen
And crafty look, that would appear to mean,
She hurried on; but turn'd again to say,
'All will be known: they anchor in the bay;
Adieu! be secret!—sailors have no home:
Blow wind, turn tide!—Be sure the fleet will come."

Grown wilder still, the frantic creature strode
With hurried feet upon the flinty road.
On her departing form I gazed with pain—
"And should you not," I cried, "her ways restrain?
What hopes the wild deluded wretch to meet?
And means she aught by this expected fleet?
Knows she her purpose? has she hope to see
Some friend to aid her in her poverty?
Why leave her thus bewilder'd to pursue
The fancy's good, that never comes in view?"

"Nay! she is harmless, and if more confined,
Would more distress in the coercion find.
Save at the times when to the coast she flies,
She rests, nor shows her mind's obliquities,
But ever talks she of the sea, and shows
Her sympathy with every wind that blows.
We think it, therefore, useless to restrain
A creature of whose conduct none complain,
Whose age and looks protect her,—should they fail,
Her craft and wild demeanour will prevail.
A soldier once attack'd her on her way—
She spared him not, but bade him kneel and pray—
Praying herself aloud—th' astonish'd man
Was so confounded, that away he ran.

Her sailor left her, with, perhaps, intent
To make her his—'t is doubtful what he meant:
But he was captured, and the life he led
Drove all such young engagements from his head.
On him she ever thought, and none beside,
Seeking her love, were favour'd or denied;
On her dear David she had fix'd her view,
And fancy judged him ever fond and true.
Nay, young and handsome—Time could not destroy—
No—he was still the same—her gallant boy!
Labour had made her coarse, and her attire
Show'd that she wanted no one to admire;
None to commend her; but she could conceive
The same of him, as when he took his leave,
And gaily told what riches he would bring,
And grace her hand with the symbolic ring.

With want and labour was her mind subdued;
She lived in sorrow and in solitude.
Religious neighbours, kindly calling, found
Her thoughts unsettled, anxious, and unsound;
Low, superstitious, querulous, and weak,
She sought for rest, but knew not how to seek;
And their instructions, though in kindness meant,
Were far from yielding the desired content.
They hoped to give her notions of their own,
And talk'd of 'feelings' she had never known;
They ask'd of her 'experience,' and they bred,
In her weak mind, a melancholy dread
Of something wanting in her faith, of some—
She knew not what—'acceptance,' that should come;
And as it came not, she was much afraid
That she in vain had served her God and pray'd.

She thought her lover dead. In prayer she named
The erring Youth, and hoped he was reclaim'd.
This she confess'd ; and trembling, heard them say,
'Her prayers were sinful—So the papists pray.
Her David's fate had been decided long,
And prayers and wishes for his state were wrong.'

Had these her guides united love and skill,
They might have ruled and rectified her will;
But they perceived not the bewilder'd mind,
And show'd her paths, that she could never find:
The weakness that was nature's they reproved,
And all its comforts from the Heart removed.

Even in this state, she loved the winds that sweep
O'er the wild heath, and curl the restless deep;
A turf-built hut beneath a hill she chose,
And oft at night in winter storms arose,
Hearing, or dreaming, the distracted cry
Of drowning seamen on the breakers by:
For there were rocks, that when the tides were low,
Appear'd, and vanish'd when the waters flow;
And there she stood, all patient to behold
Some seaman's body on the billows roll'd.

One calm, cold evening, when the moon was high,
And rode sublime within the cloudless sky,
She sat within her hut, nor seem'd to feel
Or cold or want, but turn'd her idle wheel,
And with sad song its melancholy tone
Mix'd, all unconscious that she dwelt alone.

But none will harm her—Or who, willing, can?
She is too wretched to have fear of man—
Not man! but something—if it should appear,
That once was man—that something did she fear.

No causeless terror!—In that moon's clear light
It came, and seem'd a parley to invite:
It was no hollow voice—no brushing by
Of a strange being, who escapes the eye—
No cold or thrilling touch, that will but last
While we can think, and then for ever past.
But this sad face—though not the same she knew,
Enough the same to prove the vision true—
Look'd full upon her!—starting in affright
She fled, her wildness doubling at the sight;
With shrieks of terror, and emotion strong,
She pass'd it by, and madly rush'd along
To the bare rocks—While David, who, that day,
Had left his ship at anchor in the bay,
Had seen his friends who yet survived, and heard
Of her who loved him—and who thus appear'd—
He tried to soothe her, but retired afraid
T' approach, and left her to return for aid.

None came! and Rachel in the morn was found
Turning her wheel, without its spindles, round,
With household look of care, low singing to the
sound.

Since that event, she is what you have seen,
But time and habit make her more serene,
The edge of anguish blunted—yet, it seems,
Sea, ships, and sailors' miseries are her dreams."

TALE V.

VILLARS.

Poet.—Know you the fate of Villars?—
Friend.—What! the lad
At school so fond of solitude, and sad;
Who broke our bounds because he scorn'd a guide,
And would walk lonely by the river's side?
P.—The same!—who rose at midnight to behold
The moonbeams shedding their ethereal gold;
Who held our sports and pleasures in disgrace,
For Guy of Warwick, and old Chevy Chase.—

F.—Who sought for friendships, gave his generous heart
To every boy who chose to act the part;
Or judged he felt it—not aware that boys
Have poor conceit of intellectual joys:
Theirs is no season for superfluous friends,
And none they need, but those whom Nature lends.

P.—But he, too, loved?—
F.—Oh! yes: his friend betray'd
The tender passion for the angel-maid.
Some child, whose features he at church had seen
Became his bosom's and his fancy's queen;
Some favourite look was on his mind impress'd—
His warm and fruitless fondness gave the rest.

P.—He left his father?—
F.—Yes! and rambled round
The land on foot—I know not what he found.
Early he came to his paternal land,
And took the course he had in rambling plann'd.
Ten years we lost him: he was then employ'd
In the wild schemes that he, perhaps, enjoy'd.
His mode of life, when he to manhood grew,
Was all his own—its shape disclosed to few.

Our grave, stern dames, who know the deeds of all,
Say that some damsels owe to him their fall;
And, though a Christian in his creed profess'd,
He had some heathen notions in his breast.
Yet we may doubt; for women, in his eyes,
Were high and glorious, queens and deities;
But he, perhaps, adorer and yet man,
Transgress'd yet worshipp'd. There are those who can.

Near him a Widow's mansion he survey'd—
The lovely mother of a lovelier Maid;
Not great their wealth; though they were proud to claim
Alliance with a house of noblest name.

Now, had I skill, I would right fain devise
To bring the highborn spinster to your eyes.
I could discourse of lip, and chin, and cheek,
But you would see no picture as I speak.
Such colours cannot—mix them as I may—
Paint you this nymph—We'll try a different way.

First take Calista in her glowing charms,
Ere yet she sank within Lothario's arms,
Endued with beauties ripe, and large desires,
And all that feels delight, and that inspires:
Add Cleopatra's great, yet tender soul,
Her boundless pride, her fondness of control,
Her daring spirit, and her wily art,
That, though it tortures, yet commands the heart;
Add woman's anger for a lover's slight,
And the revenge, that insult will excite;
Add looks for veils, that she at will could wear,
As Juliet fond, as Imogen sincere,—
Like Portia grave, sententious, and design'd
For high affairs, or gay as Rosalind—
Catch, if you can, some notion of the dame,
And let Matilda serve her for a name.

Think next how Villars saw th' enchanting maid,
And how he loved, pursued, adored, obey'd—
Obey'd in all, except the dire command,
No more to dream of that bewitching hand.
His love provoked her scorn, his wealth she spurn'd,
And frowns for praise, contempt for prayer return'd;
But, proud yet shrewd, the wily sex despise
The would-be husband—yet the votary prize.
As Roman conquerors, of their triumph vain,
Saw humbled monarchs in their pompous train,
Who, when no more they swell'd the show of pride,
In secret sorrow'd, or in silence died;
So, when our friend adored the Beauty's shrine,
She mark'd the act, and gave the nod divine;
And strove with scatter'd smiles, yet scarcely strove,
To keep the lover, while she scorn'd his love.

These, and his hope, the doubtful man sustain'd;
For who that loves believes himself disdain'd?—
Each look, each motion, by his fondness read,
Became Love's food, and greater fondness bred;
The pettiest favour was to him the sign
Of secret love, and said, "I 'll yet be thine!"
One doleful year she held the captive swain,
Who felt and cursed, and wore and bless'd, the chain;
Who pass'd a thousand galling insults by,
For one kind glance of that ambiguous eye.

P.—Well! time, perhaps, might to the coldest heart
Some gentle thought of one so fond impart;
And pride itself has often favour shown
To what it governs, and can call its own.

F.—Thus were they placed, when to the village came
That lordly stranger, whom I need not name;
Known since too well, but then as rich and young,
Untried his prowess, and his crimes unsung.
Smooth was his speech, and show'd a gentle mind,
Deaf to his praise, and to his merits blind;
But raised by woman's smile, and pleased with all mankind.

At humble distance he this fair survey'd,
Read her high temper, yet adored the Maid;
Far off he gazed, as if afraid to meet,
Or show the hope her anger would defeat:
Awful his love, and kept a guarded way,
Afraid to venture, till it finds it may.

And soon it found! nor could the Lady's pride
Her triumph bury, or her pleasure hide.

And jealous Love, that ever looks to spy
The dreaded wandering of a lady's eye,
Perceived with anguish, that the prize long sought
A sudden rival from his hopes had caught.
Still Villars loved; at length, with strong despair,
O'er-tortured possion thus preferr'd its prayer:—
"Life of my life! at once my fate decree—
I wait my death, or more than life, from thee:
I have no arts, nor powers, thy soul to move,
But doting constancy, and boundless love;
This is my all: had I the world to give,
Thine were its throne—now bid me die or live!"

"Or die or live"—the gentle Lady cried—
"As suits thee best; that point thyself decide;
But if to death thou hast thyself decreed,
Then like a man perform the manly deed;
The well-charged pistol to the ear apply,
Make loud report, and like a hero die:
Let rogues and rats on ropes and poison seize-
Shame not thy friends by petty death like these;
Sure we must grieve at what thou think'st to do,
But spare us blushes for the manner too!"

Then with inviting smiles she turn'd aside,
Allay'd his anger, and consoled his pride.

Oft had the fickle fair beheld with scorn
The unhappy man bewilder'd and forlorn,
Then with one softening glance of those bright eyes
Restored his spirit, and dispersed his sighs.
Oft had I seen him on the lea below,
As feelings moved him, walking quick or slow:
Now a glad thought, and now a doleful came,
And he adored or cursed the changeful dame,
Who was to him as cause is to effect—
Poor tool of pride, perverseness, and neglect!
Upon thy rival were her thoughts bestow'd,
Ambitious love within her bosom glow'd;
And oft she wish'd, and strong was her desire,
The Lord could love her like the faithful Squire
But she was rivall'd in that noble breast—
He loved her passing well, but not the best,
For self reign'd there; but still he call'd her fair,
And woo'd the muse his passion to declare.
His verses all were flaming, all were fine;
With sweetness, nay with sense, in every line—
Not as Lord Byron would have done the thing,
But better far than lords are used to sing.
It pleased the Maid, and she, in very truth,
Loved, in Calista's love, the noble youth;
Not like sweet Juliet, with that pure delight,
Fond and yet chaste, enraptured and yet right;
Not like the tender Imogen, confined
To one, but one! the true, the wedded mind;
True, one preferr'd our sighing nymph as these,
But thought not, like them, one alone could please

Time pass'd, nor yet the youthful peer proposed
To end his suit, nor his had Villars closed;
Fond hints the one, the other cruel bore;
That was more cautious, this was kind the more:
Both for soft moments waited—that to take
Of these advantage; fairly this to make.

These moments came—or so my lord believed—
He dropp'd his mask; and both were undeceived.
She saw the vice that would no longer feign,
And he an angry beauty's pure disdain.

Villars that night had in my ear confess'd,
He thought himself her spaniel and her jest.
He saw his rival of his goddess sure,
"But then," he cried, "her virtue is secure;
Should he offend, I haply may obtain
The high reward of vigilance and pain;
Till then I take, and on my bended knee,
Scraps from the banquet, gleanings of the tree."

Pitying, I smiled; for I had known the time
Of Love insulted—constancy my crime.
Not thus our friend: for him the morning shone
In tenfold glory, as for him alone;
He wept, expecting still reproof to meet,
And all that was not cruel count as sweet.
Back he return'd, all eagerness and joy,
Proud as a prince, and restless as a boy.
He sought to speak, but could not aptly find
Words for his use, they enter'd not his mind;
So full of bliss, that wonder and delight
Seem'd in those happy moments to unite.
He was like one who gains, but dreads to lose,
A prize that seems to vanish as he views:
And in his look was wildness and alarm—
Like a sad conjurer who forgets his charm,
And, when the demon at the call appears,
Cannot command the spirit for his fears:
So Villars seem'd by his own bliss perplex'd,
And scarcely knowing what would happen next.

But soon, a witness to their vows, I saw
The maiden his, if not by love, by law;
The bells proclaim'd it—merry call'd by those
Who have no foresight of their neighbours' woes.
How proudly show'd the man his lovely bride,
Demurely pacing, pondering, at his side!
While all the loving maids around declared,
That faith and constancy deserved reward.
The baffled Lord retreated from the scene
Of so much gladness, with a world of spleen;
And left the wedded couple, to protest,
That he no fear, that she no love possess'd,
That all his vows were scorn'd, and all his hope a jest.

Then fell the oaks to let in light of day,
Then rose the mansion that we now survey,
Then all the world flock'd gaily to the scene
Of so much splendour, and its splendid queen;
But whether all within the gentle breast
Of him, of her, was happy or at rest,—
Whether no lonely sigh confess'd regret,
Was then unknown, and is a secret yet;
And we may think, in common duty bound,
That no complaint is made where none is found.

Then came the Rival to his villa down,
Lost to the pleasures of the heartless town;
Famous he grew, and he invited all
Whom he had known to banquet at the Hall;
Talk'd of his love, and said, with many a sigh,
"'T is death to lose her, and I wish to die."

Twice met the parties; but with cool disdain
In her, in him with looks of awe and pain.
Villars had pity, and conceived it hard
That true regret should meet with no regard—
"Smile, my Matilda! virtue should inflict
No needless pain, nor be so sternly strict."

The Hall was furnish'd in superior style,
And money wanted from our sister isle;
The lady-mother to the husband sued—
"Alas! that care should on our bliss intrude!
You must to Ireland; our possessions there
Require your presence, nay, demand your care.
My pensive daughter begs with you to sail;
But spare your wife, nor let the wish prevail."

He went, and found upon his Irish land
Cases and griefs he could not understand.
Some glimmering light at first his prospect cheer'd.
Clear it was not, but would in time be clear'd;
But when his lawyers had their efforts made,
No mind in man the darkness could pervade;
'T was palpably obscure: week after week
He sought for comfort, but was still to seek.
At length, impatient to return, he strove
No more with law, but gave the rein to love;
And to his Lady and their native shore
Vow'd to return, and thence to turn no more.

While yet on Irish ground in trouble kept,
The Husband's terrors in his toils had slept;
But he no sooner touch'd the British soil,
Than jealous terrors took the place of toil—
"Where has she been? and how attended? Who
Has watch'd her conduct, and will vouch her true?
She sigh'd at parting, but methought her sighs
Were more profound than would from nature rise;
And though she wept as never wife before,
Yet were her eyelids neither swell'd nor sore.
Her lady-mother has a good repute,
As watchful dragon of forbidden fruit;
Yet dragons sleep, and mothers have been known
To guard a daughter's secret as their own;
Nor can the absent in their travel see
How a fond wife and mother may agree.

Suppose the lady is most virtuous!—then,
What can she know of the deceits of men?
Of all they plan, she neither thinks nor cares;
But keeps, good lady! at her books and prayers.

In all her letters there are love, respect,
Esteem, regret, affection, all correct—
Too much—she fears that I should see neglect;
And there are fond expressions, but unlike
The rest, as meant to be observed and strike;
Like quoted words, they have the show of art,
And come not freely from the gentle heart—
Adopted words, and brought from memory's store,
When the chill faltering heart supplies no more
'T is so the hypocrite pretends to feel,
And speaks the words of earnestness and zeal.

Hers was a sudden, though a sweet consent,
May she not now as suddenly repent?
My rival's vices drove him from the door;
But hates she vice as truly as before?

How do I know, if he should plead again,
That all her scorn and anger would remain?

Oh! words of folly—is it thus I deem
Of the chaste object of my fond esteem?
Away with doubt! to jealousy adieu!
I know her fondness, and believe her true.

Yet why that haste to furnish every need,
And send me forth with comfort, and with speed?
Yes; for she dreaded that the winter's rage
And our frail boy should on the seas engage.

But that vile girl! I saw a treacherous eye
Glance on her mistress! so demure and sly,
So forward too—and would Matilda's pride
Admit of that, if there was naught beside?"

Such, as he told me, were the doubt, the dread,
By jealous fears on observations fed.

Home he proceeded: there remain'd to him
But a few miles—the night was wet and dim;
Thick, heavy dews descended on the ground,
And all was sad and melancholy round.

While thinking thus, an inn's far gleaming fire
Caused new emotions in the pensive Squire.
"Here I may learn, and seeming careless too,
If all is well, ere I my way pursue.
How fare you, landlord?—how, my friend, are all?—
Have you not seen—my people at the Hall?
Well, I may judge——"
"Oh! yes, your Honour, well,
As Joseph knows; and he was sent to tell."—
How! sent—I miss'd him—Joseph, do you say?
Why sent, if well?—I miss'd him on the way."

There was a poacher on the chimney-seat,
A gipsy, conjurer, smuggler, stroller, cheat.
The Squire had fined him for a captured hare,
Whipp'd and imprison'd—he had felt the fare,
And he remember'd: "Will your Honour know
How does my Lady? that myself can show.
On Monday early—for your Honour sees
The poor man must not slumber at his ease,
Nor must he into woods and coverts lurk,
Nor work alone, but must be seen to work:
'T is not, your Honour knows, sufficient now
For us to live, but we must prove it—how.
Stay, please your Honour,—I was early up,
And forth without a morsel or a sup.
There was my Lady's carriage—Whew! it drove
As if the horses had been spurr'd by Love."

"A poet, John!" said Villars—feebly said,
Confused with fear, and humbled and dismay'd—
"And where this carriage?—but, my heart! enough—
Why do I listen to the villain's stuff?
And where wert thou? and what the spur of thine,
That led thee forth?—we surely may divine!"

"Hunger, your Honour! I and my poor wife
Have now no other in our wane of life.
Were Phœbe handsome, and were I a Squire,
I might suspect her, and young Lords admire."—
"What! rascal——"—"Nay, your Honour, on my word,
I should be jealous of that fine young Lord;
Yet him my Lady in the carriage took,
But innocent—I'd swear it on the book."

"You villain, swear!"—for still he wish'd to stay,
And hear what more the fellow had to say.
"Phœbe, said I, a rogue that had a heart
To do the deed would make his Honour smart—
Says Phœbe, wisely, 'Think you, would he go,
If he were jealous, from my Lady?—No.'"

This was too much! poor Villars left the inn,
To end the grief that did but then begin.
"With my Matilda in the coach!—what lies
Will the vile rascal in his spleen devise?
Yet this is true, that on some vile pretence
Men may entrap the purest innocence.
He saw my fears—alas! I am not free
From every doubt—but no! it cannot be."

Villars moved slow, moved quick, as check'd by fear,
Or urged by Love, and drew his mansion near.
Light burst upon him, yet he fancied gloom,
Nor came a twinkling from Matilda's room.
"What then? 't is idle to expect that all
Should be produced at jealous fancy's call;
How! the park-gate wide open! who would dare
Do this, if her presiding glance were there?
But yet, by chance—I know not what to think,
For thought is hell! and I'm upon the brink!
Not for a thousand worlds, ten thousand lives,
Would I——Oh! what depends upon our wives!
Pains, labours, terrors, all would I endure,
Yes, all but this—and this, could I be sure——"

Just then a light within the window shone,
And show'd a lady, weeping and alone.
His heart beat fondly—on another view,—
It beat more strongly, and in terror too—
It was his Sister!—and there now appear'd
A servant creeping like a man that fear'd.
He spoke with terror—"Sir, did Joseph tell?
Have you not met him?"—
"Is your Lady well?"
"Well? Sir—your Honour——"
"Heaven and earth! what mean
Your stupid questions? I have nothing seen,
Nor heard, nor know, nor—Do, good Thomas, speak!
Your mistress——"
"Sir, has gone from home a week—
My Lady, Sir, your sister——"

But, too late
Was this—my Friend had yielded to his fate.
He heard the truth, became serene and mild,
Patient and still, as a corrected child;
At once his spirit with his fortune fell
To the last ebb, and whisper'd—It is well.

Such was his fall; and grievous the effect!
From henceforth all things fell into neglect—
The mind no more alert, the form no more erect.

Villars long since, as he indulged his spleen
By lonely travel on the coast, had seen

A large old mansion suffer'd to decay
In some law-strife, and slowly drop away.
Dark elms around the constant herons bred,
Those the marsh dykes, the neighbouring ocean, fed;
Rocks near the coast no shipping would allow,
And stubborn heath around forbad the plough;
Dull must the scene have been in years of old,
But now was wildly dismal to behold—
One level sadness! marsh, and heath, and sea,
And, save these high dark elms, nor plant nor tree.

In this bleak ruin Villars found a room,
Square, small, and lofty—seat of grief and gloom;
A sloping skylight on the white wall threw,
When the sun set, a melancholy hue;
The Hall of Vathek has a room so bare,
So small, so sad, so form'd to nourish care.
"Here," said the Traveller, "all so dark within,
And dull without, a man might mourn for sin,
Or punish sinners—here a wanton wife
And vengeful husband might be cursed for life."

His mind was now in just that wretched state,
That deems Revenge our right, and crime our fate.
All other views he banish'd from his soul,
And let this tyrant vex him and control;
Life he despis'd, and had that Lord defied,
But that he long'd for Vengeance ere he died.
The law he spurn'd, the combat he declined,
And to his purpose all his soul resign'd.

Full fifteen months had pass'd, and we began
To have some hope of the returning man;
Now to his steward of his amall affairs
He wrote, and mention'd leases and repairs;
But yet his soul was on its scheme intent,
And but a moment to his interest lent.

His faithless wife and her triumphant peer
Despis'd his vengeance, and disdain'd to fear;
In splendid lodgings near the town they dwelt,
Nor fears from wrath, nor threats from conscience felt.

Long time our friend had watch'd, and much had paid
For vulgar minds, who lent his vengeance aid.
At length one evening, late returning home,
Thoughtless and fearless of the ills to come,
The Wife was seized, when void of all alarm
And vainly trusting to a footman's arm;
Death in his hand, the Husband stood in view,
Commanding silence, and obedience too;
Forced to his carriage, sinking at his side,
Madly he drove her—Vengeance was his guide.

All in that ruin Villars had prepared,
And meant her fate and sorrow to have shared;
There he design'd they should for ever dwell,
The weeping pair of a monastic cell.

An ancient couple from their cottage went,
Won by his pay, to this imprisonment;
And all was order'd in his mind—the pain
He must inflict, the shame she must sustain;
But such his gentle spirit, such his love,
The proof might fail of all he meant to prove.

Features so dear had still maintain'd their sway,
And looks so lov'd had taught him to obey;
Rage and Revenge had yielded to the sight
Of charms that waken wonder and delight;
The harsher passions from the heart had flown,
And LOVE regain'd his Subject and his Throne.

[The next Tale, and a number of others, were originally designed for a separate volume, to be entitled "The Farewell and Return." In a letter to Mrs. Leadbetter, written in 1823, the poet says—"In my 'Farewell and Return' I suppose a young man to take leave of his native place, and to exchange *farewells* with his friends and acquaintance there—in short, with as many characters as I have fancied I could manage. These, and their several situations and prospects, being briefly sketched, an interval is supposed to elapse; and our youth, a youth no more, *returns* to the scene of his early days. Twenty years have passed; and the interest, if there be any, consists in the completion, more or less unexpected, of the history of each person to whom he had originally bidden farewell."

The reader will find the tales written on this plan, divided each into two or more sections; and will easily perceive where the *farewell* terminates, and the *return* begins.]

TALE VI.

THE FAREWELL AND RETURN.

I.

I AM of age, and now, no more the Boy,
Am ready fortune's favours to enjoy,
Were they, too, ready; but, with grief I speak,
Mine is the fortune that I yet must seek.
And let me seek it; there 's the world around—
And if not sought it never can be found.
It will not come if I the chase decline;
Wishes and wants will never make it mine.
Then let me shake these lingering fears away;
What one day must be, let it be to-day;
Lest courage fail ere I the search commence,
And resolution pall upon suspense.

Yet, while amid these well-known scenes I dwell,
Let me to friends and neighbours bid Farewell.

First to our men of wealth—these are but few—
In duty bound I humbly bid adieu.
This is not painful, for they know me not,
Fortune in different states has placed our lot;
It is not pleasant, for full well I know
The lordly pity that the rich bestow—
A proud contemptuous pity, by whose aid
Their own triumphant virtues are display'd.—

"Going, you say; and what intends the Lad,
To seek his fortune? Fortune! is he mad?
Has he the knowledge? is he duly taught?
I think we know how Fortune should be sought.
Perhaps he takes his chance to sink or swim,
Perhaps he dreams of Fortune's seeking him?
Life is his lottery, and away he flies,
Without a ticket to obtain his prize:
But never man acquired a weighty sum,
Without foreseeing whence it was to come."

Fortunes are made, if I the facts may state,—
Though poor myself, I know the fortunate:
First, there's a knowledge of the way from whence
Good fortune comes—and that is sterling sense;
Then perseverance, never to decline
The chase of riches till the prey is thine;
And firmness, never to be drawn away
By any passion from that noble prey—
By love, ambition, study, travel, fame,
Or the vain hope that lives upon a name.

The whistling Boy that holds the plough,
Lured by the tale that soldiers tell,
Resolves to part, yet knows not how
To leave the land he loves so well.
He now rejects the thought, and now
Looks o'er the lea, and sighs "Farewell!"

Farewell! the pensive maiden cries,
Who dreams of London, dreams awake—
But when her favourite Lad she spies,
With whom she loved her way to take,
Then Doubts within her soul arise,
And equal Hopes her bosom shake!

Thus, like the Boy, and like the Maid,
I wish to go, yet tarry here,
And now resolved, and now afraid:
To minds disturb'd old views appear
In melancholy charms array'd,
And once indifferent, now are dear.
How shall I go, my fate to learn—
And, oh! how taught shall I return?

II.

Yes!—twenty years have pass'd, and I am come,
Unknown, unwelcom'd, to my early home,
A stranger striving in my walks to trace
The youthful features in some aged face.
On as I move, some curious looks I read;
We pause a moment, doubt, and then proceed:
They're like what once I saw, but not the same,
I lose the air, the features, and the name.
Yet something seems like knowledge, but the change
Confuses me, and all in him is strange:
That bronzed old Sailor, with his wig awry—
Sure he will know me! No, he passes by.
They seem like me in doubt; but they can call
Their friends around them! I am lost to all.

The very place is alter'd. What I left
Seems of its space and dignity bereft:
The streets are narrow, and the buildings mean;
Did I, or Fancy, leave them broad and clean?
The ancient church, in which I felt a pride,
As struck by magic, is but half as wide;
The tower is shorter, the sonorous bell
Tells not the hour as it was wont to tell;
The market dwindles, every shop and stall
Sink in my view; there 's littleness in all.
Mine is the error; prepossess'd I see;
And all the change I mourn is change in me.

One object only is the same; the sight
Of the wide Ocean by the moon's pale light
With her long ray of glory, that we mark
On the wild waves when all beside is dark:
This is the work of Nature, and the eye
In vain the boundless prospect would descry:
What mocks our view cannot contracted be;
We cannot lessen what we cannot see.

Would I could now a single Friend behold,
Who would the yet mysterious facts unfold,
That Time yet spares, and to a stranger show
Th' events he wishes, and yet fears to know!

Much by myself I might in list'ning glean,
Mix'd with the crowd, unmark'd if not unseen,
Uninterrupted I might ramble on,
Nor cause an interest, nor a thought, in one;
For who looks backward to a being tost
About the world, forgotten long, and lost,
For whom departing not a tear was shed,
Who disappear'd, was missing, and was dead!
Save that he left no grave, where some might pass,
And ask each other who that being was.

I, as a ghost invisible, can stray
Among the crowd, and cannot lose my way;
My ways are where the voice of man is known,
Though no occasion offers for my own;
My eager mind to fill with food I seek,
And, like the ghost, await for one to speak.

See I not One whom I before have seen?
That face, though now untroubled and serene,
That air, though steady now, that look, though tame,
Pertain to one, whom though I doubt to name,
Yet was he not a dashing youth and wild,
Proud as a man, and haughty when a child?
Talents were his; he was in nature kind,
With lofty, strong, and independent mind;
His father wealthy, but, in very truth,
He was a rash, untamed, expensive youth;
And, as I now remember the report,
Told how his father's money he would sport:
Yet in his dress and manner now appears
No sign of faults that stain'd his earlier years;
Mildness there seems, and marks of sober sense,
That bear no token of that wild expense
Such as to ruin leads!—I may mistake,
Yet may, perchance, a useful friendship make!
He looks as one whom I should not offend,
Address'd as him whom I would make a friend.

Men with respect attend him.—He proceeds
To yonder public room—why then he reads.

Suppose me right—a mighty change is wrought;
But Time ere now has care and caution taught.

May I address him? And yet, why afraid?
Deny he may, but he will not upbraid,
Nor must I lose him, for I want his aid.

Propitious fate! beyond my hope I find
A being well-inform'd, and much inclined
To solve my many doubts, and ease my anxious mind.

Now shall we meet, and he will give reply
To all I ask!—How full of fears am I;
Poor, nervous, trembling! what have I to fear?
Have I a wife, a child, one creature here,
Whose health would bring me joy, whose death would claim a tear?

This is the time appointed, this the place:
Now shall I learn, how some have run their race
With honour, some with shame; and I shall know
How man behaves in Fortune's ebb and flow;—
What wealth or want, what trouble, sorrow, joy,
Have been allotted to the girls and boy
Whom I left laughing at the ills of life,—
Now the grave father, or the lawful wife.
Then shall I hear how tried the wise and good!
How fallen the house that once in honour stood!
And moving accidents, from war and fire and flood!

These shall I hear, if to his promise true;
His word is pledged to tell me all he knew
Of living men; and memory then will trace
Those who no more with living men have place,
As they were borne to their last quiet homes—
This shall I learn!—And lo! my Teacher comes.

TALE VII.

THE SCHOOL-FELLOW.

[Farewell and Return.]

I.

Yes! I must leave thee, brother of my heart,
The world demands us, and at length we part;
Thou whom that heart, since first it felt, approved—
I thought not why, nor question'd how I loved;
In my first thoughts, first notions, and first cares,
Associate: partner in my mind's affairs,
In my young dreams, my fancies ill-express'd
But well conceived, and to the heart address'd.
A fellow-reader in the books I read,
A fellow-mourner in the tears I shed,
A friend, partaking every grief and joy,
A lively, frank, engaging, generous boy.

At school each other's prompters, day by day
Companions in the frolic or the fray;
Prompt in disputes—we never sought the cause,
The laws of friendship were our only laws;
We ask'd not how or why the strife began,
But David's foe was foe to Jonathan.

In after-years my Friend, the elder boy,
Would speak of Love, its tumult and its joy;

A new and strong emotion thus imprest,
Prepared for pain to come the yielding breast;
For though no object then the fancy found,
She dreamt of darts, and gloried at the wound;
Smooth verse and tender tales the spirit moved,
And ere the Chloes came the Strephons loved.

This is the Friend I leave; for he remains
Bound to his home by strong but viewless chains:
Nor need I fear that his aspiring soul
Will fail his adverse fortunes to control,
Or lose the fame he merits: yet awhile
The clouds may lour—but then his sun will smile.
Oh! Time, thou teller of men's fortunes, lend
Thy aid, and be propitious to my Friend!
Let me behold him prosperous, and his name
Enroll'd among the darling sons of Fame;
In love befriend him, and be his the bride,
Proud of her choice, and of her lord the pride.
"So shall my little bark attendant sail,"—
(As Pope has sung)—and prosperous be the gale!

II.

He is not here: the Youth I loved so well
Dwells in some place where kindred spirits dwell:
But I shall learn. Oh! tell me of my Friend,
With whom I hoped life's evening-calm to spend:
With whom was spent the morn, the happy morn!
When gay conceits and glorious views are born;
With whom conversing I began to find
The early stirrings of an active mind,
That, done the tasks and lessons of the day,
Sought for new pleasures in our untried way;
And stray'd in fairy land, where much we long'd to stray.

Here he abides not! could not surely fix
In this dull place, with these dull souls to mix;
He finds his place where lively spirits meet,
And loftier souls from baser kind retreat.

First, of my early Friend I gave the name,
Well known to me, and, as I judg'd, to Fame;
My grave informer doubted, then replied,
"That Lad!—why, yes!—some ten years since he died."

P.—Died! and unknown! the man I lov'd so well!
But is this all? the whole that you can tell
Of one so gifted?—
F.—Gifted! why, in truth,
You puzzle me: how gifted was the Youth?
I recollect him, now—his long, pale face—
He dress'd in drab, and walk'd as in a race.

P.—Good Heaven! what did I not of him expect?
And is this all indeed you recollect—
Of wit that charm'd me, with delightful ease—
And gay good-humour that must ever please—
His taste, his genius! know you naught of these?

F.—No, not of these:—but stop! in passing near
I've heard his flute—it was not much to hear:
As for his genius—let me not offend:
I never had a genius for a friend,
And doubt of yours; but still he did his best,
And was a decent Lad—there let him rest!

He lies in peace, with all his humble race,
And has no stone to mark his burial place;
Nor left he that which to the world might show
That he was one that world was bound to know,
For aught he gave it.—Here his story ends!

P.—And is this all?—This character my Friend's!
That may, alas! be mine——"*a decent Lad!*"—
The very phrase would make a Poet mad!
And he is gone!—Oh! proudly did I think
That we together at that fount should drink,
Together climb the steep ascent of Fame,
Together gain an ever-during name,
And give due credit to our native home—
Yet here he lies, without a name or tomb!
Perhaps not honour'd by a single tear,
Just enter'd in a parish-register,
With common dust, forgotten to remain—
And shall I seek, what thou couldst not obtain—
A name for men when I am dead to speak?—
Oh! let me something more substantial seek;
Let me no more on man's poor praise depend,
But learn one lesson from my buried Friend.

TALE VIII.

BARNABY; THE SHOPMAN.

[*Farewell and Return.*]

I.

Farewell! to *him* whom just across my way,
I see his shop attending day by day!
Save on the Sunday, when he duly goes
To his own church, in his own Sunday clothes.
Young though he is, yet careful there he stands,
Opening his shop with his own ready hands;
Nor scorns the broom that to and fro he moves,
Cleaning his way, for cleanliness he loves—
But yet preserves not: in his zeal for trade
He has his shop an ark for all things made;
And there, in spite of his all-guarding eye,
His sundry wares in strange confusion lie—
Delightful token of the haste that keeps
Those mingled matters in their shapeless heaps:
Yet ere he rests, he takes them all away,
And order smiles on the returning day.

Most ready tradesman he of men! alive
To all that turns to money—he must thrive,
Obsequious, civil, loath t' offend or trust,
And full of awe for greatness—thrive he must;
For well he knows to creep, and he in time,
By wealth assisted, will aspire to climb.

Pains-taking lad he was, and with his slate
For hours in useful meditation sate;
Puzzled, and seizing every boy at hand,
To make him—hard the labour!—understand;
But when of learning he enough possess'd
For his affairs, who would might learn the rest;
All else was useless when he had obtain'd
Knowledge that told him what he lost or gain'd.
He envied no man for his learning; he
Who was not rich, was poor with Barnaby:
But he for envy has no thought to spare,
Nor love nor hate—his heart is in his ware.

Happy the man whose greatest pleasure lies
In the fair trade by which he hopes to rise.
To him how bright the opening day, how blest
The busy noon, how sweet the evening rest!
To him the nation's state is all unknown,
Whose watchful eye is ever on his own.
You talk of patriots, men who give up all,
Yea, life itself, at their dear country's call!
He look'd on such as men of other date,
Men to admire, and not to imitate;
They as his Bible-Saints to him appear'd,
Lost to the world, but still to be revered.

Yet there's a Widow, in a neighbouring street,
Whom he contrives in Sunday-dress to meet;
Her's house and land; and these are more delight
To him than learning, in the proverb's spite.

The Widow sees at once the Trader's views,
And means to soothe him, flatter, and refuse;
Yet there are moments when a woman fails
In such design, and so the man prevails.
Love she has not, but, in a guardless hour,
May lose her purpose, and resign her power;
Yet all such hazard she resolves to run,
Pleased to be woo'd, and fearless to be won.

Lovers like these, as dresses thrown aside,
Are kept and shown to feed a woman's pride.
Old-fashion'd, ugly, call them what she will,
They serve as signs of her importance still.
She thinks they might inferior forms adorn,
And does not love to hear them used with scorn;
Till on some day when she has need of dress,
And none at hand to serve her in distress,
She takes the insulted robe, and turns about;
Long-hidden beauties one by one peer out.
"'T is not so bad! see, Jenny—I declare
'T is pretty well, and then 't is lasting wear;
And what is fashion?—if a woman's wise,
She will the substance, not the shadow prize;
'T is a choice silk, and if I put it on,
Off go these ugly trappings every one."
The dress is worn, a friendly smile is raised,
But the good lady for her courage praised—
Till wonder dies.—The dress is worn with pride,
And not one trapping yet is cast aside.

Meanwhile the man his six-day toil renews,
And on the seventh he worships Heaven, and woos

I leave thee, Barnaby; and if I see
Thee once again, a Burgess thou wilt be.

II.

But how is this? I left a thriving man,
Hight Barnaby! when he to trade began—
Trade his delight and hope; and, if alive,
Doubt I had none that Barnaby would thrive:
Yet here I see him, sweeping as before
The very dust from forth the very door.

So would a miser! but, methinks, the shop
Itself is meaner—has he made a stop?

I thought I should at least a burgess see,
And lo! 't is but an older Barnaby;
With face more wrinkled, with a coat as bare
As coats of his once begging kindred were,
Brush'd to the thread that is distinctly seen,
And beggarly would be, but that 't is clean.

Why, how is this? Upon a closer view,
The shop is narrow'd: it is cut in two.
Is all that business from its station fled?
Why, Barnaby! the very shop is dead!
Now, what the cause my Friend will soon relate—
And what the fall from that predicted fate.

F. A common cause: it seems his lawful gains
Came slowly forth, and came with care and pains.
These he, indeed, was willing to bestow,
But still his progress to his point was slow,
And might be quicken'd, "could he cheat the eyes
Of all those rascal officers and spies,
The Customs' greedy tribe, the wolves of the Excise."

Tea, coffee, spirits, laces, silks, and spice,
And sundry drugs that bear a noble price,
Are bought for little, but ere sold, the things
Are deeply charged for duty of the king's.
Now, if the servants of this king would keep
At a kind distance, or would wink or sleep,
Just till the goods in safety were disposed,
Why then his labours would be quickly closed.
True! some have thriven,—but they the laws defied,
And shunn'd the powers they should have satisfied.

Their way he tried, and finding some success,
His heart grew stouter, and his caution less;
Then—for why doubt, when placed in Fortune's way?—
There was a bank, and that was sure to pay.
Yes, every partner in that thriving bank
He judged a man of a superior rank.
Were *he* but one in a concern so grand—
Why! he might build a house, and buy him land;
Then, too, the Widow, whom he loved so well,
Would not refuse with such a man to dwell;
And, to complete his views, he might be made
A Borough-Justice, when he ceased to trade;
For he had known—well pleased to know—a mayor
Who once had dealt in cheese and vinegar.

Who hastens to be rich, resembles him
Who is resolved that he will quickly swim,
And trusts his full-blown bladders! He, indeed,
With these supported, moves along with speed;
He laughs at those whom untried depths alarm,
By caution led, and moved by strength of arm;
Till in mid-way, the way his folly chose,
His full-blown bladder bursts, and down he goes!
Or, if preserved, 't is by their friendly aid
Whom he despised as cautious and afraid.

Who could resist? Not Barnaby. Success
Awhile his pride exalted—to depress.
Three years he pass'd in feverish hopes and fears,
When fled the profits of the former years;
Shook by the Law's strong arm, all he had gain'd
He dropp'd—and hopeless, penniless remain'd.

The cruel Widow, whom he yet pursued,
Was kind but cautious, then was stern and rude.
"Should wealth, now hers, from that dear man which came,
Be thrown away to prop a smuggler's fame?"

She spake insulting; and with many a sigh,
The fallen Trader pass'd her mansion by.

Fear, shame, and sorrow, for a time endured,
Th' adventurous man was ruin'd, but was cured—
His weakness pitied, and his once-good name
The means of his returning peace became.

He was assisted, to his shop withdrew,
Half let, half rented, and began anew,
To smile on custom, that in part return'd,
With the small gains that he no longer spurn'd.
Warn'd by the past, he rises with the day,
And tries to sweep off Sorrow.—*Sweep away!*

TALE IX.

JANE.

[*Farewell and Return.*]

I.

Known but of late, I yet am loath to leave
The gentle Jane, and wonder why I grieve—
Not for her wants, for she has no distress,
She has no suffering that her looks express,
Her air or manner—hers the mild good sense
That wins its way by making no pretence.

When yet a child, her dying mother knew
What, left by her, the widow'd man would do,
And gave her Jane, for she had power, enough
To live in ease—of love and care a proof.
Enabled thus, the maid is kind to all—
Is pious too, and that without a call.
Not that she doubts of calls that Heaven has sent—
Calls to believe, or warnings to repent;
But that she rests upon the Word divine,
Without presuming on a dubious sign;
A sudden light, the momentary zeal
Of those who rashly hope, and warmly feel
These she rejects not, nor on these relies,
And neither feels the influence nor denies.
Upon the sure and written Word she trusts,
And by the Law Divine her life adjusts;
She blames not her who other creed prefers,
And all she asks is charity for hers.
Her great example is her gracious Lord,
Her hope his promise, and her guide his Word;
Her quiet alms are known to God alone,
Her left hand knows not what her right has done

Her talents, not the few, she well improves,
And puts to use in labour that she loves.

Pensive, though good, I leave thee, gentle maid—
In thee confiding, of thy peace afraid,
In a strange world to act a trying part,
With a soft temper, and a yielding heart!

II.

P.—How fares my gentle Jane, with spirit meek,
Whose fate with some foreboding care I seek;
Her whom I pitied in my pride, while she,
For many a cause more weighty, pitied me;
For she has wonder'd how the idle boy
His head or hands would usefully employ—
At least for thee his grateful spirit pray'd,
And now to ask thy fortune is afraid.—
——How fares the gentle Jane?—

F.—Know first, she fares
As one who bade adieu to earthly cares;
As one by virtue guided, and who, tried
By man's deceit, has never lost her guide.

Her age I knew not, but it seem'd the age
When Love is wont a serious war to wage
In female hearts,—when hopes and fears are strong,
And 't is a fatal step to place them wrong;
For childish fancies now have ta'en their flight,
And love's impressions are no longer light.

Just at this time—what time I do not tell—
There came a Stranger in the place to dwell;
He seem'd as one who sacred truth reveres,
And like her own his sentiments and years;
His person manly, with engaging mien,
His spirit quiet, and his looks serene.
He kept from all disgraceful deeds aloof,
Severely tried, and found temptation-proof:
This was by most unquestion'd, and the few
Who made inquiry, said report was true.

His very choice of our neglected place
Endear'd him to us—'t was an act of grace;
And soon to Jane, our unobtrusive maid,
In still respect was his attention paid;
Each in the other found what both approved,
Good sense and quiet manners: these they loved.

So came regard, and then esteem, and then
The kind of friendship women have with men:
At length 't was love, but candid, open, fair,
Such as became their years and character.

In their discourse, religion had its place,
When he of doctrines talk'd, and she of grace.
He knew the different sects, the varying creeds,
While she, less learned, spake of virtuous deeds;
He dwelt on errors into which we fall,
She on the gracious remedy for all;
So between both, his knowledge and her own,
Was the whole Christian to perfection shown.
Though neither quite approved the other's part—
Hers without learning, his without a heart—
Still to each other they were dear, were good,
And all these matters kindly understood:
For Jane was liberal, and her friend could trust,—
"He thinks not with me! but is fair and just."

Her prudent lover to her man of law,
Show'd how he lived: it seem'd without a flaw;
She saw their moderate means—content with what
she saw.

Jane had no doubts—with so much to admire,
She judged it insult farther to inquire.
The lover sought—what lover brooks delay?—
For full assent, and for an early day—
And he would construe well the soft consenting
Nay!

The day was near, and Jane, with book in hand,
Sat down to read—perhaps might understand:
For what prevented?—say, she seem'd to read;
When one there came, her own sad cause to plead;
A stranger she, who fearless named that cause,
A breach in love's and honour's sacred laws.

"In a far country, Lady, bleak and wild,
Report has reach'd me! how art thou beguiled!
Or dared he tell thee that for ten sad years
He saw me struggling with fond hopes and fears?

From my dear home he won me, blest and free!
To be his victim."——"Madam, who is *he?*"
"Not yet thy husband, Lady: no! not yet;
For he has first to pay a mighty debt."

"Speaks he not of religion?"—"So he speaks,
When he the ruin of his victim seeks.
How smooth and gracious were his words, how
sweet—
The fiend his master prompting his deceit!
Me he with kind instruction led to trust
In one who seem'd so grave, so kind, so just.
Books to amuse me, and inform, he brought,
Like that old serpent with temptation fraught;
His like the precepts of the wise appear'd,
Till I imbibed the vice I had not fear'd.
By pleasant tales and dissertations gay,
He wiled the lessons of my youth away.

Of moral duties he would talk, and prove
They gave a sanction, and commanded love;
His sober smile at forms and rites was shown,
To make my mind depraved, and like his own.

But wilt thou take him! wilt thou ruin take,
With a grave robber, a religious rake?
'T is not to serve thee, Lady, that I came—
'T is not to claim him, 't is not to reclaim—
But 't is that he may for my wrongs be paid,
And feel the vengeance of the wretch he made.

Not for myself I thy attention claim:
My children dare not take their father's name;
They know no parent's love—love will not dwell
with shame.
What law would force, he not without it gives,
And hates each living wretch, because it lives!
Yet, with these sinful stains, the man is mine:
How will he curse me for this rash design!
Yes—I will bear his curse, but him will not resign.

I see thee grieved; but, Lady, what thy grief?
It may be pungent, but it must be brief.
Pious thou art; but what will profit thee,
Match'd with a demon, woman's piety?

Not for thy sake my wrongs and wrath I tell,
Revenge I seek! but yet, I wish thee well.
And now I leave thee! Thou art warn'd by one,
The rock on which her peace was wreck'd to shun."

The Lover heard; but not in time to stay
A woman's vengeance in its headlong way:
Yet he essay'd, with no unpractised skill,
To warp the judgment, or at least the will;
To raise such tumults in the poor weak heart,
That Jane, believing all—yet should not dare to part.

But there was Virtue in her mind that strove
With all his eloquence, and all her love;
He told what hope and frailty dared to tell,
And all was answer'd by a stern *Farewell!*

Home with his consort he return'd once more;
And they resumed the life they led before.
Not so our maiden. She, before resign'd,
Had now the anguish of a wounded mind—
And felt the languid grief that the deserted find;
On him she had reposed each worldly view,
And when he fail'd, the world itself withdrew,
With all its prospects. Nothing could restore
To life its value; hope would live no more:
Pensive by nature, she can not sustain
The sneer of pity that the heartless feign;
But to the pressure of her griefs gives way,
A quiet victim, and a patient prey:
The one bright view that she had cherish'd dies,
And other hope must from the future rise.

She still extends to grief and want her aid,
And by the comfort she imparts, is paid:
Death is her soul's relief: to him she flies
For consolation that this world denies.
No more to life's false promises she clings,
She longs to change this troubled state of things,
Till every rising morn the happier prospect brings.

TALE X.

THE ANCIENT MANSION.

[*Farewell and Return.*]

I.

To part is painful; nay, to bid adieu
Even to a favourite spot is painful too.
That fine old Seat, with all those oaks around,
Oft have I view'd with reverence so profound,
As something sacred dwelt in that delicious ground.

There, with its tenantry about, reside
A genuine English race, the country's pride;
And now a Lady, last of all that race,
Is the departing spirit of the place.
Hers is the last of all that noble blood,
That flow'd through generations brave and good;
And if there dwells a native pride in her,
It is the pride of name and character.

True, she will speak, in her abundant zeal,
Of stainless honour; that she needs must feel;
She must lament, that she is now the last
Of all who gave such splendour to the past.

Still are her habits of the ancient kind;
She knows the poor, the sick, the lame, the blind
She holds, so she believes, her wealth in trust;
And being kind, with her, is being just.
Though soul and body she delights to aid,
Yet of her skill she 's prudently afraid:
So to her chaplain's care she *this* commends,
And when *that* craves, the village doctor sends.

At church attendance she requires of all,
Who would be held in credit at the Hall;
A due respect to each degree she shows,
And pays the debt that every mortal owes;
'T is by opinion that respect is led,
The rich esteem because the poor are fed.

Her servants all, if so we may describe
That ancient, grave, observant, decent tribe,
Who with her share the blessings of the Hall,
Are kind but grave, are proud but courteous all—
Proud of their lucky lot! behold, how stands
That grey-hair'd butler, waiting her commands;
The Lady dines, and every day he feels
That his good mistress falters in her meals.
With what respectful manners he entreats
That she would eat—yet Jacob little eats;
When she forbears, his supplicating eye
Intreats the noble dame once more to try.
Their years the same; and he has never known
Another place; and this he deems his own,—
All appertains to him. Whate'er he sees
Is *ours!*—"our house, our land, our walks, our trees!"

But still he fears the time is just at hand,
When he no more shall in that presence stand;
And he resolves, with mingled grief and pride,
To serve no being in the world beside.
"He has enough," he says, with many a sigh,
"For him to serve his God, and learn to die:
He and his lady shall have heard their call,
And the new folk, the strangers, may have all."

But, leaving these to their accustom'd way,
The Seat itself demands a short delay.
We all have interest there—the trees that grow
Near to that seat, to that their grandeur owe;
They take, but largely pay, and equal grace bestow
They hide a part, but still the part they shade
Is more inviting to our fancy made;
And, if the eye be robb'd of half its sight,
Th' imagination feels the more delight.
These giant oaks by no man's order stand,
Heaven did the work; by no man was it plann'd.

Here I behold no puny works of art,
None give me reasons why these views impart
Such charm to fill the mind, such joy to swell the heart.
These very pinnacles, and turrets small,
And windows dim, have beauty in them all.

How stately stand yon pines upon the hill,
How soft the murmurs of that living rill,
And o'er the park's tall paling, scarcely higher,
Peeps the low Church and shows the modest spire.
Unnumber'd violets on those banks appear,
And all the first-born beauties of the year.
The grey-green blossoms of the willows bring
The large wild bees upon the labouring wing.
Then comes the summer with augmented pride,
Whose pure small streams along the valleys glide:
Her richer Flora their brief charms display;
And, as the fruit advances, falls away.
Then shall th' autumnal yellow clothe the leaf,
What time the reaper binds the burden'd sheaf:
Then silent groves denote the dying year,
The morning frost, and noon-tide gossamer;
And all be silent in the scene around,
All save the distant sea's uncertain sound,
Or here and there the gun whose loud report
Proclaims to man that Death is but his sport:
And then the wintry winds begin to blow,
Then fall the flaky stars of gathering snow,
When on the thorn the ripening sloe, yet blue,
Takes the bright varnish of the morning dew;
The aged moss grows brittle on the pale,
The dry boughs splinter in the windy gale,
And every changing season of the year
Stamps on the scene its English character.

Farewell! a prouder mansion I may see,
But much must meet in that which equals thee!

II.

I LEAVE the town, and take a well-known way,
To that old Mansion in the closing day,
When beams of golden light are shed around,
And sweet is every sight and every sound.
Pass but this hill, and I shall then behold
The Seat so honour'd, so admired of old,
And yet admired———
Alas! I see a change,
Of odious kind, and lamentably strange.
Who had done this? The good old lady lies
Within her tomb: but, who could this advise?
What barbarous hand could all this mischief do,
And spoil a noble house to make it new?
Who had done this? Some genuine Son of Trade
Has all this dreadful devastation made;
Some man with line and rule, and evil eye,
Who could no beauty in a tree descry,
Save in a clump, when station'd by his hand,
And standing where his genius bade them stand;
Some true admirer of the time's reform,
Who strips an ancient dwelling like a storm,
Strips it of all its dignity and grace,
To put his own dear fancies in their place.
He hates concealment: all that was enclosed
By venerable wood, is now exposed,
And a few stripling elms and oaks appear,
Fenced round by boards, to keep them from the deer.

I miss the grandeur of the rich old scene,
And see not what these clumps and patches mean!
This shrubby belt that runs the land around
Shuts freedom out · what being likes a bound?
The shrubs indeed, and ill-placed flowers, are gay,
And some would praise; I wish they were away,
That in the wild-wood maze I as of old might stray
The things themselves are pleasant to behold,
But not like those which we beheld of old,—
That half-hid mansion, with its wide domain,
Unbound and unsubdued!—but sighs are vain;
It is the rage of Taste—The rule and compass reign.

As thus my spleen upon the view I fed,
A man approach'd me, by his grandchild led—
A blind old man, and she a fair young maid,
Listening in love to what her grandsire said.

And thus with gentle voice he spoke—
"Come lead me, lassie, to the shade,
Where willows grow beside the brook;
For well I know the sound it made,
When dashing o'er the stony rill,
It murmur'd to St. Osyth's Mill."

The Lass replied—"The trees are fled,
They 've cut the brook a straighter bed:
No shades the present lords allow,
The miller only murmurs now;
The waters now his mill forsake,
And form a pond they call a lake."

"Then, lassie, lead thy grandsire on,
And to the holy water bring;
A cup is fasten'd to the stone,
And I would taste the healing spring,
That soon its rocky cist forsakes,
And green its mossy passage makes."

"The holy spring is turn'd aside,
The rock is gone, the stream is dried,
The plough has levell'd all around,
And here is now no holy ground."

"Then, lass, thy grandsire's footsteps guide,
To Bulmer's Tree, the giant oak,
Whose boughs the keeper's cottage hide,
And part the church-way lane o'erlook;
A boy, I climb'd the topmost bough,
And I would feel its shadow now.

Or, lassie, lead me to the west,
Where grow the elm-trees thick and tall,
Where rooks unnumber'd build their nest—
Deliberate birds, and prudent all:
Their notes, indeed, are harsh and rude,
But they 're a social multitude."

"The rooks are shot, the trees are fell'd,
And nest and nursery all expell'd;
With better fate the giant-tree,
Old Bulmer's Oak, is gone to sea.
The church-way walk is now no more,
And men must other ways explore;
Though this indeed promotion gains,
For this the park's new wall contains;
And here I fear we shall not meet
A shade—although, perchance, a seat."

"O then, my lassie, lead the way
To Comfort's Home, the ancient inn

That something holds, if we can pay—
 Old David is our living kin;
A servant once, he still preserves
His name, and in his office serves."

"Alas! that mine should be the fate
Old David's sorrows to relate:
But they were brief; not long before
He died, his office was no more.
The kennel stands upon the ground,
With something of the former sound."

"O then," the grieving Man replied,
 "No further, lassie, let me stray;
Here 's nothing left of ancient pride,
 Of what was grand, of what was gay:
But all is changed, is lost, is sold—
All, all that's left is chilling cold.
I seek for comfort here in vain,
Then lead me to my cot again."

TALE XI.

THE MERCHANT.

[*Farewell and Return.*]

I.

Lo! one appears, to whom if I should dare
To say *farewell*, the lordly man would stare,
Would stretch his goodly form some inches higher,
And then, without a single word, retire;
Or from his state might haply condescend
To doubt his memory—"Ha! your name, my friend!"

He is the master of these things we see,
Those vessels proudly riding by the quay;
With all those mountain heaps of coal that lie,
For half a county's wonder and supply.
Boats, cables, anchors, all to him pertain,—
A swimming fortune, all his father's gain.
He was a porter on the quay, and one
Proud of his fortune, prouder of his son;—
Who was ashamed of him, and much distress'd
To see his father was no better dress'd.
Yet for this parent did the son erect
A tomb—'t is whisper'd, he must not expect
The like for him, when he shall near it sleep,—
Where we behold the marble cherubs weep.

There are no merchants who with us reside
In half his state,—no wonder he has pride;
Then he parades around that vast estate,
As if he spurn'd the slaves that make him great;
Speaking in tone so high, as if the ware
Was nothing worth—at least not worth his care;
Yet should he not these bulky stores contemn,
For all his glory he derives from them;
And were it not for that neglected store,
This great rich man would be extremely poor.

Generous, men call him, for he deigns to give;
He condescends to say the poor must live:
Yet in his seamen not a sign appears,
That they have much respect, or many fears;
With inattention they their patron meet,
As if they thought his dignity a cheat;
Or of himself as, having much to do
With their affairs, he very little knew;
As if his ways to them so well were known,
That they might hear, and bow, and take their own.

He might contempt for men so humble feel,
But this experience taught him to conceal;
For sailors do not to a lord at land
As to their captain in submission stand;
Nor have mere pomp and pride of look or speech,
Been able yet respect or awe to teach.

Guns, when with powder charged, will make a noise,
To frighten babes, and be the sport of boys;
But when within men find there's nothing more,
They shout contemptuous at the idle roar.
Thus will our lofty man to all appear,
With nothing charged that they respect or fear.

His Lady, too, to her large purse applies,
And all she fancies at the instant buys.
How bows the market, when, from stall to stall,
She walks attended! how respectful all!
To her free orders every maid attends,
And strangers wonder what the woman spends.

There is an auction, and the people shy,
Are loath to bid, and yet desire to buy.
Jealous they gaze with mingled hope and fear,
Of buying cheaply, and of paying dear.
They see the hammer with determined air
Seized for despatch, and bid in pure despair!
They bid—the hand is quiet as before,—
Still stands old Puff till one advances more.—
Behold great madam, gliding through the crowd:
Hear her too bid—decisive tone and loud!
"Going! 't is gone!" the hammer-holder cries—
"Joy to you, Lady! you have gain'd a prize."

Thus comes and goes the wealth, that, saved or spent,
Buys not a moment's credit or content.

Farewell! your fortune I forbear to guess;
For chance, as well as sense, may give success.

II.

P.—Say, what yon buildings, neat indeed, but low,
So much alike, in one commodious row?

F.—You see our Alms-house: ancient men, decay'd,
Are here sustain'd, who lost their way in trade;
Here they have all that sober men require—
So thought the Poet—"meat, and clothes, and fire."
A little garden to each house pertains,
Convenient each, and kept with little pains.
Here for the sick are nurse and medicine found,
Here walks and shaded alleys for the sound;

Books of devotion on the shelves are placed,
And not forbidden are the books of taste.
The Church is near them—in a common seat
The pious men with grateful spirit meet:
Thus from the world, which they no more admire,
They all in silent gratitude retire.

P.—And is it so? Have all, with grateful mind,
The world relinquish'd, and its ways resign'd?
Look they not back with lingering love and slow,
And fain would once again the oft-tried follies know?

F.—Too surely some! We must not think that all,
Call'd to be hermits, would obey the call;
We must not think that all forget the state
In which they moved, and bless their humbler fate;
But all may here the waste of life retrieve,
And, ere they leave the world, its vices leave.

See yonder man, who walks apart, and seems
Wrapt in some fond and visionary schemes;
Who looks uneasy, as a man oppress'd
By that large copper badge upon his breast.
His painful shame, his self-tormenting pride,
Would all that's visible in bounty hide;
And much his anxious breast is swell'd with wo,
That where he goes his badge must with him go.

P.—Who then is he? Do I behold aright?
My lofty merchant in this humble plight!
Still has he pride?

F.——If common fame be just,
He yet has pride,—the pride that licks the dust;
Pride that can stoop, and feed upon the base
And wretched flattery of this humbling place;
Nay, feeds himself! his failing is avow'd,
He of the cause that made him poor is proud;
Proud of his greatness, of the sums he spent,
And honours shown him wheresoe'er he went.

Yes! there he walks, that lofty man is he,
Who was so rich; but great he could not be.
Now to the paupers who about him stand,
He tells of wonders by his bounty plann'd,
Tells of his traffic, where his vessels sail'd,
And what a trade he drove—before he fail'd;
Then what a failure, not a paltry sum,
Like a mean trader, but for half a plum;
His Lady's wardrobe was apprised so high,
At his own sale, that nobody would buy!—
"But she is gone," he cries, "and never saw
The spoil and havock of our cruel law;
My steeds, our chariot that so roll'd along,
Admired of all! they sold them for a song.
You all can witness what my purse could do,
And now I wear a badge like one of you,
Who in my service had been proud to live,—
And this is all a thankless town will give.
I, who have raised the credit of that town,
And gave it, thankless as it is, renown—
Who've done what no man there had done before,
Now hide my head within an Alms-house door—
Deprived of all—my wife, my wealth, my vote,
And in this blue defilement—*Curse the Coat!*"

TALE XII.

THE BROTHER BURGESSES.

[*Farewell and Return.*]

I.

Two busy BROTHERS in our place reside,
And wealthy each, his party's boast and pride,
Sons of one father, of two mothers born,
They hold each other in true party scorn.

JAMES is the one who for the people fights,
The sturdy champion of their dubious rights;
Merchant and [illegible]man rough, but not the less
Keen in pursu[illegible] of his own happiness;
And what his happiness?—to see his store
Of wealth increase, till Mammon groans, "No more!"

JAMES goes to church, because his father went,
But does not hide his leaning to dissent;
Reasons for this, whoe'er may frown, he'll speak—
Yet the old pew receives him once a week.

CHARLES is a churchman, and has all the zeal
That a strong member of his church can feel;
A loyal subject is the name he seeks;
He of "his King and Country" proudly speaks:
He says, his brother and a rebel-crew,
Minded like him, the nation would undo,
If they had power, or were esteem'd enough
Of those who had, to bring their plans to proof.

JAMES answers sharply—"I will never place
My hopes upon a Lordship or a Grace!
To some great man you bow, to greater he,
Who to the greatest bends his supple knee,
That so the manna from the head may drop,
And at the lowest of the kneelers stop.
Lords call you loyal, and on them you call
To spare you something from our plunder'd all:
If tricks like these to slaves can treasure bring,
Slaves well may shout them hoarse for 'Church and King!'"

"Brother!" says Charles,—"yet brother is a name
I own with pity, and I speak with shame,—
One of these days you'll surely lead a mob,
And then the hangman will conclude the job."

"And would you, Charle[illegible] in that unlucky case
Beg for his life whose deat[illegible] would bring disgrace,
On you, and all the loyal of our race?
Your worth would surely from the halter bring
One neck, and I a patriot then might sing—
A brother patriot I—God save our noble king."

"James!" said the graver man, in manner grave—
"Your neck I could not, I your soul would save;
Oh! ere that day, alas, too likely! come,
I would prepare your mind to meet your doom,
That then the priest, who prays with that bad race
Of men, may find you not devoid of grace."

These are the men who, from their seats above,
Hear frequent sermons on fraternal love;
Nay, each approves, and answers—"Very true!
Brother would heed it, were he not a Jew."

II.

P.—Read I aright? beneath this stately stone
The Brothers rest in peace, their grave is one!
What friend, what fortune interfered, that they
Take their long sleep together, clay with clay?
How came it thus?—

F.—It was their own request,
By both repeated, that they thus might rest.

P.—'T is well! Did friends at length the pair unite?
Or was it done because the deed was right?
Did the cool spirit of enfeebling age
Chill the warm blood, and calm the party rage,
And kindly lead them, in their closing day,
To put their animosity away,
Incline their hearts to live in love and peace,
And bid the ferment in each bosom cease?

F.—Rich men have runners, who will to and fro
In search of food for their amusement go;
Who watch their spirits, and with tales of grief
Yield to their melancholy minds relief;
Who of their foes will each mishap relate,
And of their friends the fall or failings state.

One of this breed—the Jackal who supplied
Our Burgess Charles with food for spleen and pride—
Before he utter'd what his memory brought,
On its effect, in doubtful matters, thought,
Lest he, perchance, in his intent might trip,
Or a strange fact might indiscreetly slip;—
But he one morning had a tale to bring,
And felt full sure he need not weigh the thing;
That must be welcome! With a smiling face
He watch'd th' accustom'd nod, and took his place.

"Well! you have news—I see it—Good, my friend,
No preface, Peter. Speak, man, I attend."

"Then, sir, I'm told, nay, 't is beyond dispute,
Our Burgess James is routed horse and foot;
He'll not be seen; a clerk for him appears,
And their precautions testify their fears;
Before the week be ended you shall see,
That our famed patriot will a bankrupt be."

"Will he by——! No, I will not be profane,
But *James* a bankrupt! Boy, my hat and cane.
No! he'll refuse my offers—Let me think!
So would I his: here, give me pen and ink.
There! that will do.—What! let my father's son,
My brother, want, and I—away! and run,
Run as for life, and then return—but stay
To take his message—now, away, away!"

The pride of James was shaken as he read—
The Brothers met—the angry spirit fled:
Few words were needed—in the look of each
There was a language words can never reach;
But when they took each other's hand and press'd,
Subsiding tumult sank to endless rest;

32

Nor party wrath with quick affection strove,
Drown'd in the tears of reconciling love.

Affairs confused, and business at a stand,
Were soon set right by Charles's powerful hand;
The rudest mind in this rude place enjoy'd
The pleasing thought of enmity destroy'd,
And so destroy'd, that neither spite nor spleen,
Nor peevish look from that blest hour were seen;
Yet each his party and his spirit kept,
Though all the harsh and angry passions slept.

P.—And they too sleep! and, at their joint request,
Within one tomb, beneath one stone, they rest!

TALE XIII.

THE DEAN'S LADY.

[*Farewell and Return.*]

I.

Next, to a Lady I must bid adieu—
Whom some in mirth or malice call a "*Blue.*"
There needs no more—when that same word is said,
The men grow shy, respectful and afraid;
Save the choice friends who in her colour dress,
And all her praise in words like hers express.

Why should proud man in man that knowledge prize,
Which he affects in woman to despise?
Is he not envious when a lady gains,
In hours of leisure, and with little pains,
What he in many a year with painful toil obtains?
For surely knowledge should not odious grow,
Nor ladies be despised for what they know;
Truth to no sex confined, her friends invites,
And woman, long restrain'd, demands her rights.
Nor should a light and odious name be thrown
On the fair dame who makes that knowledge known—
Who bravely dares the world's sarcastic sneer,
And what she is, is willing to appear.

"And what she is not!" peevish man replies,
His envy owning what his pride denies:
But let him, envious as he is, repair
To this sage Dame, and meet conviction there.

Miranda sees her morning levee fill'd
With men in every art and science skill'd—
Men who have gain'd a name, whom she invites,
Because in men of genius she delights.
To these she puts her questions, that produce
Discussion vivid, and discourse abstruse:
She no opinion for its boldness spares,
But loves to show her audience what she dares
The creeds of all men she takes leave to sift,
And, quite impartial, turns her own adrift.

Her noble mind, with independent force,
Her Rector questions on his late discourse·

Perplex'd and pain'd, he wishes to retire
From one whom critics, nay, whom crowds, admire—
From her whose faith on no man's dictate leans,
Who her large creed from many a teacher gleans;
Who for herself will judge, debate, decide,
And be her own "philosopher and guide."

Why call a lady *Blue*? It is because
She reads, converses, studies for applause;
And therefore all that she desires to know
Is just as much as she can fairly show.
The real knowledge we in secret hide,
It is the counterfeit that makes our pride.
"A little knowledge is a dangerous thing"—
So sings the Poet, and so let him sing:
But if from little learning danger rose,
I know not who in safety could repose.
The evil rises from our own mistake,
When we our ignorance for knowledge take;
Or when the little that we have, through pride,
And vain poor self-love view'd, is magnified.
Nor is your deepest Azure always free
From these same dangerous calls of vanity.

Yet of the sex are those who never show,
By way of exhibition, what they know.
Their books are read and praised, and so are they,
But all without design, without display.
Is there not One who reads the hearts of men,
And paints them strongly with unrivalled pen?
All their fierce Passions in her scenes appear,
Terror she bids arise, bids fall the tear;
Looks in the close recesses of the mind,
And gives the finish'd portraits to mankind,
By skill conducted, and to Nature true,—
And yet no man on earth would call JOANNA Blue!

Not so MIRANDA! She is ever prest
To give opinions, and she gives her best.
To these with gentle smile her guests incline,
Who come to hear, improve, applaud,—and dine.

Her hungry mind on every subject feeds;
She Adam Smith and Dugald Stewart reads;
Locke entertains her, and she wonders why
His famous Essay is consider'd dry.
For her amusement in her vacant hours
Are earths and rocks, and animals and flowers:
She could the farmer at his work assist,
A systematic agriculturist.
Some men, indeed, would curb the female mind,
Nor let us see that they themselves are blind;
But—thank our stars—the liberal times allow,
That all may think, and men have rivals now.

Miranda deems all knowledge might be gain'd—
"But she is idle, nor has much attain'd;
Men are in her deceived: she knows at most
A few light matters, for she scorns to boast.
Her mathematic studies she resign'd—
They did not suit the genius of her mind.
She thought indeed the higher parts sublime,
But then they took a monstrous deal of time!"

Frequent and full the letters she delights
To read in part; she names not him who writes—
But here and there a precious sentence shows,
Telling what literary debts she owes.
Works, yet unprinted, for her judgment come,
"Alas!" she cries, "and I must seal their doom.
Sworn to be just, the judgment gives me pain—
Ah! why must truth be told, or man be vain?"

Much she has written, and still deigns to write,
But not an effort yet must see the light.
"Cruel!" her friends exclaim; "unkind, unjust!"
But, no! the envious mass she will not trust;
Content to hear that fame is due to her,
Which on her works the world might not confer—
Content with loud applauses while she lives:
Unfelt the pain the cruel critic gives.

II.

P.—Now where the Learned Lady? Doth she live,
Her dinners yet and sentiments to give—
The Dean's wise consort, with the many friends,
From whom she borrows, and to whom she lends
Her precious maxims?

F.—Yes, she lives to shed
Her light around her, but her Dean is dead.
Seen her I have, but seldom could I see:
Borrow she could not, could not lend to me.
Yet, I attended, and beheld the tribe
Attending too, whom I will not describe—
Miranda Thomson! Yes, I sometimes found
A seat among a circle so profound;
When all the science of the age combined
Was in that room, and hers the master-mind.
Well I remember the admiring crowd,
Who spoke their wonder and applause aloud;
They strove who highest should her glory raise,
And cramm'd the hungry mind with honey'd praise—
While she, with grateful hand a table spread,
The Dean assenting—but the Dean is dead;
And though her sentiments are still divine,
She asks no more her auditors to dine.

Once from her lips came wisdom; when she spoke,
Her friends in transport or amazement broke.
Now to her dictates there attend but few,
And they expect to meet attention too;
Respect she finds is purchased at some cost,
And deference is withheld, when dinner's lost.

She, once the guide and glory of the place,
Exists between oblivion and disgrace;
Praise once afforded, now,—they say not why,
They dare not say it—fickle men deny;
That buzz of fame a new Minerva cheers,
Which our deserted queen no longer hears.
Old, but not wise, forsaken, not resign'd,
She gives to honours past her feeble mind,
Back to her former state her fancy moves,
And lives on past applause, that still she loves;
Yet holds in scorn the fame no more in view,
And flies the glory that would not pursue
To yon small cot, a poorly jointured *Blue*.

TALE XIV.

THE WIFE AND WIDOW.

[*Farewell and Return.*]

I.

I leave Sophia; it would please me well,
Before we part, on so much worth to dwell:
'T is said of one who lived in times of strife,
There was no boyhood in his busy life;
Born to do all that mortal being can,
The thinking child became at once the man;
So this fair girl in early youth was led,
By reason strong in early youth, to wed.

In her new state her prudence was her guide,
And of experience well the place supplied;
With life's important business full in view,
She had no time for its amusements too;
She had no practised look man's heart t' allure,
No frown to kill him, and no smile to cure;
No art coquettish, nothing of the prude;
She was with strong yet simple sense endued,
Intent on duties, and resolved to shun
Nothing that ought to be, and could be, done.

A Captain's wife, with whom she long sustain'd
The toil of war, and in a camp remain'd;
Her husband wounded, with her child in arms,
She nursed them both, unheeded all alarms:
All useless terror in her soul supprest—
None could discern in hers a troubled breast.

Her wounded soldier is a prisoner made,
She hears, prepares, and is at once convey'd
Through hostile ranks:—with air sedate she goes,
And makes admiring friends of wondering foes.
Her dying husband to her care confides
Affairs perplex'd; she reasons, she decides;
If intricate her way, her walk discretion guides.

Home to her country she returns alone,
Her health decay'd, her child, her husband, gone;
There she in peace reposes, there resumes
Her female duties, and in rest reblooms;
She is not one at common ills to droop,
Nor to vain murmuring will her spirit stoop.

I leave her thus: her fortieth year is nigh,
She will not for another captain sigh;
Will not a young and gay lieutenant take,
Because 't is pretty to reform a rake;
Yet she again may plight her widow'd hand,
Should love invite, or charity demand;
And make her days, although for duty's sake,
As sad as folly and mischance can make.

II.

P.—Lives yet the Widow, whose firm spirit bore
Ills unrepining?—

F.—Here she lives no more,
But where—I speak with some good people's leave—
Where all good works their due reward receive;
Though what reward to our best works is due
I leave to them,—and will my tale pursue.

Again she married, to her husband's friend,
Whose wife was hers; whom going to attend,
As on her death-bed she, yet young, was laid,
The anxious parent took her hand and said,
"Prove *now* your love; let these poor infants be
As thine, and find a mother's love in thee!"

"And must I woo their father?"—"Nay, indeed;
He no encouragement but hope will need;
In hope too let me die, and think my wish decreed."

The wife expires; the widow'd pair unite;
Their love was sober, and their prospect bright.
She train'd the children with a studious love,
That knew full well to encourage and reprove;
Nicely she dealt her praise and her disgrace,
Not harsh and not indulgent out of place,
Not to the forward partial—to the slow
All patient, waiting for the time to sow
The seeds that, suited to the soil, would grow.

Nor watch'd she less the Husband's weaker soul,
But learn'd to lead him who abhorr'd control,
Who thought a nursery, next a kitchen, best
To women suited, and she acquiesced;
She only begg'd to rule in small affairs,
And ease her wedded lord of common cares,
Till he at length thought every care was small,
Beneath his notice, and she had them all.
He on his throne the lawful monarch sate,
And she was by—the minister of state:
He gave assent, and he required no more,
But sign'd the act that she decreed before

Again, her fates in other work decree
A mind so active should experienced be.

One of the name, who roved the world around,
At length had something of its treasures found,
And childless died, amid his goods and gain,
In far Barbadoes on the western main.
His kinsman heard, and wish'd the wealth to share,
But had no mind to be transported there:—
"His wife could sail—her courage who could doubt?—
And she was not tormented with the gout."

She liked it not; but for his children's sake,
And for their father's, would the duty take.
Storms she encounter'd, ere she reach'd the shore,
And other storms when these were heard no more,—
The rage of lawyers forced to drop their prey,—
And once again to England made her way.

She found her Husband with his gout removed,
And a young nurse, most skilful and approved;
Whom—for he yet was weak—he urged to stay,
And nurse him while his consort was away:—
"She was so handy, so discreet, so nice,
As kind as comfort, though as cold as ice!
Else," he assured his lady, "in no case,
So young a creature should have fill'd the place.

It has been held—indeed, the point is clear,
"None are so deaf as those who will not hear:"
And, by the same good logic, we shall find,
"As those who will not see, are none so blind."
The thankful Wife repaid the attention shown,
But now would make the duty all her own.

Again the gout return'd; but seizing now
A vital part, would no relief allow.

The Husband died, but left a will that proved
He much respected whom he coolly loved.
All power was hers; nor yet was such her age,
But rivals strove her favour to engage:
They talk'd of love with so much warmth and zeal,
That they believed the woman's heart must feel;
Adding such praises of her worth beside,
As vanquish prudence oft by help of pride.

In vain! her heart was by discretion led—
She to the children of her Friend was wed;
These she establish'd in the world, and died,
In ease and hope, serene and satisfied.

And loves not man that woman who can charm
Life's grievous ills, and grief itself disarm?—
Who in his fears and troubles brings him aid,
And seldom is, and never seems afraid?

No! ask of man the fair one whom he loves,
You 'll find her one of the desponding doves,
Who tender troubles as her portion brings,
And with them fondly to a husband clings—
Who never moves abroad, nor sits at home,
Without distress, past, present, or to come—
Who never walks the unfrequented street,
Without a dread that death and she shall meet:
At land, on water, she must guarded be,
Who sees the danger none besides her see,
And is determined by her cries to call
All men around her: she will have them all.

Man loves to think the tender being lives
But by the power that his protection gives:
He loves the feeble step, the plaintive tone,
And flies to help who cannot stand alone:
He thinks of propping elms, and clasping vines,
And in her weakness thinks her virtue shines;
On him not one of her desires is lost,
And he admires her for this care and cost.

But when afflictions come, when beauty dies,
Or sorrows vex the heart, or danger tries—
When time of trouble brings the daily care,
And gives of pain as much as he can bear—
'T is then he wants, if not the helping hand,
At least a soothing temper, meek and bland—
He wants the heart that shares in his distress,
At least the kindness that would make it less;
And when instead he hears the eternal grief
For some light want, and not for his relief—
And when he hears the tender trembler sigh,
For some indulgence he can not supply—
When, in the midst of many a care, his "dear"
Would like a duchess at a ball appear—
And, while he feels a weight that wears him down,
Would see the prettiest sight in all the town,—
Love then departs, and if some Pity lives,
That Pity half despises, half forgives,
'T is join'd with grief, is not from shame exempt,
And has a plenteous mixture of contempt.

TALE XV.

BELINDA WATERS.

[*Farewell and Return.*]

I.

Of all the beauties in our favoured place,
Belinda Waters was the pride and grace.
Say ye who sagely can our fortunes read,
Shall this fair damsel in the world succeed?

A rosy beauty she, and fresh and fair,
Who never felt a caution or a care;
Gentle by nature, ever fond of ease,
And more consenting than inclined to please.
A tame good nature in her spirit lives—
She hates refusal for the pain it gives:
From opposition arguments arise,
And to prevent the trouble, she complies.
She, if in Scotland, would be *fashed* all day,
If call'd to any work or any play;
She lets no busy, idle wish intrude,
But is by nature negatively good.

In marriage hers will be a dubious fate:
She is not fitted for a high estate:—
There wants the grace, the polish, and the pride;
Less is she fitted for a humble bride:
Whom fair Belinda weds—let chance decide!

She sees her father oft engross'd by cares,
And therefore hates to hear of men's affairs:
An active mother in the household reigns,
And spares Belinda all domestic pains.
Of food she knows but this, that we are fed:—
Though, duly taught, she prays for daily bread,
Yet whence it comes, of hers is no concern—
It comes! and more she never wants to learn.

She on the table sees the common fare,
But how provided is beneath her care.
Lovely and useless, she has no concern
About the things that aunts and mothers learn;
But thinks, when married,—if she thinks at all,—
That what she needs will answer to her call.

To write is business, and, though taught to write
She keeps the pen and paper out of sight:
What once was painful she cannot allow
To be enjoyment or amusement now.
She wonders why the ladies are so fond
Of such long letters, when they correspond.
Crowded and cross'd by ink of different stain,
She thinks to read them would confuse her brain,
Nor much mistakes; but still has no pretence
To praise for this, her critic's indolence.

Behold her now! she on her sofa looks
O'er half a shelf of circulating books.
This she admired, but she forgets the name,
And reads again another, or the same.
She likes to read of strange and bold escapes,
Of plans and plottings, murders and mishaps,
Love in all hearts, and lovers in all shapes.
She sighs for pity, and her sorrows flow
From the dark eyelash on the page below;
And is so glad when, all the misery past,
The dear adventurous lovers meet at last—
Meet and are happy; and she thinks it hard,
When thus an author might a pair reward—
When they, the troubles all dispersed, might wed—
He makes them part, and die of grief instead!

Yet tales of terror are her dear delight,
All in the wintry storm to read at night;
And to her maid she turns in all her doubt,—
"This shall I like? and what is that about?"

She had "Clarissa" for her heart's dear friend—
Was pleased each well-tried virtue to commend,
And praised the scenes that one might fairly doubt,
If one so young could know so much about:
Pious and pure, th' heroic beauty strove
Against the lover and against the love;
But strange that maid so young should know the strife,
In all its views, was painted to the life!
Belinda knew not—nor a tale would read,
That could so slowly on its way proceed;
And ere Clarissa reach'd the wicked town,
The weary damsel threw the volume down.
"Give me," she said, "for I would laugh or cry,
'Scenes from the Life,' and 'Sensibility;'
'Winters at Bath,'—I would that I had one!
'The Constant Lover,' the 'Discarded Son,'
'The Rose of Raby,' 'Delmore,' or 'The Nun.'
These promise something, and may please, perhaps,
Like 'Ethelinda,' and the dear 'Relapse.'"
To these her heart the gentle maid resign'd,
And such the food that fed the gentle mind.

II.

P.—Knew you the fair Belinda, once the boast
Of a vain mother, and a favourite toast
Of clerks and young lieutenants, a gay set
Of light admirers?—Is she married yet?

F.—Yes! she is married; though she waited long,
Not from a prudent fear of choosing wrong,
But want of choice.—She took a surgeon's mate,
With his half-pay, that was his whole estate.

Fled is the charming bloom that nature spread
Upon her cheek, the pure, the rosy red—
This, and the look serene, the calm, kind look, are fled.
Sorrow and sadness now the place possess,
And the pale cast of anxious fretfulness.

She *wonders* much—as, why they live so ill,—
Why the rude butcher brings his weekly bill,—
She wonders why that baker will not trust,—
And says, most truly says,—"Indeed, he must."

She wonders where her former friends are gone,—
And thus, from day to day, she wonders on.

Howe'er she can—she dresses gaily yet,
And then she wonders how they came in debt.
Her husband loves her, and in accent mild,
Answers, and treats her like a fretted child;
But when he, ruffled, makes severe replies,
And seems unhappy—then she pouts, and cries
"She wonders when she'll die!"—She faints, but never dies.

"How well my father lived!" she says.—"How well,
My dear, your father's creditors could tell!"
And then she weeps, till comfort is applied,
That soothes her spleen or gratifies her pride:
Her dress and novels, visits and success
In a chance-game, are softeners of distress.

So life goes on!—But who that loved his life,
Would take a fair Belinda for his wife?
Who thinks that all are for their stations born,
Some to indulge themselves, and to adorn;
And some, a useful people, to prepare,
Not being rich, good things for those who are,
And who are born, it cannot be denied,
To have their wants and their demands supplied.

She knows that money is a needful thing,
That fathers first, and then that husbands bring;
Or if those persons should the aid deny,
Daughters and wives have but to faint and die,
Till flesh and blood can not endure the pain,
And then the lady lives and laughs again.

To wed an ague, and to feel, for life,
Hot fits and cold succeeding in a wife;
To take the pestilence with poison'd breath,
And wed some potent minister of death,
Is cruel fate—yet death is then relief;
But thus to wed is ever-during grief.

Oft have I heard, how blest the youth who weds
Belinda Waters!—rather he who dreads
That fate—a truth her husband well approves,
Who blames and fondles, humours, chides, and loves.

TALE XVI.

THE DEALER AND CLERK.

[*Farewell and Return.*]

I.

Bad men are seldom cheerful; but we see
That, when successful, they can merry be.
One whom I leave, his darling money lends,
On terms well known, to his unhappy friends,
He farms and trades, and in his method treats
His guests, whom first he comforts, then he cheats
He knows their private griefs, their inward groans,
And then applies his leeches and his loans,

To failing, falling families—and gets,
I know not how, with large increase, their debts.

He early married, and the woman made
A losing bargain; she with scorn was paid
For no small fortune. On this slave he vents
His peevish slights, his moody discontents.
Her he neglects, indulging in her stead,
One whom he bribed to leave a husband's bed—
A young fair mother too, the pride and joy
Of him whom her desertion will destroy.

The poor man walks by the adulterer's door,
To see the wife whom he must meet no more:
She will not look upon the face of one
Whom she has blighted, ruin'd, and undone.
He feels the shame; his heart with grief is rent;
Hers is the guilt, and his the punishment.

The cruel spoiler to his need would lend
Unsought relief—his need will soon have end:
Let a few wintry months in sorrow pass,
And on his corse shall grow the vernal grass.
Neighbours, indignant, of his griefs partake,
And hate the villain for the victim's sake;
Wondering what bolt within the stores of heaven
Shall on that bold, offending wretch be driven.

Alas! my grieving friends, we cannot know
Why Heaven inflicts, and why suspends the blow.
Meanwhile the godless man, who thus destroys
Another's peace, in peace his wealth enjoys,
And, every law evaded or defied,
Is with long life and prosperous fortune tried:
"How long?" the Prophet cried, and we, "how long?"
But think how quick that Eye, that Arm how strong,
And bear what seems not right, and trust it is not wrong.

Does Heaven forbear? then sinners mercy find—
Do sinners fall? 't is mercy to mankind.
Adieu! can one so miserable be,
Rich, wretched man! to barter fates with thee?

II.

Yet, ere I go, some notice must be paid
To John, his Clerk, a man full sore afraid
Of his own frailty—many a troubled day
Has he walk'd doubtful in some close by-way,
Beseeching Conscience on her watch to keep,
Afraid that she one day should fall asleep.

A quiet man was John: his mind was slow;
Little he knew, and little sought to know.
He gave respect to worth, to riches more,
And had instinctive dread of being poor.
Humble and careful, diligent and neat,
He in the Dealer's office found a seat:
Happy in all things, till a fear began
To break his rest—He served a wicked man;
Who spurn'd the way direct of honest trade,
But praised the laws his cunning could evade.

This crafty Dealer of religion spoke,
As if design'd to be the wise man's cloak,
And the weak man's incumbrance, whom it awes,
And keeps in dread of conscience and the laws;
Yet, for himself, he loved not to appear
In her grave dress; 't was troublesome to wear.

This Dealer play'd at games of skill, and won
Sums that surprised the simple mind of John:
Nor trusted skill alone; for well he knew,
What a sharp eye and dexterous hand could do:
When, if suspected, he had always by
The daring oath to back the cunning lie.

John was distress'd, and said, with aching heart,
I from the vile, usurious man must part;
For if I go not—yet I mean to go—
This friend to me will to my soul be foe.
I serve my master: there is naught to blame;
But whom he serves, I tremble but to name.

From such reflections sprung the painful fear,—
The Foe of Souls is too familiar here:
My master stands between: so far, so good;
But 't is at best a dangerous neighbourhood."

Then livelier thoughts began his fear to chase,—
"It is a gainful, a convenient place:
If I should quit—another takes the pen,
And what a chance for my preferment then?
Religion nothing by my going gains;
If I depart, my master still remains.
True, I record the deeds that I abhor,
But these that master has to answer for.
Then say I leave the office! his success,
And his injustice, will not be the less;
Nay, would be greater—I am right to stay;
It checks him, doubtless, in his fearful way.
Fain would I stay, and yet be not beguiled;
But pitch is near, and man is soon defiled."

III.

P.—Such were the Man and Master,—and I now
Would know if they together live, and how.

To such inquiries, thus my Friend replied:—
F.—The Wife was slain, or, say at least, she died.
But there are murders, that the human eye
Cannot detect,—which human laws defy:
There are the wrongs insulted fondness feels,
In many a secret wound that never heals;
The Savage murders with a single blow;
Murders like this are secret and are slow.

Yet, when his victim lay upon her bier,
There were who witness'd that he dropp'd a tear;
Nay, more, he praised the woman he had lost,
And undisputed paid the funeral cost.

The Favourite now, her lord and master freed,
Prepared to wed, and be a wife indeed.
The day, 't was said, was fix'd, the robes were bought,
A feast was ordered; but a cold was caught,
And pain ensued, with fever—grievous pain,
With the mind's anguish that disturb'd the brain,—
Till nature ceased to struggle, and the mind
Saw clearly death before, and sin behind.

Priests and physicians gave what they could give;
She turn'd away, and, shuddering, ceased to live.

The Dealer now appear'd awhile as one
Lost; with but little of his race to run,
And that in sorrow: men with one consent,
And one kind hope, said, "Bonner will repent."
Alas! we saw not what his fate would be,
But this we fear'd,—no penitence had he;
Nor time for penitence, nor any time,
So quick the summons, to look back on crime.

When he the partner of his sin entomb'd,
He paused awhile, and then the way resumed,
Even as before: yet was he not the same;
The tempter once, he now the dupe became.
John long had left him, nor did one remain
Who would his harlot in her course refrain;
Obsequious, humble, studious of his ease,
The present Phœbe only sought to please.
"With one so artless, what," said he, "to fear,
Or what to doubt, in one who holds me dear?
Friends she may have, but me she will not wrong;
If weak her judgment, yet her love is strong;
And I am lucky now in age to find
A friend so trusty, and a nurse so kind."

Yet neither party was in peace: the man
Had restless nights, and in the morn began
To cough and tremble; he was hot and cold—
He had a nervous fever, he was told.
His dreams—'t was strange, for none reflected less
On his past life—were frightful to excess;
His favourite dinners were no more enjoy'd,
And, in a word, his spirits were destroy'd.

And what of Phœbe? She her measures plann'd;
All but his money was at her command:
All would be hers when Heaven her Friend should call;
But Heaven was slow, and much she long'd for all:—
"Mine when he dies, mean wretch! and why not mine,
When it would prove him generous to resign
What he enjoys not?"—Phœbe at command
Gave him his brandy with a liberal hand.
A way more quick and safe she did not know,
And brandy, though it might be sure, was slow.
But more she dared not, and she felt a dread
Of being tried, and only wish'd him dead.
Such was her restless strife of hope and fear—
He might cough on for many a weary year;
Nay, his poor mind was changing, and when ill,
Some foe to her may wicked thoughts instil!
Oh! 'tis a trial sore to watch a Miser's will.
Thus, though the pair appear'd in peace to live,
They felt that vice has not that peace to give.

There watch'd a cur before the Miser's gate,
A very cur, whom all men seem'd to hate;
Gaunt, savage, shaggy, with an eye that shone
Like a live coal, and he possess'd but one;
His bark was wild and eager, and became
That meagre body and that eye of flame;
His master prized him much, and *Fang* his name.
His master fed him largely; but not that,
Nor aught of kindness made the snarler fat.
Flesh he devour'd, but not a bit would stay;
He bark'd, and snarl'd, and growl'd it all away.
His ribs were seen extended like a rack,
And coarse red hair hung roughly o'er his back.
Lamed in one leg, and bruised in wars of yore,
Now his sore body made his temper sore.
Such was the friend of him, who could not find
Nor make him one, 'mong creatures of his kind.
Brave deeds of Fang his master often told,
The son of Fury, famed in days of old,
From Snatch and Rabid sprung; and noted they
In earlier times—each dog will have his day.

The notes of Fang were to his master known,
And dear—they bore some likeness to his own;
For both convey'd to the experienced ear,
"I snarl and bite, because I hate and fear."
None pass'd unheeded by the master's door,
Fang rail'd at all, but chiefly at the poor;
And when the nights were stormy, cold, and dark,
The act of Fang was a perpetual bark;
But though the master loved the growl of Fang,
There were who vow'd the ugly cur to hang;
Whose angry master, watchful for his friend,
As strongly vow'd his servant to defend.

In one dark night, and such as Fang before
Was ever known its tempests to outroar,
To his protector's wonder now express'd
No angry notes—his anger was at rest.
The wondering master sought the silent yard,
Left Phœbe sleeping, and his door unbarr'd;
No more return'd to that forsaken bed—
But lo! the morning came, and he was dead.
Fang and his master side by side were laid
In grim repose—their debt of nature paid!
The master's hand upon the cur's cold chest
Was now reclined, and had before been press'd,
As if he search'd how deep and wide the wound
That laid such spirit in a sleep so sound;
And when he found it was the sleep of death,
A sympathising sorrow stopp'd his breath.
Close to his trusty servant he was found,
As cold his body, and his sleep as sound.

We know no more; but who on horrors dwell
Of that same night have dreadful things to tell:
Of outward force, they say, was not a sign—
The hand that struck him was the Hand Divine
And then the Fiend, in that same stormy night,
Was heard—as many thought—to claim his right
While grinning imps the body danced about,
And then they vanish'd with triumphant shout

So think the crowd, and well it seems in them
That even their dreams and fancies vice condemn
That not alone for virtue Reason pleads,
But nature shudders at unholy deeds;
While our strong fancy lists in her defence,
And takes the side of Truth and Innocence.

IV.

P.—But, what the fortune of the Man, whose fear
Inform'd his Conscience that the foe was near;
But yet whose interest to his desk confined
That sober Clerk of indecisive mind?

F.—John served his master, with himself at strife,
For he with Conscience lived like man and wife;
Now jarring, now at peace,—the life they led
Was all contention, both at board and bed:
His meals were troubled by his scruples all,
And in his dreams he was about to fall
Into some strong temptation—for it seems
He never could resist it in his dreams.

At length his Master, dealer, smuggler, cheat,
As John would call him in his temper's heat,
Proposed a something—what, is dubious still—
That John resisted with a stout good-will.
Scruples like his were treated with disdain.
Whose waking conscience spurn'd the offer'd gain.
"Quit then my office, scoundrel! and be gone."
"I dare not do it," said the affrighten'd John.
"What fearest thou, driveller! can thy fancy tell?"
"I doubt," said John—"I'm sure there is a hell."
"No question, wretch! thy foot is on the door;
"To be in hell, thou fool! is to be poor:
Wilt thou consent?"—But John, with many a sigh,
Refused, then sank beneath his stronger eye,
Who with a curse dismiss'd the fool that dared
Not join a venture which he might have shared.

The worthy Clerk then served a man in trade,
And was his friend and his companion made—
A sickly man, who sundry wares retail'd,
Till, while his trade increased, his spirit fail'd.
John was to him a treasure, whom he prov'd,
And, finding faithful, as a brother lov'd.
To John his views and business he consign'd,
And forward look'd with a contented mind:
As sickness bore him onward to the grave,
A charge of all things to his friend he gave.

But neighbours talk'd—'t was idle—of the day
When Richard Shale should walk the dark highway—
And whisper'd—tatlers!—that the wife received
Such hints with anger, but she nothing grieved.

These whispers reach'd the man, who, weak and ill
In mind and body, had to make his will;
And though he died in peace, and all resign'd,
'T was plain he harbour'd fancies in his mind.
With jealous foresight, all that he had gain'd
His widow's was, while widow she remain'd;
But if another should the dame persuade
To wed again, farewell the gains of trade:
For if the widow'd dove could not refrain,
She must return to poverty again.

The man was buried, and the will was read,
And censure spared them not, alive or dead!
At first the Widow, and the clerk, her friend,
Spent their free days, as prudence bade them spend.
At the same table they would dine, 't is true,
And they would worship in the self-same pew:
Each had the common interest so at heart,
It would have grieved them terribly to part;
And as they both were serious and sedate,
'T was long before the world began to prate:
But when it prated,—though without a cause,—
It put the pair in mind of breaking laws,
Led them to reason what it was that gave
A husband power, when quiet in his grave.
The marriage contract they had now by heart—
"Till death!"—you see, no longer—"do us part."
"Well! death has loosed us from the tie, but still
The loosen'd husband makes a binding will:
Unjust and cruel are the acts of men."
Thus they—and then they sigh'd—and then—and then,
"'T was snaring souls," they said; and how he dared
They did not know—they wander'd—and were snared.

"It is a marriage, surely! Conscience might
Allow an act so very nearly right:
Was it not witness to our solemn vow,
As man and wife? it must the act allow."
But Conscience, stubborn to the last, replied,
"It cannot be! I am not satisfied:
'T is not a marriage: either dare be poor,
Or dare be virtuous—part, and sin no more."

Alas! they many a fond evasion made;
They could relinquish neither love nor trade.
They went to church, but thinking, fail'd to pray;
They felt not ease or comfort at a play:
If times were good,—"We merit not such times,"
If ill,—"Is this the produce of our crimes?"
When sick—"'T is thus forbidden pleasures cease."
When well—they both demand, "Had Zimri peace?
For though our worthy master was not slain,
His injured ghost has reason to complain."

Ah, John! bethink thee of thy generous joy,
When Conscience drove thee from thy late employ;
When thou wert poor, and knew not where to run,
But then could say, "The will of God be done!"
When thou that will, and not thine own obey'd,—
Of Him alone, and not of man afraid:
Thou then hadst pity on that wretch, and, free
Thyself, couldst pray for him who injured thee.
Then how alert thy step, thyself how light
All the day long! thy sleep how sound at night!

But now, though plenty on thy board be found,
And thou hast credit with thy neighbours round,
Yet there is something in thy looks that tells,
An odious secret in thy bosom dwells:
Thy form is not erect, thy neighbours trace
A coward spirit in thy shifting pace.
Thou goest to meeting, not from any call,
But just to hear that we are sinners all,
And equal sinners, or the difference made
'Twixt man and man has but the slightest shade;
That reformation asks a world of pains,
And, after all, must leave a thousand stains;
And, worst of all, we must the work begin
By first attacking the prevailing sin!—

These thoughts the feeble mind of John assail,
And o'er his reason and his fears prevail:
They fill his mind with hopes of gifts and grace,
Faith, feelings!—something that supplies the place
Of true conversion—this will he embrace;
For John perceives that he was scarcely tried
By the first conquest, that increased his pride,

When he refused his master's crime to aid,
And by his self-applause was amply paid;
But now he feels the difference—feels it hard
Against his will and favourite wish to guard:
He mourns his weakness, hopes he shall prevail
Against his frailty, and yet still is frail.

Such is his life! and such the life must be
Of all who will be bound, yet would be free;
Who would unite what God to part decrees—
The offended conscience, and the mind at ease,
Who think, but vainly think, to sin and pray,
And God and Mammon in their turn obey.
Such is his life!—and so I would not live
For all that wealthy widows have to give.

TALE XVII.

DANVERS AND RAYNER.

[*Farewell and Return.*]

I.

The purest Friendship, like the finest ware,
Deserves our praises, but demands our care.
For admiration we the things produce,
But they are not design'd for common use;
Flaws the most trifling from their virtue take,
And lamentation for their loss we make:
While common Friendships, like the wares of clay,
Are a cheap kind, but useful every day:
Though crack'd and damaged, still we make them do,
And when they 're broken, they 're forgotten too.

There is within the world in which we dwell
A Friendship, answering to that world full well;
An interchange of looks and actions kind,
And, in some sense, an intercourse of mind;
A useful commerce, a convenient trade,
By which both parties are the happier made;
And, when the thing is rightly understood,
And justly valued, it is wise and good.

I speak not here of Friendships that excite
In boys at school such wonder and delight,—
Of high heroic Friends, in serious strife,
Contending which should yield a forfeit life—
Such wondrous love, in their maturer days,
Men, if they credit, are content to praise.

I speak not here of Friendships true and just,
When friend can friend with life and honour trust;
Where mind to mind has long familiar grown,
And every failing, every virtue known:
Of these I speak not: things so rich and rare,
That we degrade with jewels to compare,
Or bullion pure and massy.—I intend
To treat of one whose Neighbour call'd him Friend,
Or call'd him Neighbour; and with reason good—
The friendship rising from the neighbourhood:
A sober kind, in common service known;
Not such as is in death and peril shown:
Such as will give or ask a helping hand,
But no important sacrifice demand;
In fact, a friendship that will long abide,
If seldom rashly, never strongly, tried.
Yes! these are sober friendships, made for use,
And much convenience they in life produce;
Like a good coat, that keeps us from the cold,
The cloth of frieze is not a cloth of gold;
But neither is it piebald, pieced, and poor;
'T is a good useful coat, and nothing more.

Such is the Friendship of the world approved,
And here the Friends so loving and so loved:—
Danvers and Rayner, equals, who had made
Each decent fortune, both were yet in trade;
While sons and daughters, with a youthful zeal,
Seem'd the hereditary love to feel:
And even their wives, though either might pretend
To claim some notice, call'd each other friend.

While yet their offspring boys and girls appear'd,
The fathers ask'd, "What evil could be fear'd?"
Nor is it easy to assign the year,
When cautious parents should begin to fear.
The boys must leave their schools, and, by and by,
The girls are sure to grow reserved and shy;
And then, suppose a real love should rise,
It but unites the equal families.

Love does not always from such freedom spring;
Distrust, perhaps, would sooner cause the thing.
"We will not check it, neither will we force"—
Thus said the fathers—"Let it take its course."

It took its course:—young Richard Danvers' mind
In Phœbe Rayner found what lovers find—
Sense, beauty, sweetness; all that mortal eyes
Can see, or heart conceive, or thought devise.
And Phœbe's eye, and thought, and heart could trace
In Richard Danvers every manly grace—
All that e'er maiden wish'd, or matron prized—
So well these good young people sympathised.

All their relations, neighbours, and allies,
All their dependants, visitors, and spies,
Such as a wealthy family caress,
Said here was love, and drank to love's success.

'T is thus I leave the parties, young and old,
Lovers and Friends. Will Love and Friendship hold?
Will Prudence with the children's wish comply,
And Friendship strengthen with that new ally?

II.

P.—I see no more within our borough's bound
The name of Danvers! Is it to be found?
Were the young pair in Hymen's fetters tied,
Or did succeeding years the Friends divide?

F.—Nay! take the story, as by time brought forth,
And of such Love and Friendship judge the worth
While the lad's love—his parents call'd it so—
Was going on, as well as love could go,
A wealthy Danvers, in a distant place,
Left a large fortune to his favour'd race.

To that same place the father quickly went,
And Richard only murmur'd weak dissent.

Of Richard's heart the parent truly guess'd:—
"Well, my good lad! then do what suits thee best;
No doubt thy brothers will do all they can
T' obey the orders of the good old man:
Well, I would not thy free-born spirit bind;
Take, Dick, the way to which thou 'rt most inclined."

No answer gave the youth; nor did he swear
The old man's riches were beneath his care;
Nor that he would with his dear Phœbe stay,
And let his heartless father move away.
No! kind and constant, tender, faithful, fond,—
Thus far he 'd go—but not one step beyond!
Not disobedient to a parent's will—
A lover constant—but dependent still.

Letters, at first, between the constant swain
And the kind damsel banish'd all their pain:
Both full and quick they were; for lovers write
With vast despatch, and read with vast delight—
So quick they were,—for Love is never slow,
So full, they ever seem'd to overflow.
Their hearts are ever fill'd with grief or joy,
And these to paint is every hour's employ:
Joy they would not retain; and for their grief,
To read such letters is a sure relief.

But, in due time, both joy and grief suppress'd,
They found their comfort in a little rest.
Mails went and came without the accustom'd freight,
For Love grew patient, and content to wait—
Yet was not dead, nor yet afraid to die;
For though he wrote not, Richard wonder'd why.
He could not justly tell how letters pass'd,
But, as to him appear'd, he wrote the last:
In this he meant not to accuse the maid—
Love, in some cases, ceases to upbraid.

Yet not indifferent was our Lover grown,
Although the ardour of the flame was flown;
He still of Phœbe thought, her lip, her smile—
But grew contented with his fate the while.
Thus, not inconstant were the youthful pair—
The Lad remember'd still the Lass was fair;
And Phœbe still, with half-affected sigh,
Thought it a pity that such love should die;
And had they then, with this persuasion, met,
Love had rekindled, and been glowing yet.

But times were changed: no mention now was made
By the old Squire, or by the young, of trade.
The worthy Lady, and her children all,
Had due respect—The People at the Hall.
His Worship now read Burn, and talk'd with skill
About the poor-house, and the turnpike-bill;
Lord of a manor, he had serious claims,
And knew the poaching rascals by their names:
And if the father thus improved his mind,
Be sure the children were not far behind:
To rank and riches what respect was due,
To them and theirs what deference, well they knew;
And, from the greatest to the least, could show
What to the favouring few the favour'd many owe.

The mind of man must have whereon to work,
Or it will rust—we see it in the Turk;
And Justice Danvers, though he read the news,
And all of law that magistrates peruse,—
Bills about roads and charities,—yet still
Wanted employ his vacant mind to fill;
These were not like the shipping, once his pride,
Now, with his blue surtout, laid all aside.

No doubt, his spirits in their ebb to raise,
He found some help in men's respect and praise—
Praise of his house, his land, his lawn, his trees—
He cared not what—to praise him was to please:
Yet though his rural neighbours call'd to dine,
And some might kindly praise his food and wine,
This was not certain, and another day,
He must the visit and the praise repay.

By better motives urged—we will suppose—
He thus began his purpose to disclose
To his good lady:—"We have lived a year,
And never ask'd our friends the Rayners here:
Do let us ask them—as for Richard's flame,
It went, we see, as idly as it came—
Invite them kindly—here 's a power of room,
And the poor people will be glad to come.
Outside and in, the coach will hold them all,
And set them down beside the garden wall."

The Lady wrote, for that was all he meant,
Kind soul! by asking for his wife's assent:
And every Rayner was besought to come
To dine in Hulver Hall's grand dining-room.

About this time old Rayner, who had lost
His Friend's advice, was by misfortune cross'd:
Some debtors fail'd, when large amounts were due,
So large, that he was nearly failing too;
But he, grown wary, that he might not fail,
Brought to in adverse gales, and shorten'd sail:
This done, he rested, and could now attend
The invitation of his distant Friend.

"Well! he would go; but not, indeed, t' admire
The state and grandeur of the new-made Squire;
Danvers, belike, now wealthy, might impart
Some of his gold; for Danvers had a heart,
And may have heard, though guarded so around,
That I have lost the fortune he has found:
Yes! Dick is kind, or he and his fine seat
Might go to——where we never more should meet."
Now, lo! the Rayners all at Hulver Place,—
Or Hulver Hall—'t is not a certain case;
'T is only known that Ladies' notes were sent
Directed both ways, and they always went.

We pass the greetings, and the dinner pass,
All the male gossip o'er the sparkling glass,
And female when retired:—The Squire invites
His Friend, by sleep refresh'd, to see his sights—
His land and lions, granary, barns and crops,
His dairy, piggery, pinery, apples, hops;—
But here a hill appears, and Peter Rayner stops.

"Ah! my old Friend, I give you joy," he cries.
"But some are born to fall, and some to rise;

You 're better many a thousand, I the worse—
Dick, there 's no dealing with a failing purse;
Nor does it shame me (mine is all mischance)
To wish some friendly neighbour would advance"—
——But here the guest on such a theme was low.
His host, meantime, intent upon the show,
In hearing heard not—they came out to see,—
And pushing forward—"There 's a view," quoth he;
"Observe that ruin, built, you see, to catch
The gazer's eye; that cottage with the thatch—
It cost me—guess you what!"—that sound of *cost*
Was accidental, but it was not lost.

"Ah! my good Friend, be sure such things as these
Suit well enough a man who lives at ease:
Think what 'The Betsy' *cost*, and think the shock
Of losing her upon the Dodder-Rock:
The tidings reach'd me on the very day
That villain robb'd us, and then ran away.
Loss upon loss! now if——"

"Do stay a bit;"
Exclaim'd the Squire, "these matters hardly fit
A morning ramble—let me show you now
My team of oxen, and my patent plough.
Talk of your horses!—I the plan condemn—
They eat us up—but oxen! we eat them;
For first they plough and bring us bread to eat,
And then we fat and kill them—there 's the meat.
What 's your opinion?"—

—"I am poorly fed,
And much afraid to want both meat and bread,"
Said Rayner, half indignant; and the Squire
Sigh'd, as he felt he must no more require
A man, whose prospects fail'd, his prospects to admire.

Homeward they moved, and met a gentle pair,
The poor man's daughter, and the rich man's heir:
This caused some thought; but on the couple went,
And a soft hour in tender converse spent.
This pair, in fact, their passion roused anew,
Alone much comfort from the visit drew.

At home the Ladies were engaged, and all
Show'd or were shown the wonders of the Hall;
From room to room the weary guests went on,
Till every Rayner wish'd the show was done.

Home they return'd: the Father deeply sigh'd
To find he vainly had for aid applied:
It hurt him much to ask—and more to be denied.

The younger Richard, who alone sustain'd
The dying Friendship, true to love remain'd:
His Phœbe's smiles, although he did not yet
Fly to behold, he could not long forget;
Nor durst he visit, nor was love so strong,
That he could more than think his Father wrong;
For, wrong or right, that father still profess'd
The most obedient son should fare the best.

So time pass'd on; the second spring appear'd,
Ere Richard ventured on the deed he fear'd:—
He dared at length; and not so much for love,
I grieve to add, but that he meant to prove
He had a will:—His father, in reply,
This known, had answer'd, "So my son, have I."
But Richard's courage was by prudence taught,
And he his nymph in secret service sought.
Some days of absence—not with full consent,
But with slow leave—were to entreaty lent;
And forth the Lover rode, uncertain what he meant.

He reach'd the dwelling he had known so long,
When a pert damsel told him, "he was wrong;
Their house she did not just precisely know,
But he would find it somewhere in *the Row;*
The Rayners now were come a little down,
No more the topmost people in the town;"
She might have added, they their life enjoy'd,
Although on things less hazardous employ'd.

This was not much; but yet the damsel's sneer
And the Row-dwelling of a lass so dear,
Were somewhat startling. He had heard, indeed,
That Rayner's business did not well succeed:
But what of that? They lived in decent style,
No doubt, and Phœbe still retain'd her smile;
And why," he asked, "should all men choose to dwell
In broad cold streets?—the Row does just as well,
Quiet and snug;" and then the favourite maid
Rose in his fancy, tastefully array'd,
Looking with grateful joy upon the swain,
Who could his love in trying times retain.

Soothed by such thoughts, to the new house he came,
Survey'd its aspect, sigh'd, and gave his name.
But ere they open'd, he had waited long,
And heard a movement—Was there somewhat wrong?
Nay, but a friendly party, he was told,
And look'd around, as wishing to behold
Some friends—but these were not the friends of old

Old Peter Rayner, in his own old mode,
Bade the Squire welcome to his new abode,
For Richard had been kind, and doubtless meant
To make proposals now, and ask consent.
Mamma and misses too, were civil all;
But what their awkward courtesy to call,
He knew not; neither could he well express
His sad sensations at their strange address.
And then their laughter loud, their story-telling,
All seem'd befitting to that Row and dwelling;
The hearty welcome to the various treat
Was lost on him—he could nor laugh nor eat.

But one thing pleased him, when he look'd around,
His dearest Phœbe could not there be found:
"Wise and discreet," he says, "she shuns the crew
Of vulgar neighbours, some kind act to do;
In some fair house, some female friend to meet,
Or take at evening prayer in church her seat."

Meantime there rose, amid the ceaseless din
A mingled scent, that crowded room within,
Rum and red-herring, Cheshire cheese and gin

Pipes, too, and punch and sausages, with tea,
Were things that Richard was disturb'd to see.
Impatient now, he left them in disdain,
To call on Phœbe, when he call'd again;
To walk with her, the morning fair and bright,
And lose the painful feelings of the night.

All in the Row, and tripping at the side
Of a young Sailor, he the nymph espied,
As homeward hastening with her happy boy,
She went to join the party, and enjoy.
"Fie!" Phœbe cried, as her companion spoke,
Yet laugh'd to hear the fie-compelling joke;—
Just then her chance to meet, her shame to know,
Her tender Richard, moving sad and slow,
Musing on things full strange, the manners of the Row.

At first amazed, and then alarm'd, the fair
Late-laughing maid now stood in dumb despair:
As when a debtor meets in human shape
The foe of debtors, and cannot escape,
He stands in terror, nor can longer aim
To keep his credit, or preserve his name,
Stood Phœbe fix'd! "Unlucky time and place!
An earlier hour had kept me from disgrace!"
She thought—but now the sailor, undismay'd,
Said, "My dear Phœbe, why are you afraid?
The man seems civil, or he soon should prove
That I can well defend the girl I love.
Are you not mine?" She utter'd no reply;
"Thine I must be," she thought; "more foolish I?"
While Richard at the scene stood mute and wondering by.

His spirits hurried, but his bosom light,
He left his Phœbe with a calm "good night."
So Love like Friendship fell! The youth awhile
Dreamt, sorely moved, of Phœbe's witching smile—
But learn'd in daylight visions to forego
The Sailor's laughing Lass, the Phœbe of the Row.

Home turn'd young Richard, in due time to turn,
With all old Richard's zeal, the leaves of Burn;
And home turn'd Phœbe—in due time to grace
A tottering cabin with a tatter'd race.

TALE XVIII.

THE BOAT RACE.

[*Farewell and Return.*]

I.

The man who dwells where party spirit reigns,
May feel its triumphs, but must wear its chains;
He must the friends and foes of party take
For his, and suffer for his honour's sake;
When once enlisted upon either side,
He must the rude septennial storm abide—
A storm that when its utmost rage is gone,
In cold and angry mutterings murmurs on:
A slow unbending scorn, a cold disdain,
Till years bring the full tempest back again.

Within our Borough two stiff sailors dwelt,
Who both this party storm and triumph felt;
Men who had talents, and were both design'd
For better things, but anger made them blind.

In the same year they married, and their wives
Had pass'd in friendship their yet peaceful lives,
And, as they married in a time of peace,
Had no suspicion that their love must cease.
In fact it did not; but they met by stealth,
And that perhaps might keep their love in health,
Like children watch'd, desirous yet afraid,
Their visits all were with discretion paid.

One Captain, so by courtesy we call
Our hoy's commanders—they are captains all—
Had sons and daughters many; while but one
The rival Captain bless'd—a darling son.
Each was a burgess to his party tied,
And each was fix'd, but on a different side;
And he who sought his son's pure mind to fill
With wholesome food, would evil too instil.
The last in part succeeded—but in part—
For Charles had sense, had virtue, had a heart;
And he had soon the cause of Nature tried
With the stern father, but this father died;
Who on his death-bed thus his son address'd:—
"Swear to me, Charles, and let my spirit rest—
Swear to our party to be ever true,
And let me die in peace—I pray thee, do."

With some reluctance, but obedience more,
The weeping youth reflected, sigh'd, and swore;
Trembling, he swore for ever to be true,
And wear no colour but the untainted Blue:
This done, the Captain died in so much joy,
As if he'd wrought salvation for his boy.

The female friends their wishes yet retain'd,
But seldom met, by female fears restrain'd;
Yet in such town, where girls and boys must meet,
And every house is known in every street,
Charles had before, nay since his father's death,
Met, say by chance, the young Elizabeth;
Who was both good and graceful, and in truth
Was but too pleasing to th' observing youth;
And why I know not, but the youth to her
Seem'd just that being that she could prefer.
Both were disposed to think that party-strife
Destroy'd the happiest intercourse of life;
Charles, too, his growing passion could defend—
His father's foe he call'd his mother's friend.
Mothers, indeed, he knew were ever kind;
But in the Captain should he favour find?
He doubted this—yet could he that command
Which fathers love, and few its power withstand.

The mothers both agreeed their joint request
Should to the Captain jointly be address'd;
And first the lover should his heart assail,
And then the ladies, and if all should fail,
They'd singly watch the hour, and jointly might prevail.

The Captain's heart, although unused to melt,
A strong impression from persuasion felt;
His pride was soften'd by the prayers he heard,
And then advantage in the match appear'd.

At length he answer'd,—"Let the lad enlist
In our good cause, and I no more resist;
For I have sworn, and to my oath am true,
To hate that colour, that rebellious Blue.
His father once, ere master of the brig,
For that advantage turn'd a rascal Whig:
Now let the son—a wife 's a better thing—
A Tory turn, and say, God save the King!
For I am pledged to serve that sacred cause,
And love my country, while I keep her laws."

The women trembled; for they knew full well
The fact they dare not to the Captain tell;
And the poor youth declared, with tears and sighs,
"My oath was pass'd; I dare not compromise."

But Charles to reason made his strong appeal,
And to the heart—he bade him think and feel:
The Captain answering, with reply as strong,—
"If you be right, then how can I be wrong?
You to your father swore to take his part;
I to oppose it ever, head and heart;
You to a parent made your oath, and I
To God! and can I to my Maker lie?
Much, my dear lad, I for your sake would do,
But I have sworn, and to my oath am true."

Thus stood the parties when my fortunes bore
Me far away from this my native shore:
And who prevail'd, I know not—Young or Old;
But, I beseech you, let the ta'e be told.

II.

P.—How fared these lov-rs? Many a time I thought
How with their ill-starred passion Time had wrought.
Did either party from his oath recede,
Or were they never from the bondage freed?

F.—Alas! replied my Friend—the tale I tell
With some reluctance, ncr can do it well.
There are three females in the place, and they,
Like skilful painters, could the facts portray,
In their strong colours—all that I can do
Is to present a weak imperfect view;
The colours I must leave—the outlines shall be true.

Soon did each party see the other's mind,
What bound them both, and what was like to bind;
Oaths deeply taken in such time and place,
To break them now was dreadful—was disgrace.

"That oath a dying father bade me take,
Can I—yourself a father—can I break?"

"That oath which I a living sinner took,
Shall I make void, and yet for mercy look?"

The women wept; the men, themselves distress'd,
The cruel rage of party zeal confess'd:
But solemn oaths, though sprung from party zeal,
Feel them we must, as Christians ought to feel.

Yet shall a youth so good, a girl so fair,
From their obedience only draw despair?
Must they be parted? Is there not a way
For them both love and duty to obey?
Strongly they hoped; and by their friends around
A way, at least a lover's way, was found.

"Give up your vote; you 'll then no longer be
Free in one sense, but in the better free."
Such was of reasoning friends the kind advice,
And how could lovers in such case be nice?
A man may swear to walk directly on
While sight remains; but how if sight be gone?
"Oaths are not binding when the party's dead;
Or when the power to keep the oath is fled:
If I 've no vote, I 've neither friend nor foe,
Nor can be said on either side to go."
They were no casuists:—"Well!" the Captain cried,
"Give up your vote, man, and behold your bride!"

Thus was it fix'd, and fix'd the day for both
To take the vow, and set aside the oath.
It gave some pain, but all agreed to say,
"You 're now absolved, and have no other way:
'T is not expected you should love resign
For man's commands, for love's are all divine."

When all is quiet and the mind at rest,
All in the calm of innocence are blest;
But when some scruple mixes with our joy,
We love to give the anxious mind employ.

In autumn late, when evening suns were bright,
The day was fix'd the lovers to unite;
But one before the eager Captain chose
To break, with jocund act, his girl's repose,
And, sailor-like, said, "Hear how I intend
One day, before the day of days, to spend!
All round the quay, and by the river's side,
Shall be a scene of glory for the bride.
We 'll have a Race, and colours will devise
For every boat, for every man a prize:
But that which first returns shall bear away
The proudest pendant—Let us name the day."

They named the day, and never morn more bright
Rose on the river, nor so proud a sight:
Or if too calm appear'd the cloudless skies,
Experienced seamen said the wind would rise.
To that full quay from this then vacant place
Throng'd a vast crowd to see the promised Race,
'Mid boats new painted, all with streamers fair,
That flagg'd or flutter'd in that quiet air—
The Captain's boat that was so gay and trim,
That made his pride, and seem'd as proud of him—
Her, in her beauty, we might all discern,
Her rigging new, and painted on the stern,
As one who could not in the contest fail,
"Learn of *the little Nautilus* to sail."

So forth they started at the signal gun,
And down the river had three leagues to run,
This sail'd, they then their watery way retrace,
And the first landed conquers in the race

The crowd await till they no more discern,
Then parting, say, "At evening we return."

I could proceed, but you will guess the fate,
And but too well my tale anticipate.

P.—True! yet proceed—

F.—The lovers had some grief
In this day's parting, but the time was brief;
And the poor girl, between his smiles and sighs,
Ask'd, "Do you wish to gain so poor a prize?"

"But that your father wishes," he replied,
"I would the honour had been still denied:
It makes me gloomy, though I would be gay,
And oh! it seems an everlasting day."
So thought the lass, and as she said, Farewell!
Soft sighs arose, and tears unbidden fell.

The morn was calm, and even till noon the strong
Unruffled flood moved quietly along;
In the dead calm the billows softly fell,
And mock'd the whistling sea-boy's favourite spell:
So rests at noon the reaper, but to rise
With mightier force and twofold energies.
The deep, broad stream moved softly, all was hush'd,
When o'er the flood the breeze awakening brush'd;
A sullen sound was heard along the deep,
The stormy spirit rousing from his sleep;
The porpoise rolling on the troubled wave,
Unwieldy tokens of his pleasure gave;
Dark, chilling clouds the troubled deep deform,
And led by terror downward rush'd the storm.

As evening came, along the river's side,
Or on the quay, impatient crowds divide,
And then collect; some whispering, as afraid
Of what they saw, and more of what they said,
And yet must speak: how sudden and how great
The danger seem'd, and what might be the fate
Of men so toss'd about in craft so small,
Lost in the dark, and subject to the squall.
Then sounds are so appalling in the night,
And, could we see, how terrible the sight;
None knew the evils that they all suspect,
And Hope at once they covet and reject.

But where the wife, her friend, her daughter, where?
Alas! in grief, in terror, in despair—
At home, abroad, upon the quay. No rest
In any place, but where they are not, best.
Fearful they ask, but dread the sad reply,
And many a sailor tells the friendly lie—
"There is no danger—that is, we believe,
And think—and hope"—but this does not deceive,
Although it soothes them; while they look around,
Trembling at every sight and every sound.

Let me not dwell on terrors——It is dark,
And lights are carried to and fro, and hark!
There is a cry—"a boat, a boat at hand!"
What a still terror is there now on land!
"Whose, whose?" they all inquire, and none can understand.

At length they come—and oh! how then rejoice
A wife and children at that welcome voice:
It is not theirs—but what have these to tell?
"Where did you leave the Captain—were they well?"
Alas! they knew not, they had felt an awe
In dread of death, and knew not what they saw.
Thus they depart.—The evening darker grows,
The light shakes wildly, and as wildly blows
The stormy night-wind: fear possesses all,
The hardest hearts, in this sad interval.

But hark again to voices loud and high!
Once more that hope, that dread, that agony,
That parting expectation! "Oh! reveal
"What must be known, and think what pangs we feel!"

In vain they ask! The men now landed speak
Confused and quick, and to escape them seek.
Our female party on a sailor press,
But nothing learn that makes their terror less;
Nothing the man can show, or nothing will confess.
To some, indeed, they whisper, bringing news
For them alone, but others they refuse;
And steal away, as if they could not bear
The griefs they cause, and if they cause must share.

They too are gone! and our unhappy Three,
Half wild with fear, are trembling on the quay.
They can no ease, no peace, no quiet find,
The storm is gathering in the troubled mind;
Thoughts after thoughts in wild succession rise,
And all within is changing like the skies.
Their friends persuade them, "Do depart, we pray!"
They will not, must not, cannot go away,
But chill'd with icy fear, for certain tidings stay.

And now again there must a boat be seen—
Men run together! It must something mean!
Some figure moves upon the ousy bound
Where flows the tide—Oh! what can he have found—
What lost? And who is he?—The only one
Of the loved three—the Captain's younger son.
Their boat was fill'd and sank—He knows no more,
But that he only hardly reach'd the shore.
He saw them swimming—for he once was near—
But he was sinking, and he could not hear;
And then the waves curl'd round him, but at length,
He struck upon the boat with dying strength,
And that preserved him: when he turn'd around,
Naught but the dark, wild, billowy flood was found—
That flood was all he saw, that flood 's the only sound—
Save that the angry wind, with ceaseless roar,
Dash'd the wild waves upon the rocky shore.

The Widows dwell together—so we call
The younger woman; widow'd are they all:
But she, the poor Elizabeth, it seems
Not life in her—she lives not, but she dreams;
She looks on Philip, and in him can find
Not much to mark in body or in mind—
He who was saved; and then her very soul
Is in that scene!—Her thoughts beyond control,
Fix'd on that night, and bearing her along,
Amid the waters terrible and strong;

Till there she sees within the troubled waves
The bodies sinking in their watery graves,
When from her lover yielding up his breath,
There comes a voice,—Farewell, Elizabeth!

Yet Resignation in the house is seen,
Subdued Affliction, Piety serene,
And Hope for ever striving to instil
The balm for grief—"It is the Heavenly will:"
And in that will our duty bids us rest,
For all that Heaven ordains is good, is best;
We sin and suffer—this alone we know,
Grief is our portion, is our part below;
But we shall rise, that world of bliss to see,
Where sin and suffering never more shall be.

TALE XIX.

MASTER WILLIAM; OR, LAD'S LOVE.

[*Farewell and Return.*]

I.

I have remembrance of a Boy, whose mind
Was weak: he seem'd not for the world design'd,
Seem'd not as one who in that world could strive,
And keep his spirits even and alive—
A feeling Boy, and happy, though the less,
From that fine feeling, form'd for happiness.
His mother left him to his favourite ways,
And what he made his pleasure brought him praise.

Romantic, tender, visionary, mild,
Affectionate, reflecting when a child,
With fear instinctive he from harshness fled,
And gentle tears for all who suffer'd shed;
Tales of misfortune touch'd his generous heart,
Of maidens left, and lovers forced to part.

In spite of all that weak indulgence wrought,
That love permitted, or that flattery taught,
In spite of teachers who no fault would find,
The Boy was neither selfish nor unkind.
Justice and truth his honest heart approved,
And all things lovely he admired and loved.
Arabian Nights, and Persian Tales, he read,
And his pure mind with brilliant wonders fed.
The long Romances, wild Adventures fired
His stirring thoughts: he felt like Boy inspired.
The cruel fight, the constant love, the art
Of vile magicians, thrill'd his inmost heart:
An early Quixote, dreaming dreadful sights
Of warring dragons, and victorious knights:
In every dream some beauteous Princess shone,
The pride of thousands, and the prize of one.

Not yet he read, nor reading, would approve,
The Novel's hero, or its ladies' love.
He would Sophia for a wanton take,
Jones for a wicked, nay a vulgar rake.
He would no time on Smollett's page bestow;
Such men he knew not, would disdain to know:
And if he read, he travell'd slowly on,
Teased by the tame and faultless Grandison.
He in that hero's deeds could not delight—
"He loved two ladies, and he would not fight."
The minor works of this prolific kind
Presented beings he could never find;
Beings, he thought, that no man should describe,
A vile, intriguing, lying, perjured tribe,
With impious habits, and dishonest views;
The men he knew, had souls they fear'd to lose;
These had no views that could their sins control,
With them nor fears nor hopes disturb'd the soul.

To dear Romance with fresh delight he turn'd,
And vicious men, like recreant cowards, spurn'd.

The Scripture Stories he with reverence read,
And duly took his Bible to his bed.
Yet Joshua, Samson, David, were a race
He dared not with his favourite heroes place.
Young as he was, the difference well he knew
Between the Truth, and what we fancy true.
He was with these entranced, of those afraid,
With Guy he triumph'd, but with David pray'd.

II.

P.—Such was the Boy, and what the man would be,
I might conjecture, but could not foresee.

F.—He has his trials met, his troubles seen,
And now deluded, now deserted, been.
His easy nature has been oft assail'd
By grief assumed, scorn hid, and flattery veil'd.

P.—But has he, safe and cautious, shunn'd the snares
That life presents?—I ask not of its cares.

F.—Your gentle Boy a course of life began,
That made him what he is, the gentle-man,
A man of business. He in courts presides
Among their Worships, whom his judgment guides
He in the Temple studied, and came down
A very lawyer, though without a gown;
Still he is kind, but prudent, steady, just,
And takes but little what he hears on trust;
He has no visions now, no boyish plans;
All his designs and prospects are the man's,
The man of sound discretion—?

P.—How so made?
What could his mind to change like this persuade—
What first awaken'd our romantic friend—
For such he is—

F.—If you would know, attend.

In those gay years, when boys their manhood prove,
Because they talk of girls, and dream of love,
In William's way there came a maiden fair,
With soft, meek look, and sweet retiring air;
With just the rosy tint upon her cheek,
With sparkling eye, and tongue unused to speak
With manner decent, quiet, chaste, that one,
Modest himself, might love to look upon,
As William look'd; and thus the gentle Squire
Began the Nymph, albeit poor, t' admire

She was, to wit, the gardener's niece; her place
Gave to her care the Lady's silks and lace,
With other duties of an easy kind;
And left her time, as much she felt inclined,
T' adorn her graceful form, and fill her craving
mind;
Nay, left her leisure to employ some hours
Of the long day, among her uncle's flowers—
Myrtle and rose, of which she took the care,
And was as sweet as pinks and lilies are.

Such was the damsel whom our Youth beheld
With passion unencouraged, unrepell'd:
For how encourage what was not in view?
Or how repel what strove not to pursue?

What books inspired, or glowing fancy wrought,
What dreams suggested, or reflection taught,
Whate'er of love was to the mind convey'd,
Was all directed to his darling maid.
He saw his damsel with a lover's eyes,
As pliant fancy wove the fair disguise;
A Quixote he, who in his nymph could trace
The high-born beauty, changed and—out of place.
That William loved, mamma, with easy smile,
Would jesting say; but love *might* grow the while;
The damsel's self, with unassuming pride,
With love so led by fear was gratified.

What cause for censure? Could a man reprove
A child for fondness, or miscall it love?
Not William's self; yet well informed was he,
That love it was, and endless love would be.
Month after month the sweet delusion bred
Wild feverish hopes, that flourish'd, and then fled,
Like Fanny's sweetest flower, and that was lost
In one cold hour, by one harsh morning frost.

In some soft evenings, 'mid the garden's bloom,
Would William wait, till Fanny chanced to come;
And Fanny came, by chance it may be; still,
There was a gentle bias of the will,
Such as the soundest minds may act upon,
When motives of superior kind are gone.
There then they met, and Master William's look
Was the less timid, for he held a book;
And when the sweetness of the evening hours,
The fresh soft air, the beauty of the flowers,
The night-bird's note, the gently falling dew,
Were all discuss'd, and silence would ensue,
There were some lovely Lines—if she could stay—
And Fanny rises not to go away.

"Young Paris was the shepherd's pride,
As well the fair Ænone knew;
They sat the mountain's stream beside,
And o'er the bank a poplar grew.

Upon its bark this verse he traced,—
Bear witness to the vow I make;
Thou, Xanthus, to thy source shalt haste,
Ere I my matchless maid forsake.

No prince or peasant lad am I,
Nor crown nor crook to me belong;
But I will love thee till I die,
And die before I do thee wrong.

Back to thy source now, Xanthus, run,
Paris is now a prince of Troy:
He leaves the Fair his flattery won,
Himself and country to destroy.

He seizes on a sovereign's wife,
The pride of Greece, and with her flies,
He causes thus a ten years' strife,
And with his dying parent dies.

Oh! think me not this Shepherd's Boy,
Who from the Maid he loves would run;
Oh! think me not a Prince of Troy,
By whom such treacherous deeds are done."

The Lines were read, and many an idle word
Pronounced with emphasis, and underscored,
As if the writer had resolved that all
His nouns and verbs should be emphatical.
But what they were the damsel little thought,
The sense escaped her, but the voice she caught;
Soft, tender, trembling, and the gipsy felt
As if by listening she unfairly dealt:
For she, if not mamma, had rightly guess'd,
That William's bosom was no seat of rest.

But Love's young hope must die.—There was a
day,
When nature smiled, and all around was gay;
The Boy o'ertook the damsel as she went
The village road—unknown was her intent;
He, happy hour, when lock'd in Fanny's arm,
Walk'd on enamour'd, every look a charm;
Yet her soft looks were but her heart's disguise,
There was no answering love in Fanny's eyes:
But, or by prudence or by pity moved,
She thought it time his folly was reproved;
Then took her measures, not perchance without
Some conscious pride in what she was about.

Along the brook, with gentle pace they go,
The Youth unconscious of th' impending wo;
And oft he urged the absent Maid to talk,
As she was wont in many a former walk;
And still she slowly walk'd beside the brook,
Or look'd around—for what could Fanny look?
Something there must be! What, did not appear;
But William's eye betray'd the anxious fear;
The cause unseen!——

But who, with giant-stride,
Bounds o'er the brook, and is at Fanny's side?
Who takes her arm? and oh! what villain dares
To press those lips? Not even her lips he spares!
Nay, she herself, the Fanny, the divine,
Lip to his lip can wickedly incline!
The lad, unnerved by horror, with an air
Of wonder quits her arm and looks despair;
Nor will proceed. Oh no! he must return,
Though his drown'd sight cannot the path discern.

"Come, Master William! come, Sir, let us on.
What can you fear? You 're not afraid of John?"

"What ails our youngster?" quoth the burly
swain,
Six feet in height—but he inquires in vain.

William, in deep resentment, scans the frame
Of the fond giant, and abhors his name;
Thinks him a demon of th' infernal brood,
And longs to shed his most pernicious blood.

Again the monster spake in thoughtless joy,—
"We shall be married soon, my pretty Boy!
And dwell in Madam's cottage, where you 'll see
The strawberry-beds, and cherries on the tree."

Back to his home in silent scorn return'd
Th' indignant Boy, and all endearment spurn'd.
Fanny perforce with Master takes her way,
But finds him to th' o'erwhelming grief a prey,
Wrapt in resentful silence, till he came
Where he might vent his woes, and hide his shame.

Fierce was his strife, but with success he strove,
And freed his troubled breast from fruitless love;
Or what of love his reason fail'd to cool
Was lost and perish'd in a public school,—
Those seats and sources both of good and ill,
By what they cure in Boys, and what they kill.

TALE XX.

THE WILL.

[*Farewell and Return.*]

I.

Thus to his Friend an angry Father spoke—
"Nay, do not think that I the Will revoke.
My cruel Son in every way I 've tried,
And every vice have found in him but pride;
For he, of pride possess'd, would meaner vices hide.
Money he wastes, I will not say he spends;
He neither makes the poor nor rich his friends—
To those he nothing gives, to these he never lends.

'T is for himself each legal pale he breaks;
He joins the miser's spirit to the rake's:
Like the worst Roman in the worst of times,
He can be guilty of conflicting crimes;
Greedy of others' wealth, unknown the use,
And of his own contemptuously profuse.

To such a mind shall I my wealth confide,
That you to nobler, worthier ends, may guide?
No! let my Will my scorn of vice express,
And let him learn repentance from distress."

So said the Father; and the Friend, who spurn'd
Wealth ill-acquired, his sober speech return'd—
"The youth is faulty, but his faults are weigh'd
With a strong bias, and by wrath repaid;
Pleasure deludes him, not the vain design
Of making vices unallied combine.
He wastes your wealth, for he is yet a boy;
He covets more, for he would more enjoy.
For, my good fiiend, believe me, very few,
At once are prodigals and misers too—
The spendthrift vice engrafted on the Jew.
Leave me one thousand pounds; for I confess
I have my wants, and will not tax you less.
But your estate let this young man enjoy;
If he reforms, you 've saved a grateful boy,
If not, a father's cares and troubles cease,
You 've done your duty, and may rest in peace."

The Will in hand, the Father musing stood,
Then gravely answer'd, "Your advice is good;
Yet take the paper, and in safety keep;
I 'll make another Will before I sleep;
But if I hear of some atrocious deed,
That deed I 'll burn, and yours will then succeed.
Two thousand I bequeath you. No reproof!
And there are small bequests—he 'll have enough;
For if he wastes, he would with all be poor,
And if he wastes not, he will need no more."

The Friends then parted: this the Will possess'd,
And that another made—so things had rest.

George, who was conscious that his Father grew
Sick and infirm, engaged in nothing new;
No letters came from injured man or maid,
No bills from wearied duns, that must be paid,
No fierce reproaches from deserted fair,
Mix'd with wild tenderness of desperate prayer;
So hope rose softly in the parent's breast,
He dying call'd his son and fondly blest,
Hail'd the propitious tear, and mildly sunk to rest.

Unhappy Youth! ere yet the tomb was closed,
And dust to dust convey'd in peace reposed,
He sought his father's closet, search'd around,
To find a Will! the important Will was found.

Well pleased he read, "These lands, this manor all,
Now call me master!—I obey the call."
Then from the window look'd the valley o'er,
And never saw it look so rich before.
He view'd the dairy, view'd the men at plough,
With other eyes, with other feelings now,
And with a new-form'd taste found beauty in a cow
The distant swain who drove the plough along
Was a good useful slave, and passing strong!
In short, the view was pleasing, nay, was fine,
"Good as my father's, excellent as mine!"

Again he reads,—but he had read enough;
What follow'd put his virtue to a proof.
"How this? to David Wright two thousand pounds!
A monstrous sum! beyond all reason!—zounds!
This is your friendship running out of bounds.

Then here are cousins Susan, Robert, Joe,
Five hundred each. Do they deserve it? No!
Claim they have none—I wonder if they know
What the good man intended to bestow!
This might be paid—but Wright's enormous sum
Is—I 'm alone—there 's nobody can come—
'T is all his hand, no lawyer was employ'd
To write this prose, that ought to be destroy'd!
To no attorney would my father trust:
He wish'd his son to judge of what was just;

As if he said, 'My boy will find the Will,
And, as he likes, destroy it or fulfil.'
This now is reason, this I understand—
What was at his, is now at my command.
As for this paper, with these cousins' names,
I—'t is *my* Will—commit it to the flames.
Hence! disappear! now am I lord alone;
They 'll groan, I know, but, curse them, let them groan.
Who wants his money like a new-made heir,
To put all things in order and repair?
I need the whole the worthy man could save,
To do my father credit in his grave:
It takes no trifle to have squires convey'd
To their last house with honour and parade.
All this, attended by a world of cost,
Requires, demands, that nothing should be lost.
These fond bequests cannot demanded be—
Where no Will is, can be no legacy;
And none is here! I safely swear it—none!—
The very ashes are dispersed and gone.
All would be well, would that same sober Friend,
That Wright, my father on his way attend:
My fears—but why afraid?—my troubles then would end."

In triumph, yet in trouble, meets our Squire
The friends assembled, who a Will require.
"There is no Will," he said—They murmur and retire.

Days pass away, while yet the Heir is blest
By pleasant cares, and thoughts that banish rest;
When comes the Friend, and asks, in solemn tone,
If he may see the busy Squire alone.

They are in private—all about is still—
When thus the Guest:—"Your father left a Will,
And I would see it."—Rising in reply,
The youth beheld a fix'd and piercing eye,
From which his own receded; and the sound
Of his own words was in disorder drown'd.
He answer'd softly,—"I in vain have spent
Days in the search; I pray you be content;
And if a Will——" The pertinacious man,
At *if* displeased, with steady tone began,—
"There *is* a Will—produce it, for you can."—

"Sir, I have sought in vain, and what the use?
What has no being, how can I produce?"

"Two days I give you; to my words attend,"
Was the reply, "and let the business end."

Two days were past, and still the same reply
To the same question—"Not a Will have I."
More grave, more earnest, then the Friend appear'd;
He spoke with power, as one who would be heard,—
"A Will your father made! I witness'd one."
The Heir arose in anger—"Sir, begone!
Think you my spirit by your looks to awe?
Go to your lodgings, friend, or to your law:
To what would you our easy souls persuade?
Once more I tell you, not a Will was made:
There 's none with me, I swear it—now, deny
This if you can!"—
"That, surely, cannot I;
Nay, I believe you, and as no such deed
Is found with you, *this* surely will succeed!"—

He said, and from his pocket slowly drew
Of the first testament a copy true,
And held it spread abroad, that he might see it too
"Read, and be sure; your parent's pleasure see—
Then leave this mansion and these lands to me."

He said, and terror seized the guilty youth;
He saw his misery, meanness, and the truth;
Could not before his stern accuser stand,
Yet could not quit that hall, that park, that land;
But when surprise had pass'd away, his grief
Began to think in law to find relief.

"While courts are open, why should I despair
Juries will feel for an abandon'd heir:
I will resist," he said, impell'd by pride:—
"I must submit," recurring fear replied.
As wheels the vane when winds around it play,
So his strong passions turn'd him every way;
But growing terrors seized th' unhappy youth:
He knew the Man, and more, he knew—the Truth
When, stung by all he fear'd, and all he felt,
He sought for mercy, and in terror knelt.

Grieved, but indignant,—"Let me not despise
Thy father's son," replied the Friend: "arise!
To my fix'd purpose your attention lend,
And know, your fate will on yourself depend.

Thou shalt not want, young man! nor yet abound,
And time shall try thee, if thy heart be sound;
Thou shalt be watch'd till thou hast learn'd to know
Th' All-seeing Watcher of the world below,
And worlds above, and thoughts within; from Whom
Must be thy certain, just, and final doom.
Thy doors all closely barr'd, thy windows blind,
Before all silent, silent all behind—
Thy hand was stretch'd to do whate'er thy soul
In secret would—no mortal could control.
Oh, fool! to think that thou thy act couldst keep
From that All-piercing Eye, which cannot sleep!

Go to thy trial! and may I with thee,
A fellow-sinner, who to mercy flee—
That mercy find, as justly I dispense
Between thy frailty and thy penitence.

Go to thy trial! and be wise in time,
And know that no man can conceal a crime.
God and his Conscience witness all that 's done,
And these he cannot cheat, he cannot shun.
What, then, could fortune, what could safety give,
If He with these at enmity must live?

Go!"—and the young man from his presence went,
Confused, uncertain of his own intent—
To sin, if pride prevail'd; if soften'd, to repent.

II.

P.—LIVES yet the Friend of that unhappy Boy,
Who could the WILL that made him rich destroy,
And made him poor? And what the after-plan,
For one so selfish, of that stern, good man?

F.—"Choose," said this Friend, "thy way in life, and I
Will means to aid thee in thy work supply."
He will the army, thought this guardian, choose,
And there the sense of his dishonour lose.

Humbly he answer'd,—"With your kind consent,
Of your estate I would a portion rent,
And farm with care——"

"Alas! the wretched fruit
Of evil habit! he will hunt and shoot."

So judged the Friend, but soon perceived a change,
To him important, and to all men strange.
Industrious, temperate, with the sun he rose,
And of his time gave little to repose:
Nor to the labour only bent his will,
But sought experience, and improved with skill;
With cautious prudence placed his gains to use,
Inquiring always, "What will this produce?"

The Friend, not long suspicious, now began
To think more kindly of the alter'd man—
In his opinion alter'd, but, in truth,
The same the spirit that still ruled the youth:
That dwelt within, where other demons dwell,
Avarice unsated, and insatiable.

But this Wright saw not: he was more inclined
To trace the way of a repenting mind;
And he was now by strong disease assail'd,
That quickly o'er the vital powers prevail'd:
And now the son had all, was rich beyond
His fondest hope, and he, indeed, was fond.

His life's great care has been his zeal to prove,
And time to dotage has increased his love.
A Miser now, the one strong passion guides
The heart and soul: there 's not a love besides.
Where'er he comes, he sees in every face
A look that tells him of his own disgrace.
Men's features vary, but the mildest show
"It is a tale of infamy we know."
Some with contempt the wealthy miser view,
Some with disgust, yet mix'd with pity too;
A part that looks of wrath and hatred wear,
And some, less happy, lose their scorn in fear.

Meanwhile, devoid of kindness, comfort, friends,
On his possessions solely he depends.

Yet is he wretched; for his fate decrees
That his own feelings should deny him ease.
With talents gifted, he himself reproves,
And can but scorn the vile pursuit he loves;
He can but feel that there abides within
The secret shame, the unrepented sin,
And the strong sense, that bids him to confess
He has not found the way to happiness.

But 't is the way where he has travell'd long,—
And turn he will not, though he feels it wrong;
Like a sad traveller, who, at closing day,
Finds he has wander'd widely from his way,
Yet wanders on, nor will new paths explore,
Till the night falls, and he can walk no more.

TALE XXI.

THE COUSINS.

[*Farewell and Return.*]

I.

P.—I LEFT a frugal Merchant, who began
Early to thrive, and grew a wealthy man:
Retired from business with a favourite Niece,
He lived in plenty, or if not—in peace.
Their small affairs, conforming to his will,
The maiden managed with superior skill.
He had a nephew too, a brother's child,—
But James offended, for the lad was wild:
And Patty's tender soul was vex'd to hear,
"Your Cousin James will rot in gaol, my dear;
And now, I charge you, by no kind of gift
Show him that folly may be help'd by thrift."
This Patty heard, but in her generous mind
Precept so harsh could no admission find.

Her Cousin James, too sure in prison laid,
With strong petitions plied the gentle maid,
That she would humbly on their uncle press
His deep repentance, and his sore distress;
How that he mourn'd in durance night and day,
And which remov'd, he would for ever pray.

"Nought will I give his worthless life to save,"
The Uncle said; and nought in fact he gave;
But the kind maiden from her pittance took
All that she could, and gave with pitying look;
For soft compassion in her bosom reign'd,
And her heart melted when the Youth complain'd.
Of his complaints the Uncle loved to hear,
As Patty told them, shedding many a tear;
While he would wonder how the girl could pray
For a young rake, to place him in her way,
Or once admit him in his Uncle's view;
"But these," said he, "are things that women do."

Thus were the Cousins, young, unguarded, fond,
Bound in true friendship—so they nam'd the bond—
Nor call'd it love—and James resolv'd, when free,
A most correct and frugal man to be.
He sought her prayers, but not for heavenly aid:
"Pray to my Uncle," and she kindly pray'd—
"James will be careful," said the Niece; "and I
Will be as careful," was the stern reply.

Thus he resisted, and I know not how
He could be soften'd—Is he kinder now?
Hard was his heart; but yet a heart of steel
May melt in dying, and dissolving feel.

II.

F.—WHAT were his feelings I cannot explain,
His actions only on my mind remain.
He never married, that indeed we know,
But childless was not, as his foes could show—
Perhaps his friends—for friends as well as foes,
Will the infirmities of man disclose.

When young, our Merchant, though of sober fame,
Had a rude passion that he could not tame;
And, not to dwell upon the passion's strife,
He had a Son, who never had a wife;
The father paid just what the law required,
Nor saw the infant, nor to see desired.
That infant, thriving on the parish fare,
Without a parent's love, consent, or care,
Became a sailor, and sustain'd his part
So like a man, it touch'd his father's heart:—
He for protection gave the ready pay,
And placed the seaman in preferment's way;
Who doubted not, with sanguine heart, to rise,
And bring home riches, gain'd from many a prize.
But Jack—for so we call'd him—Jack once more,
And never after, touch'd his native shore:
Nor was it known if he in battle fell,
Or sickening died—we sought, but none could tell.
The father sigh'd—as some report, he wept;
And then his sorrow with the Sailor slept;
Then age came on; he found his spirits droop,
And his kind Niece remain'd the only hope.

Premising this, our story then proceeds—
Our gentle Patty for her Cousin pleads;
And now her Uncle, to his room confined,
And kindly nursed, was soften'd and was kind.
James, whom the law had from his prison sent,
With much contrition to his Uncle went,
And, humbly kneeling, said, "Forgive me, I repent."
Reproach, of course, his humble spirit bore;
He knew for pardon anger opes the door;
The man whom we with too much warmth reprove,
Has the best chance our softening hearts to move;
And this he had—"Why, Patty, love! it seems,"
Said the old man, "there's something good in James:
I must forgive; but you, my child, are yet
My stay and prop; I cannot this forget.
Still, my dear Niece, as a reforming man,
I mean to aid your Cousin, if I can."
Then Patty smiled, for James and she had now
Time for their loves, and pledged the constant vow.

James the fair way to favouring thoughts discern'd—
He learn'd the news, and told of all he learn'd;
Read all the papers in an easy style,
And knew the bits would raise his Uncle's smile;
Then would refrain, to hear the good man say,
"You did not come as usual yesterday:
I must not take you from your duties, lad,
But of your daily visits should be glad!"

Patty was certain that their Uncle now
Would their affection all it ask'd allow;
She was convinced her lover now would find
The past forgotten and old Uncle kind.
"It matters not," she added, "who receives
The larger portion; what to one he leaves
We both inherit! let us nothing hide,
Dear James, from him in whom we both confide."

"Not for your life!" quoth James. "Let Uncle choose
Our ways for us, or we the way shall lose.
For know you, Cousin, all these miser men——"
"Nay, my dear James!"—
"Our worthy Uncle, then,
And all like Uncle, like to be obey'd
By their dependants, who must seem afraid
Of their own will:—If we to wed incline,
You'll quickly hear him peevishly repine,
Object, dispute, and sundry reasons give,
To prove we ne'er could find the means to live;
And then, due credit for his speech to gain,
He'll leave us poor—lest wealth should prove it vain.
Let him propose the measure, and then we
May for his pleasure to his plan agree.
I, when at last assenting, shall be still
But giving way to a kind Uncle's will;
Then will he deem it just, amends to make
To one who ventures all things for his sake;
So, should you deign to take this worthless hand,
Be sure, dear Patty, 't is at his command."

But Patty question'd—Is it, let me ask,
The will of God that we should wear a mask?"
This startled James: he lifted up his eyes,
And said with some contempt, besides surprise,
"Patty, my love! the will of God, 't is plain,
Is that we live by what we can obtain;
Shall we a weak and foolish man offend,
And when our trial is so near an end?"

This hurt the maiden, and she said, "'Tis well!
Unask'd I will not of your purpose tell,
But will not lie."—
"Lie! Patty, no, indeed,
Your downright lying never will succeed!
A better way our prudence may devise,
Than such unprofitable things as lies.
Yet, a dependant, if he would not starve,
The way through life must with discretion carve,
And, though a lie he may with pride disdain,
He must not every useless truth maintain.
If one respect to these fond men would show,
Conceal the facts that give them pain to know;
While all that pleases may be placed in view,
And if it be not, they will think it true."

The humble Patty dropp'd a silent tear,
And said, "Indeed, 't is best to be sincere."
James answer'd not—there could be no reply
To what he would not grant, nor could deny:
But from that time he in the maiden saw
What he condemn'd; yet James was kept in awe;
He felt her virtue, but was sore afraid
For the frank blunders of the virtuous maid.

Meanwhile he daily to his Uncle read
The news, and to his favourite subjects led:
If closely press'd, he sometimes staid to dine,
Eat of one dish, and drank one glass of wine;
For James was crafty grown, and felt his way
To favour, step by step, and day by day;
He talk'd of business, till the Uncle prized
The lad's opinion, whom he once despised,
And glad to see him thus his faults survive,
"This Boy," quoth he, "will keep our name alive
Women are weak, and Patty, though the best
Of her weak sex, is woman like the rest:
An idle husband will her money spend,
And bring my hard-earn'd savings to an end."

Far as he dared, his Nephew this way led,
And told his tales of lasses rashly wed,
Told them as matters that he heard,—"He knew
Not where," he said: "they might be false or true;
One must confess that girls are apt to dote
On the bright scarlet of a coxcomb's coat;
And that with ease a woman they beguile
With a fool's flattery, or a rascal's smile;
But then," he added, fearing to displease,
"Our Patty never saw such men as these."

"True! but she may—some scoundrel may command
The girl's whole store, if he can gain her hand:
Her very goodness will itself deceive,
And her weak virtue help her to believe;
Yet she is kind; and, Nephew! go, and say,
I need her now—You 'll come another day."

In such discourses, while the maiden went
About her household, many an hour was spent,
Till James was sure that when his Uncle died,
He should at least the property divide:
Nor long had he to wait—the fact was quickly tried.

The Uncle now to his last bed confined,
To James and Patty his affairs resign'd;
The doctor took his final fee in hand,
The man of law received his last command;
The silent priest sat watching in his chair,
If he might wake the dying man to prayer,—
When the last groan was heard; then all was still,
And James indulged his musings—on the Will.

This in due time was read, and Patty saw
Her own dear Cousin made the heir-by-law.
Something indeed was hers, but yet she felt
As if her Uncle had not kindly dealt;
And but that James was one whom she could trust,
She would have thought it cruel and unjust.
Even as it was, it gave her some surprise,
And tears unbidden started in her eyes;
Yet she confess'd it was the same to her,
And it was likely men would men prefer.
Loath was the Niece to think her Uncle wrong;
And other thoughts engaged her—"Is it long
That custom bids us tarry ere we wed,
When a kind Uncle is so lately dead?
At any rate," the maiden judged, "'tis he
That first will speak—it does not rest with me."

James to the Will his every thought confined,
And found some parts that vex'd his sober mind.
He, getting much, to angry thoughts gave way,
For the poor pittance that he had to pay,
With Patty's larger claim. Save these alone,
The weeping heir beheld the whole his own;
Yet something painful in his mind would dwell,—
"It was not likely, but was possible:"—
No—Fortune lately was to James so kind,
He was determined not to think her blind:
"She saw his merit, and would never throw
His prospects down by such malicious blow."

Patty, meanwhile, had quite enough betray'd
Of her own mind to make her James afraid
Of one so simply pure: his hardening heart
Inclined to anger—he resolved to part:
Why marry Patty?—if he look'd around,
More advantageous matches might be found
But though he might a richer wife command,
He first must break her hold upon his hand.

She with a spinster-friend retired awhile,
"Not long," she said, and said it with a smile.
Not so had James determined:—He essay'd
To move suspicion in the gentle maid.
Words not succeeding, he design'd to pass
The spinster's window with some forward lass.
If in her heart so pure no pang was known,
At least he might affect it in his own.
There was a brother of her friend, and he,
Though poor and rude, might serve for jealousy.
If all should fail, he, though of schemes bereft,
Might leave her yet!—They fail'd, and she was left.

Poor Patty bore it with a woman's mind,
And with an angel's, sorrowing and resign'd.
Ere this in secret long she wept and pray'd,
Long tried to think her lover but delay'd
The union, once his hope, his prayer, his pride;—
She could in James as in herself confide:
Was he not bound by all that man can bind,
In love, in honour, to be just and kind?
Large was his debt, and when their debts are large,
The ungrateful cancel what the just discharge;
Nor payment only in their pride refuse,
But first they wrong their friend, and then accuse.
Thus Patty finds her bosom's claims denied,
Her love insulted, and her right defied.
She urged it not; her claim the maid withdrew,
For maiden pride would not the wretch pursue:
She sigh'd to find him false, herself so good and true.

Now all his fears, at least the present, still,—
He talk'd, good man! about his uncle's will,—
"All unexpected," he declared,—"surprised
Was he—and his good uncle ill-advised:
He no such luck had look'd for, he was sure,
Nor such deserved," he said, with look demure;
"He did not merit such exceeding love,
But his, he meant, so help him God, to prove."
And he has proved it! all his cares and schemes
Have proved the exceeding love James bears to James.

But to proceed,—for we have yet the facts
That show how Justice looks on wicked acts;
For, though not always, she at times appears—
To wake in man her salutary fears.

James, restless grown—for no such mind can rest—
Would build a house, that should his wealth attest;
In fact, he saw, in many a clouded face,
A certain token of his own disgrace;
And wish'd to overawe the murmurs of the place.

The finish'd building show'd the master's wealth,
And noisy workmen drank his Honour's health—
"His and his heirs"—and at the thoughtless word
A strange commotion in his bosom stirr'd.

"Heirs . said the idiots?"—and again that clause
In the strange Will corrected their applause.

Prophetic fears! for now reports arose
That spoil'd "his Honour's" comforts and repose.
A stout young Sailor, though in battle maim'd,
Arrived in port, and his possessions claim'd.
The Will he read: he stated his demand,
And his attorney grasp'd at house and land.
The Will provided—"If my son survive,
He shall inherit!" and lo! Jack 's alive!
Yes! he was that lost lad, preserved by fate,
And now was bent on finding his estate.
But claim like this the angry James denied,
And to the law the sturdy heir applied.
James did what men when placed like him would do—
Avow'd his right, and fee'd his lawyer too:
The Will, indeed, provided for a son;
But was this Sailor youth the very one?

Ere Jack's strong proofs in all their strength were shown,
To gain a part James used a milder tone;
But the instructed tar would reign alone.

At last he reign'd: to James a large bequest
Was frankly dealt; the Seaman had the rest—
Save a like portion to the gentle Niece,
Who lived in comfort, and regain'd her peace.
In her neat room her talent she employ'd,
With more true peace than ever James enjoy'd.
The young, the aged, in her praise agreed—
Meek in her manner, bounteous in her deed;
The very children their respect avow'd:
"'T was the good lady," they were told and bow'd.

The merry Seaman much the maid approved,—
Nor that alone—he like a seaman loved;
Loved as a man who did not much complain,
Loved like a sailor, not a sighing swain;
Had heard of wooing maids, but knew not how—
"Lass, if you love me, prithee tell me now,"
Was his address—but this was nothing cold—
"Tell if you love me;" and she smiled and told.

He brought her presents, such as sailors buy,
Glittering like gold, to please a maiden's eye,
All silk, and silver, fringe and finery:
These she accepted in respect to him,
And thought but little of the missing limb.
Of this he told her, for he loved to tell
A warlike tale, and judged he told it well:—
"You mark me, love! the French were two to one,
And so, you see, they were asham'd to run;
We fought an hour; and then there came the shot
That struck me here—a man must take his lot;—
A minute after, and the Frenchman struck:
One minute sooner had been better luck;
But if you can a crippled cousin like,
You ne'er shall see him for a trifle strike."

Patty, whose gentle heart was not so nice
As to reject the thought of loving twice,
Judged her new Cousin was by nature kind,
With no suspicions in his honest mind,
Such as our virtuous ladies now and then
Find strongly floating in the minds of men.
So they were married, and the lasses vow'd
That Patty's luck would make an angel proud:
"Not but that time would come when she must prove
That men are men, no matter how they love:"—
"And she has proved it; for she finds her man
As kind and true as when their loves began.

James is unhappy; not that he is poor,
But, having much, because he has no more;
Because a rival's pleasure gives him pain;
Because his vices work'd their way in vain;
And more than these, because he sees the smile
Of a wrong'd woman pitying man so vile.

He sought an office, serves in the excise,
And every wish, but that for wealth, denies;
Wealth is the world to him, and he is worldly wise.
But disappointment in his face appears;
Care and vexation, sad regret and fears
Have fix'd on him their fangs, and done the work of years.

Yet grows he wealthy in a strange degree,
And neighbours wonder how the fact can be:
He lives alone, contracts a sordid air,
And sees with sullen grief the cheerful pair;
Feels a keen pang, as he beholds the door
Where peace abides, and mutters,—"*I am poor!*"

TALE XXII.

PREACHING AND PRACTICE.

[*Farewell and Return.*]

I.

P.—What I have ask'd are questions that relate
To those once known, that I might learn their fate.
But there was One, whom though I scarcely knew,
Much do I wish to learn his fortunes too.
Yet what expect?—He was a rich man's Heir,
His conduct doubtful, but his prospects fair;
Thoughtless and brave, extravagant and gay,
Wild as the wind, and open as the day;
His freaks and follies were a thousand times
Brought full in view: I heard not of his crimes.
Like our Prince Hal, his company he chose
Among the lawless, of restraint the foes;
But though to their poor pleasures he could stoop
He was not, rumour said, their victim-dupe.

His mother's Sister was a maiden prim,
Pious and poor, and much in debt to him.
This she repaid with volumes of reproof,
And sage advice, till he would cry "Enough!"

His father's Brother no such hints allow'd,—
Peevish and rich, and insolent and proud,
Of stern, strong spirit: Him the youth withstood
At length, "Presume not (said he) on our blood;
Treat with politeness him whom you advise,
Nor think I fear your doting prophecies;"

And fame has told of many an angry word,
When anger this, and that contempt had stirr'd.

"Boy! thou wilt beg thy bread, I plainly see."—
"Upbraid not, Uncle! till I beg of thee."

"Oh! thou wilt run to ruin and disgrace."—
'What! and so kind an Uncle in the place?"

"Nay, for I hold thee stranger to my blood."—
"Then must I treat thee as a stranger would:
For if you throw the tie of blood aside,
You must the roughness of your speech abide."

"What! to your father's Brother do you give
A challenge?—Mercy! in what times we live!"

Now, I confess, the youth who could supply
Thus that poor Spinster, and could thus defy
This wealthy Uncle:—who could mix with them
Whom his strong sense and feeling must condemn,
And in their follies his amusement find,
Yet never lose the vigour of his mind—
A youth like this, with much we must reprove,
Had something still to win esteem and love.
Perhaps he lives not; but he seem'd not made
To pass through life entirely in the shade.

F.—Suppose you saw him,—does your mind retain
So much, that you would know the man again?
Yet hold in mind, he may have felt the press
Of grief or guilt, the withering of distress;
He now may show the stamp of wo and pain,
And nothing of his lively cast remain.

Survey these features—see if nothing there
May old impressions on your mind repair!
Is there not something in this shatter'd frame
Like to that——

P.—No! not like it, but the same;
That eye so brilliant, and that smile so gay,
Are lighted up, and sparkle through decay.

But may I question? Will you that allow?
There was a difference, and there must be now;
And yet, permitted, I would gladly hear
What must have pass'd in many a troubled year.

F.—Then hear my tale; but I the price demand;
That understood, I too must understand
Thy wanderings through, or sufferings in the land;
And, if our virtues cannot much produce,
Perhaps our errors may be found of use.

To all the wealth my father's care laid by,
I added wings, and taught it how to fly.
To him that act had been of grievous sight,
But he survived not to behold the flight.
Strange doth it seem to grave and sober minds,
How the dear vice the simple votary blinds,
So that he goes to ruin smoothly on,
And scarcely feels he 's going, till he 's gone.

I had made over, in a lucky hour,
Funds for my Aunt, and placed beyond my power:
The rest was flown, I speak it with remorse,
And now a pistol seem'd a thing in course.

But though its precepts I had not obey'd,
Thoughts of my Bible made me much afraid
Of such rebellion, and though not content,
I must live on when life's supports were spent;
Nay, I must eat, and of my frugal Aunt
Must grateful take what gracious she would grant;
And true, she granted, but with much discourse;
Oh! with what words did she her sense enforce!
Great was her wonder, in my need that I
Should on the prop myself had raised rely—
I, who provided for her in my care,
"Must be assured how little she could spare!"

I stood confounded, and with angry tone,
With rage and grief, that blended oath and groan,
I fled her presence—yet I saw her air
Of resignation, and I heard her prayer;
"Now Heaven," she utter'd, "make his burden light!"—
And I, in parting, cried, "Thou Hypocrite!"

But I was wrong—she might have meant to pray;
Though not to give her soul—her cash—away.

Of course, my Uncle would the spendthrift shun,
So friends on earth I now could reckon none.

One morn I rambled, thinking of the past,
Far in the country—Did you ever fast
Through a long summer's day? or, sturdy, go
To pluck the crab, the bramble, and the sloe,
The hyp, the cornel, and the beech, the food
And the wild solace of the gypsy brood?
To pick the cress embrown'd by summer sun,
From the dry bed where streams no longer run?
Have you, like school-boy, mingling play and toil,
Dug for the ground-nut, and enjoy'd the spoil?
Or chafed with feverish hand the ripening wheat,
Resolved to fast, and yet compell'd to eat?

Say, did you this, and drink the crystal spring,
And think yourself an abdicated king,
Driven from your state by a rebellious race?
And in your pride contending with disgrace,
Could you your hunger in your anger lose,
And call the ills you bear the ways you choose?

Thus on myself depending, I began
To feel the pride of a neglected man;
Not yet correct, but still I could command
Unshaken nerves, and a determined hand.

"Lo! men at work!" I said, "and I a man
Can work! I feel it is my pride, I can."
This said, I wander'd on, and join'd the poor,
Assumed a labourer's dress and was no more
Than labour made—Upon the road I broke
Stones for my bread, and startled at the stroke;
But every day the labour seem'd more light,
And sounder, sweeter still the sleep of every night

"Thus will I live," I cried, "nor more return
To herd with men, whose love and hate I spurn
All creatures toil; the beast, if tamed or free,
Must toil for daily sustenance like me;

The feather'd people hunt as well as sing,
And catch their flying food upon the wing.
The fish, the insect, all who live, employ
Their powers to keep on life, or to enjoy,
Their life th' enjoyment; thus will I proceed,
A man from man's detested favours freed."

Thus was I reasoning, when at length there came
A gift, a present, but without a name.
"That Spinster-witch, has she then found a way
To cure her conscience, and her Nephew pay,
And sends her pittance? Well, and let it buy
What sweetens labour; need I this deny?
I thank her not; it is as if I found
The fairy-gift upon this stony ground."

Still I wrought on; again occurred the day,
And then the same addition to my pay.

Then, lo! another Friend, if not the same,
For that I knew not, with a message came—
"Canst keep accounts?" the man was pleased to ask—
"I could not cash!—but that the harder task."
"Yet try," he said; and I was quickly brought,
To Lawyer Snell, and in his office taught.
Not much my pay, but my desires were less,
And I for evil days reserved th' excess.

Such day occurr'd not; quickly came there one,
When I was told my present work was done:
My Friend then brought me to a building large,
And gave far weightier business to my charge.
There I was told I had accounts to keep,
Of those vast Works, where wonders never sleep,
Where spindles, bobbins, rovings, threads, and pins,
Made up the complex mass that ever spins.

There at my desk, in my six feet of room,
I noted every power of every loom;
Sounds of all kinds I heard from mortal lungs—
Eternal battle of unwearied tongues,
The jar of men and women, girls and boys,
And the huge Babel's own dull whirring grinding noise.

My care was mark'd, and I had soon in charge
Important matters, and my pay was large.
I at my fortune marvell'd; it was strange,
And so the outward and the inward change,
Till to the power who "gives and takes away"
I turn'd in praise, and taught my soul to pray.

Another came! "I come," he said, "to show
Your unknown Friend—have you a wish to know?"
Much I desired, and forth we rode, and found
My Uncle dying, but his judgment sound.
The good old man, whom I abused, had been
The guardian power, directing but unseen;
And thus the wild but grateful boy he led
To take new motives at his dying bed.

The rest you judge—I now have all I need—
And now the tale you promised!—Come, proceed.

P.—'T is due, I own, but yet in mercy spare:
Alas! no Uncle was my guide—my care
Was all my own; no guardian took a share.
I, like Columbus, for a world unknown—
'T was no great effort—sacrificed my own—
My own sad world, where I had never seen
The earth productive, or the sky serene.

But this is past—and I at length am come
To see what changes have been wrought at home;
Happy in this, that I can set me down
At worst a stranger in my native town.

F.—Then be it so! but mean you not to show
How time has pass'd? for we expect to know;
And if you tell not, know you we shall trace
Your movements for ourselves from place to place,
Your wants, your wishes, all you 've sought or seen,
Shall be the food for our remark and spleen.
So, warn'd in time, the real page unfold,
And let the Truth, before the Lie, be told.

P.—This might be done; but wonders I have none;
All my adventures are of Self alone.

F.—What then? I grant you, if your way was clear,
All smooth and right—We 've no desire to hear;
But if you 've lewd and wicked things to tell,
Low passions, cruel deeds, nay crimes—'t is well:
Who would not listen?——
P.—Hark! I hear the bell.
It calls to dinner with inviting sound,
For now we know where dinners may be found,
And can behold and share the glad repast,
Without a dread that we behold our last.

F.—Come then, shy friend, let doleful subjects cease,
And thank our God that we can dine in peace.

THE END OF CRABBE'S POEMS.

THE

POETICAL WORKS

OF

REGINALD HEBER, D.D.

LORD BISHOP OF CALCUTTA.

Contents.

MEMOIR

OF THE

Right Rev. Reginald Heber, D.D.

SECOND BISHOP OF CALCUTTA.

Among the distinguished men of the present age, the late Bishop Heber, of Calcutta, deserves a high rank, as a most accomplished poet, as an acute, discriminating, pious, and learned divine; as a traveller possessing the talent of accurate observation and perseverance in a very high degree; but, especially, as a most disinterested and devoted Christian bishop and missionary, he has left behind nim an imperishable memory.

Reginald Heber was the second son of the Rev. Reginald Heber, and was born on the 21st of April, 1783, at Malpas, in Cheshire, England, where his father then held a pastoral charge. His mother was Mary Allanson, daughter of the Rev. Dr. Allanson, of the same county. So that he may be said to have been of Levitical descent: a circumstance which, probably, was not without influence upon his mind from a very early period. The earliest dawnings of his mind are said to have given promise of those christian graces, with which he was, through all the stages of his illustrious life, so richly endowed; and of those talents, which eventually gave him an eminent rank among the literary characters of the age. In his childhood, the eagerness with which he read the Bible, and the accuracy with which he treasured up large portions of it in his memory, were such as to excite observation; and this first application of his powers undoubtedly laid the foundation of that masterly knowledge of the Scriptures, which he subsequently attained; and to the perfecting of which, almost all his reading was made, directly or indirectly, to contribute. His literary education was commenced at the grammar school of Whitchurch, pursued under Dr. Bristowe, a teacher near London, and was completed at Brazen-nose college, Oxford, where he was entered in 1800. "At the university," said his early friend, Sir Charles Grey, at the time of his decease Chief-justice of Calcutta, "he was, beyond all question or comparison, the most distinguished student of his time. The name of Reginald Heber was in every mouth; his society was courted by young and old; he lived in an atmosphere of favour, admiration, and regard, from which I have never known any one but himself, who would not have derived, and for life, an unsalutary influence."

The next year he gained the chancellor's prize at the university, by his Latin verse, "Carmen Seculare." In 1803, when but little more than nineteen years of age, occurred one of those happy coincidences which occasionally make the paths of duty and of pleasure the way to enduring fame; a prize subject, for English verse, was that year assigned, which awaked "all that was within him,"—*Palestine.* Upon this theme he wrote, and with signal success. It was recited, as usual, in the theatre, with much diffidence on the part of the author, to a greatly admiring audience, among whom was his aged father, whose feelings were so overcome by the applause bestowed upon his son, that, immediately after the recitation, he mounted his horse, and returned to his home. The poem produced a great sensation. It procured the prize, was set to music, and brought to its author public and universal praise. The knowledge it displays of Scripture and of the Holy Land, its copious and flowing language, its beautifully diversified figures, and the exact discrimination, accurate conception, and pure taste which it displays throughout, have given it a deservedly high rank among the literature of the age. It has been said by an English critic, that this is almost the only university poem that has maintained its honours unimpaired, and entitled itself, after the lapse of years to be considered the property of the nation. In 1805, Mr. Heber obtained a third prize for an English essay, *On the Sense of Honour.*

Shortly after this, he left England in company with Mr. John Thornton, to make the tour of the eastern parts of Europe. The war, at that time prevailing between England and France, excluded English travellers from a large portion of the continent. Mr. Heber and his friend were, therefore, only able to visit some parts of Germany, Russia, and the Crimea. He made a copious journal of his travels; but as he did not think proper to present his observations to the public in his own name, when Dr. E. D. Clarke sent his volume of travels through Russia, Tartary, and Turkey, to the press, he allowed him the free use of his journal, of which Dr. Clarke availed himself to a considerable extent in the form of notes to his work, by which its value was certainly largely increased.

Dr. Clarke, in his preface, and in various parts of his volume, pays a well merited tribute to "the zealous attention to accuracy which appears in every statement" of Mr. Heber. Of the closeness and discrimination of his observations, the vivid recollection of Russian buildings, language, and incidents, which appear in his Indian journals, written nearly twenty years later, afford very striking proofs. What he saw in Hindoostan is repeatedly compared with what he recollected to have seen in Russia. He seems, at times, almost convinced that several Indian practices must have had a Russian origin, and he frequently detected himself in mingling Russian words with Hindoostanee when addressing the natives of India.* It was during this journey, and while in the city of Dresden, that he began a poem on *Europe*, which, however, he did not complete till after his return, and which he published in 1809. In the same year he published his poem of *Palestine*, to which he added another poem of a few lines, on the passage of the Israelites through the Red Sea.

He returned from the continent in 1807, and soon afterwards was admitted to holy orders, and inducted into his patrimonial preferment of Hodnet in Shropshire, estimated at 3000*l.* per annum, comprising the estate of his ancestors, which had been held by his father during the last years of his life. The patronage of this living had become vested in his family by a marriage with an heiress of the Vernon family. He now married Amelia, the daughter of Dr. Shipley, Dean of St. Asaph, and thenceforward willingly devoted himself to the enjoyment of the domestic charities, and to the discharge of those unobtrusive duties which fill up the life of a country clergyman. He was here surrounded by his relatives, and an intelligent and agreeable society. He possessed as many of the ingredients which make up the sum of human happiness as he could desire. The love of fame, however valuable in the eyes of most men, appears never to have had any strong hold upon his feelings, and, at this period, probably had none whatever. His society was indeed courted by the world which he was so well qualified to attract and gratify; but he had set before himself, in the spirit of the truest and noblest ambition, a course of secret virtue and self-denying diligence, in pursuing which, he rightly estimated, that it was the way to the purest earthly happiness, and that its brilliant termination would be richly worth every sacrifice, should he be called to any, which he could make for it. Devoted to his profession, he considered it his most honourable distinction to become the friend, the pastor, the spiritual guide of those whose spiritual interests had been committed to his charge. "He laboured to accommodate his instructions," says one of his friends, "to the comprehension of all; a labour by no means easy to a mind stored with classic elegance, and an imagination glowing with a thousand images of sublimity and beauty. He rejoiced to form his manners, his habits, and his conversation, to those who were entrusted to his care, that he might gain the confidence and affection of even the poorest among his flock; so that he might more surely win their souls to God, and finally, in the day of the last account, present every man faultless before his presence with exceeding joy. He was, above all, singularly happy in his visitation of the sick, and in administering consolation to those that mourned; and his name will long be dear, and his memory most precious, in the cottages of the poor, by whose sick beds he has often stood as a ministering angel." "His sermons," says another of his friends, "were very original—sometimes expanding into general views of the scheme and doctrines of revelation, collected from an intimate acquaintance, not with commentators, but with the details

* We may introduce here Mr. Heber's account of a visit which Mr. Thornton and himself paid to the celebrated Plato, archbishop of Moscow, taken from Dr. Clarke's travels, to which it is annexed as a note.

"There is a passage in Mr. Heber's journal very characteristic of this extraordinary man. Mr. Heber, with his friend Mr. Thornton, paid him a visit in the convent of Befania; and, in his description of the monastery, I find the following account of the archbishop. 'The space beneath the rocks is occupied by a small chapel, furnished with a stove, for winter devotion; and on the right hand is a little, narrow cell, containing two coffins, one of which is empty, and destined for the present archbishop; the other contains the bones of the founder of the monastery, who is regarded as a saint. The oak coffin was almost bit to pieces by different persons afflicted with the tooth-ach, for which a rub on this board is a specific. Plato laughed as he told us this; but said, 'As they do it *de bon cœur*, I would not undeceive them.' This prelate has been long very famous in Russia, as a man of ability. His piety has been questioned; but from his conversation we drew a very favourable idea of him. Some of his expressions would rather have singed the whiskers of a very orthodox man; but the frankness and openness of his manners, and the liberality of his sentiments, pleased us highly. His frankness on the subjects of politics pleased us highly. The clergy throughout Russia are, I believe, inimical to their government; they are more connected with the peasants than most other classes of men, and are strongly interested in their sufferings and oppressions; to many of which they themselves are likewise exposed. They marry very much among the daughters and sisters of their own order, and form almost a caste. I think Buonaparte rather popular among them. Plato seemed to contemplate his success as an inevitable and not very alarming prospect. He refused to draw up a form of prayer for the success of the Russian arms. 'If,' said he, 'they are really penitent and contrite, let them shut up their places of public amusement for a month, and I will then celebrate public prayers.' His expressions of dislike to the nobles and wealthy classes were strong and singular; as also the manner in which he described the power of an emperor of Russia, the dangers which surround him, and the improbability of any rapid improvement. 'It would be much better,' said he, 'had we a constitution like that of England.' Yet I suspect he does not wish particularly well to us in our war with France."—*Heber's MS. Journal.*

of holy writ itself, frequently drawing ingenious lessons for christian conduct, from the subordinate parts of a parable, a miracle, or a history, which a less imaginative mind would have overlooked—often enlivened by moral stories, with which his multifarious reading supplied him; and occasionally by facts which had come, perhaps, under his own observation, and which he thought calculated to give spirit or perspicuity to the truths he was imparting: a practice which, when judiciously restrained, is well adapted to secure the rustic hearer from the fate of Eutychus, without giving offence even to nicer brethren: of which the powerful effect is discoverable (though the figures may be grosser than the times would now admit) in the sermons of Latimer and the Reformers; subsequently, in those of Taylor and South; and still more recently in the popular harangues of Whitfield and Wesley; and a practice we will add, which derives countenance and authority from the use of parables in the preaching of our Lord." Both in the pulpit and in his ordinary conversation, his language was polished, yet seldom above the reach of a country congregation; and when occasion required, was dealt out to them in a way it was impossible to misunderstand. Frequently he indulged in bold and striking metaphors, and he was always attractive in the happy adoption of expressions from the pure and undefiled English of the Bible, with which his mind was thoroughly imbued, and which he could call up at will.

It was while engaged in this way, that he found time for the occasional composition of some hymns, of which he originally intended to prepare a series, adapted to the English Church service throughout the year, for the use of his own parish. A few of them were first published in the Christian Observer for 1811 and 1812, introduced by a brief statement of the motives which led to their composition, which were correct in themselves, and highly creditable to the author.* From some cause he never completed the task which he had set for himself; but among those which he did prepare, there are some very beautiful specimens of devotional poetry, which would alone be sufficient to preserve his memory from decay. Some of them, as his missionary hymn, have obtained a very just celebrity; and there are few readers of poetry who are not familiar with that beautiful piece, beginning *Brightest and best of the sons of the morning*.†

* This statement may be found preceding the Hymns in this volume.

† While on his primary visitation, at Meerut, in the heart of India, he was delightfully surprised at hearing some of these hymns sung in the church where he was preaching. "I had the gratification," he says in his journal, "of hearing my own hymns, 'Brightest and best of the sons of the morning,' and that for St. Stephen's day, sung better than I ever heard them in church before."

In 1812 he published a small volume of poems, including, beside those we have already alluded to, with the exception of the hymns, some translations of Pindar, and one or two smaller pieces.

In 1815, he was chosen, though still young, and only in the first eligible degree, to deliver the Bampton Lectures before the university of Oxford. The lectures, conformably to the directions of the founder, were published the ensuing year, under the title of "The Personality and Office of the Christian Comforter asserted and explained in a course of Sermons on John xvi. 7." Of these lectures it has been said by a judicious and able critic, that the author "has displayed much depth and accuracy of investigation; an extensive acquaintance with the hidden stores of learning, whether laid up in the writings of the ancient philosophers and poets, the Christian fathers of the Greek and Latin churches, or the still more recondite Rabbinical compilers; and a richness and *grandiloquism* of expression, which, to say the least of it, is fully as appropriate to the poet of Palestine as to the Bampton lecturer. The immense mass of learning introduced into this volume is doubtless very creditable to the powers and industry of Mr. Heber."

A few critical essays, both theological and literary, which appeared in the periodical publications of the day, without his name, and an ordination sermon, printed at the request of the Bishop of Chester, before whom it was delivered, comprise all his literary labours from the date last named, till 1822, when he again appeared before the public, as the editor of an edition of the works of Jeremy Taylor, to which he annexed an account of the life of Bishop Taylor, and a review of his writings from his own eloquent pen. While this work exhibits advancement to a more ripened knowledge, and improvement in taste and style, it derives a great interest, from the evident sympathy with which Mr. Heber regards the life and writings of that heavenly-minded man. Taylor and Heber have, indeed, been thought to possess much in common, a poetical habit of mind, disgust at intolerance, great simplicity of character and feeling, a hatred of every thing sordid and contracted, a love for practical rather than speculative religion, and a degree of faith, not the less bright and towering, because connected with a lofty imagination.

It was about the same time, that he was elected preacher at Lincoln's Inn, which, requiring his residence for a short period of each year in London, brought him occasionally into more conspicuous society, and withdrew him, in a measure, from that retirement, and even obscurity, which he had appeared to court, and brought out his many virtues in a light more fitted to show forth their value, and to give them the influence they might reasonably challenge. The greater part of the year was, however, still spent by him at Hodnet, where he had now erected a dwelling for his permanent residence.

In this manner upwards of fifteen years had passed away since he had settled at Hodnet, during which he was in the enjoyment of all the benefits of refined society, and all the blessings of domestic life, which no one could more highly appreciate. His income was much more than competent to all his wants, and his pure and well balanced mind was satisfied with his enjoyments. He sought not distinction, but gifted as he was with the means of being useful to mankind, it was beyond his power to avoid it. If he had desired eminence, the way was plainly open before him, and he had only to put forth those powers with which he was so liberally endowed, to reach it. If ambition had been his object, he would have been fully justified in indulging sanguine hopes of advancement in England. Among the whole bench of English prelates, if talents and virtues constitute a claim, there was none better entitled to his seat, or more capable of adorning it, than Reginald Heber would have been.

On the death of Dr. Middleton, the first English Bishop of Calcutta, the diocesan charge of the English Churches in India was offered to him. Reluctance to leave his aged mother, and his country, made him at once decline the offer. But its acceptance was pressed upon him by friends, whose opinions he highly estimated; and after the lapse of a week, spent in devout meditation and prayer to Him who holds the destinies of man, he desired that this station, of which *the honour* most certainly, to use the language of Jeremy Taylor, *would not pay the burthen*, if not already disposed of, might be entrusted to him. He bent himself holily to that overruling Providence, which, in all the incidents of his life, he never ceased to regard as working all things for good. And when the appointment was, at length, given him, a distrustful and uneasy sensation, which had distressed his mind at the apprehension that he might have shrunk, in too cowardly a spirit, from the obvious dictates of duty, passed away, and he acquired new confidence in himself, from the conviction that he had acted rightly. "I can say with confidence," he wrote to a friend at this time, "that I have acted for the *best;* and even now, that the die is cast, I feel no regret at the resolution I have taken, nor any distrust of the mercies and goodness of Providence, who may protect both me and mine, and, if he sees best for us, bring us back again, and preserve our excellent friends to welcome us."*

When Mr. Heber's acceptance of the bishopric of Calcutta was announced to his friends, the intelligence was received with surprise by some, and with deep regret by many, whose personal feelings were too powerful to be altogether excluded from the question. Satisfied, as they were, that a bright career was open for him at home, and not taking the enlarged view of human duty which was familiar to him, they suffered their own selfish delight in his society and honours to interfere with his ardent desire *to do good to all men.* Bishop Middleton, too, it was well known, had sunk under the heavy duties of the station, joined to the debilitating effects of a tropical clime; and to many of Mr. Heber's friends, it seemed that he was too ready to go, crowned indeed with flowers, like a victim to the sacrifice. It was, moreover, believed, by some of those who would have dissuaded him from the duty, that his character possessed some points, which, however amiable in themselves, were calculated to prevent that eminent degree of success, which could atone for the sacrifice he was to make, and the hazard he was certainly to encounter. It was thought, too, that the striking simplicity of his taste and manners would be little suited to a country where the object chiefly sought was wealth, and where pomp and show were universal idols. There was, too, about him, notwithstanding all he had seen and read of human life and human character, a prodigality of kindness and confidence in his nature, which would render it very difficult for him, it was supposed, to oppose himself with sufficient decision to the many obstacles which he might meet with, in a course of government, yet barely tried upon those who were to be the subjects of it, and among whom many conflicting interests were likely to appear. No misgivings, however, of this kind, ever occurred to his own mind. He knew, and had weighed well the various difficulties with which Christianity had to contend in India, and, modest and humble as he was, he had anxiously studied the quality and bent of his own resources in regard to them. The more he thought of the matter in this light, the more strongly was he convinced that India was the proper field for his Christian labours, and having brought his mind to this result, he determined that no sense of personal gratification or comfort, nor any hope of future dignity, should interfere with a conviction, which he deliberately regarded as a voice from heaven, speaking to his conscience.

On Sunday, the twentieth of April, he took leave of his congregation, in a discourse which has been repeatedly published, in the close of which he bade them farewell, in the following pious,

* In explanation of this expression, it is stated, that in consequence of the peculiarity of the service in India, the bishops and chaplains of the Anglo-Indian Church are allowed to return to England after a certain term of service

beautiful, and even eloquent expressions, the universal admiration of which has been amply proved by the frequency with which they have appeared in print:

"My ministerial labours among you must have an end; I must give over into other hands, the task of watching over your spiritual welfare; and many, very many, of those with whom I have grown up from childhood, in whose society I have passed my happiest days, and to whom it has been, during more than fifteen years, my duty and my delight (with such ability as God has given me) to preach the gospel of Christ, must, in all probability, see my face in the flesh no more. Under such circumstances, and connected with many who now hear me by the dearest ties of blood, of friendship, and of gratitude, some mixture of regret is excusable, some degree of sorrow is holy. I can not, without some anxiety for the future, forsake, for an untried and arduous field of duty, the quiet scenes, where, during so much of my past last life, I have enjoyed a more than usual share of earthly comfort and prosperity; I can not bid adieu to those with whose idea almost every recollection of past happiness is connected, without many earnest wishes for their welfare, and (I will confess it) without some severe self-reproach, that, while it was in my power, I have done so much less than I ought to have done, to render that welfare eternal. There are, indeed, those here who know, and there is *One*, above all, who knows better than any of you, how earnestly I have desired the peace and the holiness of his church; how truly I have loved the people of this place; and how warmly I have hoped to be the means, in his hand, of bringing many among you to glory. But I am at this moment but too painfully sensible, that in many things, yea in all, my performance has fallen short of my principles; that neither privately nor publicly have I taught you with so much diligence as now seems necessary in my eyes: nor has my example set forth the doctrines in which I have, however imperfectly, instructed you; yet, if my zeal has failed in steadiness, it never has been wanting in sincerity. I have expressed no conviction which I have not deeply felt; have preached no doctrine which I have not steadfastly believed: however inconsistent my life, its leading object has been your welfare—and I have hoped, and sorrowed, and studied, and prayed for your instruction, and that you might be saved. For my labours, such as they were, I have been indeed most richly rewarded, in the uniform affection and respect which I have received from my parishioners; in their regular and increasing attendance in this holy place, and at the table of the Lord; in the welcome which I have never failed to meet in the houses both of rich and poor; in the regret (beyond my deserts, and beyond my fullest expectations) with which my announced departure has been received by you; in your expressed and repeated wishes for my welfare and my return; in the munificent token of your regard, with which I have been this morning honoured;* in your numerous attendance on the present occasion, and in those marks of emotion which I witness around me, and in which I am myself well nigh constrained to join. For all these accept such thanks as I can pay—accept my best wishes—accept my affectionate regrets—accept the continuance of the prayers which I have hitherto offered up for you daily, and in which, whatever or wherever my sphere of duty may hereafter be, my congregation of Hodnet shall (believe it!) never be forgotten."

His consecration to the office of bishop took place in May, 1823. A few days previous to this event, he wrote to a friend in the country: "My consecration is fixed for next Sunday; and, as the time draws near, I feel its awfulness very strongly —far more, I think, than the parting which is to follow a fortnight after. I could wish to have the prayers of my old congregation, but know not how to express the wish in conformity with custom, or without seeming to court notoriety."

Shortly after his consecration, a special meeting of the ancient Society for Promoting Christian Knowledge, which had for some years been engaged in active benevolent operations in India, and which comprises many of the most eminent members of the Church of England, was called, for the purpose of giving Bishop Heber a public dismissal and farewell. There were present on this occasion, the Archbishop of Canterbury, several of the Bishops, and a large and highly respectable attendance of the fair, the wise, and the pious of the realm. The Bishop of Bristol pronounced a valedictory address to him in the name of that venerable body, at once dignified, impressive, and affectionate. From this address the following passage is extracted, and while it does no more than justice to the motives of Bishop Heber, it will at the same time be gratifying to the reader.

"My Lord—The Society for promoting Christian Knowledge desire to offer to your Lordship their sincere congratulations upon your elevation to the Episcopal See of Calcutta.

"They derive from your appointment to this high office the certain assurance, that all the advantages which they have anticipated from the formation of a Church Establishment in India, will be realized; and that the various plans for the diffusion of true religion among its inhabitants, which have been so wisely laid and so auspiciously commenced by your lamented predecessor, will, under your superintendence and control, advance

* A piece of plate had been given Mr. Heber by his parishioners.

with a steady and uninterrupted progress. They ground this assurance upon the rare union of intellectual and moral qualities which combine to form your character. They ground it upon the steadfastness of purpose, with which, from the period of your admission into the ministry, you have exclusively dedicated your time and talents to the peculiar studies of your sacred profession; abandoning that human learning in which you had already shown that you were capable of attaining the highest excellence, and renouncing the certain prospect of literary fame. But, above all, they ground this assurance upon the signal proof of self-devotion, which you have given by your acceptance of the episcopal office. With respect to any other individual, who had been placed at the head of the Church Establishment in India, a suspicion might have been entertained that some worldly desire, some feeling of ambition, mingled itself with the motives by which he was actuated; but, in your case, such a suspicion would be destitute even of the semblance of truth: every enjoyment which a well regulated mind can derive from the possession of wealth, was placed within your reach: every avenue to professional distinction and dignity, if these had been the objects of your solicitude, lay open before you. What then was the motive which could incline you to quit your native land?—to exchange the delights of home for a tedious voyage to distant regions?—to separate yourself from the friends with whom you had conversed from your earliest years? What, but an ardent wish to become the instrument of good to others—a holy zeal in your Master's service—a firm persuasion, that it was your bounden duty to submit yourself unreservedly to his disposal; to shrink from no labour which he might impose; to count no sacrifice hard which he might require?"

In his reply the Bishop expressed "the settled purpose of his soul," to devote his best talents "to the great cause in which all their hearts were engaged, and for which it was not their duty only but their illustrious privilege to labour," and that he looked forward with pleasure to "the time when he should be enabled to preach to the natives of India in their own language." About the same time the University of Oxford conferred on him the Degree of Doctor in Divinity, by diploma.

On the sixteenth of June, he embarked for Calcutta; accompanied to the ship by a large number of his personal friends, who, as he modestly remarks in his Journal, were willing to let him see as much of them as possible before his departure. One of his first thoughts after the ship had sailed, was to propose daily evening prayers, and he was gratified at the readiness with which the captain assented to the proposal. He accordingly officiated as chaplain to the ship, reading prayers in the cuddy daily during the voyage. He read prayers and preached regularly once on each Sunday; and on one occasion, having on the previous Sunday discoursed to the passengers and crew, in the way of preparation, he administered the Lord's Supper, and was highly pleased; having been told to expect only one or two, that he had twenty-six or twenty-seven participants; and his gratification was much increased when he observed in the course of the evening of the same day, that "all the young men who had participated, had religious books in their hands, and that they appeared, indeed, much impressed."

The following incidents are extracted from his journal of the voyage as tending to show the character of his feelings at this interesting crisis. A few days after they had left land, a vessel passed the ship homeward bound. On this event he remarks, "my wife's eyes swam with tears as this vessel passed us, and there were one or two of the young men who looked wishfully after her. For my own part, I am well convinced all my firmness would go, if I allowed myself to look back, even for a moment. Yet, as I did not leave home and its blessings without counting the cost, I do not, and I trust in God, that I shall not, regret the choice I have made. But knowing how much others have given up for my sake, should make me more studious to make the loss less to them; and also, and above all, so to discharge my duty, as that they may never think that these sacrifices have been made in vain." Again; about a month after his departure, he writes—"How little did I dream at this time last year, that I should ever be in my present situation! How strange it now seems to me to recollect the interest which I used to take in all which related to southern seas and distant regions, to India and its oceans, to Australasia and Polynesia! I used to fancy I should like to visit them, but that I ever should, or could do so, never occurred to me. Now, that I shall see many of these countries, if life is spared to me, is not improbable. God grant that my conduct in the scenes to which he has appointed me may be such as to conduce to his glory, and to my own salvation through his Son." Such was the spirit in which this holy man denied himself, took up his cross, and followed Christ.

He arrived at Calcutta early in October, 1823, and immediately entered upon the duties of his office. That he did so with satisfaction to himself is proved by a letter to Mr. Wynn, his friend and connexion, who had anxiously pressed him to accept the office, written soon after his arrival. He says, "you will judge from my description that I have abundant reason to be satisfied with my present and future prospects; and that in the field which seems opened to me for extensive usefulness and active employment, I have more and more reason to be obliged to the friend who has placed me here."

In the following spring (May, 1824) he collected around him the Episcopal clergy of the presidency of Calcutta, and held a visitation. The number was but small, but he experienced much pleasure in bringing them together for mutual acquaintance, and in particular, that he might himself be enabled to acquire a knowledge of their characters and views. At this time he had the pleasure of ordaining the first native convert who was admitted to the ministry of the English Church, "in the person of Christian David, a black catechist of Ceylon, and a pupil of the celebrated Schwartz." On this occasion he delivered to the clergy an eloquent charge, in which he expatiated at large upon the qualities, principles, and habits, which to him appeared to be necessary to the usefulness of those who should undertake the labours of an Indian missionary. Delighting, through the whole of the time he passed in India, to be considered simply as its chief missionary, it may easily be believed that he dwelt on those topics *con amore*. In the following passage of that charge, he pours forth his soul in a strain of awful and indignant rebuke against the Abbe Dubois, and other opposers of Christian missions, which is scarcely to be paralleled in our language.

"Nor can it be a matter of reasonable surprise to any of us, that the exertions (missionary) of this kind, which the last fifteen years have witnessed, should have excited a mingled feeling of surprise and displeasure in the minds, not only of those who are strangers to the powerful and peculiar emotions which send forth the Missionary to his toil, but of those who, though themselves not idle, could not endure that God should employ other instruments besides; and were ready to speak evil of the work itself, rather than that others who followed not with them should cast out devils in the name of their common Master. To the former of these classes may be referred the louder opposition, the clamours, the expostulation, the alarm, the menace and ridicule which, some few years ago, were systematically and simultaneously levelled at whatever was accomplished or attempted for the illumination of our Indian fellow-subjects. We can well remember, most of us, what revolutions and wars were predicted to arise from the most peaceable preaching and argument; what taunts and mockery were directed against scholars who had opened to us the gates of the least accessible oriental dialects; what opprobrious epithets were lavished on men of whom the world was not worthy. We have heard the threats of the mighty; we have heard the hisses of the fool; we have witnessed the terrors of the worldly wise, and the unkind suspicions of those from whom the Missionary had most reason to expect encouragement. Those days are, for the present, gone by. Through the Christian prudence, the Christian meekness, the Christian perseverance, and indomitable faith of the friends of our good cause, and through the protection, above all, and the blessing of the Almighty, they are gone by! The angel of the Lord has, for a time, shut the mouths of these fiercer lions, and it is the false brother now, the pretended fellow-soldier in Christ, who has lift up his heel against the propagation of the Christian gospel.

"But thus it is that the power of antichrist hath worked hitherto and doth work. Like those spectre forms which the madness of Orestes saw in classical mythology, the spirit of religious party sweeps before us in the garb and with the attributes of pure and evangelical religion. The cross is on her shoulders, the chalice is in her hand, and she is anxiously busied, after her manner, in the service of Him by whose holy name she is also called. But outstrip her in the race, but press her a little too closely, and she turns round on us with all the hideous features of envy and of rage. Her hallowed taper blazes into a sulphurous torch, her hairs bristle into serpents, her face is as the face of them that go down to the pit, and her words are words of blasphemy!

"What other spirit could have induced a Christian minister, after himself, as he tells us, long labouring to convert the heathen, to assert that one hundred millions of human beings—a great, a civilized, an understanding, and most ancient people, are collectively and individually under the sentence of reprobation from God, and under a moral incapacity of receiving that gospel which the God who gave it hath appointed to be made known to all?

"What other spirit could have prompted a member of that church which professes to hold out the greatest comfort to sinners, to assert of a nation with whom, whatever are their faults, I, for one, should think it impossible to live long without loving them, that they are not only enslaved to a cruel and degrading superstition, but that the principal persons among them are sold to all manner of wickedness and cruelty; without mercy to the poor; without natural affection for each other; and this with no view to quicken the zeal of Christians, to release them from their miserable condition, but that Christians may leave them in that condition still, to the end that they may perish everlastingly?

"What other spirit, finally, could have led a Christian missionary, (with a remarkable disregard of truth, the proofs of which are in my hands,) to disparage the success of the different Protestant missions; to detract from the numbers, and vilify the good name of that ancient Sy rian church, whose flame, like the more sacred fire of Horeb, sheds its lonely and awful brightness over the woods and mountains of Malabar, and to assure us, (hear, Oh Israel!) in the same treatise, and almost in the same page, that the Christians of India are the most despised and wretched of its inhabitants; that whoever takes up the cross, takes up the hatred of his own people, the contempt of Europeans, loss of goods, loss of employment, destitution, and often beggary; and yet that it is *interest alone*, and a love of this world, which has induced, in any Hindu, even a temporary profession of the gospel?

"And this is the professed apologist of the people of India! My brethren, I have known the sharpness of censure, and I am not altogether without experience in the suffering of undeserved and injurious imputations. And, let the righteous smite me friendly, I shall receive it (I trust in God) with gratitude. Let my enemy write a book, so he be my open enemy, I trust (through the same Divine aid) to bear it or to answer it. But whatever reproofs I may deserve; to whatever calumnies I may be subjected; may the mercy of Heaven defend me from having a false friend for my vindicator!"

Soon after this he commenced his first visitation, accompanied by his friend and chaplain, the Rev. Martin Stowe, who had followed him from England. As it was late in the season before he could leave his family, which at first he intended should also accompany him, he was obliged to travel by water in preference to the then hazardous journey by land. He accordingly left Calcutta in a pinnace for Upper India, and ascended the Ganges as high as Allahabad, upwards of six hundred miles from Calcutta; stopping at all the principal places, and particularly wherever any official duty awaited him, or a congregation of Christians could be collected, however small; and though obliged to preach, as was often the case, within the contracted rooms of a temporary Indian dwelling house. At Dacca, he was called to the painful trial, for such his journal proves it to have been, of parting with his friend Stowe; who, from imprudent exposure, brought on himself a disease of the climate, which in a few days destroyed his life. Bishop Heber, in giving an account, which is pathetically descriptive of his loss, to Mrs. Heber, mentions incidentally, what he had not otherwise alluded to, that from the very beginning of the journey they had prayed and read together daily, and that, on the last Sunday which he saw, they had received the sacrament together; and adds, "I trust I shall never forget the deep contrition and humility, the earnest prayer, or the earnest faith in the mercies of Christ, with which he commended himself to God." And his pious habit of drawing instruction from every event, is finely illustrated in the following passage of the same letter. "One lesson has been very deeply imprinted on my heart by these few days. If this man's innocent and useful life (for I have no doubt that the greater part of his life has been both innocent and useful) offered so many painful recollections, and called forth such deep contrition, when in the hour of death he came to examine every instance of omission or transgression, how careful must we be to improve every hour, and every opportunity of grace, and so to remember God while we live, that we may not be afraid to think on him when dying! And, above all, how blessed and necessary is the blood of Christ to us all, which was poor Stowe's only and effectual comfort!" Any man might be proud of such an eulogy as he gave to the memory of his friend, which, indeed, he dwells upon in successive letters to Mrs. Heber, as if unable to abandon the subject. This lingering over the recollection of a deserving object evinces the strength of his attachment, and the more powerfully because alluded to incidentally, and in a way which he could not have supposed would meet any other eyes than those for whose special perusal the letters were intended.* In the same manner did he show the strength of his domestic feelings, when, a few days before the decease of Stowe, after indulging himself in a description of the beautiful scenery of the river in his journal, he suddenly, and, as if exultingly, remarks—"To-day I had the delight of hearing again from my wife, and this is worth all the scenery in the world!"

It was understood between the Bishop and Mrs. Heber, that they were to meet at Boglipoor, a place on the river some distance above Dacca, but the dangerous sickness of their children compelled Mrs. Heber to remain at Calcutta, and this feeling and sensitive man was doomed to be disappointed of the happy meeting he was anticipating, and to be deprived of the company of his beloved wife, in a journey which was yet to be extended through a whole year! In a letter to her at this period he says, "your joining me is out of the question;" and adds, "I am strangely tempted to come to you. But I fear it might be a compromise of my duty and a distrust of God! I feel most grateful indeed to him for the preservation of our invaluable treasures." And having said this he went on his way, in the path to which duty called.

From Allahabad he travelled on horseback, with, as is usual, and even necessary in that country, a considerable suite, to Almorah in the Himalaya mountains, and from thence across the country to Surat, where he embarked for Bombay; at

* His letter to Miss Stowe on the death of her brother is a fine specimen of the manner in which a feeling and Christian heart, though wounded, could pour consolation into a bosom more deeply wounded still.

which place he arrived on the 19th of April; and in a few days he had the delight of meeting his family, who came thither by sea from Calcutta, after an absence of more than ten months. On the route from Allahabad to Surat, he visited several small congregations of Christians; not a few of whom were native converts, concerning whom his journal contains many interesting anecdotes. He visited also each of the native courts which lay in his route, but, as he asserts in one of his letters, never went out of his way for objects of curiosity. He found, nevertheless, sufficient employment to keep his attention fully awake, for he says, "In every ride which I have taken, and in every wilderness in which my tent has been pitched, I have as yet found enough to keep my mind from sinking into the languor and apathy which have been regarded as natural to a tropical climate."

From Bombay he went with his family to Ceylon, where he remained several weeks, visiting the churches and performing the duties of his episcopal office. He held a visitation of his clergy at Colombo, and addressed them: among those present were two natives, one of whom was Christian David, who had been ordained by Bishop Heber himself, as before mentioned—the other had been educated at Cambridge, in England, and had married a respectable English woman; both these were chaplains on the colonial establishment. While here he exerted himself much to procure the reestablishment of the general system of schools and religious instruction, which the Dutch government had originated while in possession of the island, and which he was anxious to restore. Another object, which at the same time engrossed much of his attention, was a plan for furnishing facilities for literary and theological education to the native catechists, or "proponents," so as gradually to fit them for admission to holy orders, and make them the groundwork of a regular parochial clergy. To this end he suggested to some of the clergy, the translation of a few of the most popular English works into the Cingalese and Tamul languages. At Candy he was waited on by a deputation of the Bhuddist priests, whom Mrs. Heber describes as "dressed in long yellow robes, with the right arm and shoulder bare, and their heads and eye-brows closely shaven." On his return to Calcutta, after an absence of about fifteen months, which had been consumed in this visitation, he had the gratification of ordaining another native christian, Abdul Museeh, whom he describes as a venerable old man, a native of Lucknow, and an elegant Persian and Hindoostanee scholar. "He greatly impressed us all," says Bishop Heber, "with his deep apparent emotion, his fine voice and elegant pronunciation, as well as his majestic countenance and long white beard."

An individual who was present at the meeting of a missionary association at Calcutta, at which Bishop Heber presided, at this time, remarked of him, "It was truly encouraging to witness the kind spirit of Bishop Heber; there he was, some considerable time before the business of the evening began: in fact, the impression which his conduct made on my mind, was, that he felt as though every individual who attended the meeting conferred a personal favour on him."

In January, 1826, he again left Calcutta and his family, "with a heavy heart," on a visit to the churches in the Indian peninsula, and the now well known Syrian churches, of the Malabar coast. The following note in his journal, made while yet in the river, is interesting in its relation to his character, "We proceeded to the Sandheads, and dismissed the pilot. I was glad to learn from him, that a poor man who had once taken us up the river, and got miserably drunk on that occasion, had been greatly impressed with some good advice I had given him, and had since remained a water drinker. I wish my good counsels were always equally successful!"

During his stay at Madras he was gratified by the attention shown him by the Armenians in that city, and particularly with the presence, on one occasion, when he held a Confirmation, of their Archbishop Athanasius and two other dignified ecclesiastics, in his congregation. It is very evident from his journals, that a friendly and even brotherly intercourse with the ancient churches of the East lay very near his heart, and that he availed himself of every proper occasion to cultivate it. At one of his visitations, at Calcutta, he invited several of the principal Armenian ecclesiastics to meet his clergy at dinner at his own house; and he certainly excited in many of the members of that church a very high degree of respect for his person and character.

While at Madras he visited the Prince Azeem Khan, uncle and guardian to the Nawab of the Carnatic, accompanied by his clergy in their robes. They were received with as much state as this little court could muster; the prince being surrounded with a crowd of "Ullemah" or learned men. While the Bishop was conversing with the prince, some of these learned men expressed to Mr. Robinson, the Bishop's chaplain, their astonishment that the Bishop was without a beard, observing, (the Bishop says, with much truth,) that learned men lost much dignity and authority there by the effeminate custom of shaving. They also asked if the Bishop was the head of all the English church; and being told that he was the head in India, but that there was in England another clergyman superior to him, the question was repeated, "And does he not wear a beard?"

The time he spent in Madras was about a fortnight, and in this space he preached eleven times, besides presiding at a large society meeting, giving two large dinner parties, (for he was habitually given to hospitality,) and receiving and paying "visits innumerable." Circumstances which sufficiently show his love of action, and his disposition to fill up every moment of his time, with the duties belonging to his station.

On leaving Madras he passed the spot where, tradition says, the apostle St. Thomas was martyred. Bishop Heber thought this tradition well founded, and noted in his journal that he left the spot behind with regret, and should visit it, if he returned to Madras, with a reverent, though, he hoped, not a superstitious interest and curiosity. He reached Tanjore on the 25th of March, and on the 26th (Easter Sunday) preached an eloquent and impressive sermon on the resurrection, in the church, which, at the request of the native members of the congregation, he promised to have translated into the Tamul language and printed. In concluding the sermon, he in the most feeling manner impressed the duty of brotherly love upon all present, without regard to rank or colour. Divine service was performed the same evening in the Tamul language, when, to the agreeable surprise of all present, he pronounced the Apostolic benediction in that language. On Monday he held a confirmation. In the evening divine service was held in the chapel in the mission garden. At the conclusion, he addressed the missionaries present in an affectionate and animated manner; observing to them, that it was probably the last time that all present could expect to meet in this world; and exhorted them to diligence and perseverance by the example of Schwartz, near whose remains he was then standing. On the 28th, attended by his chaplain, and several missionaries of the district, he paid a visit of ceremony to the Rajah of Tanjore. On the 29th and 30th he visited and inspected the mission school and premises. On the 31st he departed for Trichonopoly. Of the feelings which governed him during this brief visit, a glowing but evidently not exaggerated description, has been given by the chaplain who accompanied him, Mr. Robinson. "The missions at Tanjore and this place," (Madras,) says Mr. Robinson, "awakened, in a most powerful degree, and beyond any thing he had previously seen, the affections of his heart; and to devise and arrange a plan for their revival and more extended prosperity, was the object which occupied him for many days; and to the last hour of his life, his anxious thoughts, his earnest prayers, and the concentrated energies of his mind. Again and again did he repeat to me that all which he had witnessed in the native congregations of these missions, their numbers, their general order, their devout attendance on the service of the church, exceeded every expectation he had formed; and that in their support and revival he saw the fairest hope of extending the Church of Christ. Never shall I forget the warm expressions of his delight, when on Easter-day he gathered them around him as his children, as one family with ourselves, administered to them the body and blood of our common Saviour, and blest them in their native tongue: and when in the evening of that day, he had seen before him no less than THIRTEEN HUNDRED* natives of those districts rescued from idolatry and superstition, and joining as with one heart and voice in the prayers and praises of our church,—I can never forget his exclamation, that *he would gladly purchase that day with years of life!*"

Bishop Heber arrived at Trichonopoly on the 1st of April; on the following day (Sunday), he preached to a crowded audience, and in the evening confirmed forty young persons, and the next morning at 6 o'clock he repeated this rite for the benefit of some native Christians. He returned home to breakfast; but, before sitting down, went into a cold bath, as he had done the two preceding days. His attendant, thinking that he staid more than the usual time, entered the apartment, and found his body at the bottom of the water, with the face downwards, and lifeless. The usual restoratives were immediately but ineffectually tried. The spirit had returned to God who gave it. On examination, it was discovered that a vessel had burst upon the brain, in consequence, as the medical attendants agreed, of the sudden plunge into the cold water, while he was warm and exhausted. His mortal remains were deposited on the north side of the altar of St. John's church, Trichonopoly.

The melancholy intelligence of this overwhelming calamity was communicated, in the most cautious manner, to his amiable and accomplished but unfortunate widow, by Lord Combermere, her relative. Bishop Heber left two children only, both of whom were daughters. He died in the forty-third year of his age.

Though his death is thus to be imputed to an apparent accident, yet there was reason to believe that his constitution, like that of his predecessor, gradually yielding to the effects of a tropical cli-

* Bishop Heber, in one of his letters, mentions the same number as being present on this occasion, and adds, "This however, is only in the city of Tanjore. There are scattered congregations, to the number of many thousand Protestant Christians, in all the neighbouring cities and villages; and the wicker-bound graves, each distinguished by a little cross of cane, of the poor people by the road side, are enough to tell even the most careless traveller that the country is, in a great measure, Christian."

mate, combined with active habits of exertion formed in a more temperate clime, and leading him to frequent, and somewhat too heedless an exposure of his person, even at times and in circumstances in which he is obliged to admit in his journals, that it was but a matter of ordinary prudence to leave his family behind, rather than to expose them. When he first ascended the Ganges, and before he had reached the termination of his voyage, Abdullah, a native convert, and faithful servant, whom he had first met in England, and who had accompanied him to India, on one occasion cautioned him tenderly against the exposure to which his habits of exertion constantly led him, concluding with the remark, "This has caused your hair to turn so gray since your arrival in India;" a period less than a year. In Oude, when on his way to the Himalaya mountains, he was taken ill on the road, with the country fever, brought on him, doubtless, by exposure to rain, and various changes of the atmosphere, which he had just before been compelled to endure on horseback. He was at this time without any companions but natives, and probably two days' ride from any physician. It pleased Providence to bless the remedies which he used, as he admits, in utter ignorance; and he was cheered during the three or four days in which he lay, almost hopeless, in his palanquin, at the road side, by the affectionate attentions, and kind consideration of his native servants. To such an extent did they carry this last particular, that, if any noise was made, even accidentally, within his hearing, several voices would softly urge "silence!" upon the involuntary offender. At this time he wrote to his mother and sister under the strong impression of impending death. His natural buoyancy of mind, and the ardour of his spirit, combined with the novel character of the circumstances in which he was placed, were probably the causes which made him thus thoughtless of himself. He knew, moreover, what extensive hopes of the regeneration of India had been made to rest upon him:—he knew that he was looked to as a powerful instrument in the hand of God to this end; that from his talents, his disposition, his personal habits, his principles, and above all his almost enthusiastic devotion, likening him in all these respects to the very chiefest of the apostles, much more than he could reasonably expect to accomplish, was anticipated. He had set before him, and never allowed to be absent from his mind, the maxim of his Divine Master,—*I must work the works of him that sent me while it is day; the night cometh when no man can work.* There was one, however, who watched with an anxious eye over his welfare, from whom it could not be concealed that, before the attack which proved fatal to him, decay had commenced its work, and that his personal appearance had undergone no trifling change. Indeed, it would seem to be but a waste of human life and human talent, to place any competent person, of sufficient age, whose habits have been formed in Europe, in the oversight of such a diocese as British India, with Polynesia and Australasia, forms. And yet this was Bishop Heber's lot.*

Of his death it has been beautifully said, that "His sun was in its meridian power; and its warmth most genial when it was suddenly eclipsed, forever. He fell as the standard bearer of the cross should ever wish to fall, by no lingering decay, but in the firmness and vigour of his age, and in the very act of combat and triumph. His Mas-

* Of the extent and burthensome character of the business details of his office he gave the following account in a letter to his friend and successor at Hodnet, the Rev. J. J. Blunt.

"I do not think, that, in the regular and ordinary functions of my diocese, there is more, or even so much to be done, as in any of the more extensive bishoprics of England; the small number of the clergy must prevent this being the case. But on the other hand, every thing which is done must be done by myself, both in its spirit and its details; and partly owing to the manner in which we are scattered, and partly to the general habit of the country, all must be done in writing. Questions, which in England would not occupy more than five minutes conversation, may here sometimes call for a letter of six or eight pages; and as nothing, or almost nothing, which concerns the interests or duties of the clergy, can be settled without a reference to Government, I have, in fact, at least two sets of letters to write and receive, in every important matter which comes before me. As visiter of Bishop's College, I receive almost every week six or seven sheets of close writing on the subject. I am called on to give an opinion on the architecture, expense, and details of every church which is built, or proposed to be built, in India; every application for salary of either clerk, sexton, schoolmaster, or bell-ringer, must pass through my hands, and be recommended in a letter to Government. I am literally the conductor of all the missions in the three presidencies; and what is most serious of all, I am obliged to act in almost every thing from my own single judgment, and on my own single responsibility, without any more experienced person to consult, or any precedent to guide me. I have, besides, not only the Indian clergy and the Indian government to correspond with, but the religious societies at home, whose agent I am, and to whom I must send occasional letters, the composition of each of which occupies me many days: while in the scarcity of clergy which is, and must be felt here, I feel myself bound to preach, in some one or other of the churches or stations, no less frequently than when I was in England.

"All this, when one is stationary at Calcutta, may be done, indeed, without difficulty: but my journeys throw me sadly into arrears; and you may easily believe, therefore, not only that I am obliged to let slip many opportunities of writing to my friends at home, but that my leisure for study amounts to little or nothing; and that even the native languages, in which it has been my earnest desire to perfect myself, I am compelled to acquire very slowly, and by conversation more than by reading. With all this, however, in spite of the many disadvantages of climate and banishment, I am bound to confess that I like both my employments and my present country."

ter came suddenly, and found him faithful in his charge, and waiting for his appearing. His last hour was spent in his Lord's service, and in ministering to the humblest of his flock. He had scarcely put off the sacred robes with which he served at the altar of his God on earth, when he was suddenly admitted to his sanctuary on high, and clothed with the garments of immortality."

Immediately on the intelligence of his death, public meetings were called at Calcutta, at Madras, and at Bombay, in which eulogies were pronounced upon his character, by those who had known him long,* and who gave to his memory the highest expressions of their praise.

It has been determined to erect monuments to the memory of Bishop Heber at Calcutta, at Madras, and in St. Paul's cathedral, London, and at Oxford. Several scholarships have been founded in Bishop's College, near Calcutta, which, from the same motive, are to bear his name. The monument at Madras has been already erected.

* The chief justices of the three presidencies who were present at these meetings, were by a singular coincidence his contemporaries at college.

Tributes to the memory of Bishop Heber.

BY FELICIA HEMANS.

If it be sad to speak of treasures gone,
Of sainted genius called too soon away,
Of light, from this world taken while it shone,
Yet kindling onward to the perfect day—
How shall our grief, if mournful these things be,
Flow forth, O guide and gifted friend! for thee?

Hath not thy voice been here amongst us heard?
And that deep soul of gentleness and power,
Have we not felt its breath in every word,
Wont from thy lip, as Hermon's dew, to shower?
Yes! in our hearts thy fervent thoughts have burned—
Of heaven they were, and thither are returned.

How shall we mourn thee?—With a lofty trust,
Our life's immortal birthright from above!
With a glad faith, whose eye, to track the just,
Through shades and mysteries lifts a glance of love,
And yet can weep!—for Nature so deplores
The friend that leaves us, though for happier shores.

And one high tone of triumph o'er thy bier,
One strain of solemn rapture be allowed!
Thou that, rejoicing on thy mid-career,
Not to decay, but unto death hast bowed!
In those bright regions of the rising sun,
Where Victory ne'er a crown like thine hath won.

Praise, for yet one more name, with power endowed,
To cheer and guide us onward as we press,
Yet one more image on the heart bestowed,
To dwell there—beautiful in holiness!
Thine! Heber, thine! whose memory from the dead
Shines as the star, which to the Saviour led.

BY AMELIA OPIE.

How well I remember the day I first met thee!
'T was in scenes long forsaken, in moments long fled,
Then little thought I that a WORLD would regret thee!
And Europe and Asia *both* mourn for thee dead.

Ah! little I thought in those gay social hours,
That around thy young head e'en the laurel would twine,
Still less that a crown of the amaranth's flowers,
Enwreathed with the *palm*, would, O Heber! be thine.

We met in the world, and the light that shone round thee
Was the dangerous blaze of wit's meteor ray,
But e'en then, though unseen, mercy's angel had found thee,
And the bright star of Bethlehem was marking thy way.

To the banks of the Isis, a far fitter dwelling,
Thy footsteps returned, and thy hand to its lyre,
While thy heart with the bard's bright ambition was swelling,
But holy the theme was that wakened its fire.

Again in the world and with worldlings I met thee,
And then thou wert welcomed as *Palestine's bard*,
They had *scorned* at the task which the Saviour had set thee,
The Christian's rough labour, the martyr's reward.

Yet,* the one was my calling, thy portion the other;
The far shores of India received thee, and blest,
And its lowliest of teachers dared greet as a brother,
And love thee, though clad in the prelate's proud vest.

In the meek humble Christian forgot was thy greatness,
The follower they saw of a crucified Lord,
For thy zeal showed his spirit, thy accents his sweetness,
And the heart of the heathen drank deep of the word.

Bright as short was thy course, when "a coal from the altar"
Had touched thy blest lip, and the voice bade thee "Go,"
Thy haste could not pause, and thy step could not falter,
Till o'er India's wide seas had advanced thy swift prow.

In vain her fierce sun, with its cloudless effulgence,
Seemed arrows of death to shoot forth with each ray;
Thy faith gave to fear and fatigue no indulgence,
But *on to the goal* urged thy perilous way!

And, martyr of zeal! thou e'en *here* wert rewarded,
When the dark sons of India came round thee in throngs,
While thee as a father they fondly regarded,
Who taught them and blessed in their own native tongues.

When thou heard'st them, their faith's awful errors disclaiming,
Profess the pure creed which the Saviour had given,
Those moments thy mission's blest triumph proclaiming,
Gave joy which to thee seemed a foretaste of Heaven.†

Still "On," cried the voice, and surrounding their altar,
Trichonopoly's sons hailed thy labours of love:
Ah me! with no fear did thine accents then falter;
No secret forebodings thy conscious heart move?

* At first he refused the appointment, but, "after devout prayer" he accepted it, thinking it was his duty to do so.

† When they gathered round him on Easter-day evening to the number of thirteen hundred, and he blessed them in their native tongue, he exclaimed, "that he would gladly purchase that day with years of his life."—*Robinson's Sermon.*

Thou hadst ceased—having taught them what rock to rely on,
And had doft the proud robes which to prelates belong,
But the next robe for thee was the *white robe of Zion*,*
The next hymn thou heard'st was "the seraphim's song."

Here hushed be my lay for a far sweeter verse—
Thy requiem I'll breathe in thy numbers alone,
For the bard's votive offering to hang on thy hearse,
Should be formed of no language less sweet than thy own.

† "Thou art gone to the grave, but we will not deplore thee,
Since God was thy refuge, thy ransom, thy guide;
He gave thee, He took thee, and He will restore thee,
And death has no sting, since the Saviour has died."

ANONYMOUS.

How beautiful upon the mountains are the feet of him that bringeth good tidings, that publisheth peace; that bringeth good tidings of good, that publisheth salvation!—*Isaiah*, lii. 7.

How bright and glorious are the sun's first gleams
Above yon blue horizon!—Darkness flies
Before his presence.—Mountains, vallies, trees,
Glow with resplendent beauty.—And the streams
Reflect the lustre of his orient beams.
So *Heber* shone—for unto him was given
To spread the tidings of salvation round,
Whilst heathen nations caught the joyful sound,
And learned to kneel before the shrine of Heaven;
That "cross surmounted shrine," where Faith and Prayer
Point to the crown of bliss, reserved there
For those whom Jesus loves—but his bright sun
Of glory set, ere yet its race was run,
And he *that* bliss has gained—that crown has won!

* He had scarcely put off his robes in which he officiated at the altar, when he was suddenly called away 'to be clothed with immortality."—*Robinson's Sermon.*

† Written by Bishop Heber on the death of a friend See page 27.

THE

POETICAL WORKS

OF

REGINALD HEBER, D.D.

LORD BISHOP OF CALCUTTA.

Palestine;

A PRIZE POEM, RECITED IN THE THEATRE, OXFORD.

IN THE YEAR MDCCCIII.

REFT of thy sons, amid thy foes forlorn,
Mourn, widowed queen, forgotten Sion, mourn!
Is this thy place, sad City, this thy throne,
Where the wild desert rears its craggy stone?
While suns unblest their angry lustre fling,
And way-worn pilgrims seek the scanty spring?—
Where now thy pomp, which kings with envy viewed?
Where now thy might, which all those kings subdued?
No martial myriads muster in thy gate;
No suppliant nations in thy Temple wait;
No prophet bards, thy glittering courts among,
Wake the full lyre, and swell the tide of song:
But lawless Force, and meagre Want is there,
And the quick-darting eye of restless Fear;
While cold Oblivion, 'mid thy ruins laid,
Folds his dank wing(1) beneath the ivy shade.

Ye guardian saints! ye warrior sons of heaven,(2)
To whose high care Judæa's state was given!
O wont of old your nightly watch to keep,
A host of gods, on Sion's towery steep!(3)
If e'er your secret footsteps linger still
By Siloa's fount, or Tabor's echoing hill;
If e'er your song on Salem's glories dwell,
And mourn the captive land you loved so well;
(For oft, 'tis said, in Kedron's palmy vale
Mysterious harpings(4) swell the midnight gale,
And, blest as balmy dews that Hermon cheer,
Melt in soft cadence on the pilgrim's ear;)
Forgive, blest spirits, if a theme so high
Mock the weak notes of mortal minstrelsy!
Yet, might your aid this anxious breast inspire
With one faint spark of Milton's seraph fire,
Then should my Muse(5) ascend with bolder flight,
And wave her eagle-plumes exulting in the light.

O happy once in heaven's peculiar love,
Delight of men below, and saints above!
Though, Salem, now the spoiler's ruffian hand
Has loosed his hell-hounds o'er thy wasted land;
Though weak, and whelmed beneath the storms of fate,
Thy house is left unto thee desolate;(6)
Though thy proud stones in cumbrous ruin fall,
And seas of sand o'ertop thy mouldering wall;
Yet shall the Muse to Fancy's ardent view
Each shadowy trace of faded pomp renew:
And as the Seer(7) on Pisgah's topmost brow
With glistening eye beheld the plain below,
With prescient ardour drank the scented gale,
And bade the opening glades of Canaan hail;
Her eagle eye shall scan the prospect wide,
From Carmel's cliffs to Almotana's tide;(8)
The flinty waste, the cedar-tufted hill,
The liquid health of smooth Ardeni's rill;
The grot, where, by the watch-fire's evening blaze,
The robber riots, or the hermit prays;(9)
Or, where the tempest rives the hoary stone,
The wintry top of giant Lebanon.

Fierce, hardy, proud, in conscious freedom bold,
Those stormy seats the warrior Druses hold;(10)
From Norman blood their lofty line they trace,
Their lion courage proves their generous race.
They, only they, while all around them kneel
In sullen homage to the Thracian steel,
Teach their pale despot's waning moon to fear(11)
The patriot terrors of the mountain spear.

Yes, valorous chiefs, while yet your sabres shine,
The native guard of feeble Palestine,
O, ever thus, by no vain boast dismayed,
Defend the birthright of the cedar shade!

What though no more for you th' obedient gale
Swells the white bosom of the Tyrian sail;
Though now no more your glittering marts unfold
Sidonian dyes and Lusitanian gold;(12)
Though not for you the pale and sickly slave
Forgets the light in Ophir's wealthy cave;
Yet yours the lot, in proud contentment blest,
Where cheerful labour leads to tranquil rest.
No robber rage the ripening harvest knows;
And unrestrained the generous vintage flows:(13)
Nor less your sons to manliest deeds aspire,
And Asia's mountains glow with Spartan fire.
So when, deep sinking in the rosy main,
The western sun forsakes the Syrian plain,
His watery rays refracted lustre shed,
And pour their latest light on Carmel's head.
Yet shines your praise, amid surrounding gloom,
As the lone lamp that trembles in the tomb:
For few the souls that spurn a tyrant's chain,
And small the bounds of freedom's scanty reign.
As the poor outcast on the cheerless wild,
Arabia's parent,(14) clasped her fainting child,
And wandered near the roof no more her home,
Forbid to linger, yet afraid to roam:
My sorrowing Fancy quits the happier height,
And southward throws her half-averted sight.
For sad the scenes Judæa's plains disclose,
A dreary waste of undistinguished woes:
See War untired his crimson pinions spread,
And foul Revenge, that tramples on the dead!
Lo, where from far the guarded fountains shine,(15)
Thy tents, Nebaioth, rise, and Kedar, thine!(16)
'T is yours the boast to mark the stranger's way,
And spur your headlong chargers on the prey,
Or rouse your nightly numbers from afar,
And on the hamlet pour the waste of war;
Nor spare the hoary head, nor bid your eye
Revere the sacred smile of infancy.(17)
Such now the clans, whose fiery coursers feed
Where waves on Kishon's bank the whispering reed;
And theirs the soil, where, curling to the skies,(18)
Smokes on Samaria's mount her scanty sacrifice.
While Israel's sons, by scorpion curses driven,
Outcasts of earth, and reprobate of heaven,
Through the wide world in friendless exile stray,
Remorse and shame sole comrades of their way,
With dumb despair their country's wrong behold,
And, dead to glory, only burn for gold!
O Thou, their Guide, their Father, and their Lord,
Loved for thy mercies, for thy power adored!
If at thy name the waves forgot their force, (19)
And refluent Jordan sought his trembling source;
If at thy name like sheep the mountains fled,
And haughty Sirion bowed his marble head;—
To Israel's woes a pitying ear incline,
And raise from earth thy long-neglected vine!(20)
Her rifled fruits behold the heathen bear,
And wild-wood boars her mangled clusters tear!
Was it for this she stretched her peopled reign
From far Euphrates to the western main?
For this, o'er many a hill her boughs she threw
And her wide arms like goodly cedars grew?
For this, proud Edom slept beneath her shade,
And o'er the Arabian deep her branches played?
O feeble boast of transitory power!
Vain, fruitless trust of Judah's happier hour!
Not such their hope, when through the parted main
The cloudy wonder led the warrior train:
Not such their hope, when through the fields of night
The torch of heaven diffused its friendly light
Not, when fierce Conquest urged the onward war
And hurled stern Canaan from his iron car:
Nor, when five monarchs led to Gibeon's fight,
In rude array, the harnessed Amorite:(21)
Yes—in that hour, by mortal accents stayed,
The lingering sun his fiery wheels delayed;
The moon, obedient, trembled at the sound,
Curbed her pale car, and checked her mazy round!
Let Sinai tell—for she beheld his might,
And God's own darkness veiled her mystic height:
(He, cherub-borne, upon the whirlwind rode,
And the red mountain like a furnace glowed:)
Let Sinai tell—but who shall dare recite
His praise, his power,—eternal, infinite?—
Awe-struck I cease; nor bid my strains aspire,
Or serve his altar with unhallowed fire.(22)
Such were the cares that watched o'er Israel's fate,
And such the glories of their infant state.
—Triumphant race! and did your power decay?
Failed the bright promise of your early day?
No:—by that sword, which, red with heathen gore,
A giant spoil, the stripling champion bore;
By him, the chief to farthest India known,
The mighty master of the iv'ry throne;(23)
In heaven's own strength, high towering o'er her foes,
Victorious Salem's lion banner rose:
Before her footstool prostrate nations lay,
And vassal tyrants crouched beneath her sway.
—And he, the kingly sage, whose restless mind
Through nature's mazes wandered unconfined;(24)
Who ev'ry bird, and beast, and insect knew,
And spake of every plant that quaffs the dew;
To him were known—so Hagar's offspring tell—
The powerful sigil and the starry spell,
The midnight call, hell's shadowy legions dread,
And sounds that burst the slumbers of the dead.
Hence all his might; for who could these oppose?
And Tadmor thus, and Syrian Balbec rose.(25)
Yet e'en the works of toiling Genii fall,
And vain was Estakhar's enchanted wall.
In frantic converse with the mournful wind,
There oft the houseless Santon(26) rests reclined;

Strange shapes he views, and drinks with wondering ears
The voices of the dead, and songs of other years.
Such, the faint echo of departed praise,
Still sound Arabia's legendary lays;
And thus their fabling bards delight to tell
How lovely were thy tents, O Israel!(27)
For thee his iv'ry load Behemoth bore,(28)
And far Sofala teemed with golden ore;(29)
Thine all the arts that wait on wealth's increase,
Or bask and wanton in the beam of peace.
When Tyber slept beneath the cypress gloom,
And silence held the lonely woods of Rome;
Or ere to Greece the builder's skill was known,
Or the light chisel brushed the Parian stone;
Yet here fair Science nursed her infant fire,
Fanned by the artist aid of friendly Tyre.
Then towered the palace, then in awful state
The temple reared its everlasting gate.(30)
No workman steel, no pond'rous axes rung;(31)
Like some tall palm the noiseless fabric sprung.
Majestic silence!—then the harp awoke,
The cymbal clanged, the deep-voiced trumpet spoke;
And Salem spread her suppliant arms abroad,
Viewed the descending flame, and blessed the present God!(32)
Nor shrunk she then, when, raging deep and loud,
Beat o'er her soul the billows of the proud.(33)
E'en they who, dragged to Shinar's fiery sand,
Tilled with reluctant strength the stranger's land;
Who sadly told the slow-revolving years,
And steeped the captive's bitter bread with tears;
Yet oft their hearts with kindling hopes would burn,
Their destined triumphs, and their glad return,
And their sad lyres, which, silent and unstrung,
In mournful ranks on Babel's willows hung,
Would oft awake to chant their future fame,
And from the skies their ling'ring Saviour claim.
His promised aid could every fear control;
This nerved and warrior's arm, this steeled the martyr's soul!
Nor vain their hope:—Bright beaming through the sky,
Burst in full blaze the Day-spring from on high;
Earth's utmost isles exulted at the sight,
And crowding nations drank the orient light.
Lo, star-led chiefs Assyrian odours bring,
And bending Magi seek their infant King!
Marked ye, where, hov'ring o'er his radiant head,
The dove's white wings celestial glory shed?
Daughter of Sion! virgin queen! rejoice!
Clap the glad hand, and lift the exulting voice!
He comes,—but not in regal splendour drest,
The haughty diadem, the Tyrian vest;
Not armed in flame, all glorious from afar,
Of hosts the chieftain, and the lord of war:
Messiah comes: let furious discord cease:
Be peace on earth before the Prince of Peace!
Disease and anguish feel his blest control,
And howling fiends release the tortured soul;
The beams of gladness hell's dark caves illume,
And Mercy broods above the distant gloom.
Thou palsied earth, with noonday night o'erspread!
Thou sick'ning sun, so dark, so deep, so red!
Ye hov'ring ghosts, that throng the starless air,
Why shakes the earth? why fades the light? declare!
Are those his limbs, with ruthless scourges torn?
His brows, all bleeding with the twisted thorn?
His the pale form, the meek forgiving eye
Raised from the cross in patient agony?
—Be dark, thou sun—thou noonday night arise
And hide, oh hide, the dreadful sacrifice!
Ye faithful few, by bold affection led,
Who round the Saviour's cross your sorrows shed,
Not for his sake your tearful vigils keep;— [(34)
Weep for your country, for your children weep!
—Vengeance! thy fiery wing their race pursued;
Thy thirsty poniard blushed with infant blood.
Roused at thy call, and panting still for game,
The bird of war, the Latian eagle came.
Then Judah raged, by ruffian Discord led,
Drunk with the steamy carnage of the dead;
He saw his sons by dubious slaughter fall,
And war without, and death within the wall.
Wide-wasting Plague, gaunt Famine, mad Despair,
And dire Debate, and clamorous Strife were there:
Love, strong as Death, retained his might no more,
And the pale parent drank her children's gore.(35)
Yet they, who wont to roam th' ensanguined plain,
And spurn with fell delight their kindred slain;
E'en they, when, high above the dusty fight,
Their burning Temple rose in lurid light,
To their loved altars paid a parting groan,
And in their country's woes forgot their own.
As 'mid the cedar courts, and gates of gold,
The trampled ranks in miry carnage rolled,
To save their Temple every hand essayed,
And with cold fingers grasped the feeble blade:
Through their torn veins reviving fury ran,
And life's last anger warmed the dying man!
But heavier far the fettered captive's doom!
To glut with sighs the iron ear of Rome:
To swell, slow-pacing by the car's tall side,
The stoic tyrant's philosophic pride;(36)
To flesh the lion's rav'nous jaws, or feel
The sportive fury of the fencer's steel;
Or pant, deep plunged beneath the sultry mine,
For the light gales of balmy Palestine.
Ah! fruitful now no more, an empty coast,
She mourned her sons enslaved, her glories lost:

In her wide streets the lonely raven bred,
There barked the wolf, and dire hyænas fed.
Yet midst her towery fanes, in ruin laid,
The pilgrim saint his murmuring vespers paid;
'T was his to climb the tufted rocks, and rove
The chequered twilight of the olive grove;
'T was his to bend beneath the sacred gloom,
And wear with many a kiss Messiah's tomb:
While forms celestial filled his tranced eye,
The day-light dreams of pensive piety,
O'er his still breast a tearful fervour stole,
And softer sorrows charmed the mourner's soul.
Oh, lives there one, who mocks his artless zeal?
Too proud to worship, and too wise to feel?
Be his the soul with wintry Reason blest,
The dull, lethargic sovereign of the breast!
Be his the life that creeps in dead repose,
No joy that sparkles, and no tear that flows![(37)
Far other they who reared yon pompous shrine,
And bade the rock with Parian marble shine.(38)
Then hallowed Peace renewed her wealthy reign,
Then altars smoked, and Sion smiled again.
There sculptured gold and costly gems were seen,
And all the bounties of the British queen; (39)
There barb'rous kings their sandaled nations led,
And steel-clad champions bowed the crested head,
There, when her fiery race the desert poured,
And pale Byzantium feared Medina's sword,(40)
When coward Asia shook in trembling wo,
And bent appalled before the Bactrian bow;
From the moist regions of the western star
The wand'ring hermit waked the storm of war.(41)
Their limbs all iron, and their souls all flame,
A countless host, the red-cross warriors came:
E'en hoary priests the sacred combat wage,
And clothe in steel the palsied arm of age;
While beardless youths and tender maids assume
The weighty morion and the glancing plume.(42)
In sportive pride the warrior damsels wield
The pond'rous falchion, and the sun-like shield,
And start to see their armour's iron gleam
Dance with blue lustre in Tabaria's stream.(43)
The blood-red banner floating o'er their van,
All madly blithe the mingled myriads ran:
Impatient Death beheld his destined food,
And hovering vultures snuffed the scent of blood.
Not such the numbers, nor the host so dread,
By northern Brenn or Scythian Timur led,(44)
Nor such the heart-inspiring zeal that bore
United Greece to Phrygia's reedy shore!
There Gaul's proud knights with boastful mien advance,(45)
Form the long line,(46) and shake the cornel lance;
Here, linked with Thrace, in close battalions stand
Ausonia's sons, a soft inglorious band;
There the stern Norman joins the Austrian train,
And the dark tribes of late-reviving Spain;
Here in black files, advancing firm and slow,
Victorious Albion twangs the deadly bow:—
Albion,—still prompt the captive's wrong to aid,
And wield in freedom's cause the freeman's generous blade!
Ye sainted spirits of the warrior dead,
Whose giant force Britannia's armies led!(47)
Whose bickering falchions, foremost in the fight,
Still poured confusion on the Soldan's might;
Lords of the biting axe and beamy spear,(48)
Wide-conquering Edward, lion Richard, hear!
At Albion's call your crested pride resume,
And burst the marble slumbers of the tomb!
Your sons behold, in arm, in heart the same,
Still press the footsteps of parental fame,
To Salem still their generous aid supply,
And pluck the palm of Syrian chivalry!
When he, from towery Malta's yielding isle,
And the green waters of reluctant Nile,
Th' apostate chief,—from Misraim's subject shore
To Acre's walls his trophied banners bore;
When the pale desert marked his proud array,
And Desolation hoped an ampler sway;
What hero then triumphant Gaul dismayed?
What arm repelled the victor renegade?
Britannia's champion!—bathed in hostile blood,
High on the breach the dauntless seaman stood:
Admiring Asia saw th' unequal fight,—
E'en the pale crescent blessed the Christian's might.
Oh day of death! Oh thirst, beyond control,
Of crimson conquest in th' invader's soul!
The slain, yet warm, by social footsteps trod,
O'er the red moat supplied a panting road;
O'er the red moat our conquering thunders flew,
And loftier still the grisly rampire grew.
While proudly glowed above the rescued tower
The wavy cross that marked Britannia's power
Yet still destruction sweeps the lonely plain
And heroes lift the generous sword in vain.
Still o'er her sky the clouds of anger roll,
And God's revenge hangs heavy on her soul.
Yet shall she rise;—but not by war restored,
Not built in murder,—planted by the sword.
Yes, Salem, thou shalt rise: thy Father's aid
Shall heal the wound his chastening hand has made;
Shall judge the proud oppressor's ruthless sway,
And burst his brazen bonds, and cast his cords away.(49) [(50)
Then on your tops shall deathless verdure spring;
Break forth, ye mountains, and, ye valleys, sing!
No more your thirsty rocks shall frown forlorn,
The unbeliever's jest, the heathen's scorn;
The sultry sands shall tenfold harvests yield,
And a new Eden deck the thorny field.
E'en now, perchance, wide-waving o'er the land,
That mighty Angel lifts his golden wand,
Courts the bright vision of descending power,(51)
Tells every gate, and measures every tower;(52)

And chides the tardy seals that yet detain
Thy Lion, Judah, from his destined reign!
And who is He? the vast, the awful form,(53)
Girt with the whirlwind, sandaled with the storm?
A western cloud around his limbs is spread,
His crown a rainbow, and a sun his head.
To highest heaven he lifts his kingly hand,
And treads at once the ocean and the land;
And, hark! his voice amid the thunder's roar,
His dreadful voice, that time shall be no more!
Lo! cherub hands the golden courts prepare,
Lo! thrones arise, and every saint is there;(54)
Earth's utmost bounds confess their awful sway,
The mountains worship, and the isles obey;
Nor sun nor moon they need,—nor day, nor night;
God is their temple, and the Lamb their light:(55)
And shall not Israel's sons exulting come,
Hail the glad beam, and claim their ancient home?
On David's throne shall David's offspring reign,
And the dry bones be warm with life again.(56)
Hark! white-robed crowds their deep hosannas raise,
And the hoarse flood repeats the sound of praise;
Ten thousand harps attune the mystic song,
Ten thousand thousand saints the strain prolong;
"Worthy the Lamb! omnipotent to save,
"Who died, who lives, triumphant o'er the grave!"

NOTES.

Note 1, page 1, col. 1.

Folds his dank wing.

Alluding to the usual manner in which Sleep is represented in ancient statues. See also Pindar, Pyth. I. v. 16, 17. *κνωσσων υγρον νωτον αιωρει.*"

Note 2, page 1, col. 1.

Ye warrior sons of heaven.

Authorities for these celestial warriors may be found, Josh. v. 13. 2 Kings vi. 2. 2 Macc. v. 3. Ibid. xi. Joseph. Ed. Huds. vi. p. 1282. et. alibi passim.

Note 3, page 1, col. 1.

Sion's towery steep.

It is scarcely necessary to mention the lofty site of Jerusalem. "The hill of God is a high hill, even a high hill as the hill of Bashan."

Note 4, page 1, col. 1.

Mysterious harpings.

See Sandys, and other travellers into Asia.

Note 5, page 1, col. 1.

Then should my Muse.

Common practice, and the authority of Milton, seem sufficient to justify using this term as a personification of poetry.

Note 6, page 1, col. 2.

Thy house is left unto thee desolate.

St. Matthew, xxiv. 38.

Note 7, page 1, col. 2.

The seer.

Moses.

Note 8, page 1, col. 2.

Almotana's tide.

Almotana is the oriental name for the Dead Sea, as Ardeni is for Jordan.

Note 9, page 1, col. 2.

The robber riots, or the hermit prays.

The mountains of Palestine are full of caverns, which are generally occupied in one or other of the methods here mentioned. Vide Sandys, Maundrel, and Calmet, Passim.

Note 10, page 1, col. 2.

Those stormy seats the warrior Druses hold.

The untameable spirit, feodal customs, and affection for Europeans, which distinguished this extraordinary race, who boast themselves to be a remnant of the Crusaders, are well described in Pagés. The account of their celebrated Emir, Facciardini, in Sandys, is also very interesting. Puget de S. Pierre compiled a small volume on their history; Paris, 1763. 12mo.

Note 11, page 1, col. 2.

Teach their pale despot's waning moon to fear.

"The Turkish Sultans, whose moon seems fast approaching to its wane." Sir W. Jones's 1st Discourse to the Asiatic Society.

Note 12, page 2, col. 1.

Sidonian dyes and Lusitanian gold.

The gold of the Tyrians chiefly came from Portugal, which was probably their Tarshish.

Note 13, page 2, col. 1.

And unrestrained the generous vintage flows.

In the southern parts of Palestine the inhabitants reap their corn green, as they are not sure that it will ever be allowed to come to maturity. The oppression to which the cultivators of vineyards are subject throughout the Ottoman empire is well known.

Note 14, page 2, col. 1.

Arabia's parent.

Hagar.

Note 15, page 2, col. 1.

The guarded fountains shine.

The watering places are generally beset with Arabs, who exact toll from all comers. *See Harmer and Pagés.*

Note 16, page 2, col. 1.

Thy tents, Nebaioth, rise, and, Kedar, thine!

See Ammianus Marcellinus, lib. xiv. p. 43. Ed. Vales.

Note 17. page 2, col. 1.

Nor spare the hoary head, nor bid your eye
Revere the sacred smile of infancy.

"Thine eye shall not spare them."

Note 18, page 2, col. 1.

Smokes on Samaria's mount her scanty sacrifice.

A miserable remnant of Samaritan worship still exists on Mount Gerizim. Maundrell relates his conversation with the high priest.

Note 19, page 2, col. 1.

And refluent Jordan sought his trembling source.

Psalm cxiv.

Note 20, page 2, col. 1.

To Israel's woes a pitying ear incline,
And raise from earth thy long-neglected vine!

See Psalm lxxx. 8—14.

Note 21, page 2, col. 2.

The harnessed Amorite.

Josh. x.

Note 22, page 2, col. 2.

Or serve his altar with unhallowed fire.

Alluding to the fate of Nadab and Abihu.

Note 23, page 2, col. 2.

The mighty master of the iv'ry throne.

Solomon. Ophir is by most geographers placed in the Aurea Chersonesus. See Tavernier and Raleigh.

Note 24, page 2, col. 2.

Through nature's mazes wandered unconfined.

The Arabian mythology respecting Solomon is in itself so fascinating, is so illustrative of the present state of the country, and on the whole so agreeable to Scripture, that it was judged improper to omit all mention of it, though its wildness might have operated as an objection to making it a principal object in the poem.

Note 25, page 2, col. 2.

And Tadmor thus, and Syrian Balbec rose.

Palmyra ("Tadmor in the desert") was really built by Solomon, (1 Kings ix. 2 Chron. viii.) and universal tradition marks him out, with great probability, as the founder of Balbec. Estakhar is also attributed to him by the Arabs. See the Romance of Vathek, and the various Travels into the East, more particularly Chardin's, in which, after a minute and interesting description of the majestic ruins of Estakhar, or Persepolis, the ancient capital of Persia, an account follows of the wild local traditions just alluded to. Vol. ii. p. 190. Ed. Amst. 1735, 4to. Vide also Sale's Koran; D'Herbelot, Bibl. Orient. (article Soliman Ben Dao ud); and the Arabian Nights' Entertainments, passim.

Note 26, page 2, col. 2.

Houseless Santon.

It is well known that the Santons are real or affected madmen, pretending to extraordinary sanctity, who wander about the country, sleeping in caves or ruins.

Note 27, page 3, col. 1.

How lovely were thy tents, O Israel!

Numbers xxiv. 5.

Note 28, page 3, col. 1.

For thee his iv'ry load Behemoth bore.

Behemoth is sometimes supposed to mean the elephant, in which sense it is here used.

Note 29, page 3, col. 1.

And far Sofala teemed with golden ore.

An African port to the south of Bab-el-mandeb, celebrated for gold mines.

Note 30, page 3, col. 1.

The temple reared its everlasting gate.

Psalm xxiv. 7.

Note 31, page 3, col. 1.

No workman steel, no pond'rous axes rung.

"There was neither hammer, nor axe, nor any tool of iron, heard in the house while it was in building." 1 Kings vi. 7.

Note 32, page 3, col. 1.

Viewed the descending flame, and blessed the present God.

"And when all the children of Israel saw how the fire came down, and the glory of the Lord upon the house, they bowed themselves with their faces to the ground upon the pavement, and worshipped." 2 Chron. vii. 3.

Note 33, page 3, col. 1.

Beat o'er her soul the billows of the proud.

Psalm cxxiv. 4.

Note 34, page 3, col. 2.

Weep for your country, for your children weep.

Luke xxiii. 27, 28.

Note 35, page 3, col. 2.

And the pale parent drank her children's gore.

Josephus vi. p. 1275. Ed. Huds.

Note 36, page 3, col. 2.

The stoic tyrant's philosophic pride.

The Roman notions of humanity can not have been very exalted when they ascribed so large a share to Titus. For the horrible details of his conduct during the siege of Jerusalem and after its capture, the reader is referred to Josephus. When we learn that so many captives were crucified, that *δια το πληθος χωρα τε ενελειπετο τοις σταυροις και σταυροι τοις σωμασιν*; and that after all was over, in cold blood and merriment, he celebrated his brother's birthday with similar sacrifices; we can hardly doubt as to the nature of that untold crime, which disturbed the dying moments of the "darling of the human race." After all, the cruelties of this man are probably softened in the high priest's narrative. The fall of Jerusalem nearly resembles that of Zaragoza, but it is a Morla who tells the tale.

Note 37, page 4, col. 1.

Yon pompous shrine.

The temple of the Sepulchre.

Note 38, page 4. col. 1.

And bade the rock with Parian marble shine.

See Cotovicus, p. 179, and from him Sandys.

Note 39, page 4, col. 1.

The British queen.

St. Helena, who was, according to Camden, born at Colchester. See also Howel's History of the World.

Note 40, page 4, col. 1.

And pale Byzantium feared Medina's sword.

The invasions of the civilized parts of Asia by the Arabian and Turkish Mahometans.

Note 41, page 4, col. 1.

The wandering hermit waked the storm of war.

Peter the hermit. The world has been so long accustomed to hear the Crusades considered as the height of phrenzy and injustice, that to undertake their defence might be perhaps a hazardous task. We must however recollect, that, had it not been for these extraordinary exertions of generous courage, the whole of Europe would perhaps have fallen, and Christianity been buried in the ruins. It was not, as Voltaire has falsely or weakly asserted, a conspiracy of robbers; it was not an unprovoked attack on a distant and inoffensive nation; it was a blow aimed at the heart of a most powerful and active enemy. Had not the Christian kingdoms of Asia been established as a check to the Mahometans, Italy, and the scanty remnant of Christianity in Spain, must again have fallen into their power; and France herself have needed all the heroism and good fortune of a Charles Martel to deliver her from subjugation.

Note 42, page 4, col. 1.

While beardless youths and tender maids assume
The weighty morion and the glancing plume.

See Vertot. Hist. Chev. Malthe. liv. 1.

Note 43, page 4, col. 1.

Tabaria's stream.

Tabaria (a corruption of Tiberias) is the name used for the Sea of Galilee in the old romances.

Note 44, page 4, col. 1.

By northern Brenn, or Scythian Timur led.

Brennus, and Tamerlane.

Note 45, page 4, col. 1.

There Gaul's proud knights with boastful mien advance.

The insolence of the French nobles twice caused the ruin of the army; once by refusing to serve under Richard Cœur de Lion, and again by reproaching the English with cowardice in St. Louis's expedition to Egypt. See Knollee's History of the Turks.

Note 46, page 4, col. 1.

Form the long line.

The line (*combat a la haye*), according to Sir Walter Raleigh, was characteristic of French tactics; as the column (*herse*) was of the English. The English at Créci were drawn up thirty deep.

Note 47, page 4, col. 2.

Whose giant force Britannia's armies led.

All the British nations served under the same banner.

Sono gl' Inglesi sagittarii ed hanno
Gente con lor, ch' è più vicina al polo,
Questi da l'alte selve irsuti manda
La divisa dal mondo, ultima Irlanda.
Tasso, Gierusal. lib. i. 44.

Ireland and Scotland, it is scarcely necessary to observe, were synonymous.

Note 48, page 4, col. 2.

Lords of the biting axe and beamy spear.

The axe of Richard was very famous. See Warton's Hist. of Anc. Poetry.

Note 49, page 4, col. 2.

And burst his brazen bonds, and cast his cords away.

Psalm ii. 3. cvii. 16.

Note 50, page 4, col. 2.

Then on your tops shall deathless verdure spring.

"I will multiply the fruit of the tree, and the increase of the field, that ye shall receive no more the reproach of famine among the heathen."—And they shall say, This land that was desolate is become like the garden of Eden," &c. Ezek. xxxvi.

Note 51, page 4, col. 2.

Courts the bright vision of descending power.

"That great city, the holy Jerusalem, descending out of heaven from God, having the glory of God." Rev. xxi. 10.

Note 52, page 4, col. 2.

Tells every gate and measures every tower.

Ezekiel xl.

Note 53, page 5, col. 1.

And who is He? the vast, the awful form.

Rev. x.

Note 54, page 5, col. 1.

Lo! thrones arise, and every saint is there.

Rev. xx.

Note 55, page 5, col. 1.

God is their temple, and the Lamb their light.

And I saw no temple therein: for the Lord God Almighty and the Lamb are in the temple of it. And the city had no need of the sun, neither of the moon, to shine in it: for the glory of God did lighten it, and the Lamb is the light thereof." Rev. xxi. 22.

Note 56, page 5, col. 1.

And the dry bones be warm with life again.

"Thus saith the Lord God unto these bones, Behold I will cause breath to enter into you, and ye shall live."—"Then he said unto me, Son of man, these bones are the whole house of Israel." Ezek. xxxvii.

Europe.

LINES ON THE PRESENT WAR.

WRITTEN IN 1809.

ID. QVANDO. ACCIDERIT. NON. SATIS. AVDEO
EFFARI. SIQVIDEM. NON. CLARIVS. MIHI
PER. SACROS. TRIPODES. CERTA. REFERT. DEVS
NEC. SERVAT. PENITVS. FIDEM

QVOD. SI. QVID. LICEAT. CREDERE. ADHVC. TAMEN
NAM. LAEVVM. TONVIT. NON. FVERIT. PROCVL.
QVAERENDVS. CELERI. QVI. PROPERET. GRADV
ET. GALLVM. REPRIMAT. FEROX

PETRVS. CRINITVS. IN. CARMINE
AD. BER. CARAPHAM.

At that dread season when th' indignant North
Poured to vain wars her tardy numbers forth,
When Frederic bent his ear to Europe's cry,
And fanned too late the flame of liberty;
By feverish hope oppressed, and anxious thought,
In Dresden's grove the dewy cool I sought.(1)
Through tangled boughs the broken moonshine played,
And Elbe slept soft beneath his linden shade:—
Yet slept not all;—I heard the ceaseless jar,
The rattling wagons, and the wheels of war;
The sounding lash, the march's mingled hum,
And, lost and heard by fits, the languid drum;
O'er the near bridge the thundering hoofs that trode,
And the far-distant fife that thrilled along the road.
Yes, sweet it seems across some watery dell
To catch the music of the pealing bell;
And sweet to list, as on the beach we stray,
The ship-boy's carol in the wealthy bay:
But sweet no less, when Justice points the spear,
Of martial wrath the glorious din to hear,
To catch the war-note on the quivering gale,
And bid the blood-red paths of conquest hail.
Oh! song of hope, too long delusive strain!
And hear we now thy flattering voice again?
But late, alas! I left thee cold and still,
Stunned by the wrath of heaven, on Pratzen's hill,(2)
Oh! on that hill may no kind month renew
The fertile rain, the sparkling summer dew!
Accursed of God, may those bleak summits tell
The field of anger where the mighty fell.
There youthful Faith and high-born Courage rest,
And, red with slaughter, Freedom's humbled crest;(3)
There Europe, soiled with blood her tresses gray,
And ancient Honour's shield—all vilely thrown away.
Thus mused my soul, as in succession drear
Rose each grim shape of Wrath and Doubt and Fear;
Defeat and shame in grizzly vision passed,
And Vengeance, bought with blood, and glorious Death the last.

Then as my gaze their waving eagles met,
And through the night each sparkling bayonet,
Still memory told how Austria's evil hour
Had felt on Praga's field a Frederic's power,
And Gallia's vaunting train,(4) and Mosco's horde,
Had fleshed the maiden steel of Brunswic's sword.
Oh! yet, I deemed, that Fate, by justice led,
Might wreathe once more the veteran's silver head;
That Europe's ancient pride would yet disdain
The cumbrous sceptre of a single reign;
That conscious right would tenfold strength afford,
And Heaven assist the patriot's holy sword,
And look in mercy through the auspicious sky,
To bless the saviour host of Germany.
And are they dreams, these bodings, such as shed
Their lonely comfort o'er the hermit's bed?
And are they dreams? or can the Eternal Mind
Care for a sparrow, yet neglect mankind?
Why, if the dubious battle own his power,
And the red sabre, where he bids, devour,
Why then can one the curse of worlds deride,
And millions weep a tyrant's single pride?
Thus sadly musing, far my footsteps strayed,
Rapt in the visions of the Aonian maid.
It was not she, whose lonely voice I hear
Fall in soft whispers on my love-lorn ear;
My daily guest, who wont my steps to guide
Through the green walks of scented even-tide,
Or stretched with me in noonday ease along,
To list the reaper's chaunt, or throstle's song:
But she of loftier port; whose grave control
Rules the fierce workings of the patriot's soul;
She, whose high presence, o'er the midnight oil,
With fame's bright promise cheers the student's toil;
That same was she, whose ancient lore refined
The sober hardihood of Sydney's mind.
Borne on her wing, no more I seemed to rove
By Dresden's glittering spires, and linden grove;
No more the giant Elbe, all silver bright,
Spread his broad bosom to the fair moonlight,
While the still margent of his ample flood
Bore the dark image of the Saxon wood—
(Woods happy once, that heard the carols free
Of rustic love, and cheerful industry;
Now dull and joyless lie their alleys green,
And silence marks the track where France has been.)
Far other scenes than these my fancy viewed:
Rocks robed in ice, a mountain solitude;
Where on Helvetian hills, in godlike state,
Alone and awful, Europe's Angel sate:
Silent and stern he sate; then, bending low,
Listened the ascending plaints of human wo.
And waving as in grief his towery head,
"Not yet, not yet the day of rest," he said;
"It may not be. Destruction's gory wing
Soars o'er the banners of the younger king,
Too rashly brave, who seeks with single sway
To stem the lava on its destined way.
Poor, glittering warriors, only wont to know
The bloodless pageant of a martial show;
Nurselings of peace; for fiercer fights prepare,
And dread the step-dame sway of unaccustomed war!
They fight, they bleed!—Oh! had that blood been shed
When Charles and Valour Austria's armies led;
Had these stood forth the righteous cause to shield,
When victory wavered on Moravia's field;
Then France had mourned her conquests made in vain,
Her backward beaten ranks, and countless slain;
Then had the strength of Europe's freedom stood,
And still the Rhine had rolled a German flood!
"Oh! nursed in many a wile, and practised long,
To spoil the poor, and cringe before the strong;
To swell the victor's state, and hovering near,
Like some base vulture in the battle's rear,
To watch the carnage of the field, and share
Each loathsome alms the prouder eagles spare:
A curse is on thee Brandenburgh! the sound
Of Poland's wailings drags thee to the ground;
And, drunk with guilt, thy harlot lips shall know
The bitter dregs of Austria's cup of wo.
"Enough of vengeance! O'er the ensanguined plain
I gaze and seek their numerous host in vain;
Gone like the locust band when whirlwinds bear
Their flimsy regions through the waste of air.
Enough of vengeance!—By the glorious dead,
Who bravely fell where youthful Lewis led;(5)
By Blucher's sword in fiercest danger tried,
And the true heart that burst when Brunswic died;
By her whose charms the coldest zeal might warm,(6)
The manliest firmness in the fairest form—
Save, Europe, save the remnant!—Yet remains
One glorious path to free the world from chains.
Why, when your northern band in Eylau's wood
Retreating struck, and tracked their course with blood,
While one firm rock the floods of ruin stayed,
Why, generous Austria, were thy wheels delayed?
And Albion!"—Darker sorrow veiled his brow—
"Friend of the friendless—Albion! where art thou?
Child of the Sea, whose wing-like sails are spread,
The covering cherub of the ocean's bed!(7)
The storm and tempest render peace to thee,
And the wild-roaring waves a stern security.
But hope not thou in Heaven's own strength to ride,
Freedom's loved ark, o'er broad oppression's tide;
If virtue leave thee, if thy careless eye
Glance in contempt on Europe's agony.

Alas! where now the bands who wont to pour
Their strong deliverance on th' Egyptian shore?
Wing, wing your course, a prostrate world to save,
Triumphant squadrons of Trafalgar's wave.
"And thou, blest star of Europe's darkest hour,
Whose words were wisdom, and whose counsels power,
Whom earth applauded through her peopled shores!
(Alas! whom earth too early lost deplores;—)
Young without follies, without rashness bold,
And greatly poor amidst a nation's gold!
In every veering gale of faction true,
Untarnished Chatham's genuine child, adieu!
Unlike our common suns, whose gradual ray
Expands from twilight to intenser day,
Thy blaze broke forth at once in full meridian sway,
O, proved in danger! not the fiercest flame
Of Discord's rage thy constant soul could tame;
Not when, far-striding o'er thy palsied land,
Gigantic Treason took his bolder stand;
Not when wild Zeal, by murderous Faction led,
On Wicklow's hills, her grass-green banner spread;
Or those stern conquerors of the restless wave
Defied the native soil they wont to save.—
Undaunted patriot! in that dreadful hour,
When pride and genius own a sterner power;
When the dimmed eyeball, and the struggling breath,
And pain, and terror, mark advancing death;—
Still in that breast thy country held her throne,
Thy toil, thy fear, thy prayer were hers alone,
Thy last faint effort hers, and hers thy parting groan.
"Yes, from those lips while fainting nations drew
Hope ever strong, and courage ever new;—
Yet, yet, I deemed, by that supporting hand
Propped in her fall might Freedom's ruin stand;
And purged by fire, and stronger from the storm,
Degraded Justice rear her reverend form.
Now, hope, adieu!—adieu the generous care
To shield the weak, and tame the proud in war!
The golden chain of realms, when equal awe
Poised the strong balance of impartial law;
When rival states as federate sisters shone,
Alike, yet various, and though many, one;
And, bright and numerous as the spangled sky,
Beamed each fair star of Europe's galaxy—
All, all are gone, and after-time shall trace
One boundless rule, one undistinguished race;
Twilight of worth, where nought remains to move
The patriot's ardour, or the subject's love.
"Behold, e'en now, while every manly lore
And ev'ry muse forsakes my yielding shore;
Faint, vapid fruits of slavery's sickly clime,
Each tinsel art succeeds, and harlot rhyme!
To gild the vase, to bid the purple spread
In sightly foldings o'er the Grecian bed,
Their mimic guard where sculptured gryphons keep,
And Memphian idols watch o'er beauty's sleep;
To rouse the slumbering sparks of faint desire
With the base tinkling of the Teian lyre;
While youth's enervate glance and gloating age
Hang o'er the mazy waltz, or pageant stage;
Each wayward wish of sickly taste to please,
The nightly revel and the noontide ease—
These, Europe, are thy toils, thy trophies these!
"So, when wide-wasting hail, or whelming rain,
Have strewed the bearded hope of golden grain,
From the wet furrow, struggling to the skies,
The tall, rank weeds in barren splendour rise;
And strong, and towering o'er the mildewed ear,
Uncomely flowers and baneful herbs appear;
The swain's rich toils to useless poppies yield,
And Famine stalks along the purple field.
"And thou, the poet's theme, the patriot's prayer!
Where, France, thy hopes, thy gilded promise where;
When o'er Montpelier's vines, and Jura's snows,
All goodly bright, young Freedom's planet rose?
What boots it now, (to our destruction brave,)
How strong thine arm in war? a valiant slave
What boots it now that wide thine eagles sail,
Fanned by the flattering breath of conquest's gale?
What, that, high-piled within yon ample dome,
The blood-bought treasures rest of Greece and Rome?
Scourge of the highest, bolt in vengeance hurled
By Heaven's dread justice on a shrinking world!
Go, vanquished victor, bend thy proud helm down
Before thy sullen tyrant's steely crown.
For him in Afric's sands, and Poland's snows,
Reared by thy toil the shadowy laurel grows;
And rank in German fields the harvest springs
Of pageant councils and obsequious kings.
Such purple slaves, of glittering fetters vain,
Linked the wide circuit of the Latian chain;
And slaves like these shall every tyrant find,
To gild oppression, and debase mankind.
"Oh! live there yet whose hardy souls and high
Peace bought with shame, and tranquil bonds defy?
Who, driven from every shore, and lords in vain
Of the wide prison of the lonely main,
Cling to their country's rights with freeborn zeal,
More strong from every stroke, and patient of the steel?
Guiltless of chains, to them has Heaven consigned
Th' entrusted cause of Europe and mankind!
Or hope we yet in Sweden's martial snows
That Freedom's weary foot may find repose?
No;—from yon hermit shade, yon cypress dell,
Where faintly peals the distant matin-bell;
Where bigot kings and tyrant priests had shed
Their sleepy venom o'er his dreadful head;
He wakes, th' avenger—hark! the hills around,
Untamed Austria bids her clarion sound;
And many an ancient rock, and fleecy plain,
And many a valiant heart returns the strain:

Heard by that shore, where Calpe's armed steep
Flings its long shadow o'er th' Herculean deep,
And Lucian glades, whose hoary poplars wave
In soft, sad murmurs over Inez' grave.(8)
They bless the call who dared the first withstand(9)
The Moslem wasters of their bleeding land,
When firm in faith, and red with slaughtered foes,
Thy spear-encircled crown, Asturia(10) rose,
Nor these alone; as loud the war-notes swell,
La Mancha's shepherd quits his cork-built cell;
Alhama's strength is there, and those who till
(A hardy race!) Morena's scorched hill;
And in rude arms through wide Gallicia's reign,
The swarthy vintage pours her vigorous train.
"Saw ye those tribes? not theirs the plumed boast,
The sightly trappings of a marshalled host;
No weeping nations curse their deadly skill,
Expert in danger, and inured to kill:
But theirs the kindling eye, the strenuous arm;
Theirs the dark cheek, with patriot ardour warm,
Unblanched by sluggard ease, or slavish fear,
And proud and pure the blood that mantles there.
Theirs from the birth is toil;—o'er granite steep,
And heathy wild, to guard the wandering sheep;
To urge the labouring mule, or bend the spear
'Gainst the night-prowling wolf, or felon bear;
The bull's hoarse rage in dreadful sport to mock,
And meet with single sword his bellowing shock.
Each martial chant they know, each manly rhyme,
Rude, ancient lays of Spain's heroic time.(11)
Of him in Xere's carnage fearless found,(12)
(His glittering brows with hostile spear-heads bound;)
Of that chaste king whose hardy mountain train(13)
O'erthrew the knightly race of Charlemagne;
And chiefest him who reared his banner tall(14)
(Illustrious exile!) o'er Valencia's wall;
Ungraced by kings, whose Moorish title rose
The toil-earned homage of his wondering foes.
"Yes; every mould'ring tower and haunted flood,
And the wild murmurs of the waving wood;
Each sandy waste, and orange-scented dell,
And red Buraba's field, and Lugo,(15) tell,
How their brave fathers fought, how thick the invaders fell.
Oh! virtue long forgot, or vainly tried,
To glut a bigot's zeal, or tyrant's pride;
Condemned in distant climes to bleed and die
'Mid the dank poisons of Tlascala's(16) sky;
Or when stern Austria stretched her lawless reign,
And spent in northern fights the flower of Spain;
Or war's hoarse furies yelled on Ysell's shore,
And Alva's ruffian sword was drunk with gore.
Yet dared not then Tlascala's chiefs withstand
The lofty daring of Castilia's band;
And weeping France her captive king(17) deplored,
And cursed the deathful point of Ebro's sword.
Now, nerved with hope, their night of slavery past,
Each heart beats high in freedom's buxom blast;
Lo! Conquest calls, and beck'ning from afar,
Uplifts his laurel wreath, and waves them on to war.
—Wo to th' usurper then, who dares defy
The sturdy wrath of rustic loyalty!
Wo to the hireling bands, foredoomed to feel
How strong in labour's horny hand the steel!(18)
Behold e'en now, beneath yon Bœtic skies
Another Pavia bids her trophies rise;—
E'en now in base disguise and friendly night
Their robber-monarch speeds his secret flight;
And with new zeal the fiery Lusians rear,
(Roused by their neighbour's worth,) the long-neglected spear.
"So when stern winter chills the April showers,
And iron frost forbids the timely flowers;
Oh! deem not thou the vigorous herb below
Is crushed and dead beneath the incumbent snow;
Such tardy suns shall wealthier harvests bring
Than all the early smiles of flattering spring."
Sweet as the martial trumpet's silver swell,
On my charmed sense th' unearthly accents fell;
Me wonder held, and joy chastised by fear,
As one who wished, yet hardly hoped to hear.
"Spirit," I cried, "dread teacher, yet declare,
In that good fight, shall Albion's arm be there?
Can Albion, brave, and wise, and proud, refrain
To hail a kindred soul, and link her fate with Spain?
Too long her sons, estranged from war and toil,
Have loathed the safety of the sea-girt isle;
And chid the waves which pent their fire within
As the stalled war-horse woos the battle's din.
Oh, by this throbbing heart, this patriot glow,
Which, well I feel, each English breast shall know;
Say, shall my country, roused from deadly sleep,
Crowd with her hardy sons yon western steep;
And shall once more the star of France grow pale,
And dim its beams in Roncesvalles' vale?(19)
Or shall foul sloth and timid doubt conspire
To mar our zeal, and waste our manly fire?"
Still as I gazed, his lowering features spread,
High rose his form, and darkness veiled his head;
Fast from his eyes the ruddy lightning broke,
To heaven he reared his arm, and thus he spoke.
"Wo, trebly wo to their slow zeal who bore
Delusive comfort to Iberia's shore!
Who in mid conquest, vaunting, yet dismayed,
Now gave and now withdrew their laggard aid;
Who, when each bosom glowed, each heart beat high,
Chilled the pure stream of England's energy

And lost in courtly forms and blind delay
The loitered hours of glory's short-lived day.
"O peerless island, generous, bold, and free,
Lost, ruined Albion, Europe mourns for thee!
Hadst thou but known the hour in mercy given
To stay thy doom, and ward the ire of Heaven;
Bared in the cause of man thy warrior breast,
And crushed on yonder hills th' approaching pest,
Then had not murder sacked thy smiling plain,
And wealth, and worth, and wisdom, all been vain.
"Yet, yet awake! while fear and wonder wait,
On the poised balance, trembling still with fate!(20)
If aught their worth can plead, in battle tried,
Who tinged with slaughter Tajo's curdling tide;
(What time base truce the wheels of war could stay,
And the weak victor flung his wreath away;)—
Or theirs, who, doled in scanty bands afar,
Waged without hope the disproportioned war,
And cheerly still, and patient of distress,
Led their forwasted files on numbers numberless!(21)
"Yes, through the march of many a weary day,
As yon dark column toils its seaward way;
As bare, and shrinking from th' inclement sky,
The languid soldier bends him down to die;
As o'er those helpless limbs, by murder gored,
The base pursuer waves his weaker sword,
And, trod to earth, by trampling thousands pressed,
The horse-hoof glances from that mangled breast;
E'en in that hour his hope to England flies,
And fame and vengeance fire his closing eyes.
"Oh! if such hope can plead, or his, whose bier
Drew from his conquering host their latest tear;
Whose skill, whose matchless valour, gilded flight;
Entombed in foreign dust, a hasty soldier's rite;—
Oh! rouse thee yet to conquer and to save,
And Wisdom guide the sword which Justice gave!
"And yet the end is not! from yonder towers
While one Saguntum(22) mocks the victor's powers;
While one brave heart defies a servile chain,
And one true soldier wields a lance for Spain;
Trust not, vain tyrant, though thy spoiler band
In tenfold myriads darken half the land;
(Vast as that power, against whose impious lord
Bethulia's matron(23) shook the nightly sword;)
Though ruth and fear thy woundless soul defy,
And fatal genius fire thy martial eye;
Yet trust not here o'er yielding realms to roam,
Or cheaply bear a bloodless laurel home!
"No! by His viewless arm whose righteous care
Defends the orphan's tear, the poor man's prayer;
Who, Lord of nature, o'er this changeful ball
Decrees the rise of empires, and the fall;
Wondrous in all his ways, unseen, unknown,(24)
Who treads the wine-press of the world alone;
And robed in darkness, and surrounding fears,
Speeds on their destined road the march of years!
No!—shall yon eagle, from the snare set free,
Stoop to thy wrist, or cower his wing for thee?
And shall it tame despair, thy strong control,
Or quench a nation's still reviving soul?—
Go, bid the force of countless bands conspire
To curb the wandering wind, or grasp the fire!
Cast thy vain fetters on the troublous sea!—
But Spain, the brave, the virtuous, shall be free."

NOTES.

Note 1, page 8, col. 1.

In Dresden's grove the dewy cool I sought.

The opening lines of this poem were really composed in the situation (the Park of Dresden), and under the influence of the feelings, which they attempt to describe. The disastrous issue of King Frederic's campaign took away from the author all inclination to continue them, and they remained neglected till the hopes of Europe were again revived by the illustrious efforts of the Spanish people.

Note 2, page 8, col. 2.

Pratzen's hill.

The hill of Pratzen was the point most obstinately contested in the great battle which has taken its name from the neighbouring town of Austerlitz; and here the most dreadful slaughter took place, both of French and Russians. The author had, a few weeks before he wrote the above, visited every part of this celebrated field.

Note 3, page 8, col. 2.

And, red with slaughter, Freedom's humble crest.

It is necessary perhaps to mention, that, by freedom, in this and in other passages of the present poem, political liberty is understood in opposition to the usurpation of any single European state. In the particular instance of Spain, however, it is a hope which the author has not yet seen reason to abandon, that a struggle so nobly maintained by popular energy, must terminate in the establishment not only of national independence, but of civil and religious liberty.

Note 4, page 9, col. 1.

Gallia's vaunting train.

The confidence and shameful luxury of the French nobles, during the seven years' war, are very sarcastically noticed by Templeman.

Note 5, page 9, col. 2.

Where youthful Lewis led.

Prince Lewis Ferdinand of Prussia, who fell gloriously with almost the whole of his regiment.

Note 6, page 9, col. 2.

By her whose charms, &c.

The Queen of Prussia; beautiful, unfortunate, and unsubdued by the severest reverses.

Note 7, page 9, col. 2.

The covering cherub, &c.

"Thou art the anointed cherub that coverest."—Addressed to Tyre, by Ezekiel, xxviii. 14.

Note 8, page 11, col. 1.

Inez' grave.

Inez de Castro, the beloved mistress of the Infant Don Pedro, son of Alphonso IV. King of Portugal, and stabbed by the orders, and, according to Camoens, in the presence of that monarch. A fountain near Coimbra, the scene of their loves and misfortunes, is still pointed out by tradition, and called Amores.—*De la Clede, Hist. de Portugalle*, 4to. tom. i. page 282-7:—and *Camoens' Lusiad*, canto 3, stanza cxxxv.

Note 9, page 11, col 1.

——Who dared the first withstand
The Moslem waters of their bleeding land.

The Asturians, who under Pelagius first opposed the career of Mahometan success.

Note 10, page 11, col. 1.

Thy spear-encircled crown, Asturia.

"La couronne de fer de Dom Pélage,—cette couronne si simple mais si glorieuse, dont chaque fleuron este 'formé du fer d'une lance arrachée aux Chevaliers Maures que se heros avoit fait tomber sous ses coups."—'*Roman de Dom Ursino le Navarin, Tressan*, tom. ix. 52.

Note 11, page 11, col. 1.

Rude ancient lays of Spain's heroic time.

See the two elegant specimens given by Bishop Percy in his Reliques; and the more accurate translations of Mr. Rodd in his Civil Wars of Grenada.

Note 12, page 11, col. 1.

Him in Xeres' carnage fearless found.

The Gothic monarchy in Spain was overthrown by the Mussulmans at the battle of Xeres, the Christian army being defeated with dreadful slaughter, and the death of their King, the unhappy and licentious Roderigo. Pelagius assembled the small band of those fugitives who despised submission, amid the mountains of the Asturias, under the name of King of Oviedo.

Note 13, page, 11, col. 1.

Of that chaste king, &c.

Alonso, surnamed the Chaste, with ample reason, if we believe his historians; who defeated, according to the Spanish romances, and the graver authority of Mariana, the whole force of Charlemagne and the twelve peers of France at Roncesvalles. Bertrand del Carpio, the son of Alonzo's sister, Ximena, was his general; and according to Don Quixote (no incompetent authority on such a subject) put the celebrated Ordando to the same death as Hercules inflicted on Antæus. His reason was, that the nephew of Charlemagne was enchanted, and like Achilles only vulnerable in the heel, to guard which he wore always iron shoes. See Mariana, l. vii. c. xi.; Don Quixote, book i. c. l.; and the notes on Mr. Southey's Chronicle of the Cid; a work replete with powerful description, and knowledge of ancient history and manners, and which adds a new wreath to one, who "nullum fere scribendi genus intactum reliquit, nullum quod tetigit non ornavit."

Note 14, page 11, col. 1.

Chiefest him who reared his banner tall, &c.

Rodrigo Diaz, of Bivar, surnamed the Cid by the Moors.—See Mr. Southey's Chronicle

Note 15, page 11, col. 1.

Red Buraba's field, and Lugo—

Buraba and Lugo were renowned scenes of Spanish victories over the Moors, in the reigns of Bermudo, or, as his name is Latinized, Veremundus, and Alonso the Chaste. Of Lugo the British have since obtained a melancholy knowledge.

Note 16, page 11, col. 1.

Tlascala.

An extensive district of Mexico; its inhabitants were the first Indians who submitted to the Spaniards under Cortez.

Note 17, page 11, col. 2.

Her captive king.

Francis I. taken prisoner at the battle of Pavia.

Note 18, page 11, col. 2.

Yon Bœotic skies.

Andalusia forms a part of the ancient Hispania Boetica.

Note 18, page 11, col. 2.

Roncesvalles' vale.

See the former note on Alonso the Chaste.

Note 20, page 12, col. 1.

The poised balance trembling still with fate.

This line is imitated from one of Mr. Roscoe's spirited verses on the commencement of the French revolution.

Note 21, page 12, col. 1.

Numbers numberless.

"He looked and saw what numbers numberless."
Milton, Paradise Regained.

Note 22, page 12, col. 1.

One Saguntum.

The ancient siege of Saguntum has been now rivalled by Zaragoza. The author is happy to refer his readers to the interesting narrative of his friend Mr. Vaughan.

Note 23, page 12, col. 1.

Bethulia's matron.

Judith.

Note 24, page 12, col. 1.

Who treads the wine-press of the world alone.

"I have trodden the wine-press alone, and of the people there was none with me, for I will tread them in mine anger, and trample them in my fury."—Isaiah lxiii. 3.

Hymns

WRITTEN FOR THE WEEKLY CHURCH SERVICE

OF THE YEAR.

Several of these hymns were originally published in the Christian Observer, in the years 1811 and 1812, and were then accompanied by the following prefatory notice, which it is thought due to the author, should be here preserved.

"The following Hymns are part of an intended series, appropriate to the Sundays, and principal holidays of the year; connected in some degree with their particular Collects and Gospels, and designed to be sung between the Nicene Creed and the Sermon. The effect of an arrangement of this kind, though only partially adopted, is very striking in the Romish liturgy; and its place should seem to be imperfectly supplied by a few verses of a Psalm, entirely unconnected with the peculiar devotions of the day, and selected at the discretion of a clerk or organist. On the merits of the present imperfect essays, the author is unaffectedly diffident; and as his labours are intended for the use of his own congregation, he will be thankful for any suggestion which may advance or correct them. In one respect, at least, he hopes the following poems will not be found reprehensible;—no fulsome or indecorous language has been knowingly adopted: no erotic addresses to him whom no unclean lip can approach, no allegory ill understood, and worse applied. It is not enough, in his opinion, to object to such expressions that they are fanatical; they are positively profane. When our Saviour was on earth and in great humility conversant with mankind; when he sat at the tables, and washed the feet, and healed the diseases of his creatures; yet did not his disciples give him any more familiar name than *Master* or *Lord*. And now at the right hand of his Father's majesty, shall we address him with ditties of embraces and passion, or language which it would be disgraceful in an earthly sovereign to endure? Such expressions, it is said, are taken from Scripture; but even if the original application, which is often doubtful, were clearly and unequivocally ascertained, yet, though the collective Christian church may very properly be personified as the spouse of Christ, an application of such language to individual believers is as dangerous as it is absurd and unauthorized. Nor is it going too far to assert, that the brutalities of a common swearer can hardly bring religion into more sure contempt, or more scandalously profane the Name which is above every name in heaven and earth, than certain epithets applied to Christ in our popular collections of religious poetry."

Bishop Heber subsequently arranged these hymns, with some others by various writers, in a regular series adapted to the services of the Church of England throughout the year, and it was his intention to publish them soon after his arrival in India; but the arduous duties of his station left little time, during the short life there allotted to him, for any employment not immediately connected with his diocese. This arrangement of them has been published in England since his death, and republished in this country.

ADVENT SUNDAY.

MATT. XXI.

HOSANNA to the living Lord!
Hosanna to the incarnate Word!
To Christ, Creator, Saviour, King,
Let earth, let heaven, Hosanna sing!
  Hosanna! Lord! Hosanna in the highest!

Hosanna, Lord! thine angels cry;
Hosanna, Lord! thy saints reply;
Above, beneath us, and around,
The dead and living swell the sound;
  Hosanna! Lord! Hosanna in the highest!

Oh, Saviour! with protecting care,
Return to this thy house of prayer!
Assembled in thy sacred name,
Where we thy parting promise claim
  Hosanna! Lord! Hosanna in the highest!

But chiefest, in our cleansed breast,
Eternal! bid thy spirit rest,
And make our secret soul to be
A temple pure, and worthy thee!
  Hosanna! Lord! Hosanna in the highest!

So, in the last and dreadful day,
When earth and heaven shall melt away,
Thy flock, redeemed from sinful stain,
Shall swell the sound of praise again,
  Hosanna! Lord! Hosanna in the highest!

SECOND SUNDAY IN ADVENT.

JOHN I.

THE Lord will come! the earth shall quake,
The hills their fixed seat forsake;
And, withering, from the vault of night
The stars withdraw their feeble light.

The Lord will come! but not the same
As once in lowly form he came,
A silent lamb to slaughter led,
The bruised, the suffering, and the dead.

The Lord will come! a dreadful form,
With wreath of flame, and robe of storm,
On cherub wings, and wings of wind,
Anointed Judge of human-kind!

Can this be Thee who wont to stray
A pilgrim on the world's highway;
By power oppressed and mocked by pride?
Oh, God! is this the crucified?

Go, tyrants! to the rocks complain!
Go, seek the mountain's cleft in vain!
But faith, victorious o'er the tomb,
Shall sing for joy—the Lord is come!

SECOND SUNDAY IN ADVENT.

LUKE XXI.

IN the sun and moon and stars
Signs and wonders there shall be;
Earth shall quake with inward wars,
Nations with perplexity.

Soon shall ocean's hoary deep,
Tossed with stronger tempests, rise:
Darker storms the mountain sweep,
Redder lightning rend the skies.

Evil thoughts shall shake the proud,
Racking doubt and restless fear;
And amid the thunder cloud
Shall the Judge of men appear.

But though from that awful face
Heaven shall fade and earth shall fly,
Fear not ye, his chosen race,
Your redemption draweth nigh!

THIRD SUNDAY IN ADVENT.

MATT. XI.

OH, Saviour, is thy promise fled?
No longer might thy grace endure,
To heal the sick and raise the dead,
And preach thy gospel to the poor?

Come, Jesus! come! return again;
With brighter beam thy servants bless,
Who long to feel thy perfect reign,
And share thy kingdom's happiness!

A feeble race, by passion driven,
In darkness and in doubt we roam,
And lift our anxious eyes to Heaven,
Our hope, our harbour, and our home!

Yet mid the wild and wint'ry gale,
When Death rides darkly o'er the sea,
And strength and earthly daring fail,
Our prayers, Redeemer! rest on Thee.

Come, Jesus! come! and, as of yore
The prophet went to clear thy way,
A harbinger thy feet before,
A dawning to thy brighter day:

So now my grace with heavenly shower
Our stony hearts for truth prepare;
Sow in our souls the seed of power,
Then come and reap thy harvest there!

THE FOURTH SUNDAY IN ADVENT.

THE world is grown old, and her pleasures are past;
The world is grown old, and her form may not last;
The world is grown old, and trembles for fear;
For sorrows abound and judgment is near!

The sun in the heaven is languid and pale;
And feeble and few are the fruits of the vale;
And the hearts of the nations fail them for fear,
For the world is grown old, and judgment is near!

The king on his throne, the bride in her bower,
The children of pleasure all feel the sad hour;
The roses are faded, and tasteless the cheer,
For the world is grown old, and judgment is near!

The world is grown old!—but should we complain,
Who have tried her and know that her promise is vain?
Our heart is in heaven, our home is not here,
And we look for our crown when judgment is near!

CHRISTMAS DAY.

OH, Saviour, whom this holy morn
Gave to our world below;
To mortal want and labour born,
And more than mortal wo!

Incarnate Word! by every grief,
By each temptation tried,
Who lived to yield our ills relief,
And to redeem us died!

If gaily clothed and proudly fed,
In dangerous wealth we dwell,
Remind us of thy manger bed,
And lowly cottage cell!

If prest by poverty severe,
In envious want we pine,
Oh may thy spirit whisper near,
How poor a lot was thine!

Through fickle fortune's various scene
From sin preserve us free!
Like us thou hast a mourner been,
May we rejoice with Thee!

ST. STEPHEN'S DAY.

The Son of God goes forth to war,
A kingly crown to gain;
His blood-red banner streams afar!
Who follows in his train?
Who best can drink his cup of wo,
Triumphant over pain,
Who patient bears his cross below,
He follows in his train!

The martyr first, whose eagle eye
Could pierce beyond the grave;
Who saw his Master in the sky,
And called on him to save.
Like Him, with pardon on his tongue
In midst of mortal pain,
He prayed for them that did the wrong;
Who follows in his train?

A glorious band, the chosen few,
On whom the spirit came;
Twelve valiant saints, their hope they knew,
And mocked the cross and flame.
They met the tyrant's brandished steel,
The lion's gory mane:
They bowed their necks the death to feel!
Who follows in their train?

A noble army—men and boys,
The matron and the maid,
Around the Saviour's throne rejoice,
In robes of light arrayed.
They climbed the steep ascent of Heaven,
Through peril, toil, and pain!
Oh, God! to us may grace be given
To follow in their train!

ST. JOHN THE EVANGELIST'S DAY.

Oh, God! who gav'st thy servant grace,
Amid the storms of life distrest,
To look on thine incarnate face,
And lean on thy protecting breast:

To see the light that dimly shone,
Eclipsed for us in sorrow pale,
Pure Image of the Eternal One!
Through shadows of thy mortal veil!

Be ours, oh, King of Mercy! still
To feel thy presence from above,
And in thy word, and in thy will,
To hear thy voice and know thy love;

And when the toils of life are done,
And nature waits thy dread decree,
To find our rest beneath thy throne,
And look, in humble hope, to Thee!

INNOCENT'S DAY.

Oh weep not o'er thy children's tomb,
Oh, Rachel, weep not so!
The bud is cropt by martyrdom
The flower in heaven shall blow!

Firstlings of faith! the murderer's knife
Has missed its deadliest aim:
The God for whom they gave their life,
For them to suffer came!

Though feeble were their days and few,
Baptized in blood and pain,
He knows them, whom they never knew,
And they shall live again.

Then weep not o'er thy children's tomb,
Oh, Rachel, weep not so!
The bud is cropt by martyrdom,
The flower in heaven shall blow!

SUNDAY AFTER CHRISTMAS; OR CIRCUMCISION.

Lord of mercy and of might!
Of mankind the life and light!
Maker, teacher infinite!
Jesus! hear and save!

Who, when sin's tremendous doom
Gave Creation to the tomb,
Didst not scorn the Virgin's womb,
Jesus! hear and save!

Mighty monarch! Saviour mild!
Humbled to a mortal child,
Captive, beaten, bound, reviled,
Jesus! hear and save!

Throned above celestial things,
Borne aloft on angel's wings,
Lord of Lords, and King of kings!
Jesus! hear and save!

Who shall yet return from high,
Robed in might and majesty,
Hear us! help us when we cry!
Jesus! hear and save!

EPIPHANY.

Brightest and best of the sons of the morning!
Dawn on our darkness and lend us thine aid!
Star of the East, the horizon adorning,
Guide where our infant Redeemer is laid!

Cold on his cradle the dew drops are shining,
Low lies his head with the beasts of the stall,
Angels adore him in slumber reclining,
Maker and Monarch and Saviour of all!

Say, shall we yield him, in costly devotion,
Odours of Edom and offerings divine?
Gems of the mountain and pearls of the ocean,
Myrrh from the forest or gold from the mine?

Vainly we offer each ample oblation;
Vainly with gifts would his favour secure:
Richer by far is the heart's adoration;
Dearer to God are the prayers of the poor.

Brightest and best of the sons of the morning!
Dawn on our darkness and lend us thine aid!
Star of the East, the horizon adorning,
Guide where our infant Redeemer is laid!

FIRST SUNDAY AFTER EPIPHANY.

LUKE II.

Abashed be all the boast of age!
Be hoary learning dumb!
Expounder of the mystic page,
Behold an Infant come!

Oh, Wisdom, whose unfading power
Beside th' Eternal stood,
To frame, in nature's earliest hour,
The land, the sky, the flood;

Yet didst not Thou disdain awhile
An infant form to wear;
To bless thy mother with a smile,
And lisp thy faltered prayer.

But, in thy Father's own abode,
With Israel's elders round,
Conversing high with Israel's God,
Thy chiefest joy was found.

So may our youth adore thy name!
And, Saviour, deign to bless
With fostering grace the timid flame
Of early holiness!

FIRST SUNDAY AFTER EPIPHANY

By cool Siloam's shady rill
How sweet the lily grows!
How sweet the breath beneath the hill
Of Sharon's dewy rose!

Lo! such the child whose early feet
The paths of peace have trod;
Whose secret heart, with influence sweet,
Is upward drawn to God!

By cool Siloam's shady rill
The lily must decay;
The rose that blooms beneath the hill
Must shortly fade away.

And soon, too soon, the wint'ry hour
Of man's maturer age
Will shake the soul with sorrow's power,
And stormy passion's rage!

O Thou, whose infant feet were found
Within thy Father's shrine!
Whose years, with changeless virtue crowned,
Were all alike divine,

Dependent on thy bounteous breath,
We seek thy grace alone,
In childhood, manhood, age and death,
To keep us still thine own!

SECOND SUNDAY AFTER EPIPHANY

Oh, hand of bounty, largely spread,
By whom our every want is fed,
Whate'er we touch, or taste, or see,
We owe them all, oh Lord! to Thee;
The corn, the oil, the purple wine,
Are all thy gifts, and only thine!

The stream thy word to nectar dyed,
The bread thy blessing multiplied,
The stormy wind, the whelming flood,
That silent at thy mandate stood,
How well they knew thy voice divine,
Whose works they were, and only thine!

Though now no more on earth we trace
Thy footsteps of celestial grace,
Obedient to thy word and will
We seek thy daily mercy still;
Its blessed beams around us shine,
And thine we are, and only thine!

FOR THE SAME.

Incarnate Word, who, wont to dwell
In lowly shape and cottage cell,
Didst not refuse a guest to be
At Cana's poor festivity:

Oh, when our soul from care is free,
Then, Saviour, may we think on Thee,
And seated at the festal board,
In Fancy's eye behold the Lord.

Then may we seem, in Fancy's ear,
Thy manna-dropping tongue to hear,
And think,—even now, thy searching gaze
Each secret of our soul surveys!

So may such joy, chastised and pure,
Beyond the bounds of earth endure;
Nor pleasure in the wounded mind
Shall leave a rankling sting behind!

FOR THE SAME.

When on her Maker's bosom
The new-born earth was laid,
And nature's opening blossom
Its fairest bloom displayed;

When all with fruit and flowers
The laughing soil was drest,
And Eden's fragrant bowers
Received their human guest;

No sin his face defiling,
The heir of Nature stood,
And God, benignly smiling,
Beheld that all was good!

Yet in that hour of blessing,
A single want was known;
A wish the heart distressing;
For Adam was alone!

Oh, God of pure affection!
By men and saints adored,
Who gavest thy protection
To Cana's nuptial board.

May such thy bounties ever
To wedded love be shown,
And no rude hand dissever
Whom thou hast linked in one

THIRD SUNDAY AFTER EPIPHANY.

Matt. viii.

Lord! whose love, in power excelling,
Washed the leper's stain away.
Jesus! from thy heavenly dwelling,
Hear us, help us, when we pray!

From the filth of vice and folly,
From infuriate passion's rage,
Evil thoughts and hopes unholy,
Heedless youth and selfish age;

From the lusts whose deep pollutions
Adam's ancient taint disclose,
From the tempter's dark intrusions,
Restless doubt and blind repose;

From the miser's cursed treasure,
From the drunkard's jest obscene,
From the world, its pomp and pleasure,
Jesus! Master! make us clean!

FOURTH SUNDAY AFTER EPIPHANY.

When through the torn sail the wild tempest is streaming,
When o'er the dark wave the red lightning is gleaming,
Nor hope lends a ray the poor seamen to cherish,
We fly to our Maker—"Help, Lord! or we perish!"

Oh, Jesus! once tossed on the breast of the billow,
Aroused by the shriek of despair from thy pillow,
Now, seated in glory, the mariner cherish,
Who cries in his danger—"Help, Lord! or we perish!"

And oh, when the whirlwind of passion is raging,
When hell in our heart his wild warfare is waging,
Arise in thy strength thy redeemed to cherish,
Rebuke the destroyer—"Help, Lord! or we perish!"

SEPTUAGESIMA SUNDAY.

The God of glory walks his round,
From day to day, from year to year,
And warns us each with awful sound,
"No longer stand ye idle here!

"Ye whose young cheeks are rosy bright,
Whose hands are strong, whose hearts are clear,
Waste not of hope, the morning light!
Ah, fools! why stand ye idle here?

"Oh, as the griefs ye would assuage
That wait on life's declining year,
Secure a blessing for your age,
And work your Maker's business here!

"And ye, whose locks of scanty gray
Foretell your latest travail near,
How swiftly fades your worthless day!
And stand ye yet so idle here?

"One hour remains, there is but one!
But many a shriek and many a tear
Through endless years the guilt must moan
Of moments lost and wasted here!"

Oh, Thou, by all thy works adored,
To whom the sinner's soul is dear,
Recall us to thy vineyard, Lord!
And grant us grace to please thee here!

SEXAGESIMA SUNDAY.

Oh, God! by whom the seed is given;
By whom the harvest blest;
Whose word like manna showered from heaven,
Is planted in our breast;

Preserve it from the passing feet,
And plunderers of the air;
The sultry sun's intenser heat,
And weeds of worldly care;

Though buried deep or thinly strewn,
Do thou thy grace supply;
The hope in earthly furrows sown
Shall ripen in the sky!

QUINQUAGESIMA.

Lord of mercy and of might,
Of mankind the life and light,
Maker, teacher, infinite,
Jesus, hear and save!

Who, when sin's primæval doom
Gave creation to the tomb,
Didst not scorn a Virgin's womb,
Jesus, hear and save!

Strong, Creator, Saviour mild,
Humbled to a mortal child,
Captive, beaten, bound, reviled,
Jesus, hear and save!

Throned above celestial things,
Borne aloft on angels' wings,
Lord of lords, and King of kings,
Jesus, hear and save!

Soon to come to earth again,
Judge of angels and of men,
Hear us now, and hear us then,
Jesus, hear and save!

THIRD SUNDAY IN LENT.

Virgin-born! we bow before thee!
Blessed was the womb that bore thee!
Mary, mother meek and mild,
Blessed was she in her child!

Blessed was the breast that fed thee!
Blessed was the hand that led thee!
Blessed was the parent's eye
That watched thy slumbering infancy!

Blessed she by all creation,
Who brought forth the world's salvation!
And blessed they, for ever blest,
Who love thee most and serve thee best!

Virgin-born! we bow before thee!
Blessed was the womb that bore thee!
Mary, mother meek and mild,
Blessed was she in her child!

FOURTH SUNDAY IN LENT.

Oh, King of earth and air and sea!
The hungry ravens cry to thee;
To thee the scaly tribes that sweep
The bosom of the boundless deep;

To thee the lions roaring call,
The common Father, kind to all!
Then grant thy servants, Lord! we pray,
Our daily bread from day to day!

The fishes may for food complain;
The ravens spread their wings in vain;
The roaring lions lack and pine;
But God! thou carest still for thine!

Thy bounteous hand with food can bless
The bleak and lonely wilderness;
And thou hast taught us, Lord! to pray
For daily bread from day to day!

And oh, when through the wilds we roam
That part us from our heavenly home;
When, lost in danger, want, and wo,
Our faithless tears begin to flow;

Do thou thy gracious comfort give,
By which alone the soul may live;
And grant thy servants, Lord! we pray,
The bread of life from day to day!

FIFTH SUNDAY IN LENT.

Oh Thou, whom neither time nor space
Can circle in, unseen, unknown,
Nor faith in boldest flight can trace,
Save through thy Spirit and thy Son!

And Thou that from thy bright abode,
To us in mortal weakness shown,
Didst graft the manhood into God,
Eternal, co-eternal Son!

And Thou whose unction from on high
By comfort, light, and love is known
Who, with the parent Deity,
Dread Spirit! art for ever one!

Great First and Last! thy blessing give!
And grant us faith, thy gift alone,
To love and praise thee while we live,
And do whate'er thou would'st have done!

SIXTH SUNDAY IN LENT.

The Lord of might, from Sinai's brow,
Gave forth his voice of thunder;
And Israel lay on earth below,
Outstretched in fear and wonder.
Beneath his feet was pitchy night,
And, at his left hand and his right,
The rocks were rent asunder!

The Lord of love, on Calvary,
A meek and suffering stranger,
Upraised to heaven his languid eye,
In nature's hour of danger.
For us he bore the weight of wo,
For us he gave his blood to flow,
And met his Father's anger.

The Lord of love, the Lord of might,
The king of all created,
Shall back return to claim his right,
On clouds of glory seated;
With trumpet-sound and angel-song,
And hallelujahs loud and long
O'er Death and Hell defeated!

GOOD FRIDAY.

Oh more than merciful! whose bounty gave
Thy guiltless self to glut the greedy grave!
Whose heart was rent to pay thy people's price,
The great High-priest at once and sacrifice!
Help, Saviour, by thy cross and crimson stain,
Nor let thy glorious blood be spilt in vain!

When sin with flow'ry garland hides her dart,
When tyrant force would daunt the sinking heart,
When fleshly lust assails, or worldly care,
Or the soul flutters in the fowler's snare,—
Help, Saviour, by thy cross and crimson stain,
Nor let thy glorious blood be spilt in vain!

And chiefest then, when nature yields the strife,
And mortal darkness wraps the gate of life,
When the poor spirit, from the tomb set free,
Sinks at thy feet and lifts its hope to thee—
Help, Saviour, by thy cross and crimson stain!
Nor let thy glorious blood be spilt in vain!

EASTER DAY.

God is gone up with a merry noise
Of saints that sing on high;
With his own right hand and his holy arm
He hath won the victory!

Now empty are the courts of death,
And crushed thy sting, despair:
And roses bloom in the desert tomb,
For Jesus hath been there!

And he hath tamed the strength of hell,
And dragged him through the sky,
And captive behind his chariot wheel,
He hath bound captivity!

God is gone up with a merry noise
Of saints that sing on high;
With his own right hand and his holy arm
He hath won the victory!

FIFTH SUNDAY AFTER EASTER

Life nor Death shall us dissever
From his love who reigns for ever!
Will he fail us? Never! never!
When to him we cry!

Sin may seek to snare us,
Fury passion tear us!
Doubt and fear, and grim despair,
Their fangs against us try;

But his might shall still defend us,
And his blessed Son befriend us,
And his Holy Spirit send us
Comfort ere we die!

ASCENSION DAY, AND SUNDAY AFTER.

"Sit thou on my right hand, my Son!" saith the Lord.
"Sit thou on my right hand, my Son!
Till in the fatal hour
Of my wrath and my power,
Thy foes shall be a footstool to thy throne!

"Prayer shall be made to thee, my Son!" saith the Lord.
"Prayer shall be made to thee, my Son!
From earth and air and sea,
And all that in them be,
Which thou for thine heritage hast won!"

"Daily be thou praised, my Son!" saith the Lord.
"Daily be thou praised, my Son!
And all that live and move,
Let them bless thy bleeding love,
And the work which thy worthiness hath done!"

WHITSUNDAY.

Spirit of Truth! on this thy day
To thee for help we cry;
To guide us through the dreary way
Of dark mortality!

We ask not, Lord! thy cloven flame,
Or tongues of various tone;
But long thy praises to proclaim
With fervour in our own.

We mourn not that prophetic skill
Is found on earth no more;
Enough for us to trace thy will
In Scripture's sacred lore.

We neither have nor seek the power
Ill demons to control;
But thou in dark temptation's hour,
Shall chase them from the soul.

No heavenly harpings sooth our ear,
No mystic dreams we share;
Yet hope to feel thy comfort near,
And bless thee in our prayer.

When tongues shall cease, and power decay,
And knowledge empty prove,
Do thou thy trembling servants stay
With Faith, with Hope, with Love!

TRINITY SUNDAY.

HOLY, holy, holy, Lord God Almighty,
Early in the morning our song shall rise to thee;
Holy, holy, holy, merciful and mighty!
God in three persons, blessed Trinity!

Holy, holy, holy! all the saints adore thee,
Casting down their golden crowns around the glassy sea;
Cherubim and seraphim falling down before thee,
Which wert and art and evermore shall be!

Holy, holy, holy! though the darkness hide thee,
Though the eye of sinful man thy glory may not see,
Only thou art holy, there is none beside thee,
Perfect in power, in love, and purity!

Holy, holy, holy, Lord God Almighty!
All thy works shall praise thy name in earth and sky and sea.
Holy, holy, holy, merciful and mighty!
God in three persons, blessed Trinity!

FIRST SUNDAY AFTER TRINITY.

ROOM for the proud! Ye sons of clay,
From far his sweeping pomp survey,
Nor, rashly curious, clog the way
His chariot wheels before!

Lo! with what scorn his lofty eye
Glances o'er age and poverty,
And bids intruding conscience fly
Far from his palace door!

Room for the proud! but slow the feet
That bear his coffin down the street:
And dismal seems his winding sheet
Who purple lately wore!

Ah! where must now his spirit fly
In naked, trembling agony?
Or how shall he for mercy cry
Who showed it not before!

Room for the proud! in ghastly state,
The lords of hell his coming wait,
And flinging wide the dreadful gate,
That shuts to ope no more.

"Lo here with us the seat," they cry,
"For him who mocked at poverty,
And bade intruding conscience fly
Far from his palace door!"

FOR THE SAME.

THE feeble pulse, the gasping breath,
The clenched teeth, the glazed eye,
Are these thy sting, thou dreadful death!
O grave, are these thy victory?

The mourners by our parting bed,
The wife, the children, weeping nigh,
The dismal pageant of the dead,—
These, these are not thy victory!

But, from the much-loved world to part,
Our lust untamed, our spirit high,
All nature struggling at the heart,
Which, dying, feels it dare not die!

To dream through life a gaudy dream
Of pride and pomp and luxury,
Till wakened by the nearer gleam
Of burning, boundless agony;

To meet o'er soon our angry king,
Whose love we past unheeded by;
Lo this, O Death, thy deadliest sting.
O Grave, and this thy victory!

O Searcher of the secret heart,
Who deigned for sinful man to die!
Restore us ere the spirit part,
Nor give to hell the victory!

SECOND SUNDAY AFTER TRINITY

FORTH from the dark and stormy sky,
Lord, to thine altar's shade we fly;
Forth from the world, its hope and fear
Saviour, we seek thy shelter here:
Weary and weak, thy grace we pray;
Turn not, O Lord! thy guests away!

Long have we roamed in want and pain,
Long have we sought thy rest in vain;
Wildered in doubt, in darkness lost,
Long have our souls been tempest-tost;
Low at thy feet our sins we lay;
Turn not, O Lord! thy guests away!

THIRD SUNDAY AFTER TRINITY.

There was joy in heaven!
There was joy in heaven!
When this goodly world to frame
The Lord of might and mercy came:
Shouts of joy were heard on high,
And the stars sang from the sky—
"Glory to God in heaven!"

There was joy in heaven!
There was joy in heaven!
When the billows, heaving dark,
Sank around the stranded ark,
And the rainbow's watery span
Spake of mercy, hope to man,
And peace with God in Heaven!

There was joy in heaven!
There was joy in heaven!
When of love the midnight beam
Dawned on the towers of Bethlehem;
And along the echoing hill
Angels sang—"On earth good will,
And glory in the Heaven!"

There is joy in heaven!
There is joy in heaven!
When the sheep that went astray
Turns again to virtue's way;
When the soul, by grace subdued,
Sobs it prayer of gratitude,
Then is there joy in Heaven!

FOURTH SUNDAY AFTER TRINITY.

I praised the earth, in beauty seen
With garlands gay of various green;
I praised the sea, whose ample field
Shone glorious as a silver shield;
And earth and ocean seemed to say,
"Our beauties are but for a day!"

I praised the sun, whose chariot rolled
On wheels of amber and of gold;
I praised the moon, whose softer eye
Gleamed sweetly through the summer sky!
And moon and sun in answer said,
"Our days of light are numbered!"

O God! O good beyond compare!
If thus thy meaner works are fair!
If thus thy bounties gild the span
Of ruined earth and sinful man,
How glorious must the mansion be
Where thy redeemed shall dwell with Thee!

FIFTH SUNDAY AFTER TRINITY.

Creator of the rolling flood!
On whom thy people hope alone;
Who cam'st, by water and by blood,
For man's offences to atone;

Who from the labours of the deep
Didst set thy servant Peter free,
To feed on earth thy chosen sheep,
And build an endless church to thee.

Grant us, devoid of worldly care,
And leaning on thy bounteous hand
To seek thy help in humble prayer,
And on thy sacred rock to stand:

And when, our livelong toil to crown,
Thy call shall set the spirit free,
To cast with joy our burthen down,
And rise, O Lord! and follow thee!

SEVENTH SUNDAY AFTER TRINITY.

When spring unlocks the flowers to paint the laughing soil;
When summer's balmy showers refresh the mower's toil;
When winter binds in frosty chains the fallow and the flood,
In God the earth rejoiceth still, and owns his Maker good.

The birds that wake the morning, and those that love the shade;
The winds that sweep the mountain or lull the drowsy glade;
The sun that from his amber bower rejoiceth on his way,
The moon and stars, their Master's name in silent pomp display.

Shall man, the lord of nature, expectant of the sky,
Shall man, alone unthankful, his little praise deny?
No, let the year forsake his course, the seasons cease to be,
Thee, Master, must we always love, and, Saviour, honour thee.

The flowers of spring may wither, the hope of summer fade,
The autumn droop in winter, the birds forsake the shade;

The winds be lulled—the sun and moon forget their old decree,
But we in nature's latest hour, O Lord! will cling to thee.

TENTH SUNDAY AFTER TRINITY.

JERUSALEM, Jerusalem! enthroned once on high,
Thou favoured home of God on earth, thou heaven below the sky!
Now brought to bondage with thy sons, a curse and grief to see,
Jerusalem, Jerusalem! our tears shall flow for thee.

Oh! hadst thou known thy day of grace, and flocked beneath the wing
Of him who called thee lovingly, thine own anointed King,
Then had the tribes of all the world gone up thy pomp to see,
And glory dwelt within thy gates, and all thy sons been free!

'And who art thou that mournest me?" replied the ruin gray,
'And fear'st not rather that thyself may prove a castaway?
I am a dried and abject branch, my place is given to thee;
But wo to every barren graft of thy wild olive-tree!

"Our day of grace is sunk in night, our time of mercy spent,
For heavy was my children's crime, and strange their punishment;
Yet gaze not idly on our fall, but, sinner, warned be,
Who spared not his chosen seed may send his wrath on thee!

"Our day of grace is sunk in night, thy noon is in its prime;
Oh! turn and seek thy Saviour's face in this accepted time!
So, Gentile, may Jerusalem a lesson prove to thee,
And in the new Jerusalem thy home for ever be!"

THIRTEENTH SUNDAY AFTER TRINITY.

"Who yonder on the desert heath,
Complains in feeble tone?"
—"A pilgrim in the vale of death,
Faint, bleeding, and alone!"

"How cam'st thou to this dismal strand
Of danger, grief, and shame?"
-"From blessed Sion's holy land,
By folly led, I came!"

"What ruffian hand hath stript thee bare?
Whose fury laid thee low?"
—"Sin for my footsteps twined her snare,
And death has dealt the blow!"

"Can art no medicine for thy wound,
Nor nature strength supply?"
—"They saw me bleeding on the ground,
And passed in silence by!"

"But, sufferer! is no comfort near
Thy terrors to remove?"
—"There is to whom my soul was dear,
But I have scorned his love."

"What if his hand were nigh to save
From endless death thy days?"
—"The soul he ransomed from the grave
Should live but to his praise!"

"Rise then, O rise! his health embrace,
With heavenly strength renewed;
And such as is thy Saviour's grace,
Such be thy gratitude!"

FIFTEENTH SUNDAY AFTER TRINITY.

Lo! the lilies of the field,
How their leaves instruction yield!
Hark to nature's lesson given
By the blessed birds of Heaven!
Every bush and tufted tree
Warbles sweet philosophy;
"Mortal, fly from doubt and sorrow:
God provideth for the morrow!

"Say, with richer crimson glows
The kingly mantle than the rose?
Say, have kings more wholesome fare
That we, poor citizens of air?
Barns nor hoarded grain have we,
Yet we carol merrily.
Mortal, fly from doubt and sorrow!
God provideth for the morrow!

"One there lives whose guardian eye
Guides our humble destiny;
One there lives who, Lord of all,
Keeps our feathers lest they fall:
Pass we blithely, then, the time,
Fearless of the snare and lime,
Free from doubt and faithless sorrow;
God provideth for the morrow!"

SIXTEENTH SUNDAY AFTER TRINITY.

WAKE not, oh mother! sounds of lamentation!
Weep not, oh widow! weep not hopelessly!
Strong is his arm, the bringer of salvation,
Strong is the word of God to succour thee!

Bear forth the cold corpse, slowly, slowly bear him:
Hide his pale features with the sable pall:
Chide not the sad one wildly weeping near him:
Widowed and childless, she has lost her all!

Why pause the mourners? Who forbids our weeping?
Who the dark pomp of sorrow has delayed?
"Set down the bier—he is not dead but sleeping!
"Young man, arise!"—He spake, and was obeyed!

Change, then, oh sad one! grief to exultation,
Worship and fall before Messiah's knee.
Strong was his arm, the bringer of salvation,
Strong was the word of God to succour thee!

NINETEENTH SUNDAY AFTER TRINITY.

Oh blest were the accents of early creation,
When the word of Jehovah came down from above;
In the clods of the earth to infuse animation,
And wake their cold atoms to life and to love!

And mighty the tones which the firmament rended,
When on wheels of the thunder, and wings of the wind,
By lightning, and hail, and thick darkness attended,
He uttered on Sinai his laws to mankind.

And sweet was the voice of the First-born of heaven,
(Though poor his apparel, though earthly his form,)
Who said to the mourner, "Thy sins are forgiven!"
"Be whole!" to the sick,—and "Be still!" to the storm.

Oh, Judge of the world! when, arrayed in thy glory,
Thy summons again shall be heard from on high,
While nature stands trembling and naked before thee,
And waits on thy sentence to live or to die;

When the heaven shall fly fast from the sound of thy thunder,
And the sun, in thy lightnings, grow languid and pale,
And the sea yield her dead, and the tomb cleave asunder,
In the hour of thy terrors, let mercy prevail!

TWENTY-FIRST SUNDAY AFTER TRINITY.

The sound of war! In earth and air
The volleying thunders roll:
Their fiery darts the fiends prepare,
And dig the pit, and spread the snare,
Against the Christian's soul
The tyrant's sword, the rack, the flame,
The scorner's serpent tone,
Of bitter doubt, the barbed aim,
All, all conspire his heart to tame:
Force, fraud, and hellish fires assail
The rivets of his heavenly mail,
Amidst his foes alone.

Gods of the world! ye warrior host
Of darkness and of air,
In vain is all your impious boast,
In vain each missile lightning tost,
In vain the tempter's snare!
Though fast and far your arrows fly,
Though mortal nerve and bone
Shrink in convulsive agony,
The Christian can your rage defy;
Towers o'er his head salvation's crest,
Faith, like a buckler, guards his breast,
Undaunted, though alone.

'T is past! 't is o'er! in foul defeat
The demon host are fled!
Before the Saviour's mercy-seat,
(His live-long work of faith complete,)
Their conqueror bends his head.
"The spoils thyself hast gained, Lord!
I lay before thy throne:
Thou wert my rock, my shield, my sword;
My trust was in thy name and word:
'T was in thy strength my heart was strong;
Thy spirit went with mine along;
How was I then alone?"

TWENTY-SECOND SUNDAY AFTER TRINITY.

Oh God! my sins are manifold, against my life they cry,
And all my guilty deeds foregone, up to thy temple fly;
Wilt thou release my trembling soul, that to despair is driven?
"Forgive!" a blessed voice replied, "and thou shalt be forgiven!"

My foemen, Lord! are fierce and fell, they spurn me in their pride,
They render evil for my good, my patience they deride;

Arise, oh King! and be the proud to righteous ruin driven!
"Forgive!" an awful answer came, "as thou would'st be forgiven!"

Seven times, Oh Lord! I pardoned them, seven times they sinned again;
They practice still to work me wo, they triumph in my pain;
But let them dread my vengeance now, to just resentment driven!
'Forgive!" the voice of thunder spake, "or never be forgiven!"

TWENTY-THIRD SUNDAY AFTER TRINITY.

From foes that would the land devour;
From guilty pride, and lust of power;
From wild sedition's lawless hour;
From yoke of slavery;
From blinded zeal by faction led;
From giddy change by fancy bred;
From poisonous error's serpent head,
Good Lord, preserve us free!

Defend, oh God! with guardian hand,
The laws and ruler of our land,
And grant our church thy grace to stand
In faith and unity!
The spirit's help of thee we crave,
That thou whose blood was shed to save,
May'st, at thy second coming, have
A flock to welcome thee!

TWENTY-FOURTH SUNDAY AFTER TRINITY.

To conquer and to save, the Son of God
Came to his own in great humility,
Who wont to ride on cherub wings abroad,
And round him wrap the mantle of the sky.
The mountains bent their necks to form his road;
The clouds dropt down their fatness from on high;
Beneath his feet the wild waves softly flowed,
And the winds kissed his garment tremblingly!

The grave unbolted half his grisly door,
(For darkness and the deep had heard his fame,
Nor longer might their ancient rule endure;)
The mightiest of mankind stood hushed and tame:
And, trooping on strong wing, his angels came
To work his will, and kingdom to secure:
No strength he needed save his Father's name;
Babes were his heralds, and his friends the poor!

4*

FOR ST. JAMES'S DAY.

Though sorrows rise and dangers roll
In waves of darkness o'er my soul,
Though friends are false and love decays,
And few and evil are my days,
Though conscience, fiercest of my foes,
Swells with remembered guilt my woes,
Yet ev'n in nature's utmost ill,
I love thee, Lord! I love thee still!

Though Sinai's curse, in thunder dread,
Peals o'er mine unprotected head,
And memory points, with busy pain,
To grace and mercy given in vain,
Till nature, shrieking in the strife,
Would fly to hell, to 'scape from life,
Though every thought has power to kill,
I love thee, Lord! I love thee still!

Oh, by the pangs thyself hast borne,
The ruffian's blow, the tyrant's scorn;
By Sinai's curse, whose dreadful doom
Was buried in thy guiltless tomb:
By these my pangs, whose healing smart
Thy grace hath planted in my heart;
I know, I feel thy bounteous will!
Thou lovest me, Lord! thou lovest me still!

MICHAELMAS DAY.

Oh, captain of God's host, whose dreadful might
Led forth to war the armed Seraphim,
And from the starry height,
Subdued in burning fight,
Cast down that ancient dragon, dark and grim!

Thine angels, Christ! we laud in solemn lays,
Our elder brethren of the crystal sky,
Who, 'mid thy glory's blaze,
The ceaseless anthem raise,
And gird thy throne in faithful ministry!

We celebrate their love, whose viewless wing
Hath left for us so oft their mansion high
The mercies of their king,
To mortal saints to bring,
Or guard the couch of slumbering infancy.

But thee, the first and last, we glorify,
Who, when thy world was sunk in death and sin,
Not with thine hierarchy,
The armies of the sky,
But didst with thine own arm the battle win,

Alone didst pass the dark and dismal shore
Alone didst tread the wine-press, and alone,
All glorious in thy gore,
Didst light and life restore,
To us who lay in darkness and undone!

Therefore, with angels and archangels, we
To thy dear love our thankful chorus raise,
And tune our songs to thee
Who art, and ought to be,
And, endless as thy mercies, sound thy praise!

IN TIMES OF DISTRESS AND DANGER.

Oh God, that madest earth and sky, the darkness and the day,
Give ear to this thy family, and help us when we pray!
For wide the waves of bitterness around our vessel roar,
And heavy grows the pilot's heart to view the rocky shore!

The cross our master bore for us, for him we fain would bear,
But mortal strength to weakness turns, and courage to despair!
Then mercy on our failings, Lord! our sinking faith renew!
And when thy sorrows visit us, oh send thy patience too!

INTENDED TO BE SUNG

ON OCCASION OF HIS PREACHING A SERMON FOR THE CHURCH MISSIONARY SOCIETY, IN APRIL, 1820.

From Greenland's icy mountains,
From India's coral strand,
Where Afric's sunny fountains
Roll down their golden sand;
From many an ancient river,
From many a palmy plain,
They call us to deliver
Their land from error's chain!

What though the spicy breezes
Blow soft o'er Ceylon's isle,
Though every prospect pleases,
And only man is vile:
In vain with lavish kindness
The gifts of God are strown,
The heathen, in his blindness,
Bows down to wood and stone!

Can we, whose souls are lighted
With wisdom from on high,
Can we to men benighted
The lamp of life deny?
Salvation! oh salvation!
The joyful sound proclaim,
Till each remotest nation
Has learned Messiah's name!

Waft, waft, ye winds, his story,
And you, ye waters, roll,
Till, like a sea of glory,
It spreads from pole to pole;
Till o'er our ransomed nature,
The lamb for sinners slain,
Redeemer, King, Creator,
In bliss returns to reign!

AN INTROIT

TO BE SUNG BETWEEN THE LITANY AND COMMUNION SERVICE.

Oh most merciful!
Oh most bountiful!
God the Father Almighty!
By the Redeemer's
Sweet intercession
Hear us, help us when we cry!

BEFORE THE SACRAMENT.

Bread of the world, in mercy broken!
Wine of the soul in mercy shed!
By whom the words of life were spoken,
And in whose death our sins are dead!

Look on the heart by sorrow broken,
Look on the tears by sinners shed,
And be thy feast to us the token
That by thy grace our souls are fed!

AT A FUNERAL.

Beneath our feet and o'er our head
Is equal warning given;
Beneath us lie the countless dead,
Above us is the heaven!

Their names are graven on the stone,
Their bones are in the clay;
And ere another day is done,
Ourselves may be as they.

Death rides on every passing breeze,
He lurks in every flower;
Each season has its own disease,
Its peril every hour!

Our eyes have seen the rosy light
Of youth's soft cheek decay,
And Fate descend in sudden night
On manhood's middle day.

Our eyes have seen the steps of age
Halt feebly towards the tomb,
And yet shall earth our hearts engage,
And dreams of days to come?

Turn, mortal, turn! thy danger know;
Where'er thy foot can tread
The earth rings hollow from below,
And warns thee of her dead!

Turn, Christian, turn! thy soul apply
To truths divinely given;
The bones that underneath thee lie
Shall live for hell or heaven!

STANZAS

ON THE DEATH OF A FRIEND.

Thou art gone to the grave! but we will not deplore thee,
Though sorrows and darkness encompass the tomb:
Thy Saviour has passed through its portal before thee,
And the lamp of his love is thy guide through the gloom!

Thou art gone to the grave! we no longer behold thee,
Nor tread the rough paths of the world by thy side;
But the wide arms of Mercy are spread to enfold thee,
And sinners may die, for the SINLESS has died!

Thou art gone to the grave! and, its mansion forsaking,
Perchance thy weak spirit in fear lingered long;
But the mild rays of paradise beamed on thy waking,
And the sound which thou heardst was the seraphim's song!

Thou art gone to the grave! but we will not deplore thee,
Whose God was thy ransom, thy guardian and guide;
He gave thee, he took thee, and he will restore thee,
And death has no sting, for the Saviour has died!*

* The following stanzas were written as an addition to the above hymn, by an English clergyman, on hearing of the decease of the author.

Thou art gone to the grave! and whole nations bemoan thee,
Who caught from thy lips the glad tidings of peace:
Yet grateful, they still in their hearts shall enthrone thee,
And ne'er shall thy name from their memories cease.

Thou art gone to the grave! but thy work shall not perish,
That work which the spirit of wisdom hath blest;
His strength shall sustain it, his comforts shall cherish,
And make it to prosper, though thou art at rest.

ON RECOVERY FROM SICKNESS.

Oh, Saviour of the faithful dead,
With whom thy servants dwell,
Though cold and green the turf is spread
Above their narrow cell,—

No more we cling to mortal clay,
We doubt and fear no more,
Nor shrink to tread the darksome way
Which thou hast trod before!

'Twas hard from those I loved to go,
Who knelt around my bed,
Whose tears bedewed my burning brow,
Whose arms upheld my head!

As fading from my dizzy view,
I sought their forms in vain,
The bitterness of death I knew,
And groaned to live again.

'Twas dreadful when th' accuser's power
Assailed my sinking heart,
Recounting every wasted hour,
And each unworthy part:

But, Jesus! in that mortal fray,
Thy blessed comfort stole,
Like sunshine in a stormy day,
Across my darkened soul!

When soon or late this feeble breath
No more to thee shall pray,
Support me through the vale of death,
And in the darksome way!

When clothed in fleshly weeds again
I wait thy dread decree,
Judge of the world! bethink thee then
That thou hast died for me.

Translations of Pindar.

THE FIRST OLYMPIC ODE.

TO HIERO OF SYRACUSE, VICTOR IN THE HORSE RACE.

CAN earth, or fire, or liquid air,
With water's sacred stream compare?
Can aught that wealthy tyrants hold
Surpass the lordly blaze of gold?—
Or lives there one, whose restless eye
Would seek along the empty sky,
Beneath the sun's meridian ray,
A warmer star, a purer day?—
O thou, my soul, whose choral song,
Would tell of contests sharp and strong,
Extol not other lists above
The circus of Olympian Jove;
Whence borne on many a tuneful tongue,
So Saturn's seed the anthem sung,
With harp, and flute, and trumpet's call,
Hath sped to Hiero's festival.—

Over sheep-clad Sicily
Who the righteous sceptre beareth,
Every flower of virtue's tree
Wove in various wreath he weareth.—
But the bud of poesy
Is the fairest flower of all;
Which the bards, in social glee,
Strew round Hiero's wealthy hall.—
The harp on yonder pin suspended,
Seize it, boy, for Pisa's sake;
And that good steed's, whose thought will wake
A joy with anxious fondness blended:—
No sounding lash his sleek side rended;—
By Alpheus' brink, with feet of flame,
Self-driven, to the goal he tended:
And earned the olive wreath of fame
For that dear lord, whose righteous name
The sons of Syracusa tell:—
Who loves the generous courser well:
Beloved himself by all who dwell
In Pelop's Lydian colony.—
—Of earth-embracing Neptune, he
The darling, when, in days of yore,
All lovely from the caldron red
By Clotho's spell delivered,
The youth an ivory shoulder bore.—

Well!—these are tales of mystery!—
And many a darkly-woven lie
With men will easy credence gain;
While truth, calm truth, may speak in vain;
For eloquence, whose honeyed sway
Our frailer mortal wits obey,
Can honour give to actions ill,
And faith to deeds incredible;—
And bitter blame, and praises high,
Fall truest from posterity.—

But, if we dare the deeds rehearse
Of those that aye endure,
'T were meet that in such dangerous verse
Our every word were pure.—
Then, son of Tantalus, receive
A plain unvarnished lay!—
My song shall elder fables leave,
And of thy parent say,
That, when in heaven a favoured guest,
He called the gods in turns to feast
On Sipylus, his mountain home:—
The sovereign of the ocean foam,
—Can mortal from such favour prove?
Rapt thee on golden car above
To highest house of mighty Jove;
To which, in after day,
Came golden-haired Ganymede,
As bard in ancient story read,
The dark-winged eagle's prey.—

And when no earthly tongue could tell
The fate of thee, invisible;—
Nor friends, who sought thee wide in vain,
To soothe thy weeping mother's pain,
Could bring the wanderer home again;
Some envious neighbour's spleen,
In distant hints, and darkly, said,
That in the caldron hissing red,
And on the god's great table spread,
Thy mangled limbs were seen.—
But who shall tax, I dare not, I,
The blessed gods with gluttony?—
Full oft the sland'rous tongue has felt
By their high wrath the thunder dealt;—
And sure, if ever mortal head
Heaven's holy watchers honoured,
That head was Lydia's lord.—
Yet, could not mortal heart digest
The wonders of that heavenly feast;
Elate with pride, a thought unblest
Above his nature soared.—
And now, condemned to endless dread,—
(Such is the righteous doom of fate,)
He eyes, above his guilty head,
The shadowy rocks' impending weight:—
The fourth, with that tormented three(1)
In horrible society!—

For that, in frantic theft,
The nectar cup he reft,
And to his mortal peers in feasting poured
For whom a sin it were
With mortal life to share
The mystic dainties of th' immortal board:
And who by policy
Can hope to 'scape the eye
Of him who sits above by men and gods adored?

For such offence, a doom severe,
Sent down the sun to sojourn here
Among the fleeting race of man;—
Who, when the curly down began
To clothe his cheek in darker shade,
To car-borne Pisa's royal maid(2)
A lover's tender service paid.—
But, in the darkness first he stood
Alone, by ocean's hoary flood,
And raised to him the suppliant cry,
The hoarse earth-shaking deity.—

Nor called in vain, through cloud and storm
Half-seen, a huge and shadowy form,
The god of waters came.—
He came, whom thus the youth addressed—
"Oh thou, if that immortal breast
Have felt a lover's flame,
A lover's prayer in pity hear,
Repel the tyrant's brazen spear
That guards my lovely dame!—
And grant a car whose rolling speed
May help a lover at his need;
Condemned by Pisa's hand to bleed
Unless I win the envied meed
In Elis' field of fame!—

For youthful knights thirteen
By him have slaughtered been,
His daughter vexing with perverse delay.—
Such to a coward's eye
Were evil augury;—
Nor durst a coward's heart the strife essay!
Yet, since alike to all
The doom of death must fall,
Ah! wherefore, sitting in unseemly shade,
Wear out a nameless life,
Remote from noble strife,
And all the sweet applause to valour paid?—
Yes!—I will dare the course! but, thou,
Immortal friend, my prayer allow!"—

Thus, not in vain, his grief he told—
The ruler of the wat'ry space
Bestowed a wondrous car of gold,
And tireless steeds of winged pace.—
So, victor in the deathful race,
He tamed the strength of Pisa's king,
And, from his bride of beauteous face,
Beheld a stock of warriors spring,
Six valiant sons, as legends sing.—
And now, with fame and virtue crowned,
Where Alpheus' stream in wat'ry ring,
Encircles half his turfy mound,
He sleeps beneath the piled ground;(3)
Near that blest spot where strangers move
In many a long procession round
The altar of protecting Jove.—
Yet chief, in yonder lists of fame,
Survives the noble Pelop's name;
Where strength of hands and nimble feet
In stern and dubious contest meet;
And high renown and honeyed praise,
And following length of honoured days,
To victor's weary toil repays.—

But what are past or future joys?
The present is our own!
And he is wise who best employs
The passing hour alone.—
To crown with knightly wreath the king,
(A grateful task,) be mine;
And on the smooth Æolian string
To praise his ancient line!
For ne'er shall wandering minstrel find
A chief so just,—a friend so kind;
With every grace of fortune blest;
The mightiest, wisest, bravest, best!—

God, who beholdeth thee and all thy deeds,(4)
Have thee in charge, king Hiero!—so again
The bard may sing thy horny-hoofed steeds
In frequent triumph o'er the Olympian plain;
Nor shall the Bard awake a lowly strain,
His wild notes flinging o'er the Cronian steep
Whose ready muse, and not invoked in vain,
For such high mark her strongest shaft shall keep

Each hath his proper eminence!
To kings indulgent, Providence
(No farther search the will of Heaven)
The glories of the earth hath given.—
Still may'st thou reign! enough for me
To dwell with heroes like to thee,
Myself the chief of Grecian minstrelsy.—

II.

TO THERON OF AGRAGAS, VICTOR IN THE CHARIOT RACE.

O song! whose voice the harp obeys,
Accordant aye with answering string;
What god, what hero wilt thou praise,
What man of godlike prowess sing?—
Lo, Jove himself is Pisa's king;
And Jove's strong son the first to raise
The barriers of th' Olympic ring.—
And now, victorious on the wing

Of sounding wheels, our bards proclaim
The stranger Theron's honoured name,
The flower of no ignoble race,(5)
And prop of ancient Agragas!—
His patient sires, for many a year,
Where that blue river rolls its flood,
Mid fruitless war and civil blood
Essayed their sacred home to rear,—
Till time assigned, in fatal hour,
Their native virtues, wealth and power;
And made them from their low degree,
The eye of warlike Sicily.

And, may that power of ancient birth,
From Saturn sprung, and parent Earth,
Of tall Olympus' lord,
Who sees with still benignant eye
The games' long splendour sweeping by
His Alpheus' holy ford:—
Appeased with anthems chanted high,
To Theron's late posterity
A happier doom accord!—
Or good or ill, the past is gone,
Nor time himself, the parent one,
Can make the former deeds undone
But who would these recall,—
When happier days would fain efface
The memory of each past disgrace,
And, from the gods, on Theron's race
Unbounded blessings fall?—

Example meet for such a song,
The sister queens of Laius' blood;
Who sorrow's edge endured long,
Made keener by remembered good!—
Yet now, she breathes the air of Heaven
(On earth by smouldering thunder riven.)
Long-haired Semele:—
To Pallas dear is she;—
Dear to the sire of gods, and dear
To him, her son, in dreadful glee
Who shakes the ivy-wreathed spear.—

And thus, they tell that deep below
The sounding ocean's ebb and flow,
Amid the daughters of the sea,
A sister nymph must Ino be,
And dwell in bliss eternally:—
But, ignorant and blind,
We little know the coming hour;
Or if the latter day shall lower;
Or if to nature's kindly power
Our life in peace resigned,
Shall sink like fall of summer eve,
And on the face of darkness leave
A ruddy smile behind.—
For grief and joy with fitful gale
Our crazy bark by turns assail,
And, whence our blessings flow,
That same tremendous Providence
Will oft a varying doom dispense,
And lay the mighty low.—

To Theban Laius that befell,
Whose son, with murder dyed,
Fulfilled the former oracle,
Unconscious parricide!—
Unconscious!—yet avenging hell
Pursued th' offender's stealthy pace,
And heavy, sure, and hard it fell,
The curse of blood, on all his race!—
Spared from their kindred strife,
The young Thersander's life,
Stern Polynices' heir, was left alone:
In every martial game,
And in the field of fame,
For early force and matchless prowess known.
Was left, the pride and prop to be
Of good Adrastus' pedigree.
And hence, through loins of ancient kings,
The warrior blood of Theron springs;
Exalted name! to whom belong
The minstrel's harp, the poet's song,
In fair Olympia crowned;
And where, mid Pythia's olives blue,
An equal lot his brother drew:
And where his twice-twain coursers flew
The isthmus twelve times round.—
Such honour, earned by toil and care,
May best his ancient wrongs repair,
And wealth, unstained by pride,
May laugh at fortune's fickle power,
And blameless in the tempting hour
Of syren ease abide:—
Led by that star of heavenly ray,
Which best may keep our darkling way
O'er life's unsteady tide!—

For, whoso holds in righteousness the throne,
He in his heart hath known
How the foul spirits of the guilty dead,
In chambers dark and dread,
Of nether earth abide, and penal flame
Where he, whom none may name,(6)
Lays bare the soul by stern necessity;
Seated in judgment high;
The minister of God whose arm is there,
In heaven alike and hell, almighty every where!

But, ever bright, by day, by night,
Exulting in excess of light;
From labour free and long distress,
The good enjoy their happiness.—
No more the stubborn soil they cleave,
Nor stem for scanty food the wave;
But with the venerable gods they dwell:—
No tear bedims their thankful eye,
Nor mars their long tranquillity;
While those accursed howl in pangs unspeakable

But, but who the thrice-renewed probation
Of either world may well endure;
And keep with righteous destination
The soul from all transgression pure;
To such and such alone is given,
To walk the rainbow paths of heaven,
To that tall city of almighty time,
Where Ocean's balmy breezes play,
And, flashing to the western day,
The gorgeous blossoms of such blessed clime,
Now in the happy isles are seen
Sparkling through the groves of green;
And now, all glorious to behold,
Tinge the wave with floating gold.—

Hence are their garlands woven—hence their hands
Filled with triumphal boughs;—the righteous doom
Of Rhadamanthus, whom, o'er these his lands,
A blameless judge in every time to come,
Chronos, old Chronos, sire of gods hath placed;
Who with his consort dear,
Dread Rhea, reigneth here,
On cloudy throne with deathless honour graced.

And still, they say, in high communion,
Peleus and Cadmus here abide;
And, with the blest in blessed union,
(Nor Jove has Thetis' prayer denied.)(7)
The daughter of the ancient sea
Hath brought her warrior boy to be;
Him whose stern avenging blow
Laid the prop of Ilium low,
Hector, trained to slaughter, fell,
By all but him invincible;—
And sea-born Cycnus tamed; and slew
Aurora's knight of Ethiop hue.—

Beneath my rattling belt I wear
A sheaf of arrows keen and clear,
Of vocal shafts, that wildly fly,
Nor ken the base their import high,
Yet to the wise they breathe no vulgar melody.
Yes, he is wise whom nature's dower
Hath raised above the crowd.—
But, trained in study's formal hour,
There are who hate the minstrel's power,(8)
As daws who mark the eagle tower,
And croak in envy loud!—
So let them rail! but thou, my heart!
Rest on the bow thy levelled dart;
Nor seek a worthier aim
For arrow sent on friendship's wing,
Than him the Agragantine king
Who best thy song may claim.—
For, by eternal truth I swear,
His parent town shall scantly bear
A soul to every friend so dear,
A breast so void of blame;
Though twenty lustres rolling round
With rising youth her nation crowned,
In heart, in hand, should none be found
Like Theron's honoured name.—
Yes! we have heard the factious lie!—
But let the babbling vulgar try
To blot his worth with tyranny.—
Seek thou the ocean strand!—
And when thy soul would fain record
The bounteous deeds of yonder lord,
Go—reckon up the sand!

III.

TO THE SAME.

MAY my solemn strain ascending
Please the long-haired Helen well,
And those brave twins of Leda's shell
The stranger's holy cause defending!
With whose high name the chorus blending
To ancient Agragas shall rise,
And Theron for the chariot prize
Again, and not in vain, contending.—
The muse, in numbers bold and high,
Hath taught my Dorian note to fly,
Worthy of silent awe, a strange sweet harmony.
Yes!—as I fix mine eager view
On yonder wreath of paly blue,
That olive wreath, whose shady round
Amid the courser's mane is bounded;
I feel again the sacred glow
That bids my strain of rapture flow,
With shrilly breath of Spartan flute,
The many-voiced harp to suit;
And wildly fling my numbers sweet,
Again mine ancient friend to greet.—
Nor, Pisa, thee I leave unstrung;
To men the parent of renown.
Amid whose shady ringlets strung,
Etolia binds her olive crown;
Whose sapling root from Scythia down
And Ister's fount Alcides bare,(9)
To deck his parent's hallowed town;
With placid brow and suppliant prayer
Soothing the favoured northern seed,
Whose horny-hoofed victims bleed
To Phœbus of the flowing hair.

A boon from these the hero prayed:
One graft of that delightful tree;
To Jove's high hill a welcome shade,
To men a blessed fruit to be,
And crown of future victory.—
For that fair moon, whose slender light
With inefficient horn had shone,
When late on Pisa's airy height
He reared to Jove the altar stone;

Now, through the dappled air, alone,
In perfect ring of glory bright,
Guided her golden-wheeled throne;
The broad and burning eye of night.—
And now the days were told aright,
When Alpheus, from his sandy source,
Should judge the champion's eager might,
And mark of wheels the rolling force.—
Nor yet a tree to cheer the sight
The Cronian vale of Pelops bore;—
Obnoxious to the noonday weight
Of summer suns, a naked shore.—

But she who sways the silent sky,
Latona's own equestrian maid,
Beheld how far Alcides strayed,
Bound on adventure strange and high:
Forth from the glens of Arcady
To Istrian rocks in ice arrayed
He urged th' interminable race,
(Such penance had Eurystheus laid,)
The golden-horned hind to chase,
Which, grateful for Diana's aid,
By her redeemed from foul embrace,
Old Atlas' daughter hallowed.—(10)
Thus, following where the quarry fled,
Beyond the biting North he past,
Beyond the regions of the blast,
And, all unknown to traveller's tread,
He saw the blessed land at last.—
He stopt, he gazed with new delight,
When that strange verdure met his sight;
And soft desire enflamed his soul
(Where twelve-times round the chariots roll,)
To plant with such the Pisan goal.

But now, unseen to mortal eyes,
He comes to Theron's sacrifice;
And with him brings to banquet there
High-bosomed Leda's knightly pair.—
Himself to high Olympus bound,
To these a latest charge he gave,
A solemn annual feast to found,
And of contending heroes round
To deck the strong, the swift, the brave.—
Nor doubt I that on Theron's head,
And on the good Emmenides,
The sons of Jove their blessings shed;
Whom still, with bounteous tables spread,
That holy tribe delight to please;
Observing with religious dread
The hospitable god's decrees.—

But, wide as water passeth earthy clay,
Or sun-bright gold transcendeth baser ore;
Wide as from Greece to that remotest shore
Whose rock-built pillars own Alcides' sway;
Thy fame hath past thine equals!—To explore
The further ocean all in vain essay,
Or fools or wise;—here from thy perilous way
Cast anchor here, my bark! I dare no more!—

IV.

TO PSAUMIS OF CAMARINA.

Oh, urging on the tireless speed
Of Thunder's elemental steed,
Lord of the world, Almighty Jove!
Since these thine hours have me forth
The witness of thy champions' worth,
And prophet of thine olive grove;—
And since the good thy poet hear,
And hold his tuneful message dear;—
Saturnian Lord of Etna hill!—
Whose storm-cemented rocks encage
The hundred-headed rebel's rage;
Accept with favourable will
The Muses' gift of harmony;
The dance, the song, whose numbers high
Forbid the hero's dame to die,
A crown of life abiding still!—

Hark! round the car of victory,
Where noble Psaumis sits on high,
  The cheering notes resound;
Who vows to swell with added fame
His Camarina's ancient name;
  With Pisan olive crowned.—
And thou, oh father, hear his prayer!
For much I praise the knightly care
  That trains the warrior steed:—
Nor less the hopitable hall
Whose open doors the stranger call;—
Yet, praise I Psaumis most of all
  For wise and peaceful rede,
And patriot love of liberty.—
—What?—do we wave the glozing lie?—
Then whoso list my truth to try,
  The proof be in the deed!—

To Lemnos's laughing dames of yore,
Such was the proof Ernicus bore,(11)
  When, matchless in his speed,
All brazen-armed the racer hoar,
Victorious on the applauding shore,
  Sprang to the proffered meed;—
Bowed to the queen his wreathed head;—
"Thou seest my limbs are light," he said;
  "And, lady, may'st thou know,
That every joint is firmly strung,
And hand and heart alike are young;
Though treacherous time my locks among
  Have strewed a summer snow!"

V.

TO THE SAME.

Accept of these Olympian games the crown,
Daughter of Ocean, rushy Camarine!—
The flower of knightly worth and high renown,
Which car-borne Psaumis on thy parent shrine

(Psaumis, the patriot, whom thy peopled town
Its second author owns,) with rite divine
Suspends!—His praise the twice six altars tell
Of the great gods whom he hath feasted well
With blood of bulls; the praise of victory,
Where cars and mules and steeds contest the prize;
And that green garland of renown to thee
He hallows, virgin daughter of the sea!
And to his sire and household deities—
Thee too, returning home from Pelops' land,
Thee, guardian Pallas, and thy holy wood,
He hails with song; and cool Oanus' flood;
And of his native pool the rushy strand;
And thy broad bed, refreshing Hipparis,
Whose silent waves the peopled city kiss;
That city which hath blest his bounteous hand,
Rearing her goodly bowers on high.—(12)
That now, redeemed from late disgrace,
The wealthy mother of a countless race,
She lifts her front in shining majesty.—

'Tis ever thus! by toil, and pain,
And cumbrous cost, we strive to gain
Some seeming prize whose issues lie
In darkness and futurity.
And yet, if conquest crown our aim,
Then, foremost in the rolls of fame,
Even from the envious herd a forced applause we claim.
O cloud-enthroned, protecting Jove,
Who sitt'st the Cronian cliffs above,
And Alpheus' ample wave,
And that dark gloom hast deigned to love
Of Ida's holy cave!
On softest Lydian notes to thee
I tune the choral prayer,
That this thy town, the brave, the free,
The strong in virtuous energy,
May feel thine endless care.—
And, victor thou, whose matchless might
The Pisan wreath hath bound;
Still, Psaumis, be thy chief delight
In generous coursers found.—
Calm be thy latter age, and late
And gently fall the stroke of fate,
Thy children standing round!—
And know, when favouring gods have given
A green old age, a temper even,
And wealth and fame in store,
The task were vain to scale the heaven;—
—Have those immortals more?

VI.

TO AGESIAS OF SYRACUSE.

Who seeks a goodly bower to raise,
Conspicuous to the stranger's eye,
With gold the lintel overlays,
And clothes the porch in ivory.—

So bright, so bold, so wonderful,
The choicest themes of verse I cull,
To each high song a frontal high!—
But, lives there one whose brows around
The green Olympian wreath is bound;
Prophet and priest in those abodes
Where Pisans laud the sire of gods;
And Syracusa's denizen?—
Who, 'mid the sons of mortal men,
While envy's self before his name
Abates her rage, may fitlier claim
Whate'er a bard may yield of fame?

For sure to no forbidden strife,
In hallowed Pisa's field of praise,
He came, the priest of blameless life!—
Nor who in peace hath past his days,
Marring with canker sloth his might,
May hope a name in standing fight
Nor in the hollow ship to raise!—
By toil, illustrious toil alone,
Of elder times the heroes shone;
And, bought by like emprize, to thee,
Oh warrior priest, like honour be!—
Such praise as good Adrastus bore
To him, the prophet chief(13) of yore,
When, snatched from Thebes' accursed fight
With steed and car and armour bright,
Down, down he sank to earthly night.

When the fight was ended,
And the sevenfold pyres
All their funeral fires
In one sad lustre blended.

The leader of the host
Murmured mournfully,
"I lament for the eye
Of all mine army lost!—
To gods and mortals dear,
Either art he knew;
Augur tried and true,
And strong to wield the spear!"
And by the powers divine,
Such praise is justly thine,
Oh Syracusian peer,
For of a gentle blood thy race is sprung,
As she shall truly tell, the muse of honeyed tongue.

Then yoke the mules of winged pace,
And, Phintis, climb the car with me;(14)
For well they know the path to trace
Of yonder victor's pedigree!—
Unbar the gates of song, unbar!—
For we to day must journey far,
To Sparta, and to Pitane.—

She, mournful nymph, and nursing long
Her silent pain and virgin wrong,

To Neptune's rape a daughter fair,
Evadne of the glossy hair,
(Dark as the violet's darkest shade,)
In solitary sorrow bare.
Then to her nurse the infant maid
She weeping gave, and bade convey
To high Phersana's hall away:
Where woman-grown, and doomed to prove
In turn a god's disastrous love,
Her charms allured the lord of day.

Nor long the months, ere, fierce in pride,
The painful tokens of disgrace
Her foster-father sternly eyed,
Fruit of the furtive god's embrace.—
He spake not, but, with soul on flame,
He sought th' unknown offender's name,
At Phœbus' Pythian dwelling place.—

But she, beneath the greenwood spray,
Her zone of purple silk untied;
And flung the silver clasp away
That rudely pressed her heaving side;(15)
While, in the solitary wood,
Lucina's self to aid her stood,
And fate a secret force supplied.—

But, who the mother's pang can tell
As sad and slowly she withdrew,
And bade her babe a long farewell,
Laid on a bed of violets blue?
When ministers of Heaven's decree,
(Dire nurses they and strange to see,)
Two scaly snakes of azure hue
Watched o'er his helpless infancy,
And, rifled from the mountain bee,
Bare on their forky tongues a harmless honey dew.—

Swift roll the wheels! from Delphos home
Arcadia's car-borne chief is come;
But, ah, how changed his eye!—
His wrath is sunk, and past his pride,
"Where is Evadne's babe," he cried,
"Child of the deity?
"'T was thus the augur god replied,
"Nor strove his noble seed to hide;
"And to his favoured boy, beside,
"The gift of prophecy,
"And power beyond the sons of men
"The secret things of fate to ken,
"His blessing will supply."—

But, vainly, from his liegemen round,
He sought the noble child;
Who, naked on the grassy ground,
And nurtured in the wild,
Was moistened with the sparkling dew
Beneath his hawthorn bower;
Where morn her wat'ry radiance threw,
Now golden bright, now deeply blue,
Upon the violet flower.—

From that dark bed of breathing bloom
His mother gave his name;
And Iamus, through years to come,
Will live in lasting fame;
Who, when the blossom of his days,
Had ripened on the tree,
From forth the brink where Alpheus strays,
Invoked the god whose sceptre sways
The hoarse resounding sea;
And, whom the Delian isle obeys,
The archer deity.—
Alone amid the nightly shade,
Beneath the naked heaven he prayed,
And sire and grandsire called to aid;
When lo, a voice that loud and dread
Burst from the horizon free;
"Hither!" it spake, "to Pisa's shore!
"My voice, oh son, shall go before,
"Beloved, follow me!"—

So, in the visions of his sire, he went
Where Cronium's scarred and barren brow
Was red with morning's earliest glow
Though darkness wrapt the nether element.—
There, in a lone and craggy dell,
A double spirit on him fell,
Th' unlying voice of birds to tell,
And, (when Alcmena's son should found
The holy games in Elis crowned,)
By Jove's high altar evermore to dwell,
Prophet and priest!—From him descend
The fathers of our valiant friend,
Wealthy alike and just and wise,
Who trod the plain and open way;
And who is he that dare despise
With galling taunt the Cronian prize,
Or their illustrious toil gainsay,
Whose chariots whirling twelve times round
With burning wheels the Olympian ground
Have gilt their brow with glory's ray?
For, not the steams of sacrifice
From cool Cyllene's height of snow,(16)
Nor vainly from thy kindred rise
The heaven-appeasing litanies
To Hermes, who to men below,
Or gives the garland or denies:—
By whose high aid, Agesias, know,
And his, the thunderer of the skies,
The olive wreath hath bound thy brow!—

Arcadian! Yes, a warmer zeal
Shall whet my tongue thy praise to tell!
I feel the sympathetic flame
Of kindred love;—a Theban I,
Whose parent nymph from Arcady
(Metope's daughter, Thebe) came.—
Dear fountain goddess, warrior maid,
By whose pure rills my youth hath played;

Who now assembled Greece among,
To car-borne chiefs and warriors strong,
Have wove the many-coloured song.—

Then, minstrel! bid thy chorus rise
To Juno, queen of deities,(17)
Parthenian lady of the skies!
For, live there yet who dare defame
With sordid mirth our country's name;
Who tax with scorn our ancient line,
And call the brave Bœotians swine;—
Yet, Æneas, sure thy numbers high
May charm their brutish enmity;
Dear herald of the holy muse,
And teeming with Parnassian dews,
Cup of untasted harmony!—
That strain once more!—The chorus raise
To Syracusa's wealthy praise,
And his the lord whose happy reign
Controls Trincria's ample plain,
Hiero, the just, the wise,
Whose steamy offerings rise
To Jove, to Ceres, and that darling maid,
Whom, rapt in chariot bright,
And horses silver-white,
Down to his dusky bower the lord of hell conveyed!

Oft hath he heard the muses' string resound
His honoured name; and may his latter days,
With wealth and worth, and minstrel garlands crowned,
Mark with no envious ear a subject praise,(18)
Who now from fair Arcadia's forest wide
To Syracusa, homeward, from his home
Returns, a common care, a common pride,—
(And, whoso darkling braves the ocean foam,
May safeliest moored with twofold anchor ride.)
Arcadia, Sicily, on either side
Guard him with prayer; and thou who rulest the deep,
Fair Amphitrite's lord! in safety keep
His tossing keel,—and evermore to me
No meaner theme assign of poesy!

NOTES.

Note 1, page 28, col. 2.

The fourth with that tormented three.

The three were Sisyphus, Tityus, and Ixion. The author of the Odyssey, or, at least, of that passage which describes the punishments of Tantalus, assigns him an eternity of hunger, thirst, and disappointment. Which of these opinions is most ancient, is neither very easy nor very material to decide. The impending rock of Pindar is perhaps a less appropriate, but surely, a more picturesque mode of punishment.

Note 2, page 29, col. 1.

Car-borne Pisa's royal maid.

Œnomaus, king of Pisa, had promised his daughter, the heiress of his states, in marriage to any warrior who should excel him in the chariot race, on condition however that the candidates should stake their lives on the issue. Thirteen had essayed and perished before Pelops.

Note 3, page 29, col. 2.

Sleeps beneath the piled ground.

Like all other very early tombs, the monument of Pelops was a barrow or earthen mound. I know not whether it may still be traced. The spot is very accurately pointed out, and such works are not easily obliterated.

Note 4, page 29, col. 2.

God who beholdeth thee and all thy deeds,

The solemnity of this prayer contrasted with its object, that Hiero might again succeed in the chariot race, is ridiculous to modern ears. I do not indeed believe that the Olympic and other games had so much importance attached to them by the statesmen and warriors of Greece, as is pretended by the sophists of later ages; but where the manners are most simple, public exhibitions, it should be remembered, are always most highly estimated, and religious prejudice combined with the ostentation of wealth to give distinction to the Olympic contests.

Note 5, page 30, col. 1.

The flower of no ignoble race.

Theron was a descendant of Œdipus, and consequently of Cadmus. His family had, through a long line of ancestors, been remarkable, both in Greece and Sicily, for misfortune; and he was himself unpopular with his subjects and engaged in civil war. Allusions to these circumstances often occur in the present ode.

Note 6, page 30, col. 2.

—He whom none may name.

In the original "τις," "a certain nameless person." The ancients were often scrupulous about pronouncing the names of their gods, particularly those who presided over the region of future hopes and fears; a scruple corresponding with the Rabbinical notions of the ineffable word. The pictures which follow present a striking discrepancy to the mythology of Homer, and of the general herd of Grecian poets, whose Zeus is as far inferior to the one supreme divinity of Pindar, as the religion of Pindar himself falls short of the clearness and majesty of Revelation. The connexion of these Eleusinian doctrines with those of Hindustan, is in many points sufficiently striking.

Southey and Pindar might seem to have drunk at the same source.

Note 7, page 31, col. 1.

Nor Jove has Thetis' prayer denied.

I know not why, except for his brutality to the body of Hector, Achilles is admitted with so much difficulty into the islands of the blessed. That this was considered in the time of Pindar as sufficient to exclude him without particular intercession, shows at least that a great advance had been made in moral feeling since the days of Homer.

Note 8, page 31, col. 1.

Trained in study's formal hour,
There are who hate the minstrel's power.

It was not likely that Pindar's peculiarities should escape criticism, nor was his temper such as to bear it with a very even mind. He treats his rivals and assailants with at least a sufficient portion of disdain as servile adherents to rule, and mere students without genius. Some of their sarcasms passed however into proverbs. "Διος Κορινθος," an expression in ridicule of Pindar's perpetual recurrence to mythology and antiquities, is preserved in the Phædon: while his occasional mention of himself and his own necessities, is parodied by Aristophanes. I can not but hope, however, that the usual conduct of Pindar himself, was less obtrusive and importunate than that of the Dithyrambic poet who intrudes on the festival of Nephelocoggugia, like the Gælic bard in "Christ's kirk o' the green."

Note 9, page 31, col. 2.

Whose sapling root from Scythian down
And Ister's fount Alcides bare.

There seems to have been, in all countries, a disposition to place a region of peculiar happiness and fertility among inaccessible mountains, and at the source of their principal rivers. Perhaps, indeed, the Mount Meru of Hindustan, the blameless Ethiopians at the head of the Nile, and the happy Hyperborean regions at the source of the Ister, are only copies of the garden and river of God in Eden. Some truth is undoubtedly mixed with the tradition here preserved by Pindar. The olive was not indigenous in Greece, and its first specimens were planted near Pisa. That they ascribed its introduction to the universal hero, Hercules, and derived its stock from the land of the blessed, need not be wondered at by those who know the importance of such a present. The Hyperborean or Atlantic region, which continually receded in proportion as Europe was explored, still seems to have kept its ground in the fancies of the vulgar, under the names of the island of St. Brandan, of Flath Innis, or the fortunate land of Cockayne, till the discovery of America peopled the western ocean with something less illusive.

Note 10, page 32, col. 1.

Old Atlas' daughter hallowed.

Taygeta.

Note 11, page 32, col. 2.

To Lemnos' laughing dames of yore,
Such was the proof Ernicus bore.

Ernicus was one of the Argonauts, who distinguished himself in the games celebrated at Lemnos by its hospitable queen Hypsipile, as victor in the foot-race of men clothed in armour. He was prematurely gray-headed, and therefore derided by the Lemnian women before he had given this proof of his vigour. It is not impossible that Psaumis had the same singularity of appearance.

There is a sort of playfulness in this ode, which would make us suspect that Pindar had no very sincere respect for the character of Psaumis. Perhaps he gave offence by it; for the following poem to the same champion is in a very different style.

Note 12, page 33, col. 1.

Rearing her goodly towers on high.

Camarina had been lately destroyed by fire, and rebuilt in a great measure by the liberality of Psaumis.

Note 13, page 33, col. 2.

Such praise as good Adrastus bore
To him the prophet chief.——

The prophet chief is Amphiaraus, who was swallowed up by the earth before the attack of Polynices and his allies on Thebes, either because the gods determined to rescue his virtues from the stain of that odious conflict; or according to the sagacious Lydgate, because, being a sorcerer and a pagan "byshoppe," the time of his compact was expired, and the infernal powers laid claim to him.

Note 14, page 33, col. 2.

Then yoke the mules of winged pace,
And Phintis climb the car with me.

Agesias had been victor in the Apene or chariot drawn by mules; Phintis was, probably, his charioteer.

Note 15, page 34, col. 1.

And flung the silver clasp away
That rudely prest her heaving side.

I venture in the present instance to translate "καλπις" a clasp, because it was undoubtedly used for the stud or buckle to a horse's bit, as "καλπαζειν" signifies to run by a horse's side holding the bridle. The "καλυξ" too, appended to the belt of Hercules, which he left with his Scythian mistress, should seem, from the manner in which Herodotus mentions it, to have been a clasp or stud, nor can I in the present passage understand why the pregnant Evadne should encumber herself with a water-pot, or why the water-pot and zone should be mentioned as laid aside at the same time. But the round and cup-like form of an antique clasp may well account for such names being applied to it.

Note 16, page 34, col. 2.

——Cool Cyllene's height of snow.

Cyllene was a mountain in Arcadia dedicated to Mercury.

Note 17, page 35, col. 1.

Then, minstrel! bid thy chorus rise
To Juno queen of deities.

Such passages as this appear to prove, first, that the Odes of Pindar, instead of being danced and chaunted by a chorus of hired musicians and actors, in the absurd and impossible manner pretended by the later Grecian writers, (whose ignorance respecting their own antiquities, is in many instances apparent,) were recited by the poet himself sitting, (his iron chair was long preserved at Delphos,) and accompanied by one or more musicians, such as the Theban Æneas whom he here compliments. Secondly, what will account at once for the inequalities of his style and the rapidity of his transitions, we may infer that the Dincæan swan was, often at least, an "improvisatore." I know not the origin of the Bœotian agnomen of swine. In later times we find their region called "vervecum patria."

Note 18, page 35, col. 1.

Mark with no envious ear a subject's praise.

Either the poet was led by his vanity to ascribe a greater consequence to his verses than they really possessed, when he supposes that the praise of Agesias may move his sovereign to jealousy; or we may infer from this little circumstance that the importance attached to the Olympic prize has not been so greatly overrated by poets and antiquaries, and that it was indeed "a gift more valuable than a hundred trophies."

TRANSLATIONS
FROM THE
HINDOOSTANEE.

SONNET BY THE LATE NAWAB OF OUDE, ASUF UD DOWLA.

In those eyes the tears that glisten as in pity for my pain,
Are they gems, or only dew-drops? can they, will they long remain?

Why thy strength of tyrant beauty thus, with seeming ruth, restrain?
Better breathe my last before thee, than in lingering grief remain!

To yon planet, Fate has given every month to wax and wane;
And—thy world of blushing brightness—can it, will it, long remain?

Health and youth in balmy moisture on thy cheek their seat maintain;
But—the dew that steeps the rose-bud—can it, will it long remain?

Asuf! why, in mournful numbers, of thine absence thus complain,
Chance had joined us, chance has parted!—nought on earth can long remain.

In the world, may'st thou, beloved! live exempt from grief and pain!
On my lips the breath is fleeting, can it, will it long remain?

FROM THE GULISTAN.

"Brother! know the world deceiveth!
Trust on Him who safely giveth!
Fix not on the world thy trust,
She feeds us—but she turns to dust,
And the bare earth or kingly throne
Alike may serve to die upon!"

FROM THE SAME.

"The man who leaveth life behind,
May well and boldly speak his mind;
Where flight is none from battle field,
We blithely snatch the sword and shield;
Where hope is past, and hate is strong,
The wretch's tongue is sharp and long;
Myself have seen, in wild despair,
The feeble cat the mastiff tear."

FROM THE SAME.

"Who the silent man can prize,
If a fool he be or wise?
Yet, though lonely seem the wood,
Therein may lurk the beast of blood,
Often bashful looks conceal
Tongue of fire and heart of steel,
And deem not thou in forest gray,
Every dappled skin thy prey;
Lest thou rouse, with luckless spear,
The tiger for the fallow-deer!"

Miscellaneous Poems.

THE PASSAGE OF THE RED SEA.

With heat o'erlaboured and the length of way,
On Ethan's beach the bands of Israel lay.
'T was silence all, the sparkling sands along,
Save where the locust trilled her feeble song,
Or blended soft in drowsy cadence fell
The wave's low whisper or the camel's bell.—
'T was silence all!—the flocks for shelter fly
Where, waving light, the acacia shadows lie;
Or where, from far, the flattering vapours make
The noon-tide semblance of a misty lake:
While the mute swain, in careless safety spread,
With arms enfolded, and dejected head,
Dreams o'er his wondrous call, his lineage high,
And, late revealed, his children's destiny.
For, not in vain, in thraldom's darkest hour,
Had sped from Amram's sons the word of power;
Nor failed the dreadful wand, whose god-like sway
Could lure the locust from her airy way;
With reptile war assail their proud abodes,
And mar the giant pomp of Egypt's gods.
Oh helpless gods! who nought availed to shield
From fiery rain your Zoan's favoured field!—
Oh helpless gods! who saw the curdled blood
Taint the pure lotus of your ancient flood,
And fourfold-night the wondering earth enchain,
While Memnon's orient harp was heard in vain!—
Such musings held the tribes, till now the west
With milder influence on their temples prest;
And that portentous cloud which, all the day,
Hung its dark curtain o'er their weary way,
(A cloud by day, a friendly flame by night,)
Rolled back its misty veil, and kindled into light!—
Soft fell the eve:—But, ere the day was done,
Tall, waving banners streaked the level sun;
And wide and dark along th' horizon red,
In sandy surge the rising desert spread.—
"Mark, Israel, mark!"—On that strange sight intent,
In breathless terror, every eye was bent;
And busy faction's undistinguished hum
And female shrieks arose, "They come, they come!"
They come, they come! in scintillating show
O'er the dark mass the brazen lances glow;
And sandy clouds in countless shapes combine,
As deepens or extends the long tumultuous line;—
And fancy's keener glance e'en now may trace
The threatening aspects of each mingled race;
For many a coal-black tribe and cany spear,
The hireling guards of Misraim's throne, were there.
From distant Cush they trooped, a warrior train,
Siwah's(1) green isle and Sennaar's marly plain:
On either wing their fiery coursers check
The parched and sinewy sons of Amalek:
While close behind, inured to feast on blood,
Decked in Behemoth's spoils, the tall Shangalla(2) strode.
'Mid blazing helms and bucklers rough with gold
Saw ye how swift the scythed chariot rolled?
Lo, these are they whom, lords of Afric's fates,
Old Thebes had poured through all her hundred gates,
Mother of armies!—How the emeralds(3) glowed,
Where, flushed with power and vengeance, Pharaoh rode!
And stoled in white, those brazen wheels before,
Osiris' ark his swarthy wizards bore;
And still responsive to the trumpet's cry
The priestly sistrum murmured—Victory?—
Why swell these shouts that rend the desert's gloom?
Whom come ye forth to combat?—warriors, whom?—
These flocks and herds—this faint and weary train—
Red from the scourge and recent from the chain?
God of the poor, the poor and friendless save!
Giver and Lord of freedom, help the slave!—
North, south, and west the sandy whirlwinds fly,
The circling horns of Egypt's chivalry.
On earth's last margin throng the weeping train:
Their cloudy guide moves on:—"And must we swim the main?"
'Mid the light spray their snorting camels stood,
Nor bathed a fetlock in the nauseous flood—
He comes—their leader comes!—the man of God
O'er the wide waters lifts his mighty rod,
And onward treads—The circling waves retreat
In hoarse deep murmurs, from his holy feet;
And the chased surges, inly roaring, show
The hard wet sand and coral hills below.
With limbs that falter, and with hearts that swell,
Down, down they pass—a steep and slippery dell
Around them rise, in pristine chaos hurled,
The ancient rocks, the secrets of the world;
And flowers that blush beneath the ocean green,
And caves, the sea-calves' low-roofed haunt, are seen.
Down, safely down the narrow pass they tread;
The beetling waters storm above their head:
While far behind retires the sinking day,
And fades on Edom's hills its latest ray.

Yet not from Israel fled the friendly light,
Or dark to them, or cheerless came the night,
Still in their van, along that dreadful road,
Blazed broad and fierce the brandished torch of God.
Its meteor glare a tenfold lustre gave
On the long mirror of the rosy wave:
While its blest beams a sunlike heat supply,
Warm every cheek and dance in every eye—
To them alone—for Misraim's wizard train
Invoke for light their monster-gods in vain:
Clouds heaped on clouds their struggling sight confine,
And tenfold darkness broods above their line.
Yet on they fare by reckless vengeance led,
And range unconscious through the ocean's bed.
Till midway now—that strange and fiery form
Showed his dread visage lightening through the storm;
With withering splendour blasted all their might,
And brake their chariot-wheels, and marred their coursers' flight.
"Fly, Misraim, fly!"—The ravenous floods they see,
And, fiercer than the floods, the Deity.
"Fly, Misraim, fly!"—From Edom's coral strand
Again the prophet stretched his dreadful wand:—
With one wild crash the thundering waters sweep,
And all is waves—a dark and lonely deep—
Yet o'er those lonely waves such murmurs past,
As mortal wailing swelled the nightly blast:
And strange and sad the whispering breezes bore
The groans of Egypt to Arabia's shore.
Oh! welcome came the morn, where Israel stood
In trustless wonder by th' avenging flood!
Oh! welcome came the cheerful morn, to show
The drifted wreck of Zoan's pride below;
The mangled limbs of men—the broken car—
A few sad relics of a nation's war:
Alas, how few!—Then, soft as Elim's well,(3)
The precious tears of new-born freedom fell.
And he, whose hardened heart alike had borne
The house of bondage and th' oppressor's scorn,
The stubborn slave, by hope's new beams subdued,
In faltering accents sobbed his gratitude—
Till kindling into warmer zeal, around
The virgin timbrel waked its silver sound:
And in fierce joy, no more by doubt supprest,
The struggling spirit throbbed in Miriam's breast.
She, with bare arms, and fixing on the sky,
The dark transparence of her lucid eye,
Poured on the winds of heaven her wild sweet harmony.
"Where now," she sang, "the tall Egyptian spear?
"On's sunlike shield, and Zoan's chariot, where?
"Above their ranks the whelming waters spread.
"Shout, Israel, for the Lord has triumphed!"—
And every pause between, as Miriam sang,
From tribe to tribe the martial thunder rang,
And loud and far their stormy chorus spread,—
"Shout, Israel, for the Lord hath triumphed!"

LINES

SPOKEN IN THE THEATRE, OXFORD, ON LORD GRENVILLE'S INSTALLATION AS CHANCELLOR.

Ye viewless guardians of these sacred shades,(4)
Dear dreams of early song, Aonian maids!—
And you, illustrious dead! whose spirits speak
In every flush that tints the student's cheek,
As, wearied with the world, he seeks again
The page of better times and greater men;
If with pure worship we your steps pursue,
And youth, and health, and rest forget for you,
(Whom most we serve, to whom our lamp burns bright
Through the long toils of not ingrateful night,)
Yet, yet be present!—Let the worldly train
Mock our cheap joys, and hate our useless strain,
Intent on freighted wealth, or proud to rear
The fleece Iberian or the pampered steer;—
Let sterner science with unwearied eye
Explore the circling spheres and map the sky;
His long-drawn mole let lordly commerce scan,
And of his iron arch the rainbow span:
Yet, while, in burning characters imprest,
The poet's lesson stamps the youthful breast
Bids the rapt boy o'er suffering virtue bleed,
Adore a brave or bless a gentle deed,
And in warm feeling from the storied page
Arise the saint, the hero, or the sage;
Such be our toil!—Nor doubt we to explore
The thorny maze of dialectic lore,
To climb the chariot of the gods, or scan
The secret workings of the soul of man;
Upborne aloft on Plato's eagle flight,
Or the slow pinion of the Stagyrite.
And those gray spoils of Herculanean pride,
If aught of yet untasted sweets they hide;—
If Padua's sage be there, or art have power
To wake Menander from his secret bower.
Such be our toil!—Nor vain the labour proves,
Which Oxford honours, and which Grenville loves!
—On, eloquent and firm!—whose warning high
Rebuked the rising surge of anarchy,
When, like those brethren stars to seamen known,
In kindred splendour Pitt and Grenville shone;
On in thy glorious course! not yet the wave
Has ceased to lash the shore, nor storm forgot to rave.
Go on! and oh, while adverse factions raise
To thy pure worth involuntary praise;
While Gambia's swarthy tribes thy mercies bless,
And from thy counsels date their happiness;

Say, (for thine Isis yet recalls with pride
Thy youthful triumphs by her leafy side,)
Say, hast thou scorned, mid pomp, and wealth, and power,
The sober transports of a studious hour?—
No, statesman, no!—thy patriot fire was fed
From the warm embers of the mighty dead;
And thy strong spirit's patient grasp combined
The souls of ages in a single mind.
—By arts like these, amidst a world of foes,
Eye of the earth, th' Athenian glory rose;—
Thus, last and best of Romans, Brutus shone;
Our Somers thus, and thus our Clarendon;
Such Cobham was; such, Grenville, long be thou,
Our boast before—our chief and champion now!

EPITAPH ON A YOUNG NAVAL OFFICER,

DESIGNED FOR A TOMB IN A SEAPORT TOWN IN NORTH WALES.

Sailor! if vigour nerve thy frame,
If to high deeds thy soul is strung,
Revere this stone that gives to fame
The brave, the virtuous, and the young!—(5)

For manly beauty decked his form,
His bright eye beamed with mental power;
Resistless as the winter storm,
Yet mild as summer's mildest shower.

In war's hoarse rage, in ocean's strife,
For skill, for force, for mercy known;
Still prompt to shield a comrade's life,
And greatly careless of his own.—

Yet youthful seaman, mourn not thou
The fate these artless lines recall;
No, Cambrian, no, be thine the vow,
Like him to live, like him to fall!—

But hast thou known a father's care,
Who sorrowing sent thee forth to sea;
Poured for thy weal th' unceasing prayer,
And thought the sleepless night on thee?

Has e'er thy tender fancy flown,
When winds were strong and waves were high,
Where, listening to the tempest's moan,
Thy sisters heaved the anxious sigh?

Or, in the darkest hour of dread,
Mid war's wild din, and ocean's swell,
Hast mourned a hero brother dead,
And did that brother love thee well?—

Then pity those whose sorrows flow
In vain o'er Shipley's empty grave!—
Sailor, thou weep'st:—Indulge thy wo;
Such tears will not disgrace the brave!—

AN EVENING WALK IN BENGAL

Our task is done! on Gunga's breast(6)
The sun is sinking down to rest;
And moored beneath the tamarind bough,
Our bark has found its harbour now.
With furled sail and painted side,
Behold the tiny frigate ride.
Upon her deck, 'mid charcoal gleams,
The Moslems' savoury supper steams,
While all apart, beneath the wood,
The Hindoo cooks his simpler food.
Come walk with me the jungle through;
If yonder hunter told us true,
Far off, in desert dank and rude,
The tiger holds his solitude;
Nor (taught by secret charm to shun
The thunders of the English gun,)
A dreadful guest but rarely seen,
Returns to scare the village green.
Come boldly on! no venomed snake
Can shelter in so cool a brake:
Child of the sun! he loves to lie
'Mid nature's embers parched and dry,
Where o'er some tower in ruin laid,
The peepul spreads its haunted shade,
Or round a tomb his scales to wreathe,
Fit warder in the gate of death!
Come on! yet pause! behold us now
Beneath the bamboo's arched bough,
Where gemming oft that sacred gloom,
Glows the geranium's scarlet bloom,
And winds our path through many a bower
Of fragrant tree and giant flower;
The ceiba's crimson pomp displayed
O'er the broad plaintain's humbler shade,
And dusk anana's prickly blade;
While o'er the brake, so wild and fair,
The betel waves his crest in air.
With pendent train and rushing wings,
Aloft the gorgeous peacock springs;
And he, the bird of hundred dyes,(7)
Whose plumes the dames of Ava prize.
So rich a shade, so green a sod,
Our English fairies never trod;
Yet who in Indian bower has stood,
But thought on England's "good green wood?"
And blessed beneath the palmy shade,
Her hazel and her hawthorn glade,
And breathed a prayer, (how oft in vain!)
To gaze upon her oaks again?
A truce to thought! the jackal's cry
Resounds like sylvan revelry;
And through the trees, yon failing ray
Will scantly serve to guide our way.
Yet, mark! as fade the upper skies,
Each thicket opes ten thousand eyes.
Before, beside us, and above,
The fire-fly lights his lamp of love,

Retreating, chasing, sinking, soaring,
The darkness of the copse exploring;
While to this cooler air confest,
The broad Dhatura bares her breast,
Of fragrant scent, and virgin white,
A pearl around the locks of night!
Still as we pass in softened hum,
Along the breezy valleys come
The village song, the horn, the drum.
Still as we pass, from bush and briar,
The shrill cigala strikes his lyre;
And, what is she whose liquid strain
Thrills through yon copse of sugar-cane?
I know that soul-entrancing swell!
It is,—it must be,—Philomel!
Enough, enough, the rustling trees
Announce a shower upon the breeze,—
The flashes of the summer sky
Assume a deeper, ruddier dye;
Yon lamp that trembles on the stream,
From forth our cabin sheds its beam;
And we must early sleep to find
Betimes the morning's healthy wind.
But O! with thankful hearts confess,
Ev'n here there may be happiness;
And HE, the bounteous Sire, has given
His peace on earth, his hope of heaven!

LINES WRITTEN TO HIS WIFE,

WHILE ON A VISIT TO UPPER INDIA.

IF thou wert by my side, my love!
How fast would evening fail
In green Bengala's palmy grove,
Listening the nightingale!

If thou, my love! wert by my side,
My babies at my knee,
How gaily would our pinnace glide
O'er Gunga's mimic sea!

I miss thee at the dawning gray,
When, on our deck reclined,
In careless ease my limbs I lay,
And woo the cooler wind.

I miss thee when by Gunga's stream
My twilight steps I guide,
But most beneath the lamp's pale beam,
I miss thee from my side.

I spread my books, my pencil try,
The lingering noon to cheer,
But miss thy kind approving eye
Thy meek attentive ear.

But when of morn and eve the star
Beholds me on my knee,
I feel, though thou art distant far,
Thy prayers ascend for me.

Then on! Then on! where duty leads,
My course be onward still,
On broad Hindostan's sultry meads,
O'er black Almorah's hill.

That course, nor Delhi's kingly gates,
Nor mild Malwah detain,
For sweet the bliss us both awaits,
By yonder western main.

Thy towers, Bombay, gleam bright, they say,
Across the dark blue sea,
But never were hearts so light and gay,
As then shall meet in thee!

HAPPINESS.

ONE morning in the month of May,
I wandered o'er the hill;
Though nature all around was gay,
My heart was heavy still.

Can God, I thought, the just, the great,
These meaner creatures bless,
And yet deny to man's estate
The boon of happiness?

Tell me, ye woods, ye smiling plains,
Ye blessed birds around,
In which of nature's wide domains
Can bliss for man be found.

The birds wild carolled over head,
The breeze around me blew,
And nature's awful chorus said—
No bliss for man she knew.

I questioned love, whose early ray,
So rosy bright appears,
And heard the timid genius say
His light was dimmed by tears.

I questioned friendship: Friendship sighed,
And thus her answer gave—
The few whom fortune never tried
Were withered in the grave!

I asked if vice could bliss bestow?
Vice boasted loud and well,
But fading from her withered brow,
The borrowed roses fell.

I sought of feeling, if her skill
Could sooth the wounded breast;
And found her mourning, faint and still
For others' woes distressed!

I questioned virtue: virtue sighed,
No boon could she dispense—
Nor virtue was her name, she cried
But humble penitence.

I questioned death—the grisly shade
Relaxed his brow severe—
And "I am happiness," he said,
"If Virtue guides thee here."

THE MOONLIGHT MARCH.

I SEE them on their winding way,
About their ranks the moonbeams play;
Their lofty deeds and daring high
Blend with the notes of victory.
And waving arms, and banners bright,
Are glancing in the mellow light:
They 're lost—and gone, the moon is past,
The wood's dark shade is o'er them cast;
And fainter, fainter, fainter still
The march is rising o'er the hill.

Again, again, the pealing drum,
The clashing horn—they come, they come;
Through rocky pass, o'er wooded steep
In long and glittering files they sweep.
And nearer, nearer, yet more near,
Their softened chorus meets the ear;
Forth, forth, and meet them on their way;
The trampling hoofs brook no delay;
With thrilling fife and pealing drum,
And clashing horn, they come, they come.

LINES.

REFLECTED on the lake I love
To see the stars of evening glow;
So tranquil in the heavens above,
So restless in the wave below.

Thus heavenly hope is all serene,
But earthly hope, how bright so e'er,
Still fluctuates o'er this changing scene,
As false and fleeting as 'tis fair.

FAREWELL.

WHEN eyes are beaming
What never tongue might tell,
When tears are streaming
From their crystal cell;
When hands are linked that dread to part,
And heart is met by throbbing heart,
Oh! bitter, bitter is the smar
Of them that bid farewell!

When hope is chidden
That fain of bliss would tell,
And love forbidden
In the breast to dwell;
When fettered by a viewless chain,
We turn and gaze, and turn again,
Oh! death were mercy to the pain
Of them that bid farewell!

VESPERS.

GOD that madest Earth and Heaven,
Darkness and light!
Who the day for toil hast given,
For rest the night!
May thine angel guards defend us,
Slumber sweet thy mercy send us,
Holy dreams and hopes attend us,
This livelong night!

TO LIEUTENANT-GENERAL, SIR ROWLAND HILL, K. B.

HILL! whose high daring with renewed success
Hath cheered our tardy war, what time the cloud
Of expectation, dark and comfortless,
Hung on the mountains; and yon factious crowd
Blasphemed their country's valour, babbling loud!
Then was thine arm revealed, to whose young might,
By Toulon's leaguered wall, the fiercest bowed
Whom Egypt honoured, and the dubious fight
Of sad Corunna's winter, and more bright
Douro, and Talavera's gory bays;
Wise, modest, brave, in danger foremost found.—
O still, young warrior, may thy toil-earned praise,
With England's love, and England's honour crowned,
Gild with delight thy Father's latter days!

IMITATION OF AN ODE BY KOODRUT, IN HINDOOSTANEE.

AMBITION'S voice was in mine ear, she whispered yesterday,
"How goodly is the land of Room,(9) how wide the Russian sway!
How blest to conquer either realm, and dwell through life to come,
Lulled by the harp's melodious string, cheered by the northern drum!"
But Wisdom heard; "O youth," she said, "in passion's fetter tied,
O come and see a sight with me shall cure thee of thy pride!"
She led me to a lonely dell, a sad and shady ground,
Where many an ancient sepulchre gleamed in the moonshine round.

And "Here Secunder(10) sleeps," she cried;—
"this is his rival's stone;
And here the mighty chief reclines who reared the
Median throne.(11)
Inquire of these, doth aught of all their ancient
pomp remain,
Save late regret, and bitter tears for ever, and in
vain?
Return, return, and in thy heart engraven keep
my lore;
The lesser wealth, the lighter load,—small blame
betides the poor."

NOTES.

Note 1, page 38, col. 2.

Siwah.

Oasis. Sennaar.—Meroe.

Note 2, page 38, col. 2.

Shangalla.

The black tribes whom Bruce considers as the aboriginal Nubians, are so called. For their gigantic stature, and their custom of ornamenting themselves and their houses with the spoils of the elephant, see the account he gives of the person and residence of one of their chiefs whom he visited on his departure from Ras el Feel.

Note 3, page 38, col. 2.

Emeralds.

The emerald, or whatever the ancients dignified by the name of smaragdus, is said to have been found in great quantities in the mountain now called Gebul Zumrud (the mount of emeralds.)

Note 4, page 39, col. 1.

Elim's well.

It is interesting to observe with what pleasure and minuteness Moses, amid the Arabian wilderness, enumerates the "twelve wells of water," and the "threescore and ten palm-trees," of Elim.

Note 5, page 39, col. 2.

Ye viewless guardians of these sacred shades.

These lines were spoken (as is the custom of the university on the installation of a new chancellor) by a young nobleman, whose diffidence induced him to content himself with the composition of another. Of this diffidence his friends have reason to complain, as it suppressed some elegant lines of his own on the same occasion.

Note 6, page 40, col. 1.

The brave, the virtuous, and the young.

Captain Conway Shipley, third son to the dean of St. Asaph, perished in an attempt to cut out an enemy's vessel from the Tagus with the boats of his majesty's frigate La Nymphe, April 22, 1808, in the 26th year of his age, and after nearly sixteen years of actual service; distinguished by every quality both of heart and head which could adorn a man or an officer. Admiral Sir Charles Cotton, and the captains of his fleet, have since erected a monument to his memory in the neighbourhood of Fort St. Julian.

Note 7, page 40, col. 2.

On Gunga's breast.

These lines were written at a small village on the banks of the Ganges, which he was ascending in a pinnace, on his first visitation of his diocese, in August, 1824.

Note 8, page 40, col. 2.

The bird of hundred dyes.

"The Mucharunga—many coloured. I learned at Dacca, that while we were at peace with the Burmans, many traders used to go over all the eastern provinces of Bengal, buying up these beautiful birds for the Golden Zennanah; at Ummerapoora it was said that they were sometimes worth a gold mohur each."

Note 9, page 42, col. 2.

The land of Room.

The oriental name of the Turkish Empire.

Note 10, page 43, col. 1.

Secunder.

Alexander the Great.

Note 11, page 43, col. 1.

The mighty Chief who reared the Median throne.

The founder of the Median throne was Ky Kaoos, or Deiioces.

THE END OF HEBER'S POEMS.

THE

COURSE OF TIME,

A POEM, IN TEN BOOKS.

BY ROBERT POLLOK, A. M.

THE

COURSE OF TIME.

A Poem.

BOOK I.

Eternal Spirit! God of Truth! to whom
All things seem as they are; Thou, who of old
The prophet's eye unscaled, that nightly saw,
While heavy sleep fell down on other men,
In holy vision tranced, the future pass
Before him, and to Judah's harp attuned
Burdens which made the pagan mountains shake,
And Zion's cedars bow,—inspire my song;
My eye unscale; me what is substance teach,
And shadow what, while I of things to come,
As past, rehearsing, sing the Course of Time,
The second birth, and final doom of man.
  The muse, that soft and sickly wooes the ear
Of love, or chanting loud in windy rhyme
Of fabled hero, raves through gaudy tale
Not overfraught with sense, I ask not: such
A strain befits not argument so high.
Me thought, and phrase severely sifting out
The whole idea, grant, uttering as 'tis
The essential truth—time gone, the righteous saved,
The wicked damned, and providence approved.
  Hold my right hand, Almighty! and me teach
To strike the lyre, but seldom struck, to notes
Harmonious with the morning stars, and pure
As those by sainted bards and angels sung,
Which wake the echoes of Eternity;
That fools may hear and tremble, and the wise,
Instructed, listen, of ages yet to come.
  Long was the day, so long expected, past
Of the eternal doom, that gave to each
Of all the human race his due reward.
The sun, earth's son, and moon, and stars, had ceased
To number seasons, days, and months, and years
To mortal man. Hope was forgotten, and fear:
And time, with all its chance, and change, and smiles,
And frequent tears, and deeds of villany,
Or righteousness, once talked of much, as things
Of great renown, was now but ill remembered;
In dim and shadowy vision of the past
Seen far remote, as country, which has left
The traveller's speedy step, retiring back
From morn till even; and long Eternity
Had rolled his mighty years, and with his years
Men had grown old. The saints, all home returned
From pilgrimage, and war, and weeping, long
Had rested in the bowers of peace, that skirt
The stream of life; and long—alas, how long
To them it seemed!—the wicked, who refused
To be redeemed, had wandered in the dark
Of hell's despair, and drunk the burning cup
Their sins had filled with everlasting wo.
  Thus far the years had rolled, which none but God
Doth number, when two sons, two youthful sons
Of Paradise, in conversation sweet,—
For thus the heavenly muse instructs me, wooed
At midnight hour with offering sincere
Of all the heart, poured out in holy prayer,—
High on the hills of immortality,
Whence goodliest prospect looks beyond the walls
Of heaven, walked, casting oft their eye far through
The pure serene, observant if, returned
From errand duly finished, any came,
Or any, first in virtue now complete,
From other worlds arrived, confirmed in good.
  Thus viewing, one they saw, on hasty wing
Directing towards heaven his course; and now
His flight ascending near the battlements
And lofty hills on which they walked, approached
For round and round, in spacious circuit wide,
Mountains of tallest stature circumscribe
The plains of Paradise, whose tops, arrayed
In uncreated radiance, seem so pure,
That naught but angel's foot, or saint's, elect
Of God, may venture there to walk. Here oft
The sons of bliss take morn or evening pastime,
Delighted to behold ten thousand worlds
Around their suns revolving in the vast
External space, or listen the harmonies
That each to other in its motion sings.
And hence, in middle heaven remote, is seen
The mount of God in awful glory bright.
Within, no orb create of moon, or star,
Or sun, gives light; for God's own countenance

Beaming eternally, gives light to all.
But farther than these sacred hills, his will
Forbids it flow, too bright for eyes beyond.
This is the last ascent of Virtue; here
All trial ends, and hope; here perfect joy,
With perfect righteousness, which to these heights
Alone can rise, begins, above all fall.
  And now, on wing of holy ardour strong,
Hither ascends the stranger, borne upright,—
For stranger he did seem, with curious eye
Of nice inspection round surveying all,—
And at the feet alights of those that stood
His coming, who the hand of welcome gave,
And the embrace sincere of holy love;
And thus, with comely greeting kind, began.
  Hail, brother! hail, thou son of happiness,
Thou son beloved of God, welcome to heaven,
To bliss that never fades! thy day is past
Of trial, and of fear to fall. Well done,
Thou good and faithful servant; enter now
Into the joy eternal of thy Lord.
Come with us, and behold far higher sight
Than e'er thy heart desired, or hope conceived.
See, yonder is the glorious hill of God,
'Bove angel's gaze in brightness rising high.
Come, join our wing, and we will guide thy flight
To mysteries of everlasting bliss,
The tree, and fount of life, the eternal throne,
And presence-chamber of the King of kings.
But what concern hangs on thy countenance,
Unwont within this place? Perhaps thou deemst
Thyself unworthy to be brought before
The always Ancient One? So are we too
Unworthy; but our God is all in all,
And gives us boldness to approach his throne.
  Sons of the Highest! citizens of heaven!
Began the new arrived, right have ye judged:
Unworthy, most unworthy is your servant,
To stand in presence of the King, or hold
Most distant and most humble place in this
Abode of excellent glory unrevealed.
But God Almighty be for ever praised,
Who, of his fulness, fills me with all grace
And ornament, to make me in his sight
Well pleasing, and accepted in his court.
But, if your leisure waits, short narrative
Will tell, why strange concern thus overhangs
My face, ill seeming here; and haply, too,
Your elder knowledge can instruct my youth,
Of what seems dark and doubtful, unexplained.
  Our leisure waits thee. Speak; and what we can,
Delighted most to give delight, we will;
Though much of mystery yet to us remains.
  Virtue, I need not tell, when proved, and full
Matured, inclines us up to God and heaven,
By law of sweet compulsion strong and sure;
As gravitation to the larger orb
The less attracts, through matter's whole domain.
Virtue in me was ripe. I speak not this
In boast; for what I am to God I owe,
Entirely owe, and of myself am naught.
Equipped and bent for heaven, I left yon world,
My native seat, which scarce your eye can reach,
Rolling around her central sun, far out
On utmost verge of light. But first, to see
What lay beyond the visible creation,
Strong curiosity my flight impelled.
Long was my way, and strange. I passed the bounds
Which God doth set to light, and life and love;
Where darkness meets with day, where order meets
Disorder, dreadful, waste, and wild; and down
The dark, eternal, uncreated night
Ventured alone. Long, long on rapid wing,
I sailed through empty, nameless regions vast,
Where utter Nothing dwells, unformed and void.
There neither eye, nor ear, nor any sense
Of being most acute, finds object; there
For aught external still you search in vain.
Try touch, or sight, or smell; try what you will,
You strangely find naught but yourself alone.
But why should I in words attempt to tell
What that is like, which is, and yet is not?
This passed, my path descending led me still
O'er unclaimed continents of desert gloom
Immense, where gravitation shifting turns
The other way; and to some dread, unknown,
Infernal centre downward weighs: and now,—
Far travelled from the edge of darkness, far
As from that glorious mount of God to light's
Remotest limb,—dire sights I saw, dire sounds
I heard; and suddenly before my eye
A wall of fiery adamant sprung up,
Wall mountainous, tremendous, flaming high
Above all flight of hope. I paused, and looked;
And saw, where'er I looked upon that mound,
Sad figures traced in fire, not motionless,
But imitating life. One I remarked
Attentively; but how shall I describe
What naught resembles else my eye hath seen?
Of worm or serpent kind it something looked,
But monstrous, with a thousand snaky heads,
Eyed each with double orbs of glaring wrath;
And with as many tails, that twisted out
In horrid revolution, tipped with stings;
And all its mouths, that wide and darkly gaped,
And breathed most poisonous breath, had each a sting,
Forked, and long, and venomous, and sharp;
And, in its writhings infinite, it grasped
Malignantly what seemed a heart, swollen, black,
And quivering with torture most intense;
And still the heart, with anguish throbbing high,
Made effort to escape, but could not; for,
Howe'er it turned, and oft it vainly turned,
These complicated foldings held it fast.
And still the monstrous beast with sting of head

Or tail transpierced it, bleeding evermore.
What this could image, much I searched to know;
And while I stood, and gazed, and wondered long,
A voice, from whence I knew not, for no one
I saw, distinctly whispered in my ear
These words: This is the worm that never dies.
Fast by the side of this unsightly thing
Another was portrayed, more hideous still:
Who sees it once shall wish to see't no more.
For ever undescribed let it remain!
Only this much I may or can unfold.
Far out it thrust a dart that might have made
The knees of terror quake, and on it hung,
Within the triple barbs, a being pierced
Through soul and body both. Of heavenly make
Original the being seemed, but fallen,
And worn and wasted with enormous wo.
And still around the everlasting lance,
It writhed, convulsed, and uttered mimic groans;
And tried, and wished, and ever tried and wished
To die; but could not die. Oh, horrid sight!
I trembling gazed, and listened, and heard this voice
Approach my ear: This is Eternal Death.
Nor these alone. Upon that burning wall
In horrible emblazonry, were limned
All shapes, all forms, all modes of wretchedness,
And agony, and grief, and desperate wo.
And prominent in characters of fire,
Where'er the eye could light, these words you read:
"Who comes this way, behold, and fear to sin!"
Amazed I stood; and thought such imagery
Foretokened, within, a dangerous abode.
But yet to see the worst a wish arose.
For virtue, by the holy seal of God
Accredited and stamped, immortal all,
And all invulnerable, fears no hurt.
As easy as my wish, as rapidly,
I through the horrid rampart passed, unscathed
And unopposed; and, poised on steady wing,
I hovering gazed. Eternal justice! sons
Of God! tell me, if ye can tell, what then
I saw, what then I heard. Wide was the place,
And deep as wide, and ruinous as deep.
Beneath, I saw a lake of burning fire,
With tempest tost perpetually, and still
The waves of fiery darkness 'gainst the rocks
Of dark damnation broke, and music made
Of melancholy sort; and over head
And all around, wind warred with wind, storm howled
To storm, and lightning forked lightning crossed,
And thunder answered thunder, muttering sounds
Of sullen wrath; and far as sight could pierce,
Or down descend in caves of hopeless depth,
Through all that dungeon of unfading fire,
I saw most miserable beings walk,
Burning continually, yet unconsumed;

6*

For ever wasting, yet enduring still;
Dying perpetually, yet never dead.
Some wandered lonely in the desert flames,
And some in fell encounter fiercely met,
With curses loud, and blasphemies, that made
The cheek of darkness pale; and as they fought,
And cursed, and gnashed their teeth, and wished to die,
Their hollow eyes did utter streams of wo.
And there were groans that ended not, and sighs
That always sighed, and tears that ever wept,
And ever fell, but not in Mercy's sight.
And Sorrow, and Repentance, and Despair,
Among them walked, and to their thirsty lips
Presented frequent cups of burning gall.
And as I listened, I heard these beings curse
Almighty God, and curse the Lamb, and curse
The earth, the resurrection morn, and seek,
And ever vainly seek, for utter death.
And to their everlasting anguish still,
The thunders from above responding spoke
These words, which, through the caverns of perdition
Forlornly echoing, fell on every ear:
"Ye knew your duty, but ye did it not."
And back again recoiled a deeper groan.
A deeper groan! Oh, what a groan was that!
I waited not, but swift on speediest wing,
With unaccustomed thoughts conversing, back
Retraced my venturous path from dark to light.
Then up ascending, long ascending up,
I hasted on; though whiles the chiming spheres,
By God's own finger touched to harmony!
Held me delaying, till I here arrived,
Drawn upward by the eternal love of God,
Of wonder full and strange astonishment,
At what in yonder den of darkness dwells,
Which now your higher knowledge will unfold.
They answering said. To ask and to bestow
Knowledge, is much of heaven's delight; and now
Most joyfully what thou requirest we would;
For much of new and unaccountable
Thou bringst. Something indeed we heard before,
In passing conversation slightly touched,
Of such a place; yet, rather to be taught,
Than teaching, answer, what thy marvel asks,
We need; for we ourselves, though here, are but
Of yesterday, creation's younger sons.
But there is one, an ancient bard of Earth,
Who, by the stream of life, sitting in bliss,
Has oft beheld the eternal years complete
The mighty circle round the throne of God;
Great in all learning, in all wisdom great
And great in song; whose harp in lofty strain
Tells frequently of what thy wonder craves,
While, round him gathering, stand the youth of heaven,
With truth and melody delighted both.

To him this path directs, an easy path,
And easy flight will bring us to his seat.
  So saying, they linked hand in hand, spread out
Their golden wings, by living breezes fanned,
And over heaven's broad champaign sailed serene.
O'er hill and valley, clothed with verdure green,
That never fades; and tree, and herb, and flower,
That never fades; and many a river, rich
With nectar, winding pleasantly, they passed;
And mansion of celestial mould, and work
Divine. And oft delicious music, sung
By saint and angel bands that walked the vales,
Or mountain tops, and harped upon their harps,
Their ear inclined, and held by sweet constraint
Their wing; not long, for strong desire awaked
Of knowledge that to holy use might turn,
Still pressed them on to leave what rather seemed
Pleasure, due only when all duty's done.
  And now beneath them lay the wished-for spot,
The sacred bower of that renowned bard;
That ancient bard, ancient in days and song;
But in immortal vigour young, and young
In rosy health; to pensive solitude
Retiring oft, as was his wont on earth.
  Fit was the place, most fit, for holy musing.
Upon a little mount, that gently rose,
He sat, clothed in white robes; and o'er his head
A laurel tree of lustiest, eldest growth,
Stately and tall, and shadowing far and wide,—
Not fruitless, as on earth, but bloomed, and rich
With frequent clusters, ripe to heavenly taste,—
Spread its eternal boughs, and in its arms
A myrtle of unfading leaf embraced—
The rose and lily, fresh with fragrant dew,
And every flower of fairest cheek, around
Him, smiling flocked. Beneath his feet, fast by,
And round his sacred hill, a streamlet walked,
Warbling the holy melodies of heaven;
The hallowed zephyrs brought him incense sweet,
And out before him opened, in prospect long,
The river of life, in many a winding maze
Descending from the lofty throne of God,
That with excessive glory closed the scene.
  Of Adam's race he was, and lonely sat,
By chance that day, in meditation deep,
Reflecting much of time, and earth, and man.
And now to pensive, now to cheerful notes,
He touched a harp of wondrous melody.
A golden harp it was, a precious gift,
Which, at the day of judgment, with the crown
Of life, he had received from God's own hand,
Reward due to his service done on earth.
  He sees their coming, and with greeting kind,
And welcome, not of hollow forged smiles,
And ceremonious compliment of phrase,
But of the heart sincere, into his bower
Invites. Like greeting they returned. Not bent
In low obeisancy, from creature most
Unfit to creature; but with manly form
Upright they entered in; though high his rank,
His wisdom high, and mighty his renown.
And thus, deferring all apology,
The two their new companion introduced.
  Ancient in knowledge! bard of Adam's race!
We bring thee one, of us inquiring what
We need to learn, and with him wish to learn.
His asking will direct thy answer best.
  Most ancient bard! began the new arrived,
Few words will set my wonder forth, and guide
Thy wisdom's light to what in me is dark.
  Equipped for heaven, I left my native place.
But first beyond the realms of light I bent
My course; and there, in utter darkness, far
Remote, I beings saw forlorn in wo,
Burning continually, yet unconsumed.
And there were groans that ended not, and sighs
That always sighed, and tears that ever wept
And ever fell, but not in Mercy's sight.
And still I heard these wretched beings curse
Almighty God, and curse the Lamb, and curse
The earth, the resurrection morn, and seek
And ever vainly seek, for utter death.
And from above the thunders answered still,
"Ye knew your duty, but ye did it not."
And every where throughout that horrid den,
I saw a form of excellence, a form
Of beauty without spot, that naught could see
And not admire, admire and not adore.
And from its own essential beams it gave
Light to itself, that made the gloom more dark.
And every eye in that infernal pit
Beheld it still; and from its face—how fair!
O, how exceeding fair!—for ever sought,
But ever vainly sought, to turn away.
That image, as I guess, was Virtue; for
Naught else hath God given countenance so fair
But why in such a place it should abide?
What place it is? What beings there lament?
Whence came they? and for what their endless groan?
Why curse they God? why seek they utter death?
And chief, what means the resurrection morn?
My youth expects thy reverend age to tell?
  Thou rightly deem'st, fair youth, began the bard.
The form thou saw'st was Virtue, ever fair.
Virtue, like God, whose excellent majesty,
Whose glory virtue is, is omnipresent.
No being, once created rational,
Accountable, endowed with moral sense,
With sapience of right and wrong endowed,
And charged, however fallen, debased, destroyed;
However lost, forlorn, and miserable;
In guilt's dark shrouding wrapped, however thick;
However drunk, delirious, and mad,
With sin's full cup; and with whatever damned,
Unnatural diligence it work and toil,
Can banish Virtue from its sight, or once
Forget that she is fair. Hides it in night,

In central night; takes it the lightning's wing,
And flies for ever on, beyond the bounds
Of all; drinks it the maddest cup of sin;
Dives it beneath the ocean of despair;
It dives, it drinks, it flies, it hides in vain.
For still the eternal beauty, image fair,
Once stamped upon the soul, before the eye
All lovely stands, nor will depart; so God
Ordains; and lovely to the worst she seems,
And ever seems; and as they look, and still
Must ever look, upon her loveliness,
Remembrance dire of what they were, of what
They might have been, and bitter sense of what
They are, polluted, ruined, hopeless, lost,
With most repenting torment rend their hearts.
So God ordains, their punishment severe,
Eternally inflicted by themselves.
'Tis this, this Virtue hovering evermore
Before the vision of the damned, and in
Upon their monstrous moral nakedness
Casting unwelcome light, that makes their wo,
That makes the essence of the endless flame.
Where this is, there is hell, darker than aught.
That he, the bard three-visioned, darkest saw.
  The place thou sawst was hell; the groans thou heardst
The wailings of the damned, of those who would
Not be redeemed, and at the judgment day,
Long past, for unrepented sins were damned.
The seven loud thunders which thou heardst, declare
The eternal wrath of the Almighty God.
But whence, or why they came to dwell in wo,
Why they curse God, what means the glorious morn
Of resurrection, these a longer tale
Demand, and lead the mournful lyre far back
Through memory of sin and mortal man.
Yet haply not rewardless we shall trace
The dark disastrous years of finished Time.
Sorrows remembered sweeten present joy.
Nor yet shall all be sad; for God gave peace,
Much peace, on earth, to all who feared his name.
  But first it needs to say, that other style
And other language than thy ear is wont,
Thou must expect to hear, the dialect
Of man. For each in heaven a relish holds
Of former speech, that points to whence he came.
But whether I of person speak, or place,
Event or action, moral or divine;
Or things unknown compare to things unknown;
Allude, imply, suggest, apostrophize;
Or touch, when wandering through the past, on moods
Of mind thou never feltst; the meaning still,
With easy apprehension, thou shalt take.
So perfect here is knowledge, and the strings
Of sympathy so tuned, that every word
That each to other speaks, though never heard
Before, at once is fully understood,
And every feeling uttered, fully felt.
  So shalt thou find, as from my various song,
That backward rolls o'er many a tide of years,
Directly or inferred, thy asking, thou,
And wondering doubt, shalt learn to answer, while
I sketch in brief the history of man.

BOOK II.

THIS said, he waked the golden harp, and thus,
While on him inspiration breathed, began.
  As from yon everlasting hills that gird
Heaven northward, I thy course espied, I judge
Thou from the arctic regions came? Perhaps
Thou noticed on thy way a little orb,
Attended by one moon, her lamp by night,
With her fair sisterhood of planets seven,
Revolving round their central sun; she third
In place, in magnitude the fourth. That orb,
New made, new named, inhabited anew,—
Though whiles we sons of Adam visit still,
Our native place, not changed so far but we
Can trace our ancient walks, the scenery
Of childhood, youth, and prime, and hoary age
But scenery most of suffering and wo,—
That little orb, in days remote of old,
When angels yet were young, was made for man,
And titled Earth, her primal virgin name;—
Created first so lovely, so adorned
With hill, and dale, and lawn, and winding vale,
Woodland, and stream, and lake, and rolling seas,
Green mead, and fruitful tree, and fertile grain,
And herb and flower; so lovely, so adorned
With numerous beasts of every kind, with fowl
Of every wing and every tuneful note,
And with all fish that in the multitude
Of waters swam; so lovely, so adorned,
So fit a dwelling place for man, that, as
She rose, complete, at the creating word,
The morning stars, the sons of God, aloud
Shouted for joy; and God, beholding, saw
The fair design, that from eternity
His mind conceived, accomplished, and, well pleased,
His six days finished work most good pronounced,
And man declared the sovereign prince of all.
  All else was prone, irrational, and mute,
And unaccountable, by instinct led.
But man he made of angel form erect,
To hold communion with the heavens above;
And on his soul impressed his image fair,
His own similitude of holiness,
Of virtue, truth, and love; with reason high
To balance right and wrong, and conscience quick
To choose or to reject; with knowledge great,
Prudence and wisdom, vigilance and strength,

To guard all force or guile; and, last of all,
The highest gift of God's abundant grace,
With perfect, free, unbiased will. Thus man
Was made upright, immortal made, and crowned
The king of all; to eat, to drink, to do
Freely and sovereignly his will entire.
By one command alone restrained, to prove,
As was most just, his filial love sincere,
His loyalty, obedience due, and faith.
And thus the prohibition ran, expressed,
As God is wont, in terms of plainest truth.
Of every tree that in the garden grows
Thou mayest freely eat; but of the tree
That knowledge hath of good and ill, eat not,
Nor touch; for in the day thou eatest, thou
Shalt die. Go, and this one command obey,
Adam, live and be happy, and, with thy Eve,
Fit consort, multiply and fill the earth.
Thus they, the representatives of men,
Were placed in Eden, choicest spot of earth.
With royal honour and with glory crowned,
Adam, the Lord of all, majestic walked,
With godlike countenance sublime, and form
Of lofty towering strength; and by his side
Eve, fair as morning star, with modesty
Arrayed, with virtue, grace, and perfect love:
In holy marriage wed, and eloquent
Of thought and comely words, to worship God
And sing his praise, the Giver of all good:
Glad, in each other glad, and glad in hope;
Rejoicing in their future happy race.
O lovely, happy, blest, immortal pair!
Pleased with the present, full of glorious hope.
But short, alas, the song that sings their bliss!
Henceforth the history of man grows dark!
Shade after shade of deepening gloom descends;
And Innocence laments her robes defiled.
Who farther sings, must change the pleasant lyre
To heavy notes of wo. Why! dost thou ask,
Surprised? The answer will surprise thee more.
Man sinned; tempted, he ate the guarded tree;—
Tempted of whom thou afterwards shalt hear;—
Audacious, unbelieving, proud, ungrateful,
He ate the interdicted fruit, and fell;
And in his fall, his universal race;
For they in him by delegation were,
In him to stand or fall, to live or die.
Man most ingrate! so full of grace, to sin,
Here interposed the new arrived, so full
Of bliss, to sin against the Gracious One!
The holy, just, and good! the Eternal Love!
Unseen, unheard, unthought of wickedness!
Why slumbered vengeance? No, it slumbered not.
The ever just and righteous God would let
His fury loose, and satisfy his threat.
That had been just, replied the reverend bard,
But done, fair youth, thou ne'er hadst met me here;
I ne'er had seen yon glorious throne in peace.
Thy powers are great, originally great,
And purified even at the fount of light.
Exert them now, call all their vigour out;
Take room, think vastly, meditate intensely,
Reason profoundly; send conjecture forth,
Let fancy fly, stoop down, ascend; all length,
All breadth explore, all moral, all divine;
Ask prudence, justice, mercy ask, and might;
Weigh good with evil, balance right with wrong;
With virtue vice compare, hatred with love;
God's holiness, God's justice, and God's truth,
Deliberately and cautiously compare
With sinful, wicked, vile, rebellious man;
And see if thou canst punish sin, and let
Mankind go free. Thou failst; be not surprised.
I bade thee search in vain. Eternal love,
Harp, lift thy voice on high! eternal love,
Eternal, sovereign love, and sovereign grace,
Wisdom, and power, and mercy infinite,
The Father, Son, and Holy Spirit, God,
Devised the wondrous plan, devised, achieved,
And in achieving made the marvel more.
Attend, ye heavens! ye heaven of heavens! attend,
Attend and wonder, wonder evermore!
When man had fallen, rebelled, insulted God;
Was most polluted, yet most madly proud;
Indebted infinitely, yet most poor;
Captive to sin, yet willing to be bound:
To God's incensed justice and hot wrath
Exposed, due victim of eternal death
And utter wo—Harp, lift thy voice on high!
Ye everlasting hills! ye angels! bow,
Bow, ye redeemed of men!—God was made flesh
And dwelt with man on earth! the Son of God,
Only begotten, and well beloved, between
Men and his Father's justice interposed;
Put human nature on; His wrath sustained;
And in their name suffered, obeyed, and died,
Making his soul an offering for sin;
Just for unjust, and innocence for guilt,
By doing, suffering, dying, unconstrained,
Save by omnipotence of boundless grace,
Complete atonement made to God appeased;
Made honourable his insulted law,
Turning the wrath aside from pardoned man.
Thus Truth and Mercy met, and Righteousness,
Stooping from highest heaven, embraced fair Peace,
That walked the earth in fellowship with Love.
O love divine! O mercy infinite!
The audience here in glowing rapture broke,
O love, all height above, all depth below,
Surpassing far all knowledge, all desire,
All thought! The Holy One for sinners dies!
The Lord of life for guilty rebels bleeds,
Quenches eternal fire with blood divine!
Abundant mercy! overflowing grace!
There, whence I came, I something heard of men
Their name had reached us, and report did speak
Of some abominable horrid thing,
Of desperate offence they had committed.

And something too of wondrous grace we heard.
And oft of our celestial visitants
What man, what God had done, inquired; but they,
Forbid, our asking never met directly,
Exhorting still to persevere upright,
And we should hear in heaven, though greatly blest
Ourselves, new wonders of God's wondrous love.
This hinting, keener appetite to know
Awaked; and as we talked, and much admired
What new we there should learn, we hasted each
To nourish virtue to perfection up,
That we might have our wondering resolved
And leave of louder praise to greater deeds
Of loving kindness due. Mysterious love!
God was made flesh, and dwelt with men on earth!
Blood holy, blood divine for sinners shed!
My asking ends, but makes my wonder more.
Saviour of men! henceforth be thou my theme;
Redeeming love, my study day and night.
Mankind were lost, all lost, and all redeemed!
  Thou errst again, but innocently errst,
Not knowing sin's depravity, nor man's
Sincere and persevering wickedness.
All were redeemed? Not all, or thou hadst heard
No human voice in hell. Many refused,
Although beseeched, refused to be redeemed,
Redeemed from death to life, from wo to bliss!
  Canst thou believe my song when thus I sing?
When man had fallen, was ruined, hopeless, lost—
Ye choral harps! ye angels that excel
In strength! and loudest, ye redeemed of men!
To God, to Him that sits upon the throne
On high, and to the Lamb, sing honour, sing
Dominion, glory, blessing sing, and praise!—
When man had fallen, was ruined, hopeless, lost,
Messiah, Prince of Peace, Eternal King,
Died, that the dead might live, the lost be saved.
Wonder, O heavens! and be astonished, earth!
Thou ancient, thou forgotten earth! ye worlds admire!
Admire and be confounded! and thou hell,
Deepen thy eternal groan!—men would not be
Redeemed,—I speak of many, not of all,—
Would not be saved for lost, have life for death!
  Mysterious song! the new arrived exclaimed,
Mysterious mercy! most mysterious hate!
To disobey was mad, this madder far,
Incurable insanity of will!
What now but wrath could guilty men expect?
What more could love, what more could mercy do?
  No more, resumed the bard, no more they could.
Thou hast seen hell. The wicked there lament:
And why? for love and mercy twice despised.
The husbandman, who sluggishly forgot
In spring to plough and sow, could censure none,
Though winter clamoured round his empty barns.
But he who, having thus neglected, did
Refuse, when autumn came, and famine threatened,
To reap the golden field that charity
Bestowed; nay, more obdurate, proud, and blind,
And stupid still; refused, though much beseeched,
And long entreated, even with Mercy's tears,
To eat what to his very lips was held,
Cooked temptingly,—he certainly, at least,
Deserved to die of hunger, unbemoaned.
So did the wicked spurn the grace of God;
And so were punished with the second death.
The first, no doubt, punition less severe
Intended; death, belike, of all entire.
But this incurred, by God discharged, and life
Freely presented, and again despised,
Despised, though bought with Mercy's proper blood,
'Twas this dug hell, and kindled all its bounds
With wrath and inextinguishable fire.
  Free was the offer, free to all, of life
And of salvation; but the proud of heart,
Because 'twas free, would not accept; and still
To merit wished; and choosing, thus unshipped,
Uncompassed, unprovisioned, and bestormed,
To swim a sea of breadth immeasurable,
They scorned the goodly bark, whose wings the breath
Of God's eternal Spirit filled for heaven,
That stopped to take them in, and so were lost.
  What wonders dost thou tell? To merit, how!
Of creature meriting in sight of God,
As right of service done, I never heard
Till now. We never fell; in virtue stood
Upright, and persevered in holiness;
But stood by grace, by grace we persevered.
Ourselves, our deeds, our holiest, highest deeds
Unworthy aught; grace worthy endless praise.
If we fly swift, obedient to his will,
He gives us wings to fly; if we resist
Temptation, and ne'er fall, it is his shield
Omnipotent that wards it off; if we,
With love unquenchable, before him burn,
'Tis he that lights and keeps alive the flame.
Men surely lost their reason in their fall,
And did not understand the offer made.
  They might have understood, the bard replied;
They had the Bible. Hast thou ever heard
Of such a book? The author, God himself;
The subject, God and man, salvation, life
And death—eternal life, eternal death—
Dread words! whose meaning has no end, no bounds—
Most wondrous book! bright candle of the Lord!
Star of eternity! the only star
By which the bark of man could navigate
The sea of life, and gain the coast of bliss
Securely! only star which rose on Time,
And on its dark and troubled billows, still,
As generation, drifting swiftly by,

Succeeded generation, threw a ray
Of heaven's own light, and to the hills of God,
The eternal hills, pointed the sinner's eye.
By prophets, seers, and priests, and sacred bards,
Evangelists, apostles, men inspired,
And by the Holy Ghost anointed, set
Apart and consecrated to declare
To Earth the counsels of the Eternal One,
This book, this holiest, this sublimest book,
Was sent. Heaven's will, Heaven's code of laws entire,
To man, this book contained; defined the bounds
Of vice and virtue, and of life and death;
And what was shadow, what was substance taught.
Much it revealed; important all; the least
Worth more than what else seemed of highest worth,
But this of plainest, most essential truth:
That God is one, eternal, holy, just,
Omnipotent, omniscient, infinite;
Most wise, most good, most merciful and true;
In all perfection most unchangeable:
That man, that every man of every clime
And hue, of every age and every rank,
Was bad, by nature and by practice bad;
In understanding blind, in will perverse,
In heart corrupt; in every thought, and word,
Imagination, passion, and desire,
Most utterly depraved throughout, and ill,
In sight of Heaven, though less in sight of man;
At enmity with God his maker born,
And by his very life an heir of death:
That man, that every man was, farther, most
Unable to redeem himself, or pay
One mite of his vast debt to God; nay, more,
Was most reluctant and averse to be
Redeemed, and sin's most voluntary slave:
That Jesus, Son of God, of Mary born
In Bethlehem, and by Pilate crucified
On Calvary, for man thus fallen and lost,
Died; and, by death, life and salvation bought,
And perfect righteousness, for all who should
In his great name believe: That He, the third
In the eternal Essence, to the prayer
Sincere should come, should come as soon as asked,
Proceeding from the Father and the Son,
To give faith and repentance, such as God
Accepts; to open the intellectual eyes,
Blinded by sin; to bend the stubborn will,
Perversely to the side of wrong inclined,
To God and his commandments, just and good;
The wild, rebellious passions to subdue,
And bring them back to harmony with heaven;
To purify the conscience, and to lead
The mind into all truth, and to adorn
With every holy ornament of grace,
And sanctify the whole renewed soul,
Which henceforth might no more fall totally,
But persevere, though erring oft, amidst
The mists of Time, in piety to God,
And sacred works of charity to men:
That he who thus believed, and practised thus,
Should have his sins forgiven, however vile;
Should be sustained at mid-day, morn, and even
By God's omnipotent, eternal grace:
And in the evil hour of sore disease,
Temptation, persecution, war, and death,—
For temporal death, although unstinged, remained,—
Beneath the shadow of the Almighty's wings
Should sit unhurt, and at the judgment-day,
Should share the resurrection of the just,
And reign with Christ in bliss for evermore:
That all, however named, however great,
Who would not thus believe, nor practise thus,
But in their sins impenitent remained,
Should in perpetual fear and terror live;
Should die unpardoned, unredeemed, unsaved;
And, at the hour of doom, should be cast out
To utter darkness in the night of hell,
By mercy and by God abandoned there
To reap the harvests of eternal wo.

This did the book declare in obvious phrase,
In most sincere and honest phrase, by God
Himself selected and arranged, so clear,
So plain, so perfectly distinct, that none,
Who read with humble wish to understand,
And asked the Spirit, given to all who asked,
Could miss their meaning, blazed in heavenly light.

This book, this holy book, on every line
Marked with the seal of high divinity,
On every leaf bedewed with drops of love
Divine, and with the eternal heraldry
And signature of God Almighty stamped
From first to last, this ray of sacred light,
This lamp, from off the everlasting throne,
Mercy took down, and in the night of Time
Stood, casting on the dark her gracious bow;
And evermore beseeching men, with tears
And earnest sighs, to read, believe, and live.
And many to her voice gave ear, and read,
Believed, obeyed; and now, as the Amen,
True, Faithful Witness swore, with snowy robes
And branchy palms, surround the fount of life,
And drink the streams of immortality,
For ever happy, and for ever young.

Many believed; but more the truth of God
Turned to a lie; deceiving and deceived;
Each with the accursed sorcery of sin,
To his own wish and vile propensity
Transforming still the meaning of the text.

Hear, while I briefly tell what mortals proved,
By effort vast of ingenuity,
Most wondrous, though perverse and damnable,
Proved from the Bible, which, as thou hast heard,
So plainly spoke that all could understand.
First, and not least in number, argued some,
From out this book itself, it was a lie,

A fable framed by crafty men to cheat
The simple herd, and make them bow the knee
To kings and priests. These in their wisdom left
The light revealed, and turned to fancies wild;
Maintaining loud, that ruined, helpless man,
Needed no Saviour. Others proved that men
Might live and die in sin, and yet be saved,
For so it was decreed; binding the will,
By God left free, to unconditional,
Unreasonable fate. Others believed
That he who was most criminal, debased,
Condemned, and dead, unaided might ascend
The heights of virtue; to a perfect law
Giving a lame, half-way obedience, which
By useless effort only served to show
The impotence of him who vainly strove
With finite arm to measure infinite;
Most useless effort, when to justify
In sight of God it meant, as proof of faith
Most acceptable and worthy of all praise.
Another held, and from the Bible held,
He was infallible, most fallen by such
Pretence; that none the Scriptures, open to all,
And most to humble-hearted, ought to read,
But priests; that all who ventured to disclaim
His forged authority, incurred the wrath
Of Heaven; and he who, in the blood of such,
Though father, mother, daughter, wife, or son,
Imbrued his hands, did most religious work,
Well pleasing to the heart of the Most High.
Others in outward rite devotion placed,
In meats, in drinks, in robe of certain shape,
In bodily abasements, bended knees;
Days, numbers, places, vestments, words, and names;
Absurdly in their hearts imagining,
That God, like men, was pleased with outward show.
Another, stranger and more wicked still,
With dark and dolorous labour, ill applied,
With many a gripe of conscience, and with most
Unhealthy and abortive reasoning,
That brought his sanity to serious doubt,
'Mong wise and honest men, maintained that He,
First Wisdom, Great Messiah, Prince of Peace,
The second of the uncreated Three,
Was naught but man, of earthly origin:
Thus making void the sacrifice divine,
And leaving guilty men, God's holy law
Still unatoned, to work them endless death.
These are a part; but to relate thee all
The monstrous, unbaptized fantasies,
Imaginations fearfully absurd,
Hobgoblin rites, and moon-struck reveries,
Distracted creeds, and visionary dreams,
More bodiless and hideously misshapen
Than ever fancy, at the noon of night,
Playing at will, framed in the madman's brain,
That from this book of simple truth were proved,
Were proved, as foolish men were wont to prove,
Would bring my word in doubt, and thy belief
Stagger, though here I sit and sing, within
The pale of truth, where falsehood never came.
The rest, who lost the heavenly light revealed,
Not wishing to retain God in their minds,
In darkness wandered on. Yet could they not,
Though moral night around them drew her pall
Of blackness, rest in utter unbelief.
The voice within, the voice of God, that naught
Could bribe to sleep, though steeped in sorceries
Of hell, and much abused by whisperings
Of evil spirits in the dark, announced
A day of judgment and a Judge, a day
Of misery or bliss: and, being ill
At ease, for gods they chose them stocks and stones,
Reptiles, and weeds, and beasts, and creeping things,
And spirits accursed, ten thousand deities!
Imagined worse than he who craved their peace;
And, bowing, worshipped these, as best beseemed,
With midnight revelry obscene and loud,
With dark, infernal, devilish ceremonies,
And horrid sacrifice of human flesh,
That made the fair heavens blush. So bad was sin;
So lost, so ruined, so depraved was man,
Created first in God's own image fair.
Oh, cursed, cursed Sin! traitor to God,
And ruiner of man! mother of Wo,
And Death, and Hell! wretched, yet seeking worse;
Polluted most, yet wallowing in the mire;
Most mad, yet drinking Frenzy's giddy cup;
Depth ever deepening, darkness darkening still;
Folly for wisdom, guilt for innocence;
Anguish for rapture, and for hope despair;
Destroyed, destroying; in tormenting, pained;
Unawed by wrath, by mercy unreclaimed;
Thing most unsightly, most forlorn, most sad,
Thy time on earth is passed, thy war with God
And holiness. But who, oh, who shall tell,
Thy unrepentable and ruinous thoughts!
Thy sighs, thy groans! who reckon thy burning tears,
And damned looks of everlasting grief,
Where now, with those who took their part with thee,
Thou sitt'st in hell, gnawed by the eternal Worm,
To hurt no more, on all the holy hills!
That those, deserting once the lamp of truth,
Should wander ever on, from worse to worse
Erroneously, thy wonder needs not ask:
But that enlightened, reasonable men,
Knowing themselves accountable, to whom
God spoke from heaven, and by his servants warned,
Both day and night, with earnest pleading voice,
Of retribution equal to their works,

Should persevere in evil, and be lost,—
This strangeness, this unpardonable guilt,
Demands an answer, which my song unfolds,
In part, directly; but, hereafter, more,
To satisfy thy wonder thou shalt learn,
Inferring much from what is yet to sing.
Know, then, of men who sat in highest place,
Exalted, and for sin by others done
Were chargeable, the king and priests were chief.
Many were faithful, holy, just, upright,
Faithful to God and man, reigning renowned
In righteousness, and, to the people, loud
And fearless, speaking all the words of life.
These, at the judgment-day, as thou shalt hear,
Abundant harvest reaped. But many, too,
Alas, how many! famous now in hell,
Were wicked, cruel, tyrannous, and vile;
Ambitious of themselves, abandoned, mad;
And still from servants hasting to be gods,
Such gods as now they serve in Erebus.
I pass their lewd example by, that led
So many wrong, for courtly fashion lost,
And prove them guilty of one crime alone.
Of every wicked ruler, prince supreme,
Or magistrate below, the one intent,
Purpose, desire, and struggle, day and night,
Was evermore to wrest the crown from off
Messiah's head, and put it on his own;
And in His place give spiritual laws to men;
To bind religion, free by birth, by God
And nature free, and made accountable
To none but God, behind the wheels of state;
To make the holy altar, where the Prince
Of life, incarnate, bled to ransom man,
A footstool to the throne. For this they met,
Assembled, counselled, meditated, planned;
Devised in open and in secret; and for this
Enacted creeds of wondrous texture, creeds
The Bible never owned, unsanctioned too,
And reprobate in heaven; but by the power
That made,—exerted now in gentler form,
Monopolizing rights and privileges,
Equal to all, and waving now the sword
Of persecution fierce, tempered in hell,—
Forced on the conscience of inferior men:
The conscience, that sole monarchy in man,
Owing allegiance to no earthly prince;
Made by the edict of creation free;
Made sacred, made above all human laws;
Holding of heaven alone; of most divine
And indefeasible authority;
An individual sovereignty, that none
Created might, unpunished, bind or touch;
Unbound, save by the eternal laws of God,
And unamenable to all below.
Thus did the uncircumcised potentates
Of earth debase religion in the sight
Of those they ruled, who, looking up, beheld
The fair celestial gift despised, enslaved;
And, mimicking the folly of the great,
With prompt docility despised her too.
The prince or magistrate, however named
Or praised, who, knowing better, acted thus,
Was wicked, and received, as he deserved,
Damnation. But the unfaithful priest, what tongue
Enough shall execrate? His doctrine may
Be passed, though mixed with most unhallowed leaven,
That proved, to those who foolishly partook,
Eternal bitterness. But this was still.
His sin, beneath what cloak soever veiled,
His ever growing and perpetual sin,
First, last, and middle thought, whence every wish
Whence every action rose, and ended both:
To mount to place, and power of worldly sort;
To ape the gaudy pomp and equipage
Of earthly state, and on his mitred brow
To place a royal crown. For this he sold
The sacred truth to him who most would give
Of titles, benefices, honours, names;
For this betrayed his Master; and for this
Made merchandize of the immortal souls
Committed to his care. This was his sin.
Of all who office held unfairly, none
Could plead excuse; he least and last of all.
By solemn, awful ceremony, he
Was set apart to speak the truth entire,
By action and by word; and round him stood
The people, from his lips expecting knowledge.
One day in seven, the Holy Sabbath termed,
They stood; for he had sworn, in face of God
And man, to deal sincerely with their souls;
To preach the gospel for the gospel's sake;
Had sworn to hate and put away all pride,
All vanity, all love of earthly pomp;
To seek all mercy, meekness, truth, and grace:
And being so endowed himself, and taught,
In them like works of holiness to move;
Dividing faithfully the word of life.
And oft indeed the word of life he taught;
But practising as thou hast heard, who could
Believe? Thus was Religion wounded sore
At her own altars, and among her friends.
The people went away, and, like the priest,
Fulfilling what the prophet spoke before,
For honour strove, and wealth, and place, as if
The preacher had rehearsed an idle tale.
The enemies of God rejoiced, and loud
The unbeliever laughed, boasting a life
Of fairer character than his, who owned,
For king and guide, the undefiled One.
Most guilty, villanous, dishonest man!
Wolf in the clothing of the gentle lamb!
Dark traitor in Messiah's holy camp!
Leper in saintly garb! assassin masked
In Virtue's robe! vile hypocrite accursed,
I strive in vain to set his evil forth.
The words that should sufficiently accurse

And execrate such reprobate, had need
Come glowing from the lips of eldest hell.
Among the saddest in the den of wo,
Thou sawst him saddest, 'mong the damned, most damned.
But why should I with indignation burn,
Not well beseeming here, and long forgot?
Or why one censure for another's sin?
Each had his conscience, each his reason, will,
And understanding, for himself to search,
To choose, reject, believe, consider, act.
And God proclaimed from heaven, and by an oath
Confirmed, that each should answer for himself:
And as his own peculiar work should be,
Done by his proper self, should live or die.
But sin, deceitful and deceiving still,
Had gained the heart, and reason led astray.
A strange belief, that leaned its idiot back
On folly's topmost twig,—belief that God,
Most wise, had made a world, had creatures made,
Beneath his care to govern and protect,—
Devoured its thousands. Reason, not the true,
Learned, deep, sober, comprehensive, sound;
But bigoted, one-eyed, short-sighted Reason,
Most zealous, and sometimes, no doubt, sincere,
Devoured its thousands. Vanity to be
Renowned for creed eccentrical, devoured
Its thousands; but a lazy, corpulent,
And over-credulous faith, that leaned on all
It met, nor asked if 'twas a reed or oak;
Stepped on, but never earnestly inquired
Whether to heaven or hell the journey led,
Devoured its tens of thousands, and its hands
Made reddest in the precious blood of souls.
In Time's pursuits men ran till out of breath.
The astronomer soared up, and counted stars,
And gazed, and gazed upon the heaven's bright face,
Till he dropped down dim-eyed into the grave.
The numerist, in calculations deep,
Grew gray. The merchant at his desk expired.
The statesman hunted for another place,
Till death o'ertook him, and made him his prey.
The miser spent his eldest energy
In grasping for another mite. The scribe
Rubbed pensively his old and withered brow,
Devising new impediments to hold
In doubt, the suit that threatened to end too soon.
The priest collected tithes, and pleaded rights
Of decimation to the very last.
In science, learning, all philosophy,
Men laboured all their days, and laboured hard,
And, dying, sighed how little they had done.
But in religion, they at once grew wise.
A creed in print, though never understood;
A theologic system on the shelf,
Was spiritual lore enough, and served their turn;
But served it ill. They sinned, and never knew.
For what the Bible said of good and bad,
Of holiness and sin, they never asked.
Absurd, prodigiously absurd, to think
That man's minute and feeble faculties,
Even in the very childhood of his being,
With mortal shadows dimmed and wrapped around,
Could comprehend at once the mighty scheme,
Where rolled the ocean of eternal love·
Where wisdom infinite its master-stroke
Displayed; and where omnipotence, oppressed,
Did travail in the greatness of its strength;
And everlasting justice lifted up
The sword to smite the guiltless Son of God;
And mercy smiling bade the sinner go!
Redemption is the science and the song
Of all eternity. Archangels day
And night into its glories look. The saints,
The elders round the Throne, old in the years
Of heaven, examine it perpetually;
And, every hour, get clearer, ampler views
Of right and wrong; see virtue's beauty more;
See vice more utterly depraved and vile;
And this, with a more perfect hatred, hate;
That daily love with a more perfect love.
But whether I for man's perdition blame
Office administered amiss, pursuit
Of pleasure false, perverted reason blind,
Or indolence that ne'er inquired; I blame
Effect and consequence, the branch, the leaf.
Who finds the fount and bitter root, the first
And guiltiest cause whence sprung this endless wo,
Must deep descend into the human heart,
And find it there. Dread passion! making men
On earth, and even in hell, if Mercy yet
Would stoop so low, unwilling to be saved,
If saved by grace of God. Hear, then, in brief,
What peopled hell, what holds its prisoners there.
Pride, self-adoring pride, was primal cause
Of all sin passed, all pain, all wo to come.
Unconquerable pride! first, eldest sin,
Great fountain-head of evil! highest source,
Whence flowed rebellion 'gainst the Omnipotent
Whence hate of man to man, and all else ill.
Pride at the bottom of the human heart
Lay, and gave root and nourishment to all
That grew above. Great ancestor of vice!
Hate, unbelief, and blasphemy of God;
Envy and slander, malice and revenge;
And murder, and deceit, and every birth
Of damned sort, was progeny of pride.
It was the ever-moving, acting force,
The constant aim, and the most thirsty wish
Of every sinner unrenewed, to be
A god; in purple or in rags, to have
Himself adored. Whatever shape or form

His actions took, whatever phrase he threw
About his thoughts, or mantle o'er his life,
To be the highest, was the inward cause
Of all; the purpose of the heart to be
Set up, admired, obeyed. But who would bow
The knee to one who served and was dependent?
Hence man's perpetual struggle, night and day,
To prove he was his own proprietor,
And independent of his God, that what
He had might be esteemed his own, and praised
As such. He laboured still and tried to stand
Alone, unpropped, to be obliged to none;
And in the madness of his pride, he bade
His God farewell, and turned away to be
A god himself: resolving to rely,
Whatever came, upon his own right hand.
  O desperate frenzy! madness of the will!
And drunkenness of the heart! that naught could quench
But floods of wo, poured from the sea of wrath,
Behind which mercy set. To think to turn
The back on life original, and live!
The creature to set up a rival throne
In the Creator's realm! to deify
A worm! and in the sight of God be proud!
To lift an arm of flesh against the shafts
Of the Omnipotent, and, midst his wrath,
To seek for happiness!—insanity
Most mad! guilt most complete! Seest thou those worlds
That roll at various distance round the throne
Of God, innumerous, and fill the calm
Of heaven with sweetest harmony, when saints
And angels sleep? As one of these, from love
Centripetal, withdrawing, and from light,
And heat, and nourishment cut off, should rush
Abandoned o'er the line that runs between
Create and increate, from ruin driven
To ruin still, through the abortive waste;
So pride from God drew off the bad; and so
Forsaken of him, he lets them ever try
Their single arm against the second death;
Amidst vindictive thunders lets them try
The stoutness of their hearts, and lets them try
To quench their thirst amidst the unfading fire;
And to reap joy where he has sown despair;
To walk alone, unguided, unbemoaned,
Where Evil dwells, and Death, and moral Night;
In utter emptiness to find enough;
In utter dark find light; and find repose,
Where God with tempest plagues for evermore.
For so they wished it, so did pride desire.
  Such was the cause that turned so many off
Rebelliously from God, and led them on
From vain to vainer still, in endless chase.
And such the cause that made so many cheeks
Pale, and so many knees to shake, when men
Rose from the grave; as thou shalt hear anon.

BOOK III.

Beholdst thou yonder, on the crystal sea,
Beneath the throne of God, an image fair,
And in its hand a mirror large and bright?
'Tis truth, immutable, eternal truth,
In figure emblematical expressed.
Before it Virtue stands, and smiling sees,
Well pleased, in her reflected soul, no spot.
The sons of heaven, archangel, seraph, saint,
There daily read their own essential worth;
And, as they read, take place among the just;
Or high, or low, each as his value seems.
There each his certain interest learns, his true
Capacity; and, going thence, pursues,
Unerringly, through all the tracts of thought,
As God ordains, best ends by wisest means.
  The Bible held this mirror's place on earth.
But, few would read, or, reading, saw themselves.
The chase was after shadows, phantoms strange,
That in the twilight walked of Time, and mocked
The eager hunt, escaping evermore.
Yet with so many promises and looks
Of gentle sort, that he whose arms returned
Empty a thousand times, still stretched them out,
And, grasping, brought them back again unfilled.
  In rapid outline thou hast heard of man,
His death, his offered life, that life by most
Despised, the Star of God, the Bible, scorned,
That else to happiness and heaven had led,
And saved my lyre from narrative of wo.
Hear now more largely of the ways of Time
The fond pursuits and vanities of men.
  "Love God, love Truth, love Virtue, and be happy;
These were the words first uttered in the ear
Of every being rational made, and made
For thought, or word, or deed accountable.
Most men the first forgot, the second none.
Whatever path they took, by hill or vale,
By night or day, the universal wish,
The aim, and sole intent, was happiness.
But, erring from the heaven-appointed path,
Strange tracks indeed they took through barren wastes.
And up the sandy mountain climbing toiled,
Which pining lay beneath the curse of God,
And nought produced. Yet did the traveller look
And point his eye before him greedily,
And if he saw some verdant spot, where grew
The heavenly flower, where sprung the well of life,
Where undisturbed felicity reposed;
Though Wisdom s eye no vestige could discern,
That Happiness had ever passed that way.
  Wisdom was right, for still the terms remained
Unchanged, unchangeable, the terms on which

True peace was given to man, unchanged as God,
Who, in his own essential nature, binds
Eternally to virtue happiness,
Nor lets them part through all his universe.
Philosophy, as thou shalt hear, when she
Shall have her praise, her praise and censure too,
Did much, refining and exalting man;
But could not nurse a single plant that bore
True happiness. From age to age she toiled,
Shed from her eyes the mist that dimmed them still,
Looked forth on man, explored the wild and tame,
The savage and polite, the sea and land,
And starry heavens; and then retired far back
To meditation's silent, shady seat;
And there sat pale, and thoughtfully, and weighed
With wary, most exact, and scrupulous care,
Man's nature, passions, hopes, propensities,
Relations, and pursuits, in reason's scale;
And searched and weighed, and weighed and searched again,
And many a fair and goodly volume wrote,
That seemed well worded too, wherein were found
Uncountable receipts, pretending each,
If carefully attended to, to cure
Mankind of folly, to root out the briers,
And thorns, and weeds, that choked the growth of joy;
And showing too, in plain and decent phrase,
Which sounded much like Wisdom's, how to plant,
To shelter, water, culture, prune, and rear
The tree of happiness; and oft their plans
Were tried; but still the fruit was green and sour.
Of all the trees that in Earth's vineyard grew,
And with their clusters tempted man to pull
And eat, one tree, one tree alone, the true
Celestial manna bore, which filled the soul,
The tree of holiness, of heavenly seed,
A native of the skies; though stunted much
And dwarfed, by Time's cold, damp, ungenial soil,
And chilling winds, yet yielding fruit so pure,
So nourishing and sweet, as, on his way,
Refreshed the pilgrim; and begot desire
Unquenchable to climb the arduous path
To where her sister plants, in their own clime,
Around the fount, and by the stream of life,
Blooming beneath the Sun that never sets,
Bear fruit of perfect relish fully ripe.
To plant this tree, uprooted by the fall,
To earth the Son of God descended, shed
His precious blood; and on it evermore,
From off his living wings, the Spirit shook
The dews of heaven, to nurse and hasten its growth.
Nor was this care, this infinite expense,
Not needed to secure the holy plant.
To root it out, and wither it from earth,
Hell strove with all its strength, and blew with all
Its blasts! and Sin, with cold, consumptive breath,
Involved it still in clouds of mortal damp.
Yet did it grow, thus kept, protected thus;
And bear the only fruit of true delight;
The only fruit worth plucking under heaven.
But, few, alas! the holy plant could see,
For heavy mists that Sin around it threw
Perpetually; and few the sacrifice
Would make, by which alone its clusters stooped,
And came within the reach of mortal man.
For this, of whom who would approach and eat,
Was rigorously exacted to the full:
To tread and bruise beneath the foot the world
Entire; its prides, ambitions, hopes, desires;
Its gold and all its broidered equipage;
To loose its loves and friendships from the heart,
And cast them off; to shut the ear against
Its praise, and all its flatteries abhor;
And, having thus behind him thrown what seemed
So good and fair, then must he lowly kneel,
And with sincerity, in which the Eye
That slumbers not, nor sleeps, could see no lack,
This prayer pray: "Lord, God! thy will be done,
Thy holy will, howe'er it cross my own."
Hard labour this for flesh and blood! too hard
For most it seemed. So, turning, they the tree
Derided as mere bramble, that could bear
No fruit of special taste; and so set out
Upon ten thousand different routes to seek
What they had left behind, to seek what they
Had lost. For still as something once possessed
And lost, true happiness appeared. All thought
They once were happy; and even while they smoked
And panted in the chase, believed themselves
More miserable to-day than yesterday,
To-morrow than to-day. When youth complained
The ancient sinner shook his hoary head,
As if he meant to say, Stop till you come
My length, and then you may have cause to sigh.
At twenty, cried the boy, who now had seen
Some blemish in his joys, How happily
Plays yonder child that busks the mimic babe,
And gathers gentle flowers, and never sighs!
At forty, in the fervour of pursuit,
Far on in disappointment's dreary vale,
The grave and sage-like man looked back upon
The stripling youth of plump unseared hope,
Who galloped gay and briskly up behind,
And, moaning, wished himself eighteen again.
And he, of threescore years and ten, in whose
Chilled eye, fatigued with gaping after hope,
Earth's freshest verdure seemed but blasted leaves,
Praised childhood, youth, and manhood; and denounced
Old age alone as barren of all joy.
Decisive proof that men had left behind
The happiness they sought, and taken a most
Erroneous path; since every step they took

Was deeper mire. Yet did they onward run,
Pursuing Hope that danced before them still,
And beckoned them to proceed; and with their hands,
That shook and trembled piteously with age,
Grasped at the lying Shade, even till the earth
Beneath them broke, and wrapped them in the grave.
Sometimes indeed, when wisdom in their ear
Whispered, and with its disenchanting wand,
Effectually touched the sorcery of their eyes,
Directly pointing to the holy tree,
Where grew the food they sought, they turned, surprised.
That they had missed so long what now they found
As one upon whose mind some new and rare
Idea glances, and retires as quick,
Ere memory has time to write it down;
Stung with the loss, into a thoughtful cast,
He throws his face, and rubs his vexed brow;
Searches each nook and corner of his soul
With frequent care; reflects, and re-reflects,
And tries to touch relations that may start
The fugitive again; and oft is foiled;
Till something like a seeming chance, or flight
Of random fancy, when expected least,
Calls back the wandered thought, long sought in vain;
Then does uncommon joy fill all his mind;
And still he wonders, as he holds it fast,
What lay so near he could not sooner find:
So did the man rejoice, when from his eye
The film of folly fell, and what he, day
And night, and far and near, had idly searched,
Sprung up before him suddenly displayed;
So wondered why he missed the tree so long.
But, few returned from folly's giddy chase,
Few heard the voice of Wisdom, or obeyed.
Keen was the search, and various, and wide,
Without, within, along the flowery vale,
And up the rugged cliff, and on the top
Of mountains high, and on the ocean wave.
Keen was the search, and various, and wide,
And ever and anon a shout was heard:
"Ho! here's the tree of life! come, eat, and live!"
And round the new discoverer quick they flocked
In multitudes, and plucked, and with great haste,
Devoured; and sometimes in the lips 'twas sweet,
And promised well: but, in the belly gall.
Yet after him that cried again, Ho! here's
The tree of life! again they ran, and pulled,
And chewed again, and found it bitter still.
From disappointment on to disappointment,
Year after year, age after age, pursued,
The child, the youth, the hoary headed man,
Alike pursued, and ne'er grew wise. For it
Was folly's most peculiar attribute,
And native act, to make experience void.
But hastily, as pleasures tasted, turned
To loathing and disgust, they needed not
Even such experiment to prove them vain.
In hope or in possession, Fear, alike,
Boding disaster, stood. Over the flower
Of fairest sort, that bloomed beneath the sun,
Protected most, and sheltered from the storm,
The Spectre, like a dark and thunderous cloud,
Hung dismally, and threatened, before the hand
Of him that wished, could pull it, to descend,
And o'er the desert drive its withered leaves;
Or, being pulled, to blast it unenjoyed,
While yet he gazed upon its loveliness,
And just began to drink its fragrance up.
Gold many hunted, sweat and bled for gold;
Waked all the night, and laboured all the day.
And what was this allurement dost thou ask?
A dust dug from the bowels of the earth,
Which, being cast into the fire, came out
A shining thing that fools admired, and called
A god; and in devout and humble plight
Before it kneeled, the greater to the less;
And on its altar sacrificed ease, peace,
Truth, faith, integrity: good conscience, friends,
Love, charity, benevolence, and all
The sweet and tender sympathies of life;
And, to complete the horrid murderous rite,
And signalize their folly, offered up
Their souls and an eternity of bliss,
To gain them—what?—an hour of dreaming joy,
A feverish hour that hasted to be done,
And ended in the bitterness of wo.
Most, for the luxuries it bought, the pomp,
The praise, the glitter, fashion, and renown,
This yellow phantom followed and adored.
But there was one in folly farther gone,
With eye awry, incurable, and wild,
The laughing-stock of devils and of men,
And by his guardian angel quite given up,—
The miser, who with dust inanimate
Held wedded intercourse. Ill guided wretch!
Thou mightst have seen him at the midnight hour,
When good men slept, and in light winged dreams
Ascended up to God,—in wasteful hall,
With vigilance and fasting worn to skin
And bone, and wrapped in most debasing rags,—
Thou mightst have seen him bending o'er his heaps,
And holding strange communion with his gold;
And as his thievish fancy seemed to hear
The night-man's foot approach, starting alarmed,
And in his old, decrepit, withered hand,
That palsy shook, grasping the yellow earth
To make it sure. Of all God made upright,
And in their nostrils breathed a living soul,
Most fallen, most prone, most earthy, most debased;
Of all that sold Eternity for Time,
None bargained on so easy terms with Death.
Illustrious fool! nay, most inhuman wretch!

He sat among his bags, and, with a look
Which hell might be ashamed of, drove the poor
Away unalmsed, and midst abundance died,
Sorest of evils! died of utter want.
Before this Shadow, in the vales of earth,
Fools saw another glide, which seemed of more
Intrinsic worth. Pleasure her name; good name,
Though ill applied. A thousand forms she took,
A thousand garbs she wore; in every age
And clime, changing, as in her votaries changed
Desire; but, inwardly, the same in all.
Her most essential lineaments we trace;
Her general features everywhere alike.
Of comely form she was, and fair of face;
And underneath her eyelids sat a kind
Of witching sorcery that nearer drew
Whoever, with unguarded look, beheld;
A dress of gaudy hue loosely attired
Her loveliness; her air and manner frank,
And seeming free of all disguise; her song
Enchanting; and her words, which sweetly dropped,
As honey from the comb, most large of promise,
Still prophesying days of new delight,
And rapturous nights of undecaying joy;
And in her hand, where'er she went, she held
A radiant cup that seemed of nectar full;
And by her side, danced fair, delusive Hope.
The fool pursued. enamoured; and the wise
Experienced man, who reasoned much and thought,
Was sometimes seen laying his wisdom down,
And vying with the stripling in the chase.
Nor wonder thou, for she was really fair,
Decked to the very taste of flesh and blood,
And many thought her sound within, and gay
And healthy at the heart: but thought amiss.
For she was full of all disease: her bones
Were rotten; Consumption licked her blood, and drank
Her marrow up; her breath smelled mortally,
And in her bowels plague and fever lurked;
And in her very heart, and reins, and life,
Corruption's worm gnawed greedily unseen.
Many her haunts. Thou mightst have seen her now
With indolence, lolling on the mid-day couch,
And whispering drowsy words; and now at dawn,
Loudly and rough, joining the sylvan horn;
Or sauntering in the park, and to the tale
Of slander giving ear; or sitting fierce,
Rude, blasphemous, malicious, raving, mad,
Where fortune to the fickle die was bound.
But chief she loved the scene of deep debauch,
Where revelry, and dance, and frantic song,
Disturbed the sleep of honest men; and where
The drunkard sat, she entered in, well pleased,
With eye brimful of wanton mirthfulness,
And urged him still to fill another cup.
And at the shadowy twilight, in the dark
And gloomy night, I looked, and saw her come
Abroad, arrayed in harlot's soft attire;
And walk without in every street, and lie
In wait at every corner, full of guile:
And as the unwary youth of simple heart,
And void of understanding, passed, she caught
And kissed him, and with lips of lying said,
I have peace-offerings with me; I have paid
My vows this day; and therefore came I forth
To meet thee, and to seek thee diligently,
To seek thy face, and I have found thee here.
My bed is decked with robes of tapestry,
With carved work and sheets of linen fine;
Perfumed with aloes, myrrh, and cinnamon.
Sweet are stolen waters! pleasant is the bread
In secret eaten! the goodman is from home.
Come, let us take our fill of love till morn
Awake; let us delight ourselves with loves.
With much fair speech, she caused the youth to yield;
And forced him with the flattering of her tongue.
I looked, and saw him follow to her house,
As goes the ox to slaughter; as the fool
To the correction of the stocks; or bird
That hastes into the subtle fowler's snare,
And knows not, simple thing, 'tis for its life.
I saw him enter in, and heard the door
Behind them shut; and in the dark, still night,
When God's unsleeping eye alone can see,
He went to her adulterous bed. At morn
I looked, and saw him not among the youths.
I heard his father mourn, his mother weep,
For none returned that went with her. The dead
Were in her house, her guests in depths of hell.
She wove the winding-sheet of souls, and laid
Them in the urn of everlasting death.
Such was the Shadow fools pursued on earth,
Under the name of pleasure; fair outside,
Within corrupted, and corrupting still.
Ruined and ruinous, her sure reward,
Her total recompense, was still, as he,
The bard, recorder of Earth's Seasons, sung,
"Vexation, disappointment, and remorse."
Yet at her door the young and old, and some
Who held high character among the wise,
Together stood, and strove among themselves,
Who first should enter, and be ruined first.
Strange competition of immortal souls!
To sweat for death! to strive for misery!
But think not Pleasure told her end was death.
Even human folly then had paused at least.
And given some signs of hesitation; nor
Arrived so hot, and out of breath, at wo.
Though contradicted every day by facts
That sophistry itself would stumble o'er,
And to the very teeth a liar proved,
Ten thousand times, as if unconscious still
Of inward blame, she stood and waved her hand
And pointed to her bower, and said to all

Who passed, Take yonder flowery path, my steps
Attend; I lead the smoothest way to heaven;
This world receive as surety for the next:
And many simple men, most simple, though
Renowned for learning much, and wary skill,
Believed, and turned aside, and were undone.
 Another leaf of finished Time we turn,
And read of fame, terrestrial fame, which died,
And rose not at the resurrection morn;
Not that by virtue earned, the true renown,
Begun on earth, and lasting in the skies,
Worthy the lofty wish of seraphim,—
The approbation of the Eye that sees
The end from the beginning, sees from cause
To most remote effect. Of it we read
In book of God's remembrance, in the book
Of life, from which the quick and dead were judged;
The book that lies upon the Throne, and tells
Of glorious acts by saints and angels done;
The record of the holy, just, and good.
 Of all the phantoms fleeting in the mist
Of Time, though meagre all, and ghostly thin,
Most unsubstantial, unessential shade
Was earthly Fame. She was a voice alone,
And dwelt upon the noisy tongues of men.
She never thought, but gabbled ever on,
Applauding most what least deserved applause.
The motive, the result, was naught to her.
The deed alone, though dyed in human gore,
And steeped in widow's tears, if it stood out
To prominent display, she talked of much,
And roared around it with a thousand tongues.
As changed the wind her organ, so she changed
Perpetually; and whom she praised to-day,
Vexing his ear with acclamations loud,
To-morrow blamed, and hissed him out of sight.
 Such was her nature, and her practice such.
But, O! her voice was sweet to mortal ears,
And touched so pleasantly the strings of pride
And vanity, which in the heart of man
Were ever strung harmonious to her note,
That many thought, to live without her song
Was rather death than life. To live unknown,
Unnoticed, unrenowned! to die unpraised,
Unepitaphed! to go down to the pit,
And moulder into dust among vile worms,
And leave no whispering of a name on earth!—
Such thought was cold about the heart, and chilled
The blood. Who could endure it? who could choose
Without a struggle, to be swept away
From all remembrance, and have part no more
With living men? Philosophy failed here,
And self-approving pride. Hence it became
The aim of most, and main pursuit, to win
A name, to leave some vestige as they passed,
That following ages might discern, they once
Had been on earth, and acted something there.
 Many the roads they took, the plans they tried.
The man of science to the shade retired,
And laid his head upon his hand, in mood
Of awful thoughtfulness, and dived, and dived
Again, deeper and deeper still, to sound
The cause remote; resolved, before he died,
To make some grand discovery, by which
He should be known to all posterity.
 And in the silent vigils of the night,
When uninspired men reposed, the bard,
Ghastly of countenance, and from his eye
Oft streaming wild unearthly fire, sat up,
And sent imagination forth, and searched
The far and near, heaven, earth, and gloomy hell,
For fiction new, for thought, unthought before;
And when some curious, rare idea peered
Upon his mind, he dipped his hasty pen,
And by the glimmering lamp, or moonlight beam
That through his lattice peeped, wrote fondly down,
What seemed in truth imperishable song.
 And sometimes too, the reverend divine,
In meditation deep of holy things
And vanities of Time, heard Fame's sweet voice
Approach his ear; and hung another flower,
Of earthly sort, about the sacred truth;
And ventured whiles to mix the bitter text,
With relish suited to the sinner's taste.
 And oft-times too, the simple hind, who seemed
Ambitionless, arrayed in humble garb,
While round him, spreading, fed his harmless flock,
Sitting was seen, by some wild warbling brook,
Carving his name upon his favourite staff;
Or, in ill-favoured letters, tracing it
Upon the aged thorn, or on the face
Of some conspicuous, oft-frequented stone,
With persevering, wondrous industry;
And hoping, as he toiled amain, and saw
The characters take form, some other wight,
Long after he was dead and in the grave,
Should loiter there at noon, and read his name.
 In purple some, and some in rags, stood forth
For reputation. Some displayed a limb
Well-fashioned; some, of lowlier mind, a cane
Of curious workmanship and marvellous twist.
In strength some sought it, and in beauty more.
Long, long, the fair one laboured at the glass,
And, being tired, called in auxiliar skill,
To have her sails, before she went abroad,
Full spread and nicely set, to catch the gale
Of praise; and much she caught, and much deserved,
When outward loveliness was index fair
Of purity within: but oft, alas!
The bloom was on the skin alone; and when
She saw, sad sight! the roses on her cheek
Wither, and heard the voice of Fame retire
And die away, she heaved most piteous sighs,
And wept most lamentable tears; and whiles,
In wild delirium, made rash attempt,

Unholy mimicry of Nature's work!
To re-create, with frail and mortal things,
Her withered face. Attempt how fond and vain!
Her frame itself soon mouldered down to dust;
And, in the land of deep forgetfulness,
Her beauty and her name were laid beside
Eternal silence and the loathsome worm;
Into whose darkness flattery ventured not;
Where none had ears to hear the voice of Fame.
Many the roads they took, the plans they tried,
And awful oft the wickedness they wrought.
To be observed, some scrambled up to thrones,
And sat in vestures dripping wet with gore.
The warrior dipped his sword in blood, and wrote
His name on lands and cities desolate.
The rich bought fields, and houses built, and raised
The monumental piles up to the clouds,
And called them by their names: and, strange to tell!
Rather than be unknown, and pass away
Obscurely to the grave, some, small of soul,
That else had perished unobserved, acquired
Considerable renown by oaths profane;
By jesting boldly with all sacred things;
And uttering fearlessly whate'er occurred;
Wild, blasphemous, perditionable thoughts,
That Satan in them moved; by wiser men
Suppressed, and quickly banished from the mind.
Many the roads they took, the plans they tried.
But all in vain. Who grasped at earthly fame,
Grasped wind; nay worse, a serpent grasped, that through
His hand slid smoothly, and was gone; but left
A sting behind which wrought him endless pain.
For oft her voice was old Abaddon's lure,
By which he charmed the foolish soul to death.
So happiness was sought in pleasure, gold,
Renown, by many sought. But should I sing
Of all the trifling race, my time, thy faith
Would fail, of things erectly organized,
And having rational, articulate voice,
And claiming outward brotherhood with man,
Of him that laboured sorely, in his sweat
Smoking afar, then hurried to the wine,
Deliberately resolving to be mad;
Of him who taught the ravenous bird to fly
This way or that, thereby supremely blest;
Or rode in fury with the howling pack,
Affronting much the noble animal,
He spurred into such company; of him
Who down into the bowels of the earth
Descended deeply, to bring up the wreck
Of some old earthen ware, which having stowed,
With every proper care, he home returned
O'er many a sea and many a league of land,
Triumphantly to show the marvellous prize;
And him that vexed his brain, and theories built
Of gossamer upon the brittle winds,
Perplexed exceedingly why shells were found
Upon the mountain tops, but wondering not
Why shells were found at all, more wondrous still!
Of him who strange enjoyment took in tales
Of fairy folk, and sleepless ghosts, and sounds
Unearthly, whispering in the ear of night
Disastrous things; and him who still foretold
Calamity which never came, and lived
In terror all his days of comets rude,
That should unmannerly and lawless drive
Athwart the path of earth, and burn mankind;
As if the appointed hour of doom, by God
Appointed, ere its time should come! as if
Too small the number of substantial ills,
And real fears, to vex the sons of men.
These, had they not possessed immortal souls,
And been accountable, might have been passed
With laughter, and forgot; but, as it was,
And is, their folly asks a serious tear.
Keen was the search, and various, and wide,
For happiness. Take one example more,
So strange, that common fools looked on amazed;
And wise and sober men together drew,
And trembling stood; and angels in the heavens
Grew pale, and talked of vengeance as at hand;
The sceptic's route, the unbeliever's, who,
Despising reason, revelation, God,
And kicking 'gainst the pricks of conscience, rushed
Deliriously upon the bossy shield
Of the Omnipotent; and in his heart
Purposed to deify the idol chance;
And laboured hard,—oh, labour worse than naught!—
And toiled with dark and crooked reasoning,
To make the fair and lovely earth, which dwelt
In sight of Heaven, a cold and fatherless,
Forsaken thing, that wandered on, forlorn,
Undestined, uncompassioned, unupheld;
A vapour eddying in the whirl of chance,
And soon to vanish everlastingly.
He travailed sorely, and made many a tack,
His sails oft shifting, to arrive,—dread thought!—
Arrive at utter nothingness; and have
Being no more, no feeling, memory,
No lingering consciousness that e'er he was.
Guilt's midnight wish! last, most abhorred thought!
Most desperate effort of extremest sin!
Others, pre-occupied, ne'er saw true Hope:
He, seeing, aimed to stab her to the heart,
And with infernal chymistry to wring
The last sweet drop from sorrow's cup of gall;
To quench the only ray that cheered the earth,
And leave mankind in night which had no star.
Others the streams of Pleasure troubled; he
Toiled much to dry her very fountain head.
Unpardonable man! sold under sin!
He was the devil's pioneer, who cut
The fences down of Virtue, sapped her walls,
And opened a smooth and easy way to death.

Traitor to all existence, to all life!
Soul-suicide! determined foe of being!
Intended murderer of God, most High!
Strange road, most strange! to seek for happiness!
Hell's mad-houses are full of such, too fierce,
Too furiously insane, and desperate,
To range unbound 'mong evil spirits damned.
Fertile was earth in many things, not least
In fools, who mercy both and judgment scorned,
Scorned love, experience scorned, and onward rushed
To swift destruction, giving all reproof,
And all instruction, to the winds; and much
Of both they had, and much despised of both.
Wisdom took up her harp, and stood in place
Of frequent concourse, stood in every gate,
By every way, and walked in every street;
And, lifting up her voice, proclaimed: "Be wise,
Ye fools! be of an understanding heart;
Forsake the wicked, come not near his house,
Pass by, make haste, depart and turn away.
Me follow, me, whose ways are pleasantness,
Whose paths are peace, whose end is perfect joy."
The Seasons came and went, and went and came,
To teach men gratitude; and as they passed,
Gave warning of the lapse of Time, that else
Had stolen unheeded by. The gentle Flowers,
Retired, and, stooping o'er the wilderness,
Talked of humility, and peace, and love.
The Dews came down unseen at evening-tide,
And silently their bounties shed, to teach
Mankind unostentatious charity.
With arm in arm the forest rose on high,
And lesson gave of brotherly regard.
And, on the rugged mountain-brow exposed,
Bearing the blast alone, the ancient oak
Stood, lifting high his mighty arm, and still
To courage in distress exhorted loud.
The flocks, the herds, the birds, the streams, the breeze,
Attuned the heart to melody and love.
Mercy stood in the cloud, with eye that wept
Essential love; and, from her glorious bow,
Bending to kiss the earth in token of peace,
With her own lips, her gracious lips, which God
Of sweetest accent made, she whispered still,
She whispered to Revenge, Forgive, forgive.
The Sun, rejoicing round the earth, announced
Daily the wisdom, power, and love of God.
The Moon awoke, and from her maiden face,
Shedding her cloudy locks, looked meekly forth,
And with her virgin Stars walked in the heavens,
Walked nightly there, conversing as she walked,
Of purity, and holiness, and God.
In dreams and visions, sleep instructed much.
Day uttered speech to day, and night to night
Taught knowledge. Silence had a tongue; the grave,
The darkness, and the lonely waste, had each
A tongue, that ever said, Man! think of God!
Think of thyself! think of eternity!
Fear God, the thunders said, Fear God, the waves,
Fear God, the lightning of the storm replied.
Fear God, deep loudly answered back to deep:
And, in the temples of the Holy One,
Messiah's messengers, the faithful few,
Faithful 'mong many false, the Bible opened,
And cried, Repent! repent ye sons of men!
Believe, be saved; and reasoned awfully
Of temperance, righteousness, and judgment soon
To come, of ever-during life and death:
And chosen bards from age to age awoke
The sacred lyre, and full on Folly's ear,
Numbers of righteous indignation poured:
And God, omnipotent, when mercy failed,
Made bare his holy arm, and with the stroke
Of vengeance smote; the fountains of the deep
Broke up, heaven's windows opened, and sent on men
A flood of wrath, sent plague and famine forth;
With earthquake rocked the world beneath, with storms
Above laid cities waste, and turned fat lands
To barrenness, and with the sword of war
In fury marched, and gave them blood to drink.
Angels remonstrated, Mercy beseeched,
Heaven smiled and frowned, Hell groaned, Time fled, Death shook
His dart, and threatened to make repentance vain,—
Incredible assertion! men rushed on
Determinedly to ruin; shut their ears,
Their eyes, to all advice, to all reproof;
O'er mercy and o'er judgment, downward rushed
To misery; and,—most incredible
Of all!—to misery rushed along the way
Of disappointment and remorse, where still
At every step, adders, in pleasure's form,
Stung mortally; and Joys,—whose bloomy cheeks
Seemed glowing high with immortality,
Whose bosoms prophesied superfluous bliss,—
While in the arms received, and locked in close
And riotous embrace, turned pale, and cold,
And died, and smelled of putrefaction rank;
Turned, in the very moment of delight,
A loathsome, heavy corpse, that with the clear
And hollow eyes of death, stared horribly.
All tribes, all generations of the earth,
Thus wantonly to ruin drove alike.
We heard indeed of gold and silver days,
And of primeval innocence unstained:
A pagan tale! but by baptized bards,
Philosophers, and statesmen, who were still
Held wise and cunning men, talked of so much,
That most believed it so, and asked not why.
The pair, the family first made, were ill;
And for their great peculiar sin, incurred
The Curse, and left it due to all their race;
And bold example gave of every crime,

Hate, murder, unbelief, reproach, revenge.
A time, 'tis true, there came, of which thou soon
Shalt hear, the Sabbath Day, the Jubilee
Of earth, when righteousness and peace prevailed.
This time except, who writes the history
Of men, and writes it true, must write them bad;
Who reads, must read of violence and blood.
The man, who could the story of one day
Peruse, the wrongs, oppressions, cruelties,
Deceits, and perjuries, and vanities,
Rewarded worthlessness, rejected worth,
Assassinations, robberies, thefts, and wars,
Disastrous accidents, life thrown away,
Divinity insulted, Heaven despised,
Religion scorned,—and not been sick at night,
And sad, had gathered greater store of mirth,
Than ever wise man in the world could find.
One cause of folly, one especial cause,
Was this: Few knew what wisdom was, though well
Defined in God's own words, and printed large,
On heaven and earth in characters of light,
And sounded in the ear by every wind.
Wisdom is humble, said the voice of God.
'Tis proud, the world replied. Wisdom, said God,
Forgives, forbears, and suffers, not for fear
Of man, but God. Wisdom revenges, said
The world, is quick and deadly of resentment,
Thrusts at the very shadow of affront,
And hastes, by death, to wipe its honour clean.
Wisdom, said God, loves enemies, entreats,
Solicits, begs for peace. Wisdom, replied
The world, hates enemies, will not ask peace,
Conditions spurns, and triumphs in their fall.
Wisdom mistrusts itself, and leans on Heaven,
Said God. It trusts and leans upon itself,
The world replied. Wisdom retires, said God,
And counts it bravery to bear reproach,
And shame, and lowly poverty, upright;
And weeps with all who have just cause to weep.
Wisdom, replied the world, struts forth to gaze,
Treads the broad stage of life with clamorous foot,
Attracts all praises, counts it bravery
Alone to wield the sword, and rush on death;
And never weeps, but for its own disgrace.
Wisdom, said God, is highest, when it stoops
Lowest before the Holy Throne; throws down
Its crown, abased; forgets itself, admires,
And breathes adoring praise. There Wisdom stoops,
Indeed, the world replied, there stoops, because
It must, but stoops with dignity; and thinks
And meditates the while of inward worth.
Thus did Almighty God, and thus the world,
Wisdom define: and most the world believed,
And boldly called the truth of God a lie.
Hence, he that to the worldly wisdom shaped
His character, became the favourite
Of men, was honourable termed, a man
Of spirit, noble, glorious, lofty soul!
And as he crossed the earth in chase of dreams,
Received prodigious shouts of warm applause.
Hence, who to godly wisdom framed his life,
Was counted mean, and spiritless, and vile;
And as he walked obscurely in the path
Which led to heaven, fools hissed with serpent tongue,
And poured contempt upon his holy head,
And poured contempt on all who praised his name.
But false as this account of wisdom was,
The world's I mean, it was its best, the creed
Of sober, grave, and philosophic men,
With much research and cogitation framed,
Of men, who with the vulgar scorned to sit.
The popular belief seemed rather worse,
When heard replying to the voice of truth.
The wise man, said the Bible, walks with God;
Surveys, far on, the endless line of life;
Values his soul, thinks of eternity,
Both worlds considers, and provides for both;
With reason's eye his passions guards; abstains
From evil, lives on hope, on hope, the fruit
Of faith; looks upward, purifies his soul,
Expands his wings, and mounts into the sky;
Passes the sun, and gains his father's house,
And drinks with angels from the fount of bliss.
The multitude aloud replied,—replied
By practice, for they were not bookish men,
Nor apt to form their principles in words,—
The wise man, first of all, eradicates,
As much as possible, from out his mind,
All thought of death, God, and eternity;
Admires the world, and thinks of Time alone;
Avoids the Bible, all reproof avoids;
Rocks Conscience, if he can, asleep; puts out
The eye of Reason, prisons, tortures, binds,
And makes her thus, by violence and force,
Give wicked evidence against herself;
Lets passion loose, the substance leaves, pursues
The shadow vehemently, but ne'er o'ertakes;
Puts by the cup of holiness and joy;
And drinks, carouses deeply, in the bowl
Of death; grovels in dust, pollutes, destroys,
His soul! is miserable to acquire
More misery; deceives to be deceived;
Strives, labours, to the last, to shun the truth;
Strives, labours, to the last, to damn himself;
Turns desperate, shudders, groans, blasphemes, and dies,
And sinks—where could he else?—to endless wo;
And drinks the wine of God's eternal wrath.
The learned thus, and thus the unlearned world,
Wisdom defined. In sound they disagreed;
In substance, in effect, in end, the same;
And equally to God and truth opposed,
Opposed as darkness to the light of heaven.
Yet were there some, that seemed well-meaning men,

Who systems planned, expressed in supple words,
Which praised the man as wisest, that in one
United both; pleased God, and pleased the world;
And with the saint, and with the sinner, had,
Changing his garb, unseen, a good report.
And many thought their definition best;
And in their wisdom grew exceeding wise.
  Union abhorred! dissimulation vain!
Could Holiness embrace the harlot Sin?
Could life wed death? Could God with Mammon dwell?
Oh, foolish men! oh, men for ever lost!
In spite of mercy lost, in spite of wrath!
In spite of Disappointment and Remorse,
Which made the way to ruin, ruinous!
  Hear what they were: The progeny of Sin,
Alike, and oft combined; but differing much
In mode of giving pain. As felt the gross,
Material part, when in the furnace cast,
So felt the soul, the victim of Remorse.
It was a fire which on the verge of God's
Commandments burned, and on the vitals fed
Of all who passed. Who passed, there met Remorse;
A violent fever seized his soul; the heavens
Above, the earth beneath, seemed glowing brass,
Heated seven times; he heard dread voices speak,
And mutter horrid prophecies of pain,
Severer and severer yet to come;
And as he writhed and quivered, scorched within,
The Fury round his torrid temples flapped
Her fiery wings, and breathed upon his lips
And parched tongue the withered blasts of hell.
It was the suffering begun, thou sawst
In symbol of the Worm that never dies.
  The other, Disappointment, rather seemed
Negation of delight. It was a thing
Sluggish and torpid, tending towards death.
Its breath was cold, and made the sportive blood,
Stagnant, and dull, and heavy, round the wheels
Of life. The roots of that whereon it blew,
Decayed, and with the genial soil no more
Held sympathy; the leaves, the branches drooped,
And mouldered slowly down to formless dust;
Not tossed and driven by violence of winds,
But withering where they sprung, and rotting there
Long disappointed, disappointed still,
The hopeless man, hopeless in his main wish,
As if returning back to nothing, felt;
In strange vacuity of being hung,
And rolled and rolled his eye on emptiness,
That seemed to grow more empty every hour.
  One of this mood I do remember well.
We name him not,—what now are earthly names?—
In humble dwelling born, retired, remote;
In rural quietude, 'mong hills, and streams,
And melancholy deserts, where the Sun
Saw, as he passed, a shepherd only, here
And there, watching his little flock, or heard
The ploughman talking to his steers; his hopes,
His morning hopes, awoke before him, smiling,
Among the dews and holy mountain airs;
And fancy coloured them with every hue
Of heavenly loveliness. But soon his dreams
Of childhood fled away, those rainbow dreams,
So innocent and fair, that withered Age,
Even at the grave, cleared up his dusty eye,
And, passing all between, looked fondly back
To see them once again, ere he departed:
These fled away, and anxious thought, that wished
To go, yet whither knew not well to go,
Possessed his soul, and held it still awhile.
He listened, and heard from far the voice of fame,
Heard and was charmed; and deep and sudden vow
Of resolution, made to be renowned;
And deeper vowed again to keep his vow.
His parents saw, his parents, whom God made
Of kindest heart, saw, and indulged his hope.
The ancient page he turned, read much, thought much,
And with old bards of honourable name
Measured his soul severely; and looked up
To fame, ambitious of no second place.
Hope grew from inward faith, and promised fair.
And out before him opened many a path
Ascending, where the laurel highest waved
Her branch of endless green. He stood admiring,
But stood, admired, not long. The harp he seized,
The harp he loved, loved better than his life,
The harp which uttered deepest notes, and held
The ear of thought a captive to its song.
He searched and meditated much, and whiles,
With rapturous hand, in secret, touched the lyre,
Aiming at glorious strains; and searched again
For theme deserving of immortal verse;
Chose now, and now refused, unsatisfied;
Pleased, then displeased, and hesitating still.
  Thus stood his mind, when round him came a cloud,
Slowly and heavily it came, a cloud
Of ills, we mention not. Enough to say,
'Twas cold, and dead, impenetrable gloom.
He saw its dark approach, and saw his hopes,
One after one, put out, as nearer still
It drew his soul; but fainted not at first,
Fainted not soon. He knew the lot of man
Was trouble, and prepared to bear the worst;
Endure whate'er should come, without a sigh
Endure, and drink, even to the very dregs,
The bitterest cup that Time could measure out
And, having done, look up, and ask for more.
  He called philosophy, and with his heart
Reasoned. He called religion too, but called
Reluctantly, and therefore was not heard.
Ashamed to be o'ermatched by earthly woes,

He sought, and sought, with eye that dimmed apace
To find some avenue to light, some place
On which to rest a hope; but sought in vain.
Darker and darker still the darkness grew.
At length he sunk, and Disappointment stood
His only comforter, and mournfully
Told all was passed. His interest in life,
In being, ceased: and now he seemed to feel,
And shuddered as he felt, his powers of mind
Decaying in the spring-time of his day.
The vigorous, weak became, the clear obscure.
Memory gave up her charge, Decision reeled,
And from her flight, Fancy returned, returned
Because she found no nourishment abroad.
The blue heavens withered, and the moon, and sun,
And all the stars, and the green earth, and morn
And evening, withered; and the eyes, and smiles,
And faces, of all men and women withered;
Withered to him; and all the universe,
Like something which had been, appeared; but now
Was dead and mouldering fast away. He tried
No more to hope, wished to forget his vow,
Wished to forget his harp; then ceased to wish.
That was his last. Enjoyment now was done.
He had no hope, no wish, and scarce a fear.
Of being sensible, and sensible
Of loss, he as some atom seemed, which God
Had made superfluously, and needed not
To build creation with; but back again
To nothing threw, and left it in the void,
With everlasting sense that once it was.
Oh! who can tell what days, what nights, he spent,
Of tideless, waveless, sailless, shoreless wo!
And who can tell how many, glorious once,
To others and themselves of promise full,
Conducted to this pass of human thought,
This wilderness of intellectual death,
Wasted and pined, and vanished from the earth,
Leaving no vestige of memorial there!
It was not so with him. When thus he lay,
Forlorn of heart, withered and desolate,
As leaf of Autumn, which the wolfish winds,
Selecting from its falling sisters, chase,
Far from its native grove, to lifeless wastes,
And leave it there alone, to be forgotten
Eternally, God passed in mercy by,—
His praise be ever new!—and on him breathed,
And bade him live, and put into his hands
A holy harp, into his lips a song,
That rolled its numbers down the tide of Time.
Ambitious now but little, to be praised
Of men alone; ambitious most, to be
Approved of God, the Judge of all; and have
His name recorded in the book of life.
Such things were Disappointment and Remorse.
And oft united both, as friends severe,
To teach men wisdom; but the fool, untaught,
Was foolish still. His ear he stopped, his eyes
He shut, and blindly, deafly obstinate,
Forced desperately his way from wo to wo.
One place, one only place, there was on earth,
Where no man e'er was fool, however mad.
"Men may live fools, but fools they cannot die."
Ah! 'twas a truth most true; and sung in Time,
And to the sons of men, by one well known
On earth for lofty verse and lofty sense.
Much hast thou seen, fair youth, much heard; but thou
Hast never seen a death-bed, never heard
A dying groan. Men saw it often. 'Twas sad,
To all most sorrowful and sad; to guilt,
'Twas anguish, terror, darkness, without bow.
But, oh! it had a most convincing tongue,
A potent oratory, that secured
Most mute attention; and it spoke the truth
So boldly, plainly, perfectly distinct,
That none the meaning could mistake, or doubt
And had withal a disenchanting power,
A most omnipotent and wondrous power,
Which in a moment broke, for ever broke,
And utterly dissolved, the charms, and spells,
And cunning sorceries of earth and hell.
And thus it spoke to him who ghastly lay,
And struggled for another breath: Earth's cup
Is poisoned; her renown, most infamous;
Her gold, seem as it may, is really dust;
Her titles, slanderous names; her praise, reproach;
Her strength, an idiot's boast; her wisdom blind;
Her gain, eternal loss; her hope, a dream;
Her love, her friendship, enmity with God;
Her promises, a lie; her smile, a harlot's;
Her beauty, paint, and rotten within; her pleasures,
Deadly assassins masked; her laughter grief;
Her breasts, the sting of Death; her total sum,
Her all, most utter vanity; and all
Her lovers mad, insane most grievously,
And most insane because they know it not.
Thus did the mighty reasoner, Death declare,
And volumes more; and in one word confirmed
The Bible whole, Eternity is all.
But few spectators, few believed, of those
Who staid behind. The wisest, best of men,
Believed not to the letter full; but turned,
And on the world looked forth, as if they thought
The well-trimmed hypocrite had something still
Of inward worth. The dying man alone,
Gave faithful audience, and the words of Death,
To the last jot, believed, believed and felt;
But oft, alas! believed and felt too late.
And had Earth, then, no joys, no native sweets
No happiness, that one, who spoke the truth,
Might call her own? She had; true, native sweets,
Indigenous delights, which up the tree

Of holiness, embracing as they grew,
Ascended, and bore fruit of heavenly taste;
In pleasant memory held, and talked of oft,
By yonder Saints, who walk the golden streets
Of New Jerusalem, and compass round
The Throne, with nearest vision blessed. Of these,
Hereafter, thou shalt hear, delighted hear;
One page of beauty in the life of man.

BOOK IV.

THE world had much of strange and wonderful,
In passion much, in action, reason, will,
And much in providence, which still retired
From human eye, and led Philosophy,
That ill her ignorance liked to own, through dark
And dangerous paths of speculation wild.
Some striking features, as we pass, we mark,
In order such as memory suggests.
One passion prominent appears, the lust
Of power, which oft-times took the fairer name
Of liberty, and hung the popular flag
Of freedom out. Many, indeed, its names.
When on the throne it sat, and round the neck
Of millions riveted its iron chain,
And on the shoulders of the people laid
Burdens unmerciful, it title took
Of tyranny, oppression, despotism;
And every tongue was weary cursing it.
When in the multitude it gathered strength,
And, like an ocean bursting from its bounds,
Long beat in vain, went forth resistlessly,
It bore the stamp and designation, then,
Of popular fury, anarchy, rebellion;
And honest men bewailed all order void;
All laws annulled; all property destroyed;
The venerable, murdered in the streets;
The wise despised; streams, red with human blood;
Harvests beneath the frantic foot trod down;
Lands, desolate; and famine at the door.
These are a part; but other names it had,
Innumerous as the shapes and robes it wore.
But under every name, in nature still
Invariably the same, and always bad.
We own, indeed, that oft against itself
It fought, and sceptre both and people gave
An equal aid· as long exemplified
In Albion's isle, Albion, queen of the seas;
And in the struggle, something like a kind
Of civil liberty grew up, the best
Of mere terrestrial root; but, sickly, too,
And living only, strange to tell! in strife
Of factions equally contending; dead,
That very moment dead, that one prevailed.
Conflicting cruelly against itself,
By its own hand it fell; part slaying part.
And men who noticed not the suicide,
Stood wondering much, why earth from age to age,
Was still enslaved; and erring causes gave.
This was earth's liberty, its nature this,
However named, in whomsoever found,—
And found it was in all of woman born,—
Each man to make all subject to his will;
To make them do, undo, eat, drink, stand, move,
Talk, think, and feel, exactly as he chose.
Hence the eternal strife of brotherhoods,
Of individuals, families, commonwealths.
The root from which it grew was pride; bad root,
And bad the fruit it bore. Then wonder not,
That long the nations from it richly reaped
Oppression, slavery, tyranny, and war;
Confusion, desolation, trouble, shame.
And, marvellous though it seem, this monster, when
It took the name of slavery, as oft
It did, had advocates to plead its cause;
Beings that walked erect, and spoke like men;
Of Christian parentage descended, too,
And dipped in the baptismal font, as sign
Of dedication to the prince who bowed
To death, to set the sin-bound prisoner free.
Unchristian thought! on what pretence soe'er
Of right, inherited, or else acquired;
Of loss, or profit, or what plea you name,
To buy and sell, to barter, whip, and hold
In chains, a being of celestial make;
Of kindred form, of kindred faculties,
Of kindred feelings, passions, thoughts, desires;
Born free, and heir of an immortal hope;
Thought villanous, absurd, detestable!
Unworthy to be harboured in a fiend!
And only overreached in wickedness
By that, birth, too, of earthly liberty,
Which aimed to make a reasonable man
By legislation think, and by the sword
Believe. This was that liberty renowned,
Those equal rights of Greece and Rome, where men,
All, but a few, were bought, and sold, and scourged,
And killed, as interest or caprice enjoined;
In after times talked of, written of, so much,
That most, by sound and custom led away,
Believed the essence answered to the name.
Historians on this theme were long and warm.
Statesmen, drunk with the fumes of vain debate,
In lofty swelling phrase called it perfection.
Philosophers its rise, advance, and fall,
Traced carefully: and poets kindled still,
As memory brought it up; their lips were touched
With fire, and uttered words that men adored.
Even he, true bard of Zion, holy man!
To whom the Bible taught this precious verse,
"He is the freeman whom the truth makes free,"
By fashion, though by fashion little swayed,
Scarce kept his harp from pagan freedom's praise.

The captive prophet, whom Jehovah gave
The future years, described it best, when he
Beheld it rise in vision of the night:
A dreadful beast, and terrible, and strong
Exceedingly, with mighty iron teeth;
And, lo, it brake in pieces, and devoured,
And stamped the residue beneath its feet!
True liberty was Christian, sanctified,
Baptized, and found in Christian hearts alone;
First-born of Virtue, daughter of the skies,
Nursling of truth divine, sister of all
The graces, meekness, holiness, and love;
Giving to God, and man, and all below,
That symptom showed of sensible existence,
Their due, unasked; fear to whom fear was due;
To all, respect, benevolence, and love:
Companion of religion, where she came,
There freedom came; where dwelt, there freedom dwelt;
Ruled where she ruled, expired where she expired.
"He was the freeman whom the truth made free,"
Who, first of all, the bands of Satan broke;
Who broke the bands of sin; and for his soul,
In spite of fools, consulted seriously;
In spite of fashion, persevered in good;
In spite of wealth or poverty, upright;
Who did as reason, not as fancy, bade;
Who heard temptation sing, and yet turned not
Aside; saw Sin bedeck her flowery bed,
And yet would not go up; felt at his heart
The sword unsheathed, yet would not sell the truth;
Who, having power, had not the will to hurt;
Who blushed alike to be, or have a slave;
Who blushed at naught but sin, feared naught but God;
Who, finally, in strong integrity
Of soul, 'midst want, or riches, or disgrace,
Uplifted, calmly sat, and heard the waves
Of stormy folly breaking at his feet,
Now shrill with praise, now hoarse with foul reproach,
And both despised sincerely; seeking this
Alone, The approbation of his God,
Which still with conscience witnessed to his peace.
This, this is freedom, such as angels use,
And kindred to the liberty of God.
First-born of Virtue, daughter of the skies!
The man, the state, in whom she ruled was free;
All else were slaves of Satan, Sin, and Death.
Already thou hast something heard of good
And ill, of vice and virtue, perfect each;
Of those redeemed, or else abandoned quite;
And more shalt hear, when, at the judgment-day,
The characters of mankind we review.
Seems aught which thou hast heard astonishing?
A greater wonder now thy audience asks;
Phenomena in all the universe,
Of moral being most anomalous,
Inexplicable most, and wonderful.
I'll introduce thee to a single heart,
A human heart. We enter not the worst,
But one by God's renewing spirit touched,
A Christian heart, awaked from sleep of sin.
What seest thou here? what markst? Observe it well.
Will, passion, reason, hopes, fears, joy, distress,
Peace, turbulence, simplicity, deceit,
Good, ill, corruption, immortality;
A temple of the Holy Ghost, and yet
Oft lodging fiends; the dwelling-place of all
The heavenly virtues, charity and truth,
Humility, and holiness, and love;
And yet the common haunt of anger, pride,
Hatred, revenge, and passions foul with lust
Allied to heaven, yet parleying oft with hell;
A soldier listed in Messiah's band,
Yet giving quarter to Abaddon's troops;
With seraphs drinking from the well of life,
And yet carousing in the cup of death;
An heir of heaven, and walking thitherward,
Yet casting back a covetous eye on earth;
Emblem of strength, and weakness; loving now,
And now abhorring sin; indulging now,
And now repenting sore; rejoicing now,
With joy unspeakable, and full of glory;
Now weeping bitterly, and clothed in dust;
A man willing to do, and doing not;
Doing, and willing not; embracing what
He hates, what most he loves abandoning;
Half saint, and sinner half; half life, half death,
Commixture strange of heaven, and earth, and hell.
What seest thou here? what markst? A battle-field;
Two banners spread, two dreadful fronts of war
In shock of opposition fierce, engaged.
God, angels, saw whole empires rise in arms,
Saw kings exalted, heard them tumble down,
And others raised,—and heeded not; but here
God, angels looked; God, angels, fought; and Hell,
With all his legions, fought: here, error fought
With truth, with darkness light, and life with death;
And here, not kingdoms, reputation, worlds,
Were won; the strife was for eternity,
The victory was never-ending bliss,
The badge, a chaplet from the tree of life.
While thus, within, contending armies strove,
Without, the Christian had his troubles too.
For, as by God's unalterable laws,
And ceremonial of the Heaven of Heavens,
Virtue takes place of all, and worthiest deeds
Sit highest at the feast of bliss; on earth,
The opposite was fashion's rule polite.
Virtue the lowest place at table took,
Or served, or was shut out; the Christian still
Was mocked, derided, persecuted, slain;
And Slander, worse than mockery, or sword,

Or death, stood nightly by her horrid forge,
And fabricated lies to stain his name,
And wound his peace; but still he had a source
Of happiness, that men could neither give
Nor take away. The avenues that led
To immortality before him lay.
He saw, with faith's far reaching eye, the fount
Of life, his Father's, house, his Saviour God,
And borrowed thence to help his present want.
Encountered thus with enemies, without,
Within, like bark that meets opposing winds
And floods, this way, now that, she steers athwart,
Tossed by the wave, and driven by the storm;
But still the pilot, ancient at the helm,
The harbour keeps in eye; and after much
Of danger passed, and many a prayer rude,
He runs her safely in: so was the man
Of God beset, so tossed by adverse winds;
And so his eye upon the land of life
He kept. Virtue grew daily stronger, sin
Decayed; his enemies, repulsed, retired;
Till, at the stature of a perfect man
In Christ arrived, and with the Spirit filled,
He gained the harbour of eternal rest.
But think not virtue, else than dwells in God
Essentially, was perfect, without spot.
Examine yonder suns. At distance seen,
How bright they burn! how gloriously they shine,
Mantling the worlds around in beamy light!
But nearer viewed, we through their lustre see
Some dark behind; so virtue was on earth,
So is in heaven, and so shall always be.
Though good it seem, immaculate, and fair
Exceedingly, to saint or angel's gaze
The uncreated Eye, that searches all,
Sees it imperfect; sees, but blames not; sees,
Well pleased, and best with those who deepest dive
Into themselves, and know themselves the most;
Taught thence in humbler reverence to bow
Before the Holy One; and oftener view
His excellence, that in them still may rise,
And grow his likeness, growing evermore.
Nor think that any, born of Adam's race,
In his own proper virtue entered heaven.
Once fallen from God and perfect holiness,
No being, unassisted, e'er could rise,
Or sanctify the sin-polluted soul.
Oft was the trial made, but vainly made.
So oft as men, in earth's best livery clad,
However fair, approached the gates of heaven,
And stood presented to the eye of God,
Their impious pride so oft his soul abhorred.
Vain hope! in patch-work of terrestrial grain,
To be received into the courts above!
As vain as towards yonder suns to soar,
On wing of waxen plumage, melting soon.
Look round, and see those numbers infinite,
That stand before the Throne, and in their hands
Palms waving high, as token of victory
For battles won. These are the sons of men
Redeemed, the ransomed of the Lamb of God
All these, and millions more of kindred blood,
Who now are out on messages of love,
All these, their virtue, beauty, excellence,
And joy, are purchase of redeeming blood;
Their glory, bounty of redeeming love.
O Love divine! Harp, lift thy voice on high!
Shout, angels! shout aloud, ye sons of men!
And burn, my heart, with the eternal flame!
My lyre, be eloquent with endless praise!
O Love divine! immeasurable Love!
Stooping from heaven to earth, from earth to hell;
Without beginning, endless, boundless Love!
Above all asking, giving far, to those
Who nought deserved, who nought deserved but death!
Saving the vilest! saving me! O Love
Divine! O Saviour God! O Lamb, once slain!
At thought of thee, thy love, thy flowing blood,
All thoughts decay; all things remembered fade,
All hopes return; all actions done by men
Or angels, disappear, absorbed and lost;
All fly, as from the great white Throne which he,
The prophet, saw, in vision wrapped, the heavens
And earth, and sun, and moon, and starry host,
Confounded, fled, and found a place no more.
One glance of wonder, as we pass, deserve
The books of Time. Productive was the world
In many things, but most in books. Like swarms
Of locusts, which God sent to vex a land
Rebellious long, admonished long in vain,
Their numbers they poured annually on man,
From heads conceiving still. Perpetual birth!
Thou wonderst how the world contained them all.
Thy wonder stay. Like men, this was their doom:
"That dust they were, and should to dust return."
And oft their fathers, childless and bereaved,
Wept o'er their graves, when they themselves were green.
And on them fell, as fell on every age,
As on their authors fell, oblivious Night,
Which o'er the past lay, darkling, heavy, still,
Impenetrable, motionless, and sad,
Having his dismal, leaden plumage stirred
By no remembrancer, to show the men
Who after came what was concealed beneath.
The story-telling tribe, alone, outran
All calculation far, and left behind,
Lagging, the swiftest numbers. Dreadful, even
To fancy, was their never-ceasing birth;
And room had lacked, had not their life been short.
Excepting some, their definition take
Thou thus, expressed in gentle phrase, which leaves
Some truth behind: A Novel was a book
Three-volumed, and once read, and oft crammed full
Of poisonous error, blackening every page,
And oftener still, of trifling, second-hand

Remark, and old, diseased, putrid thought,
And, miserable incident, at war
With nature, with itself and truth at war;
Yet charming still the greedy reader on,
Till done, he tried to recollect his thoughts,
And nothing found, but dreaming emptiness.
These, like ephemera, sprung, in a day,
From lean and shallow-soiled brains of sand,
And in a day expired; yet, while they lived,
Tremendous oft-times was the popular roar;
And cries of—Live for ever! struck the skies.
One kind alone remained, seen through the gloom
And sullen shadow of the past: as lights
At intervals they shone, and brought the eye,
That backward travelled, upward, till arrived
At him, who, on the hills of Midian, sang
The patient man of Uz; and from the lyre
Of angels, learned the early dawn of Time.
Not light and momentary labour these,
But discipline and self-denial long,
And purpose stanch, and perseverance, asked,
And energy that inspiration seemed.
Composed of many thoughts, possessing each
Innate and underived vitality;
Which, having fitly shaped, and well arranged
In brotherly accord, they builded up;
A stately superstructure, that, nor wind,
Nor wave, nor shock of falling years, could move;
Majestic and indissolubly firm;
As ranks of veteran warriors in the field,
Each by himself alone and singly seen,
A tower of strength; in massy phalanx knit,
And in embattled squadron rushing on,
A sea of valour, dread, invincible.
Books of this sort, or sacred, or profane,
Which virtue helped, were titled, not amiss,
'The medicine of the mind:" who read them, read
Wisdom, and was refreshed; and on his path
Of pilgrimage, with healthier step advanced.
In mind, in matter, much was difficult
To understand. But, what in deepest night
Retired, inscrutable, mysterious, dark,—
Was evil, God's decrees, and deeds decreed,
Responsible: why God, the just and good,
Omnipotent and wise, should suffer sin
To rise: why man was free, accountable;
Yet God foreseeing, overruling all.
Where'er the eye could turn, whatever tract
Of moral thought it took, by reason's torch,
Or Scripture's led, before it still this mount
Sprung up, impervious, insurmountable,
Above the human stature rising far;
Horizon of the mind, surrounding still
The vision of the soul with clouds and gloom.
Yet did they oft attempt to scale its sides,
And gain its top. Philosophy, to climb,
With all her vigour, toiled from age to age;
From age to age, Theology, with all
Her vigour, toiled; and vagrant Fancy toiled.
Not weak and foolish only, but the wise,
Patient, courageous, stout, sound headed man,
Of proper discipline, of excellent wind,
And strong of intellectual limb, toiled hard;
And oft above the reach of common eye
Ascended far, and seemed well nigh the top;
But only seemed; for still another top
Above them rose, till, giddy grown and mad,
With gazing at these dangerous heights of God,
They tumbled down, and in their raving said,
They o'er the summit saw. And some believed,
Believed a lie; for never man on earth,
That mountain crossed, or saw its farther side.
Around it lay the wreck of many a Sage,
Divine, Philosopher; and many more
Fell daily, undeterred by millions fallen;
Each wondering why he failed to comprehend
God, and with finite measure infinite.
To pass it, was no doubt desirable;
And few of any intellectual size,
That did not, some time in their day, attempt;
But all in vain; for as the distant hill,
Which on the right or left, the traveller's eye
Bounds, seems advancing as he walks, and oft
He looks, and looks, and thinks to pass; but still
It forward moves, and mocks his baffled sight,
Till night descends, and wraps the scene in gloom,
So did this moral height the vision mock;
So lifted up its dark and cloudy head,
Before the eye, and met it evermore,
And some, provoked, accused the righteous God.
Accused of what? hear human boldness now!
Hear guilt, hear folly, madness, all extreme!
Accused of what? the God of truth accused
Of cruelty, injustice, wickedness.
Abundant sin! because a mortal man,
A worm, at best, of small capacity,
With scarce an atom of Jehovah's works
Before him, and with scarce an hour to look
Upon them, should presume to censure God,
The infinite and uncreated God!
To sit, in judgment, on Himself, his works,
His providence! and try, accuse, condemn!
If there is aught, thought or to think, absurd,
Irrational and wicked, this is more,
This most; the sin of devils, or of those
To devils growing fast. Wise men and good
Accused themselves, not God; and put their hands
Upon their mouths, and in the dust adored.
The Christian's faith had many mysteries oo;
The uncreated holy Three in One,
Divine incarnate, human in divine;
The inward call; the Sanctifying Dew
Coming unseen, unseen departing thence;
Anew creating all, and yet not heard;
Compelling, yet not felt. Mysterious these,
Not that Jehovah to conceal them wished,
Not that religion wished. The Christian faith,
Unlike the timorous creeds of pagan priests,

Was frank, stood forth to view, invited all,
To prove, examine, search, investigate,
And gave herself a light to see her by.
Mysterious these, because too large for eye
Of man, too long for human arm to mete.
Go to yon mount, which on the north side stands
Of New Jerusalem, and lifts its head
Serene in glory bright, except the hill,
The Sacred Hill of God, whereon no foot
Must tread, highest of all creation's walks,
And overlooking all, in prospect vast,
From out the ethereal blue. That cliff ascend,
Gaze thence, around thee look; nought now impedes
Thy view; yet still thy vision, purified
And strong although it be, a boundary meets;
Or rather, thou wilt say, thy vision fails
To gaze throughout illimitable space,
And find the end of infinite: and so
It was with all the mysteries of faith.
God set them forth unveiled to the full gaze
Of man, and asked him to investigate;
But reason's eye, however purified,
And on whatever tall and goodly height
Of observation placed, to comprehend
Them fully, sought in vain: in vain seeks still;
But wiser now and humbler, she concludes,
From what she knows already of his love
All gracious, that she cannot understand;
And gives him credit, reverence, praise for all.
Another feature in the ways of God,
That wondrous seemed, and made some men complain,
Was the unequal gift of worldly things.
Great was the difference, indeed, of men
Externally, from beggar to the prince.
The highest take and lowest, and conceive
The scale between. A noble of the earth,
One of its great, in splendid mansion dwelt;
Was robed in silk and gold; and every day
Fared sumptuously; was titled, honoured, served.
Thousands his nod awaited, and his will
For law received. Whole provinces his march
Attended, and his chariot drew, or on
Their shoulders bore aloft the precious man.
Millions, abased, fell prostrate at his feet:
And millions more thundered adoring praise.
As far as eye could reach, he called the land
His own, and added yearly to his fields.
Like tree that of the soil took healthy root,
He grew on every side, and towered on high,
And over half a nation, shadowing wide,
He spread his ample bows. Air, earth, and sea,
Nature entire, the brute, and rational,
To please him ministered, and vied among
Themselves, who most should his desires prevent,
Watching the moving of his rising thoughts
Attentively, and hasting to fulfil.
His palace rose and kissed the gorgeous clouds.
Streams bent their music to his will, trees sprung;
The native waste put on luxuriant robes;
And plains of happy cottages cast out
Their tenants, and became a hunting-field.
Before him bowed the distant isles, with fruits
And spices rare; the South her treasures brought,
The East and West sent; and the frigid North
Came with her offering of glossy furs.
Musicians soothed his ear with airs select:
Beauty held out her arms; and every man
Of cunning skill, and curious device,
And endless multitudes of liveried wights,
His pleasure waited with obsequious look.
And when the wants of nature were supplied,
And common-place extravagances filled,
Beyond their asking; and caprice itself,
In all its zig-zag appetites, gorged full,
The man new wants and new expenses planned
Nor planned alone. Wise, learned, sober men,
Of cogitation deep, took up his case,
And planned for him new modes of folly wild;
Contrived new wishes, wants, and wondrous means
Of spending with despatch; yet, after all,
His fields extended still, his riches grew,
And what seemed splendour infinite, increased.
So lavishly upon a single man
Did Providence his bounties daily shower.
Turn now thy eye, and look on Poverty;
Look on the lowest of her ragged sons.
We find him by the way, sitting in dust;
He has no bread to eat, no tongue to ask,
No limbs to walk, no home, no house, no friend.
Observe his goblin cheek, his wretched eye;
See how his hand, if any hand he has,
Involuntary opens, and trembles forth,
As comes the traveller's foot; and hear his groan,
His long and lamentable groan, announce
The want that gnaws within. Severely now
The sun scorches and burns his old bald head;
The frost now glues him to the chilly earth.
On him hail, rain, and tempest, rudely beat;
And all the winds of heaven, in jocular mood,
Sport with his withered rags, that, tossed about,
Display his nakedness to passers by,
And grievously burlesque the human form.
Observe him yet more narrowly. His limbs,
With palsy shaken, about him blasted lie;
And all his flesh is full of putrid sores
And noisome wounds, his bones, of racking pains.
Strange vesture this for an immortal soul!
Strange retinue to wait a lord of earth!
It seems as Nature, in some surly mood,
After debate and musing long, had tried
How vile and miserable thing her hand
Could fabricate, then made this meagre man.
A sight so full of perfect misery,
That passengers their faces turned away,

And hasted to be gone; and delicate
And tender women took another path.
This great disparity of outward things
Taught many lessons; but this taught in chief,
Though learned by few: That God no value set,
That man should none, on goods of worldly kind!
On transitory, frail, external things,
Of migratory, ever-changing sort:
And further taught, that in the soul alone,
The thinking, reasonable, willing soul,
God placed the total excellence of man;
And meant him evermore to seek it there.
But stranger still the distribution seemed
Of intellect, though fewer here complained;
Each with his share, upon the whole content.
One man there was, and many such you might
Have met, who never had a dozen thoughts
In all his life, and never changed their course;
But told them o'er, each in its customed place,
From morn till night, from youth to hoary age.
Little above the ox that grazed the field,
His reason rose; so weak his memory,
The name his mother called him by, he scarce
Remembered; and his judgment so untaught,
That what at evening played along the swamp,
Fantastic, clad in robe of fiery hue,
He thought the devil in disguise, and fled
With quivering heart and winged footsteps home.
The word philosophy he never heard,
Or science; never heard of liberty,
Necessity, or laws of gravitation;
And never had an unbelieving doubt.
Beyond his native vale he never looked;
But thought the visual line, that girt him round,
The world's extreme; and thought the silver Moon,
That nightly o'er him led her virgin host,
No broader than his father's shield. He lived,—
Lived where his father lived, died where he died,
Lived happy, and died happy, and was saved.
Be not surprised. He loved and served his God.
There was another, large of understanding,
Of memory infinite, of judgment deep,
Who knew all learning, and all science knew;
And all phenomena, in heaven and earth,
Traced to their causes; traced to the labyrinths
Of thought, association, passion, will;
And all the subtle, nice affinities
Of matter traced, its virtues, motions, laws;
And most familiarly and deeply talked
Of mental, moral, natural, divine.
Leaving the earth at will, he soared to heaven,
And read the glorious visions of the skies;
And to the music of the rolling spheres
Intelligently listened; and gazed far back
Into the awful depths of Deity;
Did all that mind assisted most could do;
And yet in misery lived, in misery died,
Because he wanted holiness of heart.

8*

A deeper lesson this to mortals taught,
And nearer cut the branches of their pride
That not in mental, but in moral worth,
God excellence placed; and only to the good,
To virtue, granted happiness, alone.
Admire the goodness of Almighty God!
He riches gave, he intellectual strength,
To few, and therefore none commands to be
Or rich, or learned; nor promises reward
Of peace to these. On all, He moral worth
Bestowed, and moral tribute asked from all.
And who that could not pay? who born so poor,
Of intellect so mean, as not to know
What seemed the best; and, knowing, might not do?
As not to know what God and conscience bade,
And what they bade not able to obey?
And he, who acted thus, fulfilled the law
Eternal, and its promise reaped of peace;
Found peace this way alone: who sought it else,
Sought mellow grapes beneath the icy Pole,
Sought blooming roses on the cheek of death,
Sought substance in a world of fleeting shades.
Take one example, to our purpose quite,
A man of rank, and of capacious soul,
Who riches had and fame, beyond desire,
An heir of flattery, to titles born,
And reputation, and luxurious life:
Yet, not content with ancestorial name,
Or to be known because his fathers were,
He on this height hereditary stood,
And, gazing higher, purposed in his heart
To take another step. Above him seemed,
Alone, the mount of song, the lofty seat
Of canonized bards; and thitherward,
By nature taught, and inward melody,
In prime of youth, he bent his eagle eye.
No cost was spared. What books he wished, he read;
What sage to hear, he heard; what scenes to see,
He saw. And first in rambling school-boy days
Britannia's mountain-walks, and heath-girt lakes,
And story telling glens, and founts, and brooks,
And maids, as dew-drops pure and fair, his soul
With grandeur filled, and melody, and love.
Then travel came, and took him where he wished.
He cities saw, and courts, and princely pomp;
And mused alone on ancient mountain-brows;
And mused on battle-fields, where valour fought
In other days; and mused on ruins gray
With years; and drank from old and fabulous wells,
And plucked the vine that first-born prophets plucked,
And mused on famous tombs, and on the wave
Of ocean mused, and on the desert waste;
The heavens and earth of every country saw.
Where'er the old inspiring Genii dwelt,
Aught that could rouse, expand, refine the soul,
Thither he went, and meditated there.

He touched his harp, and nations heard, entranced.
As some vast river of unfailing source,
Rapid, exhaustless, deep, his numbers flowed,
And opened new fountains in the human heart.
Where Fancy halted, weary in her flight,
In other men, his, fresh as morning, rose,
And soared untrodden heights, and seemed at home,
Where angels bashful looked. Others, though great,
Beneath their argument seemed struggling whiles;
He from above descending stooped to touch
The loftiest thought; and proudly stooped, as though
It scarce deserved his verse. With Nature's self
He seemed an old acquaintance, free to jest
At will with all her glorious majesty.
He laid his hand upon "the Ocean's mane,"
And played familiar with his hoary locks;
Stood on the Alps, stood on the Apennines,
And with the thunder talked, as friend to friend;
And wove his garland of the lightning's wing,
In sportive twist, the lightning's fiery wing,
Which, as the footsteps of the dreadful God,
Marching upon the storm in vengeance, seemed;
Then turned, and with the grasshopper, who sung
His evening song beneath his feet, conversed.
Suns, moons, and stars, and clouds, his sisters were;
Rocks, mountains, meteors, seas, and winds, and storms,
His brothers, younger brothers, whom he scarce
As equals deemed. All passions of all men,
The wild and tame, the gentle and severe;
All thoughts, all maxims, sacred and profane;
All creeds, all seasons, Time, Eternity;
All that was hated, and all that was dear;
All that was hoped, all that was feared, by man;
He tossed about, as tempest, withered leaves,
Then, smiling, looked upon the wreck he made.
With terror now he froze the cowering blood,
And now dissolved the heart in tenderness;
Yet would not tremble, would not weep himself;
But back into his soul retired, alone,
Dark, sullen, proud, gazing contemptuously
On hearts and passions prostrate at his feet.
So Ocean from the plains his waves had late
To desolation swept, retired in pride,
Exulting in the glory of his might,
And seemed to mock the ruin he had wrought.
As some fierce comet of tremendous size,
To which the stars did reverence, as it passed,
So he through learning and through fancy took
His flight sublime, and on the loftiest top
Of Fame's dread mountain sat; not soiled and worn,
As if he from the earth had laboured up;
But as some bird of heavenly plumage fair,
He looked, which down from higher regions came,
And perched it there, to see what lay beneath.
The nations gazed, and wondered much, and praised.
Critics before him fell in humble plight,
Confounded fell, and made debasing signs
To catch his eye, and stretched, and swelled themselves
To bursting nigh, to utter bulky words
Of admiration vast: and many, too,
Many that aimed to imitate his flight,
With weaker wing, unearthly fluttering made,
And gave abundant sport to after days.
Great man! the nations gazed, and wondered much,
And praised; and many called his evil good.
Wits wrote in favour of his wickedness,
And kings to do him honour took delight.
Thus, full of titles, flattery, honour, fame,
Beyond desire, beyond ambition, full,
He died. He died of what? Of wretchedness;—
Drank every cup of joy, heard every trump
Of fame, drank early, deeply drank, drank draughts
That common millions might have quenched; then died
Of thirst, because there was no more to drink.
His goddess, Nature, wooed, embraced, enjoyed,
Fell from his arms, abhorred; his passions died,
Died, all but dreary, solitary Pride;
And all his sympathies in being died.
As some ill-guided bark, well built and tall,
Which angry tides cast out on desert shore,
And then, retiring, left it there to rot
And moulder in the winds and rains of heaven;
So he, cut from the sympathies of life,
And cast ashore from pleasure's boisterous surge,
A wandering, weary, worn, and wretched thing,
Scorched, and desolate, and blasted soul,
A gloomy wilderness of dying thought,—
Repined, and groaned, and withered from the earth.
His groanings filled the land, his numbers filled;
And yet he seemed ashamed to groan:—Poor man!—
Ashamed to ask, and yet he needed help.
Proof this, beyond all lingering of doubt,
That not with natural or mental wealth,
Was God delighted, or his peace secured;
That not in natural or mental wealth,
Was human happiness or grandeur found.
Attempt how monstrous, and how surely vain!
With things of earthly sort, with aught but God,
With aught but moral excellence, truth, and love
To satisfy and fill the immortal soul!
Attempt, vain inconceivably! attempt,
To satisfy the Ocean with a drop,
To marry Immortality to Death,
And with the unsubstantial Shade of Time,
To fill the embrace of all Eternity!

BOOK V.

PRAISE God, ye servants of the Lord! praise God!
Ye angels strong! praise God, ye sons of men!
Praise him who made, and who redeemed your
souls;
Who gave you hope, reflection, reason, will;
Minds that can pierce eternity remote,
And live at once on future, present, past:
Can speculate on systems yet to make,
And back recoil on ancient days of Time,
Of Time, soon past, soon lost among the shades
Of buried years. Not so the actions done
In Time, the deeds of reasonable men.
As if engraven with pen of iron grain,
And laid in flinty rock, they stand, unchanged,
Written on the various pages of the past:
If good, in rosy characters of love;
If bad, in letters of vindictive fire.
God may forgive, but cannot blot them out.
Systems begin and end, Eternity
Rolls on his endless years, and men absolved
By mercy from the consequence, forget
The evil deed, and God imputes it not;
But neither systems ending nor begun,
Eternity that rolls his endless years,
Nor men absolved, and sanctified, and washed
By mercy from the consequence, nor yet
Forgetfulness, nor God imputing not,
Can wash the guilty deed, once done, from out
The faithful annals of the past; who reads,
And many read, there finds it, as it was,
And is, and shall for ever be,—a dark,
Unnatural, and loathly moral spot.
The span of Time was short, indeed; and now
Three-fourths were past, the last begun, and on
Careering to its close, which soon we sing.
But first our promise we redeem, to tell
The joys of Time, her joys of native growth;
And briefly must, what longer tale deserves.
Wake, dear remembrances! wake, childhood-
days!
Loves, friendships, wake! and wake, thou morn
and even!
Sun! with thy orient locks, night, moon, and stars!
And thou, celestial bow! and all ye woods,
And hills, and vales, first trod in dawning life,
And hours of holy musing, wake! wake, earth!
And, smiling to remembrance, come, and bring,
For thou canst bring, meet argument for song
Of heavenly harp, meet hearing for the ear
Of heavenly auditor, exalted high.
God gave much peace on earth, much holy joy;
Oped fountains of perennial spring, whence flowed
Abundant happiness to all who wished
To drink; not perfect bliss;—that dwells with us,
Beneath the eyelids of the Eternal One,
And sits at his right hand alone;—but such
As well deserved the name, abundant joy;
Pleasures, on which the memory of saints
Of highest glory, still delights to dwell.
It was, we own, subject of much debate,
And worthy men stood on opposing sides,
Whether the cup of mortal life had more
Of sour or sweet. Vain question this, when asked
In general terms, and worthy to be left
Unsolved. If most was sour, the drinker, not
The cup, we blame. Each in himself the means
Possessed to turn the bitter sweet, the sweet
To bitter. Hence, from out the self-same fount,
One nectar drank, another draughts of gall.
Hence, from the self-same quarter of the sky,
One saw ten thousand angels look and smile;
Another saw as many demons frown.
One discord heard, where harmony inclined
Another's ear. The sweet was in the taste,
The beauty in the eye, and in the ear
The melody; and in the man,—for God
Necessity of sinning laid on none,—
To form the taste, to purify the eye,
And tune the ear, that all he tasted, saw
Or heard, might be harmonious, sweet, and fair.
Who would, might groan; who would, might sing
for joy.
Nature lamented little. Undevoured
By spurious appetites, she found enough,
Where least was found; with gleanings satisfied,
Or crumbs, that from the hand of luxury fell;
Yet seldom these she ate, but ate the bread
Of her own industry, made sweet by toil;
And walked in robes that her own hand had spun;
And slept on down her early rising bought.
Frugal and diligent in business, chaste
And abstinent, she stored for helpless age,
And, keeping in reserve her spring-day health,
And dawning relishes of life, she drank
Her evening cup with excellent appetite;
And saw her eldest sun decline, as fair
As rose her earliest morn, and pleased as well.
Whether in crowds or solitudes, in streets
Or shady groves, dwelt Happiness, it seems
In vain to ask, her nature makes it vain,
Though poets much, and hermits talked, and sung
Of brooks, and crystal founts, and weeping dews,
And myrtle bowers, and solitary vales,
And with the nymph made assignations there,
And wooed her with the love-sick oaten reed;
And sages too, although less positive,
Advised their sons to court her in the shade.
Delirious babble all! Was happiness,
Was self-approving, God-approving joy,
In drops of dew, however pure? in gales,
However sweet? in wells, however clear?
Or groves, however thick with verdant shade?
True, these were of themselves exceeding fair
How fair at morn and even! worthy the walk

Of loftiest mind, and gave, when all within
Was right, a feast of overflowing bliss;
But were the occasion, not the cause of joy.
They waked the native fountains of the soul,
Which slept before; and stirred the holy tides
Of feeling up, giving the heart to drink
From its own treasures draughts of perfect sweet.
The Christian faith, which better knew the heart
Of man, him thither sent for peace, and thus
Declared: Who finds it, let him find it there;
Who finds it not, for ever let him seek
In vain; 'tis God's most holy, changeless will.
True Happiness had no localities,
No tones provincial, no peculiar garb.
Where Duty went, she went, with Justice went,
And went with Meekness, Charity, and Love.
Where'er a tear was dried, a wounded heart
Bound up, a bruised spirit with the dew
Of sympathy anointed, or a pang
Of honest suffering soothed, or injury
Repeated oft, as oft by love forgiven;
Where'er an evil passion was subdued,
Or Virtue's feeble embers fanned; where'er
A sin was heartily abjured, and left;
Where'er a pious act was done, or breathed
A pious prayer, or wished a pious wish;
There was a high and holy place, a spot
Of sacred light, a most religious fane,
Where Happiness, descending, sat and smiled.
But these apart, in sacred memory lives
The morn of life, first morn of endless days,
Most joyful morn! nor yet for nought the joy.
A being of eternal date commenced,
A young immortal then was born! and who
Shall tell what strange variety of bliss
Burst on the infant soul, when first it looked
Abroad on God's creation fair, and saw
The glorious earth and glorious heaven, and face
Of man sublime, and saw all new, and felt
All new! when thought awoke, thought never more
To sleep! when first it saw, heard, reasoned, willed,
And triumphed in the warmth of conscious life!
Nor happy only, but the cause of joy,
Which those who never tasted always mourned.
What tongue!—no tongue shall tell what bliss o'erflowed
The mother's tender heart, while round her hung
The offspring of her love, and lisped her name,
As living jewels dropped unstained from heaven,
That made her fairer far, and sweeter seem,
Than every ornament of costliest hue!
And who hath not been ravished, as she passed
With all her playful band of little ones,
Like Luna, with her daughters of the sky,
Walking in matron majesty and grace?
All who had hearts here pleasure found; and oft
Have I, when tired with heavy task,—for tasks
Were heavy in the world below,—relaxed
My weary thoughts among their guiltless sports,
And led them by their little hands a-field,
And watched them run and crop the tempting flower,—
Which oft, unasked, they brought me, and bestowed
With smiling face, that waited for a look
Of praise,—and answered curious questions, put
In much simplicity, but ill to solve;
And heard their observations strange and new.
And settled whiles their little quarrels, soon
Ending in peace, and soon forgot in love.
And still I looked upon their loveliness,
And sought through nature for similitudes
Of perfect beauty, innocence, and bliss,
And fairest imagery around me thronged:
Dew-drops at day-spring on a seraph's locks,
Roses that bathe about the well of life,
Young Loves, young Hopes, dancing on Morning's cheek,
Gems leaping in the coronet of Love!
So beautiful, so full of life, they seemed
As made entire of beams of angels' eyes.
Gay, guileless, sportive, lovely, little things!
Playing around the den of Sorrow, clad
In smiles, believing in their fairy hopes,
And thinking man and woman true! all joy,
Happy all day, and happy all the night!
Hail, holy Love! thou word that sums all bliss,
Gives and receives all bliss, fullest when most
Thou givest! spring-head of all felicity,
Deepest when most is drawn! emblem of God!
O'erflowing most when greatest numbers drink!
Essence that binds the uncreated Three,
Chain that unites creation to its Lord,
Centre to which all being gravitates,
Eternal, ever-growing, happy Love!
Enduring all, hoping, forgiving all;
Instead of law, fulfilling every law;
Entirely blest, because thou seekst no more,
Hopest not, nor fearst; but on the present livest
And holdst perfection smiling in thy arms.
Mysterious, infinite, exhaustless Love!
On earth mysterious, and mysterious still
In heaven! sweet chord, that harmonizes all
The harps of Paradise! the spring, the well,
That fills the bowl and banquet of the sky!
But why should I to thee of Love divine?
Who happy, and not eloquent of Love?
Who holy, and, as thou art, pure, and not
A temple where her glory ever dwells,
Where burn her fires, and beams her perfect eye?
Kindred to this, part of this holy flame,
Was youthful love—the sweetest boon of Earth.
Hail, Love! first Love, thou word that sums all bliss!
The sparkling cream of all Time's blessedness,
The silken down of happiness complete!
Discerner of the ripest grapes of joy,
She gathered, and selected with her hand,

All finest relishes, all fairest sights,
All rarest odours, all divinest sounds,
All thoughts, all feelings dearest to the soul;
And brought the holy mixture home, and filled
The heart with all superlatives of bliss.
But who would that expound, which words transcends,
Must talk in vain. Behold a meeting scene
Of early love, and thence infer its worth.
It was an eve of Autumn's holiest mood.
The corn fields, bathed in Cynthia's silver light,
Stood ready for the reaper's gathering hand;
And all the Winds slept soundly. Nature seemed,
In silent contemplation, to adore
Its Maker. Now and then, the aged leaf
Fell from its fellows, rustling to the ground;
And, as it fell, bade man think on his end.
On vale and lake, on wood and mountain high,
With pensive wing outspread, sat heavenly Thought,
Conversing with itself. Vesper looked forth,
From out her western hermitage, and smiled;
And up the east, unclouded, rode the Moon
With all her Stars, gazing on earth intense,
As if she saw some wonder walking there.
Such was the night, so lovely, still, serene,
When, by a hermit thorn that on the hill
Had seen a hundred flowery ages pass,
A damsel kneeled to offer up her prayer,
Her prayer nightly offered, nightly heard.
This ancient thorn had been the meeting place
Of love, before his country's voice had called
The ardent youth to fields of honour far
Beyond the wave: and hither now repaired,
Nightly, the maid, by God's all-seeing eye
Seen only, while she thought this boon alone
"Her lover's safety, and his quick return."
In holy, humble attitude she kneeled,
And to her bosom, fair as moonbeam, pressed
One hand, the other lifted up to heaven.
Her eye, upturned, bright as the star of morn,
As violet meek, excessive ardour streamed,
Wafting away her earnest heart to God.
Her voice, scarce uttered, soft as Zephyr sighs
On morning lily's cheek, though soft and low,
Yet heard in heaven, heard at the mercy-seat.
A tear-drop wandered on her lovely face;
It was a tear of faith and holy fear,
Pure as the drops that hang at dawning time,
On yonder willows by the stream of life.
On her the Moon looked steadfastly; the Stars,
That circle nightly round the eternal Throne,
Glanced down, well pleased; and Everlasting Love
Gave gracious audience to her prayer sincere.
Oh, had her lover seen her thus alone,
Thus holy, wrestling thus, and all for him!
Nor did he not; for oft-times Providence,
With unexpected joy the fervent prayer
Of faith surprised. Returned from long delay
With glory crowned of righteous actions won,
The sacred thorn, to memory dear, first sought
The youth, and found it at the happy hour,
Just when the damsel kneeled herself to pray.
Wrapped in devotion, pleading with her God,
She saw him not, heard not his foot approach;
All holy images seemed too impure
To emblem her he saw. A seraph kneeled,
Beseeching for his ward, before the Throne,
Seemed fittest, pleased him best. Sweet was the thought!
But sweeter still the kind remembrance came,
That she was flesh and blood, formed for himself,
The plighted partner of his future life.
And as they met, embraced, and sat, embowered,
In woody chambers of the starry night,
Spirits of love about them ministered,
And God, approving, blessed the holy joy!
Nor unremembered is the hour when friends
Met. Friends, but few on earth, and therefore dear;
Sought oft, and sought almost as oft in vain;
Yet always sought, so native to the heart,
So much desired, and coveted by all.
Nor wonder thou,—thou wonderest not nor needst.
Much beautiful, and excellent, and fair
Was seen beneath the sun; but nought was seen
More beautiful, or excellent, or fair,
Than face of faithful friend, fairest when seen
In darkest day; and many sounds were sweet,
Most ravishing, and pleasant to the ear;
But sweeter none than voice of faithful friend,
Sweet always, sweetest, heard in loudest storm.
Some I remember, and will ne'er forget;
My early friends, friends of my evil day;
Friends in my mirth, friends in my misery too;
Friends given by God in mercy and in love;
My counsellors, my comforters, and guides;
My joy in grief, my second bliss in joy,
Companions of my young desires; in doubt,
My oracles, my wings in high pursuit.
Oh, I remember, and will ne'er forget,
Our meeting spots, our chosen, sacred hours,
Our burning words that uttered all the soul,
Our faces beaming with unearthly love;
Sorrow with sorrow sighing, hope with hope
Exulting, heart embracing heart entire.
As birds of social feather helping each
His fellow's flight, we soared into the skies,
And cast the clouds beneath our feet, and Earth
With all her tardy, leaden-footed Cares,
And talked the speech and ate the food of heaven!
These I remember, these selectest men,
And would their names record; but what avails
My mention of their name? Before the Throne
They stand illustrious 'mong the loudest harps,
And will receive thee glad, my friend and theirs.
For all are friends in heaven, all faithful friends!
And many friendships, in the days of Time

Begun, are lasting here, and growing still;
So grows ours evermore, both theirs and mine.
Nor is the hour of lonely walk forgot,
In the wide desert, where the view was large.
Pleasant were many scenes, but most to me
The solitude of vast extent, untouched
By hand of art, where Nature sowed, herself,
And reaped her crops; whose garments were the clouds,
Whose minstrels, brooks; whose lamps, the moon and stars;
Whose organ-choir, the voice of many waters;
Whose banquets, morning dews; whose heroes, storms;
Whose warriors, mighty winds; whose lovers, flowers;
Whose orators, the thunderbolts of God;
Whose palaces, the everlasting hills;
Whose ceiling, heaven's unfathomable blue;
And from whose rocky turrets, battled high,
Prospect immense spread out on all sides round,
Lost now between the welkin and the main,
Now walled with hills that slept above the storm.
Most fit was such a place for musing men,
Happiest sometimes when musing without aim.
It was, indeed, a wondrous sort of bliss
The lonely bard enjoyed, when forth he walked,
Unpurposed; stood, and knew not why; sat down,
And knew not where; arose, and knew not when;
Had eyes, and saw not; ears, and nothing heard;
And sought—sought neither heaven nor earth—sought nought,
Nor meant to think; but ran, meantime, through vast
Of visionary things, fairer than aught
That was; and saw the distant tops of thoughts,
Which men of common stature never saw,
Greater than aught that largest words could hold,
Or give idea of, to those who read.
He entered in to Nature's holy place,
Her inner chamber, and beheld her face
Unveiled; and heard unutterable things,
And incommunicable visions saw;
Things then unutterable, and visions then
Of incommunicable glory bright;
But by the lips of after ages formed
To words, or by their pencil pictured forth;
Who, entering farther in, beheld again,
And heard unspeakable and marvellous things,
Which other ages in their turn revealed,
And left to others, greater wonders still.
The earth abounded much in silent wastes,
Nor yet is heaven without its solitudes,
Else incomplete in bliss, whither who will
May oft retire, and meditate alone,
Of God, redemption, holiness, and love;
Nor needs to fear a setting sun, or haste
Him home from rainy tempest unforeseen,
Or sighing, leave his thoughts for want of time.
But whatsoever was both good and fair,
And highest relish of enjoyment gave,
In intellectual exercise was found,
When gazing through the future, present, past,
Inspired, thought linked to thought, harmonious flowed
In poetry—the loftiest mood of mind;
Or when philosophy the reason led
Deep through the outward circumstance of things;
And saw the master-wheels of Nature move;
And travelled far along the endless line
Of certain and of probable; and made,
At every step, some new discovery,
That gave the soul sweet sense of larger room
High these pursuits, and sooner to be named,
Deserved; at present, only named, again
To be resumed, and praised in longer verse.
Abundant and diversified above
All number, were the sources of delight;
As infinite as were the lips that drank;
And to the pure, all innocent and pure;
The simplest still to wisest men the best.
One made acquaintanceship with plants and flowers,
And happy grew in telling all their names;
One classed the quadrupeds; a third, the fowls;
Another found in minerals his joy:
And I have seen a man, a worthy man,
In happy mood conversing with a fly;
And as he, through his glass, made by himself,
Beheld its wondrous eye and plumage fine,
From leaping scarce he kept, for perfect joy.
And from my path I with my friend have turned,
A man of excellent mind and excellent heart,
And climbed the neighbouring hill, with arduous step,
Fetching from distant cairn, or from the earth
Digging with labour sure, the ponderous stone,
Which, having carried to the highest top,
We downward rolled; and as it strove, at first,
With obstacles that seemed to match its force,
With feeble, crooked motion to and fro
Wavering, he looked with interest most intense,
And prayed almost; and as it gathered strength,
And straightened the current of its furious flow,
Exulting in the swiftness of its course,
And, rising now with rainbow-bound immense,
Leaped down careering o'er the subject plain,
He clapped his hands in sign of boundless bliss,
And laughed and talked, well paid for all his toil,
And when at night the story was rehearsed,
Uncommon glory kindled in his eye.
And there were too,—Harp! lift thy voice on high,
And run in rapid numbers o'er the face
Of Nature's scenery,—and there were day
And night, and rising suns and setting suns,
And clouds that seemed like chariots of saints,
By fiery coursers drawn, as brightly hued

As if the glorious, bushy, golden locks
Of thousand cherubim had been shorn off,
And on the temples hung of Morn and Even.
And there were moons, and stars, and darkness streaked
With light; and voice and tempest heard secure,
And there were seasons coming evermore,
And going still, all fair, and always new,
With bloom, and fruit, and fields of hoary grain.
And there were hills of flock, and groves of song,
And flowery streams, and garden walks embowered,
Where, side by side, the rose and lily bloomed;
And sacred founts, wild harps, and moonlight glens,
And forests vast, fair lawns, and lonely oaks,
And little willows sipping at the brook;
Old wizard haunts, and dancing seats of mirth;
Gay festive bowers, and palaces in dust;
Dark owlet nooks, and caves, and battled rocks;
And winding valleys, roofed with pendent shade;
And tall and perilous cliffs, that overlooked
The breadth of Ocean, sleeping on his waves;
Sounds, sights, smells, tastes, the heaven and earth, profuse
In endless sweets, above all praise of song:
For not to use alone did Providence
Abound; but large example gave to man
Of grace, and ornament, and splendour rich,
Suited abundantly to every taste,
In bird, beast, fish, winged and creeping thing,
In herb, and flower, and in the restless change,
Which, on the many-coloured seasons, made
The annual circuit of the fruitful earth.
Nor do I aught of earthly sort remember,—
If partial feeling to my native place
Lead not my lyre astray,—of fairer view,
And comelier walk, than the blue mountain-paths,
And snowy cliffs of Albion renowned;
Albion, an isle long blessed with gracious laws,
And gracious kings, and favoured much of Heaven,
Though yielding oft penurious gratitude.
Nor do I of that isle remember aught
Of prospect more sublime and beautiful,
Than Scotia's northern battlement of hills,
Which first I from my father's house beheld,
At dawn of life; beloved in memory still,
And standard still of rural imagery.
What most resembles them, the fairest seems,
And stirs the eldest sentiments of bliss;
And, pictured on the tablet of my heart,
Their distant shapes eternally remain,
And in my dreams their cloudy tops arise.
Much of my native scenery appears,
And presses forward to be in my song;
But must not now, for much behind awaits
Of higher note. Four trees I pass not by,
Which o'er our house their evening shadow threw,
Three ash, and one of elm. Tall trees they were,
And old, and had been old a century
Before my day. None living could say aught
About their youth; but they were goodly trees:
And oft I wondered,—as I sat and thought
Beneath their summer shade, or, in the night
Of winter, heard the spirits of the wind
Growling among their boughs,—how they had grown
So high, in such a rough, tempestuous place;
And when a hapless branch, torn by the blast,
Fell down, I mourned, as if a friend had fallen.
These I distinctly hold in memory still,
And all the desert scenery around.
Nor strange, that recollection there should dwell
Where first I heard of God's redeeming love;
First felt and reasoned, loved and was beloved
And first awoke the harp to holy song.
To hoar and green there was enough of joy.
Hopes, friendships, charities, and warm pursuit,
Gave comfortable flow to youthful blood.
And there were old remembrances of days,
When, on the glittering dews of orient life,
Shone sunshine hopes, unfailed, unperjured, then;
And there were childish sports, and school-boy feats,
And school-boy spots, and earnest vows of love,
Uttered, when passion's boisterous tide ran high,
Sincerely uttered, though but seldom kept:
And there were angel looks, and sacred hours
Of rapture, hours that in a moment passed,
And yet were wished to last for evermore;
And venturous exploits, and hardy deeds,
And bargains shrewd, achieved in manhood's prime
And thousand recollections, gay and sweet,
Which, as the old and venerable man
Approached the grave, around him, smiling, flocked,
And breathed new ardour through his ebbing veins,
And touched his lips with endless eloquence,
And cheered and much refreshed his withered heart.
Indeed, each thing remembered, all but guilt,
Was pleasant, and a constant source of joy,
Nor lived the old on memory alone.
He in his children lived a second life,
With them again took root, sprang with their hopes,
Entered into their schemes, partook their fears,
Laughed in their mirth, and in their gain grew rich.
And sometimes on the eldest cheek was seen
A smile as hearty as on face of youth,
That saw in prospect sunny hopes invite,
Hope's pleasures, sung to harp of sweetest note
Harp, heard with rapture on Britannia's hills,
With rapture heard by me, in morn of life.

Nor small the joy of rest to mortal men,
Rest after labour, sleep approaching soft,
And wrapping all the weary faculties
In sweet repose. Then Fancy, unrestrained
By sense or judgment, strange confusion made
Of future, present, past, combining things
Unseemly, things unsociable in nature,
In most absurd communion, laughable,
Though sometimes vexing sore the slumbering soul.
Sporting at will, she, through her airy halls,
With moonbeams paved, and canopied with stars,
And tapestried with marvellous imagery,
And shapes of glory, infinitely fair,
Moving and mixing in most wondrous dance,—
Fantastically walked, but pleased so well,
That ill she liked the judgment's voice severe,
Which called her home when noisy morn awoke.
And oft she sprang beyond the bounds of Time
On her swift pinion lifting up the souls
Of righteous men, on high to God and heaven,
Where they beheld unutterable things;
And heard the glorious music of the blessed,
Circling the throne of the Eternal Three;
And, with the spirits unincarnate, took
Celestial pastime, on the hills of God,
Forgetful of the gloomy pass between.
Some dreams were useless, moved by turbid course
Of animal disorder; not so all.
Deep moral lessons some impressed, that nought
Could afterwards deface: and oft in dreams,
The master passion of the soul displayed
His huge deformity, concealed by day,
Warning the sleeper to beware, awake:
And oft in dreams, the reprobate and vile,
Unpardonable sinner,—as he seemed
Toppling upon the perilous edge of hell,—
In dreadful apparition, saw, before
His vision pass, the shadows of the damned;
And saw the glare of hollow, cursed eyes
Spring from the skirts of the infernal night;
And saw the souls of wicked men, new dead,
By devils hearsed into the fiery gulf;
And heard the burning of the endless flames;
And heard the weltering of the waves of wrath;
And sometimes, too, before his fancy, passed
The Worm that never dies, writhing its folds
In hideous sort, and with eternal Death
Held horrid colloquy, giving the wretch
Unwelcome earnest of the wo to come.
But these we leave, as unbefitting song,
That promised happy narrative of joy.
But what of all the joys of earth was most
Of native growth, most proper to the soil,
Not elsewhere known, in worlds that never fell,
Was joy that sprung from disappointed wo.
The joy in grief, the pleasure after pain,
Fears turned to hopes, meetings expected not,
Deliverances from dangerous attitudes,
Better for worse, and best sometimes for worst,
And all the seeming ill ending in good,—
A sort of happiness composed, which none
Has had experience of, but mortal man;
Yet not to be despised. Look back, and one
Behold, who would not give her tear for all
The smiles that dance about the cheek of Mirth.
Among the tombs she walks at noon of night,
In miserable garb of widowhood.
Observe her yonder, sickly, pale, and sad,
Bending her wasted body o'er the grave
Of him who was the husband of her youth.
The moonbeams, trembling through these ancient yews,
That stand like ranks of mourners round the bed
Of death, fall dismally upon her face,
Her little hollow, withered face, almost
Invisible, so worn away with wo.
The tread of hasty foot, passing so late,
Disturbs her not; nor yet the roar of mirth,
From neighbouring revelry ascending loud.
She hears, sees nought, fears nought. One thought alone
Fills all her heart and soul, half hoping, half
Remembering, sad, unutterable thought!
Uttered by silence and by tears alone.
Sweet tears! the awful language, eloquent
Of infinite affection, far too big
For words. She sheds not many now. That grass,
Which springs so rankly o'er the dead, has drunk
Already many showers of grief; a drop
Or two are all that now remain behind,
And, from her eye that darts strange fiery beams,
At dreary intervals, drip down her cheek,
Falling most mournfully from bone to bone.
But yet she wants not tears. That babe, that hangs
Upon her breast, that babe that never saw
Its father—he was dead before its birth—
Helps her to weep, weeping before its time,
Taught sorrow by the mother's melting voice,
Repeating oft the father's sacred name.
Be not surprised at this expense of wo!
The man she mourns was all she called her own.
The music of her ear, light of her eye,
Desire of all her heart, her hope, her fear,
The element in which her passions lived,
Dead now, or dying all: nor long shall she
Visit that place of skulls. Night after night
She wears herself away. The moonbeam, now,
That falls upon her unsubstantial frame,
Scarce finds obstruction; and upon her bones,
Barren as leafless boughs in winter-time,
Her infant fastens his little hands, as oft,
Forgetful, she leaves him a while unheld.
But look, she passes not away in gloom.
A light from far illumes her face, a light

That comes beyond the moon, beyond the sun—
The light of truth divine, the glorious hope
Of resurrection at the promised morn,
And meetings then which ne'er shall part again.
  Indulge another note of kindred tone,
Where grief was mixed with melancholy joy.
  Our sighs were numerous, and profuse our tears,
For she, we lost, was lovely, and we loved
Her much. Fresh in our memory, as fresh
As yesterday, is yet the day she died.
It was an April day; and blithely all
The youth of nature leaped beneath the sun,
And promised glorious manhood; and our hearts
Were glad, and round them danced the lightsome blood,
In healthy merriment, when tidings came,
A child was born: and tidings came again,
That she who gave it birth was sick to death.
So swift trode sorrow on the heels of joy!
We gathered round her bed, and bent our knees
In fervent supplication to the Throne
Of Mercy, and perfumed our prayers with sighs
Sincere, and penitential tears, and looks
Of self-abasement; but we sought to stay
An angel on the earth, a spirit ripe
For heaven; and Mercy, in her love, refused,
Most merciful, as oft, when seeming least!
Most gracious when she seemed the most to frown!
The room I well remember, and the bed
On which she lay, and all the faces too,
That crowded dark and mournfully around.
Her father there and mother, bending stood;
And down their aged cheeks fell many drops
Of bitterness. Her husband, too, was there,
And brothers, and they wept; her sisters, too,
Did weep and sorrow, comfortless; and I,
Too, wept, though not to weeping given; and all
Within the house was dolorous and sad.
This I remember well; but better still,
I do remember, and will ne'er forget,
The dying eye! That eye alone was bright,
And brighter grew, as nearer death approached,
As I have seen the gentle little flower
Look fairest in the silver beam which fell,
Reflected from the thunder-cloud that soon
Came down, and o'er the desert scattered far
And wide its loveliness. She made a sign
To bring her babe—'twas brought, and by her placed.
She looked upon its face, that neither smiled
Nor wept, nor knew who gazed upon't; and laid
Her hand upon its little breast, and sought
For it, with look that seemed to penetrate
The heavens, unutterable blessings, such
As God to dying parents only granted,
For infants left behind them in the world.
"God keep my child!" we heard her say, and heard
No more. The Angel of the Covenant
Was come, and, faithful to his promise, stood,
Prepared to walk with her through death's dark vale.
And now her eyes grew bright, and brighter still,
Too bright for ours to look upon, suffused
With many tears, and closed without a cloud.
They set as sets the morning star, which goes
Not down behind the darkened west, nor hides
Obscured among the tempests of the sky,
But melts away into the light of heaven.
  Loves, friendships, hopes, and dear remembrances,
The kind embracings of the heart, and hours
Of happy thought, and smiles coming to tears,
And glories of the heaven and starry cope
Above, and glories of the earth beneath,—
These were the rays that wandered through the gloom
Of mortal life; wells of the wilderness,
Redeeming features in the face of Time,
Sweet drops, that made the mixed cup of Earth
A palatable draught—too bitter else.
  About the joys and pleasures of the world,
This question was not seldom in debate;
Whether the righteous man, or sinner, had
The greatest share, and relished them the most?
Truth gives the answer thus, gives it distinct,
Nor needs to reason long: The righteous man.
For what was he denied of earthly growth,
Worthy the name of good? Truth answers, Nought.
Had he not appetites, and sense, and will?
Might he not eat, if Providence allowed,
The finest of the wheat? Might he not drink
The choicest wine? True, he was temperate;
But then, was temperance a foe to peace?
Might he not rise, and clothe himself in gold?
Ascend, and stand in palaces of kings?
True, he was honest still and charitable:
Were, then, these virtues foes to human peace?
Might he not do exploits, and gain a name?
Most true, he trode not down a fellow's right,
Nor walked up to a throne on skulls of men:
Were justice, then, and mercy, foes to peace?
Had he not friendships, loves, and smiles, and hopes?
Sat not around his table sons and daughters?
Was not his ear with music pleased? his eye
With light? his nostrils with perfumes? his lips
With pleasant relishes? Grew not his herds?
Fell not the rain upon his meadows? reaped
He not his harvests? and did not his heart
Revel, at will, through all the charities
And sympathies of nature, unconfined?
And were not these all sweetened and sanctified
By dews of holiness, shed from above?
Might he not walk through Fancy's airy halls?
Might he not History's ample page survey?
Might he not, finally, explore the depths

Of mental, moral, natural, divine?
But why enumerate thus? One word enough.
There was no joy in all created things,
No drop of sweet, that turned not in the end
To sour, of which the righteous man did not
Partake; partake, invited by the voice
Of God, his Father's voice, who gave him all
His heart's desire: and o'er the sinner still
The Christian had this one advantage more,
That when his earthly pleasures failed,—and fail
They always did to every soul of man,—
He sent his hopes on high, looked up, and reached
His sickle forth, and reaped the fields of heaven,
And plucked the clusters from the vines of God.
Nor was the general aspect of the world
Always a moral waste. A time there came,
Though few believed it e'er should come; a time,
Typed by the Sabbath day recurring once
In seven, and by the year of rest indulged
Septennial to the lands on Jordan's banks;
A time foretold by Judah's bards in words
Of fire, a time, seventh part of time, and set
Before the eighth and last, the Sabbath day
Of all the earth, when all had rest and peace.
Before its coming many to and fro,
Ran, ran from various cause; by many sent
From various cause, upright and crooked both.
Some sent and ran for love of souls, sincere;
And more, at instance of a holy name.
With godly zeal much vanity was mixed;
And circumstance of gaudy civil pomp;
And speeches buying praise for praise; and lists,
And endless scrolls, surcharged with modest names
That sought the public eye; and stories, told
In quackish phrase, that hurt their credit, even
When true; combined with wise and prudent means.
Much wheat, much chaff, much gold, and much alloy;
But God wrought with the whole, wrought most with what
To man seemed weakest means, and brought result
Of good, from good and evil both; and breathed
Into the withered nations breath and life,
The breath and life of liberty and truth,
By means of knowledge, breathed into the soul.
Then was the evil day of tyranny,
Of kingly and of priestly tyranny,
That bruised the nations long. As yet, no state
Beneath the heavens had tasted freedom's wine,
Though loud of freedom was the talk of all.
Some groaned more deeply, being heavier tasked;
Some wrought with straw, and some without; but all
Were slaves, or meant to be; for rulers, still,
Had been of equal mind, excepting few,
Cruel, rapacious, tyrannous, and vile,
And had with equal shoulder propped the Beast.
As yet, the Church, the holy spouse of God,
In members few, had wandered in her weeds
Of mourning, persecuted, scorned, reproached,
And buffeted; and killed; in members few,
Though seeming many whiles; then fewest, oft,
When seeming most. She still had hung her harp
Upon the willow-tree, and sighed, and wept
From age to age. Satan began the war,
And all his angels, and all wicked men,
Against her fought by wile, or fierce attack,
Six thousand years; but fought in vain. She stood
Troubled on every side, but not distressed;
Weeping, but yet despairing not; cast down,
But not destroyed: for she upon the palms
Of God was graven, and precious in his sight,
As apple of his eye; and, like the bush
On Midia's mountain seen, burned unconsumed;
But to the wilderness retiring, dwelt,
Debased in sackcloth, and forlorn in tears.
As yet had sung the scarlet-coloured Whore,
Who on the breast of civil power reposed
Her harlot head, (the Church a harlot then,
When first she wedded civil power,) and drank
The blood of martyred saints,—whose priests were lords,
Whose coffers held the gold of every land,
Who held a cup of all pollutions full,
Who with a double horn the people pushed,
And raised her forehead, full of blasphemy,
Above the holy God, usurping oft
Jehovah's incommunicable names.
The nations had been dark; the Jews had pined,
Scattered without a name, beneath the Curse;
War had abounded, Satan raged, unchained;
And earth had still been black with moral gloom.
But now the cry of men oppressed went up
Before the Lord, and to remembrance came
The tears of all his saints, their tears, and groans.
Wise men had read the number of the name;
The prophet-years had rolled; the time, and times
And half a time, were now fulfilled complete;
The seven fierce vials of the wrath of God,
Poured by seven angels strong, were shed abroad
Upon the earth, and emptied to the dregs;
The prophecy for confirmation stood;
And all was ready for the sword of God.
The righteous saw, and fled without delay,
Into the chambers of Omnipotence.
The wicked mocked, and sought for erring cause
To satisfy the dismal state of things;
The public credit gone, the fear in time
Of peace, the starving want in time of wealth,
The insurrection muttering in the streets,
And pallid consternation spreading wide;
And leagues, though holy termed, first ratified
In hell, on purpose made to under-prop
Iniquity, and crush the sacred truth.
Meantime, a mighty angel stood in heaven,
And cried aloud, "Associate now yourselves,

Ye princes, potentates, and men of war,
And mitred heads, associate now yourselves,
And be dispersed; embattle, and be broken.
Gird on your armour, and be dashed to dust.
Take counsel, and it shall be brought to nought.
Speak, and it shall not stand." And suddenly
The armies of the saints, imbannered, stood
On Zion hill; and with them angels stood
In squadron bright, and chariots of fire;
And with them stood the Lord, clad like a man
Of war, and to the sound of thunder, led
The battle on. Earth shook, the kingdoms shook,
The Beast, the lying Seer, dominions, fell;
Thrones, tyrants fell, confounded in the dust,
Scattered and driven before the breath of God,
As chaff of summer threshing floor, before
The wind. Three days the battle wasting slew.
The sword was full, the arrow drunk with blood;
And to the supper of Almighty God,
Spread in Hamonah's vale, the fowls of heaven,
And every beast, invited, came, and fed
On captains' flesh, and drank the blood of kings.
And, lo! another angel stood in heaven,
Crying aloud with mighty voice, "Fallen, fallen,
Is Babylon the Great, to rise no more.
Rejoice, ye prophets! over her rejoice,
Apostles! holy men, all saints, rejoice!
And glory give to God and to the Lamb."
And all the armies of disburdened earth,
As voice of many waters, and as voice
Of thunderings, and voice of multitudes,
Answered, Amen. And every hill and rock,
And sea, and every beast, answered, Amen.
Europa answered, and the farthest bounds
Of woody Chili, Asia's fertile coasts,
And Afric's burning wastes, answered, Amen.
And Heaven, rejoicing, answered back, Amen.
Not so the wicked. They afar were heard
Lamenting. Kings, who drank her cup of whoredoms,
Captains, and admirals, and mighty men,
Who lived deliciously; and merchants, rich
With merchandize of gold, and wine, and oil;
And those who traded in the souls of men,
Known by their gaudy robes of priestly pomp;—
All these afar off stood, crying, Alas!
Alas! and wept, and gnashed their teeth, and groaned;
And, with the owl that on her ruins sat,
Made dolorous concert in the ear of Night.
And over her again the Heavens rejoiced,
And Earth returned again the loud response.
Thrice happy days! thrice blessed the man who saw
Their dawn! The Church and State, that long had held
Unholy intercourse, were now divorced;
Princes were righteous men, judges upright;
And first, in general, now—for in the worst
Of times there were some honest seers—the priest
Sought other than the fleece among his flocks,
Best paid when God was honoured most; and like
A cedar, nourished well, Jerusalem grew,
And towered on high, and spread, and flourished fair;
And underneath her boughs the nations lodged,
All nations lodged, and sung the song of peace.
From the four winds, the Jews, eased of the Curse,
Returned, and dwelt with God in Jacob's land,
And drank of Sharon and of Carmel's vine.
Satan was bound, though bound, not banished quite,
But lurked about the timorous skirts of things,
Ill lodged, and thinking whiles to leave the earth,
And with the wicked,—for some wicked were,—
Held midnight meetings, as the saints were wont,
Fearful of day, who once was as the sun,
And worshipped more. The bad, but few, became
A taunt and hissing now, as heretofore
The good; and, blushing, hasted out of sight.
Disease was none; the voice of war forgot;
The sword, a share; a pruning-hook, the spear
Men grew and multiplied upon the earth,
And filled the city and the waste; and Death
Stood waiting for the lapse of tardy Age,
That mocked him long. Men grew and multiplied,
But lacked not bread; for God his promise brought
To mind, and blessed the land with plenteous rain
And made it blessed for dews and precious things
Of heaven, and blessings of the deep beneath,
And blessings of the sun and moon, and fruits
Of day and night, and blessings of the vale,
And precious things of the eternal hills,
And all the fulness of perpetual spring.
The prison-house, where chained felons pined
Threw open his ponderous doors, let in the light
Of heaven, and grew into a church, where God
Was worshipped. None were ignorant, selfish none.
Love took the place of law; where'er you met
A man, you met a friend, sincere and true.
Kind looks foretold as kind a heart within;
Words as they sounded, meant; and promises
Were made to be performed. Thrice happy days!
Philosophy was sanctified, and saw
Perfections that she thought a fable, long.
Revenge his dagger dropped, and kissed the hand
Of Mercy; Anger cleared his cloudy brow,
And sat with Peace; Envy grew red, and smiled
On Worth; Pride stooped, and kissed Humility;
Lust washed his miry hands, and, wedded, leaned
On chaste Desire; and Falsehood laid aside
His many-folded cloak, and bowed to Truth;
And Treachery up from his mining came,
And walked above the ground with righteous Faith;
And Covetousness unclenched his sinewy hand

And opened his door to Charity, the fair;
Hatred was lost in Love; and Vanity
With a good conscience pleased, her feathers cropped;
Sloth in the morning rose with Industry;
To Wisdom Folly turned; and Fashion turned
Deception off, in act as good as word.
The hand that held a whip was lifted up
To bless; slave was a word in ancient books
Met, only; every man was free; and all
Feared God, and served him day and night in love.
How fair the daughter of Jerusalem then!
How gloriously from Zion Hill she looked!
Clothed with the sun, and in her train the moon,
And on her head a coronet of stars,
And girding round her waist, with heavenly grace,
The bow of Mercy bright; and in her hand
Immanuel's cross, her sceptre and her hope.
Desire of every land! the nations came,
And worshipped at her feet; all nations came,
Flocking like doves: Columba's painted tribes,
That from Magellan to the Frozen Bay,
Beneath the Arctic, dwelt; and drank the tides
Of Amazona, prince of earthly streams;
Or slept at noon beneath the giant shade
Of Andes' mount; or, roving northward, heard
Niagara sing, from Erie's billow down
To Frontenac, and hunted thence the fur
To Labrador: and Afric's dusky swarms,
That from Morocco to Angola dwelt,
And drank the Niger from his native wells,
Or roused the lion in Numidia's groves;
The tribes that sat among the fabled cliffs
Of Atlas, looking to Atlanta's wave;
With joy and melody, arose and came.
Zara awoke and came, and Egypt came,
Casting her idol gods into the Nile.
Black Ethiopa, that, shadowless,
Beneath the Torrid burned, arose and came.
Dauma and Medra, and the pirate tribes
Of Algeri, with incense came, and pure
Offerings, annoying now the seas no more.
The silken tribes of Asia, flocking came,
Innumerous: Ishmael's wandering race, that rode
On camels o'er the spicy tract that lay
From Persia to the Red Sea coast; the king
Of broad Cathay, with numbers infinite,
Of many lettered casts; and all the tribes
That dwelt from Tigris to the Ganges' wave,
And worshipped fire, or Brahma, fabled god;
Cashmeres, Circassians, Banyans, tender race!
That swept the insect from their path, and lived
On herbs and fruits; and those who peaceful dwelt
Along the shady avenue that stretched
From Agra to Lahore; and all the hosts
That owned the Crescent late, deluded long;
The Tartar hordes, that roamed from Oby's bank,
Ungoverned, southward to the wondrous Wall.
The tribes of Europe came: the Greek, redeemed
From Turkish thrall, the Spaniard came, and Gaul
And Britain with her ships, and, on his sledge,
The Laplander, that nightly watched the bear
Circling the Pole; and those who saw the flames
Of Hecla burn the drifted snow; the Russ,
Long-whiskered, and equestrian Pole; and those
Who drank the Rhine, or lost the evening sun
Behind the Alpine towers; and she that sat
By Arno, classic stream; Venice, or Rome,
Head quarters long of sin! first guileless now,
And meaning as she seemed, stretched forth her hands
And all the Isles of ocean rose and came,
Whether they heard the roll of banished tides,
Antipodes to Albion's wave, or watched
The Moon, ascending chalky Teneriffe,
And with Atlanta holding nightly love.
The Sun, the Moon, the Constellations, came:
Thrice twelve and ten that watched the Antarctic sleep,
Twice six that near the Ecliptic dwelt, thrice twelve
And one, that with the streamers danced, and saw
The Hyperborean Ice guarding the Pole.
The East, the West, the South, and Snowy North,
Rejoicing met, and worshipped reverently
Before the Lord, in Zion's holy hill;
And all the places round about were blessed.
The animals, as once in Eden, lived
In peace. The wolf dwelt with the lamb, the bear
And leopard with the ox. With looks of love,
The tiger and the scaly crocodile
Together met, at Gambia's palmy wave.
Perched on the eagle's wing, the bird of song,
Singing, arose, and visited the sun;
And with the falcon sat the gentle lark.
The little child leaped from his mother's arms
And stroked the crested snake, and rolled unhurt
Among his speckled waves, and wished him home;
And sauntering school-boys, slow returning, played
At eve about the lion's den, and wove,
Into his shaggy mane, fantastic flowers.
To meet the husbandman, early abroad,
Hasted the deer, and waved its woody head;
And round his dewy steps, the hare, unscared,
Sported; and toyed familiar with his dog.
The flocks and herds, o'er hill and valley spread,
Exulting, cropped the ever-budding herb,
The desert blossomed, and the barren sung.
Justice and Mercy, Holiness and Love,
Among the people walked, Messiah reigned,
And Earth kept Jubilee a thousand years.

BOOK VI.

Resume thy tone of wo, immortal Harp!
The song of mirth is past, the Jubilee
Is ended, and the sun begins to fade!
Soon passed, for Happiness counts not the hours.

To her a thousand years seem as a day;
A day, a thousand years to Misery.
Satan is loose, and Violence is heard,
And Riot in the street, and Revelry
Intoxicate, and Murder, and Revenge.
Put on your armour now, ye righteous! put
The helmet of salvation on, and gird
Your loins about with truth; add righteousness,
And add the shield of faith, and take the sword
Of God—awake and watch!—The day is near,
Great day of God Almighty and the Lamb!
The harvest of the earth is fully ripe;
Vengeance begins to tread the great wine-press
Of fierceness and of wrath; and Mercy pleads,
Mercy that pleaded long, she pleads—no more!
Whence comes that darkness? whence those yells of wo?
What thunderings are these that shake the world?
Why fall the lamps from heaven as blasted figs?
Why tremble righteous men? why angels pale?
Why is all fear? what has become of hope?
God comes! God, in his car of vengeance, comes!—
Hark! louder on the blast, come hollow shrieks
Of dissolution! in the fitful scowl
Of night, near and more near, angels of death
Incessant flap their deadly wings, and roar
Through all the fevered air! the mountains rock,
The moon is sick, and all the stars of heaven
Burn feebly! oft and sudden gleams the fire,
Revealing awfully the brow of Wrath!
The Thunder, long and loud, utters his voice,
Responsive to the Ocean's troubled growl!
Night comes, last night, the long, dark, dark, dark night,
That has no morn beyond it, and no star!
No eye of man hath seen a night like this!
Heaven's trampled Justice girds itself for fight!
Earth, to thy knees, and cry for mercy! cry
With earnest heart, for thou art growing old
And hoary, unrepented, unforgiven!
And all thy glory mourns! The vintage mourns!
Bashan and Carmel, mourn and weep! and mourn,
Thou Lebanon! with all thy cedars, mourn.
Sun! glorying in thy strength from age to age,
So long observant of thy hour, put on
Thy weeds of wo, and tell the Moon to weep;
Utter thy grief at mid-day, morn, and even;
Tell all the nations, tell the Clouds that sit
About the portals of the east and west,
And wanton with thy golden locks, to wait
Thee not to-morrow, for no morrow comes!
Tell men and women, tell the new-born child,
And every eye that sees, to come, and see
Thee set behind Eternity, for thou
Shalt go to bed to-night, and ne'er awake!
Stars! walking on the pavement of the sky,
Out-sentinels of heaven, watching the earth,
Cease dancing now; your lamps are growing dim,
Your graves are dug among the dismal clouds,
And angels are assembling round your bier!
Orion, mourn! and Mazzaroth, and thou,
Arcturus! mourn, with all thy northern sons,
Daughters of Pleiades! that nightly shed
Sweet influence, and thou, fairest of stars!
Eye of the morning, weep! and weep at eve!
Weep setting, now to rise no more, "and flame
On forehead of the dawn,"—as sung the bard,
Great bard! who used on Earth a seraph's lyre,
Whose numbers wandered through eternity,
And gave sweet foretaste of the heavenly harps!
Minstrel of sorrow! native of the dark,
Shrub-loving Philomel, that wooed the Dews,
At midnight from their starry beds, and, charmed,
Held them around thy song till dawn awoke.
Sad bird! pour through the gloom thy weeping song,
Pour all thy dying melody of grief,
And with the turtle spread the wave of wo!
Spare not thy reed, for thou shalt sing no more!
Ye holy bards!—if yet a holy bard
Remain,—what chord shall serve you now! what harp!
What harp shall sing the dying Sun asleep,
And mourn behind the funeral of the Moon!
What harp of boundless, deep, exhaustless wo,
Shall utter forth the groanings of the damned!
And sing the obsequies of wicked souls!
And wail their plunge in the eternal fire!—
Hold, hold your hands! hold, angels!—God laments,
And draws a cloud of mourning round his throne!
The Organ of Eternity is mute!
And there is silence in the Heaven of Heavens!
Daughters of beauty! choice of beings made!
Much praised, much blamed, much loved; but fairer far
Than aught beheld, than aught imagined else;
Fairest, and dearer than all else most dear;
Light of the darksome wilderness! to Time
As stars to night, whose eyes were spells that held
The passenger forgetful of his way,
Whose steps were majesty, whose words were song,
Whose smiles were hope, whose actions, perfect grace,
Whose love, the solace, glory, and delight
Of man, his boast, his riches, his renown;
When found, sufficient bliss! when lost, despair!—
Stars of creation! images of love!
Break up the fountains of your tears, your tears,
More eloquent than learned tongue, or lyre
Of purest note! your sunny raiment stain,
Put dust upon your heads, lament and weep,
And utter all your minstrelsy of wo!
Go to, ye wicked, weep and howl; for all
That God hath written against you is at hand
The cry of Violence hath reached his ear,
Hell is prepared, and Justice whets his sword.
Weep all of every name! Begin the wo,

Ye woods, and tell it to the doleful winds,
And doleful winds, wail to the howling hills;
And howling hills, mourn to the dismal vales,
And dismal vales, sigh to the sorrowing brooks,
And sorrowing brooks, weep to the weeping stream,
And weeping stream, awake the groaning deep;
And let the instrument take up the song,
Responsive to the voice, harmonious wo!
Ye Heavens, great arch-way of the universe,
Put sackcloth on; and Ocean, clothe thyself
In garb of widowhood, and gather all
Thy waves into a groan, and utter it,
Long, loud, deep, piercing, dolorous, immense.
The occasion asks it!—Nature dies, and God
And angels come to lay her in the grave!
But we have overleaned our theme; behind,
A little season waits a verse or two,
The years that followed the millennial rest.
Bad years they were; and first, as signal sure,
That at the core religion was diseased,
The sons of Levi strove again for place,
And eminence, and names of swelling pomp;
Setting their feet upon the people's neck,
And slumbering in the lap of civil power,
Of civil power again tyrannical:
And second sign, sure sign, whenever seen,
That holiness was dying in a land,
The Sabbath was profaned and set at nought;
The honest seer, who spoke the truth of God
Plainly, was left with empty walls; and round
The frothy orator, who busked his tales
In quackish pomp of noisy words, the ear
Tickling, but leaving still the heart unprobed,
The judgment uninformed,—numbers immense
Flocked, gaping wide, with passions high inflamed;
And on the way returning, heated, home,
Of eloquence, and not of truth, conversed—
Mean eloquence that wanted sacred truth.
  Two principles from the beginning strove
In human nature, still dividing man,—
Sloth and activity; the lust of praise,
And indolence that rather wished to sleep.
And not unfrequently in the same mind
They dubious contest held; one gaining now,
And now the other crowned, and both again
Keeping the field, with equal combat fought.
Much different was their voice. Ambition called
To action, Sloth invited to repose.
Ambition early rose, and, being up,
Toiled ardently, and late retired to rest;
Sloth lay till mid-day, turning on his couch,
Like ponderous door upon its weary hinge,
And, having rolled him out with much ado,
And many a dismal sigh, and vain attempt,
He sauntered out, accoutred carelessly,—
With half-oped, misty, unobservant eye,
Somniferous, that weighed the object down
On which its burden fell,—an hour or two,
Then with a groan retired to rest again.
The one, whatever deed had been achieved,
Thought it too little, and too small the praise;
The other tried to think,—for thinking so
Answered his purpose best,—that what of great
Mankind could do had been already done;
And therefore laid him calmly down to sleep.
  Different in mode, destructive both alike.
Destructive always indolence; and love
Of fame destructive always too, if less
Than praise of God it sought, content with less:
Even then not current, if it sought his praise
From other motive than resistless love;
Though base, main-spring of action in the world
And, under name of vanity and pride,
Was greatly practised on by cunning men.
It opened the niggard's purse, clothed nakedness,
Gave beggars food, and threw the Pharisee
Upon his knees, and kept him long in act
Of prayer; it spread the lace upon the fop,
His language trimmed, and planned his curious gait,
It stuck the feather on the gay coquette,
And on her finger laid the heavy load
Of jewellery; it did—what did it not?
The gospel preached, the gospel paid, and sent
The gospel; conquered nations, cities built,
Measured the furrow of the field with nice
Directed share, shaped bulls, and cows, and rams,
And threw the ponderous stone; and pitiful,
Indeed, and much against the grain, it dragged
The stagnant, dull, predestinated fool,
Through learning's halls, and made him labour much
Abortively, though sometimes not unpraised
He left the sage's chair, and home returned
Making his simple mother think that she
Had borne a man. In schools, designed to root
Sin up, and plant the seeds of holiness
In youthful minds, it held a signal place.
The little infant man, by nature proud,
Was taught the scriptures by the love of praise,
And grew religious as he grew in fame.
And thus the principle, which out of heaven
The devil threw, and threw him down to hell,
And keeps him there, was made an instrument
To moralize and sanctify mankind,
And in their hearts beget humility;
With what success it needs not now to say.
  Destructive both we said, activity
And sloth: behold the last exemplified,
In literary man. Not all at once,
He yielded to the soothing voice of sleep;
But, having seen a bough of laurel wave,
He effort made to climb; and friends, and even
Himself, talked of his greatness, as at hand,
And, prophesying, drew his future life.
Vain prophecy! his fancy, taught by sloth,

Saw, in the very threshold of pursuit,
A thousand obstacles; he halted first,
And while he halted, saw his burning hopes
Grow dim and dimmer still; ambition's self,
The advocate of loudest tongue, decayed;
His purposes, made daily, daily broken,
Like plant uprooted oft, and set again,
More sickly grew, and daily wavered more;
Till at the last, decision, quite worn out,
Decision, fulcrum of the mental powers,
Resigned the blasted soul to staggering chance;
Sleep gathered fast, and weighed him downward still;
His eye fell heavy from the mount of fame;
His young resolves to benefit the world
Perished and were forgotten; he shut his ear
Against the painful news of rising worth;
And drank with desperate thirst the poppy's juice;
A deep and mortal slumber settled down
Upon his weary faculties oppressed;
He rolled from side to side, and rolled again;
And snored, and groaned, and withered, and expired,
And rotted on the spot, leaving no name.
The hero best example gives of toil
Unsanctified. One word his history writes.
"He was a murderer above the laws,
And greatly praised for doing murderous deeds."
And now he grew, and reached his perfect growth;
And also now the sluggard soundest slept
And by him lay the uninterred corpse.
Of every order, sin and wickedness,
Deliberate, cool, malicious villany,
This age, attained maturity, unknown
Before; and seemed in travail to bring forth
Some last, enormous, monstrous deed of guilt,
Original, unprecedented guilt,
That might obliterate the memory
Of what had hitherto been done most vile.
Inventive men were paid, at public cost,
To plan new modes of sin; the holy Word
Of God was burned, with acclamations loud;
New tortures were invented for the good;—
For still some good remained, as whiles through sky
Of thickest clouds, a wandering star appeared;—
New oaths of blasphemy were framed and sworn;
And men in reputation grew, as grew
The stature of their crimes. Faith was not found.
Truth was not found, truth always scarce, so scarce
That half the misery which groaned on earth,
In ordinary times, was progeny
Of disappointment, daily coming forth
From broken promises, that might have ne'er
Been made, or, being made, might have been kept;
Justice and mercy, too, were rare, obscured
In cottage garb: before the palace door,
The beggar rotted, starving in his rags;
And on the threshold of luxurious domes,
The orphan child laid down his head, and died;
Nor unamusing was his piteous cry
To women, who had now laid tenderness
Aside, best pleased with sights of cruelty;
Flocking, when fouler lusts would give them time,
To horrid spectacles of blood, where men,
Or guiltless beasts, that seemed to look to heaven,
With eye imploring vengeance on the earth,
Were tortured for the merriment of kings.
The advocate for him who offered most
Pleaded; the scribe, according to the hire,
Worded the lie, adding, for every piece,
An oath of confirmation; judges raised,
One hand to intimate the sentence, death,
Imprisonment, or fine, or loss of goods,
And in the other held a lusty bribe,
Which they had taken to give the sentence wrong;
So managing the scale of justice still,
That he was wanting found who poorest seemed.
But laymen, most renowned for devilish deeds,
Laboured at distance still behind the priest;
He shore his sheep, and, having packed the wool,
Sent them unguarded to the hill of wolves;
And to the bowl deliberately sat down,
And with his mistress mocked at sacred things.
The theatre was, from the very first,
The favourite haunt of Sin, though honest men,
Some very honest, wise, and worthy men,
Maintained it might be turned to good account;
And so perhaps it might, but never was.
From first to last it was an evil place:
And now such things were acted there, as made
The devils blush; and from the neighbourhood,
Angels and holy men, trembling, retired:
And what with dreadful aggravation crowned
This dreary time, was sin against the light.
All men knew God, and, knowing, disobeyed
And gloried to insult him to his face.
Another feature only we shall mark.
It was withal a highly polished age,
And scrupulous in ceremonious rite.
When stranger stranger met upon the way,
First, each to each bowed most respectfully,
And large profession made of humble service,
And then the stronger took the other's purse,
And he that stabbed his neighbour to the heart,
Stabbed him politely, and returned the blade
Reeking into its sheath with graceful air.
Meantime the earth gave symptoms of her end,
And all the scenery above proclaimed,
That the great last catastrophe was near.
The Sun at rising staggered and fell back,
As one too early up, after a night
Of late debauch; then rose, and shone again,
Brighter than wont; and sicked again, and paused
In zenith altitude, as one fatigued;
And shed a feeble twilight ray at noon.

Rousing the wolf before his time to chase
The shepherd and his sheep, that sought for light,
And darkness found, astonished, terrified;
Then, out of course, rolled furious down the west,
As chariot reined by awkward charioteer;
And, waiting at the gate, he on the earth
Gazed, as he thought he ne'er might see't again.
The bow of mercy, heretofore so fair,
Ribbed with the native hues of heavenly love,
Disastrous colours showed, unseen till now;
Changing upon the watery gulf, from pale
To fiery red, and back again to pale;
And o'er it hovered wings of wrath. The Moon
Swaggered in midst of heaven, grew black, and dark,
Unclouded, uneclipsed. The Stars fell down,
Tumbling from off their towers like drunken men,
Or seemed to fall; and glimmered now, and now
Sprang out in sudden blaze and dimmed again,
As lamp of foolish virgin lacking oil.
The heavens, this moment, looked serene; the next,
Glowed like an oven with God's displeasure hot.
Nor less, below, was intimation given,
Of some disaster great and ultimate.
The tree that bloomed, or hung with clustering fruit,
Untouched by visible calamity
Of frost or tempest, died and came again.
The flower and herb fell down as sick; then rose
And fell again. The fowls of every hue,
Crowding together, sailed on weary wing;
And, hovering, oft they seemed about to light;
Then soared, as if they thought the earth unsafe.
The cattle looked with meaning face on man.
Dogs howled, and seemed to see more than their masters.
And there were sights that none had seen before;
And hollow, strange, unprecedented sounds,
And earnest whisperings ran along the hills
At dead of night; and long, deep, endless sighs,
Came from the dreary vale; and from the waste
Came horrid shrieks, and fierce unearthly groans,
The wail of evil spirits, that now felt
The hour of utter vengeance near at hand.
The winds from every quarter blew at once,
With desperate violence, and, whirling, took
The traveller up, and threw him down again,
At distance from his path, confounded, pale;
And shapes, strange shapes! in winding sheets were seen,
Gliding through night, and singing funeral songs,
And imitating sad, sepulchral rites;
And voices talked among the clouds, and still
The words that men could catch were spoken of them,
And seemed to be the words of wonder great,
And expectation of some vast event.
Earth shook, and swam, and reeled, and opened her jaws,
By earthquake tossed, and tumbled to and fro;
And, louder than the ear of man had heard,
The Thunder bellowed, and the Ocean groaned.
The race of men, perplexed, but not reformed,
Flocking together, stood in earnest crowds,
Conversing of the awful state of things.
Some curious explanations gave, unlearned;
Some tried affectedly to laugh, and some
Gazed stupidly; but all were sad and pale,
And wished the comment of the wise. Nor less
These prodigies, occurring night and day,
Perplexed philosophy. The magi tried,—
Magi, a name not seldom given to fools,
In the vocabulary of earthly speech,—
They tried to trace them still to second cause
But scarcely satisfied themselves; though round
Their deep deliberations, crowding, came,
And, wondering at their wisdom, went away,
Much quieted and very much deceived,
The people, always glad to be deceived.
These warnings passed, they, unregarded, passed,
And all in wonted order calmly moved.
The pulse of Nature regularly beat,
And on her cheek the bloom of perfect health
Again appeared. Deceitful pulse! and bloom
Deceitful! and deceitful calm! The Earth
Was old, and worn within; but, like the man,
Who noticed not his mid-day strength decline,
Sliding so gently round the curvature
Of life, from youth to age,—she knew it not.
The calm was like the calm, which oft the man,
Dying, experienced before his death;
The bloom was but a hectic flush, before
The eternal paleness. But all these were taken,
By this last race of men, for tokens of good;
And blustering public News aloud proclaimed—
News always gabbling ere they well had thought—
Prosperity, and joy, and peace; and mocked
The man who, kneeling, prayed, and trembled still,
And all in earnest to their sins returned.
It was not so in heaven. The elders round
The Throne conversed about the state of man,
Conjecturing,—for none of certain knew,—
That Time was at an end. They gazed intense
Upon the Dial's face, which yonder stands
In gold, before the Sun of Righteousness,
Jehovah, and computes time, seasons, years,
And destinies, and slowly numbers o'er
The mighty cycles of eternity;
By God alone completely understood,
But read by all, revealing much to all.
And now, to saints of eldest skill, the ray,
Which on the gnomon fell of Time, seemed sent
From level west, and hasting quickly down.
The holy Virtues, watching, saw, besides,
Great preparation going on in heaven,
Betokening great event, greater than aught
That first-created seraphim had seen.
The faithful messengers, who have for wing

The lightning, waiting, day and night, on God:
Before his face, beyond their usual speed,
On pinion of celestial light were seen,
Coming and going, and their road was still
From heaven to earth, and back again to heaven.
The angel of Mercy, bent before the Throne,
By earnest pleading, seemed to hold the hand
Of Vengeance back, and win a moment more
Of late repentance for some sinful world
In jeopardy: and, now, the hill of God,
The mountain of his majesty, rolled flames
Of fire, now smiled with momentary love,
And now again with fiery fierceness burned;
And from behind the darkness of his Throne,
Through which created vision never saw,
The living Thunders, in their native caves,
Muttered the terrors of Omnipotence,
And ready seemed, impatient to fulfil
Some errand of exterminating wrath.
Meanwhile the Earth increased in wickedness,
And hasted daily to fill up her cup.
Satan raged loose, Sin had her will, and Death
Enough. Blood trode upon the heels of blood,
Revenge, in desperate mood, at midnight met
Revenge, War brayed to War, Deceit deceived
Deceit, Lie cheated Lie, and Treachery
Mined under Treachery, and Perjury
Swore back on Perjury, and Blasphemy
Arose with hideous Blasphemy, and Curse
Loud answered Curse; and drunkard, stumbling, fell
O'er drunkard fallen; and husband husband met,
Returning each from other's bed defiled;
Thief stole from thief, and robber on the way
Knocked robber down, and Lewdness, Violence,
And Hate, met Lewdness, Violence, and Hate.
Oh, Earth! thy hour was come! the last elect
Was born, complete the number of the good,
And the last sand fell from the glass of Time.
The cup of guilt was full up to the brim;
And Mercy, weary with beseeching, had
Retired behind the sword of Justice, red
With ultimate and unrepenting wrath;
But man knew not: he o'er his bowl laughed loud,
And, prophesying, said, "To-morrow shall
As this day be, and more abundant still!"
As thou shalt hear—But, hark! the trumpet sounds,
And calls to evening song; for, though with hymn
Eternal, course succeeding course, extol
In presence of the incarnate, holy God,
And celebrate his never-ending praise,—
Duly, at morn and night, the multitudes
Of men redeemed, and angels, all the hosts
Of glory, join in universal song,
And pour celestial harmony, from harps
Above all number, eloquent and sweet,
Above all thought of melody conceived.
And now behold the fair inhabitants,
Delightful sight! from numerous business turn,
And round and round through all the extent of bliss
Towards the temple of Jehovah bow,
And worship reverently before his face!
Pursuits are various here, suiting all tastes,
Though holy all, and glorifying God.
Observe yon band pursue the sylvan stream:
Mounting among the cliffs, they pull the flower,
Springing as soon as pulled, and, marvelling, pry
Into its veins, and circulating blood,
And wondrous mimicry of higher life;
Admire its colours, fragrance, gentle shape;
And thence admire the God who made it so—
So simple, complex, and so beautiful.
Behold yon other band, in airy robes
Of bliss. They weave the sacred bower of rose
And myrtle shade, and shadowy verdant bay,
And laurel, towering high; and round their song,
The pink and lily bring, and amaranth,
Narcissus sweet, and jessamine; and bring
The clustering vine, stopping with flower and fruit,
The peach and orange, and the sparkling stream,
Warbling with nectar to their lips unasked;
And talk the while of everlasting love.
On yonder hill, behold another band,
Of piercing, steady, intellectual eye,
And spacious forehead of sublimest thought.
They reason deep of present, future, past;
And trace effect to cause; and meditate
On the eternal laws of God, which bind
Circumference to centre; and survey,
With optic tubes, that fetch remotest stars
Near them, the systems circling round immense
Innumerous. See how,—as he, the sage,
Among the most renowned in days of Time,
Renowned for large, capacious, holy soul,
Demonstrates clearly motion, gravity,
Attraction, and repulsion, still opposed;
And dips into the deep, original,
Unknown, mysterious elements of things,—
See how the face of every auditor
Expands with admiration of the skill,
Omnipotence, and boundless love of God!
These other, sitting near the tree of life,
In robes of linen flowing white and clean,
Of holiest aspect, of divinest soul,
Angels and men,—into the glory look
Of the Redeeming Love, and turn the leaves
Of man's redemption o'er, the secret leaves,
Which none on earth were found worthy to open,
And, as they read the mysteries divine,
The endless mysteries of salvation, wrought
By God's incarnate Son, they humbler bow
Before the Lamb, and glow with warmer love.
These other, there relaxed beneath the shade
Of yon embowering palms, with friendship smile,
And talk of ancient days, and young pursuits,
Of dangers passed, of godly triumphs won;

And sing the legends of their native land,
Less pleasing far than this their Father's house.
Behold that other band, half lifted up
Between the hill and dale, reclined beneath
The shadow of impending rocks, 'mong streams,
And thundering waterfalls, and waving boughs;
That band of countenance sublime and sweet,
Whose eye, with piercing, intellectual ray,
Now beams severe, or now bewildered seems,
Left rolling wild, or fixed in idle gaze,
While Fancy and the Soul are far from home;
These hold the pencil, art divine! and throw
Before the eye remembered scenes of love;
Each picturing to each the hills, and skies,
And treasured stories of the world he left;
Or, gazing on the scenery of heaven,
They dip their hand in colour's native well,
And, on the everlasting canvas, dash
Figures of glory, imagery divine,
With grace and grandeur in perfection knit.
But, whatsoe'er these spirits blessed pursue,
Where'er they go, whatever sights they see
Of glory and bliss through all the tracts of heaven
The centre, still, the figure eminent,
Whither they ever turn, on whom all eyes
Repose with infinite delight, is God,
And his incarnate Son, the Lamb once slain
On Calvary, to ransom ruined men.
None idle here. Look where thou wilt, they all
Are active, all engaged in meet pursuit;
Not happy else. Hence is it that the song
Of heaven is ever new; for daily thus,
And nightly, new discoveries are made
Of God's unbounded wisdom, power, and love,
Which give the understanding larger room,
And swell the hymn with ever-growing praise.
Behold, they cease! and every face to God
Turns; and we pause from high poetic theme,
Not worthy least of being sung in heaven;
And on unvailed Godhead look from this,
Our oft-frequented hill. He takes the harp,
Nor needs to seek befitting phrase: unsought,
Numbers harmonious roll along the lyre;
As river in its native bed, they flow
Spontaneous, flowing with the tide of thought.
He takes the harp—a bard of Judah leads,
This night, the boundless song, the bard that once,
When Israel's king was sad and sick to death,
A message brought of fifteen added years.
Before the Throne he stands sublime, in robes
Of glory; and now his fingers wake the chords
To praise, which we and all in heaven repeat.
Harps of Eternity! begin the song,
Redeemed and angel harps! begin to God,
Begin the anthem ever sweet and new,
While I extol Him, holy, just, and good.
Life, beauty, light, intelligence, and love
Eternal, uncreated, infinite!
Unsearchable Jehovah! God of truth,
Maker, upholder, governor of all!
Thyself unmade, ungoverned, unupheld!
Omnipotent, unchangeable, Great God!
Exhaustless fulness! giving unimpaired!
Bounding immensity, unspread, unbound!
Highest and best! beginning, middle, end!
All-seeing Eye! all-seeing, and unseen!
Hearing, unheard! all-knowing, and unknown!
Above all praise! above all height of thought!
Proprietor of immortality!
Glory ineffable! bliss underived!
Of old thou builtst thy throne on righteousness,
Before the morning Stars their song began,
Or silence heard the voice of praise. Thou laidst
Eternity's foundation stone. and sawst
Life and existence out of Thee begin.
Mysterious more, the more displayed, where still
Upon thy glorious Throne thou sitst alone,
Hast sat alone, and shalt forever sit
Alone, Invisible, Immortal One!
Behind essential brightness unbeheld.
Incomprehensible! what weight shall weigh,
What measure measure Thee! What know we more
Of Thee, what need to know, than Thou hast taught,
And bidst us still repeat, at morn and even?—
God! Everlasting Father! Holy One!
Our God, our Father, our Eternal All!
Source whence we came, and whither we return;
Who made our spirits, who our bodies made,
Who made the heaven, who made the flowery land,
Who made all made, who orders, governs all,
Who walks upon the wind, who holds the wave
In hollow of thy hand, whom thunders wait,
Whom tempests serve, whom flaming fires obey,
Who guides the circuit of the endless years,
And sitst on high, and makest creation's top
Thy footstool, and beholdst, below Thee, all—
All nought, all less than nought, and vanity.
Like transient dust that hovers on the scale,
Ten thousand worlds are scattered in thy breath.
Thou sitst on high, and measurest destinies,
And days, and months, and wide-revolving years;
And dost according to thy holy will;
And none can stay thy hand, and none withhold
Thy glory; for in judgment, Thou, as well
As mercy, art exalted, day and night.
Past, present, future, magnify thy name.
Thy works all praise Thee, all thy angels praise,
Thy saints adore, and on thy altars burn
The fragrant incense of perpetual love.
They praise Thee now, their hearts, their voices praise,
And swell the rapture of the glorious song.
Harp! lift thy voice on high! shout, angels, shout!
And loudest, ye redeemed! glory to God,
And to the Lamb who bought us with his blood,
From every kindred, nation, people, tongue;

And washed, and sanctified, and saved our souls;
And gave us robes of linen pure, and crowns
Of life, and made us kings and priests to God.
Shout back to ancient Time! Sing loud, and wave
Your palms of triumph! sing, Where is thy sting,
O Death! where is thy victory, O Grave!
Thanks be to God, eternal thanks, who gave
Us victory through Jesus Christ, our Lord.
Harp! lift thy voice on high! shout, angels, shout!
And loudest, ye redeemed! glory to God,
And to the Lamb, all glory and all praise,
All glory and all praise, at morn and even,
That come and go eternally, and find
Us happy still, and Thee for ever blessed!
Glory to God and to the Lamb. Amen.
For ever, and for evermore. Amen.
And those who stood upon the sea of glass,
And those who stood upon the battlements
And lofty towers of New Jerusalem,
And those who circling stood, bowing afar,
Exalted on the everlasting hills,
Thousands of Thousands, thousands infinite,
With voice of boundless love, answered, Amen.
And through Eternity near, and remote,
The worlds, adoring, echoed back, Amen.
And God the Father, Son, and Holy Ghost,
The One Eternal, smiled superior bliss!
And every eye, and every face in heaven,
Reflecting and reflected, beamed with love.
Nor did he not, the Virtue new arrived,
From Godhead gain an individual smile,
Of high acceptance, and of welcome high,
And confirmation evermore in good.
Meantime the landscape glowed with holy joy.
Zephyr, with wing dipped from the well of life,
Sporting through Paradise, and living dews;
The flowers, the spicy shrubs, the lawn, refreshed,
Breathed their selectest balm, breathed odours, such
As angels love; and all the trees of heaven,
The cedar, pine, and everlasting oak,
Rejoicing on the mountains, clapped their hands.

BOOK VII.

As one who meditates at evening tide,
Wandering alone by voiceless solitudes,
And flies in fancy, far beyond the bounds
Of visible and vulgar things, and things
Discovered hitherto, pursuing tracts
As yet untravelled and unknown, through vast
Of new and sweet imaginings; if chance
Some airy harp, waked by the gentle sprites
Of twilight, or light touch of sylvan maid,
In soft succession fall upon his ear,
And fill the desert with its heavenly tones;
He listens intense, and pleased exceedingly,
And wishes it may never stop; yet when
It stops, grieves not; but to his former thoughts
With fondest haste returns: so did the Seer,
So did his audience, after worship passed,
And praise in heaven, return to sing, to hear
Of man, not worthy less the sacred lyre,
Or the attentive ear; and thus the bard,
Not unbesought, again resumed his song.
In customed glory bright, that morn, the Sun
Rose, visiting the earth with light, and heat,
And joy; and seemed as full of youth and strong
To mount the steep of heaven, as when the Stars
Of morning sung to his first dawn, and night
Fled from his face; the spacious sky received
Him, blushing as a bride, when on her looked
The bridegroom; and, spread out beneath his eye,
Earth smiled. Up to his warm embrace, the Dews,
That all night long had wept his absence, flew.
The herbs and flowers their fragrant stores unlocked,
And gave the wanton breeze that, newly woke,
Revelled in sweets, and from its wings shook health,
A thousand grateful smells; the joyous woods
Dried in his beams their locks, wet with the drops
Of night; and all the sons of music sung
Their matin song—from arboured bower, the thrush,
Concerting with the lark that hymned on high.
On the green hill the flocks, and in the vale
The herds, rejoiced; and, light of heart, the hind
Eyed amorously the milk-maid as she passed,
Not heedless, though she looked another way.
No sign was there of change. All nature moved
In wonted harmony. Men, as they met,
In morning salutation, praised the day,
And talked of common things. The husbandman
Prepared the soil, and silver-tongued Hope
Promised another harvest. In the streets,
Each wishing to make profit of his neighbour,
Merchants, assembling, spoke of trying times,
Of bankruptcies, and markets glutted full;
Or, crowding to the beach, where, to their ear,
The oath of foreign accent, and the noise
Uncouth of trade's rough sons, made music sweet,
Elate with certain gain,—beheld the bark,
Expected long, enriched with other climes,
Into the harbour safely steer; or saw,
Parting with many a weeping farewell sad,
And blessing uttered rude, and sacred pledge,
The rich laden carack, bound to distant shore,
And hopefully talked of her coming back,
With richer fraught; or sitting at the desk,
In calculation deep and intricate
Of loss and profit balancing, relieved,
At intervals, the irksome task, with thought
Of future ease, retired in villa snug.
With subtle look, amid his parchments, sat
The lawyer, weaving his sophistries for court
To meet at mid-day. On his weary couch,
Fat Luxury, sick of the night's debauch,
Lay groaning, fretful at the obtrusive beam.

That through his lattice peeped derisively.
The restless miser had begun again
To count his heaps. Before her toilet stood
The fair, and, as with guileful skill she decked
Her loveliness, thought of the coming ball,
New lovers, or the sweeter nuptial night.
And evil men, of desperate, lawless life,
By oath of deep damnation leagued to ill
Remorselessly, fled from the face of day,
Against the innocent their counsel held,
Plotting unpardonable deeds of blood,
And villanies of fearful magnitude.
Despots, secure behind a thousand bolts
The workmanship of fear, forged chains for man.
Senates were meeting, statesmen loudly talked
Of national resources, war and peace,
And sagely balanced empires soon to end;
And faction's jaded minions, by the page
Paid for abuse and oft-repeated lies,
In daily prints, the thorough-fare of news,
For party schemes made interest, under cloak
Of liberty, and right, and public weal.
In holy conclave, bishops spoke of tithes,
And of the awful wickedness of men.
Intoxicate with sceptres, diadems,
And universal rule, and panting hard
For fame, heroes were leading on the brave
To battle. Men, in science deeply read,
And academic theory, foretold
Improvements vast; and learned sceptics proved
That earth should with eternity endure—
Concluding madly, that there was no God.
  No sign of change appeared: to every man
That day seemed as the past. From noontide path
The sun looked gloriously on earth, and all
Her scenes of giddy folly smiled secure,
When suddenly, alas, fair Earth! the sun
Was wrapped in darkness, and his beams returned
Up to the throne of God, and over all
The earth came night, moonless and starless night.
Nature stood still. The seas and rivers stood,
And all the winds, and every living thing.
The cataract, that, like a giant wroth,
Rushed down impetuously, as seized, at once,
By sudden frost, with all his hoary locks,
Stood still; and beasts of every kind stood still.
A deep and dreadful silence reigned alone!
Hope died in every breast, and on all men
Came fear and trembling. None to his neighbour spoke.
Husband thought not of wife, nor of her child
The mother, nor friend of friend, nor foe of foe.
In horrible suspense all mortals stood;
And, as they stood and listened, chariots were heard,
Rolling in heaven. Revealed in flaming fire,
The angel of God appeared in stature vast,
Blazing, and lifting up his hand on high,
By him that lives for ever, swore, that Time
Should be no more. Throughout, creation heard
And sighed; all rivers, lakes, and seas, and woods,
Desponding waste, and cultivated vale,
Wild cave, and ancient hill, and every rock,
Sighed. Earth, arrested in her wonted path,
As ox struck by the lifted axe, when nought
Was feared, in all her entrails deeply groaned.
A universal crash was heard, as if
The ribs of Nature broke, and all her dark
Foundations failed; and deadly paleness sat
On every face of man, and every heart
Grew chill, and every knee his fellow smote.
None spoke, none stirred, none wept; for horror held
All motionless, and fettered every tongue.
Again, o'er all the nations silence fell:
And, in the heavens, robed in excessive light,
That drove the thick of darkness far aside,
And walked with penetration keen, through all
The abodes of men, another angel stood,
And blew the trump of God: Awake, ye dead,
Be changed, ye living, and put on the garb
Of immortality. Awake, arise!—
The God of judgment comes! This said the voice,
And Silence, from eternity that slept
Beyond the sphere of the creating Word,
And all the noise of Time, awakened heard.
Heaven heard, and earth, and farthest hell, through all
Her regions of despair; the ear of Death
Heard, and the sleep that for so long a night
Pressed on his leaden eyelids, fled; and all
The dead awoke, and all the living changed.
  Old men, that on their staff, bending, had leaned,
Crazy and frail, or sat, benumbed with age,
In weary listlessness, ripe for the grave,
Felt through their sluggish veins and withered limbs
New vigour flow; the wrinkled face grew smooth;
Upon the head, that Time had razored bare,
Rose bushy locks; and as his son in prime
Of strength and youth, the aged father stood.
Changing herself, the mother saw her son
Grow up, and suddenly put on the form
Of manhood; and the wretch, that begging sat,
Limbless, deformed, at corner of the way,
Unmindful of his crutch, in joint and limb,
Arose complete; and he, that on the bed
Of mortal sickness, worn with sore distress,
Lay breathing forth his soul to death, felt now
The tide of life and vigour rushing back;
And, looking up, beheld his weeping wife,
And daughter fond, that o'er him, bending, stooped
To close his eyes. The frantic madman, too,
In whose confused brain reason had lost
Her way, long driven at random to and fro,
Grew sober, and his manacles fell off.
The newly-sheeted corpse arose, and stared
On those who dressed it; and the coffined dead,

That men were bearing to the tomb, awoke,
And mingled with their friends; and armies, which
The trump surprised, met in the furious shock
Of battle, saw the bleeding ranks, new fallen,
Rise up at once, and to their ghastly cheeks
Return the stream of life in healthy flow;
And as the anatomist, with all his band
Of rude disciples, o'er the subject hung,
And impolitely hewed his way, through bones
And muscles of the sacred human form,
Exposing barbarously to wanton gaze,
The mysteries of nature, joint embraced
His kindred joint, the wounded flesh grew up,
And suddenly the injured man awoke,
Among their hands, and stood arrayed complete
In immortality—forgiving scarce
The insult offered to his clay in death.
That was the hour, long wished for by the good,
Of universal Jubilee to all
The sons of bondage: from the oppressor's hand
The scourge of violence fell, and from his back,
Healed of its stripes, the burden of the slave.
The youth of great religious soul, who sat
Retired in voluntary loneliness,
In reverie extravagant now wrapped,
Or poring now on book of ancient date,
With filial awe, and dipping oft his pen
To write immortal things; to pleasure deaf,
And joys of common men, working his way
With mighty energy, not uninspired,
Through all the mines of thought; reckless of pain,
And weariness, and wasted health, the scoff
Of Pride, or growl of Envy's hellish brood;
While Fancy, voyaged far beyond the bounds
Of years revealed, heard many a future age,
With commendation loud, repeat his name,—
False prophetess! the day of change was come,—
Behind the shadow of eternity,
He saw his visions set of earthly fame,
For ever set; nor sighed, while through his veins,
In lighter current, ran immortal life;
His form renewed to undecaying health;
To undecaying health, his soul, erewhile
Not tuned amiss to God's eternal praise.
All men in field and city, by the way,
On land or sea, lolling in gorgeous hall,
Or plying at the oar; crawling in rags
Obscure, or dazzling in embroidered gold,
Alone, in companies, at home, abroad;
In wanton merriment surprised and taken,
Or kneeling reverently in act of prayer;
Or cursing recklessly, or uttering lies;
Or lapping greedily, from slander's cup,
The blood of reputation; or between
Friendships and brotherhoods devising strife;
Or plotting to defile a neighbour's bed;
In duel met with dagger of revenge;
Or casting, on the widow's heritage,
The eye of covetousness; or, with full hand,
On mercy's noiseless errands, unobserved,
Administering; or meditating fraud
And deeds of horrid barbarous intent;
In full pursuit of unexperienced hope,
Fluttering along the flowery path of youth;
Or steeped in disappointment's bitterness,
The fevered cup that guilt must ever drink,
When parched and fainting on the road of ill;
Beggar and king, the clown and haughty lord;
The venerable sage, and empty fop;
The ancient matron, and the rosy bride;
The virgin chaste, and shriveled harlot vile;
The savage fierce, and man of science, mild;
The good and evil, in a moment, all
Were changed, corruptible to incorrupt,
And mortal to immortal, ne'er to change.
And now, descending from the bowers of heaven,
Soft airs o'er all the earth, spreading, were heard,
And Hallelujahs sweet, the harmony
Of righteous souls that came to repossess
Their long-neglected bodies; and anon
Upon the ear fell horribly the sound
Of cursing, and the yells of damned despair,
Uttered by felon spirits, that the trump
Had summoned from the burning glooms of hell
To put their bodies on, reserved for wo.
Now, starting up among the living changed,
Appeared innumerous the risen dead.
Each particle of dust was claimed: the turf,
For ages trod beneath the careless foot
Of men, rose, organized in human form;
The monumental stones were rolled away;
The doors of death were opened; and in the dark
And loathsome vault, and silent charnel house,
Moving, were heard the mouldered bones that sought
Their proper place. Instinctive, every soul
Flew to its clayey part: from grass-grown mould,
The nameless spirit took its ashes up,
Reanimate; and, merging from beneath
The flattered marble, undistinguished rose
The great, nor heeded once the lavish rhyme,
And costly pomp of sculptured garnish vain.
The Memphian mummy, that from age to age,
Descending, bought and sold a thousand times,
In hall of curious antiquary stowed,
Wrapped in mysterious weeds, the wondrous theme
Of many an erring tale, shook off its rags;
And the brown son of Egypt stood beside
The European, his last purchaser.
In vale remote, the hermit rose, surprised
At crowds that rose around him, where he thought
His slumbers had been single; and the bard,
Who fondly covenanted with his friend,
To lay his bones beneath the sighing bough
Of some old lonely tree, rising, was pressed
By multitudes that claimed their proper dust
From the same spot; and he, that, richly hearsed,

With gloomy garniture of purchased wo,
Embalmed, in princely sepulchre was laid,
Apart from vulgar men, built nicely round
And round by the proud heir, who blushed to think
His father's lordly clay should ever mix
With peasant dust,—saw by his side awake
The clown that long had slumbered in his arms.
The family tomb, to whose devouring mouth
Descended sire and son, age after age,
In long, unbroken, hereditary line,
Poured forth, at once, the ancient father rude,
And all his offspring of a thousand years.
Refreshed from sweet repose, awoke the man
Of charitable life—awoke and sung:
And from his prison house, slowly and sad,
As if unsatisfied with holding near
Communion with the earth, the miser drew
His carcass forth, and gnashed his teeth, and howled
Unsolaced by his gold and silver then.
From simple stone in lonely wilderness,
That hoary lay, o'er-lettered by the hand
Of oft-frequenting pilgrim, who had taught
The willow tree to weep, at morn and even,
Over the sacred spot,—the martyr saint,
To song of seraph harp, triumphant, rose,
Well pleased that he had suffered to the death.
"The cloud-clapped towers, the gorgeous palaces,"
As sung the bard by Nature's hand anointed,
In whose capacious giant numbers rolled
The passions of old Time, fell lumbering down.
All cities fell, and every work of man,
And gave their portion forth of human dust,
Touched by the mortal finger of decay.
Tree, herb, and flower, and every fowl of heaven,
And fish, and animal, the wild and tame,
Forthwith dissolving, crumbled into dust.
Alas! ye sons of strength, ye ancient oaks,
Ye holy pines, ye elms, and cedars tall,
Like towers of God, far seen on Carmel mount,
Or Lebanon, that waved your boughs on high,
And laughed at all the winds,—your hour was come!
Ye laurels, ever green, and bays, that wont
To wreath the patriot and the poet's brow;
Ye myrtle bowers, and groves of sacred shade,
Where music ever sung, and Zephyr fanned
His airy wing, wet with the dews of life,
And Spring for ever smiled, the fragrant haunt
Of Love, and Health, and ever-dancing Mirth,—
Alas! how suddenly your verdure died,
And ceased your minstrelsy, to sing no more!
Ye flowers of beauty, penciled by the hand
Of God, who annually renewed your birth,
To gem the virgin robes of Nature chaste,
Ye smiling-featured daughters of the Sun!
Fairer than queenly bride, by Jordan's stream
Leading your gentle lives, retired, unseen;
Or on the sainted cliffs on Zion hill
Wandering, and holding with the heavenly dews,
In holy revelry, your nightly loves,
Watched by the stars, and offering, every morn,
Your incense grateful both to God and man;—
Ye lovely gentle things, alas! no spring
Shall ever wake you now! ye withered all,
All in a moment drooped, and on your roots
The grasp of everlasting winter seized!
Children of song, ye birds that dwelt in air,
And stole your notes from angels' lyres, and first
In levee of the morn, with eulogy
Ascending, hailed the advent of the dawn;
Or, roosted on the pensive evening bough,
In melancholy numbers, sung the day
To rest;—your little wings, failing, dissolved,
In middle air, and on your harmony
Perpetual silence fell! Nor did his wing,
That sailed in track of gods sublime, and fanned
The sun, avail the eagle then; quick smitten,
His plumage withered in meridian height,
And, in the valley, sunk the lordly bird,
A clod of clay. Before the ploughman fell
His steers, and in midway the furrow left.
The shepherd saw his flocks around him turn
To dust. Beneath his rider fell the steed
To ruins: and the lion in his den
Grew cold and stiff, or in the furious chase,
With timid fawn, that scarcely missed his paw:
On earth no living thing was seen but men,
New-changed, or rising from the opening tomb.
Athens, and Rome, and Babylon, and Tyre,
And she that sat on Thames, queen of the seas,
Cities once famed on earth, convulsed through all
Their mighty ruins, threw their millions forth.
Palmyra's dead, where Desolation sat,
From age to age, well pleased in solitude,
And silence, save when traveller's foot, or owl
Of night, or fragment mouldering down to dust,
Broke faintly on his desert ear,—awoke.
And Salem, holy city, where the Prince
Of Life, by death, a second life secured
To man, and with him, from the grave, redeemed,
A chosen number brought, to retinue
His great ascent on high, and give sure pledge,
That death was foiled,—her generations now,
Gave up, of kings and priests, and Pharisees:
Nor even the Sadducee, who fondly said,
No morn of resurrection e'er should come,
Could sit the summons; to his ear did reach
The trumpet's voice, and, ill prepared for what
He oft had proved should never be, he rose
Reluctantly, and on his face began
To burn eternal shame. The cities, too,
Of old ensepulchred beneath the flood,
Or deeply slumbering under mountains huge,
That Earthquake, servant of the wrath of God,
Had on their wicked population thrown;
And marts of busy trade, long ploughed and sown,

By history unrecorded, or the song
Of bard, yet not forgotten their wickedness,
In heaven;—poured forth their ancient multitudes,
That vainly wished their sleep had never broke.
From battle-fields, where men by millions met
To murder each his fellow, and make sport
To kings and heroes, things long since forgot,
Innumerous armies rose, unbannered all,
Unpanoplied, unpraised; nor found a prince,
Or general then, to answer for their crimes.
The hero's slaves, and all the scarlet troops
Of antichrist, and all that fought for rule,—
Many high-sounding names, familiar once
On earth, and praised exceedingly, but now
Familiar most in hell, their dungeon fit,
Where they may war eternally with God's
Almighty thunderbolts, and win them pangs
Of keener wo,—saw, as they sprung to life,
The widow and the orphan ready stand,
And helpless virgin, ravished in their sport,
To plead against them at the coming Doom.
The Roman legions, boasting once, how loud!
Of liberty, and fighting bravely o'er
The torrid and the frigid zone, the sands
Of burning Egypt, and the frozen hills
Of snowy Albion, to make mankind
Their thralls, untaught that he who made or kept
A slave could ne'er himself be truly free,—
That morning, gathered up their dust, which lay
Wide-scattered over half the globe; nor saw
Their eagled banners then. Sennacherib's hosts,
Embattled once against the sons of God,
With insult bold, quick as the noise of mirth
And revelry, sunk in their drunken camp,
When death's dark angel, at the dead of night,
Their vitals touched, and made each pulse stand
still,—
Awoke in sorrow; and the multitudes
Of Gog, and all the fated crew that warred
Against the chosen saints in the last days,
At Armageddon, when the Lord came down,
Mustering his host on Israel's holy hills,
And, from the treasures of his snow and hail,
Rained terror, and confusion rained, and death,
And gave to all the beasts, and fowls of heaven,
Of captains' flesh, and blood of men of war,
A feast of many days,—revived, and, doomed
To second death, stood in Hamonah's vale.
Nor yet did all that fell in battle rise,
That day, to wailing. Here and there were seen
The patriot bands that from his guilty throne
The despot tore, unshackled nations, made
The prince respect the people's laws, drove back
The wave of proud invasion, and rebuked
The frantic fury of the multitude,
Rebelled, and fought and fell for liberty
Right understood, true heroes in the speech
Of heaven, where words express the thoughts of
him
Who speaks; not undistinguished these, though
few,
That morn, arose, with joy and melody.
All woke—the north and south gave up their
dead.
The caravan, that in mid-journey sunk,
With all its merchandise, expected long,
And long forgot, ingulfed beneath the tide
Of death, that the wild Spirit of the winds
Swept, in his wrath, along the wilderness,
In the wide desert,—woke, and saw all calm
Around, and populous with risen men:
Nor of his relics thought the pilgrim then,
Nor merchant of his silks and spiceries.
And he, far voyaging from home and friends,
Too curious, with a mortal eye to peep
Into the secrets of the Pole, forbid
By nature, whom fierce Winter seized, and froze
To death, and wrapped in winding sheet of ice,
And sung the requiem of his shivering ghost,
With the loud organ of his mighty winds,
And on his memory threw the snow of ages,
Felt the long-absent warmth of life return,
And shook the frozen mountain from his bed.
All rose, of every age, of every clime.
Adam and Eve, the great progenitors
Of all mankind, fair as they seemed, that morn,
When first they met in Paradise, unfallen,
Uncursed,—from ancient slumber broke, where
once
Euphrates rolled his stream; and by them stood,
In stature equal, and in soul as large,
Their last posterity, though poets sung,
And sages proved them far degenerate.
Blessed sight! not unobserved by angels, nor
Unpraised,—that day, 'mong men of every tribe
And hue, from those who drank of Tenglio's stream,
To those who nightly saw the Hermit Cross,
In utmost south retired,—rising, were seen
The fair and ruddy sons of Albion's land,
How glad!—not those who travelled far and sailed,
To purchase human flesh, or wreath the yoke
Of vassalage on savage liberty,
Or suck large fortune from the sweat of slaves·
Or, with refined knavery, to cheat,
Politely villanous, untutored men
Out of their property; or gather shells,
Intaglios rude, old pottery, and store
Of mutilated gods of stone, and scraps
Of barbarous epitaphs defaced, to be
Among the learned the theme of warm debate,
And infinite conjecture, sagely wrong!—
But those, denied to self, to earthly fame
Denied, and earthly wealth; who kindred left,
And home, and ease, and all the cultured joys,
Conveniences, and delicate delights,
Of ripe society; in the great cause
Of man's salvation, greatly valorous,—
The warriors of Messiah, messengers

Of peace, and light, and life, whose eye, unscaled,
Saw up the path of immortality,
Far into bliss, saw men, immortal men,
Wide wandering from the way; eclipsed in night,
Dark, moonless, moral night; living like beasts,
Like beasts descending to the grave, untaught
Of life to come, unsanctified, unsaved;
Who, strong, though seeming weak; who, war-like, though
Unarmed with bow and sword; appearing mad,
Though sounder than the schools alone e'er made
The doctor's head; devote to God and truth,
And sworn to man's eternal weal, beyond
Repentance sworn, or thought of turning back;
And casting far behind all earthly care,
All countryships, all national regards,
And enmities, all narrow bourns of state
And selfish policy; beneath their feet
Treading all fear of opposition down,
All fear of danger, of reproach all fear,
And evil tongues;—went forth, from Britain went
A noiseless band of heavenly soldiery,
From out the armoury of God equipped,
Invincible, to conquer sin, to blow
The trump of freedom in the despot's ear,
To tell the bruted slave his manhood high,
His birthright liberty, and in his hand
To put the writ of manumission, signed
By God's own signature; to drive away
From earth the dark, infernal legionary
Of superstition, ignorance, and hell;
High on the pagan hills, where Satan sat,
Encamped, and o'er the subject kingdoms threw
Perpetual night, to plant Immanuel's cross,
The ensign of the Gospel, blazing round
Immortal truth; and, in the wilderness
Of human waste, to sow eternal life;
And from the rock, where Sin, with horrid yell,
Devoured its victims unredeemed, to raise
The melody of grateful hearts to Heaven:
To falsehood, truth; to pride, humility;
To insult, meekness; pardon, to revenge;
To stubborn prejudice, unwearied zeal;
To censure, unaccusing minds; to stripes,
Long suffering; to want of all things, hope;
To death, assured faith of life to come;—
Opposing. These, great worthies, rising, shone
Through all the tribes and nations of mankind,
Like Hesper, glorious once among the stars
Of twilight, and around them, flocking, stood,
Arrayed in white, the people they had saved.
Great Ocean! too, that morning, thou the call
Of restitution heardst, and reverently
To the last trumpet's voice, in silence, listened.
Great Ocean! strongest of creation's sons,
Unconquerable, unreposed, untired,
That rolled the wild, profound, eternal bass,
In Nature's anthem, and made music, such
As pleased the ear of God! original,
Unmarred, unfaded work of Deity,
And unburlesqued by mortal's puny skill,
From age to age enduring and unchanged,
Majestical, inimitable, vast,
Loud uttering satire, day and night, on each
Succeeding race, and little pompous work
Of man!—unfallen, religious, holy Sea!
Thou bowedst thy glorious head to none, fearedst none,
Heardst none, to none didst honour, but to God
Thy Maker, only worthy to receive
Thy great obeisance! Undiscovered Sea!
Into thy dark, unknown, mysterious caves,
And secret haunts, unfathomably deep,
Beneath all visible retired, none went,
And came again, to tell the wonders there.
Tremendous Sea! what time thou lifted up
Thy waves on high, and with thy winds and storms
Strange pastime took, and shook thy mighty sides
Indignantly,—the pride of navies fell;
Beyond the arm of help, unheard, unseen,
Sunk friend and foe, with all their wealth and war;
And on thy shores, men of a thousand tribes,
Polite and barbarous, trembling stood, amazed,
Confounded, terrified, and thought vast thoughts
Of ruin, boundlessness, omnipotence,
Infinitude, eternity; and thought
And wondered still, and grasped, and grasped, and grasped
Again; beyond her reach, exerting all
The soul, to take thy great idea in,
To comprehend incomprehensible;
And wondered more, and felt their littleness
Self-purifying, unpolluted Sea!
Lover unchangeable, thy faithful breast
For ever heaving to the lovely Moon,
That, like a shy and holy virgin, robed
In saintly white, walked nightly in the heavens,
And to the everlasting serenade
Gave gracious audience; nor was wooed in vain.
That morning, thou, that slumbered not before,
Nor slept, great Ocean! laid thy waves to rest,
And hushed thy mighty minstrelsy. No breath
Thy deep composure stirred, no fin, no oar;
Like beauty newly dead, so calm, so still,
So lovely, thou, beneath the light that fell
From angel-chariots, sentineled on high,
Reposed, and listened, and saw thy living change,
Thy dead arise. Charybdis listened, and Scylla;
And savage Euxine, on the Thracian beach,
Lay motionless: and every battle-ship
Stood still, and every ship of merchandise,
And all that sailed, of every name, stood still.
Even as the ship of war, full-fledged, and swift,
Like some fierce bird of prey, bore on her foe,
Opposing with as fell intent, the wind
Fell withered from her wings that idly hung;
The stormy bullet, by the cannon thrown
Uncivilly against the heavenly face

Of men, half sped, sunk harmlessly, and all
Her loud, uncircumcised, tempestuous crew,
How ill prepared to meet their God! were changed,
Unchangeable—the pilot at the helm
Was changed, and the rough captain, while he mouthed
The huge, enormous oath. The fisherman,
That in his boat, expectant, watched his lines,
Or mended on the shore his net, and sung,
Happy in thoughtlessness, some careless air,
Heard Time depart, and felt the sudden change.
In solitary deep, far out from land,
Or steering from the port with many a cheer,
Or while returning from long voyage, fraught
With lusty wealth, rejoicing to have escaped
The dangerous main, and plagues of foreign climes,—
The merchant quaffed his native air, refreshed;
And saw his native hills, in the sun's light,
Serenely rise; and thought of meetings glad,
And many days of ease and honour, spent
Among his friends—unwarned man! even then,
The knell of Time broke on his reverie,
And, in the twinkling of an eye, his hopes,
All earthly, perished all. As sudden rose,
From out their watery beds, the Ocean's dead,
Renewed; and, on the unstirring billows, stood,
From pole to pole, thick covering all the sea—
Of every nation blent, and every age.
Wherever slept one grain of human dust,
Essential organ of a human soul,
Wherever tossed, obedient to the call
Of God's omnipotence, it hurried on
To meet its fellow particles, revived,
Rebuilt, in union indestructible.
No atom of his spoils remained to Death.
From his strong arm, by stronger arm released,
Immortal now in soul and body both,
Beyond his reach, stood all the sons of men,
And saw, behind, his valley lie, unfeared.
O Death! with what an eye of desperate lust,
From out thy emptied vaults, thou then didst look
After the risen multitudes of all
Mankind! Ah! thou hadst been the terror long,
And murderer, of all of woman born.
None could escape thee! In thy dungeon house,
Where darkness dwelt, and putrid loathsomeness,
And fearful silence, villanously still
And all of horrible and deadly name,—
Thou satst, from age to age, insatiate,
And drank the blood of men, and gorged their flesh,
And with thy iron teeth didst grind their bones
To powder, treading out, beneath thy feet,
Their very names and memories. The blood
Of nations could not slake thy parched throat.
No bribe could buy thy favour for an hour,
Or mitigate thy ever-cruel rage
For human prey. Gold, beauty, virtue, youth,

Even helpless, swaddled innocency, failed
To soften thy heart of stone! the infant's blood
Pleased well thy taste, and, while the mother wept,
Bereaved by thee, lonely and waste in wo,
Thy ever-grinding jaws devoured her too.
Each son of Adam's family beheld,
Where'er he turned, whatever path of life
He trode, thy goblin form before him stand,
Like trusty old assassin, in his aim
Steady and sure as eye of destiny,
With sithe, and dart, and strength invincible,
Equipped, and ever menacing his life.
He turned aside, he drowned himself in sleep,
In wine, in pleasure; travelled, voyaged, sought
Receipts for health from all he met; betook
To business, speculate, retired; returned
Again to active life, again retired;
Returned, retired again; prepared to die,
Talked of thy nothingness, conversed of life
To come, laughed at his fears, filled up the cup,
Drank deep, refrained; filled up, refrained again;
Planned, built him round with splendour, won applause,
Made large alliances with men and things,
Read deep in science and philosophy,
To fortify his soul; heard lectures prove
The present ill, and future good; observed
His pulse beat regular, extended hope;
Thought, dissipated thought, and thought again;
Indulged, abstained, and tried a thousand schemes,
To ward thy blow, or hide thee from his eye;
But still thy gloomy terrors, dipped in sin,
Before him frowned, and withered all his joy.
Still, feared and hated thing! thy ghostly shape
Stood in his avenues of fairest hope;
Unmannerly and uninvited, crept
Into his haunts of most select delight.
Still, on his halls of mirth, and banqueting,
And revelry, thy shadowy hand was seen
Writing thy name of—Death. Vile worm, that gnawed
The root of all his happiness terrene, the gall
Of all his sweet, the thorn of every rose
Of earthly bloom, cloud of his noon-day sky,
Frost of his spring, sigh of his loudest laugh,
Dark spot on every form of loveliness,
Rank smell amidst his rarest spiceries,
Harsh dissonance of all his harmony,
Reserve of every promise, and the if
Of all to-morrows!—now, beyond thy vale,
Stood all the ransomed multitude of men,
Immortal all: and, in their visions, saw
Thy visage grim no more. Great payment day!
Of all thou ever conquered, none was left
In thy unpeopled realms, so populous once.
He, at whose girdle hang the keys of death
And life, not bought but with the blood of Him
Who wears, the eternal Son of God, that morn,
Dispelled the cloud that sat so long, so thick,

So heavy o'er thy vale; opened all thy doors,
Unopened before; and set thy prisoners free.
Vain was resistance, and to follow vain.
In thy unveiled caves, and solitudes
Of dark and dismal emptiness, thou satst,
Rolling thy hollow eyes, disabled thing!
Helpless, despised, unpitied, and unfeared,
Like some fallen tyrant, chained in sight of all
The people; from thee dropped thy pointless dart,
Thy terrors withered all, thy ministers,
Annihilated, fell before thy face,
And on thy maw eternal Hunger seized.
Nor yet, sad monster! wast thou left alone.
In thy dark den some phantoms still remained,—
Ambition, Vanity, and earthly Fame,
Swollen Ostentation, meagre Avarice,
Mad Superstition, smooth Hypocrisy,
And Bigotry intolerant, and Fraud,
And wilful Ignorance, and sullen Pride,
Hot Controversy, and the subtle ghost
Of vain Philosophy, and worldly Hope,
And sweet-lipped, hollow-hearted Flattery.
All these, great personages once on earth,
And not unfollowed, nor unpraised, were left,
Thy ever-unredeemed, and with thee driven
To Erebus, through whose uncheered wastes,
Thou mayest chase them, with thy broken sithe
Fetching vain strokes, to all eternity,
Unsatisfied, as men who, in the days
Of Time, their unsubstantial forms pursued.

BOOK VIII.

Reanimated, now, and dressed in robes
Of everlasting wear, in the last pause
Of expectation, stood the human race,
Buoyant in air, or covering shore and sea,
From east to west, thick as the eared grain,
In golden autumn waved, from field to field,
Profuse, by Nilus' fertile wave, while yet
Earth was, and men were in her valleys seen.
Still, all was calm in heaven. Nor yet appeared
The Judge, nor aught appeared, save here and there
On wing of golden plumage borne at will,
A curious angel, that from out the skies
Now glanced a look on man, and then retired.
As calm was all on earth. The ministers
Of God's unsparing vengeance, waited, still
Unbid. No sun, no moon, no star, gave light.
A blessed and holy radiance, travelled far
From day original, fell on the face
Of men, and every countenance revealed;
Unpleasant to the bad, whose visages
Had lost all guise of seeming happiness,
With which on earth such pains they took to hide
Their misery in. On their grim features, now
The plain, unvisored index of the soul,
The true, untampered witness of the heart,
No smile of hope, no look of vanity
Beseeching for applause, was seen; no scowl
Of self-important, all-despising pride,
That once upon the poor and needy fell,
Like winter on the unprotected flower,
Withering their very being to decay.
No jesting mirth, no wanton leer, was seen,
No sullen lower of braggart fortitude
Defying pain, nor anger, nor revenge;
But fear instead, and terror, and remorse;
And chief, one passion, to its answering, shaped
The features of the damned, and in itself
Summed all the rest,—unutterable despair.
What on the righteous shone of foreign light,
Was all redundant day, they needed not.
For as, by Nature, Sin is dark, and loves
The dark, still hiding from itself in gloom,
And in the darkest hell is still itself
The darkest hell, and the severest wo,
Where all is wo; so Virtue, ever fair!
Doth by a sympathy as strong as binds
Two equal hearts, well pleased in wedded love,
For ever seek the light, for ever seek
All fair and lovely things, all beauteous forms,
All images of excellence and truth;
And from her own essential being, pure
As flows the fount of life that spirits drink,
Doth to herself give light, nor from her beams,
As native to her as her own existence,
Can be divorced, nor of her glory shorn,—
Which now, from every feature of the just,
Divinely rayed, yet not from all alike;
In measure, equal to the soul's advance
In virtue, was the lustre of the face.
It was a strange assembly: none, of all
That congregation vast, could recollect
Aught like it in the history of man.
No badge of outward state was seen, no mark
Of age, or rank, or national attire,
Or robe professional, or air of trade.
Untitled, stood the man that once was called
My lord, unserved, unfollowed; and the man
Of tithes, right reverend in the dialect
Of Time addressed, ungowned, unbeneficed,
Uncorpulent; nor now, from him who bore,
With ceremonious gravity of step,
And face of borrowed holiness o'erlaid,
The ponderous book before the awful priest,
And opened and shut the pulpit's sacred gates
In style of wonderful observancy
And reverence excessive, in the beams
Of sacerdotal splendour lost, or if
Observed, comparison ridiculous scarce
Could save the little, pompous, humble man
From laughter of the people,—not from him
Could be distinguished then the priest untithed.
None levees held, those marts where princely smiles

Were sold for flattery, and obeisance mean,
Unfit from man to man; none came or went,
None wished to draw attention, none was poor,
None rich, none young, none old, deformed none;
None sought for place or favour, none had aught
To give, none could receive, none ruled, none served
No king, no subject was; unscutcheoned all,
Uncrowned, unplumed, unhelmed, unpedigreed,
Unlaced, uncoroneted, unbestarred.
Nor countryman was seen, nor citizen;
Republican, nor humble advocate
Of monarchy; nor idol worshipper,
Nor beaded papist, nor Mahometan;
Episcopalian none, nor presbyter;
Nor Lutheran, nor Calvinist, nor Jew.
Nor Greek, nor sectary of any name.
Nor, of those persons, that loud title bore,
Most high and mighty, most magnificent,
Most potent, most august, most worshipful,
Most eminent, words of great pomp, that pleased
The ear of vanity, and made the worms
Of earth mistake themselves for gods,—could one
Be seen, to claim these phrases obsolete.
It was a congregation vast of men,
Of unappendaged and unvarnished men,
Of plain, unceremonious human beings,
Of all but moral character bereaved.
His vice or virtue, now, to each remained,
Alone. All else, with their grave clothes, men had
Put off, as badges worn by mortal, not
Immortal man; alloy that could not pass
The scrutiny of Death's refining fires;
Dust of Time's wheels, by multitudes pursued
Of fools that shouted—Gold! fair painted fruit,
At which the ambitious idiot jumped, while men
Of wiser mood immortal harvests reaped;
Weeds of the human garden, sprung from earth's
Adulterate soil, unfit to be transplanted,
Though by the moral botanist, too oft,
For plants of heavenly seed mistaken and nursed;
Mere chaff, that Virtue, when she rose from earth
And waved her wings to gain her native heights,
Drove from the verge of being, leaving Vice
No mask to hide her in; base-born of Time,
In which God claimed no property, nor had
Prepared for them a place in heaven or hell.
Yet did these vain distinctions, now forgot,
Bulk largely in the filmy eye of Time,
And were exceeding fair, and lured to death
Immortal souls. But they were passed, for all
Ideal now was passed; reality
Alone remained; and good and bad, redeemed
And unredeemed, distinguished sole the sons
Of men. Each, to his proper self reduced,
And undisguised, was what his seeming showed.
The man of earthly fame, whom common men
Made boast of having seen, who scarce could pass
The ways of Time, for eager crowds that pressed
To do him homage, and pursued his car
With endless praise, for deeds unpraised above,
And yoked their brutal natures, honoured much
To drag his chariot on,—unnoticed stood,
With none to praise him, none to flatter there.
Blushing and dumb, that morning, too, was seen
The mighty reasoner, he who deeply searched
The origin of things, and talked of good
And evil, much, of causes and effects,
Of mind and matter, contradicting all
That went before him, and himself, the while,
The laughing-stock of angels; diving far
Below his depth, to fetch reluctant proof,
That he himself was mad and wicked too,
When, proud and ignorant man, he meant to prove
That God had made the universe amiss,
And sketched a better plan. Ah! foolish sage!
He could not trust the word of Heaven, nor see
The light which from the Bible blazed,—that lamp
Which God threw from his palace down to earth,
To guide his wandering children home,—yet leaned
His cautious faith on speculations wild,
And visionary theories absurd,
Prodigiously, deliriously absurd,
Compared with which, the most erroneous flight
That poet ever took when warm with wine,
Was moderate conjecturing, he saw,
Weighed in the balance of eternity,
His lore how light, and wished, too late, that he
Had staid at home, and learned to know himself,
And done, what peasants did, disputed less,
And more obeyed. Nor less he grieved his time
Misspent, the man of curious research,
Who travelled far through lands of hostile clime
And dangerous inhabitant, to fix
The bounds of empires passed, and ascertain
The burial-place of heroes, never born;
Despising present things, and future too,
And groping in the dark unsearchable
Of finished years,—by dreary ruins seen,
And dungeons damp, and vaults of ancient waste,
With spade and mattock, delving deep to raise
Old vases and dismembered idols rude;
With matchless perseverance, spelling out
Words without sense. Poor man! he clapped his hands,
Enraptured, when he found a manuscript
That spoke of pagan gods; and yet forgot
The God who made the sea and sky, alas!
Forgot that trifling was a sin; stored much
Of dubious stuff, but laid no treasure up
In heaven; on mouldered columns scratched his name,
But ne'er inscribed it in the book of life.
Unprofitable seemed, and unapproved,

That day, the sullen, self-vindictive life
Of the recluse. With crucifixes hung,
And spells, and rosaries, and wooden saints,
Like one of reason reft, he journeyed forth,
In show of miserable poverty,
And chose to beg,—as if to live on sweat
Of other men, had promised great reward;
On his own flesh inflicted cruel wounds,
With naked foot embraced the ice, by the hour
Said mass, and did most grievous penance vile;
And then retired to drink the filthy cup
Of secret wickedness, and fabricate
All lying wonders, by the untaught received
For revelations new. Deluded wretch!
Did he not know, that the most Holy One
Required a cheerful life and holy heart?
  Most disappointed in that crowd of men,
The man of subtle controversy stood,
The bigot theologian, in minute
Distinctions skilled, and doctrines unreduced
To practice; in debate how loud! how long!
How dexterous! in Christian love how cold!
His vain conceits were orthodox alone.
The immutable and heavenly truth, revealed
By God, was nought to him. He had an art,
A kind of hellish charm, that made the lips
Of truth speak falsehood, to his liking turned
The meaning of the text, made trifles seem
The marrow of salvation; to a word,
A name, a sect, that sounded in the ear,
And to the eye so many letters showed,
But did no more,—gave value infinite;
Proved still his reasoning best, and his belief,
Though propped on fancies wild as madmen's dreams,
Most rational, most scriptural, most sound;
With mortal heresy denouncing all
Who in his arguments could see no force.
On points of faith, too fine for human sight,
And never understood in heaven, he placed
His everlasting hope, undoubting placed,
And died; and, when he opened his ear, prepared
To hear, beyond the grave, the minstrelsy
Of bliss, he heard, alas! the wail of wo.
He proved all creeds false but his own, and found
At last, his own most false—most false, because
He spent his time to prove all others so.
  O love-destroying, cursed Bigotry!
Cursed in heaven, but cursed more in hell,
Where millions curse thee, and must ever curse!
Religion's most abhorred! perdition's most
Forlorn! God's most abandoned! hell's most damned!
  The infidel, who turned his impious war
Against the walls of Zion, on the rock
Of ages built, and higher than the clouds,
Sinned, and received his due reward; but she
Within her walls sinned more. Of Ignorance
Begot, her daughter, Persecution, walked
The earth, from age to age, and drank the blood
Of saints, with horrid relish drank the blood
Of God's peculiar children, and was drunk,
And in her drunkenness dreamed of doing good.
The supplicating hand of innocence,
That made the tiger mild, and in his wrath
The lion pause, the groans of suffering most
Severe, were nought to her; she laughed at groans:
No music pleased her more, and no repast
So sweet to her, as blood of men redeemed
By blood of Christ. Ambition's self, though mad,
And nursed on human gore, with her compared,
Was merciful. Nor did she always rage.
She had some hours of meditation, set
Apart, wherein she to her study went,
The Inquisition, model most complete
Of perfect wickedness, where deeds were done,
Deeds! let them ne'er be named,—and sat and planned
Deliberately, and with most musing pains,
How, to extremest thrill of agony,
The flesh, and blood, and souls of holy men,
Her victims, might be wrought; and when she saw
New tortures of her labouring fancy born,
She leaped for joy, and made great haste to try
Their force—well pleased to hear a deeper groan
  But now her day of mirth was passed, and come
Her day to weep, her day of bitter groans,
And sorrow unbemoaned, the day of grief
And wrath retributory poured in full
On all that took her part. The man of sin,
The mystery of iniquity, her friend
Sincere, who pardoned sin, unpardoned still,
And in the name of God blasphemed, and did
All wicked, all abominable things,
Most abject stood, that day, by devils hissed,
And by the looks of those he murdered, scorched;
And plagued with inward shame, that on his cheek
Burned, while his votaries, who left the earth,
Secure of bliss, around him, undeceived,
Stood, undeceivable till then; and knew
Too late, him fallible, themselves accursed,
And all their passports and certificates,
A lie: nor disappointed more, nor more
Ashamed, the Mussulman, when he saw, gnash
His teeth and wail, whom he expected judge.
All these were damned for bigotry, were damned,
Because they thought, that they alone served God,
And served him most, when most they disobeyed.
  Of those forlorn and sad, thou mightst have marked,
In number most innumerable, stand
The indolent; too lazy these to make
Inquiry for themselves, they stuck their faith
To some well-fatted priest, with offerings bribed
To bring them oracles of peace, and take
Into his management all the concerns

Of their eternity; managed how well
They knew, that day, and might have sooner known,
That the commandment was, Search, and believe
In me, and not in man; who leans on him
Leans on a broken reed, that will impierce
The trusted side. I am the way, the truth,
The life, alone, and there is none besides.
This did they read, and yet refused to search,
To search what easily was found, and, found,
Of price uncountable. Most foolish, they
Thought God with ignorance pleased, and blinded faith,
That took not root in reason, purified
With holy influence of his Spirit pure.
So, on they walked, and stumbled in the light
Of noon, because they would not open their eyes.
Effect how sad of sloth! that made them risk
Their piloting to the eternal shore,
To one who could mistake the lurid flash
Of hell for heaven's true star, rather than bow
The knee, and by one fervent word obtain
His guidance sure, who calls the stars by name
They prayed by proxy, and at second hand
Believed, and slept, and put repentance off,
Until the knock of death awoke them, when
They saw their ignorance both, and him they paid
To bargain of their souls 'twixt them and God,
Fled, and began repentance without end.
How did they wish, that morning, as they stood
With blushing covered, they had for themselves
The Scripture searched, had for themselves believed,
And made acquaintance with the Judge ere then!
Great day of termination to the joys
Of sin! to joys that grew on mortal boughs,
On trees whose seed fell not from heaven, whose top
Reached not above the clouds. From such, alone,
The epicure took all his meals. In choice
Of morsels for the body, nice he was,
And scrupulous, and knew all wines by smell
Or taste, and every composition knew
Of cookery; but grossly drank, unskilled,
The cup of spiritual pollution up,
That sickened his soul to death, while yet his eyes
Stood out with fat. His feelings were his guide.
He ate, and drank, and slept, and took all joys,
Forbid and unforbid, as impulse urged
Or appetite, nor asked his reason why.
He said, he followed Nature still, but lied;
For she was temperate and chaste, he full
Of wine and all adultery; her face
Was holy, most unholy his; her eye
Was pure, his shot unhallowed fire; her lips
Sang praise to God, his uttered oaths profane;
Her breath was sweet, his rank with foul debauch.
Yet pleaded he a kind and feeling heart,
Even when he left a neighbour's bed defiled.
Like migratory fowls, that flocking sailed
From isle to isle, steering by sense alone,
Whither the clime their liking best beseemed,
So he was guided, so he moved through good
And evil, right and wrong, but, ah! to fate
All different: they slept in dust, unpained;
He rose, that day, to suffer endless pain.
Cured of his unbelief, the sceptic stood,
Who doubted of his being while he breathed,
Than whom glossography itself, that spoke
Huge folios of nonsense every hour,
And left, surrounding every page, its marks
Of prodigal stupidity, scarce more
Of folly raved. The tyrant too, who sat
In grisly council, like a spider couched,
With ministers of locust countenance,
And made alliances to rob mankind,
And holy termed,—for still, beneath a name
Of pious sound, the wicked sought to veil
Their crimes,—forgetful of his right divine,
Trembled, and owned oppression was of hell;
Nor did the uncivil robber, who unpursed
The traveller on the high-way, and cut
His throat, anticipate severer doom.
In that assembly there was one, who, while
Beneath the sun, aspired to be a fool;
In different ages known by different names,
Not worth repeating here. Be this enough
With scrupulous care exact, he walked the rounds
Of fashionable duty, laughed when sad;
When merry, wept; deceiving, was deceived;
And flattering, flattered. Fashion was his god.
Obsequiously he fell before its shrine,
In slavish plight, and trembled to offend.
If graveness suited, he was grave; if else,
He travailed sorely, and made brief repose,
To work the proper quantity of sin.
In all submissive, to its changing shape,
Still changing, girded he his vexed frame,
And laughter made to men of sounder head.
Most circumspect he was of bows, and nods,
And salutations; and most seriously
And deeply meditated he of dress;
And in his dreams saw lace and ribbons fly.
His soul was nought; he damned it, every day,
Unceremoniously. Oh! fool of fools!
Pleased with a painted smile, he fluttered on,
Like fly of gaudy plume, by fashion driven,
As faded leaves by Autumn's wind, till Death
Put forth his hand, and drew him out of sight
Oh! fool of fools! polite to man; to God
Most rude: yet had he many rivals, who,
Age after age, great striving made to be
Ridiculous, and to forget they had
Immortal souls, that day remembered well.
As rueful stood his other half, as wan
Of cheek. Small her ambition was, but strange
The distaff, needle, all domestic cares,

Religion, children, husband, home, were things
She could not bear the thought of, bitter drugs
That sickened her soul. The house of wanton mirth
And revelry, the mask, the dance, she loved,
And in their service soul and body spent
Most cheerfully. A little admiration,
Or true or false, no matter which, pleased her,
And o'er the wreck of fortune lost, and health,
And peace, and an eternity of bliss
Lost, made her sweetly smile. She was convinced,
That God had made her greatly out of taste;
And took much pains to make herself anew.
Bedaubed with paint, and hung with ornaments
Of curious selection, gaudy toy!
A show unpaid for, paying to be seen!
As beggar by the way, most humbly asking
The alms of public gaze,—she went abroad.
Folly admired, and indication gave
Of envy, cold Civility made bows
And smoothly flattered, Wisdom shook his head,
And Laughter shaped his lip into a smile;
Sobriety did stare, Forethought grew pale,
And Modesty hung down the head and blushed,
And Pity wept, as, on the frothy surge
Of fashion tossed, she passed them by, like sail
Before some devilish blast, and got no time
To think, and never thought, till on the rock
She dashed, of ruin, anguish, and despair.
O how unlike this giddy thing in Time!
And at the day of judgment how unlike,
The modest, meek, retiring dame! Her house
Was ordered well, her children taught the way
Of life, who, rising up in honour, called
Her blessed. Best pleased to be admired at home,
And hear, reflected from her husband's praise,
Her own, she sought no gaze of foreign eye;
His praise alone, and faithful love, and trust
Reposed, was happiness enough for her.
Yet who, that saw her pass, and heard the poor
With earnest benedictions on her steps
Attend, could from obeisance keep his eye,
Or tongue from due applause. In virtue fair,
Adorned with modesty, and matron grace
Unspeakable, and love, her face was like
The light, most welcome to the eye of man;
Refreshing most, most honoured, most desired,
Of all he saw in the dim world below.
As Morning when she shed her golden locks,
And on the dewy top of Hermon walked,
Or Zion hill; so glorious was her path.
Old men beheld, and did her reverence,
And bade their daughters look, and take from her
Example of their future life; the young
Admired, and new resolve of virtue made.
And none who was her husband asked; his air
Serene, and countenance of joy, the sign
Of inward satisfaction, as he passed
The crowd, or sat among the elders, told.
In holiness complete, and in the robes
Of saving righteousness, arrayed for heaven,
How fair, that day, among the fair, she stood!
How lovely on the eternal hills her steps!
Restored to reason, on that morn, appeared
The lunatic, who raved in chains, and asked
No mercy when he died. Of lunacy,
Innumerous were the causes; humble pride,
Ambition disappointed, riches lost,
And bodily disease, and sorrow, oft
By man inflicted on his brother man;
Sorrow that made the reason drunk, and yet
Left much untasted—so the cup was filled;
Sorrow that, like an ocean, dark, deep, rough,
And shoreless, rolled its billows o'er the soul
Perpetually, and without hope of end.
Take one example, one of female wo.
Loved by a father and a mother's love,
In rural peace she lived, so fair, so light
Of heart, so good, and young, that reason, scarce
The eye could credit, but would doubt, as she
Did stoop to pull the lily or the rose
From morning's dew, if it reality
Of flesh and blood, or holy vision, saw,
In imagery of perfect womanhood.
But short her bloom, her happiness was short.
One saw her loveliness, and, with desire
Unhallowed, burning, to her ear addressed
Dishonest words; "Her favour was his life,
His heaven; her frown his wo, his night, his death."
With turgid phrase, thus wove in flattery's loom,
He on her womanish nature won, and age
Suspicionless, and ruined, and forsook.
For he a chosen villain was at heart,
And capable of deeds that durst not seek
Repentance. Soon her father saw her shame,
His heart grew stone, he drove her forth to want
And wintry winds, and with a horrid curse
Pursued her ear, forbidding all return.
Upon a hoary cliff, that watched the sea,
Her babe was found—dead. On its little cheek,
The tear that nature bade it weep, had turned
An ice-drop, sparkling in the morning beam;
And to the turf its helpless hands were frozen.
For she, the woful mother, had gone mad,
And laid it down, regardless of its fate
And of her own. Yet had she many days
Of sorrow in the world, but never wept.
She lived on alms, and carried in her hand
Some withered stalks she gathered in the spring.
When any asked the cause, she smiled and said,
They were her sisters, and would come and watch
Her grave when she was dead. She never spoke
Of her deceiver, father, mother, home,
Or child, or heaven, or hell, or God, but still
In lonely places walked, and ever gazed
Upon the withered stalks, and talked to them;
Till, wasted to the shadow of her youth

With wo too wide to see beyond, she died—
Not unatoned for by imputed blood,
Nor by the Spirit, that mysterious works,
Unsanctified. Aloud, her father cursed,
That day, his guilty pride, which would not own
A daughter, whom the God of heaven and earth
Was not ashamed to call his own; and he,
Who ruined her, read from her holy look,
That pierced him with perdition manifold,
His sentence, burning with vindictive fire.
The Judge that took a bribe; he who amiss
Pleaded the widow's cause, and by delay
Delaying ever, made the law at night
More intricate than at the dawn, and on
The morrow farther from a close, than when
The sun last set, till he who in the suit
Was poorest, by his empty coffers, proved
His cause the worst; and he that had the bag
Of weights deceitful, and the balance false;
And he that with a fraudful lip deceived
In buying or in selling;—these, that morn,
Found custom no excuse for sin, and knew
Plain dealing was a virtue, but too late.
And he that was supposed to do nor good
Nor ill, surprised, could find no neutral ground,
And learned, that to do nothing was to serve
The devil, and transgress the laws of God.
The noisy quack, that by profession lied,
And uttered falsehoods of enormous size,
With countenance as grave as truth beseemed;
And he that lied for pleasure, whom a lust
Of being heard and making people stare,
And a most steadfast hate of silence, drove
Far wide of sacred truth, who never took
The pains to think of what he was to say,
But still made haste to speak with weary tongue
Like copious stream for ever flowing on;—
Read clearly in the lettered heavens, what, long
Before, they might have read, For every word
Of folly, you, this day, shall give account;
And every liar shall his portion have
Among the cursed, without the gates of life.
With groans that made no pause, lamenting there
Were seen the duellist and suicide.
This thought, but thought amiss, that of himself
He was entire proprietor; and so,
When he was tired of Time, with his own hand,
He opened the portals of Eternity,
And sooner than the devils hoped, arrived
In hell. The other, of resentment quick,
And, for a word, a look, a gesture, deemed,
Not scrupulously exact in all respect,
Prompt to revenge, went to the cited field,
For double murder armed, his own, and his
That as himself he was ordained to love.
The first, in pagan books of early times,
Was heroism pronounced, and greatly praised.
In fashion's glossary of later days,
The last was honour called, and spirit high.
Alas! 'twas mortal spirit, honour which
Forgot to wake at the last trumpet's voice,
Bearing the signature of Time alone,
Uncurrent in Eternity, and base.
Wise men suspected this before; for they
Could never understand what honour meant,
Or why that should be honour termed, which made
Man murder man, and broke the laws of God
Most wantonly. Sometimes, indeed, the grave,
And those of Christian creed imagined, spoke
Admiringly of honour, lauding much
The noble youth, who, after many rounds
Of boxing, died, or to the pistol shot
His breast exposed, his soul to endless pain.
But they who most admired, and understood
This honour best, and on its altar laid
Their lives, most obviously were fools; and, what
Fools only, and the wicked, understood,
The wise agreed was some delusive Shade,
That with the mist of time should disappear.
Great day of revelation! in the grave
The hypocrite had left his mask, and stood
In naked ugliness. He was a man
Who stole the livery of the court of heaven,
To serve the devil in; in virtue's guise,
Devoured the widow's house and orphan's bread;
In holy phrase, transacted villanies
That common sinners durst not meddle with.
At sacred feast, he sat among the saints,
And with his guilty hands touched holiest things
And none of sin lamented more, or sighed
More deeply, or with graver countenance,
Or longer prayer, wept o'er the dying man,
Whose infant children, at the moment, he
Planned how to rob. In sermon style he bought,
And sold, and lied; and salutations made
In Scripture terms. He prayed by quantity,
And with his repetitions long and loud,
All knees were weary. With one hand he put
A penny in the urn of poverty,
And with the other took a shilling out.
On charitable lists,—those trumps which told
The public ear, who had in secret done
The poor a benefit, and half the alms
They told of, took themselves to keep them sounding,—
He blazed his name, more pleased to have it there
Than in the book of life. Seest thou the man!
A serpent with an angel's voice! a grave
With flowers bestrewed! and yet few were deceived.
His virtues being over-done, his face
Too grave, his prayers too long, his charities
Too pompously attended, and his speech
Larded too frequently and out of time
With serious phraseology,—were rents
That in his garments opened in spite of him,
Through which the well-accustomed eye could see
The rottenness of his heart. None deeper blushed,
As in the all-piercing light he stood, exposed,

No longer herding with the holy ones.
Yet still he tried to bring his countenance
To sanctimonious seeming; but, meanwhile,
The shame within, now visible to all,
His purpose balked. The righteous smiled, and even
Despair itself some signs of laughter gave,
As ineffectually he strove to wipe
His brow, that inward guiltiness defiled.
Detected wretch! of all the reprobate,
None seemed maturer for the flames of hell,
Where still his face, from ancient custom wears
A holy air which says to all that pass
Him by, "I was a hypocrite on earth."
That was the hour which measured out to each,
Impartially, his share of reputation,
Correcting all mistakes, and from the name
Of the good man all slanders wiping off.
Good name was dear to all. Without it, none
Could soundly sleep, even on a royal bed,
Or drink with relish from a cup of gold;
And with it, on his borrowed straw, or by
The leafless hedge, beneath the open heavens,
The weary beggar took untroubled rest.
It was a music of most heavenly tone,
To which the heart leaped joyfully, and all
The spirits danced. For honest fame, men laid
Their heads upon the block, and, while the axe
Descended, looked and smiled. It was of price
Invaluable. Riches, health, repose,
Whole kingdoms, life, were given for it, and he
Who got it was the winner still; and he
Who sold it durst not open his ear, nor look
On human face, he knew himself so vile,
Yet it, with all its preciousness, was due
To Virtue, and around her should have shed,
Unasked, its savoury smell; but Vice, deformed
Itself, and ugly, and of flavour rank,
To rob fair Virtue of so sweet an incense,
And with it to anoint and salve its own
Rotten ulcers, and perfume the path that led
To death,—strove daily by a thousand means:
And oft succeeded to make Virtue sour
In the world's nostrils, and its loathy self
Smell sweetly. Rumour was the messenger
Of defamation, and so swift that none
Could be the first to tell an evil tale;
And was, withal, so infamous for lies,
That he who of her sayings, on his creed,
The fewest entered, was deemed wisest man.
The fool, and many who had credit, too,
For wisdom, grossly swallowed all she said,
Unsifted; and although, at every word,
They heard her contradict herself, and saw
Hourly they were imposed upon and mocked,
Yet still they ran to hear her speak, and stared,
And wondered much, and stood aghast, and said
It could not be; and, while they blushed for shame
At their own faith, and seemed to doubt, believed,
And whom they met, with many sanctions, told.
So did experience fail to teach;—so hard
It was to learn this simple truth,—confirmed
At every corner by a thousand proofs,—
That common Fame most impudently lied.
'Twas Slander filled her mouth with lying words,
Slander, the foulest whelp of Sin. The man
In whom this spirit entered was undone.
His tongue was set on fire of hell, his heart
Was black as death, his legs were faint with haste
To propagate the lie his soul had framed,
His pillow was the peace of families
Destroyed, the sigh of innocenee reproached,
Broken friendships, and the strife of brotherhoods
Yet did he spare his sleep, and hear the clock
Number the midnight watches, on his bed,
Devising mischief more; and early rose,
And made most hellish meals of good men's names.
From door to door you might have seen him speed,
Or placed amidst a group of gaping fools,
And whispering in their ears with his foul lips.
Peace fled the neighbourhood in which he made
His haunts; and, like a moral pestilence,
Before his breath, the healthy shoots and blooms
Of social joy and happiness decayed.
Fools only in his company were seen,
And those forsaken of God, and to themselves
Given up. The prudent shunned him and his house
As one who had a deadly moral plague.
And fain would all have shunned him at the day
Of judgment; but in vain. All who gave ear
With greediness, or wittingly their tongues
Made herald to his lies, around him wailed;
While on his face, thrown back by injured men,
In characters of ever-blushing shame,
Appeared ten thousand slanders, all his own.
Among the accursed, who sought a hiding place
In vain, from fierceness of Jehovah's rage,
And from the hot displeasure of the Lamb,
Most wretched, most contemptible, most vile,—
Stood the false priest, and in his conscience felt
The fellest gnaw of the Undying Worm.
And so he might, for he had on his hands
The blood of souls, that would not wipe away.
Hear what he was. He swore, in sight of God
And man, to preach his master, Jesus Christ;
Yet preached himself: he swore that love of souls,
Alone, had drawn him to the church; yet strewed
The path that led to hell with tempting flowers,
And in the ear of sinners, as they took
The way of death, he whispered peace: he swore
Away all love of lucre, all desire
Of earthly pomp; and yet a princely seat
He liked, and to the clink of Mammon's box
Gave most rapacious ear. His prophecies,
He swore, were from the Lord; and yet, taught lies

For gain: with quackish ointment, healed the wounds
And bruises of the soul, outside, but left,
Within, the pestilent matter unobserved,
To sap the moral constitution quite,
And soon to burst again, incurable.
He with untempered mortar daubed the walls
Of Zion, saying, Peace, when there was none.
The man who came with thirsty soul to hear
Of Jesus, went away unsatisfied;
For he another gospel preached than Paul,
And one that had no Saviour in't; and yet,
His life was worse. Faith, charity, and love,
Humility, forgiveness, holiness,
Were words well lettered in his sabbath creed;
But with his life he wrote as plain, Revenge,
Pride, tyranny, and lust of wealth and power
Inordinate, and lewdness unashamed.
He was a wolf in clothing of the lamb,
That stole into the fold of God, and on
The blood of souls, which he did sell to death,
Grew fat; and yet, when any would have turned
Him out, he cried, "Touch not the priest of God."
And that he was anointed, fools believed;
But knew, that day, he was the devil's priest,
Anointed by the hands of Sin and Death,
And set particularly apart to ill,—
While on him smoked the vials of perdition,
Poured measureless. Ah me! what cursing then
Was heaped upon his head by ruined souls,
That charged him with their murder, as he stood,
With eye of all the unredeemed most sad,
Waiting the coming of the Son of Man!
But let me pause, for thou hast seen his place
And punishment, beyond the sphere of love.
Much was removed that tempted once to sin.
Avarice no gold, no wine the drunkard, saw.
But Envy had enough, as heretofore,
To fill his heart with gall and bitterness.
What made the man of envy what he was,
Was worth in others, vileness in himself,
A lust of praise, with undeserving deeds,
And conscious poverty of soul: and still
It was his earnest work and daily toil,
With lying tongue, to make the noble seem
Mean as himself. On fame's high hill he saw
The laurel spread its everlasting green,
And wished to climb; but felt his knees too weak,
And stood below, unhappy, laying hands
Upon the strong, ascending gloriously
The steps of honour, bent to draw them back,
Involving oft the brightness of their path,
In mists his breath had raised. Whene'er he heard,
As oft he did, of joy and happiness,
And great prosperity, and rising worth,
'Twas like a wave of wormwood o'er his soul
Rolling its bitterness. His joy was wo,
The wo of others. When, from wealth to want,
From praises to reproach, from peace to strife,
From mirth to tears, he saw a brother fall,
Of Virtue make a slip,—his dreams were sweet.
But chief with Slander, daughter of his own,
He took unhallowed pleasure. When she talked,
And with her filthy lips defiled the best,
His ear drew near; with wide attention gaped
His mouth; his eye, well pleased, as eager gazed
As glutton, when the dish he most desired
Was placed before him; and a horrid mirth,
At intervals, with laughter shook his sides.
The critic too, who, for a bit of bread,
In book that fell aside before the ink
Was dry, poured forth excessive nonsense, gave
Him much delight. The critics,—some, but few,—
Were worthy men, and earned renown which had
Immortal roots; but most were weak and vile.
And, as a cloudy swarm of summer flies,
With angry hum and slender lance, beset
The sides of some huge animal; so did
They buzz about the illustrious man, and fain,
With his immortal honour, down the stream
Of fame would have descended; but, alas!
The hand of Time drove them away. They were,
Indeed, a simple race of men, who had
One only art, which taught them still to say,
Whate'er was done might have been better done;
And with this art, not ill to learn, they made
A shift to live. But, sometimes too, beneath
The dust they raised, was worth a while obscured;
And then did Envy prophesy and laugh.
O Envy! hide thy bosom, hide it deep.
A thousand snakes, with black, envenomed mouths,
Nest there, and hiss, and feed through all thy heart.—
Such one I saw, here interposing, said
The new arrived, in that dark den of shame,
Whom who hath seen shall never wish to see
Again. Before him, in the infernal gloom,
That omnipresent shape of Virtue stood
On which he ever threw his eye; and, like
A cinder that had life and feeling, seemed
His face, with inward pining, to be what
He could not be. As being that had burned
Continually, in slow-consuming fire,—
Half an eternity, and was to burn
For evermore, he looked. Oh! sight to be
Forgotten! thought too horrible to think!
But say, believing in such wo to come,
Such dreadful certainty of endless pain,
Could beings of forecasting mould, as thou
Entitlest men, deliberately walk on,
Unscared, and overleap their own belief
Into the lake of ever-burning fire?
Thy tone of asking seems to make reply,
And rightly seems: They did not so believe
Not one of all thou sawst lament and wail
In Tophet, perfectly believed the word

Of God, else none had thither gone. Absurd,
To think that beings, made with reason, formed
To calculate, compare, choose, and reject,
By nature taught, and self, and every sense,
To choose the good, and pass the evil by,
Could, with full credence of a time to come,
When all the wicked should be really damned,
And cast beyond the sphere of light and love,
Have persevered in sin! Too foolish this
For folly in its prime. Can aught that thinks
And wills choose certain evil, and reject
Good, in his heart believing he does so?
Could man choose pain, instead of endless joy.
Mad supposition, though maintained by some
Of honest mind. Behold a man condemned!
Either he ne'er inquired, and therefore he
Could not believe; or, else, he carelessly
Inquired, and something other than the word
Of God received into his cheated faith;
And therefore he did not believe, but down
To hell descended, leaning on a lie.
  Faith was bewildered much by men who meant
To make it clear, so simple in itself,
A thought so rudimental and so plain,
That none by comment could it plainer make.
All faith was one. In object, not in kind,
The difference lay. The faith that saved a soul,
And that which in the common truth believed,
In essence, were the same. Hear, then, what faith,
True, Christian faith, which brought salvation, was:
Belief in all that God revealed to men;
Observe, in all that God revealed to men,
In all he promised, threatened, commanded, said,
Without exception, and without a doubt.
Who thus believed, being by the Spirit touched,
As naturally the fruits of faith produced,
Truth, temperance, meekness, holiness, and love,
As human eye from darkness sought the light.
How could he else? If he, who had firm faith
The morrow's sun should rise, ordered affairs
Accordingly; if he, who had firm faith
That spring, and summer, and autumnal days,
Should pass away, and winter really come,
Prepared accordingly; if he, who saw
A bolt of death approaching, turned aside
And let it pass;—as surely did the man,
Who verily believed the word of God,
Though erring whiles, its general laws obey,
Turn back from hell, and take the way to heaven.
  That faith was necessary, some alleged,
Unreined and uncontrollable by will.
Invention savouring much of hell! Indeed,
It was the master-stroke of wickedness,
Last effort of Abaddon's council dark,
To make man think himself a slave to fate,
And, worst of all, a slave to fate in faith.
For thus 'twas reasoned then: From faith alone,
And from opinion, springs all action; hence,
If faith's compelled, so is all action too:
But deeds compelled are not accountable;
So man is not amenable to God.
Arguing that brought such monstrous birth, though good
It seemed, must have been false. Most false it was,
And by the book of God condemned, throughout.
We freely own, that truth, when set before
The mind, with perfect evidence, compelled
Belief; but error lacked such witness, still:
And none who now lament in moral night,
The word of God refused on evidence
That might not have been set aside as false.
To reason, try, choose, and reject, was free.
Hence God, by faith, acquitted, or condemned;
Hence righteous men, with liberty of will,
Believed; and hence thou sawst in Erebus
The wicked, who as freely disbelieved
What else had led them to the land of life.

BOOK IX.

Fairest of those that left the calm of heaven,
And ventured down to man, with words of peace,
Daughter of Grace! known by whatever name,
Religion, Virtue, Piety, or Love
Of Holiness, the day of thy reward
Was come. Ah! thou wast long despised, despised
By those thou wooedst from death to endless life
Modest and meek, in garments white as those
That seraphs wear, and countenance as mild
As Mercy looking on Repentance' tear;
With eye of purity, now darted up
To God's eternal throne, now humbly bent
Upon thyself, and, weeping down thy cheek,
That glowed with universal love immense,
A tear, pure as the dews that fall in heaven;
In thy left hand, the olive branch, and in
Thy right, the crown of immortality;—
With noiseless foot, thou walkedst the vale earth,
Beseeching men, from age to age, to turn
From utter death, to turn from wo to bliss;
Beseeching evermore, and evermore
Despised—not evermore despised, not now,
Not at the day of doom; most lovely then,
Most honourable, thou appeared, and most
To be desired. The guilty heard the song
Of thy redeemed, how loud! and saw thy face
How fair! Alas! it was too late! the hour
Of making friends was passed, thy favour then
Might not be sought; but recollection, sad
And accurate, as miser counting o'er
And o'er again the sum he must lay out,

Distinctly in the wicked's ear rehearsed
Each opportunity despised and lost,
While on them gleamed thy holy look, that like
A fiery torrent went into their souls.
The day of thy reward was come, the day
Of great remuneration to thy friends.
To those, known by whatever name, who sought,
In every place, in every time, to do
Unfeignedly their Maker's will, revealed,
Or gathered else from nature's school; well pleased
With God's applause alone, that, like a stream
Of sweetest melody, at still of night
By wanderer heard, in their most secret ear
For ever whispered, Peace; and, as a string
Of kindred tone awoke, their inmost soul
Responsive answered, Peace; inquiring still
And searching, night and day, to know their duty
When known, with undisputing trust, with love
Unquenchable, with zeal, by reason's lamp
Inflamed,—performing; and to Him, by whose
Profound, all-calculating skill alone,
Results—results even of the slightest act,
Are fully grasped, with unsuspicious faith,
All consequences leaving; to abound,
Or want, alike prepared; who knew to be
Exalted how, and how to be abased;
How best to live, and how to die when asked.
Their prayers sincere, their alms in secret done,
Their fightings with themselves, their abstinence
From pleasure, though by mortal eye unseen,
Their hearts of resignation to the will
Of Heaven, their patient bearing of reproach
And shame, their charity, and faith, and hope,—
Thou didst remember, and in full repaid.
No bankrupt thou, who at the bargained hour
Of payment due, sent to his creditors
A tale of losses and mischances, long.
Ensured by God himself, and from the stores
And treasures of his wealth, at will supplied,—
Religion, thou alone, of all that men,
On earth, gave credit, to be reimbursed
On the other side the grave, didst keep thy word,
Thy day, and all thy promises fulfilled.
  As in the mind, rich with unborrowed wealth,
Where multitudes of thoughts for utterance strive,
And all so fair, that each seems worthy first
To enter on the tongue, and from the lips
Have passage forth,—selection hesitates
Perplexed, and loses time, anxious, since all
Cannot be taken, to take the best; and yet
Afraid, lest what he left be worthier still;
And grieving much, where all so goodly look,
To leave rejected one, or in the rear
Let any be obscured: so did the bard.
Though not unskilled, as on that multitude
Of men who once awoke to judgment, he
Threw back reflection, hesitating pause.
For as his harp, in tone severe, had sung
What figure the most famous sinners made,
When from the grave they rose unmasked; so did
He wish to character the good; but yet,
Among so many, glorious all, all worth
Immortal fame, with whom begin, with whom
To end, was difficult to choose; and long
His auditors, upon the tiptoe raised
Of expectation, might have kept, had not
His eye—for so it is in heaven, that what
Is needed always is at hand—beheld,
That moment, on a mountain near the throne
Of God, the most renowned of the redeemed,
Rejoicing: nor who first, who most to praise,
Debated more; but thus, with sweeter note,
Well pleased to sing, with highest eulogy,
And first, whom God applauded most,—began.
  With patient ear, thou now hast heard,—though whiles,
Aside digressing, ancient feeling turned
My lyre,—what shame the wicked had, that day,
What wailing, what remorse; so hear, in brief,
How bold the righteous stood, the men redeemed
How fair in virtue, and in hope how glad!
And first among the holy shone, as best
Became, the faithful minister of God.
  See where he walks on yonder mount that lifts
Its summit high, on the right hand of bliss,
Sublime in glory, talking with his peers
Of the incarnate Saviour's love, and passed
Affliction lost in present joy! See how
His face with heavenly ardour glows, and how
His hand, enraptured, strikes the golden lyre!
As now, conversing of the Lamb, once slain,
He speaks; and now, from vines that never hear
Of winter, but in monthly harvest yield
Their fruit abundantly, he plucks the grapes
Of life! But what he was on earth it most
Behoves to say. Elect by God himself,
Anointed by the Holy Ghost, and set
Apart to the great work of saving men;
Instructed fully in the will divine,
Supplied with grace in store, as need might ask,
And with the stamp and signature of heaven,
Truth, mercy, patience, holiness, and love,
Accredited;—he was a man, by God,
The Lord, commissioned to make known to men
The eternal counsels; in his Master's name,
To treat with them of everlasting things,
Of life, death, bliss, and wo; to offer terms
Of pardon, grace, and peace, to the rebelled;
To teach the ignorant soul, to cheer the sad;
To bind, to loose, with all authority;
To give the feeble strength, the hopeless hope,
To help the halting, and to lead the blind;
To warn the careless, heal the sick of heart,
Arouse the indolent, and on the proud
And obstinate offender to denounce
The wrath of God. All other men, what name
Soe'er they bore, whatever office held,
It lawful held;—the magistrate supreme,

Or else subordinate, were chosen by men,
Their fellows, and from men derived their power,
And were accountable, for all they did,
To men; but he, alone, his office held
Immediately from God, from God received
Authority, and was to none but God
Amenable. The elders of the church,
Indeed, upon him laid their hands, and set
Him visibly apart to preach the word
Of life; but this was merely outward rite
And decent ceremonial, performed
On all alike; and oft, as thou hast heard,
Performed on those God never sent; his call,
His consecration, his anointing, all
Were inward, in the conscience heard and felt
Thus, by Jehovah chosen, and ordained
To take into his charge the souls of men,
And for his trust to answer at the day
Of judgment,—great plenipotent of heaven,
And representative of God on earth,—
Fearless of men and devils; unabashed
By sin enthroned, or mockery of a prince,
Unawed by armed legions, unseduced
By offered bribes, burning with love to souls
Unquenchable, and mindful still of his
Great charge and vast responsibility;—
High in the temple of the living God,
He stood amidst the people, and declared
Aloud the truth, the whole revealed truth,
Ready to seal it with his blood. Divine
Resemblance most complete! with mercy now
And love, his face, illumed, shone gloriously;
And frowning now indignantly, it seemed
As if offended Justice, from his eye,
Streamed forth vindictive wrath! Men heard, alarmed.
The uncircumcised infidel believed;
Light-thoughted Mirth grew serious, and wept;
The laugh profane sunk in a sigh of deep
Repentance, the blasphemer, kneeling, prayed,
And, prostrate in the dust, for mercy called;
And cursed, old, forsaken sinners gnashed
Their teeth, as if their hour had been arrived.
Such was his calling, his commission such.
Yet he was humble, kind, forgiving, meek,
Easy to be entreated, gracious, mild;
And, with all patience and affection, taught,
Rebuked, persuaded, solaced, counselled, warned,
In fervent style and manner. Needy, poor,
And dying men, like music, heard his feet
Approach their beds; and guilty wretches took
New hope, and in his prayers wept and smiled,
And blessed him, as they died forgiven; and all
Saw in his face contentment, in his life,
The path to glory and perpetual joy.
Deep-learned in the philosophy of heaven,
He searched the causes out of good and ill,
Profoundly calculating their effects
Far past the bounds of Time; and balancing,
In the arithmetic of future things,
The loss and profit of the soul to all
Eternity. A skilful workman he
In God's great moral vineyard: what to prune
What cautious hand he knew, what to uproot;
What were mere weeds, and what celestial plants
Which had unfading vigour in them, knew;
Nor knew alone, but watched them night and day
And reared and nourished them, till fit to be
Transplanted to the Paradise above.
Oh! who can speak his praise! great, humble man!
He in the current of destruction stood
And warned the sinner of his wo; led on
Immanuel's members in the evil day;
And, with the everlasting arms embraced
Himself around, stood in the dreadful front
Of battle, high, and warred victoriously
With death and hell. And now was come his rest,
His triumph day. Illustrious like a sun,
In that assembly, he, shining from far,
Most excellent in glory, stood assured,
Waiting the promised crown, the promised throne
The welcome and approval of his Lord.
Nor one alone, but many—prophets, priests,
Apostles, great reformers, all that served
Messiah faithfully, like stars appeared
Of fairest beam; and round them gathered, clad
In white, the vouchers of their ministry—
The flock their care had nourished, fed, and saved
Nor yet in common glory blazing, stood
The true philosopher, decided friend
Of truth and man. Determined foe of all
Deception, calm, collected, patient, wise,
And humble, undeceived by outward shape
Of things, by fashion's revelry uncharmed,
By honour unbewitched,—he left the chase
Of vanity, and all the quackeries
Of life, to fools and heroes, or whoe'er
Desired them; and with reason, much despised,
Traduced, yet heavenly reason, to the shade
Retired—retired, but not to dream, or build
Of ghostly fancies, seen in the deep noon
Of sleep, ill-balanced theories; retired,
But did not leave mankind; in pity, not
In wrath, retired; and still, though distant, kept
His eye on men; at proper angle took
His stand to see them better, and, beyond
The clamour which the bells of folly made,
That most had hung about them, to consult
With nature, how their madness might be cured,
And how their true substantial comforts might
Be multiplied. Religious man! what God
By prophets, priests, evangelists, revealed
Of sacred truth, he thankfully received,
And, by its light directed, went in search
Of more. Before him, darkness fled; and all
The goblin tribe, that hung upon the breasts

Of Night, and haunted still the moral gloom
With shapeless forms, and blue, infernal lights,
And indistinct, and devilish whisperings,
That the miseducated fancies vexed
Of superstitious men,—at his approach,
Dispersed, invisible. Where'er he went,
This lesson still he taught, To fear no ill
But sin, no being but Almighty God.
All-comprehending sage! too hard alone
For him was man's salvation; all besides,
Of use or comfort, that distinction made
Between the desperate savage, scarcely raised
Above the beast whose flesh he ate, undressed,
And the most polished of the human race,
Was product of his persevering search.
Religion owed him much, as from the false
She suffered much; for still his main design,
In all his contemplations, was to trace
The wisdom, providence, and love of God,
And to his fellows, less observant, show
Them forth. From prejudice redeemed, with all
His passions still, above the common world,
Sublime in reason and in aim sublime,
He sat, and on the marvellous works of God
Sedately thought; now glancing up his eye,
Intelligent, through all the starry dance,
And penetrating now the deep remote
Of central causes in the womb opaque
Of matter hid; now with inspection nice,
Entering the mystic labyrinths of the mind,
Where thought, of notice ever shy, behind
Thought, disappearing, still retired; and still,
Thought meeting thought, and thought awakening thought,
And mingling still with thought in endless maze,—
Bewildered observation; now, with eye
Yet more severely purged, looking far down
Into the heart, where passion wove a web
Of thousand thousand threads, in grain and hue
All different; then, upward venturing whiles,
But reverently, and in his hand, the light
Revealed, near the eternal Throne, he gazed,
Philosophizing less than worshipping.
Most truly great! his intellectual strength
And knowledge vast, to men of lesser mind,
Seemed infinite; yet, from his high pursuits,
And reasonings most profound, he still returned
Home, with an humbler and a warmer heart:
And none so lowly bowed before his God,
As none so well His awful majesty
And goodness comprehended; or so well
His own dependency and weakness knew.
  How glorious now, with vision purified
At the Essential Truth, entirely free
From error, he, investigating still,—
For knowledge is not found, unsought, in heaven,—
From world to world, at pleasure, roves, on wing
Of golden ray upborne; or, at the feet
Of heaven's most ancient sages, sitting, hears
New wonders of the wondrous works of God!
  Illustrious too, that morning, stood the man
Exalted by the people, to the throne
Of government, established on the base
Of justice, liberty, and equal right;
Who, in his countenance sublime, expressed
A nation's majesty, and yet was meek
And humble; and in royal palace gave
Example to the meanest, of the fear
Of God, and all integrity of life
And manners; who, august, yet lowly; who,
Severe, yet gracious; in his very heart,
Detesting all oppression, all intent
Of private aggrandizement; and, the first
In every public duty, held the scales
Of justice, and as the law, which reigned in him,
Commanded, gave rewards; or, with the edge
Vindictive, smote, now light, now heavily,
According to the stature of the crime.
Conspicuous like an oak of healthiest bough,
Deep-rooted in his country's love, he stood,
And gave his hand to Virtue, helping up
The honest man to honour and renown;
And, with the look which goodness wears in wrath
Withering the very blood of Knavery,
And from his presence driving far, ashamed.
  Nor less remarkable, among the blessed,
Appeared the man, who, in the senate-house
Watchful, unhired, unbribed, and uncorrupt,
And party only to the common weal,
In virtue's awful age, pleaded for right,
With truth so clear, with argument so strong,
With action so sincere, and tone so loud
And deep, as made the despot quake behind
His adamantine gates, and every joint,
In terror, smite his fellow-joint relaxed;
Or, marching to the field, in burnished steel,
While, frowning on his brow, tremendous hung
The wrath of a whole people, long provoked,—
Mustered the stormy wings of war, in day
Of dreadful deeds; and led the battle on,
When Liberty, swift as the fires of heaven,
In fury rode, with all her hosts, and threw
The tyrant down, and drove invasion back.
Illustrious he—illustrious all appeared,
Who ruled supreme in righteousness; or held
Inferior place, in steadfast rectitude
Of soul. Peculiarly severe had been
The nurture of their youth, their knowledge great,
Great was their wisdom, great their cares, and great
Their self-denial, and their service done
To God and man; and great was their reward,
At hand, proportioned to their worthy deeds.
  Breathe all thy minstrelsy, immortal Harp!
Breathe numbers warm with love, while I rehearse—
Delighted theme, resembling most the songs
Which, day and night, are sung before the Lamb!

Thy praise, O Charity! thy labours most
Divine; thy sympathy with sighs, and tears,
And groans; thy great, thy god-like wish, to heal
All misery, all fortune's wounds, and make
The soul of every living thing rejoice.
O thou wast needed much in days of Time!
No virtue, half so much!—None half so fair!
To all the rest, however fine, thou gavest
A finishing and polish, without which
No man e'er entered heaven. Let me record
His praise, the man of great benevolence,
Who pressed thee closely to his glowing heart,
And to thy gentle bidding made his feet
Swift minister. Of all mankind, his soul
Was most in harmony with heaven: as one
Sole family of brothers, sisters, friends,
One in their origin, one in their rights
To all the common gifts of providence,
And in their hopes, their joys, and sorrows one,
He viewed the universal human race.
He needed not a law of state, to force
Grudging submission to the law of God.
The law of love was in his heart, alive;
What he possessed, he counted not his own;
But, like a faithful steward in a house
Of public alms, what freely he received
He freely gave, distributing to all
The helpless the last mite beyond his own
Temperate support, and reckoning still the gift
But justice due to want; and so it was,
Although the world, with compliment not ill
Applied, adorned it with a fairer name.
Nor did he wait till to his door the voice
Of supplication came, but went abroad,
With foot as silent as the starry dews,
In search of misery that pined unseen,
And would not ask. And who can tell what sights
He saw! what groans he heard, in that cold world
Below! where Sin, in league with gloomy Death,
Marched daily through the length and breadth of all
The land, wasting at will, and making earth,
Fair earth! a lazar-house, a dungeon dark,
Where Disappointment fed on ruined Hope,
Where Guilt, worn out, leaned on the triple edge
Of want, remorse, despair; where Cruelty
Reached forth a cup of wormwood to the lips
Of Sorrow, that to deeper Sorrow wailed;
Where Mockery, and Disease, and Poverty,
Met miserable Age, erewhile sore bent
With his own burden; where the arrowy winds
Of winter pierced the naked orphan babe,
And chilled the mother's heart, who had no home;
And where, alas! in mid-time of his day,
The honest man, robbed by some villain's hand,
Or with long sickness pale, and paler yet
With want and hunger, oft drank bitter draughts
Of his own tears, and had no bread to eat.
Oh! who can tell what sights he saw, what shapes
Of wretchedness! or who describe what smiles
Of gratitude illumined the face of wo,
While from his hand he gave the bounty forth!
As when the Sun, to Cancer wheeling back,
Returned from Capricorn, and showed the north,
That long had lain in cold and cheerless night,
His beamy countenance; all nature then
Rejoiced together glad; the flower looked up
And smiled; the forest, from his locks, shook off
The hoary frosts, and clapped his hands; the birds
Awoke, and, singing, rose to meet the day;
And from his hollow den, where many months
He slumbered sad in darkness, blithe and light
Of heart the savage sprung, and saw again
His mountains shine, and with new songs of love
Allured the virgin's ear: so did the house,
The prison-house of guilt, and all the abodes
Of unprovided helplessness, revive,
As on them looked the sunny messenger
Of Charity. By angels tended still,
That marked his deeds, and wrote them in the book
Of God's remembrance; careless he to be
Observed of men, or have each mite bestowed
Recorded punctually, with name and place,
In every bill of news. Pleased to do good,
He gave, and sought no more, nor questioned much,
Nor reasoned, who deserved; for well he knew
The face of need. Ah me! who could mistake?
The shame to ask, the want that urged within,
Composed a look so perfectly distinct
From all else human, and withal so full
Of misery, that none could pass, untouched,
And be a Christian, or thereafter claim,
In any form, the name or rights of man,
Or, at the day of judgment, lift his eye;
While he, in name of Christ, who gave the poor
A cup of water, or a bit of bread,
Impatient for his advent, waiting stood,
Glowing in robes of love and holiness,
Heaven's fairest dress! and round him ranged, in white,
A thousand witnesses appeared, prepared
To tell his gracious deeds before the Throne.
Nor unrenowned among the most renowned,
Nor 'mong the fairest unadmired, that morn,
When highest fame was proof of highest worth,
Distinguished stood the bard: not he, who sold
The incommunicable, heavenly gift,
To Folly, and with lyre of perfect tone,
Prepared by God himself, for holiest praise,—
Vilest of traitors! most dishonest man!—
Sat by the door of Ruin, and made there
A melody so sweet, and in the mouth
Of drunkenness and debauch, that else had croaked
In natural discordance jarring harsh,
Put so divine a song, that many turned
Aside, and entered in undone, and thought
Meanwhile, it was the gate of heaven, so like

An angel's voice the music seemed; nor he,
Who, whining grievously of damsel coy,
Or blaming fortune, that would nothing give
For doing nought, in indolent lament
Unprofitable, passed his piteous days,
Making himself the hero of his tale,
Deserving ill the poet's name: but he,
The bard, by God's own hand anointed, who,
To Virtue's all-delighting harmony,
His numbers tuned: who, from the fount of truth,
Poured melody, and beauty poured, and love,
In holy stream, into the human heart;
And, from the height of lofty argument,
Who "justified the ways of God to man,"
And sung what still he sings, approved, in heaven;
Though now with bolder note, above the damp
Terrestrial, which the pure celestial fire
Cooled, and restrained in part his flaming wing.
  Philosophy was deemed of deeper thought,
And judgment more severe, than Poetry;
To fable, she, and fancy, more inclined.
And yet, if Fancy, as was understood,
Was of creative nature, or of power,
With self-wrought stuff, to build a fabric up,
To mortal vision wonderful and strange,
Philosophy, the theoretic, claimed,
Undoubtedly, the first and highest place
In Fancy's favour. Her material souls,
Her chance, her atoms shaped alike, her white
Proved black; her universal nothing, all;
And all her wondrous systems, how the mind
With matter met; how man was free, and yet
All pre-ordained; how evil first began;
And chief, her speculations, soaring high,
Of the eternal, uncreated Mind,
Which left all reason infinitely far
Behind—surprising feat of theory!—
Were pure creation of her own, webs wove
Of gossamer in Fancy's lightest loom,
And no where, on the list of being made
By God, recorded: but her look, meanwhile,
Was grave and studious; and many thought
She reasoned deeply, when she wildly raved.
  The true, legitimate, anointed bard,
Whose song through ages poured its melody,
Was most severely thoughtful, most minute
And accurate of observation, most
Familiarly acquainted with all modes
And phrases of existence. True, no doubt,
He had originally drunk, from out
The fount of life and love, a double draught,
That gave whate'er he touched a double life:
But this was mere desire at first, and power
Devoid of means to work by; need was still
Of persevering, quick, inspective mood
Of mind, of faithful memory, vastly stored,
From universal being's ample field,
With knowledge; and a judgment, sound and clear,
Well disciplined in nature's rules of taste;
Discerning to select, arrange, combine,
From infinite variety, and still
To nature true; and guide withal, hard task,
The sacred, living impetus divine,
Discreetly through the harmony of song.
Completed thus, the poet sung; and age
To age, enraptured, heard his measures flow;
Enraptured, for he poured the very fat
And marrow of existence through his verse,
And gave the soul, that else, in selfish cold,
Unwarmed by kindred interest, had lain,
A roomy life, a glowing relish high,
A sweet, expansive brotherhood of being—
Joy answering joy, and sigh responding sigh,
Through all the fibres of the social heart.
Observant, sympathetic, sound of head,
Upon the ocean vast of human thought,
With passion rough and stormy, venturing out,
Even as the living billows rolled, he threw
His numbers over them, seized as they were,
And to perpetual ages left them fixed,
To each, a mirror of itself displayed;
Despair for ever lowering dark on Sin,
And happiness on Virtue smiling fair.
  He was the minister of fame, and gave
To whom he would renown: nor missed himself—
Although despising much the idiot roar
Of popular applause, that sudden, oft,
Unnaturally turning, whom it nursed
Itself devoured—the lasting fame, the praise
Of God and holy men, to excellence given.
Yet less he sought his own renown, than wished
To have the eternal images of truth
And beauty, pictured in his verse, admired.
'Twas these, taking immortal shape and form
Beneath his eye, that charmed his midnight watch,
And oft his soul with awful transports shook
Of happiness, unfelt by other men.
This was that spell, that sorcery, which bound
The poet to the lyre, and would not let
Him go; that hidden mystery of joy,
Which made him sing in spite of fortune's worst;
And was, at once, both motive and reward.
  Nor now among the choral harps, in this
The native clime of song, are those unknown,
With higher note ascending, who, below,
In holy ardour, aimed at lofty strains.
True fame is never lost: many, whose names
Were honoured much on earth, are famous here
For poetry, and, with arch-angel harps,
Hold no unequal rivalry in song;
Leading the choirs of heaven, in numbers high,
In numbers ever sweet and ever new.
  Behold them yonder, where the river pure
Flows warbling down before the throne of God;
And, shading on each side, the tree of life
Spreads its unfading boughs!—See how they shine,
In garments white, quaffing deep draughts of love.

And harping on their harps, new harmonies
Preparing for the ear of God, Most High!
But why should I, of individual worth,
Of individual glory, longer sing?
No true believer was, that day, obscure;
No holy soul but had enough of joy;
No pious wish without its full reward.
Who in the Father and the Son believed,
With faith that wrought by love to holy deeds,
And purified the heart, none trembled there,
Nor had by earthly guise his rank concealed;
Whether, unknown, he tilled the ground remote,
Observant of the seasons, and adored
God in the promise, yearly verified,
Of seed-time, harvest, summer, winter, day
And night, returning duly at the time
Appointed; or, on the shadowy mountain side,
Worshipped at dewy eve, watching his flocks;
Or, trading, saw the wonders of the deep,
And as the needle to the starry Pole
Turned constantly, so he his heart to God;
Or else, in servitude severe, was taught
To break the bonds of sin; or, begging, learned
To trust the Providence that fed the raven,
And clothed the lily with her annual gown.
Most numerous, indeed, among the saved,
And many, too, not least illustrious, shone
The men who had no name on earth. Eclipsed
By lowly circumstance, they lived unknown,
Like stream that in the desert warbled clear,
Still nursing, as it goes, the herb and flower,
Though never seen; or like the star, retired
In solitudes of ether, far beyond
All sight, not of essential splendour less,
Though shining unobserved. None saw their pure
Devotion, none their tears, their faith, and love,
Which burned within them, both to God and man,—
None saw but God. He, in his bottle, all
Their tears preserved, and every holy wish
Wrote in his book; and, not as they had done,
But as they wished with all their heart to do,
Arrayed them now in glory, and displayed,—
No longer hid by coarse, uncourtly garb,—
In lustre equal to their inward worth.
Man's time was passed, and his eternity
Begun. No fear remained of change. The youth,
Who, in the glowing morn of vigorous life,
High-reaching after great religious deeds,
Was suddenly cut off, with all his hopes
In sunny bloom, and unaccomplished left
His withered aims,—saw everlasting days,
Before him, dawning rise, in which to achieve
All glorious things, and get himself the name
That jealous Death too soon forbade on earth.
Old things had passed away, and all was new;
And yet, of all the new-begun, nought so
Prodigious difference made, in the affairs
And thoughts of every man, as certainty.
For doubt, all doubt, was gone, of every kind;
Doubt that erewhile, beneath the lowest base
Of mortal reasonings, deepest laid, crept in,
And made the strongest, best cemented towers
Of human workmanship, so weakly shake,
And to their lofty tops so waver still,
That those who built them, feared their sudden fall.
But doubt, all doubt, was passed; and, in its place,
To every thought that in the heart of man
Was present, now had come an absolute,
Unquestionable certainty, which gave
To each decision of the mind immense
Importance, raising to its proper height
The sequent tide of passion, whether joy
Or grief. The good man knew, in very truth,
That he was saved to all eternity,
And feared no more; the bad had proof complete,
That he was damned for ever; and believed
Entirely, that on every wicked soul
Anguish should come, and wrath, and utter wo.
Knowledge was much increased, but wisdom more.
The film of Time, that still before the sight
Of mortal vision danced, and led the best
Astray, pursuing unsubstantial dreams,
Had dropped from every eye. Men saw that they
Had vexed themselves in vain, to understand
What now no hope to understand remained;
That they had often counted evil good,
And good for ill; laughed when they should have wept,
And wept, forlorn, when God intended mirth.
But what, of all their follies passed, surprised
Them most, and seemed most totally insane
And unaccountable, was value set
On objects of a day, was serious grief
Or joy for loss or gain of mortal things.
So utterly impossible it seemed,
When men their proper interests saw, that aught
Of terminable kind, that aught, which e'er
Could die, or cease to be, however named,
Should make a human soul—a legal heir
Of everlasting years—rejoice or weep,
In earnest mood; for nothing now seemed worth
A thought, but had eternal bearing in't.
Much truth had been assented to in Time,
Which never, till this day, had made a due
Impression on the heart. Take one example.
Early from heaven it was revealed, and oft
Repeated in the world, from pulpits preached,
And penned and read in holy books, that God
Respected not the persons of mankind.
Had this been truly credited and felt,
The king, in purple robe, had owned, indeed,
The beggar for his brother; pride of rank
And office thawed into paternal love;
Oppression feared the day of equal rights,
Predicted; covetous extortion kept
In mind the hour of reckoning, soon to come;

And bribed injustice thought of being judged,
When he should stand on equal foot, beside
The man he wronged, and surely—nay, 'tis true,
Most true, beyond all whispering of doubt,
That he, who lifted up the reeking scourge,
Dripping with gore from the slave's back, before
He struck again, had paused, and seriously
Of that tribunal thought, where God himself
Should look him in the face, and ask in wrath,
"Why didst thou this? Man! was he not thy brother,
Bone of thy bone, and flesh and blood of thine?"
But, ah! this truth, by heaven and reason taught,
Was never fully credited on earth.
The titled, flattered, lofty men of power,
Whose wealth brought verdicts of applause for deeds
Of wickedness, could ne'er believe the time
Should truly come when judgment should proceed
Impartially against them, and they, too,
Have no good speaker at the Judge's ear,
No witnesses to bring them off for gold,
No power to turn the sentence from its course;
And they of low estate, who saw themselves,
Day after day, despised, and wronged, and mocked,
Without redress, could scarcely think the day
Should e'er arrive, when they, in truth, should stand
On perfect level with the potentates
And princes of the earth, and have their cause
Examined fairly, and their rights allowed.
But now this truth was felt, believed and felt,
That men were really of a common stock,
That no man ever had been more than man.
  Much prophecy—revealed by holy bards,
Who sung the will of heaven by Judah's streams—
Much prophecy, that waited long the scoff
Of lips uncircumcised, was then fulfilled;
To the last tittle scrupulously fulfilled.
It was foretold by those of ancient days,
A time should come, when wickedness should weep
Abased; when every lofty look of man
Should be bowed down, and all his haughtiness
Made low; when righteousness alone should lift
The head in glory, and rejoice at heart;
When many, first in splendour and renown,
Should be most vile; and many, lowest once,
And last in Poverty's obscurest nook,
Highest and first in honour, should be seen,
Exalted; and when some, when all the good,
Should rise to glory and eternal life;
And all the bad, lamenting, wake, condemned
To shame, contempt, and everlasting grief.
  These prophecies had tarried long, so long
That many wagged the head, and, taunting, asked,
"When shall they come?" but asked no more, nor mocked:
For the reproach of prophecy was wiped
Away, and every word of God found true.
  And, oh! what change of state, what change of rank,
In that assembly everywhere was seen!
The humble-hearted laughed, the lofty mourned,
And every man, according to his works
Wrought in the body, there took character.
Thus stood they mixed, all generations stood!
Of all mankind, innumerable throng!
Great harvest of the grave!—waiting the will
Of heaven, attentively and silent all,
As forest spreading out beneath the calm
Of evening skies, when even the single leaf
Is heard distinctly rustle down and fall;
So silent they, when from above, the sound
Of rapid wheels approached, and suddenly
In heaven appeared a host of angels strong,
With chariots and with steeds of burning fire;
Cherub, and Seraph, Thrones, Dominions, Powers,
Bright in celestial armour, dazzling, rode.
And, leading in the front, illustrious shone
Michael and Gabriel, servants long approved
In high commission,—girt that day with power,
Which nought created, man or devil, might
Resist. Nor waited, gazing, long; but, quick
Descending, silently and without song,
As servants bent to do their master's work,
To middle air they raised the human race,
Above the path long travelled by the sun;
And as a shepherd from the sheep divides
The goats; or husbandman, with reaping bands,
In harvest, separates the precious wheat,
Selected from the tares; so did they part
Mankind, the good and bad, to right and left,
To meet no more; these ne'er again to smile,
Nor those to weep; these never more to share
Society of mercy with the saints,
Nor, henceforth, those to suffer with the vile.
Strange parting! not for hours, nor days, nor months,
Nor for ten thousand times ten thousand years
But for a whole eternity!—though fit,
And pleasant to the righteous, yet to all
Strange, and most strangely felt! The sire, to right
Retiring, saw the son—sprung from his loins,
Beloved how dearly once! but who forgot,
Too soon, in sin's intoxicating cup,
The father's warnings and the mother's tears—
Fall to the left among the reprobate;
And sons, redeemed, beheld the fathers, whom
They loved and honoured once, gathered among
The wicked. Brothers, sisters, kinsmen, friends;
Husband and wife, who ate at the same board,
And under the same roof, united, dwelt,
From youth to hoary age, bearing the chance
And change of Time together, parted then
For evermore. But none, whose friendship grew
From virtue's pure and everlasting root,
Took different roads; these, knit in stricter bonds
Of amity, embracing, saw no more

Death, with his sithe, stand by; nor heard the word,
The bitter word, which closed all earthly friendships,
And finished every feast of love—Farewell.
To all, strange parting! to the wicked, sad
And terrible! New horror seized them, while
They saw the saints withdrawing, and with them
All hope of safety, all delay of wrath.
Beneath a crown of rosy light,—like that
Which once, in Goshen, on the flocks, and herds,
And dwellings, smiled, of Jacob, while the land
Of Nile was dark; or like the pillar bright
Of sacred fire, that stood above the sons
Of Israel, when they camped at midnight by
The foot of Horeb, or the desert side
Of Sinai;—now, the righteous took their place,
All took their place, who ever wished to go
To heaven, for heaven's own sake. Not one remained
Among the accursed, that e'er desired with all
The heart to be redeemed, that ever sought
Submissively to do the will of God,
Howe'er it crossed his own; or to escape
Hell, for aught other than its penal fires.
All took their place, rejoicing, and beheld,
In centre of the crown of golden beams
That canopied them o'er, these gracious words,
Blushing with tints of love: "Fear not, my saints."
To other sight of horrible dismay,
Jehovah's ministers the wicked drove,
And left them bound immoveable in chains
Of Justice. O'er their heads a bowless cloud
Of indignation hung; a cloud it was
Of thick and utter darkness, rolling, like
An ocean, tides of livid, pitchy flame;
With thunders charged, and lightnings ruinous,
And red with forked vengeance, such as wounds
The soul; and full of angry shapes of wrath,
And eddies whirling with tumultuous fire,
And forms of terror raving to and fro,
And monsters, unimagined heretofore
By guilty men in dreams before their death,
From horrid to more horrid changing still,
In hideous movement through that stormy gulf:
And evermore the Thunders, murmuring, spoke
From out the darkness, uttering loud these words,
Which every guilty conscience echoed back:
"Ye knew your duty, but ye did it not."
Dread words! that barred excuse, and threw the weight
Of every man's perdition, on himself,
Directly home. Dread words! heard then, and heard
For ever through the wastes of Erebus.
"Ye knew your duty, but ye did it not!"
These were the words which glowed upon the sword,
Whose wrath burned fearfully behind the cursed,
As they were driven away from God to Tophet.
"Ye knew your duty, but ye did it not!"
These are the words to which the harps of grief
Are strung; and, to the chorus of the damned,
The rocks of hell repeat them, evermore;
Loud echoed through the caverns of despair,
And poured in thunder on the ear of Wo.
Nor ruined men alone, beneath that cloud,
Trembled. There, Satan and his legions stood,
Satan, the first and eldest sinner,—bound
For judgment. He, by other name, held once
Conspicuous rank in heaven among the sons
Of happiness, rejoicing, day and night;
But pride, that was ashamed to bow to God,
Most high, his bosom filled with hate, his face
Made black with envy, and in his soul begot
Thoughts guilty of rebellion 'gainst the throne
Of the Eternal Father, and the Son,—
From everlasting built on righteousness.
Ask not how pride, in one created pure,
Could grow; or sin without example spring,
Where holiness alone was sown: esteem't
Enough, that he, as every being made
By God, was made entirely holy, had
The will of God before him set for law
And regulation of his life, and power
To do as bid; but was, meantime, left free,
To prove his worth, his gratitude, his love;
How proved besides? for how could service done,
That might not else have been withheld, evince
The will to serve, which, rather than the deed,
God doth require, and virtue counts alone?
To stand or fall, to do or leave undone,
Is reason's lofty privilege, denied
To all below, by instinct bound to fate,
Unmeriting, alike, reward or blame.
Thus free, the Devil chose to disobey
The will of God, and was thrown out from heaven,
And with him all his bad example stained;
Yet not to utter punishment decreed,
But left to fill the measure of his sin,
In tempting and seducing man—too soon,
Too easily seduced! And, from the day
He first set foot on earth,—of rancour full,
And pride, and hate, and malice, and revenge,—
He set himself, with most felonious aim
And hellish perseverance, to root out
All good, and in its place to plant all ill;
To rub and raze, from all created things,
The fair and holy portraiture divine,
And on them to enstamp his features grim;
To draw all creatures off from loyalty
To their Creator, and to make them bow
The knee to him. Nor failed of great success,
As populous hell, this day, can testify.
He held, indeed, large empire in the world,
Contending proudly with the King of heaven.
To him temples were built, and sacrifice
Of costly blood upon his altars flowed;

And—what best pleased him, for in show he seemed
Then likest God—whole nations, bowing, fell
Before him, worshipping, and from his lips
Entreated oracles, which he, by priests,—
For many were his priests in every age,—
Answered, though guessing but at future things,
And erring oft, yet still believed ; so well
His ignorance, in ambitious phrase, he veiled.
Nor needs it wonder, that with man once fallen,
His tempting should succeed. Large was his mind
And understanding; though impaired by sin,
Still large; and constant practice, day and night,
In cunning, guile, and all hypocrisy,
From age to age, gave him experience vast
In sin's dark tactics, such as boyish man,
Unarmed by strength divine, could ill withstand.
And well he knew his weaker side; and still,
His lures, with baits that pleased the senses, busked,
To his impatient passions offering terms
Of present joy, and bribing reason's eye
With earthly wealth, and honours near at hand.
Nor failed to misadvise his future hope
And faith, by false, unkerneled promises
Of heavens of sensual gluttony and love,
That suited best their grosser appetites.
Into the sinner's heart, who lived secure,
And feared him least, he entered at his will.
But chief, he chose his residence in courts
And conclaves, stirring princes up to acts
Of blood and tyranny; and moving priests
To barter truth, and swap the souls of men
For lusty benefices, and address
Of lofty sounding. Nor the saints elect,
Who walked with God in virtue's path sublime,
Did he not sometimes venture to molest;
In dreams and moments of unguarded thought,
Suggesting guilty doubts and fears, that God
Would disappoint their hope; and in their way
Bestrewing pleasures, tongued so sweet, and so
In holy garb arrayed that many stooped,
Believing them of heavenly sort, and fell;
And to their high professions, brought disgrace
And scandal; to themselves, thereafter long
And bitter nights of sore repentance, vexed
With shame, unwonted sorrow, and remorse.
And more they should have fallen, and more have wept,
Had not their guardian angels, who, by God
Commissioned, stood beside them in the hour
Of danger, whether craft, or fierce attack,
To Satan's deepest skill opposing skill
More deep, and to his strongest arm, an arm
More strong,—upborne them in their hands, and filled
Their souls with all discernment, quick, to pierce
His stratagems and fairest shows of sin.
Now, like a roaring lion, up and down
The world, destroying, though unseen, he raged,
And now, retiring back to Tartarus,
Far back, beneath the thick of guiltiest dark,
Where night ne'er heard of day, in council grim,
He sat with ministers whose thoughts were damned,
And there such plans devised, as, had not God
Checked and restrained, had added earth entire
To hell, and uninhabited left heaven,
Jehovah unadored. Nor unsevere,
Even then, his punishment deserved. The Worm
That never dies, coiled in his bosom, gnawed
Perpetually; sin after sin brought pang
Succeeding pang; and, now and then, the bolts
Of Zion's King, vindictive, smote his soul
With fiery wo to blast his proud designs;
And gave him earnest of the wrath to come.
And chief, when on the cross, Messiah said,
"'Tis finished," did the edge of vengeance smite
Him through, and all his gloomy legions touch
With new despair. But yet, to be the first
In mischief, to have armies at his call,
To hold dispute with God, in days of Time,
His pride and malice fed, and bore him up
Above the worst of ruin. Still, to plan
And act great deeds, though wicked, brought at least
The recompense which nature hath attached
To all activity, and aim pursued
With perseverance, good, or bad; for as,
By nature's laws, immutable and just,
Enjoyment stops where indolence begins;
And purposeless, to-morrow borrowing sloth,
Itself, heaps on its shoulders loads of wo,
Too heavy to be borne; so industry—
To meditate, to plan, resolve, perform,
Which in itself is good—as surely brings
Reward of good, no matter what be done:
And such reward the Devil had, as long
As the decrees eternal gave him space
To work. But now, all action ceased; his hope
Of doing evil perished quite; his pride,
His courage, failed him; and beneath that cloud,
Which hung its central terrors o'er his head,
With all his angels, he, for sentence, stood,
And rolled his eyes around, that uttered guilt
And wo, in horrible perfection joined
As he had been the chief and leader, long,
Of the apostate crew that warred with God
And holiness; so now, among the bad,
Lowest, and most forlorn, and trembling most,
With all iniquity deformed and foul,
With all perdition ruinous and dark,
He stood,—example awful of the wrath
Of God! sad mark, to which all sin must fall!—
And made, on every side, so black a hell,
That spirits, used to night and misery,
To distance drew, and looked another way;
And from their golden cloud, far off, the saints

Saw round him darkness grow more dark, and heard
The impatient thunderbolts, with deadliest crash
And frequentest, break o'er his head,—the sign
That Satan, there, the vilest sinner, stood.
Ah me! what eyes were there beneath that cloud!
Eyes of despair, final and certain! eyes
That looked, and looked, and saw, where'er they looked,
Interminable darkness! utter wo!
'Twas pitiful to see the early flower
Nipped by the unfeeling frost, just when it rose,
Lovely in youth, and put its beauties on.
'Twas pitiful to see the hopes of all
The year, the yellow harvest, made a heap,
By rains of judgment; or by torrents swept,
With flocks and cattle, down the raging flood;
Or scattered by the winnowing winds, that bore,
Upon their angry wings, the wrath of heaven.
Sad was the field, where, yesterday, was heard
The roar of war; and sad the sight of maid,
Of mother, widow, sister, daughter, wife,
Stooping and weeping over senseless, cold,
Defaced, and mangled lumps of breathless earth,
Which had been husbands, fathers, brothers, sons,
And lovers, when that morning's sun arose.
'Twas sad to see the wonted seat of friend
Removed by death; and sad to visit scenes,
When old, where, in the smiling morn of life,
Lived many, who both knew and loved us much,
And they all gone, dead, or dispersed abroad;
And stranger faces seen among their hills.
'Twas sad to see the little orphan babe
Weeping and sobbing on its mother's grave.
'Twas pitiful to see an old, forlorn,
Decrepit, withered wretch, unhoused, unclad,
Starving to death with poverty and cold.
'Twas pitiful to see a blooming bride,
That promise gave of many a happy year,
Touched by decay, turn pale, and waste, and die.
'Twas pitiful to hear the murderous thrust
Of ruffian's blade that sought the life entire.
'Twas sad to hear the blood come gurgling forth
From out the throat of the wild suicide.
Sad was the sight of widowed, childless age
Weeping.—I saw it once. Wrinkled with time,
And hoary with the dust of years, an old
And worthy man came to his humble roof,
Tottering and slow, and on the threshold stood.
No foot, no voice, was heard within. None came
To meet him, where he oft had met a wife,
And sons, and daughters, glad at his return;
None came to meet him; for that day had seen
The old man lay, within the narrow house,
The last of all his family; and now
He stood in solitude, in solitude
Wide as the world; for all, that made to him
Society, had fled beyond its bounds.
Wherever strayed his aimless eye, there lay
The wreck of some fond hope, that touched his soul
With bitter thoughts, and told him all was passed
His lonely cot was silent, and he looked
As if he could not enter. On his staff,
Bending, he leaned; and from his weary eye,
Distressing sight! a single tear-drop wept.
None followed, for the fount of tears was dry.
Alone and last, it fell from wrinkle down
To wrinkle, till it lost itself, drunk by
The withered cheek, on which again no smile
Should come, or drop of tenderness be seen.
This sight was very pitiful; but one
Was sadder still, the saddest seen in Time.
A man to-day, the glory of his kind,
In reason clear, in understanding large,
In judgment sound, in fancy quick, in hope
Abundant, and in promise, like a field
Well cultured, and refreshed with dews from God;
To-morrow, chained, and raving mad, and whipped
By servile hands; sitting on dismal straw,
And gnashing with his teeth against the chain,
The iron chain, that bound him hand and foot;
And trying whiles to send his glaring eye
Beyond the wide circumference of his wo;
Or, humbling more, more miserable still,
Giving an idiot laugh that served to show
The blasted scenery of his horrid face;
Calling the straw his sceptre, and the stone,
On which he, pinioned, sat, his royal throne.
Poor, poor, poor man! fallen far below the brute!
His reason strove in vain to find her way,
Lost in the stormy desert of his brain;
And, being active still, she wrought all strange,
Fantastic, execrable, monstrous things.
All these were sad, and thousands more, that sleep
Forgotten beneath the funeral pall of Time
And bards, as well became, bewailed them much
With doleful instruments of weeping song.
But what were these? What might be worse had in't,
However small, some grains of happiness;
And man ne'er drank a cup of earthly sort,
That might not hold another drop of gall;
Or, in his deepest sorrow, laid his head
Upon a pillow, set so close with thorns,
That might not hold another prickle still.
Accordingly, the saddest human look
Had hope in't; faint, indeed, but still 'twas hope.
But why excuse the misery of earth?
Say it was dismal, cold, and dark, and deep,
Beyond the utterance of strongest words;
But say that none remembered it, who saw
The eye of beings damned for evermore,
Rolling, and rolling, rolling still in vain,
To find some ray, to see beyond the gulf

Of an unavenued, fierce, fiery, hot,
Interminable, dark Futurity!
And rolling still, and rolling still in vain!
Thus stood the reprobate beneath the shade
Of terror, and beneath the crown of love,
The good; and there was silence in the vault
Of heaven; and as they stood and listened, they heard
Afar to left, among the utter dark,
Hell rolling o'er his waves of burning fire,
And thundering through his caverns, empty then
As if he preparation made, to act
The final vengeance of the fiery Lamb.
And there was heard, coming from out the Pit,
The hollow wailing of Eternal Death,
And horrid cry of the Undying Worm.
The wicked paler turned, and scarce the good
Their colour kept; but were not long dismayed.
That moment, in the heavens, how wondrous fair!
The angel of Mercy stood, and, on the bad
Turning his back, over the ransomed threw
His bow, bedropped with imagery of love,
And promises on which their faith reclined.
Throughout, deep, breathless silence reigned again;
And on the circuit of the upper spheres,
A glorious seraph stood, and cried aloud,
That every ear of man and devil heard,
"Him that is filthy, let be filthy still;
Him that is holy, let be holy still."
And, suddenly, another squadron bright,
Of high arch-angel glory, stooping, brought
A marvellous bow,—one base upon the Cross,
The other on the shoulder of the Bear,
They placed,—from south to north, spanning the heavens,
And on each hand dividing good and bad,—
Who read, on either side, these burning words,
Which ran along the arch in living fire,
And wanted not to be believed in full:
"As ye have sown, so shall ye reap this day."

BOOK X.

God of my fathers! holy, just, and good!
My God! my Father! my unfailing Hope!
Jehovah! let the incense of my praise,
Accepted, burn before thy mercy seat,
And in thy presence burn, both day and night.
Maker! Preserver! my Redeemer! God!
Whom have I in the heavens but Thee alone?
On earth, but Thee, whom should I praise, whom love?
For thou hast brought me hitherto, upheld
By thy omnipotence; and from thy grace,
Unbought, unmerited, though not unsought—
The wells of thy salvation, hast refreshed
My spirit, watering it, at morn and even;
And, by thy Spirit, which thou freely givest
To whom thou wilt, hast led by venturous song,
Over the vale and mountain tract, the light
And shade of man; into the burning deep
Descending now, and now circling the mount,
Where highest sits Divinity enthroned;
Rolling along the tide of fluent thought,
The tide of moral, natural, divine:
Gazing on past and present, and again,
On rapid pinion borne, outstripping Time,
In long excursion, wandering through the groves
Unfading, and the endless avenues,
That shade the landscape of Eternity;
And talking there with holy angels met,
And future men, in glorious vision seen!
Nor unrewarded have I watched at night,
And heard the drowsy sound of neighbouring sleep,
New thought, new imagery, new scenes of bliss
And glory, unrehearsed by mortal tongue,
Which, unrevealed, I, trembling, turned and left,
Bursting at once upon my ravished eye,—
With joy unspeakable have filled my soul,
And made my cup run over with delight:
Though in my face the blasts of adverse winds,
While boldly circumnavigating man,
Winds seeming adverse, though perhaps not so,
Have beat severely; disregarded beat,
When I, behind me, heard the voice of God,
And his propitious Spirit say, Fear not!
God of my fathers! ever present God!
This offering, more, inspire, sustain, accept;
Highest, if numbers answer to the theme;
Best answering, if thy Spirit dictate most.
Jehovah! breathe upon my soul; my heart
Enlarge; my faith increase; increase my hope,
My thoughts exalt; my fancy sanctify,
And all my passions, that I near thy throne
May venture, unreproved; and sing the day,
Which none unholy ought to name, the Day
Of Judgment! greatest day, passed or to come!
Day! which,—deny me what thou wilt, deny
Me home, or friend, or honourable name,—
Thy mercy grant, I, thoroughly prepared,
With comely garment of redeeming love,
May meet, and have my Judge for Advocate.
Come, Gracious Influence, Breath of the Lord
And touch me trembling, as thou touched the man,
Greatly beloved, when he in vision saw,
By Ulai's stream, the Ancient sit; and talked
With Gabriel, to his prayer swiftly sent,
At evening sacrifice. Hold my right hand,
Almighty! hear me, for I ask through Him,
Whom thou hast heard, whom thou wilt always hear,
Thy Son, our interceding Great High Priest!
Reveal the future, let the years to come
Pass by, and open my ear to hear the harp,

The prophet harp, whose wisdom I repeat,
Interpreting the voice of distant song;—
Which thus again resumes the lofty verse,
Loftiest, if I interpret faithfully
The holy numbers which my spirit bears.
Thus came the day, the Harp again began,
The day that many thought should never come,
That all the wicked wished should never come,
That all the righteous had expected long:
Day greatly feared, and yet too little feared,
By him who feared it most; day laughed at much
By the profane, the trembling day of all
Who laughed; day when all shadows passed, all dreams;
When substance, when reality commenced;
Last day of lying, final day of all
Deceit, all knavery, all quackish phrase;
Ender of all disputing, of all mirth
Ungodly, of all loud and boasting speech;
Judge of all judgments, Judge of every judge,
Adjuster of all causes, rights and wrongs;
Day oft appealed to, and appealed to oft
By those who saw its dawn with saddest heart;
Day most magnificent in Fancy's range,
Whence she returned, confounded, trembling, pale,
With overmuch of glory faint and blind;
Day most important held, prepared for most,
By every rational, wise, and holy man;
Day of eternal gain, for worldly loss;
Day of eternal loss for worldly gain;
Great day of terror, vengeance, wo, despair;
Revealer of all secrets, thoughts, desires;
Rein-trying, heart-investigating day,
That stood between Eternity and Time,
Reviewed all past, determined all to come,
And bound all destinies for evermore;
Believing day of unbelief; great day,
That set in proper light the affairs of earth,
And justified the Government Divine;
Great day!—what can we more? what should we more?
Great triumph day of God's incarnate Son!
Great day of glory to the Almighty God!
Day! whence the everlasting years begin
Their date, new era in eternity.
And oft referred to in the song of heaven!
Thus stood the apostate, thus the ransomed stood,
Those held by justice fast, and these by love,
Reading the fiery scutcheonry, that blazed
On high, upon the great celestial bow:
"As ye have sown, so shall ye reap this day."
All read, all understood, and all believed,
Convinced of judgment, righteousness, and sin.
Meantime the universe throughout was still.
The cope, above and round about, was calm;
And motionless, beneath them, lay the Earth,
Silent and sad, as one that sentence waits,
For flagrant crime;—when suddenly was heard,
Behind the azure vaulting of the sky,
Above, and far remote from reach of sight,
The sound of trumpets, and the sound of crowds,
And prancing steeds, and rapid chariot wheels,
That from four quarters rolled, and seemed in haste,
Assembling at some place of rendezvous;
And so they seemed to roll, with furious speed,
As if none meant to be behind the first.
Nor seemed alone: that day, the golden trump,
Whose voice, from centre to circumference
Of all created things, is heard distinct,
God had bid Michael sound, to summon all
The hosts of bliss to presence of their King;
And, all the morning, millions infinite,
That millions governed each, Dominions, Powers
Thrones, Principalities, with all their hosts,
Had been arriving, near the capital,
And royal city, New Jerusalem,
From heaven's remotest bounds. Nor yet from heaven
Alone came they, that day. The world's around,
Or neighbouring nearest, on the verge of night,
Emptied, sent forth their whole inhabitants.
All tribes of being came, of every name,
From every coast, filling Jehovah's courts.
From morn till mid-day, in the squadrons poured
Immense, along the bright celestial roads.
Swiftly they rode, for love unspeakable,
To God, and to Messiah, Prince of Peace,
Drew them, and made obedience haste to be
Approved. And now, before the Eternal Throne,
Brighter, that day, than when the Son prepared
To overthrow the seraphim rebelled,—
And circling round the mount of Deity
Upon the sea of glass, all round about,
And down the borders of the stream of life,
And over all the plains of Paradise,
For many a league of heavenly measurement,—
Assembled, stood the immortal multitudes,
Millions, above all number infinite,
The nations of the blessed. Distinguished each,
By chief of goodly stature blazing far;
By various garb, and flag of various hue
Streaming through heaven from standard lifted high—
The arms and imagery of thousand worlds.
Distinguished each, but all arrayed complete.
In armour bright, of helmet, shield, and sword;
And mounted all in chariots of fire.
A military throng, blent, not confused;
As soldiers on some day of great review,
Burning in splendour of refulgent gold,
And ornament, on purpose, long devised
For this expected day. Distinguished each,
But all accoutred as became their Lord,
And high occasion; all in holiness,
The livery of the soldiery of God.

Vested; and shining all with perfect bliss,
The wages that his faithful servants win.
Thus stood they numberless around the mount
Of presence; and, adoring, waited, hushed
In deepest silence, for the voice of God.
That moment, all the Sacred Hill on high
Burned, terrible with glory, and, behind
The uncreated lustre, hid the Lamb,
Invisible; when, from the radiant cloud,
This voice, addressing all the hosts of heaven,
Proceeded, not in words as we converse,
Each with his fellow, but in language such
As God doth use, imparting, without phrase
Successive, what, in speech of creatures, seems
Long narrative, though long, yet losing much
In feeble symbols of the thought Divine.
My servants long approved, my faithful sons,
Angels of glory, Thrones, Dominions, Powers,
Well pleased, this morning, I have seen the speed
Of your obedience, gathering round my throne,
In order due, and well-becoming garb;
Illustrious, as I see, beyond your wont,
As was my wish to glorify this day:
And now, what your assembling means, attend.
This day concludes the destiny of man.
The hour, appointed from eternity,
To judge the earth in righteousness, is come;
To end the war of Sin, that long has fought,
Permitted, against the sword of Holiness;
To give to men and devils, as their works,
Recorded in my all-remembering book,
I find; good to the good, and great reward
Of everlasting honour, joy, and peace,
Before my presence here for evermore;
And to the evil, as their sins provoke,
Eternal recompense of shame and wo,
Cast out beyond the bounds of light and love.
Long have I stood, as ye, my sons, well know,
Between the cherubim, and stretched my arms
Of mercy out, inviting all to come
To me, and live; my bowels long have moved
With great compassion; and my justice passed
Transgression by, and not imputed sin.
Long here, upon my everlasting throne,
I have beheld my love and mercy scorned;
Have seen my laws despised, my name blasphemed,
My providence accused, my gracious plans
Opposed; and long, too long, have I beheld
The wicked triumph, and my saints reproached
Maliciously, while on my altars lie,
Unanswered still, their prayers and their tears,
That seek my coming, wearied with delay;
And long, Disorder in my moral reign
Has waked rebelliously, disturbed the peace
Of my eternal government, and wrought
Confusion, spreading far and wide, among
My works inferior, which groan to be
Released. Nor long shall groan. The hour of grace,
The final hour of grace, is fully passed;
The time accepted for repentance, faith,
And pardon, is irrevocably passed;
And Justice, unaccompanied, as wont,
With Mercy, now goes forth, to give to all
According to their deeds. Justice alone,—
For why should Mercy any more be joined?
What hath not mercy, mixed with judgment, done,
That mercy, mixed with judgment and reproof,
Could do? Did I not revelation make,
Plainly and clearly, of my will entire?
Before them set my holy law, and gave
Them knowledge, wisdom, prowess to obey,
And win, by self-wrought works, eternal life?
Rebelled, did I not send them terms of peace,
Which, not my justice, but my mercy asked?—
Terms, costly to my well-beloved Son;
To them, gratuitous, exacting faith
Alone for pardon, works evincing faith?
Have I not early risen, and sent my seers,
Prophets, apostles, teachers, ministers,
With signs and wonders, working in my name?
Have I not still, from age to age, raised up
As I saw needful, great, religious men,
Gifted by me with large capacity,
And by my arm omnipotent upheld,
To pour the numbers of my mercy forth,
And roll my judgments on the ear of man?
And lastly, when the promised hour was come,—
What more could most abundant mercy do?—
Did I not send Immanuel forth, my Son,
Only begotten, to purchase, by his blood,
As many as believed upon his name?
Did he not die to give repentance, such
As I accept, and pardon of all sins?
Has he not taught, beseeched, and shed abroad
The Spirit unconfined, and given at times
Example fierce of wrath and judgment, poured
Vindictively on nations guilty long?
What means of reformation, that my Son
Has left behind, untried? what plainer words,
What arguments more strong, as yet remain?
Did he not tell them, with his lips of truth,
The righteous should be saved, the wicked damned?
And has he not, awake both day and night,
Here interceded with prevailing voice,
At my right hand, pleading his precious blood
Which magnified my holy law, and bought,
For all who wished, perpetual righteousness?
And have not you, my faithful servants, all
Been frequent forth, obedient to my will,
With messages of mercy and of love,
Administering my gifts to sinful man?
And have not all my mercy, all my love,
Been sealed and stamped with signature of heaven?
By proof of wonders, miracles, and signs

Attested, and attested more by truth
Divine, inherent in the tidings sent?
This day declares the consequence of all.
Some have believed, are sanctified, and saved,
Prepared for dwelling in this holy place,
In these their mansions, built before my face;
And now, beneath a crown of golden light,
Beyond our wall, at place of judgment, they,
Expecting, wait the promised, due reward.
The others stand with Satan bound in chains,
The others, who refused to be redeemed:
They stand, unsanctified, unpardoned, sad,
Waiting the sentence that shall fix their wo.
The others, who refused to be redeemed;
For all had grace sufficient to believe,
All who my gospel heard; and none, who heard
It not, shall by its law, this day, be tried.
Necessity of sinning, my decrees
Imposed on none; but rather, all inclined
To holiness; and grace was bountiful,
Abundant, overflowing with my word;
My word of life and peace, which to all men,
Who shall or stand or fall, by law revealed,
Was offered freely, as 'twas freely sent,
Without all money, and without all price.
Thus they have all, by willing act, despised
Me, and my Son, and sanctifying Spirit.
But now, no longer shall they mock or scorn.
The day of grace and mercy is complete,
And Godhead from their misery absolved.
So saying, He, the Father infinite,
Turning, addressed Messiah, where he sat,
Exalted gloriously, at his right hand.
This day belongs to justice and to thee,
Eternal Son, thy right for service done,
Abundantly fulfilling all my will;
By promise thine, from all eternity,
Made in the ancient Covenant of Grace;
And thine, as most befitting, since in thee
Divine and human meet, impartial Judge,
Consulting thus the interest of both.
Go then, my Son, divine similitude,
Image express of Deity unseen,
The book of my remembrance take; and take
The golden crowns of life, due to the saints;
And take the seven last thunders ruinous;
Thy armour take; gird on thy sword, thy sword
Of justice ultimate, reserved, till now,
Unsheathed, in the eternal armoury;
And mount the living chariot of God.
Thou goest not now, as once, to Calvary,
To be insulted, buffeted, and slain;
Thou goest not now, with battle and the voice
Of war, as once against the rebel hosts.
Thou goest a Judge, and findst the guilty bound;
Thou goest to prove, condemn, acquit, reward.
Not unaccompanied; all these, my saints,
Go with thee, glorious retinue, to sing
Thy triumph, and participate thy joy;
And I, the Omnipresent, with thee go:
And with thee all the glory of my throne.
Thus said the Father; and the Son beloved,
Omnipotent, Omniscient, Fellow God,
Arose, resplendent with Divinity;
And He the book of God's remembrance took;
And took the seven last thunders ruinous;
And took the crowns of life, due to the saints;
His armour took; girt on his sword, his sword
Of justice ultimate, reserved, till now,
Unsheathed, in the eternal armoury;
And up the living chariot of God
Ascended, signifying all complete.
And now the Trump, of wondrous melody,
By man or angel never heard before,
Sounded with thunder, and the march began.
Not swift, as cavalcade, on battle bent
But, as became procession of a judge,
Solemn, magnificent, majestic, slow;
Moving sublime with glory infinite,
And numbers infinite, and awful song,
They passed the gate of heaven, which, many a league,
Opened either way, to let the glory forth
Of this great march. And now, the sons of men
Beheld their coming, which, before, they heard
Beheld the glorious countenance of God!
All light was swallowed up, all objects seen
Faded; and the Incarnate, visible
Alone, held every eye upon him fixed;
The wicked saw his majesty severe;
And those who pierced Him saw his face with clouds
Of glory circled round, essential bright!
And to the rocks and mountains called in vain,
To hide them from the fierceness of his wrath:
Almighty power their flight restrained, and held
Them bound immoveable before the bar.
The righteous, undismayed and bold—best proof,
This day, of fortitude sincere,—sustained
By inward faith, with acclamations loud,
Received the coming of the Son of Man;
And, drawn by love, inclined to his approach,
Moving to meet the brightness of his face.
Meantime, 'tween good and bad, the Judge his wheels
Stayed, and, ascending, sat upon the great
White Throne, that morning founded there by power
Omnipotent, and built on righteousness
And truth. Behind, before, on every side,
In native and reflected blaze of bright,
Celestial equipage, the myriads stood,
That with his marching came; rank above rank,
Rank above rank, with shield and flaming sword.
'Twas silence all! and quick, on right and left,
A mighty angel spread the book of God's
Remembrance; and, with conscience now sincere,

All men compared the record, written there
By finger of Omniscience; and received
Their sentence, in themselves, of joy or wo;
Condemned or justified, while yet the Judge
Waited, as if to let them prove themselves.
The righteous, in the book of life displayed,
Rejoicing, read their names; rejoicing, read
Their faith for righteousness received, and deeds
Of holiness, as proof of faith complete.
The wicked, in the book of endless death,
Spread out to left, bewailing, read their names;
And read beneath them, Unbelief, and fruit
Of unbelief, vile, unrepented deeds,
Now unrepentable for evermore;
And gave approval of the wo affixed.
This done, the Omnipotent, Omniscient Judge,
Rose infinite, the sentence to pronounce,
The sentence of eternal wo or bliss!
All glory heretofore seen or conceived,
All majesty, annihilated, dropped,
That moment, from remembrance, and was lost;
And silence, deepest hitherto esteemed,
Seemed noisy to the stillness of this hour.
Comparisons I seek not, nor should find,
If sought. That silence, which all being held,
When God's Almighty Son, from off the walls
Of heaven the rebel angels threw, accursed,
So still, that all creation heard their fall
Distinctly, in the lake of burning fire,—
Was now forgotten, and every silence else.
All being rational, created then,
Around the judgment seat, intensely listened.
No creature breathed. Man, angel, devil, stood
And listened; the spheres stood still, and every star
Stood still, and listened; and every particle,
Remotest in the womb of matter, stood,
Bending to hear, devotional and still.
And thus upon the wicked, first, the Judge
Pronounced the sentence, written before of old:
"Depart from me, ye cursed, into the fire,
Prepared eternal in the Gulf of Hell,
Where ye shall weep and wail for evermore,
Reaping the harvest which your sins have sown."
So saying, God grew dark with utter wrath;
And, drawing now the sword, undrawn before,
Which through the range of infinite, all around,
A gleam of fiery indignation threw,
He lifted up his hand omnipotent,
And down among the damned the burning edge
Plunged; and from forth his arrowy quiver sent,
Emptied, the seven last thunders ruinous,
Which, entering, withered all their souls with fire.
Then first was vengeance, first was ruin seen!
Red, unrestrained, vindictive, final, fierce!
They, howling, fled to west among the dark;
But fled not these the terrors of the Lord.
Pursued, and driven beyond the Gulf, which frowns
Impassable, between the good and bad,
And downward far remote to left, oppressed
And scorched with the avenging fires, begun
Burning within them,—they upon the verge
Of Erebus, a moment, pausing stood,
And saw, below, the unfathomable lake,
Tossing with tides of dark, tempestuous wrath;
And would have looked behind; but greater wrath,
Behind, forbade, which now no respite gave
To final misery. God, in the grasp
Of his Almighty strength, took them upraised,
And threw them down, into the yawning pit
Of bottomless perdition, ruined, damned,
Fast bound in chains of darkness evermore;
And Second Death, and the Undying Worm,
Opening their horrid jaws, with hideous yell,
Falling, received their everlasting prey.
A groan returned, as down they sunk, and sunk,
And ever sunk, among the utter dark!
A groan returned! the righteous heard the groan,
The groan of all the reprobate, when first
They felt damnation sure! and heard Hell close!
And heard Jehovah, and his love retire!
A groan returned! the righteous heard the groan,
As if all misery, all sorrow, grief,
All pain, all anguish, all despair, which all
Have suffered, or shall feel, from first to last
Eternity, had gathered to one pang,
And issued in one groan of boundless wo!
And now the wall of hell, the outer wall,
First gateless then, closed round them; that which thou
Hast seen, of fiery adamant, emblazed
With hideous imagery, above all hope,
Above all flight of fancy, burning high;
And guarded evermore, by Justice, turned
To Wrath, that hears, unmoved, the endless groan
Of those wasting within; and sees, unmoved,
The endless tear of vain repentance fall.
Nor ask if these shall ever be redeemed.
They never shall! Not God, but their own sin,
Condemns them. What could be done, as thou hast heard,
Has been already done; all has been tried
That wisdom infinite, and boundless grace,
Working together, could devise; and all
Has failed. Why now succeed? Though God should stoop,
Inviting still, and send his Only Son
To offer grace in hell, the pride, that first
Refused, would still refuse; the unbelief,
Still unbelieving, would deride and mock;
Nay more, refuse, deride, and mock; for sin,
Increasing still, and growing, day and night,
Into the essence of the soul, become
All sin, makes what in time seemed probable,—
Seemed probable, since God invited then,—
For ever now impossible. Thus they,
According to the eternal laws which bind
All creatures, bind the Uncreated One,
Though we name not the sentence of the Judge,

Must daily grow in sin and punishment,
Made by themselves their necessary lot,
Unchangeable to all eternity.
What lot! what choice! I sing not, can not sing.
Here, highest seraphs tremble on the lyre,
And made a sudden pause!—but thou hast seen.
And here, the bard, a moment, held his hand,
As one who saw more of that horrid wo
Than words could utter; and again resumed.
Nor yet had vengeance done. The guilty Earth,
Inanimate, debased, and stained by sin,
Seat of rebellion, of corruption, long,
And tainted with mortality throughout,—
God sentenced next; and sent the final fires
Of ruin forth, to burn and to destroy.
The saints its burning saw, and thou mayst see.
Look yonder, round the lofty golden walls
And galleries of New Jerusalem,
Among the imagery of wonders passed;
Look near the southern gate; look, and behold—
On spacious canvas, touched with living hues—
The Conflagration of the ancient earth,
The handywork of high archangel, drawn
From memory of what he saw, that day.
See! how the mountains, how the valleys burn;
The Andes burn, the Alps, the Appenines,
Taurus and Atlas; all the islands burn;
The Ocean burns, and rolls his waves of flame.
See how the lightnings, barbed, red with wrath,
Sent from the quiver of Omnipotence,
Cross and recross the fiery gloom, and burn
Into the centre!—burn without, within,
And help the native fires, which God awoke,
And kindled with the fury of his wrath.
As inly troubled, now she seems to shake;
The flames, dividing, now a moment, fall;
And now, in one conglomerated mass,
Rising, they glow on high, prodigious blaze!
Then fall and sink again, as if, within,
The fuel, burned to ashes, was consumed.
So burned the Earth upon that dreadful day,
Yet not to full annihilation burned.
The essential particles of dust remained,
Purged by the final, sanctifying fires,
From all corruption; from all stain of sin,
Done there by man or devil, purified.
The essential particles remained, of which
God built the world again, renewed, improved,
With fertile vale, and wood of fertile bough;
And streams of milk and honey, flowing song;
And mountains cinctured with perpetual green;
In clime and season fruitful, as at first,
When Adam woke, unfallen, in Paradise.
And God, from out the fount of native light,
A handful took of beams, and clad the sun
Again in glory; and sent forth the moon
To borrow thence her wonted rays, and lead
Her stars, the virgin daughters of the sky.
And God revived the winds, revived the tides;
And touching her from his Almighty hand,
With force centrifugal, she onward ran,
Coursing her wonted path, to stop no more.
Delightful scene of new inhabitants!
As thou, this morn, in passing hither, sawst.
Thus done, the glorious Judge, turning to right,
With countenance of love unspeakable,
Beheld the righteous, and approved them thus:
"Ye blessed of my Father, come, ye just,
Enter the joy eternal of your Lord;
Receive your crowns, ascend, and sit with me,
At God's right hand, in glory evermore!"
Thus said the Omnipotent, Incarnate God
And waited not the homage of the crowns,
Already thrown before him; nor the loud
Amen of universal, holy praise;
But turned the living chariot of fire,
And swifter now,—as joyful to declare
This day's proceedings in his Father's court,
And to present the number of his sons
Before the Throne,—ascended up to heaven
And all his saints, and all his angel bands,
As, glorious, they on high ascended, sung
Glory to God and to the Lamb!—they sung
Messiah, fairer than the sons of men,
And altogether lovely. Grace is poured
Into thy lips, above all measure poured;
And therefore God hath blessed thee evermore.
Gird, gird thy sword upon thy thigh, O thou
Most Mighty! with thy glory ride; with all
Thy majesty, ride prosperously, because
Of meekness, truth, and righteousness. Thy throne,
O God, for ever and for ever stands;
The sceptre of thy kingdom still is right;
Therefore hath God, thy God, anointed thee,
With oil of gladness and perfumes of myrrh,
Out of the ivory palaces, above
Thy fellows, crowned the Prince of endless peace!
Thus sung they God, their Saviour: and themselves
Prepared complete to enter now, with Christ,
Their living Head, into the Holy Place.
Behold! the daughter of the King, the bride,
All glorious within, the bride adorned,
Comely in broidery of gold! behold,
She comes, appareled royally, in robes
Of perfect righteousness, fair as the sun,
With all her virgins, her companions fair,—
Into the Palace of the King she comes,
She comes to dwell for evermore! Awake,
Eternal harps! awake, awake, and sing!—
The Lord, the Lord, our God Almighty, reigns!
Thus the Messiah, with the hosts of bliss,
Entered the gates of heaven, unquestioned now
Which closed behind them, to go out no more;
And stood, accepted, in his Father's sight;
Before the glorious, everlasting Throne,
Presenting all his saints; not one was lost,

Of all that he in Covenant received;
And, having given the kingdom up, he sat,
Where now he sits and reigns, on the right hand
Of glory; and our God is all in all!
Thus have I sung beyond thy first request,
Rolling my numbers o'er the track of man,
The world at dawn, at mid-day, and decline;
Time gone, the righteous saved, the wicked damned,
And God's eternal government approved.

THE END OF THE COURSE OF TIME.

NEW AND COMPLETE COOK-BOOK.

THE PRACTICAL COOK-BOOK,

CONTAINING UPWARDS OF

ONE THOUSAND RECEIPTS,

Consisting of Directions for Selecting, Preparing, and Cooking all kinds of Meats, Fish, Poultry, and Game; Soups, Broths, Vegetables, and Salads. Also, for making all kinds of Plain and Fancy Breads, Pastes, Puddings, Cakes, Creams, Ices, Jellies, Preserves, Marmalades, &c. &c. &c. Together with various Miscellaneous Recipes, and numerous Preparations for Invalids.

BY MRS. BLISS.

In one volume, 12mo.

The City Merchant; or, The Mysterious Failure.

BY J. B. JONES,

AUTHOR OF "WILD WESTERN SCENES," "THE WESTERN MERCHANT," &c.

ILLUSTRATED WITH TEN ENGRAVINGS.

In one volume, 12mo.

EL PUCHERO; or, A Mixed Dish from Mexico.

EMBRACING GENERAL SCOTT'S CAMPAIGN, WITH SKETCHES OF MILITARY LIFE IN FIELD AND CAMP; OF THE CHARACTER OF THE COUNTRY, MANNERS AND WAYS OF THE PEOPLE, &c.

BY RICHARD M'SHERRY, M. D., U. S. N.,

LATE ACTING SURGEON OF REGIMENT OF MARINES.

In one volume, 12mo.

WITH NUMEROUS ILLUSTRATIONS.

MONEY-BAGS AND TITLES:

A HIT AT THE FOLLIES OF THE AGE.

TRANSLATED FROM THE FRENCH OF JULES SANDEAU.

BY LEONARD MYERS.

One volume, 12mo.

"'*Money-Bags and Titles*' is quite a remarkable work, amounts to a kindly exposure of the folly of human pride, and also presents at once the evil and the remedy. If good-natured ridicule of the impostures practised by a set of self-styled reformers, who have nothing to lose, and to whom change must be gain—if, in short, a delineation of the mistaken ideas which prevent, and the means which conduce to happiness, be traits deserving of commendation,—the reader will find much to enlist his attention and win his approbation in the pages of this unpretending, but truly meritorious publication."

WHAT IS CHURCH HISTORY?

A VINDICATION OF THE IDEA OF HISTORICAL DEVELOPMENTS,

BY PHILIP SCHAF.

TRANSLATED FROM THE GERMAN.

In one volume, 12mo.

DODD'S LECTURES.

DISCOURSES TO YOUNG MEN.

ILLUSTRATED BY NUMEROUS HIGHLY INTERESTING ANECDOTES.

BY WILLIAM DODD, LL. D.,

CHAPLAIN IN ORDINARY TO HIS MAJESTY GEORGE THE THIRD.

FIRST AMERICAN EDITION, WITH ENGRAVINGS.

One volume, 18mo.

THE IRIS:

AN ORIGINAL SOUVENIR.

With Contributions from the First Writers in the Country.

EDITED BY PROF. JOHN S. HART.

With Splendid Illuminations and Steel Engravings. Bound in Turkey Morocco and rich Papier Mache Binding.

IN ONE VOLUME, OCTAVO.

Its contents are entirely original. Among the contributors are names well known in the republic of letters; such as Mr. Boker, Mr. Stoddard, Prof. Moffat, Edith May, Mrs. Sigourney, Caroline May, Mrs. Kinney, Mrs. Butler, Mrs. Pease, Mrs. Swift, Mr. Van Bibber, Rev. Charles T. Brooks, Mrs. Dorr, Erastus W. Ellsworth, Miss E. W. Barnes, Mrs. Williams, Mary Young, Dr. Gardette, Alice Carey, Phebe Carey, Augusta Browne, Hamilton Browne, Caroline Eustis, Margaret Junkin, Maria J. B. Browne, Miss Starr, Mrs. Brotherson, Kate Campbell, &c.

Gems from the Sacred Mine;

OR, HOLY THOUGHTS UPON SACRED SUBJECTS.

BY CLERGYMEN OF THE EPISCOPAL CHURCH.

EDITED BY THOMAS WYATT, A. M.

In one volume, 12mo.

WITH SEVEN BEAUTIFUL STEEL ENGRAVINGS.

The contents of this work are chiefly by clergymen of the Episcopal Church. Among the contributors will be found the names of the Right Rev. Bishop Potter, Bishop Hopkins, Bishop Smith, Bishop Johns, and Bishop Doane; and the Rev. Drs. H. V. D. Johns, Coleman, and Butler; Rev. G. T. Bedell, M'Cabe, Ogilsby, &c. The illustrations are rich and exquisitely wrought engravings upon the following subjects:—"Samuel before Eli," "Peter and John healing the Lame Man," "The Resurrection of Christ," "Joseph sold by his Brethren," "The Tables of the Law," "Christ's Agony in the Garden," and "The Flight into Egypt." These subjects, with many others in prose and verse, are ably treated throughout the work.

HAW-HO-NOO:

OR, THE RECORDS OF A TOURIST.

BY CHARLES LANMAN,

Author of "A Summer in the Wilderness," &c. In one volume, 12mo.

"In the present book, '*Haw-ho-noo*,' (an Indian name, by the way, for America,) the author has gathered up some of the relics of his former tours, and added to them other interesting matter. It contains a number of carefully written and instructive articles upon the various kinds of fish in our country, whose capture affords sport for anglers; reminiscences of unique incidents, manners, and customs in different parts of the country; and other articles, narrative, descriptive, and sentimental. In a supplement are gathered many curious Indian legends. They are related with great simplicity and clearness, and will be of service hereafter to the poem-makers of America. Many of them are quite beautiful."—*National Intelligencer.*

LONZ POWERS; Or, The Regulators.

A ROMANCE OF KENTUCKY.

FOUNDED ON FACTS.

BY JAMES WEIR, ESQ.

IN TWO VOLUMES.

The scenes, characters, and incidents in these volumes have been copied from nature, and from real life. They are represented as taking place at that period in the history of Kentucky, when the Indian, driven, after many a hard-fought field, from his favourite hunting-ground, was succeeded by a rude and unlettered population, interspersed with organized bands of desperadoes, scarcely less savage than the red men they had displaced. The author possesses a vigorous and graphic pen, and has produced a very interesting romance, which gives us a striking portrait of the times he describes.

THE WESTERN MERCHANT.

A NARRATIVE,

Containing useful Instruction for the Western Man of Business, who makes his Purchases in the East. Also, Information for the Eastern Man, whose Customers are in the West. Likewise, Hints for those who design emigrating to the West. Deduced from actual experience.

BY LUKE SHORTFIELD, A WESTERN MERCHANT.

One volume, 12mo.

This is a new work, and will be found very interesting to the Country Merchant, &c. &c.

A sprightly, pleasant book, with a vast amount of information in a very agreeable shape. Business, Love, and Religion are all discussed, and many proper sentiments expressed in regard to each. The "moral" of the work is summed up in the following concluding sentences: "Adhere steadfastly to your business; adhere steadfastly to your first love; adhere steadfastly to the church."

A MANUAL OF POLITENESS,

COMPRISING THE

PRINCIPLES OF ETIQUETTE AND RULES OF BEHAVIOUR

IN GENTEEL SOCIETY, FOR PERSONS OF BOTH SEXES.

18mo., with Plates.

Book of Politeness.

THE GENTLEMAN AND LADY'S

BOOK OF POLITENESS AND PROPRIETY OF DEPORTMENT.

DEDICATED TO THE YOUTH OF BOTH SEXES.

BY MADAME CELNART.

Translated from the Sixth Paris Edition, Enlarged and Improved.

Fifth American Edition.

One volume, 18mo.

THE ANTEDILUVIANS; Or, The World Destroyed.

A NARRATIVE POEM, IN TEN BOOKS.

BY JAMES M'HENRY, M.D.

One volume, 18mo.

Bennett's (Rev. John) Letters to a Young Lady,

ON A VARIETY OF SUBJECTS CALCULATED TO IMPROVE THE HEART, TO FORM THE MANNERS, AND ENLIGHTEN THE UNDERSTANDING.

"That our daughters may be as polished corners of the temple."

The publishers sincerely hope (for the happiness of mankind) that a copy of this valuable little work will be found the companion of every young lady, as much of the happiness of every family depends on the proper cultivation of the female mind.

THE DAUGHTER'S OWN BOOK:

OR, PRACTICAL HINTS FROM A FATHER TO HIS DAUGHTER.

One volume, 18mo.

This is one of the most practical and truly valuable treatises on the culture and discipline of the female mind, which has hitherto been published in this country; and the publishers are very confident, from the great demand for this invaluable little work, that ere long it will be found in the library of every young lady.

THE AMERICAN CHESTERFIELD:

Or, "Youth's Guide to the Way to Wealth, Honour, and Distinction," &c. 18mo.

CONTAINING ALSO A COMPLETE TREATISE ON THE ART OF CARVING.

"We most cordially recommend the American Chesterfield to general attention; but to young persons particularly, as one of the best works of the kind that has ever been published in this country. It cannot be too highly appreciated, nor its perusal be unproductive of satisfaction and usefulness."

SENECA'S MORALS.

BY WAY OF ABSTRACT TO WHICH IS ADDED, A DISCOURSE UNDER THE TITLE OF AN AFTER-THOUGHT.

BY SIR ROGER L'ESTRANGE, KNT.

A new, fine edition; one volume, 18mo.

A copy of this valuable little work should be found in every family library.

NEW SONG-BOOK.

Grigg's Southern and Western Songster;

BEING A CHOICE COLLECTION OF THE MOST FASHIONABLE SONGS, MANY OF WHICH ARE ORIGINAL.

In one volume, 18mo.

Great care was taken, in the selection, to admit no song that contained, in the slightest degree, any indelicate or improper allusions; and with great propriety it may claim the title of "The Parlour Song-Book, or Songster." The immortal Shakspeare observes—

"The man that hath not music in himself,
Nor is not moved with concord of sweet sounds,
Is fit for treasons, stratagems, and spoils."

ROBOTHAM'S POCKET FRENCH DICTIONARY,

CAREFULLY REVISED,

AND THE PRONUNCIATION OF ALL THE DIFFICULT WORDS ADDED.

THE LIFE AND OPINIONS OF TRISTRAM SHANDY, GENTLEMAN.

COMPRISING THE HUMOROUS ADVENTURES OF

UNCLE TOBY AND CORPORAL TRIM.

BY L. STERNE.

Beautifully Illustrated by Darley. Stitched.

A SENTIMENTAL JOURNEY.

BY L. STERNE.

Illustrated as above by Darley. Stitched.

The beauties of this author are so well known, and his errors in style and expression so few and far between, that one reads with renewed delight his delicate turns, &c.

THE LIFE OF GENERAL JACKSON,

WITH A LIKENESS OF THE OLD HERO.

One volume, 18mo.

LIFE OF PAUL JONES.

In one volume, 12mo.

WITH ONE HUNDRED ILLUSTRATIONS.

BY JAMES HAMILTON.

The work is compiled from his original journals and correspondence, and includes an account of his services in the American Revolution, and in the war between the Russians and Turks in the Black Sea. There is scarcely any Naval Hero, of any age, who combined in his character so much of the adventurous, skilful and daring, as Paul Jones. The incidents of his life are almost as startling and absorbing as those of romance. His achievements during the American Revolution—the fight between the Bon Homme Richard and Serapis, the most desperate naval action on record—and the alarm into which, with so small a force, he threw the coasts of England and Scotland—are matters comparatively well known to Americans; but the incidents of his subsequent career have been veiled in obscurity, which is dissipated by this biography. A book like this, narrating the actions of such a man, ought to meet with an extensive sale, and become as popular as Robinson Crusoe in fiction, or Weems's Life of Marion and Washington, and similar books, in fact. It contains 400 pages, has a handsome portrait and medallion likeness of Jones, and is illustrated with numerous original wood engravings of naval scenes and distinguished men with whom he was familiar.

THE GREEK EXILE;

Or, A Narrative of the Captivity and Escape of Christophorus Plato Castanis,

DURING THE MASSACRE ON THE ISLAND OF SCIO BY THE TURKS.

TOGETHER WITH VARIOUS ADVENTURES IN GREECE AND AMERICA.

WRITTEN BY HIMSELF,

Author of an Essay on the Ancient and Modern Greek Languages; Interpretation of the Attributes of the Principal Fabulous Deities; The Jewish Maiden of Scio's Citadel; and the Greek Boy in the Sunday-School.

One volume, 12mo.

THE YOUNG CHORISTER;

A Collection of New and Beautiful Tunes, adapted to the use of Sabbath-Schools, from some of the most distinguished composers; together with many of the author's compositions.

EDITED BY MINARD W. WILSON.

CAMP LIFE OF A VOLUNTEER.

A Campaign in Mexico; Or, A Glimpse at Life in Camp.

BY "ONE WHO HAS SEEN THE ELEPHANT."

Life of General Zachary Taylor,

COMPRISING A NARRATIVE OF EVENTS CONNECTED WITH HIS PROFESSIONAL CAREER, AND AUTHENTIC INCIDENTS OF HIS EARLY YEARS.

BY J. REESE FRY AND R. T. CONRAD.

With an original and accurate Portrait, and eleven elegant Illustrations, by Darley.

In one handsome 12mo. volume.

"It is by far the fullest and most interesting biography of General Taylor that we have ever seen." —*Richmond (Whig) Chronicle.*

"On the whole, we are satisfied that this volume is the most correct and comprehensive one yet published." —*Hunt's Merchants' Magazine.*

"The superiority of this edition over the ephemeral publications of the day consists in fuller and more authentic accounts of his family, his early life, and Indian wars. The narrative of his proceedings in Mexico is drawn partly from reliable private letters, but chiefly from his own official correspondence."

"It forms a cheap, substantial, and attractive volume, and one which should be read at the fireside of every family who desire a faithful and true life of the Old General."

GENERAL TAYLOR AND HIS STAFF:

Comprising Memoirs of Generals Taylor, Worth, Wool, and Butler; Cols. May, Cross, Clay, Hardin, Yell, Hays, and other distinguished Officers attached to General Taylor's Army. Interspersed with

NUMEROUS ANECDOTES OF THE MEXICAN WAR,

and Personal Adventures of the Officers. Compiled from Public Documents and Private Correspondence. With

ACCURATE PORTRAITS, AND OTHER BEAUTIFUL ILLUSTRATIONS.

In one volume, 12mo.

GENERAL SCOTT AND HIS STAFF:

Comprising Memoirs of Generals Scott, Twiggs, Smith, Quitman, Shields, Pillow, Lane, Cadwalader, Patterson, and Pierce; Cols. Childs, Riley, Harney, and Butler; and other distinguished officers attached to General Scott's Army.

TOGETHER WITH

Notices of General Kearny, Col. Doniphan, Col. Fremont, and other officers distinguished in the Conquest of California and New Mexico; and Personal Adventures of the Officers. Compiled from Public Documents and Private Correspondence. With

ACCURATE PORTRAITS, AND OTHER BEAUTIFUL ILLUSTRATIONS.

In one volume, 12mo.

THE FAMILY DENTIST,

INCLUDING THE SURGICAL, MEDICAL AND MECHANICAL TREATMENT OF THE TEETH.

Illustrated with thirty-one Engravings.

By CHARLES A. DU BOUCHET, M. D., Dental Surgeon.

In one volume, 18mo.

MECHANICS FOR THE MILLWRIGHT, ENGINEER AND MACHINIST, CIVIL ENGINEER, AND ARCHITECT:

CONTAINING

THE PRINCIPLES OF MECHANICS APPLIED TO MACHINERY

Of American models, Steam-Engines, Water-Works, Navigation, Bridge-building, &c. &c. By

FREDERICK OVERMAN,

Author of "The Manufacture of Iron," and other scientific treatises.

Illustrated by 150 Engravings. In one large 12mo. volume.

WILLIAMS'S TRAVELLER'S AND TOURIST'S GUIDE

Through the United States, Canada, &c.

This book will be found replete with information, not only to the traveller, but likewise to the man of business. In its preparation, an entirely new plan has been adopted, which, we are convinced, needs only a trial to be fully appreciated.

Among its many valuable features, are tables showing at a glance the *distance, fare*, and *time* occupied in travelling from the principal cities to the most important places in the Union; so that the question frequently asked, without obtaining a satisfactory reply, is here answered in full. Other tables show the distances from New York, &c., to domestic and foreign ports, by sea; and also, by way of comparison, from New York and Liverpool to the principal ports beyond and around Cape Horn, &c., as well as *via* the Isthmus of Panama. Accompanied by a large and accurate Map of the United States, including a separate Map of California, Oregon, New Mexico and Utah. Also, a Map of the Island of Cuba, and Plan of the City and Harbor of Havana; and a Map of Niagara River and Falls.

THE LEGISLATIVE GUIDE:

Containing directions for conducting business in the House of Representatives; the Senate of the United States; the Joint Rules of both Houses; a Synopsis of Jefferson's Manual, and copious Indices; together with a concise system of Rules of Order, based on the regulations of the U. S. Congress. Designed to economise time, secure uniformity and despatch in conducting business in all secular meetings, and also in all religious, political, and Legislative Assemblies.

BY JOSEPH BARTLETT BURLEIGH, LL. D.

In one volume, 12mo.

This is considered by our Judges and Congressmen as decidedly the best work of the kind extant. Every young man in the country should have a copy of this book.

THE INITIALS; A Story of Modern Life.

THREE VOLUMES OF THE LONDON EDITION COMPLETE IN ONE VOLUME 12MO.

A new novel, equal to "Jane Eyre."

WILD WESTERN SCENES:

A NARRATIVE OF ADVENTURES IN THE WESTERN WILDERNESS.

Wherein the Exploits of Daniel Boone, the Great American Pioneer, are particularly described. Also, Minute Accounts of Bear, Deer, and Buffalo Hunts — Desperate Conflicts with the Savages — Fishing and Fowling Adventures — Encounters with Serpents, &c.

By Luke Shortfield, Author of "The Western Merchant."

BEAUTIFULLY ILLUSTRATED. One volume, 12mo.

POEMS OF THE PLEASURES:

Consisting of the PLEASURES OF IMAGINATION, by Akenside; the PLEASURES OF MEMORY, by Samuel Rogers; the PLEASURES OF HOPE, by Campbell; and the PLEASURES OF FRIENDSHIP, by M'Henry. With a Memoir of each Author, prepared expressly for this work. 18mo.

BALDWIN'S PRONOUNCING GAZETTEER.

A PRONOUNCING GAZETTEER:

CONTAINING

TOPOGRAPHICAL, STATISTICAL, AND OTHER INFORMATION, OF ALL THE MORE IMPORTANT PLACES IN THE KNOWN WORLD, FROM THE MOST RECENT AND AUTHENTIC SOURCES.

BY THOMAS BALDWIN.

Assisted by several other Gentlemen.

To which is added an APPENDIX, containing more than TEN THOUSAND ADDITIONAL NAMES, chiefly of the small Towns and Villages, &c., of the United States and of Mexico.

NINTH EDITION, WITH A SUPPLEMENT,

Giving the Pronunciation of near two thousand names, besides those pronounced in the Original Work: Forming in itself a Complete Vocabulary of Geographical Pronunciation.

ONE VOLUME 12MO.—PRICE, $1.50.

Arthur's Library for the Household.

Complete in Twelve handsome 18mo. Volumes, bound in Scarlet Cloth.

1. WOMAN'S TRIALS; OR, TALES AND SKETCHES FROM THE LIFE AROUND US.
2. MARRIED LIFE; ITS SHADOWS AND SUNSHINE.
3. THE TWO WIVES; OR LOST AND WON.
4. THE WAYS OF PROVIDENCE; OR, "HE DOETH ALL THINGS WELL."
5. HOME SCENES AND HOME INFLUENCES.
6. STORIES FOR YOUNG HOUSEKEEPERS.
7. LESSONS IN LIFE, FOR ALL WHO WILL READ THEM.
8. SEED-TIME AND HARVEST; OR, WHATSOEVER A MAN SOWETH THAT SHALL HE ALSO REAP.
9. STORIES FOR PARENTS.
10. OFF-HAND SKETCHES, A LITTLE DASHED WITH HUMOR.
11. WORDS FOR THE WISE.
12. THE TRIED AND THE TEMPTED.

The above Series are sold together or separate, as each work is complete in itself. No Family should be without a copy of this interesting and instructive Series. Price Thirty-seven and a Half Cents per Volume.

FIELD'S SCRAP BOOK.—New Edition.

Literary and Miscellaneous Scrap Book.

Consisting of Tales and Anecdotes — Biographical, Historical, Patriotic, Moral, Religious, and Sentimental Pieces, in Prose and Poetry.

COMPILED BY WILLIAM FIELDS.

SECOND EDITION, REVISED AND IMPROVED.

In one handsome 8vo. Volume. Price, $2.00.

THE ARKANSAW DOCTOR.

THE LIFE AND ADVENTURES OF AN ARKANSAW DOCTOR.

BY DAVID RATTLEHEAD, M. D.

"The Man of Scrapes."

WITH NUMEROUS ILLUSTRATIONS. PRICE FIFTY CENTS.

THE HUMAN BODY AND ITS CONNEXION WITH MAN.

ILLUSTRATED BY THE PRINCIPAL ORGANS.

BY JAMES JOHN GARTH WILKINSON,

Member of the Royal College of Surgeons of England.

IN ONE VOLUME, 12MO—PRICE $1 25.

THE CONFESSIONS OF A HOUSEKEEPER.

BY MRS. JOHN SMITH.

WITH THIRTEEN HUMOROUS ILLUSTRATIONS.

One Volume 12mo. Price 50 Cents.

Splendid Illustrated Books, suitable for Gifts for the Holidays.

THE IRIS: AN ORIGINAL SOUVENIR FOR ANY YARE.

EDITED BY PROF. JOHN S. HART.

WITH TWELVE SPLENDID ILLUMINATIONS, ALL FROM ORIGINAL DESIGNS.

THE DEW-DROP: A TRIBUTE OF AFFECTION.

WITH NINE STEEL ENGRAVINGS.

GEMS FROM THE SACRED MINE.

WITH TEN STEEL PLATES AND ILLUMINATIONS.

The Poet's Offering.

WITH FOURTEEN STEEL PLATES AND ILLUMINATIONS.

THE STANDARD EDITIONS OF THE POETS.

WITH ILLUSTRATIONS.

LORD AND LADY HARCOURT:
OR, COUNTRY HOSPITALITIES.

BY CATHARINE SINCLAIR,

Author of "Jane Bouverie," "The Business of Life," "Modern Accomplishments," &c.

One Volume 12mo. Price 50 cents, paper; cloth, fine, 75 cents.

McGOWN ON DISEASES OF THE SOUTH.

A PRACTICAL TREATISE

ON THE

MOST COMMON DISEASES OF THE SOUTH.

Exhibiting their peculiar nature and the corresponding adaptation of Treatment: to which is added an Appendix containing some Miscellaneous matter; also a Glossary, explaining the meaning of the technicalities, or medical phrases used in this work.

BY THOMPSON McGOWN, M. D.,

Graduate of Transylvania University, Member of the Lexington Medical Society, and a Practitioner of the South.

One Volume Octavo. Price Two Dollars and a Half.

The Regicide's Daughter:
A TALE OF TWO WORLDS.

BY W. H. CARPENTER,

AUTHOR OF "CLAIBORNE THE REBEL," "JOHN THE BOLD," &C., &C.

One Volume 18mo. Price Thirty-seven and a Half Cents.

WILLIAMS'S NEW MAP OF THE UNITED STATES, ON ROLLERS.

SIZE TWO AND A HALF BY THREE FEET.

A new Map of the United States, upon which are delineated its vast works of Internal Communication, Routes across the Continent, &c., showing also Canada and the Island of Cuba,

BY W. WILLIAMS.

This Map is handsomely colored and mounted on rollers, and will be found a beautiful and useful ornament to the Counting-House and Parlor, as well as the School-Room. Price Two Dollars.

VALUABLE STANDARD MEDICAL BOOKS.

DISPENSATORY OF THE UNITED STATES.

BY DRS. WOOD AND BACHE.

New Edition, much enlarged and carefully revised. One volume, royal octavo.

A TREATISE ON THE PRACTICE OF MEDICINE.

BY GEORGE B. WOOD, M. D.,

One of the Authors of the "Dispensatory of the U. S.," &c. New edition, improved. 2 vols. 8vo.

AN ILLUSTRATED SYSTEM OF HUMAN ANATOMY; SPECIAL, MICROSCOPIC, AND PHYSIOLOGICAL.

BY SAMUEL GEORGE MORTON, M. D.

With 391 beautiful Illustrations. One volume, royal octavo.

SMITH'S OPERATIVE SURGERY.

A SYSTEM OF OPERATIVE SURGERY,

BASED UPON THE PRACTICE OF SURGEONS IN THE UNITED STATES; AND COMPRISING A

Bibliographical Index and Historical Record of many of their Operations,

FOR A PERIOD OF 200 YEARS.

BY HENRY H. SMITH, M.D.

Illustrated with nearly 1000 Engravings on Steel.

MATERIA MEDICA AND THERAPEUTICS,

With ample Illustrations of Practice in all the Departments of Medical Science, and copious Notices of Toxicology.

BY THOMAS D. MITCHELL, A.M., M.D.,

Prof. of the Theory and Practice of Medicine in the Philadelphia College of Medicine, &c. 1 vol. 8vo.

THE THEORY AND PRACTICE OF SURGERY.

By George M'Clellan, M. D. 1 vol. 8vo.

EBERLE'S PRACTICE OF MEDICINE.

New Edition. Improved by GEORGE M'CLELLAN, M. D. Two volumes in 1 vol. 8vo.

EBERLE'S THERAPEUTICS.

TWO VOLUMES IN ONE.

A TREATISE ON THE DISEASES AND PHYSICAL EDUCATION OF CHILDREN,

By JOHN EBERLE, M. D., &c. Fourth Edition. With Notes and very large Additions,

By Thomas D. Mitchell, A. M., M. D., &c. 1 vol. 8vo.

EBERLE'S NOTES FOR STUDENTS—NEW EDITION,

*** These works are used as text-books in most of the Medical Schools in the United States.

A PRACTICAL TREATISE ON POISONS:

Their Symptoms, Antidotes, and Treatment. By O. H. Costill, M. D. 18mo.

IDENTITIES OF LIGHT AND HEAT, OF CALORIC AND ELECTRICITY,

BY C. CAMPBELL COOPER.

UNITED STATES' PHARMACOPŒIA,

Edition of 1851. Published by authority of the National Medical Convention. 1 vol. 8vo

SCHOOLCRAFTS GREAT NATIONAL WORK ON THE

Indian Tribes of the United States.

PART SECOND—QUARTO.

WITH EIGHTY BEAUTIFUL ILLUSTRATIONS ON STEEL,

Engraved in the first style of the art, from Drawings by Captain Eastman, U. S. A.

PRICE, FIFTEEN DOLLARS.

COCKBURN'S LIFE OF LORD JEFFREY.

LIFE OF LORD JEFFREY,

WITH A SELECTION FROM HIS CORRESPONDENCE,

BY LORD COCKBURN,

One of the Judges of the Court of Sessions in Scotland. Two volumes, demi-octavo.

"Those who know Lord Jeffrey only through the pages of the Edinburgh Review, get but a one-sided, and not the most pleasant view of his character."

"We advise our readers to obtain the book, and enjoy it to the full themselves. They will unite with us in saying that the self-drawn character portrayed in the letters of Lord Jeffrey, is one of the most delightful pictures that has ever been presented to them."—*Evening Bulletin.*

"Jeffrey was for a long period editor of the Review, and was admitted by all the other contributors to be the leading spirit in it. In addition to his political articles, he soon showed his wonderful powers of criticism in literature. He was equally at home whether censuring or applauding; in his onslaughts on the mediocrity of Southey, or the misused talents of Byron, or in his noble essays on Shakspeare, or Scott, or Burns."—*New York Express.*

PRICE, TWO DOLLARS AND A HALF.

ROMANCE OF NATURAL HISTORY;

OR, WILD SCENES AND WILD HUNTERS.

WITH NUMEROUS ILLUSTRATIONS, IN ONE VOLUME OCTAVO, CLOTH.

BY C. W. WEBBER.

"We have rarely read a volume so full of life and enthusiasm, so capable of transporting the reader into an actor among the scenes and persons described. The volume can hardly be opened at any page without arresting the attention, and the reader is borne along with the movement of a style whose elastic spring and life knows no weariness."—*Boston Courier and Transcript.*

PRICE, TWO DOLLARS.

THE LIFE OF WILLIAM PENN,

WITH SELECTIONS FROM HIS CORRESPONDENCE AND AUTOBIOGRAPHY,

BY SAMUEL M. JANNEY.

Second Edition, Revised.

"Our author has acquitted himself in a manner worthy of his subject. His style is easy, flowing, and yet sententious. Altogether, we consider it a highly valuable addition to the literature of our age, and a work that should find its way into the library of every Friend."—*Friends' Intelligencer, Philadelphia.*

"We regard this life of the great founder of Pennsylvania as a valuable addition to the literature of the country."—*Philadelphia Evening Bulletin.*

"We have no hesitation in pronouncing Mr. Janney's life of Penn the best, because the most satisfactory, that has yet been written. The author's style is clear and uninvolved, and well suited to the purposes of biographical narrative."—*Louisville Journal.*

PRICE, TWO DOLLARS.

LIPPINCOTT'S CABINET HISTORIES OF THE STATES,

CONSISTING OF A SERIES OF

Cabinet Histories of all the States of the Union,

TO EMBRACE A VOLUME FOR EACH STATE.

We have so far completed all our arrangements, as to be able to issue the whole series in the shortest possible time consistent with its careful literary production. SEVERAL VOLUMES ARE NOW READY FOR SALE. The talented authors who have engaged to write these Histories, are no strangers in the literary world.

NOTICES OF THE PRESS.

"These most tastefully printed and bound volumes form the first instalment of a series of State Histories, which, without superseding the bulkier and more expensive works of the same character, may enter household channels from which the others would be excluded by their cost and magnitude."

"In conciseness, clearness, skill of arrangement, and graphic interest, they are a most excellent earnest of those to come. They are eminently adapted both to interest and instruct, and should have a place in the family library of every American."—*N. Y. Courier and Enquirer.*

"The importance of a series of State History like those now in preparation, can scarcely be estimated. Being condensed as carefully as accuracy and interest of narrative will permit, the size and price of the volumes will bring them within the reach of every family in the country, thus making them home-reading books for old and young. Each individual will, in consequence, become familiar, not only with the history of his own State, but with that of the other States; thus mutual interests will be re-awakened, and old bonds cemented in a firmer re-union."—*Home Gazette.*

NEW THEMES FOR THE PROTESTANT CLERGY;

CREEDS WITHOUT CHARITY, THEOLOGY WITHOUT HUMANITY, AND PROTESTANTISM WITHOUT CHRISTIANITY:

With Notes by the Editor on the Literature of Charity, Population, Pauperism, Political Economy, and Protestantism.

"The great question which the book discusses is, whether the Church of this age is what the primitive Church was, and whether Christians—both pastors and people—are doing their duty. Our anthor believes not, and, to our mind, he has made out a strong case. He thinks there is abundant room for reform at the present time, and that it is needed almost as much as in the days of Luther. And why? Because, in his own words, 'While one portion of nominal Christians have busied themselves with forms and ceremonies and observances; with pictures, images, and processions; others have given to doctrines the supremacy, and have busied themselves in laying down the lines by which to enforce human belief—lines of interpretation by which to control human opinion—lines of discipline and restraint, by which to bring human minds to uniformity of faith and action. They have formed creeds and catechisms; they have spread themselves over the whole field of the sacred writings, and scratched up all the surface; they have gathered all the straws, and turned over all the pebbles, and detected the colour and determined the outline of every stone and tree and shrub; they have dwelt with rapture upon all that was beautiful and sublime; but they have trampled over mines of golden wisdom, of surpassing richness and depth, almost without a thought, and almost without an effort to fathom these priceless treasures, much less to take possession of them.'"

PRICE, ONE DOLLAR.

SIMPSON'S MILITARY JOURNAL.

JOURNAL OF A MILITARY RECONNOISSANCE FROM SANTA FE, NEW MEXICO, TO THE NAVAJO COUNTRY,

BY JAMES H. SIMPSON, A. M.,

FIRST LIEUTENANT CORPS OF TOPOGRAPHICAL ENGINEERS.

WITH SEVENTY-FIVE COLOURED ILLUSTRATIONS.

One volume, octavo. Price, Three Dollars.

TALES OF THE SOUTHERN BORDER.

BY C. W. WEBBER.

ONE VOLUME OCTAVO, HANDSOMELY ILLUSTRATED.

The Hunter Naturalist, a Romance of Sporting;

OR, WILD SCENES AND WILD HUNTERS.

BY C. W. WEBBER,

Author of "Shot in the Eye," "Old Hicks the Guide," "Gold Mines of the Gila," &c.

ONE VOLUME, ROYAL OCTAVO.

ILLUSTRATED WITH FORTY BEAUTIFUL ENGRAVINGS, FROM ORIGINAL DRAWINGS, MANY OF WHICH ARE COLOURED.

Price, Five Dollars.

NIGHTS IN A BLOCK-HOUSE;

OR, SKETCHES OF BORDER LIFE.

Embracing Adventures among the Indians, Feats of the Wild Hunters, and Exploits of Boone, Brady, Kenton, Whetzel, Fleehart, and other Border Heroes of the West

BY HENRY C. WATSON,

Author of "Camp-Fires of the Revolution."

WITH NUMEROUS ILLUSTRATIONS.

One volume, 8vo. Price, $2 00.

HAMILTON, THE YOUNG ARTIST.

BY AUGUSTA BROWNE.

WITH

AN ESSAY ON SCULPTURE AND PAINTING,

BY HAMILTON A. C. BROWNE.

1 vol. 18mo. Price, 37 1-2 cents.

THE SUGAR CAMP, and other Sketches,

BY CHARLES LANMAN.

12mo. ILLUMINATED COVERS. Price, 50 cents.

A HIT AT THE FOLLIES OF THE AGE.

TRANSLATED FROM THE FRENCH,

BY LEONARD MYERS.

One volume, 12mo. ILLUMINATED COVERS. Price, 50 cents.

MILITARY LIFE IN FIELD AND CAMP.

BY RICHARD M'SHERRY, M. D.,

LATE SURGEON OF A REGIMENT OF MARINES.

One volume, 12mo. ILLUMINATED COVERS. Price, 50 cents.

FROST'S JUVENILE SERIES.

TWELVE VOLUMES, 16mo., WITH FIVE HUNDRED ENGRAVINGS.

WALTER O'NEILL, OR THE PLEASURE OF DOING GOOD. 25 Engrav'gs.
JUNKER SCHOTT, and other Stories. 6 Engravings.
THE LADY OF THE LURLEI, and other Stories. 12 Engravings.
ELLEN'S BIRTHDAY, and other Stories. 20 Engravings.
HERMAN, and other Stories. 9 Engravings.
KING TREGEWALL'S DAUGHTER, and other Stories. 16 Engravings.
THE DROWNED BOY, and other Stories. 6 Engravings.
THE PICTORIAL RHYME-BOOK. 122 Engravings.
THE PICTORIAL NURSERY BOOK. 117 Engravings.
THE GOOD CHILD'S REWARD. 115 Engravings.
ALPHABET OF QUADRUPEDS. 26 Engravings.
ALPHABET OF BIRDS. 26 Engravings.

PRICE, TWENTY-FIVE CENTS EACH.

The above popular and attractive series of New Juveniles for the Young, are sold together or separately.

THE MILLINER AND THE MILLIONAIRE.

BY MRS. REBECCA HICKS,

(Of Virginia,) Author of "The Lady Killer," &c. One volume, 12mo.

Price, 37½ cents.

STANSBURY'S
EXPEDITION TO THE GREAT SALT LAKE.

AN EXPLORATION
OF THE VALLEY OF THE GREAT SALT LAKE
OF UTAH,

CONTAINING ITS GEOGRAPHY, NATURAL HISTORY, MINERALOGICAL RESOURCES, ANALYSIS OF ITS WATERS, AND AN AUTHENTIC ACCOUNT OF

THE MORMON SETTLEMENT.

ALSO,

A RECONNOISSANCE OF A NEW ROUTE THROUGH THE ROCKY MOUNTAINS.

WITH SEVENTY BEAUTIFUL ILLUSTRATIONS,

FROM DRAWINGS TAKEN ON THE SPOT,

AND TWO LARGE AND ACCURATE MAPS OF THAT REGION.

BY HOWARD STANSBURY,

CAPTAIN TOPOGRAPHICAL ENGINEERS.

One volume, royal octavo.

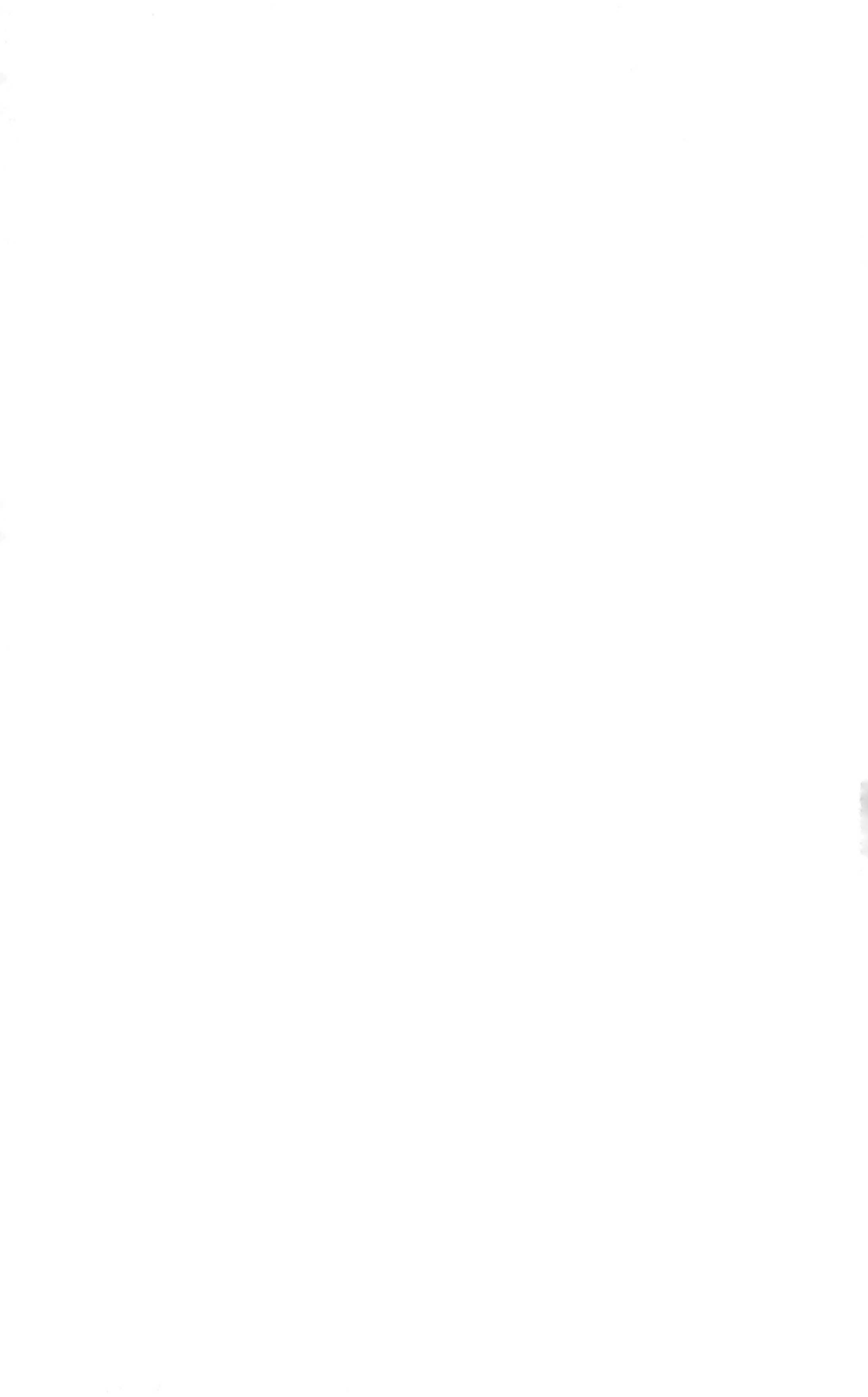

www.ingramcontent.com/pod-product-compliance
Lightning Source LLC
LaVergne TN
LVHW021243110826
845150LV00002B/400